Components of the strategic management process

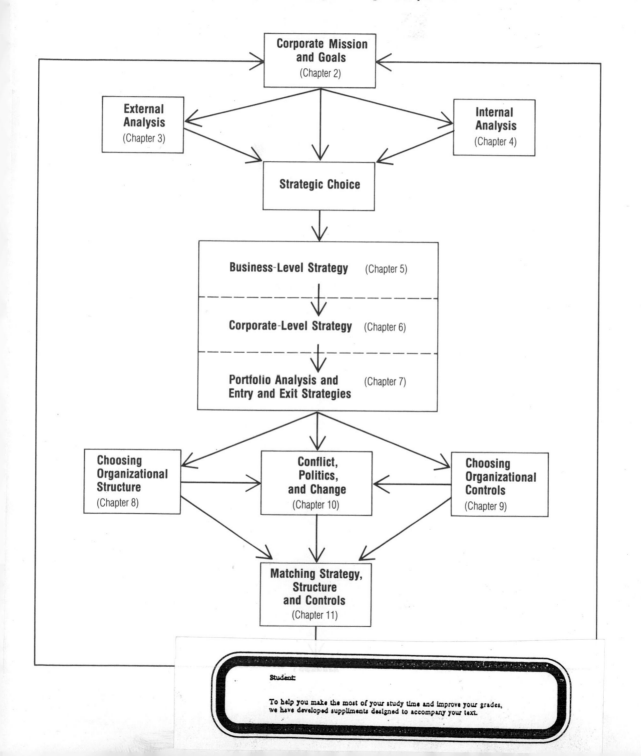

Corporate Mission
and Goals
(Chapter 2)

External
Analysis
(Chapter 3)

Internal
Analysis
(Chapter 4)

Strategic Choice

Business-Level Strategy   (Chapter 5)

Corporate-Level Strategy   (Chapter 6)

Portfolio Analysis and   (Chapter 7)
Entry and Exit Strategies

Choosing
Organizational
Structure
(Chapter 8)

Conflict,
Politics,
and Change
(Chapter 10)

Choosing
Organizational
Controls
(Chapter 9)

Matching Strategy,
Structure
and Controls
(Chapter 11)

Student:

To help you make the most of your study time and improve your grades,
we have developed suppliments designed to accompany your text.

STRATEGIC MANAGEMENT

An Integrated Approach

CHARLES W. L. HILL
University of Washington

GARETH R. JONES
Texas A & M University

For my wife Alexandra
and my daughter Elizabeth
C. W. L. H.

For my parents
Iori and Mona Jones
G. R. J.

Cover Photo: Gary Cralle/The Image Bank

Printed in the U.S.A.

Library of Congress Catalog Card Number: 88-81335

ISBN: 0-395-43411-4

ABCDEFGHIJ-DOH-9543210-898

Contents

Preface

Our objective in writing *Strategic Management: An Integrated Approach* has been to offer a book with a text that is first, accessible to undergraduate students, yet at the same time comprehensive and up-to-date in its coverage of the strategic management literature; second, balanced in its discussion of strategic issues; and third, successful at maintaining an integrated flow between chapters. We also wanted to differentiate our book by the high quality and relevance of its cases. While the market will be the ultimate judge of our success in achieving these objectives, we think that professors and students will find this book very satisfying to work with.

Comprehensive and Up-to-Date Coverage

The comprehensive and up-to-date nature of the text can be illustrated by the following examples of material that is not found in many other textbooks. In addition to the "standard" strategic management material, in this text we discuss

- alternative models of the strategy-making process (e.g. intended versus emergent strategies);
- the quality of strategic decision making and the role of devil's advocacy and dialectic inquiry in improving decisions;
- the implications that key stakeholders, such as shareholders, have for the mission and strategic development of a company;
- changes that occur in the determinants of competitive intensity as an industry evolves, such as barriers to entry and inter-company rivalry;
- the implications of strategic groups;
- the contribution of the functional components of a company's value chain, such as manufacturing, marketing, materials management, R&D, and information systems, in producing firm strengths and weaknesses;
- the role of investment strategies in supporting a company's business-level strategy;
- the sources of economic value created by vertical integration and diversification strategies;
- global versus multidomestic strategies;
- acquisitions and internal new ventures as alternative means of company growth and development;

■ an in-depth discussion of how to match a firm's structure and control systems in order to implement business- and corporate-level strategy;

■ the role of intra-organizational power and conflict in inhibiting or promoting organizational change.

Balanced Discussion of Strategic Issues

In addition to comprehensive coverage, we have also attempted to provide a balanced view of the topics discussed in this text. By this we mean going beyond uncritical presentation of material. For example, we talk at length about the strengths and weaknesses of the various approaches to portfolio planning, we critically examine the pros and cons of different vertical integration and diversification strategies, we consider why so many acquisitions and new ventures apparently fail and discuss how the risk of failure might be attenuated, we evaluate the advantages and disadvantages of different organizational structures and control systems for the management of diversity, and so on. The objective is to demonstrate to students that in the real world strategic issues are inevitably complex and necessarily involve a consideration of pros and cons.

Achieving balance also means that we have not allowed any one disciplinary orientation to determine the content of this text. In addition to the strategic management literature, we have drawn on the literature of economics, marketing, organizational theory, finance, and international business. The perspective of this text is truly strategic in that it integrates the contributions of these diverse academic disciplines into a comprehensive whole.

Achieving balance also involves giving weight to each topic in proportion to its importance. Nowhere is this more evident than with regard to strategy implementation. Treated superficially in many textbooks, strategy implementation is the focus of four of the twelve chapters in this text. The commitment to balance is also evident within chapters. For example, while many textbooks discuss diversification in some detail, most give no more than a passing mention to vertical integration. This imbalance is surprising given the extent to which vertical integration is used by American enterprises. Here, we discuss at some length the nature, benefits, and costs of vertical integration.

Integrated Progression of Topics

A comprehensive and balanced coverage of material, while extremely important, does not on its own make for a good text. To achieve this, the material must also be placed within the context of an overall framework that integrates the different topics into a conceptual whole. Accordingly, we have attempted to fit the pieces of the strategic management puzzle together in a logical fashion so that students will understand the relationships between them. Above all else, this involves laying out the book so that each chapter builds on the previous one.

We start with an overview of the strategic management process (Chapter 1). This sets down an integrated framework within which subsequent chapters can be placed. Next, in Chapter 2, we consider the importance of stakeholders and the company mission in determining the context within which strategies are formulated. In Chapter 3, we move on to look at the opportunities and threats a company faces in its external environment. This is followed by a discussion of the sources of internal strengths and weaknesses in Chapter 4. Building on this, we turn in Chapters 5 and 6 to look at the business- and corporate-level strategy options open to a company. Chapter 7 deals with different portfolio techniques available for the management of diversity, and the strategies that can be used for entering and exiting from business areas. Finally, Chapters 8–11 focus on strategy implementation. In sequence, these consider the different organizational structures with which a company can operate, the different organizational control systems that a company can use, the way in which firms should match structure and control to strategy, and the difficult implementation issues raised by intraorganizational conflict, politics, and strategic change.

Chapter 12 (Part IV) immediately precedes the cases, and is designed to provide students with an introduction to analyzing and writing case studies.

One point that should be clarified at this juncture is our decision to discuss corporate-level strategy (Chapter 6) after business-level strategy (Chapter 5). Many textbooks discuss corporate-level strategy first, the logic being that corporate-level strategy sets the context within which business-level strategy is formulated. We believe that this is a fundamental mistake. Our position is that the set of appropriate strategies at the corporate level is determined by a company's business-level *competences* and *needs*. For example, one of the ways in which related diversification can create value is from skill transfers between different businesses. A company's ability to do this, however, depends on the company having a distinctive *competence* in one or more of its business units that can be transferred. For another example, consider vertical integration; this can arise out of the *need* to gain access to low-cost inputs and may, therefore, be designed to help the company attain a low-cost position in its primary business. Thus, as these examples suggest, it is often the case that business-level competences and needs drive corporate-level strategy — not the other way around.

Cases

We have attempted to assemble a balanced selection of high-quality cases that address all the key subject areas covered in the text. Many of the cases are new, including eight that we have written ourselves. There are also a number of "classic cases" in the selection. About half of the cases focus on large companies with high name recognition (e.g. Chrysler, Compaq, Greyhound, Kodak, USX). A number of the remainder focus on small businesses (e.g. Bennett's Machine Shop, Walsh Petroleum). The cases are fairly evenly split between manufacturing and service companies. We have taken care to choose cases that are of a higher quality and richer in useful information than is the norm.

Instructors Manual

Accompanying the textbook is also a comprehensive instructors manual that offers a complete package of materials for the classroom. For each of the book's chapters there are a lecture outline, a comprehensive set of true-false and multiple choice questions, and transparency masters for most of the figures and tables. For each of the cases there are discussion questions (with answers) that can be used for homework assignments or to stimulate class discussion, and detailed teachers notes that provide comprehensive analysis of the case issues.

Acknowledgments

This book is more than the product of the two authors. Thanks are also due to the case authors for allowing us to use their material, to the Departments of Management of Michigan State and Texas A & M Universities for providing the setting and atmosphere in which the book could be written, and to the students of these same universities who reacted to and provided input for many of our ideas.

We would like to thank Mike Hitt and Bob Hoskisson for their comments during the planning of this book, and Vicky Buenger for her help in reading and commenting on the chapters. In addition, the following reviewers provided valuable suggestions for improving the original manuscript:

Gene R. Conatser
Golden Gate University

Joseph A. Schenk
University of Dayton

Eliezer Geisler
Northeastern Illinois University

Barbara Spencer
Clemson University

Lynn Godkin
Lamar University

Bobby Vaught
Southwest Missouri State

Joanna Mulholland
West Chester University of
   Pennsylvania

Finally, thanks are due to our families for their patience and understanding during the course of the book's development. We would like to thank our wives, Alexandra Hill and Jennifer George, for their support and affection.

C. W. L. H.

G. R. J.

STRATEGIC
MANAGEMENT

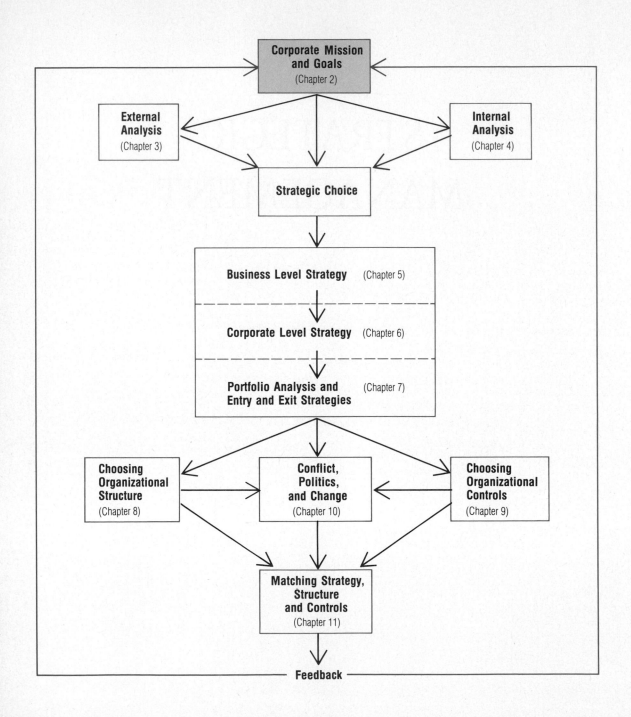

P A R T

I

INTRODUCTION

Chapter 1

THE STRATEGIC MANAGEMENT PROCESS

1.1 OPENING INCIDENT: TEXAS AIR

In 1975 Texas International was a small regional airline generating passenger revenues of $60.6 million. But its CEO, Frank Lorenzo, had aspirations for the company. He wanted to turn Texas International into a dominant force in an industry that he expected would undergo massive consolidation. Lorenzo's strategy to attain his goal involved two elements: a focus on cost cutting to make low fares profitable and the acquisition of other carriers to attain the critical mass needed for national coverage.

Lorenzo began to implement the first part of his strategy in 1975. He broke the airline unions' hold over labor costs at Texas International after a long strike and then introduced a "Fly for Peanuts" marketing campaign to attract a new class of economy-minded passengers. The strategy worked, and between 1976 and 1978 Texas International's net income grew from $3.5 million to $13.2 million, making the company the fourth largest regional carrier.

Lorenzo, however, had only just begun. In 1978 the airline industry was deregulated, leading to intensified competition. Agreements concerning fares and route structures, which had placed competition in a straight-jacket, no longer prevailed. Deregulation created opportunities to expand route structures and introduce new low fares. At the same time the increased competitive pressure threatened established airlines that had grown fat during the years of regulation. Texas International, having slashed labor costs and successfully introduced low fares, was positioned so that it could capitalize on the opportunities brought by deregulation.

In 1978 Lorenzo began the second phase of his strategy — growth by acquisition. That year he made a bid for National Airlines and in 1979 tried to buy TWA. Both bids failed, but Texas International gained a $46-million profit on the sale of the stock it had acquired in the two companies. In 1980 Lorenzo created a holding company called Texas Air Corporation. Texas International became a wholly owned subsidiary, and Lorenzo had a vehicle for future acquisitions. The same year also saw Lorenzo create New York Air in order to challenge Eastern Airlines' lucrative East Coast shuttle service.

Texas Air completed its first successful acquisition in 1982. Continental Airlines Corp., financial troubles and all, became part of Texas Air. Despite Lorenzo's best efforts, losses from the merger mounted. Lorenzo responded by filing for Chapter 11 protection for Continental and then promptly abrogated labor contracts with the company's unions. Pilots, machinists, and flight attendants walked out. Lorenzo replaced the strikers and cut the work force by two-thirds. Continental emerged from this affair as the lowest-cost national airline, well placed to survive in the developing fare war.

The acquisition of Continental was followed in 1986 by the acquisition of two other financially troubled airlines, Eastern and People Express Airlines, Inc., making Texas Air the largest domestic airline, with approximately 20 percent of the U.S. airline market. Lorenzo achieved his goal by taking advantage of strategic opportunities in the deregulated airline industry and by capitalizing on a major strength of Texas Air, its low cost structure. But Texas Air did not expand without cost. The company amassed a $4.5-billion debt by the end of 1986 — about twelve times equity. It remains to be seen whether Texas Air can now eliminate this major weakness.[1]

1.2 OVERVIEW

Why do some organizations succeed and others fail? What is it that makes some profit-seeking organizations, such as IBM, Hewlett-Packard Co., and the pharmaceutical giant Merck & Co., Inc., excellent performers year after year, while others, such as Chrysler Corp., Navistar International Corporation, and USX, have gone through periods during which they have struggled to survive? Why is it that some not-for-profit organizations, such as the United Way, have been able to build up a stable constituency of charitable givers, while others, such as Farm Aid, have been unable to sustain their operations for any length of time? An answer can be found in the subject matter of this book: strategic management. We will consider the advantages that accrue to organizations that think strategically. We will also examine how organizations that understand both their operating environment and their own internal strengths and weaknesses can identify and exploit strategies successfully.

The techniques that we will discuss in this book are relevant to many different kinds of organizations, from large, multibusiness enterprises to small, one-person enterprises, from manufacturing enterprises to service enterprises, and from publicly held profit-seeking corporations to not-for-profit organizations. Although we tend to think of strategic management as primarily concerned with profit-seeking organizations, even a small not-for-profit organization, such as a local theater or church charity, has to make decisions about how best to generate revenues, given the environment in which it is based and the organization's own strengths and weaknesses. Such decisions are, by their very nature, strategic in form and content, involving such factors as an analysis of the "competition." For example, the local church-run charity has to compete with other charities for the limited resources that individuals are prepared to give to charitable causes. Identifying how best to do so is a strategic problem.

The objective of this book is to give the reader a thorough understanding of the analytical techniques and skills necessary to identify and exploit strategies successfully. The first step toward achieving this objective involves an overview of the main elements of the strategic management process, and the way in which these elements fit together. This is the function of the present chapter. In subsequent chapters we will consider the individual elements of the strategic management process in greater detail.

1.3 DEFINING STRATEGY

The Traditional Approach

Reflecting the military roots of strategy, *Webster's New World Dictionary* defines strategy as "the science of planning and directing military operations." The *planning* theme remains an important component of most management definitions of strategy. For example, Harvard's Alfred Chandler defined strategy as "the determination of the basic long-term goals and objectives of an enterprise, and the adoption of courses of action and the allocation of resources necessary for carrying out these goals."[2] Implicit in Chandler's definition is the idea that strategy involves a *rational* planning process. The organization is depicted as choosing its goals, identifying those courses of action (or strategies) that best enable it to fulfill its goals, and allocating resources accordingly. Similarly, James B. Quinn of Dartmouth College has defined strategy as "the pattern or plan that integrates an organization's major goals, policies, and action sequences into a cohesive whole."[3] And finally, along the same lines, William F. Glueck defined strategy as "a unified, comprehensive, and integrated plan designed to ensure that the basic objectives of the enterprise are achieved."[4]

The case of Texas Air, discussed in the Opening Incident, is a good example of how the strategic planning process works. In the mid-1970s Texas International's CEO, Frank Lorenzo, correctly foresaw that deregulation of the airline industry would increase competitive pressure and price competition. Lorenzo reasoned that to survive in the long run an airline would have to have (a) low operating costs and (b) national coverage. The plan at Texas International was to pursue strategies that would enable it to attain both of these objectives. Since the mid-1970s the company has reduced operating costs by forcing through deep cuts in labor costs—often in the face of union hostility. It has also achieved national coverage by acquiring three financially troubled airlines: in

1982 Continental Airlines, and in 1986 Eastern and People Express. These acquisitions transformed Texas Air from a small, low-fare carrier with services concentrated in a few regions of the country into the largest domestic airline, with 20% of the market and national coverage. As a result, Texas Air is now well placed to become a dominant force in the rapidly consolidating airline industry.

A New Approach

For all their appeal, planning-based definitions of strategy have recently evoked criticism. As Henry Mintzberg of McGill University has pointed out, the problem with the planning approach is that it incorrectly assumes that an organization's strategy is always the outcome of a rational planning process.[5] According to Mintzberg, definitions of strategy that stress the role of planning ignore the fact that strategies can emerge from within an organization without any formal plan. That is to say, even in the absence of intent, strategies can emerge from the grassroots of an organization. Mintzberg's point is that strategy is more than what a company intends or plans to do; it is also what it actually does. With this in mind, Mintzberg has defined strategy as *"a pattern in a stream of decisions or actions,"*[6] the pattern being a product of whatever *intended* (planned) strategies are actually realized and of any *emergent* (unplanned) strategies. The scheme proposed by Mintzberg is illustrated in Figure 1.1.

Mintzberg's argument is that emergent strategies are often successful and may be more appropriate than intended strategies. Richard T. Pascale of Stanford University has described how this was the case for the entry of Honda Motor Co., Ltd. into the U.S. motorcycle market.[7] When a number of Honda executives arrived in Los Angeles from Japan in 1959 to establish an American subsidiary, their original aim (intended strategy) was to focus on selling 250cc and 305cc machines to confirmed motorcycle enthusiasts, rather than 50cc Honda Cubs, which were a big hit in Japan. Their instinct told them that the

FIGURE 1.1   Emergent and deliberate strategies

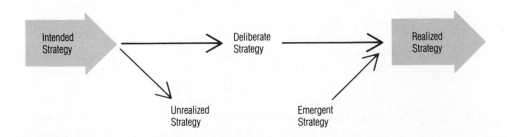

Source: Reprinted from "Strategy Formation in an Adhocracy," by Henry Mintzberg and Alexandra McHugh, published in *Administrative Science Quarterly*, Vol. 30, No. 2 (June 1985), by permission of *Administrative Science Quarterly*.

Honda 50s were not suitable for the U.S. market, where everything was bigger and more luxurious than in Japan.

However, sales of the 250cc and 305cc bikes were sluggish, and the bikes themselves were plagued by mechanical failure. It looked as if Honda's strategy was going to fail. At the same time the Japanese executives were using the Honda 50s to run errands around Los Angeles, attracting a lot of attention. One day they got a call from a Sears, Roebuck buyer who wanted to sell them to a broad market of Americans who were not necessarily already motorcycle enthusiasts. The Honda executives were very hesitant to sell the 50cc bikes for fear of alienating serious bikers who might then associate Honda with "wimp" machines. In the end they were pushed into doing so by the failure of the 250cc and 305cc models. The rest is history. Honda had stumbled on a previously untouched market segment that was to prove huge: the average American who had previously never owned a motorbike. It had also found a previously untried channel of distribution: general retailers rather than specialty motorbike stores. By 1964 nearly one out of every two motorcycles sold in the United States was a Honda.

The conventional explanation of Honda's success is that the company redefined the U.S. motorcycle industry with a brilliantly conceived *intended* strategy.[8] The fact was that Honda's intended strategy was a near disaster. The strategy that *emerged* did so not through planning but through unplanned action taken in response to unforseen circumstances. Nevertheless, credit should be given to the Japanese management for recognizing the strength of the emergent strategy and for pursuing it with vigor.

The critical point that emerges from the Honda example is that in contrast to the view that strategies are planned, successful strategies can emerge within an organization without prior planning. As Mintzberg has noted, strategies can take root in all kinds of strange places, virtually wherever people have the capacity to learn and the resources to support that capacity.

In sum, Mintzberg's revision of the concept of strategy suggests that strategy involves more than just planning a course of action. It also involves the recognition that successful strategies can emerge from deep within an organization. In practice, the strategies of most organizations are probably a combination of the intended and the emergent. The message for management is that it needs to recognize the process of emergence and to intervene when appropriate, killing off bad emergent strategies but nurturing potentially good ones. To make such decisions, however, managers must be able to judge the worth of emergent strategies. They must be able to think strategically.

1.4 COMPONENTS OF THE STRATEGIC MANAGEMENT PROCESS

The strategic management process can be broken down into a number of different components. These components are illustrated in Figure 1.2 and each forms

FIGURE 1.2   Components of the strategic management process

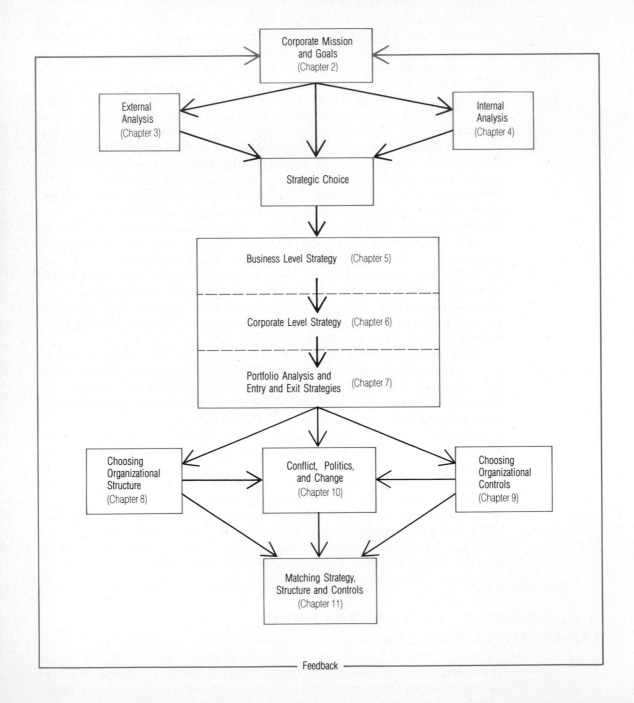

a chapter of this book. Thus the reader needs to understand how the different components fit together. The components include the selection of the corporate mission and major corporate goals, analysis of the organization's external competitive environment and internal operating environment, the selection of appropriate business and/or corporate level strategies, and the designing of organizational structures and control systems to implement the organization's chosen strategy. The task of analyzing the organization's external and internal environment and then selecting an appropriate strategy is normally referred to as **strategy formulation.** The task of designing appropriate organizational structures and control systems, given the organization's choice of strategy, is usually called **strategy implementation.**

The traditional approach has been to stress that each of the components illustrated in Figure 1.2 constitutes a *sequential* step in the strategic management process. Each *cycle* of the strategy-making process is depicted as beginning with a statement of the corporate mission and major corporate goals, followed by environmental analysis and strategic choice, and ending with the design of the organizational structure and control systems necessary to implement the organization's chosen strategy. In practice, however, this is only likely to be the case for the formulation and implementation of *intended* strategies. As noted earlier, *emergent* strategies arise from within the organization without prior planning— that is to say, without going through the steps illustrated in Figure 1.2 in a *sequential* fashion. However, top management still has to evaluate emergent strategies. Such evaluation involves comparing each emergent strategy with the organization's goals, external environmental opportunities and threats, and the organization's own internal strengths and weaknesses. The objective is to assess whether the emergent strategy *fits* the organization's needs and capabilities. In addition, Mintzberg stresses that an organization's capability to produce emergent strategies is a function of the kind of corporate culture fostered by the organization's structure and control systems.

In other words, the different components of the strategic management process are just as important from the perspective of emergent strategies as they are from the perspective of intended strategies. The essential differences between the strategic management process for intended and emergent strategies are illustrated in Figure 1.3. The formulation of intended strategies is basically a top-down process, whereas the formulation of emergent strategies is a bottom-up process.

Mission and Major Goals

The first component of the strategic management process involves defining the **mission** and **major goals** of the organization. This topic is covered in depth in Chapter 2. The mission and major goals of an organization provide the context within which intended strategies are formulated and the criteria against which emergent strategies are evaluated. The mission sets out why the organization

FIGURE 1.3   **The strategic management process for intended and emergent strategies**

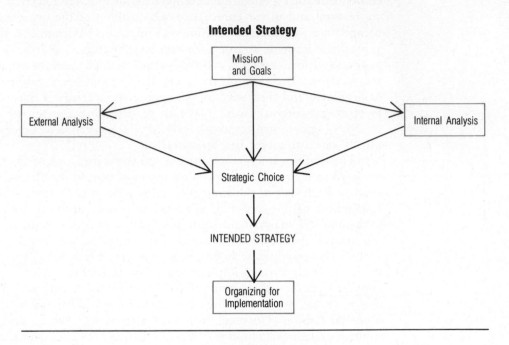

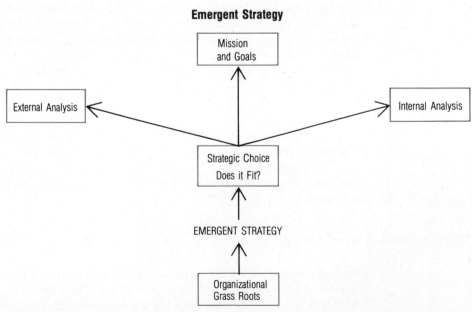

exists and what it should be doing. For example, the mission of Texas Air might be defined as satisfying the needs of individual and business travelers for high-speed transportation at a reasonable price to all the major population centers of North America. Major goals specify what the organization hopes to fulfill in the medium to long term. Most profit-seeking organizations operate with a hierarchy of goals in which the maximization of stockholder wealth is placed at the top. Secondary goals, such as Texas Air's goal of becoming one of the six major airlines in the United States, are objectives judged necessary by the company if it is to maximize stockholder wealth. Not-for-profit organizations typically have a more diverse set of goals. The major goal of Band Aid, for example, was to alleviate starvation in Ethiopia, whereas the goal of a performing arts theater might be to provide high quality cultural entertainment at a reasonable cost to the public.

External Analysis

The second component of the strategic management process is the analysis of the organization's external operating environment. This topic is covered in detail in Chapter 3. The objective of external analysis is to identify strategic **opportunities** and **threats** in the organization's operating environment. Two interrelated environments should be examined at this stage: the immediate, or industry environment in which the organization operates, and the wider macroenvironment. Analyzing the industry environment involves an assessment of the competitive structure of the organization's industry, including the competitive position of the focal organization and its major rivals, as well as the stage of industry development. Analyzing the macroenvironment consists of examining macroeconomic, social, governmental, legal, international, and technological factors that may affect the organization. Again consider Texas Air. Its external opportunities included financially troubled airlines coming up for sale, landing spots becoming available at major hubs, and its using national coverage to build brand loyalty. The threats included the possibility of another price war, rising interest rates that would place an additional burden on the company given its debt structure, and rising fuel costs.

Internal Analysis

The next component of the strategic management process, internal analysis, serves to pinpoint the **strengths** and **weaknesses** of the organization. Such analysis involves identifying the quantity and quality of resources available to the organization. These issues are considered in Chapter 4, where we use the concept of the value chain to examine the factors that determine the quantity and quality of an organization's resources in manufacturing, marketing, materials management, research and development, information systems, personnel, and finance. In addition, for the multibusiness enterprise, identifying strengths and weaknesses also involves assessing whether the balance of different businesses in its portfolio is a strength or a weakness. For example, if the company's businesses are concentrated in highly competitive and unprofitable industries, then this is a weakness. Conversely, if its businesses are concentrated in very profitable industries, then this is a strength. Assessing the corporate portfolio is an issue that we discuss in Chapter 7.

Strategic Choice

The next step involves generating a series of strategic alternatives, given the goals of the firm, its internal strengths and weaknesses, and external opportunities and threats. This issue is covered in Chapter 12. We do not deal with the issue until this stage in the text because it is necessary first to lay out the different strategic alternatives open to the firm and to familiarize the reader with the complexities of organizational structure and control systems. The reader should remember, however, that for strategic decision makers who know the full range of strategic options, strategic choice follows directly from an analysis of the organization's external and internal environments.

The process of comparing **s**trengths, **w**eaknesses, **o**pportunities, and **t**hreats is normally referred to as a **SWOT** analysis.[9] A SWOT analysis might generate a series of strategic alternatives. To choose among the alternatives, the organization has to evaluate them against each other with respect to their ability to achieve major goals. The objective is to select the strategies that ensure the best **alignment,** or **fit,** between external environmental opportunities and threats and the internal strengths and weaknesses of the organization. For the single business organization, the objective is to match a company's strengths to environmental opportunities in order to gain a competitive advantage and thus increase profits. For the multibusiness organization, the goal is to choose strategies for its portfolio of business that align the strengths and weaknesses of the portfolio with environmental opportunities and threats.

Again consider Texas Air. The strategy of acquiring financially troubled competitors can be seen as taking advantage of an opportunity to counter a potential threat. The *opportunity* was that Texas Air could become a major carrier by buying out financially troubled competitors at a relatively low price. The potential *threat* involved being squeezed out of the airline industry if the company failed to become large enough to compete as a major national carrier. The strategy also built upon a major *strength* of Texas Air: that of being an efficient low-cost carrier. Nonunionized Texas Air broke Continental's unions after its acquisition of the airline, slashing labor costs and in the process transforming Continental into a low-cost carrier. However, Texas Air's high debt raises questions about its strategy. The acquisitions have intensified rather than alleviated this *weakness*. By the end of 1986 Texas Air was highly leveraged, with

$4.5 billion in debt and lease commitments—about twelve times equity. This debt level casts a shadow over Texas Air's long-term future. Only time will tell whether the strategy of Frank Lorenzo and his colleagues was brilliantly conceived or a gamble that did not pay off. Such uncertainty as to ultimate outcomes, however, is also part of strategic management. By systematically analyzing its external environment and internal organization, the company can reduce the uncertainty it has to face, though it can never eliminate it.

Business-Level Strategy

For the organization operating in a single competitive environment (industry), the outcome of the process of strategic choice will be the identification of an appropriate business-level strategy. The different strategic alternatives are discussed in Chapter 5. In brief, the main choices are a strategy of cost leadership, a strategy of differentiation, or a strategy of focusing on a particular market niche. The organization's objective when pursuing the strategy of its choice should be to establish a sustainable competitive advantage. (Note: The strategy of Texas Air has been one of cost leadership). In addition, Chapter 5 examines the different investment strategies needed to *support* each of these main strategic alternatives. The argument developed in Chapter 5 is that a company must vary its investment strategy with the stage of development of its industry in order to make its business-level strategy successful.

Corporate-Level Strategy

An organization's corporate-level strategy must answer the question: what businesses should we be in to maximize the long-run profitability of the organization? For many organizations, the answer involves focusing the organization's full attention on continuing to compete within a single business area. However, competing successfully within a single business area also often involves **vertical integration** and/or **global expansion.** In some segments of the electronics industry, for example, global markets are necessary to generate the sales volume to achieve full economies of scale. Establishing a low-cost position within a single industry may thus require global expansion. Similar arguments can be made regarding vertical integration. Beyond this, organizations that are successful at establishing a sustainable competitive advantage may find that they are generating resources *in excess* of their investment requirements within their primary industry. For such organizations, maximizing long-run profitability may entail **diversification** into new business areas. The strategies of vertical integration, global expansion, and diversification fall under the rubric of corporate-level strategies. We consider them in depth in Chapter 6.

Portfolio Analysis and Entry and Exit Strategies

Substantially diversified companies face the problem of how best to make sense out of their many different activities. General Electric Co., for example, has more than 240 different business units. How do the different activities fit together? What is the relative contribution of each activity to corporate profitability? What is the future outlook for each activity? Portfolio analysis offers a body of techniques designed to help organizations answer such questions. In Chapter 7, we examine these techniques and consider their strengths and weaknesses.

Portfolio analysis may indicate that the company needs to leave some existing business areas or enter new ones. A number of different entry and exit strategies are available. The options for entering new businesses include acquisitions and internal new venturing. The options for exiting from an existing business include harvest, divestment, and liquidation. We discuss the merits of these various entry and exit strategies in Chapter 7.

Designing Organizational Structure

To make a strategy work, regardless of whether it is intended or emergent, the organization needs to adopt the correct structure. The main options here are reviewed in Chapter 8. Choosing a structure entails allocating task responsibility and decision-making authority within the organization. The issues covered include how best to divide the organization into subunits and how to distribute authority among the different levels of an organization's hierarchy. The options reviewed include whether the organization should function with a tall or a flat structure, how centralized or decentralized decision-making authority should be, and to what extent the organization should be divided up into semiautonomous subunits (such as product divisions).

Choosing Integration and Control Systems

Beyond an organization's choice of structure, strategy implementation involves the selection of appropriate organizational integration and control systems. The main options here are reviewed in Chapter 9. Strategy implementation often requires collective action or coordination between semiautonomous subunits (i.e., divisions or departments) within an organization. Thus we consider the different integration mechanisms that are available for achieving coordination between semiautonomous subunits. The organization must also decide how best to assess the performance and control the actions of subunits. Its options range from market and output controls to bureaucratic and clan controls, all of which we tackle in Chapter 9.

Matching Strategy, Structure, and Controls

Implementing a strategy requires the adoption of appropriate organizational structures and control systems. After reviewing various structures and control systems in Chapters 8 and 9, in Chapter 10 we consider how to achieve a *fit* among an organization's strategy, structure, and controls. Different strategies and environments place different demands on an organization and therefore require different structural responses and control systems. For example, a strategy of cost leadership demands that the organization be kept simple (so as to reduce costs) and that controls stress productive efficiency. On the other hand, a strategy of differentiating the organization's product by unique technological characteristics generates a need for integrating the activities of the organization around its technological core and for establishing control systems that reward technical creativity. The appropriate structure and control systems are very different in these two cases.

Conflict, Politics, and Change

Although in theory the strategic management process is characterized by *rational* decision making, in practice organizational politics plays a key role. Politics is endemic to organizations: different subgroups within an organization (i.e., departments or divisions) have their own agendas. Typically, the agendas of different subgroups conflict. Thus departments may compete with each other for a bigger share of an organization's finite resources. Such conflicts may be resolved as much by the relative distribution of power between subunits as by a rational evaluation of relative need. Similarly, individual managers often engage in contests with each other over what the correct policy decisions are. Power struggles and coalition building are major consequences of such conflicts and clearly play a part in the strategic management process. Strategic change tends to bring such power struggles to the fore, since by definition change entails altering the established distribution of power within an organization. In Chapter 11, we analyze the sources of organizational power and conflict and consider how organizational politics influences the strategic management process and can inhibit strategic change. In addition, we examine how an organization can manage conflicts to better fulfill its strategic mission and implement change.

Feedback

Finally, it is important to note that the strategic management process is an on-going affair. Once a strategy is implemented, its execution must be monitored to determine the extent to which strategic objectives are actually being achieved. This information passes back to the corporate level through feedback loops. Here it is fed into the next round of strategy formulation and implementation. It serves either to reaffirm existing corporate goals and strategies or to suggest changes. For example, when put into practice, a strategic objective may prove to have been too optimistic, and so the next time more conservative objectives will be set. Alternatively, feedback may reveal that strategic objectives were attainable but that implementation was poor, in which case the next round in the strategic management process may concentrate more on implementation. As it is an aspect of organizational control, feedback is considered in detail in Chapter 9.

1.5 STRATEGIC MANAGERS

To develop strategies to compete in the complex and ever-changing environment of today's world, the organization must have somebody who is responsible for managing this process. The task normally falls on the shoulders of **strategic managers.** Strategic managers are individuals who bear responsibility for the overall performance of the organization or for one of its major self-contained divisions. Their overriding concern is for the health of the *total* organization under their direction. (Many textbooks refer to such individuals as general managers). Strategic managers are distinct from **functional managers** within an organization. Functional managers bear responsibility for specific business functions, such as personnel, purchasing, production, sales, customer service, accounts, and so on. Thus their sphere of authority is generally confined to one organizational activity, whereas strategic managers oversee the operation of the whole organization. This puts strategic managers in the unique position of being able to direct the total organization in a strategic sense.

Edward Wrapp of the University of Chicago has written extensively about the characteristics of successful strategic managers.[10] In Wrapp's view, five skills are especially significant. They are summarized in Table 1.1. First, successful strategic managers keep themselves *well informed* about a wide range of operating decisions being made at different levels in the organization. They develop a network of information sources in many different parts of the organization, which enables them to remain in touch with operating realities. Second, successful strategic managers know how best to *allocate their time and energy* among different issues, decisions, or problems. They know when to delegate and when to become involved in a particular decision. Third, successful strategic managers

TABLE 1.1   **Major characteristics of successful strategic managers**

Successful strategic managers are

1. Well informed
2. Skilled at allocating their time and energy
3. Good politicians (consensus builders)
4. Experts at being imprecise
5. Able to push through programs in a piecemeal fashion

---

are *good politicians*. They play the power game with skill, preferring to build consensus for their ideas, rather than using their authority to force them through. They act as members or leaders of a coalition rather than as dictators.

Fourth, successful strategic managers are able to satisfy the organization that it has a sense of direction without actually committing themselves *publicly* to precise objectives or strategies. In other words, they are experts at *being imprecise*. At first glance this may seem curious, since so much of the received wisdom in the management literature suggests that part of the job of strategic managers is to set precise objectives and formulate detailed strategies. However, in a world where the only constant is change, there is value in being imprecise. Strategic managers would be foolish to commit themselves to a *precise* objective, given the constant state of environmental flux. Deliberate imprecision can often give both the organization and the manager room for maneuver and an enhanced ability to adapt to environmental change. This does not mean that the organization should operate without objectives but rather that the objectives should be *open ended*. Thus a strategic manager might commit the organization to becoming number one in its industry, without specifying a precise timetable for reaching this goal.

Similarly, successful strategic managers often hesitate to commit themselves *publicly* to detailed strategic plans, since in all probability the emergence of unexpected contingencies will require adaptation. Thus a successful strategic manager might commit the organization to diversification, without stating precisely how or when this will be achieved. It is also important to note that *privately* successful strategic managers often have precise objectives and strategies that they would like to see the organization pursue. However, they recognize the futility of public commitment, given the likelihood of change and the difficulties of implementation.

The fifth skill that Wrapp claims successful strategic managers possess is the *ability to push through programs in a piecemeal fashion*. Successful strategic managers recognize the futility of trying to push total packages or strategic programs through the organization, since significant objections to at least parts of such programs are likely to arise. Instead, the successful strategic manager is willing to take less than total acceptance in order to achieve modest progress toward a goal. The successful strategic manager tries to push through his or her ideas in a piecemeal fashion, so that they appear as incidentals to others, though in fact they are part of a larger program or hidden agenda that moves the organization in the direction of his or her objectives.

Wrapp thus presents a very different picture of the successful strategic manager than the rational decision maker depicted in much of the strategic management literature. In his view, successful strategic managers are skilled organizational politicians who can build coalitions that get their programs pushed through with a minimum of friction. Furthermore, successful strategic managers recognize the futility of commitment to a precise course of action in a world of constant change. Rather, they keep their options open.

1.6 LEVELS OF STRATEGIC MANAGEMENT

Within the multibusiness company, strategic managers are found not just at the apex of the organization, but also at different levels within its hierarchy. Essentially, the typical multibusiness company has three main levels of management: the corporate level, the business level, and the functional level (see Figure 1.4). Strategic managers are found at the first two of these levels but their roles differ depending on their sphere of responsibility. In addition, functional managers too, have a strategic role, though of a different kind. We now look at each of the three levels and the strategic roles assigned to managers within them.

Corporate Level

The corporate level of management consists of the chief executive officer (CEO), other senior executives, the board of directors, and corporate staff. These individuals occupy the apex of decision making within the organization. The CEO is the main strategic manager at this level. His or her strategic role is to *oversee* the development of strategies for the total organization. Typically, this involves defining its mission and goals, determining what businesses it should be in, allocating resources between the different business areas, and formulating and implementing strategies that span individual businesses.

For example, consider Fortune 500 company Owens-Illinois, Inc. Owens-Illinois is a multibusiness enterprise that in 1986 generated 26 percent of its sales from glass containers, 18 percent from forest products, 29 percent from other packaging products, 18 percent from health-care operations, and 6 percent from financial services. The main strategic responsibilities of its CEO, Robert Lanigan, include allocating resources among these different business areas, deciding whether the firm should divest itself of any of the business, and determining whether it should acquire any new business. In other words, it is up to him to

FIGURE 1.4 **Levels of strategic management**

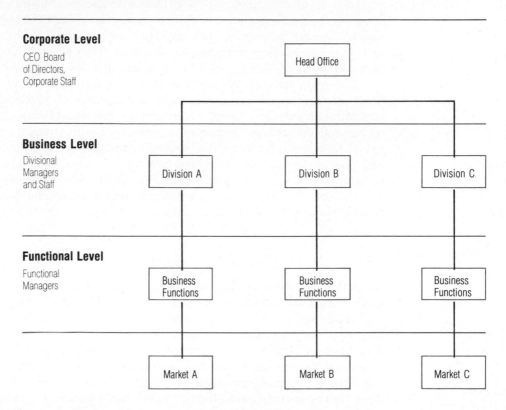

develop strategies that span individual businesses. It is not his specific responsibility, however, to develop strategies for competing in the individual business areas, such as health care. That is the responsibility of business-level strategic managers.

Besides overseeing resource allocation and managing the divestment and acquisition process, corporate-level strategic managers also provide the link between the people who oversee the strategic development of the firm (strategic managers) and those who own it (stockholders). Corporate-level strategic managers, and particularly the CEO, can be viewed as the guardians of stockholder welfare. It is their responsibility to ensure that corporate strategies pursued by the company are consistent with maximizing stockholder wealth. If they are not, then ultimately the CEO is likely to be called to account by the stockholders.

Business Level

In the multibusiness company, the business level consists of the heads of individual business units within the organization and their support staff. In the single-industry company, the business and corporate level are the same. A business unit is an organizational entity that operates in a distinct business area. Typically, it is self-contained, with its own functional departments (e.g., its own finance, buying, production, and marketing departments). Within most companies, business units are referred to as divisions. Thus General Electric has more than 240 divisions, one for each business area that the company is active in.

The main strategic managers at this level are the heads of the divisions. Their strategic role is to translate general statements of direction and intent at the corporate level into concrete strategies for individual businesses. Thus while corporate-level strategic managers are concerned with strategies that span individual businesses, business-level strategic managers are concerned with strategies that are specific to a particular business. At Owens-Illinois, for example, the corporate level might commit itself to supporting expansion in the health care business. It is then up to the strategic managers heading the health care operation to work out the details of an expansion strategy for the health care business.

Functional Level

By definition, there are no strategic managers to be found at the functional level. Functional managers bear responsibility for specific business functions, such as personnel, purchasing, production, marketing, customer service, and accounts. They are not in a position to look at the big picture. Nevertheless, they have an important strategic role, for it is their responsibility to develop functional strategies in production, marketing, purchasing, and so on that help fulfill the strategic objectives set by business- and corporate-level general managers. In the case of Owens-Illinois' health care business, for example, it would be the responsibility of marketing managers to develop marketing strategies consistent with the business-level expansion strategy. An even greater responsibility for managers at this level involves strategy implementation — the execution of corporate- and business-level decisions.

1.7 THE FLOW OF STRATEGIC INFORMATION

Goal setting, strategy formulation, and strategy implementation involve personnel at all levels within the organization. Communication among personnel at different levels is necessary to ensure that corporate-, business-, and functional-level strategies are *attainable* and *consistent* with each other and with corporate goals and objectives.

For example, strategic managers at the business level cannot hope to formulate realistic business-level strategies unless they receive input from functional-level managers concerning the strengths and weaknesses of each functional area. Without such input, business level managers might decide on a strategy that the

FIGURE 1.5   **The flow of information**

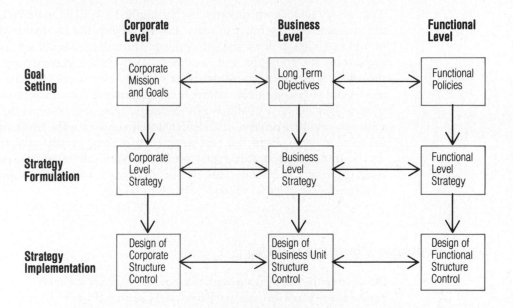

company does not have the functional resources to pursue. Similarly, corporate-level strategic managers cannot hope to formulate realistic corporate-level strategies unless they receive input from business-level managers about the strengths and weaknesses of each business unit, as well as the market opportunities and threats that each unit faces. Strategic managers also have to make certain that the strategies being pursued by different levels of the organization are consistent with overall corporate goals. This necessitates further communication among managers at the different levels.

To ensure that strategies being pursued at each level are consistent and attainable, most organizations go to some length to establish the necessary information flow among their different levels. Figure 1.5 illustrates how this process works, at least in theory. On the top axis are the levels of corporate, divisional, and functional management. On the vertical axis are the three key strategic management tasks of setting goals and mission, strategy formulation, and strategy implementation. In the boxes are the various components of the strategic management process just discussed. The arrows in the figure represent the way that information flows up and down the organization from level to level and from each part of the strategic management process to the next. Thus, looking laterally, we see how the setting of corporate goals provides the context for the development of business- and functional-level objectives and vice versa. Looking vertically, we see how for each level the goal-setting process provides the context for strategy formulation and implementation so that a fit can be achieved in this direction as well.

1.8 THE QUALITY OF STRATEGIC DECISION MAKING

The last three sections described what might be considered a rational model of the strategic management process. In this model, the company goes through a number of well-defined steps in order to formulate *intended* strategies that align organizational strengths and weakness with environmental opportunities and threats. It is pertinent to ask whether such systems work. Do they help companies establish a sustainable competitive advantage? The answer to this question would seem to be a qualified yes. Strategic planning systems do work, but as with any rational process, their efficiency is subject to the limitations of human decision makers. Even the best-designed planning system will fail to produce the desired results if corporate decision makers fail to use the information at their disposal effectively. This section examines ways of guarding against the adverse effects of poor strategic decision making.

Does Strategic Planning Work?

Do companies that go through the kind of process outlined above actually generate superior performance relative to those that do not? Clearly, we would expect planning to have some positive effects; empirical evidence does indeed suggest that *on the average* companies that plan outperform those that do not. Of fourteen studies reviewed in a recent survey by Lawrence C. Rhyne of Northwestern University, eight found varying degrees of support for the hypothesis that strategic planning improves company performance, five found no support for the hypothesis, and one study reported a negative relationship between planning and performance.[11] Moreover, an empirical study by Rhyne, reported in the same article, concluded that "firms with strategic planning systems more closely resembling strategic management theory were found to exhibit superior long-term financial performance both relative to their industry and in absolute terms."[12]

In recent years, however, the use of formal planning systems has been increasingly questioned. Thomas J. Peters and Robert H. Waterman, the best-selling authors of *In Search of Excellence,*[13] are among those who have raised doubts about the usefulness of formal planning systems. Similarly, Henry Mintzberg's revision of the concept of strategy suggests that *emergent* strategies may be just as successful as the *intended* strategies that are the outcome of a formal planning process. Moreover, it is true that business history is filled with examples of companies that have made poor decisions on the basis of a supposedly comprehensive strategic planning process.[14] An interesting example of this phenomenon concerns the 1979 acquisition of Howard Johnson Co. by Britain's Imperial Group.[15]

The Case of Imperial and Howard Johnson

Imperial is the third largest tobacco company in the world after British American Tobaccos and Philip Morris Companies, Inc. In the 1970s it began a diversification program designed to reduce its dependence on the declining tobacco market. Part of this program included a plan to acquire a major U.S. company. Imperial spent two years scanning the United States for a suitable acquisition opportunity. It was looking for an enterprise in a high-growth industry that had a high market share, a good track record, and good future growth prospects and that could be acquired at a reasonable price. Imperial scanned more than 30 industries and 200 different companies before deciding on Howard Johnson.

When Imperial announced its plans to buy Howard Johnson for close to $500 million in 1979, the company's shareholders threatened rebellion. They were quick to point out that at $26 per share Imperial was paying double what the company was worth only six months previously, when share prices stood at $13. The acquisition hardly seemed to be at a reasonable price. Moreover, the motel industry was entering a low- rather than high-growth phase, and future growth prospects were poor. Besides, Howard Johnson did not have a good track record. Imperial ignored shareholder protests and bought the lodging chain. Five years later, after persistent losses, Imperial was trying to divest itself of Howard Johnson. The acquisition had been a complete failure.

What went wrong? Why, after a two-year planning exercise, did Imperial buy a company that so patently did not fit its own criteria? The answer would seem to lie not in the planning process itself but in the quality of strategic decision making. Imperial bought Howard Johnson in spite of its planning process, not because of it. What happened at Imperial was that the CEO decided independently that Howard Johnson was a good buy. A rather authoritarian figure, the CEO surrounded himself with subordinates who agreed with him. Once he had made his choice, his advisers concurred with his judgment and shared in developing rationalizations for the choice. No one questioned the decision itself, even though information was available to show that it was flawed. Instead, strategic planning was used to justify a decision that in practice did not conform with strategic objectives.

Groupthink

The Imperial example is a case of what has been referred to by social psychologist Irving L. Janis as groupthink.[16] This occurs when a group of decision makers embarks on a course of action without questioning underlying assumptions. Typically, a group coalesces around a person or policy. It ignores or filters out information that can be used to question the policy and develops after-the-fact rationalizations for its decision. Thus commitment is based on an emotional, rather than an objective, assessment of what is the correct course of action. The consequences can be poor decisions.

This phenomenon probably explains, at least in part, why, in spite of sophisticated strategic management processes, companies often make poor strategic decisions. Janis traced many historical fiascoes to defective policy making by government leaders who received social support from their in-group of advisers. In a series of case studies, he suggested that the following three groups of policy advisers, like the group surrounding Imperial's CEO, were dominated by concurrence seeking or groupthink and collectively avoided information that challenged their assumptions.[17]

1. President Harry Truman's advisory group, whose members supported the decision to escalate the war in North Korea despite firm warnings by the Chinese Communist government that U.S. entry into North Korea would be met with armed resistance from the Chinese

2. President John Kennedy's inner circle, whose members supported the decision to launch the Bay of Pigs invasion of Cuba, even though available information showed that it would be an unsuccessful venture and would damage U.S. relations with other countries

3. President Lyndon Johnson's close advisers, who supported the decision to escalate the war in Vietnam despite intelligence reports and other information indicating that this action would not defeat the Vietcong or the North Vietnamese and would entail unfavorable political consequences within the United States

Janis observed that all these groupthink-dominated groups were characterized by strong pressures toward uniformity, which inclined their members to avoid raising controversial issues, questioning weak arguments, or calling a halt to softheaded thinking.

The groupthink phenomenon raises the problem of how to bring critical information to bear on the decision mechanism so that strategic decisions made by the company are realistic and based on thorough evaluation. Two techniques that counteract groupthink are devil's advocacy and dialectic inquiry.

Devil's Advocacy and Dialectic Inquiry

The traditional approach to strategic decision making might be called the expert approach.[18] The expert approach involves a recommended course of action based on a set of assumptions. The generation of a single plan by a knowledgeable planner or a planning committee, the members of which share common assumptions, would be an example of the expert approach. The problem with the expert approach is that it is vulnerable to the groupthink phenomenon. In addition, the assumptions are critical. If they are incorrect, then the approach is likely to generate poor decisions.

Devil's advocacy and dialectic inquiry have been proposed as two means of guarding against the weaknesses of the expert approach.[19] Devil's advocacy involves the generation of both a plan and a critical analysis of the plan. The idea is that one member of the decision-making group should act as the devil's advocate, bringing out all the reasons that might make the proposal unacceptable. In this way, decision makers can be made aware of the possible perils of recommended courses of action.

Dialectic inquiry is more complex, for it involves the generation of a plan (a thesis) and counterplan (an antithesis). According to R. O. Mason, one of the early proponents of this method in strategic management, the plan and the counterplan should reflect plausible but conflicting courses of action.[20] Corporate decision makers should consider a debate between advocates of the plan and counterplan. The purpose of the debate would be to reveal problems with definitions, recommended courses of action, and assumptions. As a result, corporate decision makers and planners would be able to form a new and more encompassing conceptualization of the problem, which would become the final plan (a synthesis).

Each of the three decision-making processes is illustrated in Figure 1.6. Logic suggests that both devil's advocacy and dialectical inquiry are likely to produce better-quality decisions than the traditional expert approach. If either of

FIGURE 1.6   **Three decision-making processes**

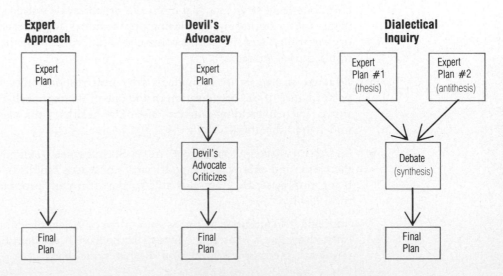

these processes had been used in the Imperial case, then it is likely that a different (and probably better) decision would have been taken. However, there is considerable dispute over which of the two nontraditional methods is better.[21] Researchers have come to conflicting conclusions, and it seems safe to say that the jury is still out on this issue. From a practical point of view, it should be observed that devil's advocacy is probably the easier method to implement, as it involves less commitment in terms of time.

1.9 SUMMARY OF CHAPTER

This chapter has provided a broad overview of the strategic management process. In discussing both the scope of the strategic management process and its complexity, we have made the following major points:

1. The techniques of strategic management are applicable to a wide range of organizations, from large, multibusiness organizations to small, one-man businesses, from manufacturing to service organizations, and from profit-seeking to not-for-profit organizations.

2. Traditional definitions of strategy stress that an organization's strategy is the outcome of a rational *planning* process.

3. Mintzberg's revision of the concept of strategy suggests that, in addition to planned *intentions,* strategy can also *emerge* from within the organization in the absence of any prior intentions.

4. The major components of the strategic management process include defining the mission and major goals of the organization; analyzing the external and internal environments of the organization; choosing business and/or corporate level strategies that align the organization's strengths and weaknesses with external environmental opportunities and threats; and adopting organizational structures and control systems to implement the organization's chosen strategy.

5. Strategic managers are individuals who bear responsibility for the overall performance of the organization or for one of its major self-contained divisions. Their overriding concern is for the health of the *total* organization under their direction.

6. Successful strategic managers are well informed, skilled at allocating their time and energy, good politicians (consensus builders), and experts at being imprecise; they are also able to push through programs in a piecemeal fashion.

7. Strategic management, as a process, embraces the whole company. Specifically, three levels of strategic management have been identified: the corporate level, the business level, and the functional level.

8. The strategic management process involves communication among individuals at different levels of the organization to ensure that the strategies being pursued are attainable and consistent.

9. In spite of systematic planning, companies may adopt poor strategies if their decision-making processes do not question underlying assumptions and guard against the dangers of groupthink.

10. Techniques for enhancing the effectiveness of the strategic decision-making process include devil's advocacy and dialectic inquiry.

Discussion Questions

1. What do we mean by strategy?

2. What are the strengths of a formal strategic planning process? What are its weaknesses?

3. Evaluate the 1987 Iran-Contra affair from a strategic decision-making perspective? Do you think different decisions would have been made if the administration had used a dialectic inquiry or devil's advocacy approach when making strategic decisions? Was the sale of arms to Iran the result of an intended or an emergent strategy?

Endnotes

1. James Norman and John Byrne, "Nice Going Frank, But Will it Fly?" *Business Week,* September 29, 1986, pp. 34–35. Chuck Hawkins and Aaron Bernstein, "Frank Lorenzo, High Flier," *Business Week,* March 10, 1986, pp. 104–112. Gregg Easterbrook, "Lorenzo Braves the Air-wars," *New York Times Magazine,* November 29, 1987, pp. 17–20, 62, 64, 68, 70. Kenneth Labich, "Winners in the Air Wars," *Fortune,* May 11, 1987, pp. 68–79.

2. Alfred Chandler, *Strategy and Structure: Chapters in the History of the American Enterprise* (Cambridge, Mass.: MIT Press, 1962)

3. James B. Quinn, *Strategies for Change: Logical Incrementalism* (Richard D. Irwin, 1980).

4. William F. Glueck, *Business Policy and Strategic Management* (New York: McGraw-Hill, 1980).

5. Henry Mintzberg, "Patterns in Strategy Formulation," *Management Science,* 24, (1978), 934–948.

6. Ibid.

7. Richard T. Pascale, "Perspectives on Strategy: The Real Story Behind Honda's Success," *California Management Review,* 26 (1984), 47–72.

8. The conventional explanation was championed by the Boston Consulting Group. See BCG, *Strategy Alternatives for the British Motorcycle Industry* (London: Her Majesty's Stationary Office, 1979).

9. K. R. Andrews, *The Concept of Corporate Strategy* (Homewood, Ill.: Dow Jones Irwin, 1971). H. I. Ansoff, *Corporate Strategy* (New York: McGraw-Hill, 1965). C. W. Hofer and D. Schendel, *Strategy Formulation: Analytical Concepts* (St. Paul, Minn.: West, 1978).

10. Edward Wrapp, "Good Managers Don't Make Policy Decisions," *Harvard Business Review* (September–October 1967).

11. For a summary of fourteen major studies up to 1985, see Lawrence C. Rhyne, "The Relationship of Strategic Planning to Financial Performance," *Strategic Management Journal,* 7 (1986), 423–436.

12. Lawrence C. Rhyne, "The Relationship of Strategic Planning to Financial Performance," *Strategic Management Journal,* 7 (1963), 432.

13. Thomas J. Peters and Robert H. Waterman, *In Search of Excellence* (New York: Harper & Row, 1982).

14. For some examples, see S. Tilles, "How to Evaluate Corporate Strategy," *Harvard Business Review,* 41 (1963), 111–121.

15. The story ran on an almost daily basis in the *Financial Times* of London during the autumn of 1979.

16. Irving L. Janis, *Victims of Groupthink,* 2nd ed. (Boston: Houghton Mifflin, 1982).

17. All these cases are discussed in detail in Janis, *Victims of Groupthink.* Further implications of the phenomenon are examined in I. L. Janis and L. Mann, *Decision Making* (New York: Free Press, 1977).

18. R. O. Mason, "A Dialectic Approach to Strategic Planning," *Management Science,* 13 (1969), 403–414.

19. R. A. Cosier and J. C. Aplin, "A Critical View of Dialectic Inquiry in Strategic Planning," *Strategic Management Journal,* 1 (1980), 343–356. I. I. Mintroff and R. O. Mason, "Structuring Ill-Structured Policy Issues: Further Explorations in a Methodology for Messy Problems," *Strategic Management Journal,* 1 (1980), 331–342.

20. Mason, "A Dialectic Approach to Strategic Planning," pp. 403–414.

21. D. M. Schweiger and P. A. Finger, "The Comparative Effectiveness of Dialectic Inquiry and Devil's Advocacy," *Strategic Management Journal,* 5 (1984), 335–350.

Chapter 2

CORPORATE MISSION, GOALS, AND STAKEHOLDERS

2.1 OPENING INCIDENT: DIAMOND SHAMROCK

In 1976 Diamond Shamrock Corp. was a profitable chemical company with a modest oil operation and a solid future. The company earned a record $140 million on sales of $1.4 billion, while its stock ended the year near its all-time high, at $34 a share. Ten years later Diamond Shamrock had become a debt-ridden energy conglomerate with large and persistent losses whose stock traded at only $14 a share. Earnings, which had been $4 per share in 1976, were transformed into a $2-per-share loss. While Wall Street was enjoying boom years, with even troubled oil stocks appreciating 125 percent over the ten-year period, Diamond Shamrock's stockholders saw the value of their holdings decline by 60 percent.

Diamond Shamrock's CEO, Bill Bricker, had attempted to turn the company from a chemical enterprise into a big-league energy company. By the time he was done, Diamond Shamrock had all the trappings of the status he aspired to: a lavish 12,000-acre ranch in Texas, a $1-million box at the Dallas Cowboy's home stadium, and a fleet of airplanes to whisk him and his directors around the world. Unfortunately, Diamond Shamrock had none of the profits of a big-league energy company.

The strategy Diamond Shamrock had pursued under Bricker's leadership had been erratic. In 1978 Diamond Shamrock sold its gasoline service stations to Sigmor Corporation. In 1983 Diamond Shamrock bought Sigmor for $162 million. Then in 1986, as part of a restructuring plan, Diamond Shamrock proposed to spin off Sigmor's refineries and service stations from the rest of the company.

Diamond Shamrock also took unusual risks for a company of its size. In 1983, when the combination of a recession and lower energy prices was beginning to hit hard, the company spent $160 million to buy drilling rights in Alaska's Beaufort Sea. The next year, in spite of stockholder opposition, Diamond Shamrock bought Natomas Company, a struggling oil company, for $1.5 billion. The drilling rights in Alaska produced nothing but a dry hole and write-offs of $200 million. It also quickly became apparent that Diamond Shamrock had paid too much for Natomas, probably twice as much as the company was actually worth, and in 1985 Diamond Shamrock was forced to write down the value of Natomas properties by $600 million. As a consequence, Diamond Shamrock's losses for 1985 totaled $605 million; stock prices plunged to $14 a share

Falling stock prices encourage takeover bids. In 1985 Occidental Petroleum Corp. made a $28-per-share bid for the company. With Diamond Shamrock's shares trading at $17 each, the deal looked good for stockholders, but Diamond Shamrock's board rejected the offer and Occidental withdrew. Then corporate raider T. Boone Pickens Jr. launched the first of two takeover attempts. Diamond Shamrock successfully fought off Pickens' bids, but at a price. Its CEO, Bricker, was forced to resign, and major shareholder Prudential Insurance Company of America was given three seats on the board in return for helping to fend off Pickens. With heavy investment in Diamond Shamrock and board representation, Prudential now seems set to bring about a much-needed change in the status quo, through dramatic cuts in top management perks and strategic retrenchment. In short, stockholder pressure has forced Diamond Shamrock to jettison its CEO and adopt strategies more consistent with maximizing stockholder wealth.[1]

2.2 OVERVIEW

Clearly, Diamond Shamrock failed to satisfy the interests of one of its major constituencies, or stakeholders: its stockholders. Most companies see their primary goal as maximizing stockholder wealth. After all, stockholders are a company's legal owners. Essentially, Diamond Shamrock pursued strategies inconsistent with maximizing stockholder wealth. In order to avoid the kind of problems that Diamond Shamrock has had to face, companies can and should identify and incorporate the claims of various stakeholder groups into the strategic decision-making process. This chapter is concerned with identifying how this can be done.

The formulation of the corporate mission statement is the first key indicator of how an organization views the claims of its stakeholders. The mission statement defines the business of the organization and states basic goals, characteristics, and guiding philosophies. Its purpose is to set the organizational context within which strategic decisions will be made — in other words, to give the organization strategic focus and direction. All strategic decisions flow from the mission statement. In examining how organizations formulate such statements, we will concentrate on the three main components that strategy writers have recommended for inclusion in a corporate mission statement:

TABLE 2.1   NCR's corporate mission statement

NCR's mission: create value for our stakeholders

NCR is a successful, growing company dedicated to achieving superior results by assuring that its actions are aligned with stakeholder expectations. Stakeholders are all constituencies with a stake in the fortunes of the company. NCR's primary mission is to create value for our stakeholders.

- ■ We believe in conducting our business activities with integrity and respect while building mutually beneficial and enduring relationships with all of our stakeholders.
- ■ We take customer satisfaction personally: we are committed to providing superior value in our products and services on a continuing basis.
- ■ We respect the individuality of each employee and foster an environment in which employees' creativity and productivity are encouraged, recognized, valued and rewarded.
- ■ We think of our suppliers as partners who share our goal of achieving the highest quality standards and the most consistent level of service.
- ■ We are committed to being caring and supportive corporate citizens within the world-wide communities in which we operate.
- ■ We are dedicated to creating value for our shareholders and financial communities by performing in a manner that will enhance returns on investments.

Source: Courtesy of National Cash Register Corporation.

1. A definition of the organization's business
2. A statement of major corporate goals
3. A statement of corporate philosophy[2]

An example of what a mission statement actually looks like appears in Table 2.1, which shows the mission statement of NCR Corporation. The six points set out major corporate commitments with respect to the following stakeholder groups: customers, stockholders, employees, suppliers, and the community.

After examining how to construct a mission statement, we consider the company's various **stakeholders,** whose interests must be taken into account when formulating a mission statement (see Figure 2.1). Stakeholders are individuals or groups, either within or outside the organization, that have some claim on it. Then we look closely at two particularly important stakeholder groups, **stockholders** and **the general public,** analyzing how stockholders can and do influence the corporate mission, and hence corporate strategies, and considering the issue of **corporate social responsibility.**

FIGURE 2.1   **The relationship between the mission, stakeholders, and strategies**

Source: Reprinted from "The Company Mission as a Strategic Tool," by John Pearce III, *Sloan Management Review*, Spring 1982, page 22, by permission of the publisher. Copyright © 1982 by the Sloan Management Review Association. All rights reserved.

2.3 DEFINING THE BUSINESS

The first component of the mission statement is a clear definition of the organization's business. Essentially, defining the business involves answering the questions "What is our business? What will it be? What should it be?"[3] The answers to these questions vary depending on whether the organization is a single-business or a diversified enterprise. A single-business enterprise is active in just one main business area. For example, U.S. Steel in the 1950s was involved just in the production of steel; it was a single-business enterprise. By the 1980s, however, U.S. Steel had become USX, a diversified company, with interests in steel, oil and gas, chemicals, real estate, transportation, and the production of energy equipment. For USX, the process of defining itself is complicated by the fact that to a large extent the concern of a multibusiness enterprise such as USX is *managing businesses*. Thus the business definition of USX involves different issues than did that of U.S. Steel. In this section, the problem of how to define the business of a single-business company is considered first. The problem of how best to define the business of a diversified enterprise follows.

The Single-Business Company

To answer the question "What is our business?" Derek F. Abell has suggested that a company should define its business in terms of three dimensions: (1) who

FIGURE 2.2   **Abell's framework**

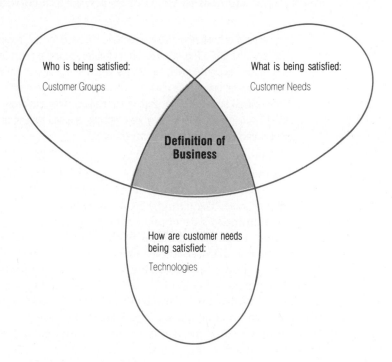

is being satisfied (what customer groups); (2) what is being satisfied (what customer needs); and (3) how are customer needs being satisfied (by what technologies).[4] Figure 2.2 illustrates these three dimensions.

Abell's approach stresses the need for a *consumer-oriented* rather than *product-oriented* business definition. A product-oriented business definition focuses just on the products sold and the markets served. Abell maintains that such an approach obscures the company's function, which is to satisfy consumer needs. A product is only the physical manifestation of applying a particular technology to satisfy a particular need for a particular consumer group. In practice, there are often different ways (technologies) of serving a particular need for a particular consumer group. Identifying these ways through a broad consumer-oriented business definition can safeguard companies from being caught unawares by major shifts in demand. Indeed, by helping anticipate future demand shifts, Abell's framework can assist companies in capitalizing on the changes in their environment. It can help answer the question "What will our business be?"

Unfortunately, the need to take a customer-oriented view of a company's business has often been ignored. Consequently, history is littered with the wreckage of once-great corporations that failed to define their business or that defined it incorrectly. These firms failed to see what their business would become and ultimately declined. Theodore Levitt described the fall of the once-mighty U.S. railroads in terms of their failure to correctly define their business:

> The railroads did not stop growing because the need for passenger and freight transportation declined. That grew. The railroads are in trouble today not because the need was filled by others (cars, trucks, airplanes, even telephones), but because it was *not* filled by the railroads themselves. They let others take customers away from them because they assumed themselves to be in the railroad business rather than in the transportation business. The reason they defined their industry wrong was because they were railroad oriented instead of transport oriented; they were product oriented instead of customer oriented.[5]

Had the railroads used Abell's framework, they might have anticipated the impact of technological change and decided that their business was transportation. In that case, they might have transferred their early strength in rail into dominance in today's diversified transport industry. Sadly, most railroads stuck to a product-oriented definition of their business and went bankrupt.

In contrast, IBM correctly foresaw what its business would be. Originally, IBM was a leader in the manufacture of typewriters and mechanical tabulating equipment using punch card technology. However, IBM viewed itself as providing a means for information processing and storage, rather than as a supplier of mechanical tabulating equipment and typewriters. Given this definition, the company's subsequent moves into computers, software systems, office systems, and copiers seem logical.

The question "What should our business be?" can also be answered using Abell's framework. Recall that IBM decided that its business should be computers, word processors, and office systems — all natural extensions of its original business. Other companies do not see as much promise in their original business, perhaps because of negative and irreversible changes in consumer needs and technologies or for other reasons. These companies decide to switch to something different, and they diversify away from their original business. In the 1960s many companies reduced their dependence on their original business by moving into unrelated areas. Conglomerates such as ITT Corporation, Gulf & Western Industries, Inc., and Textron, Inc. are a result of this diversification movement.[6]

Table 2.2 details how a number of companies define their business. Perhaps the best example of a consumer-oriented business definition in the table is that of Zale Corporation. Given this definition, it is not surprising that Zale is one of the most successful national jewelry retailers. Yet until 1980 Zale was primarily product oriented, and that outlook endangered the company's health. According to Zale's current chairman, Donald Zale,

> the first, foremost and primary change has been to acquire a consumer orientation. The company makes about half the jewelry it sells. In the past manufacturing operations largely decided what products to make. For a decade manufacturing ground out what were called mother's

TABLE 2.2   **Examples of business definitions**

Bethlehem Steel Corp.: Bethlehem is a large integrated steel producer which makes and sells a wide variety of steel mill and manufactured steel products. Bethlehem is also engaged in the production and sales of coal and other raw materials . . . in the construction and servicing of mobile offshore drilling rigs and ships . . . in the manufacture of railroad cars and parts . . . in the sale of equipment and supplies to the oil and gas industries . . . and in the manufacture of home building products and custom-molded plastic products. Bethlehem also sells technology domestically and internationally.

Litton Industries, Inc.: Litton is a technology-based company applying advanced electronics products and services to business opportunities in defense, industrial automation and geophysical markets. Research and product engineering emphasis is on developing advanced products which the company manufacturers and supplies worldwide to commerical, industrial and government customers.

Polaroid Corp. (late 1970s definition): Polaroid manufactures and sells photographic products based on inventions of the company in the field of one-step instant photography and light polarizing products, utilizing the company's inventions in the field of polarized light. The company considers itself to be engaged in one line of business.

Polaroid Corp. (mid-1980s definition): Polaroid designs, manufactures and markets worldwide a variety of products based on its inventions, primarily in the photographic field. These include instant photographic cameras and films, light polarizing filters and lenses, and diversified chemical, optical and commercial products. The principal products of the company are used in amateur and professional photography, industry, science, medicine and education.

Zale Corporation: Zale's business is speciality retailing. Retailing is a people-oriented business. The corporation's business existence and continued success are dependent upon how well it meets its responsibilities to serve critically important groups of people.

Source: Adapted from company annual reports.

rings — rings set with children's birthstones. Zale wasn't watching the market. The business died and the company was left with a worthless inventory. This forced us to rethink our business definition.[7]

Like Zale's early definition, Polaroid's business definition until the 1980s was much more product oriented, stressing the company's involvement in one-step instant photography. This myopic definition has not served Polaroid well. The development of quick-turnaround photo developing and high-quality, low-cost 35mm cameras, a product that Polaroid's founder, Edwin Land, once rejected, has taken away much of Polaroid's market. At the height of its popularity in 1978, more than eight million instant cameras were sold in the United States. Four years later the figure was closer to five million. Polaroid's net earning declined from nearly $120 million in 1978 to $23.5 million in 1982. Its problem was defining its business as one-step instant photography rather than as the recording of images and memories. In other words, its business definition was guided by the products it manufactured rather than by the needs it served. Somewhat belatedly, Polaroid realized its mistake, changed its business definition, and attempted to broaden its product base — but only with limited success.

Part of the reason for its difficulty in producing a turnaround is that its current business definition is still primarily product oriented. Polaroid still defines its business in terms of the products it manufactures and sells, rather than the customer needs it is seeking to satisfy.[8]

The Diversified Company

The diversified company faces special problems when trying to define its business because it actually operates several businesses. In essence, the corporate business is often one of managing a collection of businesses. For example, USX, formerly U.S. Steel, is still known primarily for its steel interests. A consumer-oriented definition of USX's steel interests might be something like this: "USX seeks to satisfy customers' needs for a high-strength construction and fabricating material." However, USX is, in fact, a diversified company, which in 1986 generated only 33 percent of its revenues from steel. The rest came from oil and gas, chemicals, real estate, transportation, and energy equipment. Clearly, the consumer-oriented definition given above only applies to the company's steel operations. It would not suffice as a definition of its *corporate* businesses.

Thus, in a diversified enterprise, the question "What is our business?" must be asked at two levels: the business level and the corporate level. At the business level, such as USX's steel operations, the focus should be on a consumer-oriented definition. But at the corporate level, one cannot simply aggregate the various business definitions, for that will lead to an unfocused and confusing statement. Instead, the corporate business definition should be *portfolio oriented*. A **portfolio** refers to a company's collection of businesses. A portfolio-oriented definition should include the following:

1. The purpose of the company's portfolio of businesses
2. The desired scope (diversity) of the portfolio
3. The balance desired between different businesses in the portfolio

The purpose of a portfolio—the gains that a portfolio of businesses can bring a company—is discussed in more detail in Chapters 6 and 7. At this stage, it is enough to note that a company should define its corporate business so that its strategic objective is clear. For example, in building its portfolio of businesses, USX wanted to become less dependent on its ailing steel operations. Unless it has a clear objective, a company runs the risk of building a portfolio without identifying the underlying industrial or financial logic behind its actions—indeed, without knowing why it is building a portfolio. This criticism has been leveled at the early U.S. conglomerates. A number of commentators claim that these companies built diversified portfolios for no other reason than to be fashionable.[9]

For similar reasons, a portfolio-oriented definition must include the desired scope of the portfolio; otherwise the company risks pursuing portfolio diversifi-

FIGURE 2.3   Summary of factors important in business definitions

cation for its own sake. If no constraint is placed on scope, the company can diversify too widely. Finally, the company must consider the important issue of desired balance among the different businesses in its portfolio. It must decide whether it wants a balanced portfolio of activities, with each business making an equal contribution toward corporate earnings, or an unbalanced portfolio, where the constituent businesses vary considerably in size. Most companies prefer a balanced portfolio, perhaps because an unbalanced portfolio can result in top management focusing too much attention on large businesses at the expense of the smaller ones.

A summary of factors important in the definitions of both single-business and diversified companies is given in Figure 2.3.

2.4 SETTING CORPORATE GOALS

As we indicated at the start of this chapter, the first major component of the mission statement is a definition of the company's business and the second a statement of major corporate goals. Corporate goals set out formally what the organization is trying to achieve; they give direction to the corporate mission statement and help guide strategy formulation. For example, a major corporate goal of General Electric is to be first or second in every market in which it competes. Accordingly, General Electric's businesses typically seek market leadership rather than a secure market niche and therefore center their strategies on *how* to achieve market leadership. While profit-seeking organizations may operate with a variety of major corporate goals, in theory at least, all these goals should be directed toward one end: the maximization of stockholder wealth.

Maximizing Stockholder Wealth

Stockholders provide the company with capital and expect an appropriate return on their investment in exchange. Furthermore, a company's stockholders are its legal owners. Consequently, the overriding goal of most corporations is to maximize stockholder wealth, which involves increasing the long-run returns earned by stockholders from owning shares in the corporation. Stockholders receive returns in two ways: (1) from dividend payments, and (2) from capital appreciation in the market value of a share (that is, by increases in stock market prices).

The best way for a company to maximize stockholder wealth is to pursue strategies that maximize its own return on investment, **ROI,** which is a good general indicator of a company's efficiency. In short, the more efficient a company, the better its future prospects look to stockholders and the greater its ability to pay dividends. Furthermore, higher ROI leads to greater demand for a company's shares. Demand bids up the share price and leads to capital appreciation.

Secondary Goals

However, as management theorist Peter F. Drucker and many others have pointed out, there is danger in emphasizing only ROI.[10] An over-zealous pursuit of ROI can misdirect managerial attention and encourage some of the worst management practices, such as maximizing short-run rather than long-run ROI. A short-run orientation would favor such action as cutting expenditures judged to be non-essential in that span of time—for instance, research and development, marketing expenditures, and new capital investments. Decreasing current expenditure increases current ROI but the resulting underinvestment, lack of innovation, and poor market awareness jeopardize the long-run ROI. Yet despite these negative consequences, managers do make such decisions, because the adverse effects of a short-run orientation may not materialize and become apparent to stockholders for several years. By that time, the management team responsible may have moved on, leaving others to pick up the pieces.

In a major *Harvard Business Review* article, Robert H. Hayes and William J. Abernathy argue that the widespread focus on short-run ROI has been a major factor in the long-run loss of international competitiveness by U.S. companies.[11] MIT economist Lester Thurow likewise faults the short-run orientation of many American businesses for some of their problems and cites declining R&D expenditures and reduced innovative activity within American enterprises as evidence of this orientation.[12] The household products and drug company American Home Products Corp., which manufactures Advil, is a case in point.[13] American Home has a history of impressive financial performance, regularly recording a return of more than 30 percent on equity. Since 1983, however, American Home has been showing signs of fatigue. Pretax income, which grew at double-digit rates for a decade, increased at only 3 percent annually between 1984 and 1986.

The reason for such a decline in profit growth is the company's difficulty in coming up with new products. Its tight cost controls and focus on current profitability have stunted spending on research and development. For example, in

1983 spending on R&D at American Home was only 3 percent of sales, compared with a drug industry average of 6.1 percent.[14] Moreover, American Home expects a new product to show profit in a year and a half rather than in three years or more, which is the norm for most companies. Thus American Home illustrates the adverse effects of short-run profit maximization.

To guard against short-run behavior, in addition to ROI Drucker suggests that companies adopt a number of secondary goals. These goals should be designed to balance short-run and long-run considerations. Drucker's list includes secondary goals relating to the following areas: (1) market share, (2) innovation, (3) productivity, (4) physical and financial resources, (5) manager performance and development, (6) worker performance and attitude, and (7) social responsibility. Though such secondary goals need not be part of the mission statement, sometimes the most important ones are. Recall that General Electric stresses a market-share goal: that of being first or second in every business in which it competes. Given the strong positive relationship between market share and profitability, this goal is consistent with long-run profit maximization.[15]

Even if a company does not recognize secondary goals explicitly, it must recognize them implicitly through a commitment to long-run profitability. Take Hewlett-Packard, one of the companies cited in Thomas J. Peters and Richard H. Waterman's famous management study as being an "excellent" company.[16] The following quotation from Hewlett-Packard's mission statement clearly expresses the importance of an orientation toward maximizing long-run profitability and can serve as a model:

> In our economic system, the profit we generate from our operations is the ultimate source of the funds we need to prosper and grow. It is the one absolutely essential measure of our corporate peformance *over the long term.* Only if we continue to meet our profit objective can we achieve our other corporate objectives.[17]

2.5 CORPORATE PHILOSOPHY

The third component of the mission statement is a statement of corporate philosophy, reflecting the basic beliefs, values, aspirations, and philosophical priorities that the strategic decision makers are committed to, and that guide their management of the company. It tells how the company intends to do business and often reflects the company's recognition of its social responsibility. The issue of corporate social responsibility is discussed in a later section of this chapter.

Many companies establish a philosophical creed to emphasize their own distinctive outlook on business. Thus a company's creed forms the basis for establishing its corporate culture (an issue considered in Chapter 9). Take the creed of Lincoln Electric Company. It states that productivity increases should be shared primarily by customers and employees through lower prices and higher wages. This belief distinguishes Lincoln Electric from many other enterprises, and, by all accounts, is acted on by the company in terms of its specific strategies, objectives, and operating policies.[18]

2.6 CORPORATE STAKEHOLDERS

Stakeholders and the Mission Statement

As noted earlier, stakeholders are individuals or groups that have some claim on the company. Stakeholders can be divided into internal claimants and external claimants.[19] Internal claimants are stockholders or employees, including executive officers and board members. External claimants are all other individuals and groups affected by the company's actions. Typically, they comprise customers, suppliers, governments, unions, competitors, local communities, and the general public.

All stakeholders can justifiably expect that the company will attempt to satisfy their particular demands. As John A. Pearce, a prominent strategy writer, has noted, stockholders provide the enterprise with capital and expect an appropriate return on their investment in exchange; employees provide labor and skills and in exchange expect commensurate income and job satisfaction; customers want value for money; suppliers seek dependable buyers; governments insist on adherence to legislative regulations; unions demand benefits for their members in proportion to their contributions to the company; rivals seek fair competition; local communities want companies that are responsible citizens; and the general public seeks some assurance that the quality of life will be improved as a result of the company's existence.

A company has to take these claims into account when formulating its strategies, or stakeholders may withdraw their support. Stockholders may sell their shares, employees leave their jobs, and customers buy from elsewhere. Suppliers are likely to seek more dependable buyers, whereas governments can prosecute the company. Unions may engage in disruptive labor disputes, and rivals may respond to unfair competition by anticompetitive moves of their own or by filing antitrust suits with the authorities. Communities may oppose the company's attempts to locate its facilities in their area, and the general public may form pressure groups, demanding action against companies that impair the quality of life. Any of these reactions can have a disastrous impact on the enterprise.

The mission statement enables a company to incorporate stakeholder claims into its strategic decision process and thereby reduce the risk of losing stakeholder support. The mission statement thus becomes the company's formal commitment to a stakeholder group; it carries the message that its strategies will be formulated with the claims of those stakeholders in mind. We have already discussed how stockholder claims are incorporated into the mission statement when a company decides on maximizing long-run profitability as its primary goal. Any strategies that the company generates should reflect this major corporate goal. Similarly, the mission statement should recognize additional stakeholder claims, either in terms of secondary goals or as philosophies.

Stakeholder Impact Analysis

A company cannot always satisfy the claims of all stakeholders. The claims of different groups may conflict, and in practice few organizations have the resources to manage all stakeholders. For example, union claims for higher wages can conflict with consumer demands for reasonable prices and stockholder demands for acceptable returns. Hence often the company must make choices. To do so, it must identify the most important stakeholders and give a higher priority to pursuing strategies that satisfy their needs. Stakeholder impact analysis can provide such identification. Typically, stakeholder impact analysis involves the following steps:

1. Identify stakeholders
2. Identify their interests and concerns
3. As a result, identify what claims they are likely to make on the organization
4. Identify the most important stakeholders from the perspective of the organization
5. Identify the resultant strategic challenges[20]

The process allows the company to identify the stakeholders most critical to its continued survival, and their claims should be explicitly incorporated into the mission statement. From the mission statement, they then feed down into the rest of the strategy formulation process. For example, if community involvement is identified as a critical stakeholder claim, it must be incorporated in the mission statement. Any strategies that conflict with it must be rejected.

2.7 STOCKHOLDERS, THE MISSION, AND STRATEGY

Satisfying stockholders' demands typically receives the greatest attention in many corporate mission statements. As providers of capital and owners of the corporation, stockholders play a unique role in the company. Ultimately, the enterprise exists for its stockholders. In the case of most publicly held corporations, however, stockholders delegate the job of controlling the company and determining strategies to corporate managers, who become the agents, or employees, of stockholders.[21] Accordingly, corporate managers should pursue strategies that are in the best interest of their employers, the stockholders. But managers do not always act in this fashion. Diamond Shamrock, discussed in the Opening Incident, exemplifies a company that ignored its stockholders' best interest.

Management Versus Stockholder Goals

Why should managers want to pursue other strategies than those consistent with maximizing stockholder wealth? The answer depends on the personal goals of professional managers. Many writers have argued that managers are motivated by a desire for status, power, job security, income, and the like.[22] A large company can satisfy such desire better than a small one. A manager gets more status, power, job security, and income as a senior manager at General Motors than as a senior manager in a small local enterprise. Consequently, managers are thought to favor the pursuit of corporate growth goals at the expense of long-run profitability. To quote Carl Icahn, one of the most renowned corporate raiders of the 1980s,

> ...make no mistake, a strongly knit corporate aristocracy exists in America. The top man, what's more, usually finds expanding his power more important than rewarding owners (stockholders). When Mobil and USX had excess cash, did they enrich shareholders? Of course not. They bought Marcor and Marathon—disastrous investments, but major increases in the size of the manor.[23]

Thus, instead of maximizing stockholder wealth, managers trade long-run profitability for greater growth. Figure 2.4 graphs profitability against a company's growth rate. The company that does not grow is probably missing out on some profitable opportunities.[24] A growth rate of G_0 in Figure 2.4 is not consistent with maximizing profitability ($P_1 < P_{MAX}$). A moderate growth rate of G_1, on the other hand, does allow a company to maximize profitability, producing profits equal to P_{MAX}. Past G_1, further growth involves lower profitability. Yet G_2 might be the growth rate favored by managers, for it maximizes their power and status. At this growth rate, profits are only equal to P_2. Because $P_{MAX} < P_2$, a company growing at this rate is clearly not maximizing its profitability, and hence the wealth of its stockholders. However, a growth rate of G_2 may be consistent with attaining managerial goals of power, status, and income.

The Role of the Board

Stockholder interests are guarded within the company by the board of directors. Board members are directly elected by stockholders; besides, under corporate law, the board represents the owners' interests in the company. Thus the board can be held legally accountable for the company's actions. Its position at the

FIGURE 2.4   The tradeoff between profitability and growth rate

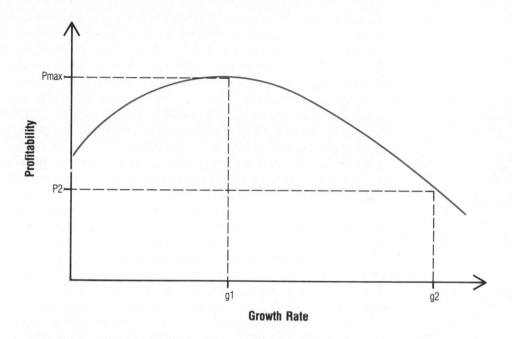

apex of decision making within the company allows the board to monitor corporate strategy decisions and to ensure that they are consistent with stockholder interests. In addition, the board has the legal authority to hire, fire, and compensate corporate employees, including, most importantly, the CEO.[25] Thus, if the board's sense is that corporate strategies are not in the best interest of stockholders, it can apply sanctions. For example, in the case of Diamond Shamrock, one of the factors that led to the resignation of the CEO, Bill Bricker, was that his strategies lost the support of the Diamond board.

However, although in theory the board should be loyal to stockholders rather than to management, in practice its role can be much more ambiguous. The typical board comprises a mix of insiders and outsiders. Since insiders are full-time employees of the company, their interests tend to be aligned with those of management. The outsiders are not full-time employees of the company. Many of them may be professional directors and hold board positions in a number of companies. Because the insiders tend to have intimate knowledge of the company's operations, they are in a position to dominate the outsiders on the board. A board dominated by insiders may pursue strategies consistent with the interests of management rather than of stockholders. In short, the board may become the captive of insiders and serve merely as a rubber stamp for management decisions, rather than as a guardian of stockholder interests.

Stock Compensation Schemes

To get around the problem of captive boards many companies have introduced stock-based compensation schemes for their senior executives. These schemes are designed to align the interests of managers with those of stockholders. In addition to their regular salary, senior executives are given stock in the firm, so that they receive a major portion of their income from dividend payments and stock price appreciations. Thus they have a direct interest in adopting strategies consistent with maximizing stockholder wealth, for as significant stockholders themselves, they will gain from such strategies. Lee Iacocca, for example, earned $20 million in 1986 from the sale of Chrysler stock that he was given when he arrived at Chrysler in 1979 to head the company. This gain can be viewed as Iacocca's reward for adopting strategies consistent with the best interests of Chrysler's stockholders.

Recent studies have confirmed that stock-based compensation schemes for senior executives can align management and stockholder interests. For instance, one study, found that managers were more likely to consider the effects of their acquisition decisions on stockholder wealth if they themselves were significant shareholders.[26] According to another study, managers were less likely to pursue diversification strategies consistent with maximizing the size of the company rather than its profitability when they themselves were significant stockholders.[27]

For all their attractions, stock-based compensation schemes have yet to be universally adopted by American companies. Some critics argue that the schemes do not always have the desired effect, since stock compensation plans can harm stockholders by diluting their interests and rewarding management unjustifiably for improvements in stock prices. They note that stock prices often increase due more to improvements in the overall economy than to managerial effort, so why should management be rewarded for this? In addition, when stock prices are falling due to factors outside the company's control, as can occur during a slump in general economic activity, then executives may see the value of their stockholdings decline rapidly. Under such circumstances, stock-based compensation schemes give managers little incentive to align their goals with those of stockholders in general.

The Takeover Constraint

If the board is loyal to management rather than to stockholders or if stock-based compensation schemes have not been adopted by the company, then as suggested in the last section, management may pursue strategies that maximize the company's growth rate rather than its profitability. Stockholders, however, still have some residual power, for they can always sell their shares. If they start doing so in large numbers, as Diamond Shamrock's stockholders did after 1980, then the price of the company's shares will decline. If the share price falls far enough, the company might be worth less on the stock market than the book value of its assets. At that point, it becomes an attractive takeover target.

This risk of being bought out is known as the **takeover constraint.** The takeover constraint effectively limits the extent to which managers can pursue strategies that put their own interests over those of stockholders, for if they ignore stockholder interests and the company is bought out, senior managers would lose their independence and probably their jobs as well.

The situation at Diamond Shamrock, presented in the Opening Incident, is one example of this process. That at Walt Disney Productions offers another. In 1984 Disney was the target of a takeover bid by Saul Steinberg. Disney had immensely valuable assets. Its real estate was worth $2.2 billion, and its film and program library and its cable television channel had a book value of $420 million. But the company's performance was poor: income before taxes declined from $248 million in 1980 to $163.4 million in 1983. Moreover, the movie division had not been able to shake the impression that it was making films for children growing up in the 1940s. In 1983 this division registered losses of $33 million. Clearly, the strategy of Walt Disney was not consistent with maximizing stockholder welfare, for it did not seem to be making the best use of its valuable assets.

Steinberg's takeover bid roused the company from its slumbers. Although the bid failed, the old management team was replaced by a more energetic team, which promptly undertook a complete review of Disney's strategy. The new management team opened Disney's vast film library, selling the rights to old films to the highest bidder. It also created a new division of the movie operations, Touchstone Films, to escape the old "Disney is for children" stigma. Touchstone soon showed success with major box office hits such as *Ruthless People, Down and Out in Beverly Hills,* and *Outrageous Fortune.* Plans for a major European theme park outside Paris were actively pursued, and aggressive marketing of the Disney channel turned it into the fastest-growing cable television operation in 1986. The stock market responded favorably to this change. One year after the initial bid, Disney's shares were trading at a price 70 percent higher than at the time of the takeover attempt, and by 1986 the company had tripled profits from its 1983 level.[28]

Corporate Raiders

Increasingly, the threat of takeover constraint is being enforced by individuals known as **corporate raiders.** The corporate raider is a phenomenon that emerged in a big way during the late 1970s and early 1980s. Corporate raiders are individuals who buy up large blocks of shares in companies that they think are pursuing strategies inconsistent with maximizing stockholder wealth. They argue that if these companies pursued different strategies they could create more wealth for stockholders. Raiders buy stock in a company either (1) to take over the business and run it more efficiently or (2) to precipitate a change in the top management, replacing the existing team with one more likely to maximize stockholder welfare.

Raiders, of course, are *not* motivated by altruism but by gain. If they succeed in their takeover bid, they can institute strategies that create value for stockholders—including themselves. Icahn's 1985 takeover of TWA for $400 million illustrates the process. TWA was in deep trouble when Icahn bought the company. Its high cost structure was pricing the airline out of lucrative international routes and out of business. Icahn cut costs by persuading pilots and machinists to agree to pay cuts of up to 26 percent. He broke a flight attendants' strike, replacing veterans with younger workers whose pay was up to 50 percent lower. By deciding not to renew leases for three Boeing 747 jumbo jets and selling a fourth, he also pared overhead costs. In all, TWA's cost reductions amounted to $600 million per year,[29] and now the company appears to be moving into profitability.

Even if a takeover bid fails, raiders can still earn millions, for their stockholdings will typically be bought out by the defending company for a hefty premium. Called **greenmail,** this source of gain has stirred much controversy and debate as to its benefits. The 1986 bid by international financier Sir James Goldsmith for The Goodyear Tire & Rubber Company, the largest U.S. tire manufacturer, provides a good example of some of the issues raised.[30]

The Raiders and Goodyear

During the slump of the late 1970s and early 1980s, like most auto-related businesses, Goodyear faced severe financial constraints.[31] The recovery of the auto industry did not help much. Between 1983 and 1985 Goodyear's tire sales rose barely 2 percent, while gross profits from tires fell 15 percent. However, between 1983 and 1985, its heavy depreciation policy helped Goodyear generate a strong positive cash flow amounting to more than $2 billion.

What did Goodyear do with that money? It lacked the confidence to invest heavily in making tires; the competition was too intense. Goodyear could have returned the money to stockholders, who could then have reinvested it in more productive companies. That at least would have been consistent with maximizing stockholder wealth. Instead Goodyear chose to expand by diversifying into the oil industry—an area that it knew nothing about. In 1983 Goodyear bought Celeron Corp., an exploration and production company in the area of oil and gas, and ended up investing $1.2 billion in this business. Stockholders were not happy. Despite a bull market, by October 1986 Goodyear's stock was trading at $32 a share, just about where it had been three years before. Moreover, Goodyear's price-to-earnings ratio was a little more than half of that of the average stock.

On their own stockholders could do little to change Goodyear's strategy. They could and did sell their shares, but since the company was not dependent on the stock market for new capital, the effect of declining share prices was minimal. Goodyear's stockholders were also too dispersed to get together and effectively pressure management to change its strategy. When Goodyear shares dropped to $32, Goldsmith saw an opportunity to make some money out of the company. He started buying shares, accumulating 12.5 million, and then offered to buy the rest for $4.7 billion. In effect, Goldsmith was saying, "I think that Goodyear is worth at least 50 percent more than the market values it—but only if I run the company myself."

Goldsmith stated his strategy for Goodyear. Specifically, he wanted the company to get back into the business it knew best, tires, and leave the business it did not know at all, oil. He also wanted Goodyear to trim back its tire operations, closing down plants and reducing capacity in order to increase efficiency. Goldsmith's bid seemed likely to succeed until the insider trader scandal concerning Ivan Boesky broke into the news. The uncertainty caused by the scandal persuaded Goldsmith to drop the bid and sell his shares back to Goodyear—for a profit of $93 million. As one commentator at the time noted,

Goodyear in effect bribed Goldsmith to take a walk. Management dipped into the corporate treasury to save its own hide. But the company also, as *The Wall Street Journal* put it, largely agreed to carry out Sir James's ideas for the company's future. It will focus again on tires, and it will sell off businesses in which it isn't expert—presumably oil and aerospace.[32]

The Goodyear case illustrates both the bad and the good aspects of the corporate raider phenomenon. Some would argue that Goldsmith blackmailed (greenmailed) Goodyear for $93 million. The resultant debt that the company incurred will burden it for years to come. Others however, might counter that without Goldsmith's intervention, inefficient management teams would have gone on pursuing their own desires for bigger size rather than maximizing stockholder welfare. In that context, the $93 million earned by Goldsmith can be considered a generous consulting fee rather than greenmail. Though these opposing views may never be reconciled, perhaps the most important conclusion is that a company would probably not have to deal with a takeover bid and its consequences if it were already maximizing stockholder wealth.

From the strategic management perspective, the important point to note about the material covered in this section is that the takeover constraint does exist and operate, though imperfectly. In theory, managers are constrained by the board of directors, stock compensation schemes, or stockholder pressures to adopt strategies consistent with maximizing stockholder welfare. In practice, however, many boards are captives of top management and tend to rubberstamp managerial decisions; stock compensation schemes are not universally adopted; and stockholders are often too dispersed to act collectively and hold managers accountable for their decisions. Such flaws give managers some leeway to pursue strategies that maximize goals other than stockholder wealth— generally, goals of greater growth rather than profitability. However, the phenomenon of corporate raiders effectively checks managers' ability to pursue such alternative goals. As Goodyear and Walt Disney exemplify, companies that dissatisfy their stockholders always run the risk of becoming the raider's target. To avoid this danger, a company must formulate strategies that focus on the overriding goal of maximizing stockholder wealth.

2.8 CORPORATE SOCIAL RESPONSIBILITY

The Concept of Social Responsibility

The concept of corporate responsibility refers to corporate actions that protect and improve the welfare of society along with the corporation's own interests.[33] Strategic decisions of large corporations inevitably involve social, as well as economic, consequences;[34] the two cannot be separated. Moreover, the social consequences of economic actions typically affect the company's outside claimants, especially local communities and the general public. For example, if a large company decides for economic reasons to close down a plant employing thousands of workers in a small community, then the social impact on that community is both direct and fundamental. Many steel towns in the Midwest have turned into ghost towns after such closings. Similarly, when a manufacturing enterprise decides to build a major plant in a rural community, it will probably change the social fabric of that community for ever. Thus, when selecting a strategy on the basis of economic criteria, a company is also making a choice that will have wider social consequences.

Why Be Socially Responsible?

Should companies be socially responsible? Should they build certain social criteria or goals into their strategic decision processes? Many companies do take this position and incorporate broad declarations of social intent into their mission statement. Indeed, there are a number of good reasons why companies should be socially responsible.

In its purest form, social responsibility can be supported for its own sake simply because it is the noble, or right, way for a company to behave. Less pure, but perhaps more practical, are arguments that socially responsible behavior is in the company's self-interest. Since economic actions have social consequences affecting the company's outside claimants, if the company wants to retain the support of the claimants, it must take those social consequences into account when formulating strategies. Otherwise it may generate ill will and opposition. For example, if the community perceives a company as having an adverse impact on the local environment, it may block the company's attempts to build new facilities in the area.

Edward H. Bowman of the University of Pennsylvania's Wharton School has taken this point further, arguing that social responsibility is actually a sound investment strategy.[35] He maintains that a company's social behavior affects the price of its stock. In other words, socially responsible policy can also benefit the company's important inside claimants, the stockholders. According to Bowman, many investors view companies that are not socially responsible as riskier investments. Moreover, many institutional investors, such as churches, universities, cities, states, and mutual funds, pay attention to corporate social behavior and thus influence the market for a company's stock.

Evidence can certainly be found in favor of Bowman's arguments. The withdrawal of American assets from South Africa by companies such as IBM and General Motors Corp. in 1986, for example, can at least in part be attributed to a desire to create a favorable impression with investors. At that time, for social or political reasons, many investors were selling any stock they held in companies that maintained a substantial presence in South Africa. Similarly, Union Carbide Corporation saw its market value plunge more then 37 percent in 1985, in the aftermath of the gas leak at its Bhopal plant in India (which killed 1,757 people and left 17,000 seriously injured) and subsequent revelations concerning poor safety procedures at many Union Carbide plants. In Union Carbide's case, the consequence was a takeover bid from GAF Corporation (which ultimately failed), extended litigation, and a negative image problem.

Bowman has also shown that companies concerned about social responsibility tend to be more profitable.[36] To test the effect of social responsibility on profits, Bowman performed a line-by-line content analysis of the 1973 annual reports of food processing companies in order to ascertain the amount of prose devoted to issues of corporate social responsibility. He then used this figure as a surrogate for actual company concern. He found that companies with some social responsibility prose performed better than those with none (14.7 percent return on equity against 10.2 percent return on equity over the previous five years).

On the other hand, there are those who argue that a company has no business pursuing social goals. Nobel laureate Milton Friedman, for one, insists that concepts of social responsibility should not enter the corporate strategic decision process.[37]

> What does it mean to say that the corporate executive has a social responsibility in his capacity as a businessman? If this statement is not pure rhetoric, it must mean that he is to act in some way that is not in the interests of his employers. For example ... that he is to make expenditures on reducing pollution beyond the amount that is in the best interests of the corporation or that is required by law in order to contribute to the social objective of improving the environment .... Insofar as his actions in accord with his social responsibility reduce returns to stockholders, he is spending their money. Insofar as his actions raise the price to customers, he is spending the customer's money. Insofar as the actions lower the wages of some employees, he is spending their money.[38]

Essentially, Friedman's position is that a business has only one kind of social responsibility: to use its resources for activities that increase its profits, *so long as it stays within the rules of the game,* which is to say, so long as it engages in open and free competition without deception or fraud.

Corporate Social Responsibility and Regulation

Friedman's views cannot be ignored, particularly in a country like the United States, where the rules of the game are well established. Our society recognizes that businesses, if left to themselves, will not always behave in a socially responsible manner. The need to generate profit can conflict with society's desire for responsible behavior. For this reason, governments, acting in the interests of society as a whole, have enacted legislation to regulate corporate behavior. Thus there are rules to safeguard consumers from abuse by companies, rules to ensure fair competition, and rules to protect the environment (from pollution, for example).

Unfortunately, companies do not always obey these rules. In a major survey of corporate crimes from 1970 to 1980, *Fortune* magazine found plenty of evidence to this effect.[39] Of 1,043 major corporations in the study, 117, or 11 percent, were involved in at least one major delinquency during the period covered. Some companies were multiple offenders. In all, 188 citations were given by *Fortune,* covering 163 separate offenses: 98 antitrust violations; 28 cases of kickbacks, bribery, or illegal rebates; 21 cases of illegal political contributions; 11 cases of fraud; and 5 cases of tax evasion.

Bethlehem Steel Corp. illustrates the kind of cases identified here. The company pleaded guilty to criminal activity over the five years 1972–1976. It was operating a kickback scheme, with the purpose of bribing representatives of shiplines to steer repair work to Bethlehem's seven shipyards. Another case involves Archer-Daniels-Midland Company, which was successfully prosecuted in 1976 for defrauding grain buyers by short weighing. Still another instance of corporate crime is offered by E. I. Du Pont de Nemours' dye group. Wanting to raise prices, in late 1970 the executives of Du Pont's dye business contacted the competition and won an agreement for a "follow the leader" scheme. In January 1971 Du Pont announced a 10 percent price increase; the competition followed suit in February and March. When charged with price fixing, the nine companies involved all pleaded no contest and were fined between $35,000 and $50,000 each.

The very fact that companies do not always behave lawfully is in itself an argument for stressing social responsibility in the mission statement of an enterprise. By expressing its commitment to "free enterprise" or to "maintaining fair relationships with our customers," the company is sending a message both to its own employees and to important stakeholders that it intends to act within the bounds of the law.

FIGURE 2.5   **Comparing profitability and social returns from strategies**

Profitability

		Negative	Low	Medium	High
Social Returns	Negative				
	Low				
	Medium			**Favored Strategies**	
	High				

The Practice of Social Responsibility

How should a company decide which social issues it will respond to and to what extent it should trade profits for social gain? The spectrum of actual corporate behavior among companies that espouse social responsibility is quite broad. It encompasses mere reaction to the strict requirements of the law, some response to direct pressure from interest groups, and commitment to incorporating wider social concerns within the corporate ethic.

Although the concept of social responsibility implies voluntary response by the company, some degree of external coercion, perhaps from government or from other pressure groups, is likely to occur in a number of situations. Such prodding may be very difficult to resist. Where no pressure exists, the incentive to adopt a social policy commitment will be less. There are, however, some criteria that a company may apply to help it choose which social action to undertake. This approach is to judge both the private and the social effects of particular strategies. A company can rank them according to their profitability and their social benefits, as shown in Figure 2.5.[40]

If this framework is used, strategies showing both high profitability and high social benefits would be the most likely to be adopted. Those with high profitability but negative social effects would worry a socially responsible company and probably would not be pursued. On the other hand, even the most socially concerned company would hesitate to adopt strategies with high social gains but negative or low profitability.

2.9 SUMMARY OF CHAPTER

The primary purpose of this chapter has been to identify various factors that constitute the organizational context within which strategies are formulated. Normally, these factors are explicitly recognized through the corporate mission statement. The mission statement thus sets the boundaries within which strategies must be contained. Specifically, the following points have been made.

1. The mission statement is the starting point of the strategic management process. It sets the context within which strategies are subsequently formulated.

2. The mission statement contains three broad elements; a definition of the company's business, a statement of the major goals of the corporation, and a statement of corporate philosophy.

3. For the single-business company, defining the business involves focusing on consumer groups to be served, consumer needs to be satisfied, and the technologies by which those needs can be satisfied. This amounts to a consumer-oriented business definition.

4. For the diversified company, defining the business involves focusing on the purpose behind owning a portfolio of businesses, the desired scope of the enterprise, and the desired balance between the constituent businesses in the portfolio.

5. A company's major corporate goal should reflect concern for the welfare of the company's owners—its stockholders. Maximizing long-run profits is the major goal consistent with maximizing stockholder wealth.

6. To avoid adverse short-run consequences of an overzealous focus on profitability, the company needs to adopt a number of secondary goals that balance short-run and long-run considerations.

7. A company's corporate philosophy makes clear how the company intends to do business. A statement of this philosophy reflects the company's basic values, aspirations, beliefs and philosophical priorities.

8. Every company has its stakeholders—individuals who have some claim on the organization. They can be divided into inside and outside claimants. The company needs to recognize their claims in its mission statement, for if it does not, it may lose their support.

9. The claims of stakeholders can conflict. Frequently, a company does not have the resources to satisfy all claimants. Therefore it has to identify the stakeholder groups that are most important to its continued survival and satisfy their claims first. It can uncover this information through a stakeholder impact analysis.

10. Stockholders are among a company's most important internal claimants. If stockholder wealth is not maximized, then the company runs the risk of becoming a takeover target. Companies sometimes fall into this trap because of managerial obsessions with the size of the business and the power and status that it brings. Corporate raiders have become a major means of disciplining such companies through takeover bids.

11. Satisfying a company's claimants often involves stressing corporate social responsibility. Social responsibility is important because a company's economic actions inevitably have social consequences that directly affect its claimants. Thus it is in the company's best interest to stress social responsibility.

12. Deciding which social issues to respond to can prove difficult for a company. However, by comparing the social impact of strategies against their economic returns, the company can identify strategies with negative or positive social consequences.

Discussion Questions

1. Why is it important for a company to take a consumer-oriented view of its businesses? What are the possible shortcomings of such a view?

2. What are the strategic implications of a focus on short-run returns? Discuss in terms of the impact on product innovation, marketing expenditure, manufacturing, and purchasing decisions.

3. Are corporate raiders a positive or negative influence on the U.S. economy? How can companies reduce the risk of takeover?

4. Companies should always be socially responsible, whatever the cost. Discuss.

Endnotes

1. For details, see "The Downfall of a CEO," *Business Week,* February 16, 1987, pp. 76–84; "Diamond Shamrock Proposes Restructuring," *The Wall Street Journal,* February 3, 1987; and "Pickens Drops Bid for.Diamond Shamrock," *The Wall Street Journal,* December 19, 1986.

2. Derek F. Abell, *Defining the Business: The Starting Point of Strategic Planning* (Englewood Cliffs, N.J.: Prentice-Hall, 1980). K. Andrews, *The Concept of Corporate Strategy* (Homewood, Ill.: Dow-Jones-Irwin, 1971). John A. Pearce, "The Company Mission as a Strategic Tool," *Sloan Management Review* (Spring 1982), 15–24.

3. These three questions were first proposed by D. F. Drucker. See Drucker, *Management: Tasks, Responsibilities, Practices* (New York: Harper & Row, 1974), pp. 74–94.

4. Abell, *Defining the Business*, p. 17.

5. Theodore Levitt, "Marketing Myopia," *Harvard Business Review* (July–August 1960), 45–56.

6. F. J. Weston and S. K. Mansinghka, "Tests of the Efficiency Performance of Conglomerate Firms," *Journal of Finance*, 26 (1971), 919–935.

7. T. Mack, "Polishing the Gem," *Forbes*, January 28, 1985, p. 64.

8. For details, see "Polaroid: Turning away from Land's one product strategy," *Business Week*, March 2, 1981, pp. 108–112; "Polaroid can't get its future in focus," *Business Week*, April 4, 1983, pp. 31–32; "Polaroid hopes to snap out of sales slump," *The Wall Street Journal*, November 11, 1985, p. 6; and "The marketing man who hopes to reform Polaroid," *International Management*, (June 1986), 35.

9. S. R. Reid, "A Reply to the Weston and Mansinghka Criticisms Dealing with Conglomerate Mergers," *Journal of Finance*, 26 (1971), 937–940.

10. Peter F. Drucker, *The Practice of Management* (New York: Harper Brothers, 1954).

11. Robert H. Hayes and William J. Abernathy, "Managing Our Way to Economic Decline," *Harvard Business Review* (July–August 1980), 67–77.

12. Lester C. Thurow, *The Zero Sum Solution* (New York: Simon and Schuster, 1985), 69–89.

13. "Too Much Penny-Pinching at American Home?" *Business Week*, December 22, 1986, pp. 64–65.

14. Figures are taken from Standard & Poor's COMPUSTAT service.

15. The evidence of the PIMS data base provides strong support for this proposition, although the direction of causation has not been proven. See R. D. Buzzell, T. G. Bradley, and R. G. M. Sultan, "Market Share: A Key to Profitability," *Harvard Business Review* (January–February 1975), 97–106.

16. T. J. Peters and R. H. Waterman, *In Search of Excellence* (New York: Harper and Row, 1982).

17. Quoted in Pearce, "The Company Mission," pp. 15–24.

18. M. D. Richards, *Setting Strategic Goals and Objectives* (St. Paul, Minn.: West, 1986).

19. Pearce, "The Company Mission," pp. 15–24.

20. I. C. Macmillan and P. E. Jones, *Strategy Formulation: Power and Politics.* (St. Paul, Minn.: West, 1986), 66.

21. M. C. Jensen and W. H. Meckling, "Theory of the Firm: Managerial Behavior, Agency Costs and Ownership Structure," *Journal of Financial Economics*, 3, (1976), 305–360.

22. For example, see R. Marris, *The Economic Theory of Managerial Capitalism* (London: Macmillan, 1964) and J. K. Galbraith, *The New Industrial State* (Boston: Houghton-Mifflin, 1970).

23. Carl Icahn, "What Ails Corporate America — And What Should be Done?" *Business Week*, October 27, 1986, p. 101.

24. E. T. Penrose, *The Theory of the Growth of the Firm* (London: Macmillan, 1958).

25. O. E. Williamson, *The Economic Institutions of Capitalism* (New York: Free Press, 1985).

26. W. G. Lewellen, C. Loderer, and A. Rosenfeld, "Merger decisions and executive stock ownership in acquiring firms," *Journal of Accounting and Economics,* 7 (1985), 209–231.

27. C. W. L. Hill and S. A. Snell, "External Control, Corporate Strategy, and Firm Performance," *Strategic Management Journal,* in press, 1989.

28. "Disney's Magic: A Turnaround Proves Wishes Can Come True," *Business Week,* March 9, 1987, pp. 62–69. "The Tinker Bell Principle," *Forbes,* December 2, 1985, pp. 102–105. "Disney Becomes Walt Disney," *The Wall Street Journal,* February 7, 1986, p. 9.

29. "Carl Icahn: Raider or Manager?" *Business Week,* October 27, 1986, pp. 98–104.

30. J. K. Glassman, "Après Ivan," *The New Republic,* December 15, 1986, pp. 11–13.

31. See "The Two Worlds of Jimmy Goldsmith," *Business Week,* December 1, 1986, pp. 98–102; "Goodyear May Be Acquired by Goldsmith," *The Wall Street Journal,* November 19, 1986, p. 2; and Glassman, "Après Ivan," p. 12.

32. Glassman, "Après Ivan," p. 12.

33. K. Davis, W. C. Frederick, and R. L. Blomstrom, *Business and Society Concepts and Policy Issues* (New York: McGraw-Hill, 1980).

34. Henry Mintzberg, "The Case for Corporate Social Responsibility," *Journal of Business Strategy* (December 1983) 3–15.

35. Edward H. Bowman, "Corporate Social Responsibility and the Investor," *Journal of Contemporary Business* (Winter 1973) 21–43.

36. Edward H. Bowman and M. Haire, "Strategic Posture Towards Corporate Social Responsibility," *California Management Review* (Winter 1975), 49–58.

37. Milton Friedman, "A Friedman Doctrine: The Social Responsibility of Business Is to Increase Its Profits," *The New York Times Magazine,* September 13, 1970, pp. 32, 33, 122, 124, and 126.

38. Ibid., p. 33.

39. I. Ross, "How Lawless Are Big Companies?" *Fortune,* December 1, 1980, pp. 56–64.

40. J. F. Pickering and T. T. Jones, "The Firm and Its Social Environment," in J. F. Pickering and T. A. J. Cockerill, *The Economic Management of the Firm* (Oxford: Philip Allan, 1984).

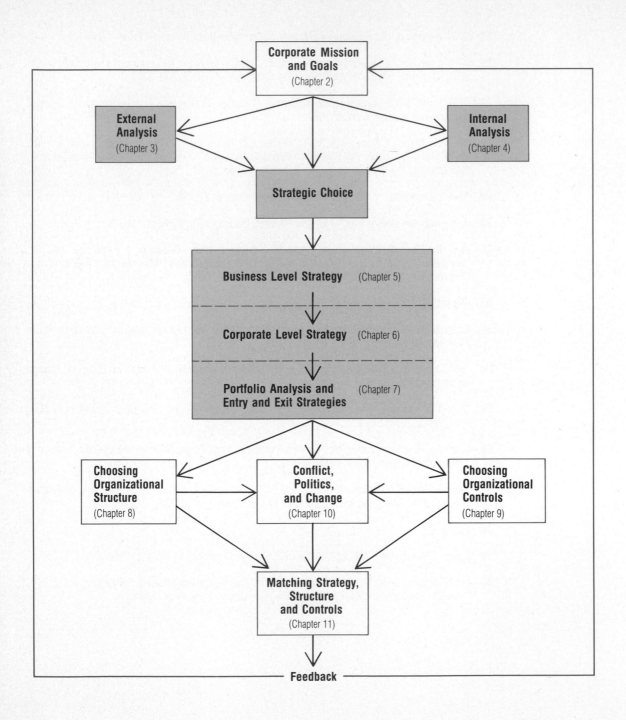

P A R T

II

STRATEGY FORMULATION

Chapter 3

Analyzing the External Environment: The Indentification of Opportunities and Threats

3.1 OPENING INCIDENT: USX

U.S. Steel, the forerunner of USX, was formed in the early 1900s by merging ten steel companies. For more than half a century U.S. Steel dominated the American steel industry. Into the 1960s the company accounted for as much as 55 percent of the industry's sales. By 1986, however, the market share of the steel-making arm of USX had fallen to 17 percent, and in that year steel operations posted enormous losses (estimated at $1.4 billion). The once-dominant force in a consolidated domestic industry found itself struggling to hold on to a dwindling market share in a highly competitive global industry.

Most of the decline in the company's market share occurred after the boom years of 1972–1974, when demand for steel was at an all-time high. Since then the American steel market has been dealt a number of blows. For instance, lowcost foreign producers, utilizing state-of-the-art production facilities, captured a large share of the domestic market. In 1980 foreign steel mills held 16 percent of the domestic market; by 1985, benefiting from a strong dollar, they had captured 22 percent of the market. In addition, new steel-making technologies, based on electric arc furnaces, have allowed domestic minimills to produce steel at a lower cost than the large integrated operations of the steel majors, which, in some cases, are still based on the technology of the 1930s. As a result, minimills and specialty steel companies increased their share of the market from 21 percent in 1980 to around 40 percent in 1985.

A further blow to the mature industry has been the growing popularity of high tech synthetic substitutes for steel, which is pushing out steel products in many market segments. For example, auto manufacturers increasingly prefer plastic rather than steel body panels. Fourth, the high costs of severance pay, pensions, and insurance for terminated workers and the low liquidation value of steel plants have made it expensive to shut down steel-making capacity. In 1983 it cost USX $1.2 billion to shut down 16 percent of its capacity and shed 15,400 jobs. These high costs of exit have made it difficult for established companies to reduce their capacity in line with demand. As a direct result, 40 percent of total domestic capacity was lying idle in 1987.

Hindsight is always 20/20, so it is easy to criticize USX for failing to respond to those market threats until it was too late. Nevertheless, there is little doubt that had USX responded to these threats as they began to emerge in the 1960s, it would not be facing problems of such magnitude today. The company could have made massive cost-reducing investments at a time when it was making good money; it could have become a major player in the minimills and specialty steel segments; or it could have diversified into the manufacture of synthetics. However, instead of formulating strategic responses to these environmental threats, USX, along with other steel majors, continued to indulge in cozy price leadership agreements and to lobby Washington for import controls. In short, USX continued to behave like a dominant company in a strong domestic industry, whereas it was fast becoming a high-cost manufacturer in a much larger, and rapidly changing, global industry.[1]

3.2 OVERVIEW

A company's external environment can be broken down into two parts: the industry environment that the company competes in and the macroenvironment. Both environments and their relationship to the company are illustrated in Figure 3.1. A company's industry environment consists of elements that directly affect the company, such as competitors, customers, and suppliers. The macroenvironment consists of the broader economic, social, demographic, political, legal, and technological setting within which the industry and the company are placed.

For a company to succeed, its strategy must be consistent with the external environment. Superior performance is the product of a good *fit* between strategy and environment. To achieve a good fit, managers must first of all understand the forces that shape competition in the external environment. This understanding enables them to identify external environmental trends and to respond by adopting appropriate strategies. In other words, they make the correct strategic choices in relation to the environment, thereby maximizing the company's prof-

FIGURE 3.1   **The external environment**

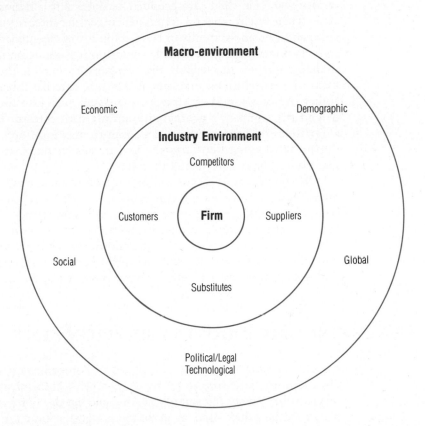

itability. In contrast, companies that fail often do so because their managers do not understand the forces that shape competition in the external environment. Consequently, they make poor strategic choices (the company's strategy does not fit the environment), and the company's profitability suffers. USX, discussed in the opening incident, is an example of a company whose strategy did not fit its environment. USX failed to anticipate the threats to its position that arose from changes in the environment of the steel industry. The strategy USX was pursuing in the early 1980s was suited to the environment of the steel industry in the 1960s, but not in the 1980s, and USX's market share and profitability declined.

The objective of this chapter is to discuss a number of models that can assist strategic managers in analyzing the external environment. The models provide a framework that can be used to identify environmental *opportunities* and *threats*. Opportunities arise when environmental trends create the potential for the company to make greater profits. For example, the baby boom of the 1950s and early 1960s gave Mothercare Stores, Inc. the opportunity to expand its maternity ware and child care products business into a national operation. Threats arise when environmental trends endanger the integrity and profitability of a company's business: trends in the steel industry threatened USX's business.

Having identified profitable opportunities, strategic managers need to formulate strategies that enable the company to exploit those opportunities and maximize its return on investment. Because external threats can squeeze profitability out of a company, strategic managers must also formulate strategies that defend the company's profitability against such threats. The different strategic alternatives that the company can adopt to maximize opportunities and counter threats are discussed in Chapters 5–7. In this chapter, we focus on the issue of identifying opportunities and threats.

We begin with a discussion of a model for analyzing the industry environment. Next we discuss the competitive implications that arise when groups of companies within an industry pursue similar strategies. We then move on to consider the nature of industry evolution. Finally, we review a number of macroenvironmental issues. By the end of this chapter, you should be familiar with the main factors strategic managers have to take into consideration when analyzing a company's external environment for opportunities and threats.

3.3 ANALYZING THE INDUSTRY ENVIRONMENT

An industry can be defined as a group of companies offering products or services that are close substitutes for each other. Close substitutes are products or services that satisfy the same basic *consumer* needs. For example, the metal and plastic body panels used in automobile construction are close substitutes for each other. Despite different production technologies, auto supply companies manufacturing metal body panels are in the same basic industry as companies manufacturing plastic body panels. They are serving the same consumer need, that of auto assembly companies for body panels.

The task facing strategic managers is to analyze competitive forces in the industry environment in order to identify the opportunities and threats that confront the company. Michael E. Porter of The Harvard School of Business Administration has developed a framework that helps managers do this.[2] Porter's framework is known as the **five forces model.** It focuses on five forces that shape competition within an industry: (1) the risk of new entry by potential competitors; (2) the degree of rivalry amongst established companies within the industry; (3) the bargaining power of buyers; (4) the bargaining power of suppliers; and (5) the closeness of substitutes to the industry's products (see Figure 3.2).

Porter's argument is that the stronger each of these forces is, the more are established companies limited in their ability to raise prices and earn greater profits. Within Porter's framework, a strong competitive force can be regarded

FIGURE 3.2   **Porter's five forces model**

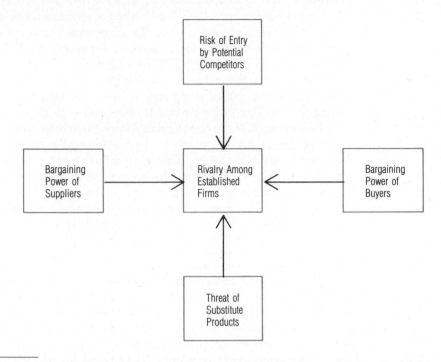

Source: Reprinted by permission of the *Harvard Business Review*. An exhibit from "How Competitive Forces Shape Strategy" by Michael E. Porter (March–April 1979). Copyright © 1979 by the President and Fellows of Harvard College; all rights reserved.

as a threat, since it depresses profits. A weak competitive force can be regarded as an opportunity, since it allows a company to earn greater profits. As you will see, the strength of the five forces may change through time due to factors beyond the company's direct control, such as industry evolution. In such circumstances, the task facing strategic managers is to recognize opportunities and threats as they arise and to formulate appropriate strategic responses. In addition, it is possible for a company through its choice of strategy, to alter the strength of one or more of the five forces to its advantage. This is part of the subject matter of the following chapters. In this chapter, we focus on understanding the impact that each of the five forces has upon a company.

Potential Competitors

Potential competitors are companies that currently are not competing in the industry but have the capability to do so if they choose. The American Telephone & Telegraph Company, for example, was regarded as a potential competitor in the personal computer industry in the early 1980s, for it had the technology, sales force, and capital necessary to manufacture and sell PCs. AT&T, in fact, did enter the industry in 1985. Established companies try to discourage potential competitors from entering, since the more companies enter an industry, the more difficult it becomes for established companies to hold their share of the market and to generate profits. Thus a high risk of entry by potential competitors represents a threat to the profitability of established companies. On the other hand if the risk of new entry is low, established companies can take advantage of this opportunity to raise prices and earn greater returns.

The strength of the competitive force of potential rivals is largely a function of the height of barriers to entry. The concept of barriers to entry implies that there are significant costs to joining an industry. The greater the costs that potential competitors must bear, the greater are the barriers to entry. High entry barriers keep potential competitors out of an industry even when industry returns are high. The classic work on barriers to entry was done by economist Joe Bain, who identified three main sources of barriers to new entry.[3]

Brand loyalty   Brand loyalty refers to the preference of buyers for the products of established companies. A company can create brand loyalty through continuous advertising of brand and company names; patent protection of products; product innovation through company research and development programs; an emphasis on high product quality; and good after-sales service. Significant brand loyalty makes it difficult for new entrants to take market share away from established companies. Thus brand loyalty reduces the threat of entry by potential competitors; they may see the task of breaking down well-established consumer preferences as too costly.

Absolute cost advantages   Lower absolute costs give established companies an advantage that is difficult for potential competitors to match. Absolute cost advantages can arise from superior production techniques as a result of past experience, patents, or secret processes; control of particular inputs required for production, be they labor, materials, equipment or management skills; or access to cheaper funds because existing companies represent lower risks than established ones. If established companies have an absolute cost advantage, then again the threat of entry is significantly reduced.

Economies of scale   Economies of scale refer to the cost advantages associated with large company size. Sources of scale economies include cost reductions gained through mass-producing a standardized output, discounts on bulk purchases of raw material inputs and component parts, the spreading of fixed costs over a larger volume, and scale economies in advertising.[4] If these cost advantages are significant, then a new entrant faces the dilemma of either entering on a small scale and suffering a significant cost disadvantage or taking a very large risk by entering on a large scale and bearing significant capital costs. A further risk of large-scale entry is that the increased supply of products will depress prices and result in vigorous retaliation by established companies. Thus, when established companies have scale economies, the threat of entry is reduced.

If established companies have built brand loyalty for their products, have an absolute cost advantage with respect to potential competitors, or have significant scale economies, then the risk of entry by potential competitors is significantly reduced. When this risk is low, established companies can charge higher prices and earn greater profits than would have otherwise been possible. Clearly, it is in the interest of companies to pursue strategies consistent with these aims. Indeed, empirical evidence suggests that the height of barriers to entry is *the most important* determinant of profit rates in an industry.[5] Examples of industries where entry barriers are significant include pharmaceuticals, household detergents, and aerospace. In the first two cases, product differentiation achieved through substantial expenditures for research and development and for advertising has built brand loyalty, making it difficult for new companies to enter these industries on a significant scale. So successful have the differentiation strategies of Procter & Gamble and Unilever been in household detergents that these two companies dominate the global industry.

In the aerospace industry, the barriers to entering the commercial airline market are primarily due to scale economies. Development costs alone can be staggering. For example, before McDonnell Douglas Corp. sold a single MD-11, the wide-bodied jetliner designed to take the company well into the twenty-first century, more than $1.5 billion was spent on development and tooling.[6] Industry analysts estimate that, just to break even on a new model like the MD-11, a company has to sell more than 200 aircraft, a figure representing 13 percent of expected industry sales of wide-bodied jets between 1990 and 2000. In addition, the cost disadvantages of not achieving an efficient scale of production are substantial in airplane manufacture. Companies that are able to achieve only half of the market share necessary to break even face a 20 percent unit cost disadvantage.[7] Clearly, in aerospace the up-front capital costs, the need to achieve a significant market share to break even, and the cost disadvantages of not achieving an efficient scale of production are likely to deter all but the most determined potential competitors from entry. In spite of this, it should be noted that Airbus Industrie, a European consortium, did manage to enter successfully the commercial aerospace industry in the 1980s, although with the help of significant government backing.

Rivalry Among Established Companies

The second of Porter's five competitive forces is the extent of rivalry among established companies within an industry. If this competitive force is weak, companies have the opportunity to raise prices and earn greater profits. If this competitive force is strong, however, significant price competition, including price wars, may result from the intense rivalry among companies. Price competition limits profitability by reducing the margins that can be earned on sales. Thus intense rivalry among established companies constitutes a strong threat to profitability. The extent of rivalry among established companies within an industry is largely a function of three factors: (1) industry competitive structure; (2) demand conditions; and (3) the height of exit barriers in the industry.

Competitive structure   Competitive structure refers to the number and size distribution of companies in an industry. Different competitive structures have different implications for rivalry. Structures vary from **fragmented** to **consolidated.** A fragmented industry contains a large number of small or medium-sized companies, none of which is in a position to dominate the industry. A consolidated industry is dominated by a small number of large companies, or in extreme cases, by just one company (a monopoly). Examples of fragmented industries include agriculture, real estate brokerage, and sun-tanning parlors. Examples of consolidated industries include aerospace, automobiles, and pharmaceuticals. The most common competitive structure in the United States is a consolidated structure—what economists call an oligopoly.[8] The range of structures and their different characteristics are illustrated in Figure 3.3.

Fragmented industries tend to be characterized by intense price competition and low profitability. With little power to influence the market, companies are forced to take whatever price the market offers. Profitability depends on how well the company can minimize operating costs. Small size makes it difficult for a company to bear the marketing and development costs of product differentiation in order to build brand loyalty. Thus companies in fragmented industries find it hard to protect themselves from competition. In other words, a fragmented industry structure constitutes a threat rather than an opportunity. Often the best strategy for a company to pursue in such circumstances is cost minimization.

FIGURE 3.3   **The continuum of industry structures**

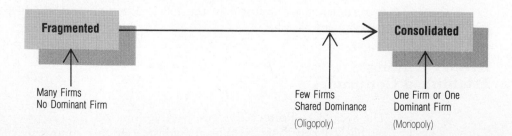

The nature and intensity of competition for consolidated industries are much more difficult to predict. The one certainty about consolidated industries is that the companies are *interdependent*. Interdependence means that the competitive actions of one company will directly effect the profitability of others in the industry. For example, General Motors' introduction of cut-rate financing deals to sell autos in 1986 had an immediate negative impact on the sales and profits of Chrysler Corp. and Ford Motor Company, which then had to introduce similar packages in order to protect their market share.

Thus, in a consolidated industry, the competitive action of one company directly affects the market share of its rivals, forcing a response from them. The consequence can be a dangerous competitive spiral, with rival companies trying to undercut each other's prices, pushing industry profits down in the process. The fare wars that racked the airline industry during the seven years after the deregulation of 1979 provide a good illustration of what can happen when companies are highly interdependent. As a result of the fare wars, in 1982 the airline industry as a whole lost over $700 million. Braniff International Corporation and Continental Airlines Corp. were pushed into bankruptcy, and Eastern and People Express sold out to Texas Air to avoid bankruptcy.

Clearly, then, the interdependence of companies in consolidated industries and the possibility of a price war constitute a major threat. Companies often attempt to reduce this threat by following the price lead set by a dominant company in the industry. However, companies must be careful, for explicit price-fixing agreements are illegal, although tacit agreements are not. (A tacit agreement is one arrived at without direct communication. Instead, companies watch and interpret each other's behavior. Normally, tacit agreements involve following the price lead set by a dominant company).[9] More generally, when price wars are a threat, companies often compete on nonprice factors such as product quality and design features. This constitutes an attempt to build brand loyalty and minimize the threat of a price war occurring. Thus extensive nonprice competition and the avoidance of price wars tend to characterize consolidated industries.

Demand conditions   Industry demand conditions are a further determinant of the intensity of rivalry among established companies. Growing demand tends to moderate competition by providing greater room for expansion. Demand grows when the market as a whole is growing through the addition of new consumers or when existing consumers are purchasing more of the industry's product. When demand is growing, companies can increase revenues without taking market share away from other companies. Thus growing demand gives a company a major opportunity to expand operations.

Conversely, declining demand results in more competition as companies fight to maintain revenues and market share. Demand declines when consumers are leaving the marketplace or when each consumer is buying less. When demand is declining, a company can attain growth only by taking market share away from other companies. Thus declining demand constitutes a major threat, for it increases the extent of rivalry between established companies. The issue of what determines demand conditions is discussed in more detail later in the chapter, when we consider industry evolution.

Exit barriers   Exit barriers are a serious competitive threat when industry demand is declining. Exit barriers are economic, strategic, and emotional factors that keep companies competing in an industry even when returns are low. If exit barriers are high, companies can become locked into an unfavorable industry. Excess productive capacity can result. In turn, excess capacity tends to lead to more intense price competition, with companies cutting prices in an attempt to get the orders necessary to utilize their idle capacity.

Common exit barriers include the following:

1. Investments in plant and equipment that have no alternative uses and cannot be sold off. Therefore, if the company wishes to leave the industry, it has to write off the book value of these assets.

2. High fixed costs of exit, such as severance pay to workers who are being made redundant.

3. Emotional attachments to an industry, such as when a company is unwilling to exit from its original industry for sentimental reasons.

4. Strategic relationships between business units. For example, within a multi-industry company, a low-return business unit may provide vital inputs for a high-return business unit based in another industry. Thus the company may be unwilling to exit from the low-return business.

5. Economic dependency on the industry, as when a company is not diversified and so relies on the industry for its income.

The steel industry illustrates the adverse competitive effects of high exit barriers. A combination of declining demand and new low-cost sources of supply have created overcapacity in the global steel industry. American companies, with their high-cost structure, are on the sharp end of this decline. Demand for American steel fell from a 1977 peak of 160 million tons to 70 million tons in 1986. The result has been excess capacity amounting to an estimated 45 million tons in 1987, or 40 percent of total productive capacity.[10] Industry profits are low, and several of the majors, including The LTV Corp. and Bethlehem Steel, face bankruptcy.

Since the steel industry is clearly unattractive, why do not companies leave or at least reduce capacity? The answer is that the costs of exit are too high. As noted in the Opening Incident, in 1983 USX shut down 16 percent of its raw steel-making capacity at a cost of $1.2 billion! USX has to write off the book value of these assets; they could not be sold. In addition, it had to cover pen-

TABLE 3.1 **Demand conditions and exit barriers as determinants of opportunities and threats in a consolidated industry**

		Demand conditions	
		Demand decline	Demand growth
Exit barriers	High	High threat of excess capacity and price wars	Opportunities to raise prices through price leadership and to expand operations
	Low	Moderate threat of excess capacity and price wars	Opportunities to raise prices through price leadership and to expand operations

sions and insurance for 15,400 terminated workers.[11] Given such high exit costs, companies such as USX have remained locked into this unprofitable industry. The effect of impeded exit has been more intense price competition than might otherwise have been the case. Thus high exit barriers are threatening the profitability of established companies within the steel industry.

The extent of rivalry among established companies within an industry is a function of competitive structure, demand conditions, and exit barriers. Particularly within a consolidated industry, it is the *interaction* of these factors that determines the extent of rivalry. For example, the environment of a consolidated industry may be favorable when demand growth is high. Under such circumstances, companies might seize the opportunity to adopt price leadership agreements. However, when demand is declining and exit barriers are high, the probable emergence of excess capacity is likely to give rise to price wars. Thus, depending on the interaction between these various factors, the extent of rivalry between established companies in a consolidated industry might constitute an opportunity or a threat. These issues are summarized in Table 3.1.

The Bargaining Power of Buyers

The third of Porter's five competitive forces is the bargaining power of buyers. Buyers can be viewed as a competitive threat when they force down prices or when they demand higher quality and better service (which increases operating costs). Alternatively, weak buyers give a company the opportunity to raise prices and earn greater returns. Whether buyers are able to make demands on a company depends on their *power* relative to that of the company. According to Porter, buyers are most powerful in the following circumstances:

1. when the supply industry is composed of many small companies, and the buyers are few in number and large. These circumstances allow the buyers to dominate supply companies.

2. when they purchase in large quantities. In such circumstances, buyers can use their purchasing power as leverage to bargain for price reductions.

3. when the supply industry depends on them for a large percentage of its total orders.

4. when they can switch orders between supply companies at a low cost, thereby playing off companies against each other to force down prices.

5. when it is economically feasible for them to purchase the input from several companies at once.

6. when they can use the threat to supply their own needs through vertical integration as a device for forcing down prices.

An example of an industry whose buyers are powerful is the auto components supply industry. Auto component suppliers are numerous and typically small in scale. Their customers, the auto manufacturers, are large in size and few in number. Chrysler, for example, does business with close to 2,000 different component suppliers and normally contracts with a number of different companies to supply the same part. The auto majors have used their powerful position to play off suppliers against each other, forcing down the price they have to pay for component parts and demanding better quality. If a component supplier objects, then the auto major uses the threat of switching to another supplier as a bargaining tool. Additionally, both Ford and GM have used the threat of manufacturing a component themselves rather than buying it from auto component suppliers as a device for keeping component prices down.

The opposite circumstances arise when a company has more power than its buyers. For example, by virtue of its patent, Xerox Corporation had a twenty-five-year monopoly in the production of photocopiers. Buyers were dependent on Xerox, which was the only source of supply. This power gave Xerox the opportunity to raise prices above those that would have been set under more competitive conditions, such as the prices currently prevailing in the industry.

The Bargaining Power of Suppliers

The fourth of Porter's competitive forces is the bargaining power of suppliers. Suppliers can be viewed as a threat when they are able to force up the price a company must pay for input or reduce the quality of goods supplied, thereby depressing the company's profitability. Alternatively, weak suppliers give a company the opportunity to force down prices and demand higher quality. As with buyers, the ability of suppliers to make demands on a company depends upon their *power* relative to the company. According to Porter, suppliers are most powerful in the following circumstances:

1. when the product that they sell has few substitutes and is important to the company.

2. when the company's industry is *not* an important customer to the suppliers. In such circumstances the health of suppliers does not depend on the company's industry. Thus suppliers have little incentive to reduce prices or improve quality.

3. when their respective products are differentiated to such an extent it is costly for a company to switch from one supplier to another. In such circumstances, the company is dependent on its suppliers and *unable* to play them off against each other.

4. when they can use the threat of vertically integrating forward into the industry and competing directly with the company as a device for raising prices.

5. when buying companies are *unable* to use the threat of vertically integrating backward and supplying their own needs as a device for reducing input prices.

For a long time the airlines exemplified an industry whose suppliers were powerful. In particular, the airline pilots and aircraft mechanics unions, as suppliers of labor, were in a very strong position with respect to the airlines. The airlines depended on union labor to fly and service their aircraft. Because of labor agreements and the probability of damaging strikes, nonunion labor was not regarded as a feasible substitute. The unions used this position to raise pilots' and mechanics' wages above the level that would have prevailed in more competitive circumstances, such as those currently found in the industry. This situation persisted until the early 1980s, when the resultant high-cost structure of the airline industry was driving many airlines into bankruptcy. The airlines then used the threat of bankruptcy to break union agreements and drive down labor costs, often by as much as 50 percent.

Substitute Products

The final element of Porter's five forces model is the competitive force of substitute products. Substitute products are the products of enterprises in industries serving similar consumer needs to a company's industry. For example, companies in the coffee industry compete indirectly with those in the tea and soft drinks industries. The prices that companies in the coffee industry can charge are limited by the existence of substitutes such as tea and soft drinks. If the price of coffee rises too much relative to that of tea or soft drinks, then coffee drinkers will start to switch from coffee to these substitutes. This phenomenon occurred when unusually cold weather destroyed much of the Brazilian coffee crop in 1975–1976. The price of coffee rose to record highs, reflecting the shortage, and consumers began to switch to tea in large numbers.

The existence of close substitutes, then, constitutes a strong competitive threat, limiting the price a company can charge and thus its profitability. However, if a company's products have few close substitutes (substitutes are a weak competitive force), then other things being equal, the company has the opportunity to raise prices and earn additional profits. Its strategies should be designed to take advantage of this fact.

3.4 IDENTIFYING GROUPS WITHIN INDUSTRIES

The Concept of Strategic Groups

So far we have had very little to say about how companies in an industry might differ from each other and what implications this might have for the opportunities and threats that they face. In practice, companies in an industry often differ from each other with respect to factors such as distribution channels used, market segments served, product quality, technological leadership, customer service, pricing policy, advertising policy, and promotions. Within most industries, it is possible to observe groups of companies, where the members follow the same basic strategy as other companies in the group but a different strategy than companies in other groups. These groups of companies are known as **strategic groups.**[12]

Normally, a limited number of groups capture the essence of strategic differences between companies within an industry. For example, the global auto industry, contains a number of different strategic groups. First, there is a group of companies that manufactures a restricted range of cars aimed at serving market segments at the bottom, or basic transportation, end of the market. These companies compete primarily on price. Their strategy involves minimizing costs through the attainment of scale economies and competitive pricing to gain market share. Members of this group include Hyundai Motor Company (of Korea) and Yugo GV (from Yugoslavia).

Second, there is a group of companies that manufactures a restricted range of cars aimed at serving segments at the top, or luxury, end of the market. For these companies, it is not so much cost as luxury, quality, and outstanding performance that are the critical competitive dimensions. The strategy of these companies involves stressing the uniqueness of their product, its outstanding quality and performance, and the status of owning such a car. Examples of such companies include BMW AG, Daimler Benz AG (Mercedes Benz), and Jaguar Cars, Inc. They command a high price for their products.

Third, there is a group of companies whose strategy involves manufacturing a comprehensive model range of cars aimed at serving the majority of market segments. This strategy focuses on minimizing cost through the realization of scale economies, so that the companies can compete on price in the lower end of the market. At the same time it stresses quality and performance, so that the companies can compete at the top end of the market on quality. General Motors, Ford, Chrysler, Nissan Motor Company, Honda, Toyota Motor Corp., and Volkswagen AG are among the companies pursuing such a strategy.

As our discussion suggests, it should be possible to plot these three strategic groups along two main dimensions: price/quality and number of market segments served. This has been done in Figure 3.4. In practice, however, there are more than three strategic groups in the auto industry. We have limited our discussion to three groups for the sake of clarity. Figure 3.4 is also a simplification, since it focuses on only two strategic dimensions.

FIGURE 3.4   **Strategic groups in the automobile industry**

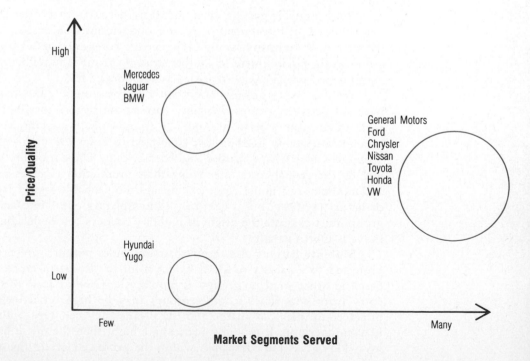

Implications of Strategic Groups

The concept of strategic groups has a number of implications for industry analysis and the identification of opportunities and threats. First, a company's immediate competitors are those in its strategic group. Since all the companies in a strategic group are pursuing similar strategies, consumers will tend to view the products of such enterprises as being direct substitutes for each other. Thus a major threat to a company's profitability can come from within its own strategic group.

Second, different strategic groups can have a different standing with respect to each of Porter's five competitive forces. In other words, the risk of new entry by potential competitors, the degree of rivalry among companies within a group, the bargaining power of buyers, the bargaining power of suppliers, and the competitive force of substitute products can all vary in intensity among different strategic groups within the same industry.

For example, in the auto industry, companies in low-volume strategic groups, such as the now defunct American Motors Company, traditionally lacked the buying power of those in high-volume strategic groups, such as General Motors. This put companies from low-volume strategic groups in a much weaker position vis-à-vis suppliers than companies in high-volume strategic groups. Thus AMC was unable to bargain down suppliers' prices in the way GM could.

Some strategic groups, then, are more desirable than others for they have a lower level of threats and/or greater opportunities. Managers must evaluate whether their company would be better off competing in a different strategic group. If the environment of another strategic group is more benign, then moving into that group can be regarded as an opportunity.

Yet this opportunity is rarely without costs, mainly because of **mobility barriers** between groups. Mobility barriers are factors that inhibit the movement of companies between groups in an industry. For example, Jaguar would encounter mobility barriers if it attempted to enter the high-volume strategic group to which GM, Chrysler, and Ford belong. These mobility barriers would include the capital costs of building mass production facilities to manufacture a comprehensive model range of cars and the probable loss of Jaguar's unique, or luxury, status. Thus a company contemplating entry into another strategic group must evaluate the height of mobility barriers before deciding whether the move is worth its while.

Mobility barriers also imply that companies within a given group may be protected to a greater or lesser extent from the threat of entry by companies based in other strategic groups. If mobility barriers are low, then the threat of entry from companies in other groups may be high, effectively limiting the prices companies can charge and the profits they can earn without attracting new competition. If mobility barriers are high, then the threat of entry will be low. This gives the companies within the protected group the opportunity to raise prices and earn higher returns without attracting entry.

3.5 COMPETITIVE CHANGES DURING INDUSTRY EVOLUTION

The Industry Life Cycle Model

Over time most industries pass through a series of well-defined stages, from initial growth, through maturity, and eventually into decline. These different stages have different implications for the nature of competition. Specifically, the strength of each of Porter's five competitive forces typically changes as an industry evolves. These changes give rise to different opportunities and threats at different stages of an industry's evolution.[13] The task facing strategic managers is to *anticipate* how the strength of each force will change with the stage of industry development and to formulate strategies that take advantage of opportunities as they arise and that counter any emerging threats.

The industry life cycle model is a useful tool for analyzing the effects of industry evolution on competitive forces. This model is similar to the product life cycle model discussed in the marketing literature.[14] Using the industry life cycle model, five different industry environments can be identified, each occurring during a distinct stage of an industry's evolution: (1) an embryonic industry environment, (2) a growth industry environment, (3) a shakeout environment, (4) a mature industry environment, and (5) a declining industry environment. Figure 3.5 illustrates them.

An *embryonic* industry is one that is just beginning to develop (e.g., the hand-held calculator industry in the late 1960s). Typically, growth at this stage

FIGURE 3.5   **Stages of the industry life cycle**

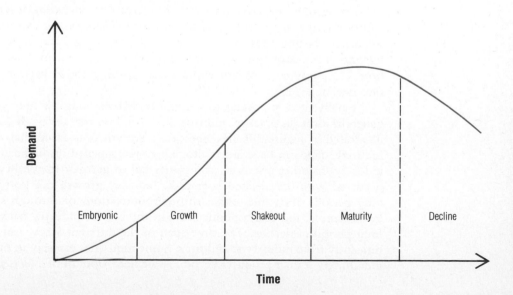

is slow, because of such factors as buyer unfamiliarity with the industry's product, high prices due to the inability of companies to reap any significant scale economies, and poorly developed distribution channels.

Once demand for the industry's product begins to take off, the industry develops the characteristics of a growth industry. A *growth* industry is one where first-time demand is expanding rapidly as many new consumers enter the market. Typically, industry growth takes off when consumers become familiar with the product, when prices fall due to the attainment of experience and scale economies, and as distribution channels develop. The personal computer industry was at this stage of development between 1981 and 1984. In the United States, 55,000 PCs were sold in 1981. By 1984 the figure had risen to 7.5 million—a 136-fold increase in just four years.[15]

Explosive growth of the type experienced by the PC industry in the early 1980s cannot be maintained indefinitely. Sooner or later the rate of growth slows down and the industry enters the shakeout stage. In the *shakeout* stage, demand approaches saturation levels. A saturated market is one where there are few potential first-time buyers left. Most of the demand is limited to replacement demand. A dramatic example of a shakeout occurred in the PC industry during 1984–1986. The average annual growth rate of demand between 1984 and 1986 was 3.3 percent, compared with an average annual growth rate of 3,000 percent between 1981 and 1984.

The shakeout stage ends when the industry enters its mature stage. A *mature* industry is one where the market is totally saturated and demand is limited to replacement demand. During this stage, growth is low or zero. What little growth there is comes from population expansion bringing new consumers into the market.

Eventually, most industries enter a decline stage. In the *decline* stage, growth becomes negative for a variety of reasons, including technological substitution (e.g., air travel for rail travel), social changes (e.g., greater health consciousness hitting tobacco sales), demographics (e.g., the declining birth rate hurting the market for baby and child products), and international competition (e.g., low-cost foreign competition pushing the American steel industry into decline).

Finally, it is important to remember that the industry life cycle model is a generalization. In practice, industry life cycles do not always follow the pattern illustrated in Figure 3.5. In some cases, growth is so rapid that the embryonic industry stage can be skipped altogether, as happened in the personal computer industry. In other instances, companies fail to get past the embryonic stage, as occurred with the ill-fated laser disk. Industry growth can be revitalized after long periods of decline, either through innovations or through social changes. For example, the health boom brought the bicycle industry back to life after a long period of decline. The time span of the different stages can also vary significantly from industry to industry. Some industries can stay in maturity almost indefinitely if their products become basic necessities of life, as is the case for the automobile industry. Others skip the mature stage altogether and go straight into decline, which is essentially what occurred in the vacuum tube industry. Vacuum tubes were replaced by transistors as a major component in electronic products while the industry was still in its growth stage.

Implications of Industry Evolution

For strategic managers, the most important aspect of industry evolution concerns its impact on Porter's five competitive forces, and through them, on opportunities and threats. Industry evolution has *major* implications for two of the five competitive forces — potential competitors and rivalry among established companies — and less substantial implications for the competitive forces of buyers, suppliers, and substitutes. We will discuss each in turn.

Potential competitors and industry evolution The way entry barriers change with industry evolution are summarized in Table 3.2. In an embryonic industry and in the early stages of a growth industry, entry barriers are usually based on the control of technological knowledge.[16] Consequently, at those stages, the threat of entry by potential competitors tends to be relatively low. However, the importance of technological knowledge as a barrier to entry is normally short-lived. Sooner or later potential rivals manage to work out the technological requirements for competing in the industry themselves, and technological barriers to entry decline in importance.

TABLE 3.2   **How barriers to entry change with industry evolution**

		Stage of industry evolution				
		Embryonic	Growth	Shakeout	Maturity	Decline
	Technology	High to medium	Medium to low	Low	Low	Low
Entry barriers	Scale economies	Low	Low to medium	Medium to high	Medium to high	Medium to high
	Brand loyalty	Low	Low to medium	Medium to high	Medium to high	Medium to high

The best thing for the company to do when technological entry barriers are high is to take advantage of the relative lack of new competition to build up market share and brand loyalty. For example, in the embryonic stage of the PC industry, Apple Computer, Inc., had a virtual monopoly of the relevant knowledge. This technological advantage allowed Apple to become the market leader. Thus, when technological entry barriers were eroded by imitators such as IBM, Apple had already established a degree of brand loyalty for its products. This enabled Apple to survive in the industry when competitive pressures increased.

Normally, the importance of control over technological knowledge as a barrier to entry declines significantly by the time the industry enters its growth stage. In addition, because few companies have yet achieved significant scale economies or have differentiated their product sufficiently to guarantee brand loyalty, other barriers to entry tend to be low at this stage. Given the low entry barriers, the threat from potential competitors is normally highest at this point. However, high growth usually means that new entrants can be absorbed into the industry without a marked increase in competitive pressure.

As an industry goes through the shakeout stage and enters maturity, barriers to entry increase and the threat of entry from potential competitors decreases. As growth slows during the shakeout, companies can no longer maintain historic growth rates merely by holding onto their market share. Competition for market share develops, driving down prices. Often the result is a price war, as happened in the airline industry during the 1980–1986 shakeout. To survive the shakeout, companies begin to focus *both* on costs minimization and on building brand loyalty. The airlines, for example, tried to cut operating costs by hiring nonunion labor and to build brand loyalty by introducing frequent-flyer programs. By the time the industry matures, the surviving companies are those that have brand loyalty and low-cost operations. As both of these factors constitute a significant barrier to entry, the threat of entry by potential competitors is greatly diminished. High entry barriers in mature industries give companies the opportunity to increase prices and profits.

Finally, as an industry enters the decline stage, entry barriers remain high and the threat of entry is low. Economies of scale and brand loyalties are by now well established. In addition, the low profitability characteristics of this stage makes the industry less attractive to potential competitors.

Rivalry among established companies and industry evolution   The extent of rivalry among established companies also changes as an industry evolves, presenting a company with new opportunities and threats. These are summarized in Table 3.3. In an embryonic industry, rivalry normally focuses on perfecting product design. This rivalry can be intense, as in the race to develop superconductors, and the company that is the first to solve design problems often has the opportunity to develop a significant market position. An embryonic industry may also be the creation of one company's innovative efforts, as happened with personal computers (Apple) or vacuum cleaners (The Hoover

TABLE 3.3   **How rivalry among established firms changes with industry evolution**

		Stage of industry evolution				
		Embryonic	Growth	Shakeout	Maturity	Decline
Competitive features	Price competition	Low	Low	High	Normally low-medium, can be high	High
	Brand loyalty	Low	Low	Medium to high	High	High
	Overall rivalry	Low	Low	High	Medium can be high	High

Company). In such circumstances, the company has a major opportunity to capitalize on the lack of rivalry and build up a strong hold on the market.

During an industry's growth stage, rivalry tends to be low. Rapid growth in demand enables companies to expand their revenues and profits without taking market share away from competitors. The company has the opportunity to expand its operations. In addition, a strategically aware company takes advantage of the relatively benign environment of the growth stage to prepare itself for the intense competition of the coming industry shakeout.

As the industry enters the shakeout stage, rivalry between companies becomes intense. The slowdown in growth at this stage means that companies cannot maintain historic growth rates without taking market share away from competitors. A battle for market share develops, driving prices and profits down. Rivalry between established companies becomes a major threat to a company's existence.

As a result of the shakeout, most industries by maturity have consolidated and become oligopolies. In the airline industry, for example, it is estimated that as a consequence of the shakeout the top five companies will control 85 percent of the industry by 1990, up from only 50 percent in 1984.[17] In mature industries, companies tend to recognize their interdependence and try to avoid price wars. Stable demand conditions give them the opportunity to enter into price leadership agreements. The net effect is to reduce the threat of intense rivalry among established companies, thereby allowing greater profitability. However, as noted earlier, the stability of a mature industry is always threatened by further price wars. A general slump in economic activity can depress industry demand. As companies fight to maintain their revenues in the face of declining demand, price leadership agreements break down, rivalry increases, and prices and profits fall. The periodic price wars that occur in the gasoline market illustrate this situation. During periods of strong demand for oil, most producers followed the price lead set by OPEC. As demand for oil weakened in the mid-1980s, however, the price lead set by OPEC broke down and severe price competition developed. Mature industries thus are characterized by long periods of price stability, when rivalry is relatively mild, interspersed with periods of intense rivalry and price wars, brought on by a general worsening of macroeconomic conditions. The threat of a price war never disappears. Given this factor, companies should look for opportunities to reduce the sensitivity of their product to price changes.

Finally, within a declining industry, the degree of rivalry amongst established companies usually increases. Depending on the speed of the decline and the height of exit barriers, competitive pressures can become as fierce as in the shakeout stage.[18] The main problem in a declining industry is that falling demand leads to the emergence of excess capacity. In an attempt to utilize this capacity, companies begin to cut prices, thus sparking a price war. As noted earlier, the American steel industry has experienced these problems due to the attempt of steel companies to utilize their excess capacity (40% of the steel industry's total productive capacity was classified as being excess in 1986).[19] Exit barriers play a part in adjusting excess capacity. The greater the exit barriers, the harder it is for companies to reduce capacity and the greater the threat of severe price competition.

Buyers, suppliers and industry evolution Industry evolution can change the nature of the relationships between an industry, and its buyers and suppliers. As an industry evolves toward maturity, it becomes both larger and more consolidated. These changes enhance the bargaining power of companies in the industry vis-à-vis suppliers and buyers in a number of ways. First, the larger the company, the more important it is to suppliers as a customer for their products and the greater its bargaining power. Second, the more consolidated an industry, the less suppliers are able to play off companies against each other in an attempt to increase prices. Third, the more consolidated an industry, the less buyers are able to play off companies against each other in an attempt to drive down prices. Hence, as an industry moves toward maturity, the competitive power of buyers and suppliers shrinks.

Substitute products and industry evolution The competitive force of substitute products depends to some extent on the ability of companies in the industry to build brand loyalty for their own products. Other things being equal, the greater the brand loyalty for an industry's products, the less likely are consumers to switch to the products of substitute industries. Generally, as an industry evolves toward maturity, companies within it begin to expend more effort on differentiating their products to create brand loyalty. This gives a company some protection not only from companies in its own industry, but also from those in substitute industries. Thus, as it moves toward maturity, an industry begins to develop a greater degree of protection against the competitive force of substitute products. However, the emergence of significant *new* substitutes may well push a mature industry into decline, as synthetic materials have done in the steel industry.

Summary: Industry Evolution

The discussion of the effects of industry evolution on competition suggests that the strength of Porter's five competitive forces varies across an industry's life cycle. Rapid expansion makes for weak competitive forces in growth industries. Opportunities for expansion and capturing market share are greatest during this stage. Competitive threats then increase sharply during the shakeout period. The threat of price competition is one of the most important problems that strategic managers have to deal with at this stage. As an industry enters maturity competitive threats tend to decline and the opportunity exists to limit price competition through price leadership agreements. Thus, mature industries tend to be characterized by relatively high profitability.[20] Nonprice competition may often play a greater role at this stage, so it is important for the company to capitalize on opportunities to differentiate its product. This situation changes again when the industry enters the decline stage. Competitive intensity increases, particularly when exit barriers are high, profits fall, and the threat of price wars once more becomes substantial.

3.6 ANALYZING THE MACROENVIRONMENT

Macroenvironmental factors are factors external to an industry that influence the level of demand within it, directly affecting company profits. Many of these factors are constantly changing, a process that in itself gives rise to new opportunities and threats. Strategic managers must understand the significance of macroenvironmental factors and be able to assess the impact of changes in the macroenvironment on their company and the opportunities and threats it faces. Six main elements of the macroenvironment are of particular importance here: the macroeconomic environment, the technological environment, the social environment, the demographic environment, the political/legal environment, and the international environment.

The Macroeconomic Environment

The state of the macroeconomic environment determines the general health and well-being of the economy. This, in turn, affects companies' ability to earn an adequate rate of return. The four most important macroeconomic indicators in this context are: the growth rate of the economy, the interest rate, currency exchange rates, and the inflation rate.

Economic growth   The rate of growth in the economy has a direct impact on the level of opportunities and threats that companies face. Because it leads to an expansion in consumer expenditure, economic growth, tends to produce a general easing of competitive pressures within an industry. This gives companies the opportunity to expand their operations. Economic decline, because it leads to a reduction in consumer expenditure, increases competitive pressures and constitutes a major threat to profitability. Economic decline frequently causes price wars in mature industries. This happened in the heavy construction equipment industry during the recession of 1979, when many of the major companies, such as International Harvester Co., came close to bankruptcy.

Although the precise level of economic growth is notoriously difficult to predict, strategic managers need to be aware of the future outlook for the economy. For example, it would make little sense to embark on an ambitious expansion strategy if most forecasters expected a sharp economic downturn. Conversely, if the economy is currently in poor shape but a general upturn in activity is forecasted, companies might be well advised to take up an expansion strategy.

Interest rates   The level of interest rates can determine the level of demand for a company's products. Interest rates are important whenever consumers routinely borrow money to finance their purchase of these products. The most obvious example is the housing market, where the mortgage rate directly affects demand, but interest rates also have an impact on auto sales, appliance sales, and capital equipment sales, to give just a few examples. For companies in such industries, rising interest rates are a threat and falling rates an opportunity.

In addition, interest rates also determine the cost of capital for a company. This cost can be a major factor in deciding whether a given strategy is feasible. For instance, a company may finance an ambitious expansion strategy with borrowed money. This course of action may make good sense if interest rates are low and are predicted to stay at that level, but it would be folly if forecasts show interest rates rising to record levels.

Currency exchange rates   Currency exchange rates refer to the value of the dollar relative to the currencies of other countries. Movement in currency exchange rates has a direct impact on the competitiveness of a company's products in the global marketplace. When the value of the dollar is low compared with other currencies, products made in the United States are relatively inexpensive, whereas products made overseas are relatively expensive. A low or declining dollar reduces the threat from foreign competitors while creating opportunities for increased sales overseas. For example, the 45 percent fall in the value of the dollar against the Japanese yen between 1985 and 1987 sharply increased the price of imported Japanese cars, giving American manufacturers some degree of protection against the Japanese threat. However, when the value of the dollar is high, as was the case during the 1984–1985 period, then imports become relatively cheap and the threat from foreign producers increases. A high dollar also limits opportunities for overseas sales because of the relatively high price of goods manufactured in the United States.

Inflation rates Inflation can destablize the economy, producing slower economic growth, higher interest rates, and volatile currency movements. If it keeps increasing, investment planning becomes a hazardous business. The key characteristic of inflation is that it makes the future less predictable. In an inflationary environment, it may be impossible to predict with any accuracy the real value of returns that can be earned from a project five years hence. Such uncertainty makes companies less willing to invest. Their holding back, in turn, depresses economic activity and ultimately pushes the economy into a slump. Thus high inflation is a threat to companies.

The Technological Environment

In the post–World War II period the pace of technological change has accelerated, unleashing a process that has been called a "perennial gale of creative destruction."[21] Technological change can make established products obsolete overnight. At the same time it can create a host of new product possibilities. Thus it is both creative and destructive—both an opportunity and a threat. Since accelerating technological change also shortens the average product life cycle,[22] organizations need to anticipate the changes that new technologies bring with them: they need to analyze their environment strategically.

Witness recent changes in the electronics industry. For forty years until the early 1960s vacuum valves were a major component in radios, and then in record players and early computers. The advent of transistors destroyed the market for vacuum valves but at the same time created new opportunities connected with transistors. Transistors took up far less space than vacuum valves, encouraging a trend toward miniaturization that still continues today.

The transistor held its position as the major component in the electronics industry for just a decade. In the 1970s microprocessors were developed, and the market for transistors declined rapidly. At the same time, however, the microprocessor created yet another set of new product opportunities—hand-held calculators (which destroyed the market for slide rules), compact disk players, and personal computers, to name just a few. The strategically aware electronics company, by anticipating the effects of change, benefited from the progression of new technologies. The unaware company went out of business.

New technologies also give rise to new ways of manufacturing established products, in other words, to new processes. In turn, these new processes give rise to opportunities and threats. Robotics, especially as applied to the automation of vehicle assembly plants, is one example of a new process technology.

Another is the steel industry's development of minimills using new electric arc smelting techniques. This particular technology took away from large, integrated steel operations, such as U.S. Steel and Bethlehem Steel, the considerable advantage they once enjoyed due to economies of scale. Thus minimills have emerged as a major threat to established American steel manufacturers. Many minimills can now turn out steel at a lower cost than large, integrated plants, which use thirty-year-old technology. Indeed, by 1985 minimills and specialty steel mills held 40 percent of the U.S. market, while domestic integrated companies had a 38–40 percent market share, down from close to 70 percent ten years earlier.[23]

The Social Environment

Like technological change, social change, too, creates opportunities and threats. One of the major social movements of the 1970s and 1980s has been the trend toward greater health consciousness. The impact of this social change has been immense, and companies that recognized the opportunities early have often reaped significant gains. Philip Morris, for example, capitalized on the growing health trend when it acquired Miller Brewing Company and then redefined competition in the beer industry with its introduction of low-calorie beer (Miller Lite). Similarly, PepsiCo was able to gain market share from its archrival, The Coca-Cola Company, by introducing diet colas and fruit-based soft drinks first. The health trend has also given rise to booming sales of mineral waters, with a market growth of 15 percent per annum during the mid-1980s. In an attempt to capitalize on this opportunity, many of the country's largest beverage companies are currently expanding into this fragmented industry. At the same time the health trend has created a threat for many industries. The tobacco industry, for example, is now in decline as a direct result of greater consumer awareness of the health implications of smoking. Similarly, the sugar industry has seen sales decline as consumers have switched to artificial sweeteners.

The Demographic Environment

The changing composition of the population is a further factor that can create both opportunities and threats. For example, as the baby boom generation of the 1960s moved through the population, it has created a host of opportunities and threats. Currently, baby boomers are getting married, and creating an upsurge in demand for the consumer appliances normally bought by couples marrying for the first time. Thus companies such as Whirlpool Corporation and General Electric are looking to capitalize on the predicted upsurge in demand for washing machines, dishwashers, spin dryers, and the like. The other side of the coin is that industries oriented toward the young, such as the toy industry, have seen their consumer base decline in recent years.

The Political and Legal Environment

Political and legal factors also have a major effect on the level of opportunities and threats in the environment. One of the most significant trends in recent years has been the move toward deregulation. By eliminating many legal restrictions, deregulation has opened up a number of industries to intense competition. The deregulation of the airline industry in 1979, for example, created the opportunity to establish low-fare carriers — an opportunity that Texas Air, People Express, and others tried to capitalize on. At the same time, the increased intensity of competition created many threats, including, most notably, the threat of prolonged fare wars, which have repeatedly thrown the airline industry into turmoil during the last decade.

Deregulation apart, companies also face serious legal constraints, which limit their potential strategic options. Antitrust laws, for example, can prevent companies from trying to achieve a dominant market position through acquisitions. In 1986 both PepsiCo and Coca-Cola attempted to buy up smaller soft drink manufacturers, Pepsi bidding for the Seven-Up Company and Coca-Cola for Dr. Pepper Co. Both acquisitions were forbidden by the Federal Trade Commission on the grounds that, if they went through, Pepsi and Coca-Cola would between them control more than 80 percent of the soft drink market. Seven-up subsequently merged with Dr. Pepper, a move that has created the possible threat (to Pepsi and Coca-Cola) of a third major company emerging in the industry.

The Global Environment

Changes in the global environment can create both opportunities for market expansion and serious threats to a company's domestic and international market share. A crucial factor in the international environment is the stage of economic development of different nation states. Developing nations, such as Brazil, China, Korea, and Taiwan, offer enormous opportunities for U.S. companies to expand their international operations. At the same time the emergence of capable competitors in these nations threatens the domestic and international market position of American companies.

American companies have a history of ignoring the implications of changes in the international environment. In particular, they have often underestimated the potential impact of emerging competitors in developing nations on their share of the domestic and international market. In the 1960s, for example, U.S. auto manufacturers seriously underrated the effect that Japanese auto manufacturers would have on their competitive position. Consequently, they failed to react to the emerging Japanese threat and continued to design and build cars the way they had always done. This myopia led directly to the crisis situation in which U.S. auto manufacturers found themselves during the late 1970s and early

1980s. Similarly, American steel manufacturers, such as USX, discounted the threat of overseas competition from such countries as Japan, Korea, and Brazil until it was too late (see Opening Incident).

3.7 SUMMARY OF CHAPTER

This chapter has detailed the framework that can be used by strategic managers to analyze the external environment of their company, enabling them to identify opportunities and threats. The major points made in the chapter are as follows:

1. Superior performance is the product of a fit between strategy and the environment. In order to achieve such a fit, strategic managers must be able to identify environmental opportunities and threats.

2. The main technique used to analyze competition in the industry environment is the Five Forces Model. The five forces are the risk of new entry by potential competitors, the extent of rivalry among established firms, the bargaining power of buyers, the bargaining power of suppliers, and the threat of substitute products. The stronger each of these forces, the more competitive is the industry and the lower the rate of return that can be earned in that industry.

3. The risk of entry by potential competitors is a function of the height of barriers to entry. The higher the barriers to entry, the lower is the risk of entry and the greater the profits that can be earned in the industry.

4. The extent of rivalry among established companies is a function of the industry's competitive structure, demand conditions, and barriers to exit. Strong demand conditions moderate the competition among established companies and create opportunities for expansion. When demand is weak, intensive competition can develop, particularly in consolidated industries with high exit barriers.

5. Buyers are most powerful when a company depends on them for business but they themselves are not dependent on the company. In such circumstances, buyers are a threat.

6. Suppliers are most powerful when a company depends on them for business, but they themselves are not dependent on the company. In such circumstances, suppliers are a threat.

7. Substitute products are the products of companies based in industries serving consumer needs similar to those served by the industry being analyzed. The closer the substitute products, the lower is the price that companies can charge without losing customers to those substitutes.

8. Most industries are composed of strategic groups. Strategic groups are groups of companies pursuing the same or a similar strategy. Companies in different strategic groups pursue different strategies.

9. The members of a company's strategic group constitute its immediate competitors. Since different strategic groups are characterized by different opportunities and threats, it may pay a company to switch strategic groups. The feasibility of doing so is a function of the height of mobility barriers.

10. Industries go through a well-defined life cycle, from an embryonic stage, through growth, shakeout, and maturity, and eventually into decline. Each stage has different implications for the competitive structure of the industry, and each stage gives rise to its own set of opportunities and threats.

11. Important components of the macroenvironment include the macroeconomic environment, the technological environment, the social environment, the demographic environment, the political/legal environment, and the international environment. Although largely outside its direct control, macroenvironmental trends can profoundly affect the magnitude of opportunities and threats facing a company.

Discussion Questions

1. Under what environmental conditions are price wars most likely to occur in an industry? What are the implications of price wars for a company? How should a company try to deal with the threat of a price war?

2. Discuss Porter's Five Forces Model with reference to what you know about the airline industry. What does the model tell you about the level of competition in this industry?

3. Identify a growth industry, a mature industry, and a declining industry. For each industry, identify the following: (a) the number and size distribution of companies, (b) the nature of barriers to entry, (c) the height of barriers to entry, and (d) the extent of product differentiation. What do these factors tell you about the nature of competition in each industry? What are the implications for the company in terms of opportunities and threats?

4. Assess the impact of macroenvironmental factors on the likely level of enrollment at your university over the next decade. What are the implications of these factors for the job security and salary level of your professors?

Endnotes

1. Sources include Business Week, "It's USX vs Everybody," October 6, 1986, pp. 26–27; Organization for Economic Co-operation and Development, Steel in the 80s (Paris: OECD, 1980); "Better 'X' than Steel," Industry Week, July 21, 1986, p. 23; Frank Koelble, "Strategies for Restructuring the US Steel Industry," 33 Metal Producing (December 1986), 28–33.

2. Michael E. Porter, *Competitive Strategy: Techniques for Analyzing Industries and Competitors* (New York: Free Press, 1980). See also Porter, *Competitive Advantage: Creating and Sustaining Superior Performance* (New York: Free Press, 1985).

3. Joe S. Bain, *Barriers to New Competition* (Cambridge, Mass.: Harvard University Press, 1956).

4. For a more complete discussion of the sources of scale economies, see Chapter 4.

5. Most of this information on barriers to entry can be found in the industrial organization economics literature. See especially the following works: Bain, *Barriers to New Competition;* M. Mann, "Seller Concentration, Barriers to Entry and Rates of Return in 30 Industries," *Review of Economics and Statistics,* 48, (1966), 296–307; and W. S. Comanor and T. A. Wilson, "Advertising, Market Structure and Performance," *Review of Economics and Statistics,* 49, (1967), 423–440.

6. S. Greenhouse, "Dicey Days at McDonnell Douglas," *The New York Times,* February 22, 1987, p. 4.

7. C. F. Pratten, *Economies of Scale in Manufacturing Industry* (London: Cambridge University Press, 1971).

8. F. M. Scherer, *Industrial Market Structure and Economic Performance* (Chicago: Rand McNally, 1981).

9. For a discussion of tacit agreements, see T. C. Schelling, *The Strategy of Conflict,* (Cambridge, Mass.: Harvard University Press, 1960).

10. Koelble, "Strategies," pp. 28–33.

11. "It's USX vs Everybody," *Business Week,* October 6, 1986, pp. 26–27.

12. The development of strategic-group theory has been a strong theme in the strategy literature during recent years. Important contributions include the following: R. E. Caves and Michael E. Porter, "From Entry Barriers to Mobility Barriers," *Quarterly Journal of Economics* (May 1977), 241–262; K. R. Harrigan "An Application of Clustering for Strategic Group Analysis," *Strategic Management Journal,* 6, (1985), 55–73; K. J. Hatten and D. E. Schendel, "Heterogeneity Within an Industry: Firm Conduct in the U.S. Brewing Industry, 1952–71," *Journal of Industrial Economics,* 26, (1977), 97–113; and Michael E. Porter, "The Structure Within Industries and Companies' Performance,"*The Review of Economics and Statistics,* 61, (1979), 214–227.

13. Indeed, Charles W. Hofer has argued that life cycle considerations may be the most important contingency when formulating business strategy. See Charles W. Hofer, "Towards a Contingency Theory of Business Strategy," *Academy of Management Journal,* 18, (1975), 784–810. There is also empirical evidence to support this view. See C. R. Anderson and C. P. Zeithaml, "Stages of the Product Life Cycle, Business Strategy, and Business Performance," *Academy of Management Journal,* 27, (1984), 5–24; and D. C. Hambrick and D. Lei, "Towards an Empirical Prioritization of Contingency Variables for Business Strategy," *Academy of Management Journal,* 28, (1985), 763–788.

14. The difference is that individual products can have their own life cycle within the broader context of an industry life cycle.

15. "The PC Wars: IBM vs the Clones," *Business Week,* July 28, 1986, pp. 62–68.

16. Porter, *Competitive Strategy,* pp. 215–236.

17. "Nice Going, Frank, But Will It Fly?" *Business Week,* September 29, 1986, pp. 34–35.

18. The characteristics of declining industries have been summarized by K. R. Harrigan "Strategy Formulation in Declining Industries," *Academy of Management Review*, 5, (1980), 599–604.

19. J. J. Innace "Slippery Footing and the Fall of the Axe," *33 Metal Producing* (December 1986), 25–27.

20. The evidence of the effect of industrial organization economics on the relationship between profitability and market structure would seem to support the idea that mature industries are characterized by high profitability. For a review, see D. A. Hay and D. J. Morris, *Industrial Economics: Theory and Evidence* (Oxford: Oxford University Press, 1979).

21. The phrase was originally coined by J. Schumpeter, *Capitalism, Socialism and Democracy* (London: Macmillan, 1950), p. 68.

22. See M. Gort and J. Klepper, "Time Paths in the Diffusion of Product Innovations," *Economic Journal* (September 1982), 630–653. Looking at the history of forty-six different products, Gort and Klepper found that the length of time before other companies entered the markets created by a few inventive companies declined from an average of 14.4 years for products introduced before 1930 to 4.9 years for those introduced after 1949.

23. Innace, "Slippery Footing," pp. 25–27.

Chapter 4

INTERNAL ANALYSIS: STRENGTHS, WEAKNESSES, AND DISTINCTIVE COMPETENCES

4.1 OPENING INCIDENT: CATERPILLAR TRACTOR CO.

Caterpillar Tractor Co.'s first half century was one of remarkable success. To quote one 1980 commentator, "Caterpillar has combined lowest-cost manufacturing with higher cost but truly outstanding distribution and after-market support to differentiate its line of construction equipment. As a result, Caterpillar, ranking as the 24th largest and 39th most profitable company in the United States, is well ahead of its competitors and most of the Fortune '500' glamour companies."[1] In essence, Caterpillar had capitalized on distinctive competences in two of its major functional areas, manufacturing and marketing, to build a strong competitive position.

In 1982, however, things suddenly went bad for Caterpillar. The company reported its first loss in forty-eight years. A dramatic slump in world demand for heavy earth-moving and construction equipment, a strong dollar that increased the costs of Caterpillar's exports, and intense new low-cost competition from Komatsu of Japan all combined to make 1982 the worst year in the company's history. Caterpillar's response to these threats was to re-examine the basis of its former competitive advantage. It found that while it still had by far the best dealer network in the industry, it had lost its cost advantage to Komatsu. Instead of having distinctive competences in two major areas, Caterpillar now only had them in one—and that was not enough.

To re-establish its former cost advantage, Caterpillar embarked on an aggressive new manufacturing strategy, involving a $1-billion plant modernization program called PWAF (Plant with a Future). New high tech machine tools (including robots) were purchased and grouped with existing machines in work areas called cells. Each cell is a self-contained work unit that undertakes a major amount of assembly work on an individual product. In an operation such as Caterpillar's PWAF, a large number of cells work in parallel. The use of cells has improved product quality, lowered inventory requirements, and strengthened employee morale; it also decreased operating costs. In addition, Caterpillar installed sophisticated computer-controlled "just-in-time" inventory systems in its PWAF, reducing the need to hold expensive inventories of parts and equipment.

The result of Caterpillar's attempts to regain its low-cost position has been impressive. Between 1982 and the end of 1986 Caterpillar cut its operating costs by 22 percent, and the company stated its aim to reduce costs by a further 15–20 percent by 1990. Although Caterpillar has a long way to go, the performance consequences of its manufacturing strategy are beginning bear fruit. After three years of losses, Caterpillar netted profits in 1985 and 1986, while continuing to hold onto its 35–40 percent share of the U.S. market.[2]

4.2 OVERVIEW

In Chapter 3, we reviewed the elements of the external environment that determine the opportunities and threats facing a company. In this chapter, we will focus on identifying a company's *strengths* and *weaknesses* and examine functional-level strategies that can build and exploit the strengths and correct the weaknesses. For example, historically, its low-cost manufacturing position has been one of Caterpillar's strengths. When Caterpillar lost this advantage to Komatsu of Japan, its manufacturing function turned into a weakness. The company's manufacturing strategy in the 1980s was designed to correct this and to build a new distinctive competence for itself in manufacturing.

The term **distinctive competence** refers to a company's strengths that competitors cannot easily match or imitate. Distinctive competences represent the *unique* strengths of a company. Building a sustainable competitive advantage involves the strategic exploitation of distinctive competences; they form the bedrock of a company's strategy. For example, Caterpillar has always exploited its distinctive competence in distribution and after-sales service to maintain buyer loyalty and protect its market share. Similarly, 3M Company has exploited its distinctive competence in research and development to produce a wide range of product innovations.

In this chapter, we consider the sources of distinctive competences. Since distinctive competences are typically found *within* individual functions of a company—functions such as marketing, manufacturing, and materials management—we also examine the role of functional-level strategies in establishing and exploiting distinctive competences. The relationships considered in this

FIGURE 4.1   **The relationships between strategic resources, distinctive competences, and functional-level strategies**

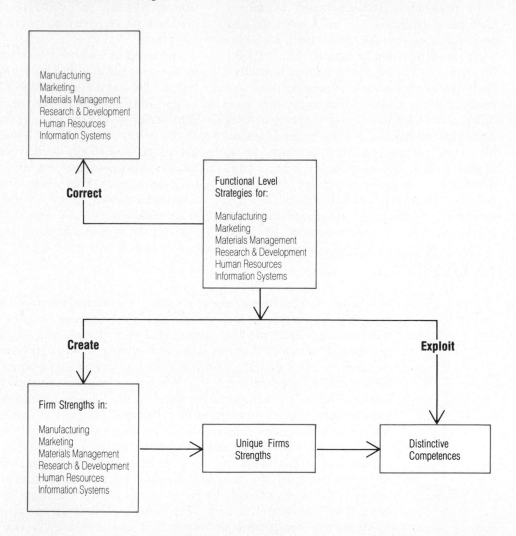

chapter are summarized in Figure 4.1. This figure indicates that unique company strengths create distinctive competences. Functional-level strategies are designed to exploit these distinctive competences. Functional-level strategies can also be used to create distinctive competences through the creation of company strengths. Thus, in a very real sense, a company's strengths are also the results of past functional strategies. Finally, functional-level strategies can be used to correct a company's weaknesses, with the aim of turning them into strengths — perhaps unique strengths or distinctive competences.

To explore the relationships set out in Figure 4.1, this chapter is structured as follows. First, we examine the concept of the **value chain** and the way in which distinctive competences help a company maximize value created through its value chain. The objective here is to show how the different functional areas referred to Figure 4.1 fit together. Second, we review each of the functional areas referred to in Figure 4.1. The objective is to identify both the sources of company-level strengths and weaknesses and basic functional strategies.

Bear in mind at this juncture that functional-level strategies are not formulated in a vacuum but in the context set by business-level strategies. Furthermore, the strategy-formulation process is not a top-down one (see Chapter 1). Distinctive competences help determine the set of feasible business-level strategies. In other words, an examination of a company's strengths and weaknesses tells management what the company *can* and *cannot* do at the business level. Thus the strategy-formulation process is an interactive one, and functional-level strategies and considerations are an integral part of it.

4.3 THE VALUE CHAIN AND DISTINCTIVE COMPETENCES

The value a company creates is measured by the amount that buyers are willing to pay for a product or service.[3] A company is profitable if the value it creates exceeds the cost of performing value-creation functions, such as procurement, manufacturing, and marketing. To gain a competitive advantage, a company must either perform value-creation functions at a lower cost than its rivals or perform them in a way that leads to differentiation and a premium price. To do either, it must have a distinctive competence in one or more of its value-creation functions. If it has significant weaknesses in any of these functions, it will be at a competitive disadvantage.

The value-creation process can be illustrated with reference to a concept called the value chain, which has recently been popularized by Professor Michael Porter of the Harvard School of Business Administration.[4] The form of the value chain is given in Figure 4.2. As you can see, the value chain is divided between *primary* activities and *support* activities. Each activity adds value to the product.

Primary activities have to do with the physical creation of the product, its marketing and delivery to buyers, and its support and after-sales service. In this chapter, we consider the activities involved in the physical creation of the product under the heading of manufacturing and those involved in marketing, delivery, and after-sales service under the heading of marketing. Thus establishing distinctive competences in primary value-creation activities means establishing them in manufacturing and marketing.

Support activities provide the inputs that allow the primary activities of manufacturing and marketing to take place. The materials management function controls the transmission of physical materials through the value chain, from

FIGURE 4.2   **The value chain**

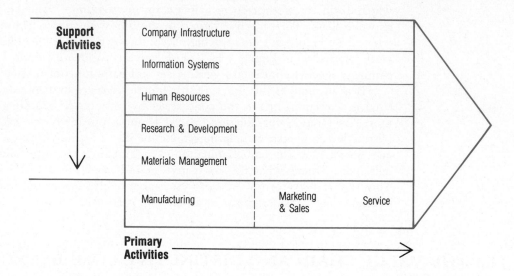

Source: Adapted with permission of The Free Press, a Division of Macmillan, Inc. from *Competitive Advantage: Creating and Sustaining Superior Performance* by Michael E. Porter. Copyright © 1985 by Michael E. Porter.

procurement through operations and into distribution. The efficiency with which this is carried out can significantly lower the cost of value creation. The R&D function develops new product and process technologies. Technological developments can lower manufacturing costs and result in the creation of more attractive products that demand a premium price. Thus R&D can affect primary manufacturing and marketing activities, and through them value creation. The human resource function ensures that the company has the right mix of people to perform its primary manufacturing and marketing activities effectively and that it meets the staffing requirements of other support activities. The information systems function makes certain that management has the information to maximize the efficiency of its value chain and to exploit information-based competitive advantages in the marketplace. Finally, company infrastructure consists of a number of activities, including general management, planning, finance, and legal and government affairs. The infrastructure embraces all other activities of the company and can be viewed as setting the context within which they take place. As with primary activities, establishing a distinctive competence in support activities can give the company a competitive advantage.

If a company can gain a distinctive competence in a primary or support value-creation function, its profit margin will increase. On the other hand, when these functions are weak, the company's value-creation process will lead to higher cost or an output that is valued less by consumers. In either case, its profit margin will be squeezed.

4.4 MANUFACTURING

With the rise of low-cost overseas competition, American companies have come to recognize the importance of manufacturing strategy. The objective of a company's manufacturing strategy should be to produce cost-competitive goods that are also sufficiently high in quality. If the company can achieve this objective, then its manufacturing function can be classified as a strength. If not, then manufacturing must be regarded as a weakness. Two concepts have played a particularly important role in the development of manufacturing strategy and in the identification of manufacturing strengths and weaknesses. The first is the experience curve, and the second, the product-process life cycle.

The Experience Curve

The concept of the experience curve was popularized by management consultants at the Boston Consulting Group (BCG) in the 1970s, although the basic idea had been around for at least thirty years before that.[5] The experience curve refers to systematic manufacturing cost reductions that have been observed to occur over the life of a product. Specifically, the BCG has noted that manufacturing costs for a product typically decline by some characteristic amount each time *accumulated* output is doubled. The relationship was first observed in the aircraft industry, where it was found that each time accumulated output of airframes was doubled unit costs typically declined to 80 percent of their previous level.[6] Thus, the fourth airframe typically cost only 80 percent of the second airframe to produce, the eighth airframe only 80 percent of the fourth, the sixteenth only 80 percent of the eighth, and so on. The outcome of this process is a relationship between unit manufacturing costs and accumulated output similar to that illustrated in Figure 4.3.

The strategic significance of the experience curve is clear. It suggests that increasing a company's product volume and market share will also bring cost advantages over the competition. Thus company A in Figure 4.3, because it is further down the experience curve, has a clear cost advantage over company B. Manufacturing is a strength for company A but a weakness for company B. Two reasons explain the cost reductions that underlie the experience curve: learning effects and plant-level economies of scale.

Learning effects   Learning effects refer to cost savings that come from learning by doing. Labor, for example, learns by repetition how best to carry out a task such as assembling airframes. In other words, labor productivity increases over time as individuals learn the most efficient way to perform a particular task. Similarly, it has been observed that in new manufacturing facilities management typically learns how best to run the new operation. Hence, production costs eventually decline due to increasing labor productivity and management efficiency.

FIGURE 4.3   A typical experience curve

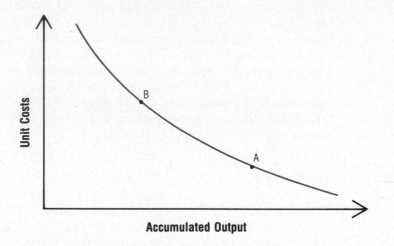

Learning effects tend to be more significant in situations where a technologically complex task is repeated, since there is more to learn. Thus learning effects will be more significant in an assembly process involving 1,000 complex steps than in an assembly process involving 100 simple steps. No matter how complex the task, however, learning effects typically die out after a limited period of time. Indeed, it has been suggested that they are really important only during the start-up period of a new process and cease after two or three years.[7] Any decline in the experience curve after such a point, therefore, is due to economies of scale.

Economies of scale   Economies of scale at the plant level refer to unit cost reductions achieved through mass production techniques. The classic example of such economies is Ford's Model T automobile. The world's first mass-produced car, the Model T-Ford, was introduced in 1923. Until then it had cost Ford approximately $3000 (in 1958 dollars) to build and assemble an automobile. By introducing mass production techniques, the company achieved greater division of labor (i.e., splitting assembly into small, repeatable tasks) and specialization, and reduced the cost of manufacturing cars to less than $900 per unit (in 1958 dollars) at large output volumes.[8]

As in the Model T case, so in many other situations plant-level scale economies lower costs. Du Pont, for example, was able to reduce the cost of rayon fiber from 53 cents per pound to 17 cents per pound in less than two decades mainly through plant-level scale economies. But these economies do not continue indefinitely. Indeed, most experts agree that after a certain **minimum efficient scale (MES)** is reached there are few, if any, plant-level scale

FIGURE 4.4   **A typical long-run unit cost curve**

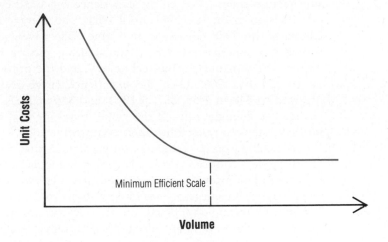

economies to be had from expanding volume.[9] (Minimum efficient scale refers to the minimum plant size necessary to gain significant economies of scale.) In other words, as shown in Figure 4.4, the long-run unit cost curve of a company is L-shaped. At outputs beyond MES in Figure 4.4, additional cost reductions are hard to come by.

Strategic implications   The experience curve concept is clearly important. If a company wishes to attain a low-cost position, it must try to ride down the experience curve as quickly as possible. This involves constructing efficient scale manufacturing facilities even before the company has the demand, and the aggressive pursuit of cost reductions from learning effects. The company probably also needs to pursue an aggressive marketing strategy, cutting prices to the bone and stressing heavy sales promotions in order to build up cumulative volume as quickly as possible. Once down the experience curve, the company is likely to have a significant cost advantage vis-à-vis its competitors, for it will have gained a distinctive competence in low-cost manufacturing.

However, the company furthest down the experience curve must not become complacent about its cost advantage for three reasons. First, since neither learning effects nor economies of scale go on forever, the experience curve is likely to bottom out at some point, and further cost reductions will be hard to come by. Thus in time other companies can catch up with the cost leader. Once this happens, a number of low-cost companies can have cost parity with each other. In such circumstances, establishing a sustainable competitive advantage must involve strategic factors in addition to the minimization of production costs.

Second, cost advantages gained from experience effects can be made obsolete by the development of new technologies. For example, the price of television picture tubes followed the experience curve pattern from the introduction of television in the late 1940s until 1963. The average unit price dropped from $34 to $8 (in 1958 dollars) in that time. The advent of color television interrupted the experience curve. Manufacturing picture tubes for color TVs required a new manufacturing technology, and the price for color TV tubes shot up to $51 by 1966. Then the experience curve reasserted itself. The price dropped to $48 in 1968, $37 in 1970, and $36 in 1972.[10] In short, technological change can alter the rules of the game, requiring that former low-cost companies take steps to re-establish their competitive edge.

A final reason for avoiding complacency is that high volume does not necessarily give a company a cost advantage. Some technologies have different cost functions. For example, the steel industry has two alternative manufacturing technologies: an integrated technology based on the basic oxygen furnace and a minimill technology based on the electric arc furnace. As illustrated in Figure 4.5, the electric arc furnace is cost efficient at relatively low volumes, whereas the basic oxygen furnace is most efficient at high volumes. Even when both operations are producing at their most efficient output levels, steel companies with basic oxygen furnaces *do not* have a cost advantage over minimills.

FIGURE 4.5   Unit production costs in an integrated steel mill and a minimill

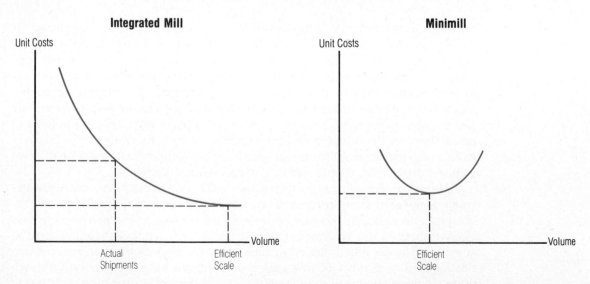

Source: Adapted from D. F. Barnett and R. W. Crandall, *Up From the Ashes: The Rise of the Steel Minimills in the United States* (Washington D.C.: Brookings Institute, 1986), p. 40. Reprinted by permission.

Consequently, the pursuit of experience economies by an integrated company using basic oxygen technology may not bring the kind of cost advantages that a naive reading of the experience curve phenomenon would lead the company to expect. Indeed, in recent years integrated companies have not been able to get enough orders to run at optimum capacity. Hence their production costs have been considerably higher than those of minimills.[11]

The Product-Process Life Cycle

The second concept that has played a role in the development of manufacturing strategy and the identification of manufacturing strengths and weaknesses is the product-process life cycle, originally developed by Harvard Business School Professors Robert H. Hayes and Steven G. Wheelwright.[12] The process-product life cycle suggests that manufacturing efficiency is optimized when a company matches its manufacturing process with its product structure.

Product-process framework   A version of Hayes and Wheelwright's framework appears in Figure 4.6. The horizontal axis summarizes a company's product structure, while the vertical axis summarizes different process technologies (process structure). Hayes and Wheelwright suggest that in the first instance manufacturing efficiency is optimized for companies on the diagonal of this matrix.

For example, typical of a company positioned in the upper left hand corner of the matrix is a commercial printer. In such a company, each job is unique and a jumbled flow, or job shop, process is usually selected as the most effective in meeting those product requirements. That is, the characteristics of the product require a flexible, job shop type of technology. Further down the diagonal, we might find a manufacturer of heavy equipment, such as Caterpillar or Navistar. These companies produce a range of different products, some of which may be customized. The fact that each item is not unique, however, allows the company to attain some economies of scale by moving from a job shop technology to a disconnected line, where batches of a given model proceed irregularly through a series of work stations.

Still further down the diagonal would be mass production operations such as high-volume auto manufacturers. The company's product structure at this stage is characterized by a limited range of high-volume products. By adopting full assembly line technology, the company can realize significant economies of scale (as in the classic example of the Model T Ford). Finally, in the right hand corner of the matrix are refinery-type operations, such as sugar refining and petroleum refining. These operations use continuous flow technology to manufacture high volumes of a standardized commodity-type product.

In Figure 4.6, the two shaded corners of the matrix are void of individual companies. The upper right-hand corner characterizes a commodity product

FIGURE 4.6 **Product and process structure**

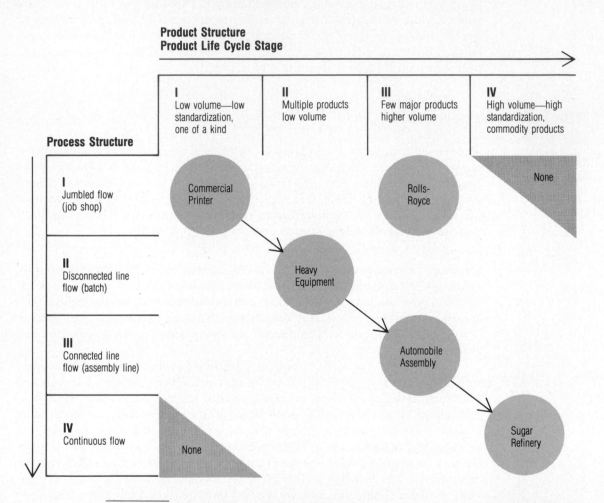

Source: Reprinted by permission of the *Harvard Business Review*. An exhibit from "Link Manufacturing Process and Product Life Cycles" by Robert H. Hayes and Steven C. Wheelwright (January–February 1979). Copyright © 1979 by the President and Fellows of Harvard College; all rights reserved.

produced by a job shop process. Such an arrangement would simply be uneconomical, if not impractical. The lower left-hand corner represents a one-of-a-kind product that is made by a continuous flow process. Again, such an arrangement would not be practical; continuous flow processes do not have the flexibility to manufacture one-of-a-kind products.

Strategic implications Hayes and Wheelwright's framework has both static and dynamic implications. From a static perspective, it suggests that matching product structure with process structure is the best way to minimize manufacturing costs. Companies off the diagonal are unlikely to be able to minimize unit costs. For example, it is not cost efficient for a company to attempt to produce a few high-volume products utilizing a disconnected line flow process. Thus, from the perspective of manufacturing costs, a match of product and process structure might be considered a company strength, while a mismatch might be considered a weakness.

However, Hayes and Wheelwright also recognize that under certain conditions it may be profitable for a company to seek a position off the diagonal. For example, Rolls Royce Motors, Ltd., makes a limited product line of automobiles using a process that is more like a job shop than an assembly line (see Figure 4.6). As a result, Rolls Royce's manufacturing costs are considerably above those of an automobile company on the diagonal, such as Ford or Chrysler. Nevertheless, because of the reputation for high quality and luxury stemming from its job shop process, Rolls Royce can charge a high enough price to cover its high manufacturing costs. In other words, Rolls Royce carries out its value-creation activities in a way that leads to differentiation and a premium price. It pays Rolls Royce to be off the diagonal because the company competes primarily on the basis of quality and image rather than cost. A company like Ford, however, has to remain on the diagonal if it is to compete effectively, because Ford competes on the basis of cost (price).

From a dynamic perspective, the main implications of the product-process framework stem from the fact that for some industries at least, industry evolution takes place down the diagonal of the matrix. The first three stages of the product structure dimension, for example, roughly correspond to the kind of product structures found within companies in the embryonic, growth, and maturity phases of an industry's evolution. The implication is that *companies competing on cost* need to match their process structure with the requirements of industry evolution. Thus in embryonic industries a jumbled flow process may be most appropriate, whereas in mature industries a connected line flow process may work best. However, these relationships are not inevitable. The heavy equipment industry, for example, has reached maturity, and yet most companies still produce a low volume of multiple products — because that is what the market demands. Nevertheless, from a dynamic perspective, the framework is of some use in predicting how a company should change its process structure to match the stage of industry evolution.

4.5 MARKETING

As with manufacturing, there has been an increasing tendency in recent years to view marketing from a strategic perspective.[13] Three key decision areas are central to strategic marketing management and the development of marketing competences: (1) the selection of target market segments that determine *where* the company will compete; (2) the design of the marketing mix (price, promotion, product, place) that determines *how* the company will compete in these target markets; and (3) positioning strategy. The company that performs each of these tasks well can create a differential advantage for itself in the marketplace. The marketing function is a strength for such a company. If the company fails to create a differential advantage, its marketing function must be regarded as a weakness.

Selection of Target Market Segments

Markets are rarely homogeneous (except in the cases of certain commodities). The typical market is made up of different types of buyers with diverse wants regarding such critical factors as product characteristics, price, distribution channels, and service. A market segment is a group of buyers with similar purchasing characteristics. For example, the auto market might be divided up into a compact segment, a status segment, a sports vehicle segment, and so on.

The critical strategic choice that a company faces is how to position itself with regard to different market segments. It has three basic alternatives (see Figure 4.7). In **undifferentiated marketing,** a single marketing mix is offered to the entire market. This rarely succeeds, given the different demands of different segments. In **differentiated marketing,** a different marketing mix is offered for each segment served. In **focused marketing,** the company competes in just one segment and develops the most effective marketing mix to serve that segment.

The classic example showing why undifferentiated marketing is normally a major weakness is the strategy Ford adopted toward its revolutionary Model T in the 1920s. To minimize production costs, Henry Ford proclaimed that consumers could have any car "as long as it is black," This strategy worked fine until Alfred Sloan of General Motors realized the potential for adopting a differentiated marketing strategy, offering different cars to different segments. Even though differentiation meant that it cost GM more than Ford to produce a car, the strategy worked because it recognized the diversity of consumer needs and wants.

One of the classic examples of a focused marketing strategy is that of Rolls Royce. By focusing on the needs of status-conscious high-income consumers, Rolls Royce has established a profitable niche for itself in the auto industry (which, as we saw in the previous section, has eliminated the need for Rolls Royce to adopt a low-cost manufacturing position).

One of the most difficult strategic choices many companies have to face is that between a focused and a differentiated marketing strategy. A differentiated strategy lets a company capture customers from many different market segments, thus permitting greater growth. Its drawback, however, is that a broader customer base may cause the company to lose the unique appeal generated by focusing on just one segment. Rolls Royce, for example, would probably lose

FIGURE 4.7   **Market segmentation and marketing strategy**

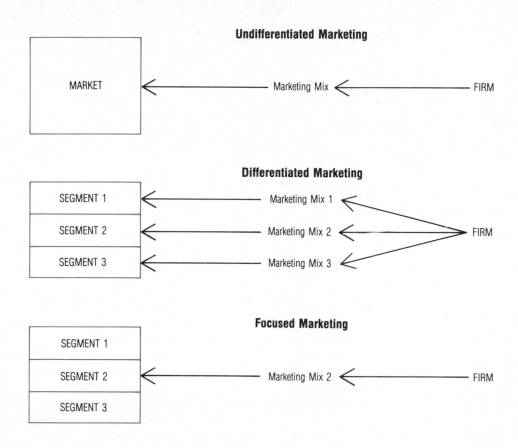

much of its prestige appeal if it began to manufacture compact cars. Making such a choice involves business-level strategy considerations, and we take up this dilemma in the next chapter.

Designing the Marketing Mix

The marketing mix is the set of choices that determine a company's offer to its target market(s). The marketing mix is normally defined in terms of the four P's of marketing: product, price, promotion, and place. Table 4.1 summarizes these main components. A company alters its marketing mix to discriminate among different segments. For example, the market for personal computers consists of a number of segments, including a segment of scientific users, an office segment, an educational segment, and a home user segment. Each segment is likely to desire different product characteristics (the scientific segment, for example, might require specialist features that other segments do not). The distribution

TABLE 4.1   **Components of the marketing mix**

Product	Price	Promotion	Place
Quality	List price	Advertising	Distributors
Features	Discounts	Sales promotions	Direct selling
Name/reputation	Allowances	Packaging	Retailers
	Credit		Locations
			Inventory
			Transport

channels utilized will also vary, as will advertising, promotional, and pricing strategies. Zenith Data Systems Corp., for example, has done well in the educational segment by offering 40 percent price discounts to colleges that buy its PC-compatible machines and by giving away free software to academic and student users as a promotional tool. IBM has excelled in the business segment by capitalizing on its reputation and using its substantial sales force to sell PCs directly to businesses. Hewlett-Packard Co. has done well in the scientific segment by designing its machines to suit the specific requirements of engineers and research scientists.

A company's objective when designing a marketing mix is to try to create a **differential advantage** or to exploit any differential advantage it already has. A differential advantage enables the company to distinguish its offer from that of its competitors in the segments in which it competes. In other words, it enables the company to establish a distinctive competence, or strength, in marketing. A differential advantage may be obtained through any element of the marketing mix: creation of a superior product or a more attractive design, better after-sales service, better advertising, more persuasive point-of-sales promotions, and so on. For example, much of IBM's differential advantage stems from name recognition. Caterpillar's comes from its dealer network, spare parts availability, and reputation for turning out a high-quality product. Anheuser-Busch, Inc., derives its differential advantage from name recognition of its Budweiser Beer brand, as well as from its competitive pricing and promotional skills. In most industries, only by creating such a differential advantage can a company ordinarily obtain high profits. Thus companies lacking any kind of differential advantage must view their marketing function as being a major weakness.

Positioning

As the final element of marketing strategy, positioning draws on the two earlier principles of marketing strategy. Positioning refers to the choice of target market segments that a company decides to focus on and the design of the marketing mix to create a differential advantage that defines how the company will compete with rivals in each segment. For example, Porsche is positioned in the prestige segment of the auto market with a differential advantage based on technical performance. Similarly, Rolls Royce is positioned in the prestige segment of the auto market with a differential advantage based on status, quality, and luxury. On the other hand, Chrysler has positioned itself in a number of different segments of the auto market, including the compact segment, midsized family car segment, and high-performance car segment. A company's success in positioning its products generally determines whether it has a distinctive competence in marketing or not.

4.6 MATERIALS MANAGEMENT

The role of the materials management function is to oversee the functions of purchasing, production planning and control, and distribution.[14] Sometimes referred to as logistics management, materials management is becoming an increasingly important function in many companies, since it can help a company establish a low-cost position. For the average U.S. manufacturing enterprise, materials and transport costs account for nearly 60 percent of sales revenues. Minimizing these costs leads to more value. In addition, according to the *Census of Manufactures,* U.S. manufacturing companies annually reinvest four or five times more capital in inventories than in new plant and equipment.[15] Efficient materials management can reduce the amount of cash a company has tied up in inventories, freeing money for investment in plant and equipment. Efficient materials management systems can therefore be regarded as a strength.

One technique specifically designed to reduce materials management costs is the just-in-time inventory system. Since under this system, parts are shipped from suppliers to manufacturers at the last possible moment, it can dramatically reduce inventory-holding costs, such as warehousing and storage, by increasing inventory turnover. Ford's switch to just-in-time inventory systems in the early 1980s reportedly brought the company a huge one-time saving of $3 billion. At Ford, minimal inventory now turns over nine times a year instead of the former six, reducing carrying costs by a third.[16]

Just-in-time systems also help improve the competitive position of many service companies. For example, Kroger, a nationwide grocery, drug, and convenience store, grades its suppliers on the timing of delivery. If goods are sent in too soon, they increase the space needed to store inventory, slow the turnover, and create the probability that goods will have to be paid for before they are resold. Kroger's grading system allows the company to track all their suppliers accurately and know which are the most reliable and the fastest.

According to materials management specialists Jeffrey G. Miller and Peter Gilmour of Harvard Business School, the concept of a materials management function reflects the fact that purchasing, production, and distribution are not separate activities but three aspects of one basic task: controlling the flow of materials and products from sources of supply through manufacturing and channels of distribution and into the hands of customers, in other words, through the value chain.[17] Tight coordination and control of the flow of materials allow a company to take advantage of cost savings, inventory reductions, and performance improvement opportunities unavailable without a materials management function. In short, materials management can assist companies such as Caterpillar in attaining a low-cost position.

FIGURE 4.8a   **Traditional reporting relationships**

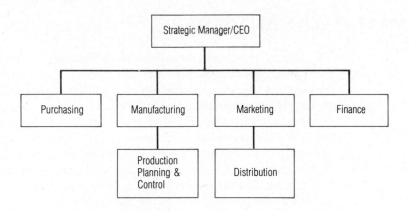

FIGURE 4.8b   **Materials management organization**

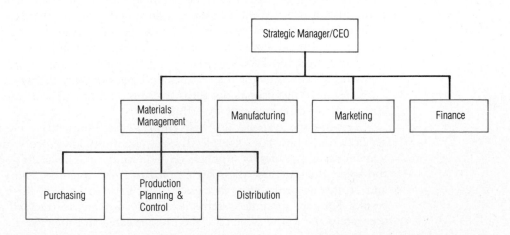

Despite the cost advantages of a materials management function, according to Miller and Gilmour, only about half of U.S. companies actually operate with such a function. Those that do not include many companies in which purchasing costs, inventories, and customer service levels are important and interdependent aspects of establishing a competitive advantage. Such companies typically operate with a traditional organization structured along the lines illustrated in Figure 4.8a. In such an organization, purchasing, planning and control, and distribution are not integrated. Indeed, planning and control are part of the manufacturing function, while distribution is seen as part of the marketing function. Such companies will be unable to establish materials management as a major strength and consequently will face higher production costs. Figure 4.8b shows what a typical materials management organization looks like. Its purchasing, planning and control, and distribution are all integrated within a single materials management function. Such an arrangement allows the company to transform materials management into an important strength or distinctive competence.

4.7 RESEARCH AND DEVELOPMENT

Of all the business functions, investment in research and development often produces the most spectacular results. Examples include Xerox's twenty-five-year domination of the photocopier market after the company's initial development of the invention; Du Pont's steady stream of inventions such as Cellophane, nylon, Freon (used in all air conditioners), and Teflon (nonstick pans); Sony Corp.'s development of the Walkman; and Bausch & Lomb Inc.'s development of contact lenses. However, research and development also involves the greatest risks of failure, with only about 12–20 percent of R&D-based projects actually generating profit when they get to the marketplace.[18] The remaining 80–88 percent fail. A couple of well-publicized recent failures were AT&T's losses taken on its venture into the computer industry (which amounted to a staggering $1.25 billion in 1986[19]) and Sony's development of Betamax video players, which have lost out to VHS systems (in 1986 Betamax had only a 5-percent share of the video player market).

Despite the high failure rate, a number of companies — for instance, 3M, Du Pont, and (despite Betamax) Sony — have managed to establish an undisputed distinctive competence in R&D. Such competence can be achieved by formulating an R&D strategy that stresses a close relationship with R&D skills.

R&D Strategy and R&D Skills

A company's R&D strategy can be broken down into three types: (1) strategies of **product innovation,** aimed at developing entirely new products ahead of competitors; (2) strategies of **product development,** aimed at improving the quality or features of existing products; and (3) strategies of **process innovation,** aimed at improving manufacturing processes to reduce costs and/or increase quality.[20] The basic R&D skills necessary to support each of these strategy types will vary along the lines illustrated in Figure 4.9. They include (1) skills in basic scientific and technological research, (2) skills in exploiting new scientific and technological knowledge, (3) skills in project management (selection and evaluation), (4) skills in prototype design and development, (5) skills in integrating R&D with manufacturing; and (6) skills in integrating R&D with marketing. Possession of these skills constitutes a strength in R&D.

Product innovation   As Figure 4.9 shows, product innovations require the most skills. The company must be able to carry out basic research, exploit the results of that research to develop new products, screen new products to select only those that have the greatest probability of success, ensure that it has the ability to manufacture these products and make certain that there is a market for them and/or that they meet market requirements.

FIGURE 4.9   **Strategy and R&D skills**

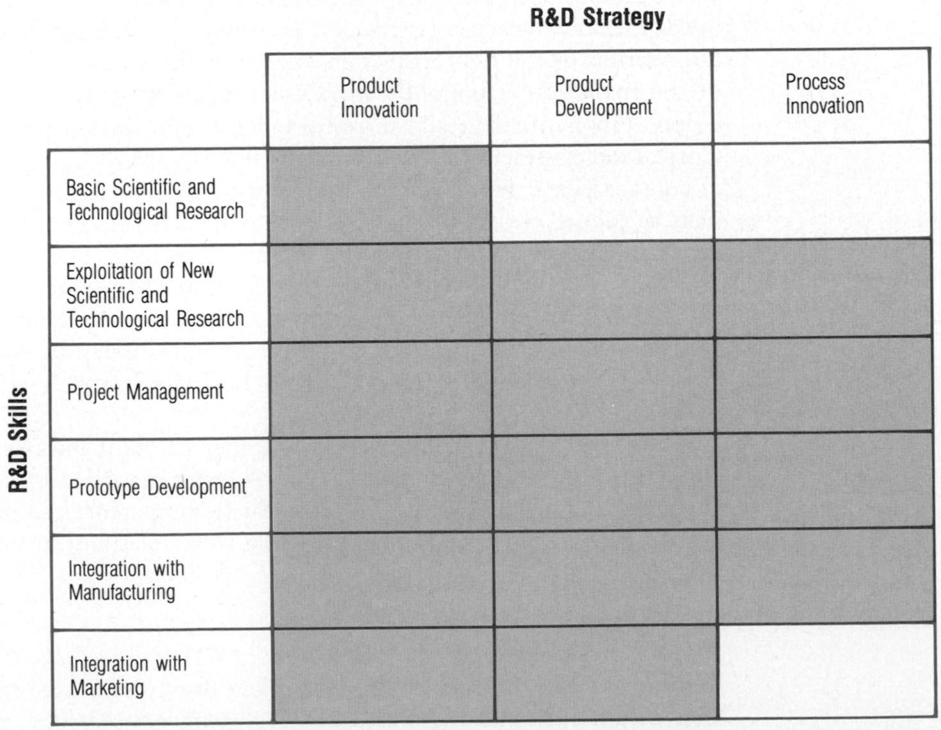

R&D Skills	Product Innovation	Product Development	Process Innovation
Basic Scientific and Technological Research	▓		
Exploitation of New Scientific and Technological Research	▓	▓	▓
Project Management	▓	▓	▓
Prototype Development	▓	▓	▓
Integration with Manufacturing	▓	▓	▓
Integration with Marketing	▓	▓	

R&D Strategy

Given the cost of establishing all these skills, only the largest companies in an industry tend to pursue a new product innovation strategy *on a continual basis* (although it is not unusual for small companies to generate important one-time innovations). Only companies such as AT&T, Du Pont, and IBM have the requisite funds to support basic research laboratories, and only they can afford to bear the risks. AT&T and IBM for example, have spent millions of dollars during the last few years in an attempt to develop superconducting materials. Yet despite spectacular advances, both companies predict that another twenty years may pass before they develop marketable products.[21] Clearly, most small and medium-sized companies cannot support research efforts on this scale.

Product development A product development strategy characteristically involves lower risks. The company is not introducing a totally new product but rather refining an existing one with a known demand. As Figure 4.10 shows, a product development strategy places significantly lower requirements on the company: it does not have to undertake basic research nor need it develop skills

FIGURE 4.10   **R&D strategy over the industry life cycle**

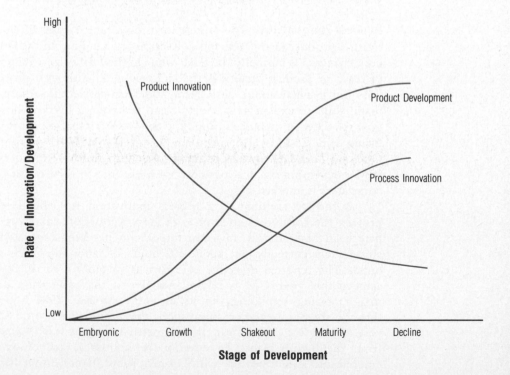

to exploit *new* scientific knowledge and technologies. Instead, the company takes an existing technology and refines or extends the products associated with it. Such companies are often classified as imitators. In the Japanese electronics industry, for example, Sony has been the traditional innovator, while Matsushita Electric Industrial Co., Ltd., with its Panasonic brand, and Sharp Electronics Corporation have been major followers or imitators.

However, product development need not mean imitation. One of the most notable cases of product development was that of Apple Computer. The original founders of Apple took existing computer technology that had originally been worked out by Intel Corp., Texas Instruments, and NASA and then used the technology to develop a dramatic extension of existing computer products — the first personal computer.

More generally, many companies undertake product development on a regular basis to continually upgrade their own product line. Nowhere is this more evident than in the automobile industry: its annual model changes involve incremental product developments. Leadership in product design, rather than the creation of new markets or imitation of market innovators, is the distinctive competence being sought here. Thus auto companies tend to stress prototype development and integration of R&D with marketing to ensure that new models appeal to consumers. The failure of General Motors to do this in recent years reduced the company's sales and market share at the end of the 1980s.

Process innovation   The motive for process innovation differs from the motive for product innovation and development strategies. In the latter cases, market expansion is normally the goal, while in the former cost reduction and/or an increase in product quality is the strategic aim. Although process innovation does not usually require basic technological and scientific research, it does demand skills to exploit new scientific and technological know-how. Because the goal is related to manufacturing efficiency, close integration between manufacturing and R&D is also called for. Caterpillar's PWAF project, cited in the Opening Incident, is one example of a cost-motivated process innovation. IBM's development of a low-cost assembly line to turn out its PS/2 personal computers is another.

A further example of a process innovation is General Motors' Saturn project: the company's attempt to produce a low-cost small car that can compete head to head with low-cost imports. It has been estimated that Japanese automakers currently put about 100 hours of labor into each small car they build. The reported objective of Saturn is to build a car in 30–40 hours. To achieve this goal, GM is relying heavily on the application of leading-edge manufacturing technology to its assembly process. GM hoped to produce through the Saturn project innovations that would slash some $2,000 from the cost of building a small car. It anticipated selling at least 400,000 cars yearly from the Saturn plant. To develop the necessary technology, in 1982 GM entered into a joint venture with Japanese robot manufacturer Fanuc (GMFanuc

Robotics Corporation) in an attempt to build supersmart machines to save on labor costs and boost product quality.[22]

For all the hype surrounding Saturn, however, many doubt that GM will be able to recoup its $5-billion investment in the project. GM has found it far from easy to develop the manufacturing technology for Saturn, and much of the equipment failed to work as well as expected. Besides, in the seven years that it took Saturn to develop a new low-cost small car, competition from Korea and Yugoslavia has forced GM executives to reorient Saturn toward the middle of the import pack, where prices are a few thousand dollars higher. GM has also lowered its expectations for Saturn. In November 1986 it decided to build only a first-phase plant, with a capacity of producing 250,000 vehicles. A second factory will be built only if sales are strong enough. In short, both the capital costs and the risks inherent in process developments as ambitious as Saturn are significant.[23]

Industry Life Cycle Factors

Industry life cycle factors also affect the propensity of companies to pursue different R&D strategies.[24] Figure 4.10 illustrates the implications of life cycle factors for R&D strategies. As shown, the rate of new product innovations is greatest in the embryonic and early growth stages of an industry, falling off thereafter. At those stages, the innovating company has the chance to set the technological context for future industry development. That was Sony's thrust when it introduced the Betamax video player, but its innovation lost out to the rival VHS system. However, had Sony succeeded in establishing Betamax as the industry standard, the company would have reaped substantial rewards.

As an industry matures, basic product characteristics become more standardized, and the significance of new innovations declines. Complementing this trend, product development strategies become more important. Detroit's obsession with annual model changes in an example of how the phenomenon manifests itself in the auto industry. At this stage, company R&D tends to be oriented less toward basic research and more toward product development and design.

A similar trend can be observed with respect to process innovations. Early in an industry's development, rapid growth permits companies with efficient and inefficient manufacturing processes to coexist, but as growth slows and competitive intensity increases, manufacturing efficiency becomes an important precondition for survival. At this stage, companies devote more attention to cost-reducing process innovations. Caterpillar's Plant with a future, IBM's high tech personal computer assembly line, and GM's Saturn project can all be seen as a natural response to the increase in competitive pressure as an industry enters a shakeout.

4.8 HUMAN RESOURCES

"Our people are our greatest resource" is one of the statements most commonly found in corporate annual reports; it is also one of the most important. Without the right people in the right positions, no strategy, however well formulated in other respects, is likely to succeed. This recognition has lead to the recent development of the field of strategic human resource management.[25] The objective of strategic human resources management is to develop a manpower plan that matches people with a company's strategic requirements, both in the short run and the long run. The critical elements of a manpower plan are (1) manpower forecasts that estimate the company's future manpower needs; (2) a manpower inventory that establishes whether there is a match between the company's current manpower resources and future manpower needs; (3) an analysis of the supply and demand for human resources; and (4) the formulation of alternative approaches to head off manpower resource imbalances.[26]

Beyond manpower planning, strategic human resource management also recognizes that people can themselves be a source of distinctive competence. The critical elements here are motivation, skills, and experience. If the company employs motivated individuals with a high degree of skills and/or experience, it is likely to be at a distinct advantage vis-à-vis competitors lacking such personnel. One of the factors underlying the rise of Domino's Pizza, Inc. as a major force in the fast food industry has been the high motivation of its branch managers. Most of these individuals are in their twenties and are motivated by the prospect of substantial profit bonuses. Similarly, the early successes of Apple in the personal computer industry can be attributed largely to the company's highly-motivated and skilled work force. We should note that corporate culture and control systems can influence employee motivation, and we consider these factors in Chapter 9.

4.9 INFORMATION SYSTEMS

We live in an information age. The sharp reduction in the cost of information systems (IS) technology has allowed computer systems to move from back office support applications to applications offering a significant competitive advantage.[27] The applications of IS technology are many and embrace all the primary and support activities of the value chain. Table 4.2 offers examples of the possible range of applications and shows that IS technology enhances a company's control over its costs, as well as helps create a differential advantage.

Specific examples of the strengths of IS technology come from a whole range of companies: Caterpillar applied IS technology in its PWAF project to manage just-in-time inventory systems and manufacturing cells; major airlines depend on computer-controlled reservation systems to create a differential advantage and capture customers; auto manufacturers rely on computer-aided de-

TABLE 4.2   **Examples of information system applications**

Activities	Applications	Implications
Manufacturing	Computer-controlled manufacturing systems	Lower costs/better quality control
Marketing	Telemarketing	Increased orders/ differential advantage
	Remote terminals for salespersons	Increased orders/ differential advantage
	Electronic market research	Increased orders/ differential advantage
Materials management	Automated warehousing/ just-in-time inventory systems	Lower costs
	Automated order processing	Lower costs
	Computer-scheduled distribution	Lower costs
Research and development	Computer-aided design	Lower costs/ differential advantage
Human resources	Automated personnel scheduling	Lower costs

sign systems to make more fuel-efficient automobiles and speed up the product development process (thereby lowering costs); and salespeople count on remote computer terminals to help them increase the scope and speed of price quotes. In addition, IS systems have fostered the growth of new products, such as credit cards. They have also enabled companies to change their competitive scope. For example, Dow Jones & Co., Inc., the publisher of *The Wall Street Journal,* pioneered a page transmission technology that links seventeen U.S. printing plants to produce a truly national newspaper. Using the same technology, Dow Jones has also started *The Asian Wall Street Journal* and *The Wall Street Journal/Europe*; it can maintain control over much of the editorial content while printing the paper in plants all over the world.

According to M. E. Porter and V. E. Millar, creating a distinctive competence in information systems and exploiting information-based competitive advantages requires the following steps[28]:

1. *Assess information intensity.*   The first task is to evaluate the existing and potential information intensity of the company's processes and products. An information-intensive manufacturing process is one that involves many complex assembly steps. Assembling an automobile, for instance, requires

the bringing together of as many as 7,500 different parts. Clearly, the scope for IS technology to reduce costs through better manufacturing coordination and control is much greater in such a case than in an assembly process involving 20 parts. An information-intensive product is one that has a high information content, for example, The Dun & Bradstreet Corp.'s service for corporate analysts.

2. *Identify how IS technology might create a competitive advantage.*   Managers need to evaluate in a systematic way how IS technology can create a competitive advantage. This requires assessing the impact of IS technology on the value chain and on industry competition (i.e., the five competitive forces discussed in Chapter 3), for the stronger the impact of IS technology on the value chain, the greater the potential change in industry competition. Many companies have succeeded in altering the basis of competition in their favor through investments in IS technology to create an IS-based distinctive competence. Citibank N.A. did so in the early 1970s with its introduction of automated teller machines, and American Airlines in the 1960s with the introduction of the first computerized reservation system.

3. *Develop a plan for taking advantage of IS technology.*   To create or exploit a distinctive competence in IS technology, a systematic IS plan must be worked out. This plan should rank the strategic investments needed in hardware and software, as well as in new product development activities that are necessary to establish a distinctive competence. Organizational changes reflecting the role that IS technology can play both within functional activities and in linking functional activities need to be recognized. In essence, the IS function needs to be closely integrated with other functions to exploit information-based competitive advantages to their full extent.

If the above steps are followed, a company may well place itself in a position where it has a distinctive competence in information systems. This support function helps it establish distinctive competences in other areas, thus contributing toward overall value creation in a number of different ways. By the same token, however, the company that does not develop a distinctive competence in information systems will find its ability to establish distinctive competences in other areas limited. Low-cost manufacturing and materials management, for example, are difficult to achieve without mastery of IS technologies. Thus strengths in information systems are becoming increasingly important. The company whose information system skills are weak will almost certainly find itself at a competitive disadvantage.

4.10 COMPANY INFRASTRUCTURE

Company infrastructure is the last support function in the value chain. It consists of the activities that set the organizational context within which other support and primary functions take place: strategic management, planning, finance, accounting, legal affairs, and government relations. These activities are often viewed as overheads — a somewhat unjust view, since they can be an important source of competitive advantage.[29] By helping a company identify its strengths, weaknesses, opportunities and threats, planning skills are in themselves often a major strength. Many strategic managers, such as Chrysler's Lee Iacocca, can be considered a company strength. Financial and accounting skills are perhaps among the most important company strengths. The ability of Texas Air to keep on growing by acquisitions in the airline industry, despite depressed profits, can largely be attributed to the company's skills in raising finance and keeping lines of credit open. Finally, legal skills and skills in governmental relations can also be an important source of competitive advantage, particularly for companies that depend on government contracts for business (e.g., defense contractors) or for companies that must negotiate with regulatory bodies on a regular basis (e.g., telephone companies).

4.11 FINANCIAL RESOURCES

As already noted, a company's financial position can constitute either a strength or weakness. Indeed, it can seriously affect the company's ability to build distinctive competences in other areas, given that doing so often requires substantial investments. The critical considerations here are cash flow, credit position, and liquidity.

Cash Flow

Cash flow — perhaps the most important financial consideration for a company — refers to the surplus of internally generated funds over expenditures. A positive cash flow enables a company to fund new investments without having to borrow money from bankers or investors. This is obviously a strength, since the company avoids paying interest or dividends. If current operations cannot generate a positive cash flow, the company is in a relatively weak financial position.

Like so much else, a company's cash flow position often depends on the industry life cycle. In the embryonic and early growth stages of an industry, most companies reinvest all their cash in operations. Companies in such industries are cash hungry. They have to construct manufacturing capacity to meet demand, undertake research to perfect basic product design, and bear marketing expenditures to expand demand for the product. Later in an industry's development, however, the necessary production facilities will have been built and basic product design features perfected. Consequently, demands for cash tend to be less substantial as an industry matures, enabling companies to generate a strong positive cash flow. Thus cash flow may move from being a weakness to a strength as the company's industry matures.

Credit Position

Even if cash flow is a weakness, a company can still establish a reasonably secure overall financial standing if it has a good credit position. A good credit position can enable the company to expand using borrowed money. To establishing good credit, a company must (a) have a low level of current debt and/or (b) be viewed by bankers and investors as having good future prospects. Many biotechnological companies, for example, have a negative cash flow but a strong overall financial position — because investors are willing to underwrite short-term losses in anticipation of big profit gains in the future from innovations in genetic engineering.

To a large extent, a company's ability to establish a good credit position depends on how it projects itself to bankers and investors. Companies based in embryonic or high-growth industries have an advantage, since the outlook for their business is generally more positive than for companies based in mature or declining industries. However, even a troubled company based in a highly competitive mature industry can establish good lines of credit if it is able to build up confidence on the part of investors. This is exactly what Lee Iacocca did when in 1979 he persuaded the U.S. government to underwrite a $1.5-billion loan for Chrysler, which was ailing.

Liquidity

A company is said to be liquid when its current assets exceed its current liabilities. Liquidity takes the form of idle working capital, such as marketable securities, or funding in reserve, such as unused lines of credit. A company's liquidity is a measure of its ability to meet unexpected contingencies, for instance, a sudden dip in demand or a price war. Companies that lack liquidity are in a weak financial position because they may be unable to meet these contingencies. Companies with major investments in fixed assets, such as steel mills or auto plants, tend to be less liquid than companies with a lower level of fixed assets. The reason is that fixed assets cannot be easily translated into cash and often require major fixed costs, which place heavy demands on the company's cash reserves in times of trouble.

4.12 THE VALUE CHAIN REVISITED

At the beginning of this chapter, we discussed the concept of the value chain as a means of identifying the important value-creation activities of a company. Here we consider the use of the value chain as an analytical tool to identify how a company might gain an advantage over its rivals, either by performing value-creation functions at a lower cost or by performing them in a way that leads to differentiation.

The Value Chain and Operating Costs

The allocation of operating costs to the different components of the value chain reveals how a company divides its costs among value-creation activities. Identifying whether a company has a strength or a weakness in each of its value-creation activities can provide pointers to the areas where significant cost savings might be found. For example, in Table 4.3 a company has apportioned its operating costs among the seven main value-creation functions discussed in this chapter. It has also assessed each activity according to whether it is a strength or a weakness from a cost perspective. As the table shows, the major contributors to operating costs are materials management (14 percent) and manufacturing (64 percent). Both of these functions have also been assessed as weaknesses. It follows that the company could substantially improve its cost position by focusing on materials management and manufacturing strategies designed to improve operating efficiency. Thus the company might introduce just-in-time inventory systems and pursue strategies consistent with the establishment of scale economies.

The Value Chain and Differentiation

Differentiation also grows out of a company's value chain. Virtually any value activity can be a potential source of uniqueness. For example, not only can an efficient materials management function be a major source of cost savings, it can also help improve product quality. In recent years the procurement staff at Chrysler has paid particular attention to the quality of the parts purchased from auto component suppliers. This helped reduce the number of warranty claims made on Chrysler's cars by more than 40 percent between 1981 and 1986. Similarly, Heineken Holland Beer takes pains to use superior and pure ingredients in its beer, in order to maintain a consistently high quality for its product. It is also

TABLE 4.3   **The distribution of operating costs over the value chain**

Value-creation activity	Operating costs	Strength	Weakness
Company infrastructure	5%	Yes	No
Information systems	1%	Yes	No
Human resources management	2%	Yes	No
Research and development	5%	Yes	No
Materials management	14%	No	Yes
Manufacturing	64%	No	Yes
Marketing and sales	9%	Yes	No

TABLE 4.4   **Value-creation activities and differentiation**

Value-creation activity	Impact upon differentiation	Strength	Weakness
Firm infrastructure	Moderate	Yes	No
Information systems	Moderate	Yes	No
Human resource management	High	Yes	No
Research and development	High	No	Yes
Materials management	Moderate	Yes	No
Manufacturing	Low	Yes	No
Marketing and sales	High	No	Yes

important to note that value-creation activities representing only a small percentage of total costs can have a major impact upon differentiation. Running information systems may only involve 1 percent of total costs. Nevertheless, information systems are important for a manufacturer such as Whirlpool, which keeps complete records of the after-sales service problems experienced by individual consumers as a way of creating uniqueness through its service function.

The task for strategic managers is to assess each of the value-creation functions in terms of (a) its potential impact upon differentiation, and (b) its being a strength or a weakness from a differentiation perspective. An example of how this might work is given in Table 4.4. Here a company has identified three value-creation activities that have a high impact on differentiation in the industry in which it competes: human resource management, research and development, and marketing. Two of these activities, R&D and marketing, are considered weaknesses. If the company wishes to differentiate its product, it must pursue strategies at the functional level designed to turn these weaknesses into strengths. For example, it may have to redesign its marketing mix to better align its product with certain market segments. In addition, it may have to improve its R&D skills so that they match the R&D requirements of a differentiation strategy.

Coordination Within the Value Chain

Establishing a competitive advantage often requires close coordination between the different activities of the value chain. We have already observed how coordination between (a) R&D and marketing, (b) R&D and manufacturing, and (c) purchasing, production and distribution through the materials management function are all important preconditions for establishing distinctive competences. More generally, meeting consumer needs almost always involves coordination among the different activities of the value chain. For example, in the auto industry, U.S. companies are trying to emulate Japanese quality standards by modifying every activity that influences product defects instead of relying on a single activity, such as inspection.

4.13 SUMMARY OF CHAPTER

This chapter has shown how distinctive competences arise out of the unique strengths found within a company's individual functions, or value-creation activities. These competences enable the company to establish a sustainable competitive advantage, whereas their lack places the company at a considerable competitive disadvantage. The pursuit of functional strategies can help the company (a) exploit existing distinctive competences, and (b) establish new distinctive competences.

The main points made in this chapter can be summarized as follows:

1. Distinctive competences derive from unique company-level strengths and are the result of past strategies. Functional strategies can be used to establish or exploit distinctive competencies and/or to correct weaknesses.

2. To gain a competitive advantage, a company must either perform value-creation activities at a lower cost than its rivals or perform them in a way that leads to differentiation and a premium price. To do either, a company must have a distinctive competence in one or more of its value-creation functions.

3. Strengths in manufacturing enable a company to minimize manufacturing costs for a given level of product quality. Establishing a distinctive competence in manufacturing involves exploiting experience curve economies and matching process structure with product structure. A company that attains both these objectives will find that its manufacturing costs are at least as low as, if not lower than, those of its nearest rivals.

4. Strengths in marketing enable a company to differentiate its product. Establishing a distinctive competence in marketing involves appropriate market segmentation and the design of a marketing mix that enables the company to establish a differential advantage. A company that achieves this will be able to increase volume sold and/or charge a higher price than a company that does not.

5. Strengths in materials management enable a company to minimize the costs of logistics functions. Establishing a distinctive competence in materials management involves creating a materials management function that oversees purchasing, production planning, and distribution activities. A company that achieves this will be able to minimize costs in each of these areas.

6. Strengths in R&D enable a company to create new market opportunities through product innovation, differentiate its product through product development, or minimize product costs for a given quality through process innovation. Establishing a distinctive competence in R&D involves matching R&D skills to the requirement of an R&D strategy. Companies that lack appropriate skills will not be able to build an R&D-based competitive advantage.

7. Strengths in human resource management enable a company to match people to strategic manpower requirements. Establishing a distinctive competence in human resources involves manpower planning to acquire individuals with the requisite mix of skills and experience, and control procedures designed to motivate people.

8. Strengths in information systems enable the company to exploit information-based competitive advantages in other business functions, from manufacturing to human resource management. Establishing a distinctive competence in information systems involves assessing the information intensity of company products and processes, identifying ways in which information systems can lead to a competitive advantage, and developing a company wide plan for taking advantage of information systems.

9. A company's infrastructure consists of activities that set the organizational context within which other support and primary functions take place. These activities include general management, planning, finance, accounting, legal affairs, and government relations. A distinctive competence in any of these areas can assist the company in obtaining a sustainable competitive advantage.

10. The most critical components of a company's financial resources are its cash flow, credit, and liquidity positions. A positive cash flow, good credit, and high liquidity constitute strengths, whereas a negative cash flow, poor credit (high debt), and low liquidity are weaknesses.

11. A company can use the value chain as a tool for identifying (a) the functions where it might gain the most from cost reductions, and (b) the functions where it might gain most from focusing on differentiation.

Discussion Questions

1. What is the purpose of the value chain? How can it assist strategic managers in identifying the company's strengths and weaknesses with respect to (a) operating costs, and (b) differentiation?

2. What functional strategies might a company pursue for each of the value-creation activities to minimize its overall operating costs?

3. What functional strategies might a company pursue for each of the value-creation activities to maximize the uniqueness of its product?

4. To what extent are the strategies you listed in response to Question 2 incompatible with the strategies you listed in responding to Question 3?

Endnotes

1. W. K. Hall "Survival Strategies in a Hostile Environment," *Harvard Business Review* (September–October 1980), 75–85.

2. "Caterpillar is Betting on Pint-sized Machines," *Business Week,* November 25, 1985, p. 41. "For Caterpillar the Metamorphosis Isn't Over," *Business Week,* August 31, 1987, pp. 72–74. "Where to Find the Top 100s," *Forbes,* July 13, 1987, p. 164.

3. Michael E. Porter, *Competitive Advantage: Creating and Sustaining Superior Performance* (New York: Free Press, 1985).

4. Ibid.

5. See W. J. Abernathy and K. Wayne, "Limits of the Learning Curve," *Harvard Business Review* (September–October 1974) 109–119; Boston Consulting Group, *Perspectives on Experience* (Boston, Mass.: The Boston Consulting Group, 1972); G. Hall and S. Howell, "The Experience Curve from an Economist's Perspective," *Strategic Management Journal,* 6 (1985), 197–212; and W. B. Hirschmann, "Profit from the Learning Curve," *Harvard Business Review* (January–February 1964).

6. A. A. Alchian, "Reliability of Progress Curves in Airframe Production," *Econometrica* 31 (1963), 679–693.

7. Hall and Howell, "The Experience Curve," pp. 197–212.

8. Abernathy and Wayne, "Limits of the Learning Curve," pp. 109–119.

9. For example, see F. M. Scherer, A. Beckenstein, E. Kaufer, and R. D. Murphy, *The Economies of Multiplant Operations* (Cambridge: Mass.: Harvard University Press, 1975).

10. Abernathy and Wayne, "Limits of the Learning Curve," pp. 109–119.

11. D. F. Barnett and R. W. Crandall, *Up from the Ashes: The Rise of the Steel Minimill in the United States* (Washington, D.C.: The Brookings Institute, 1986).

12. For example, see these three articles by Robert H. Hayes and Steven G. Wheelwright: "Link Manufacturing Process and Product Life Cycles," *Harvard Business Review* (January–February 1979), 133–153; "The Dynamics of Process-Product Life Cycles," *Harvard Business Review* (March–April 1979), 127–136; and "Competing Through Manufacturing," *Harvard Business Review* (January–February 1985), 99–109.

13. For example, see J. M. Hulbert and N. E. Toy, "A Strategic Framework for Marketing Control," *Journal of Marketing,* 41 (1977), 12–20; R. M. Johnson, "Market Segmentation: A Strategic Management Tool," *Journal of Marketing Research,* 8 (1971), 15–23.

14. D. Ammer, "Materials Management as a Profit Center," *Harvard Business Review* 47 (January–February 1969), 49–60. Jeffrey G. Miller and Peter Gilmour, "Materials Managers: Who Needs Them?," *Harvard Business Review,* (July–August 1979), 57.

15. Miller and Gilmour, "Materials Managers," p. 57.

16. "Old-Line Industry Shapes Up," *Fortune,* April 27, 1987, pp. 23–32.

17. Miller and Gilmour, "Materials Managers," p. 57.

18. These figures are averages taken from research by Edwin Mansfield and his associates. For example, see Edwin Mansfield, "How Economists See R&D," *Harvard Business Review* (November–December 1981), 98–106; and Edwin Mansfield, J. Rapoport, J. Schnee, S. Wagner, and M. Hamburger, *Research and Innovation in the Modern Corporation* (New York: Norton, 1971).

19. For details, see P. Petre, "AT&T's Epic Push into Computers," *Fortune,* May 25, 1987, pp. 42–50.

20. V. Scarpello, W. R. Boulton, and C. W. Hofer, "Reintegrating R&D into Business Strategy," *Journal of Business Strategy,* (Spring 1986), Vol. 6, pp. 49–56.

21. See "Our Life Has Changed," *Business Week,* April 6, 1987, pp. 94–100.

22. A. B. Fisher, "Behind the Hype at Saturn," *Fortune,* November 11, 1985, p. 35.

23. A. B. Fisher, "Behind the Hype at Saturn," *Fortune,* November 11, 1985, pp. 34–46. "General Motors: What Went Wrong?" March 16, 1987, pp. 102–110. J. K. Glassman "The Wreck of General Motors," *The New Republic,* December 29, 1986, pp. 21–23.

24. W. J. Abernathy and J. M. Utterback, "Patterns of Industrial Innovation," *Technology Review* 80 (1978), 1–9.

25. C. Fomrun, N. Tichy, and M. A. Devanna, *Strategic Human Resource Management* (New York: John Wiley, 1983).

26. J. Sweet, "How Manpower Development Can Support Your Strategic Plan," *Journal of Business Strategy,* (Summer 1981), Vol. 2, pp. 78–81.

27. See F. W. McFarlan, "Information Technology Changes the Way You Compete," *Harvard Business Review* (May–June 1984), 98–103. Michael E. Porter and V. E. Millar "How Information Gives You a Competitive Advantage," *Harvard Business Review* (July–August 1985), 149–160.

28. Porter and Millar, ibid.

29. Porter, *Competitive Advantage,* p. 43.

Chapter 5

BUSINESS-LEVEL
STRATEGY

5.1 OPENING INCIDENT: HOLIDAY INNS INC.

The history of the Holiday Inns Inc. motel chain is one of the greatest success stories in American business. Its founder, Kemmons Wilson, vacationing in the early 1950s, discovered that existing motels were small, expensive, and of unpredictable quality. This discovery, along with the promise of unprecedented highway travel that would come with the new interstate highway program, triggered a realization: he had uncovered an unmet customer need, a gap in the market for quality accommodations. His Holiday Inns were to meet that need. From the beginning, Holiday Inns set the standard for motel features like air conditioning and ice makers, while keeping room rates reasonable.[1] All these qualities added to the motels' popularity, and a Wilson invention, motel franchising, made rapid expansion possible. By 1960 Holiday Inns motels dotted America's landscape; they could be found in every city and on every highway. Before that decade ended, more than 1,000 of them were in full operation, and occupancy rates averaged 80 percent. The concept of mass accommodation had arrived.

By the 1970s, however, the motel chain's strategy was in trouble. The kind of service Holiday Inns offered appealed to the average traveler who wanted a standardized product (room) at an average cost. In essence, it targeted the middle of the hotel-room market segment. But travelers began to make different demands on hotels and motels: some wanted luxury and were willing to pay higher prices for better accommodations and service, while others sought low prices and accepted rock-bottom quality and service to get them. The market had fragmented into different groups of customers with different needs, but Holiday Inns was still offering an undifferentiated, average-cost, average-quality product aimed at the average customer.[2]

Holiday Inns may have missed the change in the market and thus failed to respond appropriately to it, but the competition had not. Some companies, like Hyatt Corp., siphoned off the top end of the market, where quality and service sold rooms. Other chains, like Motel 6 Inc. or Days Inn, captured the basic-quality, low-price end of the market. In between were many specialty chains that appealed to business travelers or families or self-caterers. Holiday Inns' position was attacked from all sides. The company's earnings declined as occupancy rates dropped drastically, and marginal Holiday Inns motels began to close as competition increased.

Wounded but not dead, Holiday Inns is counterattacking. The original chain has been upgraded to suit quality-oriented travelers. At the same time, to meet the needs of different kinds of travelers, the company has created new hotel and motel chains, including the luxury Holiday Inn Crowne Plazas, the Hampton Inns that serve the low-price end of the market, and the all-suite Embassy Suites. Holiday Inns has attempted to meet the demands of the many niches, or segments, in today's hotel market. However, while it is still the biggest motel operator, it has lost its leading role in the industry. Now it is simply one of the companies in a mature and overcrowded market.[3]

5.2 OVERVIEW

As the Holiday Inns example suggests, this chapter examines *how a company can compete effectively in a business or industry* and scrutinizes the various strategies that a company can adopt to maximize its competitive advantage and profitability. Chapter 3, on the industry environment, provided the concepts for analyzing industry opportunities and threats. The last chapter discussed how a company can develop distinctive competences at the functional level in order to gain a competitive edge. The purpose of this chapter is to consider the business-level strategies that a company can use to compete effectively in the marketplace.

We begin by examining the basis of all business-level strategy: the process of deciding what products to offer, what markets to compete in, and what distinctive competences to pursue. Second, we discuss the three **generic competitive business-level strategies** of cost leadership, differentiation, and focus. The discussion centers on how to organize and combine decisions regarding product, market, and distinctive competences so that a company can follow one of these generic strategies. We then look at how the industry context affects the way a company competes. Third, we examine the various **investment strategies** that a company may adopt at the business level to match its generic competitive strategies. Two factors are important in the choice of investment strategy: (1) a company's relative competitive strength in the industry, and (2) its stage in the industry life cycle. Finally, we discuss the issues involved in choosing a business-level strategy in fragmented and consolidated industries. By the end of the chapter, you will understand how the successful choice of business-level strategy is a product of matching environmental opportunities and threats, discussed in Chapter 3, to a company's strengths and weaknesses, discussed in Chapter 4.

5.3 FOUNDATIONS OF BUSINESS-LEVEL STRATEGY

In Chapter 2, on defining the business, we discussed how Abell saw the process of business definition as one involving decisions about (1) customer needs, or what is to be satisfied, (2) customer groups, or who is to be satisfied, and (3) distinctive competences, or how customer needs are to be satisfied.[4] These three decisions are at the heart of business-level strategy choice because they provide the sources of a company's competitive advantage over its rivals and determine how the company will compete in a business or industry. Consequently, we need to look in more detail at the ways in which companies can gain a competitive advantage at the business level.

Customer Needs and Product Differentiation

Customer needs are anything that can be satisfied through the characteristics of a product or service. Product differentiation is *the process of creating a competitive advantage by designing product characteristics to satisfy customer needs.* All companies must differentiate their products to a certain degree in order to satisfy some minimal level of customer needs. However, some differentiate their products to a much greater degree than others, and this difference can give them a competitive edge. For example, some companies simply offer the customer a low-price product, without engaging in much product differentiation.[5] Others seek to create something *unique* about their products so that they satisfy customer needs in ways other products cannot. This uniqueness may relate to the actual physical characteristics of the product, such as quality or reliability, or it may lie in the product's appeal to customers' psychological needs, such as need for prestige or status.[6] Thus a Japanese auto may be differentiated by its reputation for reliability, while a Corvette or a Porsche may be differentiated by its ability to satisfy customers' status needs. Alternatively, product differentiation may be achieved by the number or diversity of models in the company's product range. For example, in a recent catalogue, Sony offered twenty-four different kinds of nineteen-inch color television sets aimed at the top end of the market. Similarly, Baskin-Robbins Inc. provides at least thirty-one flavors of ice cream aimed at ice cream lovers, and Foot Locker stocks the largest selection of athletic shoes available to appeal to the greatest number of buyers. A final way to differentiate a product is through a company's distinctive competence, as we will discuss below. In practice, the form of product differentiation a company pursues is closely linked to the customer groups it serves.

Customer Groups and Market Segmentation

Market segmentation may be defined as *the way a company decides to group customers, based on important differences in their needs or preferences, in order to gain a competitive advantage.*[7] In general, a company can adopt three alternative strategies toward market segmentation.[8] First, it may choose not to recognize that different groups of customers have different needs and may adopt an approach of serving the average customer. Holiday Inns did this for much of its history. Second, it may choose to segment its market into different constituencies and develop a product to suit the needs of each group. This approach matches that of Holiday Inns after it lost market share. Third, a company can choose to recognize that the market is segmented but concentrate on servicing only one market segment, or niche.

Why would a company want to make complex product/market choices and create a different product, tailored to each market segment, rather than a single product for the whole market? The answer is that the decision to provide many products for many market niches allows a company to satisfy customer needs better. As a result, customer demand for the company's products rises and generates more revenue than if the company just offered one product for the whole market.[9] The contest between Ford and General Motors back in the 1920s illustrates this point.

Ford produced more motor cars in the 1920s than any other company. It was also the lowest-cost producer, since Henry Ford believed that one product would satisfy the entire market. This strategy worked well until GM's Alfred Sloan recognized the potential of segmenting the market and offering differentiated products.[10] Sloan developed five car divisions—Chevrolet, Pontiac, Oldsmobile, Cadillac, and Buick—each producing a wide range of different kinds of cars. Although this approach cost more, GM could recoup the costs with a differentiated pricing policy: different car models were directed at different socioeconomic market segments. Because the product policy satisfied different customer needs, it was wildly successful. GM passed Ford in market share and profit, a position it sustained until 1986. Essentially, *Ford and GM made different decisions about which customer groups and customer needs to satisfy, and as a result they obtained different competitive advantages.* Holiday Inns made the same mistake as Ford made in the 1920s. It failed to realize that a company has to respond to customer groups and needs if it is to maximize profitability.

Sometimes, however, the nature of the product or the nature of the industry does not allow much differentiation—for example, bulk chemicals or cement.[11] In these cases, there is less opportunity for obtaining a competitive advantage through product differentiation and market segmentation because there is less opportunity for serving customer needs and customer groups in different ways. Instead, price is the main criterion used by customers to evaluate the product, and the competitive advantage lies with the company providing the lowest-priced product.

Deciding on Distinctive Competences

The third issue in business-level strategy is to decide what distinctive competence to pursue in order to satisfy customer needs and groups.[12] Here we define a distinctive competence *as the means by which a company attempts to satisfy cus-*

tomer needs and groups in order to obtain a competitive advantage. Thus, for example, some companies will use their production technology to develop a manufacturing distinctive competence as a way of satisfying customer needs. The company will try to ride down the experience curve to provide customers with lower-cost products. Other companies may choose to concentrate on research and development to build a technological distinctive competence and satisfy customer needs through the design and performance characteristics of their products. Still others may decide to satisfy customer needs by the quality of their service and the responsiveness of service personnel; that is, they may focus on developing a sales and marketing competence. The point is that, in making business strategy choices, a company must decide how to *organize and combine* its distinctive competences in order to gain a competitive advantage. The source of these distinctive competences was discussed at length in the last chapter.

In sum, the use of a product/market/distinctive competence perspective provides a framework for understanding the foundations of competitive business level strategy. Each of the generic competitive strategies discussed below is the result of making different product/market/distinctive competence decisions in order to obtain a competitive advantage over industry rivals.

5.4 CHOOSING A GENERIC COMPETITIVE STRATEGY AT THE BUSINESS LEVEL

In this section, we examine the strategies available to companies to compete effectively in a business or industry. Companies pursue a business-level strategy to gain a competitive advantage that will allow them to outperform rivals and achieve above-average returns. They can choose from three basic competitive approaches at the business level: the generic competitive strategies of **cost leadership, differentiation,** and **focus.**[13] These strategies are called generic because all businesses or industries can pursue them, regardless of whether they are manufacturing, service, or not-for-profit enterprises. Each of the generic strategies results from a company's making consistent choices on product, market, and distinctive competences—choices that reinforce each other. Table 5.1 summarizes the choices appropriate for each generic strategy.

Cost Leadership Strategy

A company's goal in pursuing a cost leadership or low-cost strategy is to outperform competitors by producing goods or services at a lower cost. Two advantages accrue from this strategy. First, because of its lower costs, the cost leader is able to charge a lower price for its products than its competitors and still make the same level of profit as other companies. If companies in the industry charge similar prices for their products, the cost leader makes a higher profit

TABLE 5.1   **Product/market/distinctive competence choices and generic competitive strategy**

	Cost leadership	Differentiation	Focus
Product differentiation	Low (principally by price)	High (principally by uniqueness)	Low to high (price or uniqueness)
Market segmentation	Low (mass market)	High (many market segments)	Low (one or a few segments)
Distinctive competence	Manufacturing and materials management	Research and development sales and marketing	Any kind of distinctive competence

than its competitors because of its lower costs. Second, if price wars develop and companies start to compete on price as the industry matures, the cost leader will be able to withstand competition better than the other companies because of its lower costs. For both these reasons, cost leaders are likely to earn above-average returns. The question is how does a company become the cost leader? It achieves this position by the combination of product/market/distinctive competence choices it makes to gain a low-cost competitive advantage. Table 5.1 outlines these strategic choices.

Strategic choices   As Table 5.1 demonstrates, the cost leader chooses a low level of product differentiation. Differentiation is expensive, and if the company produces a wide range of products or expends resources to make its products unique, then its costs rise.[14] The cost leader aims for a level of differentiation not markedly inferior to that of the differentiator—the company that competes by spending resources on product development—but still a level obtainable at low cost.[15] The cost leader does not try to be the industry leader in differentiation; it waits until customers want a feature or service before providing it. For example, a cost leader does not introduce stereo sound in television sets. It adds stereo sound only when it is obvious that consumers want it.

The cost leader will also normally ignore the different market segments and aim for the average customer, again for the sake of lowest cost. Thus, in product/market terms, the company seeks a level of product differentiation that appeals to the average customer. Even though no customer may be totally happy with the product, the fact that *the company normally charges a lower price than its competitors* puts the product within a customer's range of choices.

The development of a distinctive competence in the manufacturing function is most important to a low-cost company, which will attempt to ride down the experience curve so that it can lower its manufacturing costs. Since the company charges less for its products, it can attract the extra sales volume that allows it to obtain these experience curve effects (i.e., costs go down as production output increases). Besides, cost minimization means matching product and process structure and adopting efficient materials management techniques. Consequently, the manufacturing and materials management functions are the center of attention in the cost leadership company, and the other functions will shape their distinctive competences to meet the needs of manufacturing.[16] For example, the sales function will develop the competence of capturing large, stable sets of customer orders that will allow manufacturing to make longer production runs and so reduce costs. The research and development function will specialize in process improvements to lower the costs of manufacture, as well as product improvements to make production easier. For example, Chrysler reduced the number of parts involved in manufacturing a car from 75,000 to 40,000 in order to decrease costs.

In short, the cost leader gears all its strategic product/market/distinctive competence choices to the single goal of squeezing out every cent of production costs to provide a competitive advantage. A company like Heinz is an excellent example of a cost leader. As you can imagine, beans and canned vegetables do not permit much of a markup. The profit comes from the large volume of cans sold (each can having only a small markup). Therefore the H. J. Heinz Company goes to extraordinary lengths to try to reduce costs — by even 1/20th of a cent per can — because this will lead to large cost savings and thus bigger profits over the long run. As we will see in the chapters in Part III on strategy implementation, the other source of cost savings in pursuing cost leadership is the design of the organization structure to match this strategy, since structure is a major source of a company's costs. As we discuss in Chapter 10, a low-cost strategy implies tight production controls and rigorous use of budgets to control the production process.

Advantages and disadvantages   The advantages of each of the generic strategies are best discussed in terms of Porter's five forces model introduced in Chapter 3.[17] The five forces involve threats from competitors, from powerful suppliers or powerful buyers, from substitute products, and from new entrants. As we have just shown, the cost leader is protected from prospective *competitors* by its cost advantage. Its lower costs also mean that it will be less affected than its competitors by increases in the price of inputs if there are *powerful suppliers* and less affected by a fall in the price it can charge for its products if *powerful buyers* exist. Moreover, since cost leadership usually requires a big market share, the cost leader will purchase in relatively large quantities, increasing bargaining power vis-à-vis suppliers. If *substitute products* start to come into the market, the cost leader can reduce its price to compete with these products and retain its market share. Finally, the leader's cost advantage constitutes a *barrier to entry,* since other companies will be unable to enter the industry and match the leader's costs or prices. The cost leader is therefore relatively safe as long as it can maintain its cost advantage.

The principal dangers of the cost leadership approach lurk in competitors' ability to find ways of producing at lower cost and beat the cost leader at its own game. For instance, if technological change makes experience curve economies obsolete, new companies may apply lower-cost technologies that give them a cost advantage over the cost leader. The specialty steel mills we discussed in Chapter 3 gained this advantage. Competitors may also draw a cost advantage from labor cost savings. Foreign competitors in Third World countries have very low labor costs; for example, wage costs in the United States are on the order of 600 or so percent more than in the Korea or Mexico. Many American companies now assemble their products abroad as part of their low-cost strategy; many are forced to do so simply to compete.

Competitors' ability to easily *imitate* the cost leader's methods is another threat to the cost leadership strategy. For example, the ability of IBM clone manufacturers to produce IBM-compatible products at similar cost (and, of course, they sell at a much lower price) is a major worry for IBM. Finally, cost leadership strategy carries a risk that the cost leader, in the single-minded desire to reduce costs, may lose sight of changes in customer tastes. Thus a company may make decisions that reduce costs but drastically affect demand for the product—the problem Holiday Inns experienced. Similarly, the Joseph Schlitz Brewing Co. reduced the quality of its beer's ingredients, substituting inferior grains to reduce costs. Consumers immediately caught on, and demand for the product dropped dramatically. As mentioned earlier, the cost leader cannot abandon product differentiation, and even low-priced products, such as Timex watches cannot be too inferior to the more expensive Seikos if the low-cost-and-price policy is to succeed.

Although all companies try to contain their costs, the cost leader takes an extreme position in this regard and makes all its product/market/distinctive competence choices with cost minimization in mind. Its ability to charge a lower price is a competitive advantage that allows it to be the industry price setter. However, given the huge growth in low-cost competition from abroad, it appears that cost leadership may become increasingly difficult to pursue in many industries. Even Japanese companies are now experiencing this problem, since their cost edge has been eroded by companies in Taiwan and Korea, such as Gold Star and Samsung, which are now the cost leaders. Japanese companies are increasingly looking to differentiation as a competitive strategy. Honda, for example, began building Acura to compete in the luxury car market, and Toyota and Nissan quickly responded with Nexus and Infinity, respectively.

Differentiation Strategy

The objective of the generic strategy of differentiation is to achieve a competitive advantage by creating a product or service that is *perceived* by customers to be unique in some important way. The differentiated company's ability to satisfy a customer need in a way that its competitors cannot means that it can charge a **premium price** for its product(s). It is the ability to increase revenues by charging premium prices (rather than to reduce costs like the cost leader) that allows the differentiator to outperform its competitors and make above-average returns. The premium price is usually substantially above the price charged by the cost leader, and customers pay it because they believe the product's differentiated qualities to be worth it. Consequently, the product is priced on the basis of what the market will bear.[18] Thus Mercedes autos are much more expensive in the United States than in Europe because they confer more status here. Similarly, a basic BMW is not a lot more expensive to produce than an Oldsmobile, but its price is determined by customers who perceive that the prestige of owning a BMW is something worth paying for. Similarly, Rolex watches do not cost much to produce, their design has not changed very much for years, and their gold content is only a fraction of the watch price, but customers buy the Rolex because of the unique quality they perceive in it: its ability to confer status on its wearer. In stereos, the name Bang & Olufsen of Denmark stands out, in jewelry Tiffany & Company, in airplanes Lear Jets. All these products command premium prices because of their differentiated qualities.

Strategic choices   In Table 5.1, on the dimension of product differentiation, a differentiator obviously chooses a high level of product differentiation. As noted earlier, product differentiation can be achieved in a wide variety of ways. Procter & Gamble Company claims that its product quality is high and that Ivory soap is 99.9 percent pure. The Maytag Co. stresses reliability and the best repair record of any washer on the market, while Sony emphasizes the quality of its television sets. In such technologically more complex products, technological features are the source of differentiation, and many people will pay a premium price for the items. Differentiation can be based on *service*, the ability of the company to offer comprehensive after-sales service and product repair — an especially important consideration when one buys complex products such as autos and domestic appliances, which are likely to break down periodically. Companies like IBM and Federal Express Corp. have excelled in service and reliability. In service organizations, quality of service attributes are also very important. Why can Neiman-Marcus Co. or Nordstrom, Inc. charge a premium price for their products? They offer an exceptionally high level of service. Similarly, firms of lawyers or accountants stress the service aspects of their operations to clients: their knowledge, professionalism, or reputation.

Finally, a product's appeal to customers' psychological desires can become a source of differentiation. The appeal can be to prestige or status, as with BMWs and Rolex watches, but also to patriotism, or to safety of home and family, as in the case of Prudential, or to value for money, as with Sears Roebuck and J. C. Penney Company, Inc. Differentiation can also be tailored to age groups, as well as socioeconomic groups. Indeed, the bases of differentiation are endless.

If a company pursues a differentiation strategy, it will attempt to differentiate itself along as many dimensions as possible. The less it resembles its rivals, the more it is protected from competition and the wider its market appeal. Thus BMWs are not just prestige cars; they also offer technological sophistication, luxury, and reliability, as well as good, although very expensive, repair service. All these bases of differentiation help increase sales.

Generally, the differentiator chooses to segment its market into many niches. Now and then a company offers a product designed for each market niche and chooses to be a **broad differentiator,** but a company might choose to serve just those niches where it has a specific differentiation advantage. For example, Sony produces twenty-four models of television, filling all the niches from midpriced to high-priced sets. However, its lowest-priced model is always about $100 above that of its competitors — bringing into play the premium price factor. You have to pay the extra for a Sony. Similarly, although Mercedes-Benz has recently filled niches below its old high-priced models with its 190 and 290 series, nobody would claim that Mercedes is going for every market segment. As we mentioned earlier, GM was the first company that tried to fill most of the niches, from the cheapest Chevrolet to the highest-priced Cadillac and Corvette.

Finally, in choosing which distinctive competence to pursue, the differentiated company concentrates on the organization function that provides the sources of its differentiation advantage. Differentiation on the basis of technological competence depends on the research and development function. Attempts to increase market segments are aided by the marketing function. A focus on a specific function does not mean, however, that manufacturing and the control of production costs are unimportant. The differentiator does not want to increase costs unnecessarily and tries to keep them somewhere near those of the cost leader. However, since developing the distinctive competences needed to provide a differentiation advantage is expensive, the differentiator usually has higher costs than the cost leader. Still, it must control those costs so that the price of the product does not exceed what customers are willing to pay. As we already noted, the cost of producing some differentiated products, such as Rolex watches, is relatively low and the markup is relatively high; in such cases, companies can manipulate the price to match the market segments they serve. Nevertheless, since bigger profits are earned by controlling costs, as well as by maximizing revenues, it pays to control production costs, though not to minimize them to the point of losing the source of differentiation.[19]

Advantages and disadvantages   The advantages of this strategy can now be discussed in the context of the five forces model. First, differentiation safeguards a company against *competitors* to the degree that customers develop **brand loyalty** for its products. Brand loyalty is a very valuable asset because it protects the company on all fronts. For example, *powerful suppliers* are rarely a problem because the differentiated company's strategy is geared more toward the price it can charge than toward the costs of production. Thus the differentiator can tolerate moderate increases in the prices of its inputs better than the cost leader. On the *powerful buyer* side, differentiators are unlikely to experience problems because buyers are at their mercy. Only they can supply the product, and they command brand loyalty. Differentiators can pass on price increases to customers because customers are willing to pay the premium price. Differentiation and brand loyalty also create an *entry barrier* for other companies seeking to enter the industry. New companies are forced to develop their own distinctive competence to be able to compete, and this is very expensive. Finally, the threat of *substitute products* depends on the ability of competitors' products to meet the same customer needs as the differentiator's products and to break customers' brand loyalty. This can happen, as when IBM-clone manufacturers captured a large share of the home computer market, but many people will still pay the price for an IBM, even though there are many IBM clones about. The issue is how much of a premium price the company can charge for uniqueness before customers will switch products.

The main problems with this strategy center on the company's long-term ability to maintain its perceived uniqueness in customers' eyes. We have seen in the last ten years how quickly competitors move to *imitate and copy* successful differentiators. This has happened in many industries, such as computers, autos, and home electronics. Patents and first-mover advantages — the advantages of being the first to market a product or service — last only so long, and as the overall quality of products goes up, brand loyalty declines. Furthermore, the increasing use of consumer magazines that objectively compare the quality of competing products has helped the consumer to become more educated in the marketplace. The result is that differentiators always have to be one step ahead of their imitators, or they will get left behind. No longer are consumers afraid of taking a risk. If the price is right and the features are minimally suitable, consumers will switch products, giving the cost leader an advantage over the differentiator.

One final threat to the differentiator is that the source of a company's uniqueness may be overridden by changes in consumer tastes and demands. We saw how Holiday Inns lost the source of its competitive advantage because the market had segmented into more complex niches while the company still served the needs of the average customer. It was neither low cost nor differentiated. A company must be constantly on the lookout for ways to match its unique strengths to changing product/market opportunities and threats. Otherwise it will be outperformed by its competitors. Clothing manufacturers know this well, and they change their clothes styles every year to keep up with consumers' changing tastes.

Thus the disadvantages of this strategy are the ease with which competitors can imitate the differentiator's product and the difficulty in maintaining the premium price.[20] When differentiation stems from the design or physical feature of the product, differentiators are at more risk because imitation is easier. The risk is that over time products like VCRs or stereos become *commodity-like* products, where the importance of differentiation diminishes as the price of products starts to fall. But if differentiation stems from service quality or reliability, or any *intangible source*, like the Federal Express guarantee, or the prestige of a Rolex, the company is much more secure. It is difficult to imitate these qualities. Thus the differentiator can continue to reap the benefits from this strategy in the long run.

In summary, pursuing a strategy of differentiation involves the firm developing a competitive advantage by making product/market/distinctive competence choices that reinforce one another and together increase the value of the product/service in the eyes of the consumer. When the product has uniqueness in customer's eyes, differentiators can charge a premium price for their product. However, they must watch out for imitators and be careful that they do not charge a price higher than the market will bear. Assessing the price they can charge for their uniqueness is a crucial part of this strategy because this is what determines the long run profitability of differentiation.

Focus Strategy

The third generic competitive strategy, the focus strategy, differs from the other two chiefly because it is directed toward serving the needs of *a limited customer group or segment.* In other words, a focused company concentrates on serving a particular market niche, which may be defined geographically or by type of customer or by segment of the product line.[21] For example, a geographical niche may be defined by region or even locality. Selecting a niche by type of customer might mean serving only the very rich or the very young or the very adventurous. Concentrating only on a segment of the product line means focusing only on vegetarian foods or on very fast motor cars or on designer clothes. In following a focus strategy, a company is therefore *specializing* in some way.

Having chosen its market segment, a company may pursue a focus strategy through either a differentiation *or* a low-cost approach. In essence, a focused company is a specialized differentiator or cost leader. If it uses a low-cost approach, it competes against the cost leader in those market segments where it has no cost disadvantage. For example, in local lumber or cement markets, the focuser has lower transportation costs than the low-cost national company. The focuser may also have a cost advantage because it is producing complex or custom-built products that do not lend themselves easily to economies of scale in production and therefore offer few experience curve advantages. With a focus strategy, a company concentrates on small-volume custom products, where it has a cost advantage, and leaves the large-volume standardized market to the cost leader.

If a focuser pursues a differentiation approach, then all the means of differentiation discussed above that are open to the differentiator are available to the focused company. The point is that the focused company competes with the differentiator in only one or in just a few segments. For example, Porsche, a focused company, competes against General Motors in the sports car segment of the car market but not in other market segments. Focused companies are likely to be particularly successful in developing differentiated product qualities because of their intimate knowledge of a small customer set (sports car buyers) or knowledge of a region. Furthermore, a focuser's concentration on a small product range sometimes allows it to develop innovations faster than the large differentiator. However, the focuser does not attempt to serve all market segments because this would bring it into direct competition with the differentiator. Instead, the focused company concentrates on building market share in one market segment and, if successful, may begin to serve more and more market segments and chip away at the differentiator's competitive advantage.

Strategic choices   Table 5.1 shows the specific product/market/distinctive competence choices made by the focused company. Differentiation can be high or low because the company can pursue a low-cost or a differentiation approach. As for customer groups, the company chooses a specific niche or niches in which to compete, rather than going for whole market, like the cost leader, or filling a large number of niches, like the broad differentiator. The focuser may pursue any distinctive competence because it can pursue any kind of differentiation or low-cost advantage. Thus it may seek a cost advantage and develop a low-cost manufacturing competence within a region. Or it could develop a service competence based on its ability to serve the needs of regional customers in ways that a national differentiator would find very expensive.

The many avenues that a focused company can take in developing a competitive advantage explains why there are so many small companies in relation to large ones. A company has enormous opportunity to develop its own niche and compete against the low-cost and differentiated enterprises that tend to be larger. This is the opportunity for the entrepreneur, to find the gap in the market to exploit by developing a product that customers cannot do without.[22] The small specialty steel mills discussed in the last chapter are a good example of how focused companies that specialize in one market can grow so efficient that they become the cost leaders. Many large companies started with a focus strategy, and, of course, one means by which companies can expand is to take over other focused companies. For example, Saatchi & Saatchi DFS Compton Inc., a specialist marketing company, grew by taking over several companies that were also specialists in their own market, such as Hay Associates Inc., the management consultants.

Advantages and disadvantages   The focused company's competitive advantages stem from the nature of its distinctive competence; it is protected from *rivals* to the extent that it can provide a product/service that they cannot. This ability also gives the focuser power over its *buyers,* because they cannot get the same thing from anyone else. With regard to *powerful suppliers,* however, the focused company is at a disadvantage, since it buys in small volumes, which puts it in the supplier's power. But as long as it can pass on price increases to loyal customers, this may not be a significant problem. *Potential entrants* have to overcome the hurdle of the customer loyalty that the focuser has generated, and in turn, the development of customer loyalty reduces the threat from *substitute* *products*. This protection from the five forces also allows the focuser to earn above-average returns on its investment. A further advantage of the focus strategy is that it permits a company to stay close to its customers and to respond to their changing needs. The problem that the large differentiator sometimes experiences in managing the large number of market segments in which it competes is not an issue for the focuser.

Since the focuser produces at a small volume, its production costs often exceed those of the low-cost company. Higher costs can also reduce its profitability, if it is forced to invest heavily in developing a distinctive competence—such as expensive product innovation—in order to compete with the differentiated firm. A second problem is that the focuser's niche can suddenly disappear because of technological change or changes in consumer tastes. Unlike the more generalist differentiator, the focuser cannot move easily to new niches, given its concentration of resources and competence in one or a few niches. For example, a clothing manufacturer focusing on punk rock enthusiasts will find it very difficult to shift to other segments as punk rock loses its appeal. The disappearance of their niche is one reason that so many small companies fail. Finally, there is the prospect that differentiators will compete for the focuser's niche by offering a product that can satisfy the demands of the focuser's customers; for example, GM's new top-of-the-line models are aimed at BMW. The cost leader may compete by providing a product whose low price may lure customers into switching; for example, IBM reduced its price to gain market share from the clone manufacturers. The focuser is vulnerable to attack and therefore has to constantly defend its niche.

Being Stuck in the Middle

Each of the generic strategies discussed above requires that the company make consistent product/market/distinctive competence choices to establish a competitive advantage. In other words, a company must achieve a fit among these three components of business-level strategy. Thus, for example, a low-cost company cannot go for a high level of market segmentation like the differentiator or provide a wide range of products because this would raise production costs too much, and it would lose its low-cost advantage. Similarly, a differentiator with a technological competence that tries to reduce its expenditures on research and development or one that specializes in comprehensive after-sales service and tries to economize on its sales force to reduce costs is asking for trouble because it will also lose its competitive advantage as its distinctive competence disappears.

The point is that successful business-level strategy choice involves serious attention to all elements of the competitive plan. There are many examples on record of companies that, through ignorance or through mistakes, did not do the planning necessary for success in their chosen strategy. Such companies are said to be **stuck in the middle** because they have made product/market choices in such a way that they have been unable to obtain or sustain a competitive advantage.[23] As a result, they have a below-average level of performance and will suffer when industry competition intensifies.

Paths to the middle   Sometimes these stuck-in-the-middle companies started out pursuing one of the three generic strategies but made wrong decisions or were subject to environmental changes. It is very easy to lose control of a generic strategy unless management keeps close track of the business and its environment, constantly adjusting product/market choices to suit changing industry conditions. We saw in Holiday Inns how this can happen. There are many paths to being stuck in the middle. Sometimes the low-cost company may decide to use some of its profits to diversify into product markets where it has less expertise or to invest in research and development that management thinks may bolster the prestige of the organization. Such actions are expensive and have no guarantee of success. Consequently, bad strategic decisions can quickly erode the cost leader's above-average profitability.

Quite commonly, too, a focuser can get stuck in the middle when it becomes overconfident and starts to act like a broad differentiator. People Express is a good example of a company in this kind of situation. It started out as a specialized carrier serving a narrow market niche: low-priced travel on the Eastern Seaboard. In pursuing this focus strategy based on cost leadership, it was very successful, but when it tried to expand to other geographical regions and began taking over other airlines to increase its number of planes, it lost its niche. People Express became one more carrier in an increasingly competitive market, where it had no special competitive advantage against the other national carriers. The result for People was financial troubles, and as a consequence, it was swallowed up by Texas Air and incorporated into Continental Airlines.

Differentiators, too, can fail in the market and end up stuck in the middle if competitors attack their markets with more specialized or low-cost products that blunt their competitive edge. This happened to IBM in the large-frame computer market. No company is safe in the jungle of competition, and each must be constantly on the lookout to exploit competitive advantages as they arise and to defend the advantages it already has.

In sum, managing a successful generic competitive strategy requires that strategic managers attend to two main things. First, they need to ensure that the product/market/distinctive competence decisions they make are oriented towards one specific competitive strategy. Second, managers need to monitor the environment so that they can keep firm strengths and weaknesses aligned to changing opportunities and threats.

Generic Strategies and the Industry Environment

In Chapter 3, on analyzing the industry environment, Table 3.3 summarizes how the basis of rivalry among companies changes as their industry ages. The table shows that competition by price and product differentiation becomes increasingly pronounced at later stages of the industry life cycle. This has several implications for companies pursuing a specific generic strategy. First, it implies that pursuing a cost leadership strategy is less important at early stages in the life cycle because companies can sell all they can produce. Thus while it is true that low costs will help increase profit margins, at the embryonic stage, most companies will be trying to differentiate their products in order to develop customer tastes for them.

By the growth stage, however, companies must choose which competitive strategy to follow, because the growth stage is succeeded by the shakeout stage, where only the strongest survive. Some companies will attempt to become the *cost leaders,* others will strive to become *differentiators*, while still others will *focus* their efforts on their chosen niche. Some will be better in making their product/market choices than others, so that by the shakeout stage the companies *stuck in the middle* will be the ones to exit the industry first.

By the maturity stage, an industry is composed of a *collection of companies pursuing each of the generic strategies.* This is where the strategic group concept, discussed in Chapter 3, becomes important. Essentially, all the companies pursuing a low-cost strategy can be viewed as composing one strategic group, while all those pursuing differentiation constitute another; the focusers form a third group.[24] The *mobility barrier* surrounding each group is based upon the generic business-level strategy pursued by companies in the group. That is, once a company has made an investment in one generic strategy, it is very expensive to change to another, and this restricts intraindustry competition. For example, if a company invests resources to develop a distinctive competence in cost leadership, it will find it very difficult to enter the differentiator group since it lacks the extensive sales force or advanced technological competence necessary to compete with the differentiator. Similarly, differentiators cannot enter the low-cost group unless they have the capacity to reduce their costs to the level of companies in that group because they *have* made an investment in the necessary sales force or technology. Thus, when strategic groups are based on different generic competitive strategies, there is likely to be a stable pattern of industry competition over time.

This is why the development of a cohesive set of product/market/distinctive competence choices to pursue a generic strategy is so important early on. The strategy sets the scene for profitability in later stages of the industry life cycle because the emergence of strategic groups defined by strategy type simultaneously protects companies from potential industry entrants and limits the degree to which companies pursuing different strategies can compete against each other.

Summary

The three generic strategies represent the principal ways in which organizations can compete in an industry. These strategies protect companies from the five forces of competition, and ultimately, for the companies that survive the shakeout stage, provide protection via mobility barriers. However, many companies do fail along the way. Sometimes companies do not continue to develop the functional competences necessary to sustain their dominance; sometimes they lose their product differentiation advantage to a competitor; sometimes the market changes and the niches or segments they were filling disappear. It is therefore not enough just to choose a generic competitive strategy. As many resources must be devoted to maintaining a competitive strategy as to establishing it, if above-average returns are to be consistently obtained. Consequently, if a company is to pursue a competitive strategy, it must evaluate the potential returns from the strategy against the cost of the resources that have to be invested in order to develop it. This is the issue we turn to now.

5.5 CHOOSING AN INVESTMENT STRATEGY AT THE BUSINESS LEVEL

Up to now we have discussed business-level strategy in terms of making product/market/distinctive competence choices to gain a competitive advantage. However, there is a second major choice to be made at the business level: the choice of which type of investment strategy to pursue in support of the competitive strategy.[25] An investment strategy refers to the *amount and type of resources — both human and financial — that must be invested to gain a competitive advantage.* Generic competitive strategies provide competitive advantages, but they are expensive to develop and maintain. Differentiation is the most expensive of the three because it requires that the company invest resources in many functions, such as research and development and sales and marketing, to develop distinctive competences. Cost leadership is less expensive to maintain once the initial investment in a manufacturing plant and equipment has been made. It does not require such sophisticated research and development or marketing efforts. The focus strategy is cheapest because fewer resources are needed to serve one market segment than the whole market.

In deciding on an investment strategy, a company must evaluate the potential returns from investing in a generic competitive strategy against the cost of developing the competitive strategy. In this way, it can determine if a strategy is profitable to pursue and how profitability will change as industry competition changes. Two factors are crucial in choosing an investment strategy: the strength of a company's position in an industry relative to its competitors and the stage of the industry life cycle in which the company is competing.[26]

Competitive Position

Two attributes can be used to determine the strength of a company's relative competitive position. First, the larger the company's *market share,* the stronger is its competitive position and the greater the potential returns from future investment. This is because a large market share provides experience curve economies and/or suggests that the company has developed brand loyalty. The strength and uniqueness of a company's *distinctive competences* are the second measure of competitive position. If it is difficult to imitate a company's research and development expertise, its manufacturing or marketing skills, its knowledge of particular customer segments, or its reputation or brand-name capital, the company's relative competitive position is stronger and its returns from the generic strategy increase. In general, the companies with the largest market share and strongest distinctive competence are in the best position.

These two attributes obviously reinforce one another and explain why some companies get stronger and stronger over time. A unique competence leads to higher demand for the company's products, and then, as a result of larger market share, the company has more resources to invest in developing its distinctive competence. Companies with a smaller market share and little potential for developing a distinctive competence are in a weaker competitive position.[27] Consequently, they are less attractive sources for investment.

Life Cycle Effects

The second main factor influencing the investment attractiveness of a generic strategy is the *stage of the industry life cycle*. Each life cycle stage has different opportunities and threats from the environment associated with it, and each stage, therefore, has different implications for the amount of investment of resources needed to obtain a competitive advantage. You saw earlier, for example, how competition is strongest in the shakeout stage of the life cycle and least important in the embryonic stage, so that the risks of pursuing a strategy change over time. This difference in risk explains why the potential returns from investing in a competitive strategy depend on the life cycle stage. Table 5.2 summarizes the relationship among the stage of the life cycle, competitive position, and investment strategy at the business level.

Choosing an Investment Strategy

Embryonic strategy   In the embryonic stage, all companies, weak and strong, emphasize the development of a distinctive competence and a product/market policy. During this stage, investment needs are very great because the company has to establish a competitive advantage. There are many fledgling companies in the industry seeking resources to develop a distinctive competence. Consequently, the appropriate business-level investment strategy is a **share-building strategy.** The aim is to build market share by developing a stable and unique competitive advantage to attract customers who have no knowledge of the company's products. Companies require large amounts of capital to build

TABLE 5.2   **Choosing an investment strategy at the business level**

Stage of industry life cycle	Strong competitive position	Weak competitive position
Embryonic	Share building	Share building
Growth	Growth	Market concentration
Shakeout	Share increasing	Market concentration or harvest/liquidation
Maturity	Hold and maintain or profit	Harvest or liquidation/divestiture
Decline	Market concentration, harvest, or asset reduction	Turnaround, liquidation, or divestiture

research and development competences or sales and service competences. They cannot generate much of this capital internally. Consequently, a company's success depends on its ability to demonstrate some unique competence to attract outside investors, or venture capitalists. Assuming that the company gains the resources to develop a distinctive competence, it will be in a relatively stronger competitive position. If it fails, its only option may be to exit the industry. In fact, companies in weak competitive positions at all stages in the life cycle may choose to exit the industry to cut their losses.

Growth strategies   At the growth stage, the task facing a company is to consolidate its position and provide the base it needs to survive the coming shakeout phase. Thus the appropriate investment strategy is the **growth strategy.** The goal is to maintain the company's relative competitive position in a rapidly expanding market and, if possible, to increase it — in other words, to grow with the expanding market. However, other companies will be entering the market and catching up with the industry innovators. As a result, companies require successive waves of capital infusion to maintain the momentum generated by their success in the embryonic stage. For example, differentiators will be engaging in massive research and development efforts and cost leaders will be investing in plant to obtain experience curve economies. All this investment is very expensive.

The growth stage is also the time when companies attempt to consolidate existing market niches and enter new ones so that they can increase their market share. Increasing the level of market segmentation is also expensive. A company will have to invest resources to develop a new sales and marketing competence. Consequently, the growth stage is where companies fine-tune their competitive strategy and make business-level investment decisions about the relative advantages of a differentiation, low-cost, or focus strategy, given financial needs and relative competitive position. For example, if one company has emerged as the cost leader, the other companies in the industry may decide not to compete head on with it. Instead, they will pursue a growth strategy using a differentiation or focus approach and invest resources in developing unique competences. Because companies will be spending a lot of money just to keep up with growth in the market, finding additional resources to develop new skills and competences is a difficult task for strategic managers.

Companies in a weak competitive position at this stage will engage in a **market concentration strategy** to consolidate their position. This means that they will move to specialize in some way and adopt a focus strategy in order to reduce their investment needs. If very weak, they may also choose to exit the industry.

Shakeout strategies   By the shakeout stage, demand is increasing more slowly and competition by price or product characteristics has become intense. Consequently, companies in strong competitive positions will need resources to invest in a **share-increasing strategy** to attract customers from weaker companies that are exiting the market. In other words, companies attempt to maintain and increase market share despite fierce competition. The way companies invest their resources depends on their generic strategy. For cost leaders, investment in cost control is crucial if they are to survive the shakeout stage because of the price wars that can occur. Differentiators in a strong competitive position will choose to forge ahead and become broad differentiators. Their investment is likely to be oriented toward marketing, and they are likely to develop a sophisticated after-sales service network. They will also widen the product range to match the range of customer needs.

Differentiators in a weak position will reduce the investment burden by withdrawing to a focused strategy — the market concentration strategy — in order to specialize in a particular niche or product. Finally, weak companies exiting the industry will engage in a harvest or liquidation strategy, both of which are discussed below.

Maturity strategies   By the maturity stage, a strategic group structure has emerged in the industry, and companies have learned how their competitors will react to their competitive moves. At this point companies want to reap the rewards of their previous investments in developing a generic strategy. Until now profits will have been reinvested in the business, and dividends will have been smaller. Investors in strong companies will have obtained their rewards through capital appreciation because the company will have reinvested most of its capital to maintain and increase market share. As market growth slows down in the maturity stage, a company's investment strategy will depend on the level of competition in the industry and the source of its competitive advantage.

In environments where competition is high because technological change is occurring or where barriers to entry are low, companies will need to defend their competitive position. Strategic managers will need to continue to invest heavily in maintaining the company's competitive advantage. Both low-cost companies and differentiators will adopt a **hold-and-maintain** strategy to support their generic strategies. They will expend resources to develop their distinctive competences so as to remain the market leaders. For example, differentiated companies may invest in improved after-sales service, while low-cost companies will invest in the latest production technologies, for example, robotics. This is expensive but is warranted by the revenues that will accrue from maintaining a strong competitive position.

However, when a company is protected from industry competition, it may decide to exploit its competitive advantage to the full by engaging in a **profit strategy.** A company pursuing this strategy attempts to maximize the present returns from its previous investments. Typically, it will reinvest proportionally less in its business and increase returns to shareholders. This strategy works well as long as competitive forces remain relatively *constant*, so that the company can maintain the profit margins developed by its competitive strategy. However, the company must constantly remain alert for threats from the environment and must take care not to become complacent and unresponsive to changes in the competitive environment.

All too often market leaders fail to exercise such vigilance, imagining that they are impregnable to competition. For example, GM felt secure against foreign car manufactures until changes in oil prices precipitated a crisis. Kodak Company, which had profited so long from its strengths in film processing, was slow to respond to the threat of electronic imaging techniques. Paradoxically, it is often the most successful companies that fail to sense changes in the market. For example, Holiday Inns' failure to perceive changes in customer needs was to some extent the result of its single-minded efforts to develop its existing motel chain. Developing two chains side by side would have obviously required more resources, but that was what the market demanded. A company's ability to raise capital becomes very important in such situations; otherwise its distinctive competence may disappear.

Companies in a weak competitive position at the maturity stage will use the decline strategies discussed below.

Decline strategies   The decline stage of the industry life cycle begins when demand for the industry's product starts to fall. As you saw in Chapter 3, there are many possible reasons for this, including foreign competition or product substitution. A company may lose its distinctive competence as its rivals enter with new or more efficient technologies. Therefore it must decide what investment strategy to adopt in order to deal with new industry circumstances. Table 5.2 lists the strategies that companies can resort to when their competitive position is declining.[28]

The initial strategies that companies can adopt are known as market concentration and asset reduction strategies.[29] With a **market concentration strategy,** a company attempts to consolidate its product and market choices. It narrows its product range and exits marginal niches in an attempt to redeploy its investments more efficiently and improve its competitive position. Reducing customer needs and the customer groups served may allow the company to pursue a focus strategy in order to survive the decline stage. (As noted earlier, weak companies in the growth stage will tend to adopt this strategy.) That is what International Harvester did as the demand for farm machinery fell. It now produces only medium-size trucks under the name Navistar.

An **asset reduction strategy** requires the company to limit or reduce its investment in a business and to extract, or milk, the investment as much as it can. This approach is sometimes called a **harvest strategy,** since the company reduces to a minimum the assets it employs in the business and forgoes future investment for the sake of immediate profits.[30] While a market concentration strategy generally indicates that a company is trying to turn around its business so that it can survive in the long run, a harvest strategy implies that the company will exit the industry once it has harvested all the returns it can. Low-cost companies are more likely to pursue a harvest strategy simply because a smaller market share means higher costs, and they are unable to move to a focus strategy. Differentiators, on the other hand, have a competitive advantage in this stage if they can move to a focus strategy.

Turnaround strategies may be applied at any stage of the life cycle by companies that are in weak competitive positions.[31] The question that a company has to answer is whether there is a viable way to compete in the industry and how much will such competition cost? If the company is stuck in the middle, then it must assess the investment costs of developing a generic competitive strategy. Perhaps a company pursuing a low-cost strategy has not made the right product or market choices, or a differentiator has been missing niche opportunities. In such cases, the company can redeploy resources and change its competitive strategy.

Sometimes a company's loss of competitiveness may be due to bad strategy implementation. If so, the company must move to change its structure and control systems rather than its strategy. For example, Dan Schendel, a prominent management researcher, found that 74 percent of the turnaround situations he and his colleagues studied were due to inefficient strategy implementation. The strategy-structure fit at the business level is thus very important in determining competitive strength.[32] We discuss it in detail in Chapter 10.

If a company decides that turnaround is not possible, either for competitive or life cycle reasons, then the two remaining investment alternatives are **liquidation** and **divestiture.** As the terms imply, the company moves to exit the industry either by liquidating its assets or by selling the whole business. Both can be regarded as radical forms of harvesting strategy because the company is seeking to get back as much as it can from its investment in the business. Often, however, it can only exit at a loss and take a tax write-off. Timing is important, because the earlier a company senses that divestiture is necessary, the more it can get for its assets. There are many stories about companies that buy weak or declining companies, thinking that they can turn them around, and then realize their mistake as the new acquisitions become a drain on their resources. Often these acquired companies have lost their competitive advantage and the cost of regaining it too great. However, there have also been spectacular successes, like that achieved by Iacocca, who engaged in a low-cost strategy involving the firing of more than 45 percent of the work force.

5.6 BUSINESS STRATEGY AND INDUSTRY STRUCTURE

A final factor influencing business-level strategy is the nature of the industry in which a company competes.[33] As seen in Chapter 3, industry structure varies from those industries that are *fragmented,* or have many small companies, to those that are *consolidated,* or have a few large companies. The choice of a business-level strategy is crucially affected by the kind and number of companies in the industry because these factors influence the nature of industry competition, that is, competitive forces. We next consider the appropriate strategies to pursue in these industry conditions.

Strategy in Fragmented Industries

A fragmented industry is one composed of a large number of small and medium-sized companies. An industry may consist of many small companies rather than a few large ones for several reasons.[34] If there are few economies of scale to be achieved, entry barriers into the industry may be low. Furthermore, customer needs may differ from region to region so that each particular market segment is small. These factors make it hard to obtain a cost advantage, and they make differentiation very difficult. In addition, customer needs may be so specialized that only small job lots of products are required, and thus there is no room for a large mass production operation to satisfy the market. Finally, if transportation costs are high, regional production may be the only efficient way to satisfy customer needs.

For some fragmented industries, these factors dictate the competitive strategy to pursue, and the *focus strategy* stands out as a principal choice. Companies may specialize by customer group, customer need, or geographical region, so that there is a proliferation of small specialty companies operating in local or regional market segments. All kinds of custom-made products—furniture, clothing, rifles, and so on—fall into this category, as do all small service operations that cater to particular customer needs, such as laundries or restaurants. Indeed, service companies make up a large proportion of the enterprises in fragmented industries because they provide personalized service to clients and therefore need to be close to their clients.

However, if a company can overcome the limitations of a fragmented market, it can often reap the benefits of a *differentiation* or *low-cost strategy*. Entrepreneurs are eager to gain the cost advantages of pursuing a cost leadership strategy or the sales revenue-enhancing advantages of differentiation by circumventing the problems of a fragmented industry. The returns from consolidating the fragmented industry are often huge. And, of course, during the last twenty-five years many companies have overcome industry structure problems and consolidated many fragmented industries. These companies are large retailers like Wal-Mart Stores, Inc., Sears, and J.C. Penney, fast food chains like McDonald's Corp. and Burger King, as well as chains of health clubs, repair shops, and even lawyers and consultants. What business strategies are these companies using to grow and become the industry leaders?

Those like Wal-Mart Stores, Inc. and Midas International Corporation are pursuing a low-cost strategy. The amazing buying power they possess through their nationwide store chains allows them to negotiate large price reductions. This provides their competitive advantage. Similarly, these companies overcome the barriers of high transportation costs by establishing sophisticated regional distribution centers that can economize on inventory costs and maximize responsiveness to the needs of stores, Wal-Mart's specialty. Last, but not least, they realize economies of scale by sharing managerial skills across the chain and from nationwide rather than local advertising.

For differentiated companies in fragmented industries, such as McDonald's or Century 21, the competitive advantage comes from their business strategy of **franchising.** With franchising, the local store operation is both owned and managed by the same person. When the owner is the manager, there is a strong motivation to control the business closely and make sure quality and standards are consistently high so that customer needs are always satisfied. Such motivation is particularly critical in a strategy of differentiation, where it is vitally important that the company maintain its uniqueness. One of the reasons that industries fragment has been the difficulty of maintaining control over, and the uniqueness of, the many small outlets that must be operated. Franchising avoids this problem. In addition, franchising lessens the financial burden of swift expansion, allowing rapid growth of the company. Finally, the differentiator can also reap the advantages of large-scale advertising and the purchasing, managerial, and distribution economies of the large company, as McDonald's does very efficiently.

Thus in fragmented industries, companies can pursue all three business-level strategies; focus, low-cost, and differentiation. The huge increase in franchising and the emergence of chain stores and restaurants has perhaps been the business strategy that has had the greatest impact on the consumer in the last twenty-five years. Its effect on America has been startling, as identical fast food chains and stores in every shopping mall are now part of the American scene. Similarly, it is difficult today to think of any major service activity, from consulting and accounting to those satisfying the smallest consumer need, such as beauty parlors or car repair, that have not been consolidated into chains.

Strategy in Consolidated Industries

The consolidated industry is one dominated by a small number of large companies. This is not to suggest that it does not contain either medium-sized companies or a host of small specialized ones; however, the large companies determine the structure of industry competition because they can influence the five competitive forces. Indeed, to choose appropriate business-level strategy in consolidated industries, one must understand how large companies can collectively, although *indirectly* (since explicit collusion among companies violates antitrust law) help stabilize the industry to prevent cutthroat price competition that would hurt all companies.

All industries start out fragmented, with small companies battling for market share. Then, over time, the leading players emerge, and by the maturity stage of the industry life cycle, the surviving companies begin to understand each other's competitive moves. In fact, the mechanism of **market signaling** is the first means by which companies attempt to structure industry competition and control rivalry among competitors.[35] Market signaling is the process by which companies convey their intentions to other companies about how they will compete in the future or how they will react to the competitive moves of their rivals. Companies may signal that if one company starts to cut prices aggressively, then they will respond in kind, or that if one company makes a differentiation move—for instance, extends car warranties, as GM did—then all the other companies will follow, to maintain the status quo.

Business-level strategy in a consolidated industry, then, involves developing the rules of the game to manage relationships among competitors and toward suppliers and customers. For example, because there are so few companies, suppliers cannot exert much power over them. If they do, the companies can threaten to make the product rather than buy it. Similarly, on the customer side, companies are fighting for the same set of customers, but they also want to avoid a situation where they come into head-to-head competition.

It is for this reason that **price leadership,** where one company takes the responsibility for setting industry prices, develops formally or informally among companies in the consolidated industry. By setting prices, the industry leader implicitly creates the price standards that other companies will follow. In consolidated industries, price setting is a crucial part of business-level strategy. The prices of different models in the model range indicate the customer segments that the companies are aiming for and the price range they believe this market segment can tolerate. Price leadership stabilizes industry relations by precluding head-to-head competition.

Product policy through product differentiation is a second very important means of preventing price competition in consolidated industries. Product differentiation allows companies to compete for market share by using nonprice competitive methods, such as offering products with different or superior features or applying different marketing techniques. This minimizes the risk that companies will compete by price, which will hurt everyone. Similarly, to reduce the threat of entry, companies will tailor their range of products to fill a range of niches because this will make entry by potential competitors more difficult. For example, the large U.S. car makers had not filled the small-car niche that made them so vulnerable to the Japanese. They really had no excuse for this state of things, since in their European operations they had a long history of small-car manufacturing. They should have seen the opening and filled it ten years earlier, but their view was that small cars meant small profits. Consequently, large companies in the industry all have a model in the same niche and compete head-to-head for customers. If a new niche develops, like convertibles, then the leader gets a first-mover advantage, but soon all the others catch up and once again competition is stabilized.

In sum, business strategy in consolidated industries revolves around the process of developing means by which firms can pursue the hold and maintain or profit strategies discussed above. To maximize profitability, firms rationalize their product/market choices to reduce costs and increase revenues, and develop means to stabilize industry competition so as to increase the industry's level of profitability. The two principal means are market signaling/price leadership, and the development of a non-price competitive product policy. Conditions in the macro environment such as changes in technology or foreign competition or consumer tastes complicate both these processes which is why there are periodic times of stability in an industry followed by unrest and intense competition as firms jockey for position in the changed industry environment. Managing this process is the goal of business level strategy.

5.7 SUMMARY OF CHAPTER

The purpose of this chapter has been to discuss the factors that must be considered if a company is to develop a business-level strategy that will allow it to compete effectively in the marketplace. Business-level strategy is the process of matching the opportunities and threats in the environment to the company's strengths and weaknesses by making choices about products, markets, technologies, and the investments necessary to pursue these choices. All companies, from small, one-person operations to the strategic business units of large corporations, must develop a business strategy if they are to compete effectively and maximize their long-term profitability. The chapter has made the following main points:

1. Selecting a business-level strategy involves two main decisions: (a) choosing a generic competitive strategy, and (b) choosing an investment strategy.

2. At the heart of generic competitive strategy are choices concerning product differentiation, market segmentation, and distinctive competence.

3. It is the combination of these three choices that results in the specific form of generic competitive strategy employed by the company.

4. The three generic competitive strategies are cost leadership, differentiation, and focus. Each has advantages and disadvantages, and a company must constantly manage its strategy; otherwise it risks being stuck in the middle.

5. The choice of generic competitive strategy will be affected by the stage of the industry life cycle.

6. The second choice facing the company is an investment strategy for supporting the competitive strategy. The choice of investment strategy will depend on two main factors: (a) the strength of the company's competitive position in the industry, and (b) the stage of the industry life cycle.

7. The main choices of investment strategy are share building, growth, share increasing, hold and maintain, profit, market concentration, asset reduction, harvest, turnaround, liquidation, and divestiture.

8. A company's choice of business strategy will also depend on the industry structure, and particularly whether it is fragmented or consolidated.

Discussion Questions

1. Why do each of the three generic competitive strategies require a different set of product/market/distinctive competence choices? Give examples of pairs of companies in the (a) computer, and (b) auto industries that pursue different competitive strategies.

2. How can companies pursuing cost leadership, differentiation, or focus strategy become stuck in the middle? In what ways can they regain their competitive advantage?

3. What investment strategy choices should (a) differentiators in a strong competitive position, and (b) differentiators in a weak competitive position make over the industry life cycle?

4. How does the nature of industry structure in (a) fragmented, and (b) consolidated industries affect a company's choice of business-level strategy?

Endnotes

1. "The Holiday Inns Trip: A Breeze For Decades, Bumpy Ride in the '80s," *The Wall Street Journal,* February 11, 1987, p. 1.

2. Holiday Inns, *Annual Report,* 1985.

3. U.S. Industrial Outlook, 1986, Bureau of Labor Statistics, Washington, D.C.

4. Derek F. Abell, *Defining the Business: The Starting Point of Strategic Planning* (Englewood Cliffs, N.J.: Prentice-Hall, 1980), p. 169.

5. Michael E. Porter, *Competitive Strategy: Techniques for Analyzing Industries and Competitors* (New York: Free Press, 1980).

6. P. Kotler, *Marketing Management,* 5th ed. (Englewood Cliffs, N.J.: Prentice-Hall, 1984); M. R. Darby and E. Karni, "Free Competition and The Optimal Amount of Fraud, *Journal of Law and Economics,* 16 (1973), 67–86.

7. Abell, *Defining the Business,* p. 8.

8. Michael E. Porter, *Competitive Advantage: Creating and Sustaining Superior Performance* (New York: Free Press, 1985).

9. R. D. Buzzell and F. D. Wiersema, "Successful Share Building Strategies," *Harvard Business Review,* 59 (1981), 135–144; L. W. Phillips, D. R. Chang, and R. D. Buzzell, "Product Quality, Cost Position, and Business Performance: A Test of Some Key Hypotheses," *Journal of Marketing,* 47 (1983), 26–43.

10. Alfred P. Sloan, *My Years at General Motors* (New York: Doubleday, 1972).

11. Porter, *Competitive Strategy,* p. 45.

12. Abell, *Defining the Business,* p. 15.

13. Although many other authors have discussed cost leadership and differentiation as basic competitive approaches (e.g., F. Scherer, *Industrial Market Structure and Economic Performance,* 2nd ed. (Boston: Houghton Mifflin, 1980) Porter's model (Porter, *Competitive Strategy*) has become the dominant approach. Consequently, this model will be the one developed below, and the discussion draws heavily on his definitions. The basic cost leadership–differentiation dimension has recently received substantial empirical support (e.g., D. C. Hambrick, "High Profit Strategies in Mature Capital Goods Industries; A Contingency Approach," *Academy of Management Journal,* 26 (1983), 687–707).

14. Porter, *Competitive Strategy,* p. 37.

15. Porter, *Competitive Advantage,* pp. 13–14.

16. D. Miller, "Configurations of Strategy and Structure: Towards a Synthesis," *Strategic Management Journal,* 7 (1986), 217–231.

17. Porter, *Competitive Advantage,* pp. 44–46.

18. Charles W. Hofer and D. Schendel, *Strategy Formulation: Analytical Concepts.* (St. Paul, Minn.: West Publishing, 1978).

19. W. K. Hall, "Survival Strategies in a Hostile Environment," *Harvard Business Review,* 58(5) (1980), 75–85. Hambrick, "High Profit Strategies in Mature Capital Goods Industries," pp. 687–707.

20. Porter, *Competitive Strategy,* p. 46.

21. Ibid., p. 38.

22. P. Drucker, *The Practice of Management* (New York: Harper and Row, 1954).

23. Porter, *Competitive Strategy,* p. 43.

24. G. Dess and P. Davies, "Porter's (1980) Generic Strategies as Determinants of Strategic Group Membership and Organizational Performance," *Academy of Management Journal,* 27 (1984), 467–488.

25. Hofer and Schendel, *Strategy Formulation,* pp. 102–104.

26. Our discussion of the investment, or posturing, component of business-level strategy draws heavily on Hofer and Schendel's discussion in *Strategy Formulation,* especially Chapter 6.

27. Hofer and Schendel, *Strategy Formulation,* pp. 75–77.

28. K. R. Harrigan, "Strategy Formulation in Declining Industries," *Academy of Management Review,* 5 (1980), 599–604.

29. Hofer and Schendel, *Strategy Formulation,* pp. 169–172.

30. L. P. Feldman and A. L. Page, "Harvesting; The Misunderstood Market Exit Strategy," *Journal of Business Strategy,* 4 (1985), 79–85.

31. C. W. Hofer, "Turnaround Strategies," *Journal of Business Strategy,* 1 (1980), 19–31.

32. Hofer and Schendel, *Strategy Formulation,* p. 172.

33. Porter, *Competitive Strategy,* p. 157.

34. This discussion draws heavily on Porter, *Competitive Strategy,* Chapter 9.

35. Porter, *Competitive Strategy,* pp. 76–86.

Chapter 6

CORPORATE-LEVEL STRATEGY

6.1 OPENING INCIDENT: HANSON INDUSTRIES

In 1973 Gordon White, cofounder of British conglomerate Hanson Trust PLC, arrived in the United States to start the North American arm of Hanson Trust. Thirteen years later the company he set up, Hanson Industries, was ranked ninety-seventh among the Fortune 500 Industrials. Hanson Industries' achievement in joining the elite of U.S. companies capped a twenty-two-year period during which Hanson Trust's pretax profits had grown at an average rate of 45 percent a year. This phenomenal growth was based upon a carefully thought-out corporate strategy of diversification by acquisition into many unrelated industries. Between 1984 and 1986 alone Hanson Industries bought three major U.S. companies: U.S. Industries, a building and industrial products company; SCM Corporation, a typewriter and chemicals conglomerate; and Kaiser Cement Corporation.

The basis of the company's diversification strategy has been to acquire businesses cheaply, often against the existing management's will, liquidate surplus assets, and manage what is left in such a way as to increase earnings and generate cash for the next acquisition. When seeking companies to acquire, Hanson looks for cyclical businesses that earn good returns over the long run but may be suffering from a short-term setback. It also looks for companies in which a bad division or two have depressed overall performance, as well as for once-bad companies whose stock prices do not yet reflect recent turnarounds. All these factors keep down the price of the acquisition. In addition, Hanson seeks businesses in mature industries, where demand is predictable and new capital requirements are likely to be minimal. The company deliberately steers clear of high-tech industries, where capital requirements are large and technological change makes the future uncertain.

Once Hanson acquires a company, it economizes further by selling headquarters buildings and eliminating staff jobs or pushing them down into operations. Underperforming divisions are either turned around quickly or sold. The divisions that remain are given substantial operating autonomy but are held accountable for their performance through a system of tight financial controls. Strong profit incentives are introduced to encourage divisional executives to focus on the bottom line. Hanson's objective is to markedly improve the profitability of the companies it acquires.

The working out of all these factors can produce remarkable results. For example, Hanson Industries paid $930 million for SCM in January 1986, after a bitterly contested takeover battle. By September 1986 it had sold off a number of SCM subsidiaries for more than $1 billion. Hanson held onto the typewriter and chemicals businesses, which in effect cost nothing and which earned record pretax profits of $165 million in 1987.[1]

6.2 OVERVIEW

Corporate-level strategy is concerned with answering the question: *how should we manage the growth and development of the company to maximize long-run profitability?* Answering this question involves choosing (1) the set of *businesses* and (2) the *markets* that a company is going to compete in. With regard to different businesses, the company may decide to (a) concentrate on a single business, (b) vertically integrate into adjacent businesses, or (c) diversify into new business areas. With regard to different markets, it may decide to (a) compete just within its domestic marketplace or (b) expand globally and compete in the international arena.

Table 6.1 illustrates the range of choices open to a company. In this chapter, we review in depth the decisions to concentrate on a single business, integrate vertically, diversify into new businesses, and compete domestically or expand globally. Throughout we emphasize that, to succeed, corporate strategies should *add value* to the corporation. To understand what this means, we have to go back to the concept of the value chain, introduced in Chapter 4. *To add value, a corporate strategy should enable a company, or one or more of its business units, to perform one or more of the value-creation functions at a lower cost, or perform one or more*

TABLE 6.1   Corporate-level strategy options

		Businesses		
		Single business	Vertical integration	Diversification
Markets	Domestic	e.g., Domino's Pizza, Inc.	e.g., Nucor Corporation	e.g., Southland Corporation
	Global	e.g., Holiday Inns Inc.	e.g., Exxon Corporation	e.g., Hanson Trust

of the value creation functions in a way that allows for differentiation and a premium price. Thus a company's *corporate* strategy should help in the process of establishing a distinctive competence *at the business level.*

For example, in the case of Hanson Trust's acquisition of SCM, discussed in the Opening Incident, Hanson's restructuring of that company reduced the operating costs of SCM's typewriter and chemicals businesses, thereby increasing the *value added* by each of these businesses. By eliminating excess staff and reducing corporate overheads, the value-creation functions of the businesses acquired from SCM could be performed at a lower cost.

We must emphasize at the outset that companies frequently make mistakes when pursuing corporate-level strategies and may end up reducing rather than adding value. Consequently, at the end of the chapter, we discuss strategic retrenchment and turnaround as a response to failed corporate strategies.

6.3 CORPORATE GROWTH AND DEVELOPMENT

Most companies begin as single-business enterprises competing within the confines of their domestic market. For such companies, maximizing long-run profitability means identifying how best to compete within their market. As you saw in Chapter 5, this process requires management to consider differentiation, cost leadership, and focus. However, it may also involve vertical integration, either backward, to gain a strategic advantage from owning supply sources, or forward, to gain a strategic advantage from owning distribution outlets. In addition, in today's marketplace, a company often needs a global presence in order to compete successfully. For example, global electronics manufacturers, such as Sony, have a cost advantage over domestic companies, such as Zenith and RCA Consumer Electronics Division, that comes from their huge volume and scale economies.

Beyond these considerations, the company that manages to establish a sustainable competitive advantage in its original industry may find itself generating resources *in excess* of those required to maintain its position. It must then decide how to invest the excess resources in order to maximize its long-run profitability. One option is to diversify into new business areas. Diversification can take several forms, but, to be viable, must *add value* to the corporation. In the case of Hanson Trust, value is added by restructuring acquired companies to reduce costs and generate extra profits. As you will see, diversification can also create value through resource sharing between businesses, by transferring skills from one business to another, and by operating a portfolio strategy.

Thus, the growth and development of a typical *modern* enterprise can be divided into three main stages. At stage 1, a company operates as a single business within the confines of a single national market. Stage 2 involves vertical integration and/or global expansion to strengthen the competitive position of the company's *core* activity; vertical integration and global expansion *support* a com-

FIGURE 6.1   **Stages of corporate growth and development**

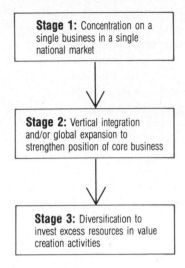

pany's business-level strategy. Stage 3 begins when the company is generating resources *in excess* of those necessary to maintain a competitive advantage in its core activity. Typically, at this stage the company looks for diversification opportunities outside its core business to generate value from the investment of excess resources. Figure 6.1 summarizes these stages.

The model proposed in Figure 6.1 differs from that offered by Alfred Chandler of MIT.[2] On the basis of historical research, Chandler suggested that most U.S. companies first grew as single businesses, then vertically integrated, then diversified into related businesses, and only at that point expanded globally. However, historical analogies are a poor guide to modern conditions, since the emergence of truly global markets and global competition is a phenomenon of the late twentieth century. Today the imperatives of global competition often force companies to become global before they diversify.

6.4 CONCENTRATION ON A SINGLE BUSINESS

All companies begin by concentrating on a single business within the confines of their domestic market. For such companies, corporate- and business-level strategy are synonymous. To maximize profitability, they must achieve low cost, differentiation, or focus. Even when a company has established a sustainable competitive advantage, however, it can still benefit from continuing to serve a single business.

Advantages

By concentrating on one operation, the single-business company can orient the total human, physical, and financial resources of the organization towards competing successfully within its market. This can be important in growth industries, where demands on the company's resources are likely to be substantial but where the long-term profits from establishing a competitive advantage are also substantial.

Besides top managers of a single business in a single national market are likely to have an intimate knowledge of the business the company is involved in, whereas in multibusiness and multinational enterprises, top managers may have to struggle just to keep abreast of the different operations of the individual subsidiary companies. Such knowledge is a major asset when the company's business is based in an intensely competitive and technologically dynamic industry that requires quick and informed top management decision making.

Disadvantages

Concentrating on just one business has significant disadvantages as well. Both vertical integration and global expansion may be necessary to establish a sustainable competitive advantage within an industry. Even in a young, technologically dynamic, high-growth industry such as the personal computer industry, companies like Apple and Compaq Computer Corporation have found that they need global markets and global manufacturing in order to generate the volume necessary to realize economies of scale and compete on costs. Similarly, IBM's strategy for establishing a competitive advantage in the PC market involves backward integration into the manufacture of proprietary components that are difficult for competitors to copy.

Beyond this, companies that concentrate on just one line of business face two other major constraints in trying to maximize profitability, and both these constraints push profit-seeking companies toward corporate diversification. First, single-business enterprises that are based in mature industries may find their growth rate limited by low industry growth. At this stage, concentrating on a single business may not be the best use of the company's resources — especially if the company has established a competitive advantage and is now generating financial resources *in excess* of those needed to maintain that advantage. To make better use of such excess resources, companies often begin to diversify into new business areas. For example, Coca-Cola, finding its growth limited by a mature soft drinks industry, recently diversified into the entertainment industry with the acquisition of Columbia Pictures Industries, Inc.

In addition, companies that concentrate on a single business also risk missing out on profitable opportunities stemming from the application of a company's distinctive competences to other industries. For example, had Philip Morris not acquired Miller Beer, it would have missed out on the opportunity to apply its distinctive competence in marketing one consumer product (cigarettes) to another consumer product (beer).

6.5 VERTICAL INTEGRATION

Vertical integration means that the company is producing its own inputs (backward integration) or is disposing of its own outputs (forward integration). The steel company that supplies its iron ore needs from company-owned iron ore mines exemplifies backward integration. The auto manufacturer that sells its cars through company-owned distribution outlets illustrates forward integration. In Figure 6.2, you see five main stages in a typical raw-material-to-consumer production chain. For a company based in the assembly stage, backward integration would involve moving into intermediate manufacturing and raw material production. Forward integration would involve movement into distribution and/or retail.

In addition to forward and backward integration, it is also possible to distinguish between **full integration** and **taper integration** (see Figure 6.3).[3] A company achieves full integration when it produces *all* of a particular input needed for its processes or when it disposes of *all* its output through its own operations. Taper integration occurs when a company buys from independent suppliers in addition to company-owned suppliers, or when it disposes of its output through independent outlets in addition to company-owned outlets. As you will see, taper integration has a number of advantages over full integration.

Creating Value Through Vertical Integration

A company pursuing vertical integration is normally motivated by a desire to strengthen the competitive position of its original, or core, business.[4] Through this strategy, the company can add value from the following sources; (1) production cost savings, (2) avoidance of market costs, (3) better quality control, and (4) protection of proprietary technology.[5] At the very least, these sources of additional value allow the company either to reduce its overall cost position in its core business or to charge a premium price for its product. Vertical integration,

FIGURE 6.2   **The different stages in the raw material to consumer chain**

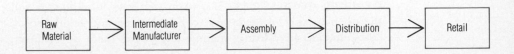

FIGURE 6.3   **Full and taper integration**

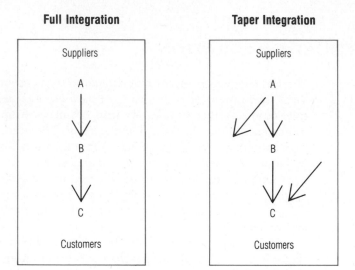

then, is consistent with a company's attempt to establish itself as the cost leader or as a differentiated player in its core business.

Production costs   When vertical integration permits technologically complementary processes to be carried out in quick succession, a company can save on production costs. For example, the ability to roll steel when hot from refining offers an advantage to steel refineries with their own rolling mills. The newly refined steel does not have to be reheated to make it malleable. Similarly, the ability to turn wood pulp into newsprint without drying and reconstituting it — as would have to be done if the pulp were to be delivered to a different organization for further processing — gives an advantage to integrated pulp and paper mills.

Further production cost savings arise from the easier planning, coordination, and scheduling of adjacent processes made possible in vertically integrated organizations. For example, in the 1920s Ford profited from the tight coordination and scheduling that is possible with backward vertical integration. Ford integrated backward into steel foundries, iron ore shipping, and iron ore mining. Deliveries at Ford were coordinated to such an extent that iron ore landed at Ford's steel foundries on the Great Lakes was turned into engine blocks within twenty-four hours. Thus Ford substantially reduced its production costs by eliminating the need to hold excessive inventories.

Avoiding market costs   If a company buys its inputs or sells its outputs on the open market, it often has to bear buying and selling costs. Many of these costs, such as advertising, maintaining a sales force, and running a procurement department, can be reduced, or even eliminated, through vertical integration. Moreover, vertical integration can also dispose of the need to pay profits to market middlemen (commodity brokers, warehouse operators, transport companies, and the like). Since it avoids market costs, a company may find it easier to become the cost leader in its core business.

Further costs of using the market arise when a company depends on a limited number of powerful suppliers for important inputs. The suppliers may take advantage of such a situation to raise prices above those that would be found in more competitive circumstances. The company ends up having to pay exorbitantly high prices for its inputs. These prices are the costs of using the market. If the company would integrate backward and supply its own inputs, it could avoid these costs. The same arguments apply when a company sells to a limited number of powerful buyers. Recognizing the company's dependence on them for orders, the buyers can squeeze down prices below those found in more competitive circumstances, costing the company potential profit. By integrating forward, the company can circumvent powerful buyers and earn greater returns on its final sales.[6]

Protection of product quality   By protecting product quality, vertical integration enables a company to become a differentiated player in its core business. The banana industry illustrates this situation. Historically, a problem with the banana industry has been the variable quality of delivered bananas, which often arrived on the shelves of American stores either too ripe or not ripe enough. To correct this problem, major American food companies, such as General Foods Corp., have integrated backward to gain control over supply sources. Consequently, they have been able to distribute bananas of a standard quality at the optimal time for consumption to American consumers. Knowing that they can rely on the quality of these brands, consumers are willing to pay more for them. Thus by integrating backward into plantation ownership, the banana companies have built consumer confidence, which enables them in turn to charge a premium price for their product.

Similar reasons can govern forward integration. Ownership of distribution outlets may be necessary if the required standards of after-sales service with complex products are to be provided. For example, in the 1920s Kodak owned retail outlets for distributing photographic equipment. The company felt that there were few established retail outlets with the skills necessary to sell and service its photographic equipment. By the 1930s, however, Kodak decided that it was no longer necessary to own its retail outlets, since other retailers had begun to provide satisfactory distribution and service for its products. The company then withdrew from retailing.

Proprietary technology   Proprietary technology is technology that is unique to a company and can give it an advantage over competitors. Proprietary technology can allow a company to establish more efficient product processes, thus reducing manufacturing costs, or it can be embodied in the design of a company's product, permitting the company to charge a premium price. Vertical integration makes good sense when a company needs to prevent its competitors from knowing too much about its technology. When proprietary technology involves an innovative process, vertical integration helps a company to protect its know-how and to establish itself as a cost leader in its core operation. When proprietary technology relates to a product innovation, vertical integration assists the company in establishing itself as a differentiated player in its core operation.

Recently, IBM integrated backward into the manufacture of microcircuits to protect the innovations incorporated in its new PS/2 personal computer system from being duplicated by competitors. The information pathways and graphics of the PS/2 machines are created by proprietary chips, manufactured by IBM itself, that will be difficult for competitors to decipher. By taking this step, IBM hopes to avoid the widespread copying of its machines that occurred in the case of the company's original PC system; that is, it hopes to differentiate itself.[7]

Disadvantages of Vertical Integration

Vertical integration has its disadvantages, however. Most important among them are (1) potential cost disadvantages, (2) disadvantages that arise when technology is changing fast, (3) disadvantages that arise when demand is unpredictable. Each of these types of disadvantages is discussed below. Because of these disadvantages, the benefits of vertical integration are not always as substantial as they might seem initially. Strategic managers need to weigh the value created by vertical integration against the disadvantages of the strategy when deciding whether to integrate. In many cases, the disadvantages are such that vertical integration may reduce rather than increase value.

Cost disadvantages   Although often undertaken to gain a cost advantage, vertical integration can bring higher costs if the company becomes committed to purchasing inputs from company-owned suppliers when low-cost external sources of supply exist. For example, currently General Motors is at a cost disadvantage in relation to Chrysler because it makes 70 percent of its own components, whereas Chrysler makes only 30 percent. GM has to pay United Auto Worker wages to workers in its own component supply operations, and these wages are generally $2 more per hour than the wages paid by independent component suppliers. Thus, as General Motors exemplifies, vertical integration can be a disadvantage when a company's own sources of supply have higher operating costs than those of independent suppliers. The problem may be less serious, however, when the company pursues taper, rather than full, integration, since the need to compete with independent suppliers can produce a downward pressure on the cost structure of company-owned suppliers.

Technological change   When technology is changing fast, vertical integration poses the hazard of tying a company to an obsolescent technology.[8] Consider the radio manufacturer who in the 1950s integrated backward and acquired a manufacturer of vacuum valves. When in the 1960s transistors replaced vacuum valves as a major component in radios, this company would have found itself tied to a technologically obsolescent business. Switching to transistors would have meant writing off its investment in vacuum valves. Thus the company might have been reluctant to change and instead might have continued to use vacuum valves in its radios while its nonintegrated competitors would have been rapidly switching to the new technology. But since it kept making an outdated product, the company would have rapidly lost market share. Thus vertical integration can inhibit a company's ability to change its suppliers or its distribution systems to match the requirements of changing technology.

Demand uncertainty   Vertical integration can also be risky in unstable or unpredictable demand conditions. When demand is stable, higher degrees of vertical integration might be managed with relative ease. Stable demand allows better scheduling and coordination of production flows among different activities. When demand conditions are unstable or unpredictable, it may be difficult to achieve close coordination among vertically integrated activities.

The problem involves balancing capacity among different stages of a process. For example, an auto manufacturer might vertically integrate backward to acquire its own supplier of carburetors that has a capacity exactly matching the auto manufacturer's needs. However, if demand for autos subsequently falls, the company will find itself locked into a business that is running below capacity. Clearly, this would be uneconomical. The auto manufacturer could avoid this situation by continuing to buy carburetors on the open market rather than making them itself.

If demand conditions are unpredictable, taper integration might be somewhat less risky than full integration. When the company provides only part of its total input requirements from company-owned suppliers, in times of low demand it can keep its in-house suppliers running at full capacity by ordering exclusively from them.

6.6 GLOBAL EXPANSION

Global expansion involves establishing significant operations and market interests outside a company's home country. We begin by examining how global expansion can create additional value for the company, thereby maximizing long-run profitability. Next, we consider whether it is better for global enterprises to recognize differences in national conditions and vary their strategy accordingly or to adopt a standardized approach to competing in the global marketplace. The former approach is referred to as a **multidomestic strategy** and the latter as a **global strategy.** Then we look at the different ways of entering a foreign market and the factors that influence the choice among different entry modes. Finally, we close this section with a discussion of the problems of managing global enterprises.

Creating Value Through Global Expansion

Global expansion enables the company to add value in a number of ways not available to domestic enterprises. These arise from the ability of global enterprises to (1) expand their market, (2) better cover investment costs, (3) realize economies of scale from global volume, and (4) base manufacturing operations in locations where operating costs are lowest.

Market expansion   Global expansion is a way of overcoming domestic limits to growth. Many companies favor it over diversification into new businesses as a method of continued growth at historic rates once their domestic market matures. Instead of diversifying, they prefer to invest any *excess* resources in a familiar line of business, even if the setting is an unfamiliar foreign country. For example, McDonald's recent push overseas can be attributed to a slowdown in the growth rate of the fast food industry in the United States. During the 1980s the U.S. fast food industry displayed all the signs of maturity. Few prime locations remained, industry growth was averaging only 1 percent, and intense competition from Burger King and Wendy's International Inc. further limited the opportunities for the profitable investment of corporate resources. In response, McDonald's stepped up its overseas expansion. Forty percent of McDonald's new openings in 1985 were overseas, up from 28 percent in 1980.[9] In such cases, value is created by transferring skills acquired in the company's domestic market to tap the profit potential of new and largely unexploited markets.

Covering investment costs   Were it not for global markets, some companies would have great difficulty recouping their investment in product development—that is, in generating value from their investment. It costs pharmaceutical companies between $50 million and $100 million to put a new drug on the market. To recoup this expenditure, pharmaceutical companies need global markets; the U.S. market alone is too small. Similarly, without global markets, aircraft manufacturers would probably be unable to cover the billions of dollars of development costs necessary to produce a new aircraft. Thus global markets may be necessary to reap the full value of investment in product development.

Realizing economies of scale   By offering a standardized product to the global marketplace and by manufacturing that product in a single location, a global company can reap scale economies from its global volume that are not available to smaller domestic enterprises. For example, by using centralized manufacturing facilities and global marketing strategies, Sony has wrested a share in the global television market from competitors such as Philips NV, RCA, and Zenith, which traditionally have based manufacturing operations in each of their major markets. Similarly, Japanese manufacturers of electronic components, such as NEC Corporation, are beginning to dominate the global market because their huge global volume for a standardized product has enabled them to ride down the experience curve and gain significant cost economies over their rivals.

Locating for low cost   It can pay a company to base its manufacturing facilities in those areas of the world where operating costs are lowest, even if that means direct exporting back into the company's home country. The main factors determining the most favorable locations for global manufacturing are (1) labor costs, (2) energy costs, (3) access to the necessary infrastructure (e.g., an educated work force, roads, rail networks, a favorable political climate, etc.), and (4) proximity to important global markets (particularly when transport costs are high). For example, in the late 1980s European subsidiaries of Ford and GM began shifting much of their European auto production from West Germany to Great Britain because labor costs in Britain were 45 percent less than those in West Germany, while productivity gains among British auto workers had been averaging 10–12 percent annually, against 8 percent in West Germany.[10] In short, GM and Ford were moving their operations from a high-cost location to a low-cost location.

Global or Multidomestic Strategy

One of the major choices global companies face is whether to compete on a *global* basis or on a *multidomestic* basis.[11] A multidomestic strategy — the time-honored way in which global companies compete — is based on the assumption that national markets differ widely with regard to consumer tastes and preferences, competitive conditions, operating conditions, and political, legal, and social structures. To deal with these differences, companies decentralize strategic and operating decisions letting national subsidiaries make them. Each subsidiary will have its own marketing function and its own manufacturing facilities and the attributes of the product will vary among nations according to the tastes and preferences of local consumers.

Though a multidomestic strategy has the advantage of recognizing differences among nations, it also has a major disadvantage. Since manufacturing is decentralized, multidomestic companies are unable to realize scale economies from centralizing manufacturing facilities and offering a *standardized* product to the global marketplace. A global strategy, on the other hand, is designed to do just that. The distinguishing feature of a global strategy is that competitive strategy is centralized. National subsidiaries are viewed as *interdependent,* rather than independent, entities in terms of both operations and competitive strategy.

In recent years a number of companies have shifted to a global strategy because global markets keep moving toward greater standardization. According to Theodore Levitt, modern communications and transport technologies have created the conditions for a convergence of the tastes and preferences of consumers from different nations.[12] The result is the emergence of enormous global markets for standardized consumer products. Worldwide acceptance of McDonald's hamburgers, Coca-Cola, Levi Strauss blue jeans, and Sony television sets, all of which are sold as standardized products, confirms the increasing homogeneity of the global marketplace.

Given these circumstances, when should a company choose a global strategy and when a multidomestic strategy? The answer depends on both the extent to which it can realize economies of scale from centralized production and the extent to which the global marketplace allows standardization. As Table 6.2 illustrates, four main strategic postures are possible.

If there are no scale economies from centralized global production and if national differences make market standardization impossible, then a multidomestic strategy is appropriate. Companies such as Unilever N.V. and CPC International Inc. are currently in such a position. If there are no scale economies from centralized production but global market standardization *is* possible, then a global marketing strategy, along with local production (to avoid transport costs), is appropriate. Levi Strauss and Coca-Cola are currently in such a posi-

TABLE 6.2   **A global or multidomestic strategy?**

	No significant scale economies	Significant scale economies
Global market standardization not possible	Local manufacturing and marketing (multi-domestic strategy) e.g., CPC International Inc. Unilever N.V.	Global component manufacturing, local final assembly and marketing e.g., Caterpillar Tractor Co.
Global market standardization possible	Global marketing and local manufacturing e.g., The Coca-Cola Company Levi Strauss	Global manufacturing and global marketing (pure global strategy) e.g., Sony Corp. Toyota

tion. If there *are* scale economies from centralized production but global standardization is not possible, global component manufacture, along with local assembly and marketing operations, is most appropriate. This is the strategy pursued by Caterpillar Tractor. Caterpillar has designed its products to use many identical components and has invested in a few large-scale component manufacturing facilities to fill global demand and realize scale economies. At the same time the company augments the centralized manufacturing of components with assembly plants in each of its major global markets. At these plants, Caterpillar adds local product features, tailoring the finished product to local needs. Thus Caterpillar is able to realize many of the benefits of global manufacturing while differentiating its product among national markets.[13] Finally, if there *are* scale economies from centralized production and global standardization *is* also possible, then global manufacturing and marketing make good sense. This is the purest form of global strategy and is currently being pursued by companies such as Sony and Toyota.

Even when a multidomestic strategy makes sense, a company should still have a global perspective. Gary Hamel of London Business School and C. K. Prahalad of the University of Michigan have argued that many multidomestic corporations are locked in a fiercely competitive global battle.[14] In the tire industry, for example, Michelin Tire Corporation, Goodyear, and Firestone Tire & Rubber Co. all manufacture and distribute in local markets, yet they are locked in a global struggle. In the early 1970s Michelin used its strong European profits to attack Goodyear's North American home market. Goodyear could have retaliated by cutting its North American prices, but because Michelin would only expose a small amount of its worldwide business in North America, Michelin had little to lose from a North American price war. Goodyear, on the other hand, would sacrifice profits in its largest market. Therefore Goodyear struck back by cutting prices and expanding its operations in Europe. The action forced Michelin to slow down its attack on Goodyear's North American market and to think again about the costs of taking market share away from Goodyear.

According to Hamel and Prahalad, the pattern of cross-subsidization engaged in by Michelin and Goodyear is the essence of global strategy. By drawing on strengths in one market to gain share in another market, a company can build up a global presence. That is what Canon Inc., Hitachi Ltd., and Seiko have done. In other words, even if there is no manufacturing or marketing interdependence among local operations, it can still pay the multinational company to build a global strategy around financial interdependence.

Choice of Entry Mode

When considering global expansion, strategic managers can choose from four different ways of serving an overseas market: exporting, licensing and franchising, entering into a joint venture with a host country company, and setting up a wholly owned subsidiary in the host country.

Exporting   Most manufacturing companies begin their international expansion as exporters and only later switch to one of the other strategies for serving a foreign market. While exporting avoids the costs of having to establish operations in the host country, it does have a number of disadvantages. They include high transportation costs, costs of tariffs, and problems associated with delegating marketing activities to a foreign agent, who may not always act in the company's best interest.[15] For one or more of these reasons many companies that start off as exporters eventually switch to one of the other ways of serving a foreign market.

Licensing and franchising   International licensing and franchising are arrangements whereby the foreign licensee (or franchisee) buys the rights to produce a company's product for a negotiated fee (normally, royalty payments on units of the product sold). The licensee then puts up most of the money to get the overseas operation going. Under this arrangement, the company does not have to bear development costs, as it must with a joint venture or wholly owned subsidiary. The advantage of licensing and franchising over other forms of direct involvement is that they are the least costly to the company.

Despite this advantage, licensing can be inappropriate if a company has a technological competence that it wishes to protect. By licensing its technology, the company can quickly lose control over it. For example, in the 1960s RCA licensed its color television technology to Japanese producers. RCAs management saw the deal as a way of making some easy money. However, the Japanese quickly assimilated the technology and then turned it to their advantage, exporting color televisions to the United States. As a result, Japanese producers now have a bigger share of the U.S. market than the RCA brand. In a similar example, Acme-Cleveland Corporation once licensed Mitsubishi Heavy Industries, Ltd., to manufacture and sell some of its machine tools in Japan, only to watch Mitsubishi become its rival in the U.S. market.[16]

Joint ventures   There are two reasons why joint ventures may be the preferred entry mode. First, a company may feel that it can benefit from a local partner's knowledge of a host country's competitive conditions. For example, for most U.S. enterprises, joint ventures have involved an American company providing the technology and a local partner providing the marketing and operating know-how necessary to compete within that country. Second, when the development costs of opening up an overseas market are very high, a company might gain by sharing these costs with a local partner. Furthermore, in many countries political factors make joint ventures the only feasible entry mode. Until the mid 1970s the Japanese prohibited U.S. companies from setting up wholly owned subsidiaries. Instead, they had to enter into joint ventures with Japanese companies. Although such regulations are less common in other developed nations, political expediency can again make joint ventures the favored entry mode.

As in licensing, however, a company entering into a joint venture runs the risk of losing control over its technology. Indeed, many companies that initially relied on joint ventures to compete in Japan have learned this to their dismay and are now establishing wholly owned subsidiaries.

Wholly owned subsidiaries   Establishing a wholly owned subsidiary is generally the most costly method of serving a foreign market. Companies doing this have to bear the full costs of setting up overseas operations (as opposed to a joint venture, where the costs are shared, or licensing, where the licensee bears the costs). However, when a company's competitive advantage is based on control over a technological competence, a wholly owned subsidiary will normally be the preferred entry method, for it reduces the risks of losing control over that competence.

In addition, executing a global strategy, particularly if that strategy is based on strong manufacturing interdependence among different national operations, normally requires that the company establishes wholly owned subsidiaries. Only wholly owned subsidiaries give the company the degree of control necessary if it is to coordinate international production. Wholly owned subsidiaries tend to be the favored entry mode in the semiconductor, electronics, and pharmaceutical industries.

In sum, the need to protect firm specific advantages in technology and the requirements of a global strategy are the critical determinants of the choice of entry mode. When technological content is low and global manufacturing interdependencies are not a consideration, licensing/franchising is normally the preferred entry mode. Thus, McDonald's is expanding overseas via franchising and many international hotel chains are based upon franchising. This is because such firms do not have a technological advantage to protect. Nor do they need to centralize control over operations in order to coordinate global manufacturing.

However, when the competitive advantage of the firm is based upon control over technology and/or there is a need for tight control to coordinate global manufacturing, the establishment of a wholly owned subsidiary makes the most sense.

Managing Global Risks

Global expansion is frequently difficult to implement and can involve high risks. Strategic managers need to be aware of a number of risks that the global corporation has to deal with. Foremost among them are political risks, economic risks, and management problems.

Political risks   Political risks stem from political turmoil, such as riots, demonstrations, terrorism, civil war, and international war. The consequences of political turmoil include economic collapse of the host country's economy (as in Lebanon), nationalization of assets without compensation by the host country's government, and prohibition of profit repatriation to the home country. For example, in 1960 Texaco lost a refinery worth $60 million ($260 million in 1986 prices) when the Castro government nationalized all foreign assets in Cuba. Similarly, many U.S. companies lost investments worth hundreds of millions of dollars after the 1979 Iranian revolution. Prohibition of profit repatriation is also fairly commonplace, even among other Western nations.

Economic risks   The chief economic risks are those associated with currency fluctuations. Fluctuations in the value of the dollar against other currencies make international planning very difficult. What may look like a good investment, given one exchange rate, may look bad a few months later, due to a change in the rate. A rising dollar can dramatically reduce the value of overseas assets and earnings. Consider the case of Mexico, where between 1976 and 1987 the value of the peso dropped from 22/dollar to 1,500/dollar. As a result, U.S.-based multinationals with operations in Mexico have seen the dollar value of their investments drop through the floor. Strategic managers need to assess currency risks when deciding whether to invest overseas.

Management problems   Management problems in multinational enterprises can be enormous. Management practices developed in the United States cannot always be easily transferred to other countries. McDonald's, for example, has based much of its success in the United States upon building close ties with its suppliers. The suppliers have geared themselves to McDonald's particular needs, enabling McDonald's to keep down costs. In turn, the suppliers have got a guaranteed customer. Few foreign companies, however, have been prepared to enter into the same kind of relationships with McDonald's, since they perceive the risks of such relationships as too great. Consequently, it cost McDonald's more to run its overseas operations than its domestic operations.[17]

There are a host of other problems associated with managing businesses in radically different cultures. Different nations have different legal, political, monetary, economic, and social systems, all of which must be taken into account when going global. Responding to these differences can require new forms of organization, new management skills, and different accounting and control systems. There are also the logistics of trying to control a global enterprise. The simple fact that the western United States is eight to ten hours behind Europe can make day-to-day business communications difficult to manage.

6.7 DIVERSIFICATION

There are two major types of diversification: **related diversification** and **unrelated diversification.** Related diversification refers to diversification into a new activity that is linked to a company's existing activity by a commonality between one or more components of each activity's value chain. Normally, these linkages are based on manufacturing, marketing, materials management, and technological commonalities. The diversification of Philip Morris into the brewing industry with the acquisition of Miller Beer is an example of related diversification, since there are marketing commonalities between the brewing and tobacco business (both are consumer-product businesses, where competitive success depends on brand-positioning skills). Unrelated diversification refers to diversification into a new activity that has no obvious commonalities with any of the company's existing activities. Hanson Trust, considered in the opening incident, is an example of an unrelated company.

In this section, we will begin by looking at how diversification can create value for a company, and then we will examine some of the pitfalls of diversification. Finally, we will consider some of the factors that determine the choice between the strategies of related diversification and unrelated diversification.

Creating Value Through Diversification

Most companies first consider diversification when they are generating financial resources *in excess* of those necessary to maintain a competitive advantage in their original or core business.[18] The question they must tackle is how to invest the excess resources in order to create value? Diversification can create value in four main ways: (1) a portfolio strategy, (2) restructuring, (3) transferring skills among businesses, and (4) sharing functions or resources.

Portfolio strategy A portfolio strategy creates value by establishing within a diversified company an internal capital market that takes over some of the functions of the stock market. In an internal capital market, the head office has three major roles: (1) to perform strategic planning functions concerning the composition of the corporate portfolio (decisions about acquisitions and divestments); (2) to set financial targets and monitor the subsequent performance of business units, intervening selectively in underperforming units to correct any problems; and (3) to allocate corporate capital among the competing claims of different business units. The business units themselves are set up as autonomous profit centers, subject only to financial controls from the head office.

Advocates of this strategy contend that the head office of a company pursuing a portfolio strategy can monitor business unit performance and allocate financial resources among units more efficiently than the stock market could do if each business unit were an independent company.[19] The reason is that the head office, as an internal investor, has access to better information about the performance of business units and is better able to use that information than could stock market investors if each business unit were independent. For example, the head office can use its authority to demand detailed information on the efficiency of a business unit's operations, whereas stock market investors have to make judgments on the basis of whatever information a company chooses to release to them. The head office can also intervene selectively in underperforming business units and fine-tune their operations (for instance, by making relatively minor management changes), whereas the stock market can only make drastic adjustments (such as a takeover). Consequently, the stock market may fail to adequately discipline underperforming management teams and may allocate too few capital resources to some companies and too many to others. The head office of a diversified company can perform both the task of disciplining underperforming management teams and of allocating resources much more effectively.

Since a company is more efficient than the stock market with regard to performance monitoring and capital allocation functions, it should acquire potentially strong but poorly managed enterprises that are undervalued by the stock market. By exposing acquired companies to the discipline of tight financial controls and efficient capital allocation, a portfolio strategy encourages and rewards aggressive profit-seeking behavior by the acquired company's management. The resultant increase in the efficiency of the acquired company adds value to the acquiring corporation.

However, the strategy has its critics. Some contend that today's computer-driven stock market is efficient at allocating resources and penalizing poorly managed companies by forcing proxy votes on key elements of corporate strategy.[20] If this is true, and it is a debatable point, the whole basis for the strategy has been destroyed. Others argue that overly tight financial controls can lead to short-run profit maximization within the business units of companies pursuing a portfolio strategy.[21] In turn, the arms-length relationship between the head office and the business units allows such behavior to go undetected until a good deal of damage has been done. The poor performance of portfolio diversifiers, such as Gulf & Western Industries, Inc., Consolidated Foods Corporation, and ITT, has lent weight to these criticisms. However, there are also some spectacular examples of how successful the strategy can be — for instance the Anglo-American conglomerate BTR Inc.[22] More than anything else, these conflicting examples suggest that the strategy is a difficult one to implement.

Restructuring A restructuring strategy has a lot in common with a portfolio strategy. The essential differences have to do with the degree to which the head office becomes involved in business unit operations. Companies that pursue a restructuring strategy seek out poorly managed, underperforming, or undeveloped companies. The objective is to acquire such companies and then intervene in a *proactive* fashion, frequently changing the acquired company's management team, developing new business-level strategies, and infusing the company with new financial or technological resources. If all goes well, the upshot is a dramatic improvement in the competitive position and financial health of the acquired company, creating value for the acquiring enterprise.

The diversification strategy of Hanson Trust, described in the Opening Incident, is based on restructuring. Hanson seeks out companies that are not maximizing stockholder wealth. Such companies are normally characterized by excess organizational slack. This means that they use more resources than necessary to run their business. For example, managers may be given expensive company cars as perks, corporate headquarters may be lavishly decorated and overstaffed, and the company may own a ranch in Texas to entertain its visiting executives or run a fleet of jets to fly its managers around the country (Diamond Shamrock did all of this under the leadership of Bill Bricker—see the Opening Incident in Chapter 2).

Because of their inefficiency, companies with a high degree of organizational slack are often undervalued by the stock market. Companies such as Hanson Trust can acquire them at a reasonable price and then reorganize them to increase their efficiency. Excess staff are likely to be laid off and the executive jets, company cars, and expensive headquarters sold. Typically, unwanted subsidiary companies are also sold at this stage. Whatever remains is then subjected to central financial controls designed to instill profit discipline and efficiency awareness. The result, as in the case of the Hanson/SCM acquisition discussed in the Opening Incident, is improved performance. Thus the acquiring company creates value for its stockholders.

Transferring skills Companies that base their diversification strategy on transferring skills seek out new businesses related to their existing business by one or more value-creation functions (e.g., manufacturing, marketing, materials management, and R&D—see Chapter 4). They want to create value by drawing on the distinctive skills in one or more of their existing value-creation functions in order to improve the competitive position of the new business.

For such a strategy to work, the skills being transferred must involve activities that are important for establishing a competitive advantage. All too often, companies assume that any commonality is sufficient for creating value. General Motors' acquisition of Hughes Aircraft, made simply because autos and auto manufacturing were going electronic and Hughes was an electronics concern, demonstrates the folly of overestimating the commonalities among businesses. To date, the acquisition has failed to realize any of the anticipated gains for GM, whose competitive position has only worsened.

Philip Morris's transfer of marketing skills to Miller Beer, discussed earlier, is one of the classic examples of how value can be created by skill transfers. Drawing on its marketing and brand-positioning skills, Philip Morris pioneered the introduction of Miller Lite, the product that redefined the brewing industry and moved Miller from number six to number two in the market. Rockwell International Corp.'s diversification into factory automation with the company's 1985 acquisition of Allen-Bradley Canada Ltd. is another example of skill transfers. In this case, skill transfers were based on technological linkages between different activities. Rockwell has given Allen-Bradley strong research and development support and Rockwell's own electronics technology, while Allen-Bradley's factory automation expertise is boosting efficiency in Rockwell's commercial and defense factories.[23]

Sharing functions   As with skill transfers, diversification to share functions is only possible when there are significant commonalities between one or more of the value-creation functions of a company's existing and new activities. One objective when sharing functions is to create value from the realization of **economies of scope.**[24] Economies of scope arise when two or more business units share manufacturing facilities, distribution channels, advertising campaigns, R&D costs, and the like. By sharing functions, each business unit has to invest fewer resources in that function. For example, the costs of General Electric's advertising, sales, and service activities in major appliances are low because they are spread over a wide range of products.

In addition, such a strategy can utilize the capacity of certain functions better. For example, by producing the components for the assembly operations of two distinct businesses, a component-manufacturing plant may be able to operate at a greater capacity, thereby realizing *economies of scale,* in addition to economies of scope.

A diversification strategy based on resource sharing can help a company attain a low-cost position in each of the businesses in which it operates. Thus diversification to share resources can be a valid way of *supporting* the generic business-level strategy of cost leadership. However, strategic managers need to be aware that the costs of coordination necessary to achieve resource sharing within a company often outweigh the value that can be created by such a strategy.[25] Consequently, the strategy should only be pursued when sharing is likely to generate a significant competitive advantage in one or more of the company's business units.

Procter & Gamble's disposable diaper and paper towel businesses offer one of the best examples of successful resource sharing. These businesses share the costs of procuring certain raw materials (such as paper) and developing the technology for new products and processes. In addition, a joint sales force sells both products to supermarket buyers, and both products are shipped via the same distribution system. This resource sharing has given both business units a cost advantage that has enabled them to undercut their less diversified competitors.[26]

The Pitfalls of Diversification

In a study that looked at the diversification of thirty-three major U.S. corporations between 1950 and 1986, Michael Porter observed that the track record of corporate diversification has been dismal.[27] Porter found that most of these companies had divested many more diversified acquisitions than they had kept. He concluded that the corporate diversification strategies of most companies have dissipated value instead of creating it. Porter's research begs the question of why diversification so often fails. Part of the answer seems to be that diversity, too, has its pitfalls, and we consider some of them below.

Diversification to pool risks   One common pitfall is to pursue diversification in order to pool risks. The benefits of risk pooling are said to come from pooling together imperfectly correlated income streams to create a more stable income stream. An example of risk pooling might be USX's diversification into the oil and gas industry in an attempt to offset the adverse effects of cyclical downturns in the steel industry. According to the advocates of risk pooling, the more stable income stream reduces the risk of bankruptcy and is in the best interests of the company's stockholders.

This argument ignores two facts. First, stockholders can easily eliminate the risks inherent in holding an individual stock by diversifying their own portfolios, and they can do so at a much lower cost than the company. Thus, far from being in the best interests of stockholders, attempts to pool risks through diversification represent an unproductive use of resources. Second, the vast majority of research on this topic suggests that corporate diversification is not a very effective way to pool risks.[28] The business cycles of different industries are not easy to predict and in any case tend to be less important than a general economic downturn that hits all industries simultaneously. International Harvester illustrates the point. By 1979 International Harvester had diversified into three major businesses: agricultural equipment, construction equipment, and trucks. These businesses were supposed to follow different business cycles, cushioning the company against severe fluctuations. In the early 1980s, however, all these businesses suffered a downturn at the same time, cumulating a $2.9-billion loss for Harvester.

Diversification for growth   Another common pitfall involves the pursuit of diversification for growth. Such diversification is not a coherent strategy since growth on its own does not create value. Growth should be the *by-product,* rather than the objective, of a diversification strategy. However, companies sometimes diversify for reasons of growth alone, rather than to gain any well-thought out strategic advantage. ITT under the leadership of Harold Geneen took this path. Geneen turned ITT from an international telecommunications company into a broadly based conglomerate consisting of more than 100 separate businesses with interests in such diverse areas as baking, car rental, defense electronics, fire hydrants, insurance, hotels, paper products, and telecommunications. The strategy seemed to have more to do with Geneen's desire to build an empire than with maximizing the company's value.[29] Since Geneen's departure in 1979, ITT's management has been trying to divest many of the businesses acquired under his leadership and to concentrate on insurance and financial services instead.

Overdiversification   Too much diversification can also lead to loss of control. This happens when top management loses touch with what is going on within the company's different businesses and stops probing deeply into their affairs. Loss of control typically occurs when top management resources are spread thinly over too many different activities, as is often the case in highly diversified companies. The main consequence of such overextension is a failure to anticipate financial crises. The danger is particularly acute during a sharp downturn in general economic activity, when the simultaneous occurrence of problems in a large number of the company's different businesses may be too much for a small central management team to cope with.[30]

Miscalculating benefits and costs   Companies often fall into the trap of overestimating the value that diversification can create. When seeking to share resources or transfer skills, companies must ascertain that the benefits they expect are tangible rather than imaginary. The benefits are more likely to be tangible when they center on critical value-creation functions. Similarly, many companies underestimate the difficulties of implementing their chosen diversification strategy. Sharing resources, for example, requires close coordination between business units. It involves costs in terms of the bureaucratic mechanisms that are necessary to share resources and the intraorganizational conflicts arising from decisions on distributing returns to a shared asset. Portfolio or restructuring strategies can also have a negative effect on a company if they lead to short-run rather than long-run profit maximization.

Thus, when pursuing a diversification strategy, a company should weigh the value created by the strategy against the costs of implementation before deciding whether to proceed.

Related or Unrelated Diversification?

One issue that a company must resolve is whether to diversify into businesses related to its existing activities by value chain commonalities or into totally new business. Even though strategic management literature has long distinguished between *related* and *unrelated* diversification, it is not immediately apparent why a company should choose unrelated diversification over related diversification.

By definition, related companies can create value by resource sharing and by transferring skills between businesses. They can also carry out some restructuring and create value by applying portfolio concepts to the management of their diverse activities. By way of contrast, since there are no commonalities between the value chains of unrelated businesses, the unrelated company cannot create value by sharing resources or transferring skills between businesses. Unrelated diversifiers can only create value by restructuring and by applying a portfolio strategy. Since related diversification can create value in more ways than unrelated ones, related diversification should be the preferred strategy. In addition, related diversification is normally perceived as involving fewer risks, since the company is moving into business areas of which the top management has some knowledge.

Probably because of the above considerations, most diversified companies display a preference for related diversification.[31] However, research suggests that the average related company is no more profitable than the average unrelated company.[32] Moreover, a significant minority of companies continue to diversify into unrelated areas, and besides some dramatic failures (such as Consolidated Foods, Gulf & Western, and ITT), there have also been some dramatic successes (for instance, BTR, Hanson Trust, and Textron Inc.).

A major reason why some companies continue to diversify into unrelated areas appears to be that, despite apparent advantages, related diversification is not always an attainable option. Related diversification is only possible if there are obvious commonalities between the skills required to compete in the company's core business and the skills needed to compete in other industrial or commercial areas. Some companies' skills are so specialized that they have few applications outside their core businesses. For example, since the commonalities between steel making and other industrial or commercial operations are few, most steel companies have diversified into unrelated industries (LTV into defense contracting, USX into oil and gas). When companies have less specialized skills, they can find many more diversification opportunities outside their core business. Examples include chemical and electrical engineering companies.

Another reason that some companies prefer unrelated diversification is the high cost of implementing a strategy of related diversification. Sharing resources or transferring skills raises difficult organizational issues, including the problem of achieving coordination between otherwise autonomous business units without jeopardizing the accountability of each, the problem of pricing skills transferred between business units (the transfer pricing problem), and the problem of allocating profits and costs among business units when significant asset sharing is involved. Unless the value created by resource sharing and skill transfers is substantial, it may not pay the company to confine its diversification to related activities alone.

In sum, the above arguments suggest that it will pay the firm to concentrate on related diversification when (a) significant commonalities exist between the value chains of the different business units, and (b) the costs of implementation do not exceed the value that can be created through resource sharing and skill transfers. For firms that do not meet these criteria, it does not follow that related diversification will be any more profitable than unrelated diversification. Indeed, in some situations unrelated diversification may be the most profitable strategy since the firm avoids the costs of implementation associated with related diversification.

6.8 RETRENCHMENT AND TURNAROUND

The strategies of vertical integration, global expansion, and diversification are strategies for profitable expansion. However, for a variety of reasons, corporate strategies sometimes fail, and corporate decline ensues. Retrenchment is not so much a corporate strategy as a strategic response to corporate decline. The objective of retrenchment is to restructure the operations of a troubled company in order to halt corporate decline and return the company to profitability. In this section, we review the causes of corporate decline and then examine the steps toward successful retrenchment and turnaround.

The Causes of Corporate Decline

Six main causes stand out in most cases of corporate decline: poor management, overexpansion, inadequate financial controls, high costs, the emergence of powerful new competition, and unforeseen shifts in demand.[33] Normally, several, if not all, of these different factors are present in a decline situation. For example, Chrysler's decline toward near bankruptcy in the 1970s was brought on by poor top management that had failed to put adequate financial controls in place. In turn, this allowed Chrysler's cost structure to get out of line, inhibiting Chrysler's ability to respond to powerful new low-cost Japanese competition. In addition, the unforeseen shift in demand toward compact and subcompact cars after the oil price hikes of 1974 and 1979 left Chrysler, as a manufacturer of intermediate and full-sized models, ill prepared to serve the market.

Poor management "Poor management" covers a multitude of sins, ranging from sheer incompetence to neglect of core businesses and an insufficient number of good managers. Although not necessarily a bad thing, one-person rule often seems to be at the root of many cases of poor management. One study found that the presence of a dominant and autocratic chief executive with a passion for empire-building strategies often seems to characterize many failing companies.[34] Examples include Bill Bricker, the former CEO of Diamond Shamrock (see the Opening Incident of Chapter 2); Harold Geneen, the former CEO of ITT; and Roy Mason, the former CEO of the one-time Fortune 500 and later bankrupt Charter Company.

Overexpansion The empire-building strategies of autocratic CEOs such as Bricker, Geneen, and Mason often involve rapid expansion and extensive diversification. Much of this diversification tends to be poorly conceived and adds little value to a company. As observed above, the consequences of too much diversification include loss of control and an inability to cope with recessionary conditions. Moreover, companies that expand rapidly tend to do so by taking on large amounts of debt financing. Adverse economic conditions can limit a company's ability to meet its debt requirements and can thus precipitate a financial crisis.

Inadequate financial controls The most common aspect of inadequate financial controls is a failure to assign profit responsibility to key decision makers within the organization.[35] A lack of accountability for the financial consequences of their actions can encourage middle-level managers to employ excess staff and spend resources beyond what is necessary for maximum efficiency. In such cases, bureaucracy may balloon and costs spiral out of control. This is precisely what happened at Chrysler during the 1970s. As Lee Iacocca later noted, Jerry Greenwald, whom Iacocca brought in to head the finance function in 1980, "had a hell of a time finding anybody who could be identified as having specific responsibility for anything. They would tell him, 'Well, everyone is responsible for controlling costs'. Jerry knew very well what that meant — in the final analysis nobody was."[36]

High costs   Inadequate financial controls can lead to high costs. Beyond this, the most common cause of a high-cost structure is low labor productivity, which may stem from union-imposed restrictive working practices (as in the case of the auto and steel industries), management's failure to invest in new labor-saving technologies, or, more often, a combination of both. Other common causes include high wage rates (a particularly important factor for companies competing on costs in the global marketplace) and a failure to realize economies of scale due to low market share.

New competition   For U.S. companies, powerful new competition typically comes from overseas, and many companies have been caught unprepared for its emergence. The auto majors initially ignored the Japanese threat; by the time they responded, they had already given up substantial market share. Similarly, U.S. manufacturers of microprocessors made the mistake of discounting Asian competition, only to see their market share plummet during the mid-1980s in the face of new low-cost competition.

Unforeseen demand shifts   Unforeseen, and often unforeseeable, shifts in demand can be brought about by major changes in technology, economic or political conditions, and social and cultural norms. Although such changes can open up market opportunities for new products, they also threaten the existence of many established enterprises, necessitating restructuring. The classic example is clearly the 1974 OPEC oil price increase that, among other things, hit the demand for autos, oil-fired central heating units, and many oil-based products, such as vinyl phonographic records. Similarly, the oil price collapse of 1983–86 devastated many oil field drilling companies, and forced them into drastic restructuring.

The Main Steps of Retrenchment and Turnaround

There is no standard model of how a company should respond to a decline situation. Indeed, there can be no such model, since every situation is unique. However, a number of common features are present in most *successful* turnaround situations. These include changing the leadership, redefining the company's strategic focus, divesting or closing unwanted assets, taking steps to improve the profitability of remaining operations, and, occasionally, making acquisitions to rebuild core operations.

New leadership   Since the old leadership bears the stigma of failure, new leadership is an essential element of most retrenchment and turnaround situations. At Chrysler Lee Iacocca replaced John Riccardo, at U.S. Steel. David Roderick replaced the autocratic Edgar Speer, and at Apple Computer John Sculley replaced the erratic, emotional, but sometimes brilliant Steve Jobs. To resolve a crisis situation, the new leader should be someone who is able to make difficult decisions, motivate lower-level managers, listen to the views of others, and delegate power when appropriate.

Redefining strategic focus   For the single-business enterprise, redefining strategic focus involves a re-evaluation of the company's business-level strategy. The failed cost leader, for example, may reorient toward a more focused or differentiated strategy. For the diversified company, redefining strategic focus means identifying the businesses in the portfolio that have the best long-term profit and growth prospects and concentrating investment there. For example, in response to the profit debacle of the early 1980s, International Harvester sold its construction and agricultural equipment businesses and concentrated on heavy and medium trucks and spare parts, in which it was number one in the United States.

Asset sales and closures   Having redefined its strategic focus, a company should divest as many unwanted assets as it can find buyers for and liquidate whatever remains. It is important not to confuse unwanted assets with unprofitable assets. Assets that no longer fit in with the redefined strategic focus of the company may be very profitable. Their sale can bring the company much-needed cash, which it can invest in improving the operations that remain.

Improving profitability   Improving the profitability of the operations that remain after asset sales and closures involves a number of steps. They may include the following: (1) layoffs of white- and blue-collar employees; (2) investments in labor-saving equipment; (3) assignment of profit responsibility to individuals and subunits within the company, by a change of organizational structure if necessary; (4) a tightening of financial controls; and (5) a cutting back on marginal products.

In a recent example, Kodak took several of these steps in an attempt to regain the market share it had lost to foreign competition. Between 1983 and 1987 Kodak cut its total work force by 20 percent, with most of the job losses affecting white-collar employees. The company scrapped an archaic organization based on centralized functions (manufacturing, R&D, marketing, and the like), and reorganized into twenty-four business units, each with its own profit and loss responsibility. In addition, a 1985 study showed that 80–90 percent of Kodak's products generated only 10–20 percent of its profits. In response, by 1987 the company had discontinued 10,000 products, reducing its total to 55,000.

Acquisitions   A somewhat surprising but quite common turnaround strategy involves making acquisitions, primarily to strengthen the competitive position of the company's remaining core operations. For example, Champion International Corporation used to be a very diversified company manufacturing a wide range of paper and wood products. After years of declining performance, in the mid-1980s Champion decided to focus on its profitable newsprint and magazine paper business. The company divested many of its other paper and wood products businesses, but at the same time it paid $1.8 billion for St. Regis Corp., one of the country's largest manufacturers of newsprint and magazine paper.

6.9 SUMMARY OF CHAPTER

The purpose of this chapter has been to examine the different corporate-level strategies that companies pursue in order to maximize their value.

1. Corporate-level strategy is concerned with answering the question of how to manage a company's growth and development in order to maximize long-run profitability. The answer involves choices of both the set of *businesses* and the *markets* that the company is going to compete in.

2. Corporate strategies should *add value* to a corporation. To add value, a corporate strategy should enable the company, or one or more of its business units, to perform one or more of the value-creation functions at a lower cost or in a way that allows for differentiation and a premium price.

3. The advantages of concentrating on a single business include focusing the company's resources on establishing a distinctive competence within one business area and keeping top management in touch with operating realities. These benefits are particularly significant in growth industries.

4. The disadvantages of concentrating on a single business are that the company may need to integrate vertically and/or expand globally in order to establish a low-cost or differentiated position in its core operation. The single-business company may also miss out on opportunities to expand its market to other nations and/or apply its distinctive competences to profit opportunities that arise in other industries.

5. Vertical integration allows a company to create value through production-cost savings and by avoiding the costs of using the market, protecting product quality, and protecting proprietary technology.

6. The disadvantages of vertical integration include cost disadvantages if the company's internal source of supply is a high-cost one and a lack of flexibility when technology is changing fast or when demand is uncertain.

7. Taper integration is normally preferable to full integration, since taper integration exposes in-house suppliers and/or distributors to some degree of competitive pressure, thereby keeping costs low. Taper integration also enables a company to adopt a more flexible posture toward uncertainties in demand.

8. Global expansion creates value through market expansion, by allowing a company to cover investment costs, realize economies of scale, or manufacture in low-cost locations.

9. The choice between a global strategy and a multidomestic strategy depends on the (a) the extent to which it is possible to standardize the global marketplace and (b) the extent to which global production generates scale economies.

10. The main factor influencing the choice of alternative entry modes for a global company is the technological basis of its competitive advantage. The more important and unusual a company's technology, the greater is the need to protect that technology from a foreign partner or licensee, and the more wholly owned subsidiaries are to be preferred to joint ventures and licensing.

11. The risks of global expansion include a company's exposure to political risks, economic risks, and the problems of managing a global business.

12. Diversification can create value through the pursuit of a portfolio strategy, restructuring, skill transfers, and resource sharing. Diversification for other reasons is unlikely to add value.

13. The pitfalls of diversification include diversifying in order to pool risks or achieve greater growth, engaging in too much diversification, and miscalculating the costs and benefits of diversification.

14. Related diversification is preferred to unrelated diversification since it enables a company to engage in more value-creation activities and is less risky. If the company's skills are not transferable, it may have no choice but to pursue unrelated diversification.

15. The causes of corporate decline include poor management, overexpansion, inadequate financial controls, high costs, the emergence of powerful new competition, and unforeseen shifts in demand.

16. Responses to corporate decline include changing the leadership, redefining the company's strategic focus, divestment or closure of unwanted assets, taking steps to improve the profitability of the operations that remain, and occasionally, acquisitions to rebuild core operations.

Discussion Questions

1. When will a company choose related diversification and when unrelated diversification? Discuss with reference to an electronics manufacturer and an ocean shipping company.

2. Why was it profitable for General Motors and Ford to integrate backward into component parts manufacturing in the past, and why are both companies now trying to buy more of their parts from outside?

3. Under what conditions might concentration on a single business be inconsistent with the goal of maximizing stockholder wealth? Why?

4. General Motors integrated vertically in the 1920s, diversified in the 1930s, and expanded overseas in the 1950s. Explain these developments with reference to the profitability of pursuing each strategy. Why do you think vertical integration is normally the first strategy to be pursued after concentration on a single business?

5. Discuss the benefits and drawbacks of a global versus a multidomestic strategy for (a) Apple Computer, (b) Chrysler Corp., and (c) PepsiCo. How many companies can you think of for which a pure multidomestic strategy makes the most sense?

Endnotes

1. Hope Lampert, "Britons on the Prowl," *The New York Times Magazine,* November 29, 1987, pp. 22–24, 36, 38, 42. Thomas Moore, "Old Line Industry Shapes Up," *Fortune,* April 27, 1987, pp. 23–32, and "Goodbye Corporate Staff," *Fortune,* December 21, 1987, pp. 65–76.

2. Alfred D. Chandler, *Strategy and Structure: Chapters in the History of the Industrial Enterprise* (Cambridge, Mass.: MIT Press, 1962).

3. K. R. Harrigan, "Formulating Vertical Integration Strategies," *Academy of Management Review,* 9 (1984), 638–652.

4. This is the essence of Chandler's argument. See his *Strategy and Structure.* The same argument is also made by Jeffrey Pfeffer and Gerald R. Salancik, *The External Control of Organizations* (New York: Harper & Row, 1978).

5. For a detailed and somewhat different look at the benefits and disadvantages of vertical integration, see K. R. Harrigan, *Strategic Flexibility* (Lexington, Mass.: Lexington Books, 1985). See also K. R. Harrigan, "Vertical Integration and Corporate Strategy," *Academy of Management Journal,* 28 (1985), 397–425; and F. M. Scherer, *Industrial Market Structure and Economic Performance* (Chicago: Rand McNally, 1981).

6. One interpretation of the dynamics involved in this type of situation can be found in resource dependence models of organizations. See Pfeffer and Salancik, *The External Control of Organizations,* pp. 113–142. Another can be found in transaction cost analysis. See Oliver E. Williamson, *Markets and Hierarchies: Analysis and Antitrust Implications* (New York: Free Press, 1975), pp. 82–131.

7. See "IBM, Clonebuster," *Fortune,* April 27, 1987, p. 225; and "How IBM Hopes to Skin the Copycats," *Business Week,* April 6, 1987, p. 40.

8. Harrigan, *Strategic Flexibility,* pp. 67–87.

9. For details, see "McWorld," *Business Week,* October 13, 1986, pp. 78–86.

10. "West German and British cars: A tale of two motor industries," *The Economist,* February 13, 1988, p. 65.

11. For example, see T. Hout, Michael E. Porter, and E. Rudden, "How Global Companies Win Out," *Harvard Business Review* (September–October 1982), 98–108; Theodore Levitt, "The Globalization of Markets," *Harvard Business Review* (May–June 1983), 92–102; and S. Ghoshal, "Global Strategy: An Organizing Framework," *Strategic Management Journal,* 8 (September–October 1987), 425–440.

12. Levitt, "The Globalization of Markets," p. 92.

13. For details, see: Hout, Porter, and Rudden, "How Global Companies Win Out," pp. 98–108.

14. Gary Hamel and C. K. Prahalad, "Do You Really Have a Global Strategy," *Harvard Business Review* (July–August 1985), 139–148.

15. For elaboration, see M. Z. Brooke and H. L. Remmers, *The Strategy of Multinational Enterprise* (London: Longman, 1970); and G. D. Newbould, P. J. Buckley, and J. Thurwell, *Going International: The Experience of Smaller Companies* (London: Associated Business Press, 1978).

16. S. Prokesch, "Stopping the High-Tech Giveaway," *The New York Times,* March 22, 1987, Business section, pp. 1 and 8.

17. For details, see "McWorld," pp. 78–86.

18. This resource-based view of diversification can be traced back to Edith Penrose's seminal book, *The Theory of the Growth of the Firm* (Oxford University Press: Oxford, 1959).

19. See, for example, G. R. Jones and C. W. L. Hill, "A Transaction Cost Analysis of Strategy-Structure Choice," *Strategic Management Journal* (March–April 1988), Vol. 9, pp. 159–172; and Williamson, *Markets and Hierarchies,* pp. 132–175.

20. See Michael E. Porter, "From Competitive Advantage to Corporate Strategy," *Harvard Business Review* (May–June 1987), 43–59.

21. See C. W. L. Hill, M. A. Hitt, and R. E. Hoskisson, "Declining U.S. Competitiveness: Reflections on a Crisis," *Academy of Management Executive,* 2 (February 1988), 51–59.

22. See C. W. L. Hill, "Profile of a Conglomerate Takeover: BTR and Thomas Tilling," *Journal of General Management,* 10 (1984), 34–50.

23. "Rockwell: Using Its Cash Hoard to Edge Away from Defense," *Business Week,* February 4, 1985, pp. 82–84.

24. D. J. Teece, "Economies of Scope and the Scope of the Enterprise," *Journal of Economic Behavior and Organization,* 3 (1980), 223–247.

25. For a detailed discussion, see C. W. L. Hill and R. E. Hoskisson, "Strategy and Structure in the Multi-product Firm," *Academy of Management Review,* 12 (1987), 331–341.

26. Michael E. Porter, *Competitive Advantage: Creating and Sustaining Superior Performance* (New York: The Free Press, 1985), p. 326.

27. Porter, "From Competitive Advantage to Corporate Strategy," pp. 43–59.

28. For a survey of the evidence, see C. W. L. Hill, "Conglomerate Performance over the Economic Cycle," *Journal of Industrial Economics,* 32 (1983), 197–212; and D. T. C. Mueller, "The Effects of Conglomerate Mergers," *Journal of Banking and Finance,* 1 (1977), 315–347.

29. Michael Brody, "Caught in the Cash Crunch at ITT," *Fortune,* February 18, 1985, pp. 63–72.

30. For empirical findings consistent with this interpretation, see Hill, "Conglomerate Performance," pp. 197–211; and S. R. Reid, "A Reply to the Weston and Mansinghka Criticisms Dealing with Conglomerate Mergers," *Journal of Finance,* 26 (1971), 937–940.

31. For example, see C. W. L. Hill, "Diversified Growth and Competition," *Applied Economics,* 17 (1985), 827–847; and R. P. Rumelt, *Strategy, Structure and Economic Performance* (Boston: Harvard Business School, 1974).

32. See H. K. Christensen and C. A. Montgomery, "Corporate Economic Performance: Diversification Strategy Versus Market Structure," *Strategic Management Journal,* 2 (1981), 327–343; and G. R. Jones and C. W. L. Hill, "A Transaction Cost Analysis of Strategy-Structure Choice," *Strategic Management Journal,* 9 (1988), pp. 159–172.

33. See J. Argenti, *Corporate Collapse: Causes and Symptoms* (New York: McGraw-Hill, 1976); D. Schendel, G. R. Patton, and J. Riggs, "Corporate Turnaround Strategies: A Study of Profit Decline and Recovery," *Journal of General Management,* 2 (1976); and S. Slatter, *Corporate Recovery: Successful Turnaround Strategies and Their Implementation* (Harmondsworth, England: Penguin Books, 1984) pp. 25–60.

34. See Slatter, *Corporate Recovery,* pp. 25–60.

35. See C. W. L. Hill and J. F. Pickering, "Divisionalization, Decentralization and Performance in Large United Kingdom Companies," *Journal of Management Studies,* 23 (January 1986), 26–50.

36. Lee Iacocca, *Iacocca: An Autobiography* (Toronto: Bantam Books, 1984), p. 254.

Chapter 7

ANALYZING AND CHANGING THE CORPORATE PORTFOLIO

7.1 OPENING INCIDENT: ROCKWELL

In 1974 Robert Anderson succeeded the legendary Willard Rockwell as chairman of the board of Rockwell International Corp., a broadly diversified group with activities in aerospace, automotive equipment, electronics, and consumer appliances. Anderson's task was to make some sense out of this portfolio of businesses. He focused resources on the businesses that had the best long-term growth and profit prospects, while divesting businesses with poor prospects. The winner in this process was the defense-oriented aerospace business.

The focus on defense began to pay big dividends in 1981, when Congress ordered 100 B-1B bombers from Rockwell, a contract worth $15 billion. As a consequence, in 1984 aerospace activities accounted for nearly 45 percent of Rockwell's revenues, up from around 30 percent five years earlier. However, this

growth brought its own problems. The B-1B contract was due to end in 1988, and with few signs of congressional eagerness to order more B-1Bs, Rockwell faced the problem of how to maintain eleven years of continuous growth. Management was also worried that Rockwell now depended too much on defense contracts. After five years of expansion, the federal defense budget could not continue to grow indefinitely, particularly given growing political unrest over the size of the federal deficit. To make matters worse, Rockwell's nondefense activities were concentrated in the mature industrial and automotive sectors, where growth prospects were low.

In short, by the mid-1980s Rockwell's portfolio was no longer balanced. Too great a percentage of earnings came from defense contracts and mature nondefense activities. If the company was to continue growing, it had to change the mix of businesses in its portfolio. In January 1985 Rockwell took a major step toward this goal with its $1.65-billion acquisition of Allen-Bradley, a leader in computerized factory automation. Allen-Bradley gave Rockwell a fifth leg to complement its four core areas — aerospace, electronics, automotive components, and industrial products. The acquisition put Rockwell in the forefront of an expanding industry, in which sales were predicted to grow from $5 billion to $20 billion between 1985 and 1990. In essence, Rockwell took the cash harvest from the B-1B bomber and invested it for the 1990s in a business with star potential.[1]

7.2 OVERVIEW

Chapter 6 reviewed the corporate-level strategies that companies pursue in order to become multibusiness enterprises. This chapter examines various techniques used by multibusiness enterprises like Rockwell to analyze their portfolio of businesses. These techniques are referred to as **portfolio techniques.** They give strategic managers an overview of the long-term prospects and competitive strengths and weaknesses of a company's various businesses, enabling them to evaluate whether the portfolio is adequate from the perspective of long-term corporate growth and profitability. For example, Rockwell's portfolio in the mid-1980s was judged by management to provide the company with too few long-term growth and profit prospects.

The objective of most companies when analyzing their portfolio is to identify what needs to be done to construct a **balanced portfolio** of businesses. A balanced portfolio can be defined as one that enables a company to achieve the growth and profit objectives associated with its corporate strategy without exposing the company to undue risks. If the company does not have the right balance of businesses in its portfolio, it needs to pursue strategies designed to correct the imbalance. Thus Rockwell acquired Allen-Bradley in an attempt to shift the balance of activities in its portfolio toward businesses with greater long-term growth and profit prospects.

In this chapter, we discuss the advantages and limitations of three different portfolio techniques: (1) a portfolio matrix developed by management consultants at the Boston Consulting Group (BCG); (2) a portfolio matrix developed originally by management consultants McKinsey & Company, Inc. for use at General Electric; and (3) an industry evolution matrix developed by Charles Hofer. We also look at the pitfalls of portfolio planning in general.[2]

After examining the different portfolio techniques, we consider the means that companies employ to change the composition of their portfolios. These means include both *entry* strategies, that is, acquisitions and internal venturing, and *exit* strategies, that is, divestments, liquidation, and harvest strategies. Acquisitions and internal venturing are alternative ways of entering new business areas, and we look at the factors that influence the choice between them. Divestment, liquidation, and harvest strategies are alternative ways of exiting from existing businesses areas, and we examine the factors that affect a company's choice in this situation.

7.3 THE BOSTON CONSULTING GROUP BUSINESS MATRIX

The main objective of the Boston Consulting Group (BCG) technique is to help strategic managers identify the cash flow requirements of the different businesses in their portfolio. The BCG approach involves three main steps: (1) dividing a company into **strategic business units (SBUs)** and assessing the long-term prospects of each; (2) comparing SBUs against each other by means of a matrix that indicates the relative prospects of each; and (3) developing strategic objectives with respect to each SBU.

Defining and Evaluating Strategic Business Units

A company must create an SBU for each economically distinct business area that it competes in. When identifying SBUs, the objective is to divide the company into the most relevant strategic entities for planning purposes. Normally, a company will define its SBUs in terms of the product markets they are competing in. For example, Rockwell divides itself up into five SBUs—aerospace, automotive components, electronics, factory automation, and industrial products—each reflecting a particular product market. Alternatively, companies that have significant vertically integrated operations might define all the businesses involved in a single vertically integrated chain of operations as one SBU. For example, the company shown in Figure 7.1 has divided itself into three SBUs. The first SBU contains three closely related operations in the chemical industry; the second, a business operating in the automotive components industry; and the third, three vertically integrated businesses in the iron ore mining, steel-refining, and steel-fabricating industries.

Having defined its SBUs, the company then assesses each according to two criteria: (1) the SBU's *relative* market share and (2) the growth rate of the SBU's industry.

Relative market share   The objective when identifying an SBU's relative market share is to establish whether that SBU's market position can be classified as a strength or a weakness. Relative market share is defined as the ratio of an SBU's market share to the market share held by the largest rival company in its industry. If an SBU has a market share of 10 percent and its largest rival has a market share of 30 percent, then its relative market share is 10/30, or 0.3. Only if an SBU is a market leader in its industry will it have a relative market share greater than 1.0. For example, if an SBU has a market share of 40 percent and

FIGURE 7.1   **The division of activities into SBUs**

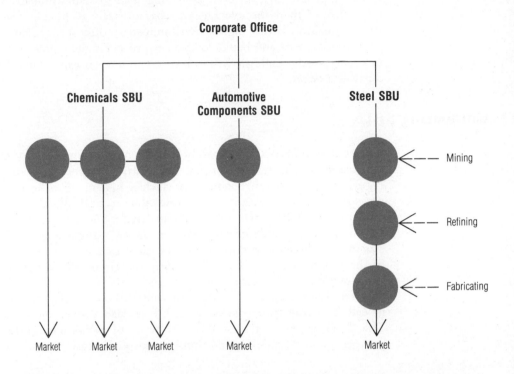

its largest rival has a market share of 10 percent, then its relative market share is $40/10 = 4.0$.

According to the BCG, market share gives a company cost advantages from economies of scale and experience effects (we discussed the details in Chapter 4). An SBU with a relative market share greater than 1.0 is assumed to be furthest down the experience curve and therefore to have a significant cost advantage over its rivals. By similar logic, an SBU with a relative market share smaller than 1.0 is assumed to be at a competitive disadvantage because it lacks the scale economies and low-cost position of the market leader. Thus a relative market share greater than 1.0 can be characterized as a *strength,* while a relative market share smaller than 1.0 is a *weakness.* The BCG characterizes SBUs with a relative market share greater than 1.0 as having a *high* relative market share and SBUs with a relative market share smaller than 1.0 as having a *low* relative market share.

Industry growth   The objective when assessing industry growth rates is to determine whether industry conditions offer opportunities for expansion, or whether they threaten the SBU (as in a declining industry). The growth rate of an SBU's industry is assessed according to whether its growth is faster or slower than that of the economy as a whole. Industries with growth rates faster than the average are characterized as having *high* growth. Industries with growth rates slower than the average are characterized as having *low* growth. The BCG's position is that high growth industries offer a more favorable competitive environment and better long-term prospects than slow growth industries. In other words, high growth industries present an *opportunity,* low growth industries a *threat.*

Comparing SBUs

The next step involves comparing SBUs against each other by means of a matrix based on the two dimensions of relative market share and high growth. Figure 7.2 provides an example of such a matrix. The horizontal dimension measures relative market share, and the vertical dimension, an industry's growth rate. Each circle represents an SBU. The center of each circle corresponds to the position of that SBU on the two dimensions of the matrix. The size of each circle is proportional to the sales revenue generated by each business in the company's portfolio. The bigger the circle, the larger is the size of an SBU relative to total corporate revenues.

The matrix is divided into four cells. SBUs in cell 1 are defined as **stars,** in cell 2 as **question marks,** in cell 3 as **cash cows,** and in cell 4 as **dogs.** The BCG argues that these different types of SBUs have different long-term prospects and different implications for corporate cash flows.

1. *Stars* Stars are the leading SBUs in the company's portfolio. They have a high relative market share and are based in high-growth industries. In the language of SWOT analysis, they have both competitive strengths and opportunities for expansion. Thus they offer excellent long-term profit and growth opportunities. Generally, the BCG predicts that established *stars* are likely to be highly profitable and therefore can generate sufficient cash for their own investment needs. Emerging *stars,* however, may require substantial cash injections to enable them to consolidate their market lead.

2. *Question marks* Question marks are SBUs that are relatively weak in competitive terms, having *low* relative market shares. However, they are based in *high*-growth industries and thus may offer opportunities for long-term profit and growth. *Question marks* can become *stars* if nurtured properly. To become market leaders, *question marks* require substantial net injections of cash; they are cash hungry. The corporate head office has to decide whether a particular *question mark* has the potential to become a *star* and therefore is worth the capital investment necessary to achieve this.

3. *Cash cows* Cash cows are in low-growth industries but have a high market share and a strong competitive position in mature industries. Their com-

FIGURE 7.2   **The Boston Consulting Group matrix**

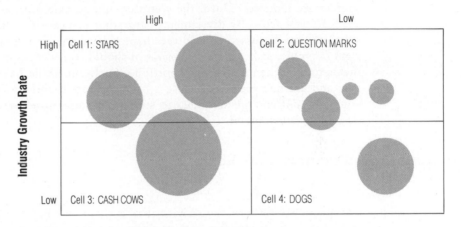

Source: Reprinted with permission from *Long Range Planning,* February 1977, B. Hedley, "Strategy and the Business Portfolio" page 12. Copyright © 1977 Pergamon Press Inc.

petitive strength comes from being furthest down the experience curve. They are the cost leaders in their industries. The BCG argues that this position enables such SBUs to remain very profitable. However, low growth is taken to imply a lack of opportunities for future expansion. As a consequence, the BCG argues that the capital investment requirements of *cash cows* are not substantial, and thus, they are depicted as generating a strong positive cash flow.

4. *Dogs* Dogs are SBUs in low-growth industries but have a low market share. They have a weak competitive position in unattractive industries and thus are viewed as offering few benefits to the company. The BCG suggests that such SBUs are unlikely to generate much in the way of a positive cash flow and indeed may become cash hogs. They may require substantial capital investments just to maintain their low market share, while offering few prospects for future growth in returns.

Strategic Implications

The objective of the BCG's portfolio is to identify how corporate cash resources can best be used to maximize a company's future growth and profitability. BCG recommendations include the following. First, use the cash surplus from any *cash cows* to support the development of selected *question marks* and to nurture emerging *stars*. The long-term objective is to consolidate the position of *stars* and to turn favored *question marks* into *stars,* thus making the company's portfolio more attractive. Second, *question marks* with the weakest or most uncertain long-term prospects are divested so that demands on the company's cash resources are reduced. Third, the company should exit from any industry where the SBU is a *dog* — by divestment, harvesting market share, or liquidation (exit strategies are discussed later in the chapter). Fourth, if the company lacks sufficient *cash cows, stars,* or *question marks,* it should consider acquisitions and divestments to build a more balanced portfolio. Such a portfolio has to contain enough *stars* and *question marks* to ensure a healthy growth and profit outlook for the company and enough *cash cows* to support the investment requirements of the *stars* and *question marks.*

Strengths and Weaknesses of the BCG Matrix

The major strength of the BCG matrix is that it focuses a company's attention on the cash flow requirements of different types of businesses and points out ways of using cash flows to optimize the value of the corporate portfolio. A second positive feature of the BCG matrix is that it indicates when a company needs to add another SBU to its portfolio and when it needs to remove an SBU.

However, the BCG matrix also has a number of significant shortcomings. First, the model is simplistic. To assess the attractiveness of an SBU in terms of just two dimensions, market share and industry growth, is misleading, since a host of other relevant factors should be taken into account. Although market share is undoubtedly an important determinant of an SBU's competitive position, you saw in Chapter 5 that companies can also establish a strong competitive position by differentiating their product to serve the needs of a particular segment of the market. Thus a low market share business can be very profitable and have a strong competitive position with regard to certain segments of the market. The auto manufacturer Rolls Royce is in this position, and yet the BCG matrix would classify Rolls Royce as a *dog,* since it is a low market share business in a low-growth industry. Similarly, industry growth is not the only factor determining industry attractiveness. As you saw in Chapter 3, many factors besides growth determine competitive intensity in an industry and thus its attractiveness.

The connection between relative market share and cost savings is not as straight-forward as the BCG suggests. Chapter 4 made clear that a high market share does not always give a company a cost advantage. In some industries, for example the U.S. steel industry, low market share companies using a low share technology (minimills) can have lower production costs than high market share companies using high share technologies (integrated mills). The BCG matrix would classify minimill operations as the *dogs* of the American steel industry, whereas in fact their performance over the last decade has characterized them as STAR businesses.[3]

Furthermore, a high market share in a low-growth industry does not necessarily result in a large positive cash flow characteristic of *cash cow* businesses. The BCG matrix would classify General Motors' auto operations as a *cash cow*. However, the capital investments needed to remain competitive are so substantial in the auto industry that the reverse is more likely to be true. Low-growth industries can be very competitive, and staying ahead in such an environment can require substantial cash investments.

The BCG approach, then, carries the risk of misclassifying businesses. The next technique was developed to counter some of its weaknesses.

7.4 THE McKINSEY MATRIX

The technique developed by management consultants McKinsey & Co. also divides a company into SBUs. As in the BCG matrix, each SBU is assessed along two dimensions, but these dimensions are based on many more factors. The dimensions are (1) the attractiveness of the industry in which an SBU is based and (2) an SBU's competitive position within that industry.

Assessing Industry Attractiveness

Assessing industry attractiveness is a four-step process, and each step can be illustrated with reference to Table 7.1. The table shows how Rockwell might assess the attractiveness of the factory automation industry, in which it now operates (see Opening Incident). The steps are as follows:

1. The company identifies a set of criteria that determine the attractiveness of an industry. This set will typically include factors commonly acknowledged to be important determinants of industry attractiveness—factors such as growth, size, capital intensity, and competitive intensity. The competitive

TABLE 7.1   **Assessing industry attractiveness: factory automation industry**

Industry attractiveness criteria	Weight	Rating	Weighted score
Industry size	0.10	3	0.30
Industry growth	0.30	5	1.50
Industry profitability	0.20	4	0.80
Capital intensity	0.05	5	0.25
Technological stability	0.10	5	0.50
Competitive intensity	0.20	3	0.60
Cyclicality	0.05	2	0.10
Totals	1.00		4.05

forces discussed in Chapter 3 are normally to be found in this kind of list, either individually or summarized by some aggregate criterion, such as competitive intensity.

2. The company then assigns a weight to each of the criteria in the set to indicate the relative importance of each criterion *to the company*. To ensure consistency, the sum of the weights should add up to 1. For example, Rockwell is shown in Table 7.1 to rank industry growth as the most important attractiveness criterion, assigning it a weight of 0.3. The rationale for this ranking is that Rockwell is currently involved in too many mature industries and needs to move into high-growth ones. Hence the company attaches great importance to considerations of industry growth.

3. Next, the company rates the attractiveness of each industry in its portfolio according to the various attractiveness criteria. Normally, a scale of 1 to 5 is used, where 1 is unattractive and 5 is very attractive. A company's decisions about the attractiveness of criteria will largely reflect its own objectives. Thus the industry growth criterion in Table 7.1 is rated 5 by Rockwell because factory automation is a high-growth industry and Rockwell is looking for high growth. Note also that an attractive criterion can be viewed as providing the company with an *opportunity* to realize its corporate objectives, while an unattractive criterion must be viewed as a *threat*.

4. Finally, the company computes a **total weighted score** for each industry in its portfolio. This is arrived at by multiplying *weight* by *rate* for each of the attractiveness criteria to get a weighted score and then adding these scores. Thus in Table 7.1, Rockwell assigns competitive intensity a weight of 0.2, and the factory automation industry is given a rating of 3 against this criterion. Therefore the weighted score is $0.2 \times 3 = 0.60$. Adding these weighted scores together gives a total weighted score for each industry in the company's portfolio. These total weighted scores are an index of how attractive each industry is to the company. The maximum value this index can have is 5 and the minimum is 1, with the average score being around 3. The total score of 4.05 for the factory automation industry indicates to Rockwell that this is an industry of above-average attractiveness.

Assessing Competitive Position

Assessing an SBU's competitive position within its industry involves four steps similar to those followed in assessing industry attractiveness. The process is illustrated in Table 7.2, which shows how Rockwell might assess the competitive position of its factory automation business (Allen-Bradley) within the factory automation industry.

1. First, the company identifies the **key success factors** in each of the industries in which it competes. In the case of Rockwell's factory automation business,

TABLE 7.2   **Assessing competitive position: factory automation SBU**

Key success factors	Weight	Rating	Weighted score
Market share	0.15	5	0.75
Technological know-how	0.25	5	1.25
Product quality	0.15	4	0.60
After-sales service/maintenance	0.20	5	1.00
Price competitiveness	0.05	2	0.10
Low operating costs	0.10	3	0.30
Productivity	0.10	3	0.30
Totals	1.00		4.30

these factors are market share, technological know-how, after-sales service/maintenance, price competitiveness, low operating costs, and productivity.

2. Next, the company assigns a weight to each success factor, indicating its relative importance for establishing a strong competitive position within the industry being considered. As before, to ensure consistency, the weights must add up to 1. Table 7.2 shows that Rockwell views technological know-how as the most important success factor in the factory automation industry, followed by after-sales service/maintenance.

3. Third, the company rates the competitive strengths of each SBU against relevant success factors in the various industries. As before, a scale of 1 to 5 is normally used, where 1 is very weak and 5 is very strong. Table 7.2 shows that Rockwell's factory automation SBU is in a very strong position with respect to market share, technological know-how, and after-sales service/maintenance—all important success factors in the factory automation industry. In other words, the *strengths* (distinctive competences) of Rockwell's factory automation business include market share, technological know-how, and service/maintenance. Its *weaknesses* include price competitiveness, operating costs, and productivity.

4. Finally, the company computes a total weighted score, which can then be used as an index of an SBU's competitive position. This score is derived by multiplying *weight* by *rate* to get a weighted score for each success factor, and then adding these to obtain the total weighted score. The value of the total weighted score will be between 5 (very strong competitive position) and 1 (very weak competitive position), with 3 being the average. Table 7.2 shows us that Rockwell's factory automation SBU is in a strong competitive position, with a total score of 4.30.

FIGURE 7.3   The McKinsey matrix

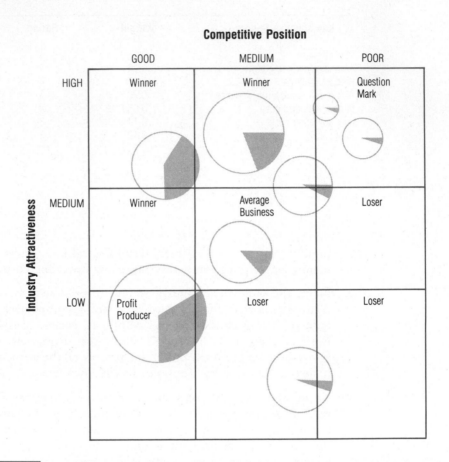

Comparing SBUs

Once the above analysis has been completed, the actual position of each SBU can be plotted on a matrix similar to that shown in Figure 7.3. Industry attractiveness is plotted on the vertical dimension and competitive position on the horizontal dimension. Each circle represents an SBU. The position of the center of each circle is determined by the score that the SBU received on the two dimensions. The size of each circle is proportional to the size of the industry in which the SBU is based (measured total industry sales). The shaded wedge indicates an SBU's market share in that industry.

The matrix is divided into nine cells. SBUs falling into three of the cells are characterized as *winners,* or the most desirable businesses. They are based in industries of medium to high attractiveness and have medium to strong competitive positions. Rockwell's factory automation business might be characterized as a *winner.* A further three cells are characterized as containing *losers.* These are the least desirable businesses. They have relatively weak competitive positions in unattractive industries.

One cell is shown to contain *question marks.* As with the BCG matrix, *question marks* have an uncertain but potentially promising future. They have a weak competitive position in an attractive industry. With proper nurturing, they could become *winners.* However, they also run the risk of developing into *losers.* One cell is shown to contain *profit producers.* Analogous to the BCG's *cash cows,* these businesses have a strong competitive position in an unattractive industry. Finally, one cell is shown to contain *average businesses.* These businesses have no great strengths, but neither are they particularly weak.

Strategic Implications

The strategic implications of the McKinsey analysis are straightforward. *Losers* should be divested, liquidated, or told to harvest market share (a process we describe in detail later in the chapter). The position of *winners* and developing *winners* should be consolidated, if necessary by net injections of cash. The company should also nurture selected *question marks* in an attempt to turn them into *winners.* Since *profit producers* are based in industries whose long-term prospects are poor, these businesses should use their strong competitive position to generate profits, which can then be invested to support *winners* and selected *question marks.* The company should either try to turn *average businesses* into winners or consider divesting these businesses, because they are unlikely to offer the best long-term returns.

One of the objectives of the McKinsey analysis is to try to identify how far removed from a **balanced portfolio** the company's portfolio actually is. In this context, a balanced portfolio can be defined as one that contains mostly *winners* and developing *winners,* with a few *profit producers* to generate the cash flow necessary to support the developing *winners* and a few small *question mark* businesses with the potential to become future *winners.*[4] Such a portfolio is balanced because it offers the company good profit and growth prospects while not straining its cash flow position.

More typically, however, a company will have an unbalanced portfolio—a portfolio that places too many demands on the company's cash flow position and/or offers inadequate prospects for future profits and growth. Table 7.3 shows several different kinds of unbalanced portfolios, along with appropriate corrective strategies. To correct an unbalanced portfolio, a company must change the composition of its portfolio, adding and/or removing SBUs. For example,

TABLE 7.3   **Four basic types of unbalanced portfolios**

Problem action	Typical symptoms	Typical corrective
Too many *losers*	Inadequate cash flow Inadequate profits Inadequate growth	Divest/liquidate/harvest losers Acquire profit producers Acquire winners
Too many *question marks*	Inadequate cash flow Inadequate profits	Divest/harvest/liquidate selected question marks
Too many *profit producers*	Inadequate growth Excessive cash flow	Acquire winners Nurture/develop selected question marks
Too many *developing winners*	Excessive cash demands Excessive demands on management Unstable growth and profits	Divest selected developing winners if necessary Acquire profit producer

Source: Adapted from C. W. Hofer and M. J. Davoust, *Successful Strategic Management*. Reprinted by permission of A. T. Kearney, Inc.

Rockwell's portfolio in the early 1980s essentially suffered from having too many *profit producers;* it was unbalanced. In order to correct this situation, Rockwell acquired a developing *winner*.

Strengths and Weaknesses of the McKinsey Matrix

The McKinsey matrix is a great improvement on the BCG approach since it is more comprehensive and avoids the simplifications and unwarranted assumptions of the BCG approach. One of its greatest strengths is its flexibility. The McKinsey matrix recognizes that different industries are characterized by different success factors and incorporates this fact into the analysis. Moreover, the analysis can cover a much greater range of strategically relevant variables.

Nevertheless, the McKinsey approach is not perfect. One of the main difficulties is that it produces numbers to give strategic decisions legitimacy but does not explicitly recognize that the numbers are all subjectively derived. Strategic managers must be careful, therefore, not to let their own subjective biases enter into the analysis. Another problem is that the analysis is basically a static one. It looks at the *current* position of SBUs but does not take into account how their *future* position might change due to industry evolution. It does not depict the position of businesses across different stages of the industry life cycle. For example, it does not depict what might happen to a *question mark* as its industry enters the growth stage or to a *winner* as its industry enters the shakeout stage. This is where the third portfolio technique becomes relevant.

7.5 THE INDUSTRY EVOLUTION MATRIX

To offset the shortcomings of the McKinsey matrix, Charles Hofer has suggested that companies use a portfolio matrix based on industry evolution.[5]

Evaluating and Comparing SBUs

Like the other approaches, the industry evolution matrix starts by dividing a company into SBUs. The next step is to assess the competitive position of each SBU using techniques similar to those of the McKinsey approach. The position of each SBU is then plotted on a fifteen-cell matrix similar to that shown in Figure 7.4. The horizontal dimension indicates an SBU's competitive position. The vertical dimension shows the different stages of industry evolution. Each circle represents an SBU. The size of the circle is proportional to the size of the industry in which the SBU is based (measured by total industry revenues), and the shaded wedge indicates the market share of the SBU.

The power of this approach lies in the story that it can tell about the distribution of a company's businesses across different stages of the industry life cycle. Using descriptive terminology similar to that of the McKinsey approach, we might characterize business A in Figure 7.4 as a high-potential *question mark*. It has a strong competitive position in the early stage of an industry's development. Thus it is well placed to capitalize on the opportunities for expansion when its industry enters the growth stage. Similarly, business B is a developing *winner*. It has a strong position in a growth industry. It, too, can capitalize on opportunities for expansion. Business C, however, although also based in a growth industry, looks like a developing *loser*. Such a business is unlikely to survive the threat of the shakeout stage. The industry in which business D is based is currently undergoing a shakeout. Although this makes the industry environment a threat, business D has a strong competitive position and will probably survive and enter into maturity as a market leader or *profit producer*. Businesses E and F look to be *profit producers,* whereas business G is a definite *loser*.

Strategic Implications

The strategic implications of this analysis center on the different stages of the life cycle at which the various businesses are found. High-potential *question*

FIGURE 7.4   **The product/industry evolution matrix**

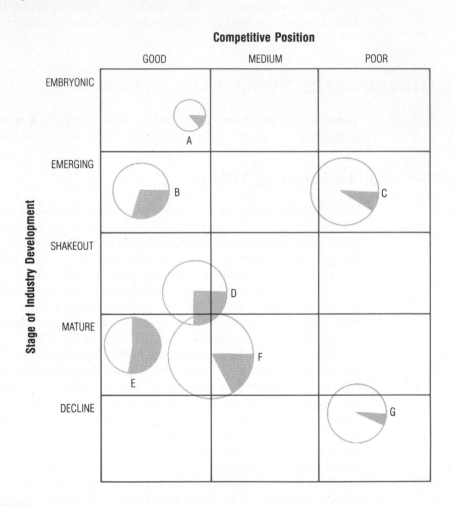

Source: Adapted from Charles W. Hofer, "Conceptual Constructs for Formulating Corporate and Business Strategies". Copyright © 1977 by Charles W. Hofer. Used by permission.

marks and developing *winners,* such as businesses A and B, should be nurtured, for they may become the established *winners* and *profit producers* of the future. Potential *losers,* such as business C, should be divested as quickly as possible. Similarly, businesses such as G have few long-term prospects. The company needs to adopt an exit strategy for such operations. Business D is unlikely to be currently earning good returns, but its future prospects are good. Businesses in this kind of position need to be supported. Businesses E and F should be managed in a way that consolidates and maintains their competitive strengths. Any surplus cash flows from these businesses should be used to support developing *winners* and companies going through a shakeout stage.

As with the McKinsey approach, the industry evolution matrix enables the company to assess whether its portfolio is balanced or unbalanced. A balanced portfolio should consist mainly of established *winners* and *profit producers,* such as businesses E and F, a few developing *winners,* such as business B, and a few high-potential *question marks,* such as business A. Most companies, however, will find that they have unbalanced portfolios similar to those depicted in Table 7.3. The additional advantage of the industry evolution matrix over the McKinsey matrix is that a company can assess how its portfolio of current operations is likely to develop over the next few years. For example, a company with a number of potential *losers* based in currently profitable high-growth emerging industries might foresee that several years down the line it could be faced with an unbalanced portfolio containing too many *losers.* By taking corrective action now, it can avoid this situation.

Strengths and Weaknesses of the Industry Evolution Matrix

The strength of the industry evolution matrix is that it shows the distribution of a company's activities across different stages of the life cycle. As a result, the company can predict how its current portfolio might develop in the future, and it can take immediate action to ensure that its portfolio is balanced. The industry evolution matrix has the additional advantage of focusing the attention of corporate-level personnel on potential *business-level* strategies. As you recall from Chapters 3 and 4, the industry life cycle is one of the most important determinants of strategic choice at the business level. For example, developing *winners,* such as business B in Figure 7.4, are at the stage of their development where the realization of cost economies from experience curve effects is most important. Thus, by using the industry evolution matrix, corporate-level personnel can perceive strategic requirements at the business level. No other approach has this advantage.

The drawback of the industry evolution matrix is that it does not focus on all the relevant factors of industry attractiveness. As the McKinsey matrix illustrates, the stage of industry evolution is a very important, but not the sole, determinant of industry attractiveness. Other factors are also significant and have an impact that is independent of the stage of industry evolution.

7.6 BENEFITS AND PITFALLS OF PORTFOLIO TECHNIQUES

Benefits of Portfolio Techniques

As a planning tool, portfolio techniques have a number of benefits. First, they enable strategic managers to analyze the diverse activities of a multibusiness company in a systematic fashion and so help make sense out of enterprise diversity. Second, these techniques highlight the different cash flow implications and requirements of different business activities. Such highlighting can assist the corporate head office in carrying out its resource allocation function.

Third, the concept of a balanced portfolio prods strategic managers to identify what kind of adjustments need to be made in the composition of the company's portfolio, so that long-term growth and profitability can be optimized. Essentially, a balanced portfolio constitutes a company *strength,* and an unbalanced portfolio a company *weakness.* Portfolio analysis can be used to identify *gaps* in the corporate portfolio that need to be filled in order to make it balanced. Thus in the early 1980s Rockwell saw the lack of any developing winners as a gap in its portfolio and filled it with the purchase of Allen-Bradley. By the same token, portfolio analysis can indicate when there are too many businesses of a certain type in a company's portfolio. Exiting from these business will correct the portfolio's imbalance.

Of the three techniques reviewed in this chapter, the BCG business portfolio matrix is perhaps the least useful, since it oversimplifies and makes unwarranted assumptions about the relation of market share and performance. Both the McKinsey technique and the industry evolution matrix are more comprehensive and realistic. A strong case can be made for using them together and giving strategic managers two different but complementary perspectives of a company's portfolio. The McKinsey technique provides the company with an overview of the attractiveness of its *current* portfolio, whereas the industry evolution matrix can be used to project how the attractiveness of that portfolio might alter in the *future.*

Pitfalls of Portfolio Techniques

The merits of the different techniques apart, it must be recognized that the whole process of portfolio planning has its own pitfalls. Although these pitfalls do not invalidate the concept of portfolio planning, they suggest that companies should be cautious about relying too heavily on portfolio planning techniques. Three major areas of concern can be identified.[6]

First, portfolio techniques explicitly assume that a company can be divided into a reasonable number of SBUs for the purpose of analysis. In practice, many companies are very diverse and have a large number of different business units. General Electric, for example, now has close to 300 businesses. Grouping such a large number of businesses into SBUs still results in a large number of SBUs to be managed by the head office. Large numbers of SBUs can create problems of **information overload** at the corporate office. It has been suggested that this starts becoming a serious problem when a company contains forty to fifty SBUs.[7] When an information overload develops, the corporate office's analysis of each SBU becomes increasingly superficial. Strategic managers at the corporate office simply do not have the time to undertake the kind of thorough analysis needed to make portfolio techniques work. Consequently, the head office may commit large sums of money to different SBUs on the basis of only superficial knowledge of the activities involved and of the different industries that the company is active in. Poor decisions and poor performance are the inevitable results of this process.

Second, when an SBU contains a number of different but related businesses, as is often the case, then conflicts of interest can develop between the internal cash flow priorities of the SBU and the cash flow priorities of the company as a whole. For example, an SBU may be defined as a *dog,* told to harvest its market share, and denied any significant capital investments. However, this SBU may contain a business unit that strategic managers at the SBU level see as a rising *star.* To realize its full potential, it needs significant capital investments, but the corporate analysis does not uncover this fact. The result can be damaging political conflict between strategic managers at the SBU level and at the corporate level over the lack of fund allocations to the potential *star.*

Third, the *naive* application of portfolio planning techniques can create problems in the case of vertically integrated companies and companies that have pursued a strategy of related diversification. In the vertically integrated company, one SBU might supply inputs to another. Portfolio planning might suggest that the supplying SBU should be divested. However, that might be absurd if benefits in the form of lower production costs can be derived from an internal source of supply. Similarly, in the related company, two SBUs might coordinate their activities in order to realize benefits from the exploitation of marketing and production synergies. If portfolio planning should suggest that one of these SBUs be divested, then the benefits from exploiting these synergies would be lost. In short, a naive application of portfolio techniques can result in strategic relationships between SBUs being ignored. This potential limitation of portfolio techniques, however, can be overcome if strategic managers take the time to weigh the conflicting considerations of achieving a balanced portfolio against the loss of valuable strategic relationships among the SBUs.

7.7 ENTRY STRATEGIES

As noted above, correcting an imbalance in a company's corporate portfolio frequently requires *entry* into new business areas, adding *question marks, winners,* or *profit producers* to the portfolio. This means adding new business areas to the company through related diversification, unrelated diversification, or international expansion. In Chapter 6, we reviewed a number of factors that influence a company's choice among these different generic corporate-level strategies. In this section, we examine the *means* of entry into a new business area (as distinct from the *type* of generic corporate-level strategy being pursued). The choice strategic managers face is between entry through **acquisition** and entry through **internal new venturing.**

Acquisitions Versus
Internal Venturing

Entry into a new business area through acquisition involves purchasing an *established* company, complete with all its facilities, equipment, and personnel. Entry into a new business area through internal venturing involves a company starting a business from scratch: building facilities, purchasing equipment, recruiting personnel, opening up distribution outlets, an so on. Such projects are often called greenfield projects, since the company starts with nothing but a green field.

The choice between acquisitions and internal venturing as the preferred entry strategy is influenced by a number of factors. The most important among them are (1) barriers to entry; (2) the relatedness of the new business to existing operations; (3) the comparative speed and development costs of the two entry modes; (4) the risks involved in the different entry modes; and (5) industry life cycle factors.[8]

Barriers to entry As you may recall from Chapter 3, the sources of barriers to entry arise from factors associated with product differentiation (brand loyalty), absolute cost advantages, and economies of scale. When barriers are substantial, a company finds it difficult to enter the industry through internal venturing. To do so, it may have to construct efficient scale manufacturing plant, undertake massive advertising to break down established brand loyalties, and quickly build up distribution outlets — all hard to achieve and likely to involve substantial expenditures. By acquiring an established enterprise, however, a company can circumvent most entry barriers. It can purchase a market leader that already benefits from substantial scale economies and brand loyalty. Thus the greater the barriers to entry, the more will acquisition be the favored entry mode.

Relatedness The more related a new business is to a company's established operations, the lower are the barriers to entry and the more likely it is that the company has accumulated experience of this type of business. These factors heighten the attractiveness of new venturing as an entry mode. For example, IBM entered the personal computer market in 1981 by new venturing. It was a very successful entry, enabling IBM to capture 35 percent of the market within two years. IBM was able to enter by this mode because of the high degree of relatedness between the PC market and IBM's established computer mainframe operations. IBM already had a well-established sales force and brand loyalty, and it had accumulated considerable expertise in the computer industry. Similarly, companies such as Du Pont and Dow Chemicals Co. have successfully entered closely related chemical businesses through internal new venturing.

In contrast, the more unrelated a new business, the more likely will entry be through acquisition. By definition, unrelated diversifiers lack the specific expertise necessary to enter a new business area through greenfield development.

The unrelated company choosing internal venturing would have to develop its own expertise regarding how to compete in the new industry. The learning process can be lengthy and involve costly mistakes before the company fully understands its new industry. In the case of acquisitions, however, the acquired business already has a management team with accumulated experience on how to compete in that particular industry. When making an acquisition, a company is also buying knowledge and experience. Thus widely diversified conglomerates such as ITT, Textron, Gulf & Western, and Hanson Trust have all expanded through acquisition.

Speed and development costs As a rule, internal venturing takes years to generate substantial profits. Establishing a significant market presence can be both costly and time-consuming. In a study of corporate new venturing, Ralph Biggadike of the University of Virginia found that on the average it takes eight years for a new venture to reach profitability and ten to twelve years before the profitability of the average venture equals that of a mature business.[9] He also found that cash flow typically remains negative for at least the first eight years of a new venture. In contrast, acquisitions represent a much quicker means of establishing a significant market presence and of generating profitability. A company can purchase a market leader in a strong cash position overnight, rather than having to spend years building up a market leadership position through internal development. Thus, when speed is important, acquisitions will be the favored entry mode.

Risks of entry New venturing tends to be a very uncertain process, with a low probability of success. A series of studies by Edwin Mansfield of the University of Pennsylvania, for example, concluded that only between 12 percent and 20 percent of R&D-based new ventures actually succeed in earning an economic profit.[10] Indeed, business history is strewn with examples of large companies that lost money through internal new venturing. For example, in 1984 AT&T entered the computer market through an internal new venture. Company officials predicted that by 1990 AT&T would rank second in data processing, behind IBM. So far there are few signs of that happening. In 1985 AT&T's computer division lost $500 million, and in 1986 it lost $1.2 billion.[11]

When it makes an acquisition, however, a company is also acquiring known profitability, known revenues, and known market share; thus it avoids uncertainty. Essentially, internal venturing involves the establishment of a *question mark* business, whereas an acquisition allows a company to buy a *winner*. Hence many companies favor acquisitions.

Industry life cycle factors We have already considered the general importance of the industry life cycle in Chapter 3. In the present context, the industry life cycle has a major impact on many of the factors that influence the choice between acquisitions and new venturing. In embryonic and growth industries, barriers to entry are typically lower than in mature industries, since in the former, established companies are still going through a learning process. They do not have the same experience advantages as the established companies in a mature industry environment. Given these factors, entry by internal venture during the early stage of the industry life cycle means lower risks and development costs, as well as fewer penalties in terms of expansion speed, than entry into a mature industry environment. Consequently, internal venturing tends to be the favored entry mode in embryonic and growth industries, whereas acquisition tends to be the favored mode in mature industries. Indeed, many of the most successful internal ventures have been associated with entry into emerging industries — for instance, IBM's entry into the personal computer arena and John Deere Company's entry into the snowmobile business.

Summary   In sum, internal venturing would seem to make most sense when the following conditions exist: when the industry to be entered is in its embryonic or growth stage; when barriers to entry are low; when the industry is closely related to the firm's existing operations (the firm's strategy is one of related diversfication); and when the firm is willing to accept the time frame, development costs, and risks involved in the venture process. In portfolio terms, new venturing makes most sense when a company needs more *question marks* in its portfolio or when it sees a strong possibility of establishing an *emerging winner* in an embryonic or growth industry. On the other hand, acquisitions make the most sense when a company needs more *established winners* or *profit producers* in its portfolio. Table 7.4 summarizes these situations.

In contrast, acquisitions make most sense when the following conditions exist: when the industry to be entered is mature; when barriers to entry are high; when the industry is not closely related to the firm's existing operations (the strategy is one of unrelated diversification); and when the firm is unwilling to accept the time frame, development costs, and risks of new venturing.

Pitfalls of Acquisitions

Despite the popularity of acquisitions as the preferred means of entry into a new business area, they often do not bring the gains predicted.[12] For example, management consultants McKinsey & Co. recently put fifty-eight major acquisitions undertaken between 1972 and 1983 to two tests: did the return on the total amount invested in the acquisitions exceed the cost of capital, and did they help their parent companies outperform the competition in the stock market? Twenty-eight out of the fifty-eight clearly failed both tests, and six others failed one.[13]

In terms of the generic corporate strategies discussed in Chapter 6, these test results indicate that many acquisitions fail to establish the *strategic advantages* that a company's managers originally planned for. Consequently, far from acquiring an *established winner* or a *profit producer,* a company may find that it has added a *dog* to its portfolio. Why does this happen? Why do so many acquisitions fail?

TABLE 7.4   **Portfolio gaps and entry strategies**

Portfolio gap	Entry strategy
Insufficient cash cows	Acquire companies in mature industries
Insufficient winners	Acquire companies in mature industries
Insufficient question marks or developing winners	Internal venture in growth or embryonic industry

There appear to be four major reasons: (1) companies often experience difficulties when trying to integrate divergent corporate cultures; (2) companies overestimate the potential gains from synergy; (3) acquisitions tend to be very expensive; and (4) companies often do not adequately screen their acquisition targets.

Integration   Having made an acquisition, the acquiring company has to integrate the acquired one into its own organizational structure. This can entail the adoption of common management and financial control systems, the joining together of operations from the acquired and the acquiring company, or the establishment of linkages to share information and personnel between different businesses. When integration is attempted, many unexpected problems can occur. Often they stem from differences in corporate cultures. Many acquired companies experience high management turnover after an acquisition because their personnel do not like the acquiring company's way of doing things. The loss of management talent and expertise can set back the realization of gains from an acquisition by several years, to say nothing of the damage from constant tensions between the businesses. For example, four years after Fluor bought St. Joe Minerals Corporation in one of the largest acquisitions of 1981, only seven of the twenty-two senior managers who ran St. Joe before the acquisition remained. Instead of reaping gains from an established *winner,* Fluor found itself struggling to transform a business that was fast becoming a *loser.* The crux of the problem was that Fluor, a very centralized and autocratic organization, and St. Joe, a decentralized company, clashed in their corporate cultures. St. Joe's senior management resented the centralized management style at Fluor, and many managers left in protest.[14]

Overestimated synergies   Even when they achieve integration, companies often overestimate the extent of synergy between the different businesses. They overestimate the strategic advantages that can be derived from the acquisition and consequently pay more for the target company than it is probably worth. For example, Coca-Cola once thought that it could use its marketing skills to dominate the U.S. wine industry. It reasoned that a beverage is a beverage. But after buying three wine companies and enduring seven years of marginal profits, Coca-Cola finally conceded that wine and soft drinks are very different products, with different kinds of appeal, pricing systems, and distribution networks. In 1983 Coke sold its wine operations to Joseph E. Seagram and Sons, Inc., for $210 million—the price it had paid for the purchases and a substantial loss when adjusted for inflation.[15]

The expense of acquisition   Acquisitions of companies whose stock is publicly traded tend to be very expensive. When a company bids to acquire the stock of another enterprise, the stock price frequently gets bid up by speculators hoping to gain from the acquisition. Thus the acquiring company often must pay a premium over the current market value of the target. In the early 1980s acquiring companies paid an average premium of 40–50 percent over current stock prices for an acquisition. The debt taken on to finance the acquisition can later become a noose around the acquiring company's neck, particularly if interest rates rise.

Preacquisition screening   Many companies make acquisition decisions without thoroughly analyzing the potential benefits and costs. Consequently, they often find that instead of a *winner* or *profit producer* they have bought a *dog*. Philip Morris, for example, thought it could apply the same brand-management skills that it had used so successfully with cigarettes and beer to turn Seven-Up into another Coca-Cola. After investing eight years and hundreds of millions of dollars, Philip Morris finally faced up to something Seven-Up researchers had known all along: that lemon-lime soft drinks have limited appeal. The company was sold. Had Philip Morris screened Seven-Up thoroughly before acquiring the company, it could have saved itself a lot of money.

Guidelines for Acquisition Success

To avoid pitfalls and make acquisitions successful, companies need to take a structured approach that involves three main components: (1) target identification and preacquisition screening, (2) bidding strategy, and (3) integration.[16]

Screening   Thorough preacquisition screening increases a company's knowledge about potential takeover targets, leads to a more realistic assessment of the problems involved in executing an acquisition and integrating the new business into the company's organizational structure, and lessens the risk of purchasing a *dog*. The screening process should begin with a detailed assessment of the strategic rationale for making the acquisition and the identification of the kind of company that would make an ideal acquisition candidate. Hanson Trust exemplifies a company that has a very clear idea of its ideal acquisition candidate (see the Opening Incident in Chapter 6).

Next, the company should scan a target population of potential acquisition candidates, evaluating each according to a detailed set of criteria that focus on the following: (1) financial position, (2) product market position, (3) management capabilities, and (4) corporate culture. Such an evaluation should enable the company to identify the strengths and weaknesses of each candidate, the extent of potential synergies between the acquiring and the acquired company, any potential integration problems, and the compatibility of the different corporate cultures of the acquiring and the acquired company.

The company should then reduce the list of candidates to the most favored ones and evaluate them further. At this stage, it should sound out third parties, such as investment bankers, whose opinions may be important and who may be able to give valuable insights as to the efficiency of target companies. The company that comes out best from this process should be the acquisition target.

Bidding strategy   The objective of bidding strategy is to reduce the price that a company must pay for an acquisition candidate. The essential element of a good bidding strategy is timing. Hanson Trust, for example, always looks for essentially sound businesses that are suffering from short-term problems due to cyclical industry factors or localized problems in one division. Such companies will typically be undervalued by the stock market and thus can be picked up without payment of the standard 40–50-percent premium over current stock prices. With good timing, a company can make a *bargain* purchase.

Integration   Despite good screening and bidding, an acquisition will fail unless positive steps are taken to integrate the acquired company into the organizational structure of the acquiring one. Integration should center on the source of the potential strategic advantages from the acquisition — for instance, marketing, manufacturing, procurement, R&D, financial, or management synergies. Integration should also be accompanied by steps to eliminate any duplication of facilities or functions. In addition, any unwanted activities of the acquired company should be sold. Finally, if the different business activities are closely related, they will require a high degree of integration. In the case of a company like Hanson Trust, the level of integration can be minimal, for the company's strategy is one of unrelated diversification. But a company such as Rockwell requires greater integration because its strategy is one of related diversification.

Pitfalls of Internal Venturing

Science-based companies that use their technology to create market opportunities in related areas tend to favor internal venturing as an entry strategy. Du Pont, for example, has created whole new markets for the chemical industry with products such as Cellophane, nylon, Freon, and Teflon — all internally generated innovations. Another company, 3M, has a near-legendary knack of shaping new markets from internally generated ideas. Internal new venturing, however, need not be based on radical innovations. Although IBM was an imitator rather than innovator, it successfully entered the PC market in 1981 through a venture-based strategy rather than by acquisition. Similarly, The Gillette

Company successfully diversified into the manufacture of felt-tip pens, and John Deere into snowmobiles, through internal venturing.

As noted earlier, internal ventures often fail, and even when they succeed, it may take years before they become profitable. To a certain extent, these factors are inherent in the venturing process. In terms of the portfolio approach, new ventures are by definition *question marks*. However, management can reduce the probability of failure by avoiding three common pitfalls in the internal venturing process: (1) entering on too small a scale, (2) poor commercialization of the new venture, and (3) poor corporate management of the venture process.

Scale of entry   Research suggests that large-scale entry into a new business is the best way for an internal venture to succeed. Although in the short run large-scale entry means significant development costs and substantial losses, in the long run (that is, after eight to twelve years) it brings greater returns than small-scale entry.[17] Figure 7.5 plots the relationships among scale of entry, profitability, and cash flow over time for successful small-scale and large-scale ventures. As can be seen, successful small-scale entry involves lower losses, but in the long run large-scale entry generates greater returns. However, perhaps because

FIGURE 7.5   **The impact of large-scale versus small-scale entry on profitability and cash flow**

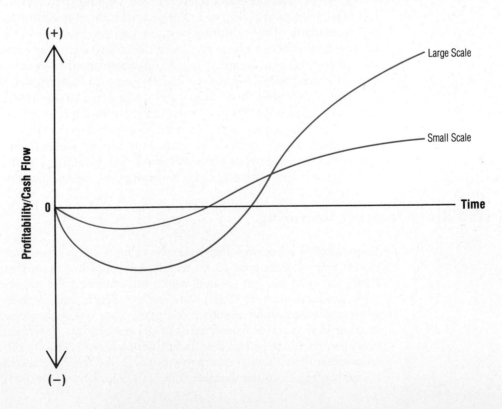

of the costs of large-scale entry, many companies prefer a small-scale entry strategy. This can be a major mistake, for the company fails to build up the market share necessary for long-term success.

Commercialization   To be commercially successful, science-based innovations must be developed with market requirements in mind. Many new ventures fail when a company ignores the basic needs of the market. The company can become blinded by the technological possibilities of a new product and fail to analyze the market opportunities properly. Thus a new venture may fail due to lack of commercialization, as happened when the British and French governments underwrote the development of the Concorde supersonic jet airplane.

Poor implementation   Managing the new venture process raises difficult organizational issues.[18] Though we will deal with the specifics of implementation in later chapters, we must note some of the most common mistakes here. The shotgun approach of supporting many different internal new venture projects can be a major error, for it places great demands on the company's cash flow and can result in the best ventures being starved of the cash they need for success. Another mistake involves a failure by corporate management to set the strategic context within which new venture projects should be developed. Simply taking a team of research scientists and allowing them to do research in their favorite field may produce novel results, but these results may have little strategic or commercial value. Failure to anticipate the time and costs involved in the venture process constitutes a further mistake. Many companies have unrealistic expectations of the time frame involved. Reportedly, some companies operate with a philosophy of killing new businesses if they do not turn a profit by the end of the third year—a clearly unrealistic view, given Biggadike's evidence that it can take eight to twelve years before a venture generates substantial profits.

Guidelines for Internal Venture Success

As with acquisitions, to avoid the pitfalls just discussed a company should adopt a structured approach to managing the venture process. New venturing typically begins with R&D. To make effective use of its R&D capacity, a company must first spell out its strategic objectives and then communicate them to its scientists and engineers. Research, after all, only makes sense when it is undertaken in areas relevant to strategic goals.[19]

To increase the probability of commercial success, the company should foster close links between R&D and marketing personnel, as this is the best way of ensuring that research projects address the needs of the market. The company should also foster close links between R&D and manufacturing personnel, so as to ensure that the company has the capability to manufacture any proposed new products. Many companies achieve close integration between different functions by setting up project teams. These are comprised of the representatives of the various functional areas. The task of these teams is to oversee the development of new products. For example, the success that Compaq Computers has had in introducing new products in the personal computer industry has been linked to its use of project teams that oversee the development of the new product from its inception through to its market introduction.

A further advantage of such teams is that they can significantly reduce the time it takes to develop a new product. Thus, while R&D personnel are working on the design, manufacturing personnel can be setting up facilities, and marketing personnel can be developing their plans. Due to such integration, it took Compaq only six months to take the first portable personal computer from an idea on a drawing board to a marketable product.

To use resources to the best effect, the company must also devise a selection process for choosing only those ventures that demonstrate the greatest probability of commercial success. Picking future *winners,* however, is a tricky business, since by definition new ventures are *question marks* with an uncertain future. A study by Edwin Mansfield and G. Beardsley, for example, found that the uncertainty surrounding new ventures was so great that a company typically took four to five years after launching the venture before it could reasonably estimate its future profitability.[20] Nevertheless, some kind of selection process is necessary if the company is not to spread its resources too thinly over too many projects.

Once a project is selected, management needs to monitor the progress of the venture closely. The evidence suggests that the most important criterion for evaluating a venture during its first four to five years is market share growth rather than cash flow or profitability. In the long run, the most successful ventures will be those that increase their market share. The company should have clearly defined market share objectives for a new venture and decide to retain or kill a venture in its early years on the basis of its ability to achieve market share goals. Only in the medium term should profitability and cash flow begin to take on greater importance.

Finally, the association of large-scale entry with greater long-term profitability suggests that a company can increase the probability of success for its new venture by thinking big. This involves construction of efficient scale manufacturing facilities ahead of demand, large marketing expenditures, and a commitment on the part of corporate management to accept initial large losses so long as market share is expanding.

7.8 EXIT STRATEGIES

Just as building a balanced portfolio requires entry into new business areas, so it also requires exit from existing business areas. As Table 7.3 suggested earlier, exit is normally required when a company has too many *losers* or *question marks* and sometimes when it has too many *developing winners.* (It is not unusual for a company to sell a *developing winner* if the business does not fit the basic strategic thrust of the corporation.) Exit strategies are also normally a critical component of corporate retrenchment strategies. How should a company deal with the exit problem? In essence, it has three choices: divest, harvest, or liquidate. Which strategy is best in a given situation largely depends on two factors: the characteristics of the relevant industry and the characteristics of the business to be divested.

Divestment, Harvest, and Liquidation

Divestment   Divestment involves selling a business to another company or to the management of that business. As an exit option, divesture is becoming an increasing popular strategy. In 1986 the number of divestments in the United States reached an all-time high of 1,317.[21] Divestment makes sense if the future prospects for the business to be sold seem good — that is, if the business to be divested is a *developing winner* or a particularly promising *question mark*. In these circumstances, the unit to be divested can command a high price. Divestment can be difficult to implement if the prospects for the business are poor, as in the case of a *loser*. For example, when The Bendix Corporation decided to exit from the troubled machine tool industry in 1984, it could only get $74 million for its operation. Yet five years earlier, when the machine tool industry was booming, Bendix had paid $300 million to acquire just part of the business it sold in 1984.[22]

Harvest   A harvest exit strategy involves controlled disinvestment in a business unit to optimize cash flow as the company exits from that industry. To increase cash flow, management eliminates or severely curtails new investment, cuts maintenance of facilities, and reduces advertising and research while reaping the benefits of past good will.[23] The effects are illustrated in Figure 7.6. The business unit loses market share, but in the short run cash flow out of the business increases markedly. The cash generated by the harvest strategy can be invested elsewhere in the corporation. Once the cash flow begins to decline, then liquidation is normally considered. Divestment is difficult because by this time the business is run down and its long-term prospects are poor.

The trouble with a harvest strategy is that it can be very difficult to implement. It creates motivational problems in the business being harvested and can lead to a lack of confidence on the part of customers and suppliers once they perceive what is occurring. Thus the strategy may be administratively more difficult to manage than it is worth.

Liquidation   Liquidation involves closing down an operation. Liquidation is normally the exit option of last resort. It is selected only when all other options have failed because, by definition, the company must take substantial write-offs on the closure of an operation and bear the fixed costs of exit, such as severance pay to employees.

FIGURE 7.6   **The impact of a harvest strategy on cash flow**

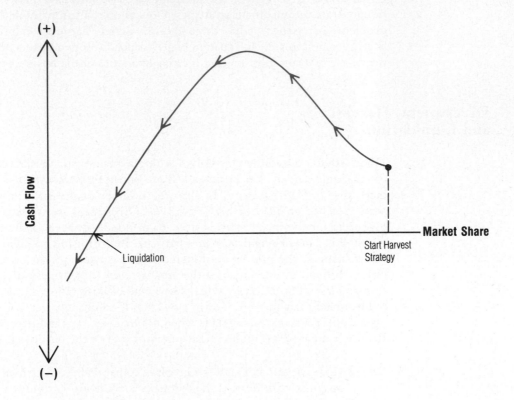

Choice of Exit Strategy

The choice of exit strategy is governed by the characteristics of the business unit to be sold and the competitive intensity of the industry in which it is based. The characteristics of the business unit to be sold can be summarized by its portfolio category: *developing winner, question mark,* or *loser.* Relevant industry characteristics include those factors that determine competitive intensity—such as barriers to entry, life cycle factors, exit barriers, product characteristics, and so on (we have reviewed the details in Chapter 3). An industry's characteristics can be summarized by its overall competitive prospects, which are either *favorable* or *unfavorable*.

Other things being equal, a company will choose the exit strategy that maximizes the payoffs of exit. Given that liquidation normally has a negative payoff, the preferred choice is between divestment and harvest. Within this framework, the range of preferred exit strategies is illustrated in Table 7.5. By definition, *developing winners* are most likely to be found in industries with

TABLE 7.5   **Exit strategies**

Business characteristic	Favorable industry	Unfavorable industry
Developing winner	Divest	
Loser	Harvest/divest	Harvest/liquidate
Question mark	Divest	Liquidate

favorable prospects. Divestment makes most sense in these circumstances, since an abundance of buyers will bid up the purchase price.

Losers can be found in industries with both favorable and unfavorable prospects. The poor competitive position of *losers* makes it unlikely that they can be divested at a reasonable price. When an industry's prospects are favorable, then a harvest strategy may be preferred. Even in such circumstances, however, difficulties associated with implementing a harvest strategy may prompt a company to divest *losers* at a bargain price rather than try to manage decline.

When industry prospects are unfavorable, divestment may be out of the question for *losers,* since there would be no buyers. The preferred strategy will be harvest. However, if the industry is facing rapid decline in sales, then even a harvest strategy may not generate much in the way of positive cash flow. Liquidation will be the only option in such circumstances.

For *question marks* operating in a favorable industry environment, divestment will be the favored option. In such cases, a company can often sell the business to its managers through a leveraged buyout. When the industry environment is unfavorable, however, few buyers are likely to be found. A harvest strategy will not work, since the market share of most *question marks* is typically too low to make the strategy viable. Thus liquidation may be the only option.

7.9 SUMMARY OF CHAPTER

This chapter has reviewed three main techniques for analyzing the portfolio of a multibusiness company. The rationale for undertaking such an analysis is to identify what needs to be done to build a *balanced* portfolio. Building a balanced portfolio typically involves entry and exit strategies. The choice between different entry and exit strategies, and the pitfalls involved, have also been reviewed. The following points have been made:

1. There are three main portfolio techniques that companies can use: the Boston Consulting Group's matrix, McKinsey's matrix, and Hofer's industry evolution matrix.

2. The strength of the BCG matrix is its focus on cash flow requirements. Weaknesses include the simplistic categorization of businesses and unten-

able assumptions concerning relationships among market share, growth, and profitability.

3. The strength of the McKinsey matrix is its ability to incorporate a wide range of strategically relevant variables into the analysis. The main weakness is that the analysis is essentially static and tells us little about how industry evolution might change business attractiveness.

4. The strength of the industry evolution matrix lies in what it tells about the distribution of a company's businesses across different stages of the industry life cycle. The weakness of the technique is that it ignores many strategically relevant industry factors.

5. In general, portfolio analysis helps companies conceptualize their diversity, assists in the allocation of corporate cash, and identifies the adjustments necessary to achieve a balanced portfolio. However, it has the following weakness: the assumption that a company can be divided into a reasonable number of strategic business units; a tendency to ignore potential conflicts of interest that might emerge between corporate cash flow priorities and cash flow priorities within an SBU; and a tendency to ignore interrelationships among business units.

6. Correcting an imbalance in a corporate portfolio typically requires entry strategies (acquisitions and internal new venturing) and exit strategies (divestments, liquidation, and harvest).

7. The choice of an appropriate entry strategy is influenced by barriers to entry, relatedness, speed and development costs of entry, risks of entry, and industry life cycle considerations. In general, internal venturing makes the most sense when the strategic goal is to establish *question marks* or perhaps developing *winners*. Acquisitions make the most sense when the strategic goal involves establishing *profit producers* or *winners*.

8. Many acquisitions fail because of poor postacquisition integration, overestimation of the potential gains from synergy, the high cost of acquisitions, and poor preacquisition screening. Guarding against failure involves structured screening, good bidding strategies, and positive attempts to integrate the acquired company into the organization of the acquiring one.

9. Many internal ventures fail because of entry on too small a scale, poor commercialization, and poor corporate management of the internal venture process. Guarding against failure involves a structured approach toward project selection and management, integration of R&D and marketing to improve commercialization of a venture idea, and entry on a significant scale.

10. Exit strategies include divestment, harvest, and liquidation. The choice of exit strategy is governed by the characteristics of the relevant business unit and the competitive intensity of the relevant industry.

Discussion Questions

1. Why might diversified companies that use portfolio analysis techniques have an advantage over diversified companies that do not? How do you think cash flows are allocated in companies that do not use portfolio analysis techniques?

2. Under what circumstances might it be best to enter a new business area by acquisition, and under what circumstances might internal venturing be the preferred entry mode?

3. In the face of the obvious difficulties of succeeding with acquisitions, why do so many companies continue to make them?

4. What are the main pitfalls of portfolio planning? How might these pitfalls be overcome?

Endnotes

1. For details, see "Rockwell: Using Its Cash Hoard to Edge Away From Defense," *Business Week*, February 4, 1985, pp. 82–84; "Bob Anderson has New Miracles to Work at Rockwell," *Business Week*, March 31, 1986, pp. 64–65; and "Rockwell's Hard Place," *Business Week*, February 29, 1988, pp. 46–47.

2. For further details of portfolio techniques, see R. A. Bettis and W. K Hall, "Strategic Portfolio Management in the Multibusiness Firm," *California Management Review*, 24 (1981), 23–38; P. Haspeslagh, "Portfolio Planning: Uses and Limits," *Harvard Business Review*, 60 (January–February 1983), 58–73; B. Hedley, "Strategy and the Business Portfolio," *Long Range Planning*, 10 (1977), 9–15; and Charles W. Hofer and Dan Schendel, *Strategy Formulation: Analytical Concepts* (St. Paul, Minn. West, 1978).

3. For evidence, see D. F. Barnett and R. W. Crandall, *Up From the Ashes: The Rise of the Steel Minimill* (Washington, D.C.: The Brookings Institution, 1986), pp. 1–17.

4. As defined by Hofer and Schendel, *Strategy Formulation*, p. 82.

5. Charles W. Hofer, *Conceptual Constructs for Formulating Corporate and Business Strategies* (Boston: Intercollegiate Case Clearing House, #9-378-754, 1977).

6. For details, see R. A. Bettis and W. K. Hall, "The Business Portfolio Approach: Where it Falls Down in Practice," *Long Range Planning*, 12 (1983), 95–105; Haspeslagh, "Portfolio Planning," pp. 58–73.

7. Bettis and Hall, "The Business Portfolio Approach," pp. 95–105.

8. For further details, see H. I. Ansoff, *Corporate Strategy* (New York: McGraw-Hill, 1965). E. R. Biggadike, *Corporate Diversification: Entry, Strategy and Performance* (Cambridge, Mass.: Division of Research, Harvard Business School, 1979); M. S. Salter and W. A. Weinhold, *Diversification Through Acquisition: Strategies for Creating Economic Value* (New York: Free Press, 1979); and G. S. Yip, "Diversification Entry: Internal Development Versus Acquisition," *Strategic Management Journal*, 3 (1982), 331–345.

9. E. R. Biggadike, "The Risky Business of Diversification," *Harvard Business Review*, 57 (May–June 1979), 103–111.

10. Edwin Mansfield, "How Economists see R&D," *Harvard Business Review,* 59 (November–December 1981), 98–106.

11. Peter Petre, "AT&T's Epic Push Into Computers," *Fortune,* May 25, 1987, pp. 42–50.

12. See D. C. Mueller, "The Effects of Conglomerate Mergers: A Survey of the Empirical Evidence," *Journal of Banking and Finance,* 1 (1977), 315–342, and *The Determinant and Effects of Mergers* (Cambridge, Mass.: Oelgeschlager, Gunn & Hain, 1980). See also M. H. Lubatkin, "Merger and the Performance of the Acquiring Firm," *Academy of Management Review,* 8 (1983), 218–225.

13. "Do Mergers Really Work?" *Business Week,* June 3, 1985, pp. 88–100.

14. "Fluor: Compounding Fractures from Leaping Before Looking," *Business Week,* June 3, 1985, pp. 92–93.

15. "Coca-Cola: A Sobering Lesson from its Journey into Wine," *Business Week,* June 3, 1985, pp. 96–98.

16. For views on this issue, see L. L. Fray, D. H. Gaylin, and J. W. Down, "Successful Acquisition Planning," *Journal of Business Strategy,* 5 (1984), 46–55; C. W. L. Hill, "Profile of a Conglomerate Takeover: BTR and Thomas Tilling," *Journal of General Management,* 10 (1984), 34–50; and D. R. Willensky, "Making it Happen: How to Execute an Acquisition," *Business Horizons* (March–April 1985), 38–45.

17. Biggadike, "The Risky Business of Diversification," pp. 103–111.

18. R. A. Burgelman, "A Process Model of Internal Corporate Venturing in the Diversified Major Firm," *Administrative Science Quarterly,* 28 (1983), 223–244.

19. I. C. MacMillan and R. George, "Corporate Venturing: Challenges for Senior Managers," *Journal of Business Strategy,* 5 (1985), 34–43.

20. G. Beardsley and Edwin Mansfield, "A Note on the Accuracy of Industrial Forecasts of the Profitability of New Products and Processes," *Journal of Business* (1978), 127–130.

21. "1986 Profile," *Mergers and Acquisitions,* 21 (1986), 57–61.

22. "Bendix: A Buy that Really Was Too Good To Be True," *Business Week,* June 3, 1985, pp. 93–94.

23. K. R. Harrigan and Michael E. Porter, "End-game Strategies for Declining Industries," *Harvard Business Review,* 61 (July–August 1983), 111–120.

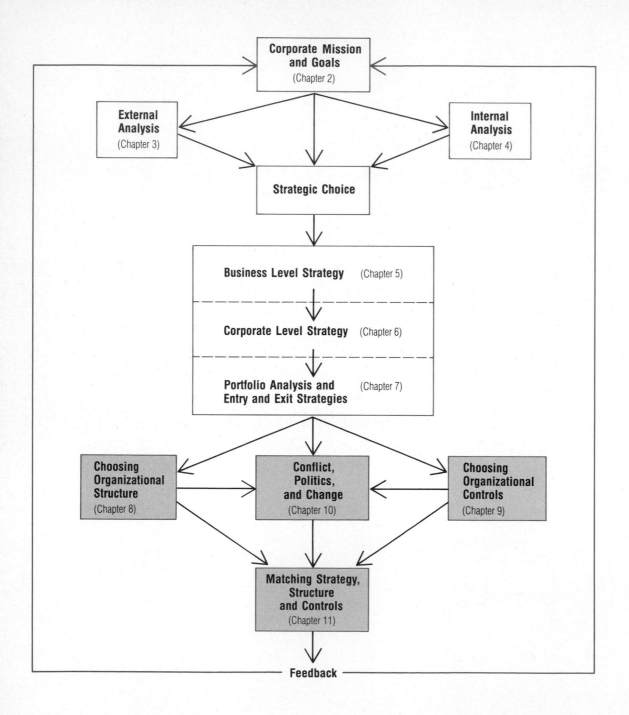

III

STRATEGY
IMPLEMENTATION

Chapter 8

DESIGNING
ORGANIZATIONAL
STRUCTURE

8.1 OPENING INCIDENT: APPLE COMPUTER

Incorporated in 1977, Apple Computer, Inc., designs, manufactures, and markets personal computers for use in business, education, and the home.[1] The structure of Apple Computer was created in 1976, when two engineers, Steven Jobs and Steven Wozniak, collaborated on producing a computing board for personal use. As early orders for their system increased, Jobs and Wozniak realized that they needed to create an organization with a structure that could handle capital acquisitions, marketing, management and strategic planning, engineering and production. In essence, they needed to formalize the functions necessary in any complex business. In true entrepreneurial fashion, they created a flat, decentralized structure designed to allow people to be creative, flexible, and responsive to the uncertainty Apple was experiencing in the new home computer industry. The organization had few rules and only a vague hierarchy, and it operated on the basis of personal contact between people in different functions through teams and task forces, many of which were chaired by Jobs and Wozniak.

By 1982 Apple was taller, with more levels of management. A new chief executive, Hugh Sculley, had been hired to take control of the management side of the business. Fast growth and the introduction of a wider range of products—the Lisa and Macintosh computers, as well as the old Apple IIe—led to greater organizational differentiation. As a result, Apple moved to a divisional structure, where each product was manufactured in a self-contained division and each division had its own set of specialist functions like marketing, research and development, and product engineering. Problems arose with this structure, however.[2] Jobs championed Macintosh against Lisa for development and triggered hostile competition for resources among the divisions. Overhead costs rose dramatically because specialist functions were duplicated in each division. Furthermore, Sculley's role and the role of top managers in running the business became unclear in the organization because all direction seemed to come from the divisions and especially from Jobs. The unsettling outcome of these traumas was that IBM overtook Apple as leader in the personal computer industry.

By 1985 the recession in the computer industry had exacerbated these problems and made reorganization imperative. Sculley took total control of the company and once again changed its structure.[3] He created a structure in which one set of specialist functions served the needs of all the various product lines — a product structure. The production system was also changed so that products were not manufactured in separate divisions by different

managers, but in one central production department, where one management team had overall control. This change reduced costs massively, and centralized management control allowed the company to respond more quickly to market developments. In addition, company-based, rather than division-based, plans for achieving corporate objectives were adopted.

Paradoxically, a company that had started out with a flat, decentralized functional structure had moved to a second form, the divisional structure, which then inhibited its development and growth. Today Apple uses a more centralized product structure and is in good financial shape. Its streamlined management team is able to address the strategic and operational needs of the business as it seeks to expand its market share.

8.2 OVERVIEW

As the discussion of Apple suggests, this chapter deals with the creation of the right organizational structure for managing a company's strategy. In the first chapter of this book, we defined strategy implementation as the way in which a company creates the organizational arrangements that allow it to put its strategic plan into operation most efficiently and to achieve its objectives. Strategy is implemented through organizational design. Organizational design involves selecting the combination of organizational structure and control systems that lets a company pursue its strategy most efficiently. Different kinds of structure and control systems provide strategic planners with alternative means of pursuing different strategies because they lead the company and the people within it to act in different ways.

In this chapter, the organizational structures available to strategic managers are examined. In Chapter 9, we consider the integration mechanisms that companies use to coordinate the structure, as well as the control systems through which they monitor and evaluate corporate, divisional, and functional performance. Chapter 10 traces the ways in which different strategy choices lead to the use of different kinds of structure and control systems. After reading this section of the book, you will be able to choose the right organizational design for implementing a company's strategy. You will understand why Apple Computer chose to change organizational structures as it grew and developed over time.

8.3 DESIGNING ORGANIZATIONAL STRUCTURES

After formulating a company's strategy, the management must make designing the structure its next priority, for strategy can only be implemented through organizational structure. The activities of organizational personnel are meaningless unless some type of structure is used to assign people to tasks and to connect the activities of different people or functions.[4] The terms used to describe the characteristics of organizational structure are differentiation and integration. The term **differentiation** refers to the way in which a company allocates people and resources to organizational tasks.[5] First, it deals with choices about how to distribute *decision-making authority* in the organization—choices about **vertical differentiation.**[6] Second, it deals with choices about the division of labor in the organization and the *grouping of organizational tasks* — choices about **horizontal differentiation.** The term **integration** refers to the means by which a company seeks to coordinate people and functions to accomplish organizational tasks.[7] These means include the use of integrating mechanisms and the whole apparatus of organizational control. In short, differentiation refers to the way in which a company divides itself up into parts, and integration refers to the way in which the parts are then combined. Together the two processes determine how an organizational structure will operate and how successfully managers will be able to implement their chosen strategies.

As a comparison, consider the structure of a chemical compound like water. It consists of different types of atoms, two of hydrogen and one of oxygen. It also comprises bonds between the atoms. The properties of the chemical—the way it functions—are a consequence both of its individual atoms (differentiation) and the way these are bonded or connected (integration). The same is true of organizational structure: the way it functions depends on what it is made up of and how it is put together—its differentiation and integration. Strategic managers must design the organization correctly if it is to be effective for a particular strategy.

8.4 VERTICAL DIFFERENTIATION

The aim of vertical differentiation is to specify the reporting relationships that will link together people, tasks, and functions at all levels of a company. Fundamentally, this means choosing the appropriate number of hierarchical levels and the correct span of control for implementing a company's strategy most effectively. The organizational hierarchy establishes the authority structure from the top to the bottom of the organization. The span of control is defined as the number of subordinates a manager directly manages.[8] The basic choice is whether to aim for a **flat structure,** with few hierarchical levels and thus a relatively wide span of control, or a **tall structure,** with many levels and thus a

FIGURE 8.1   **Tall and flat structures**

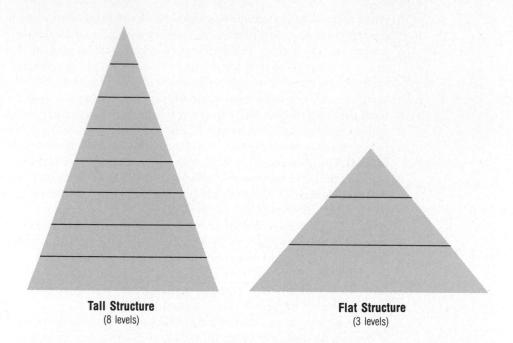

Tall Structure
(8 levels)

Flat Structure
(3 levels)

relatively narrow span of control (Figure 8.1). Tall structures have many hierarchical levels relative to size; flat structures have few levels relative to size.[9] For example, research suggests that the average number of hierarchical levels for a company employing 3,000 people is seven. Thus an organization having nine levels would be called tall, whereas one having four would be called flat. With its 4,000 employees and four hierarchical levels, Liz Claiborne, for instance, has a relatively flat structure. On the other hand, before reorganization, Westinghouse, with its ten levels in the hierarchy, had a relatively tall structure. Now it has seven levels — the average for a large organization.

Companies choose the number of levels they need on the basis of their strategy and the functional tasks necessary to achieve their strategy. For example, manufacturing companies often pursue a low-cost strategy in order to minimize production costs and increase operating efficiency. As a result, these companies are usually very tall, with many levels in the hierarchy and very prescribed areas of authority, so that managers can exert tight control over personnel and resources.[10] On the other hand, high tech companies often pursue a strategy of differentiation based on service and quality. Consequently, these companies are usually very flat, giving employees wide discretion to meet customers' demands without having to refer constantly to supervisors.[11] We discuss this subject further in Chapter 10. The crux of the matter is that the allocation of authority and responsibility in the organization must match the needs of corporate-, business-, and functional-level strategy.

Disadvantages of Tall Hierarchies

As a company grows and diversifies, choosing the right number of levels for managing its business becomes very important, since research shows that the number of hierarchical levels relative to company size is predictable as the size increases.[12] This finding demonstrates an interesting lesson in organization design concerning the correct choice of the number of hierarchical levels. The relationship between size and number of levels is presented in Figure 8.2. At about 1,000 employees, companies usually have four levels in the hierarchy: chief executive officer, departmental vice presidents, first-line supervisors, and shop-floor employees. By 3,000 employees, they have increased their level of vertical differentiation by raising the number of levels to seven or eight. However, beyond 3,000 employees, something interesting happens: even when companies grow to 10,000 employees or more, the number of hierarchical levels rarely increases beyond eight or nine. As organizations grow, managers apparently try to limit the number of hierarchical levels. For when companies become too tall,

FIGURE 8.2   **Relationship between company size and number of hierarchical levels**

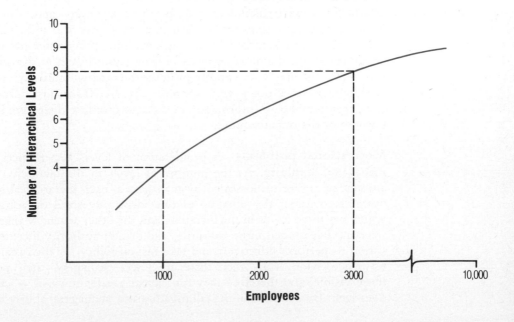

problems crop up, making strategy more difficult to implement and the company less efficient in pursuing its mission.[13]

Communication problems   Too many hierarchical levels impede communication. Communication between the top and the bottom of the hierarchy takes much longer as the chain of command lengthens. This leads to inflexibility and the loss of valuable time in bringing a new product to market or in keeping up with technological developments.[14] For Federal Express, communication is vital in its business; the company therefore allows a maximum of only five layers of management between any employee and the CEO in order to avoid communication problems.[15] On the other hand, because of its very tall hierarchy, Procter & Gamble needed twice as much time as its competitors to introduce new products—until it recently moved to streamline its structure.[16]

More subtle, but just as important, are the problems of information distortion that accompany the transmission of information up and down the hierarchy. Going down the hierarchy, the problem is that managers at different levels—for example, divisional or corporate managers—may misinterpret information, either through accidental garbling of messages or on purpose, to suit their own interests. In either case, information from the top may not reach its destination intact. For instance, a request to share divisional knowledge among divisions in order to achieve gains from synergy may be overlooked by divisional managers or it may be ignored by divisional managers who perceive it as a threat to their autonomy and power. This attitude among managers was one of the problems that led Iacocca to reorganize Chrysler in order to coordinate cost-cutting measures across divisions.

Information transmitted upward in the hierarchy may also be distorted. Subordinates may transmit to their superiors only the information that improves their own standing in the organization. The greater the number of hierarchical levels, the more scope there is for subordinates to distort facts, so that top managers may lose control over the hierarchy. Similarly, managers may compete with each other, and, when they are free from close corporate supervision, they may hoard information in order to promote their own interests at the expense of the organization's.

Motivational problems   A proliferation of levels also reduces the scope of managerial authority. As the number of levels in the hierarchy increases, the amount of authority possessed by managers at each hierarchical level falls. For example, consider the situation of two identically sized organizations, one of which has three levels in the hierarchy and the other seven. Managers in the flat structure have much more authority, and greater authority increases their motivation to perform effectively and take responsibility for the organization's performance. Moreover, when there are fewer managers, their performance is more visible, and therefore they can expect greater rewards when the business does well. By contrast, in the tall organization, managers' ability to exercise authority is limited, and their decisions are being constantly scrutinized by their superiors. As a result, the tendency is for managers to pass the buck and refuse to take the risks that are often necessary when pursuing new strategies. The shape of the organization's structure strongly affects the behavior of people within it, and thus the way in which strategy is implemented.[17]

Costs of operation   Another problem facing very tall structures is the simple fact that many hierarchical levels imply many managers, and employing managers is very expensive. Managerial salaries, benefits, offices, and secretaries are a huge expense for an organization. If the average middle manager costs a company $200,000 a year in total, then employing 100 surplus managers will cost $20 million a year. U.S. oil companies recognized this fact when oil prices fell in 1986. When these companies made billions in profits, they had no incentive to control the number of levels in the hierarchy and the number of managers. However, once they grew aware of the cost of these managers, companies like ARCO and Exxon Corporation ruthlessly purged the hierarchy, reducing the number of levels, and thus of managers, in order to reduce costs and restore profitability.

To offer another example, when companies grow and are successful, they often hire personnel and create new positions without much regard for the effect of these actions on the organizational hierarchy. Later, when managers review that structure, it is quite common to see the number of levels reduced because of the disadvantages discussed above. Deregulation also quite often prompts a reduction in levels and personnel. In a deregulated environment, companies have to respond to increased competition. After deregulation, AT&T, as well as a number of airline companies, reduced costs and streamlined their structure so that they could respond more rapidly to opportunities and threats brought about by increased competition. An examination of the nature of vertical differentiation in an organization is one means by which strategic planners are able to assess organizational *strengths* and *weaknesses*.

In sum, there are many problems that arise when firms become too tall and the chain of command becomes too long. Strategic managers tend to lose control over the hierarchy which means that they lose control over their strategies. Disaster often follows. However, one way that such problems can be partially overcome is by the decentralization of authority. That is, authority is vested in lower levels in the hierarchy as well as at the top. Since this is one of the most important implementation decisions a firm can make it needs to be discussed in more detail.

Centralization or Decentralization?

Centralization of authority exists in those situations where managers at the upper levels of the organizational hierarchy retain the authority to make the most important decisions. When authority is decentralized, it is delegated to divisions, functional departments, and managers at lower levels in the organization. If top management delegates authority to lower levels in the hierarchy, the communication problems described earlier are avoided because information does not have to be constantly sent to the top of the organization for decisions to be made. There are several other advantages to the decentralization or delegation of authority. First, if strategic managers delegate **operational decision making** to lower levels, they can spend more time on **strategic decision making.** As a result, they make more effective decisions and are better at long-time planning. Second, decentralization also promotes flexibility and responsiveness, since lower-level managers can make on-the-spot decisions. Thus the bottom layers in the organization can more easily adapt to the local situation. As IBM has demonstrated, this can be an enormous advantage for business strategy. For example, IBM has a very tall structure, but it is famous for the amount of authority it delegates to lower levels. Operational personnel can respond quickly to customer needs and so ensure superior service, which is a major source of IBM's competitive advantage. Similarly, to revitalize its product strategy, Westinghouse has massively decentralized its operations to give divisions more autonomy and to encourage risk taking and quick response to customer needs.[18]

If decentralization is so effective, why do not all companies decentralize decision making and avoid the problems of tall hierarchies? The answer is that centralization has its advantages, too. Centralized decision making allows easier coordination of the organizational activities needed to pursue a company's strategy. If managers at all levels can make their own decisions, planning becomes very difficult, and the company may lose control of its decision making. Centralization also means that decisions fit broad organizational objectives. For example, when its branch operations were getting out of hand, Merrill Lynch & Co., Inc., increased centralization by installing more information systems to give corporate managers greater control over branch activities. Similarly, Hewlett-Packard centralized research and development responsibility at the corporate level to provide a more directed corporate strategy. Furthermore, in times of crisis, centralization of authority permits strong leadership because authority is focused in one person or group. This allows for speedy decision making and a concerted response by the whole organization. Perhaps Iacocca personifies the meaning of centralization in times of crisis. He provided the vision and energy for Chrysler managers to respond creatively to Chrysler's problems and designed a cohesive plan for restoring its profitability.

Summary

It is difficult and expensive to manage the strategy-structure relationship when the number of hierarchical levels becomes too great. Depending on a firm's specific situation, the problems of tall hierarchies can be avoided by decentralization. However, as firm size increases decentralization becomes less effective. How, therefore, as firms grow and diversify can they maintain control over their structures and strategies without becoming taller or more decentralized? That is, how can a firm like Exxon control 300,000 employees without becoming too tall and inflexible? There must be alternative ways to create organizational arrangements to achieve corporate objectives. The first of these ways is through the choice of form of horizontal differentiation: by deciding on the correct way to group organizational activities and tasks.

8.5 HORIZONTAL DIFFERENTIATION

Whereas vertical differentiation concerns the division of authority, horizontal differentiation focuses on the *division and grouping of tasks to meet the objectives of the business*.[19] Because, to a large degree, an organization's tasks are a function of its strategy, the dominant view is that companies choose a form of horizontal differentiation or structure to match their organizational strategy. Perhaps the first person to address this issue formally was the Harvard business historian Alfred D. Chandler.[20] After studying the organizational problems experienced by large U.S. corporations such as Du Pont and General Motors as they grew and diversified in the early decades of this century, Chandler reached two conclusions: (1) that in principle organizational structure follows the growth strategy of a company, or, in other words, the range and variety of tasks it chooses to pursue; and (2) that American enterprises go through a sequence of strategy and structure changes in stages as they grow and diversify. In other words, a company's structure changes as its strategy changes in a predictable way.[21] The kinds of structure that companies adopt are discussed in this section.

Simple Structure

The simple structure is normally used by the small, entrepreneurial company involved in producing one or a few related products for a specific market segment. Often in this situation, one person, the entrepreneur, takes on most of the managerial tasks. No formal organization arrangements exist, and horizontal differentiation is low because employees perform multiple duties. A classic example of this structure is Apple in its earliest stage, as a venture between two people, Steven Jobs and Steven Wozniak, working in a garage together to perform all the tasks necessary to market their personal computer. The success of their product, however, made this simple structure outdated almost as soon as it was adopted. In order to grow and perform all the tasks required by a rapidly expanding company, Apple needed a more complex form of horizontal differentiation.

Functional Structure

As companies grow, two things happen. First, the range of tasks that must be performed expands. For example, it suddenly becomes apparent that the services of a professional accountant or production manager are needed to take control of specialized tasks. Second, no one person can successfully perform more than one organizational task without becoming overloaded: for example, the entrepreneur can no longer simultaneously produce and sell the product. The issue arises, then, as to what grouping of activities, or what form of horizontal differentiation, can most efficiently handle the needs of the growing company. The answer for most companies is the **functional structure.** In functional structures, people are grouped together on the basis of their common expertise and experience or because they use the same resources.[22] For example, engineers are grouped together in a function because they perform the same tasks and use the same skills or equipment. Figure 8.3 shows a typical functional structure. Here, each of the triangles represents a different functional specialization — manufacturing, marketing, research and development, and so on — and each function concentrates on its own task specialization.

The functional structure has several advantages. First, if people who perform similar tasks are grouped together, they can learn from one another and

FIGURE 8.3   **Functional structure**

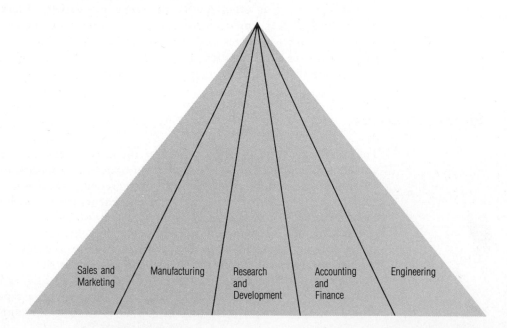

Sales and Marketing   Manufacturing   Research and Development   Accounting and Finance   Engineering

become better at what they do, that is, more specialized and productive. Second, they can monitor one another and make sure others are doing their tasks effectively and not shirking their responsibilities. As a result, the work process becomes more efficient, reducing costs and increasing operational flexibility.

The other important advantage of the functional structure derives from its ability to give managers more control of organizational activities. As already noted many difficulties arise when the number of levels in the hierarchy increases. However, if you group people into different functions, each with its own managers, then *several different hierarchies* are created, and the company can avoid becoming too tall. For example, there will be one hierarchy in manufacturing and others in sales and finance. It is much easier to manage the business when different groups specialize in different organizational tasks and are managed separately.

In adopting a functional structure, a company increases its level of horizontal differentiation in order to handle more complex task requirements. The structure allows it to keep control of its activities as it grows. This structure serves the company well until it begins to grow and diversify. If the company becomes very diverse geographically and begins operating in many locations or if it starts producing a wide range of products, control problems arise. Specifically, **control loss** problems develop in the functional structure, and the company is no longer able to coordinate its activities.[23]

Problems with a Functional Structure

Communications problems   As functional hierarchies evolve, functions grow more remote from one another. As a result, it becomes increasingly difficult to communicate across functions to implement strategy. This communication problem stems from **functional orientations**.[24] With increasing differentiation, the various functions develop different orientations to the problems and issues facing the organization. Different functions have different time or goal orientations. Some functions, like manufacturing, see things in a short time framework and are concerned with achieving short-run goals, such as reducing manufacturing costs. Others, like research and development, see things from a long-term point of view, and their goals (that is, product development) may have a time horizon of several years. Moreover, different functions may have different interpersonal orientations—a further impediment to good communication. As a result of all these factors, each function may develop a different view of the strategic issues facing the company. For example, manufacturing may see the problem as the need to reduce costs, while sales may see it as the need to increase responsiveness to customer needs and research and development as the need to introduce new products. In such cases, the functions find it difficult to communicate and coordinate with one another, and implementation suffers.

Measurement problems As the number of its products proliferates, a company may find it difficult to measure the contributions of one or a group of products to its overall profitability. Consequently, the company may be turning out some unprofitable products without realizing it and may also be making poor decisions on resource allocation. In essence, the company's measurement systems are not complex enough to serve its needs.

Location problems Location factors may also hamper coordination and control. If a company is producing or selling in many different regional areas, then the centralized system of control provided by the functional structure no longer suits it, since managers in the various regions must be flexible enough to respond to the needs of these regions. Thus the functional structure is not complex enough to handle regional diversity.

Strategic problems Sometimes the combined effect of all these factors is that long-term strategic considerations are ignored because management is preoccupied with solving communication and coordination problems. As a result, a company may lose direction and fail to take advantage of new opportunities.

Experiencing these problems is a sign that the company does not have an appropriate level of differentiation to achieve its objectives. It must change its mix of vertical and horizontal differentiation to accommodate more complex organizational tasks. To this end, many companies reorganize to a product or geographical structure.

Product or Geographical Structure

In the product or geographical structure, activities are grouped either by product lines or by geographical location. In the product structure, the production function is broken down into different product lines based on the similarities and differences among the products. Figure 8.4 presents a product structure typical of a drug or pharmaceutical company. In this company, products are grouped in terms of their being wet drugs, dry drugs, or powders. Inside each product group, there may be many similar products manufactured.

Since three different product groupings now exist, the degree of horizontal differentiation in this structure is higher than in the functional structure. The specialized support functions, such as accounting or sales, are centralized at the top of the organization, but each support function is divided in such a way that personnel tend to specialize in one of the different product categories, so as to avoid communication problems. Thus there may be three groups of accountants, one for each of the three product categories. In sales, separate sales forces dealing with the different product lines may emerge, but because a single sales function brings economies of scale to selling and distribution, these groups will coordinate their activities. Unisys Corporation, for example, recently moved to

FIGURE 8.4   **Product or geographical structure**

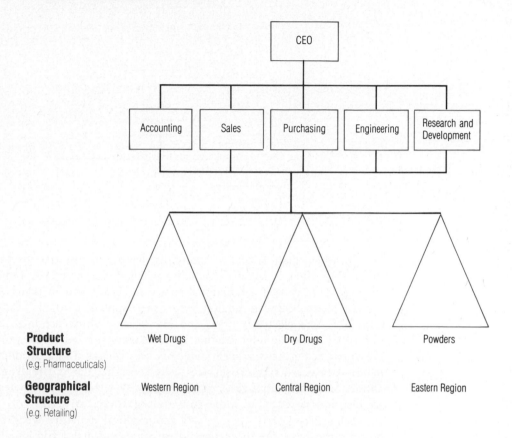

**Product
Structure**
(e.g. Pharmaceuticals)

**Geographical
Structure**
(e.g. Retailing)

a product structure based on serving the product needs of different customer groups, for instance, the commercial and the public sector. Unisys's salespeople specialize in one customer group, but all groups coordinate their sales and software activities to ensure good communication and the transfer of knowledge among product lines.

The use of a product structure, then, reduces the problems of control and communication associated with the functional structure. It pushes aside barriers among functions because the product line, rather than each individual function, becomes the focus of attention. In addition, the profit contribution of each product line can be clearly identified, and resources can be allocated more efficiently. Note also that this structure has one more level in the hierarchy than the functional structure — that of the product line manager. This increase in vertical differentiation allows managers at the level of the production line to concentrate on day-to-day operations and gives top managers more time to take a longer-term look at business opportunities.

FIGURE 8.5   **Maytag's product structure**

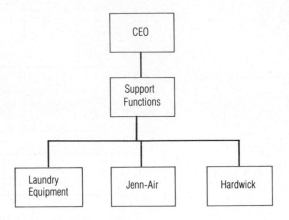

Another example of a company that adopted a product structure to manage its product lines is Maytag. Initially, when it manufactured only washers and dryers, Maytag used a functional structure. However, in trying to increase its market share, Maytag bought two other appliance manufacturers, Jenn-Air, known for its electric ranges, and Hardwick, which produces gas ranges. In order to handle the new product lines, Maytag moved to the product structure presented in Figure 8.5. Each company was operated as a product line, and the major specialized support services were centralized as in the drug company example. Maytag continued to diversify, however, and, as you will see in the next section, it was forced to move to a multidivisional structure.

When a company operates as a geographical structure, geographical regions become the basis for the grouping of organizational activities. Thus the three parts in Figure 8.5 might be named Western Region, Central Region and Eastern Region. The same range of products are manufactured in each region. Like a product structure, a geographical structure provides more control than a functional structure because there are essentially three regional hierarchies carrying out the work previously performed by a single centralized hierarchy. A company like Federal Express clearly needs to operate a geographical structure to fulfill its corporate goal—next-day mail. Large merchandising organizations, such as Neiman-Marcus, also moved to a geographic structure soon after they started building stores across the country. With a geographical structure, different regional clothing needs—sun wear in the West, down coats in the East—can be handled as required. At the same time, since the purchasing function remains centralized, one central organization can buy for all regions. Thus a company both achieves economies of scale in buying and distribution and reduces coordination and communication problems.

Once again, however, the usefulness of the product or geographical structure depends on the size of the company and its range of products and regions.

If a company starts to diversify into unrelated products or to integrate vertically into new industries, the product structure would not be capable of handling the increased diversity. The reason is that it does not provide managers with enough control over organizational activities to allow them to manage the company effectively; it is not complex enough to deal with the needs of the large, multibusiness company. At this point in its development, a company would normally adopt the multidivisional structure.

Multidivisional Structure

The multidivisional structure possesses two main innovations that let a company grow and diversify while overcoming control loss problems. First, each distinct product line or business unit is placed in its *own self-contained unit or division with all support functions.* For example, Pepsi-Cola has three major divisions, the soft drinks, snack foods, and restaurant divisions, and each division has its own marketing, research and development, and other functions. The result is a higher level of horizontal differentiation. Second, the office of corporate headquarters' staff is created to monitor interdivisional activities and to exercise financial control over each of the divisions.[25] This staff contains corporate managers who oversee all divisional and functional activities, and it constitutes an additional level in the organizational hierarchy. Hence there is a higher level of vertical differentiation in a multidivisional structure than in a product structure. Figure 8.6 presents a typical divisional structure found in a large chemical company, such as Du Pont. Although this company might easily have seventy operating divisions, only three — the oil, drugs, and plastics divisions — are represented here.

As a self-contained business unit, each division possesses a full array of support services. That is, each has a self-contained accounting, sales, and personnel department, etc. Each division functions as a profit center, making it much easier for corporate headquarters staff to monitor and evaluate the activities of each.[26]

Each division is also able to adopt the structure that best suits its needs. Thus Figure 8.6 shows the oil division as having a functional structure because its activities are very standardized, whereas the drug division has a product structure for reasons discussed earlier. The third division, the plastics, has a matrix structure, a structure that is discussed in detail below. Similarly, General Motors operates the whole corporation through a multidivisional structure, but each auto division operates a product structure, where product lines are based on the type of auto produced.

Going back to the Maytag example noted earlier, we mentioned that Maytag continued to diversify its operations. It purchased two more appliance manufacturers, Magic Chef Company, which produces a wide variety of air conditioners and refrigerators, and Toastmaster Inc., a maker of small appliances. Management originally intended to operate the businesses as product lines through a product structure but soon realized that it would be infeasible to

FIGURE 8.6   **Multidivisional structure**

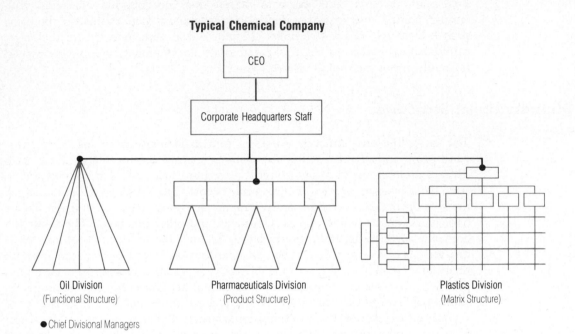

Typical Chemical Company

Oil Division
(Functional Structure)

Pharmaceuticals Division
(Product Structure)

Plastics Division
(Matrix Structure)

● Chief Divisional Managers

market several different brands in every category of the appliance industry with centralized support services.[27] Therefore the company reorganized to a multidivisional structure, utilizing three autonomous divisions, each of which was given its own support functions. Then, within each division, a product structure was used. This was a very efficient change in structure. Figure 8.7 shows the present structure.

In the multidivisional structure, day-to-day operations of a division are the responsibility of divisional management; that is, divisional management has **operating responsibility.** However, corporate headquarters staff, which includes members of the board of directors, as well as top executives, is responsible for overseeing long-term plans and providing the guidance for interdivisional projects. This staff has **strategic responsibility.** Such a combination of self-contained divisions with a centralized corporate management represents a higher level of both vertical and horizontal differentiation, as we noted earlier. These two innovations provide the extra control necessary to manage growth and diversification. Because this structure is now adopted by 60 percent of all large U.S. corporations, we need to consider its advantages and disadvantages in more detail.

FIGURE 8.7   Maytag's multidivisional structure

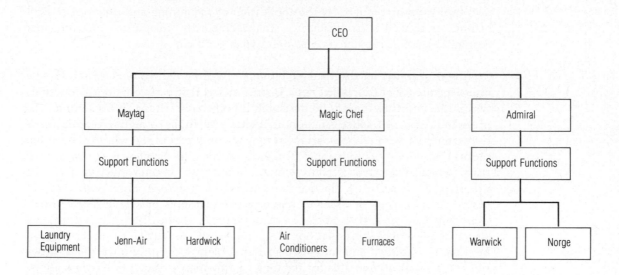

Advantages of the Multidivisional Structure

Enhanced corporate financial control   The profitability of different business divisions is clearly visible in the multidivisional structure.[28] Because each division is its own profit center, financial controls can be applied to each business on the basis of profit criteria. Typically, this involves establishing targets, monitoring performance on a regular basis, and selectively intervening when problems arise. Corporate headquarters is also in a better position to allocate corporate financial resources among competing divisions. The new visibility of divisional performance also means that corporate headquarters can identify the divisions where investment of funds would yield the greatest long-term returns. In a sense, the corporate office is in a position to act as the investor or banker in an internal capital market, channeling funds to high-yield uses.

Enhanced strategic control   The new structure frees corporate staff from operating responsibilities. The staff thus gains time for contemplating wider strategic issues and for developing responses to environmental changes. The new structure also gives headquarters the proper information to perform strategic planning functions. For example, separating individual businesses is a necessary prerequisite for the application of portfolio planning techniques.

Growth   The new structure enables the company to overcome an organizational limit to its growth. By reducing information overload at the center, headquarters personnel can now handle a greater number of businesses. They can consider opportunities for further growth and diversification. Communication problems are reduced by the application of accounting and financial control techniques as well as by policies of "management by exception," meaning that corporate headquarters intervenes only when problems arise.

Stronger pursuit of internal efficiency   Within a functional structure, the interdependence of functional departments means that performance of functions within the company cannot be measured by objective criteria. For example, the profitability of the finance function, marketing function, or manufacturing function cannot be assessed in isolation, as they are only part of the whole. This often means that within the functional structure considerable degrees of organizational slack can go undetected. Resources might be absorbed in unproductive uses. For example, the head of the finance function might employ a larger staff than required for efficiency in order to reduce work pressures inside the department. Generally, a larger staff also brings a manager higher status. But since a divisional structure prescribes divisional operating autonomy, the divisions' efficiency can be directly observed and measured in terms of profit. Autonomy makes divisional managers accountable for their own performance; they can have no alibis. The general office is thus in a better position to identify inefficiencies.

A multidivisional structure then, has a number of powerful advantages. No doubt that is why this structure appears to be the preferred choice of most large diversified enterprises today. Indeed, research suggests that large business companies that adopt this structure outperform those that retain the functional structure.[29] But a multidivisional structure has its disadvantages as well. Good management can eliminate some of them, but others are inherent in the way the structure operates, and require constant attention. They are discussed in the next section.

Disadvantages of the Multidivisional Structure

Establishing the divisional–corporate authority relationship   The authority relationship between corporate headquarters and the divisions must be correctly established. The multidivisional structure introduces a new level in the hierarchy — the corporate level. The problem is to decide how much authority and control to assign to the operating divisions and how much authority to retain at corporate headquarters. This problem was first noted by Alfred Sloan, the founder of General Motors. He introduced the multidivisional structure into GM, which became the first company to adopt it.[30] It was he who created the familiar five-automobile divisions in GM — Oldsmobile, Buick, Pontiac, Chevrolet, and Cadillac. The problem he noted was that when headquarters retained too much power and authority, the operating divisions lacked sufficient autonomy to develop the business strategy that might best meet the needs of the division. However, when too much power was delegated to the divisions, then they pursued divisional objectives with little heed to the needs of the whole corporation. For example, all the potential gains from synergy discussed earlier would not be achieved. Thus the central issue in managing the multidivisional structure is *how much authority should be centralized at corporate headquarters and how much should be decentralized to the divisions?* This question has to be answered by each company in reference to the nature of its business and its corporate-level strategies. There are no easy answers, and over time, as the environment changes or the company alters its strategies, the balance between corporate and divisional control will also change.

Distortion of information If corporate headquarters puts too much emphasis on divisional return on investment, for instance, by setting very high and stringent ROI targets, divisional managers may choose *to distort the information they supply top management* and paint a very rosy picture of the present situation at the expense of future profits. That is, divisions may maximize short-run profits — perhaps by cutting research and product development or new investments or marketing expenditures. This may cost the company dearly in the future. The problem stems from too tight financial control. GM has suffered from this problem in recent years, as declining performance has made managers attempt to make their divisions look good to corporate headquarters. On the other hand, if the divisional level exerts too much control, powerful divisional managers may resist attempts to use their profits to strengthen other divisions and therefore disguise their performance. Thus managing the corporate-divisional interface involves coping with very subtle power issues.

Competition for resources The third problem of managing the divisional structure is that the *divisions themselves may compete for resources,* and this rivalry will prevent gains from synergy from emerging. For example, the pot of money that corporate personnel have to distribute to the divisions is fixed in size. Generally, the divisions that can demonstrate the highest ROI will get the lion's share of the money. But that large share strengthens them in the next time period, and so the strong divisions grow stonger. Consequently, divisions may actively compete for resources, and by doing so, reduce interdivisional coordination. For example, at Procter & Gamble, the struggle among divisions for resources has actually led to a loss in market share because resources had been inefficiently distributed due to competition.

Transfer pricing Divisional competition may also lead to battles over **transfer pricing.** As discussed in Chapter 7, one of the problems with vertical integration or related diversification is setting transfer prices between divisions. Rivalry among divisions increases the problem of setting fair prices. Each supplying division tries to set the highest price for its outputs to maximize its own ROI. Such competition can completely undermine the corporate culture and make the corporation a battleground. Many companies seem to have a history of competition among divisions. Some, of course, may encourage competition, if managers believe that it leads to maximum performance.

Operations costs   Since each division possesses its own specialized functions, such as finance or research and development, these structures are very expensive to run and manage. Research and development is especially costly, and so some companies centralize such functions at the corporate level to serve all divisions, as is done in the product structure. The duplication of specialist services, however, is not a problem if the gains from having separate specialist functions outweigh the costs. Again, management must decide if duplication is financially justified. Activities are often centralized in times of downturn or recession — particularly advisory services and planning functions. Divisions, however, are retained as profit centers.

The advantages of divisional structures must be balanced against their disadvantages, but, as already noted, the disadvantages can be managed by an observant, professional management team that is aware of the issues involved. The fact that this structure is the dominant one today clearly suggests its usefulness as the means of managing the multibusiness corporation.

Strategic Business Unit (SBU) Structure

As corporations have grown and developed, new variants of the multidivisional structure have emerged. The increased size of many companies has resulted in the use of a structure with an even higher level of horizontal differentiation: the strategic business unit structure (SBU). When a company has 200 to 300 different divisions, as in the case of Beatrice Foods Company or General Electric, corporate management finds it almost impossible to retain control over the organization. As noted earlier, problems of information overload at the center can emerge, and with 300 divisions to control, corporate staff may not have the time to examine the operations of each division very thoroughly.

To simplify this control problem, the organizational response has been to introduce yet another level in the hierarchy and to split up the company into groups of divisions operating in similar areas. The idea is to group divisions together in order to realize synergies among them. Typically, these groups are referred to as strategic business units (SBUs), and each SBU is controlled by an SBU headquarters staff. Each SBU, as well as each division inside each SBU, becomes a profit center, and it is the SBU headquarters staff's job to maximize the profitability of its SBU. For example, in Beatrice Foods, one strategic business group comprises all the divisions that produce in the food industry, and another all those in the consumer products industry; each SBU is operated independently and evaluated separately.

As originally conceived, the role of the SBU office is to control the divisions inside the SBU and allocate resources among them. The role of corporate headquarters thus becomes to control the SBUs and allocate resources among them. As a result the corporation becomes more manageable. However, SBUs are not ideal solutions, and the arguments for and against their creation are similar to those for the multidivisional structure.

On the positive side, SBUs do reduce the work of corporate personnel by decreasing the span of control to a manageable level and permitting the decentralization of authority. Moreover, the SBU structure can provide an effective integrating device for coordinating the needs of companies inside a group. SBU personnel are more in touch with the needs and interests of those companies than a corporate office is likely to be. They are able to promote gains from synergy between companies in their group.

On the down side, since the corporate office is now more remote, it can lose touch with individual operating divisions inside an SBU because the SBU structure intervenes between it and the operating divisions. Corporate staff may not realize the seriousness of divisional problems until it is too late for counteractive measures. Besides, conflicts of interest may arise between the SBU and the corporate staff over funds for development. For example, using the BCG matrix, the corporate office may define the SBU as a *dog* and limit its access to corporate capital. However, the SBU may also contain a *star* business, which would now be starved for cash. If the SBU staff starts challenging the authority of corporate staff, that would further weaken integration and accountability. Finally, the introduction of the SBU level in the organizational hierarchy may slow down information transfers and communication and reduce the flexibility of the company as a whole.

On balance, then, it appears that the usefulness of this structure depends on the strategy with which the company is operating. The SBU structure is only appropriate for the companies that can group their divisions into separate, distinct categories, so that the benefits of this form of structure can be exploited. Such companies are likely to be related diversifiers.

Conglomerate Structure

The conglomerate structure is the other main variant of the multidivisional form.[31] Whereas the SBU structure works best when commonalities link the various divisions or businesses in the company's portfolio, the conglomerate structure is used when there are *no commonalities among divisions*. The conglomerate form functions as a holding company, and *each* division is evaluated as a totally autonomous profit center. Textron is a good example of a company that pursues unrelated diversification and uses a conglomerate structure. The role of the corporate staff in a conglomerate structure is purely to perform portfolio analyses of the company's businesses. Decisions to acquire or divest businesses are linked to the goal of maximizing the profitability of the *corporate portfolio*. In contrast to the ordinary multidivisional or SBU structure, here problems of control and communication are at a minimum, since the corporate staff makes no attempt to intervene in divisional strategy. This structure is therefore very economical to manage because, even if the corporate staff does control 300 businesses, the same portfolio matrix techniques can be applied to each business. For example, American Express Company operates its divisions very loosely and treats its businesses as autonomous and self-financing fund generators. American Express believes that to attract able managers, its divisions must be given independence, and management views the divisions as "players" and the parent company as "referee." Corporate headquarters is active, however, in setting objectives, reviewing performance, and allocating capital to divisions.

Matrix Structure

A matrix structure differs from the structures discussed so far in that the matrix is based on two forms of horizontal differentiation rather than on one, as in the functional or product structure.[32] In the usual matrix design, on the vertical axis activities are grouped by *function,* so that we get a familiar differentiation of tasks into functions such as production, research and development, and engineering. However, superimposed on this vertical pattern is a horizontal pattern based on differentiation by *product or project*. The result is a complex network of reporting relationships among projects and functions, as depicted in Figure 8.8.

This structure also employs an unusual kind of vertical differentiation. Although matrix structures are flat, with few hierarchical levels, employees inside the matrix have two bosses: a **functional boss,** who is the head of a function, and a **project boss,** who is responsible for managing the individual projects. Employees work in a project team with specialists from other functions and report to the project boss on project matters and the functional boss on matters relating to functional issues. These employees are called **subproject managers** and are responsible for managing coordination and communication among the functions and projects.

Matrix structures were first developed by companies in high technology industries like aerospace and electronics — by companies such as TRW Information Services and Apple Computer. These companies were developing radically new products in uncertain, competitive environments, where speed of product development was the crucial consideration. They needed a structure that could respond to this strategy, but existing functional and product structures were too inflexible to allow the complex role and task interactions necessary to meet new product development requirements. Moreover, employees in these companies tend to be very highly qualified, professional employees who perform best in autonomous, flexible working conditions, and the matrix structure provides such conditions. For example, this structure requires a minimum of direct hierarchical control by supervisors. Employees control their own behavior, and participation in project teams allows them to monitor other team members and

FIGURE 8.8   **Matrix structure**

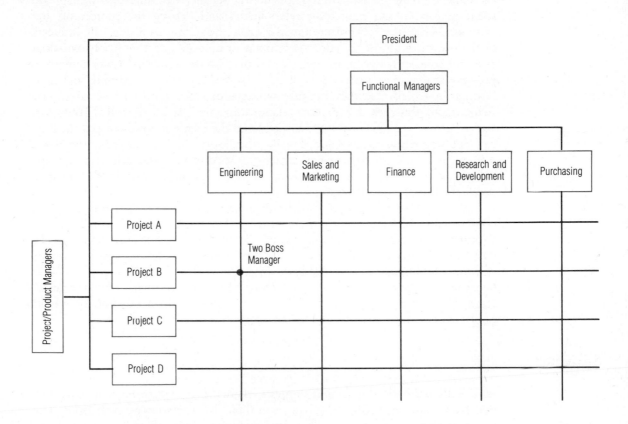

learn from each another. A further advantage on the employee dimension is that, as the project goes through its different phases, different specialists from the various functions are required. Thus, for example, at the first stage the services of research and development specialists may be needed, and then at the next stage there will be a need for engineers and marketing specialists to make cost and marketing projections. As the demand for the type of specialist changes, employees can be moved to other projects that need their services. As a result, the matrix structure can make maximum use of employee skills as existing projects are completed and new ones come into existence. Finally, the freedom given by the matrix not only provides the autonomy to motivate employees; but also leaves top management free to concentrate on strategic issues, since they do not have to become involved in operating matters. On all these counts, the matrix is an excellent tool for creating the flexibility necessary for quick reactions to competitive conditions.

There are disadvantages to the matrix, however.[33] First, it is expensive to operate compared with a functional structure. Employees tend to be highly skilled, and therefore both salaries and overheads are high. Second, the constant movement of employees around the matrix means that time and money are spent in establishing new team relationships and getting the project off the ground. Third, the subproject manager's role, balancing as it does the interests of the project with the function, is difficult to manage and care has to be taken to avoid conflict between functions and projects over resources. Over time, it is possible that project managers will take the leading role in planning and goal setting, in which case the structure works more like a product or divisional structure. If function and project relationships are left uncontrolled, they can lead to power struggles among managers and the result is not increased flexibility, but stagnation and decline. Finally, the larger the organization, the more difficult it is to operate a matrix structure, because task and role relationships become very complex. In such cases, the only option may be to change to a product or divisional structure.

Given these advantages and disadvantages, the matrix is generally used only when a company's strategy warrants it. There is no point in using a more complex structure than necessary because it will only cost more to manage. In dynamic product/market environments, the benefits of the matrix in terms of flexibility and innovation are likely to exceed the extra cost of using it, and so it becomes an appropriate choice of structure. However, companies in the mature stage of the industry life cycle or those pursuing a low-cost strategy would rarely choose this structure. We discuss it further in Chapter 10.

Summary

As the discussion in this section suggests, there are a large number of structures that firms can adopt to match changes in their size and strategy over time. The structure that a firm selects will be the one whose logic of grouping activities, that is, its form of horizontal differentiation best meets the needs of the firm's business or businesses. What the firm must do is to match its form of horizontal differentiation to vertical differentiation. That is, it must choose a structure and then make choices about levels in the hierarchy and degree of centralization or decentralization. It is the combination of both kinds of differentiation which produce its internal organizational arrangements. However, as noted above, once the firm has divided itself into parts it must then integrate itself. This is discussed in the next chapter.

8.6 GLOBAL CONSIDERATIONS

So far, in examining the choice of organizational structure, we have not discussed the global dimension. However, in earlier chapters we noted how most large companies have an international, or global, dimension to their strategy because they produce and sell their products in international markets. For example, Procter & Gamble, and food companies like Heinz, Kellogg Co., and Nestle Company Inc. have production operations throughout the world, as do the large auto companies and computer makers. In this section, we examine how the need to manage foreign operations affects a company's choice of structure and how a company will change its structure as it expands internationally.

In general, the choice of structure for managing a global business is a function of two factors. The first is the need to choose a level of vertical differentiation that provides effective supervision of foreign operations. Companies operating in international markets must create a hierarchy of authority that clarifies the responsibilities of domestic management for handling the sale of products abroad and also allocates responsibility for foreign operations between domestic *and* foreign management. Second, such companies must choose a level of horizontal differentiation that groups foreign operation tasks with domestic operations in a way that allows the company to market its products abroad and serve the needs of foreign customers in the most effective way. In practice, a company's choice of structure is a function of the complexity and the extent of its foreign operations.

When a company sells only domestically made products in foreign markets, problems of coordinating foreign and domestic operations are minimal. Companies like Mercedes-Benz or Jaguar, for example, make no attempt to produce in the foreign market; rather they sell or distribute their domestic products internationally. Such companies usually just add a **foreign operations department** to their existing structure. If a company is using a functional structure, this department has the responsibility for coordinating manufacturing, sales, and research and development activities according to the needs of the foreign market. In the foreign country, the company usually establishes a subsidiary to deal with sales and distribution. For example, Mercedes-Benz's foreign subsidiaries have the responsibility for allocating dealerships, organizing supplies of spare parts, and, of course, selling cars.

A company with many different products or businesses operating from a multidivisional structure has a more serious coordination problem: to coordinate the flow of different products across different countries. In order to manage these transfers, many companies create an **international division,** which they add to their existing divisional structure.[34] International operations are managed as a separate divisional business whose managers are given the authority and responsibility for coordinating domestic product divisions and foreign markets. The international division also controls the foreign subsidiaries that market the products and decides how much authority to delegate to foreign management. This arrangement permits the company to handle more complex foreign operations.

The next level of complexity arises when companies establish **foreign subsidiaries** to produce goods and services abroad. In terms of vertical differentiation, the problem for the company is how to allocate responsibility for foreign operations between management in the United States and management in the foreign country. Clearly, the lines of communication and chain of command lengthen in managing foreign production operations. The company has to maintain control of the strategy of the foreign subsidiary while giving the management of the foreign branch the flexibility it needs to deal with its own unique situation. Because strategic managers are much farther away from the scene of operations, it makes sense to decentralize control and grant decision-making authority to managers in the foreign operations. Many companies adopt the policy of creating autonomous foreign operating divisions, which, like home divisions, are evaluated on the basis of their rate of return. Chrysler and GM both did just that when they moved into Europe and began developing, producing, and marketing cars to suit Europeans' particular needs.

When synergies can be obtained from cooperation between a company's home divisions and its autonomous foreign subsidiaries, a structure to exploit these synergies must be chosen. One solution lies in grouping foreign subsidiaries into world regions; the domestic divisions then coordinate with world regions rather than with individual subsidiaries. For example, when a company makes and sells the same products in many different markets, it often groups its foreign subsidiaries into world regions to simplify the coordination of products across countries; Europe might be one region, the Pacific Basin another, and the Middle East a third. This sort of grouping across world markets results in **a global SBU structure** where subsidiaries inside each SBU are grouped together on the basis of geographical region. This allows synergies from dealing with broadly similar cultures to be obtained. For example, consumer preferences regarding product design and marketing are likely to be more similar among countries in one world region than among countries in different world regions.

Sometimes the potential gains from sharing product, marketing or research and development knowledge between home and foreign operations are so great that companies adopt a **global matrix structure** for organizing their international activities. Such a structure appears in Figure 8.9. The figure represents the structure adopted by a large chemical company like Du Pont. On the vertical axis, instead of functions, are the company's *product divisions,* which provide product and marketing information to the foreign subsidiaries. For example, these might be the petroleum, plastics, drug, or fertilizer divisions. On the horizontal axis are the company's foreign subsidiaries in the various *countries* or *world regions* in which it operates. Managers in the foreign subsidiary control foreign operations and report to divisional personnel back in the United States. They are also responsible, together with U.S. divisional personnel, for sharing marketing or research and development information to achieve gains from synergies. This structure therefore both provides a great deal of local flexibility and gives divisional personnel in the United States considerable access to information about local affairs. Additionally, the matrix form allows knowledge and experience to be transferred among geographical regions and among divisions and regions. Club Med Inc. exploits these synergies to the full in the way it manages its holiday resorts. The matrix also allows each home division to rationalize (i.e.

FIGURE 8.9   A multinational matrix structure

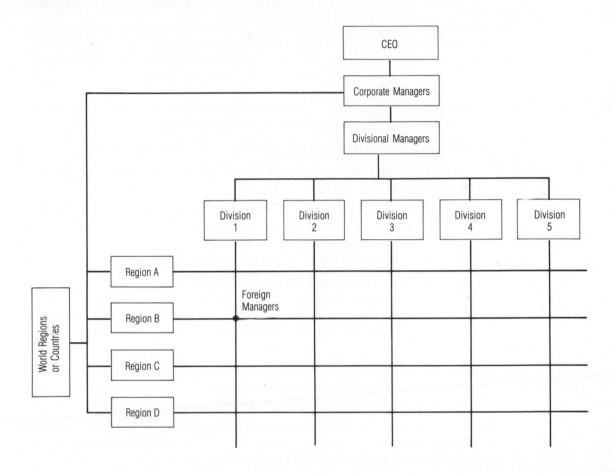

balance) production so that, for example, a lack of demand in one world region can be compensated by increased demand in another. Philip Morris does this with cigarettes. Slumping demand in the United States is countered by supplying regions where cigarette sales are expanding. Similarly, Japanese car manufacturers plan their international strategy to compensate for import restrictions or currency changes in the world market.

Most large companies have a global component in their organizational structures. The issue with multinational companies, as with all others, is to adopt the structure that best meets the needs of their strategy. The need to implement multinational strategy successfully has put an increasing burden on corporate managers to design the company's structure to respond to the challenges of the world market.

8.7 SUMMARY OF CHAPTER

This chapter has introduced the issues involved in designing a structure to meet the needs of a company's strategy. The reasons that Apple changed its structure over time and the problems that can arise when companies make such changes should now be clear. We have stressed the following points:

1. Implementing a strategy successfully depends on selecting the right structure and control system to match a company's strategy.

2. The basic tool of strategy implementation is organizational design.

3. Differentiation and integration are the two design concepts that decide how a structure will work.

4. Differentiation has two aspects: (a) vertical differentiation, which refers to how a company chooses to allocate its decision-making authority; and (b) horizontal differentiation, which refers to the way that a company groups organizational activities into functions or departments or divisions.

5. The basic choice in vertical differentiation is whether to have a flat or a tall structure. Very tall hierarchies have a number of disadvantages, such as problems with communication, information transfer, motivation, and cost. However, the decentralization or delegation of authority can solve some of these problems.

6. The structures that a company can adopt as it grows and diversifies include the functional, product, and multidivisional forms. Each structure has advantages and disadvantages associated with it.

7. Other specialized kinds of structures include the matrix, conglomerate, and Strategic Business Unit (SBU) forms. Each has a specialized use, and to be chosen, must match the needs of the organization.

8. As companies grow and enter foreign markets, multinational considerations affect their choice of structure. Consequently, companies develop foreign divisions to operate in these markets. When there are gains to be derived from synergy, companies often adopt a global matrix form to trade knowledge and expertise.

Discussion Questions

1. What is the difference between vertical and horizontal differentiation? Rank the various structures discussed in this chapter along these two dimensions.

2. What kind of structure best describes the way this (a) business school and (b) university operates? Why is the structure appropriate? Would another structure fit better?

3. When would a company decide to change from a functional to a product structure and when from a product to a multidivisional structure?

4. When would a company choose a matrix structure and when a multinational matrix structure? What are the problems in managing these structures?

Endnotes

1. "Apple Computer, Inc.,-Background History," *Apple Computer, Inc.,* 1986.

2. "Apple takes on its Biggest Test Yet," *Business Week,* January 31, 1983, p. 79.

3. Bro Uttal, "Behind the Fall of Steve Jobs," *Fortune,* August 5, 1985, pp. 20–24.

4. J. R. Galbraith, *Designing Complex Organizations* (Reading, Mass.: Addison-Wesley, 1973).

5. J. Child, *Organization: A Guide for Managers and Administrators* (New York: Harper & Row, 1977), pp. 50–72.

6. R. H. Miles, *Macro Organizational Behavior* (Santa Monica, Calif.: Goodyear, 1980), pp. 19–20.

7. Galbraith, *Designing Complex Organizations.*

8. V. A. Graicunas, "Relationship in organization," in *Papers on the Science of Administration,* ed. L. Gulick and L. Urwick, (New York: Institute of Public Administration, 1937), pp. 181–185; J. C. Worthy, "Organizational Structure and Company Morale," *American Sociological Review,* 15 (1950), 169–179.

9. Child, *Organization,* pp. 50–52.

10. G. R. Jones, "Organization-Client Transactions and Organizational Governance Structures," *Academy of Management Journal,* 30 (1987), 197–218.

11. H. Mintzberg, *The Structuring of Organizations* (Englewood Cliffs, N. J.: Prentice-Hall, 1979), p. 435.

12. Child, *Organizations,* p. 51.

13. R. Carzo Jr. and J. N. Yanousas, "Effects of Flat and Tall Organization Structure," *Administrative Science Quarterly,* 14 (1969), 178–191.

14. A. Gupta and V. Govindarajan, "Business Unit Strategy, Managerial Characteristics, and Business Unit Effectiveness at Strategy Implementation," *Academy of Management Journal,* 27 (1984), 25–41. R. T. Lenz, "Determinants of Organizational Performance: An Interdisciplinary Review," *Strategic Management Journal,* 2 (1981), 131–154.

15. W. H. Wagel, "Keeping the Organization Lean at Federal Express," *Personnel* (March 1984), 4.

16. J. Koter, "For P&G Rivals, the New Game is to Beat the Leader, Not Copy It," *Wall Street Journal,* May 6, 1985, p. 35.

17. G. R. Jones, "Task Visibility, Free Riding and Shirking: Explaining the Effect of Organization Structure on Employee Behavior," *Academy of Management Review,* 4 (1984), 684–695.

18. "Operation Turnaround — How Westinghouse's New Chairman Plans to Fire Up An Old Line Company," *Business Week,* December 14, 1983, pp. 124–133.

19. R. L. Daft, *Organizational Theory and Design,* 2nd ed. (St. Paul, Minn.: West, 1986), p. 215.

20. Alfred D. Chandler, *Strategy and Structure* (Cambridge, Mass.: MIT Press, 1962).

21. The discussion draws heavily on Chandler, *Strategy and Structure,* and B. R. Scott, "Stages of Development," (Cambridge, Mass.: Intercollegiate Clearing House, Harvard Business School, 1971).

22. J. R. Galbraith and R. K. Kazanjian, *Strategy Implementation: Structure System and Process,* 2nd. ed. (St. Paul, Minn.: West, 1986); Child, *Organization;* R. Duncan, "What is the right organization structure," *Organizational Dynamics* (Winter 1979), 59–80.

23. O. E. Williamson, *Markets and Hierarchies: Analysis and Antitrust Implications* (New York: Free Press, 1975).

24. P. R. Lawrence and J. Lorsch, *Organization and Environment* (Boston: Division of Research, Harvard Business School, 1967).

25. Chandler, *Strategy and Structure;* Williamson, *Markets and Hierarchies;* L. Wrigley, "Divisional Autonomy and Diversification," Ph.D. dissertation, Harvard Business School, 1970.

26. R. P. Rumelt, *Strategy, Structure, and Economic Performance* (Boston: Division of Research, Harvard Business School, 1974; Scott, *Stages of Corporate Development;* Williamson, *Markets and Hierarchies.*

27. *Business Week,* February 16, 1987.

28. The discussion draws on each of the sources cited in endnotes 20–27, and also on G. R. Jones and C. W. L. Hill, "Transaction Cost Analysis of Strategy-Structure Choice," *Strategic Management Journal,* 9 (1988), pp. 159–172.

29. H. O. Armour and D. J. Teece, "Organizational Structure and Economic Performance: A Test of the Multidivisional Hypothesis," *Bell Journal of Economics,* 9 (1978), 106–122.

30. Alfred Sloan, *My Years at General Motors* (New York: Doubleday, 1983), Ch. 3.

31. N. A. Berg, "Strategic Planning in Conglomerate Companies," *Harvard Business Review,* 43 (1965), 79–92; K. N. M. Dundas and P. R. Richardson, "Implementing the Unrelated Product Strategy," *Strategic Management Journal,* 3 (1982), 287–301.

32. S. M. Davis and P. R. Lawrence, *Matrix* (Reading, Mass.: Addison-Wesley, 1977); J. R. Galbraith, "Matrix Organization Designs: How to Combine Functional and Project Forms," *Business Horizons,* 14 (1971), 29–40.

33. R. Duncan, "What is the Right Organizational Structure?," *Organizational Dynamics* (Winter 1979), pp. 59–80; S. M. Davis and P. R. Lawrence, *Matrix.*

34. J. Stopford and L. Wells, *Managing the Multinational Enterprise* (London: Longmans, 1972).

Chapter 9

Choosing
Integration
and Control
Systems

9.1 OPENING INCIDENT: TRW

TRW Information Services, one of America's most successful high tech companies, was heavily involved in the ICBM research program and has continued to be a leader in electronics, defense, and space program development. It was one of the first companies to introduce the matrix structure as a means of coordinating and integrating its complex and constantly changing product lines. To make the matrix structure work, TRW also adopted a variety of integration and control systems to encourage high performance and to increase the level of coordination between functions. First, it relied heavily on the recruitment and selection of highly skilled, professional employees with strong internal motivation to perform.[1] Second, it established project teams in which employees were able to work and integrate with employees in other functions. In addition, TRW

reinforced employee commitment to high performance by avoiding employee layoffs and by developing a decentralized, freewheeling organization culture that rewarded risk taking, innovation, and creativity. Its innovative strategic organization design brought TRW huge success. It grew from a $500,000 company in 1965 to one valued at over $6 billion in 1988.[2]

With rapid growth, however, came some major problems. Each project group inside its matrix structure developed into a full-fledged division within a multidivisional structure. As a result, integration among divisions dissipated, and the kind of controls that the company could use when it was small and decentralized no longer suited a high tech giant. In fact, the company was running into the very integration problems that it had sought to avoid by developing a matrix structure. The various divisions in TRW—defense, electronics, and automotive products—were not cooperating with one another and were sharing their research and development know-how less and less. Actually, they were competing.[3] This was an enormous problem for a company that depended on technological advances for its future growth and success.

The reason for the lack of integration was that divisional managers were saying, "Why should I spend billions of dollars investing in research for my own product lines and then this other division can just come along and get the knowledge free and apply it to its own products: especially when I am evaluated on bottom line performance?" In other words, divisions were competing rather than cooperating because the old kind of controls used by TRW were no longer appropriate, and the company had not yet developed a new set of controls to coordinate its new organizational structure. Rube Mettler, TRW's chairman, faced the problem of finding new ways to integrate divisions and new control systems that would encourage cooperation among them and prepare the corporation for future growth.

TRW attempted to improve integration by introducing new types of incentive schemes to stimulate cooperation rather than competition. For example, divisional managers' bonuses, promotions, and pay raises were linked to the results of cooperation among divisions. The company also developed a transfer pricing scheme that allowed divisions to charge a fair price for technology transferred to other divisions. In addition, to improve performance, it tried to develop a corporate culture based on cooperative corporate values rather than competitive divisional values. These efforts were just one part of TRW's overall control system, which also monitored costs, productivity, quality, and all the other indicators of organizational performance.

9.2 OVERVIEW

In the last chapter, we discussed the various kinds of structures available to companies when they implement their strategies. As the example of TRW suggests, here we consider the various kinds of integrating mechanisms and control systems that companies use to make these structures operate efficiently. **Integrating mechanisms** coordinate the various functions and divisions of the business. More complex structures require the use of more complex kinds of integrating mechanisms. Through **control systems,** organizations can monitor, evaluate, and change their performance. These systems provide information on how well a company's strategy is working and how well the structure used to implement the strategy is working. **Strategic control** is the process of selecting the types of controls at the corporate, business, and functional levels in a company that allow strategic managers to evaluate whether the company's strategy and structure are achieving organizational objectives.

We first take up the kinds of integrating mechanisms that companies can activate. Then we outline the process of strategic control and examine in detail the types of control that companies can use. These include market control, output control, bureaucratic control, and clan control and culture. Finally, we discuss how the design of reward systems is an important element of the strategic control process. In the next chapter, we consider in detail how to match organizational structure and control to corporate-, business-, and functional-level strategy.

9.3 INTEGRATION AND INTEGRATING MECHANISMS

Matching Differentiation with Integration

As discussed in Chapter 8, an organization must choose the appropriate form of differentiation to match its strategy. Greater diversification, for example, requires that a company move from a product structure to a divisional structure. Differentiation, however, is only the first design decision to be taken. The second one concerns the level of integration necessary to make the structure work effectively. Integration is defined as *the extent to which the organization seeks to coordinate the various activities of the organization and make them interdependent.* The design issue can be summed up very simply: the higher a company's level of differentiation (that is, the more complex its structure), the higher is the level of integration needed to make the structure perform effectively.[4] Thus, if a company adopts a more complex form of differentiation, it requires a more complex form of integration to accomplish its goals. For example, Federal Express needs an enormous amount of integration and coordination to allow it to fulfill its promise of delivering the mail the next day. It is renowned for its innovative use of integrating mechanisms, such as customer liaison personnel, to manage its transactions quickly and efficiently. Similarly, if managers adopt a multidivisional structure to manage a strategy of related diversification, they must establish means to integrate across divisions to achieve the gains from synergy. Take the problem facing Texas Air, the nation's biggest airline company. Its acquisition of Eastern Airlines, People Express, and New York Air doubled its size, and integrating these airlines with Continental caused enormous problems for the company. It is still in the process of selecting integrating mechanisms to coordinate the airlines.

Forms of Integrating Mechanism

Jay R. Galbraith, a prominent management theorist, has identified a series of integration mechanisms that a company can use to increase its level of integration as its level of differentiation increases.[5] These mechanisms—on a continuum from simplest to most complex—are listed in Table 9.1 together with the examples of the individuals or groups that might perform these integrating roles.

Direct contact The aim behind establishing direct contact among managers is to set up a context within which managers from different divisions or functional

TABLE 9.1   **Types and examples of integrating mechanisms**

Direct contact	Sales and production managers
Liaison roles	Assistant sales and plant managers
Task forces	Representatives from sales, production, and research and development
Teams	Organizational executive committee
Integrating roles	Assistant vice president for strategic planning or vice president without portfolio
Integrating departments	Corporate headquarters staff
Matrix	All roles are integrating roles

departments can work together to solve mutual problems. However, as the TRW example suggests, there are several problems associated with establishing contact among managers in different functional departments or divisions. Managers from different functional departments have different subunit orientations but equal authority and so may tend to compete rather than cooperate when conflicts arise. For example, in a typical functional structure, the heads of each of the functions have equal authority; the nearest common point of authority is the CEO. Consequently, if disputes arise, there is no mechanism to resolve the conflicts apart from the authority of the boss. In fact, one sign of conflict in organizations is the number of problems sent up the hierarchy for managers above to solve. This wastes management time and effort, slows down strategic decision making, and makes it difficult to create a cooperative culture in the company. For this reason, companies choose more complex integrating mechanisms to coordinate interfunctional and divisional activities.

Interdepartmental liaison roles   A company can improve its interfunctional coordination through the mechanism of the interdepartmental liaison role. When the volume of contacts between two departments or functions increases, one of the ways of improving coordination is to give one person in *each* division or function the responsibility for coordinating with the other. These people may meet daily, weekly, monthly, or as needed. Figure 9.1a depicts the nature of the liaison role, the small circle representing the individual inside the functional department who has responsibility for coordinating with the other function. The responsibility for coordination is part of an individual's full-time job, but through these roles, a permanent relationship forms between the people involved, greatly easing strains between departments. Furthermore, it offers a way of transferring information across the organization—a very important factor in large, anonymous organizations, where people may know no one outside their immediate department.

FIGURE 9.1   **Forms of integrating mechanisms**

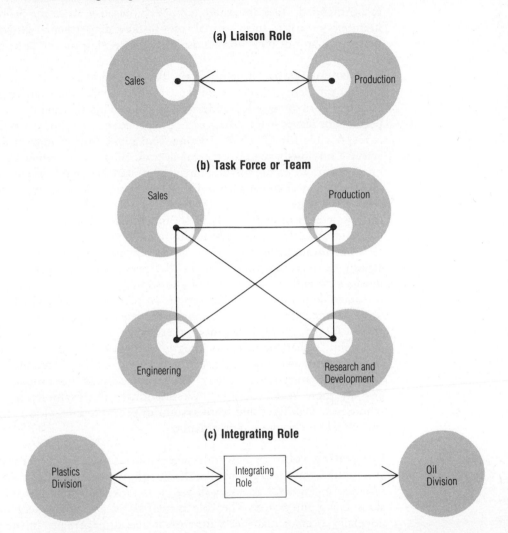

(a) Liaison Role

Sales — Production

(b) Task Force or Team

Sales   Production

Engineering   Research and Development

(c) Integrating Role

Plastics Division ⟷ Integrating Role ⟷ Oil Division

● Indicates manager with responsibility for integration

Temporary task forces   When more than two functions or divisions share common problems, then direct contact and liaison roles are of limited value because they do not provide enough coordination. The solution is to adopt a more complex form of integrating mechanism called a task force. The nature of the task force is represented diagrammatically in Figure 9.1b. One member of each function or division is assigned to a task force created to solve a specific problem. Essentially, task forces are *ad hoc committees,* and members are responsible for reporting back to their departments on the issues addressed and solutions recommended. Task forces are temporary because, once the problem is solved, members return to their normal roles in their departments. However, they also perform many of their normal duties while serving on the task force.

Permanent teams   In many cases, the issues addressed by a task force are recurring problems. To deal with these problems effectively, an organization must establish permanent integrating mechanisms. This is when the company creates permanent teams — for instance, a new product development committee, which is responsible for the choice, design, and marketing of new products. Such an activity obviously requires a great deal of integration among functions, if new products are to be successfully introduced, and the establishment of a permanent integrating mechanism accomplishes this. Intel, for instance, emphasizes teamwork. It formed a council system based on some ninety cross-organizational groups, which meet regularly to set functional strategy in engineering, marketing, and other areas, and develop business-level strategy.

The importance of teams in the management of the organizational structure cannot be overemphasized. Essentially, permanent teams are the organization's *standing committees,* and much of the strategic direction of the organization is formulated in these meetings. For example, Henry Mintzberg, in a study of how the managers of corporations spend their time discovered that they spend almost 60 percent of their time in these committees.[6] The reason is not bureaucracy, but rather the fact that integration is possible only in intensive, face-to-face sessions, where managers can understand others' viewpoints and develop a cohesive organizational strategy. The more complex the company, the more important these teams become. Westinghouse, for example, has established a whole new task force and team system to promote integration among divisions and improve corporate performance.

Integrating roles   A new role whose only function is to prompt integration among divisions or departments, the integrating role, is a full-time job. It is represented in Figure 9.1c. As you see, it is independent of the subunits or divisions being integrated. The role is staffed by an independent expert, who is normally a senior manager with a great deal of experience in the joint needs of the two departments. The job is to coordinate the decision process among departments or divisions to allow the synergetic gains from cooperation to be obtained. One study found that Du Pont had created 160 integrating roles in order to provide coordination among the different divisions of the company and improve corporate performance.[7] Once again, the more differentiated the company, the more common are these roles. Often people in these roles take the responsibility for chairing task forces and teams, and this provides additional integration.

Integrating departments   Sometimes the number of integrating roles becomes so high that a permanent integrating department is established at corporate headquarters. Normally, this occurs only in large, diversified corporations, which see the need for integration among divisions. This department consists mainly of strategic planners and may indeed be called the strategic planning department. Corporate headquarters staff in a divisional structure can also be viewed as an integrating department from the divisional perspective.

Matrix structure   Finally, when differentiation is very high and the company must be able to respond quickly to the environment, a matrix structure becomes the appropriate integrating device. The matrix contains many of the integrating mechanisms already discussed: the subproject managers integrate among functions and projects, and the matrix is built on the basis of temporary task forces.

Summary

It is clear that firms have a large number of options open to them when they increase their level of differentiation as a result of increased growth or diversification. The implementation issue is for managers to match differentiation with the level of integration to meet organizational objectives. Note that while too much differentiation and not enough integration will lead to failure of implementation, the converse is also true. That is, the combination of low differentiation and high integration will lead to an overcontrolled bureaucratized organization where flexibility and speed of response is reduced and not enhanced by the level of integration. Also, integration is very expensive for the firm because it raises management costs. For these reasons the goal is to decide on the optimum amount of integration necessary for meeting organizational goals and objectives. It is in this connection that strategic control becomes important because it allows managers to assess whether their integration mechanisms are coordinating their structures.

9.4 STRATEGY IMPLEMENTATION AND CONTROL

In the last chapter, we mentioned that implementation involves selecting the right combination of structure *and* control for achieving a company's strategy. Structure assigns people to tasks and roles (differentiation) and specifies how these are to be coordinated (integration). However, it does not of itself provide the mechanism through which people can be *motivated* to make the structure work. Hence the need for control. Put another way, management can develop *on paper* an elegant organization structure with the right integrating mechanisms, but only appropriate control systems will make this structure work. For example, in TRW, top management established a complex system of teams and integrating roles to link the various divisions in the company and solve the problem of cooperation. Although this seemed a good solution on paper, in practice, management found that different divisional teams were not cooperating because the company offered no rewards for cooperation. Top management had to establish a monitoring system to evaluate the divisions' attempts at cooperating with each other and also had to introduce rewards for cooperation. For a company like TRW, the right control system was vital for achieving the gains from synergy on which the company's dominance in the high tech field depends.

This example demonstrates that a structure will not work without the complex web of controls that allow a company to monitor, evaluate, and reward its parts—divisions, functions, and individual personnel. In the rest of this chapter, we discuss the various options open to companies in designing such a control system. First, however, we need to examine in more detail what a control system is.

9.5 STRATEGIC CONTROL SYSTEMS

Strategic control systems are the formal target-setting, monitoring, evaluation, and feedback systems that provide management with information about whether the organization's strategy and structure are meeting strategic performance objectives. An effective control system should have three characteristics: it should be *flexible enough* to allow managers to respond as necessary to unexpected events; it should provide *accurate* information, giving a true picture of organizational performance; and it should provide managers with the information in a *timely manner,* since making decisions on the basis of outdated information is a recipe for failure.[8] As Figure 9.2 shows, designing an effective strategic control system requires four steps.[9]

1. *Establish the standards or targets against which performance is to be evaluated.* The standards or targets that managers select are the ways in which a company chooses to evaluate its performance. Generally, these targets are derived from the strategy pursued by the company. For example, if a company is pursuing a low-cost strategy, then "reducing costs by 7 percent a year" might be a target. If the company is a service organization like McDonald's, its standards might include time targets for serving customers or guidelines for food quality.

2. *Create the measuring or monitoring systems that indicate whether the targets are being achieved.* The company establishes procedures for assessing whether work goals at all levels in the organization are being achieved. In many cases, measuring performance is a difficult task because the organization is engaged in many complex activities. For example, managers can measure quite easily how many customers their employees serve: they can count the number of receipts from the cash register. However, how can they judge how well their research and development department is doing when it may take five years for products to be developed? Or how can they measure the

FIGURE 9.2   **Steps in designing an effective control system**

Establish Standards and Targets

Create Measuring and Monitoring Systems

Compare Actual Performance Against
the Established Targets

Evaluate Result and Take Action if Necessary

company's performance when the company is entering new markets and serving new customers? Or how can they evaluate how well divisions are integrating? The answer is that they need to use various types of control, which we discuss later in this chapter.

3. *Compare actual performance against the established targets.* Managers evaluate whether — and to what extent — performance deviates from the targets developed in step 1. If performance is higher, management may decide that it had set the standards too low and may raise them for the next time period. The Japanese are renowned for the way they use targets on the production line to control costs. They are constantly trying to raise performance, and they constantly raise the standards to provide a goal for managers to work toward. On the other hand, if performance is too low, managers must decide whether to take remedial action. This decision is easy when the reasons for poor performance can be identified — for instance, high labor costs. More often, however, the reasons for poor performance are hard to uncover. They may involve external factors, such as a recession. Or the cause may be internal. For instance, the research and development laboratory may have underestimated the problems it would encounter or the extra costs of doing unforeseen research. For any form of action, however, step 4 is necessary.

4. *Evaluate the result and initiate corrective action when it is decided that the target is not being achieved.* If managers decide to begin corrective action, they have two choices. They *can alter the control systems* being used to measure and monitor the performance of divisions, departments, or individuals — for example they may change budgets or replace rules. In adopting this response, managers are acting on the work system itself to correct the deviation, and they may push for more creative decision making or try to increase productivity by offering better bonuses. The other option available to managers is

to *act on the target itself.* Perhaps a target was set wrongly—for example, a sales target was too optimistic or too high. In this situation, the objective would be to change the target rather than the type of control being used to achieve it. Essentially, then, managers can act on the *means,* that is, the actual types of controls used, or the *ends,* that is, the standards or targets.

The simplest example of a control system is the thermostat in a home. By setting the thermostat, you establish the standard with which actual temperature is to be compared. The thermostat contains a sensing or monitoring device, which measures the actual temperature against the desired temperature. Whenever there is a difference between them, the furnace or air-conditioning unit is activated, to bring the temperature back to the standard: in other words, corrective action is initiated. Note that this is a simple control system, for it is entirely self-contained and the target (temperature) is easy to measure.

Obviously, establishing targets and designing measurement systems is much more difficult in the strategic arena because there are many different targets or standards to choose from. This is the issue we turn to next.

9.6 SELECTING PERFORMANCE STANDARDS

In selecting performance standards, managers are deciding what criteria they will use to evaluate the organization's performance. Standards or measures of a company's performance fall into four basic categories.[10] These are summarized in Table 9.2, along with the individual kinds of measures within each category.

The first category contains standards that measure a company's ability *to meet efficiency goals.* Thus standards relating to productivity, cost, or quality of production are set up and used as the base-line measures for evaluating performance. The second category consists of standards that deal with *the measurement of human resources* in an organization. A company creates targets concerning the

TABLE 9.2   Types and examples of performance targets

Efficiency targets	Productivity, profit, quality, output, costs
Human resource targets	Absenteeism, turnover, job satisfaction, morale, commitment, cooperation
Internal functioning targets	Flexibility, planning, goal-setting, communication, conflict management
Environmental targets	External constituency building, political legitimacy, control of scarce inputs and outputs

FIGURE 9.3   **Levels of organizational control**

Corporate-Level Managers
(set controls which provide context for)

Divisional-Level Managers
(set controls which provide context for)

Functional-Level Managers
(set controls which provide context for)

First-Level Managers

level of absenteeism, turnover, or job satisfaction that is acceptable in the organization. Much more difficult to formulate are standards pertaining to the *internal functioning and responsiveness* of the organization, which make up the third category. Here managers are concerned with factors such as creativity, flexibility, decision making, and organizational communication. In the fourth, and last, category standards relate to an organization's ability to *exploit the environment and obtain scarce resources.* Hence such measures as ability to respond to changes in the environment or to manage external constituencies, such as stockholders, customers, or the government, are important. These standards, too, are also difficult to devise.

Generally, performance is measured at four levels in the organization: the corporate, divisional, functional, and individual levels. Managers at the corporate level are most concerned with overall and abstract measures of organizational performance, such as profit, return on investment, or total labor force turnover. The aim is to choose performance standards that measure overall corporate performance. Similarly, managers at the other levels are most concerned with developing a set of measures that can evaluate business- or functional-level performance. The issue is to tie these measures as closely as possible to the work activities needed to meet strategic objectives at each level. However, care must be taken to ensure that the standards used at each level do not cause problems at the other levels—for example, that divisions' attempts to improve their performance do not conflict with corporate performance. Furthermore, controls at each level should provide the basis on which managers at the levels below can select their control systems. Figure 9.3 illustrates these links.

Problems with Selecting Standards

Selecting the appropriate standards for evaluating performance is one of the most important decisions strategic managers can make, since these standards determine what the company should be doing, that is, its strategic mission. But managers must watch out for some problems.

1. Since there are so many different kinds of standards available, assessments of a company's performance can vary according to the measures selected. If managers choose measures that emphasize productivity but ignore those concerning the environment, they may end up with conflicting impressions of a company's performance. A classic case is that of the large American car makers at the time of high oil prices. The car makers were very efficient: they could produce large cars at low cost. However, they were hardly effective, since nobody wanted to buy large cars. Thus they were not satisfying their outside constituencies—customers or shareholders. Thus, through the measures they select and try to control, managers can create a misleading impression of a company's performance. It is vital, therefore, that they measure the right things.

2. The four categories of measures are not always consistent and may be incompatible. That is, pursuing one type of standard may stop a company from achieving another. For example, a company's attempts to minimize cost and maximize productivity often lead to higher employee absenteeism and turnover, since employees must work under more intense pressure. As another example, companies often like to maintain large inventories of spare parts or components in order to ride out shortages in stocks of finished goods and respond properly to customer needs. However, maintaining buffer stocks and inventory is expensive and therefore raises costs. In such a situation, a company is trading off efficiency against its internal flexibility.

   An important tradeoff at the heart of this problem is that between *short-run efficiency* and *long-term effectiveness*. For example, the competitive advantage that the Japanese have over American manufacturers is often attributed to their long-term planning, large investments of funds in research and development, and expectation of a slower payoff, or return on investment. American corporations, on the other hand, are so concerned with maximizing short-run returns that they limit investment in research and development and, in general, try to reduce costs in the short run. As a result, they suffer in the long run because they have not made the investment for the future. The kind of measures management adopts to evaluate its performance can strongly influence whether or not this will occur, and large companies like GM are now building long-term quality standards into their control system. For example, in the attempt to catch up, GM has increased its research and development budgets. In the last five years, it has spent so much that it could have easily bought Toyota on the stock exchange and still have had money to spare. The issue is to design a control system that can evaluate whether a company is meeting all the objectives necessary to accomplish its strategic mission.

3. The measures chosen to evaluate performance may depend on whose interests are at stake. You saw in Chapter 1 that a company's primary function is to maximize stockholder wealth. What path should be pursued to achieve this, however? Suppose some stockholders prefer short-term dividends whereas others prefer long-term capital appreciation. Which measure of performance should management adopt? Furthermore, if it adopts the standard of maximizing long-term wealth, how should it move toward this goal? Should it reduce costs, maximize its ability to deal with the environment, maximize employee welfare to encourage productivity, or maximize spending on research and development? These are all possible targets, but there are no easy rules for determining which of them are best. Some companies are more successful than others simply because they adopt the right kind of measures.

Management needs to use all four categories of standards to create the mix of standards necessary to pursue a successful long-term strategy. Specifically, management must *minimally* satisfy all the constituencies that have an interest in the company.[11] As identified in Chapter 1, the constituencies in question included shareholders, customers, and the company's employees. In satisfying their interests, management will be balancing the needs of short-run operating efficiency against long-run strategic effectiveness.

9.7 TYPES OF CONTROL SYSTEMS

The control systems that managers can use range from those measuring **organizational outputs** to those measuring and controlling **organizational behaviors.**[12] In general, outputs are much easier to measure than behaviors because outputs are relatively tangible or objective. Hence output controls tend to be the first type that a company employs. In many situations, however, organizational outputs cannot be easily measured or evaluated. For example, it is very difficult to measure organizational creativity or flexibility objectively. In addition, the more complex the organizational tasks, the harder it is to use output control, since it is both difficult and expensive to evaluate the work of people such as research and development personnel or strategic planners. Similarly, the higher the interdependence among functions or divisions — for instance, when a company is seeking to achieve gains from synergy — the tougher it is for a company to pinpoint divisional contributions to performance.

In these situations, a company usually adopts control systems that shape the behaviors necessary to reach its targets.[13] Although such behavior control systems are generally more expensive to employ, they are often the only means a

TABLE 9.3   **Types of control systems**

Market control	Output control	Bureaucratic control	Clan control
Stock price	Divisional goals	Rules and procedures	Norms
ROI	Functional goals	Budgets	Values
Transfer pricing	Individual goals	Standardization	Socialization

company has to monitor and evaluate performance when organizational activities are complex. Table 9.3 presents the various types of control systems along this output-to-behavior control continuum. We will discuss each of these types in turn and also consider the use of different kinds of control mechanisms at the various organizational levels—corporate, divisional, functional, and individual.

Market Control

Market control is the most objective kind of output control. It is achieved by setting a *system of prices* to monitor and evaluate performance. Market control can therefore be used only when an organization is able to establish objective financial measures of performance. In practice, this means that there must be *competition* of some kind, because only through a competitive market mechanism can a fair price be established. There are three common forms of market control: stock market price, return on investment, and transfer pricing.

Stock market price   Stock price is a useful measure of a company's performance primarily because the price of the stock is determined competitively by the number of buyers and sellers in the market. Movements in the price of a stock provide top management with feedback on its performance. They act as a powerful means of control because managers tend to be sensitive to falls in stock market prices, since their compensation is often related to stock price. Falls in stock price may also stimulate takeover attempts, and this factor also serves to control managerial action. Finally, because stock price reflects the long-term future return from the stock, it can be regarded as an indicator of the company's long-run potential.

Return on investment   Return on investment (ROI), determined by dividing net income by invested capital, is another form of market control. At the corporate level, the performance of the whole company can be evaluated *against* other companies, and it is in this sense that ROI acts as a market control. However, this measure can also be used *inside* the company, at the divisional level, to evaluate the relative performance of one operating division either against similar free-standing businesses or against other internal divisions. For example, one reason for selecting the multidivisional structure is that each division can be evaluated as a self-contained profit center. Consequently, management can directly measure the performance of one division against the next. This was one of the reasons for GM's original move to a divisional structure. ROI is a powerful form of market control at the divisional level when managers are concerned with the performance of the whole corporation.

Transfer pricing   Transfer pricing involves establishing the price at which one division will transfer outputs (goods or services) to another — for example, the price at which the oil division will transfer petroleum products to the chemical division, as in Conoco Inc., or the price at which the aerospace division at TRW will transfer research and development knowledge to the vehicle division. There are two basic methods of setting transfer prices. The **market-based method** is the more objective one, since the price charged in the external market is the guage. Competitors' prices are commonly used to set the internal price. In the **cost-based method,** on the other hand, prices are set relative to some standard-cost or full-cost method, but the problem lies in determining the markup to be charged to the buying division.

Both methods are used pretty equally, and each has its drawbacks.[14] With the cost-based method, the issue is determining how much profit the supplying division should earn. Internal transfer prices between divisions can be difficult to set, and sometimes divisions fight over prices to be charged, creating additional problems for corporate managers. When the market-based method is used, the price may be set too high, since the supplying division may have a cost advantage over its competitors. This doubly penalizes the buying divisions: not only are they paying more to the selling division than is really necessary, but, as a result, they may have to charge a price in the market for their product that would rob them of sales. The conflicts stemming from transfer price decisions are among the hardest problems that a vertically integrated and related company must face. Unrelated companies, obviously, are spared these difficulties, since there are no transactions between divisions.[15]

Problems with Market Controls

The use of market controls such as ROI and transfer pricing are two prime ways in which strategic managers can evaluate corporate and divisional performance. As this section has already suggested, however, market control is appropriate only under one condition: when some form of comparison system exists. In comparisons with other companies, market controls such as ROI or stock market price function well. But whether or not market control can work at the divisional level depends on the skills of managers and their willingness to reach equitable solutions over transfer prices for products. Finally, failure to meet stock price or ROI targets also indicates that corrective action is necessary. It signals the need for corporate reorganization in order to meet corporate objectives, and such reorganization could involve a change in structure or liquidation and divestiture of businesses.

Output Control

The next most objective method of organizational control is output control. When no market system can be devised to allocate and price organizational resources because no system of comparison (between companies or divisions) exists, companies must turn to alternative methods of control. The easiest and cheapest kind of control available is **output control.** In order to apply output control, a company must be able to estimate or forecast appropriate targets for its various divisions, departments, or personnel. The most common forms of output controls are discussed below.

Divisional goals   In creating divisional goals, corporate management is setting the standards against which divisional performance will be judged. Such standards include sales, productivity, growth, and market share goals. Divisional managers use the standards as the basis for designing the organizational structure to meet the objectives. Generally, corporate managers try to raise these standards over time, in order to force divisions to adopt more efficient forms of structure. Goal setting is also used to evaluate divisions' attempts to cooperate for the sake of achieving synergies or to measure the efficiency of scheduling of resources among divisions. Thus divisional goals are a way of assessing the alignment of structure with strategy.

Functional goals   Output control at the functional level is achieved by setting goals for each function. For example, sales goals are the typical means through which managers control the sales function. Sales targets are established for the whole function, and then individual personnel are given specific goals, which they in turn are required to achieve. Functions and individuals are then evaluated on the basis of achieving or not achieving their goals, and, of course, compensation is pegged to achievement. As at the divisional level, functional goals are established to encourage development of functional competences that provide the company with a competitive advantage at the business level. The achievement of these goals is a sign that the company's strategy is working and meeting organizational objectives.

Individual goals   Output control at the individual level is also very common. You have already seen how sales compensation is normally based on individual performance. In general, whenever employee performance can be easily monitored and evaluated, output controls are usually appropriate. Thus, for example, piece-rate systems, where individuals are paid on exactly how much they produce, are characteristic output control systems. For many jobs, output control is impossible because individuals' performance cannot be evaluated. For example, if individuals work in teams, it is impossible or very expensive to measure their individual outputs. Similarly, if their work is extremely complex, such as in research and development, it makes little sense to control people on the basis of how much they produce. In general, to prevent problems, it is important to set individual goals with the functional strategy in mind.

Problems with Output Control

The inappropriate use of output control at all levels in the organization can lead to unintended and unfortunate consequences. For instance, the wrong goals may be used to evaluate divisions, functions, or individuals. If short-term measures of performance, such as quantity produced, are used, they can conflict with quality goals. In a classic example of the unintended consequence of output control, an employment placement agency rewarded its workers on the basis of how many people they placed weekly in new jobs. The result, of course, was that they directed prospective applicants to job positions for which they were totally unsuited — for instance, they sent accountants to production line jobs. Realizing its mistake, the agency changed the reward system to emphasize how long new employees stayed in their positions after placement. The moral of the story is clear: monitoring, evaluating, and rewarding employee behavior requires the right set of controls.

The same is true at the functional and divisional levels. The use of the wrong reward system can have the unintended effect of producing conflict among departments, which start to compete for resources, as in TRW. To give another example, F. W. Whyte, a famous researcher, was studying the effect of reward systems on the relation between the production function and packaging and distribution in a manufacturing organization. Management introduced a new output control system for production personnel. Performance rose sharply, and employee salaries increased proportionately. However, these unskilled workers were now making more than those in packaging and distribution, which were semiskilled positions. Chaos ensued when the other workers insisted that their salaries be raised above those being paid to the production people. Since such raises would have led to very high salary levels, management responded by removing the output control system, and all the gains from productivity were forfeited as production workers reverted to their previous performance levels.

We have already noted clashes over transfer prices at the divisional level. In general, setting across-the-board output targets, such as ROI targets, for divisions can lead to destructive results if divisions single-mindedly try to maximize divisional profits at the expense of corporate objectives. Moreover, to reach output targets, divisions may start to distort the numbers and engage in strategic manipulation of their figures to make their divisions look good.[16] Thus strategic managers need to design output controls that stimulate divisions to pursue long-run profitability goals at the divisional and corporate levels. In practice, output or market controls must be used in conjunction with bureaucratic (and clan) controls, if the right strategic behaviors are to be achieved.

Bureaucratic Control

Market and output controls require that relatively objective, measurable standards exist for monitoring and evaluating performance. When measurable standards are difficult or expensive to develop, and when they are not sufficient to fulfill corporate objectives, managers must turn to **bureaucratic control.** Bureaucratic control is control through the establishment of a comprehensive *system of rules and procedures* to direct the actions or behavior of divisions, functions, and individuals.[17] In using bureaucratic control, the intention is not to specify the goals, but the best *means* to reach the goals. Types of bureaucratic control include not only impersonal rules and procedures, but also budgets, and the standardization of activities. The specific types of bureaucratic control chosen by an organization to direct employee behavior will be the ones best matched to its particular strategy. As strategy changes over time, the kinds of rules and procedures a company uses also change. The point is to devise a system of rules and procedures that will accomplish the activities necessary to pursue a particular strategy. Each of the various types of bureaucratic control available to strategic planners is discussed below.

Rules and procedures   Rules and procedures are important sources of control in most organizations. The power of the rule is that it standardizes behavior. If employees follow the rules, then actions or decisions are performed the same way time and time again. The result is *predictability* and *accuracy,* which are the goals of all control systems. Rules are essentially guides to action that can be followed in all routine situations. However, the more unusual the situation, the less useful are the rules, for if frequent exceptions have to be made, the rules cease to serve the purpose of a simple guide to action. Nevertheless, much of the routine business is done through written rules, which specify how different functions are to coordinate their behavior and how people are to perform their tasks and roles.

Budgets   Budgets are a second source of bureaucratic control. Budgets are essentially *collections of rules for allocating resources,* principally financial resources.[18] Organizations establish budgets for divisions, functions, and individuals. Then they organize their behavior around the rules the budget establishes.[19] For example, the research and development department normally has a budget for new product development. Managers know that, if they spend too much on one project, they will have less to spend on other projects. Hence they modify their behavior to suit the budget. Similarly, sales personnel have budgets that indicate how much money they can spend on advertising or distributing their products. These rules control the behavior of salespeople and lead to decisions about the best way to use scarce resources to meet the company's strategy. The main types of budgets are (1) operating budgets, which specify what the company intends to produce and the resources needed to produce it; (2) sales budgets, which focus on the revenue the company expects to earn from sales per time period; and (3) expense budgets, which specify the resources that managers in various functions have to conduct activities and meet their goals.[20] Merck, the chemical company, is well known for its innovative design and use of budgets in manufacturing to squeeze out costs and by these means has gained a major cost advantage over competitors.

As with the other means of control, care must be taken to design the budget so that it does not lead to conflict or competition among functions. Such feuding frequently occurs in sales/production relationships. For example, production is often evaluated on its ability to reduce production costs and come in under budget. Therefore production managers try to reduce costs by lengthening production runs, which lowers costs, since less time is spent on changing the production line specifications to turn out other products. However, while such action allows production managers to beat their budgets (and get appropriately rewarded), it often hurts the sales function, since it can reduce its costs only by selling more and can sell more only by being able to respond quickly to customer demands. However, production personnel will not respond to sales' needs, since rescheduling production to satisfy sales customers will increase production costs. The result is that the two functions frequently clash because each follows the needs of its own budget, and the company as a whole suffers.

The budget thus becomes the *goal* to be strived for rather than remaining a set of rules that simply guide decision making. Managers are driven into short-term behavior paths in order to meet the budget, and the performance of the whole organization suffers. Changes in the environment can worsen this problem, if management cannot respond creatively to changing circumstances because an inflexible budget has put it in a straightjacket. On the plus side, however, budgets do provide the guidelines that let managers monitor their own behavior effectively and enable superiors to measure functional activities accurately. They also provide a natural means through which the company can link functional and divisional activities to the corporate mission. The goals of the organization — for instance, high-quality products or customer service — can be built into the size of the budgets allocated to each function, and such action aligns employee behavior with the company's strategy.

Standardization   Standardization is a very potent weapon that organizations can use to influence behaviors.[21] Indeed, to a large degree, bureaucratic control is based on standardization. Rules are a part of the standardization process, but only one part of it. In practice, there are three things that an organization can standardize: its *inputs,* its *throughput activities,* or its *outputs.*

Standardization of inputs   One way in which an organization can control the behavior of both people and resources is by standardizing the inputs into the organization. What this means is that the organization screens inputs and allows only those that meet its standards to enter. For example, if employees are the input in question, then one way of standardizing them is to recruit and select only those people who possess the qualities or skills needed by the organization. Arthur Andersen & Company, the accounting firm, is very selective in the way it recruits people into the organization, and so are most prestigious organizations. If the inputs in question are raw materials or component parts, then the same considerations apply. The Japanese are renowned for the high quality and precise tolerances they demand from component parts, in order to minimize problems with the product at the manufacturing stage.

Standardization of throughput activities The aim of standardization of throughputs is to program work activities so that they are done the same way time and time again. The goal is predictability. As already noted, the use of bureaucratic controls such as rules and procedures is one main way in which organizations can standardize throughputs. Another way is to organize production tasks to facilitate the movement of semifinished goods from one stage to the next and to reduce the time and resources needed to produce outputs. The goal is to improve the efficiency with which goods are produced and to find improved ways to control and standardize production. Output controls are very important because they provide the means by which management monitors and evaluates the success of its efforts.

Standardization of outputs The goal of standardizing outputs is to specify what the performance characteristics of the final product or service should be — for example, what the dimensions or tolerances of the product should conform to. To ensure that their products are standardized companies apply quality control and use various criteria to measure this standardization. One criterion might be the number of goods returned from customers or the number of customer complaints. On production lines, periodic sampling of products can indicate whether they are meeting performance characteristics. Given the intensity of foreign competition, companies are devoting extra resources to standardizing outputs, not just to reduce costs but to retain customers, since companies will retain their customers' business if the product's performance satisfies the customers. For example, if you buy a Japanese car and have no problems with its performance, which car are you most likely to buy next time? That is why companies like the American car makers have been emphasizing the quality dimension of their products. They know how important standardizing outputs is in a competitive market.

McDonald's is an excellent example of a company that uses all three types of standardization. First, the quality of its inputs is standardized though controlling food supplies and franchise holders, then, at the throughput phase, its food operations are totally standardized, and so, at the output phase, we get uniform burgers and strict output control over employee behavior. In general, fast food restaurants, convenience stores, and all types of service-oriented chain stores use standardization as a main means of control.

Problems with Bureaucratic Control

As with the other kinds of controls, the use of bureaucratic control is accompanied by problems, which have to be managed if the organization is to avoid unforeseen difficulties. Since bureaucratic control is central to the operation of all large organization structures, these problems deserve to be considered in more detail.

First, management must be careful to monitor and evaluate the usefulness of bureaucratic controls over time. Rules lead to standardized, predictable behavior and constrain people's behaviors. However, rules are always easier to establish than to get rid of, and over time the number of rules an organization uses tends to increase. However, as new developments lead to additional rules, often the old rules are not discarded, and the company becomes overly bureaucratized. Consequently, the organization and the people in it become inflexible and therefore unable to deal effectively with changing or unusual circumstances. Such inflexibility hampers strategy implementation and makes the company slow to react. Managers must therefore continually be on the alert for reducing the number of rules and procedures necessary to manage the business and should always prefer to discard a rule rather than use a new one.

The second major problem is *the cost of using bureaucratic controls*. Just as structure is expensive, so is bureaucratic control. To give a dramatic example, according to a recent estimate, 20 percent of the cost of health care is spent on managing the paperwork necessary to satisfy organizational and government health care rules and procedures. This amount runs to billions of dollars a year. Hence reducing the number of rules and procedures to the essential minimum is very important. Management frequently neglects this task, however, and often only a change in strategic leadership brings the company back on course.

Bureaucratic control costs much more than market or output control, since outputs are relatively easy to evaluate, but behaviors are not. For this reason, output controls are selected first and bureaucratic controls second. They are most useful when combined, as in a divisional structure, where market controls are used to monitor divisional performance, but then inside the division, bureaucratic controls such as budgets or standardization become appropriate. To prevent short-term profit-seeking behaviors from emerging because of the sole emphasis on output control, it is necessary to apply bureaucratic controls to evaluate other aspects of a division's or function's performance.

When rules are used, authority is delegated to lower levels in the hierarchy. However, if subordinates are not monitored closely, functions or divisions may develop their own goals at the expense of organizational goals. This is the control loss phenomenon, discussed in Chapter 8. Care must be taken that the rules corporate headquarters devise minimize control loss problems; otherwise the structure will not work, as managers may start to distort information or even compete with other divisions for resources.

Managers must realize that much of the decision making and work that gets done in the organization gets done not formally through prescribed bureaucratic controls, but *through managers themselves meeting and communicating informally*. Indeed, in many cases a third form of control is being used in the organization—a very subtle form, often taken for granted by people who fail to realize the important effect it has on their behavior. This is control through the development of common norms and values.

Clan Control and Culture

Clan control is control through the *establishment of an internal system of organizational norms and values*.[22] The goal of clan control is self-control, where individuals feel responsible for working to the best of their ability in the interests of the organization. With clan control, employees are not controlled by some external system of constraint, such as direct supervision, outputs, or rules and procedures. Rather, employees are said to internalize the norms and values of the organization and make them part of their own value system.[23] Just as we internalize the values of society—for instance, "thou shalt not steal"—so in organizations employees internalize the expectations of the organization and act in terms of them. The value of clan control for an organization is its ability to specify the beliefs, norms, and values that govern employee behavior.[24] Wal-Mart is a good example of a company that actively promotes organizational norms and values. Its employees are called "associates" and are encouraged to take initiative as partners in the organization.

Clan control is initially expensive to use, since it requires a great amount of time and resources to generate norms and values strong enough to control employee behavior. Consequently, clan control is used particularly in small companies or in departments staffed by professional employees, who, through their training, have already developed a professional orientation toward their job. In fact, clan control is used most often in conjunction with standardization of inputs. In other words, first the company recruits experts or professionals, and then it allows them to develop their own codes of behavior to guide their work activities. That is why in professional contexts, such as research and development teams, you find a common code of dress or language in the group. For example, clan control is most likely to thrive in a matrix structure, or in an organization such as Apple Computer, where employees were guided by the common vision of creating a desk-top computer, or in IBM, where a commitment to service is a major value.

Much of the most recent research, however, does not talk about clan control, but rather about the development of an organizational culture for managing a company's strategy. The terms clan control and culture are very similar and are used interchangeably below.

Culture refers to that specific collection of norms, standards, and values that are shared by members of an organization and affect the way an organiza-

FIGURE 9.4   **Ways of transmitting culture**

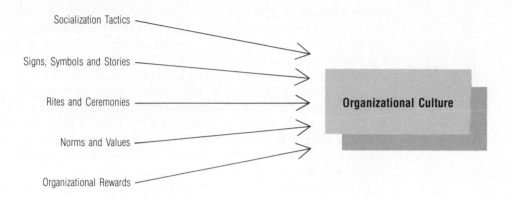

Socialization Tactics

Signs, Symbols and Stories

Rites and Ceremonies → **Organizational Culture**

Norms and Values

Organizational Rewards

tion does business.[25] The principal difference between the way this concept controls behavior and, say, the organization's mission statement, is that culture is implicit in the way people act in the organization; it does not need to be written down to be understood. Socialization is the term used to describe how people learn organizational culture. Through socialization, people internalize the norms and values of the culture and learn to act like existing personnel.[26] Control through culture is so powerful because, once these values are internalized, they become a part of the individual, and the individual follows organizational values without thinking about them. As shown in Figure 9.4, culture may be transmitted in the organization by several means.

Several scholars in the field have tried to uncover the common traits that strong corporate cultures share and to find out whether there is a particular set of values that dominates strong cultures but is missing from the weak. Perhaps the best-known attempt is T. J. Peters and R. H. Waterman's account of the norms and values characteristic of successful organizations and their cultures.[27] First, successful companies have values promoting *a bias for action*. The emphasis is on autonomy and entrepreneurship, and employees are encouraged to take risks — for example, to create new products, even though there is no assurance that these products will be winners. Another component of the process is that employees have a "hands-on, value-driven approach." Similarly, managers are closely involved in the day-to-day operations of the company and do not simply make strategic decisions isolated in some "ivory tower."

The second set of values stems from *the nature of the organization's mission*. The company must stick with what it does best and maintain control over its core activities. A company can easily get side-tracked into pursuing activities outside its area of expertise just because they seem to promise a quick return. Management should cultivate values so that a company "sticks to the knitting," which means staying with the businesses it knows best. A company must also establish close relations with the customer as a way of improving its competitive position. After all, who knows better about a company's performance than those who use its products or services? By emphasizing customer-oriented values, organizations are able to learn customer needs and improve their ability to develop products and services customers desire. All these management values are strongly represented in IBM, Hewlett-Packard, Toyota, and other companies that are sure of their mission and take constant steps to maintain it.

The third set of values bears on *how to operate the organization*. A company should try to establish an organizational design that will motivate employees to do their best. The first of these values is the belief that productivity is obtained through people and that respect for the individual is the primary means by which a company can create the right atmosphere for productive behavior. As William Ouchi has noted, a very similar philosophy pervades the culture of Japanese companies.[28] Many American companies also pay this kind of attention to their employees — for instance, Kodak, Procter & Gamble, and Levi-Strauss. An emphasis on entrepreneurship and respect for the employee leads to establishing a structure that gives employees the latitude to make decisions and motivates them to succeed. Since a simple form and a lean staff best fit this situation, the choice should be the structure with only the number of managers and hierarchical levels that are necessary to get the job done. The organization should also be sufficiently decentralized to permit employee participation but centralized enough for management to make sure that the company pursues its strategic mission and that cultural values are still being followed.

These three main sets of values are at the heart of an organization's culture, and the management transmits and maintains them through stories, myths, symbols, and socialization. Pursuing these values is not enough to ensure organizational success, however, and over time cultural values should change to suit the environment in which the company is operating. A company needs to establish the values that are good for it and base its organizational structure and control system on them. When that is accomplished, only those people who fit the values are recruited into the organization, and, through training, they become a part of the organization's culture. Thus the types of control systems chosen should reinforce and build upon one another in a cohesive way. Although, as we noted earlier, culture is difficult and expensive to develop, it is a powerful form of control. However, it is not free of problems, and we now consider its debit side.

Problems with Clan Control

The development of unique systems of norms and values at the divisional and functional levels can lead to communications problems across divisions and functions. Thus, when clan control is used, care must be taken that integration does not suffer because of such failures in communication. Moreover, clan control is not suitable where rapid growth or changes in the environment do not provide a context within which stable norms and values can develop. A classic case of clan control failing under these conditions is People Express, which started off with a system based on a team structure, where clan control was used as the main means of getting the work done. As the company grew quickly through its takeover of other airlines and rapid increase in flights, it could not maintain control of its operations, and its costs rose dramatically.

Clan control is also not appropriate where turnover of employees is high, since there is no time to develop a stable system of values and the costs rise dramatically with increased turnover. Consequently, it is of little use in most production line systems. The Japanese, however, can use clan control in their factories, since turnover there is typically low, and if lifetime employment exists, turnover is negligible.

Finally, organizational culture cannot by itself control organizational performance and make structure work. It must be backed by output and bureaucratic controls and matched to a reward system, so that employees will in fact cultivate organizational norms and values and modify their behavior to organizational objectives. Because of the expense involved, many companies abandon culture in favor of tight objective control and close supervision of behavior.

Summary

Choosing a control system to match the firm's strategy and structure offers management a number of important challenges. The issue is to find that selection of controls which provides the framework which allows for the accurate monitoring, measurement, and evaluation of the standards or targets organizations choose to achieve their strategic objectives at stage one in the control process. Market and output controls are the cheapest and easiest to use, but they must be backed up with bureaucratic and clan control to ensure that the firm is achieving its goals in the most efficient way possible. In general, these controls should reinforce one another and care must be taken to ensure that they do not result in unforeseen consequences such as competition between functions, divisions, and individuals.

9.8 STRATEGIC REWARD SYSTEMS

A final way in which organizations attempt to control employee behavior is by linking reward systems to their control systems.[29] An organization must decide which behaviors it wishes to reward, adopt a control system to measure these behaviors, and then link the reward structure to them. How to relate rewards to performance is a crucial strategic decision because it affects the way managers and employees at all levels in the organization behave. For example, in designing a pay system for salespeople, the choice would be whether to employ salespeople on the basis of straight salary or salary, plus a bonus based on how much is sold. For example, Neiman-Marcus, the luxury retailer, pays employees a straight salary because it wants to encourage high-quality service but discourage hard sell. Thus there are no incentives based on quantity sold. On the other hand, the pay system for rewarding car salespeople typically contains a high bonus component for the number of cars sold.

What behaviors to reward is therefore an important decision, tied closely to a company's business-level strategy, as you will see in Chapter 10. Now we need to consider the types of reward systems available to strategic managers.[30] Generally, reward systems are found at the individual and group or total organizational levels. Often these systems are used in combination; for example, merit raises at the individual level may be accompanied by a bonus based on divisional or plant performance. Within each type, several forms of reward systems are available.

Individual Reward Systems

Piecework plans Piecework plans are used when outputs can be objectively measured. Essentially, employees are paid on the basis of some set amount for each unit of output produced. Piecework plans are most commonly found in production line situations, where individuals work alone and their performance can be directly measured. Since this system encourages quantity rather than quality, the company normally applies stringent quality controls to make sure that the quality is acceptable.

Commission systems Commission systems resemble piecework systems, except that they are normally tied not to what is produced but to how much is sold. Thus they are most commonly found in sales-type situations. Often the salaries of salespeople are based principally on commission, to encourage superior performance. Thus it is common for first-rate salespeople to earn more than $1 million per year.

Bonus plans Bonus plans at the individual level generally reward the performance of a company's key individuals, such as the CEO or senior vice presidents. The performance of these people is very visible to the organization as a whole and to stakeholders such as shareholders. Consequently, there is a strong rationale for paying these individuals according to some measure of functional or divisional performance. A company must proceed carefully, however, if it is to avoid problems such as an emphasis on short-run rather than long-term objectives. For example, paying bonuses based on quarterly or yearly ROI rather than on, say, five-year growth can have a markedly different effect on the way strategic managers behave.

Group and Organizational Reward Systems

Group and organizational reward systems provide additional ways in which companies can relate pay to performance. In general, the problem with these systems is that the relationship is less direct and more difficult to measure than in the case of individually based systems. Consequently, they are viewed as less motivating. The most common reward systems at these levels involve group bonuses, profit sharing, employee stock options, and organization bonuses.

Group-based bonus systems   Sometimes a company can establish project teams, or work groups, where the group performs all the operations needed to turn out a product or provide a service. This arrangement makes it possible to measure group performance and to offer rewards on the basis of group productivity. The system can be highly motivating, since employees are allowed to develop the best work procedures for doing the job and are responsible for improving their own productivity. For example, Wal-Mart supports a group bonus plan based on controlling shrinkage (i.e. employee theft).

Profit-sharing systems   Profit-sharing plans are designed to reward employees on the basis of the profit a company earns in any one time period. Such plans encourage employees to take a broad view of their activities and feel connected with the company as a whole. Wal-Mart uses this method as well to develop its organizational culture.

Employee stock option systems   Rather than reward employees on the basis of short-term profits, a company sometimes allows them to buy its shares at below-market prices, heightening employee motivation. As shareholders, the employees will focus not only on short-term profits, but also on long-term capital appreciation, for they are now the company's owners. Over time, if enough employees participate, they can control a substantial stock holding, as in the case of Eastern Airlines, and thus become vitally interested in the company's performance.

Organization bonus systems   Profit is not the only basis on which a company can reward organization-wide performance. Rewards are also commonly based on cost savings, quality increases, or production increases obtained in the last time period. Since these systems usually require that outputs be measured accurately, they are most common in production line organizations or in service companies, where it is possible to cost out the price of the services of personnel. The systems are mainly a back-up to other forms of pay systems. In rare situations, however, such as at The Lincoln Electric Company, a company renowned for the success of its cost-savings group plan, they become the principal means of control.

Control through organizational reward systems complements all the other forms of control we have discussed in this chapter. The reward systems help determine how output or clan control, for example, will work. Rewards act as the oil for making a control system function effectively. To ensure that the right strategic behaviors are being rewarded, rewards should be closely linked to an organization's strategy. Moreover, they should be so designed that they do not lead to conflicts among divisions, functions, or individuals.

9.9 SUMMARY OF CHAPTER

The purpose of this chapter has been to discuss the types of integrating mechanisms and control systems available to strategic planners to influence organizational performance. Companies must use more complex integrating mechanisms when they adopt more complex structures. They must also select the combination of controls that will make the structure work and meet the company's strategic objectives. Companies may use a variety of controls, since different types of controls may suit different divisions or functions or different types of employees.

The essential task for companies is to select controls that are consistent with one another and also match the organizational structure. Companies with a high level of differentiation and integration require a more complex set of controls than those with a low degree of differentiation and integration. For example, as you saw earlier, in the discussion of TRW, controls should spur divisions to cooperate rather than compete. The control system has to provide rewards for cooperation based on establishing a fair price for each division's technological know-how and rewards, such as group bonus plans, for sharing knowledge. In the case of simple functional structures, on the other hand, output controls can monitor each function's performance separately from the others, making control much easier to achieve. In the next chapter, we will consider in detail how structure and control should be jointly matched to the company's corporate- and business–level strategies.

The chapter has made the following main points:

1. The more complex the company and the higher its level of integration, the higher is the level of integration that it needs in order to manage its structure.

2. The kinds of integrating mechanisms available to a company range from direct control to matrix structure. The more complex the mechanism, the greater are the costs of using it. A company should take care to match these mechanisms to its strategic needs.

3. Organizational control is the process of setting targets, monitoring, evaluating, and rewarding organizational performance.

4. Control takes place at all levels in the organization: corporate, divisional, functional, and individual.

5. Effective control systems are flexible, accurate, and able to provide quick feedback to strategic planners.

6. There are four steps to designing an effective control system: establishing performance standards, creating measuring systems, evaluating performance, and taking corrective action.

7. Many kinds of performance standards are available for strategy implementation. The kinds of measures managers choose affect the way a company operates.

8. Control systems range from those directed at measuring outputs or productivity to those measuring behaviors or actions.

9. The three main forms of *market control* are stock market price, return on investment, and transfer pricing.

10. Output control establishes goals for divisions, functions, and individuals. It can be used only when outputs can be objectively measured.

11. Bureaucratic control is used to control behaviors when it is impossible to measure outputs. The main forms of bureaucratic control are rules and procedures, budgets, and standardization.

12. When neither outputs nor behaviors can be monitored and evaluated, organizations turn to clan control. Clan control is control through a system of norms and values that individuals internalize as they are socialized into the organization. Organizational culture is a collection of the norms and values that govern the way in which people act and behave inside the organization.

13. An organization's reward systems constitute the final form of control. A company links its reward systems to organizational goals and objectives to provide an incentive for employees to perform well.

14. Organizations use all these forms of controls simultaneously. The point is to select and combine those that are consistent with each other and with the strategy and structure of the organization.

Discussion Questions

1. What are the relationships among differentiation, integration, and strategic control systems? Why are these relationships important?

2. For each of the structures discussed in Chapter 8, outline the integrating mechanisms and control systems most suitable for matching them.

3. What kinds of integration and control systems does this (a) business school, and (b) university employ to operate its structure and control personnel?

4. List the kinds of integration and control systems you would be likely to find in (a) a small manufacturing company, (b) a chain store, (c) a gourmet restaurant, and (d) a big five accounting firm.

Endnotes

1. *Fortune,* February 1963, p. 95.

2. TRW Inc., Annual Report, 1988.

3. *Business Week,* November 15, 1982, p. 124.

4. P. R. Lawrence and J. Lorsch, *Organization and Environment* (Homewood, Ill.: Irwin, 1967), pp. 50–55.

5. J. R. Galbraith, *Designing Complex Organizations* (Reading, Mass.: Addison-Wesley, 1977), Ch. 1. J. R. Galbraith and R. K. Kazanjian, *Strategy Implementation: Structure, System, and Process* (St. Paul, Minn.: West, 1986), Ch. 7.

6. Henry Mintzberg, *The Nature of Managerial Work* (Englewood Cliffs, N. J.: Prentice-Hall, 1973), Ch. 10.

7. Lawrence and Lorsch, *Organization and Environment,* p. 55.

8. W. G. Ouchi, "The Transmission of Control Through Organizational Hierarchy," *Academy of Management Journal,* 21 (1978), 173–192. W. H. Newman, *Constructive Control* (Englewood Cliffs, N. J.: Prentice-Hall, 1975).

9. K. A. Merchant, *Control in Business Organizations* (Marshfield, Mass.: Pitman, 1985). E. E. Lawler III and J. G. Rhode, *Information and Control in Organizations* (Pacific Palisades, Calif.: Goodyear, 1976).

10. J. P. Campbell, "On the Nature of Organizational Effectiveness," in *New Perspectives on Organizational Effectiveness,* ed. P. S. Goodman and J. M. Pennings (San Francisco: Jossey-Bass, 1977), pp. 13–55.

11. T. Connolly, E. J. Conlon, and S. J. Deutsch, "Organizational Effectiveness: A Multiple-Constituency Approach," *Academy of Management Review,* 5 (1980), 211–217; R. E. Quinn and J. Rohrbaugh, "A Spatial Model of Effectiveness Criteria: Towards a Competing Values Approach to Organizational Analysis," *Management Science,* 29 (1983), 33–51.

12. W. G. Ouchi, "The Relationship Between Organizational Structure and Organizational Control," *Administrative Science Quarterly,* 22 (1977), 95–113.

13. J. D. Thompson, *Organizations in Action* (New York: McGraw-Hill, 1967), Ch. 10. W. G. Ouchi, "A Conceptual Framework for the Design of Organizational Control Systems," *Management Science,* 25 (1979), 833–848.

14. R. F. Vancil, *Decentralization: Managerial Ambiguity by Design* (Homewood, Ill.: Dow-Jones Irwin, 1978).

15. R. G. Eccles, *The Transfer Pricing Problem* (Lexington, Mass.: Lexington Books, 1985), Ch. 2.

16. E. Flamholtz, "Organizational Control Systems as a Managerial Tool," *California Management Review* (Winter 1979), 50–58.

17. O. E. Williamson, *Markets and Hierarchies* (New York: Free Press, 1975). W. G. Ouchi, "Markets, Bureaucracies, and Clans," *Administrative Science Quarterly,* 25 (1980), 129–141.

18. P. Lorange, *Corporate Planning* (Englewood Cliffs, N. J.: Prentice-Hall, 1980). G. A. Welsch, *Budgeting: Profit Planning and Control,* 4th ed. (Englewood Cliffs, N. J.: Prentice-Hall, 1976).

19. C. S. Trapani, "Six Critical Areas in the Budgeting Process," *Management Accounting,* 64 (1982), 52–58.

20. Trapani, "Six Critical Areas," p. 54.

21. H. Mintzberg, *The Structuring of Organizations* (Englewood Cliffs, N. J.: Prentice-Hall, 1979), pp. 5–9.

22. Ouchi, "Markets, Bureaucracies, and Clans," p. 130.

23. G. R. Jones, "Socialization Tactics, Self-Efficacy, and Newcomers' Adjustments to Organizations," *Academy of Management Journal,* 29 (1986), 262–279.

24. M. R. Louis, "Surprise and Sensemaking: What Newcomers Experience in Entering Unfamiliar Settings," *Administrative Science Quarterly,* 25 (1980), 226–251.

25. L. Smircich, "Concepts of Culture and Organizational Analysis," *Administrative Science Quarterly,* 28 (1983), 339–358.

26. J. Van Maanen and E. H. Schein, "Towards a Theory of Organizational Socialization," in *Research in Organizational Behavior,* ed. B. M. Staw (Greenwich, Conn.: JAI Press, 1979), I, 209–264.

27. T. J. Peters and R. H. Waterman, *In Search of Excellence: Lessons from America's Best-Run Companies* (New York: Harper and Row, 1982).

28. W. G. Ouchi, *Theory Z: How American Business Can Meet the Japanese Challenge* (Reading, Mass.: Addison-Wesley, 1981).

29. E. E. Lawler III, *Motivation in Work Organizations* (Monterey, Cal.: Brooks/Cole, 1973). Galbraith and Kazanjian, *Strategy Implementation,* Ch. 6.

30. E. E. Lawler III, "The Design of Effective Reward Systems," in *Handbook of Organizational Behavior,* ed. J. W. Lorsch (Englewood Cliffs, N. J.: Prentice-Hall, 1987), pp. 386–422. R. Mathis and J. Jackson, *Personnel,* 2nd ed. (St. Paul, Minn.: West, 1979), p. 456.

Chapter 10

MATCHING STRUCTURE AND CONTROL TO STRATEGY

10.1 OPENING INCIDENT: TEXAS INSTRUMENTS

Texas Instruments (TI) was started by two entrepreneurs, Clarence Karcher and Eugene McDermott, who invented the technique of using sound waves to map underground strata. This technique became the dominant way for oil companies to prospect for oil, and its applications for sonar and radar in the military became evident. The real breakthrough for TI, however, came in the 1950s, when it pioneered transistors small enough for use in radios and developed silicon transistors for use in military operations. Miniaturization of electronic circuits became TI's chief competitive advantage and allowed the company to grow rapidly, even when companies like GE and RCA entered the market. It solidified its competitive advantage by emphasizing efficiency and emerged as the lowest-cost producer of these circuits.[1]

To maintain its technological edge, TI adopted a decentralized matrix structure, so that product and technological knowledge could be shared across its many divisions. Divisional sharing gave TI a leading edge in two fast-growing and highly profitable businesses, computers and consumer electronics. In controlling the matrix, the president of TI at this time, Patrick E. Haggerty, decentralized decision making to the divisional level. He made little attempt to interfere in the various divisions' business-level strategy. He saw the role of the corporate center as one of managing a portfolio of investments and instituted a strict set of financial controls to evaluate divisional performance. Under his leadership, and then under J. Fred Bucy's, the company prospered and grew.[2] However, by 1983 the company was experiencing problems.

TI faced substantial competition from Japanese companies that had imitated many of TI's products and technical innovations, while usurping its cost leadership position. In addition, the company received a major blow to its morale when its consumer products business reported record losses and plunged TI into its first quarterly loss ever. Bucy, in a statement to stockholders, explained the company's downturn: "TI is suffering from the problems of the company's success. As it passes through phases of corporate life, it must accommodate its organization and structures to these phases as it grows. This failure to adjust affected operating and strategic structures."[3]

TI realized that it had to alter its structure and control system as its competitive position changed over time. To restore profitability, TI abandoned its matrix structure because it had begun to fragment both people and resources, making it almost impossible for management to exert effective control over divisional operations. TI moved to a more centralized, divisional structure, where control could be exercised more easily. In the new structure, divisional managers were evaluated on their division's performance as a profit center. In addition, corporate-level personnel designed new control systems to promote the sharing of information and knowledge across divisions more efficiently and to promote synergies. In essence, TI went to an SBU structure, which, when coupled with the right mix of integrating mechanisms and divisional controls, put the company back on track.

TI realized that its structure had to match its business- and corporate-level strategy. It recognized, too, that as changes in the competitive environment caused changes in its strategy, the management would have to keep moving quickly to implement the structure and control system best suited to its objectives.

10.2 OVERVIEW

At Texas Instruments, strategic managers moved to implement the right mix of structure and control systems to allow the company to deal with changes in its strategy and the competitive environment. In this chapter, we discuss how strategic choice at the corporate, business, and functional levels affects the choice of structure and control systems—in other words, how to match different forms of structure and control to strategy. As we emphasized in Chapter 1, the issue facing strategic managers is to match strategy formulation with strategy implementation. All the tools of strategy formulation and implementation have been discussed in previous chapters. Now we put the two sides of the equation together and examine the issues involved in greater detail.

First, we consider how functional-level strategy affects structure and control and then how a company's choice of generic business-level strategy affects the choice of structure and control for implementing the strategy. Next, we take up the special problems that different kinds of corporate-level strategy pose for strategic managers in designing a structure and note how changes in corporate-level strategy over time affect the form of structure and control systems adopted by a company. Finally, we examine the problems relating to the two entry strategies we discussed in Chapter 7: managing mergers and acquisitions and providing the setting that encourages internal venturing. By the end of this chapter, you will understand why TI and all companies go through a series of transitions in structure and control as they attempt to deal with the changing nature of their strategy and environment.

10.3 STRUCTURE AND CONTROL AT THE FUNCTIONAL LEVEL

In Chapter 4, dealing with strategy formulation at the functional level, we emphasized that a company must develop distinctive competences to give it a competitive advantage. We discussed how different competences could be developed in each function and then, in Chapter 5, we noted that at the business level different competitive strategies require the development of different types of distinctive competences. In this section, we consider how a company can create a structure and control system that permits the development of various distinctive functional competences or skills.

Decisions at the functional level fall into two categories: choices about the level of vertical differentiation and choices about monitoring and evaluation systems (choices about horizontal differentiation are not relevant here because we are considering each function individually). The choices made depend on the distinctive competence that a company is pursuing.

Manufacturing

In manufacturing, functional strategy usually centers on reducing production costs. A company must create an organizational setting where managers can learn from experience curve effects how to economize on costs. To move down the experience curve quickly, the company must exercise tight control over work activities and employees, so that it can squeeze out costs wherever possible. This is why manufacturing generally has the tallest structure of all the functions.

However, besides supervision from the hierarchy, manufacturing also relies on bureaucratic and output control to reduce costs. Standardization is frequently used to squeeze out costs. For example, human inputs are standardized through the recruitment and training of personnel; the work process is standardized or programmed to reduce costs; and quality control is used to make sure that outputs are being produced correctly. In addition, managers are closely monitored and controlled through output control and production budgets.

Finally, in some manufacturing settings, especially those run on Japanese-style principles, companies attempt to develop a production culture. Employees are given benefits that normally only management receives; quality control circles are created to exchange information and suggestions about problems and work procedures; and workers share in the increases in output through some form of bonus system. The aim is to match structure and control so that they jointly create a low-cost competence and the function achieves its strategy.

Research and Development

In contrast, the functional strategy for a research and development department is to develop a technological distinctive competence. Consequently, the structure should produce a setting where personnel can develop innovative products or processes. In practice, research and development departments have flatter structures than any other function in an organization. That is, they usually have the fewest number of hierarchical levels relative to their size. Flatter structures give research and development personnel the freedom and autonomy to be innovative. Furthermore, since supervisors can rarely evaluate what research and development personnel are doing anyway, adding layers of hierarchy would waste resources.[4]

Controlling the research and development function is somewhat problematical because it is very difficult to monitor employee behavior. Using output controls for the purpose is difficult and expensive. The solution, therefore, is to use input control and only recruit highly trained employees. Research and development departments also rely heavily on *small teams and clan control* to reinforce innovation, and a professional culture emerges to control employee behavior.

Sales

Like research and development, the sales function usually has a very flat structure. Most commonly, three hierarchical levels—sales director, regional or product sales managers, and individual salespeople—can accommodate even very large sales forces. Flat structures are possible because the organization does not depend on direct supervision for control. Salespeople's activities are often complex; moreover, since they are dispersed in the field, these employees are difficult to monitor. Rather than depend on the hierarchy, the sales function usually implements *output and behavioral controls*. These take the form of specific sales goals, as well as detailed reports that salespeople must file describing their interactions with customers.[5] Supervisors can then review salespeoples's performance easily.

Similar considerations apply to the other functions, such as accounting, finance, engineering, or personnel. Managers must select the right combination of structure and control mechanisms to achieve functional objectives. Table 10.1 lists the appropriate choices of structure and control for all the principal organizational functions.

TABLE 10.1   **Structure and control at the functional level**

Function	Type of structure	Main type of control
Production	Tall/centralized	Output control e.g., cost targets
Materials management	Flat/centralized	Output control e.g., inventory and purchasing targets
Research and development	Flat/decentralized	Clan control e.g., norms, values, and culture
Sales	Flat/decentralized	Output control e.g., sales targets
Accounting/finance	Tall/decentralized	Bureaucratic control e.g., budgets
Human resources	Flat/centralized	Bureaucratic control e.g., standardization

10.4 STRUCTURE AND CONTROL AT THE BUSINESS LEVEL

Generic Business-Level Strategies

Designing the right mix of structure and control at the business level is a continuation of designing a company's functional departments. Having implemented the right structure and control system for each individual function, the company must then implement the organizational arrangements so that all the functions can be managed together to achieve business-level strategy objectives. Because the focus is on managing interfunctional relationships, the choice of *horizontal differentiation* (division of organizational activities) and *integration* for achieving business-level strategies becomes very important.[6] Control systems must also be selected with the monitoring and evaluating of interfunctional activities in mind. Table 10.2 summarizes the appropriate organizational structure and control systems that companies can use when following a low-cost, differentiation, or focused strategy.

Cost-leadership strategy and structure   The aim of the cost-leadership strategy is to make the company pursuing it the lowest-cost producer in the market.[7] At the business level, this means reducing costs not just in production, but across *all* functions in the organization—including research and development and sales and marketing.

If a company is following a cost-leadership strategy, its research and development efforts probably focus on process engineering rather than on the more expensive product research, which carries no guarantee of success. That is, the

TABLE 10.2   Generic strategy, structure, and control

| | Strategy | | |
	Cost leadership	Differentiation	Focus
Appropriate structure	Functional or product	Product or matrix	Functional
Integrating mechanisms	Center on manufacturing	Center on R&D or marketing	Center on product or customer
Output control	Great use e.g., cost control	Some use e.g., quality goals	Some use e.g., cost and quality
Bureaucratic control	Some use e.g., budgets, standardization	Great use e.g., rules, budgets	Some use e.g., budgets
Clan control	Little use e.g., quality control circles	Great use e.g., norms and culture	Great use e.g., norms and culture

company stresses research that lowers the cost of making existing products. Similarly, the company tries to decrease the cost of sales and marketing by offering a standard product to a mass market rather than by offering different products aimed at different market segments.[8]

To implement such a strategy, the cost leader chooses the simplest structure—the one with the lowest level of differentiation that can meet the needs of the strategy. Simple structures are the least expensive to operate and thus match the needs of the low-cost strategy. In practice, the structure chosen is normally a functional or perhaps a product structure. Each of these structures allows manufacturing activities to be programmed or standardized, a major source of cost saving.[9] The two structures are also relatively easy to manage, since they require a low degree of integration. The company does not need to coordinate as many new products or innovations and so avoids the expense of creating task forces or teams. Seagate Technology, the hard disk maker, is an example of a cost leader that continually streamlines its structure to maintain a competitive advantage. It periodically reduces levels in the hierarchy and institutes strict production controls to minimize costs. This process puts it substantially ahead of its Japanese competitors.

To reduce costs, cost-leadership companies want to use the cheapest and easiest forms of control available. Therefore they choose output controls. For each function, a company adopts output controls that allow it to monitor and evaluate functional performance closely, so that waste is curtailed and cost savings maximized. In the production function, for example, the company imposes tight controls and stresses meeting budgets based on production or cost targets.[10] In research and development, too, the emphasis falls on the bottom line. Research and development personnel concerned with demonstrating their contribution to saving costs may focus their efforts on improving process technology, where actual savings are calculable. Heinz Foods clearly illustrates such efforts. In following a cost-leadership strategy, it places enormous emphasis on production improvements that can reduce the cost of a can of beans. Like manufacturing and research and development, the sales function is closely monitored, and sales targets are usually very challenging. Cost-leadership companies, however, are likely to reward employees by generous incentive and bonus schemes to encourage high performance. Often their culture is based on values that emphasize the bottom line, such as in Heinz, Lincoln Electric, and PepsiCo.

In short, pursuing a successful cost-leadership strategy requires close attention to the design of structure and control in order to economize on costs. Managers, rules, and any kind of organizational control mechanism cost money, and low-cost companies must try to economize when implementing their structures. When a company's competitive advantage depends on achieving and maintaining a low-cost advantage, adopting the right organizational arrangements is vital.

Differentiation strategy and structure   To pursue a differentiation strategy, a company has to develop a distinctive competence in a function such as research and development or marketing and sales. To give its product uniqueness in the eyes of the customer, the differentiated company must design its structure and control systems around the *particular source* of its competitive advantage.[11] As a result, the differentiated company usually employs a more complex structure, that is, a structure with a higher level of differentiation and integration than the cost leader.

For example, suppose the differentiator's strength lies in technological competence; the company has the cutting-edge technology. In this case, the company's structure and control systems should be designed around the research and development function. Implementing a *matrix structure,* as TI and TRW have done, helps develop technological innovations, for it allows the cross-fertilization of ideas among functions. Integrating mechanisms, such as tasks forces and teams, help to transfer knowledge among functions and are designed around the research and development function. For example, since sales, marketing, and production targets are geared to research and development goals, marketing devises advertising programs that focus on technological possibilities, and salespeople are evaluated on their understanding of new product characteristics and their ability to inform potential customers about them. Stringent sales targets are unlikely to be set in this situation, since the goal is quality of service.

When the source of the differentiator's advantage is in the breadth of its product range or the number of different market segments it serves, a different structure is required. In such cases, companies design a structure around their products, and thus a *product* or *geographical structure* fits best. Consequently, if a company manufactures a distinctive range of products, research and development or sales are organized by product, and task forces and teams have a product, not a research, orientation. If designed around types of customers, the company may have a structure based on regional needs or even on different types of customers, such as businesses, individual consumers, or the government. For example, both Compaq and Rockwell have recently reorganized their structures to concentrate on the needs of specific customers or regions in order to gain a competitive advantage.

The control systems used to match the structure are also geared to the company's distinctive competence. For the differentiator, it is important that the various functions do not pull in different directions; indeed, cooperation among the various functions is vital. But when functions work together, output controls become much harder to use. In general, it is much more difficult to measure the performance of people in different functions when they are engaged in cooperative efforts. As a result, a company must rely more on behavior controls and clan control when pursuing a strategy of differentiation. That is why companies pursuing a differentiation strategy often have a very different kind of culture than those pursuing a low-cost strategy. Because the quality of human resources is often the source of differentiation — good scientists, designers, or marketing people — these organizations have a culture based on professionalism and collegiality, a culture that emphasizes the distinctiveness of the human resource rather than the high pressure of the bottom line.[12] Hewlett-Packard, IBM, and Frito-Lay, Inc., all of which emphasize some kind of distinctive competence, exemplify companies with professional cultures.

The structure and control system of the differentiator is more expensive than the cost leader's, but the benefits are also greater, if companies reap the rewards of a premium price.

Focus strategy and structure   In Chapter 5, we defined a focus strategy as one that was directed at a particular customer segment. A company focuses on a product or range of products directed at one sort of customer or region. This strategy tends to have higher production costs than the other two strategies because output levels are lower, making it harder to obtain substantial economies of scale. As a result, a focused company must exercise cost control. On the other hand, because some attribute of its product usually gives the focused company its unique advantage—possibly its ability to provide customers with high-quality, personalized service—a focuser has to develop a unique competence. For both these reasons, the structure and control system adopted by the focused company have to be inexpensive to operate but flexible enough to allow a distinctive competence to emerge.

A focused company normally adopts a functional structure to meet these needs. This structure is appropriate because it is complex enough to manage the activities necessary to serve the needs of the market segment or produce a narrow range of products. At the same time, a functional structure is also relatively easy to control, and there is less need for complex, expensive integrating mechanisms. This structure permits more personal control and flexibility than the other two, and so reduces the costs of control, while fostering the development of a distinctive competency.[13] Given its small size, a focused company can rely less on bureaucratic control and more on clan control and culture, which are vital to the development of a service competence. Although output controls need to be used in production and sales, this form of control, as with clan control, is inexpensive in a small organization.

The combination of functional structure and low cost of control helps to offset the higher costs of production while still allowing a company to develop unique strengths. It is little wonder, then, that there are so many focused companies. Additionally, since a focuser's competitive advantage is often based on personalized service, the flexibility of this kind of structure allows a company to respond quickly to customer needs and change its products in response to customer requests. The structure, then, backs up the strategy and helps the company develop and maintain its distinctive competence.

Au Bon Pain Company, Inc., a fast food chain specializing in fancy coffees and croissants, is a good example of a company that recognized the need to design a structure and control system to match a focused strategy aimed at an upscale customer group. To encourage franchises to perform highly and satisfy customer needs, it decentralized control to each franchise, making each a self-contained functional unit. Then, through a profit-sharing plan that rewarded cost cutting and quality, it gave each franchise manager the incentive to create a set of control arrangements that minimized costs but maximized quality of service. The result was a strategy-structure fit that led to a massive increase in franchise profits.

Although research corroborates that the forms of structure and control we have been discussing are appropriate for the different kinds of strategies, these forms are ideals. Many companies do *not* use the right forms. Quite likely, they are not as successful and may not survive as long as those that do match their strategy, structure, and control systems.[14] In Chapter 11, we discuss some of the problems that companies may encounter when they attempt to change their structures or strategies, and we also examine the reasons that their structures do not match their strategies.

Business Strategies and the Industry Life Cycle

Although the choice of generic strategy is at the heart of a company's business-level strategy, the stage of the industry life cycle that the company is in also influences its business strategy. Table 10.3 shows the relationships between industry life cycle strategy and form of structure and control.

Embryonic stage strategy and structure   In the embryonic industry stage, the principal problem facing companies at the business level is to perfect the product and to educate the customer about the product. The computer industry in the early 1970s is a good example of the embryonic stage. At this stage, a share-building strategy is the appropriate choice, since the company's objective is to establish a reputation and market share. Generally, because the company is very small at this stage, it has a flat structure, and its founder probably exercises a great deal of centralized control.

In terms of horizontal differentiation, a functional structure is likely to emerge as a company establishes its goals and objectives and begins to group activities by function. Developing market share depends primarily on product development; hence the research and development and the marketing functions take precedence in the new structure. Integration, in turn, is organized around the function providing the distinctive competence that the company is trying to develop.

Companies in embryonic industries are likely to be entrepreneurial, with a fast-moving culture that stems mainly from a technological or marketing orientation. Clan control, like that used by Apple in its early years, is the main type of control because the company is essentially discovering how to do things right. These companies settle for loose control because output controls or stringent rules and procedures do not suit a company that does not know as yet what targets it can achieve. In fact, establishing targets can hurt the company by lowering aspirations and stifling creativity. Thus structure and control are best kept simple and fluid.

Growth-stage strategy and structure   By the time it reaches the growth stage of the life cycle, an organization has learned how to do the right things in the right way. It therefore adopts a *growth strategy* to retain its share of the rapidly expanding market.[15] By now, it has established a relatively stable grouping of functional activities, and functional managers have emerged to take control of the functions, lessening the burden on the founding entrepreneur. Consequently, the company is also taller, with a higher level of vertical differentiation. More managerial control results as well. These changes mean that the company is operating with a fully developed functional structure that gives it a firm foundation on which to build. The boundaries among functions are still likely to be

TABLE 10.3   Life cycle strategy and structure and control

Life cycle strategy	Appropriate structure	Integrating mechanisms	Type of control		
			Output	Bureaucratic	Clan
Embrionic	Simple	Personal and group meetings	Little use	Little use (e.g. sales targets)	Great use (e.g. entrepreneurial culture)
Growth	Functional, product, or matrix	Liaison roles task forces and teams (e.g. product innovation committee)	Little use	Little use	Little use
Shakeout	Product or matrix (depends on generic strategy)	Fully developed teams and task forces (e.g. product development committee)	Some to great use	Some to great use (depends on generic strategy)	Some to great use
Maturity	Product/ functional	Teams and task forces (e.g. process development committee)	Some to great use	Some to great use (depends on generic strategy)	Some to great use
Decline	Move to simplify structure (e.g. product to functional)	Streamline integrating mechanisms	Great use	Great use	Some use

fluid, however, and cross-functional communication that integrates the organization persists. As the company grows and becomes more complex, it increasingly uses teams and task forces. At this stage, the company's goal should be to perfect its manufacturing operations in order to ride down the experience curve, and to design its structure to suit its distinctive competence.

However, problems can occur at this stage when companies do not change their structures and controls to suit future contingencies. Because of the large increase in market growth, many companies neglect their costs, since they can still sell all they can produce. As there is no pressure to cut costs, a company has a lot of slack, and there is little incentive for it to exert tight control over itself. Often companies develop complex structures with little concern for their cost. You saw earlier in the Apple and TI examples how lax control was in these companies during their period of unprecedented growth. Apple thought it had the luxury to develop the expensive divisional structure that duplicated design, research and development, and marketing activities for each product line. When the next stage of the life cycle, the shakeout stage, arrived, Apple scrambled to restructure itself more efficiently. Similarly, at TI managers recognized the consequences of using an expensive matrix structure in a maturing market. Organizational design during growth almost inevitably determines a company's success in future stages.

Shakeout strategy and structure   In the shakeout stage, a *share-maintaining* or *share-increasing strategy* is the appropriate choice. In a shakeout, the market is increasing, but at a decreasing rate: excess capacity develops throughout the industry as demand growth slows. To survive, a company must hold onto its share of the market. The companies that have perfected their manufacturing systems and streamlined their structures are in the best position because they have accumulated more experience and lowered costs faster than the others. Companies that paid close attention to adopting the right organizational structure and controls in the growth stage now find themselves in the best position to develop their generic business-level strategy and to sustain their competitive advantage in the shakeout. Such companies control their structures and can choose the right organizational arrangements to capitalize on generic strategy. As discussed earlier, companies at this stage are forced to decide what kind of structure they need because *cost leadership and differentiation have very different kinds of structure and control requirements*.

To increase market share and reduce costs, both low-cost and differentiated companies usually adopt a product structure based on product lines or market segments. This structure allows a low-cost company to control its production system efficiently. For a differentiator, such a structure helps increase market share, since the company can group its activities to mirror its market segments and different kinds of customers. The integration mechanisms used can be closely tied to the company's product lines, which also makes coordination easier. Apple's reorganization to a product structure as it went after the school market, home market, and so on, illustrates this point. Similarly, Hewlett-Packard, faced with increasing competition from the Japanese, reorganized its structure around six product/market segments to achieve a fit between its strategy and structure.

A company's controls also change. Managers quite likely are more attentive to the bottom line and develop tough performance standards for the various functions. Standardization of inputs, throughputs, and outputs is the chief concern. Bonuses for key employees in the management team and for salespeople are usually linked to increases in market share. The culture of the organization probably changes as well, to reflect the more competitive and uncertain industry environment. Management must become less freewheeling and more efficiency oriented, and rewards are tied to cost effectiveness. Marketing, not just selling, is emphasized. If the company is a differentiator, customers have to be convinced of its dedication to product quality, reliability, or after-sales service.[16]

Thus a marked shift in the kind of controls companies use occurs at this stage in the industry life cycle. Dealing with the new reality of the competitive environment is hard on strategic managers, and consequently, many organizations go into decline and fail. Companies undergo major changes in competitive position and advantage as they are forced to readjust their structure and control system to the new competitive conditions.

Maturity strategies and structure In the maturity stage, *hold-and-maintain* market share and *profit strategies* are most likely. Companies try to exploit the benefits of having made the right strategy-structure choices at the previous stages and enjoy their competitive advantage. At this stage, the goals of the research and development and production functions are to keep up with incremental product and process innovations. Products have been standardized, and a company's principal concern is to increase the product range to suit different kinds of customers and iron out any distribution difficulties to maximize sales. Its competitive strategy determines how the company strives to hold and maintain its position at this stage and to reap profits.

With a strategy of differentiation, a hold-and-maintain position means concentrating resources on developing the customer base. Companies use resources to improve marketing, distribution, and after-sales service. Decentralization occurs, and autonomy is granted to lower-level employees so that they can respond creatively and flexibly to customer needs. A high level of interfunctional communication is emphasized. The sales force feeds information to research and product development personnel so that they can make product refinements to enhance customer satisfaction, and research and development coordinates with manufacturing to bring new products on line. Since it needs as much integration as possible, the company frequently relies on task forces to trade and share information. Structure is buttressed by a culture that stresses service and customer satisfaction. IBM is renowned for its cultural values which allow it to respond effectively to customer needs.

Although a company may be following a differentiation strategy, costs are still a concern, especially if a profit strategy is being pursued. In production, strict cost control is likely to be stringently enforced, and in fact, production may be contracted out to third world countries with lower labor costs.

If the company is following a low-cost strategy, both the hold-and-maintain and profit strategies require continuing attention to materials management and the regulation of procurement, production, and distribution in order to control costs. Thus control is likely to become increasingly stringent. These companies also develop tall structures, with rigid rules and procedures that standardize organizational activities. Output controls increase and include strict accounting procedures and quantitative and qualitative measures of performance.[17] The culture of a company pursuing a profit strategy will combine a rigid cost-cutting mentality with a heavy managerial emphasis on the bottom line. Bonus systems linked directly to cost reduction or sales targets tied to increases in the customer base dominate the reward system and reinforce the production culture.[18] The combined result of all these measures is an organization that is a far cry from the decentralized and flexible differentiating company. It reaps profits from its meticulous attention to cost cutting. Crown Cork & Seal Company, Inc. is the epitome of a company in the mature stage and has remained the cost leader in the bottling and capping market for many years because of its innovative cost-cutting methods.

Decline strategies and structure   As all the decline strategies discussed in Chapter 7 — harvest, asset reduction, divestiture, and others — suggest, companies choosing to remain in the industry must shift to a structure and control system that reduces their total costs of production. Otherwise, they cannot respond to the inevitable fall in demand in a declining industry. Since the industry has excess capacity, companies must change their structure and move rapidly to remove excess capacity by closing down plants. If they operate with a product structure, product lines should be trimmed and consolidated. GM did so, though very belatedly, when the demand for its vehicles declined. It shut down plants across the country, streamlined its structure, and cut costs by reducing the numbers of white-collar employees. Similarly, Kodak responded to increasing competition and a stagnating market by reducing capacity and combining many of its operating facilities both at home and abroad.

The move to streamline structure is often accompanied by a centralization of authority at the top levels in the organization.[19] That is, management moves to reassert tight personal control over lower levels in the hierarchy. Increased control is often attended by a reduction in the number of hierarchical levels as the company streamlines its structure. After deregulation, AT&T eliminated two levels in the hierarchy and recentralized control.

Obviously, decline is very difficult for companies to manage. Employees, accustomed to prosperity, find that promotion opportunities and bonuses have dried up and that layoffs may ensue. Layoffs threaten morale and exacerbate the problems that the company is trying to deal with. Corporate culture deteriorates. Large oil companies suffered these consequences when they terminated thousands of employees during the oil price slump. During decline, top management continually tightens control, autonomy at lower levels is reduced, and any function or activity that cannot demonstrate bottom line results is in danger. Output controls work in a punitive fashion and are reinforced by strict accounting procedures and bureaucratic control.

The resulting structure is far less costly to operate, and the company is in a better position to survive. If the company is pursuing a low-cost strategy, its only option is to move quickly to reduce costs even further. The cost leader may be able to survive comfortably for many years as other, less efficient, companies are driven out of the market. For the differentiator in a declining situation, cost cutting will mean reducing distribution costs. Although it must protect its distinctive competence, the differentiator may have room to reduce its product range or trim marginal customer segments in order to reduce costs without hurting revenues too much. In essence, it pursues a strategy of market concentration, which lowers costs but permits the company to retain its differentiated appeal. Many companies may also decide to specialize in one niche and essentially move to a focused strategy, serving one customer segment. These companies can streamline and simplify their structure because they have simplified their strategies. They can reduce the costs of coordination and control by selecting a simplified structure that has a lower level of differentiation and integration.

Summary

Firms must match their structures and control systems to their business level strategies if they are to survive and prosper in competitive environments. Not only does the basic choice between a low cost and a differentiation strategy require the firm to make a different set of choices, but choices of structure and control must be continually changed and modified to suit the nature of the industry life cycle. This is a complex job for strategic managers and one that many firms do not do well. The evidence suggests that firms that do not alter their structures do not perform as well as those that do, so that there is a strong link between strategy, structure and firm performance at the business level.

10.5 STRUCTURE AND CONTROL AT THE CORPORATE LEVEL

At the corporate level, a company needs to choose the organizational structure that will let it operate efficiently in a number of different businesses. Although product structures are sometimes used to manage the multibusiness company, the structure normally chosen at the corporate level is the multidivisional structure or one of its variants, discussed in Chapter 8. The larger and more diverse the businesses in the corporate portfolio, the more likely is the company to have a divisional structure. The reason is that each division requires the services of full-scale specialist support functions and that a headquarters corporate staff is needed to oversee and evaluate divisional operations. Once it selects a divisional structure, a company must make two more choices: the right mix of integrating mechanisms to match the particular divisional structure and the right control systems to make the divisional structure work.

In Chapter 6, we discussed the various types of corporate strategy that a company can pursue. For the first of these types — concentration on a single business — the corporate- and the business-level strategies are identical. Thus the discussion of structure and business-level strategy above covers the issue of choice of structure and control for the single-business firm. We discuss below how the corporate-level strategies of vertical integration, related diversification, and unrelated diversification affect the choice of structure and control systems.

As we discussed in Chapter 6, the main reason a company pursues vertical integration is to achieve *economies of integration* among divisions.[20] For example, the company can coordinate resource scheduling decisions among divisions to reduce costs. For instance, locating a rolling mill next to a steel furnace saves the costs of reheating steel ingots. Similarly, the chief gains from related diversification come from obtaining *synergies* among divisions: divisions benefit by sharing distribution and sales networks or research and development knowledge. With both these strategies, the benefits to the company come from some transfer of resources among divisions. To secure these benefits, the company must coordinate activities between divisions. Consequently, *structure and control must be designed to handle the transfer of resources among divisions.*

However, in the case of unrelated diversification, the benefits to the company come from the possibility of achieving an *internal capital market,* which allows corporate personnel to make better allocations of capital than the external capital market. With this strategy, there are no transactions or exchanges among divisions; each operates separately. Therefore *structure and control must be designed to allow each division to operate independently.*

A company's choice of structure and control mechanisms thus depends on the degree to which the company must control the interactions among divisions. The more interdependent the divisions — that is, the more they depend on each other for resources — the more *complex are the structure and control mechanisms required to make the strategy work.*[21]

Table 10.4 indicates what forms of structure and control companies should adopt to manage the three corporate strategies. We examine them in detail below.

Unrelated Diversification

Since there are *no linkages* among divisions, unrelated diversification is the easiest and cheapest strategy to manage. The main requirement of the structure and control system is that it let corporate personnel easily and accurately evaluate

TABLE 10.4   Corporate strategy and structure and control

Corporate strategy	Appropriate structure	Need for integration	Type of control		
			Market	Bureaucratic	Clan
Unrelated diversification	Conglomerate	Low (no exchanges between divisions)	Great use (e.g. ROI)	Some use (e.g. budgets)	Little use
Vertical integration	Multidivisional	Medium (scheduling resource transfers)	Great use (e.g. ROI, transfer pricing)	Great use (e.g. stan-dardization, budgets)	Some use (e.g. shared norms and values)
Related diversification	Multidivisional SBU	High (achieve synergies between divisions by integrating roles)	Little use	Great use (e.g. rules, budgets)	Great use (e.g. develop corporate culture)

divisional performance. Thus the *conglomerate structure,* discussed earlier, is the appropriate choice, and market and bureaucratic controls are used with it. Each division is evaluated by strict ROI criteria, and each division is given a budget in relation to its return on investment. The company also applies sophisticated accounting controls in order to obtain information quickly from the divisions, so that corporate managers can readily compare divisions on whatever dimensions corporate personnel choose. Textron is a good example of a company that operates a conglomerate structure through the use of sophisticated computer networks and accounting controls, which allow it almost daily access to divisional performance.

Divisions in the conglomerate structure usually have considerable autonomy, unless they fail to reach their ROI objectives. Generally, corporate headquarters is not interested in the types of business-level strategy pursued by each division unless there are problems. If problems arise, corporate headquarters may step in to take corrective action, perhaps replacing managers or providing more financial resources, depending on the reason for the problem. However, if they see no possibility of a turnaround, corporate personnel may just as easily decide to divest the division. This structure, therefore, allows the unrelated company to operate its businesses as a portfolio of investments, which can be bought and sold as business conditions change. Usually, managers in the various divisions do not know one another, and they may not know what companies are in the corporate portfolio.

The use of market controls to manage a company means that no integration among divisions is necessary. Thus the costs of managing an unrelated company are low. The biggest problem facing corporate personnel is to decide on capital allocations to the various divisions, in order to maximize the overall profitability of the portfolio. They also have to oversee divisional management and make sure that divisions are achieving ROI targets.

Vertical Integration

Vertical integration is a more expensive strategy to manage because *sequential* resource flows from one division to the next must be coordinated. The multidivisional structure effects such coordination. This structure provides the centralized control necessary for the vertically integrated company to achieve benefits from the control of resource transfers. Corporate personnel assume the responsibility for devising market and bureaucratic controls to promote the efficient transfer of resources among divisions. Complex rules and procedures are instituted to manage interdivisional relationships and to specify how exchanges are to be made. In addition, an internal transfer pricing system is created to allow one division to sell its products to the next. As we have already noted, these complex links can lead to ill will among divisions, and so corporate personnel must try to minimize divisional conflicts.

Centralizing authority at corporate headquarters must be done with care in vertically related companies. It carries the risk of involving corporate personnel in operating issues at the business level to the point where the divisions lose their autonomy and motivation. As noted in Chapter 8, the company must strike the right balance of centralized control at corporate headquarters and decentralized control at the divisional level, if it is to implement this strategy successfully.

Because their interests are at stake, divisions need to have input into scheduling and resource transfer decisions. For example, the plastics division in a chemical company has a vital interest in the activities of the oil division, for the quality of the products it gets from the oil division determines the quality of its own products. Divisional integrating mechanisms can bring about direct coordination and information transfers among divisions.[22] To handle communication among divisions, the company can set up task forces or teams for the purpose. At the very least, it should establish liaison roles; in high tech and chemical companies, integrating roles among divisions are very common. Thus a strategy of vertical integration is managed through a combination of corporate and divisional controls. Although the organizational arrangements for managing this strategy cost more than those for operating unrelated diversification, the benefits derived from vertical integration often outweigh its costs.

Related Diversification

In the case of related diversification, divisions share research and development knowledge, information, customer bases, and goodwill in order to obtain gains from synergy. The process is difficult to manage, and so a multidivisional structure is used to facilitate the transfer of resources to obtain synergies. Even with this structure, however, high levels of resource sharing and joint production by divisions make it very hard for corporate managers to measure the performance of each individual division. Besides, you saw as in the TRW example in Chapter 8, the divisions themselves may not want to exchange products or knowledge because transfer prices — inherently difficult to set — are perceived as unfair. If a related company is to obtain gains from synergy, it has to adopt complicated forms of integration and control at the divisional level to make the structure work efficiently.

First, since market control is impossible because resources are shared, the company needs to develop a corporate culture that stresses cooperation among divisions, along with corporate, rather than divisional, goals. Second, corporate managers must establish sophisticated integrating devices to ensure coordination among divisions. Integrating roles and teams become crucial because they provide the context in which managers from different divisions can meet and develop a common vision of corporate goals. Hewlett-Packard, for example, created three new high-level integrating teams to make certain that the new products developed by its technology group made their way quickly to its product divisions.

The right mix of incentives and rewards for cooperation is also essential to a multidivisional structure if it is to achieve gains from synergy. With unrelated diversification, divisions operate autonomously, and the company can quite easily reward managers on their division's individual performance. With related diversification, however, rewarding divisions is more difficult since they are engaged in joint production, and strategic managers must be sensitive and alert to achieving equity in rewards among divisions.

In this situation, the strategic business unit (SBU) structure, discussed in earlier chapters, can prove useful. If the company designs its structure around the basic commonalities among divisions, it can evaluate divisional performance more easily. Thus, for example, one SBU could be operated around one customer group, such as chain stores, while another SBU could be operated around technological similarities. SBUs make it easier to integrate and control the performance of the company and allow management to sense opportunities and threats, as well as to develop the company's distinctive competences. The aim always is to design the structure so that it can maximize the benefits from the strategy at the lowest management cost.

Managing a strategy of related diversification also raises the issue of how much authority to centralize and how much to decentralize. Corporate managers need to take a close look at how their controls affect divisional performance and autonomy. If corporate managers get too involved in the day-to-day operations of the divisions, they can endanger divisional autonomy and undercut divisional managers in their decision making on their divisions' future. Corporate managers, after all, see everything from a corporate, rather than a divisional, perspective. For example, in the Heinz case, mentioned, management attempted to develop one form of competitive advantage, low-cost advantage, in every division.[23] While this approach may work well for Heinz, it may be totally inappropriate to a company that is operating a totally diverse set of businesses, each of which needs to develop its own unique competence. Too much corporate control can put divisional managers in a *straightjacket,* and performance suffers.

10.6 CHANGES IN CONTROLS AND STRUCTURE

As you saw in Chapter 8, the main growth path for American corporations is from vertical integration to related diversification. Given the previous discussion, this means that, to succeed, a company has to alter its structure and control systems as it changes from one strategy to another. It must change the controls that were appropriate when it was pursuing a strategy of vertical integration to those that suit a strategy of related diversification. In practice, this means moving from transfer prices and output controls to bureaucratic and clan control.

However, often corporate and divisional managers do not grasp the fact that the benefits from related diversification cannot be achieved using the old market controls. Managers do not foresee the new pattern of relationships successfully and do not choose controls matched to the new strategy.[24] As a result, companies fail to realize the benefits from their new strategy. The Greyhound Corporation is an example of a company that is experiencing problems in managing its new acquisition strategy because it seems to be unable to decide if it is pursuing related or unrelated diversification.

Mixing two strategies leads to similar problems. For example, companies pursuing a strategy of related diversification often buy unrelated businesses and pursue both related and unrelated diversification simultaneously. What often happens is that managers tend to apply the same types of controls across all divisions. Thus, if they control their unrelated companies using controls appropriate for related ones their new unrelated businesses perform badly. That is the situation at Greyhound. Strategic managers have not put the right controls in place to achieve internal capital market gains.

Switching strategies in midstream thus creates some very serious implementation problems that have to be dealt with. Managers must be sensitive to the need to readjust their controls and form of divisional structure in order to achieve their objectives. Mixed structural forms such as the strategic business unit (SBU) structure are very useful for this purpose because this structure can be designed to allow companies to pursue different strategies together. For example, an SBU structure permits companies to manage the strategies of vertical integration, related diversification, and unrelated diversification simultaneously because divisions can be grouped into business units based on the similarities or differences among their businesses. When companies are grouped according to the types of benefit expected from the strategy, the costs of managing them are reduced and many of the problems outlined above are avoided. In the next sections, we look in more detail at the strategy implementation problems that emerge when companies acquire new businesses and/or develop new businesses through internal corporate venturing.

10.7 MERGERS, ACQUISITIONS, AND STRUCTURE

In Chapter 7, we noted that mergers and acquisitions are principal vehicles by which companies enter new product markets and expand the size of their operations.[25] We have already discussed the advantages and disadvantages of mergers and acquisitions from the strategy side. We now consider how to design structure and control systems to manage the new acquisitions. This issue is important because, as we noted earlier, many acquisitions are unsuccessful, and one of the main reasons is that many companies do a very poor job of integrating the new divisions into their corporate structure.[26]

The first factor that makes it difficult to manage the new acquisitions is the nature of the businesses that a company acquires. If a company acquires businesses related to its existing businesses, it should find it fairly easy to integrate these businesses into its corporate structure. The controls already being used in the related company can be adapted to the new divisions. To achieve gains from synergies, the company can expand its task forces or increase the number of integrating roles, so that the new divisions are drawn into the existing divisional structure.

If managers do not understand how to develop connections among divisions to permit gains from synergy, the new businesses will perform poorly. Some authors have recently argued that that is why the quality of management is so important. A company must employ managers who have the ability to recognize synergies among apparently different businesses and so derive benefits from acquisitions and mergers.[27] For instance, Porter cites the example of Philip Morris, the tobacco maker, which took over Miller Brewing Company.[28] On the surface these seem to be very different businesses. However, when their products are viewed as consumer products that are often bought and consumed together, the possibility of sales, distribution, and marketing synergies becomes clearer. Since both businesses require the same kind of managerial skills, even management synergies are feasible. Because it is usually easier to see the potential synergies between very similar businesses, companies should take over only related businesses, where they have the knowledge and expertise to manage the new acquisitions and make them profitable.

However, if companies acquire businesses for the sake of capital market gains alone, strategy implementation is easier. If companies acquire unrelated businesses and seek to operate them only as a portfolio of investments, they should have no trouble managing the acquisitions. Implementation problems are likely to arise only when corporate managers try to interfere in businesses that they know little about or when they use inappropriate structure and controls to manage the new business and attempt to achieve the wrong kind of benefits from the acquisition. For example, if managers try to integrate unrelated companies with related ones, or apply the wrong kinds of controls at the divisional level, or interfere in business-level strategy, corporate performance suffers. These mistakes explain why related acquisitions are sometimes more successful than unrelated ones.[29]

Strategic managers therefore need to be very sensitive to the problems involved in taking over new businesses through mergers and acquisitions. As outsiders, they rarely appreciate the real issues inherent in managing the new business until they have to deal with them personally. Even in the case of acquiring closely related businesses, new managers must realize that each business has a unique culture or way of doing things. Such idiosyncrasies have to be understood to manage the new organization. Over time new management can change the culture and alter the internal workings of the company, but this is a difficult implementation task, as we will discuss in the next chapter, when politics and strategic change are considered.

10.8 INTERNAL NEW VENTURES AND STRUCTURE

The main alternative to growth through acquisition or merger is for a company to develop new businesses internally. In Chapter 7, we called this strategy the new venturing process, and we discussed its advantages for growth and diversification. Now we consider the design of the appropriate internal arrangements for encouraging the development of new ventures. At the heart of this design process must be the realization by corporate managers that internal new venturing is a form of entrepreneurship. The design should encourage creativity and give new venture managers the opportunity and resources to develop new products or markets. Hewlett–Packard, for example, gives managers a great deal of latitude in this respect. In order to encourage innovation, it allows them to work on informal projects while they carry out their assigned tasks.[30] More generally, the point is to choose the appropriate structure and controls for operating new ventures.[31]

One of the main design choices is the creation of **new venture divisions.** To provide new venture managers with the autonomy to experiment and take risks, the company sets up a new venture division separate from other divisions and makes it a center for new product or project development. Away from the day-to-day scrutiny of top management, divisional personnel pursue the creation of new business like external entrepreneurs. The division is operated by controls that reinforce the entrepreneurial spirit. Thus market and output controls are inappropriate because they can inhibit risk taking. Instead, the company uses clan control and develops a culture for entrepreneurship in this division to provide a climate for innovation. However, care must be taken to institute bureaucratic controls that put some limits on freedom of action. Otherwise costly mistakes may be made and resources wasted on frivolous ideas.

In managing the new venture division, it is very important to use integrating mechanisms such as task forces and teams to screen new ideas. Managers from research and development, sales and marketing, and product development are heavily involved in this screening process. Generally, there is a formal evaluation committee, consisting of proven entrepreneurs and experienced managers from the other divisions, before whom the champions of new products must defend their projects in order to have to secure the resources for developing them. Firms like 3M, IBM, and Texas Instruments are examples of successful companies that use this method for creating opportunities internally.

Care must be taken to preserve the autonomy of the new venture division. As mentioned earlier, the costs of research and development are high and the rewards uncertain. After spending millions of dollars, corporate managers often become concerned about the division's performance and introduce tight output controls or strong budgets to increase accountability. All this hurts the entrepreneurial culture.

Sometimes, however, after creating a new invention, the new venture division wants to reap the benefits by producing and marketing it. If this happens, then the division becomes an ordinary operating division and entrepreneurship declines.[32] Strategic managers must take steps to provide a structure that can sustain the entrepreneurial spirit.[33] Hewlett-Packard has a novel way of dealing with new venturing. In the operating divisions, as soon as a new, self-supporting product is developed, a new division is formed to turn out and market the product. By spinning off the product in this fashion, the company keeps all its divisions small and entrepreneurial. The arrangement also provides a good climate for innovation. In the last few years, however, Hewlett-Packard found that having many new venture divisions was too expensive and so has merged some of them. The company appears to be moving toward the creation of a single new venture division.

Internal new venturing is an important means by which large, established companies can maintain their momentum and grow from within.[34] The alternative is to acquire small businesses that have already developed some technological competence and to pump resources into them. This approach can also succeed, and it obviously lessens the management's burden if the company operates the new business as an independent entity. In recent years Kodak has taken this path to diversification, buying a share in many small companies. In practice, companies are likely to operate in both ways, acquiring some new businesses and developing others internally. Recently, many companies have done so when increasing competition from abroad has threatened their dominance in existing businesses and has forced them to evaluate opportunities for maximizing long-term growth in new businesses.

10.9 SUMMARY OF CHAPTER

The purpose of this chapter has been to bring together strategy formulation and strategy implementation and to examine how a company's choice of strategy affects the form of its structure and control systems. The cause of TI's problems with its structure should now be clear: its structure no longer fit the strategy that the company had to pursue in order to regain its competitive advantage. The following are the main points made in the chapter.

1. At the functional level, each function requires a different kind of structure and control system to achieve its functional objectives.

2. At the business level, the structure and control system must be designed to achieve business-level objectives. This involves managing the relationships among all the functions to permit the company to develop a distinctive competence.

3. A cost-leadership and a differentiation strategy require different structures and control systems if the company is to develop a competitive advantage.

4. The form of the company's structure and control systems varies at different stages of the industry life cycle.

5. At the corporate level, the company must choose the structure and control system that will allow it to operate a collection of businesses.

6. Related diversification, unrelated diversification, and vertical integration require different forms of structure and control if the benefits of pursuing the strategy are to be realized.

7. As companies change their corporate strategies over time, they must change their structures, since different strategies have to be managed in different ways.

8. The profitability of mergers and acquisitions depends on the structure and control systems that companies adopt to manage them and the way a company integrates them into its existing businesses.

9. To encourage internal new venturing, companies must design a structure that gives the new venture division the autonomy needed for developing new products and protects it from excessive interference by corporate managers.

Discussion Questions

1. How should (a) a high tech company, (b) a fast food franchise, and (c) a small manufacturing company design its functional structure and control systems to implement a generic strategy?

2. How should (a) a differentiated company and (b) a low-cost company alter its structure and control systems over the industry life cycle?

3. If a related company begins to buy unrelated businesses, in what ways should it change its structure or control mechanisms to manage the acquisitions?

4. How would you design a structure and control system to encourage entrepreneurship in a large, established corporation?

Endnotes

1. "Texas Instruments Inc.," *Moody's Industrial Manual*, 2 (1986), 6120.

2. "TI: Shot Full of Holes and Trying to Recover," *Business Week*, March 6, 1984, pp. 82–84.

3. "Texas Instruments Cleans Up Its Act," *Business Week*, September 19, 1983, p. 56.

4. W. G. Ouchi, "The Relationship Between Organizational Structure and Organizational Control," *Administrative Science Quarterly*, 22 (1977), 95–113.

5. K. M. Eisenhardt, "Control: Organizational and Economic Approaches," *Management Science,* 16 (1985), 134–148.

6. J. R. Galbraith, *Designing Complex Organizations* (Reading, Mass.: Addison-Wesley, 1973). P. R. Lawrence and J. W. Lorsch, *Organization and Environment* (Cambridge, Mass.: Harvard University Press, 1967). D. Miller, "Strategy Making and Structure: Analysis and Implications for Performance," *Academy of Management Journal,* 30 (1987), 7–32.

7. Michael E. Porter, *Competitive Strategy: Techniques for Analyzing Industries and Competitors* (New York: Free Press, 1980). D. Miller, "Configurations of Strategy and Structure," *Strategic Management Journal,* 7 (1986), 233–249.

8. D. Miller and P. H. Freisen, *Organizations: A Quantum View* (Englewood Cliffs, N.J.: Prentice Hall, 1984).

9. J. Woodward, *Industrial Organization: Theory and Practice* (London: Oxford University Press, 1965). Lawrence and Lorsch, *Organization and Environment.*

10. R. E. White, "Generic Business Strategies, Organizational Context and Performance: An Empirical Investigation," *Strategic Management Journal,* 7 (1986), 217–231.

11. Porter, *Competitive Strategy.* Miller, "Configurations of Strategy and Structure".

12. T. E. Deal and A. A. Kennedy, *Corporate Cultures* (Reading, Mass.: Addison-Wesley), "Corporate Culture," *Business Week,* October 27, 1980, pp. 148–160.

13. Miller, "Configurations of Strategy and Structure". R. E. Miles and C. C. Snow, *Organizational Strategy, Structure, and Process* (New York: McGraw-Hill, 1978).

14. Lawrence and Lorsch, *Organization and Environment.*

15. C. W. Hofer and D. Schendel, *Strategy Formulation: Analytical Concepts* (St. Paul, Minn.: West Publishing, 1978).

16. Porter, *Competitive Strategy.*

17. T. Burns and G. M. Stalker, *The Management of Innovation* (London: The Tavistock Institute, 1961) Lawrence and Lorsch, *Organization and Environment.*

18. G. R. Jones, "Transaction Costs, Property Rights, and Organizational Culture: An Exchange Perspective," *Administrative Science Quarterly,* 28 (1983), 454–467.

19. D. A. Whetten, "Sources, Responses, and Effects of Organizational Design," in J. R. Kimberly and R. H. Miles, eds. *The Organizational Life Cycle.* (San Francisco: Jossey-Bass, 1980).

20. G. R. Jones and C. W. L. Hill, "Transaction Cost Analysis of Strategy-Structure Choice," *Strategic Management Journal,* 9 (1988), 159–172.

21. Jones and Hill, "Transaction Cost Analysis of Strategy-Structure Choice".

22. Lawrence and Lorsch, *Organization and Environment.* Galbraith, *Designing Organizational Structure.* Porter, *Competitive Advantage: Creating and Sustaining Superior Performance.*

23. Porter, *Competitive Advantage.*

24. C. K. Prahalad and R. A. Bettis, "The Dominant Logic: A New Linkage Between Diversity and Performance," *Strategic Management Journal,* 7 (1986), 485–501.

25. M. S. Salter and W. A. Weinhold, *Diversification Through Acquisition* (New York: Free Press, 1979).

26. F. T. Paine and D. J. Power, "Merger Strategy: An Examination of Drucker's Five Rules for Successful Acquisitions," *Strategic Management Journal,* 5 (1984), 99–110.

27. Prahalad and Bettis, "The Dominant Logic." Porter, *Competitive Advantage.*

28. Ibid.

29. H. Singh and C. A. Montgomery, "Corporate Acquisitions and Economic Performance," unpublished manuscript, 1984.

30. T. J. Peters and R. H. Waterman Jr., *In Search of Excellence* (New York: Harper and Row, 1982).

31. R. A. Burgelman, "Managing the New Venture Division: Research Findings and the Implications for Strategic Management," *Strategic Management Journal,* 6 (1985), 39–54.

32. N. D. Fast, "The Future of Industrial New Venture Departments," *Industrial Marketing Management,* 8 (1979), 264–279.

33. Burgleman, "Managing the New Venture Division".

34. R. A. Burgelman, "Corporate Entrepreneurship and Strategic Management: Insights from a Process Study," *Management Science,* 29 (1983), 1349–1364.

Chapter 11

CONFLICT, POLITICS, AND CHANGE IN STRATEGY-STRUCTURE CHOICE

11.1 OPENING INCIDENT: CBS INC.

CBS Inc. is a diversified entertainment and information company engaged in the principal businesses of broadcasting, recorded music, and publishing. One of America's most prestigious organizations, CBS experienced much turmoil in recent years. Its troubles began when outside investors, deciding that the company's profitability and return on assets were under par, led several takeover attempts against it. In successive attacks, Jesse Helms, a senator from North Carolina, Ivan Boesky the arbitrager, and finally Ted Turner, the founder of Turner Broadcasting System, Inc., announced takeover attempts.[1] CBS realized that it had to take these takeover attempts seriously if it wanted to remain independent.

First, Thomas Wyman, the chairman of CBS at the time, authorized a repurchase of CBS stock for $150 a share (Turner's offer was only $130). This increased CBS's debt from $510 million to $1.4 billion. Next, CBS searched for a white knight who would buy a major portion of CBS stock in the event that a hostile bid seemed likely to succeed. Laurence Tisch of Loews Corporation agreed to play this role. However, by 1986 Tisch had purchased 25 percent of CBS stock, making him the largest stockholder, and board members, including Wyman, began to fear he would take over CBS. Tisch did nothing to stop these rumors.[2]

Tisch began to take a more active role in CBS to question or disagree with Wyman's policies. Wyman himself was now suffering on two fronts. Although he had been brought in by the legendary founder of CBS, William Paley, Paley had become increasingly disturbed that Wyman was not consulting him on CBS policy, particularly because CBS was going through bad times. Tensions increased, and at a board meeting at the end of 1986 Wyman revealed that he had been secretly negotiating with Coca-Cola for the sale of CBS to the soft drink company. Board members were shocked and withdrew their support. Wyman resigned, Paley became acting chairman, and Tisch became acting CEO.

After this power struggle, the pressing issue facing the company became to change CBS's strategy and structure to increase its ratings. The CBS news division posed a problem. It had been CBS's most prestigious operation since the golden days of Edward Murrow and Walter Cronkite, but the recruitment of a new president for the division, Van Gordon Sauter, had led to conflict between management and staff. Sauter believed that the news should be entertaining, in order to earn the highest ratings, whereas the news staff believed that the news should remain free of entertainment value, as in the past. In the ensuing conflict, Dan Rather, Bill Moyers, and Don Hewitt,

executive producer of "60 Minutes", all offered to buy the news division and take it out of CBS. The offer was refused, but Tisch decided to remove Sauter in order to restore stability to the division.[3]

The next problem was reorganizing CBS's structure and control systems. The trend in all the three main networks was for downsizing and reducing staff and costs to make the company more efficient. Tisch, as the CEO of CBS, began this change process by laying off staff. He eliminated more than 1,500 employees, about 9 percent of the CBS work force; this number included 150 people from the news division. He also severely cut expense accounts and reduced the slack that CBS personnel had previously enjoyed. Tisch's goal was to change CBS so that it functioned like a company in the maturity stage of the industry life cycle and to attain a 12 percent ROI goal.[4] However, this change process caused more conflict and further hurt morale at CBS, and particularly in the news division.

11.2 OVERVIEW

As the example of CBS suggests, this chapter is about organizational politics, conflict, and the problems that occur when companies attempt to change their strategy and structure. Until now in our study of strategic management, we have treated strategy formulation and implementation from an impersonal, rational perspective, where decisions are made coldly and logically. In reality, this is an incomplete picture of how companies make decisions, since politics and conflict influence the decision-making process and the selection of organizational objectives. CBS most likely would not have made the tough choices it did if Tisch, an outsider with concern for the bottom line, had not approached the problems facing CBS's broadcasting division with a fresh perspective — one that was not colored by years spent in a CBS culture, where this division's dominance was taken for granted and the bottom line got scant attention.

The power struggle at CBS for control of the corporation indicates the importance of politics at the company. Wyman's failure to share power with Tisch and Paley and their subsequent removal of him is an example of the use of power in organizations to change organizational objectives. The problems in the news division underscore not only the issue of power, but also that of conflict between different interests—between a manager who wanted high ratings by being entertaining and a news staff that wanted ratings based on the quality of the news broadcasts. The time it took to recognize the need for organizational change and the difficulties CBS had in pushing changes through exemplify the problems of implementing strategic change.

In this chapter, we look at each of these issues. We probe the sources of organizational politics and discuss how individuals, departments, and divisions seek to increase their power so that they can influence organizational decision making. Then we examine the nature of organizational conflict and note how managers must deal with conflict to make better strategy-structure choices. Finally, we consider why it is difficult to change organizations, and we outline ways in which managers can direct organizational change so that their company's strategy and structure matches new competitive environments.

11.3 ORGANIZATIONAL POLITICS AND POWER

So far, we have assumed that in formulating the corporate mission and setting policies and goals strategic managers strive to maximize corporate wealth. This picture of the strategic decision-making process is known as the **rational view.** It suggests that managers achieve corporate goals by following a calculated, rational plan, where only shareholders' interests are considered. In reality, the process of strategic decision making is very different. Often, strategic managers' decisions further their personal, functional, or divisional interests. In this **political view** of decision making, goals and objectives are set through compromise, bargaining, and negotiation.[5] Top-level managers constantly clash over what the correct policy decisions should be, and as at CBS, power struggles and coalition building are a major part of strategic management. As in the public sphere, politics is the name given to the process in which different individuals or groups in the organization try to influence the strategic management process to further their own interests.

In this section, we examine the nature of organizational politics and the process of political decision making. **Organizational politics** is defined as the process by which self-interested but interdependent individuals and groups seek to obtain power and use power to influence the goals and objectives of the organization to further their own interests.[6] First, we consider the sources of politics and why politics is a necessary part of the strategic management process. Second, we look at how managers or divisions can increase their power so that they can influence the company's strategic direction. Third, we explore the ways in which the organization can manage politics to help it fulfill its strategic mission.

Sources of Organizational Politics

According to the political view of organizational decision making, several factors foster politics in corporate life. Figure 11.1 contrasts these factors with those underlying the rational view of organizational decision making.

The rational view assumes that complete information is available and no uncertainty exists about outcomes, but the political view suggests that strategic managers can never be sure that they are making the best decisions.[7] From a political perspective, decision making always takes place in an uncertain context, where the outcomes of actions are difficult to predict. According to the rational view, moreover, managers lack consensus about appropriate organizational *goals* and the appropriate *means,* or strategies, for achieving these goals. According to the political view, on the other hand, the choice of goals and means is linked to each individual's, function's, or division's pursuit of self-interest. Disagreement over the best course of action is inevitable in the political view because the strategic decisions made by the organization necessarily help some individuals or divisions more than others. For example, if managers decide to invest in resources to promote and develop one product, other products will not be created. Some managers win, and others lose.

Given this point of view, strategy choices are never right or wrong; they are simply better or worse ones. As a result, managers have to promote their

FIGURE 11.1   Rational and political views of the decision-making process

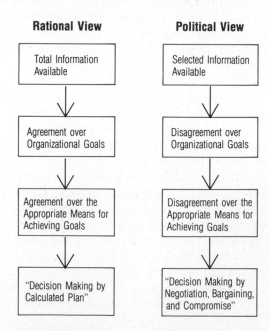

ideas and try to lobby support from other managers so that they can build up backing for a course of action. Thus coalition building is vital in strategic decision making.[8] Managers join coalitions to lobby for their interests, because in doing so they increase their political muscle in relation to their organizational opponents.

Managers also engage in politics for personal reasons. Since organizations are shaped like pyramids, individual managers realize that the higher they rise the more difficult it is to climb the next position.[9] However, if their views prevail and the organization follows their lead, *and* if their decisions bear results, they reap rewards and promotions. Thus, by being successful at politics, they increase their visibility in the organization and make themselves contenders for high organizational office.

The assumption that personal, rather than shareholder or organizational, interest governs corporate actions is what gives the word *politics* bad connotations in many people's minds. However, since no one knows for certain what decision is truly best, letting people pursue their own interest may in the long run mean that the organization's interests are being followed. Competition among managers stemming from self-interest may improve strategic decision making, with successful managers moving to the top of the organization over time. If a company can maintain checks and balances in its top management circles, politics can be a healthy influence, for it can prevent managers from becoming complacent about the status quo and thus avert organizational decline.

However, if politics grows rampant and if powerful managers gain such dominance that they can suppress the views of managers who oppose their interests, major problems may arise. Checks and balances fade, debate is restricted, and performance suffers. For example, at Gulf & Western, as soon as its founder died, the company sold off fifty businesses that the new top management saw as his pet projects (and therefore his political preferences) and not suited to the company's portfolio. Ultimately, the companies that let politics get so out of hand that shareholder interests suffer are taken over by aggressive new management teams, as happened at Diamond Shamrock. (See Chapter 2).

If kept in check, politics can be a useful management tool in making strategic decisions. The best CEOs are those who recognize this fact and create a strategic context in which managers can fight for their ideas and reap the rewards from their lobbying efforts. For example, 3M is well known for its top management committee structure, where divisional managers who request new funds and new venture managers who champion new products must present their projects to the entire top management team and lobby for support for their ideas. All top managers in 3M experienced this learning process, and presumably the ones in the top management team are those who succeeded best at mobilizing support and commitment for their concepts.

In order to play politics, managers must have *power*. Power can be defined as the ability of one individual, function, or division, to cause another individual, function, or division to do something that it would not otherwise have done.[10] Power differs from authority, which stems from holding a formal position in the hierarchy. Power comes from the ability to influence informally the way other parties behave. Perhaps the simplest way to understand power is to look at its sources.

Sources of Power

To a large degree, the relative power of organizational functions and divisions derives from a company's corporate- and business-level strategies. Different strategies make some functions or divisions more important than others in achieving the corporate mission. We will consider sources of power at the *functional or divisional level,* rather than at the individual level, because we are primarily interested in the links between politics and power and business- and corporate-level strategy. Figure 11.2 lists the sources of power that we discuss below.

Ability to cope with uncertainty A function or division gains power if it can *reduce uncertainty on behalf of another function or division.*[11] Let us suppose that a company is pursuing a strategy of vertical integration. A division that controls the supply and quality of inputs to another division has power over it because it controls the uncertainty facing the second division. At the business level, in a company pursuing a low-cost strategy, sales has power over production because sales provides information about customer needs necessary to minimize production costs. In a company pursuing a differentiation strategy, research and development have power over marketing at the early stages in the product life cycle because it controls product innovations. However, once innovation problems are solved, marketing is likely to be the most powerful function because it supplies research and development with information on customer needs. Thus a function's power depends on the degree to which other functions rely on it.

FIGURE 11.2   **Sources of power**

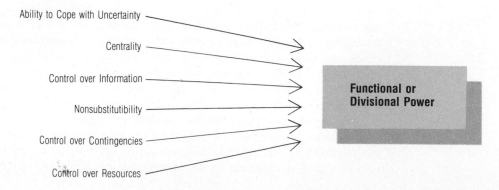

- Ability to Cope with Uncertainty
- Centrality
- Control over Information
- Nonsubstitutibility
- Control over Contingencies
- Control over Resources

Functional or Divisional Power

Centrality   Power also derives from the **centrality** of a division or function.[12] Centrality refers to the extent to which a division or function is at the center of resource transfers among divisions. For example, in a chemical company, the division supplying specialized chemicals is likely to be very central because its activities are critical both to the petroleum division, which supplies its inputs, and to the end-using divisions like plastics or pharmaceuticals, which depend on its outputs. Its activities are central to the production process of all the company's businesses. Therefore it can exert pressure on corporate headquarters to pursue policies in its own interest.

At the functional level, the function that has the most centrality, and therefore power, is the one that provides the distinctive competence on which a company's business-level strategy is based. For example, in Apple the function with the greatest centrality is research and development because the company's competitive advantage rests on a technical competence. On the other hand, in Wal-Mart the purchasing and distribution function is the most central, since Wal-Mart's competitive advantage depends on its ability to provide a low-cost product.

Control over information   Functions and divisions are also central if they are at the heart of the information flow — that is, if they can control the flow of information to other functions or divisions, or both.[13] Information is a power resource, since by giving or withholding information, one function or division can cause others to behave in certain ways. For example, sales can control the way production operates. If sales manipulates information to satisfy its own goals — for instance, responsiveness to customers — production costs will rise, but production may be unaware that costs could be lowered with a different sales strategy. Similarly, research and development can shape managers' attitudes to the competitive prospects of different kinds of products by supplying favorable information on the attributes of the products it prefers and by downplaying others.

In a very real sense, managers in organizations are playing a subtle information game when they form policies and set objectives. We discussed in Chapter 8 how divisions can disguise their performance by providing only positive information to corporate managers. The more powerful a division, the easier it can do this. In both strategy formulation and implementation, by using information to develop a power base, divisions and functions can strongly influence policy in their own interests.

Nonsubstitutability   A function or division can accrue power proportionately to the degree to which its activities are **nonsubstitutable**, that is, cannot be duplicated.[14] For example, if a company is vertically integrated, supplying divisions are nonsubstitutable to the extent that the company cannot buy what they produce in the marketplace. Thus the petroleum products division is not very powerful if a large supply of oil is available from other suppliers. In an oil crisis, the opposite would be true. On the other hand, the activities of a new venture division—a division where new products are developed—are nonsubstitutable to the extent that a company cannot buy another company that possesses similar knowledge or expertise. If knowledge or information can be bought, the division is substitutable.

The same holds true at the functional level. A function and the managers inside that function are powerful to the extent that no other function can perform their task. As in the case of centrality, which function is nonsubstitutable depends on the nature of a company's business-level strategy. If the company is pursuing a low-cost strategy, then production is likely to be the key function, and research and development or marketing have less power. But if the company is pursuing a strategy of differentiation then the opposite is likely to be the case.

Thus the power that a function or division gains by virtue of its centrality or nonsubstitutability derives from the strategy that the company is engaged in. Eventually, as a company's strategy changes, we would expect to see changes in the relative power of the functions and divisions. This is the next source of power that we discuss.

Control of contingencies   Over time, the nature of the contingencies, that is, the opportunities and threats, facing a company from the competitive environment will change as the environment changes.[15] The functions or divisions that can deal with the problems confronting the company and allow it to achieve its objectives gain power. Conversely, the functions that can no longer manage the contingency lose power. To give an example, if you look at which functional executives rose to top management positions during the last fifty years, you find that, generally, the executives who reached the highest posts did so from functions or divisions that were able to deal with the opportunities and threats facing the company.[16]

In the 1950s, for example, the main contingency problem a company confronted was to produce goods and services. Pent up demand from the years of World War II led to a huge increase in consumer spending for autos, homes, and durable goods. Goods needed to be produced quickly and cheaply to meet demand, and during this period the managers who rose to the top were from the *manufacturing* function or consumer products divisions. In the 1960s, the problem changed. Most companies had increased their productive capacity, and the market was saturated. Producing goods was not as difficult as selling them. Hence, *marketing and sales* functions rose to prominence. The rise of executives in companies reflected this critical contingency, for greater numbers of them emerged from the sales function and from marketing-oriented divisions than from any other groups. In the 1970s companies began to realize that competitive conditions were permanent. They had to streamline their strategies and structures to survive in an increasingly hostile environment. As a result, *accounting and finance* became the function that supplied most of the additions to the top management team. Today a company's business- and corporate-level strategy determines which group gains pre-eminence.

Control of resources   The final source of power that we need to examine is the ability to control and allocate scarce resources.[17] This source gives corporate-level managers their clout. Obviously, the power of corporate managers depends to a large extent on their ability to allocate capital to the operating divisions and to allot cash to or take it from a division on the basis of their expectations of its future success.

However, power from this source is not just a function of the ability to allocate resources immediately; it also comes from the ability to *generate resources in the future*. Thus individual divisions that can generate resources will have power in the corporation. For example, if the Boston Consulting Group matrix is used to categorize divisions, rising stars have power because of the future resources they are expected to generate, whereas cash cows have power because of their ability to generate resources right away. This balance of power between the stars and cash cows explains why corporate management must intervene to allocate resources. Left to themselves, the divisions would never agree on the correct price to charge for capital or on the most efficient way to allocate capital among divisions. Obviously, from a resource perspective, dogs have no power at all, and cash cows are in a very weak position, unless they have a strong corporate champion. At the functional level, the same kinds of considerations apply. The ability of sales and marketing to increase customer demand and generate revenues explains their power in the organization. In general, the function that can generate the most resources has the most power.

The most powerful division or function in the organization, then, is the one that can reduce uncertainty for others, is most central and nonsubstitutable, has control over resources and can generate them, and is able to deal with the critical external strategic contingency facing the company. In practice, each division in the corporation has power from one or more of these sources, and so there is a distribution of power among divisions. This condition gives rise to organizational politics, for managers form coalitions to try to get other power holders on their side and thus gain control over the balance of power in the organization.

Effects of Power and Politics on Strategy-Structure Choice

Power and politics strongly influence a company's choice of strategy and structure because the company has to maintain an organizational context that is responsive both to the aspirations of the various divisions, functions, and managers and to changes in the external environment. The problem companies face is that the internal structure of power always lags behind changes in the environment because, in general, the environment changes faster than companies can respond. Those in power never voluntarily give it up, but excessive politicking and power struggles reduce a company's flexibility and may erode its competitive advantage.

For example, if power struggles proceed unchecked, divisions start to compete and to hoard information or knowledge in order to maximize their own returns. This condition prevailed at TRW as we noted in Chapter 8. It also occurred at Digital Equipment Corp. when its product groups became self-contained units that cared more about protecting their interests than about achieving organizational goals. In such situations, exchanging resources among divisions becomes expensive and gains from synergy are difficult to obtain. These factors in turn lower a company's profitability and reduce organizational growth. Similar problems arise at the functional level: if one function starts to exercise its political muscle, the other functions are likely to retaliate by decreasing their cooperation with the function in question and not responding to its demands. For example, in a company pursuing a low-cost strategy, if the manufacturing function starts to exploit its position and ignores the need of sales to be responsive to customers, over the long run sales can hurt manufacturing by accepting bigger orders but at lower prices or even by seeking many small customer accounts to deliberately elevate production costs and so squeeze profits for the manufacturing function.

Managing Organizational Politics

In order to manage its politics, a company must devise organizational arrangements that create a **power balance** among the various divisions or functions so that no single one of them dominates the whole enterprise. In the divisional structure, the corporate headquarters staff play the balancing role, since they can exert power even over strong divisions and force them to share resources for the good of the whole corporation. In a single-business company, a strong chief executive officer is important because he or she must replace the corporate center and balance the power of the strong functions against the weak. The forceful CEO takes the responsibility for giving the weak functions an opportunity to air their concerns and interests and tries to avoid being railroaded into decisions by the strong function pursuing its own interests.

The CEO of a large divisional corporation also has great potential for exerting power. However, here the CEO plays another important role, that of arbiter of acceptable political decision making. Politics pervade all companies, but the CEO and top-level managers can shape its character. In some organizations, power plays are the norm because that is the way the CEOs themselves garnered power. However, other companies—especially those founded by entrepreneurs who believed in democracy or in decentralized decision making—may not tolerate power struggles, and a very different kind of political behavior becomes acceptable. It is based on a function or division manager's competence or expertise rather than on her or his ability to form powerful coalitions. At Pepsi-Cola, politics is of the cutthroat power play variety, and there is a rapid turnover of managers who fail to meet organizational aspirations. However, at Coca-Cola, ideas and expertise are much more important in politics than power plays directed at maximizing functional or divisional self-interest. Similarly, Intel Corporation does not tolerate politicking or lobbying for personal gain; instead, it rewards risk taking and makes promotion contingent on performance, not seniority.

To design an organizational structure that creates a power balance, strategic managers can use the tools of implementation that we discussed in Chapters 8 and 9. First of all, they must create the right mix of integrating mechanisms to allow functions or divisions to share information and ideas. A multidivisional structure offers one means of balancing power among divisions, and the matrix structure among functions. A company can then develop norms, values, and a common culture that emphasize corporate, rather than divisional, interests and that stress the company's mission. In companies such as IBM or 3M, for instance, culture serves to harmonize divisional interests with the achievement of corporate goals. Finally, as already noted, strong hierarchical control by a gifted CEO can also create the organizational context where politics can be put to good use and its destructive consequences avoided. When CEOs use their expert knowledge as their power, they provide the strong leadership that allows a company to achieve its corporate mission. Indeed, it should be part of the strategic managers' job to learn how to manage politics and power to further corporate interests because politics is an essential part of the process of efficiently allocating scarce organizational resources.

11.4 ORGANIZATIONAL CONFLICT

Politics implies an attempt by one party to influence the goals and decision-making process of the organization in order to further its own interests. Sometimes, however, the attempt of one group to further its interests thwarts another group's ability to attain its goals. The result is conflict within the organization. **Conflict** can be defined as a situation that arises when the goal-directed behavior of one organizational group blocks the goal-directed behavior of another.[18] In the discussion that follows, we examine (1) the effect of conflict on organizational performance, (2) the sources of conflict, (3) the ways in which the conflict process operates in the organization, and (4) the ways in which strategic managers can regulate the conflict process so that—just as in the case of politics—it yields benefits rather than costs.

Conflict: Good or Bad?

The effect of conflict on organizational performance is a continually debated question. In the past, conflict was viewed as always bad, or dysfunctional, because it leads to lower organizational performance.[19] According to that view, conflict occurs because managers have not implemented strategy correctly and have not designed the appropriate structure that would make functions or divisions cooperate to achieve corporate objectives. Without doubt, bad implementation can cause conflict and good design can prevent it. However, if carefully managed, conflict can increase organizational performance.[20] The graph in Figure 11.3 indicates the effect of organizational conflict on performance.

The graph shows that to a point conflict increases organizational performance. The reason is that conflict leads to needed organizational change, since it exposes weaknesses in organizational design. Managers can respond by changing structure and control systems, thus realigning the power structure of the organization and shifting the balance of power in favor of the group that can best meet the organization's needs. Conflict signals the need for change. However, after the optimum point, a rise in conflict leads to a decline in performance, for conflict gets out of control and the organization fragments into competing interest groups. Astute managers prevent conflict from passing the optimum point and therefore can use it to increase organizational performance. Managing conflict, then, like managing politics, is a means of improving organizational decision making and of allocating resources and responsibilities. However, politics

FIGURE 11.3   Effect of conflict on performance

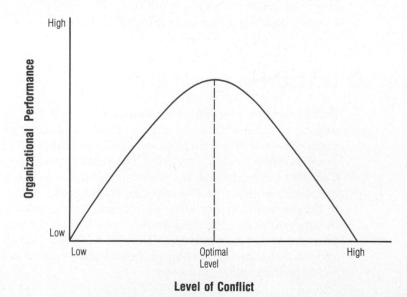

FIGURE 11.4   **Sources of organizational conflict**

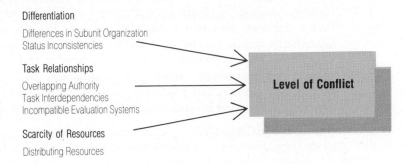

Differentiation

Differences in Subunit Organization
Status Inconsistencies

Task Relationships

Overlapping Authority
Task Interdependencies
Incompatible Evaluation Systems

Scarcity of Resources

Distributing Resources

Level of Conflict

does not necessarily stir up conflict and effective management of the political process is a way of avoiding destructive clashes among groups. Conflict in organizations has many sources, and strategic managers need to be aware of them, so that when conflict does occur it can be quickly controlled or resolved.

Sources of Conflict

As we have already noted, conflict arises when the goals of one organizational group thwart those of another. Many factors inherent in the way organizations operate can produce conflict among functions, divisions, and individuals.[21] We will focus on three main sources of organizational conflict, and they are summarized in Figure 11.4.

Differentiation   In Chapter 8, we defined differentiation as the way in which a company divides authority and task responsibilities. The process of splitting the organization into hierarchical levels and functions or divisions may produce conflict because it brings to the surface the differences in the goals and interests of groups inside the organization. This kind of conflict has two main causes.

Differences in subunit orientations   As differentiation leads to the emergence of different functions or subunits in a company, each group develops a unique orientation toward the organization's major priorities, as well as its own view of what needs to be done to increase organizational performance. Goals of the various functions naturally differ. For example, production generally has a very short-term, cost-directed efficiency orientation. Research and development is oriented toward long-term, technical goals and sales toward satisfying customer needs. Thus production may see the solution to a problem as one of reducing costs, sales as one of increasing demand, and research and development as product innovation. Differences in subunit orientation make strategy hard to formulate and implement because they slow a company's response to changes in the competitive environment and reduce its level of integration.

Differences in orientation are also a major problem at the divisional level. For example, cash cow divisions emphasize marketing goals, while stars promote technological possibilities. Consequently, it is very difficult for them to find a common way of viewing the problem. In large corporations, such disagreements can do considerable harm, for they reduce the level of cohesion and integration among divisions, hamper cooperation and synergy, and thus lower corporate performance. Many large companies, such as DEC International, Inc., Westinghouse, and Procter & Gamble, have had to cope with this handicap; they responded by reorganizing their structure and improving integration.

Status inconsistencies   In a differentiated company, over time some functions or divisions come to see themselves as more vital to its operations than others. As a result, they make little attempt to adapt their behaviors to the needs of other functions, thus blocking the goals of the latter. For example, at the functional level, production usually sees itself as the linchpin in the organization and the other functions as mere support services. This leads to line and staff conflict, where production, or line, personnel thwart the goals of staff, or support, personnel.[22] The kind of business-level strategy that a company adopts may intensify line and staff conflict because it increases the status of some functions relative to others. In low-cost companies, production is particularly important, and in differentiators, marketing or research and development are most important.

At the divisional level, the divisions that are more central to the company's operations, for example, those that supply resources to the end-using divisions, may come to see themselves as the system's linchpins. They also may pay little attention to the needs of the end users, for example, to developing new products for the end users. The end users may retaliate by buying in the marketplace or, more typically, by fighting over transfer prices, which, as we discussed earlier, is a major sign of conflict among divisions. Thus the relationships among divisions must be handled carefully by corporate headquarters to prevent conflicts from flaring up and damaging interdivisional relationships.

Task relationships   As discussed in Chapter 8, several features of task relationships may generate conflict among functions and divisions.[23]

Overlapping authority   If two different functions or divisions claim authority and responsibility for the same task, then conflict may develop in the organization. This often happens when the organization is growing, and thus functional or divisional relationships are not yet fully worked out. Likewise, when changes occur in task relationships, for instance, when divisions start to share sales and distribution facilities to reduce costs, disputes over who controls what emerge. As a result, divisions may fight for control of the resource and thus spawn conflict.

Task interdependences   In order to develop or produce goods and services, the work of one function flows horizontally to the next so that each function can build on the contributions of the others.[24] If one function does not do its job well, then the function next in line is seriously hampered in its work, and this too, generates conflict. For example, the ability of manufacturing to reduce costs on the production line depends on how well research and development has designed the product for cheap manufacture and how good a job sales has done in attracting large, stable customer accounts. At the divisional level, when divisions are trading resources, the quality of the products supplied by one division to the next affects the quality of the next division's products.

The potential for conflict is great when functions or divisions are very interdependent. In fact, the higher the level of interdependence, the higher is the potential for conflict among functions or divisions.[25] Interdependence among functions, and the consequent need to prevent conflict from arising, is the reason that managing a matrix structure is so expensive. Similarly, managing a strategy of related diversification is expensive because conflicts over resource transfers arise and have to be continually dealt with. Conversely, with unrelated diversification, the potential for interdivisional conflict is minimal because divisions do not trade resources.

The merger between Burroughs Corporation and Sperry Corporation to create Unisys Corporation is an example of the problems that must be managed to prevent conflict due to task interdependence. The CEO of Burroughs, W. M. Blumenthal, has taken enormous pains to manage new task interdependences in order to avoid major conflicts among divisions and has used a variety of integrating mechanisms to bring the two companies together. The problem is so severe because each company has the same set of functions, which, in the long run, must be merged.

Incompatible evaluation systems   We mentioned in Chapter 9 that a company has to design its evaluation and reward systems so that they do not interfere with task relationships among functions and divisions. Inequitable performance evaluation systems stir up conflict.[26] Typical problems include finding a way of jointly rewarding sales and production to avoid scheduling conflicts and setting budgets and transfer prices so that they do not lead to competition among divisions. Again, the more complex the task relationships, the harder it is to evaluate each function's or division's contribution to revenue, and the more likely is conflict to arise.

Scarcity of resources   Competition over scarce resources also produces conflict.[27] This kind of conflict most often occurs among divisions, and between divisions' and corporate management, over the allocation of capital, although budget fights among functions can also be fierce when resources are scarce. As discussed in previous chapters, divisions resist attempts to transfer their profits to other divisions and may distort information in order to retain their resources. Other organizational stakeholders also have an interest in the way a company allocates scarce resources. For example, shareholders care about the size of the dividends, and unions and employees want to maximize their salaries and benefits.

Given so many potential sources of conflict in organizations, conflict of one kind or another is always present in strategic decision making. We need to consider how a typical conflict process works itself out in the organization and whether there are any guidelines that corporate managers can use to try to direct conflict and turn its destructive potential to good strategic use. A model developed by Lou R. Pondy, a famous management theorist, helps show how the conflict process operates in organizations.[28] We discuss this in the next section.

The Organizational Conflict Process

Conflict is so hard to manage strategically because it is usually unexpected. The sources of conflict that we have just discussed often inhere in a company's mode of operation. The first stage in the conflict process, then, is *latent conflict* — potential conflict that can flare up when the right conditions arise. (The stages in the conflict process appear in Figure 11.5.) Latent conflicts are frequently activated by changes in an organization's strategy or structure that affect the relationship among functions or divisions. For example, if a company has been pursuing a dominant product strategy using a functional structure to implement the strategy, it might decide to widen its product range. To overcome problems of coordinating a range of specialist services over many products, the company perhaps adopts a product structure. The new structure changes task relationships among product managers, and this in turn changes the relative status and areas of authority of the different functional and product managers. Conflict between functional and product managers or among product managers is likely to ensue.

Since every change in a company's strategy and structure alters the organizational context, conflict can arise very easily unless the situation is carefully managed to avoid it. But avoidance is not always possible. Consequently, the latent stage of the conflict process quickly leads to the next stage: the *perceived conflict stage*.

Perceived conflict means that managers become aware of the clashes. After a change in strategy and structure, managers discover that the actions of another function or group are obstructing the operations of their group. Managers start to react to the situation, and from the perceived stage, they go quickly to the *felt conflict stage*. Here managers start to personalize the conflict. Opinions polarize, as one function or division starts to blame the others for causing the conflict. Production might blame the inefficiency of sales for a fall in orders, while sales might blame production for a fall in product quality. Typically, there is a marked lack of cooperation at this stage, and integration among functions or divisions breaks down as the groups start to polarize and develop an "us versus them" mentality. If not managed, this stage in the conflict process leads very quickly to the next stage, the *manifest conflict stage*.

At this point, the conflict among functions or divisions comes into the open, and each group strives to thwart the goals of the other. Groups compete

FIGURE 11.5   **Stages in the conflict process**

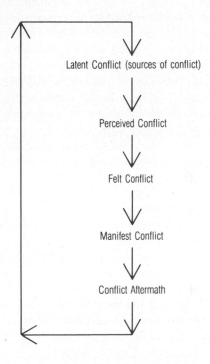

Latent Conflict (sources of conflict)

Perceived Conflict

Felt Conflict

Manifest Conflict

Conflict Aftermath

to protect their own interests and block the interests of other groups. Manifest conflict can take many forms. The most obvious is open aggression among top managers as they start to blame other functions or divisions for causing the problem. Other forms of manifest conflict are transfer pricing battles and knowledge hoarding. Defamatory information about other divisions is also likely to be circulated at this stage in the conflict process. These actions are much worse than political maneuvering because divisions are trying not simply to promote their interests, but also to damage the performance of the other divisions. As a result, the company cannot achieve any gains from scheduling resource transfers or from developing synergy between divisions.

At the functional level, the effects of conflict can be equally devastating. A company cannot pursue a low-cost strategy if the functions are competing. If sales makes no attempt to keep manufacturing informed about customer demands, manufacturing cannot maximize the length of production runs. Similarly, a company cannot successfully differentiate if marketing does not inform research and development about changes in consumer preferences or if product engineering and research and development are competing over product specifications. Companies have experienced each of these conflicts at one time or another and suffered a loss in performance and competitive advantage because of them.

The long-term effects of manifest conflict emerge in the last stage of the conflict process, the *conflict aftermath*. Suppose that in one company a change in strategy leads to conflict over transfer prices. Then divisional managers, with the help of corporate personnel, resolve the problem to everyone's satisfaction and re-establish good working relationships. In another company, however, the conflict between divisions over transfer prices is resolved only by the intervention of corporate managers, who *impose* a solution on divisional managers. A year later, a change in the environment occurs that makes the transfer pricing system in both companies no longer equitable, and prices must be renegotiated. How will the two companies react to this situation? The managers in the company where the conflict was settled amicably will approach this new round of negotiations with a cooperative, and not an adversarial, attitude. However, in the company where divisions never really established an agreement, there is likely to be a new round of intense clashes, with a resulting fall in organizational performance.

In each company, then, there was a different conflict aftermath because in one case conflict had been resolved successfully and in the other it had not. The conflict aftermath sets the scene for the next round of conflict that will certainly occur, since conflict is inherent in the ways companies operate and since the environment is constantly changing. The reason that some companies have a long history of bad relations among functions or divisions is that their conflict has never been managed successfully. In companies where strategic managers have resolved the conflict, a cohesive organizational culture obtains. In those companies, managers adopt a cooperative, not a competitive, attitude when conflict occurs. The question we need to tackle, however, is how best to manage the conflict process strategically in order to avoid its bad effects and make transitions in strategy-structure choice as smooth as possible.

Managing Conflict Strategically

Given the way the conflict process operates, the goal of strategic managers should be to intervene as early as possible in this process so that conflict does not reach the felt, and particularly the manifest, stage. At the manifest stage, conflict is very difficult to resolve successfully and is much more likely to lead to a bad conflict aftermath. At what point, then, should managers intervene?

Ideally, managers should intervene at the latent stage and act on the sources of conflict.[29] Good strategic planning early on can prevent many of the problems that occur later. For example, when managers are changing a company's strategy, they should be consciously thinking about the effects of these changes on group relationships later on. Similarly, when changing organizational structure, strategic managers should anticipate the effects the changes will have on functional and divisional relationships. Many large organizations do act in this way and require that the potential effect of strategy-structure changes on the organization be included in the strategic planning process to prevent conflict from arising later on.

However, often it is impossible to foresee the ramifications of changes in strategy. Organizations are complex, and many unexpected things can happen as managers go about changing organizations. Consequently, managers cannot always intervene at the latent stage to prevent conflict from arising. Thus changes in strategy or structure may lead to failure, as when Apple went to a divisional structure or when Kodak's instant camera proved a financial disaster.

Frequently, intervention is only possible between the felt and the manifest stage. It is here that managers may have the best chance to find a solution to the problem. There are a number of different solutions, or conflict resolution strategies, that managers can adopt, and we consider them next.

Conflict Resolution Strategies

Using authority   As we discussed in Chapter 9, integration among functions and divisions is such a problem because they have equal authority and thus cannot control each other. When functions cannot solve their problems, these problems are often passed on to corporate managers or to the CEO, who has the authority to impose a solution on parties. In general, there are two ways of using authority to manage conflict. First, the CEO or corporate managers can play the role of arbiters and impose a solution on the parties in conflict. Second, they can act as a mediators and try to open up the situation so that the parties in conflict can find their own solution. Research shows that the latter approach works better because it leads to a good conflict aftermath.

Change task relationships   In this approach, the aim is to change the interdependence among functions or divisions so that the source of the conflict is removed. There are two ways of altering task relationships. First, strategic managers can *reduce* the degree of dependence among the parties. For example, they can develop a structure in which integration among groups is easier to accomplish. Thus a shift from a functional to a divisional structure can reduce the potential for conflict. Similarly, establishing a strategic business unit structure can lessen the chances of conflict among divisions.

On the other hand, conflict may arise because the correct integrating mechanisms for managing task interdependence have not been adopted. In this case, managing the conflict means *increasing* integration among divisions and functions. Thus, in high tech companies, where functions are very highly task interdependent, managers can use a matrix structure to provide the integration necessary to resolve conflict. In a divisional structure, managers may use integrating roles and establish integrating departments to allow divisions to price and transfer resources. At Hewlett-Packard, corporate staff created three integrating committees to allow divisions to share resources and to minimize conflict over product development. Increased integration prevents conflicts from emerging. Managers also use structure through the process of strategy implementation to solve conflicts.

Changing controls   Conflict can also be managed by altering the organization's control and evaluation systems. For example, in some cases it may be possible to develop joint goals among functions and divisions and to create a reward system based on the achievement of these joint goals. For example, sales and production may be jointly rewarded on the basis of how much revenue they generate. Similarly, corporate evaluation systems may be created to measure the degree to which divisions cooperate with one another. We discussed earlier how TRW attempted to develop such evaluation systems so that divisions could share information and knowledge while being appropriately rewarded for it. Finally, to some degree, conflict is the result of managers in one function not appreciating the position of those in another. To give managers a broader perspective and to overcome differences in subunit orientations, managers can be rotated among divisions and given assignments at the corporate level to show them the problems faced by managers elsewhere in the company.

Summary

Conflict is an ever present organizational phenomenon that has to be managed if the firm is to achieve its objectives. The whole process of strategy-structure choice creates the potential for conflict and in a rapidly changing environment conflict is much more likely. It is a part of the strategic manager's job to develop the personal skills and abilities needed to solve conflict problems. This involves first, the ability to analyze the organizational context to pinpoint the source of the problem, and second, the development of the personal skills necessary to handle managers who are in conflict. It is possible now to consider the process of managing organizational change.

11.5 MANAGING CHANGES IN STRATEGY-STRUCTURE CHOICE

In the modern corporation, change rather than stability is the order of the day. Rapid changes in technology, the competitive environment, and customer demands have increased the rate at which companies have to alter their strategies in order to survive in the marketplace.[30] Consequently, companies have to go through rapid structural reorganizations as they outgrow their structures. E. F. Hutton, for example, estimates that well over half of the top 800 major corporations have undergone major restructuring in recent years.[31] In this section, we discuss the problems associated with managing such changes in strategy and structure.

Steps in the Change Process

The management of strategic change involves a series of distinct steps that managers must follow if the change process is to succeed. These steps are listed in Figure 11.6.

Determining the need for change   The first step in the change process involves strategic managers determining the need for change. Sometimes this change is obvious, as when divisions are fighting or competitors introduce a product that is clearly superior to anything that the company has in production. More often, however, managers have trouble determining that something is going wrong in the organization. Problems may develop very gradually, and organizational performance may be slipping for a number of years before it becomes obvious. At CBS, for example, profitability fell, but because it was a reputable stock, the fall caused little stir. However, after a lapse of time, investors realized that the stock had been undervalued and that CBS could be made to perform better. In other words, outside investors realized sooner than inside management did that there was a need for change.

Thus the first step in the change process occurs when the company's strategic managers or others in a position to take action recognize that there is a gap between *desired company performance and actual performance*.[32] Using measures such as falls in stock price or market share as indicators that change is needed, managers can start looking for the source of the problem. To discover it, they conduct a SWOT analysis. First, they examine the company's strengths and weaknesses. For example, management conducts a strategic audit of the functions and divisions and looks at their contribution to profitability over time. Perhaps some divisions have become dogs without management realizing it or the company has too many rising stars. Management also analyzes the company's level of differentiation and integration to make sure that it is appropriate

FIGURE 11.6   Stages in the change process

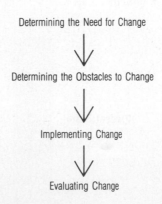

Determining the Need for Change

↓

Determining the Obstacles to Change

↓

Implementing Change

↓

Evaluating Change

for its strategy. Perhaps a company does not have the integrating mechanisms in place to achieve gains from synergy. Management then examines environmental opportunities and threats that might explain the problem. For instance, the company may have had intense competition from substitute products without being aware of it, or a shift in consumer tastes or technology may have caught it unawares.

Once the source of the problem has been identified, the next step is to decide on the direction the company should take, that is, how it should change its strategy and structure. A company may decide, like CBS, to lower its costs by streamlining its operation. Or, like GM, it may increase its research and development budget or diversify into new products in order to increase its future profitability. Essentially, strategic managers apply the conceptual tools that this book has described to work out the best choice of strategy and structure to maximize profitability. The choice they make is specific to each individual company, and as noted earlier, there is no way that managers can determine its correctness in advance. This is the adventure of strategic management.

Thus the first step in the change process involves determining the need for change, analyzing the organization's current position, and determining the ideal future state that strategic managers would like it to attain. This process is diagrammed in Figure 11.7.

Determining the obstacles to change   The second step in the change process involves determining the obstacles to change.[33] Strategic managers must analyze the factors that may prevent the company from reaching its ideal future state. Obstacles to change are found at four levels in the organization: corporate, divisional, functional, and individual levels.

At the corporate level, there are several potential obstacles to consider. First, changing strategy or structure even in seemingly trivial ways may significantly affect a company's behavior. For example, suppose that to reduce costs

FIGURE 11.7   A model of change

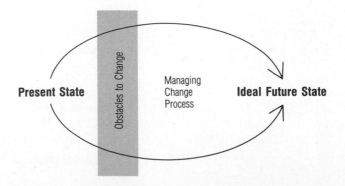

the company decides to centralize all divisional purchasing and sales activities at the corporate level. Such consolidation could severely damage each division's ability to develop a unique strategy for its own individual markets. Or suppose that in response to low-cost foreign competition the company decides to pursue a policy of differentiation. This action would change the balance of power among functions and lead to politicking and even conflict as functions start fighting to retain their status in the organization. The fact is that a *company's present structure and strategy are powerful obstacles to change*. They produce a massive amount of inertia that has to be overcome before change can take place. This is why change is usually such a slow process.

The *type of structure* a company uses can also impede change. For example, it is much easier to change strategy if a company is using a matrix, rather than a functional, structure, or if it is decentralized rather than centralized, or if it has a high, rather than a low, level of integration. Decentralized, matrix structures are more flexible than highly controlled functional structures. It is easier to change subunit orientations, and thus there is a lower potential for conflict.

Some *corporate cultures* are easier to change than others. For example, change is notoriously difficult in the military because everything is geared to obedience and the following of orders. However, some cultures, such as Hewlett-Packard's, are based on values that emphasize flexibility or change itself. Consequently, they are much easier to change when change becomes necessary.

Similar factors operate at the divisional level. Change is difficult at the divisional level if divisions are *highly interrelated and trade resources,* since a shift in one division's operations will affect other divisions. Consequently, it is more difficult to manage change if a company is pursuing a strategy of related, rather than unrelated, diversification. Furthermore, changes in strategy affect divisions in different ways because change generally favors the interests of some divisions over those of others. Divisions may thus have different attitudes to change, and some will not support the changes in strategy that the company makes. Existing divisions may resist establishing new product divisions because they will lose resources and their status inside the organization may fall.

The same obstacles to change exist at the functional level as well. Like divisions, different functions have different strategic orientations and react differently to the changes management proposes. For example, in a decline situation, sales will resist attempts to cut back on sales expenditures to reduce costs if it believes the problem stems from inefficiency in manufacturing. At the individual level, too, people are notoriously resistant to change because change implies uncertainty, which breeds insecurity and the fear of the unknown.[34] Since managers are people, this individual resistance reinforces the tendency of each function and division to oppose changes that may have uncertain effects on them.

All these obstacles make it very difficult to change organizational strategy or structure quickly. That is why American car manufacturers took so long to respond to the Japanese challenge. They were accustomed to a situation of complete dominance and had developed inflexible, centralized structures that inhibited risk taking and quick reaction. Paradoxically, companies that experience the greatest uncertainty may become best able to respond to it. When they have been forced to change often, they develop the ability to handle change easily.[35]

Strategic managers must understand all these potential obstacles to change as they design a company's new strategy and structure. All these factors are potential sources of conflict and politics that can dramatically affect a company's ability to move quickly to exploit new strategic opportunities. Obstacles to change must be recognized and incorporated into the strategic plan. The larger and more complex the organization, the harder it is to implement change.

Implementing Change

Implementing—that is, introducing and managing—change raises several questions. For instance, who should actually carry out the change: internal managers or external consultants? Although internal managers may have the most experience or knowledge about a company's operations, they may lack perspective, since they are too much a part of the organization's culture. They also run the risk of appearing to be politically motivated and of having a personal stake in the changes they recommend. Companies therefore often turn to external consultants, who can view the situation more objectively. However, outside consultants must spend a lot of time learning about the company and its problems before they can propose a plan of action. Thus the issue of who should manage the change is complex, and most companies create a task force consisting of both internal managers and external consultants. In this way, companies can get the benefits of inside information and the external perspective.

Generally, there are two main approaches to change that a company can take: **top-down change** or **bottom-up change.**[36] With top-down change, the change task force analyzes how to alter strategy and structure, recommends a course of action, and then moves quickly to implement change in the organization. The emphasis is on speed of response and management of problems as they occur. In the case of bottom-up change, however, the process is much more gradual. The change task force consults with managers at all levels in the organization. Then, over time, it develops a detailed plan for change, with a timetable of events and stages that the company will go through. The emphasis here is on participation and on keeping people informed about the situation, so that uncertainty is minimized.

The advantage of bottom-up change is that it removes some of the obstacles to change by incorporating them into the stategic plan. In addition, the aim of consulting with managers at all levels is to reveal potential problems. The disadvantage of bottom-up change is its slowness. On the other hand, in the case of the much speedier top-down change, the problems may emerge later and may be very difficult to solve. In general, the type of change that companies adopt depends on the nature of the situation they are dealing with. Companies that are used to change and have flexibility risk fewer problems with top-down change. For corporate lumbering giants, bottom-up change may be the only way of getting anything done because managers are so unaccustomed to, and threatened by, change.

Evaluating Change

The last step in the change process is to evaluate the effects of the changes in strategy and structure on organizational performance. A company must compare the way it operates after implementing change with the way it operated before. Managers use indices such as changes in stock market price or market share to assess the effects of change in strategy. However, it is much more difficult to assess the effects of changes in structure on company performance because they are so much more difficult to measure. Whereas companies can easily measure the increased revenue from increased product differentiation. They do not have any sure means of evaluating the effects that moving from a product to a divisional structure has had on performance. However, managers can be surveyed, and over time it may become obvious that organizational flexibility and the company's ability to manage its strategy have increased. Managers can also assess whether the change has decreased the level of politicking and conflict and strengthened cooperation among the divisions and functions.

Organizational change is a very complex and difficult process for firms to manage successfully. The problem starts from the beginning in getting managers to realize that change is necessary and to admit that there is a problem. Once the need for change is recognized managers can go about the process of recommending a course of action and analyze potential obstacles to change. Depending on the organization, and the nature of the problem the firm is dealing with, either bottom-up or top-down change is appropriate. However, in both cases it is best to use a mix of internal managers and external consultants to implement the change. After implementing change, managers assess its effects on organizational performance and then the whole process is repeated as firms strive to increase their level of performance. This is why those firms in which change is a regular occurrence find it much easier to manage than those firms where complacent managers only start a change effort when the firm is already in trouble.

11.6 SUMMARY OF CHAPTER

The purpose of this chapter has been to examine the political side of strategy formulation and implementation and to discuss the problems that can arise in managing changes in strategy and structure. It should now be apparent that organizations are not just rational decision-making systems, where managers coldly calculate the potential returns from their investments. Organizations are arenas of power, where individuals and groups fight for prestige and possession of scarce resources. In the pursuit of their interests, managers compete and come into conflict. The very nature of the organization makes this inevitable. Managers have to deal with politics and conflict creatively to achieve organizational benefits from them. They also have to manage the process of organizational change so that the company can maximize its ability to exploit the environment. The most successful companies are those in which change is regarded as the norm and where managers are constantly seeking to improve organizational strengths and eliminate weaknesses so that they can maximize future profitability. This chapter has made the following main points:

1. Organizational decision making is a combination of both rational and political processes. Formation of coalitions, compromise, and bargaining are integral parts of the strategic management process.

2. Organizational politics occurs because different groups have different interests and different perceptions of the appropriate means to further their interests.

3. In order to play politics, managers must have power. Power is the ability of one party to cause another party to act in the first party's interest.

4. The sources of power available to strategic managers include coping with uncertainty, centrality and nonsubstitutability, and control of contingencies and resources.

5. Politics must be managed, if the company is to obtain benefits from the process, and one of the best ways of doing so is to create a power balance in the organization. A strong CEO or a well-designed structure can create a power balance.

6. When divisions, functions, or individuals go beyond competition and strive to thwart each other's goals, organizational conflict exists. Conflict may be defined as a situation that occurs when the goal-directed behavior of one group blocks the goal-directed behavior of another.

7. Whether conflict is good or bad for the organization depends on the way it is managed. In general, conflict is useful in exposing organizational weaknesses, but it must be managed quickly, before it gets out of hand.

8. Conflict is inherent in the nature of an organization's design. The sources of conflict include differentiation, task relationships, and scarcity of resources.

9. Conflict can be regarded as a process with a series of stages. These stages are latent conflict, perceived conflict, felt conflict, manifest conflict, and the conflict aftermath.

10. Organizational change is the process by which companies alter their strategy and structure in order to improve performance.

11. Organizational change is also managed through a series of stages. First, the need for change must be recognized, and the company must decide on its ideal future state. Then the obstacles to change must be analyzed and incorporated into the change plan, and change must be implemented. Finally, the change process must be evaluated to assess its effects on organizational performance.

12. Well-run organizations are constantly aware of the need to monitor their performance, and they institutionalize change so that they can realign their structures to suit the competitive environment.

Discussion Questions

1. How can managing (a) politics and (b) conflict in organizations lead to improved organizational decision making? How might a company create a system of checks and balances in the organization through the design of its structure and control systems?

2. How might conflict and politics affect the formulation and implementation of (a) generic competitive strategies, (b) corporate-level strategies?

3. What are some of the political problems a company may encounter if it takes over a related business and tries to integrate it into its organizational structure? (Hint: use the sources of power to frame your answer).

4. Discuss how you would set up a plan for change for an unrelated company that is starting to pursue a strategy of related diversification. What problems will the company encounter? How should it deal with them?

Endnotes

1. "Corporate Shoot-Out at Black Rock," *Time,* September 22, 1986, pp. 68–72.

2. "Civil War at CBS," *Newsweek,* September 15, 1986, pp. 46–54.

3. P. W. Barnes, "Tisch wins praise for fast action at CBS," *The Wall Street Journal,* October 28, 1986, p. 5.

4. P. J. Boyers, "Three New Bosses are Slashing Operations and Putting Nearly Everyone's Job on the Line," *The New York Times,* November 2, 1986, p. 26.

5. A. M. Pettigrew, *The Politics of Organizational Decision Making* (London: Tavistock, 1973).

6. R. H. Miles, *Macro Organizational Behavior* (Santa Monica, Calif.: Goodyear 1980).

7. J. G. March and H. A. Simon, *Organizations* (New York: Wiley, 1958).

8. J. G. March, "The Business Firm as a Coalition," *The Journal of Politics,* 24 (1962), 662–678. D. J. Vredenburgh and J. G. Maurer, "A Process Framework of Organizational Politics," *Human Relations,* 37 (1984), 47–66.

9. T. Burns, "Micropolitics: Mechanism of Institutional Change," *Administrative Science Quarterly,* 6 (1961), 257–281.

10. R. A. Dahl, "The Concept of Power," *Behavioral Science,* 2 (1957), 201–215. G. A. Astley and P. S. Sachdeva, "Structural Sources of Intraorganizational Power," *Academy of Management Review,* 9 (1984), 104–113.

11. This section draws heavily on D. J. Hickson, C. R. Hinings, C. A. Lee, R. E. Schneck, and D. J. Pennings, "A Strategic Contingencies Theory of Intraorganizational Power," *Administrative Science Quarterly,* 16 (1971) 216–227; and C. R. Hinings, D. J. Hickson, J. M. Pennings, and R. E. Schneck, "Structural Conditions of Interorganizational Power," *Administrative Science Quarterly,* 19 (1974), 22–44.

12. Hickson et al., "A Strategic Contingencies Theory."

13. Pettigrew, *The Politics of Organizational Decision Making.*

14. Hickson et al., "A Strategic Contingencies Theory." Pettigrew, *The Politics of Organizational Decision Making.*

15. Hickson et al., "A Strategic Contingencies Theory."

16. H. A. Landsberger, "The Horizontal Dimension in Bureaucracy," *Administrative Science Quarterly,* 6 (1961), 299–232.

17. G. R. Salancik and J. Pfeffer, "The Bases and Use of Power in Organizational Decision Making: The Case of a University," *Administrative Science Quarterly,* 19 (1974), 453–473.

18. J. A. Litterer, "Conflict in Organizations: A Reexamination," *Academy of Management Journal,* 9 (1966), 178–186. S. M. Schmidt and T. A. Kochan, "Conflict: Towards Conceptual Clarity," *Administrative Science Quarterly,* 13 (1972), 359–370. Miles, *Macro Organizational Behavior.*

19. Miles, *Macro Organizational Behavior.*

20. S. P. Robbins, *Managing Organizational Conflict: A Nontraditional Approach* (Englewood Cliffs, N.J.: Prentice-Hall, 1974. L. Coser, *The Functions of Social Conflict* (New York: Free Press, 1956).

21. This discussion owes much to the seminal work of the following authors: Lou R. Pondy, "Organizational Conflict: Concepts and Models," *Administrative Science Quarterly,* 2 (1967), 296–320, and R. E. Walton and J. M. Dutton, "The Management of Interdepartmental Conflict: A Model and Review," *Administrative Science Quarterly,* 14 (1969), 62–73.

22. M. Dalton, *Men Who Manage* (New York: Wiley, 1959). Walton and Dutton, "The Management of Interdepartmental Conflict."

23. Walton and Dutton, "The Management of Interdepartmental Conflict." J. McCann and J. R. Galbraith, "Interdepartmental relationships," in *Handbook of Organizational Design,* ed. P. C. Nystrom and W. H. Starbuck (New York: Oxford University Press, 1981).

24. J. D. Thompson, *Organizations in Action* (New York: McGraw-Hill, 1967).

25. Walton and Dutton, "The Management of Interdepartmental Conflict," p. 65.

26. Ibid., p. 68.

27. Pondy, "Organizational Conflict," p. 300.

28. Ibid., p. 310.

29. Ibid., p. 316.

30. T. J. Peters and R. H. Waterman Jr., *In Search of Excellence* (New York: Harper & Row, 1982).

31. J. Thackray, "Restructuring Is The Name of The Hurricane," *Euromoney* (February 1987), 106–108.

32. R. Beckhard, *Organizational Development* (Reading, Mass.: Addison Wesley, 1969). W. L. French and C. H. Bell Jr., *Organization Development,* 2nd ed. (Englewood Cliffs, N.J.: Prentice-Hall, 1978).

33. L. C. Coch and R. P. French Jr., "Overcoming Resistance to Change," *Human Relations* (August 1948), 512–532. P. R. Lawrence, "How to Deal with Resistance to Change," *Harvard Business Review,* (January–February 1969), 4–12.

34. P. Kotter and L. A. Schlesinger, "Choosing Strategies for Change," *Harvard Business Review* (March–April 1979), 106–114.

35. J. R. Galbraith, "Designing the Innovative Organization," *Organization Dynamics* (Winter 1982), 5–25.

36. M. Beer, *Organizational Change and Development* (Santa Monica, Calif.: Goodyear, 1980). L. E. Greiner, "Patterns of Organizational Change," *Harvard Business Review* (May–June 1967), 3–5.

CASE STUDY ANALYSIS

Chapter 12

ANALYZING AND WRITING A CASE STUDY

12.1 WHAT IS CASE STUDY ANALYSIS?

Case study analysis is an integral part of a course in strategic management. The purpose of a case study is to provide students with experience of the strategic management problems faced by actual organizations. A case study presents an account of what happened to a business or industry over a number of years. It chronicles the events that managers had to deal with, such as changes in the competitive environment, and charts the managers' response, which usually involved changing the business- or corporate-level strategy. The cases in Part V of this book cover a wide range of issues and problems that managers have had to confront. Some cases are about finding the right business-level strategy to compete in changing industry conditions. Some are about companies that grew by acquisition, with little concern for the rationale behind their growth, and how this affected their future profitability. Each case is different because each organization is different. The underlying thread in all the cases, however, is the use of strategic management techniques to solve business problems.

Cases prove valuable in a strategic management course for several reasons. First, cases provide you, the student, with experience of organizational problems that you probably have not had the opportunity to experience firsthand. In a relatively short period of time, a semester, you will have the chance to appreciate and analyze the problems faced by many different companies and to understand how managers tried to deal with them.

Second, cases illustrate the theory and content of strategic management — that is, all the information that we have presented to you in the previous eleven chapters of this book. This information has been collected, discovered, and distilled from the observations, research, and experience of managers and academics. The meaning and implication of this information are made clearer when they are applied to case studies. The theory and concepts help reveal what is going on in the companies studied and allow you to evaluate the solutions that specific companies adopted to deal with their problems. Consequently, when you analyze cases, you will be like a detective who, with a set of conceptual tools, probes what happened and what or who was responsible, and then marshals the evidence that provides the solution. Top managers enjoy the thrill of testing their problem-solving abilities in the real world. After all, it is important to remember that no one knows what the right answer is. All that managers can do is to make the best guess. In fact, managers say repeatedly that they are happy if they are right only half the time in solving strategic problems. Strategic management is an uncertain game, and using cases to see how theory can be put to practice is one way of improving your skills in diagnostic investigation.

The third advantage of case studies is that they provide you the opportunity to participate in class and gain experience in presenting your ideas. Sometimes the instructor will call on students as a group to identify what was going on in a case, and through classroom discussion the issue and solutions to the problem in the case will reveal themselves. In this situation, you will have to organize your views and conclusions so that you can present them to the class. Be prepared for a discussion of your ideas. Since your classmates may have analyzed the issues differently from you, they will want you to argue your points before you can convince them, and so be prepared for debate. This mode of discussion is an example of the dialectical approach to decision making that you may recall from Chapter 1. This is how decisions are made in the actual business world. Sometimes instructors will assign an individual, or more commonly a group, to analyze the case before the whole class. The individual or group will probably be responsible for a thirty-forty-minute presentation of the case to the class, and in that presentation must cover the issues involved, the problems facing the company, and a series of recommendations for resolving those problems. Then the discussion will be thrown open to the class, and you will have to defend your ideas. Through such discussions and presentations, you will experience how to convey your ideas effectively to others. Remember that a great deal of managers' time is spent in these kinds of situations, presenting their ideas and engaging in discussion with other managers, who have their own views about what is going on. Thus you will experience in the classroom the actual process of strategic management, and this will serve you well in your future career.

If you work in groups to analyze case studies, you will also learn about the group process involved in joint work. When people work in groups, it is often difficult to schedule time and allocate responsibility for the case analysis. There will always be group members who shirk or who are so sure of their own ideas that they try to dominate the group's analysis. However, most of strategic management takes place in groups, and it is best if you learn about these problems now.

12.2 ANALYZING A CASE STUDY

As mentioned above, the purpose of the case study is to let you apply the concepts of strategic management when you analyze the issues facing a specific company. Thus, to analyze a case study, it is necessary to examine very closely the issues with which the company is involved. This will often take several readings of the case: a first reading, to grasp the overall picture of what is happening to a company, and then subsequent readings, to discover and grasp the specific problems.

Generally speaking, detailed analysis of a case study should include eight areas:

1. The history, development and growth of the company over time

2. The identification of the company's internal strengths and weaknesses

3. The nature of the external environment surrounding the company

4. A SWOT analysis

5. The kind of corporate-level strategy pursued by a company

6. The nature of the company's business-level strategy

7. The company's structure and control systems and how they match its strategy

8. Recommendations

In order to analyze a case, you need to apply the course concepts to each of these areas. Which concepts to use is obvious from the chapter titles. For example, to analyze the company's environment, you would use Chapter 3, on environmental analysis. To help you further, we offer below a brief guide to some of the main strategic management concepts that can be used to analyze the case material for each of the points we have just noted.

1. *Analyzing the company's, history, development and growth* A convenient way of investigating how a company's past strategy and structure affect it in the present is to chart the critical incidents in its history, that is, the events that were the most unusual or the most essential for its development into the company it is today. Some of the events have to do with its founding, its initial products, how it made new product market decisions, and how it

developed and chose functional competences to pursue. Its entry into new businesses and shifts in its main lines of business are also important milestones to consider.

2. *Identification of the company's internal strengths and weaknesses* Once the historical profile is completed, you can begin the SWOT analysis. Take all the incidents you have charted and use them to develop an account of the company's strengths and weaknesses as they have emerged historically. Examine each of the value creation functions of the company, and identify the functions where the company is currently strong and those where it is currently weak. Some companies might be weak in marketing, and some strong in research and development. Make lists of these strengths and weaknesses. Table 12.1 gives examples of what might go in these lists.

3. *Environmental analysis* The next step is to identify environmental opportunities and threats. Here you should apply all the concepts from Chapter 3, on industry and macroenvironments, to analyze the environment the company is confronting. Of particular importance at the industry level is Porter's five forces model and the stage of the life cycle model. Which factors in the macroenvironment will appear salient depends on the specific company being analyzed. However, use each concept in turn — for instance, demographic factors — to see if it is relevant for the company in question.

   Having done this analysis, you will have generated both an analysis of the company's environment and a list of opportunities and threats. Table 12.1 also lists some common environmental opportunities and threats that you might look for. However, the list you generate will be specific to your company.

4. *The SWOT analysis* Having identified the company's external opportunities and threats, as well as its internal strengths and weaknesses, you need to consider what your findings mean. In other words, you need to balance strengths and weaknesses against opportunities and threats. Is the company in an overall strong competitive position? Can it continue to pursue its current business- or corporate-level strategy profitably? What can the company do to turn weaknesses into strengths and threats into opportunities? Can it develop new functional, business, or corporate strategies to accomplish this change? *Never merely generate the SWOT analysis and then put it aside.* Since it provides a succinct summary of the company's condition, a good SWOT analysis is the key to all the analyses that follow.

5. *Analyzing corporate-level strategy* To analyze a company's corporate-level strategy, you first need to define the company's mission and goals. Sometimes the mission and goals will be stated explicitly in the case; at other times you will have to infer them from available information. The information you need to collect in order to find out the company's corporate strategy includes such factors as its line(s) of business and the nature of its

TABLE 12.1   **A SWOT checklist**

Potential internal strengths	Potential internal weaknesses
Many product lines?	Obsolete, narrow product lines?
Broad market coverage?	Rising manufacturing costs?
Manufacturing competence?	Decline in R&D innovations?
Good marketing skills?	Poor marketing plan?
Good materials management systems?	Poor materials management systems?
R&D skills and leadership?	Loss of customer good will?
Information system competences?	Inadequate information systems?
Human resource competences?	Inadequate human resources?
Brand name reputation?	Loss of brand name capital?
Portfolio management skills?	Growth without direction?
Cost or differentiation advantage?	Bad portfolio management?
New venture management expertise?	Loss of corporate direction?
Appropriate management style?	Infighting among divisions?
Appropriate organizational structure?	Loss of corporate control?
Appropriate control systems?	Inappropriate organizational structure and control systems?
Ability to manage strategic change?	High conflict and politics?
Well-developed corporate strategy?	Poor financial management?
Good financial management?	Others?
Others?	

Potential environmental opportunities	Potential environmental threats
Expand core business(es)?	Attacks on core business(es)?
Exploit new market segments?	Increases in domestic competition?
Widen product range?	Increase in foreign competition?
Extend cost or differentiation advantage?	Change in consumer tastes?
Diversify into new growth businesses?	Fall in barriers to entry?
Expand into foreign markets?	Rise in new or substitute products?
Apply R&D skills in new areas?	Increase in industry rivalry?
Enter new related businesses?	New forms of industry competition?
Vertically integrate forward?	Potential for takeover?
Vertically integrate backward?	Existence of corporate raiders?
Enlarge corporate portfolio?	Increase in regional competition?
Overcome barriers to entry?	Changes in demographic factors?
Reduce rivalry among competitors?	Changes in economic factors?
Make profitable new acquisitions?	Downturn in economy?
Apply brand name capital in new areas?	Rising labor costs?
Seek fast market growth?	Slower market growth?
Others?	Others?

subsidiaries and acquisitions. It is very important to analyze the relationship among the company's businesses. Do they trade or exchange resources? Are there gains to be achieved from synergy? Or is the company just running a portfolio of investments? This analysis should enable you to define the corporate strategy that the company is pursuing (for example, related or unrelated diversification, or a combination of both) and also to conclude whether the company operates in just one core business. Then take your SWOT analysis and debate the merits of this strategy. Is it appropriate, given the environment the company is in? Could a change in corporate strategy provide the company with new opportunities or transform a weakness into a strength? For example, should the company diversify from its core business into new businesses?

There are other issues to be considered as well. How has the company's strategy changed over time? Why? What is the claimed rationale for the change? Often it is a very good idea to apply a *portfolio matrix technique* to the company's businesses or products in order to analyze its situation and identify which divisions are stars or dogs. It is also useful to explore how the company has built its portfolio over time. Did it acquire new businesses or did it internally venture its own? All these factors provide clues about the company and indicate ways of improving its future performance.

6. *Analyzing business-level strategy* Once you know the company's corporate-level strategy and have done the SWOT analysis, the next step is to identify the company's business-level strategy. If the company is a single-business company, then its business-level strategy is identical to its corporate-level strategy. If the company is in many businesses, then each business will have its own business-level strategy. You will need to identify the company's generic competitive strategy — differentiation, low cost, or focus — and its investment strategy, given the company's relative competitive position and the stage of the life cycle. The company may also market different products using different business-level strategies: for example, it may offer a low-cost product range and a line of differentiated products. You should be sure to give a full account of a company's business-level strategy to show how it competes.

Identifying the functional strategies that a company pursues to achieve its business-level strategy is very important. The SWOT analysis will have provided you with information on the company's functional competences. You should further investigate production, marketing, or research and development strategy to gain a picture of where the company is going. For example, pursuing a low-cost or a differentiation strategy successfully requires a very different set of competences. Has the company developed the right ones? If it has, how can it exploit them further?

The SWOT analysis is especially important at this point if the industry analysis, particularly Porter's model, has revealed the threats to the company from the environment. Can the company deal with these threats?

How should it change its business-level strategy to counter them? To evaluate the potential of a company's business-level strategy, you must first perform a thorough SWOT analysis that captures the essence of its problems.

Once you complete this analysis, you will have a full picture of the way the company is operating and be in a position to evaluate the potential of its strategy. Thus you will be able to make recommendations concerning the pattern of its future actions. But first you need to consider strategy implementation, or the way the company tries to achieve its strategy.

7. *Analyzing structure and control systems* The aim of the analysis here is to identify what structure and control systems the company is using to implement its strategy and to evaluate whether that structure is the appropriate one for the company. As you saw in Chapter 10, different corporate and business strategies require different structures. The chapter, and particularly Tables 10.2, 10.3, and 10.4, provide you with the conceptual tools to determine *the degree of fit between the company's strategy and structure.* For example, you need to assess whether the company has the right level of vertical differentiation (for instance, does it have the appropriate number of levels in the hierarchy or decentralized control?), or horizontal differentiation (does it use a functional structure when it should be using a product structure?). Similarly, is the company using the right integration or control systems to manage its operations? Are managers being appropriately rewarded? Are the right rewards in place for encouraging cooperation among divisions? These are all issues that should be considered.

In some cases, there will be little information on these issues, whereas in others there will be a lot. Obviously, in writing each case, you should gear the analysis toward its most salient issues.

In some cases, organizational conflict, power, and politics will be important issues. Try and analyze why these problems are occurring. Is it because of bad strategy formulation or bad strategy implementation? Organizational change is an issue in most of the cases since companies in the cases are attempting to alter their strategies or structures to solve strategic problems. Thus, as a part of the analysis, you might suggest an action plan that the company in question could use to achieve its goals. For example, you might list the steps it would need to go through to alter its business-level strategy from differentiation to focus in a logical sequence.

8. *Making recommendations* The last part of the case analysis process involves making recommendations based on your previous analysis of the case. Obviously, the quality of your recommendations is a direct result of the thoroughness with which you prepared the case analysis. The work you put into the case analysis is very obvious to the professor from the nature of your recommendations. Recommendations are directed at solving whatever strategic problem the company is facing and at increasing its future profitability. Your recommendations should be in line with the previous analysis,

that is, should follow logically from the previous discussion. For example, your recommendations will generally center on the specific ways of changing functional, business, and corporate strategy and organizational structure and control in order to improve business performance. The set of recommendations will be specific to each case, and so it is difficult to discuss these recommendations here. However, such recommendations might include an increase in spending on specific research and development projects; the divesting of certain businesses; a change from a strategy of unrelated to related diversification; an increase in the level of integration among divisions by using task forces and teams; or a move to a different kind of structure to implement a new business-level strategy. Again, make sure your recommendations are mutually consistent and are written in the form of an action plan. The plan might contain a timetable that sequences the actions for changing the company's strategy and a description of how changes at the corporate level will necessitate changes at the business level and subsequently at the functional level.

After following all these stages, you will have performed a thorough analysis of the case and will be in a position to join in class discussion or present your ideas to the class, depending on the format used by your professor. Remember that you must tailor your analysis to suit the specific issue discussed in your case. In some cases, you might omit completely one of the stages of the analysis because it is not relevant to the situation you are considering. You must be sensitive to the needs of the case and not apply the framework we have discussed in this section blindly. The framework is meant only as a guide, and not as an outline that you must use to do a successful analysis.

12.3 WRITING A CASE STUDY

Often, as part of your course requirements, you will need to write up one or more of the cases and present your instructor with a written case analysis. Sometimes this will be an individual report, and at other times it will be a group report. Whatever the situation, there are certain guidelines to follow in writing a case that will improve the evaluation that your analysis will receive from your teacher. Before we discuss these guidelines, and before you use them, make sure that they do not conflict with any instructions your teacher may have given you.

The main point is how to structure the writing of a case study. Generally, if you follow the stages of analysis discussed above, *you will already have a good structure for your written discussion.* All reports begin with an *introduction* to the case. In it, you outline briefly what the company does, how it developed historically, what problems it is experiencing, and how you are going to approach the issues in the case write-up. Do this sequentially, saying, "first, we discuss environment of Company X . . . third, we discuss Company X's business level strategy . . . Last, we provide recommendations for turning around Company X's business.

In the second part of the case, the strategic analysis section, do the SWOT analysis, analyze and discuss the nature and problems of the company's business-level and corporate strategy, and then analyze its structure and control systems. Make sure you use plenty of headings and subheadings to structure your analysis. For example, have separate sections on any important conceptual tool you use. Thus you might have a section on Porter's five forces model as part of your analysis of the environment. Or you might offer a separate section on portfolio techniques when analyzing a company's corporate strategy. Tailor the sections and subsections to the specific issue of importance in the case.

Then, in the third part of the case write-up, present your solutions and recommendations. Be comprehensive, do this in line with the previous analysis so that the recommendations fit together, and move logically from one to the next. The recommendations section is very revealing because, as we mentioned earlier, your teacher will have a good idea of how much work you put into the case from the quality of your recommendations.

Following this framework will provide a good structure for most written reports, though obviously it must be shaped to fit the individual case being considered. Some cases are about excellent companies experiencing no problems. In such instances, it is hard to write recommendations. Instead, you can focus on analyzing why the company is doing so well and using that analysis to structure the discussion. There are some minor points to note that can also affect the evaluation you receive.

1. Do not repeat in summary form large pieces of factual information from the case and feed them back to the instructor in the report. The instructor has also read the case and knows what is going on. Rather, use the information in the case to illustrate your statements, to defend your arguments, or to make salient points. Beyond the brief introduction to the company, you must avoid being *descriptive;* instead, you must be *analytical.*

2. Make sure the sections and subsections of your discussion flow logically and smoothly from one to the next. That is, try to build on what has gone before so that the case study builds to a climax. This is particularly important for group cases. With group cases there is a tendency for people to split up the work and say, "I'll do the beginning, you take the middle, and I'll do the end." The result is bad because the parts of the analysis do not flow from one to the next, and it is obvious to the instructor that no real group work has been done.

3. Avoid grammatical and spelling errors. They make the paper seem sloppy.

4. Some cases dealing with well known companies end in 1986 or 1987 because no later information was available when the case was written. If possible, do

a library search for more information on what has happened to the company since then. Below are sources of information for performing this search.

Datext is a service on compact disk that gives an amazing amount of good information.

F&S Predicasts provide a listing on a yearly basis of all the articles written about a particular company. Simply reading the titles gives an indication of what has been happening in the company.

10K annual reports often provide an organizational chart.

Write to the company for information.

Fortune and *Business Week* have many articles on companies featured in the cases in this book.

Standard & Poor's industry reports provide detailed information about the competitive conditions facing the company's industry.

5. Sometimes the instructor will hand out questions for each case to help you in your analysis. Use these as a guide for analyzing and writing the case because they often illuminate the important issues that have to be covered in the discussion.

  If you follow the guidelines in this section, you should be able to write a thorough and effective evaluation.

12.4 THE ROLE OF FINANCIAL ANALYSIS IN CASE STUDY ANALYSIS

Another significant aspect of analyzing and writing a case study is the role and use of financial information. A careful analysis of the company's financial condition immensely improves a case write-up. After all, these figures represent the concrete results of the company's strategy and structure. Many useful financial performance ratios can be derived from a company's balance sheet and profit and loss accounts. These can be broken down into four different subgroups: profit ratios, liquidity ratios, leverage ratios, and shareholder-return ratios. In addition to these performance ratios, a company's *cash flow* position is of critical importance and should be assessed.

Profit Ratios

Profit ratios measure the efficiency with which the company uses its resources. The more efficient the company, the greater is its profitability. It is useful to compare a company's profitability against that of its major competitors in its industry. Such a comparison will tell you whether the company is operating more or less efficiently than its rivals. In addition, the change in a company's profit ratios over time will tell you whether its performance is improving or declining.

There are a number of different profit ratios that can be used, each of them purporting to measure a different aspect of a company's performance. The most commonly used profit ratios are given below.

1. *Gross profit margin* The gross profit margin gives an indication of the total margin available to cover operating expenses and yield a profit. It is a measure of the value a company creates net of the cost of performing value creation activities. It is defined as follows:

$$\text{Gross Profit Margin} = \frac{\text{Sales Revenue} - \text{Cost of Goods Sold}}{\text{Sales Revenue}}$$

2. *Return on total assets* This is a measure of the return earned on the total investment in a company. It is defined as follows:

$$\text{Return on Total Assets} = \frac{\text{Profits After Tax} + \text{Interest}}{\text{Total Assets}}$$

Total assets refer to fixed assets, plus current assets. Interest payments are added back to after-tax profits in order to account for the fact that current assets are financed by creditors.

3. *Return on stockholders' equity* Often referred to as return on net worth, this is a measure of the rate of return on stockholders' investment in the company. In theory, a company attempting to maximize the wealth of its stockholders should be trying to maximize this ratio. It is defined as follows:

$$\text{Return on Stockholders' Equity} = \frac{\text{Profit After Tax and Interest}}{\text{Total Stockholders' Equity}}$$

Liquidity Ratios

A company's liquidity is a measure of its ability to meet unexpected contingencies—such as a prolonged strike or price war. An asset is termed "liquid" if it can be quickly converted into cash. A company's current assets are liquid assets. Liquidity can be in the form of idle working capital, marketable securities, or funding in reserve, such as unused lines of credit. A company that lacks liquidity is in a weak financial position. For example, if a company whose sales revenues are hurt by a strike lacks liquidity, it might not be able to generate the cash necessary to meet the claims of short-term creditors, such as banks. Bankruptcy could ultimately result from such a scenario. Companies with major investment in fixed assets, such as steel mills or auto plants, tend to be less liquid than companies with a lower level of fixed assets. This is because fixed assets cannot be easily translated into cash and because they often necessitate major fixed costs, which place heavy demands on a company's cash reserves in times of trouble.

Two commonly used liquidity ratios are given below.

1. *Current ratio*   The current ratio measures the extent to which the claims of short-term creditors are covered by assets that can be quickly converted into cash. If a company's current ratio declines to less than 1, the company could be in serious trouble should an unexpected contingency arise. The ratio is defined as follows:

$$\text{Current Ratio} = \frac{\text{Current Assets}}{\text{Current Liabilities}}$$

2. *Quick ratio*   The quick ratio measures a company's ability to pay off the claims of short-term creditors without relying on the sale of its inventories. This is a valuable measure since in practice the sale of inventories is often difficult. It is defined as follows:

$$\text{Quick Ratio} = \frac{\text{Current Assets} - \text{Inventories}}{\text{Current Liabilities}}$$

Leverage Ratios

A company is said to be highly leveraged when it relies on external sources of funds rather than internally generated funds to finance its investments. In some situations, it may make good sense for a company to be highly leveraged. For example, many successful high tech start-ups have relied almost entirely on external sources of funds to finance their initial investments. On the other hand, high leverage can become a terminal weakness, particularly when rising interest rates increase the cost of debt beyond a company's ability to service that debt. Generally, a highly leveraged company is more vulnerable to changes in the cost of finance than a company that funds its investments from internally generated cash.

Three commonly used leverage ratios appear below.

1. *Debt-to-assets ratio*   The debt-to-assets ratio is the most direct measure of the extent to which borrowed funds have been used to finance a company's investments. It is defined as follows:

$$\text{Debt-to-Assets} = \frac{\text{Total Debt}}{\text{Total Assets}}$$

Total debt is the sum of a company's current liabilities and its long-term debt, and total assets are the sum of fixed assets and current assets.

2. *Long-term debt-to-equity ratio* The long-term debt-to-equity measure indicates the balance between debt and equity in a company's long-term capital structure. This is perhaps the most widely used measure of a company's leverage. It is defined as follows:

$$\text{Debt-to-Equity} = \frac{\text{Long-term debt}}{\text{Total Stockholders' Equity}}$$

3. *Times-covered ratio* The times-covered ratio measures the extent to which a company's gross profit covers its annual interest payments. If the times-covered ratio declines to less than 1, then the company is unable to meet its interest costs and is technically insolvent. The ratio is defined as follows:

$$\text{Times-covered Ratio} = \frac{\text{Profits Before Interest and Tax}}{\text{Total Interest Charges}}$$

Shareholder-Return Ratios

Shareholder-return ratios measure the return earned by shareholders from holding stock in the company. Given the goal of maximizing stockholder wealth, providing their shareholders with an adequate rate of return is a primary objective of most companies. As with profit ratios, it can be helpful to compare a company's shareholder returns against those of similar companies. This will give you a yardstick for determining how well the company is satisfying the demands of this particularly important group of organizational constituents. Two commonly used ratios are given below.

1. *Total shareholder returns* Total shareholder returns measure the returns earned by time t + 1 on an investment in a company's stock made at time t. (*Time t* is the time at which the initial investment is made.) Total shareholder returns include both dividend payments and appreciation in the value of the stock (adjusted for stock splits) and are defined as follows:

$$\text{Total Shareholder Returns} = \frac{\text{Stock Price(t + 1)} - \text{Stock Price(t)} + \text{Sum of Annual Dividends per Share}}{\text{Stock Price(t)}}$$

Thus if a shareholder invests $2 at time t, and at time t + 1 the share is worth $3, while the sum of annual dividends for the period t to t + 1 has amounted to $0.2, total shareholder returns are equal to (3 − 2 + 0.2)/2 = 0.6, that is a 60-percent return on an initial investment of $2 made at time t.

2. *Dividend yield* The dividend yield measures the return to shareholders received in the form of dividends. It is defined as follows:

$$\text{Dividend Yield} = \frac{\text{Dividends per Share}}{\text{Market Price per Share}}$$

Market price per share can be calculated for the first of the year, in which case the dividend yield refers to the return on an investment made at the beginning of the year. Alternatively, the average share price over the year may be used. A word of caution: a company that pays out high annual dividends may leave itself with too few cash reserves to meet its investment needs and may have to borrow more than it would choose to do from external sources of finance. In turn, the subsequent high level of debt may depress the market value of a company's stock. Thus a high dividend yield is not always a good thing.

Cash Flow

A company's cash flow position is an important indicator of its financial status. Cash flow refers to the surplus of internally generated funds over expenditure. Some businesses are cash hungry, while others are net generators of cash. Cash flow is important for what it tells us about a company's financing needs. A strong positive cash flow enables a company to fund future investments without having to borrow money from bankers or investors. This is desirable, since the company avoids the need to pay out interest or dividends. A weak or negative cash flow means that a company has to turn to external sources to fund future investments. Generally speaking, companies in high-growth industries often find themselves in a poor cash flow position (since their investment needs are substantial), whereas successful companies based in mature industries find themselves in a strong cash flow position.

A company's internally generated cash flow is calculated by adding back its depreciation provision to profits after interest, taxes, and dividend payments. If this figure is insufficient to cover proposed new investment expenditures, the company has little choice but to borrow funds to make up the shortfall—or curtail investments. If this figure exceeds proposed new investments, the company can use the excess to build up its liquidity (that is, through investments in financial assets) or to repay existing loans ahead of schedule.

12.5 CONCLUSION

When evaluating a case, it is important to be *systematic*. Analyze the case in a logical fashion, beginning with the identification of operating and financial strengths and weaknesses and environmental opportunities and threats. Move on to assess the value of a company's current strategies only when you are fully conversant with the SWOT of the company. Ask yourself whether the company's current strategies make sense, given the SWOT. If they do not, what changes need to be made? What are your recommendations? Above all, link any strategic recommendations you may make to the SWOT analysis. State explicitly how the strategies you identify take advantage of company strengths to exploit environmental opportunities, how they rectify company weaknesses, and how they counter environmental threats. And do not forget to outline what needs to be done to implement your recommendations.

CASES

BUSINESS-LEVEL STRATEGY:

FORMULATION AND IMPLEMENTATION

BEER AND
WINE INDUSTRIES:
BARTLES & JAYMES

INTRODUCTION

At the end of 1986, Bartles & Jaymes conquered the number one position in the wine cooler industry after coming in second to California Coolers since this product hit the consumer goods market. Going into 1987, Bartles & Jaymes and its corporate parent, Ernest & Julio Gallo Winery, were faced with the task of maintaining this market position and increasing sales of its newest product—the wine cooler.

HISTORY OF THE FIRM

Ernest and Julio Gallo Winery, the world's largest, began in 1938 at a tragic point in the brothers' lives. They had just inherited their father Joseph's vineyard after he shot his wife, reportedly chased Ernest and Julio with a shotgun, and committed suicide. Suddenly they were faced with operating the vineyard where they grew up and had gone to work upon completing their education (high school for Julio and junior college for Ernest). The business of growing grapes was all they knew. Joseph Gallo, an immigrant from Italy, came to Modesto, California, and began his small grape-producing company. The fledgling company survived Prohibition due to the fact that the government allowed

This case was prepared by Professor Per V. Jenster, McIntire School of Commerce, University of Virginia. The author gratefully acknowledges the assistance of students Morlon Bell, Michele Goggins, and Mary May, as well as the support provided by the McIntire Foundation. Copyright 1987.

wine production for medicinal and religious use. The Depression dealt the small company a somewhat more devastating blow. It was at this company low point that Joseph decided on such a dramatic solution to his problems. Though he may have solved his problems, Joseph left his relatively young sons a burden of responsibility and decision-making. Shortly after their parents' deaths, Prohibition was repealed and the brothers decided to move from grape growing to wine producing. With two pamphlets on wine-making from the local public library and less than $6000 in hand, the ambitious Gallos began their empire.

Gallo's climb to its dominant position in the wine industry (see Exhibit 1) began slowly. In the 1930's and 1940's, Ernest developed his acute marketing sense and Julio cultivated and refined his wine-making expertise. Initially they sold their product in bulk to bottlers on the east coast, but in 1938 they decided it would be more profitable to bottle the wine under a Gallo label. In the 1950's Gallo greatly increased its success with a high-alcohol, low-price product called Thunderbird. This product became exceptionally popular on skid rows and increased Gallo's profitability, but it may have done irreparable damage by saddling Gallo with a "gutter" image. In the 1960's and early 1970's Gallo's image, not sales, was further tarnished by the "pop-wine" craze of which it was a leader with such products as Boone's Farm and Spanada wines. In the mid-1970's, Ernest Gallo became conscious of and concerned about the fact that even though it had formidable sales, it also had a "brown bag," jug wine image. At that time the company decided to attempt to upgrade its image and at the same time maintain its market share and sales. In this attempt it began to produce premium table wines such as Zinfandel, Sauvignon Blanc, Ruby Cabernet, and French Colombard. This push to improve its image continued to be a dominating theme for Gallo.

As Gallo grew, it not only developed its wine sales but became extensively vertically integrated. It had divisions in virtually every step of the wine-producing process. The brothers owned one of the largest intrastate trucking companies in California, which was used to haul wine, grapes, raw materials, sand, lime, etc. Gallo was the only wine producer who made its own bottles, and its Midcal Aluminum Company supplied it with screw tops. Unlike most other wine pro-

EXHIBIT 1   **1985 Share of U.S. wine market**

E. & J. Gallo Winery	26.1%
Seagram & Sons	8.3%
Canandaigua Wine	5.4%
Brown-Forman	5.1%
National Distillers	4.0%
Heublein	3.7%
Imports	23.4%
All others	24.0%

Source: Reprinted from *Advertising Age*, March 24, 1986, by permission.

ducers, Gallo took an active role in the marketing of its products. Typical wineries would turn their products over to independent distributors who represented several producers and expected the distributor to get the product to the consumer. These distributors, on the other hand, felt their job consisted of taking orders and making deliveries. Gallo owned many of its distributors and the independent distributors it used had to be willing to submit to Gallo's regimentation. Gallo was known to "encourage" its independent distributors to exclusively distribute Gallo products. Ten years ago the Federal Trade Commission took offense at this, charging Gallo with unfair competition and forcing Gallo to sign a consent order. In 1984 the FTC removed the order due to the fact that the wine industry had become more competitive.

In its fifty-year history Gallo developed an extensive product line. It had products geared toward the low-price, jug wine market (Carlo Rossi, Chablis Blanc, etc.). It also had a replete category of premium wine, selling more than any competitor, but growth in this market was limited due to the fact that Gallo did not have snob appeal. In 1984 Gallo entered the wine cooler category (a carbonated drink with half white wine and half citrus juice) with its Bartles & Jaymes wine cooler. Gallo followed the lead of such industry innovators as California Cooler, Sun Country Coolers, etc., which fit well with its strategy of building market share through skillful marketing and sales, but not introducing inventive new products. Bartles & Jaymes was marketed in 12-oz. green bottles similar to those used for Michelob beer and aimed at a more sophisticated consumer than its competitors. To help promote this upgrade image, Gallo tried to distance itself from Bartles & Jaymes, and many consumers did not know that Gallo wine was used to make the coolers. In the summer of 1986, Bartles & Jaymes took over the number one position in the wine cooler market with a share of 22.1%.

With that initial $6000, some ingenuity, a little luck, and a lot of spunk, the Gallo brothers built the world's preeminent wine dynasty. Because Gallo was a private, tightly-held company there was no public financial data, but it was estimated that it had annual sales of $1 billion and yearly earnings of $50 million. In comparison, Joe E. Seagram and Sons, the second largest winery, had revenues of $350 million and lost money on its best-selling table wines in 1985.

BACKGROUND ON KEY EXECUTIVES

E. & J. Gallo was a private company owned and operated by the Gallo brothers, Ernest and Julio. Julio, the 77-year-old president of the firm, and Ernest, chairman of the board at 78, ran their company in a very dichotomous manner. Julio was in charge of producing the wine and Ernest marketed and distributed it. They operated in their separate worlds and often did not have daily contact. It seemed to be a game—Julio trying to produce more than Ernest could sell and Ernest trying to sell more than Julio could produce. But the game apparently worked and provided the company with good returns.

Julio, the more easy-going of the two, described himself as a "farmer at heart." He spent much of his time in the fields and overseeing the wine-making. Though definitely not a pushover, Julio was not the hard-core, intense business-man that his brother Ernest was. Ernest ruled over the company and usually made the final decisions. He was characterized as being polite, but blunt. He could not bear to relinquish power and control, and it was at his insistence that everything about the operations of the firm was kept secret. He could be a very demanding, driving boss, and when asked about the secret to Gallo's success, he remarked it was a "constant striving for perfection in every aspect of our business."

A looming concern, though not openly addressed or dealt with at Gallo, was the brothers' advancing age. Julio seemed to be training and grooming his son, Robert, and his son-in-law, James Coleman, in his area of expertise. Ernest, on the other hand, had no heir apparent. Two of his sons, David and Joseph, worked with him but neither was viewed as having the ability to take over their father's job. Joseph was felt to give uneven decisions, and David was described as "occasionally bizarre." The firm had many intelligent, able, top-level executives, but they had no power to make decisions and predominantly strove to please Ernest. The deaths of Ernest and Julio, which were inevitable, could prove to be devastating for the firm.

INTERNAL OPERATIONS

Because Gallo was so tightly held and secretive it was hard to determine how and why things were done the way they were—maybe only Ernest knew. A few loyal senior managers ran the divisions of the vertically integrated firm and reported to Ernest. He had a hand in all major decisions and procedures and went so far as to help write a 300-page very detailed training manual for sales representatives. Gallo was so secretive that at times even its own employees did not know what was happening. According to Diana Kelleher, former marketing manager at Gallo, "I never saw a profit-and-loss statement; Ernest wouldn't tell anyone the cost of raw materials, overhead, or packaging."

INDUSTRY HISTORY & ANALYSIS

It would be difficult to pinpoint exactly when the wine cooler industry emerged. Three separate events were cited to mark the beginning of this prosperous industry. In 1977, Joseph Bianchi, owner of Bianchi Vineyards, observed people at a summer party mixing Seven-Up with wine. In 1981, Thomas Steidl, owner of Canada Dry/Graf's Bottling Company, formulated his own wine cooler recipe. The event which was commonly viewed as the beginning of this industry stemmed from the concoction of Michael M. Crete and R. Stuart Bewley produced by California Cooler.

Crete and Bewley's drink was initially served in 1972 to their friends. Little did they know that this new refresher would be a huge success a decade later. Batches of white wine and fruit juice were mixed in a beer barrel and served from a plastic hose. Labels were stuck on by hand and an average workday consisted of bottling 100 to 150 cases. As this product was marketed in the early 1980's, sales began to increase steadily. This campaign spurred national attention toward the new market.

At the point of the cooler's entry, other sectors of the beverage industry were experiencing declining sales. The wine industry had experienced declining table wine sales for two years in a row at the beginning of the 1980's. Likewise, the beer industry was faced with declining sales. It was costing both industries more in advertising to keep their regular customers. Several factors caused such a response in the consumer market. First, drunken driving laws and the crackdown on drinking that they spurred led to more awareness about the negative effects of alcohol. Public interest groups such as MADD (Mothers Against Drunk Driving) played a key role in changing the consumer's perceptions of drinking. Second, there was growing concern for fitness. As the health conscious consumers grew in number, the tendency to indulge in alcoholic beverages declined. Third, the raising of the legal drinking age presented obstacles to increasing sales. Since younger adults consumed a significant percentage of the alcohol sold, the change in age cut out some sales originally anticipated by beer and wine producers. Fourth, the lobbying to remove liquor advertising from television showed wineries and breweries as the villains in society.

In view of societal factors, a method was needed to help the alcoholic industries survive. Thus, an alternative to beer and wine appeared to be the solution in the eyes of Crete and Bewley. They saw the potential and seized the opportunity to capitalize on the venture. In order to achieve a successful outcome, however, the product had to be positioned properly. The wine cooler was a fruity-tasting, slightly cloudy beverage made from chablis, blended citrus-pineapple juice, fructose and a slight amount of carbonation. Its targeted consumers were young adults from legal drinking age to 34 years old, both male and female. The cooler was marketed in the same manner as beer, particularly its "cold-box," refrigerator bottling. It was to be less of an elitist drink than wine. It contained more alcohol than beer but less alcohol than wine.

In order for the wine cooler industry to succeed, several characteristics had to be present. Taste was an important factor to provide a basis for differentiation between products. Points of difference were sought to make individual brands stand out by varying fruit flavors, packaging, or advertising techniques. Another major characteristic was merchandising, which was relevant to the success of any consumer market. In the wine industry particularly, price was the key to merchandising. It could be extremely difficult for competitors to come up with original ideas to differentiate their product, so most relied on price to help them capture a reasonable percentage of the market.

Several viewpoints have been given about wine coolers. The single service focus was the major thrust of the cooler's marketing plan. It could be carried easily (exactly like beer) and did not concentrate heavily on the jug mentality of wineries. Coolers also cut across beverage boundaries by "touting the fizz of soft drinks, the popularity of white wine, the freshness of citrus juice, plus a bit of fructose to satisfy the sweet tooth." The cooler fit the desires of the current pluralistic consumer society. It was viewed as "wine for the common man" because it appealed to the beer drinker who wanted a little more alcohol, the wine drinker who wanted a little less, the calorie- and taste-conscious and the first-time wine drinkers put off by the snobbery of the wine elite. The marketing module appeared to contain all the elements of success — "a firm product identity; a well defined package and price image; a powerful distribution channel that stressed cold box merchandising to capitalize on its 'cool' perception and enhance its full price and profit positioning; and advertising that communicated a refreshing message to the public." This segment showed second generation development. Three trends were cited in the existing industry. One trend focused on the low-alcohol content of approximately 6%. This aspect was probably influenced by the anti-drunk driving campaigns. Sales of coolers were said to have been spurred by this concern. Another trend was geared toward its thirst-quenching characteristic. Its refreshing health perspective was the focus of the last trend. Coolers were professed to be healthier since they contained half citrus juice.

The wine cooler industry appeared particularly attractive because the product offered high margins and a low base with no capital requirements. It generated better gross dollar margins than beer or wine. The expected annual growth rate was projected to be 13% until 1993. The expected growth rate in 1986 was 69%. Cooler sales were estimated to account for 17 to 20 percent of total wine sales in 1986 as compared to only 1 percent in 1984.

In 1986 the cooler industry was faced with various trends in the beverage world. First, it was reported that Americans were drinking more soft drinks (April 1986). The alcohol industry was still faced with overall declines but the wine industry was better than the beer industry due to the success of the wine cooler. It was predicted that the wine cooler industry would soon be viewed separately from the wine industry. The second area of concern involved the steadily increasing cost of competing. The fight for wholesale and retail distribution was intensifying. This led marketers to cut prices to acquire more shelf space and visibility. Also, coupons were used to increase distribution. As of August 1986, the dollar level was low and the investment spending was high.

The wine cooler industry consisted of approximately 40 producers and 154 individual labels during the summer of 1986. Because of the high barriers to entry, competition from other segments, particularly the breweries and wineries, did not appear to be substantial. Since the beer and wine markets were mature, the success achieved in the wine cooler industry caused them to take a second look at this area for potential profits. Even though breweries and wineries experienced decreasing sales, only a small portion was attributed to the boom in the wine cooler industry. The soft drink industry, on the other hand, proved to be a minor problem for coolers due to increased consumption by consumers. The effect of the competition was not significantly shown in the sales figures for coolers but the potential loomed in the background. Experts raised questions concerning the cooler sales. Declines were predicted based on a speculated consumer interest in a variety of flavored drinks. Were coolers a fad or a new and growing industry?

COMPETITION

When California Cooler began peddling its wine cooler, the competition was sparse and far from formidable. Initially, the cost of entry into the new market was relatively low. But by the first quarter of 1986, the world's largest winery, brewery, and distillery were all vying for the top spot and all three were holding fat bankrolls. The cost of entry into the market had risen to $10 million just for advertising. Cooler marketers and industry observers were confident this category would continue to grow steadily for the next few years. It was estimated that 60 to 65 million cases of coolers — including malt-based coolers — would have been sold by the end of 1987, up from 41 million cases in 1985. In 1987, more than 150 kinds of wine coolers were competing with the top seven coolers, which controlled about 90% of the market — E. & J. Gallo Winery's Bartles & Jaymes, Brown-Forman Corporation's California Cooler, Canandaigua Wine Co.'s Sun Country, Joseph Victori Wines' Calvin Cooler, Stroh Brewery Co.'s malt-based White Mountain cooler, and Joe E. Seagram and Sons' Premium and Golden coolers. (See Exhibit 2.)

EXHIBIT 2   **Top 10 cooler brands share of the market**

	1986*	1985
1. Bartles & Jaymes	22.1%	17.5%
2. California Cooler	18.0	26.8
3. Sun Country	13.1	11.7
4. White Mountain	12.4	7.5
5. Calvin Cooler	8.3	6.5
6. Seagram's Golden	6.9	—
7. Seagram's Premium	5.5	9.3
8. Dewey Stevens	2.8	—
9. 20/20	2.5	3.7
10. La Croix	1.5	1.9

*estimate

Source: Impact Databank, 1986. Reprinted by permission of M. Shanken Communications, Inc.

Bartles & Jaymes

By October of 1986, Gallo's Bartles & Jaymes wine cooler was the largest selling cooler in the nation with a 22.1% market share. Its standing was quite remarkable in light of Bartles & Jaymes' relatively narrow product line. Gallo produced only one flavor of wine cooler (6% alcohol). This clear, less sweet cooler came in sleek 12 oz. green bottles like those of imported beers and was available in the standard four-pack.

Two key factors, advertising and distribution, differentiated the industry leader from its competitors. In 1986, Gallo budgeted $30 million for advertising expenditures for Bartles & Jaymes (see Exhibit 3). The majority of this money was spent on an ad campaign in which Gallo chose to distance its cooler from the parent corporation by creating fictional proprietors named Frank Bartles and Ed Jaymes, who sat on their front porch while Frank delivered low-key comic monologues about the product. An advertiser with the Bartles & Jaymes campaign said, "Most of the competition was using youthful music and showing young people doing all the predictable things. We thought that if we got into all those clichés, we'd get lost." This was all part of a cold, hard-edged effort on Gallo's part to maintain a sense of warm, down-home, folksy legitimacy around the TV spots that obviously had many Americans believing there really were a Frank Bartles and an Ed Jaymes.

Some observers, including a few of Gallo's competitors, were not as amused by Gallo's marketing strategy as most of America seemed to be. Tom Gibbs, director of marketing for California Coolers, saw the ads as downright deceptive. "Yuppies are not Gallo drinkers, so they (Gallo) have tried to disassociate their names from this market." Mr. Gibbs said the public did not know Frank and Ed were not on the level and believed consumers would turn away from the product if they knew the truth. He claimed his company had done interviews after which people quit drinking Bartles & Jaymes once they learned it was a Gallo product—a name, he says, "people equate with jug wines."

Jon Fredrikson, an industry analyst with San Francisco-based wine industry consultants Gomberg, Fredrikson & Associates, said the public might react

EXHIBIT 3   1986 advertising budgets

Bartles & Jaymes	$30,000,000
Seagram's	30,000,000
California Cooler	25,000,000
Dewey Stevens	20,000,000
Sun Country	20,000,000
White Mountain	12,000,000
Calvin Cooler	10,000,000

Source: Reprinted from *Advertising Age*, March 24, 1986, by permission.

negatively if the truth got out on a widespread basis, but added that wasn't likely.

Aileen Fredrikson, also with Gomberg, said the campaign had the dual effect of helping beer drinkers relate to the wine cooler market. "Young people can always be convinced to try something once," she said, "but this may be a way to get hard-core beer drinkers to try it, since it's two good ole boys selling it."

The channel of distribution chosen by Gallo was the second key factor in differentiating Bartles & Jaymes from its competitors. Unlike other wine cooler producers who distributed their products through beer distributors, Bartles & Jaymes used Gallo's extensive wine distributorship. Ernest Gallo hand-picked each of these distributors and then planned strategies with them down to the last detail, analyzing traffic patterns in every store in the district and the number of Gallo cases each should stock. Ernest Gallo encouraged distributors to hire a separate sales force to sell his products alone. He also tried to persuade distributors to sell his wine exclusively.

California Cooler

Stuart Bewley and Michael Crete were partners who founded California Cooler Co., Stockton, California, just five years ago. The two childhood friends created the product when they started filling washtubs at beach parties with their special mixture—half white wine and half citrus juice. In September 1985, Brown-Forman, a Louisville-based distiller, bought out the segment leader California Cooler for $63 million in cash plus millions more in incentive payments based on future sales.

California Coolers contained 6% alcohol and came in a variety of flavors including tropical, orange and the original citrus flavor. Crucial to California Cooler's initial success was that it was marketed more as a beer than as a wine. From the beginning, Crete and Bewley wanted a quality package and, from their beer-drinking days, they felt nothing beat a Heineken bottle. So they packaged California Cooler in a green tinged twist-top, short-neck bottle, added a gold foil top, and sold it in four-packs for under $4. This, they figured, might draw some beer drinkers. Subsequently, to counter competition, California Cooler introduced several new packages, including 2-liter bottles, 198-ml. bottles and in some areas quarter and half barrels.

In another important step, they left the natural fruit pulp in the bottle and stressed it on the label. California Cooler was thus further removed from the clear, sipping wine category. California Cooler hoped to get the younger, natural-thinking consumers. The product was positioned as an informal, mainstream American drink, targeted toward males and females from 18 to 35 years old.

Once the company broke even in early 1983, the co-founders began looking for an advertising agency to help broaden sales from its Northern California base. Its only advertising up until that point was a spot radio jingle sung to the tune of the Beach Boys' hit "California Girls." The new advertising campaign adopted positioned California Cooler not as a beer, not as a wine, but "beyond ordinary refreshment." These ads were funny putdowns by outsiders who were slightly envious of the hot tubs, health food fetishes and all around casual lifestyles of Californians—including their namesake drink, California Cooler. Other ads featured young people and 1960's rock 'n roll. Brown-Forman Corp. spent over $20 million on this ad campaign in 1986, yet still lost its top standing to Bartles & Jaymes. In 1986, California Cooler had an 18.0% market share, down from 26.8% in 1985 (see Exhibit 2).

Unlike Bartles & Jaymes, California Coolers was distributed by beer distributors, not wine wholesalers. The founders of California Coolers wanted their cooler to be in the "cold box" or refrigerator of a sales account. They felt the movement in beverages was out of the cold box, not the racks. Beer distributors were chosen because: they typically had more accounts than their wine counterparts; beer distributors carried fewer products compared to the huge portfolios of wine wholesalers; and as "good ole boys" beer distributors represented their informal product better. More recently though, to counter Gallo's tremendous distribution strength, California Cooler tried to take advantage of Brown-Forman's distribution muscle—it handled the popular Jack Daniels whiskey—and worked at broadening the overall market for coolers.

Sun Country

Sun Country coolers, produced by Canandaigua Wine, were the third largest selling wine coolers with a 13.1% market share. Sun Country coolers were very similar to California Coolers: both contained six percent alcohol, both retained the fruit pulp which gave them a cloudy character, both were available in citrus, tropical, and orange flavors, and both were packaged in green bottles and sold in convenient four-packs or 2-liter bottles.

To help differentiate their product, Canandaigua expanded Sun Country's product line to include two new flavors, cherry and peach. They also pumped up advertising with a $25 million budget and celebrity spokespeople including Charo, Cathy Lee Crosby, and The Four Tops. The ads targeted both men and women between the ages of 21 and 34.

Canandaigua also hoped to capitalize on exports of Sun Country, already available in Canada, Japan, South Africa, and the U.K. As of 1986, about 600,000 of 10 million cases were exported.

White Mountain

Recognizing the appeal of wine coolers, several brewers entered the market with malt-based products. As of 1986, only Stroh's White Mountain cooler showed any real success and significant sales. White Mountain cooler had a market share of 12.4%, up from 7.5% in 1985. The majority of its sales came from states where it had a tax and distribution advantage over wine coolers. Several states like Pennsylvania, White Mountain's leading market, barred the sale of wine-based products in supermarkets and other food stores.

White Mountain cooler bore a closer resemblance to beer than to wine. It was derived from malt, but unless the consumers looked closely at the label or the advertising they wouldn't know it, and that was how the brewer wanted it. Rather than attempt to create a market for a subcategory of malt-based coolers, which could be misconstrued as a flavored beer, the brewers simply sold their products as "coolers," taking advantage of the imagery of the wine-based products. White Mountain's label said it was an "alcohol beverage with natural fruit juices" and 5% alcohol content by weight.

White Mountain cooler was packaged in 12-oz. bottles and sold in six-packs like beer. Stroh's had over a $12 million ad budget behind White Mountain, targeting mainly 21 to 40 year olds. Stroh's also distributed its cooler through its existing beer distributors.

Seagram

Joe E. Seagram & Sons produced both Seagram's Premium and Seagram's Golden wine coolers. Combined, these two coolers made up 12.4% of the market. Seagram's coolers were a clear liquid, not cloudy like Sun Country and California Cooler. They came in 12-oz. glass bottles and were available in four-packs. Unlike the industry leaders, Bartles & Jaymes and California Cooler, which contained 6% alcohol, Seagram's coolers had just 4% alcohol. The Premium cooler came in a variety of flavors including citrus, peach, wild berry, and apple cranberry.

Seagram's original ads for the Premium cooler were fast-paced scenes of young people playing outdoor sports, with energetic background music. The cooler ad was intentionally like a beer commercial because Seagram's was aiming its product at beer drinkers and encouraging them to switch. Though men consumed 80% of the beer sold, they tended to be skeptical of coolers. But since women consumed almost four times as much beer as wine, Seagram's hoped that women who switched would encourage men to join them.

The citrus-based Premium wine cooler did not receive the market leverage observers had expected. As a result, the company then backed Golden wine coolers, a new line, with a $25 million ad campaign. The campaign starred "Moonlighting" star Bruce Willis, who played the same roguish character he portrayed on the hit ABC-TV series. These ads were once again targeted toward women between the ages of 21 and 35.

Seagram's also introduced a new product into the market — Seagram's Golden Spirits. It was the first line of spirit-based drinks modeled after the wine cooler. It was sold in four-packs of 375-ml. bottles that closely resembled the

Golden wine cooler. The line's four flavors—Mandarin Vodka, Peach Melba Rum, Spiced Canadian (whiskey) and Sunfruit Gin—each contained 5.1% alcohol. These flavors were proprietary; consumers could not replicate them in their homes.

The spirit coolers were expected to appeal more to men and to an older audience than wine coolers did. "They're positioned somewhat more serious," said Thomas McInerney, executive vp-marketing, Seagram Distillers. "They are not being given the beach-party image of wine coolers."

Calvin

Calvin Cooler, produced by New York based Joseph Victori Wines, was the fifth largest selling cooler. The company broke into early dominance in New York City, thanks to a state law that allowed only New York state liquor products to be sold in grocery stores, when its cooler hit the market in 1984. As of 1986, Calvin Cooler had an 8.3% market share and distributed nearly 6 million cases to every state but South Dakota.

However, the cooler still sat behind competitors with stronger distribution channels and two or three times Calvin's $10 million ad budget.

Calvin coolers came in a full line of flavors, including raspberry, one of its most popular flavors. The product was available in both four-packs and 2-liter bottles.

Dewey Stevens

Dewey Stevens Premium Light, produced by Anheuser-Busch, was the first product of its kind. The wine cooler was sold in four-packs of 12-oz. bottles, each containing 4% alcohol and only 135 calories. Most wine coolers contained 5% to 6% alcohol and more than 200 calories. Dewey Stevens contained no artificial sweeteners; Anheuser-Busch cut the calories by cutting its wine content and adding water.

The ad campaign for the cooler made an appeal to active, young women and placed emphasis on the product's lower calorie content.

Selected References

William Dunn, "Coolers Add Fizz to Flat Wine Market," *American Demographics* (March 1986), 19–20.

Scott Hume, "Drop In Consumption a Sour Note for Industries," *Advertising Age*, April 7, 1986, p. 23.

J. D. Stacy, "The Wine Cooler Phenomenon," *Beverage World* (December 1984), 49–50.

Patricia Winters, "Predict Big Chill for Wine Coolers," *Advertising Age*, August 11, 1986, p. 23.

BENNETT'S MACHINE SHOP, INC.

"This won't even be a one-page month," said Pat Bennett. "Worst month we've ever had." Pat was the owner of Bennett's Machine Shop, an automotive engine rebuilder in Lake Charles, Louisiana. He went on to explain what he meant by a "one-page" month: "We write each engine job order on one line of a 32-line yellow legal pad. Last year, we figured out that a breakeven point was about sixty engines a month. If we have three pages in a month, we have really made some money. A single page? We should have gone fishing."

Bennett's engine sales for July 1987 were $57,000, down from $80,000 to $90,000 a year earlier. Pat said, "We install about 40 percent of the engines we rebuild, at about $1,250 a shot. The carry-outs average about $750. So I don't expect sales in August to even reach $30,000."

Pat saw his problem as "too little sales to support the overhead cost." He said, "Because of this, we have a day-to-day cash flow problem." After receiving his July financial statement from the accountant, Pat had laid off all the office help (a secretary/bookkeeper and a clerk/parts runner). Pat had released four mechanics and a helper earlier in the year.

Pat himself had been spending most of his time on a tool modification and sharpening contract with Boeing of Louisiana, Inc. (BLI). Bennett's had begun doing this work in February 1987, shortly after Boeing opened its new Louisiana facility, where Air Force KC-135 tankers (a variation of the Boeing 707) were reworked. In July, Boeing had begun returning Bennett's invoices, with a rubber-stamped note that they exceeded the $75,000 contract amount. By mid-August, unpaid billings to Boeing totaled over $60,000. Pat said, "I've cut about everything I can cut and sold about as much as I can sell. I even took out a second mortgage on my condo. If Boeing doesn't pay pretty soon, or a miracle

This case was prepared by Arthur Sharplin, McNeese State University, Lake Charles, Louisiana. Reprinted by permission of the author.

doesn't happen in the machine shop, we're going to be history." Appendix A contains excerpts from an interview with Pat Bennett conducted in mid-September 1987.

COMPANY BACKGROUND

In 1972, Pat Bennett earned a Bachelor of Science degree in mechanical engineering at McNeese University in Lake Charles. Recalling his senior year, Pat said, "I knew then I would not stick with my engineering career. Besides going through just a real burnout, I already had this machine shop idea. There were just three automotive machine shops in Lake Charles. And all the operators were in their late fifties. I knew there would be an excellent opportunity for a new shop in just a few years."

After graduation, Pat took a job with a chemical plant contractor as a designer/draftsman. The contract was completed in six months and Pat's employer offered him a chance to move to St. Louis. Instead, he quit and hired on at a local Cities Service plant as a "field engineer." Since all he actually did at the plant was drafting, Pat felt he had been misled. He stuck out his one-year contract — all except the last four hours. Pat said, "On the 365th day when the boss went to lunch, I said 'Goodbye' to the man sitting beside me, took just the drafting equipment I could hold in my hand, and walked out the back door." Pat's impetuosity cost him the one week of vacation pay he had accumulated.

For the next year (1974–75), Pat commuted 60 miles to Beaumont, Texas, where he worked for Stubbs-Overbeck, Inc., a petroleum refinery engineering firm. According to Pat, this was "my first real engineering job." He explained,

> My first day on the job, they fired the civil engineer. I was sitting there feeling inadequate, worrying what my assignment would be and if I would remember how to do it. I heard the office manager ask two other guys, "Who are we going to get to run the theodolite (a sophisticated surveying instrument) so the design crew can get going?" I got their attention and timidly said, "I know how to run a theodolite." They questioned why a mechanical engineer would know how to do that. I told them I had worked for a civil engineer while in college.

At about the same time, Pat bought a boring bar (a tool used to recondition cylinders in engine blocks) from a farmer for $50. He also sold his wife's washer and dryer for $100 to get the down payment on a valve grinding machine, the other piece of equipment required for the most rudimentary engine rebuilder. At night and on weekends, Pat rebuilt engines in a six-by-eight-foot shack next to the trailer house where he lived with his wife, Cheryl. Customers gave Pat money to buy parts, and he charged them only for his labor.

Pat told of his big entrepreneurial decision:

> I worked ten hours in Beaumont and drove an hour each way in addition to the time I spent doing engines. The drive just got too dangerous. I was sleepy most of the time and kept dozing

at the wheel. Finally, one morning on the way to work I almost ran off the road. I had to pull over and sleep and didn't get to work until 9:30. When I got home that evening, Cheryl and I talked it over and decided I should quit my job and try the machine shop business full time.

Pat rented a small Quonset hut as his first shop, paying the owner $75 for the month he used it. Then he moved to a stall in a service station about a block from the trailer park. There, his rent was one-third of all labor charges. The service station owner made additional profit on engine parts. Pat said, "I could not get any discount on parts. I had no business license. We did not even have a name. But the fellow who ran the service station bought parts at jobber prices."

Near the end of 1975, a local garage owner asked Pat if he would split the rent on a larger building the garage owner was considering. Pat would pay $150 of the $400 monthly rent. Pat agreed, and the arrangement lasted about two years. During that time Pat hired a helper (a pre-med student) and bought a cylinder head grinder and two other specialized machines (all on credit).

In 1977, Pat incorporated his business as Bennett's Machine Shop, Inc. and moved it to a rented building on Prien Lake Road, a busy commercial street. Sales and profits continued to expand through 1979, when his landlord, whom Pat had nicknamed "The Iron Maiden," ordered him to move because of the growing pile of used engines and parts next to the shop building. The shop flooded frequently anyway, and the fire department had complained about the oily rinse water Bennett's discharged into the city storm drains. Pat said, "I told the Iron Maiden that this was about as clean as it was going to get and made plans to move."

"I arranged to borrow $80,000 from Gulf National Bank," said Pat, adding, "I found a two-acre lot on the old Chennault air base for $57,000. I built a 4,000-square-foot building with the other $23,000, plus $3,000 I had saved." Bennett's Machine Shop moved to the new location in December 1979.

Pat said, "The first year we really had any extra money was 1981. We bought eleven pieces of property. We put 20 percent down on all of it and borrowed the rest, about $80,000." That year and the next, Pat added 6,000 square feet to the machine shop and built another shop building, all without borrowing. For the first time in 1981, Bennett's began to do "over-the-fender" work, installing engines and some minor general repair work. At about this time, Pat and Cheryl bought a "real house" in nearby Westlake and moved from their mobile home. By 1985, Pat had bought a new condominium in Lake Charles and a 38-foot cabin cruiser. Cheryl was using the Westlake home as a cat sanctuary, and the sixty cats she had taken in required much of her time. Pat had collected 22 "muscle cars" and his personal car was a 1984 Jaguar XJS coupe.

"Then we made our big blunder," said Pat. "I thought it was time to open a new location, not to rebuild engines, but to install them. We bought the back half of an old Dodge dealership on Ryan Street [about three miles from Bennett's Machine Shop]. A Firestone tire store was in the front. Cheryl often reminds me how stupid it was to think I could run the business long-distance."

Pat opened the new shop as Lake Charles Motor Exchange, Inc. He assigned four of his people there. He said, "For fourteen months, I pumped money into the new operation." Pat closed the Ryan Street location and sold the facility—he said at a $25,000 profit—in March 1986. "I never realized how personalized the business was," said Pat. He added, "By the way, we proved it again this summer, while I was fooling with Boeing. Things really got out of hand."

OPERATIONS

In late 1987, Bennett's Machine Shop was involved in three types of work: engine rebuilding, "over-the-fender" work, and tool sharpening and modification (the Boeing contract). Exhibit 1 shows the layout of Bennett's facilities.

Engine Rebuilding

Rebuilding engines is highly technical work. "The heart of it," said Pat, "is don't let the customer talk you into skipping the machine work. You've got to start with an empty, bare block." An actual case will illustrate the steps involved. Exhibit 2 provides an exploded view of a typical engine.

On August 9, 1987, Thomas Winkles, maintenance manager for a local dry cleaning firm and a personal friend of Pat's, ordered a "1974 250 Chevy short block." (A "short block" is a basic engine core, without the cylinder head, oil pan, oil pump, and several other parts which can be reused. These accounted for about 20 percent of the engines Bennett sold.) Pat felt Winkles was qualified to install the engine. "Otherwise," Pat said, "I would have questioned the customer to make sure the job could be done right. Replacing an engine is major surgery. It must not be done by amateurs."

Pat recorded the order on the yellow legal pad mentioned earlier and checked the *Four-Star Engine Catalog* (published by a national engine rebuilder) for casting numbers of 250 cubic-inch 1974 Chevrolet engines. He found there were two. Notes Pat had made in the catalog revealed that one used a straight and the other an offset starter motor. After having Winkles look to see which he had, Pat wrote the distinguishing feature, "straight starter," above the record on the legal pad.

Pat told the "tear-down man," Lac Xuan Huyn, he had added an order to the list. That day, Lac checked the order record and located the appropriate used engine among the several thousand piled here and there around the shop. (To augment the supply of exchange engines from previous jobs, Bennett bought some from a travelling used-engine dealer and from individuals who called or came by from time to time.) Lac disassembled the engine, distributing parts to the crankshaft grinding area (crankshaft, pistons, and connecting rods) and the headwork area (cylinder heads). Lac placed the block near the two cleaning machines—which work like large dishwashers but use caustic soda (lye) instead of

EXHIBIT 1   **Layout of Bennett's facilities**

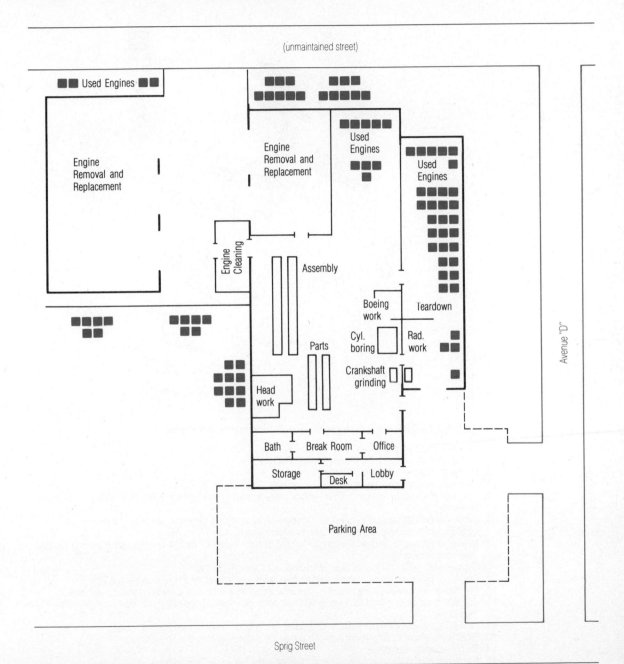

EXHIBIT 2   **Exploded view of General Motors V-6 engine**

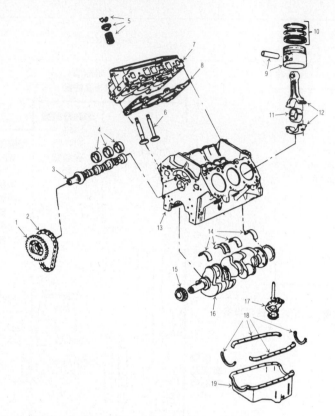

Nomenclature for Exhibit 2:   Exploded View of General Motors V-6 Engine

1. Camshaft gear (drives camshaft).
2. Timing chain (connects camshaft gear to crankshaft gear).
3. Camshaft (operates linkage to intake and exhaust valves).
4. Camshaft bearings (steel sleeves with soft metal inner surfaces).
5. Valve spring assembly (two per cylinder—holds intake or exhaust valve closed except when linkage to camshaft opens it).
6. Intake and exhaust valves (two valves per cylinder—open and close to control flow of air-gas mixture into cylinders and burned gases out of cylinders to exhaust system).
7. Cylinder head (two required on this engine—bolted to block to seal off tops of cylinders above pistons; contains intake and exhaust valves).
8. Cylinder head gasket (seals joint between cylinder head and cylinder block).
9. Piston and piston pin (six of each required on this engine—pin connects piston to connecting rod).
10. Piston rings (springy metal rings maintain seal between piston and cylinder as piston moves up and down).
11. Connecting rod bearing (split steel sleeve with soft metal inner surface, separated from crankshaft journal by thin layer of oil).
12. Connecting rod and cap (cap bolted to connecting rod, holding connecting rod bearing tightly).
13. Block (main engine casting—cylinders and certain flat surfaces machined to smoothness).
14. Main crankshaft bearings.
15. Crankshaft gear (pulls timing chain so that camshaft turns half as fast as crankshaft).
16. Crankshaft (heavy steel shaft with four main bearing journals concentric with shaft axis and six connecting rod bearing journals off center—the shaft is drilled to allow oil to flow from holes in the block to the main bearings and from there to the connecting rod bearings).

17. Oil pump (gear-type pump which takes a suction from the oil pan and discharges to holes drilled through the block to all points requiring oil under pressure).
18. Oil pan gaskets (cork and rubber pieces which maintain seal between oil pan and bottom of cylinder block).
19. Oil pan (sheet metal pan which collects motor oil returning from the various lubricated points).

regular detergent. He put the camshaft in a wood box. The contents of the box were shipped periodically to Cam-Recon, a shop in Houston, Texas, for regrinding. Bolts and valve pushrods were placed in appropriate bins. The oil pan and timing cover were set aside for reuse on this or another engine. And certain parts, mostly sheetmetal items such as rocker-arm covers, were discarded.

Bennett's machinists were responsible for checking the legal pad record of orders and making sure parts were available for jobs listed there. There were no written procedures, about this or anything else, and the machinists often failed to verify parts availability. Still, the system worked about as intended for the Winkles engine. Dale LeBlanc, who operated the cylinder boring machines, checked to see that the correct pistons and rings were on hand. He found that the ring set was not in stock. Curtis Manuel, who ground crankshafts and sized connecting rods, located a crankshaft for the engine—as usual, not the one Lac had just delivered. Curtis checked the crankshaft with a micrometer to see how far he would have to grind it and then confirmed that he had all main and connecting rod bearings, in the correct undersizes. Byron Woods, the assembler, checked the parts bins for the following items: gasket set, oil pump, matched camshaft and crankshaft gears, camshaft, camshaft bearings, and valve lifters. No gasket set was in stock. Dale and Byron, separately, called a Bennett's supplier in Houston and ordered needed parts, confirming that parts would arrive by bus or UPS the next day.

Dale washed the engine block in one of the cleaning machines. Then, he took the block to the cylinder boring area and "magnafluxed" it. This involves sprinkling iron filings over unmachined surfaces and placing a large electromagnet at strategic points. Any crack would have been indicated by a string of concentrated iron filings. None existed. Dale selected a box of six 0.030″ oversize 250 Chevrolet pistons. After measuring one of the pistons with a micrometer, he proceeded to bore the cylinders, to 0.001″ larger than the piston size, manually checking cylinder diameters with a hand-held "bore gauge" after each cut. He visually inspected each cylinder for cracks. Then, the block was placed in a "honing tank," where, in a bath of number 2 jet fuel, the cylinders were honed to 0.002″–0.003″ beyond the piston size. Dale cleaned the engine again, this time finishing with a steam cleaner. Finally, he sprayed the cylinder walls with light oil and delivered the block to the assembly area.

Still on August 9, Curtis Manuel cleaned the crankshaft he had checked for Winkles' engine. He then positioned it on the crankshaft grinder set up to grind main bearing journals (the shiny surfaces which turn in the main bearings). During grinding, Curtis carefully observed the "Arnold gauge," which he had positioned to indicate the undersize dimension, in ten-thousandths of an inch. After grinding the main journals to 0.010″ undersize, Curtis moved the shaft to the other grinding machine in an adjacent room, and left it set up to do connecting rod journals (Pat said the two machines were located across a wall from each other "to keep from having to rig another electric box"). There, he machined the connecting rod journals to 0.020″ undersize. The whole operation took about one hour. Curtis then cleaned and oiled the crankshaft, as Dale had done for the block, and placed the shaft in a plastic tube. It, too, was taken to the assembly area.

Not through yet, Curtis searched the waist-high pile of connecting rods and pistons at his work station for six Chevrolet 250 connecting rods. Unsure of his selection, he called Byron, the assembler, to help verify he had the right ones. Byron confirmed Curtis' choice. Curtis then pressed out each piston pin (the short shaft which joins the piston to the connecting rod). Then, he placed each rod in a rod vise, and, using a torque wrench (a wrench which indicates the amount of twisting force being applied), tightened the nuts which secure the rod cap. Next, Curtis measured the inside dimension at the crankshaft end of each rod. Finding all measurements to be within specifications (plus or minus 0.0005″), he cleaned the rods. He got the box of pistons Dale had used in sizing the cylinders and installed them on the rods. The pistons with rods attached were taken to the assembly area.

If Winkles had ordered a complete engine, instead of just a short block, Scott McConathy or Martin Simmons, the machinists who recondition cylinder heads, would have been involved. Reconditioning a cylinder head mainly consists of resizing the valve guides, grinding valves and valve seats, and regrinding the cylinder head surface. After these operations, the cylinder head is cleaned, reassembled, and painted.

At about 3:00 p.m., Byron finished his previous job and began assembling the Winkles engine. He visually checked each cylinder for cracks. Then, he painted the surfaces of the block which would be exposed to oil with "Cast Blast," a grey paint which seals cast iron surfaces and minimizes sludge buildup. Byron also painted the exterior surfaces of the block the appropriate original color. Next, he installed the plugs in the block which seal holes required for certain casting and machining operations. After that, he manually installed the piston rings on the pistons. Byron then installed the major parts in the block — bearings, camshaft, crankshaft, and pistons — tightening all bolts to specified tightness and checking each part for free movement. Finally, he performed a careful inspection of the entire engine, recording the results on a specially designed form — kiddingly referred to as "the birth certificate."

The finished short block was placed in a bag and banded to a small pallet. The next day, Thomas Winkles picked up his new engine. A few days later, he dropped his old one by Bennett's.

Over-the-Fender Work

Over-the-fender work at Bennett's mainly involved removing and replacing engines. Of course, this often required replacing water hoses, vee belts, and other items which were worn or damaged at the time of the engine job. The engine warranty (12,000 miles or six months) was conditioned upon an exhaust gas analysis, which often revealed the need for carburetor work. Radiator disassembly and cleaning were also required as a condition of warranty, even for carry-out engines. In addition to work related to engine replacement, Bennett's accepted general automobile repair work, such as carburetor rebuilding and air-conditioning component replacement.

Unlike the machinists discussed above, the mechanics furnished their own hand tools. Bennett's provided testing equipment, hoists, a pressurized air system, floor jacks and stands, hydraulic lifts, and cleaning equipment. Each mechanic had a separate work stall.

"We had a terrible, terrible parts situation," said Pat. "The situation was so out of control, I was actually looking at parts purchases as overhead and not as a profit producer. Items were either not getting on the tickets, or not getting on the cars." To solve this, Pat assigned one mechanic, his best, as checker, to make sure every part put on each car was on the respective invoice. He also closed all charge accounts with parts suppliers, requiring mechanics to come to Pat or his shop coordinator, Jack Beard, to get a check for any parts purchase. "Now we've got some control over it," said Pat.

Bennett's kept an inventory of common engine filters, ignition components, vacuum hoses and fittings, and nuts and bolts. Mechanics were required to order and pick up other required parts. Pat said, "We don't stock any radiator hoses, belts, or water pumps because there are just too many different ones."

Richard Hardesty, one of the mechanics Pat had laid off in July, leased one of the company's three buildings and the equipment in it to do general automotive repair, engine installations, and exhaust system repairs. Pat explained, "Our whole objective was to get the payroll down. Payroll taxes are a burden. And the $675 lease payment will come in handy. I was able to rent the building to Richard so cheaply because we don't owe anything on it."

Tool Sharpening and Modification

Boeing's operations in Lake Charles involved a great deal of drilling and reaming, especially of rivet holes in the skins of the KC-135s. Many screwed fasteners required countersunk holes to preserve a flush exterior surface. The thousands of drill bits, reamers, and countersinks used by Boeing required frequent modifications and/or sharpening. There were also numerous occasions when specialized tools such as reamer extensions had to be made, modified, or repaired. When Boeing had trouble locating a local supplier for these services, Pat Bennett volunteered to do the work and negotiated a single-source supply contract with Boeing procurement.

Gearing up to do this highly technical work consumed most of Pat's energy and time from February to August 1987. A 1,000-square-foot area of the machine shop building was enclosed and modified to house the tool work. A large horizontal lathe, a cylindrical grinder, two form relief grinders, two tool and cutter grinders, and a drill bit sharpening machine were purchased and installed in the temperature-controlled enclosure. To find these machines, Pat traveled to Wichita, Cincinnati, Dallas, and Houston.

Boeing was on an extremely tight schedule on its own contract with the Air Force and there were frequent emergencies, often involving innovative solutions to unique problems. For example, Pat stayed up all one night sharpening and resharpening a special cobalt drill bit then being used to drill through a titanium alloy engine mount. Much experimentation was required on this and other jobs, and Pat worked many nights and weekends to solve problems.

Generally, Pat Bennett picked up the tools to be modified at the Boeing plant, a few hundred yards from the machine shop, and returned them there. Because of a Boeing procedure, the tools only needing sharpening were picked up at a Boeing warehouse at the Lake Charles Port, four miles away. Each batch of tools to be serviced was accompanied by a work order providing instructions for the work to be done. For nonstandard modifications, Pat frequently had to call or visit the supervisor who wrote the order and get clarification of the instructions.

Five machinists, three on days and two on evenings, were hired to do the Boeing work. Two only sharpened drill bits, while the others did the work on countersinks, reamers, and special tools. James Smith, the machinist Pat charged with quality control for the Boeing contract, did most of the particularly innovative operations. For example, James designed and made a number of torque wrench extensions which allowed tightening nuts which were not directly accessible.

Pat personally trained the machinists to do the repetitive operations. "The most difficult operation to perfect," said Pat, "was grinding the flutes of a piloted reamer so that they would cut. We were finally able to do it on a German form-relief grinder. Everything on it was written in German. We couldn't read any of the buttons except the one which said 'halt.'" The machine came to be used solely for grinding the cutting edges on piloted reamers. A large magnifying glass was installed so the machinist could see the tiny flutes. With his left hand, the machinist would orientate one of the six flutes on a reamer. Then, with his right hand he would move the grinding head into the reamer flute and back, grinding the tiny cutting edge at precisely ten degrees. This was repeated on each of the six flutes. Because of the exactness required, the grinding wheel had to be reshaped daily with a diamond "dresser."

Drill bit sharpening is a fairly standard operation, although the Boeing specification added some complexity. Bennett's drill bit sharpening machine was hardly state of the art—requiring several manual manipulations of each bit sharpened. Still, sharpening each bit took only about 45 seconds.

The two-way form relief grinder used to sharpen countersinks was almost completely automatic. Once the machinist orientated a countersink to be ground, the machine did the rest. This took about four minutes per countersink.

A great deal of skill was required to set up each of the operations described above and especially to do the custom tool making. But, according to Pat, a person of average dexterity could learn any of the repetitive jobs in a day or two.

PERSONNEL

In late 1987, Bennett's employed sixteen people in addition to Pat and Jack Beard, the Shop Coordinator. There were five machinists and a radiator repairman in the automotive machine shop, five mechanics in the service department, and five machinists in the tool grinding shop.

Jack Beard had been with Bennett's four years. He was about 29 years old. A hard worker, Jack often spent ten hours a day at the shop, including every Saturday — except during hunting season, when Jack and Byron, the assembler, alternated Saturdays. On a weekend in August, Jack rebuilt the engine in a Chevrolet Citation he had just bought. The following Monday, he told Pat, "I can see how they have such a hard time getting any motors built. There is only one air hose, tools are scattered everywhere, and the place is filthy dirty."

Pat observed that Jack was right. He had tried several ways to get the workers to keep the shop clean, at one point assigning each person "just one little area" to clean. "Nothing worked," said Pat, "so that morning I just pulled the main breaker. When everything shut down and the men came to see why, I told them I would restore the power when the shop was clean." Pat said two of the "main culprits" came in to punch in on the time clock — they were on piece rates — so they would be paid for doing the cleaning. Pat objected to paying them "for cleaning up a mess they had a big part in creating," and they both quit. Asked how he replaced the men, Pat replied, "They weren't worth replacing."

The automotive machinists, Lac, Dale, Curtis, Scott, Martin, and Byron, were mentioned earlier. None had been automotive machinists when Bennett hired them, although Curtis had taken a regular machinist course at a local trade school. Lance Hammack, the radiator repairman, also learned his trade at Bennett's. He had been a welder. "It is much easier to teach a person a new trade than to get a person who already knows a trade to change bad work habits," said Pat.

Lac, a Vietnamese, was hired in 1985. Pat said, "He had to bring an interpreter to apply for the job, he could speak so little English. But his attitude — he just seemed so eager. He learned very rapidly. Meticulous. Pays attention to detail. Terribly dependable. I don't know that he ever missed a day — never even asks for time off."

Dale, Curtis, Martin, and Lance had all been with Bennett's less than six months. Dale was a construction worker before Pat hired him. "Couldn't even read a micrometer," said Pat. "He had some kind of hangup about reading the dial. I got him a micrometer with a digital readout and three days later he was operating the cylinder boring machine." Curtis knew how to run a lathe when he was hired. "So we put him on our crankshaft grinder," said Pat. (The two machines have similarities but are far from identical.) Martin had been a paint and body technician before Pat hired him. "He turns out the prettiest paint jobs on cylinder heads you ever saw," Pat kidded. Martin worked most Saturdays, in addition to full days during the week. Radiator work was not a full-time job at Bennett's, so Lance helped out in the office, drove the delivery truck, and did other tasks.

Scott and Byron had been hired about four years earlier, Scott right out of high school, Byron off the unemployment line. According to Pat, Scott had a strong interest in cars. "He was easy to train, always thinking," said Pat. "I could just give him a few pointers and he would go with it. He is very thorough. I don't have to check anything he tells me. He doesn't mind staying late during the week, but he likes his Saturdays off." Pat said that Scott did almost all the "really difficult head jobs—the overhead cams, heads that need new valve seats." Byron, young and unskilled, had started doing engine "teardowns." "Most machinists are too proud to do that," said Pat. "They think that is the low-class job in the shop. Byron was so easy-going. There was nothing he wouldn't try to learn, if you needed him to do it."

Next Byron had mastered the cylinder-boring machine. Pat told how Byron got his next job: "I was grinding the crankshafts at that time. You should have seen me—an Extendaphone on my belt and a Sony Walkman under my shirt. People thought the Walkman was part of the machine. But I was grooving, listening to 'fifties' music while I watched the cranks go round and round." Pat's wife, Cheryl, was "acting secretary" (the regular secretary had left due to illness) at the time. She quit after Pat threw a can of blue engine paint at her, so he had to take over the office. Another man, later fired for suspected theft, took over the boring machine, and Byron moved to the crankshaft grinder, relieving Pat. "That was a major accomplishment for Byron," Pat said. "He had never even run a lathe." Byron stayed with that job until March 1987, when he started assembling engines.

The five mechanics were Ronnie Smith, Tim "Tamale" Authemont, Kenneth Thornton, Clyde Brown, and Kevin "Goat" Gauthreaux. Ronnie, in his fourth year at Bennett's, was responsible for inspecting and test driving every vehicle repaired, regardless of who did the work. He also did mechanic work himself—all the carburetor work, certain diesel-to-gasoline conversions, and most of the computer checks. But Ronnie refused to do engine replacements in front-wheel-drive cars. Tim was a helper, supervised and paid by Ronnie. Tim had been with Bennett's over two years, but had worked as Ronnie's helper only about six months.

Kenneth Thornton was the longest-tenured employee Pat had, having hired on eight years earlier, when the shop was on Prien Lake Road. He did most of the engine replacements on front-wheel-drive cars, certain diesel-to-gasoline conversions, and regular repair work.

Clyde and Kevin had only worked at Bennett's a couple of months. Both did all kinds of engine replacements as well as a wide range of other mechanic work. Both were in their early thirties, married, with children. Pat said, "I am really impressed with their attitudes. Unlike many mechanics, they are not afraid of this new generation of cars—mostly transverse engined, fuel injected, and computer controlled."

The machinists who did the tool work were James Smith (Ronnie's brother), James McManus, Craig McMichael, John Shearer, and Billy Lambert. James Smith had worked on and off for Bennett's for about five years, doing various construction jobs. He had hired on full-time in March 1987. Pat said, "In the early weeks of the Boeing job, I was running that German form-relief grinder while James was building the room around me." As the Boeing work had begun to increase, Pat had taught James to run the grinder. Pat said, "I would run it on the weekends, he'd do it during the week." James had paid his own way to go with Pat and locate other machines to buy.

James McManus and Billy worked evenings. Craig and John worked days. James and Craig did reamers and countersinks. Billy and John sharpened drill bits. All four were in their early twenties. Pat recruited James and Craig through Sowela Tech, a local vo-tech school, and James continued as a co-op student there. John's father, who worked at the Boeing port warehouse, had recommended his unemployed son to Pat one day as Pat picked up an order. John had later recommended Billy.

The automotive machinists, except for Curtis (who operated the crankshaft grinder), were paid on a piece-rate basis, so much for each type of operation and each model of engine. Each had an established hourly rate as well, which was applied to other than normally assigned work. Curtis was paid on an hourly basis.

The mechanics were paid a combination of piece-rates, commissions, and hourly rates. Piece-rates applied to engine replacements. Most other automotive work was done on a commission basis — each mechanic got one-half of all labor charges that mechanic generated. Hourly rates were paid for warranty work which was not the mechanic's fault. Pat said, "We don't do like the dealerships and guarantee the mechanics a weekly minimum."

The machinists who did the tool grinding were all paid by the hour. At first, Pat set the machinists' wages according to the Boeing pay scale. But when Boeing tried to hire some of his people, he hiked the rate by about 40 percent. "I pay James Smith more than the rest," said Pat, "but he and I have an agreement that he doesn't get any overtime pay when he works over forty hours."

Jack Beard, the Shop Coordinator, and Lance Hammack, the radiator repairman, were also paid by the hour.

Bennett's provided limited fringe benefits. There was a group health plan, paid entirely by the employees. Several chose not to participate. Each employee received six paid holidays each year (after a 90-day waiting period) and a one-week paid vacation each year after the first. Bennett's paid all over one dollar a day of uniform costs per employee, although workers were not required to wear them. "I also let the men work on their personal and family cars in the shop after hours and on weekends," said Pat.

MARKETING

Exhibit 3 provides demographic and economic data for Bennett's market area.

Sprig Street, where Bennett's was located, was "off the beaten path and far from the business district," according to Pat. He said, "The best thing about the

EXHIBIT 3 Geographic and demographic data

	Lake Charles	Calcasieu Parish (County)	Southwest Louisiana*	State of Louisiana	United States
Population, 7/80	77,400	167,223	259,809	4,206,000	226,546,000
Per capita income, 1985	$10,183	$10,224	$8,806	$10,741	$12,772
Change in *real* per capita income, 1980–85 (percent change for period)	1.2	1.3	1.6	2.3	2.8
Work force employed in manufacturing, 3/87 (percent)	7.4	17.3	16.2	11.2	18.8
Work force employed in construction, 3/87 (percent)	8.7	9.4	9.0	6.2	3.0
Land area (square miles)	27	1,082	5,083	44,521	3,539,289

*Southwest Louisiana Parishes — Allen, Beauregard, Calcasieu, Cameron, and Jefferson Davis.

location is it's one block outside the city limits. No one bothers us out here, no matter how messy it gets." It was messy. Except for concreted areas, grass and weeds were everywhere. Piles of greasy used engines were here and there— even next to the street behind the facility. Inside the machine shop building, half the space was occupied by stacks—no, piles—of engines and useless remnants of others long deceased. Individual blocks, heads, and other parts, as well as several derelict cars, littered the property, especially around the edges of driveways and other concreted areas. Everywhere there was grease and oil. Two large pitch-coated septic tanks and a stack of rusting metal shelves added confusion. A dingy, although lighted, 3′ × 4′ sign near the lobby and office area announced "Bennett's Machine Shop—Engine Rebuilding."

Thirty-second television spots featuring Pat Bennett ran throughout the year at a cost of about $350 per month. A feature article written by Pat appeared in the *American Press,* the local paper, once a month, at a cost of $114 per month. Once a year, when business was slow, a Bennett's supplement would be distributed with the 48,000-circulation newspaper. The cost was $1,600 for each distribution. The supplement offered discounts, good for two months with presentation of the flyer, on reconditioned engines — $50 on carryouts, $100 on installations. "The first time we did this, two years ago," said Pat, "we had to shut down and just answer the phones and take orders for two days. We sold 28 engines, almost a whole page, that time."

A form letter was sent to engine customers, thanking them for the business and asking for referrals to other prospective customers. Once a year, during the local festival called "Contraband Days," Bennett's subscribed to a radio advertising special. A thirty-second spot was run sixty times during a ten-day period at a cost of $450. Pat said, "I've never seen a sale directly related to radio advertising. We did it one time, and they hounded us the next year till I agreed to do it."

Bennett's major competitors for engine sales were Dimick Supply Company, 100,000 Auto Parts, and Hi-Lo Auto Parts. None of these did installations and all bought their engines from large remanufacturers. No local automobile service shop other than Bennett's specialized in rebuilt engines, although most bought and installed them from time to time. Periodically, Pat Bennett checked the prices competitors charged for engines, often by simply calling and asking. He also kept current catalogs and price sheets for the engine remanufacturers who supplied Bennett's competitors. "We get their catalogs because we're a jobber," Pat said, "and sometimes we sell truck engines we buy from others — because the risk is so high if a truck engine fails."

Asked where he set his prices relative to the competition, Pat replied, "We make sure we're a little under everybody except Hi-Lo. They sell almost nothing but short blocks remanufactured in Texas. They are ridiculously low."

Pat said the quality of all the engines was about the same. "But if you have a problem with a Four-Star or a Roadrunner (the brands sold by Bennett's competitors) you bought from, say, Dimick," Pat said, "you have to take it out and wait for them to send it back to Texas. And they normally don't help you with labor." In contrast, he said, a Bennett's customer who has problems "can just bring the car to my front gate, and it's taken care of — if it's within warranty and hasn't been overheated or run out of oil." Pat complained, "Carryout customers will go to somebody else if there is just a $20 difference. It bothers me that customers will bring us their car if anything goes wrong, expecting us to fix it free. They wouldn't think of doing this at Hi-Lo or Dimick." He explained that parts-and-labor warranties, in general, only apply to situations where the labor is supplied by the vendor. "Sometimes," said Pat, "a customer will even call me for advice about some trouble with an engine he bought from a parts house. I tell him to call the parts house."

Mechanic labor at Bennett's was based on the time estimates in the *Chilton Flat-Rate Manual* (a book which gives estimated times to do all kinds of repair operations for most automobiles and light trucks), priced at $30 per hour. Most good mechanics can beat the flat-rate times significantly, more so on some types of work than on others. Bennett's priced most parts, other than engines, at locally competitive retail. The local parts houses gave Bennett's a 20 percent discount off retail. "List" prices, usually about 40 percent above retail, are shown on parts house invoices. Pat said, "If we think the list price is fair and the customer is unlikely to check with a parts house, we often use list instead of retail."

For the Boeing work, prices were set according to contract. Drill bit sharpening was at so much per item. The other operations were done by the hour. At first, Boeing allowed Bennett's to charge very profitable prices. After the work had totalled about $137,000, Boeing audited Bennett's costs and revised the prices downward, by more than 50 percent. The audit was conducted by Boeing's Vendor Cost Analysis (VCA) group and involved many lengthy meetings with four different teams of auditors. In fact, Bennett's initial contract was apparently so remunerative that Boeing assigned a "security investigator" who asked many questions implying possible collusion between Pat and various Boeing officials.

Boeing held up payment on past invoices while pressure was exerted on Bennett's to re-price previously submitted invoices at the VCA-determined rates. Pat refused to do that and successfully insisted that the invoices be paid as submitted. Pat did decide to accept the VCA prices during month-to-month renewals of the contract, while Boeing made plans to let the work out for bids. Meanwhile, Pat was trying to decide how to bid the work. He was making money at the new rates. Profits on the earlier contract had more than paid for all his machines. So he was tempted to bid even a little below the VCA numbers. But he knew Boeing was having trouble finding other vendors with even minimal competence to do the work. And he had served Boeing faithfully, and at great cost to his other business, for several difficult months.

FINANCE

Exhibits 4 and 5 give financial summaries for Bennett's Machine Shop, Inc. For ten years, Pat Bennett had employed a local accounting firm, Management Services, Inc., to keep financial records, prepare financial statements and sales and income tax returns, submit business license applications, and so forth. During the 1987 tax season, Bennett's was not able to get Management Services to prepare the usual monthly profit and loss statements. Pat explained, "They said they couldn't get to it. So I changed to a real CPA firm in the Lakeside Plaza Building — and that was worse. This guy had less time than Management Services did for us. When he finally, after sixty days, got the first month done, he asked me to come in at nine o'clock one day. I got there at 9:15, and nobody except the secretary was at work. I passed him on the sidewalk with his briefcase and his three-piece suit. That's the last time I saw him."

After firing his new accountant, Pat talked with Dorothy McConathy, who had been assigned his work at Management Services, and asked whom he could get to do his bookkeeping. Pat said, "Dorothy had already told her boss she was going to quit when she got one more account on the side. She already had two, so she agreed to keep my books and gave Management Services notice."

EXHIBIT 4   **Bennett's Machine Shop, Inc., income statements**

	Fiscal year 1985*	Fiscal year 1986*	Fiscal year 1987*	4 mos. 1988**
REVENUE				
Automotive	926,243	1,091,890	971,950	140,131
Aircraft Tool	0	0	13,318	140,679
Total revenue	926,243	1,091,890	985,268	280,810
EXPENSES				
Direct costs				
Materials	456,828	570,372	504,811	64,939
Labor	248,833	316,164	271,858	53,693
Freight	0	0	0	1,031
Total direct costs	705,661	886,536	776,669	119,663
Gross profit	220,582	205,354	208,599	161,147
G & A expenses				
Advertising	10,697	15,831	17,828	1,193
Depreciation	33,550	42,240	29,220	7,359
Equipment leasing	5,680	950	1,657	0
Insurance	23,100	39,298	35,528	11,359
Interest	22,060	24,044	26,504	8,841
Miscellaneous	4,867	7,205	7,020	4,438
Office labor	6,815	11,420	13,300	3,961
Office supplies	5,883	7,015	6,458	2,129
Professional fees	3,696	8,373	6,622	1,175
Taxes	5,623	4,852	5,926	245
Utilities and telephone	15,871	30,767	27,933	8,830
Total G & A expenses	137,842	191,995	177,996	49,530
Net income	82,740	13,359	30,603	111,617
Withdrawals***	(61,500)	(53,389)	(70,755)	(17,109)
Earnings reinvested	21,240	(40,030)	(40,152)	94,508

*Fiscal years end April 30 of years shown.
**May–August 1987.
***Includes funds to pay income taxes. The corporation is taxed as a partnership/proprietorship under Subchapter S of the Internal Revenue Code.

After buying the boring bar when he first started rebuilding engines in 1972, Pat never directly contributed any more equity funds to the business. Equipment vendors furnished financing for most of the machines Pat bought. When Pat started to buy a used crankshaft grinder, which he found at a shop in Plaquemine Parish, he approached the bank that handled his checking account.

EXHIBIT 5   **Bennett's Machine Shop, Inc., balance sheets, April 30**

	1985	1986	1987	1988*
ASSETS				
Current assets				
Cash	11,698	1,206	3,475	5,385
A/R, trade	0	1,255	16,662	65,436
N/R, stkhdr.	0	22,568	22,568	22,569
Inventory	37,548	45,436	45,436	45,436
Total c/a	49,246	70,465	88,141	138,826
Fixed assets				
Furniture & equip.	205,292	165,886	193,432	212,209
Buildings	305,657	155,657	155,657	155,657
Total depr.	510,949	321,543	349,089	367,866
Less accu. depr.	(133,559)	(134,067)	(143,834)	(155,081)
Net depr. assets	377,390	187,476	205,255	212,785
Land	126,418	90,000	90,000	90,000
Total fixed assets	503,808	277,476	295,255	302,785
Other assets				
Deposits	492	342	342	342
Total assets	553,546	348,283	383,738	441,953
LIABILITIES AND CAPITAL				
Current liabilities				
A/P, trade & other	12,727	25,062	29,407	31,242
N/P, current	103,160	16,385	60,299	57,775
Accrued payroll,				
taxes, interest	0	0	3,223	1,571
Total c/1	115,887	41,447	92,929	90,588
Long-term liabilities				
Notes payable	266,720	175,897	200,052	166,099
Stockholders' equity				
Common stock	10,000	10,000	10,000	10,000
Retained earnings	160,939	120,909	80,757	175,265
Total capital	170,939	130,909	90,757	185,265
Total liabilities				
and capital	553,546	348,253	383,738	441,952

*August 31, 1987.

Pat had taken out a few small personal loans at the bank, but the loan officer who had approved them was gone at the time. The bank president refused to loan Pat the $6,400 he needed to buy the machine.

"I got my little file from him and went over to the new American Bank of Commerce," said Pat. "There, I was a total stranger, but I got the loan." Three years later, Pat needed the $80,000 loan to buy the Chennault property. "American Bank of Commerce wouldn't make a decision," said Pat, "so, I went back to Gulf National. My friend Lloyd Rion, the loan officer who was gone that day three years earlier, was there. He gave me the money, and I moved our checking account back." The loan was a ten-year, fixed-rate loan at 10 percent interest.

From 1980 to 1985, Pat took out several 90-day loans to make additions to the shop facilities. The bank allowed him to roll the loans over once. "Those were super productive years. We never had any money problems," said Pat.

When Pat bought the Ryan Street shop in 1985, which he sold 14 months later, the seller financed the whole $180,000, for ten years at 10–14 percent variable rate. "That's when our trouble started," said Pat. "We loaded up the company with operating loans — a $25,000 three-year loan, a $24,000 five-year loan, and another three-year loan for $12,000, all from Calcasieu Marine Bank. I also let the work force run up to 22 people. It was a real runaway situation."

Pat described 1986 as "one helluva bad year." "That's when we could have used some input from the bookkeeper," said Pat. "I didn't realize that payroll and the taxes related to it were having such a devastating effect. We had almost the same sales as in 1984. Just the *increase* in payroll-based taxes was $70,000. What really ticked me off was that I had to figure this out and show him (the bookkeeper)." Pat had to refinance the ten-year loan on the Chennault property. "I put off laying off the extra people from January to August," said Pat. "That cost me another $40,000 and made me have to redo the loan." Bennett's showed a $12,000 profit in November that year. Pat said, "It was our first three-page month in a long time. I was scared to death. If we had not made a profit with that kind of sales, I didn't know what else to do." On the way to a New Year's Eve party, Pat made himself a promise: "I will not go through another year like that." A friend asked, "What are you going to do to prevent that — as if you have some control over it?" "I'm going to work my tail off," Pat replied.

The machinery to do the Boeing work was all financed with $37,000 in 90-day notes at Calcasieu Marine. There were no other financial crises until August, when Boeing was holding up payment and engine sales collapsed. Pat was able to sell enough assets to meet the payroll and pay operating expenses, but he was unable to pay maturing loans. So Pat mortgaged his condominium and consolidated the three term loans into one $45,000, five-year mortgage. Boeing paid its account up to date in early September, and Pat paid off the $37,000 in 90-day notes.

Until 1987, all the loans mentioned above were in Pat's and Cheryl's personal names, although entered on the company books and sometimes secured by company assets. The $45,000 mortgage loan from Calcasieu Marine was put in the company name, "So we could deduct the interest under the new tax law," according to Pat. But Pat and Cheryl had to personally endorse the note and sign continuing guaranty agreements with the bank.

Appendix

Excerpts from interview with Pat Bennett

Q: What is your main objective for this year?

A: I guess the goal we're all in business for is to make it profitable, and it hasn't been for the past two years. We've had a real bad downward trend. We might not make a real big profit this year, but I hope we can stop the downward trend and turn it around. That would be a major accomplishment.

Q: What about the longer term?

A: I would like the business to be successful to the point that I would have some freedom to do some of the things I want to do. Travel some, sports in the winter — before I get decrepit. Until recently, I dreamed of having a nicer shop near the downtown area, but that seems out the window now.

Q: Can you be a little more specific about what the business would have to do to satisfy you?

A: If we got back to where net profit, including my total compensation, was $70,000–$100,000 a year — and we've been there — I would think that was okay.

Q: Do you mean in ten years? Twenty years?

A: I'm not really that patient a person. I mean in the next two to three years. That is very obtainable.

Q: Do you think about twenty-five years from now, when you will be almost sixty-five?

A: No.

Q: Do you feel responsible to make the business support anyone else but you and Cheryl, in the long or short term?

A: Sure, I probably have more loyalty to some of those guys than I should.

Q: Which ones? Or do you mean all of the workers?

A: I mean as a whole. My dad was a union man his entire life. We grew up with the idea that the company had to provide benefits — medical care, retirement, vacations, days off. Retirement is a big thing Dad always talked about. He always talked about the days before Roosevelt, when there wasn't any Social Security, not much to look forward to.

Q: Do the workers look out for your interests?

A: Sometimes I think they do. But on days like today I wonder.

Q: What happened today?

A: Everybody screwed up. Jack has trouble ordering anybody to do anything. Someday he's got to learn he isn't "one of the gang" anymore. Dale loaded the wrong engine on a customer truck. Lance spent the whole day chasing his tail, pretending to go get parts. One of my good customers asked for his car at 1:00 — and it wasn't out until 4:00. Know what I'm going to do? I'm moving my desk right out to the middle of the shop, right by the boring bars. They'll be nervous with me watching every move. But I'm going to get this mess under control. [Within three weeks, Pat had built a 6' × 8' office in the center of the shop near the assembly area. It had one-way windows so that Pat could observe the machinists but could not be seen by them.]

Q: What major changes in the business do you foresee?

A: More diversity. Wait! I mean more diversification. We've had all the diversity we can stand.

Q: What do you mean by diversification?

A: There still are several areas of the engine business that are untouched in Lake Charles. I just did a catalog so we'll be ready to do the parts house business. The closest production shops are in Baton Rouge and Houston, both over two hours away. We've got the whole west side of the state. And the crack repair business, cylinder head cracks mainly, is just untapped. I visited a big diesel shop in Houston that does this. The whole system, really nothing more than a big fire-bricked oven, would cost only a couple of thousand dollars. This is an especially good business with today's thin-wall castings on engines. There are tremendous numbers of heads thrown away. A plain old six-cylinder Chevrolet head is $400 new, bare. I also think we have a good opportunity in the aircraft industry — the tool work, a heat treating facility. And Boeing is about to certify us for "level II" work, allowing us to make parts which stay on the plane. No more gravy train — we'll have to bid everything. Level II will also let us bid on the work for the big Strategic Petroleum Reserve. They have to send their work 80 miles to New Iberia.

THE UNITED STATES AUTO INDUSTRY: OUTLOOK FOR THE 1990S

INTRODUCTION

In 1965 the United States auto industry was a secure domestic industry dominated by the oligopolistic trio of General Motors, Ford, and Chrysler. Foreign competition was negligible, with imports of passenger cars and trucks taking only 5.6 percent of total U.S. sales. The industry was enjoying a record year, with domestic producers selling 10.3 million new vehicles. The big three could look back on fifteen years of steady growth, when motor vehicle sales by domestic producers had increased by 170 percent. In short, the view from Detroit was a splendid one in 1965.

Ten years later the story was very different. Domestic producers sold only 9.3 million vehicles in 1975, down 26 percent from two years earlier, while imports accounted for 16.2 percent of the market. The fourfold increase in the price of oil introduced by OPEC after the Arab-Israeli conflict of 1973 had changed the rules of the game in the auto industry. The days of cheap gasoline were over. Consumers responded by purchasing smaller, more fuel-efficient cars in growing numbers. These cars, however, were not manufactured by Detroit but by Honda and Toyota of Japan and Volkswagen of West Germany. In truth Detroit had never given much thought to the compact and subcompact end of the market, believing such cars to be unsuited for American conditions. The events of 1973 proved this assumption to be dreadfully wrong.[1]

This case was prepared by Charles W. L. Hill, University of Washington.

[1]The figures are taken from Motor Vehicle Manufacturers Association of the United States, *Ward's Auto World,* and Standard & Poor's Auto Industry Survey.

The story of the U.S. auto industry since 1975 has been one of often painful adjustment in response to a growing realization that the U.S. market is no longer isolated from the rest of the world, but instead just one part of the global auto industry. Unlike the oligopolistic U.S. industry of the 1960s, the global industry of today is characterized by intense competition, slow growth, the emergence of excess capacity, and the frequent entry into the market of new producers from low-cost developing nations such as South Korea, Yugoslavia, and Brazil.[2] United States manufacturers have responded to the threat inherent in this new competitive environment by the vigorous, and often impressive, pursuit of cost-reducing and quality-improving strategies. While results have been mixed and mistakes have been made, there is little doubt that the U.S. manufacturers are in a better position to meet foreign competition than they were ten years ago. Nevertheless, serious questions as to the long-term health of the domestic manufacturers remain, given likely future market conditions. In particular, it is likely that the period between now and the year 2000 will be characterized by only moderate growth and excess capacity.

THE CHANGING INDUSTRY ENVIRONMENT

Demand Conditions

The 1950s and 1960s were the golden years for the U.S. auto industry. The U.S. market had not yet approached saturation and grew at a healthy rate for most of the two decades. Things began to change after the OPEC oil price increases of 1973. Since that period the industry has exhibited many of the characteristics of maturity. Growth has been modest, although the trend has been upward. Total U.S. registrations and trend demand figures for the 1975–1987 period are given in Exhibit 1.

The industry gives every indication of continuing to grow at a modest pace through the 1990s, primarily due to demographics. The baby boom generation of the 1950s will be found in the major car-buying thirty- to fifty-four age bracket during the 1990s, and this should stimulate demand. In addition, rising disposable incomes and a propensity to scrap cars more often should help to keep up demand.

However, despite a modest growth trend, pronounced cyclical fluctuations can be expected. Demand for passenger cars is particularly sensitive to macro-economic conditions and the impact of the business cycle upon personal disposable income. For example, in response to recessionary conditions, between 1978 and 1982 total sales of passenger cars in the U.S. slumped from 11.3 million to 8.0 million, a decline of over 22 percent. During the same period total U.S.

[2]See Standard & Poor's Industry Survey, *Autos-Auto Parts*, October 30, 1986, and "Overcapacity," *Ward's Auto World*, June 1987, 28–39.

EXHIBIT 1   **U.S. registrations and trend demand — cars and trucks (in millions)**

Year	U.S. cars	Imported cars	Trucks	Total sales	Trend demand*	Above or below trend
1987*	7.8	3.2	4.4	15.4	14.8	+0.6
1986*	8.4	3.1	4.7	16.2	14.6	+1.6
1985	8.2	2.8	4.7	15.7	14.4	+1.3
1984	8.0	2.4	4.0	14.4	14.2	+0.2
1983	6.8	2.4	3.0	12.2	14.0	−1.8
1982	5.8	2.2	2.4	10.4	13.7	−3.3
1981	6.2	2.2	2.2	10.6	13.5	−2.9
1980	6.6	2.3	2.5	11.4	13.2	−1.8
1979	8.3	2.3	3.5	14.1	13.0	+1.1
1978	9.3	2.0	4.0	15.3	12.7	+2.6
1977	9.1	2.1	3.5	14.7	12.5	+2.2
1976	8.6	1.5	3.1	13.2	12.3	+0.9
1975	7.1	1.6	2.4	11.1	12.0	−0.9

*Standard & Poor's estimates.

Source: Bureau of Public Roads. Standard & Poor's figures reprinted by permission from *Autos-Auto Parts*.

sales of cars and trucks combined slumped from 15.3 million to 10.4 million, a decline of 32 percent. The other side of this phenomenon is that demand can become pent up during recessionary periods. After the end of the recession, auto sales rebounded impressively in 1984–1986, hitting an all-time high of 16.2 million vehicles sold in 1986. Other factors of importance in determining demand include the availability, cost, and maturity of credit. On this point, record levels of consumer debt in 1985 and 1986 do not portend too well for future auto sales.

A breakdown of demand for passenger cars by segment is given in Exhibit 2 for the 1972–1985 period. The U. S. passenger car market is split into five main segments: subcompact, compact, intermediate, full-sized standard, and luxury. As can be seen, intermediate and compact cars are the most popular. The big loser in recent years has been the full-sized standard segment, with sales slumping from 35.4 percent of the U.S.-produced total in 1972, to 9.8 percent of the U.S. total in 1985. The biggest sales gains have been in the luxury segment, up from 3.8 percent of the total in 1972 to 7.4 percent in 1985. To some extent, the figures in Exhibit 2 are also a little misleading, since imports are not counted into the segments. If this was done, then the figures for subcompact, compact, and luxury sales would be still higher. Future sales growth is predicted to be strongest in the compact, intermediate, and luxury segments, primarily due to the purchasing preferences of the baby boom generation.

EXHIBIT 2   **U.S. passenger car sales by segment**

Year	Subcompact	Compact	Intermediate	Standard	Luxury	Imports
1985	10.6%	22.0%	22.5%	9.8%	7.4%	27.7%
1984	14.0%	18.1%	25.5%	10.6%	8.3%	23.5%
1983	12.7%	16.4%	26.5%	12.7%	5.7%	26.0%
1982	16.7%	17.5%	19.0%	13.4%	5.6%	27.8%
1981	17.1%	20.2%	20.4%	10.2%	4.9%	27.3%
1980	15.4%	21.0%	21.4%	11.1%	4.5%	26.7%
1979	12.9%	20.9%	23.8%	15.1%	5.5%	21.9%
1978	8.8%	22.9%	26.6%	18.4%	5.6%	17.7%
1977	8.5%	21.2%	26.4%	20.4%	5.0%	18.5%
1976	9.9%	24.1%	27.8%	18.8%	4.7%	14.8%
1975	12.3%	22.9%	23.9%	17.9%	4.7%	18.2%
1974	10.6%	22.7%	24.4%	22.7%	3.7%	15.8%
1973	10.7%	16.8%	23.4%	29.8%	3.9%	15.3%
1972	8.2%	15.3%	22.6%	35.4%	3.8%	14.7%

Source: Reprinted from *Automotive News Market Data Book*, 1986, by permission of Crain Automotive Group.

As can be seen from Exhibit 1, the brightest spot in the auto industry has been in the truck segment. Between 1981 and 1986, while sales of passenger cars increased by 35 percent, sales of trucks increased by a remarkable 113 percent. Most of the increase in truck sales has been due to rapid growth in the sales of light trucks; including pickups, minivans, and sport/utility vehicles.[3] The growth in light trucks seems to be the consequence of a change in life style, new products, and refocused marketing. Light trucks are being bought increasingly by city dwellers — partly because of their low price relative to passenger cars. Minivans have replaced station wagons as second vehicles for families (women drive half of all minivans and often choose which model to buy), while four-wheel-drive utility vehicles have become trendy amongst young, outdoorsy, and yuppie buyers and increasingly are being offered as an alternative to passenger cars.

The Import Challenge

While total new registrations reached 11.5 million in 1986 (the highest level since the 1973 record of 13.1 million), 26.7 percent of these vehicles were imports. This represented a rise of 14 percent from the 23.5 percent of the market taken by imports in 1984. As shown in Exhibit 1, projections for 1987 are worse still, with an estimated 29 percent of the market going to imports.[4] Of those who

[3]"Why All Those City Folks Are Buying Pickups," *Business Week*, April 27, 1987, pp. 102–103.
[4]Estimates by Standard & Poor's Industry Survey, *Autos-Auto Parts*, April 23, 1987.

export to the United States, by far the most significant competitors are Japan and West Germany. In 1985 the Japanese accounted for more than 78.3 percent of all cars imported into the United States. The major Japanese exporters were Nissan, 19.2 percent; Toyota, 19.1 percent; Honda, 17.8 percent; Mazda, 8.8 percent; and Subaru, 5.6 percent. West Germany accounted for 15 percent of all imports in the same year.

Between 1972 and 1986 Japanese penetration of the U.S. passenger car market increased from 5.7 percent to 20.0 percent. This growing demand reflected the lower price, perceived higher quality, and more attractive design features of Japanese cars. Although a decline in the value of the yen from 250 per dollar in May 1985 to 169 per dollar in October 1986 virtually eliminated the price advantage previously enjoyed by Japanese manufacturers, it is unlikely Japanese imports will slump as much as either expected or hoped. Part of the reason is that the Japanese have strengthened their market position by moving into the midrange higher-priced segments of the market in recent years, leaving the low-priced end of the market, which they once dominated, to new entries. Another factor is that many of the baby boom generation who initially bought Japanese for price reasons in the 1970s were so impressed by the quality and reliability of their purchases that they are now reluctant to change to the products of domestic companies and are prepared to pay a premium price. This perception is certainly founded in fact. A recent survey by J. D. Power & Associates found that Japanese manufacturers average 30–50 fewer defects per 100 cars during their first 90 days of ownership than the cars of domestic companies. Finally, to some extent Japanese producers and their U.S. dealers have been able to absorb the currency appreciation by taking smaller margins.

As the Japanese have moved away from the low-priced end of the market, new producers have begun to take their place. In the year after their introduction in February 1986, newcomers Hyundai from Korea and Yugo from Yugoslavia sold more than 200,000 cars in the United States, far exceeding their own expectations. What is more worrisome is that industry analysts are predicting further low-priced entry from companies based in Taiwan, Spain, Greece, Rumania, Czechoslovakia, India, and Malaysia by 1990. The combined sales volume of these potential entrants has been tentatively put at a minimum of 750,000.[5]

While the market share of U.S. producers has been squeezed from below by low-priced Asian imports, it has also been squeezed from above by European imports. Sales of luxury European cars costing $20,000 and over almost doubled between 1977 and 1987, whereas the number of luxury cars sold by U.S. producers has remained about flat. Detroit has responded by attempting to produce more European-looking cars for the top end of the market. However, the Europeans show no signs of standing still either. Jaguar, which increased U.S. sales eightfold between 1980 and 1986, has plans to launch an all-new successor to its classic sedan, the XJ6. BMW overhauled its entire line in 1987 in an

[5]Standard & Poor's, *Autos-Auto Parts,* April 23, 1987.

attempt to become the number one luxury exporter to the United States, and the ever-present Japanese are also moving into the luxury segment. The Japanese debut was the Honda Acura Legend sedan, launched in 1986, followed by the Legend coupe, launched in 1987.[6]

The Transplant Challenge

The rising import tide has raised fears of U.S. protectionism among many foreign exporters, and particularly the Japanese. Foreign manufacturers have responded by building manufacturing facilities in the United States. The trend was started by Volkswagen in 1979. More recently Honda, Nissan, and Toyota have built facilities in the United States. In the first five months of 1986 these foreign-owned plants, called "transplants," accounted for about 4 percent of U.S. auto output. The figure for the first five months of 1987 was about 7.5 percent, and the trend will continue upward as new plants are built.[7] Estimates suggest that by 1990 the U.S. plants of Asian car makers will have a combined capacity of 2 million vehicles per year, or about 17 percent of total projected U.S. capacity for 1990.[8] These estimates have two implications: that Detroit may not benefit as much as hoped from the expected falloff in Japanese imports after the appreciation of the yen and that the additional capacity may produce a situation of overcapacity.

Emerging Overcapacity

The combination of the extra capacity added by transplants, additions to global capacity due to the emergence of new producers in developing nations, and only moderate growth in demand until the end of the century raises the prospect of overcapacity in the U.S. auto industry. Estimates differ as to how much extra capacity will be around in the 1990s. A Harvard study has predicted that in 1990 Chrysler, Ford, and General Motors will among them have a combined capacity of 10.5 million vehicles per year. Of this, 33 percent is expected to be excess capacity. The president of Ford, Harold A. Poling, predicts an even greater excess for North American car makers, including transplants — up to 6 million units by 1990. Others predict that this figure will be at least 7 million by the mid-1990s.[9]

The problem of excess capacity stems from the size of the U.S. market: it is the largest in the world, and everyone between Tokyo and Detroit wants to get a bigger piece of the pie. To do so, car makers have to sell more vehicles. To sell more vehicles they have to be prepared to build more, which means that ca-

[6]Alexander Taylor, "Detroit vs. New Upscale Imports," *Fortune*, April 27, 1987, pp. 69–78.
[7]Value Line Industry Survey, *The Auto Industry*, June 26, 1987.
[8]Harry A. Stack, "Forecast," *Ward's Auto World*, June 1987, p. 29.
[9]Quoted in "Overcapacity," *Ward's Auto World*, June 1987, p. 29.

pacity has to be constructed in advance of sales. Thus individual auto companies are increasing their capacity on the basis of the additional sales they think they can achieve in the United States, but since everybody else is doing the same, the result is significant excess capacity.

Market Structure and Profitability

The changes we have just discussed have affected the market structure of the auto industry in recent years. In the 1960s the auto industry was a stable oligopoly, dominated by General Motors with a market share of more than 50 percent. Since imports were negligible, GM's dominance allowed the company to act as a price leader, and Ford and Chrysler normally followed GM's lead. The lack of significant price competition made for a profitable industry. By 1980 General Motors still dominated the auto industry, but low-cost Japanese imports had changed the rules of the game. Price competition was now intense. Although General Motors still acted as the *domestic* price leader, it was forced to set its prices so that it could compete with the Japanese imports, thereby depressing industry profits. In 1980 General Motors had a 48.1 percent share of the U.S. passenger car market, followed by Ford with 15.3 percent and Chrysler with 7.6 percent (see Exhibit 3). As can be seen from Exhibit 4, however, the deep recessionary conditions of 1980 and depressed demand meant that none of the three major U.S. companies made any money that year.

Despite a healthy revival in demand, by 1986 the persistence of import competition, along with gains made by Ford and Chrysler, reduced GM's market share to below 40 percent for the first time in the postwar period. Nor is the outlook for GM particularly promising. Most analysts predict further falls in GM's market share as the company grapples with substantial restructuring problems. These problems have arisen from a failure of ambitious plans, made in 1979, to yield forecasted efficiency gains. The consequence at GM has been

EXHIBIT 3   **U.S. market share for passenger cars, 1980–1986**

Company	1980	1981	1982	1983	1984	1985	1986
General Motors	48.1%	46.4%	46.1%	44.7%	46.2%	42.1%	39.6%
Ford	15.3%	15.5%	16.7%	17.3%	16.9%	18.8%	18.1%
Chrysler	7.6%	8.8%	8.5%	9.8%	11.3%	10.3%	10.3%
AMC	2.2%	1.5%	1.0%	2.2%	2.0%	1.2%	0.6%
Imports	26.7%	27.3%	27.8%	26.0%	23.5%	27.7%	28.3%

Source: Reprinted by permission from *Autos-Auto Parts*, 10/30/86 for 1980–1985 figures; 4/23/87 for 1986 figures.

EXHIBIT 4   **Return on assets of auto companies quoted on the New York Stock Exchange, 1980–1986**

Company	1980	1981	1982	1983	1984	1985	1986
General Motors	NM	0.9%	2.4%	8.5%	9.2%	6.9%	4.3%
Ford	NM	NM	NM	8.1%	11.2%	8.6%	9.6%
Chrysler	NM	NM	NM	3.7%	18.9%	16.2%	10.6%
AMC	NM	NM	NM	NM	0.5%	NM	NM
Honda	3.0%	10.4%	5.8%	5.9%	6.6%	8.1%	10.6%

Note: NM means "not meaningful," i.e., the company had a loss.

Source: Company annual reports.

not only declining market share, but also declining profitability. In 1986, for example, Chrysler's pretax profit per vehicle was $1,058, Ford's was $847, while GM only managed $170 per vehicle. Similarly, the turnarounds achieved at Chrysler and Ford have been impressive, allowing these companies to increase both their profitability and their market share.

The midget among U.S. auto manufacturers was the American Motors Corp. The 1980s was a period of desperate struggle for AMC. The company's market share never rose above 2.2 percent, and the company made a profit only in 1984. In 1986 AMC's market share slumped to 0.6 percent, an all-time low, while the company lost $91.3 million. AMC's struggle for survival ended in 1987, when the company was acquired by third-placed Chrysler. The acquisition of AMC gave Chrysler the additional capacity it needed, AMC's profitable Jeep line, and an additional 1,400 dealers. However, it also brought problems: two of AMC's plants are outdated; aside from Jeep, AMC's passenger car operations have consistently lost money in recent years; and skeptics question the quality of many of AMC's dealers.[10] Whether the acquisition will enhance Chrysler's competitive position, therefore, is an open question.

DEALER AND SUPPLIER RELATIONSHIPS

Dealers

Auto dealerships enter into long-term arrangements with specific auto manufacturers through franchising agreements. Other things being equal, the larger the number of dealerships a company franchises, the greater a company's sales. Thus auto manufacturers try to get as many financially sound dealers on their

[10]Burt Stoddard, "How Much Is That Jeep in the Window?" Ward's Auto World, April 1987, p. 36.

books as possible. The number is restricted only by the necessity of generating enough sales volume to give each outlet a reasonable chance of making a profit. A lack of dealers can choke a company's expansion plans. Part of the rationale underlying Chrysler's acquisition of AMC in 1987, for example, was to gain control of AMC's 1,420 dealers, thereby giving Chrysler the potential to increase its sales.

As might be expected, General Motors leads the way with dealerships. In January 1, 1986, GM had 9,830 U.S. dealers, Ford had 5,515, and Chrysler 4,000. All of the majors have seen a reduction in their dealer networks in recent years, partly due to a natural consolidation of the retail industry. The dealer count has fallen as small marginal dealers left the business to be replaced by fewer but larger outlets that stress high unit volume. In addition, the majors have also attempted to improve the quality of their dealerships, weeding out those that fall below standard. As a consequence of these changes, the number of domestic dealers handling domestic cars has dropped from around 40,000 in 1955 to about 20,000 today.

Suppliers

Traditionally, the U.S. auto supply industry has been in a weak position vis-a-vis the auto majors. The auto supply industry is fragmented, whereas the domestic auto manufacturing industry is consolidated. In the past Ford and General Motors in particular were known for their ability to play suppliers off against each other in order to push down the prices of auto parts. Both companies also used the threat that they would make parts themselves as a further means of depressing prices. Indeed, both companies undertook substantial vertical integration in an effort to cut out suppliers and increase profit margins in the end market. At one stage, this process was followed to such an extent at Ford that the company found itself involved in sheep farming and rubber plantations. Sheep wool was used for the filling in automobile seats (which Ford also manufactured), while rubber had numerous applications including tires, hoses, and brake shoes. Ford also owned steel mills, iron ore mining operations, and Great Lakes steamers to ship the ores to the mills.

However, what was rational in the relatively benign competitive environment of earlier years is not rational in the intense competitive environment of the modern auto industry. Vertical integration, by giving in-house suppliers a captive market and eliminating the incentive for in-house suppliers to make a profit, can depress efficiency. At least that is what seems to have occurred in the auto industry. The current trend is toward greater out-sourcing. Independent auto suppliers have been found to have two major advantages over in-house suppliers: lower labor costs and greater efficiency, both of which allow them to produce specific parts at a much lower cost than the auto makers can. In 1987 GM outsourced about 30 percent of its car parts, Ford an estimated 50 percent, and Chrysler 70 percent. This is an important factor explaining the superior profitability of Chrysler over GM.

In addition to the trend toward greater outsourcing, the auto companies have also been trying to reduce the number of suppliers that they have to deal with by weeding out weaker vendors. The changes at Chrysler are indicative of the industry trend. Chrysler plans to reduce its suppliers from 2,700 in 1985 to 1,500 by 1990.[11] Much closer ties are being built with the remaining vendors, who have to meet strict specifications regarding quality, delivery, and cost. These specifications enable the majors to improve the quality of their product, to operate just-in-time delivery systems (thereby reducing inventory holding costs), and, generally, to keep a lid on cost levels. The need for cost savings in this area is of paramount importance since it constitutes part of the cost advantage enjoyed by Japanese manufacturers. According to estimates for comparable $6,000 small cars, U.S. manufacturers spend an average of $3,350 on parts, materials, and services, whereas in Japan the figure is $2,750—a cost saving of $600 achieved largely through more efficient vendor relations.[12]

In an interesting footnote to buyer-supplier relations in the auto industry, Japanese auto parts companies are following Japanese auto manufacturers in building new, efficient facilities in the United States. Their initial objective in doing this is to serve the Japanese transplants; but it is also clear that they will be interested in capturing a share of the business of supplying parts to GM, Ford, and Chrysler. This suggests that a significant increase in competitive pressures in the U.S. auto supply industry may develop in the next few years.

COMPETITIVE RESPONSES

The U.S. auto manufacturers have not been blind to the changes taking place in the auto industry. They have responded to the increasingly competitive environment with a series of steps aimed at reducing operating costs, improving quality, and stimulating sales. As already discussed, at Chrysler and Ford these efforts have met with some success, while at General Motors the results have been less than promising.

Operating Costs and Productivity

Operating costs have been cut and productivity raised through a number of strategies. A major part of the cost advantage of Japanese automakers comes from lower labor cost and higher productivity. In 1985 the Japanese on the average spent $700 on wages and salaries in order to build a $6,000 small car; U.S. companies spent, on the average, $2,000 on wages and salaries to build a comparable $6,000 car.[13] The average Japanese compact took 14 worker hours to assemble, compared with an average of 33 worker hours in the United States.

[11]"Lee Iacocca's Production Whiz," *Fortune*, June 22, 1987, pp. 36–42.
[12]"Behind the Hype at GM's Saturn," *Fortune*, November 11, 1985, pp. 34–46.
[13]"Behind the Hype," pp. 34–46.

Building a Japanese engine required 2.8 worker hours compared with 6.8 hours in the United States. And finally, stamping out body parts required 2.9 worker hours in Japan versus 9.5 hours in the United States.

To try and close the cost/productivity gap, U.S. auto companies have embarked on programs aimed at cutting manpower and boosting productivity through greater automation. All the auto majors have substantially reduced manpower. At Chrysler the work force was cut in half during the early 1980s, from 160,000 to 80,000—including a 19,000-cut in white collar manpower.[14] Additionally, General Motors and Ford have both announced plans to reduce the number of white collar employees by 20–25 percent by 1990, while GM plans to close at least three manufacturing plants.

Productivity has improved through the widespread adoption of robots for assembly operations, machine loading, spot and fusion welding, body painting, and parts transfer. As recently as 1980 General Motors had only 300 robots in use. By the middle of 1986 the company's robot population numbered 6,000, and it is projected to reach 15,000 by 1990. Ford had 3,000 robots in operation in early 1986, and may have as many as 7,000 in operation by 1990. Chrysler increased its robot population from 300 in 1982 to 1,242 in 1986.

However, the adoption of robots has not always resulted in anticipated efficiency gains being realized. Many unanticipated problems have been encountered. Employees have been poorly trained to handle the new high tech equipment. The robots themselves have had teething problems, frequently breaking down and sometimes bringing a whole production line grinding to an expensive halt (a production line can generate $10 million a day in revenues when running, and so breakdowns are very expensive). Moreover, experience has shown that some tasks targeted for automation are too complicated for robots to perform, necessitating an expensive changeback to manual methods. Finally, generating efficiency gains from robots has been severely handicapped by the "tower-of-Babel problem:" the fact that different robots built by different companies speak different computer languages and hence they cannot communicate with each other. General Motors is currently leading the way in developing a system that will allow all pieces of automated hardware to communicate with each other regardless of vendor. However, as of 1987 considerable technical difficulties still need to be resolved before such a system can be fully implemented.[15]

As noted earlier, the adoption of just-in-time parts delivery systems has also brought major cost reductions. These systems require close coordination between vendor and manufacturer to ensure that parts arrive just when they are needed. Such systems can dramatically reduce inventories, save shipping time and costs, reduce storage space requirements (allowing for smaller plants), and quickly reveal any deficiencies in parts supplied by the vendor.

[14]Lee A. Iacocca, "The Rescue and Resuscitation of Chrysler," *Journal of Business Strategy*, Vol. 4 (Summer 1983), 67–69.
[15]"MAP: It Will Survive, but Will It Thrive?" *Ward's Auto World*, May 1987, 52–53.

Quality Control

The problem of inferior quality relative to Japanese imports has bedeviled U.S. auto companies. Poor quality hurts auto companies both directly, by putting buyers off, and indirectly, by raising operating costs. Studies have shown that the typical U.S. factory invests a staggering 20–25 percent of its operating budget in finding and fixing mistakes. In some industries, as many as one-quarter of all factory hands do not produce anything; they just fix things that were not produced correctly the first time around.[16] Historically, the U.S. auto industry has been one of the worst offenders in this respect.

In recent years costs have been reduced and quality improved in the auto industry through the adoption of sophisticated statistical quality control techniques. These are aimed at insuring that a job is performed correctly the first time around. The techniques gauge the performance of the manufacturing process by carefully monitoring changes in whatever is being produced. The goal is to detect potential problems before they result in poor-quality products, then pinpoint the reasons for the variation and adjust the process to make it more stable. The techniques have minimized product variations and reduced the need for inspections and waste.

The auto makers have also borrowed the idea of quality circles from the Japanese in their attempts to improve quality. Quality circles comprise groups of workers who gather to discuss ways of improving efficiency and quality in the areas where they work. Adoption of ideas suggested by such groups has helped the auto companies improve their control over quality while increasing the commitment of workers to the company and its product. For example, at General Motor's facility in Lansing, Michigan, workers are organized into teams rather than on a traditional assembly line basis. Each team is given specific responsibility for a range of assembly line tasks. The members are allowed to define their own jobs and they are expected to monitor the quality of their output on a daily basis. The self monitoring enabled the plant to reduce the number of quality inspection jobs by over one third between 1985 and 1987, while the higher productivity of teams has reduced the costs of manufacturing a car by 21 percent.[17]

In the search for greater quality and efficiency, some companies are also experimenting with the modular manufacturing methods. Under these methods workers are organized into production teams and perform more extensive operations than on moving assembly lines. The method is supposed to enhance quality through an increase in the commitment of workers to the product. Furthermore, productivity gains arise from the greater flexibility of the work force and from pay systems tied to modular output. Currently, the most extensive application of this method can be found at GM's new Saturn plant in Spring Hill, Tennessee.

[16]"The Push for Quality," *Business Week,* June 8, 1987, pp. 130–143.
[17]"Why Image Counts: A Tale of Two Industries," *Business Week,* June 8, 1987, pp. 138–140.

Finally, quality has been improved through building closer ties with suppliers to ensure that component parts meet requisite quality standards and through reducing the number of parts in the manufacturing process. For example, Ford recently redesigned an instrument panel for its Escort model so that it contained only six parts, rather than the twenty-two parts found in older panels. As a consequence, Ford reported that material costs fell by close to 30 percent and labor costs by over 80 percent, while the number of problems with instrument panels declined by 10 percent.[18] In short, simpler products are easier to assemble and leave less room for error.

Stimulating Sales

Domestic auto manufacturers have attempted to stimulate sales in recent years through two main strategies: better auto design and quality aimed at closing the perceived gap between U.S. and foreign cars, and cut-rate financing deals. In an apparent attempt to reverse their image as producers of blandly-styled vehicles that all resemble each other, domestic auto makers seem finally to be starting to introduce models that match the design features of foreign manufacturers. In 1987 the prestigious magazine *Ward's Auto World* ranked U.S. cars and trucks ahead of foreign competition in six out of the eight price/size/style categories that it looked at.[19] General Motors did particularly well, capturing the top spot in four of the eight categories. Nevertheless, problems remain, particularly at General Motors, where by 1987 the company had proved unable to differentiate design features among its 175 models. Many critics note that GM's large cars look like its small cars, and its Chevrolets and Pontiacs look much like its Buicks, Oldsmobiles, and Cadillacs. As a result, GM is competing against itself and has difficulty achieving break-even output levels for individual models.

Cut-rate financing deals have always been a way of stimulating sales to cut inventories in the auto industry. In the late 1980s, however, cut-rate financing deals reached new levels, depressing profits for the whole industry. The problem started at General Motors, which found itself producing more cars than it could sell in 1985. Inventories started to rise, and General Motors responded by introducing 7.7 percent retail financing to trim inventories and try to bring its sales in line with production. The ploy worked, but only for a short period. The following year GM was again forced to offer cut-rate financing deals to bring sales in line with production, only this time it needed a 2.9 percent rate to achieve the same effect — amounting to a $1,500 rebate on each vehicle sitting in the dealers' lots. Ford and Chrysler, which had no problem selling all the cars they could produce in 1986, were forced to follow suit just to stay competitive. Hence all three auto majors saw their profits depressed as a result of GM's introduction of 2.9 percent financing. The financing ended in December 1986 with

[18]"Why Image Counts," pp. 138–140.
[19]"BMW M6 Rises to the Top," *Ward's Auto World,* April 1987, 39–41.

predictable results: sales of domestic cars plunged 40 percent in January 1987. Moreover, there are worrying signs that consumers have become so accustomed to financing deals that they now regard them as normal. If this has indeed happened, then Detroit could find itself in a position of having to run ever faster just to stay still.

CONCLUSION

Clues to the potential future of the U.S. auto industry were revealed in August 1987, when accountants Arthur Andersen & Company released the results of a detailed study of the industry's outlook between 1987 and 1995.[20] The study, based on a poll of 650 respondents among Canadian and U.S. vehicle makers and parts suppliers, highlighted a number of important factors that may adversely affect the future of the domestic industry. The conclusions of the study included the following:

1. The main reason for the success of foreign-owned plants in the United States is the management practices of overseas companies.
2. The U.S. car market will remain flat at between 8.3 million and 8.5 million units, but nearly a third will come from transplant companies, cutting the share of traditional U.S. automakers.
3. The Japanese will maintain a $500–$800 price advantage over U.S. car makers by 1995.
4. Japanese suppliers are willing to accept lower profit margins than U.S. companies.
5. The engineering and design staffs of U.S. car makers are not as tuned into the competitive pressures of the industry as they should be.
6. The time it takes to develop a new U.S. car will be cut from about four years to three by 1990, while the Japanese will reduce the time from the current three years to two and a half by then.
7. Some companies, discouraged by unanticipated problems, are already giving up on or de-emphasizing automation and technology. The report notes that this may be a mistake.

On the same day the Industrial Bank of Japan issued a report predicting that "the American auto market may face an oversupply of 1.4 million cars in 1990 because of the increasing number of Japanese automakers building their products in the United States."[21]

[20]"Study Predicts Cutbacks in Auto Industry in Face of Competition," *Investor's Daily*, August 5, 1987, p. 29.
[21]"Oversupply Seen for U.S. Auto Market by '90," *Investor's Daily*, August 4, 1987, p. 29.

CHRYSLER CORPORATION: TURNAROUND AND BEYOND

INTRODUCTION

Sterling Heights, Michigan, November 1984. Lee Iacocca drives onto the spotlights in a glistening silver Dodge Lancer. As Iacocca steps out of the car, the plant's 2,300 hourly workers let out a roar "worthy of the crowds in Latin American soccer stadiums when their national team takes the field."[1] The occasion was the introduction of Chrysler Corporation's new H car, to which Iacocca had invited the plant's hourly workers, in addition to the usual collection of industry bigwigs, politicians, and journalists. The roar was one of appreciation for the man who had masterminded one of the most dramatic business turnarounds in American history. Five years earlier Chrysler had been forced to go cap in hand to the government to beg for a $1.5-billion loan in guarantees to save the company from certain bankruptcy. In 1980 Chrysler had lost $771 million on revenues of $9.23 billion and had seen its market share decline to a dismal 7.6 percent, down from 16.2 percent ten years earlier. Now Chrysler was on the rebound, soon to report record year-end profits of $2.79 billion on revenues of $19.57 billion and a market share of 11.3 percent.

The story of Chrysler's transformation between 1979 and 1984 is one of a relentless drive to reduce costs, improve quality, and produce exciting new car

This case was prepared by Charles W. L. Hill, University of Washington.

[1] S. Flax, "Can Chrysler Keep Rolling Along?" *Fortune*, January 7, 1985, pp. 34–39.

designs. The success of the turnaround had left Chrysler in a better position to survive and prosper in an industry that was becoming ever more competitive. Yet at the same time fresh clouds were already appearing on the horizon. Although Chrysler could now build cars for $500 less than Ford and General Motors, many foreign producers still enjoyed a formidable cost advantage. With imports predicted to rise, market growth to slow, and excess capacity to emerge in the industry by 1990 Chrysler could not afford to sit back and enjoy the successes of 1984. Indeed, although revenues continued to rise through 1985 and 1986, Chrysler's profits began to slip back from their 1984 level as significant price competition developed in the auto industry. There seemed to be little doubt, at least in Lee Iacocca's mind, that come 1995 the global auto industry would be even more competitive than in 1985. The question for Chrysler was how best to respond.

HISTORICAL BACKGROUND[2]

The Chrysler corporation was founded in 1924 by Walter Percy Chrysler. W. P. Chrysler was a former General Motors executive who, like Iacocca, developed a reputation for performing turnarounds. He had retired from General Motors in 1919, a millionaire at the age of forty-five, after having transformed GM's Buick division from a position close to extinction into the company's top profit producer. Two years later the postwar slump threatened to wipe out Willys-Overland Inc. and Maxwell Motor Corporation. Induced by the companies' bankers, Chrysler came out of retirement to try to save them both. It was at Willys-Overland that Chrysler met the innovative design team of Fred Zender, Carl Breer, and Owen Skelton. The three so impressed Chrysler that he persuaded them to come to work for him at Maxwell Motor Car. There in 1923 they developed a medium-priced car known as the Chrysler Six. It featured a high-compression engine, plus hydraulic brakes, replaceable oil filters, aluminum pistons, and shock absorbers — all items that had previously been found only in higher-priced cars.

Introduced in 1924, the Chrysler Six broke all industry records for a first-year car with sales of 32,000 units. Buoyed by this success, W. P. Chrysler went ahead with plans to set up the Chrysler Corp. in 1925, taking over the Maxwell Motor Car Company in the process. The following year Chrysler introduced four models: the 50, the 60, the 70, and the Imperial 80. (The numbers signified the speed each model could reach.) Chrysler took off, selling 192,000 cars in 1927 and reaching number five in the industry. In 1928 Chrysler advanced further still with the acquisition of Dodge Brothers Corporation. In the same year

[2]For further details on historical development, see M. Y. Gordon, *The Iacocca Management Technique* (New York: Dodd, Mead, 1985); and R. B. Reich and J. D. Donahue, *New Deals: The Chrysler Revival and the American System* (New York: Times Books, 1985).

Chrysler introduced the Plymouth car, aimed at the low end of the market. The basic line-up of cars assembled at this time—Chrysler, Dodge, Plymouth—continues to constitute Chrysler's basic offering today.

Chrysler's strategy after 1928 was one of conservative growth coupled with innovative product developments. W. P. Chrysler did not believe in striving for domination and insisted that the company should grow by no more than 10 percent per annum. The strategy enabled Chrysler to ride through the Great Depression and come out stronger than ever, with a market share of 25 percent in 1936.

In 1935 W. P. Chrysler stepped down from the presidency and promoted K. T. Keller to the position. Keller practiced the founder's hands-on management style, which was becoming increasingly unsuited to an organization of Chrysler's size. Unlike the founder, however, Keller resisted product innovation. By 1956, when Keller retired, Chrysler's products were hopelessly outdated and the company had lost second place in the industry to Ford. However, worse was in store. The 1958 recession sent Chrysler into a tailspin. Sales declined by 50 percent in a year, and market share slumped to 11.3 percent, from 20 percent six years earlier.

Largely as a result of Chrysler's failure to come to grips with conditions in the postwar period, forty-two-year-old Lynn Townsend was appointed to the presidency in 1961. Townsend oversaw the transformation of Chrysler. Costs were cut, capital investment increased, a new line of cars more in keeping with the ethos of the period was introduced in 1963, and decision making was decentralized. Early in 1963 the company announced a ten-year expansion plan, with a $700-million budget, which was increased to $1.7 billion by 1965. The company revitalized its neglected dealer network, built major new factories, diversified into aerospace, marine engineering, and real estate, and, perhaps more significantly, began to expand internationally, both in Europe and Latin America. In 1961 only 4 percent of Chrysler's vehicles were made outside the United States; in 1967 the figure was 24 percent.

Chrysler's ambitious expansion plans, however, drained cash reserves and raised debt, leaving little room for maneuver. This was all right so long as the economy continued to expand, but in 1970 things started to change for the worse. Inflation and unemployment began to rise. In 1969 the economy entered a recession, which deepened in 1970. Furthermore, in 1970 new auto safety and emission standard regulations were introduced, and the auto makers had to comply with them by 1975; that required substantial new investments and design changes. Chrysler responded by halting expansion plans, adopting tight cost controls, and rationalizing the product line. Between 1971 and 1973 Chrysler cut overheads by several hundred million dollars and reduced its model range by 30 percent.

By the first half of 1973 Chrysler was on the way up again, carried along by the biggest auto boom in history. Then, just as the future was looking bright for Chrysler, the company was hit by a number of body blows. A series of wildcat strikes during the summer of 1973 delayed the launching of its new line of C-body cars. In September an all-out strike shut down Chrysler's plant for nine days. In October Israel and Egypt went to war. The Arab countries declared an oil embargo on the United States and other allies of Israel. The price of gasoline increased sharply and overall car sales decreased, while small fuel-efficient cars surged to capture the market. Unfortunately for Chrysler, the company had just spent $450 million on restyling all its large cars. In the following year things only got worse as the United States entered its most severe postwar depression.

By mid-1974 Chrysler was in deep financial difficulty. In response, Chrysler's lead bank, Manufacturers Hanover Trust Co., organized a consolidation of the company's network of loan agreements into a single $455-million credit agreement. This first bailout amounted to a contract between Chrysler and about eighty major banks, each of which was prepared to lend the company specified sums on demand.

With Chrysler's finances stabilized, Lynn Townsend felt it was a good time to leave. He was replaced by his right-hand man, John Riccardo. Riccardo introduced a new strategy, which represented a sharp departure from the Townsend years. Instead of growth, Riccardo was interested in making a steady profit. Under his direction, parts of Chrysler that did not fit or that lost money were sold off. Management controls were tightened in an effort to reduce inventories and bring production in line with sales potential. The company's product strategy was redefined, with attempts being made to move upmarket and attract a more affluent clientele. In 1976 the benefits of these changes began to show as Chrysler bounced back once more with a 31 percent increase in sales (versus 22 percent for the industry as a whole) and record profits.

However, in November 1977 Chrysler once more ran into bad luck when it was obliged to recall more than one million vehicles to check for defects that could have caused brake failure. Two more recalls followed in December, one for engine stalling and one for bad hood latches. At the same time Chrysler was laying plans for a massive $7.5-billion retooling program. This had been made necessary in part by new federal emission and fuel-economy regulations and in part by Chrysler's decision to switch to front-wheel drive for its new flagship car, code-named the K-car.

The debt necessary to finance such a program made Chrysler particularly vulnerable to falling demand. In 1978 the worst happened as sales slumped and Chrysler reported a first quarter loss of $120 million. In the second quarter Chrysler managed to generate a $30.4 million profit, but that was not nearly enough to finance the retooling program. The need for cash was now paramount. Riccardo responded by selling off Chrysler's international operations. First to go were the company's Australian and Brazilian subsidiaries, and in August Peugeot-Citroen took over Chrysler's French, British, and Spanish plants for $432 million. Then, in November, Chrysler reported record third-quarter losses of $159 million. On the same day as these results were announced, the Chrysler board announced that it had decided on a new helmsman. Only months after he had been fired from the presidency of Ford, Lee Iacocca became Chrysler's president and chief operating officer.

LEE IACOCCA

Lee Iacocca was born to Italian immigrant parents in Allentown, Pennsylvania, on October 14, 1924. His father, Nick, was an entrepreneur whose interests included the food retail business, one of the earliest car rental agencies, and real estate. Nick Iacocca's businesses survived the Great Depression, but just barely, and the hard times of that era instilled in young Lee a desire to be rich enough not to have to worry about money.

Lee excelled in high school, graduating with straight A's. However, in his senior year at high school, Lee experienced one of the great disappointments of his life. It was 1941, and the Japanese had just attacked Pearl Harbor. America was at war, and, like many young men of his age, Iacocca rushed to join up. To his enormous disappointment, he was turned down. Iacocca was classified 4 F — a medical deferment — which meant that he could not join the Air Corps and fight in the war. Iacocca attributed the deferment to a bout with rheumatic fever when he was fourteen, which had weakened his heart. Whatever the reason for the deferment, Iacocca felt disgraced, and there is little doubt that his failure here motivated him to prove himself in other ways.

Iacocca attended Lehigh University, from which he graduated with a B.S. in engineering and a 3.53 grade-point average. He went on to get a master's degree in engineering from Princeton before joining Ford in 1946. Iacocca initially worked as an engineer at Ford but soon found himself bored by the technical side of the business and requested a transfer to sales. Ford agreed, provided Iacocca could find an opening for himself. As luck would have it, the company was looking for a truck salesman at its Chester, Pennsylvania, office. Iacocca was hired and soon caught the eye of his superiors with his energy, commitment, and knack for selling. His rapid rise within Ford's sales division began, culminating with his appointment in December 1960 as general manager of the division at the age of thirty-six.

As head of the sales division, Iacocca took over some responsibilities from Ford's ex-president Robert McNamara, who had left to join the Kennedy administration. McNamara had introduced the Ford Falcon in 1959, the first American compact — an extremely successful venture, with sales of 417,000 units in the first year. The Falcon, however, was a basic nuts-and-bolts car. While it sold well, it did not make a great deal of money, due to the small profit margin that could be earned on cars aimed at the low end of the market. Iacocca saw the possibility of developing a sporty version of the Falcon, with a pepped-up engine, whitewall tires, air conditioning, automatic transmission, and the like, which would appeal to a more upscale market and allow a greater profit margin. Under Iacocca's direction, a development team that included Hal Sperlich, who was later to play an important role at Chrysler under Iacocca, set to work on the idea. The result was the launching of the Ford Mustang in April 1964. The Mustang broke all records at Ford, ending up with a first-year volume of 417,174 units sold. In its first two years the Mustang generated what was then a staggering $1.1 billion for Ford in net profits, securing for Iacocca a reputation as one of the auto industry's best marketers.

Iacocca continued at Ford until 1978, reaching the rank of president in 1970. The relationship between Iacocca and the company's chairman, Henry Ford II, however, was never an easy one. In his autobiography, Iacocca paints a picture of a dictatorial and "somewhat paranoid" Henry Ford, who resented Iacocca as an Italian interloper and felt threatened by Iacocca's ambition, competence, and popularity in the company. Things eventually came to a head in 1978, when Ford fired Iacocca, for "personal reasons," right on top of the two best years in the company's history. Shortly afterwards Iacocca was hired by Chrysler.

TURNAROUND AND CONSOLIDATION, 1979–1987

When Iacocca joined Chrysler, it was a company that was fast going under. Costs were out of control, the products were out of touch with the market, sales were falling, inventories were high, inefficiency was rampant, cash flow was negative, and the management of the company was, in Iacocca's words, in a state of anarchy. In 1979 Chrysler was set to lose $489 million, followed by a further $771 million in 1980. Yet in just four short years sales revenues would double and profits surge to a record $2.79 billion (see Exhibit 1). Many factors

EXHIBIT 1   **Chrysler's performance, 1977–1986 (in millions of dollars)**

Year	Revenues	Operating income	Return on assets	Return on equity
1986	22,586	2,338	10.6%	30.0%
1985	21,256	2,424	16.2%	46.9%
1984	19,573	2,790	18.9%	65.5%
1983	13,240	1,356	3.7%	109.0%
1982	10,045	518	NM	NM
1981	10,822	250	NM	NM
1980	9,225	−771	NM	NM
1979	12,002	−489	NM	NM
1978	13,618	144	NM	NM
1977	16,708	710	1.7%	4.3%

Notes: NM means "not meaningful." ROA and ROE are calculated using net income.

Source: Company annual reports. Reprinted by permission.

contributed to this turnaround, but among the most important were government support, organizational and management changes, the success of new car designs, cost reductions, and quality controls.

Bailout or Bankruptcy

In mid-1979 Chrysler's second-quarter loss reached $207 million, while 75,000 cars stood unsold on dealers' lots. In the long run, Chrysler couldn't survive without investing cash to boost productivity and develop new models. With plummeting sales and mounting losses, Chrysler could not itself generate the necessary cash, and the banks were not too keen to lend to Chrysler. Unless the government stepped in to help, Chrysler was finished: it was bailout or bankruptcy. After intensive lobbying in Washington, Iacocca persuaded Congress to pass the Loan Guarantee Act at the end of 1979, which guaranteed government support for a further $1.5 billion in loans to the troubled corporation. The act was unprecedented in the United States and politically controversial, with many feeling that it amounted to "state socialism." The loans did not have to be repaid until 1990, but Chrysler was able to pay back in August 1983 all of the $1.2 billion that it had eventually borrowed.[3]

Organization and Management

When Iacocca arrived for his first day at Chrysler, the situation he found there was one of anarchy. As he later noted in his autobiography:

> I soon stumbled upon my first major revelation: Chrysler didn't really function like a company at all. Chrysler in 1978 was like Italy in the 1860s — the company consisted of a lot of little duchies, each one run by a prima donna. It was a bunch of mini-empires with nobody giving a damn about what anyone else was doing. . . . There was no real committee setup. . . no system of meetings to get people to talk to each other. I couldn't believe, for example, that the guy running the engineering department wasn't in constant touch with his counterpart in manufacturing. But that's how it was. . . . The manufacturing guys would build cars without even checking with the sales guys. They just built them, stuck them in a yard, and then hoped that somebody would take them out of there. We ended up with a huge inventory and a financial nightmare.[4]

Iacocca moved fast to solve Chrysler's organizational problems. His prime objectives were to instill a sense of accountability and control within the organization, to break down the empires, and to get people talking to each other. Until Iacocca took over, evaluation of the individual functions at Chrysler had been at best haphazard. He was determined to undertake a complete review

[3]"Why Chrysler's Cash Handles Like a Dream," *Business Week,* June 8, 1987, p. 116.
[4]Lee A. Iacocca, *Iacocca: An Autobiography* (Toronto: Bantam Books, 1984), pp. 152–153.

of all Chrysler operations. He had little faith in the existing senior management, regarding it to be too much a part of the old status quo. (During the next three years Iacocca fired thirty-three of Chrysler's thirty-five top corporate officials.)

One of Iacocca's first steps involved bringing in Gerald Greenwald from Ford in November 1978 to try to make sense out of Chrysler's haphazard financial controls. Greenwald's last post at Ford was as head of its manufacturing and sales operations in Venezuela, where he had carved out the biggest market share of any Ford subsidiary. In addition, Iacocca promoted ex-Ford design man Hal Sperlich to group vice president for product planning, design, and engineering. Sperlich was an old friend of Iacocca's from his Ford days and one of the few Chrysler insiders that he trusted. Sperlich orchestrated Chrysler's K-car program and was father to its enormously successful minivan—a concept that he had first pushed unsuccessfully at Ford in the 1970s.

Iacocca then turned to three retired Ford executives and persuaded them to join him at Chrysler: Gar Laux, who had headed sales and marketing at Ford; Paul Bergmoser, the one-time purchasing chief at Ford; and Hans Matthias, who had been in charge of manufacturing at Ford. Matthias, who had retired from Ford in 1972, functioned as an outside consultant and undertook a review of Chrysler's manufacturing operations. Bergmoser initially did the same, preparing a report on Chrysler's purchasing operations for Iacocca. Laux, too, initially accepted a consulting role and undertook a review of Chrysler's sales operations.

The task of these three ex-Ford men was to identify ways to reduce costs, increase quality, and get the organization pulling together. They uncovered one inefficiency after another. For example, Matthias noted that Chrysler had more than 100 separate driveshaft combinations on trucks and thousands of paint combinations, all of which was very expensive. Laux found that Chrysler's dealer systems desperately needed overhauling. Dealers had been allowed to stay in business, or to expand, without regard to changes in neighborhoods. In many metropolitan markets, this translated into extensive competition among Chrysler's dealers. In addition, Laux found that Chrysler had nearly 200 company-owned dealerships engaged in wasteful competition with the privately owned dealers (by 1985 all but a handful of these had been sold off or closed down). After they had made their recommendations, in the spring of 1979 Iacocca persuaded Matthias, Bergmoser, and Laux to join Chrysler on a full-time basis, so that they could implement these recommendations.

Meanwhile, Greenwald had found that central financial controls were almost nonexistent in the accounts payable area, with bills being paid from about thirty different locations. In addition, to his dismay, he discovered that the people at the controller's office had no idea of how to evaluate what management was doing from a financial perspective. Nor could they project the financial consequences of corporate decisions. As Iacocca himself later observed, "He [Greenwald] had a hell of a time finding anybody who could be identified as having specific responsibility for anything. They would tell him: 'Well, everyone is responsible for controlling costs.' Jerry knew very well what that meant—in the final analysis nobody was."[5]

An experience indicative of the lack of control at Chrysler concerned Greenwald's attempt to get a grip on warranty costs, which at that time were running at around $350 million per year. When, in an attempt to uncover the sources of the costs, Greenwald asked for a list of the top ten warranty problems, no one could tell him what they were. The requisite systems were simply not in place.

Despite such obstacles, by the middle of 1979 Greenwald had straightened out much of the mess in the controller's office. Financial control had been centralized and systems introduced to increase accountability. In addition, close to 8,500 deadwood white-collar finance staff had been sacked or retired early. At this stage, Greenwald was moved up to become chairman of Chrysler's main subsidiary, Chrysler Motors Corporation. To replace Greenwald as controller, yet another ex-Ford man was recruited, Steve Miller, who had been Greenwald's main financial man in Venezuela.

With initial management problems solved and Iacocca's Ford recruits busy looking at ways to improve efficiency, Iacocca's next order of business was to get information flowing throughout the company. In the old Chrysler, the people at the top were hopelessly out of touch with what was going on at lower levels in the organization. The financial control systems introduced by Greenwald partly solved this problem. In addition, drawing directly on techniques worked out while at Ford, Iacocca formed five-to-seven-member teams at every level of the corporation. The lower-level teams would meet each quarter with their supervisor to set goals and evaluate past performance. The supervisor of each team would in turn be a member of a higher team. The higher teams, too, would meet with their supervisors. The teams would continue to meet up the hierarchy until they reached the top group of which Iacocca was the leader. This system facilitated the flow of information upward within the organization and ensured that problems at the lower levels received the attention of top management. A further innovation that Iacocca introduced at Chrysler was the creation of committees and management positions designed to stimulate the flow of information among divisions, groups, and departments. The objective here was to get people in different functions to talk to each other.

The K-Car Concept

When Hal Sperlich arrived at Chrysler in 1977, he began working on a series of cars called the K-car. Since its introduction in 1980, all of Chrysler's new models have been a variation on this single theme. Working with one basic engine, transmission, and underbody structure, the company has spun off no fewer than

[5]Iacocca, *Iacocca*, p. 170.

ten models from the basic K-car concept. Introduced initially as the Dodge Aries and Plymouth Reliant, subsequent K-car spinoffs have ranged in size from the compact Dodge Shadow to the full-sized Chrysler New Yorker. The basic platform has also yielded specialty vehicles as diverse as Chrysler's highly successful minivans and the sporty Chrysler TC, designed by Maserati.[6]

The single platform strategy of the K-car was born out of economic necessity. Financially strapped, Chrysler was simply not able to afford all-new models. So Sperlich designed the basic K-car platform, which could then be used to produce a wide variety of different models. By using many of the same parts in different models, Chrysler found a way to keep its costs down and achieve greater scale economies. The success of this concept has given Chrysler a unique advantage over its competitors. While General Motors produces 19 distinct body platforms for its 175 models, Chrysler only has to deal with 1 platform — greatly reducing the complexity of manufacturing operations.

The use of the same basic parts in different K-car models has improved Chrysler's position with respect to component suppliers. Chrysler is now able to order parts in much larger volumes than in the 1970s, enabling it to get quotes akin to those offered to GM or Ford. Indeed, Chrysler is sometimes a more important customer to the component suppliers than GM or Ford. This leverage has enabled Chrysler to bargain down the prices that it pays for inputs. In 1984, for example, Chrysler purchased and installed more than 104,000 turbochargers from auto supplier Garrett, whereas GM and Ford have turned to outside suppliers for far fewer — less than one-quarter — of these parts.[7]

Manufacturing apart, the K-car had other advantages that helped make it and its spin-offs a successful line of products. The basic K-car was a fuel-efficient, front-wheel drive, comfortable, and roomy compact. In short, it held the promise of being able to hold its own against Japanese imports. In addition, the K-car came at a time when competition from other American manufacturers, and Ford in particular, was weakened by a lack of comparable vehicles.

Despite all its advantages, the K-car very nearly turned into a disaster for Chrysler. The launch date for the initial Aries and Reliant models was set for October 1980. A good launch requires at least 35,000 cars in the show rooms, but by October Chrysler had only 10,000. The company had run into some unexpected problems with its high tech robotic welders, resulting in production snags. To boot, Chrysler made a big mistake with its initial pricing strategy. The basic K-car had been priced at $5,880, to undercut the main domestic competition, GM's Citation, which sold for $6,270. At this price, Chrysler was not going to make much money, and so it tried to widen margins by producing a large number of cars fully loaded with extras — which added about $2,000 to the price. This proved to be a mistake. Sales fizzled when consumers, who had expected a good buy, saw the $8,000–$9,000 price sticker. Fortunately for

[6]"The Chrysler Guidebook to Creative Packaging," *Fortune*, June 22, 1987, p. 39.
[7]"Can Chrysler Keep Rolling Along?" *Fortune*, January 7, 1985, p. 37.

Chrysler, the pricing mistake was soon discovered, and the company rushed to get as many low-priced K-cars into the show rooms as possible.[8]

Since 1981 the basic K-cars have sold well. As the figures in Exhibit 2 show, the two versions of the K-car initially dominated the American-manufactured compact market. Although market share declined with the introduction of new models from Ford in 1983 and renewed efforts by GM, volume remained stable between 1982 and 1985, despite a switch by Chrysler back to higher-priced (and more profitable), fully loaded versions of the cars.

The success of the initial K-cars gave Chrysler the cash it so desperately needed to develop further variants of the K-car basic platform. Of these the most successful to date has been the innovative minivan — the front-wheel-drive hybrid of a car and a van that has created a new market niche. The minivan concept was originally developed by Sperlich at Ford in the early 1970s, but the project was shelved by Ford when market research did not indicate sales of at least 60,000 per year. When Iacocca came to Chrysler, Sperlich reminded him of the project. Iacocca, who in marked contrast to his predecessors had plowed money into product development since arriving in 1979, was prepared to take the chance that Ford was not and allocated $700 million to develop the vehicle.

Chrysler was rewarded with the impressive sales of 148,000 minivans under the names of Dodge Caravan and Plymouth Voyager in 1984. GM and Ford were not in the market, and Toyota, constrained by import quotas, sold only 46,593 minivans. Using many K-car parts, including engines, transaxles, and some steering parts, helped keep costs down and enabled Chrysler to make more than $2,000 per vehicle on those loaded with options. The minivan is also helping Chrysler in other respects. Along with sporty cars such as the Dodge Daytona, the minivan is helping Chrysler gain customers who are younger and

EXHIBIT 2   **Market share among American-manufactured compacts, 1982–1985 (unit sales)**

Brand	1982	1983	1984	1985
Chevrolet Cavalier (GM)	118,110	249,697	372,206	419,697
Pontiac 2000 (GM)	55,720	85,435	124,123	115,183
Buick Skyhawk (GM)	44,986	71,501	119,314	85,411
Ford Tempo (Ford)	.....	124,060	254,437	278,475
Mercury Topaz (Ford)	.....	36,106	73,879	73,554
Plymouth Reliant (Chrysler)	145,216	154,679	134,562	137,213
Dodge Aries (Chrysler)	111,646	117,988	109,256	114,289

Source: Standard & Poor's Industry Surveys, *Autos and Auto-Parts,* October 30, 1986. Reprinted by permission.

[8]Iacocca, *Iacocca,* p. 254.

richer than the fifty-five-year-old blue-collar worker who used to be the typical buyer. According to Chrysler's research, some forty percent of minivan buyers say that they have never been in a Chrysler dealership before their purchase.

The attempt by Chrysler to shift its products upmarket has been underscored by two further developments. First, Chrysler acquired a 15-percent stake in Italian sports car manufacturer Maserati with a view to establishing cooperation on the design of new Chrysler sports cars and importing Maserati vehicles into the United States. This has borne fruit in the shape of Chrysler's sporty TC, which features bodywork designed by Maserati Automobiles Inc., combined with a K-car platform. Second, Chrysler acquired two high-performance sports car manufacturers in 1986, Lamborghini SpA of Italy and Group Lotus Plc. of England, with a view to tapping their design and high-performance engineering expertise. In addition, the agreement between Chrysler and Maserati leaves open the option for Chrysler to acquire total control of the Italian company by 1995.

Costs and Productivity

In 1979 Chrysler's break-even point was 2.4 million vehicles. By 1984 the break-even point had been reduced to 1.1 million vehicles. In 1981 it took 175 man-hours to build a vehicle at Chrysler. By 1986 the number of man-hours required had been cut to 102. Chrysler now builds vehicles for $500 less per unit than General Motors and Ford and has cut in half the cost advantage enjoyed by Japanese manufacturers in 1980.[9] These changes are the consequence of a series of measures taken at Chrysler in the early 1980s to reduce costs and raise productivity. They included layoffs, salary cuts, plant closings, the adoption of new manufacturing technologies and techniques, and the use of interchangeable parts.

Iacocca's first step was to cut salaried expenses by more than half. Executive salaries were cut by up to 10 percent, which had never been done in the auto industry before. Only the secretaries were left alone, as Iacocca felt that "they deserved every cent they made."[10] Next, Chrysler turned to cutting blue-collar pay. With the prospect of job loss looming large, the United Auto Workers Union was prepared to make some major concessions. During a year-and-a-half period paychecks were cut by $2 per hour, amounting to a $6,000-per-year pay cut. The impact of these wage and salary changes was an annual cost saving of $1.2 billion.

Then there were massive layoffs. In the first four years under Iacocca, the company's total work force was reduced by half from 160,000 to 80,000. White-collar employees were not immune from this process. They saw their numbers

[9]"Lee Iacocca's Production Whiz," *Fortune*, June 22, 1987, pp. 36–44. "The Next Act at Chrysler," *Business Week*, November 3, 1986, pp. 66–72.
[10]Iacocca, *Iacocca*, p. 232.

fall from 40,000 to 21,000 over the same period. At the same time, Chrysler shut down twenty of its oldest plants and modernized the remaining forty to make them among the most efficient in the industry. As a consequence of these plant closures, fixed costs were reduced by $2 billion per year.[11]

Getting such painful concessions out of the work force was not an easy job. However, a number of factors reduced friction to a minimum. First, the UAW representatives knew that they had no choice. It was a case of either concessions or bankruptcy. Second, Iacocca started by cutting his own salary to $1 per year. Third, Doug Fraser, the chief UAW man at Chrysler, was made a member of the board. From this vantage point, Fraser could see just how serious Chrysler's condition was. Fourth, under the terms of the federal loan guarantees, a stock ownership scheme was introduced for the workers. Although this cost Chrysler $40 million a year for the first four years, it made good economic sense, since letting workers share in profits increases employee motivation. Finally, Iacocca spent a good deal of time during 1980 going round the plants explaining to the workers what had to be done and why.

The plants that were not closed down were quickly modernized. To oversee the process, Iacocca again recruited outsiders, including Dick Dauch from Volkswagen, who now heads manufacturing at Chrysler. Automation quickly became a priority. Automation has the twin advantages of economizing on labor costs and increasing quality control. Between 1982 and 1986 the number of robots at Chrysler had increased from 300 to 1,242, with the number expected to reach 2,225 by 1990. However, as Chrysler found out the hard way in the early days of K-car production, merely adding robots does not necessarily improve productivity. The robots also have to work efficiently. Learning from the K-car experience, Dauch insisted that before he took delivery all robots had to run for fifty consecutive hours without breaking down. Surprisingly, 25 percent failed the test. This quickly got suppliers to turn their attention to improving the reliability of their machines.[12]

To get the most out of the new technology, the assembly line itself was also modified. Scrambling between work stations has been eliminated. Instead, the workers remain fixed, and the line brings the cars to the workers. Chrysler also used to divert faulty bodies into repair bays, a process that was both costly and inefficient. Now, except in the most extreme cases, cars must stay on the line for the whole of their two-day, ten-mile trips. The process, called in-line sequencing, forces workers to build cars right the first time and eliminates repair bays.

In-line sequencing also makes possible the implementation of a sophisticated just-in-time inventory system. Under this system, parts are shipped to assembly lines from suppliers at the last possible moment. The Japanese have been using the system for decades. Its advantages are that it dramatically reduces inventory holding costs by increasing inventory turnover. (See Exhibit 3.) As a

[11]"Lee A. Iacocca, "The Rescue and Resuscitation of Chrysler," *Journal of Business Strategy*, Vol. 4, (Summer 1983), 67–69.
[12]"Lee Iacocca's Production Whiz," *Fortune*, pp. 36–44.

EXHIBIT 3   Inventory turnover rates, 1981–1985

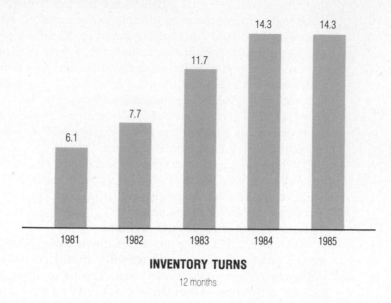

INVENTORY TURNS
12 months

Source: Company annual reports. Reprinted by permission.

result of these systems, Chrysler's inventory turnover increased from 6.1 times per year in 1981 to 14.3 times in 1985. Moreover, improvements are still being registered. In 1986 some 70 percent of the company's parts arrived just in time, compared with 46 percent in 1985.

Chrysler has further reduced costs by decreasing the number of parts used in the assembly process. It accomplished this decrease by relying on interchangeable parts as a central feature of the K-car concept and by limiting the number of options offered per vehicle from about sixty in 1980 to twenty-five in 1986. As a consequence of these changes, Chrysler has managed to cut back the number of different parts used in its manufacturing system from 75,000 to 40,000. At the plant level, this translates into a reduction in the number of parts that must be handled from about 8,000 to 5,000.[13] Reducing the number of parts lessens the complexity of the manufacturing process and lowers the inventory that has to be held. This action alone lowered inventory costs by about $1 billion per year.[14]

Much of Chrysler's cost advantage over its competitors comes from shopping around for cheap sources of components, instead of making the parts itself. Chrysler currently buys about 70 percent of its parts from outsiders, compared with 50 percent at Ford and only 30 percent at General Motors. Although

[13]"The Next Act at Chrysler," *Business Week*, November 3, 1986, pp. 66–72.
[14]Iacocca, "The Rescue," pp. 67–69.

Chrysler bought about the same proportion of parts from outsiders in 1978, the company has become much more aggressive in demanding price reductions from its suppliers since then. In the early days under Iacocca, it was pointed out to the suppliers that unless they cut their prices Chrysler would go out of business. Not willing to lose such a major customer, the suppliers complied. Since the early 1980s the shift to a common-parts strategy has given Chrysler much greater buying power, enabling it to pressure suppliers to keep down costs. For example, in 1987 Greenwald told the company's suppliers to reduce their prices by 2.5 percent. Greenwald also suggested that the suppliers should reduce their production costs by 5 percent—and pass on half the savings to Chrysler. The suppliers have been willing to comply, for they can see that Chrysler is decreasing the number of parts suppliers it deals with. The company cut its parts suppliers from 2,700 in 1985 to 2,424 in 1987 and expects to have only 1,500 by 1991.

Quality Improvements

In 1978 Chrysler was beset by quality problems. Since then quality improvements have been dramatic. Many of the quality improvements have come from the close relations Chrysler has built with its suppliers in recent years. To keep Chrysler's business, suppliers have to meet strict specifications for quality, in addition to cost and delivery. Furthermore, Chrysler has worked together with select suppliers on ways of improving quality. For example, PPG Industries, Inc., Chrysler's paint supplier, worked closely with Chrysler to design and build an elaborate new high tech paint facility at Chrysler's Sterling Heights Plant, which produces high-quality finishes. Chrysler also worked with suppliers to develop body panels made from corrosion-resistant precoated steels. Consequently, Chrysler got to introduce the technology faster. In 1984 Chrysler used the technology in 85 percent of its body panels, compared with 40 percent at General Motors and 30 percent at Ford. The innovation has markedly reduced the rust problem in Chrysler cars.[15]

Further quality improvements have come from the reduction in the number of parts used in the manufacturing process. Assembling two pieces is always easier and more reliable than assembling three. Thus when Chrysler decreased the average number of parts used in an assembly operation from 8,000 to 5,000, it also significantly reduced the chances of poor assembly. As Iacocca himself once observed, "easy to manufacture—that's the key to quality."[16]

Chrysler has also attempted to make quality considerations a part of the consciousness of the workers in the plants. Chrysler has used quality circles to get plant workers much more involved in the manufacturing process. Like just-in-time inventory, the concept of quality circles was borrowed from the Japanese.

[15]"Can Chrysler Keep Rolling Along?" pp. 34–39.
[16]Iacocca, *Iacocca*, p. 175.

The idea behind quality circles is to seek the workers' opinions as to the efficiency of an operation. A process that might look fine on paper from an engineering perspective might not work too well in practice. So workers are encouraged to try new ideas and then report back through the quality circles to give their opinions as to how well an operation works, and how it might be improved. The significance of the concept lies as much in the suggestions received from workers as in the notion that their suggestions are being listened to by management and, when appropriate, acted upon.

Largely as a result of these steps, Chrysler registered an impressive improvement in the quality of its vehicles. For example, between 1982 and 1984 model years, the company claimed to have (1) reduced the number of demerits per car by 35 percent; (2) reduced warranty costs per average car by 25 percent; (3) reduced repairs in the field by 21 percent; and (4) reduced scheduled maintenance costs to a level $20 to $200 below the competition.[17]

Chrysler in 1987

Chrysler in 1987 was a much stronger corporation than Chrysler in 1977, yet it was still a company facing many challenges. Unlike General Motors and Ford, Chrysler was now primarily a domestic enterprise, with 97 percent of earnings being generated from the United States and Canada. General Motors and Ford, respectively, generated 89 percent and 75 percent of their earnings from the United States and Canada. This makes Chrysler more dependent on competitive conditions in North America than its two domestic rivals.

There were signs in early 1987 that the North American market was entering a period of intense competition. With Japanese manufacturers constructing new production plants in the United States, new competition from developing nations such as Korea and Yugoslavia threatening to capture the low-priced end of the market, and total demand projected to grow only slowly until the end of the century, the emergence of both excess capacity and significant price competition was a real possibility. (For details of the environmental conditions likely to face the U.S. industry in the 1990s, see Case 3.)

Market and Financial Position

Chrysler's market position has improved considerably since 1979, when it held only 6.4 percent of the United States passenger car market. Its share of this market increased to 11.3 percent in 1984, before slipping back slightly to 10.3 percent in 1986. Comparable market share figures for the three other main U.S. manufacturers in 1986 were as follows: General Motors, 39.6 percent; Ford, 18.1 percent; and American Motors Corp., 0.6 percent. Imports took

---

[17]Iacocca, "The Rescue and Resuscitation of Chrysler," p. 69.

28.3 percent of the market.[18] Chrysler's market share figures are somewhat higher when truck and cars are combined — reflecting the success of the minivans. In 1985 Chrysler held 12.2 percent of the combined North American car and truck market, before seeing its share decline slightly to 11.5 percent in 1986.

The fall in Chrysler's market share in 1986 was more a reflection of the strong demand in the United States auto market than of any underlying weakness at Chrysler. Indeed, Chrysler's nine assembly plants were running at full capacity during 1986, and the company was negotiating with American Motors to lease some of that organization's excess capacity. In 1986 the company manufactured 1.86 million cars and trucks in the U.S. and Canada, a figure virtually unchanged from the 1.87 million in 1985. (See Exhibit 4.)

Another indication of a company's market strength in the auto industry is its dealer network. Other things being equal (such as quality and location), the more dealers a company has, the more customers it can reach. At the start of 1987 Chrysler had 4,025 U.S. dealers. This compares with General Motors' 9,700 U.S. dealers, Ford's 5,450 U.S. dealers, and American Motors' 1,400 U.S. dealers.

EXHIBIT 4   **Chrysler's production of passenger cars and trucks, 1980–1986**

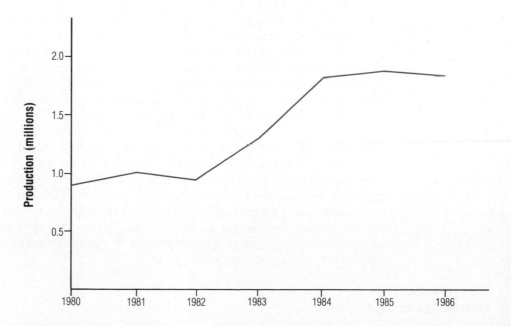

Source: Company annual reports.

[18]The figures are taken from Standard & Poor's Industry Survey, *Autos and Auto-Parts,* April 23, 1987.

Financially, Chrysler has come a long way since the loan guarantee days of 1981. Although 1986 operating earnings of $2.33 billion represented a decline from the record $2.79-billion earnings of 1984, this decline must be seen against the background of a price war initiated by General Motors' introduction of cut-rate financing deals in late 1985 and 1986. Net revenues continued to advance between 1984 and 1986, reaching a record $22.6 billion. Financial statements and summaries are presented in Exhibits 5, 6, and 7.

Investments to Reduce Costs and Increase Quality

Chrysler shows no signs of slowing down its drive to cut costs and increase quality. In 1986 Chrysler embarked on a $12.5-billion, five-year product and capital spending program — about twice what it spent in the previous five years — designed to bring the company in line with Japanese productivity levels. Despite recent advances, the executives at Chrysler recognize that they still have a long way to go. Toyota, for example, made sixty cars per worker per year in 1985, whereas Chrysler made only twenty.

An important component of this investment program is Project Liberty. The objective of this project is to decrease by $2,500 the cost of building small cars made in America by 1991. Project Liberty will rely heavily upon flexible manufacturing technologies to achieve its objective. Flexible manufacturing is designed to reduce hard automation such as welding presses — huge assemblages of welding machines designed to turn out long runs of specific cars — and replace them with reprogrammable robots. It should speed up welding and make model changeovers faster. Increasing use of this technique should raise Chrysler's robot population to around 2,225 by 1990.

A further objective at Chrysler is to continue reducing vehicle defects, primarily through a continuation of the programs begun in 1979. Dauch, manufacturing boss at Chrysler Motors, wants to reduce defects by 56 percent between 1986 and 1991. He notes that removing production defects entirely from the manufacturing process could save Chrysler as much as $4 billion.[19] The aim is to increase quality by sticking to less complex manufacturing operations, reducing still further the number of parts needed in assembly operations, adopting advanced statistical quality control procedures, and continuing to work with suppliers to increase the quality of parts.

Cooperation with Other Manufacturers

Chrysler has two important cooperative ventures under way. First, the company has bought a 15-percent stake in Maserati of Italy, primarily with a view to tapping Maserati's design expertise. The agreement between Chrysler and

---

[19]"Lee Iacocca's Production Whiz," pp. 36–44.

EXHIBIT 5　　Consolidated statement of earnings — Chrysler Corporation and consolidated subsidiaries

	Year ended December 31		
	1986	1985	1984
	(In millions of dollars)		
Net sales	$22,586.3	$21,255.5	$19,572.7
Equity in earnings of unconsolidated subsidiaries	298.6	255.9	126.1
Other income	120.7	41.7	18.4
	23,005.6	21,553.1	19,717.2
Costs, other than items below	18,635.2	17,467.7	15,528.2
Depreciation of plant and equipment	236.8	263.7	271.6
Amortization of special tools	306.8	212.6	282.8
Selling and administrative expenses	1,376.8	1,144.4	987.7
Pension plans	236.3	219.8	267.3
Interest (income) expense — net	32.7	(124.9)	(50.7)
Gain on sale of investment in Peugeot S.A.	(144.3)	—	—
	20,680.3	19,183.3	17,286.9
EARNINGS BEFORE TAXES AND EXTRAORDINARY ITEM	2,325.3	2,369.8	2,430.3
Taxes on income	921.7	734.6	934.2
EARNINGS BEFORE EXTRAORDINARY ITEM	1,403.6	1,635.2	1,496.1
Extraordinary item — effect of utilization of tax loss carryforwards	—	—	883.9
NET EARNINGS	$ 1,403.6	$ 1,635.2	$ 2,380.0
	(In dollars or shares)		
Per share data (restated to reflect stock splits)			
Primary			
Earnings before extraordinary item	$ 6.31	$ 6.25	$ 5.22
Net earnings	6.31	6.25	8.39
Average number of shares of common stock used in primary computation (in thousands)	222,324	261,426	278,643
Common stock dividends declared	$ 0.80	$ 0.44	$ 0.38

Source: Company annual report (1986). Reprinted by permission.

EXHIBIT 6   Consolidated balance sheet—Chrysler Corporation and consolidated subsidiaries

Assets			Liabilities and shareholders' equity		
	December 31			December 31	
	1986	1985		1986	1985
	(In millions of dollars)			(In millions of dollars)	
CURRENT ASSETS			CURRENT LIABILITIES		
Cash and time deposits	$ 285.1	$ 147.6	Accounts payable	$ 2,958.3	$ 2,504.5
Marketable securities—at cost which approximates market	2,394.3	2,649.9	Short-term debt	82.2	195.3
Accounts receivable (less allowance for doubtful accounts: 1986—$19.9 million; 1985—$17.3 million)	372.5	207.5	Payments due within one year on long-term debt	119.8	101.6
			Accrued liabilities and expenses	1,960.7	1,927.8
Inventories	1,699.6	1,862.7	TOTAL CURRENT LIABILITIES	5,121.0	4,729.2
Prepaid pension expense	348.9	260.0	ACCRUED EMPLOYEE BENEFITS	289.6	298.4
Prepaid insurance, taxes and other expenses	263.6	185.8	OTHER NONCURRENT LIABILITIES	661.3	604.5
TOTAL CURRENT ASSETS	5,364.0	5,313.5	DEFERRED TAXES ON INCOME	712.4	391.8
			LONG-TERM DEBT	2,334.1	2,366.1
INVESTMENTS AND OTHER ASSETS			COMMITMENTS	—	—
Investments in associated companies	317.7	283.0			
Investments in and advances to unconsolidated subsidiaries	1,989.6	1,787.4	SHAREHOLDERS' EQUITY (issued and treasury stock restated to reflect stock splits)		
Other noncurrent assets	674.1	581.8	Common stock—$1 per share par value; authorized 300,000,000 shares; issued:		
TOTAL INVESTMENTS AND OTHER ASSETS	2,981.4	2,652.2	229,802,603 shares	229.8	—
			229,842,968 shares	—	153.2
PROPERTY, PLANT, AND EQUIPMENT:			Additional paid-in capital	1,866.6	1,943.2
Land, buildings, machinery, and equipment	7,081.5	5,942.0	Retained earnings	3,567.5	2,153.3
Less accumulated depreciation	2,767.5	2,664.8	Treasury stock—common stock, at cost:		
	4,314.0	3,277.2	13,109,477 shares	(319.1)	—
Unamortized special tools	1,803.8	1,362.4	2,039,661 shares	—	(34.4)
NET PROPERTY, PLANT, AND EQUIPMENT	6,117.8	4,639.6	TOTAL SHAREHOLDERS' EQUITY	5,344.8	4,215.3
TOTAL ASSETS	$14,463.2	$12,605.3	TOTAL LIABILITIES AND SHAREHOLDERS' EQUITY	$14,463.2	$12,605.3

Source: Company annual report (1986). Reprinted by permission.

EXHIBIT 7   **Ten year financial summary—Chrysler Corporation and consolidated subsidiaries**

	1987*	1986*	1985*	1984*	1983*	1982	1981	1980	1979	1978
					(Dollars in millions)					
Operating Data*										
Motor vehicles sold (in thousands of units)	2,260	2,198	2,157	2,034	1,494	1,182	1,283	1,225	1,796	2,212
Net sales	$ 26,277	22,586	21,256	19,573	13,264	10,057	9,972	8,600	11,377	13,049
Interest expense	$ 380	302	180	132	210	295	334	333	275	166
Maintenance and repairs	$ 662	674	540	475	339	229	221	289	314	420
Other taxes	$ 492	455	432	382	281	233	220	230	269	299
Research and development	$ 798	732	609	452	365	307	250	278	358	344
Depreciation	$ 464	237	264	272	183	196	233	261	180	153
Amortization of special tools	$ 412	307	213	283	274	237	218	306	220	198
Taxes on income (credit)	$ 890	908	711	44	2	1	17	29	(15)	(114)
Earnings (loss) from continuing operations	$ 1,290	1,389	1,610	1,489	302	(69)	(555)	(1,772)	(1,153)	(259)
A common share (in dollars)**	$ 5.90	6.25	6.16	5.20	1.04	(0.57)	(3.69)	(11.97)	(8.01)	(1.97)
Net earnings (loss)	$ 1,290	1,389	1,610	2,373	701	170	(476)	(1,710)	(1,097)	(205)
A common share (in dollars)**	$ 5.90	6.25	6.16	8.37	2.57	0.82	(3.19)	(11.55)	(7.63)	(1.57)
Average shares outstanding (in thousands)**	218,612	222,324	261,426	278,643	261,089	172,575	158,175	150,461	147,492	138,779
Common stock dividends declared	$ 219	176	116	105	—	—	—	—	13	52
A share (in dollars)**	$ 1.00	0.80	0.44	0.38	—	—	—	—	0.09	0.38
Net earnings (loss) as a percent of sales	4.9%	6.2%	7.6%	12.1%	5.3%	1.7%	(4.8%)	(19.9%)	(9.6%)	(1.6%)
Expenditures for facilities other than special tools	$ 1,281	1,312	1,043	800	643	147	242	440	407	338
Expenditures for special tools	$ 655	749	492	447	415	227	214	395	342	333
Financial Position—Year End										
Current assets	$ 6,171	5,364	5,314	3,980	2,754	2,369	2,601	2,861	3,121	3,562
Current liabilities	$ 6,638	5,121	4,729	4,116	3,454	2,112	2,419	3,029	3,232	2,486
Working capital	$ (467)	243	585	(136)	(700)	257	182	(168)	(111)	1,076
Current ratio	0.93	1.05	1.12	0.97	0.80	1.12	1.08	0.94	0.97	1.43
Net property, plant and equipment	$ 8,312	6,118	4,640	3,713	3,055	2,474	2,447	2,520	2,349	2,023
Total assets	$ 19,945	14,400	12,556	9,039	6,755	6,264	6,270	6,618	6,653	6,981
Long-term debt	$ 3,333	2,334	2,366	760	1,104	2,189	2,075	2,502	992	1,203
Shareholders' equity	$ 6,503	5,281	4,166	3,282	1,126	(330)	(540)	(104)	1,605	2,710
Shares of common stock outstanding (in thousands)**	220,778	216,043	226,531	273,312	274,077	178,820	164,550	150,690	150,084	143,177
Number of shareholders	193,054	132,422	131,999	151,298	168,527	187,241	212,525	211,587	206,854	209,153

*Restated to reflect retroactive adoption of SFAS No. 91 by CFC (see Note 14).
**Restated to reflect the three-for-two stock splits.
***1981 and prior are restated to exclude certain operating data for the sale and deconsolidation of Chrysler Defense, Inc.

Source: Chrysler Corporation Report to Shareholders 1987, page 35. Reprinted by permission.

Maserati calls for cooperation on design and for Chrysler to import Maserati sports cars into the United States. By 1987 the venture had already borne fruit with Chrysler's TC. Designed by Maserati and built around a K-car platform, the TC is a sporty limited-production convertible, which retails for about $30,000.

The second area of cooperation is with Japan's Mitsubishi International Corporation. Chrysler purchased 15 percent of Mitsubishi back in 1971 and arranged to import some of its small cars into the United States under the Dodge and Chrysler names (one of the most successful was the Dodge Colt). Chrysler increased its holding in Mitsubishi to 24 percent in 1985, agreed to increase the number of Mitsubishi cars and engines it imports, and entered into a joint venture. The joint venture, called Diamond Star Corporation, is scheduled to begin building small cars in Illinois by 1988 and aims to produce up to 180,000 vehicles per year for sale in the United States.

Acquisitions of Auto Companies

In 1986–1987 Chrysler acquired three auto companies. Two of these, Lotus of Great Britain and Lamborghini of Italy, were small-volume, high-performance sports car manufacturers. Chrysler acquired them for their design and high-performance engineering skills. Whereas both of these acquisitions were small, the third was a major one. In early 1987 Chrysler made an agreed takeover bid tentatively valued at $1.5 billion for American Motors Corp. (AMC), the fourth-largest auto manufacturer in the United States.[20]

American Motors had long been the poor man of the United States auto industry. During much of the 1980s the company had struggled to make a profit and to hold onto its small market share. In 1986 its U.S. market share was only 0.7 percent for passenger cars, down from 1.2 percent in 1985 and 2.0 percent in 1984. The one bright spot in the company was the profitable Jeep line. In 1986 the Jeep brand held 12.9 percent of the U.S. market for four-wheel-drive utility and recreational vehicles (unchanged from 1985) and 0.9 percent of the two-wheel-drive light truck market (up from 0.4 percent in 1985).[21] At the time of the acquisition, 46.1 percent of AMC's common stock was held by the French company Renault Inc., and AMC was manufacturing Renault cars for sale in the United States.

The acquisition of AMC has its supporters and its critics. On the positive side, Chrysler gained the popular brand name of the Jeep. Chrysler previously lacked the proven four-wheel-drive technology that Jeep brings. Jeep's 4.5 percent market share in the light truck market also swells Chrysler's penetration in the segment to 17.3 percent (based upon 1986 figures). Another major attraction is AMC's 1,400 U.S. dealers. Iacocca has for a long time wanted another distribution channel, but it would have been both difficult and costly

[20]"Now for Chrysler's Next Trick," *Business Week*, March 23, 1987, pp. 32–33. "AMC Deal Shocks Execs...With Decisiveness," *Ward's Auto World*, April 1987, 34–36, 79.
[21]Standard & Poor's NYSE Stock Report, *American Motors*, June 5, 1987.

for Chrysler to have built additional stores itself. On the manufacturing side, Chrysler acquired four additional assembly plants, including a brand-new plant at Bramalea, Ontario, reportedly the most modern in North America. In 1986 Chrysler was short of capacity and already leasing plant space from AMC, and so the additional capacity may be welcome.

The acquisition also has potential international advantages. AMC has a much publicized Jeep-making joint venture in China, along with manufacturing plants in Egypt and Venezuela. This gives Chrysler its first international operations since 1979. In addition, Chrysler may enter into cooperative agreements with Renault, whose 46.1 percent stake in AMC it has purchased. Chrysler may want to tap Renault as a source of vehicles and components for the United States—a line of cars to go with its domestic brands and Mitsubishi imports. There is also the possibility of Chrysler using Renault's dealer network to distribute its cars through Europe.

On the downside, critics claim that Chrysler may well find itself with too much capacity. The acquisition boosts Chrysler's capacity by one third. With demand softening, imports increasing, and AMC's brands apart from Jeep selling poorly, the risk of excess capacity seems real. In addition, AMC's Kenosha plant in Wisconsin is undeniably antiquated, while its Toledo plant in Ohio is both outdated and known for labor militancy. The critics also note that, although Jeep is profitable, competition in the four-wheel-drive specialty field is fast increasing, with recent entries from Japanese and British companies. Finally, some argue that the AMC dealer network is of questionable value. Many of AMC's dealers have a poor reputation, and there is a fair degree of overlap between AMC and Chrysler dealers.

Diversification

In recent years Chrysler had adopted a strategy of diversifying into industries and businesses that can supplement its existing auto operations. The company has justified these moves as a hedge against the cyclical nature of the world auto industry. The two major growth areas to date have been in aerospace and finance. In 1985 Chrysler acquired Gulfstream Aerospace Corporation for $642 million. Gulfstream has a strong reputation as one of the world's premier manufacturers of corporate jets. At the end of 1985 Gulfstream had a record-breaking order backlog of $1.3 billion for the manufacture of eighty-seven corporate jets. Chrysler hopes to finance the sale of corporate jets through its own financing subsidiary, Chrysler Financial Corporation.

Chrysler Financial Corporation (CFC) has been the focus of Chrysler's second area of diversification. In 1983 CFC had assets of $5 billion and was wholly dedicated to financing car and truck sales. By the end of 1986 CFC had tripled in size and offered a much broader range of commercial and retail financial services. This growth has been fueled by two major acquisitions in 1985, that of E. F. Hutton Credit Corp. for $125 million and a financial service subsidiary from Bank of America for $405 million. These acquisitions have helped make CFC the fourth-largest nonbank financial company in America.

Another diversification plan has yet to get off the ground in any significant way, although Chrysler has already created a subsidiary—Chrysler Technologies Corp.—to oversee its development. Chrysler is reportedly looking primarily for high tech defense companies costing less than $1 billion. By early 1987, however, the search had yet to yield a suitable takeover target.[22]

Organization

Reflecting the new diversity of the corporation, in November 1985 Iacocca announced a reorganization of Chrysler and its major component operations, the creation of a new corporate executive committee, and several new personnel assignments. (See Exhibit 8.) Under this plan, the corporation was reorganized into four separate operating groups: automotive operations, known as Chrysler Motors; Chrysler Financial Corporation; Gulfstream Aerospace Corporation; and Chrysler Technologies. Each became an autonomous unit of Chrysler Corp., with its own management. The members of the executive committee are given in Exhibit 9. As can be seen, they are exclusively ex-Ford.[23]

EXHIBIT 8   **Chrysler's organizational structure, 1985**

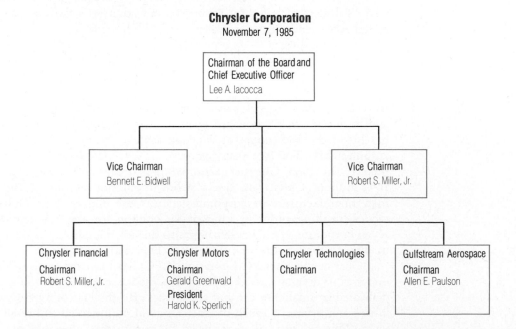

Chrysler Corporation
November 7, 1985

Chairman of the Board and Chief Executive Officer
Lee A. Iacocca

Vice Chairman
Bennett E. Bidwell

Vice Chairman
Robert S. Miller, Jr.

Chrysler Financial
Chairman
Robert S. Miller, Jr.

Chrysler Motors
Chairman
Gerald Greenwald
President
Harold K. Sperlich

Chrysler Technologies
Chairman

Gulfstream Aerospace
Chairman
Allen E. Paulson

[22]"The Next Act at Chrysler," pp. 66–72.
[23]"The Men Who Make Chrysler Work," *Business Week*, November 3, 1986, p. 69.

EXHIBIT 9   **Chrysler executive committee—1986**

Lee Iacocca   Chairman of the board and chief executive officer. Former president of Ford, Iacocca joined Chrysler in 1978 and has been chief architect of the subsequent turnaround. He is sixty-two years old.

Gerald Greenwald   Chairman of the auto subsidiary Chrysler Motors Corp. Greenwald, aged fifty-one, is front runner to succeed Iacocca. He holds the most powerful position in the company after Iacocca. A graduate of Princeton (B.A. in economics), Greenwald made his name as head of Ford's Venezuela operation. He joined Chrysler in 1978.

Robert Lutz   Executive vice president. Lutz, aged fifty-four, joined Chrysler in June 1986 after heading Ford's European operations. Iacocca hired Lutz to oversee the company's top three growth priorities: trucks, international development, and component operations. Lutz was born in Switzerland and maintains dual citizenship.

Bennett Bindwell   Vice chairman of Chrysler Corp. Bindwell, at fifty-nine, has a reputation as Detroit's most intuitive marketing expert. He left Ford in 1981 to run Hertz but willingly returned to the auto industry in 1983 to work for Iacocca. Bindwell is responsible for Washington lobbying, personnel, public affairs, corporate planning, and marketing strategies.

Harold Sperlich   President of auto subsidiary Chrysler Motors Corp. Sperlich, aged fifty-six, is Chrysler's product development expert. He worked closely with Iacocca on the Mustang at Ford before being fired by the erratic Henry Ford II. Sperlich joined Chrysler in 1977 and has overseen the development on the K-car program and the minivan.

Robert Miller   Vice chairman of Chrysler Corp. At forty-four, Miller is the youngest member of Chrysler's top echelon. Educated at Stanford and Harvard, he worked under Greenwald at Ford and was recruited by him to join Chrysler in 1979 as assistant controller. His rise through the corporation since then has been meteoric.

Organizational changes have also been taking place within Chrysler's automotive operations. With a view to establishing a more keenly focused marketing strategy, in 1986 Chrysler realigned its product and marketing staff within Chrysler Motors. Now each staff is divided into four groups, one for each of the company's brands. Their mandate is to develop and market vehicles around key themes for each line: Plymouth for value and integrity, Dodge for performance, Chrysler for luxury and comfort, and Dodge trucks for quality and toughness.

CHRYSLER IN THE FUTURE

Chrysler in 1987 was a company that had completed one of the most impressive turnarounds in American business history. In an ever-changing competitive environment, however, the company needed to make decisions as to its future direction. What part was Chrysler going to play in the U.S. auto industry of the 1990s? Should it aspire to greater market share and challenge the dominance of Ford and General Motors? How should the company respond to the likely increase in competition in the U.S. auto industry during the 1990s? What kind of product mix should the company adopt? How should it deal with the AMC operations it had recently acquired? What stance should it take toward international operations? Should it try to recapture its global position of the 1970s, or should it remain primarily a North American auto manufacturer? It was these issues that Lee Iacocca and his executive committee were having to deal with in the fall of 1987.

COMPAQ COMPUTER CORPORATION: AMERICA'S MOST SUCCESSFUL NEW VENTURE

THE ESTABLISHMENT AND GROWTH OF COMPAQ

The Compaq Portable

In the hot Houston summer of 1981 three Texas Instruments executives, Bill Murto, Jim Harris, and Rod Canion, decided it was time that they struck out on their own. Initially, they had no clear idea of the type of business they wanted to set up. Their first idea — to build plug-in hard disks for IBM personal computers — was vetoed by prospective investors, because too many companies were already competing in that market. A month later Rod Canion and Jim Harris were eating dinner in a Houston restaurant when suddenly they got a better idea: why not build a portable version of IBM's personal computer?

This time around investors were more interested. In January 1982, Canion persuaded Sevin Rosen Management Company, the venture capital company that had financed the premier software company Lotus, to put up $20,000 to develop a prototype. The management team had six months to get a working model ready to show prospective dealers. If the reaction was favorable, Sevin Rosen promised further funding. A five-man engineering team began working

This case was prepared by Charles W. L. Hill, University of Washington.

day and night to complete the design. The prototype was finally finished only hours before its demonstration to dealers.

Initial dealer reaction was strong. Unlike most IBM compatibles at the time, Compaq Corporation's machine could run most IBM PC software straight out of the package. Just as important from the dealers' perspective, IBM was proving unable to meet the huge demand that it had created for the PC following its 1981 introduction. In 1983 IBM produced 600,000 PCs, twice its original plan. Even so, most of IBM's dealers were on allocation. Unless the dealers could find a machine to fill the gap, many of them stood to lose money. Compaq's portable looked as if it would do the job.

On the basis of the favorable dealer reaction, Sevin Rosen raised a further $30 million for Compaq. The company saw a window of opportunity in the personal computer market created by IBM's short-run inability to meet demand. Compaq's original business plan was aggressive. It called for the recruitment of experienced executives from large corporations and the construction of a manufacturing plant capable of producing 5,000 machines per month. The hope was that by reaching high-volume production quickly Compaq would be able to penetrate major retail stores before other PC-compatible manufacturers had a chance.

To handle the finances of the new company, Compaq recruited another former Texas Instruments man, John Gribi. Gribi was appointed chief financial officer and given the task of setting up an accounting system that would be able to cope with Compaq's ambitious growth objectives. To oversee manufacturing, Compaq recruited John Walker. A former senior manufacturing executive at Datapoint Corporation, Walker was given the job of establishing a manufacturing system that could maintain quality control for high volumes of a mass produced output. Another early recruit was H. L. "Sparky" Sparks. A former IBM employee, Sparks had played a leading role in the marketing and service of IBM's personal computer line. At Compaq he was to head the marketing function.

Thanks to the open architecture of IBM's PC, Compaq was able to buy most components of the IBM machine off the shelf, including some of the Microsoft operating system and the Intel 8088 microprocessor chip that was the PC's brain. However, special instructions copyrighted by IBM were built into a microchip to make the operating system run. Compaq's software engineers had to mimic this program without violating the terms of the copyright. A team of fifteen programmers worked for nine months and spent $1 million to get the job done.

After urging by Sparks, Compaq pursued an aggressive dealership strategy that guaranteed high margins for dealers. Compaq planned to price its product so that dealers could gross 38 percent on sales made at the suggested retail price, rather than the 32 percent dealers could gross on sales of IBM's computers. Compaq also planned to sell its machine exclusively through dealers rather than set up its own direct sales force that would skim off business with large corporations.

With extensive dealer support, Compaq's twenty-eight-pound portable computer sold well following its introduction in early 1983. The machine retailed at $2,995, about $400 less than IBM's PC system. In its first year of sales, Compaq sold over 50,000 units and reported sales of $111 million, an all-time record for a new start-up. By comparison, Apple Computer took four years to reach the $100-million mark. IBM responded by introducing a portable of its own in early 1984, but to no avail. IBM's portable actually ran fewer IBM PC programs than Compaq's and was two pounds heavier. By the end of 1984 Compaq was outselling IBM's portable 5 to 1. In mid-1984 the company moved to new manufacturing facilities capable of turning out 10,000 machines a month, while 1984 sales tripled to $325 million.

The Deskpro and the Deskpro 286

Compaq realized that the niche it had created would not be sufficient for future growth. Following the instant success of the portable machine, Compaq set to work to produce a nonportable IBM-compatible machine. The result was the Deskpro—a family of four machines based on Intel Corporation's 8086 microprocessor—which was introduced in mid-1984. The Intel chip used in the Deskpro range was more than twice as fast as the chip used in the Compaq portable and IBM PC. Compaq's research had revealed that many PC programs, such as spread sheets, took a long time to run on the older machines and that users were hungry for more power.

However, toward the end of 1984 IBM introduced the AT personal computer. The AT ran on Intel's 80286 microprocessor, which was significantly faster than the 8086 chip used in the original Deskpros. The AT was in great demand by scientists and engineers, who require quick processing speeds to run complicated programs. The AT was also a multiuser machine that allowed several people to operate remote terminals at the same time. Significantly, though, the AT was incompatible with some of the best-selling software running on the PC and Compaq machines at the time.

Compaq's response to IBM's move was to design an upgrade of the Deskpro range that could utilize Intel's new 80286 microprocessor. Another former Texas Instruments executive, Kevin Ellington, was given the job of developing the new machines. Ellington set up a multi-department team comprising personnel from engineering, manufacturing, marketing, and finance. By working in tandem, the team was able to move the new machines from the drawing board to the market within six months. Thus, while engineers were working out the design of the new computers, manufacturing personnel were already establishing production facilities, marketing personnel were developing a marketing plan, and the finance personnel were busy arranging funding. Regular meetings of the team kept the members informed of each others' requirements and allowed them to keep to a tight time table.

Meanwhile, manufacturing and quality control problems held up production of IBM's AT, allowing Compaq to once again take advantage of a market that IBM had created but was unable to satisfy. To fill this demand Compaq shipped 10,000 units of the new 286 range in the first three months of production, surpassing the company's own expectations.

The Deskpro 386

In 1986 Intel had introduced another microprocessor, the 80386, that promised personal computer speeds far exceeding those of the IBM AT and Compaq's Deskpro 286 range. Rumors abounded that IBM was working on a new line of personal computers, to be introduced in early 1987, that would use the 80386 chip and replace the original IBM PC line. Against this background, on September 9, 1986, Compaq unveiled the Deskpro 386, the first computer based on Intel's 80386 chip. Compaq had beaten IBM to the market by six months in what many characterized as a gutsy bid to seize the technological lead.

The Deskpro 386 quickly emerged as the most powerful personal computer on the market. The machine runs IBM PC software two to three times faster than the IBM AT and can use ten times the internal memory. With this capacity, the machine is capable of handling jobs previously run on minicomputers. For example, the power of the Deskpro 386 makes it possible to perform sophisticated scientific and engineering design tasks on a personal computer. Although at $6,499 and $8,799, the two models of the Deskpro 386 initially retailed for two to three times the price of most personal computers, they were half the price of the smallest minicomputers.

Despite fears that many buyers might wait to see IBM's new systems before purchasing an 80386 machine, early sales of the Deskpro 386 were better than expected. The company sold 75,000 Deskpro 386s in its first full year. More importantly, the 386 established Compaq as the technological leader and opened up the door to many large corporations and new applications. According to Compaq, 40 percent of the Deskpro 386s it has sold are being used for nontraditional PC jobs such as computer-aided design, and 15 percent have stolen work from minicomputers or mainframes.

Compaq Telecommunications Corporation

The one notable failure in Compaq's short history has been Compaq Telecommunications Corporation. After the breakup of the AT&T system in 1984, many believed that products combining phones and personal computers would be at the forefront of the next wave of the microcomputer revolution. Compaq Telecommunications was set up in 1984 to develop a line of such products. In March 1985, the subsidiary introduced six models of the Telecompaq PC/phone, priced between $4,194 and $6,395 — about twice the cost of a regular PC.

Unfortunately for Compaq, the buyers it had in mind — middle-level managers — saw no reason to pay twice the cost of a regular personal computer for a

EXHIBIT 1   **Key financial statistics 1983–1986 and 1987 estimates for Compaq Computer Corporation**

	1983	1984	1985	1986	1987*
		(in millions of dollars)			
Sales	111.2	329.0	503.9	625.2	1065.0
Operating margin	5.4%	7.3%	12.2%	16.1%	20.2%
Depreciation	1.4	4.2	9.3	14.6	18.0
Net profit	2.6	12.9	26.6	42.9	115.0
Working cap	75.0	67.7	140.4	141.0	350.0
Long-term debt	—	—	75.0	72.8	150.0
Net worth	90.7	109.1	136.6	183.3	370.0

*1987 figures are Value Line estimates.

Telecompaq. Electronic mailing and automatic telephone dialing, two of Telecompaq's key features, could be accomplished just as easily with a $500 fax terminal and an inexpensive speed dialer. The Telecompaqs were often hard to hook up because of differences in phone systems. Until new software came along in 1987, they could only send electronic mail to another Telecompaq. And on top of all this, as of 1987 the machines were still using Intel's 8086 microprocessor, rather than the much faster 80286 and 80386 chips found in Compaq's regular personal computers.

ORGANIZATION AND MANAGEMENT

The themes of teamwork and consensus management are central to Compaq's culture. To promote teamwork, the company is divided up into product teams, each of which has its own marketing, manufacturing, engineering, and accounting staff. A team takes a product through from start to finish. The team approach at Compaq is based on the idea that personnel from different functions are able to make important contributions to each other's work. Thus, for example, marketing managers might have valuable insights to give engineers that can then be fed into the design process. At the same time Compaq recognizes the need for coordination among the different product areas of the company. To achieve this, superimposed on the product teams are four main functional groups; marketing, engineering, sales, and manufacturing. By centralizing marketing, for example, the company can make sure a new model does not prematurely kill off any of Compaq's current PCs.

Teamwork is reinforced by an open management style and an emphasis on consensus management that encourages individuals at all levels in the company to express their opinions. The idea is to counteract any tendency for a top down or authoritarian management style to develop within the company. An interesting example of how this works occurred in 1983. At that time Rod Canion was championing the idea of a small lab-top computer. From a technological perspective, such a product might have placed Compaq at the leading edge of the personal computer industry. Despite support for the idea among many senior executives however, a low-level market researcher concluded that there was little demand for a lab-top computer. After this negative assessment of likely demand had been presented a number of times, Canion felt he had little choice but to drop the project. In the event, this seems to have been the correct decision. Lab-top computers subsequently introduced by a number of other companies in 1983–1984 generated little demand.

A further feature of Compaq that is unusual for a new start-up is the experience of its management team. Compaq has made a point of hiring people with big company experience. Each manager in the start-up team already had years of relevant experience with major corporations. Of Compaq's twenty-one officers in 1987, seventeen were Texas Instruments alumni who had as much as twenty-one years of experience. Similarly, programmers had an average of fifteen years' outside experience before joining Compaq. All Compaq's employees also get stock options when they join the company. As Rod Canion once explained: "When we left Texas Instruments we were determined to start a company with people who could work in a Fortune 500 company. We wanted to combine the discipline of a big company with an environment where people felt they could participate in success. We wanted the best of both worlds. And we wanted to do it right."[1]

DISTRIBUTION

By 1987 Compaq had built up a network of dealers that stretched around the globe. With nearly 3,000 stores on their books, Compaq has a larger dealer network than IBM. Unlike IBM and Apple, however, Compaq has no direct sales force and does not compete with its retailers. Many dealers have criticized IBM and Apple for allowing their factory sales teams to compete with authorized dealers. Even though it has been approached by customers wanting to buy directly from the company, Compaq has continued to sell only through authorized dealers. This dedication to retailers has produced a level of dealer loyalty unequaled in the industry.

On the other hand, overdistribution in some areas has led to heavy discounting from list prices and smaller dealer profit margins on Compaq products. Stores are adding lower-priced clones and house brands in hopes of finding

[1]Joel Kotkin, "The Smart Team at Compaq Computer," *INC*, February 1986, p. 50.

greater profit margins. Without a direct sales force of its own, Compaq has nothing to fall back on if its dealers start to defect.

THE MICROCOMPUTER MARKET

The term *microcomputer* covers a wide range of products: inexpensive home computers on which children play games; the personal computers found on office desktops and in students' dormitory rooms; and costly workstations used by engineers and scientists for computer-aided design (CAD) and computer-aided manufacturing (CAM). The common feature of all these machines is the central processing unit or microprocessor.

Market Trends

Since its inception in 1979 with the introduction of Apple Computer's pioneering machine, the microcomputer market has mushroomed into a $74-billion global industry. Microcomputers have become the growth sector of the computer industry, with micros taking on tasks that previously could only be performed on minicomputers or mainframes. In 1986 microcomputers accounted for 31 percent of the dollar value of worldwide computer shipments by U.S. manufacturers, up from only 10 percent in 1981. Between 1981 and 1986 unit shipments of microcomputers by U.S. manufacturers grew at an annual compounded rate of 56 percent. One market research firm, International Data Sciences, Inc., was predicting that unit growth would level off to around 5.7 percent annually during the 1986–1991 period. By the end of 1987, however, this figure seemed unduly conservative, given a 20 percent plus increase in global unit shipments of micros during 1987.

The 1986 market share figures for the major manufacturers of microcomputers are given in Exhibit 2. The notable trend in recent years has been the decline in IBM's share, from 45 percent to 28 percent between 1984 and 1986. Much of this decline has been due to the rise of IBM-compatible PCs produced by Compaq, Zenith Data Systems Corp., Tandy Corporation, and a host of global competitors, from Britain to Korea. The IBM-compatible PCs, or clones, like IBM's PC line, operate under Microsoft's disk operating system (MS-DOS) which has become the standard in the personal computer industry. IBM's share of MS-DOS-compatible PCs fell from 65 percent of global unit shipments in 1985 to 48 percent in 1986.

IBM's PS/2 System

Despite a recent decline in market share, IBM still drives competition in the microcomputer market. The most important market event in 1987 was the

EXHIBIT 2   **Market share of microcomputers by value and unit shipments for 1986**

Company	Value ($)	Units
IBM	27.3%	17.3%
Apple	9.8%	11.4%
Hewlett-Packard	7.6%	2.3%
Commodore	6.8%	29.5%
Tandy	4.6%	8.8%
Zenith	3.6%	1.5%
Compaq	3.2%	1.7%
Atari	2.4%	5.6%
Unisys	2.4%	NA
Digital	1.8%	NA
Texas Instruments	NA	3.3%
Sinclair	NA	2.9%
Others	30.5%	15.6%

Source: Standard & Poor's Industry Survey, *Computers and Office Equipment: Basic Analysis,* October 1, 1987. Reprinted by permission.

launching of IBM's new Personal System 2 range of microcomputers. Since IBM's dramatic entry into the micro market in 1981, the IBM PC computer has set the standards in the micromarket. IBM adopted open architecture for its PC computer, primarily to facilitate the growth of software that could run on the PC. However, this decision also made the PC easy to copy, and a host of clones sprang up. To retain control of the market, IBM realized that its next generation of computers would have to be more difficult to copy.

Introduced in April 1987, the first four models of the new PS/2 system contained more proprietary technology, including the pathways by which data are moved back and forth inside the computer, graphics chips, and a one megabyte random-access memory chip. The new line sports three-and-a-half-inch disk drives, departing from the industry standard of five-and-a-quarter-inch drives. IBM has also erected a thicket of patents and copyrights to try to protect the system from clone makers. It has announced its intention to take legal action against companies that infringe on its copyrights.

The PS/2 system consists of four basic models: the Model 30, Model 50, Model 60, and Model 80. They range in price from $1,695 to $10,995. The Model 30 uses Intel's 8086 microprocessor and is designed to replace the original IBM PC. The Models 50 and 60 use Intel's 80286 microprocessor, originally used in the IBM AT. The Model 80 uses Intel's 80386 microprocessor. IBM has acknowledged that it will be phasing out the entire PC line, including the XT and AT models. The attractions of the PS/2 system include rapid processing, advanced graphics, and an ability to share complex software with IBM mainframes across company-wide networks.

The emergence of the PS/2 system has created considerable confusion among buyers. Should they switch to the PS/2 system or should they continue to buy the old PCs, based on established standards? Getting PC owners to switch to the PS/2 system may not be easy. The PS/2 computers use a different kind of floppy disk from the PCs, making it difficult to transfer programs and files to the new machine. The PS/2 computers cannot use the add-on circuit cards designed for existing PCs. And although the PS/2 computers are more powerful than their predecessors, the OS/2 software that will let them use that power won't exist until mid-1988 at the earliest.

The early indications are that the PS/2 system has met with moderate success. IBM shipped 250,000 PS/2 machines in the second quarter of 1987, and by June 1987 had an order backlog of 500,000. Initial indications are that the most popular machine is the Model 50. It is possible that the Model 50 could become the basic workstation in many offices. It has the advantage of having twice the speed of IBM's old AT models, while a price sticker of $3,845 makes it competitive with the most powerful of the AT clones. However, the Model 30, which replaced IBM's original PC machine, is doing poorly. It offers few of the hardware and software advantages of the Model 50 machines, while a price sticker of $1,945 makes it seem expensive when compared with Far Eastern clones that retail for as little as $1,000. Interestingly enough, the launch of the PS/2 system did not initially affect either PC-compatible vendors or other personal computer players. In the first six months of 1987, Compaq's revenues surged 64 percent, while Apple Computer's revenues were up 41 percent. Demand for Compaq's Deskpro 386 machines and Apple's new Macintosh machines was reportedly at an all-time high.

Despite the proprietary technology built into the PS/2 system and despite IBM's threat to take legal action against companies infringing on its copyright, many observers believe the PS/2 system can be copied. Most clonemakers have stated that they will be able to copy the PS/2 system, although the cloning process is likely to be more expensive and time consuming than was the case with the original PC. Industry observers expect to see the first PS/2 clones appearing toward the middle of 1988.

The OS/2 Operating System

With the exception of the Model 30, IBM PS/2 models have been designed to run on the new OS/2 operating system. This system, developed by Microsoft, takes full advantage of the computing power of Intel's 80286 and 80386 microprocessors; something that MS-DOS does not do. In particular, OS/2 breaks through the 640K memory ceiling of MS-DOS. This will allow microcomputers to run more sophisticated applications than has been the case to date.

New software applications written under OS/2 will run on the PS/2 machines, but they will not be able to execute on the older PC line, with the exception of the AT, which is based on the 80386 microprocessor. Like MS-DOS, the OS/2 operating system is not proprietary to IBM and can run on any micro based on Intel's 80286 and 80386 chips. Microsoft and IBM have been slow in getting OS/2 to the market. The first version of OS/2, Standard Edition 1.0, was issued in December 1987. However, the full potential of the PS/2 machines and OS/2 will not be known until mid-1988 at the earliest, when Extended Edition 1.1 of OS/2 is scheduled for release.

Market Segments

There are four main segments in the microcomputer market: the business market, the home market, the scientific market, and the educational market. The largest of these is the business market, which in 1986 accounted for 64 percent by value of all U.S. computer shipments. The figures for the other segments are as follows: the home market, 14.8 percent; the scientific market, 14.9 percent; and the educational market, 5.8 percent.[2]

Business market   The role of the microcomputer is expanding rapidly in the business market. Introduced originally as a stand-alone productivity tool, the personal computer is evolving into a general-purpose workstation connected to a companywide network on which it can communicate with other PCs, and with mainframes. Currently, about one in seven office workers has a PC on his or her desk. In 1986 IBM claimed about 34 percent of the business market, followed by Apple (10 percent), Tandy (9 percent), Compaq (6.5 percent), AT&T (5.4 percent), and Leading Edge Products (4.2 percent).[3]

Home market   According to *Computer and Software News,* some 16 percent of U.S. homes had computers in March 1987, up from 8 percent in September 1984. The market has been boosted by the emergence of low-cost PC compatibles, such as Tandy's basic system, which sells for under $600. As of March 1987 Commodore Business Machines Inc. held 23 percent of the home market, followed by Apple (21 percent), IBM (16 percent), Tandy (11 percent), and Atari (6 percent).[4] Home computers are used primarily for computer games, educational purposes, and word processing.

Scientific market   The scientific market places the greatest demands on microcomputer power. Until recently, the scientific market has been dominated by technical workstations. These are machines characterized by a thirty-two-bit microprocessor (such as Intel's 80386 microprocessor), the UNIX operating system, greater storage capacity, more sophisticated graphics, more powerful software, and the ability to function in a network. The market for such machines is

[2]Standard & Poor's, *Computers and Office Equipment: Basic Analysis,* Industry Surveys, October 1, 1987.
[3]Ibid.
[4]Ibid.

one of the fastest-growing niches in the overall computer market. Dataquest has predicted that the market will expand from $1.5 billion in 1986 to $4.5 billion in 1990. The leading manufacturers of technical workstations are Apollo Computers Inc., Sun Microsystems Inc., and Hewlett-Packard. Their machines retail at between $5,000 and $42,000.

The launching of 80386 machines by IBM, Compaq, and others poses a threat to the existing manufacturers of technical workstations. Many of the tasks that previously could be carried out only on a workstation can now be run on machines like Compaq's 386 Deskpro. The manufacturers of workstations are responding to this threat by cutting their prices and marketing their computers to major business users such as banks, brokerage houses, and insurance companies.

Education market   Currently, there is about one computer for every thirty public school students. Teachers are pushing for a ratio of one computer for every five students, and so there is room for substantial growth. Link Systems has projected that the kindergarten through high school segment will grow to 3.57 million units in 1991, from 1.63 million units in 1986. Apple dominates this segment with a 58 percent share, followed by Tandy (17 percent), and Commodore International Ltd. (12 percent). The market is software driven and very price competitive.

COMPAQ'S RESPONSE TO THE PS/2 SYSTEM

Immediately after the launching of IBM's PS/2 system in April 1987, Compaq stated that it saw no reason to revamp its models to match the new standards set by IBM. Compaq seems to be positioning itself to take advantage of IBM's discontinuation of the old PC line of computers. In a speech given in mid-1987, Compaq's chairman, Rod Canion, pointed out that customers have sunk more than $80 billion into IBM PCs, PC clones, and the hardware options and software that work with them. Canion's belief is that IBM cannot redirect that movement, at least not quickly. In the meantime, IBM PCs are in short supply because IBM has curtailed shipments in the hope of quickly converting customers to the PS/2 system. It thus created a temporary gap in the market that Compaq is well placed to fill.

In late 1987 Compaq underlined its continuing commitment to the pre-PS/2 industry standard by introducing two new models based on that standard: the Portable III, a lighter and higher-power version of Compaq's original portable, and an updated version of the innovative Deskpro 386. At the same time Compaq is aggressively expanding into overseas markets. The company is building new manufacturing plants in Singapore and Scotland and has plans to increase its overseas revenues from 19 percent to 45 percent by 1990. Most market analysts have reacted favorably to Compaq's strategy. For example, the investment house Goldman Sachs & Company has forecast a jump in sales from

$1.2 billion in 1987 to $1.7 billion in 1988. To reach those numbers, they are predicting that Compaq will sell 160,000 of its Deskpro 386s in 1988—nearly double the 1987 total.

On the other hand, some critics feel that Compaq is setting itself up as a defender of the old standard simply because it does not have its own version of the PS/2 to sell. As one analyst noted, "The strategy is to slam the PS/2 now because Compaq doesn't have one to sell. Meanwhile, they are madly cloning the PS/2 in their labs."[5] Canion, however, insists that the company has no plans to clone the PS/2 unless it becomes a widely accepted standard.

Bibliography

Rod Canion, "Creating a Strong Management Team," Keynote Address by Rod Canion, CEO, Compaq Computer Corporation. Annual Meeting, Houston, Texas, May 15, 1985.

Jo Ellen Davis and Geoff Lewis, "Who's Afraid of IBM?," *Business Week*, June 29, 1987, pp. 68–74.

Jo Ellen Davis, "Will Compaq Be Dethroned as the King of the Compatibles?," *Business Week*, July 28, 1986, p. 67.

Paul Duke, "Compaq's Two New Models Help Lift Stock," *Wall Street Journal*, October 8, 1987, p. 62.

Paul Duke, "Powerful 386 Personal Computers Show Promise, but Software Lags," *Wall Street Journal*, January 19, 1988, p. 20.

Thomas Hayes, "Compaq's Explosive Growth," *The New York Times*, February 22, 1986, p. 31.

Joel Kotkin, "The Smart Team at Compaq Computer," *INC*, February 1986, pp. 48–56.

Geoff Lewis, "The Verdict on IBM's System/2: Clonemakers Are Still in the Game," *Business Week*, May 4, 1987, pp. 118–121.

Peter Lewis, "Whether or When to Buy OS/2," *The New York Times*, December 27, 1987, p. 8.

Brian O'Reilly, "Compaq's Grip on IBM's Slippery Tail," *Fortune*, February 18, 1985, pp. 74–83.

David Sanger, "One Computer Maker Is Hot: Compaq Scores in a Weak Field," *The New York Times*, August 13, 1985, p. 29.

Standard & Poor's, *Computers and Office Equipment: Basic Analysis*, Industry Surveys, October 1, 1987.

[5] Jo Ellen Davis and Geoff Lewis, "Who's Afraid of IBM?" *Business Week*, June 29, 1987, p. 69.

GENICOM
CORPORATION

GENICOM CORPORATION

Curtis W. Powell, President of Genicom Corporation, faced the morning of June 18, 1985, with uncertainty. His upcoming meeting with the labor union at the firm's Waynesboro, Virginia, facility was one that raised some disturbing questions about the company's future, and even its past.

Prior to today's meeting, Genicom had proposed wage and benefit reductions, which resulted in increasing confrontation with union representatives. Mr. Powell pondered what strategic alternatives the company should pursue if the union did not accept the proposed reductions. And even if the union did make the concessions needed, what strategy should Genicom follow in the competitive computer printer market over the next three to five years?

Background

Genicom was founded in June 1983, as a result of a leveraged buyout of General Electric's (GE) Data Communication Products Business Department in Waynesboro, a relatively self-contained entity that produced computer printers and relay components. The department operated as one of GE's strategic business units.

GE came to Waynesboro, a small town in central Virginia, in 1954 as part of a major decentralization effort that also included establishing facilities nearby in Lynchburg and Salem, Virginia. Between 1954 and 1974, the Waynesboro plant produced a wide variety of highly sophisticated electromechanical devices such

This case was prepared by Per V. Jenster, John M. Gwin, and David B. Croll, McIntire School of Commerce, University of Virginia.
This case was originally used in the fifth McIntire Commerce Invitational (MCI V) held at the University of Virginia on February 13–15, 1986. We gratefully acknowledge the General Electric Foundation for support of the MCI and the writing of this case. Copyright 1986.

as process controls, numerical controls, and aircraft controls, many of which are now produced by other GE divisions.

Products once manufactured in the Waynesboro facility accounted for several hundred milion dollars in annual sales revenues for GE. As a result, the Waynesboro factory had a long-standing reputation for its skill in electromechanical design and engineering and for its ability to solve difficult design tasks in its highly vertically integrated facilities.

The first electromechanical printer was created by GE in Waynesboro as a result of the firm's own dissatisfaction with the performance of the Teletype 33 printers. The new GE printer was three times faster than the Teletype 33 and gained quick popularity. In 1969, a send-receive printer was introduced with such success that it evolved into one of GE's fastest-growing product lines. Other products were added using the same technology, and by 1977 the business in Waynesboro had attained annual revenues of $100,000,000 while being very profitable.

In 1980 GE changed corporate leadership. The new GE Chairman, John F. Welch, initiated a major review of the corporation's businesses to determine which ones were critical to GE's future strategies. Businesses with products that did not rank number one or number two in their served industries or did not have the technological leadership to become first or second required special review. The Waynesboro products did not rank number one or number two in their served industry, nor were they critical to GE's long-term strategies, and in 1981 the department's Strategic Planning process investigated the possibility of divestiture as an alternative course of action.

During 1981 the then current General Manager resigned and Curtis Powell, the Financial Manager and long-time GE employee, was appointed the new General Manager.[1]

During the same time frame the printer business' line of reporting was dismantled; the General Manager, the Division Manager and his superior, the Group Vice President, left GE and the Executive Vice President and Sector Executive retired. As a result, there were no administrative levels between the Waynesboro facility and a newly appointed Sector Executive. Mr. Powell received the dual task of (1) positioning the business for divestiture and (2) making it viable if no acceptable buyers could be found. To accomplish these two objectives, Mr. Powell implemented programs to improve the competitiveness of the Department's printer products and productivity programs to reduce the cost of operations. To support aggressive new product design efforts, funding of research and development activities was increased by $1.0MM per year. The first product, the new 3000 Series printer, was introduced in the latter part of 1981. By 1982, the 3000 Series product had received an excellent reception in the marketplace. Variable cost had been reduced by 28%, primarily as a result of

---

[1]In this respect, it is important to understand GE's organizational structure. GE was organized as follows: The chairman, three vice-chairmen, seven industry sectors, numerous groups and divisions, each containing many departments. The Waynesboro factory was a department.

the relocation of 300 jobs from Waynesboro to the Department's Mexican facility, fixed costs had been reduced by 25% and net assets in the business had been reduced by $14.0MM. Despite the successful introduction of the new printer product and rapidly increasing orders, GE was still interested in divesting the business.

After several months of meetings with potential acquirers, GE had not received an acceptable offer. During the fourth quarter of 1982, Mr. Powell and a group of plant managers offered to purchase the Waynesboro-based business from GE.

The Buyout of Genicom

During early 1983, GE agreed to sell the business as a leveraged buyout, but required a substantial cash payment. In order to complete the transaction, the Management team was joined by two New York–based venture capital firms who provided the financial resources needed to purchase the business.

The price agreed upon for the business was net depreciated value plus $8.0MM (note that the business had been in Waynesboro since 1954 and the net depreciated value was significantly less than the appraised value). The purchase price amounted to less than six months' sales revenue.

The assets purchased included every printer ever designed by the Waynesboro facility, all customers and contracts, all patents and cross licenses, tools, and buildings, as well as the Relay business. The purchase agreement was signed October 23, 1983, at which time GE received approximately 75% of the purchase price in cash and subordinated notes for the balance. The purchase amount was financed through sale of shares to the venture capital firms and to local management (approximately 45 of the top managers received stock or stock options). Twelve million dollars were borrowed against fixed assets in the business, and a revolving credit line was secured against equipment leases, receivables, and selected inventory. Given the assessed value of the firm, Genicom had not exceeded 65% of its borrowing capacity.

The Genicom Corporation

By 1983, Genicom was one of the larger independent computer printer companies that manufactured teleprinters (i.e., keyboard send/receive units), dot-matrix printers, and line printers. These printers were primarily industrial grade, and thus were not widely used for personal computer output. They served a wide variety of data processing and telecommunication needs, with printing speeds ranging from 60 cps (characters per second) in the teleprinter version to 400 lpm (lines per minute) in their line printer series. Genicom was also the industry leader in crystal relays sold to defense, space, and other industries where there was a need for highly reliable electrical switches.

Genicom was also a multi-national company with production facilities in Waynesboro (1300 employees) and Mexico (700 employees). Approximately 20% of the 1984 sales revenue of $140.0MM was derived from international customers, primarily Original Equipment Manufacturers (OEM's). Genicom was in the process of establishing its own sales affiliates in the United Kingdom, France, Germany, and Sweden in order to further serve its foreign customers.

Prior to the change in ownership, Genicom's management negotiated a comprehensive benefits package that was essentially the same as GE's. Furthermore, a new agreement with the union was settled, and customers and suppliers were briefed. All but fifteen current employees were offered positions with Genicom at the same salary and similar benefits as provided by GE and all accepted. According to Mr. Powell:

> Everything considered, the buyout went extremely well. 1984 was an excellent year, a very successful year for Genicom. We are still trying to change the culture we inherited from GE, where people feel they have unlimited resources to a small company climate, a climate in which costs must be contained. Some of our people in Waynesboro believe that the success we had in 1984 will continue forever. They don't realize that in our industry product life cycles are short and even if your products are doing well today, you need to prepare for tomorrow. This transition from GE to Genicom has been difficult.

> When we were a part of GE all employees were paid GE wages and salaries. Other firms in our industry and other firms in Waynesboro paid considerably less than GE rates.

As part of the two largest employers in Waynesboro, Genicom's actions when dealing with its employees became public very soon.

> We have a very quality conscious work force in Waynesboro and quality has always been extemely important to us. But in our competitive market quality is not enough, we must be cost competitive also.

Management and Structure

Genicom's management inherited an organizational structure and an information system that reflected GE's standards and procedures. Consequently, Genicom was probably the most vertically integrated printer company in the world (largely encouraged by GE's capital budgeting and performance evaluation system), making almost everything in-house, from tools to printer ribbons to sales brochures. This high degree of vertical integration enabled Genicom to respond quickly to specific requests for redesign of products to suit individual customer needs.

The firm's information system was also aligned with GE's reporting system, which led one outside observer to conclude that he "had never seen an organization with such a sophisticated information system which used it so little." As an illustration, Exhibit 1 shows Genicom's MIS budget *vis-à-vis* industry

EXHIBIT 1   **Comparisons with industry averages**

	Manufacturing (electronics, electrical)			Genicom		
	($1,000)*	% of revenue	% of MIS budget	($1,000)	% of revenue	% of MIS budget
Total revenue	$75,590	100	N/A	$165,000	100	N/A
MIS operating budget	723	1.01	100	2,567.4[1]	1.56	100
Personnel	308	.43	42.5	1,271.0	.77	49.5
Hardware	208	.29	28.4	400.6[2]	.24	15.6
System software	21	.03	3.1	27.5	.02	1.1
Application software	36	.05	4.9	76.5	.05	3.0
Supplies	57	.08	7.8	110.3	.07	4.2
Outside services	36	.05	7.8	559.0	.34	21.8
Communications	21	.03	3.3	19.8	.01	0.8
Other	36	.05	5.0	102.7[3]	.06	4.0

Survey of 642 firms conducted for Datamaton, and published March 15, 1985, shows that firms averaging $200 million in revenue employ an average of 20.1 people in data processing (equivalent to IS&S at Genicom without office services). This provides an index of average revenue of $9,950,200 per data processing employee.

*Represents average amounts reported in source survey.

[1]Genicom's IS&S actual expenses January–May 1985 have been annualized and have been modified to (1) remove office services expenses and to (2) add estimated hardware depreciation expense and estimated occupancy expense in order to correlate to survey figures.

[2]This category includes equipment rental, maintenance, and depreciation expense. Depreciation expense is drawn from Genicom's fixed asset register and includes annual depreciation (book) for all assets acquired through December 1984.

[3]This category includes occupancy expense estimated at 4 percent of total MIS expense budget.

Sources: Infosystems 25th and 26th annual salary surveys, June 1984 and June 1983. Reprinted by permission of Hitchcock Publishing Company.

averages. Exhibit 2 compares Genicom's data processing department with a similar organization in the industry. According to Coopers and Lybrand, a consulting firm retained by Genicom, the cost problem, highlighted in these two exhibits, could also be found in other areas: Finance, Materials, Shop Operations, Manufacturing Engineering, Quality Control, Marketing, Product Engineering, and Relays.

The management team of Genicom (April 1985) consists of the following members:

1. *Curtis W. Powell, President/Chief Executive Officer*
   Mr. Powell graduated from Lynchburg College, Lynchburg, Virginia in 1961 with a BA degree in Business Administration — Economics. Prior to the purchase of the Waynesboro business by Genicom, Mr. Powell had served 22 years in various General Electric assignments; the last two as Department General Manager of the Waynesboro business.

EXHIBIT 2   **Comparison of Genicom and other firm**

Listed below is a personnel information comparison for a data processing department with some similarities to Genicom.

	Genicom	Other firm
Hardware	5 H-P 3000's	4 H-P 3000's
Number of data centers	1 current, 1 planned	2
Annual revenues of organization	$165,000,000 (1985 budget)	$500,000,000 (1985 budget)
Type of business	Manufacturing	Manufacturing
Number of employees in MIS	34 (includes staff at one data center)	44 (includes staff at both data centers)
Salary expense	$1,051,300	$1,075,200 (1984 + 5%)
Processing characteristics	In-house plus heavy use of remote computing service	In-house plus heavy use of remote computing service
Company revenues per MIS employee	$4,852,900	$12,500,000

2. *John V. Harker, Executive Vice President*
   Mr. Harker was responsible for the Sales and Marketing functions, including Product Planning, Market and New Business Development, Marketing Administration, Customer Service, Domestic Sales and International Operations. He formerly held positions as Senior Vice President for Marketing and Corporate Development at Dataproducts, Vice President of Booz, Allen, and Hamilton, Inc., a Management Consulting firm, and with IBM in various Marketing capacities. Upon joining Genicom, he initiated the hiring of six new Marketing and Sales Executives from the computer peripherals industry.

3. *Robert C. Bowen, Vice President & Chief Financial Officer*
   Mr. Bowen has served in various financial capacities with GE since 1964, and with Genicom's predecessor for the past ten years.

4. *W. Douglas Drumheller, Vice President of Manufacturing*
   Mr. Drumheller joined GE's Manufacturing Management Program in 1970 and was appointed Vice President at Genicom in 1983.

5. *Dennie J. Shadrick, Vice President of Engineering*
   Mr. Shadrick recently joined Genicom after seventeen years with Texas Instruments, where he served in a variety of Engineering and Management positions in the terminal and printer business unit.

6. *Charles A. Ford, Vice President of Relay Operations*
    Mr. Ford has had a long career with GE and Genicom serving in the areas of Manufacturing, Engineering, and General Management.

7. *Robert B. Chapman, Treasurer*
    Mr. Chapman has been with Genicom since 1984, after holding positions with Centronics Data Computer Corporation, Honeywell, Inc., and the Datapoint Corporation, where he was Assistant Treasurer.

> Part of our GE heritage was a strong Engineering and Manufacturing orientation and this is a valuable asset. However, as a new and independent company, we needed to establish a Marketing presence, we needed a new and aggressive approach to our Marketing and Sales Activities. One of our first action items was to recruit the best Marketing and Sales executives we could locate. Genicom's strategy for developing marketing strengths has been to bring experienced and capable people from other firms in the computer peripherals industry.

Financial Statements

The 1984 financial statements and footnotes are included in Exhibits 3–6. Due to the time period constraints associated with any financial statements, Genicom's balance sheet for December 30, 1984, did not include the subsequent private placement of stock that took place on January 3, 1985. Genicom sold 353,000 shares of its unissued common stock for $5 per share. If these shares had been issued at December 30, 1984, unaudited *pro forma* stockholders' equity would have been $16,993,000.

The two period comparisons used in the financials entitled "December 30, 1984" and "January 1, 1984" are not true comparisons since the time periods covered are not equal. The first column for the year ending December 30, 1984, represents a 12-month period, but the second column for the year ending January 1, 1984, represents only a two-month, ten-day period.

The remaining statements and ten footnotes are complete and self-explanatory. The strong financial orientation of the management is evident in the statement presentation.

Cost Accounting

A major cost accounting issue was that Genicom's product costs were well above those of their competitors. Genicom's willingness to customize their products to meet their customers' individual needs allowed them to charge a premium price. The costs that seemed disproportionately high were salary and hourly wages. Genicom's salary and wage structures were established over many years while it was a part of GE. General Electric traditionally provided its employees with both a generous base salary and a generous fringe package. As wages and benefits were negotiated with the union on an overall corporate basis, the printer department had avoided serious conflicts with the union.

EXHIBIT 3   **GENICOM Corporation and subsidiaries—consolidated balance sheet**

	December 30, 1984	January 1, 1984
	(amount in thousands)	
ASSETS		
Current assets		
Cash	$ 451	$ 3,023
Accounts receivable, less allowance for doubtful accounts of $958 and $483	21,224	22,459
Inventories	26,917	24,343
Prepaid expenses and other assets	1,368	356
Total current assets	**49,960**	**50,181**
Property plant, and equipment	27,821	27,314
Other assets	239	180
Total assets	**$78,020**	**$77,675**
LIABILITIES AND CAPITAL		
Current liabilities		
Current portion of long-term debt	1,600	11,841
Accounts payable and accrued expenses	16,104	15,682
Deferred income	1,519	1,359
Income taxes	5,579	
Total current liabilities	**$24,802**	**$28,882**
Long-term debt, less current portion	36,400	44,500
Deferred income taxes	1,590	504
Redeemable preferred stock, $1 par value; 32,000 shares issued and outstanding at January 1, 1984; stated at liquidation value of $100/share		3,200
Stockholders' equity		
Common stock, $.01 par value; 20,000,000 shares authorized; shares outstanding: 12/30/84 — 10,995,500 1/1/84 — 8,575,000	110	86
Additional paid-in capital	9,297	772
Retained earnings (deficit)	5,821	(269)
	15,228	589
Total liabilities and capital	**$78,020**	**$77,675**

EXHIBIT 4   **Genicom Corporation and subsidiaries — consolidated statement of income**

	Year ended December 30, 1984	October 21, 1983, to January 1, 1984
	(amount in thousands)	
Net sales	$136,661	$26,752
Cost of goods sold	90,647	20,403
Gross profit	**$ 46,014**	**$ 6,349**
Expenses		
Selling, general & administration	22,442	3,965
Engineering, research and product development	4,795	890
Interest	6,900	1,386
Total expenses	**$ 34,137**	**$ 6,241**
Income before income taxes	11,877	108
Income tax expense	5,787	377
Net income (loss)	$ 6,090	$ (269)
Net income (loss) per common share and common share equivalent		
Primary	$ .61	$ (.03)
Fully diluted	$ .59	$ (.03)
Weighted average number of common shares and common share equivalents		
Primary	$ 9,967	$ 8,753
Fully diluted	$ 10,292	$ 8,892

Consultants from Coopers and Lybrand were hired by Genicom to evaluate the firm's cost structure. Although the study was not completed, preliminary research had focused on this labor cost problem. The preliminary findings suggested that most areas of the firm seemed overstaffed and salary and wage levels exceeded both industry norms and local community standards (e.g., see Exhibits 1 & 2).

An interesting point was that Genicom's wage and salary differential over other local companies was so great that it proved detrimental to some laid-off employees. Other companies in the region had reported that they were hesitant to hire a laid-off Genicom employee knowing that, as soon as an opening existed, the employee would be lost back to Genicom.

EXHIBIT 5   Genicom Corporation and subsidiaries — consolidated statement of changes in capital accounts

For the year ended 12/30/84 and the period from 10/21/83 (commencement of operations) to 1/1/84

	Redeemable preferred stock	Common stock	Additional paid-in capital	Retained earnings
		(dollar amounts in thousands)		
Issued in connection with acquisition:				
32,000 shares of redeemable preferred stock	$ 3,200			
8,000,000 shares of common stock		$ 80	$ 721	
Issuance of 525,000 shares of common stock		5	47	
Exercise of stock options		1	4	
Net loss				$ (269)
Balance, January 1, 1984	**3,200**	**86**	**772**	**(269)**
Issuance of 1,297,000 shares of common stock		13	5,288	
Redemption of preferred stock	(3,200)	6	3,194	
Exercise of stock options		5	43	
Net income				$6,090
Balance, December 30, 1984		**$110**	**$9,297**	**$5,821**

Union Negotiations

Negotiations with Local 124 of the United Electrical Radio and Machine Workers (UE) of America started on April 23, 1985. Management's primary goal was to reduce the average costs of an applied direct labor hour by four dollars. Included in the employee benefit package were vacation (five weeks maximum), holidays (ten days), comprehensive medical benefits, life insurance, temporary disability, overtime premium, pension, breaks, night-shift bonus, paid sick days/personal time, and job structures which included seventeen pay grades. Appendices 1–5 provide a picture of the negotiations as the confrontation grew.

Earlier in April, a different local of UE in a nearby Virginia town had been involved in an almost identical situation. A former department of Westinghouse which had been sold to outside interests, confronted with wage and benefit structures originally negotiated at the national level, attempted to win major financial concessions from its work force in order to become cost competitive in its market. The local refused to accept any cutbacks in its package and, after

EXHIBIT 6   **Genicom Corporation and subsidiaries — consolidated statement of changes in financial position**

	Year ended December 30, 1984	10/21/83 to 1/1/84
	(amounts in thousands)	
Sources of working capital		
From operations:		
Net income (loss)	$ 6,090	$ (269)
Charges to income not affecting working capital:		
Depreciation	4,664	630
Amortization	49	
Deferred income taxes	1,086	504
Working capital from operations	11,889	865
Issued or assumed in connection with acquisition:		
Redeemable preferred stock		3,200
Common stock		801
Long-term debt		57,841
Proceeds from issuance of common stock	8,501	52
Exercise of options	48	5
Other, net	357	(189)
Total sources	**$20,795**	**$62,575**
Applications of working capital		
Additions to property, plant, and equipment	5,636	918
Noncurrent assets purchased in acquisition		27,017
Reduction of long-term debt	8,100	13,341
Redemption of preferred stock	3,200	
Total applications	**$16,936**	**$41,276**
Analysis of working capital components		
Increase (decrease) in current assets:		
Cash	(2,572)	3,023
Accounts receivable	(1,235)	22,459
Inventories	2,574	24,343
Prepaid expenses and other assets	1,012	356
Totals	**$ 221**	**$ 50,181**

EXHIBIT 6   Genicom Corporation and subsidiaries—consolidated statement of changes in financial position (*cont.*)

	Year ended December 30, 1984	10/21/83 to 1/1/84
	(amounts in thousands)	
Increase (decrease) in current liabilities:		
Current portion of long-term debt	(10,241)	11,841
Accounts payable and accrued expenses	422	15,682
Deferred income	160	1,359
Income taxes	5,579	
Totals	**$ (4,080)**	**$ 28,882**
Increase in working capital	3,859	21,299
Working capital, beginning of period	21,299	
Working capital, end of period	**$ 25,158**	**$ 21,299**

several months of negotiation, went on strike. Two days later the company announced it would begin hiring permanent replacements for the striking workers on the following Monday and placed help wanted ads in the local newspapers. On Sunday afternoon, in a close vote, the union members voted to end the strike and accept management's proposals.

The Printer Industry

The demand for printer hardware is derived from the demand for computing machinery. As the demand for computing capability shifted from mainframe computers to minicomputers to microcomputers, so did the demand for printing capacity shift from output capability to output quality. Similarly, the attributes of printers that determined their success in the marketplace changed from reliability and performance when dealing with mainframe applications to price and capability when dealing with microcomputer applications. At the same time, as business applications of microcomputers moved into networking situations, where a number of microcomputers are linked to a central database and a single printer, the demands placed on the printer hardware changed from the demands of a stand-alone microcomputer.

In addition to the changes that took place in the printer industry as a result of changes in the computer industry, there was change in the competitive structure of the marketplace. The presence of the Japanese manufacturers had altered the competitive nature of the industry. As had been the strategy in other industries, Japanese manufacturers entered the market at the bottom of the price structure. Because of lower labor rates and efficient production capability, the Japanese products forced extreme price pressure into the market. Once established, the Japanese manufacturers then began to "trade up" through product improvement and brand extension. As a result, the Japanese printer manufacturers became a formidable force in the marketplace, particularly in the micro-printer (for personal computer use) segment. This set of competitors was a force all U.S. manufacturers of printers must have accounted for in the formulation of new product introductions and pricing strategies. A number of U.S. manufacturers had licensed "off-shore" (Mexican, Korean, Taiwanese, and Japanese) manufacturers to produce price competitive products under the U.S. manufacturer brand names as a means of competing with the Japanese manufacturers.

The Market

The total market for printers of all types was predicted to be $10.44 billion in 1986. The breakdown of sales by printer type is shown in Exhibit 7. The market was segmented by impact (printers that use a printhead that actually strikes the paper) and non-impact (printers that do not strike the paper, but apply ink in

EXHIBIT 7   **The U.S. printer market**

	1983				1986			
	units	(% share)	$ value	(% share)	units	(% share)	$ value	(% share)
Serial daisy wheel	712,000	25	1.37 billion	25	2,000,000	24	2.4 billion	23
Serial dot matrix	1,857,000	66	2.28 billion	41	4,600,000	54	4.14 billion	40
Serial* nonimpact	132,000	5	162 million	3	1,600,000	19	990 million	9
Nonimpact** page printers	5,200	0	222 million	4	150,000	2	1 billion	10
Fully formed line printers	86,000	3	1.13 billion	21	100,000	1	1.4 billion	13
Dot matrix line printers	31,000	1	318 million	6	55,000	0	510 million	5
Totals:	**2,823,000**		**5,482 billion**		**8,505,000**		**10.44 billion**	

*Inkjet and thermal transfer printers
**Laser and similar printers

Source: Reprinted by permission of Datek Information Services, Waltham, MA.

some other fashion). Within the impact market, printers were also segmented by dot matrix (printers that use dots to form the characters printed) and fully formed (printers that print an entire character at once, such as a "daisy wheel" printer). This market was further segmented according to whether a printer was a serial printer (one that prints character by character in a serial fashion) or a line printer (one that prints an entire line at a time—in general, line printers are called "high speed" and print faster than serial printers, but often at a lower quality); finally, the impact market segment was subdivided according to speed of printing. The non-impact segment was divided further according to printer technology (electrostatic, ink jet, laser), and by speed (in characters per second). Certain non-impact printers were also segmented as page printers (those that print a complete page at a time). All non-impact printers were considered to have fully formed characters. A schematic representation of the complete market for printers is shown in Exhibit 8.

Besides print quality, different classes of printers had advantages and disadvantages for end users. Fully formed character printers, whether daisy wheel or band line, offered no graphics capability since they were limited to alphanumeric characters. These printers also were very noisy while printing unless special quietized enclosures were used to surround them. Additionally, daisy wheel printers, which were found almost exclusively in offices for word processing applications, were extremely slow.

The primary drawback to dot matrix printers was perceived print quality, although a number of technological developments had improved their performance. These printers, however, supplied excellent adaptability to applications needs—graphics, spreadsheets, data and word processing, for instance—and prices had been dropping very rapidly in this market segment.

Non-impact printers offered much of the best aspects of performance—quiet operation, flexible application, and outstanding print quality—but drawbacks included high prices, inability to print multiple copies simultaneously (i.e., continuous multipart forms printing), higher cost of operation because of their utilization of consumable supplies such as toner, and some perception of the part of users that non-impact printers, like the copiers their technology was derived from, were less reliable.

As advances in technology decreased the cost of non-impact printers, the growth of sales in these segments was expected to increase. The prices of non-impact printers were still high relative to impact offerings, and the impact printers still enjoyed a speed advantage. However, the non-impact printers were much quieter than their impact counterparts, and the quality of their output was at least as high as the best fully formed impact output. Exhibit 9 shows the characteristics of printer types, as compared against the "ideal" printer.

Genicom Product Line

By April of 1985, Genicom primarily produced dot matrix impact printers, though $6,000,000 in 1984 revenue was derived from a 300 lpm fully formed

EXHIBIT 8   **Electronic printer market breakdown**

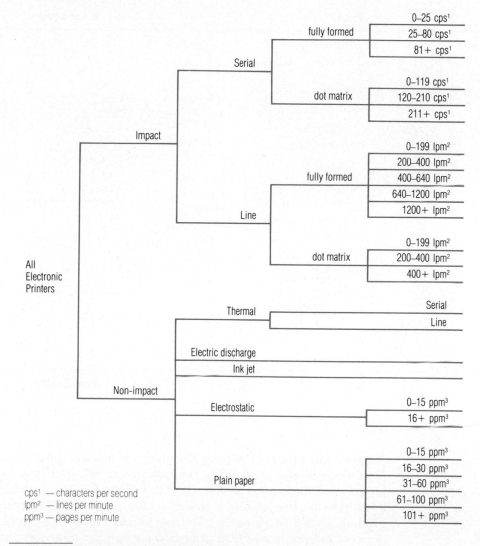

cps[1] — characters per second
lpm[2] — lines per minute
ppm[3] — pages per minute

Source: Used by permission of Dataquest, Inc., San José, CA.

EXHIBIT 9   **Personal computer printer trends: characteristics by technology**

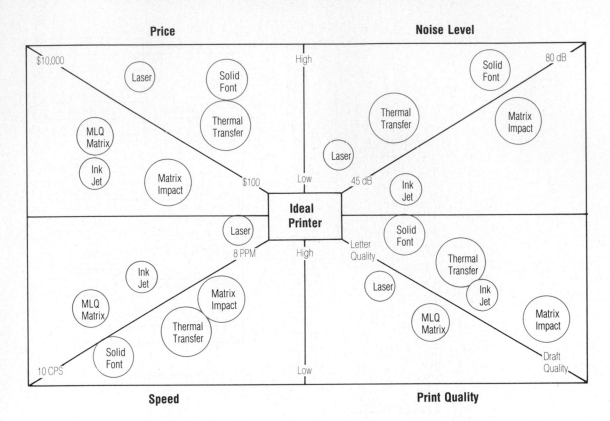

Source: Used by permission of Future Computing/Datapro, Dallas, TX.

character line printer. The company produced line and serial printers that could print from 60 cps in an office environment to 600 lpm in a high speed line printer used for volume production. Most of the Genicom product line also offered letter-quality printing at slower speeds, so the machines were flexible, depending on the user's needs. Genicom offered branded printers as peripheral devices, and produced OEM printers for a number of major customers. Genicom's products generally were more expensive than those of their major competitors, but had higher performance capabilities and greater durability. Genicom sales by product for 1984 are shown in Exhibit 10.

Genicom Competitors

Genicom had a number of major competitors in each of the market segments it served. Its two major U.S. competitors were Centronics and Dataproducts, both competing essentially head on with Genicom in almost every market seg-

EXHIBIT 10   **Genicom sales—1984**

Printers	Dollar amount (in thousands)	Units
340/510	5,980	1,749
200	8,564	4,016
2030	6,131 ⎱	
2120	5,011 ⎰	9,623
3000	30,924	20,495
3014/3024	3,879	5,036
4000	—	—
Other	399	—
Subtotal	60,888	31,296
Parts	16,962	
Ribbons	7,846	
Lease	18,140	
Service	9,380	
Printer Business Total	113,216	
Relays	23,426	
Company Total	**$136,642**	

ment. There were other, smaller competitors for special applications and certain of Genicom's market segments. Exhibit 11 offers market share estimates for major competitors in each major segment.

End User

The end user for Genicom products was faced with a complex decision process in the choice of a printer. The current products operated faster, printed more legibly, and cost less than those of a few years ago. However, there were more machines to choose from, so the choice needed to be carefully made.

GENICOM MARKETING STRATEGY

Genicom's general marketing strategy had been one of improving current products and expanding product lines rather than developing entirely new products or diversifying into new technologies. The strategy could have been characterized as "evolutionary" rather than "revolutionary." Gencicom's main distinctive

EXHIBIT 11   **Market share (units), U.S. serial impact printer market—1984**

Country of manufacture	Manufacturer	% Share	Fully formed	Dot matrix
Japan	Epson	20.1		X
	C. Itoh (TBC)	13.9	X	X
	Okidata	11.4		X
	Star	3.2		X
	NEC	2.4	X	X
	Brother	2.0	X	X
	Ricoh	2.0	X	
	Toshiba	1.1		X
	Canon	0.9		X
	Juki	0.9	X	
	Fujitsu	0.6	X	X
	Subtotal	**58.5**		
United States	Xerox	3.2	X	
	IBM	3.0	X	
	Texas Instruments	2.2		X
	DEC	2.2		X
	Teletype	2.0		X
	Qume	2.0	X	
	Centronics	1.6		X
	Genicom	1.1		X
	Anadex	0.6		X
	Datasouth	0.4		X
	Dataproducts	1.6	X	X
	Subtotal	**19.9**		
Europe	Mannesmann	0.9		X
	Facit	0.5	X	X
	Philips	0.3		X
	Hermes	0.2		X
	Subtotal	**1.9**		
Other		**19.7**		

competencies in the market had been flexibility in production and the quality of its products. They had traditionally been on the upper end of price points for similar products and had sought to gain market share by stressing the advantages their machines offered relative to the competition. Each of Genicom's products offered some distinct advantage—speed, print quality, quietness, or flexibility—which was thought to offset price disadvantages.

Genicom had an important presence in the OEM market, offering those customers a wide variety of choices regarding specifications for products. The Genicom presence in the branded printer market was not so strong, though efforts were underway to increase the importance of that market.

EXHIBIT 11   Market share (units), U.S. serial impact printer market — 1984 (*cont.*)

Country of manufacture	Manufacturer	% Share	Page	Thermal	Ink jet
Japan	Canon	17.3	X		X
	Okidata	17.0		X	X
	Star	12.8		X	
	Sharp	8.5		X	X
	Brother	4.5		X	
	Subtotal	**60.1**			
United States	IBM	8.0	X	X	X
	Hewlett-Packard	4.5		X	X
	Xerox	3.6	X	X	X
	Texas Instruments	2.5		X	
	Subtotal	**18.6**			
Europe	Simmons	3.5	X		X
	Honeywell	1.0	X		
	Subtotal	**4.5**			
Other		**16.8**			

Country of manufacture	Manufacturer	% Share	Fully formed	Dot matrix
United States	Dataproducts	31.0	X	
	IBM	23.0	X	X
	Teletype	8.0	X	
	Centronics	7.0	X	
	Hewlett-Packard	6.0		X
	Printronix	6.0	X	X
	Genicom	1.5	X	
	Subtotal	**82.5**		
Japan	NEC	4.1	X	
	Fujitsu	1.6	X	
	Hitachi	0.7	X	X
	Subtotal	**6.4**		
Europe	Mannesmann	2.1	X	
Other		**8.0**		

The product positioning of the Genicom line had been for the professional user. Both for data processing and for word processing, the strength of Genicom's product line had been in the commercial rather than the personal segments. The current product line was more durable, had more capability, and was more expensive than the bulk of the personal printer market. The Genicom products could be compared to IBM office typewriters; they were generally considered "over-engineered" for the home market. Genicom was giving some consideration to the personal printer market, to compete with Epson, Okidata, Toshiba, and others. It recognized that among other factors a new product line, rather than modification of an existing product, would be necessary to compete in this highly price-competitive market.

Distribution

In early 1985, Genicom products were distributed through a distributor network that focused on industrial users and on wholesale/retail distributors who serviced end user needs. Consideration was given to entering retail distributorship relations with large companies or with independently owned and franchised chains.

The Genicom distribution system was not vertically integrated at that time. Although Genicom had been contemplating expanding the distributor network slightly to effect better geographic coverage of markets, other plans suggested

EXHIBIT 12   **Domestic multi-tier distribution channels**

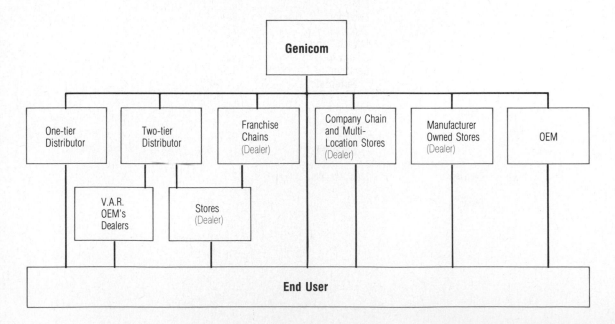

that they develop recognition of authorized dealers through the current distributor network. A schematic representation of the Genicom distribution system is presented in Exhibit 12.

While prices and margins for dot matrix impact printers had been dropping as market pressures grew, the future could be said to be nothing but certain. Curtis Powell considered the union negotiations a critical turning point in the firm's history.

Appendix 1   **The United Effort (a union newsletter)**

Negotiations Report

On Tuesday afternoon the negotiating committee met with Relations and a lawyer to start contract talks. Right away, without putting paperwork on the table, this lawyer wanted us to tell him ways management can cut *four dollars an hour* off the cost of labor. According to him, the cost per hour, including wages and benefits, is fourteen dollars an hour and this is "significantly higher" than other workers are making in Waynesboro and must drop to ten dollars total of wages and benefits. He was even so helpful as to offer selections, like a smorgasbord, if you will, of items from which *we* could decide where to make the cuts.

For our consideration he laid out: rate cuts, night shift differential pay, vacation time cuts and other paid time off, give up bump rights, retraining, premium pay for some overtime, call in pay, medical benefits and the list goes on. All he wants *us* to do is decide where to cut to come up with a four dollar price cut. He pointed out that the wages in the lower job rates are much too high and will have to be cut to make us more comparable with other wage earners in Waynesboro.

Based on the claim that Genicom needs for us to cough up four dollars worth of wages and benefits, we naturally figured the company was going broke, so we asked a question about the financial condition of the business. The reply was contrary to what you might suspect based on them wanting cost cuts. It turns out that the company is *making* money but wants to make *more* money and in order to do that they want to get into our pocket.

Just as we figured, when the word got out in the plant, you became furious to think that the company would be so greedy as to come after the wages and benefits you have worked years for and some of you even walked a picket line for a hundred and two days in 1969 to get. There is a growing demand from the union membership to hold work stoppages to protest these unrealistic demands by management and it appears the time will come for that kind of action! The next meeting with management is scheduled for May 6th and Boris "Red"

Block will be here for that meeting. We will have a full membership meeting the next day, Tuesday, May 7th, to let you know what is going on and how negotiations are progressing. At that time we will be *led by the membership* about what action you want to take.

After we listened to what management had to say about their thoughts we laid out our proposals and informed them that the list was only a partial list of what we think is needed in a new contract. Some of what we are looking at includes strong job security language, improvement in pensions, and downward adjustments in our contributions to the pension plan, a better severance pay clause, insurance coverage to be nothing less than we now have, improvements in S&A benefits, cost of living clause, contract language improvements, and a general wage increase. And, as we pointed out, there are other things we are looking at which we will lay on the table later. What happens in negotiations and what we are able to do is directly dependent on you and how much support you are willing to give.

It's your Local and "The Members Run This Union!"

Appendix 2   The United Effort (a union newsletter)

The Members Decide

At the end of the second session of negotiations, management still insists on demanding a $4.00 an hour wage and benefit concession from you. They set the record straight so there would be no mistake in anyone's mind we were told "we are taking it." We asked time and time again what they would do with the $4.00 if they can take it and we were told rather matter of factly, "we are going to put it in our pockets." It's not that Genicom didn't make a profit last year, it's just plain and simple they just want to add an additional $3,200 an hour to their pockets (300 employees × $4.00 per hr. = $3,200.00 an hour) at your expense.

At a full house special membership meeting, 1st and 2nd shift, the committee was instructed to take a secret ballot strike vote. We normally keep the meetings to one hour but due to the number of members who wanted to speak, the meeting lasted well over the normal length of time and then a vote was taken, which was in favor of a strike action. As we have said before, this local doesn't have a history of strike action but the workers at Genicom feel they have no choice but to fight on the issues of wages and working conditions in this plant. Management some time ago decided to cut the rate of the mold machine operators from R13 to R9 and it seems this only whet their appetite to want to take even more. We filed a grievance and processed it through the required steps of

Source: Content of Appendix 2 reprinted by permission of The United Effort, Waynesboro, VA.

the grievance procedure and we will be taking action on that grievance at the proper time of which you will be notified.

We don't need to tell you how important it is for everyone to support the strike action. The issue is over a rate cut on one job but remember the bigger issue is now management is saying they are going to cut $4.00 off of everyone in wages and benefits. Whether they can get away with it or not depends on you and everyone in the plant. The stakes are high and it's up to you to decide. Do you just fork over the $4.00 in wages and benefits or do you join your fellow workers and fight?

Shop Steward Election

There will be a meeting at Jim Durcin's desk today, five minutes before the end of lunch break, to nominate and elect a shop steward.

Appendix 3   **Genicom Printer Flash (a local press clipping)**

Date: May 31, 1985   No. 85–6

TO ALL EMPLOYEES:
In response to the excessive amount of publicity in the local press concerning Genicom's negotiations with the UE Local 124, the following advertisement will appear in tomorrow's Waynesboro News-Virginian and Sunday's Staunton News Leader. We felt you, as Genicom employees, should be the first to have this information.

What's Really Happening at Genicom

Genicom and its negotiations with Local 124 have been the subject of much discussion in our community and among Genicom employees in recent weeks. All the information to this point has come from the Union. Since so much is at stake for Genicom, its employees, and our community, we believe management should do its best to assure that the people who may be affected understand what is happening and why.

Genicom is a Waynesboro company that is dedicated to remaining a Waynesboro company. That dedication is reflected in Genicom's proposals to UE Local 124 to establish a wage and benefit program that will allow Genicom to meet competition while providing Genicom workers with wages and benefits in line with community standards.

As part of the negotiations process, Genicom provided wage survey data to Local 124 on both Genicom's national competition and its Waynesboro neighbors. Reflecting that data, Genicom's proposal includes job rates from $6.50 to

$12.00 per hour, three weeks paid vacation, eight holidays, medical and dental insurance at a cost of $4 per week to employees, a defined benefit pension plan with limited contributions by employees, as well as company paid life and disability programs.

Starting in 1954, and for nearly 30 years, General Electric Company conducted manufacturing operations at the current Genicom facility in Waynesboro. Under General Electric, wages were negotiated on a national basis. As a result, Waynesboro wage and salary costs reached levels which are out of line with the electronics industry and with the Waynesboro community. Genicom Corporation was formed to operate the business purchased from G.E. Genicom is now managed by people who are committed to establishing and maintaining a successful and profitable business—because it is our only business. In the 19 months since Genicom acquired its business, it has been operated on a profitable basis. This was particularly true in 1984, when the market for computers and related equipment was robust. The Business is less profitable now that its market has become much softer and competition for sales of electronic products such as Genicom's has become very intense. Genicom management is determined and committed to reducing costs and competing.

These costs reductions can be accomplished either by moving operations to Genicom's existing lower cost locations or by lowering costs in Waynesboro. Genicom has decided to stay in Waynesboro. The wage and benefit concessions requested will make Waynesboro a competitive manufacturing location—a manufacturing location with a future. These concessions will not be easy or insignificant for Genicom workers to accept, but they are not unreasonable. Competitive wages will make operations in Waynesboro much more economically attractive for Genicom and increase Genicom's incentive to maintain and expand those operations, thus offering more job security to Waynesboro workers and greater stability to the Waynesboro community.

C. W. Powell
President and Chief Executive Officer
Genicom Corporation

Appendix 4   **The United Effort (a union newsletter)**

Genicom Should Tell It Like It Is, Instead of Wanting to Pocket 6½ Million Dollars of Its Employees And the Community

That's what Genicom wants in concessions from the hourly workers. Genicom said that's not all. They are going to get a like amount from the lower paid salary workers and supervisors.

Not once have they said they are going to cut top paid Genicom employees such as Mr. Powell.

Genicom says they are dedicated to remaining in Waynesboro. If that is so, why have they moved over 600 jobs to Mexico, and continue to move jobs out of Waynesboro? They say they need concessions from their employees to do this. But they refuse to put in writing to the Union that these concessions will keep jobs in Waynesboro.

Instead the Company tells us they want to "put the money in their pockets." They go on to say they will use some of this money to buy other plants in other states. This will not bring jobs to Waynesboro. The Company is going to run the plants where they buy them. Not once has the Company said they would bring jobs back from Mexico with the $4 per hour concessions that they want.

The Truth Is!

The Company proposal to the Union means 2 less paid holidays per year, it means that more employees would lose 2 weeks paid vacation per year. All employees would take pay cuts. So Genicom families would take cuts of $12,000 per year. As for the pensions and the insurance, the proposal is to leave it as it is now. The Company proposal would take away all of the night shift bonus, the few sick days workers have now, and would do away with rest breaks.

If the Company really means that they will bring more jobs to Waynesboro they should be willing to put it in writing.

If the Company really means to have greater stability for the Community they should reinvest the extra profits in the Genicom Waynesboro plant. Not take the money and buy plants in other states.

Genicom would like the Community to believe that GE negotiated the last Union contract. *THAT IS NOT SO. GENICOM NEGOTIATED THE LAST CONTRACT*. Mr. Stoner of Genicom Management was part of the last negotiations and he is part of this negotiation. Mr. Stoner plays a big part in negotiations.

The Company admits in their paid ad that they made money with the last Union Contract. They could make money with the new contract that has no cuts.

It's time for Genicom to put in writing to its employees that the Company will keep jobs in Waynesboro. Genicom is making a profit. They should let the employees keep what they have. There should be NO CUTS. Workers should keep their 6½ million dollars. This would keep the money in the Community. Not take it to other states and Mexico.

If Genicom takes this money and "puts it in their pockets" merchants will lose, taxes for other people in the community will go up and everyone in the community will lose.

Only top management like Mr. Powell will gain when they line their pockets with our money at community expense.

Source: Content of Appendix 4 reprinted by permission of The United Effort, Waynesboro, VA.

Appendix 5

June 13, 1985

This letter was mailed to all hourly employees on 6/14/85. This copy is for your information.

TO: OUR GENICOM EMPLOYEES AND THEIR FAMILIES

I would like to take this opportunity to express my appreciation for the patience being displayed by the majority of our employees during a very difficult time in which we are negotiating a new labor agreement.

Genicom and its management team remain dedicated to the resolution of differences with UE Local 124 and the adoption of a new collective bargaining agreement through the negotiation process. Nevertheless, in reflecting on Local 124's recent newsletter concerning strike preparations, we feel compelled to offer our thoughts on some questions and other appropriate subjects that should be addressed by the Union's lawyer at Sunday's meeting.

Q: Is the Company required to pay wages to strikers during an economic strike?

A: No, the Company is not required to pay wages to economic strikers.

Q: Is the Company required to pay the premiums to continue health insurance, life insurance and other benefits for strikers during an economic strike?

A: No, the Company is not required to continue payments for benefits to economic strikers.

Q: Are the economic strikers eligible for Virginia unemployment benefits during an economic strike?

A: No, state law disqualifies employees involved in a "labor dispute."

Q: Is it possible for the UE to guarantee that Genicom will change its proposals because of strike action?

A: No, negotiations are a give and take process that may remain unchanged in the face of employee strikes or Company lockouts.

Q: If there is no agreement for a new contract by June 23rd, is the Company required to keep the current contract in effect?

A: No, at that time the Company may unilaterally implement its final proposal.

Q: Can economic strikers be permanently replaced by new workers if the Company decides to continue operations without them?

A: Yes, federal law allows a company to continue operations with new employees. The law also does not require the Company to discharge those employees to allow returning strikers to resume their jobs. Replaced strikers who indicate they wish to return to work on the Company's terms may fill open positions if any exist or be placed on a hiring list ahead of non-employees.

Once again let me say we, as Genicom's Management team, remain dedicated to reaching agreement with UE Local 124 *without* any strike action. However, we are also dedicated to continue the growth of a viable business in Waynesboro. In order to accomplish this, we *must* reduce our cost structure to a level that will allow Genicom to meet our competition.

Currently, the demand for our printers is poor due to a downturn in the computer market and foreign competition. This market situation, and Genicom's decision to maintain Waynesboro as our primary production location, demand the changes we have proposed to the UE.

We have furnished wage data on Waynesboro and our national competition to the Union negotiating committee establishing that our proposals are competitive with both Waynesboro and national rates.

Under one proposal, wages would run between $6.00 per hour and $11.50 per hour and benefits would remain at current levels or slightly better. In recognition of the economic impact that such concessions may have, we have offered alternative proposals such as eliminating sick days, night shift differential and afternoon breaks. These reductions would increase the wage proposal to between $6.50 and $12.00 per hour. All other benefits would remain the same or slightly better.

We hope that our employees, their families and their collective bargaining representatives will consider all these factors before taking any action that could be injurious to both Employees and the Company.

Sincerely,

Curtis W. Powell
President/Chief Executive Officer

Case 7

HARLEY-DAVIDSON, INC.: THE EAGLE SOARS ALONE

In May 1987, Vaughn Beals, chief executive of Harley-Davidson, Inc., and Thomas Gelb, vice-president of operations, made a difficult decision. They had turned Harley-Davidson around on a dime and were now poised for continued success with a fine-tuned production process and an exciting new product line. However, in a continued effort to maintain low costs, Beals and Gelb were forced to give a contract for eight electronically controlled machining centers worth $1.5 million to Japanese-owned Toyoda Machine Works. Even though the Toyoda production site for the machining centers was in Illinois, Beals would have preferred to buy from an American company. But he was constrained because of the Japanese company's ability to deliver both high quality and low price.

Beals was well aware of the implications of the decision. He had previously toured several Japanese motorcycle plants during Harley's turnaround. And he understood the pressure foreign competition had put on his company as well as on other manufacturing-intensive companies in the United States. Nonetheless, the decision reflected Harley's commitment to quality and reliability, and also indicated the company's willingness to change with the competitive environment.

This case was prepared by Stuart C. Hinrichs, Iowa State University; Charles B. Shrader, Iowa State University; and Alan N. Hoffman, Bentley College. Reprinted by permission.

This case was written to illustrate various management principles and concepts for class discussion, and was not intended to be an example of either effective or ineffective company practices. The authors thank Linda Zorzi, assistant to Vaughn L. Beals (CEO and Chairman of Harley-Davidson, Inc.); Kathryn Molling, Public Relations Director, Harley-Davidson, Inc.; and Don Wright, Vice President of Corporate Services, Holiday Rambler Corporation, for information they provided in preparing this manuscript. The authors also thank Michael Melvin and Blain Ballantine for providing helpful information.

Beals and his small management team turned around a company whose product—Harley-Davidson motorcycles—embodied the American values of freedom and rugged individualism. Beals had put Harley back as the market leader in the super heavyweight (more than 851cc) motorcycle market. Harley owned 33.3 percent of that market in 1986, compared to Honda's 30.1 percent. As of August 1987, Harley had 38 percent of the large cycle market, and total company sales were expected to rise from under $300 million in 1986 to over $600 million in 1987.

Yet Beals knew that his company needed to diversify in order to stabilize performance. The Milwaukee-based company manufactured motorcycles and motorcycle accessories, as well as bomb casings and other defense products for the military. In 1986, Harley acquired Holiday Rambler Corporation, a recreational vehicle company, a business that Beals felt fit perfectly with the others, and one that was in an industry free from Japanese competitors.

Beals knew that to remain strong competitively Harley had to continue to improve both production and human resource management techniques. He also realized his company's basic product, super heavyweight ("hog") motorcycles, had the loyal customers and brand image upon which successful competitive and diversification strategies could be built. The company's nonmotorcycle businesses were performing well and the Holiday Rambler acquisition looked promising. The challenge Beals faced was how to keep the company moving down the road at high speed.

HISTORY[1]

The Harley-Davidson story began in 1903 when William Harley, age 21, a draftsman at a Milwaukee manufacturing firm, designed and built a motorcycle with the help of three Davidson brothers: Arthur, a pattern maker at the same company as Harley; Walter, a railroad mechanic; and William, a tool maker. At first, they tinkered with ideas, motors, and old bicycle frames. Legend has it that their first carburetor was fashioned from a tin can. Still they were able to make a three-horsepower, 25-cubic-inch engine and successfully road test their first motorcycle.

Operating out of a shed in the Davidson family's backyard, the men built and sold three motorcycles. Production was expanded to eight in 1904, and in 1906 the first building was erected on the current Juneau Avenue site of the main Milwaukee offices. On September 17, 1907, Harley-Davidson Motor Company was incorporated.

Arthur Davidson set off to recruit dealers in New England and in the South. William Harley completed a degree in engineering, specializing in inter-

[1]David K. Wright, *The Harley-Davidson Motor Company: An Official Eighty-Year History*, 2nd ed. (Osceola, Wisc.: Motorbooks International, 1987).

nal combustion engines, and quickly applied his expertise in the company by developing the first V-twin engine in 1909. He followed this with a major breakthrough in 1912—the first commercially successful motorcycle clutch, which made possible the use of a roller chain to power the motorcycle. The first three-speed transmission was offered in 1915.

During the early 1900s the U.S. experienced rapid growth in the motorcycle industry, with firms such as Excelsior, Indian, Merkel, Thor, and Yale growing and competing. However, with the exception of Harley-Davidson and Indian, most of the early U.S. motorcycle companies turned out shoddy, unreliable products. Early continued success in racing and endurance made Harleys favorites among motorcyclists. The company's V-twin engines became known for power and reliability.

During World War I, Harley-Davidson supplied the military with many motorcycles. By virtue of very strong military and domestic sales, Harley-Davidson became the largest motorcycle company in the world in 1918.[2] The company built a 300,000-square-foot plant in Milwaukee, Wisconsin, in 1922, making it one of the largest motorcycle factories in the world.[3]

In the late 1930s Harley-Davidson dealt a strong competitive blow to the Indian motorcycle company by introducing the first overhead valve engine. The large, 61-cubic-inch engine became very popular and was thereafter referred to as the "Knucklehead." Indian could not make a motorcycle to compete with these Harleys.

Harley introduced major innovations in the suspensions of its cycles in the 1940s. However, in 1949 Harley first met with international competition. British companies, such as Norton and Triumph, were making motorcycles that were cheaper, lighter, easier to handle, and just as fast, even though they had smaller engines.

Harley-Davidson countered the British threat by making further design improvements in the engines, thereby increasing the horsepower of their heavier cycles. The changes produced, in 1957, what some consider to be the first of the modern superbikes: the Harley Sportster. During the fifties Harley also developed the styling that made it famous.

As the 1950s drew to a close, new contenders from Japan entered the lightweight (250cc and below) motorcycle market. Harley welcomed the little bikes because it was thought that small bike customers would quickly move to larger bikes as the riders became more experienced. The Japanese cycles proved to be popular with riders, however, and Japanese products began to successfully penetrate the off-road and street cycle markets. In the 1960s Japan entered the middleweight (250 to 500cc) market.

As Harley entered the 1960s, it made an attempt to build smaller, lightweight bikes in the U.S. However, the company found it difficult to build small machines and still be profitable. As a result, Harley acquired 50% of Aermacchi,

[2]Wright, *The Harley-Davidson Motor Company*, p. 17.
[3]Wright, *The Harley-Davidson Motor Company*, p. 17.

an Italian cycle producer, and built small motorcycles for both street and off-road use. The first Aermacchi/Harleys were sold in 1961.[4]

The Italian venture endured until 1978, but was never considered to be highly successful. Few took Harley's small cycles seriously, including some Harley dealers who refused to handle them. In the meantime, Japanese cycles dominated the small and middleweight markets. Harley seemed trapped in the heavyweight segment.

In an attempt to expand production capacity and raise capital, Harley went public in 1965. The company merged with the conglomerate AMF, Inc., in 1969. AMF, a company known for its leisure and industrial products, expanded production capacity from 15,000 units in 1969 to 40,000 units in 1974.[5] With the expanded capacity, AMF pursued a milking strategy, favoring short-term profits rather than investment in research and development, and retooling. The Japanese products continued to improve, while Harley began to turn out heavy, noisy, vibrating, poorly finished machines.

In 1975, AMF was faced with a serious Japanese threat to the heavyweight market. Honda Motor Company introduced the "Gold Wing," which quickly became the standard for large touring motorcycles, a segment Harley previously dominated. At the time, Harley's top-of-the-line touring bike sold for almost $9,000, while the comparable Honda Gold Wing was approximately $7,000.[6] Not only did Japanese cycles sell for less than comparable Harleys, but Japanese manufacturing techniques yielded operating costs that were 30 percent lower than Harley-Davidson's.

Motorcycle enthusiasts more than ever began to go with Japanese products because of the cycles' price/performance advantages. Even some loyal Harley owners and police department contracts were lost. The company was rapidly losing ground both technologically and in the market.

Starting in 1975 and continuing through the middle 1980s, the Japanese companies penetrated the big bore custom motorcycle market, producing Harley look-alikes with V-twin engines.[7] The Honda "Magna" and "Shadow," the Suzuki "Intruder," and the Yamaha "Virago" were representative of the Japanese imitations. In a short time Japanese companies captured a significant share of the large cycle segment and controlled nearly 90 percent of the total motorcycle market.[8]

During AMF's ownership of Harley, motorcycles were strong on sales but relatively weak on profits. AMF did put a great deal of money into Harley, and production went as high as 75,000 units in 1975.[9] But motorcycles never seemed to be AMF's priority. For example, in 1978, motorcycles accounted for 17 percent of revenues but for only 1 percent of profits. AMF was more inclined to emphasize its industrial products and services.

[4]Wright, *The Harley-Davidson Motor Company*, p. 35.
[5]Wright, *The Harley-Davidson Motor Company*, pp. 282–283.
[6]"Uneasy Rider: Harley pleads for relief," *Time*, December 13, 1982, p. 61.
[7]Wright, *The Harley-Davidson Motor Company*, pp. 244–262.
[8]"Trade Protection: Mind my (motor) bike," *The Economist*, 264 (July 1977), 82.
[9]Wright, *The Harley-Davidson Motor Company*, p. 281.

THE TURNAROUND[10]

Vaughn Beals served as Harley's top manager during its last six years under AMF control. Beals was uncomfortable with AMF's short-term orientation and unwillingness to confront problems caused by imports. Consequently, in June 1981, a subgroup of Harley Management, including Beals, completed a leveraged buyout of Harley-Davidson from AMF. To celebrate, Beals and the management team made a Pennsylvania-to-Wisconsin motorcycle ride, proclaiming, "The Eagle Soars Alone."

Beals knew reversing Harley's momentum would not be easy, especially without the help of the former parent. Indeed, things began to get worse. Harley suffered its first operating loss in 1981. In 1982, many motorcycles were coming off the assembly line with defects, registrations for motorcycles were falling, and the Japanese were continuing to penetrate Harley's market segments. Company losses for the year totalled over $25 million.[11] Several Japanese companies built up inventories in the face of a declining market and engaged in aggressive price discounting.

Beals petitioned the International Trade Commission (ITC) for temporary protection from Japanese "dumping" practices in 1982. He accused the Japanese of dumping large quantities of bikes in the U.S. and selling them for prices much below what they were in Japan. The U.S. Treasury had previously found the Japanese guilty of excess inventory practices, but the ITC ruled that the practices had not adversely affected the sales of Harley-Davidson motorcycles. Therefore, no sanctions were placed on the Japanese companies. The Japanese continued price competition, and many thought Harley would soon buckle from the pressure.

In 1983, with the help of many public officials, including Senator John Heinz of Pennsylvania, Harley was able to obtain protection from the excess inventory practices of the Japanese. In April 1983, President Reagan, on the recommendation of the ITC, imposed a declining five-year tariff on the wholesale prices of Japanese heavyweight (over 700cc) motorcycles. The tariff schedule was as follows:

1983   45 percent
1984   35 percent
1985   20 percent
1986   15 percent
1987   10 percent

The effects of the tariff were mixed. Much of the Japanese inventory was already in the U.S. when the tariff went into effect. Dealers selling Japanese cycles sharply reduced prices on older models, which hurt the sale of new bikes.

[10]Wright, *The Harley-Davidson Motor Company,* pp. 244–262.
[11]Dean Witter Reynolds, *Prospectus, Harley-Davidson, Inc.,* July 8, 1986, p. 8.

On the other hand, the tariff signaled that Japanese overproduction would not be tolerated, giving Harley some breathing room and management a chance to reposition the company. Beals and others inside the company felt that the dumping case and the tariff protection helped focus the company on developing competitive strengths and on improving the production process. They also felt that the tariffs were the result of the government's recognition of Harley's overall revitalization effort, which had begun several years prior to the imposition of the tariff.

Improving Production[12]

In the early years Harley had been successfully run by engineers. Beal's background was in engineering as well, and as president he began to focus on the beleaguered production process. Until 1982, the company used a batch production system in which only one model was produced at a time. The final line work force would shift from 90 to 140 people, depending on which model was being produced on a given day.

To make the production system more efficient, Beals, Thomas Gelb, and others on the management team implemented what they called their productivity triad: materials-as-needed, a just-in-time inventory method; statistical process control; and employee involvement. The materials-as-needed (MAN) system stabilized the production schedule and helped reduce inventory. Production worked with marketing to make more accurate demand forecasts for each model. Precise production schedules were established for a given month and were not allowed to vary by more than 10 percent in subsequent months. A production method was adopted in which a different mix of models was produced every day. This was referred to as the "jelly bean" method.

Under the MAN system, Harley required its suppliers to comply with its quality requirements. Harley offered long-term contracts to suppliers who conformed to its quality requirements and who delivered only the exact needed quantity for a given period of time. Harley also integrated backward into transporting materials from suppliers. The Harley-Davidson transportation company made scheduled pickups from suppliers, which in turn allowed Harley greater control over the shipments, thereby cutting costs.

Prior to the 1983 tariff, Beals, Gelb, and others visited several Japanese motorcycle plants and learned the importance of employee development and involvement. As a result, rigorous training programs were developed. By 1986, over one-third of the employees were trained in statistical process control, the ability to sample and analyze data while performing a job. Setup times were re-

---

[12]Rod Willis, "Harley-Davidson comes roaring back," *Management Review* (October 1986), 20–27.

duced by implementing ideas gleaned from quality circles and problem-solving sessions involving workers, managers, and engineers.

Further improvements in the production process were made by Walter Anderson, senior production engineer, with the help of Harley employees and management. Instead of running components down straight lines, Anderson organized workers into a series of "work cells." Work cells consisted of a few workers in a small area with all the machines and tools they needed to complete a job. The work cells were often arranged in U-shaped configurations, which allowed intensive work within a cell and reduced the total movement of components through the process. The cells also improved employee efficiency and job satisfaction in that while workers stayed at the same work station all day, they enjoyed variety in their tasks.

A "simultaneous engineering" system implemented by Beals also helped to improve production. In simultaneous engineering, the design and manufacture of products were combined from the start. The process facilitated the use of statistical design control and helped generate products more efficiently.

Harley also invested heavily in research and development. A computer-aided design system was developed by the research and development group. The CAD system allowed management to make changes in the entire product line while maintaining the traditional styling. In 1983 the company developed a more efficient engine, and in 1984, a new suspension. Harley was soon thereafter recognized to be an industry leader in various areas of production including belt drive technology, vibration isolation, and steering geometry. Since 1981, the company has allocated a major portion of revenues to R & D each year.

Beal's emphasis on production brought big payoffs for the company. In 1986, 99 percent of the Harleys were coming off the production line free of defects. The company also lowered its breakeven point from 53,000 units in 1982 to 35,000 units in 1986.[13] Many companies now visit Harley for seminars and advice on how to improve efficiency.

Perhaps one of the greatest indicators of Harley's production turnaround was evidenced through one of their oldest pieces of equipment—a huge sheet metal–forming machine known simply as "the Tool." The Tool, originally built in Milwaukee but later moved to the plant in York, Pennsylvania, was used to forge the "Fat Bob" gas tanks for all the FX and FXR series bikes. There was no operating manual nor maintenance book for the Tool, yet the company still used this old legendary machine to crank out modern, high-quality products.

In March 1987, Vaughn Beals appeared before a Washington, D.C. news conference and offered to give up the tariff protection that was to last until the middle of 1988. Congress praised the announcement and commended the company for its success. President Reagan even visited the York plant in celebration of the event.

[13]Willis, "Harley-Davidson comes roaring back".

Corporate Structure[14]

According to Beals, one of the most important contributions to the company's turnaround was the savings obtained by reducing the number of salaried staff. Staff jobs were reduced drastically by Beals as a result of his experience with leaner Japanese companies. The number of managers at each plant was reduced, and each manager was given responsibility for one function at the plant, such as hiring, operations, productivity, and so on.

The number of line employees was also reduced. Line employees were given responsibility to inspect products for defects, apply quality control, determine quotas and goals, and make production decisions.

A majority of the company's employees participated actively in quality circle programs. The quality circles were used not only to improve efficiency but also to address other issues, such as job security. An outcome of the turnaround was a growing fear among employees of being laid off. Both the reduction in staff and the increased productivity caused workers to worry about the security of their jobs. However, the quality circles came up with the idea to move some sourcing and fabricating of parts in-house. In-house sourcing made it possible for many employees, who may have otherwise been laid off, to retain their jobs.

Harley's corporate staff was made very lean and the structure was simple. Top executive officers were put in charge of functional areas. Under top management, the company was basically organized into two divisions—motorcycles and defense. Holiday Rambler Corporation became a wholly owned subsidiary in 1986.

Top Management[15]

Vaughn L. Beals, Jr., was appointed as the chief executive officer and chairman of the board of directors of Harley-Davidson Motor Company. He earned an engineering degree from the Massachusetts Institute of Technology and worked as a logging machine manufacturer and as an engine maker before joining AMF in 1975. In 1981, along with one of the grandsons of the founder and 12 other individuals, he led the leveraged buyout of the Harley-Davidson Motor Company. He was known throughout the company for his devotion to and enthusiasm for motorcycles. He owned a Harley deluxe Electra-Glide and rode it on business trips whenever possible.

Harley's top management always demonstrated their willingness to take a "hog" on the road for a worthy cause. On one occasion, in 1985, Beals and product designer, William G. Davidson (known as "Willie G") led a caravan of

---

[14]Willis, "Harley-Davidson comes roaring back".
[15]Jeff Baily, "Beals takes Harley-Davidson on new road," *The Wall Street Journal*, March 20, 1987, p. 39.

Harleys from California to New York in an effort to raise money for the Statue of Liberty renovation. At the conclusion of the ride, Beals presented a check to the Statue of Liberty Foundation for $250,000.

Beals claimed that his major responsibility was for product quality improvements. On one occasion, during a business trip, Beals noticed a defect in a 1986 model's seat. He stopped long enough to call the factory about the problem. The workers and test riders, however, had already found and corrected the flaw.

Beals made an all-out effort to keep managerial levels in the company to a minimum. The Board of Directors was composed of six officers, four of whom came from outside the company. The CEO often communicates with everyone in the company through memos known as "Beals'-grams."

Because of the company's success, and in an effort to provide additional capital for growth, Harley went public with an offering of approximately six million shares in the summer of 1986. Beals owned nearly 16 percent of Harley stock, which was increasing in value.

Human Resource Management[16]

Harley-Davidson employed approximately 2,336 people in 1986, down from 3,840 in 1981. Under chief executive Beals, the company made great strides in developing a participative, cooperative, less hierarchical work climate. Employees wrote their own job descriptions and actively participated in on-the-job training. Employees learned that they were not only responsible for their own jobs, but also for helping others learn. Performance was evaluated through a peer review program.

The company developed many career and placement opportunity programs as a response to employee concern over job security. Harley entered into a cooperative placement agreement with other Wisconsin unions. The company even developed a voluntary layoff program in which senior workers volunteered to be laid off first in down times to protect the jobs of newer workers. Harley offered sophisticated health and retirement benefits, and has also developed employee wellness and college tuition funding programs.

Financial Performance

Harley was purchased through a leveraged buyout from AMF in 1981 for approximately $65 million.[17] The buyout was financed with a $30 million term loan and $35 million in revolving credit from institutional lenders. AMF also received $9 million of securities in the form of preferred stock. In 1984, an agreement was reached between the two companies whereby the preferred stock held

[16]Willis, "Harley-Davidson comes roaring back," pp. 20–27.
[17]Dean Witter Reynolds, *Prospectus, Harley-Davidson, Inc.*, July 8, 1986, p. 8.

by AMF was cancelled and payments where to be made directly to AMF from future Harley-Davidson profits.

In 1985, Harley negotiated an exchange of common stock for forgiveness of a portion of the loans. The company offered $70 million in subordinated notes and $20 million in stock for public sale in 1986. The proceeds were used to re-pay a portion of the debt to AMF, refinance unfavorable loans, provide financing for the Holiday Rambler acquisition, and provide working capital.

Holiday Rambler Corporation was a privately held company until its acquisition by Harley in 1986. Holiday Rambler performed very well in its first year as part of Harley-Davidson. It had total sales of approximately $257 million through September 1987 compared with $208 million for the same period in 1986, nearly a 24 percent increase.

While Harley-Davidson's net sales and profitability improved during the years 1982 to 1986, net income and earnings per share fluctuated in that period. The motorcycle division's sales decreased as a percentage of the total because of the rapid increase in the defense division. In the years following the 1981 buy-out, the company relied greatly on credit for working capital.

Marketing Strategy

Harley-Davidson's marketing efforts centered around the use of the Harley name. The company emphasized that its name was synonymous with quality, reliability, and styling. Company research indicated a 90% repurchase rate, or loyalty factor, on the part of Harley owners.

Harley's marketing concentrated on dealer promotions, magazine advertising, direct mail advertising, sponsorship of racing activities, and the organization of the Harley owners group (HOG). The HOG club had enrolled 77,000 members by 1987 and permitted the company close contact with customers.

In addition, Harley sponsored or cosponsored organizations such as the Ellis Island Statue of Liberty Foundation and the Muscular Dystrophy Association.

The company was also the first motorcycle manufacturer to offer a national program of demonstration rides. Some dealers felt the program, introduced in 1984, resulted in a large number of Harley motorcycle purchases.

A major form of advertising was accomplished through Harley's licensing operation. The licensing of the Harley name was very profitable and served to promote the company's image.

The company directed a portion of its marketing expenditures toward expanding the field sales force in an effort to assist the domestic dealer network. In some areas the sales force developed local marketing programs to train dealers.

The Harley Image

Few companies could elicit the name recognition and brand loyalty of Harley-Davidson. Harley's appeal was based on the thrill and prestige of owning and riding the king of the big bikes. A Harley has traditionally been known as a sturdy, powerful, macho bike, definitely not for wimps or kids, and a true bike for the open road.

A worrisome problem with the Harley image, however, was the perceptual connection of Harleys exclusively with "outlaw" biker groups. The negative "Road Warrior" image affected sales in some areas to such a degree that the company initiated a public relations campaign. The company gently attacked the biker image by directing much of its advertising toward young professionals. The message was that Harley-Davidson represented fun, recreation, and reliability. The company heralded the fact that famous professionals such as Malcolm Forbes and Reggie Jackson rode Harleys. The campaign seemed to work. More doctors, lawyers, and dentists began to purchase Harleys.

Harley also put tighter controls on licensing its name, ensuring that it was not used in obscene ways. Advertisements picturing Reggie Jackson and Malcolm Forbes atop their "hogs" further helped the company's image.

A related problem was that Harley had not attracted very many women customers. This was due to the image and to the size of the bikes. Harleys were very big and heavy. The Harley low-rider series was attracting some women customers because the bikes were lower and easier to get on. Notwithstanding, some Japanese companies introduced smaller, lighter, low-riding, and inexpensive Harley look-alikes in a straightforward attempt to attract women buyers. Honda's "Rebel" (250cc) was one such bike that became fairly successful with women.

Harley was careful not to alienate their loyal biker customers, however. The company continued to promulgate its tough image and even attempted to enhance the image through certain forms of advertising in motorcycle magazines. For example, one ad pictured a group of rather tough-looking bikers and had a caption that read: "Would you sell an unreliable bike to these guys? We Don't!" Another ad showed a junkyard filled with scrapped Japanese bikes. The caption was: "Can you find a Harley in here?"

Perhaps the most objective indicator of the strength of the Harley image came from an unlikely source—Japan itself! Japanese companies made numerous attempts to copy Milwaukee's designs.[18] For example, Suzuki's 1987 "Intruder" (1400cc) went to great lengths to hide the radiator, because Harleys were air cooled. Some analysts felt that Japanese imitations only served to strengthen the mystique of the original. The more the Japanese tried to make look-alike bikes, the more the real thing increased in value. Beals agreed. He maintained that Harleys were built to last longer and have a higher resale than other bikes.

Diversification Strategy

Since the early years of the company, Harley-Davidson specialized in the heavy-weight motorcycle market segment. Heavyweight bikes were divided into three

---

[18]"Why Milwaukee won't die," *Cycle*, 38 (June 1987), 35–41.

categories: touring/custom, standard street, and performance motorcycles. Harley was never totally successful in building smaller bikes. Beals was even quoted at one time as saying that Harley would not build small bikes.

Harley's motorcycle product line was very narrow, therefore, compared with that of its competitors. The company's management thought about expanding international operations and penetrating other markets. The largest export markets for Harley were Canada, Australia, and West Germany.

The company purchased a small three-wheeler firm named "Trihawk" in 1984. Shortly thereafter the company realized it could not make a go of it in this market because of high start-up costs, and the project was terminated.

Under Beals the company moved into the manufacturing of casings for artillery shells and rocket engines for military target drones. The defense business proved to be very profitable for Harley. In an attempt to diversify the company, Beals set corporate goals to increase the level of defense-related business. The company became very active in making bids for the design, development, and manufacture of defense products.

Accessories, bike parts, clothing and "leathers," and even furniture associated with the Harley name were big business for the company. Brand-name licensing and related accessories generated about as much income as did the motorcycles.

But Beals wanted to move the company into other businesses not related to the rather narrow motorcycle line and not in competition with Japanese companies. He felt Harley needed to diversify in order to be a truly stable performer. Thus Harley acquired the Holiday Rambler Corporation in December 1986. Beals saw the fit as a good one because Holiday produced recreational vehicles and was what he called "manufacturing intensive" just like Harley.

Holiday Rambler manufactured premium motorhomes, specialized commercial vehicles, and travel trailers. The company employed 2,300 people and was headquartered in Wakarusa, Indiana. At the time of the acquisition Holiday was the largest privately owned maker of recreational vehicles, recognized as a leader in the premium class motorhome and towable trailer markets. In 1986 Holiday Rambler ranked fourth in market share in the motorhome market and fifth in towable recreational vehicles. Its products were gaining share in the industry as a whole.

A Holiday subsidiary, Utilimaster, built truck trailers and bodies for commercial uses. The company had contracts with companies such as Purolator Courier and Ryder Truck Rentals. Other Holiday subsidiaries produced office furniture, custom wood products, custom tools, van conversions, and park trailers.

Even with the Holiday Rambler acquisition and with the success in defense-related products, Harley looked for other means of diversifying. In September 1986, a tobacco company purchased a license to test market Harley-Davidson brand cigarettes.

THE FUTURE

Because of Harley's success in the face of stiff competition, the company came to be viewed as an example of what can be accomplished by using modern production and personnel management techniques. Top management was committed to keeping the company lean and viable. Yet they knew they needed to diversify and change. Beals felt that his company needed to become as tough as its image.

Beals had focused his turnaround effort on the internal operating efficiency of the company. Now he needed to provide leadership for a newly acquired subsidiary and plan for growth in the defense division. He also faced the challenge of breaking the company out of its narrow market segment in its bread-and-butter division: motorcycles. Should he plan for growth and market penetration in the motorcycle industry? Or should he be content with maintaining Harley as a big bike company only?

Since 1903, 150 American motorcycle companies had come and gone. Harley-Davidson Motor Company, with Vaughn Beals at the helm, was the only one that survived. The eagle continues to soar alone.

EXHIBIT 1   **Harley-Davidson, Inc. — sales and income by business segment**

	1983	1984	1985
	(In thousands)		
Net sales:			
Motorcycles and related products	$229,412	$260,745	$240,631
Defense and other businesses	24,093	33,080	46,845
	$253,505	$293,825	$287,476
Income from operations:			
Motorcycles and related products	$ 16,513	$ 15,489	$ 9,980
Defense and other businesses	3,566	7,012	9,390
General corporate expenses	(6,606)	(6,969)	(6,457)
	13,473	15,532	12,913
Interest expense	(11,782)	(11,256)	(9,412)
Other	188	(311)	(338)
Income before income taxes, extraordinary items and cumulative effect of change in accounting principle	$ 1,879	$ 3,965	$ 3,163

Source: Dean Witter Reynolds, *Prospectus, Harley-Davidson, Inc.*, July 8, 1986. Reprinted by permission.

EXHIBIT 2   **Harley-Davidson, Inc. — consolidated balance sheet**

	1984	1985	1986
	(In thousands, December 31)		
ASSETS			
Current assets			
Cash	$ 2,056	$ 9,070	$ 7,345
Temporary investments	—	4,400	20,500
Accounts receivable net of			
allowance for doubtful accounts	27,767	27,313	36,462
Inventories	32,736	28,868	78,630
Prepaid expenses	2,613	3,241	5,812
Total current assets	65,172	72,892	148,758
Property, plant and equipment, at cost,			
less accumulated depreciation and			
amortization	33,512	38,727	90,932
Deferred financing costs	—	2,392	3,340
Intangible assets	—	—	82,114
Other assets	523	81	2,052
	$99,207	$114,092	$327,196
LIABILITIES AND STOCKHOLDERS' EQUITY			
Current liabilities			
Notes payable	$ —	$ —	$ 14,067
Current maturities of long-term debt	2,305	2,875	4,023
Accounts payable	21,880	27,521	29,587
Accrued expenses and other liabilities	24,231	26,251	61,144
Total current liabilities	48,416	56,647	108,821
Long-term debt, less current maturities	56,258	51,504	191,594
Long-term pension liability	856	1,319	622
Stockholder's equity			
Common stock 6,200,000 issued in 1986			
and 4,200,000 in 1985	42	42	62
Class B common stock, no shares issued	—	—	—
Additional paid-in capital	9,308	10,258	26,657
Deficit	(15,543)	(5,588)	(717)
Cumulative foreign currency			
translation adjustment	—	40	287
	(6,193)	4,752	26,289
Less treasury stock (520,000 shares)			
at cost	(130)	(130)	(130)
Total stockholder's equity	(6,323)	4,622	26,159
	$99,207	$114,092	$327,196

Sources: Harley-Davidson, Inc., *1986 Annual Report;* Dean Witter Reynolds, *Prospectus, Harley-Davidson, Inc.,*
July 8, 1986. Reprinted by permission.

EXHIBIT 3   **Harley-Davidson, Inc.—consolidated statement of income**

	1982	1983	1984	1985	1986
	(Year ended December 31, in thousands except per share amounts)				
Income statement data					
Net sales	$ 210,055	$ 253,505	$ 293,825	$ 287,476	$ 295,322
Cost of goods sold	174,967	194,271	220,040	217,222	219,167
Gross profit	35,088	59,234	73,785	70,254	76,155
Operating expenses:					
Selling and administrative	37,510	36,441	47,662	47,162	51,060
Engineering, research and development	13,072	9,320	10,591	10,179	8,999
Total operating expenses	50,582	45,761	58,253	57,341	60,059
Income (loss) from operations	(15,494)	13,473	15,532	12,913	16,096
Other income (expenses):					
Interest expense	(15,778)	(11,782)	(11,256)	(9,412)	(8,373)
Other	(1,272)	188	(311)	(388)	(388)
	(17,050)	(11,594)	(11,567)	(9,750)	(8,761)
Income (loss) before provision (credit) for income taxes, extraordinary items, and cumulative effect of change in accounting principle	(32,544)	1,879	3,965	3,163	7,335
Provision (credit) for income taxes	(7,467)	906	1,077	526	3,028
Income (loss) before extraordinary items and cumulative effect of change in accounting principle	(25,077)	973	2,888	2,637	4,307
Extraordinary items and cumulative effect of change in accounting principle	—	7,795	3,578	7,318	564
Net income (loss)	$ (25,077)	$ 8,768	$ 6,466	$ 9,955	$ 4,871
Average number of common shares outstanding	4,016,664	3,720,000	3,680,000	3,680,000	5,235,230
Per common share:					
Income (loss) before extraordinary items and cumulative effect of change in accounting principle	$ (6.61)	$ .26	$ .79	$ .72	$ .82
Extraordinary items and cumulative effect of change in accounting principle	—	2.10	.97	1.99	.11
Net income (loss)	$ (6.61)	$ 2.36	$ 1.76	$ 2.71	$ .93

Source: Harley-Davidson, Inc., *1986 Annual Report*. Reprinted by permission.

EXHIBIT 4   **Harley-Davidson executive officers**

Name	Age	Position	Years with company*	Annual compensation
Vaughn L. Beals, Jr.	58	Chairman and CEO	10	$207,217
Richard F. Teerlink	49	Vice President, Chief Finance Officer	5	$143,375
Jeffrey L. Bleustein	46	Vice President Parts and Accessories	15	$118,387
Thomas A. Gelb	50	Vice President Operations	21	$132,666
James H. Paterson	38	Vice President Marketing	15	$ 95,728
Peter L. Profumo	39	Vice President Program Management	17	$129,521

*Years with Harley-Davidson or AMF, Inc.

Source: Dean Witter Reynolds, *Prospectus, Harley-Davidson, Inc.,* July 8, 1986. Reprinted by permission.

EXHIBIT 5   **Board of directors, Harley-Davidson, Inc.**

Vaughn L. Beals, Jr.	Chairman, president, and chief executive officer, Harley-Davidson, Inc., Milwaukee, Wisconsin
Frederick L. Brengel	Chairman and chief executive officer, Johnson Controls, Inc., Milwaukee, Wisconsin
F. Trevor Deeley	Chairman and chief executive officer, Fred Deeley Imports, Richmond, British Columbia, Canada
Dr. Michael J. Kami	President, Corporate Planning, Inc., Lighthouse Point, Florida
Richard Hermon-Taylor	Management consultant, South Hamilton, Massachusetts
Richard F. Teerlink	Vice-president, treasurer, and chief financial officer, Harley-Davidson, Inc., Milwaukee, Wisconsin

Source: Harley-Davidson, Inc., *1986 Annual Report.* Reprinted by permission.

EXHIBIT 6   **Harley-Davidson's U.S. market share — super heavyweight motorcycles (850cc +)**

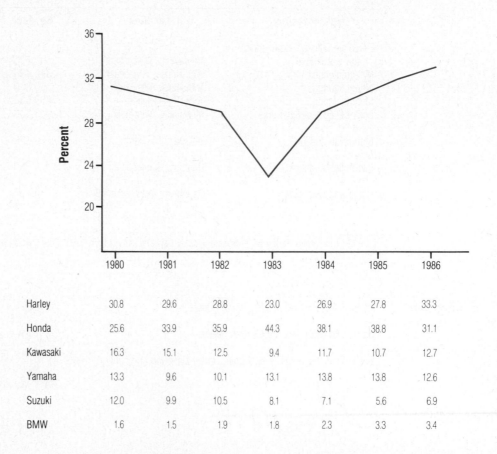

	1980	1981	1982	1983	1984	1985	1986
Harley	30.8	29.6	28.8	23.0	26.9	27.8	33.3
Honda	25.6	33.9	35.9	44.3	38.1	38.8	31.1
Kawasaki	16.3	15.1	12.5	9.4	11.7	10.7	12.7
Yamaha	13.3	9.6	10.1	13.1	13.8	13.8	12.6
Suzuki	12.0	9.9	10.5	8.1	7.1	5.6	6.9
BMW	1.6	1.5	1.9	1.8	2.3	3.3	3.4

Source: Harley-Davidson, Inc., *1986 Annual Report*. Reprinted by permission.

EXHIBIT 7   **Harley-Davidson, Inc. — facilities**

Type of facility	Location	Sq. feet	Status
Executive offices, engineering and warehouse	Milwaukee, Wisconsin	502,720	Owned
Manufacturing	Wauwatosa, Wisconsin	342,430	Owned
Manufacturing	Tomahawk, Wisconsin	50,600	Owned
Manufacturing	York, Pennsylvania	869,580	Owned
Engineering test laboratory	Milwaukee, Wisconsin	6,500	Lease expiring 1991
Motorcycle testing	Talladega, Alabama	9,326	Lease expiring 1988
International offices	Danbury, Connecticut	2,850	Lease expiring 1988
Office and workshop	Raunheim, West Germany	4,300	Lease expiring 1989

Source: Dean Witter Reynolds, *Prospectus, Harley-Davidson, Inc.,* July 8, 1986. Reprinted by permission.

Bibliography   Harley-Davidson, Inc. *1986 Annual Report.*

Harley-Davidson, Inc. *1986 10-K Report.*

Dean Witter Reynolds, *Prospectus, Harley-Davidson, Inc.,* July 8, 1986.

KITCHEN MADE PIES

INTRODUCTION

In late 1981, Paul Dubicki, owner and president of Kitchen Made Pies, was faced with a difficult problem. Company sales had stagnated since 1975, and the firm was about to suffer its fourth straight year of losses. Further compounding the problem were unfavorable economic and industry conditions, both nationally and locally, as well as difficulties with certain customers and creditors. In addition, the firm's financial condition had deteriorated, which served to limit the range of feasible alternatives available to turn the situation around. In spite of these concerns, Mr. Dubicki was determined to return the business to profitability; and, in fact, was confident that this task could be accomplished if he could only get away from day-to-day decision making.

When commenting on the current situation at Kitchen Made, Mr. Dubicki emphasized volume as the key to success. "We must increase our customer base and we must somehow encourage our present distributors to provide the promotional support retailers need to sell our products. One well-publicized special can sell more pies in one day than can be sold in a normal week without one. That's what I'd like to concentrate on, but every day something else comes up around here."

COMPANY HISTORY

Kitchen Made Pies is a regional producer of a wide variety of pies, as well as other bakery products. Located in Peoria, Illinois, the firm traces its history back 30 years. The firm was founded by Frank Dubicki, the father of the current owner, and was run like most family businesses. Paul Dubicki grew up in

This case was prepared by James J. Chrisman, of the University of South Carolina, and Fred L. Fry, of Bradley University.

the bakery business, but was not really very interested in the firm in his earlier years. After leaving the business for a while to pursue other activities, Paul returned in 1968 to work and later become, along with David Dubicki, a minority stockholder. During this time, he was dissatisfied because he never could get away from the operational aspects of the business. Later, however, Paul was running the business. In early 1981, the elder Dubicki was persuaded to sell out, though he did retain ownership of the company's land and facilities. This sale was actually a redemption of Frank Dubicki's stock by the corporation in a transaction that also eliminated his debt to the corporation. During the same period, David exited from the business, leaving Paul as the sole owner. Upon assuming control, Paul immediately set about changing and updating the firm's operations (i.e., revised inventory stocking measures) and for the first time, established a commitment to strategic planning. Unfortunately, at the same time, problems building up over a long period of time began to surface.

PRODUCT LINE

Kitchen Made Pies, as the name implies, is primarily engaged in pie baking. The company makes a full line of pies, some on a regular basis, some seasonally. Exhibit 1, presented below, lists all major sizes and flavors of pies currently produced by Kitchen Made, as well as other bakery products which the firm makes.

Kitchen Made sells both fresh and frozen pies, though the former are preferred due to better turnover and more predictable ordering on the part of the customers. Another problem restricting frozen pie sales is limited freezer space. Kitchen Made can currently freeze only 3,500 pies at one time. Since this represents the maximum amount of pies per day it can freeze, frozen pie sales are limited.

Kitchen Made has long been proud of the fact that it uses only the highest-quality ingredients in its products. Many would agree that Kitchen Made pies taste better than competitors' products. Of course, this also means that Kitchen Made pies are usually more expensive. Mr. Dubicki views this quality as a major strength, especially to maintain repeat business. Still, he concedes that many times customers are more concerned with price; but in the end, Mr. Dubicki believes, quality will win out.

MARKETS/CUSTOMERS

The majority of Kitchen Made's sales are to food/bakery distributors who basically supply two major markets. The first is the institutional market, which consists of restaurants, as well as university, hospital, corporate, and government cafeterias. The second is the retail market, which includes grocery stores and convenience outlets. The institutional market accounts for the majority of cake

EXHIBIT 1   **Pie categories**

4-inch	8-inch	9-inch	Other
Apple	Apple	Apple	Shortcake
Pineapple	Applecrumb	Applecrumb	10″ cakes
Cherry	Peach	Peach	8″ cakes
Blackberry	Pineapple	Pineapple	Sheet cakes
Lemon	Lemon	Blackberry	
Coconut	Coconut	Black raspberry	
Chocolate	Chocolate	Walnut	
Peach	Black raspberry	Cherry	
	Pumpkin	Lemon meringue	
	Cherry	Coconut meringue	
	High-top meringues	Chocolate meringue	
	Regular meringues	Banana meringue	
		Pumpkin	
		Chocolate Boston	
		Boston	
		Lemon whip	
		Coconut whip	
		Chocolate whip	
		Banana whip	
		Pumpkin whip	

and 9″ pie sales, while the retail market buys mainly 4″ and 8″ pies. Most distributors concentrate on one market or the other, thus determining the type of products they buy. Buying motives for both markets vary depending upon the customer and market area involved. Some customers are very conscious of price, especially in institutional markets, while others — most notably restaurants and grocers — can be more interested in quality or promotional support.

Most of Kitchen Made's products are sold in the Peoria and St. Louis areas, but the firm also serves customers in other parts of Missouri and Illinois, as well as in Iowa and Wisconsin. Major distributors of Kitchen Made products, as well as the markets they serve, are included in Exhibit 2, presented below.

Besides the differences in buying motives and the type of products purchased by the two end markets, there are several other distinguishing features which differentiate them from each other. Institutional markets frequently prefer frozen pies because of buying habits (institutional customers often buy to satisfy monthly needs) which prevent extensive use of fresh varieties. On the other hand, in the grocery business, turnover is a way of life, and thus, customers usually prefer to make weekly or biweekly purchases. Retail customers like fresh pies better because they can be put directly on the shelf, which eliminates storage, thawing, and the extra work involved in moving and stocking products twice. However, fresh pies in the grocery stores sell best through the in-store bakeries since the connotation of "freshness" lies in this area.

EXHIBIT 2   **Customers**

Dean's Distributing	40%	(institutional)
McCormick Distributing	10%	(institutional)
Lowenberg	11%	(retail)
Eisner's	8%	(retail)
Master Snack & New Process	13%	(retail)
Edward's	4%	(retail)
Other (including Schnuck's)	16%	(retail)

Unlike institutional markets, retailers depend heavily upon promotional assistance for sales. One reason Dean's Distributing has become a less important customer for Kitchen Made is that it refuses to offer grocers this type of support. As a result, Dean's, and therefore Kitchen Made, have lost much of their retail grocer business in recent years, especially in the Peoria area. Today, most of Dean's pie distribution business done in the Peoria vicinity, as well as in other markets, is institutional.

Distributors use two basic methods to sell products to grocers. Some distributors sell on a guaranteed basis, with unsold products returned to the dealer at no charge. Others sell products unguaranteed, or in other words, grocers take full responsibility for all products they buy. Naturally, profit margins for the methods differ. Grocers usually make about 23–25% on guaranteed sales, while unguaranteed sales yield margins of approximately 35–40%. However, because of the inherent risks involved in unguaranteed purchases, most grocers prefer the lower-but-safer profit margins of guaranteed arrangements when dealing with "door-to-store" distributors such as Dean's. Non-guaranteed sales work well through efficient drop shipment techniques that may be used by bread bakers.

There is a basic difference between the two distribution methods. Door-to-store distributors accumulate individual orders on a daily basis and deliver merchandise direct from the pie baker to the grocer. On the other hand, drop shipments involve larger orders, which are taken first to warehouses for later delivery to individual stores. For example, drop ship distributors, such as Eisner's, sell direct to their own or an affiliated grocery chain, and thus enjoy profits on both the delivery and retail end. This can be an important competitive advantage, since 40–50% of the product cost is in distribution. Thus, Mr. Dubicki has expressed a desire to focus on these direct distributors because of the reduced price for retailers, and hence consumers. This, he feels, could help circumvent the higher prices charged for Kitchen Made products on the wholesale end. Furthermore, since drop shippers order larger quantities, longer production runs and, therefore, lower costs are possible.

In addition to sales to bakery wholesalers, Kitchen Made also operates its own delivery truck, which is used primarily to deliver specialty or rush orders. No plans have been made to expand this portion of the operation.

THE BAKING INDUSTRY

Though the outlook for the baking industry has been helped by softening of flour and sugar prices, overall prospects have been unfavorable and should continue to be so as long as economic conditions remain depressed. The baking industry, and particularly the pie and cake segment, is more susceptible to cyclical economic variabilities than other foodstuffs due to the discretionary nature of purchases. Pies and cakes are more or less luxury foods; thus, sales are dependent upon the disposable incomes of consumers. When times are rough, it is these discretionary items that consumers cut back on first. Further dampening the outlook for the industry is the national swing toward nutrition. Sweets and sugar intake have decreased because too much is considered unhealthy, besides, of course, being very fattening. Additionally, because of demographic changes, the average age of the population is higher. Historically, younger individuals account for a large portion of the consumption of pies, cakes, and other desserts.

The frozen segment of the bakery industry is doing even worse. Consumers view frozen foods as being more expensive, and sales have therefore suffered. No relief appears in sight here, at least in the near future.

In addition to the conditions previously cited, other developments are occurring in the industry. Between 1972 and 1977 the number of firms included under SIC code 2051 dropped from 3,323 to 3,062, but at the same time, the number of establishments employing fewer than 20 workers increased. This, of course, has widened the gap between the large and the small bakeries. A major contributor to this trend was the energy shortage, which made transportation costs, already high due to the perishable nature of bakery products, even higher, thus providing cost advantages to the huge firms with internal delivery capabilities and the smaller firms which emphasize local business. Medium-sized firms which were unable to maintain their own delivery function and depended on a more diffuse range of customers were hurt most by this event.

Other factors which could affect the performance of the industry in the future are recent trends toward eating out and the emerging popularity of pre-prepared foods. In today's fast-paced world people no longer have as much time to cook their own meals. The increasing participation of women in the work force has also been a contributor to this turn of events. It should be noted that these fast food chains that are gaining popularity usually use desserts on a nation-wide basis and do not like to buy from local dessert manufacturers.

Overall, the bakery industry is very mature. There has been little real growth in sales over the past few years. However, prices and costs have risen substantially, reflecting inflationary conditions and shortages of certain ingredients. Since ingredient costs represent a major expense (approximately 50% of total costs), recent price declines (e.g., sugar prices fell from $.55 per pound in November 1980 to $.26 per pound in October 1981) have given bakers the opportunity to improve profit margins. Changes in several food and bakery prices, both wholesale and retail, as well as the Consumer Price Index, for the past six years are provided in Exhibit 3.

EXHIBIT 3   **Food price changes**

	1975	1976	1977	1978	1979	1980
RETAIL						
Cereal and bakery products	+11.3%	−2.2%	+1.6%	+8.9%	+10.1%	+11.9%
All foods	+8.5%	+3.1%	+6.3%	+10.0%	+10.9%	+8.6%
Consumer Price Index	+9.1%	+5.8%	+6.5%	+7.7%	+11.3%	+13.5%
WHOLESALE						
Cereal and bakery products	+4.0%	−3.3%	+0.1%	+9.8%	+10.5%	+12.2%
All foods	+6.7%	+3.8%	+4.4%	+10.5%	+9.6%	+8.2%

Source: Department of Labor.

THE LOCAL ECONOMY

Changes in the retail market, prompted by changing demographics and a fluctuating economy, may have a dramatic effect on Kitchen Made. The retail segment of Kitchen Made's market is susceptible to changes in the economy, as is the institutional side. However, some segments of the institutional market, such as hospital cafeterias, do not always reflect economic variabilities.

The Peoria area, like most Midwestern cities, has shown little or no growth in the past decade, as the U.S. population shifts to the Southwest. Peoria itself showed a population decline, according to the 1980 census, although the number of households increased. The economy in Peoria has traditionally been solid due to the dominant impact of Caterpillar Tractor Co., a Pabst Brewing Co. plant, a Hiram-Walker distillery, a number of other medium-sized manufacturing facilities, and a host of small plants — many of which are suppliers of Caterpillar. As a result, Peoria wage rates have consistently ranked in the top 20 cities in the nation. Many have stated that "Peoria doesn't have recessions."

That appears to have changed in the last few years. Caterpillar endured a twelve-week strike in the fall of 1979 that idled many of the 30,000 Peoria area Caterpillar workers and did far more damage to the many suppliers and other businesses that depended either directly or indirectly on the firm. In addition, the Hiram-Walker plant closed in 1981, the Pabst plant is scheduled to close in March of 1982, and Caterpillar, for the first time in twenty years, laid off substantial amounts of workers in 1981 and 1982. These events could have a significant impact on the sale of pies and other desserts in the Peoria area. For instance, Caterpillar uses less than half as many pies today as it did ten years ago. Similar problems are expected in other markets.

COMPETITION

Kitchen Made competes against a variety of firms who do business both nationally and locally. Some rivals make a full line of pies. Additionally, some firms are also diversified into breads and other bakery products. Other have been successful concentrating on specific sizes or types of pies, which allows longer production runs, lower inventories, and thus, lower costs, in some cases. Mr. Dubicki feels, however, that Kitchen Made's full line of pies gives the firm an advantage over competitors in attracting new customers, and protects sales from changes in customer taste.

Kitchen Made has no direct competition in the Peoria area although it does compete against a variety of regional rivals. In some cases, the firm must compete against its own customers who possess in-house baking capabilities. Exhibit 4, presented below, provides a list of some of Kitchen Made's major competitors, as well as available information concerning product lines, major customer segments, and market areas.

PRODUCTION

Baking and production techniques at Kitchen Made are relatively uncomplex, though not without their own special problems. In most instances, pie crusts and fillings are made via the assembly-line method. One person operates the dough machine, which flattens the dough and rolls enough out to make one

EXHIBIT 4   **Competitors**

Company	Location	Markets	Product lines
Lloyd Harris (div. of Fasano)	Chicago	East of Rockies (in and re)	Fresh 9" pies Frozen 8" and 10"
Chef Pierre		Nationwide (in)	Frozen 8" and 10"
Mrs. Smith		(in)	Frozen 8" and 10"
Bluebird Baking	Dayton	Midwest (re)	Fresh 4" and 8"
Shenandoah Pie	St. Louis	St. Louis (in and re)	Full line fresh

Notes: (re) = retail customers
(in) = institutional customers and in-store bakeries
10" pies compete with Kitchen Made's 9" variety.

crust. The dough is passed to a second person, who places it into a pie pan. The machine then presses the dough into the pan. Afterward, the crust passes under a filling machine, which is set according to the size of pie being made. After the crust is filled with the desired ingredients, the pie passes under another station, where the top crust is molded onto the sides of the pie pan and the excess dough removed. This excess is transported by conveyor back to the dough machine. Once the pies are assembled, they are placed on racks and wheeled over to the ovens for baking (All fresh pies are baked. However, frozen pies may or may not be, depending on customer preference.) It should be mentioned that a more efficient pie machine is available, but would be expensive ($150,000), and would require long production runs to be efficient.

A major problem associated with production is the frequent conversions required each time the size or the flavor is changed. It takes approximately 15–20 minutes to changeover pie size, and 4–5 minutes to change the type of ingredient. Size changes usually occur twice a day (from 4″ to 8″ to 9″), but ingredients must be changed 20–25 times per day depending upon the production schedule.

All fruit pies are put together by the method described above, but currently cream pies are filled by hand. Mr. Dubicki intends to make all of Kitchen Made's pie products on the assembly line in the near future.

One way to greatly reduce production costs, of course, would be to limit the numbers of different types of pies made. However, Mr. Dubicki is concerned that this move could hurt the firm because many retail and institutional buyers prefer to buy full-lines of products from the same supplier. Despite this perceived concern, substantial savings are available by limiting pie varieties. For example, with full crews, Kitchen Made currently bakes about $30,000 worth of pies and cakes per week. In some instances, when the firm receives a special order, a half crew will be brought in on an unscheduled shift. On these days, production has reached as high as $10,000. In other words, if sales potential was exploited on a limited number of varieties, the changeover time savings would generate cost savings.

Recently, the first production manager, not a member of the Dubicki family, was appointed. Despite opening up this new position, Mr. Dubicki has continued to spend a significant portion of his time in the shop. The production manager has helped, and Mr. Dubicki expresses confidence in her ability, but sometimes fails to delegate. Another problem is that all of the aspects of the operation have not been completely worked out and some are in the midst of changes.

One positive development has been the ability of Mr. Dubicki to reduce inventory. Though done as much out of necessity as out of design, the move has, nonetheless, helped in many respects. In the past, ingredients were often bought in six-month quantities. Today, the firm tries to buy only what it needs for one or two weeks, except in special cases, when supplies are hard to find or favorable price breaks can be obtained.

FINANCIAL INFORMATION

Given Kitchen Made's current product mix, sales of approximately $35,000 per week ($1,820,000 per year) are needed to break even, according to Mr. Dubicki. Variable expenses are estimated to be about 15% of sales revenue. Exhibit 5 provides a breakdown of sales and operating profits by product line in percentages and dollar amounts. The 4″ pies and the cakes appear to be the biggest moneymakers, with margins on the 8″ and 9″ varieties substantially lower.

Prices have not changed much at Kitchen Made in recent months, and in fact, are the same as they were the year before. Exhibit 6 shows the relative prices for the various types of pies made by Kitchen Made.

Management is particularly pleased with the high-top meringue pie. Because of its superior looks and acceptance by consumers, it is priced much higher than the regular meringue, but costs are almost identical. Thus, profit margins are significantly higher.

Because of weak sales over the past several years, the financial condition of Kitchen Made has deteriorated. Exhibit 7 provides the operating results for the years 1971 through 1981. Exhibit 8 shows the balance sheet for 1981.

EXHIBIT 5   **Sales/operating profits by product lines***

	Sales		**Operating profits**		**Profit margin**
	%	(in thousands of dollars)	%	(in thousands of dollars)	%
Four-inch	33.5	(536)	61.5	(147.6)	27.5
Eight-inch	18.5	(296)	10.3	(24.7)	8.3
Nine-inch	44.0	(704)	21.0	(50.4)	7.2
Other	4.0	(64)	7.2	(17.3)	27.0
TOTAL	100.0	(1600)	100.0	(240.0)	15.0

EXHIBIT 6   **Wholesale pie prices**

4″ pies	$.25	8″ regular meringue	$.90	9″ fruit	$1.30
		8″ high-top meringue	$1.40	9″ whip	$1.30
		8″ fruit	$1.00	9″ meringue	$1.25
				9″ specialty	$1.60
				9″ walnut	$2.00
				9″ cherry	$2.25

*Mr. Dubicki's estimates.

EXHIBIT 7   **Operating results 1971–1981**

	Sales	Profits	Materials	Labor	Selling	Admin.	Production
	(in thousands of dollars)				(costs %)		
1971	844	14 (1.7%)	51.2%	30.0%	2.9%	9.9%	7.6%
1972	955	8 (.8%)	50.5%	29.3%	2.8%	9.5%	7.1%
1973	1246	24 (1.9%)	52.7%	24.6%	2.8%	9.2%	8.9%
1974	1453	18 (1.2%)	57.0%	22.3%	2.5%	7.7%	9.3%
1975	1604	110 (6.9%)	53.9%	20.7%	2.2%	6.9%	9.4%
1976	1580	109 (6.9%)	48.8%	23.0%	2.6%	7.4%	11.3%
1977	1642	7 (.4%)	48.9%	26.0%	2.7%	8.5%	13.5%
1978	1608	−24	50.9%	26.3%	2.2%	9.4%	12.7%
1979	1601	−58	50.6%	27.0%	2.8%	10.0%	13.1%
1980	1506	−91	51.3%	28.3%	3.3%	10.3%	12.8%
1981	1635	−178	54.3%	27.7%	4.1%	11.2%	13.5%

Note: All cost figures are not comparable due to changes in allocation procedures.

Besides the apparent financial problems implied by these statements, several other events have served to increase their seriousness. The most immediate problem relates to the bank note which has currently come due. Kitchen Made had an agreement with a local financial institution which allowed it to borrow $70,000 on a program resembling revolving credit. Kitchen Made paid only interest on this loan, with the principal due in lump sum at the end of the borrowing period. Mr. Dubicki had hoped to refinance the loan, but the attitude of the bank caused him great concern and dissatisfaction. One major complaint was that despite keeping $20,000–$30,000 in cash in its bank account, Kitchen Made received no interest relief. Furthermore, when discussing the possibility of refinancing the loan, Mr. Dubicki was informed that in the future he would be required to sign a second mortgage on his house to secure the note. Without renewal, the firm would be faced with a considerable liquidity problem. However, Mr. Dubicki was hopeful that other institutions would welcome his business if his present bank does not choose to continue their current relationship. It must be understood that this note is not secured in any way, and arrangements to place the bank in a secured position with options for renewal may be possible.

Another problem causing concern was slow payments by some customers. Most firms paid on time, however. Lowenberg and Eisner's consistently take advantage of discounts for early payment (usual terms are 2%/10 days, net/30 days), for example. The major delinquent was Dean's Distributing. Dean's currently owes over six months' back payments, amounting to $60,000. Mr. Dubicki feels that most of this account is uncollectible, but has not, as of yet, written this amount off the company's books. Mr. Dubicki has expressed a desire to eliminate or substantially cut back on the business done with this customer, but despite its unfavorable relations and payment record, Dean's still accounts for a

EXHIBIT 8   **Balance sheet — 1981**

Assets (in thousands of dollars)

CURRENT
Cash	$ 2
Accounts receivable	163
Inventory	137
Prepaid expenses	17
Total current assets	$319

FIXED ASSETS (after depreciation)
Leasehold improvements	$ 1
Machinery and equipment	48
Autos and trucks	28
Total fixed assets	77
Total assets	$396

Liabilities and equity (in thousands of dollars)

CURRENT
Accounts payable	$291
Unsecured bank note	70
Accrued payroll and taxes	25
Note — F. Dubicki	8
Total current liabilities	$394

LONG-TERM LIABILITIES
Note on truck	$ 15
Note on equipment	12
Total long-term liabilities	$ 27
Total liabilities	$421
Equity (deficit)	$ (25)
Total liabilities and equity	$396

large portion of sales. Thus, Kitchen Made must continue to rely upon this customer to maintain sales levels. However, all dealings are conducted strictly on a cash basis with this firm today.

In spite of these financial difficulties, Kitchen Made has been able to keep current on most of their current payables and pay small amounts on older accounts. Thus, while the situation is far from ideal and the firm is very vulnerable to unforeseen events, liquidity is probably not a life-or-death concern at the moment. However, Mr. Dubicki realizes that any further decline in this condition could be extremely hazardous and potentially fatal.

PERSONNEL

Most of the managerial activities at Kitchen Made Pies are handled directly by Mr. Dubicki. Besides the production manager, Ms. Barbara Britt, the only other management personnel are Ms. Charolette Watson, office manager, and Mr. Lonnie Beard, the sales promotion manager. Mr. Beard is responsible for making sure products are stocked and advertised properly at the individual stores, which he visits periodically. Mr. Dubicki, besides being president and owner, also acts as general manager and sales and distribution manager, as well as performing a variety of other functions. Mr. Dubicki prepares projected cash flow statements, searches for new accounts, and, of course, handles many other day-to-day activities. He also is the only person involved in strategic planning, and really is the only person who completely understands all aspects of the business. About the only activity he is not directly involved with is the actual assembly of the pies.

Kitchen Made currently employs about 30 production workers, as well as a half-dozen office workers. The shop is unionized and pays wages comparable to other like-sized area firms. In addition to production and office personnel, Kitchen Made also employs several maintenance workers and a truck driver.

CONCLUSIONS

Though the current situation at Kitchen Made Pies is far from ideal, there are several indications that the situation is not hopeless. Mr. Dubicki is committed to the planning process and has made some long needed improvements in operations. Furthermore, the owner has developed good employee relations, which should facilitate some of the changes being considered. Naturally, there are many questions yet to be answered, such as: Would lengthening production runs really reduce costs? How important is a full product line? Would more equipment decrease costs or increase production, and if so, what equipment should be acquired? How do customers actually perceive quality/price differences in their buying habits? and What type of product mix will maximize sales and, more importantly, profits? The answers to questions such as these will determine the company's fate in the future.

Again, despite all the problems, Mr. Dubicki remains confident. "I'm optimistic about our future, but then again, isn't that the only way I can feel?" Whether this confidence can be turned into results remains to be seen. However, if hard work and dedication are enough, the future should begin to show some improvements.

MERABANK

MeraBank is one of the oldest and largest financial institutions in the Southwest. Formerly First Federal Savings and Loan, MeraBank changed its name creating a new corporate identity to support and enhance its strong commitment to customer service and to facilitate new strategic thrusts. Now, MeraBank must consider the impact of its name and identity change, its expansion and repositioning strategies, and its basic services marketing challenges.

BACKGROUND

On January 1, 1986, First Federal Savings and Loan of Arizona gave banking a great new name, MeraBank (see Exhibit 1). The rich history of First Federal was a foundation and catalyst for the emergence of MeraBank.

Brief History of MeraBank

Arizona was a frontier state in 1925 when State Building and Loan opened its doors for business. State Building and Loan was a forward-thinking company, an enthusiastic group of business people determined to grow with the needs of the nation's newest state. In 1938, the company became First Federal Savings and Loan, and continued to grow becoming the state's oldest and largest thrift.

First Federal was an appropriate name for this innovative company that achieved a long list of "firsts." For example, First Federal was the first Arizona savings and loan to open a branch office. This was achieved in 1948 when a

This case was prepared by Michael P. Mokwa, John A. Grant, and Richard E. White of Arizona State University, in cooperation with MeraBank and the First Interstate Center for Services Marketing at Arizona State University. The case was developed as a basis for discussion rather than to illustrate either effective or ineffective management practice. The help of Robba Benjamin, Margaret B. McGuckin, and Barry Iselin of MeraBank is gratefully acknowledged.

EXHIBIT 1   The MeraBank logo

branch office was opened in Yuma. First Federal was the first savings and loan in Arizona to exceed a billion dollars in assets. It was the first savings and loan to acquire other savings and loans with the acquisitions in 1981 of American Savings in Tucson, Mohave Savings in north and northwestern parts of Arizona, and the acquisition in 1982 of Mutual Savings in El Paso, Texas. After becoming a public company in 1983, First Federal was the first Arizona savings and loan to be listed on the New York and Pacific Stock Exchanges.

In 1984 and 1985, First Federal's growth accelerated, primarily due to the injection of capital from the stock conversion. The company progressed with its mission clearly defined — to be a leading real estate–based financial institution in the Southwest. To achieve its mission, activity centered on diversification with a real estate focus. Three companies were acquired — Realty World, a realty franchising business; First Service Title, a title and escrow service; and F.I.A. Associates, an investment consulting and advisory company. Consumer loan operations were expanded throughout eight western states. In 1985, the company changed its charter from a savings and loan association to a federal savings bank. First Federal officially became MeraBank on January 1, 1986.

In December 1986, MeraBank was acquired by Pinnacle West, formerly AZP, Incorporated. Pinnacle West is Arizona's largest corporation. Pinnacle West is a diversified group of subsidiaries that include: Arizona Public Service Company, a public utility; Suncor Development Company, a real estate development company; El Dorado Investment Company, which invests through limited partnerships in private companies with significant growth potential; and Malapai Resources Company, which locates and develops fuel and uranium reserves. MeraBank with its $6.3 billion in assets and banking presence could be expected to improve short-term earnings and growth potential for the diversified Pinnacle West.

MeraBank's Business Lines

Throughout all of its changes, MeraBank has positioned itself as a family-oriented financial institution, capitalizing on its real estate expertise. For over 15 years, MeraBank has set the pace in residential mortgage lending in Arizona with a market share nearly double that of its closest competitor. The company also has been a significant originator and syndicator of commercial real estate development and construction loans on a national basis. As illustrated in Exhibit 2, MeraBank's operations span eight western states. It is the 25th largest thrift in the United States, the largest thrift in Arizona, and the second largest financial institution in Arizona.

MeraBank has five major business lines: (1) retail banking; (2) consumer lending; (3) real estate lending and mortgage banking; (4) corporate banking; and (5) real estate development.

MeraBank has a well-established retail banking presence. The company offers the convenience of 78 branches including 9 in Texas. Aside from MeraBank's commitment to the Texas region, expansion is being planned for other geographic areas in the Southwest. MeraBank's core products relate to checking and savings, but utilization of electronics and the potential for cross selling are providing new opportunities in retail banking. Currently, MeraBank is a part of the largest ATM (automatic teller machine) system in the state of Arizona.

Phoenix is the largest and strongest area of operation for MeraBank's retail banking. As illustrated in Exhibit 3, MeraBank's market penetration is nearly 18% in Phoenix, which is significantly greater than in the smaller metropolitan areas of Tucson and El Paso. The Phoenix area accounts for over 45% of the bank's business while Tucson is about 10.4% and El Paso is 8.8%. Other parts of Arizona account for 12.8% of the business, other areas of Texas are 4.1%, and other states are 18.2%. By reaching 15% of the Arizona market, MeraBank has a 7.1% share of the total deposit market. Exhibit 4 illustrates MeraBank's

EXHIBIT 2   **MeraBank's areas of operation**

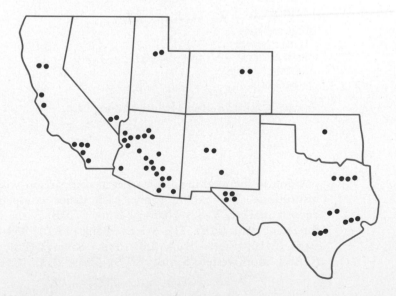

EXHIBIT 3   **Retail household penetration**

Total	3Q85: 231,949
	3Q86: 251,195
	3Q87: 280,663

Total accounts   677,240

Total deposit dollars $2.4 billion

Market penetration	Arizona	15.0%
	Phoenix	17.8%
	Tucson	10.7%
	El Paso	12.2%

EXHIBIT 4   **Major competitors**

Arizona financial market (1986)

Competitor	AZ branches	Assets	Loans	Deposits
		($ In billions)		
Banks				
Valley National	272	$10.7	$7.3	$9.2
First Interstate	183	6.5	4.3	5.7
Arizona Bank	119	4.5	3.2	3.8
United Bank	47	2.7	1.8	2.2
MeraBank	68	6.3	5.1	4.0
Savings and loans				
Western Savings	82	5.5	3.0	3.8
Great American*	32	3.2	2.5	1.4
Southwest Savings	50	2.1	1.7	1.5
Pima Savings	28	2.6	1.8	1.3

*Estimated: AZ operations combined with parent company.

position in the total deposit market in comparison with other Arizona financial institutions. The exhibit shows each major competitor's share of the total deposit market. Valley National Bank (VNB) is the leader, followed by First Interstate Bank (FIB), The Arizona Bank (TAB), Western Savings (WS), Mera-Bank (MB), United Bank (UB), Pima Savings (PS), Great American Savings (GAS), Southwestern Saving (SWS), Chase Bank (CH), and CitiBank (CB).

In consumer lending, MeraBank offers customers a variety of secured and unsecured loans, including home equity lines of credit, car loans, RV loans, and boat loans. Credit cards and lines of credit are also important dimensions of the consumer lending package. MeraBank views consumer lending as an expansion area and has opened new consumer lending offices called MeraFinancial Services Corporation in key expansion areas of Colorado, California, and Texas. The bank's goal in this area is to create as large a consumer loan portfolio as possible, commensurate with sound underwriting. The consumer lending group has instituted a detailed program of monthly loan reviews that will keep management well-informed on the status of the portfolio and how it is meeting underwriting standards.

A strong core of MeraBank's expertise lies in real estate financing. The mortgage lending operations originate and service more loans in Arizona than any other finance company. Additionally, Meracor Mortgage Corporation offices operate in Arizona, California, Colorado, Nevada, New Mexico, Texas, and Utah. They handle residential, commercial, and construction loans. A further presence of MeraBank in the real estate lending market is the marketing of its realty brokerage office franchises. Meracor Realty Corporation holds the license for a large segment of the West and Southwest, having franchised more than 135 Realty World offices. Realty World brokers can offer MeraBank mortgages and services to clients, enabling the bank to reach new customers without adding its own branch office. Through ReaLoan, a computerized mortgage application system, a home buyer and broker can use a computer terminal to analyze the dozens of mortgages available through MeraBank.

In 1985, MeraBank expanded into title insurance. This service was designed to provide customers with title insurance and escrow services from national title insurance companies. Further expansion of the mortgage banking business is sought as MeraBank continues to pursue a program of nationwide lending to strengthen its position as a major force nationally in commercial and construction lending. F.I.A. Associates, the bank's real estate advisory and management company, manages over $1.5 billion in real estate properties and is viewed as a way of diversifying in the real estate business through institutional investors.

Corporate banking provides both deposit and lending services to companies throughout the Southwest. MeraBank offers corporate clients a wide variety of deposit, checking, and lending services as well as financing, secured by accounts receivable and inventory. The bank finances equipment acquisition and plant expansions as well. Cash management accounts and high-yield bonds are products that were designed to meet the needs of the corporate banking customers. Corporate banking is a new area for savings institutions, and the bank is branching into this new and challenging business prudently.

MeraBank is also a significant competitor in real estate joint ventures, which includes the marketing and property management of joint venture projects. This fifth business line, real estate development, is achieved through Meracor Development Corporation, the bank's joint venture and development company. Meracor activities focus on the management of profitable, high-quality projects in Arizona, and to a lesser extent in Texas, California, Colorado, and New Mexico. Management has made a strategic decision to reduce dependence on this area and to limit the size of joint venture development in the future to assure that MeraBank retains a conservative level of leverage.

The Competitive Market Environment

Competition in financial markets is expanding and intensifying as many new institutions are entering and as traditional market and service boundaries are eroding. The basic financial market in Arizona, MeraBank's largest area of operations, can be segmented fundamentally into (1) banks, and (2) savings and loans. Information about MeraBank's major competitors in each of the segments can be found in Exhibit 4. In 1985, savings and loans totaled about a 24% share of the Arizona deposit market, while banks maintained the largest overall market share with 70% of the deposits.

With product deregulation, savings and loan institutions have been given freedom to expand much more into consumer banking services. This has allowed savings and loan institutions to compete directly with the banks, which has resulted in a blurring of the distinction between banks and savings and loan institutions. Through mergers and acquisitions that have taken place as a result of geographical deregulation, larger national and international bank holding companies have moved into the Arizona competitive environment and made their presence known. Of the six largest banks in Arizona, four changed hands in 1986. The two largest banks that have not changed hands during this period are Valley National Bank and First Interstate Bank.

Despite increased competition and activity, total deposits in the Arizona market have begun to decline. As illustrated in Exhibit 5, Arizona's deposit base increased by $11.2 billion from 1983 through 1986, reaching a peak of $33.4 billion. However, in 1987, total deposits declined from 1986. Exhibit 6 shows that the leading financial institutions saw a stable or declining market share trend. First Interstate's market share dropped from 19% to 15.4%, while Valley National and MeraBank's market shares declined 2.5 and 1.4 points, respectively. Exhibit 7 shows that all competitors experienced a positive annual growth rate between 1983 and 1986. But in 1987, all but two competitors had a drop in the average deposit per branch from the first quarter of 1987 through the third quarter of 1987. This is illustrated in Exhibit 8.

The decline in bank deposits appears to stem from consumers' desire for higher return investments. As the stock market enjoyed a record bull market period in the first three quarters of 1987, conservative banking products had a continuing decline, as seen in Exhibit 9. Certificates of deposit (CDs), which offer a guaranteed rate of return for a specified period of deposit time, declined while Money Market Accounts (MMA), which offer a varying rate of interest with no time commitment on the deposit, exhibited a dramatic increase in sales.

EXHIBIT 5   **Trend of Arizona's total consumer banking deposits, 1983–1987/Q3**

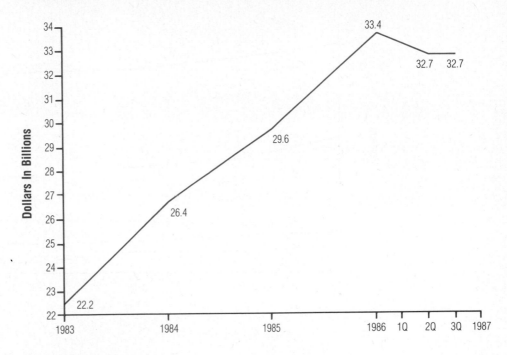

Passbook savings (PB) and interest-bearing checking accounts (NOW) steadily declined in 1987.

The Major Competitors

In the Arizona market, the most formidable competitor has been Valley National Bank with nearly 10 billion dollars in assets. Valley National remains as the only bank that is headquartered in Phoenix. Valley has 277 branches in Arizona. Valley National's 24.1% share of the total deposit market is maintained with 25% of the branches. Valley National's strategy seems centered on intense penetration and physical presence, supported by regional expansion.

Valley National is also the leader in the Arizona market for electronic banking and is planning further expansion. At present, the Valley National debit card is the most widely accepted in the Arizona market and can be used to make purchases at grocery stores, service stations, convenience stores, even department stores. This electronic funds transfer card has become known as a POS (point of sale). It allows a debit of the customer's bank account as payment for a purchase. The POS is expected to be expanded into more retail outlets by Valley National.

In the lending end of the business, Valley National has instituted a Loan by Phone program. The bank promises answers to loans in 30 minutes. These are

EXHIBIT 6   **Market share trend—total consumer banking deposits, 1983–1987/3Q**

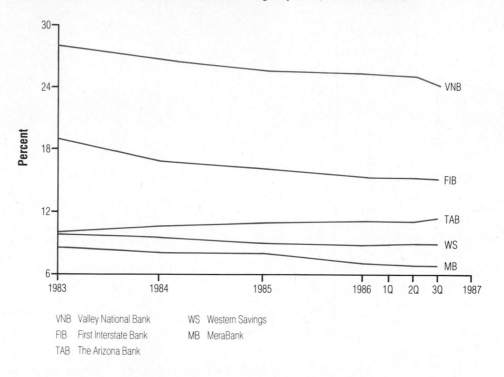

VNB Valley National Bank	WS Western Savings
FIB First Interstate Bank	MB MeraBank
TAB The Arizona Bank	

some of the services that Valley focuses on in its advertising to create its image as "The Leader in Your Banking Needs."

First Interstate Bank has been very close in asset size to MeraBank, but has over twice as many branch locations in Arizona. First Interstate has 15.2% of the deposit market share and 16.4% of the branches. The bank is also involved in POS capability with their debit card being accepted at all but grocery store locations. First Interstate is an affiliate of First Interstate Bancorp, which is the eighth-largest retail banking organization in the nation. First Interstate is a relatively new name for a long-standing competitor. Their advertising theme is "Serving Arizona for 110 years." First Interstate customers are the highest users of the automatic teller machines (ATMs) in Arizona, and First Interstate plans to continue to expand its ATMs, POS, and branches to stay on the leading edge in convenience banking.

The Arizona Bank is another competitor close to MeraBank in asset size, with just under 5 billion dollars. The Arizona Bank with 126 branches in Arizona was acquired in October of 1986 by Security Pacific Corporation, the sixth-largest bank holding company in the United States. The bank's image is tied closely with the state it serves. To convey an Arizona image, a native American Indian is used in the bank's logo with the slogan "The Bank Arizona

EXHIBIT 7   **Growth in total deposits by major competitors**

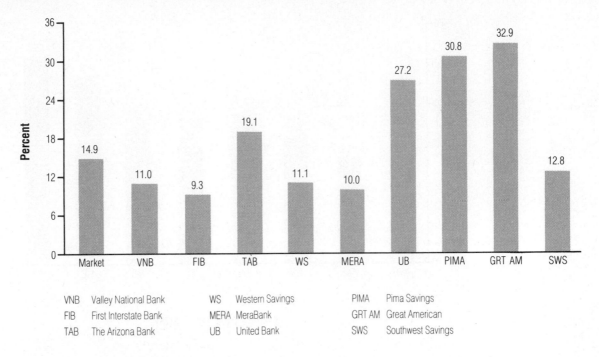

VNB	Valley National Bank	WS	Western Savings	PIMA	Pima Savings
FIB	First Interstate Bank	MERA	MeraBank	GRT AM	Great American
TAB	The Arizona Bank	UB	United Bank	SWS	Southwest Savings

Source: *Deposit Institution Performance Directory.*

Turns To" and "Count on Us." The bank's plans include expansion of more branches in the Phoenix metropolitan area and some outlying communities.

The United Bank of Arizona has been a smaller competitor with only 47 branch operations. It has maintained over 2 billion dollars in assets. United Bank has a 5.7 percent share of the total deposits with only 3.9% share of the branches. United Bank was acquired by Union Bancorp in January of 1987. Union Bancorp is a holding bank in Los Angeles, a subsidiary of Standard Chartered PLC, an International Banking Network. United Bank has had the fastest percentage growth in assets, deposits, and loans of all major Arizona banks in the last 5 years. The bank's focus has been on responsiveness to the needs of the middle market, growing businesses. This is reflected in the advertising theme, "Arizona's Business Bank for Over 25 Years." Citicorp has been very interested in United Bank and would like to acquire it to enhance their presence in Arizona.

In the savings and loan segment, the largest competitor has been Western Savings, with approximately 5.8 billion dollars in assets. Headquartered in Phoenix, Western Savings has begun expansion into Tucson and Flagstaff. In their major markets, Western Savings has located branch offices in popular grocery stores. To develop their image as "The Foresight People," Western Savings

EXHIBIT 8   **Average consumer banking deposits/branch, third quarter 1987**

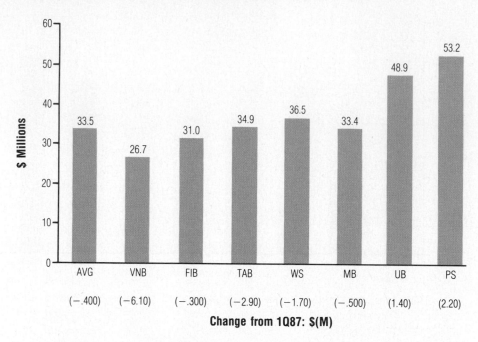

EXHIBIT 9   **Deposit product mix, 1983–1987/3Q**

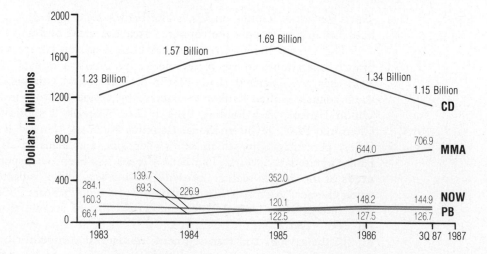

plans to continue to expand products and services. The company experienced about a 2% drop in CDs but has seen an increasing volume of retail deposits. Western Savings is the only thrift currently involved in POS. It has only been able to have its POS card accepted by about 200 Mobil service stations.

Great American, though substantially smaller, has been aggressively expanding in the Phoenix area following a similar location strategy to that of Western Savings. Headquartered in San Diego, the company plans continued expansion in the Phoenix area, targeting high-income growth markets. Great American has experienced the largest increases in the MMAs and has seen a strong increase in the volume of retail deposits in the last year. They present themselves in the image of a bank, trying to stress the name Great American, "Your Advantage Bank."

Southwest Savings is a smaller institution with 53 branch operations. It has been an independent and closely held organization. Southwest has committed themselves to serving the growing senior citizen population in Arizona. Southwest Savings has experienced the industry trend in product performance with about a 2% drop in CDs, while MMAs were up sharply. However, overall total deposits have been down.

Pima Savings has operated out of Tucson, where they have a 40 percent share of the total savings and loan deposits in Pima County. Pima Savings has a 5.9 percent market share of the total deposits in Arizona with only 3.7 percent of the total branches. Pima Savings has seen continued growth in total deposits and in CDs. The company is viewed in the industry as the investment rate leader. Pima is rapidly expanding branches in the Phoenix area, frequently using Safeway grocery stores as their outlets. Pima is owned by Pima Financial Corporation, which is a subsidiary of Heron Financial Corporation, a U.S. holding company for one of Europe's largest privately owned companies.

To gain insight into the competitive environment, 10 additional exhibits have been included. Exhibit 10 illustrates the net worth of the Arizona financials as a percent of their assets. The composition of loan services is expressed in terms of real estate and consumer loans for the banks in Exhibit 11, and for the savings and loan associations in Exhibit 12.

Other major competitors in the Arizona financial market began to arrive with reinstatement of interstate banking in 1986. Among the newest financial institutions are: Citibank, which took over Great Western Bank & Trust of Arizona and is a subsidiary of Citicorp, the largest bank holding company in the United States; and Chase Bank of Arizona, a division of Chase, the second largest holding company in the country. Chase took over the former Continental Bank. These acquisitions should have an impact on the Arizona financial market in the near future. Interstate banking has provided the opportunity for the acquisition of Arizona's financial institutions by out-of-state companies and could continue to be a factor in the competitive environment. Also considered as competitors in some segments of MeraBank's lines of business are insurance companies, finance companies, investment companies, money market

EXHIBIT 10   **GAAP net worth as a percent of unconsolidated assets**

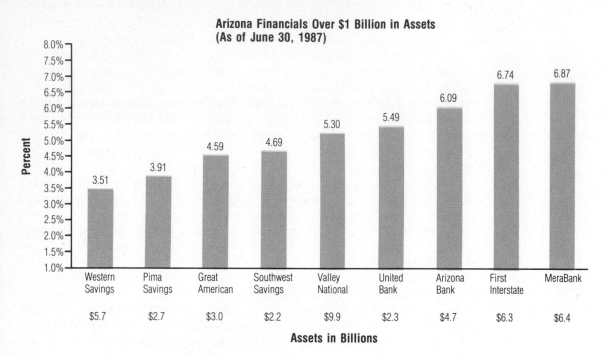

Arizona Financials Over $1 Billion in Assets
(As of June 30, 1987)

Western Savings	Pima Savings	Great American	Southwest Savings	Valley National	United Bank	Arizona Bank	First Interstate	MeraBank
3.51	3.91	4.59	4.69	5.30	5.49	6.09	6.74	6.87
$5.7	$2.7	$3.0	$2.2	$9.9	$2.3	$4.7	$6.3	$6.4

Assets in Billions

funds, credit unions, and pension funds. Overall, many organizations are entering financial service markets.

THE NAME AND IDENTITY CHANGE

In 1985, the total population of Arizona was 3.2 million. The state had experienced a five-year increase in its total population, an increase of nearly 25%. Growth had been projected to continue. MeraBank's other dominant market, Texas, also had been growing. In 1985, it had a much larger population than Arizona, over 15 million people. At that time, First Federal operated 12 offices located throughout Texas, in El Paso, Dallas, Austin, Houston, and Fort Worth.

Even though First Federal was well-positioned in its highly competitive markets, banking deregulation and legislative changes were opening doors to interstate banking and to charter changes for thrift institutions. New products and services would soon be available and a significant challenge confronted First Federal. Although First Federal offered a full range of products and services, most consumers perceived banks to be better—more full-service and service-oriented—than savings and loans.

EXHIBIT 11   Major competitors for loan services, banks, 9/30/86

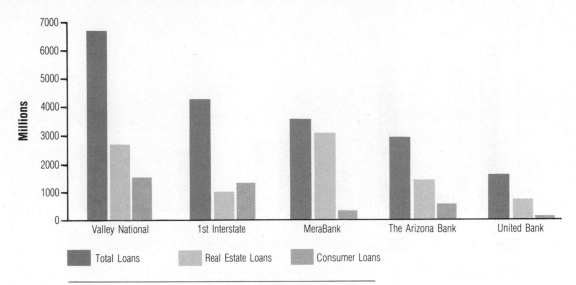

Dollars (Millions)		
	Total Loans	Real Estate Loans	Consumer Loans
Valley National	6718	2740	1538
1st Interstate	4307	1078	1345
MeraBank	3595	3138	352
The Arizona Bank	2942	1466	569
United Bank	1632	754	118

Source: *Deposit Institution Performance Directory.*

First Federal perceived a name change as a necessity, but the corporate priorities in 1985 were complex. The company hoped to demonstrate superior financial performance, while making customer service its most effective marketing tool. Moreover, the company hoped to protect its current market share from the threat of new competition, while increasing retail banking coverage in Texas and expanding beyond Arizona and Texas.

The board of directors had been considering a name change since the company went public in 1983. The name First Federal was a very common name in financial institutions. There were over 89 First Federals in Texas alone. If expansion was to be considered, the company needed a name it could grow with. Aside from expanding under one name and distinguishing itself to stockholders, the board wanted to include the word "bank" in its name and position itself as a bank in the market.

EXHIBIT 12   Major competitors for loan services, savings associations, 9/30/86

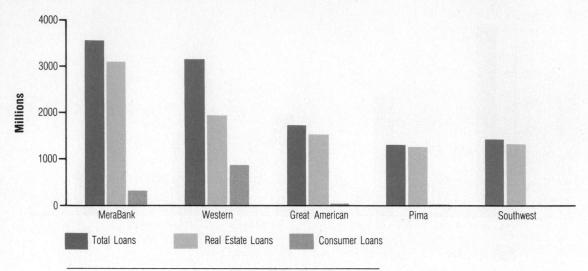

Dollars (Millions)

	Total Loans	Real Estate Loans	Consumer Loans
MeraBank	3595	3138	352
Western	3180	1978	919
Great American	1773	1571	90
Pima	1345	1286	58
Southwest	1477	1343	34

Source: *Deposit Institution Performance Directory.*

A market research company from New York was retained to help determine what the new name and bank image should be. However, the board felt the process would be easy, simply changing some signs and forms. The board decided that the First Federal logo could be maintained by simply changing the name to FedBank. The board dismissed the market research team, and by 1984, they were ready to make the change. In August, a new senior Vice President was given the task of implementing the name change. The initial step was to check out regulations regarding the use of the word "bank" in the name of a chartered savings and loan association. However, it was discovered in the legal search that the proposed use of FED in the new name would violate law. There is a regulation banning private organizations from using a name that sounds like a federal agency. In this case, the proposed FedBank name was very similar to the federal bank known as the "FED."

The task of changing the name would have to start over. The first market research company had left with some ill feelings. So in 1985, a new consulting firm, S & O Consultants from San Francisco, was contracted for the project. S & O specialized in corporate identity. They had recently done the name change for First Interstate Bank in Arizona and were familiar with the financial institution market in the area.

The Project Objectives

Objectives were established at the beginning of the project. These objectives are outlined in Exhibit 13. The primary objective was to select a name that conveyed a positive image and new identity. The name needed to be legally available in all 50 states. It needed to fit all the business lines — everything from the title company to retail banking to real estate joint ventures. A distinctive identity was to be developed as well. The First Federal logo was very similar to other existing corporate identities and offered little value to the company as an identity. The new name needed to create excitement and set the tone for continued innovation and leadership. It needed to increase the employees' morale and help generate new business. However, the company did not have unlimited resources. So, a very important objective was to accomplish everything within a strict, tight budget and a short time frame.

The Process

Distinct phases were identified in the change process. First, the name itself had to be generated and selected. Second, the logo and identity surrounding the name had to be developed. Third, the identity needed to be communicated in a clear and concise way, and finally, evaluation must be undertaken.

Selecting the name was the first step. Criteria for the new name were established. These included implying stature and strength, and being distinctive, memorable, and easy to pronounce. All the criteria were ranked and weighted in terms of perceived importance. The criteria of conveying a service-oriented bank and of implying stature and strength were ranked as the two most important criteria for the new name.

After a positioning statement was developed for the name itself, the process of generating the name began. Over 800 names were evaluated and critiqued. The top 20 names were further evaluated using a mathematical scoring system, and all the top 20 names were legally searched in all 50 states. The final five that were considered were: First Mark Savings Bank, Interprize Savings Bank, Landmark Savings Bank, Merit Savings Bank, and Pace Savings Bank.

An early favorite was Merit Savings Bank. However, this name was being used elsewhere, particularly in California. And it was associated with a brand of cigarettes. However, the name had some interesting roots. After an arduous series of executive interviews, brainstorming sessions, and stormy meetings, a consensus was reached. The name MeraBank was selected.

EXHIBIT 13   **Name objectives**

The new name for First Federal of Arizona's retail bank should accomplish the following (percentages indicate weights given to each objective when evaluating names):

1. Convey an honest, hard-working, service-oriented bank. (30%)
2. Imply stature and strength. (30%)
3. Appeal to the mass-market retail banking audience. (20%)
4. Be distinctive, memorable, and easy to pronounce. (20%)
5. Be compatible with a range of financial services including retail banking, real estate development, construction lending, mortgage banking, corporate lending, etc.
6. Make no specific reference to Arizona, but may incorporate southwestern flavor.
7. Be available and legally protectable.

In phase two, the logo and identity were developed. The company desired a design that would uniquely identify them and reach across all their business lines. The logo had to be instantly recognizable, even before the name was seen. The company wanted something that would emphasize a commitment to comprehensive financial services. The logo would have to be modern, make a strong retail statement, and incorporate a taste of southwestern imagery, but not limit the bank to Arizona.

Choices were narrowed, and focus group testing began. In Exhibit 14, the leading choices are represented. Focus group reaction favored C, a multicolored logo. Group participants described the identity as "progressive," "modern," and "large." Obviously, this met the company's objectives. The colors were described as being "attractive" and "southwestern." The vibrant yellow-gold and orange-red of the sunrise with the royal purple of the mountains were well-understood southwestern images.

Several modifications were made to the logo based on focus group work. For example, the company has had a substantial senior citizen customer base. They expressed some very strong dissatisfaction with the proposed typeface. They perceived the logo as very contemporary, but the typeface was perceived as very different and too modern. What resulted was a new and much more conservative typeface with the same multicolored contemporary logo. Perceptions were much more favorable.

Effective communication of the name and imagery were vital to establishing the identity and accomplishing performance-oriented objectives. A strategic decision was made to communicate the change from the inside out. To accomplish this, a large task force was assembled internally to cover literally every aspect of the identity change. The name change task force began working in July of 1985. It included a project manager, 7 project leaders, and 30 employees. The task force was responsible for the signage, forms, merchant notification, employee notification and promotion, media notification and promotion, and customer notification and promotion.

EXHIBIT 14   **Proposed MeraBank logos**

A)

B)

C)

To direct and guide the task force, several objectives and strategic thrusts were outlined. The first objective was to gain employee awareness and enthusiasm for the name change. Employee support was essential to communicate the name from the inside out. A second objective of the task force was to develop a graphic plan and standards manual that clearly spelled out the proper representation and usage of the new logo. A high priority was given to the delicate task of communicating the change to primary stakeholders, including board members and the stockholders. A major undertaking involved identification and revision of all forms. The effort uncovered the opportunity to reduce by 30% the number of forms used.

The task force also needed to develop an advertising campaign and related promotions for customer notification. A TV spot would provide only 30 seconds to communicate the new identity; a billboard would provide less time. A very complex message had to be refined to its strongest, simplest components. Also, the task force needed to develop branch employee training and information sessions including the revision of the branch operations manuals. Finally, the task force had to be prepared to handle any of the legal questions that could arise concerning the name change. Thus, one of the task force members was a staff attorney.

The plans to generate employee awareness and enthusiasm were initiated within tight time and resource constraints. The task force knew that employee support was essential to market acceptance. The name, but not the logo, was first announced to all employees at the company's big 60th birthday celebration in September 1985. Further internal communication was initiated through a new publication called "The MeraBanker." The employee campaign even included a "mystery shopper" who went into the field asking employees questions about the name change.

A customer awareness program began in November with a teaser advertising campaign. By December, more than 1200 stationery forms and collateral pieces had been redesigned and printed. On January 1, 1986, the new signs and the major campaign theme, "First Federal Gives Banking a Great New Name," were unveiled. Throughout the customer awareness program, the "MeraBanker" term was consistently used for name and identity–related internal communication.

Extensive work was done with the press. Hundreds of press releases were sent out. Early releases included a question and answer piece that did not include the full identity. Later in the program, the logo, the name, and the advertising campaign were released to the press.

MeraBank wanted its identity to be comprehensive and wanted to maintain the integrity and power of the identity. So for the first time in the company's history, a graphic standards manual was developed to state how and for what purposes the logo could be used. This was necessary to determine proper use for advertising, promotions, and brochures, as well as use on checks, credit cards, debit cards, ATM cards, all banking forms, and annual reports. MeraBank even changed their hot-air balloon.

Results of the Name Change

The impact of the name change was very positive. Employees were enthusiastic about the change and scored extremely well on the mystery shopper quizzes. Over 96% of all employees answered questions about the new name correctly. The extensive amount of employee involvement in the name change stimulated a renewed sense of pride in the company. Moreover, the name change was the catalyst generating a new orientation: employees and management perceived themselves as a bank.

Market studies were undertaken to determine consumer response. Consumers were positive about the new name. Over two-thirds recalled the new name, their primary source being television advertising. Fifty-five percent of consumers could identify the new name as MeraBank, and very few people perceived the name change as negative. Overall, post–name change advertising was perceived as more meaningful than previous advertising. In fact, advertising recall doubled and achieved a significant breakthough in terms of consumer scoring.

The new advertising was very successful in promoting the new MeraBank image. When surveys were conducted after the name change, people began to list MeraBank in the bank category and not with the savings and loan institutions. The ad campaign also helped to promote the trial of MeraBank. Of those surveyed who were likely to try MeraBank, most were impressed with the name change advertising and rated it as being very meaningful to them. Those who were willing to try MeraBank described the company as "progressive" and having a "high level of customer service."

In Exhibit 15, there is a comparison of performance figures. A year after the name change, MeraBank's assets were up 20%, and its advertising recall was up almost 100%. MeraBank's retail banking and mortgage lending market share had dropped slightly. This was planned through new pricing strategies that were undertaken to reduce the overall cost of funds. MeraBank, now positioned as a bank, lowered interest rates, getting these more in line with bank competitors versus savings and loan competitors.

THE NEW MERABANK

MeraBank began thinking of itself as a bank after the name change. Customers, employees, and the financial market began to refer to MeraBank as a bank, not as a thrift. However, changing the charter and creating new advertising campaigns were just the beginning. A complete repositioning in the market would be necessary to educate, attract, and serve "bank" customers. Changes in products, advertising, service, and facilities would be needed to complete the identity metamorphosis.

EXHIBIT 15   **Year-end performance comparison**

	December 1985	December 1986	3Q 1987
Assets	$5.2 Billion	$6.3 Billion	6.4 Billion
Retail Banking Market Share	9.1%	8.5%	8.1%
Mortgage Lending Market Share	6.6%*	6.4%*	5.4%*
Advertising Awareness	18.0%*	33.0%*	20.1%*

*Phoenix and Tucson metro combined.

Several strategic changes occurred in conjunction with the name change. Advertising positioned MeraBank directly against the banks. Management dropped interest rates on savings deposits to bring them in line with bank rates. In the six months following the name change, the six-month CD rate dropped 1.1%. Through December 1987, the overall interest expense had been reduced by over $20 million as a result of this strategy. Interest rates and fees on credit cards were increased to be aligned with the pricing policies of banks. Customer service did not appear to suffer as a result of these changes. As seen in Exhibit 3, the number of total retail households served by MeraBank increased by 9% the first six months after the name change. By December 1987, the number of households served was up 22%.

The Marketing Group

Overall, changes were initiated to build a new corporate culture emphasizing service and measuring performance against both banks and thrifts. Strategy implementation became the major responsibility of the marketing group. As a result of the successful name change, the Senior Vice President of Marketing was promoted to Executive Vice President and Chief Administrative Officer in charge of marketing, human resources, and long-range planning. She recruited a new senior vice president for the marketing group.

The basic structure of the marketing organization is presented in Exhibit 16. Headed by a senior vice president, the department is organized into four major divisions. The first division, Market Planning, Research and Development, works on analyzing and segmenting the market and on keeping an accurate account of MeraBank's position in the financial market. Marketing Services develops and manages products, promotions, advertising, and print production for the company. Corporate Communications is responsible for public relations activities, audio/visual productions, and employee communications. The fourth division, Direct Marketing, oversees direct mail campaigns, telemarketing, customer service, and training. Though the reporting structure is set clearly, the functions interface frequently, and informal relationships appear to be very cooperative.

Consumer Market Segments

The primary demographic factors related to financial product usage appear to be age and income. Financial consumers for the banking industry often are segmented using these two criteria. Segments with the strongest potential for heavy financial product usage are: mid-age middle income; mid-age affluent; pre-retired middle income; pre-retired affluent; and retired higher income groups. These segments represent 57% of the Phoenix metropolitan population and 47% of the Tucson area, as seen in Exhibit 17.

EXHIBIT 16   **Organization structure of the marketing group**

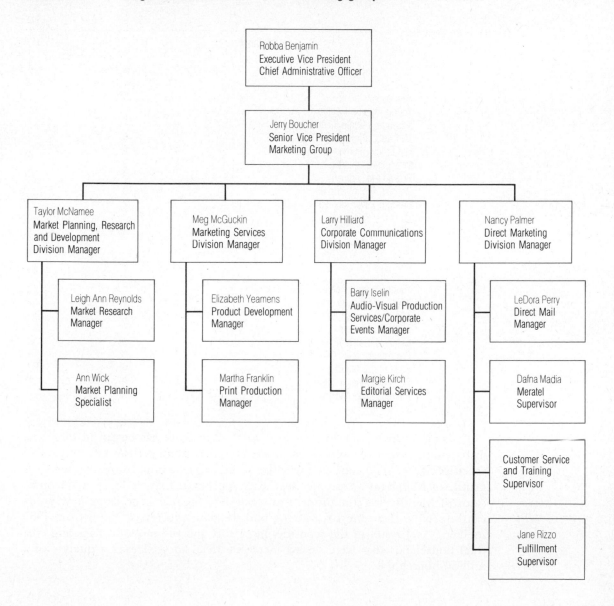

EXHIBIT 17   **MeraBank segment penetration**

Phoenix

	Population
Young, low income	9%
Young, middle income	21
Mid-age, middle income	17
Mid-age, affluent	16
Older, low income	6
Pre-retired, middle income	9
Pre-retired, affluent	5
Retired, higher income	10
Retired, lower income	7

Tucson

	Population
Young, low income	16%
Young, middle income	21
Mid-age, middle income	15
Mid-age, affluent	11
Older, low income	9
Pre-retired, middle income	8
Pre-retired, affluent	4
Retired, higher income	9
Retired, lower income	8

Using segmentation profiles as a base, MeraBank has begun to target its distribution system as well as its products and communication efforts toward specific market segments, in particular more affluent population segments. A profile of MeraBank's customer segments appears in Exhibit 18. A major indicator of MeraBank's commitment to reach new segments and serve new needs can be seen in their direct marketing budget, which increased 200% from 1985 to 1986. As a result of the repositioning effort and the move to targeting, the total households that were served increased 15%, to well over a quarter of a million households.

Service and Product Development

MeraBank launched two new retail banking services since the name change: the Passport Certificate Account and the Working Capital Account. These new accounts have brought in new deposits at a time when total deposits have been declining. Many existing product lines, such as CDs, have seen a decline in sales.

EXHIBIT 18   **Market segmentation profiles**

Mid-Age, Middle Income — These households will be hard to target as an entire segment, because they are widely distributed across all financial styles and thus vary greatly in their attitudes toward financial matters. Households in this segment are family oriented. Much of their financial behavior is focused on protecting their families and planning for their children's future.

Mid-Age, Affluent — A large portion of this segment are "Achievers" and have the most-in-command financial style. They are likely to be receptive to marketing approaches that appeal to their self-image as successful, knowledgeable, and decisive people.

Households in this segment are value sensitive. They are receptive to distinctive product features, and are able to make price/feature trade-offs. While households in this segment are price sensitive, they are willing to pay for services that they don't have time for, especially the dual earner households. They have positive attitudes toward using electronics and are likely to own computers and other electronic/high technology products.

Pre-Retired, Middle Income — Half of the households in this segment are "Belongers." Their financial style is predominantly more-safe-and-simple. Many of these households will be receptive to marketing approaches that stress traditional, conservative values and emphasize the safety of the institution. In their efforts to minimize taxes and accumulate funds for retirement, these households will require conservative, lower risk products.

Many of these households are shifting their focus away from their children to their own future retirement. Though the family is still important, these households' goals are changing as they enter a new life stage. They place a high value on the reputation of the financial institutions they use and on having trust in them.

Pre-Retired, Affluent — The financial styles of the pre-retired affluent households are predominantly most-in-command and most-comfortable. They are oriented toward the present and are concerned about retaining their present lifestyles during their retirement. They are sophisticated in their approach to financial matters. These households like having access to people that they perceive as competent, but are receptive to using the telephone for financial dealings.

Retired, Higher Income — Households in this segment are the most-safe-and-simple and prefer to keep financial affairs uncomplicated and are generally unexperimental. Other households, called most-comfortable, are sophisticated in their approach to their financial affairs. They view themselves as prosperous and financially secure. They highly value security and involvement in financial affairs. These retired households are likely to be receptive to social seminar-type events, because they have the time to attend and the interest in learning.

MeraBank has suffered a loss of about 2% of its CD deposits. Passbook savings accounts have also been on a decline. However, MeraBank has increased its share of interest-bearing checking accounts—a conventional "bank" product—despite increases in the minimum balance of the NOW account from $100 to $500. Similarly, an increase in credit card fees has had only a minimal effect on the number of credit card accounts and card usage.

The Passport Certificate is targeted to the 55+ age group. The advertising campaign has used primarily newspaper. The core product is very traditional, a certificate of deposit. But the CD is augmented with free checking as well as free and discounted travel services such as car rentals, insurance, and even a

24-hour travel center. The account is made more tangible by giving each customer a wallet-size passport card with the account number and the package benefits included.

The Working Capital Account is targeted to the affluent, middle-aged market segment. It is patterned after a money market account. It is a liquid investment with a very high yield tied to the one-year treasury bill. The account requires a high minimum balance of $10,000, but permits unlimited access to the money. The investor can gain a high-yield CD rate, but maintain checking privileges and access to the money. Once again, newspaper was the primary advertising medium for the product. The Working Capital Account provides its subscribers with monthly statements of the investment and the checking accounts. The account is the only product of its type in the Arizona market. In the first nine months after introduction, it generated a half billion dollars.

MeraBank has a strong commitment to customer service and convenience that goes beyond the traditional branch structure. The direct marketing division supervises the operations of Meratel, which is a customer service hotline and "telephone bank." Customers can open an account, obtain information, or transact business by calling 1-800-MERATEL. This convenience to customers has been well received. Call volume increased 300% during the year following the name change. The effectiveness of the Meratel operation can be evaluated using Exhibit 19. To further improve the level of service performance, MeraBank has initiated direct marketing campaigns to retail customers, contacting them by mail and telephone. The intention is to expand this operation and begin a regular program of calling retail customers to enhance convenience.

MeraBank's management believes that its success is dependent on the capabilities and performance of employees. The company is recruiting and developing employees who are more sales-oriented. Employees are expected to produce superior levels of performance, be customer-oriented, have high standards of integrity, and work in unison with a team spirit. To insure these service standards, a comprehensive training program has been instituted for the sales staff with an incentive compensation system for frontline personnel. The commission program has resulted in doubling the cross-sales ratio at the front line. The training process has also been revised to reflect more product training and to

EXHIBIT 19   **Meratel**

	Deposit acquisition	Number of calls
1984	$37,600,000	7,831
1985	$58,014,800	22,319
1986	$51,435,700	75,222
1987	$80,234,630	266,000

amend a thrift vocabulary by incorporating banking terms. Periodically, the company will sponsor a contest to encourage high-quality service and improve morale. Internal newsletters provide employees with communication and inspiration to maintain quality service.

Community service also is an important orientation at MeraBank. In 1987, MeraBank contributed over $1.2 million to charity, and many of its employees work in behalf of civic and charitable endeavors. Contributions are divided among worthy cultural, civic, educational, health, and social welfare programs. In one project, MeraBank teamed with Realty World brokers to create a "Dream House." This project benefits victims of cerebral palsy. Strong community spirit is perceived to be a direct expression of MeraBank's service philosophy and culture.

Advertising and Promotion

Advertising and promotional strategy play a key role in positioning MeraBank. Following the name change, advertising objectives emphasized creating awareness and educating the public to the new identity. These objectives have evolved to emphasize increasing both deposits and branch traffic. The initial name change campaign required an increase in promotional expenditures. However, the current advertising budget is only slightly more than it was for First Federal Savings. The primary medja used are television and newspaper, while radio is used to a lesser extent. TV advertising is targeted at the 35+ age customer, while newspaper ads are aimed at an older 55+ customer. Direct mail and billboard campaigns are used less often, but have been effective for some products.

MeraBank television advertising has incorporated the new identity of the institution, while maintaining the First Federal campaign theme of "We'll Be There." This theme has been used since 1985, and there are no plans to change the theme for general TV ads. However, MeraBank has tried to develop more sophisticated messages and imagery in their ads. Also, they run special promotional campaigns using television as the primary medium. For example, MeraBank became involved in an advertising campaign promoting CDs and a contest linked with ABC television stations and the 1988 Winter Olympics.

This campaign capitalized on patriotic interest in the Olympics and offered a free trip to the games in Canada as the grand prize. The winner of the contest was announced at the half time of the 1988 Super Bowl. Additional prizes were large interest rates on CDs with MeraBank. TV, newspaper, and direct mail were utilized in this campaign. The campaign also included a contest for employees. Employee Olympics were held to spur interest in the promotion and to encourage outstanding service. Employees were able to nominate peers for sportsmanship, team spirit, and customer service. Given the perceived success of the winter campaign, MeraBank planned to extend this strategy to include the summer games.

Merchandising and Facility Management

Extending the emphasis placed on promotion, MeraBank has given more attention to branch merchandising. The entire point-of-sale "look" has been revised to reflect the new corporate identity. Signage, brochures, and point-of-purchase material incorporate the company logo and identity color scheme. Though thought has been given to a standardized interior appearance, there is not a uniform branch configuration. However, the newer and remodeled facilities reflect an interior design that is more open and modular in construction. Partitions are utilized to provide a flexible lobby setup. Interior decor and career apparel that would embody MeraBank's corporate identity through style and color schemes both have been under serious consideration. The basic design and exterior of branch locations also is under review.

MeraBank has essentially three prototypes for branch facilities: (1) a large regional center; (2) an intermediate-size complex; or (3) a small shopping center style. However, a pilot project is being undertaken with the Circle K convenience stores. A MeraBank branch and Circle K convenience store are sharing the same building. Though no direct internal connection was made between bank and store, the two facilities share a parking lot and the same foundation. This approach is viewed as a way of saving on construction costs for new branches as well as providing added security to the customers who use the ATM machine outside of the branch, as the convenience store is always open. It is not, however, regarded as an expansion strategy into retail grocery outlets— a strategy that has been popular with competitors.

MeraBank is planning a new corporate headquarters. The new office building is being designed based on a careful study of the company's history and image. The building is to personify the new positioning thrust and corporate culture of MeraBank.

Emerging Technology

MeraBank belongs to an automatic teller machine network that provides its customers with the most extensive coverage of any financial institution in Arizona. Expansion of the ATM machines and a nationwide hookup are being planned. This could lead toward a future where most banking transactions could be done electronically at home using a computer terminal. Home banking appears to be a long-term technological goal of the banking industry.

The current trend in convenience bank merchandising is electronic fund transfers. Electronic fund transfers are used by many banks in the Phoenix area in the form of a debit card, POS. Though it looks like a credit card, it is used to facilitate payment at retail locations. Using the POS, a transaction is automatically debited to an account. While POS has been limited to market tests in most states, penetration in Arizona has been substantial.

A recent survey found the overall rate of POS acceptance to be 26% among financial service consumers. The response varied by age groups. Younger age brackets had higher usage ratings. While the ratings may not seem impressive, they are when compared with the early ratings of ATM acceptance. Investment in POS technology is very high. However, market penetration might generate transaction volumes that reduce transaction costs considerably. Though many of the larger financial institutions have been involved in POS, MeraBank is taking a conservative stance toward electronic technology and is waiting to see how others fare before they follow.

Profitability Perspectives

Examining the profit picture of MeraBank, it is easiest to consider loans as the assets of the bank and deposits as the liabilities. A key to profitability is the diversity of the bank's assets and liabilities. MeraBank attempts to spread its investment risks and not invest too heavily in any one particular business line. Currently, the retail banking, consumer lending, real estate lending, and mortgage banking lines of business contribute most significantly. Corporate banking contributes to a lesser extent. On a limited basis, the real estate development line is profitable.

MeraBank is very competitive in consumer loans such as auto loans, student loans, and RV and boat loans. Home and mortgage loans are a particular strength. The home equity loan is the fastest growing loan in the Arizona market. Commercial loans are a smaller segment of MeraBank's loan operations. Given that commercial interest rates vary on a case-by-case basis, it is difficult to generalize profitability in this line of business.

One area of consumer loans that could be developed into a more profitable position is credit cards. Profit in this area relates to volume and use of the card. Since the name change, MeraBank has offered the first year of the card with no fee, but has added a $15 annual fee for each year after the first. The interest rate paid by the customer is 17.9%, which is comparable to other Arizona banks. Anyone may apply for a MeraBank credit card. The program is not tied to a deposit in the bank. Changes in the credit card program have brought MeraBank in line with the pricing policies of the major banks. However, credit card customers decreased when the changes were initiated. This is not thought to be a long-term setback.

On the liability side of the balance sheet, MeraBank offers several products that vary widely in their profit contribution. Certificates of deposits are the most profitable deposits. A bank can guarantee a certain return on the deposit, then pool them together and invest them at a higher rate. Passbook savings accounts would rank second in profitability potential. Low interest rate returns are the sacrifice for demand deposit accounts. Other less profitable deposit products would be IRAs, followed by money market accounts. The least profitable deposit account is the interest-bearing checking account, which serves as a loss leader to attract customers and to "cross-sell" other more profitable accounts. Automatic teller cards and point-of-sale cards also are only marginally profitable and serve mainly as loss leaders.

Financial planning, sales of securities, estate planning, administering trusts, and private bankers are services provided by many major banks. These services are very competitive in the Arizona market and require experienced personnel with established performance. However, MeraBank has not expanded into these areas. Though these services have been studied, MeraBank views them as marginally profitable and does not consider them as a hedge against the risk of any loan segment going soft.

Expansion

The objective of reaching new consumers and offering convenience to all consumers drive the expansion of branch locations. Since the name change, new branches have been added in the existing service areas of Arizona and Texas. And further penetration of these states is being actively pursued.

Other expansion efforts seem to be evolving within the current eight-state southwest region that already is served by divisions of MeraBank. The southwest imagery that is projected in the corporate identity should fit well into such states as Colorado and California. Moreover, MeraBank management believes that their identity and the imagery of their logo would be acceptable to all parts of the country in any future expansion.

FUTURE CHALLENGES

MeraBank is no longer a small savings and loan. It has grown in sophistication, as its markets and competitors have. MeraBank aspires to continue its tradition of innovation and leadership. The financial services market will become more complex and turbulent. Diversification and expansion present significant opportunities, but also tough questions. MeraBank envisions establishing and sustaining a competitive advantage in terms of its customer service and service marketing strategies across its business lines and diverse geographic markets. With many different facilities, employees, and markets, setting appropriate objectives while creating the best strategies and programs to service its markets will be challenging.

MeraBank envisions using its identity as a means to powerfully exhibit who they are as a company and to provide evidence of their marketing presence. MeraBank believes that their identity can differentiate them from competitors and provide a distinct position in the market to generate sales and performance. They recognize the problems of being a service provider with many intangibilities to manage and market. Their identity must be considered all the way throughout service design, development, and delivery.

Increasingly, MeraBank has begun to consider fundamental service marketing challenges, such as: making its services more tangible for its publics; controlling its service quality; developing its service culture; enhancing the productivity of its service encounters and environments; and protecting its new identity. MeraBank's new management orientation and renewed employee enthusiasm have generated a new strategic thrust and uncovered new challenges.

NUCOR CORPORATION

INTRODUCTION

Nuclear Corporation of America had been near bankruptcy in 1965, when a fourth reorganization put a 39-year-old division manager, Ken Iverson, into the president's role. Iverson began a process that resulted in Nucor, a steel mini-mill and joist manufacturer that rated national attention and reaped high praise.

In a 1981 article subtitled "Lean living and mini-mill technology have led a one-time loser to steel's promised land," *Fortune* stated:

> Although Nucor didn't build its first mill until 1969, it turned out 1.1 million tons of steel last year, enough to rank among the top 20 U.S. producers. Not only has Nucor been making a lot of steel, it's been making money making steel—and a lot of that as well. Since 1969, earnings have grown 31% a year, compounded, reaching $45 million in 1980 on sales of $482 million. Return on average equity in recent years has consistently exceeded 28%, excellent even by Silicon Valley's standards and almost unheard of in steel. The nine-fold increase in the value of Nucor's stock over the last five years—it was selling recently at about $70 a share—has given shareholders plenty of cause for thanksgiving.

The Wall Street Journal commented, "The ways in which management style combines with technology to benefit the mini-mill industry is obvious at Nucor Corp., one of the most successful of the 40 or more mini-mill operators." Ken Iverson was featured in an NBC special, "If Japan Can, Why Can't We?" for his management approach. As *The Wall Street Journal* commented, "You thought steel companies are only a bunch of losers, with stodgy management, outmoded plants and poor profits? Well, Nucor and Iverson were different."

However, the challenges hadn't stopped. The economy made the 1980s a horrible time for the steel industry. All companies reported sales declines, most lost profitability and some, in both major and mini-mill operations, closed or

This case was prepared by Professor Frank C. Barnes of the University of North Carolina at Charlotte as a basis for class discussion. Used by permission of Frank C. Barnes.

restructured. Nucor's 30% plus return on equity hit 9%. Iverson, however, was one of 52 recipients of the bronze medal from *Financial World* in 1983 for holding onto profitability; they kept costs down but not at the expense of laying off their people—a near-religious commitment at Nucor.

By 1987 Nucor was the ninth-largest steel producer in the U.S. and number 372 on the Fortune 500 list. But the easy gains scored by the new mini-mill operations over the integrated mills were over. The historical steel companies were arousing from their twenty-year slumber, adding modern technology, renegotiating with their equally aged unions, and closing some mills. They were determined to fight back. Mini-mill was fighting mini-mill, as well as imports, and a number had closed. Thus the industry faced a picture of excess capacity that would be the backdrop in the battle for survival and success over the next years.

Iverson and Nucor knew how to fight the battle. By 1986 they had $185 million in cash at their disposal. An expansion program in steel was started. Analysts, however, moved away from their stock, worrying about expansion in an industry facing overcapacity and intense competition. Among their moves, Nucor announced a revolutionary new steel mill based on an advanced technology unique in the world, planned a joint-venture mill with a Japanese steel company, and shocked analysts by entering the fastener business, which had become 90% imported. "We're going to bring that business back." The battle was joined.

BACKGROUND

Nucor was the descendant of a company that manufactured the first Oldsmobile in 1897. After seven years of success, R. E. Olds sold his first company and founded a new one to manufacture the Reo. Reo ran into difficulties and filed for voluntary reorganization in 1938. Sales grew 50 times over the next 10 years, based on defense business, but declined steadily after World War II. The motor division was sold and then resold in 1957 to the White Motor Corporation, where it operates as the Diamond Reo Division. Reo Motors' management planned to liquidate the firm, but before this could be done, a new company gained control through a proxy fight. A merger was arranged with Nuclear Consultants, Inc., and the stock of Nuclear Corporation of America was first traded in 1955. Nuclear acquired a number of companies in high-tech fields but continued to lose money until 1960 when an investment banker in New York acquired control. New management proceeded with a series of acquisitions and dispositions; they purchased U.S. Semi-Conductor Products, Inc.; Valley Sheet Metal Co., an air conditioner contractor in Arizona; and Vulcraft Corp., a Florence, South Carolina, steel joist manufacturer. Over the next four years, sales increased five times, but losses increased seven times. In 1965, a New York investor purchased a controlling interest and installed the fourth management team. The new president was Ken Iverson, who had been in charge of the Vulcraft division.

Ken Iverson had joined the Navy upon graduation from a Chicago-area high school in 1943. The Navy first sent him to Northwestern University for an officer training program but then decided it needed aeronautical engineers and transferred him to Cornell. This had been "fine" with Iverson because he enjoyed engineering. Upon receiving his Bachelors degree in 1945 at age 20, he served in the Navy for six months, completing his four-year obligation.

He wasn't too excited about an A.E. career because of the eight years of drafting required for success. Metals and their problems in aircraft design had intrigued him, so he considered a Masters degree in metallurgy. An uncle had attended Purdue, so he chose that school. He married during this time, gave up teaching geometry so he could finish the program in one year, and turned down an offer of assistance toward a Ph.D. to "get to work."

At Purdue he had worked with the new electron microscope. International Harvester's research physics department had just acquired one and hired Iverson as Assistant to the Chief Research Physicist. Iverson stayed there five years and felt he was "set for life." He had great respect for his boss, who would discuss with him the directions businesses took and their opportunities. One day the Chief Physicist asked if that job was what he really wanted to do all his life. There was only one job ahead for Iverson at International Harvester and he felt more ambition than to end his career in that position. At his boss's urging he considered smaller companies.

Iverson joined Illium Corporation, 120 miles from Chicago, as Chief Engineer (Metallurgist). Illium was a 60-person division of a major company but functioned like an independent company. Iverson was close to the young president and was impressed with his good business skill; this man knew how to manage and had the discipline to run a tight ship, to go in the right direction with no excess manpower. The two of them proposed an expansion that the parent company insisted they delay three to four years until it could be handled without going into debt.

After two years at Illium, Iverson joined Indiana Steel Products as Assistant to the Vice President of Manufacturing, for the sole purpose of setting up a spectrographic lab. After completing this within one year, he could see no other opportunity for himself in the company, because it was small and he could get no real responsibility. A year and a half later, Iverson left to join Cannon Muskegon as Chief Metallurgist.

The next seven years were "fascinating." This small ($5–6 million in sales and 60–70 people) family company made castings from special metals which were used in every aircraft made in the U.S. The company was one of the first to get into "vacuum melting" and Iverson, because of his technical ability, was put in charge of this. Iverson then asked for and got responsibility for all company sales. He wasn't dissatisfied but realized that if he was to be really successful he needed broader managerial experience.

Cannon Muskegon sold materials to Coast Metals, a small, private company in New Jersey that cast and machined special alloys for the aircraft industry. The president of Coast got to know Iverson and realized his technical expertise would be an asset. In 1960 he joined Coast as Executive Vice President, with responsibility for running the whole company.

Nuclear Corporation of America wished to buy Coast; however, Coast wasn't interested. Nuclear's president then asked Iverson to act as a consultant to find metal businesses Nuclear could buy. Over the next year, mostly on weekends, he looked at potential acquisitions. He recommended buying a joist business in South Carolina. Nuclear said it would, if he would run it. Coast was having disputes among its owners and Iverson's future there was clouded. He ended his two years there and joined Nuclear in 1962 as a vice president, Nuclear's usual title, in charge of a 200-person joist division.

By late 1963 he had built a second plant in Nebraska and was running the only division making a profit. The president asked him to become a group vice president, adding the research chemicals (metals) and contracting businesses, and to move to the home office in Phoenix. In mid-1965 the company defaulted on two loans and the president resigned. During that summer Nuclear sought some direction out of its difficulty. Iverson knew what could be done, put together a pro-forma statement, and pushed for these actions. It was not a unanimous decision when he was made president in September 1965.

The new management immediately abolished some divisions and went to work building Nucor. According to Iverson the vice presidents of the divisions designed Nucor in hard-working, almost T-group type, meetings. Iverson was only another participant and only took charge whenever the group couldn't settle an issue. This process identified Nucor's strengths and set the path for Nucor.

By 1966 Nucor consisted of the two joist plants, the Research Chemicals division, and the Nuclear division. During 1967 a building in Ft. Payne, Alabama was purchased for conversion into another joist plant. According to Iverson, "We got into the steel business because we wanted to be able to build a mill that could make steel as cheaply as we were buying it from foreign importers or from offshore mills." In 1968 Nucor opened a steel mill in Darlington, South Carolina, and opened a joist plant in Texas. Another joist plant was added in Indiana in 1972. Steel plant openings followed in Nebraska in 1977 and in Texas in 1975. The Nuclear division was divested in 1976. A fourth steel plant was opened in Utah in 1981 and a joist plant was opened in Utah in 1982. By 1984 Nucor consisted of six joist plants, four steel mills, and a Research Chemicals division.

In 1983, in testimony before the Congress, Iverson warned of the hazards of trade barriers, that they would cause steel to cost more and that manufacturers would move overseas to use the cheaper steel shipped back into this country. He commented, "We have seen serious problems in the wire industry and the fastener industry." *Link* magazine reported that in the last four years, 40 domestic fastener plants had closed and that imports had over 90 percent of the market.

In 1986 Nucor began construction of a $25 million plant in Indiana to manufacture steel fasteners. Iverson told the *Atlanta Journal,* "We are going to bring that business back." He told *Inc.* magazine, "We've studied for a year now, and we decided that we can make bolts as cheaply as foreign producers and make a profit of it." He explained that in the old operation two people, one simply required by the union, made one hundred bolts a minute. "But at Nucor, we'll have an automated machine which will manufacture 400 bolts a minute. The automation will allow an operator to manage four machines." Hans Mueller, a steel industry consultant at East Tennessee State University, told the *Journal,* "I must confess that I was surprised that Iverson would be willing to dive into that snake pit. But he must believe that he can do it because he is not reckless."

Before making the decision, a Nucor task force of four people traveled the world to examine the latest technology. The management group was headed by a plant manager who joined Nucor after several years' experience as general manager of a bolt company in Toronto. The manager of manufacturing was previously plant manager of a 40,000-ton melt-shop for Ervin Industries. The sales manager was a veteran of sales, distribution, and manufacturing in the fastener industry. The plant's engineering manager transferred from Nucor R & D in Nebraska. The Touche-Ross accountant who worked on the Nucor account joined the company as controller. The first crew of production employees received three months of in-depth training on the bolt-making machines, with extensive cross-training in tool making, maintenance, and other operations.

In what the *New York Times* called their "most ambitious project yet," Nucor signed an agreement in January 1987 to form a joint venture with Yamato Kogyo, Ltd., a small Japanese steelmaker, to build a steel mill on the Mississippi River with a 600,000 ton per year capacity. The two hundred million dollar plant would make very large structural products, up to 24 inches. Structural steel products are those used in large buildings and bridges. Iverson noted, "These are now only made by the Big Three integrated steel companies." The Japanese company, which would own 49% of the stock, had expertise in continuous-casting in which Nucor was interested. Their 1985 sales totaled $400 million, with approximately 900 workers. They would provide the continuous casting technology while Nucor would provide the melting technology and management style.

In August 1986, Iverson told Cable News Network, "We are talking about within the next two years perhaps building a steel mill to make flat roll products, that would be the first time a mini-mill has been in this area." It was expected that approximately $10 million would be needed to develop this process. The thin-slab would also produce feed stock for Vulcraft's 250,000 tons per year steel deck operation. Although the project was considered pure research at the time and projected for "late 1988," the Division Manager stated, "The more we look into it, the more we feel we'll be able to successfully cast those slabs." This process would be the most significant development in the steel industry in decades and would open up the auto and appliance businesses to the mini-mills. Then in January 1987 plans were announced to build the $200 million, 800,000-ton mill for the production of high-grade flat rolled steel by the first half of 1989. Iverson stated: "We've tested numerous approaches... this one is commercially feasible. It's been tested and it can do the job."

In December 1986 Nucor announced its first major acquisition, Genbearco, a steel bearings manufacturer. At a cost of more than $10 million, it would add $25 million in sales and 250 employees. Iverson called it "a good fit with our business, our policies and our people." It was without a union and tied pay to performance.

Nucor's innovation was not limited to manufacturing. In the steel industry, it was normal to price an order based on the quantity ordered. In 1984, Nucor broke that pattern. As Iverson stated, "Sometime ago we began to realize that with computer order entry and billing, the extra charge for smaller orders was not cost justified. We found the cost of servicing a 20 ton order compared with a 60 ton order was about 35 cents a ton and most of that was related to credit and collection. We did agonize over the decision, but over the long run we are confident that the best competitive position is one that has a strong price to cost relationship." He noted that this policy would give Nucor another advantage over foreign suppliers in that users could maintain lower inventories and order more often. "If we are going to successfully compete against foreign suppliers, we must use the most economical methods for both manufacturing and distribution."

THE STEEL INDUSTRY

The early 1980s had been the worst years in decades for the steel industry. Data from the American Iron and Steel Institute showed shipments falling from 100.2 million tons in 1979 to the mid-80 levels in 1980 and 1981. Slackening in the economy, particularly in auto sales, led the decline. In 1986, when industry capacity was at 130 million tons, the outlook was for a continued decline in per-capita consumption and movement toward capacity in the 90–100 million ton range. The Chairman of Armco saw "millions of tons chasing a market that's not there; excess capacity that must be eliminated."

The large, integrated steel firms, such as U.S. Steel and Armco, which made up the major part of the industry, were the hardest hit. *The Wall Street Journal* stated, "The decline has resulted from such problems as high labor and energy costs in mining and processing iron ore, a lack of profits and capital to modernize plants, and conservative management that has hesitated to take risks."

These companies produced a wide range of steels, primarily from ore processed in blast furnaces. They had found it difficult to compete with imports, usually from Japan, and had given up market share to imports. They sought the protection of import quotas. Imported steel accounted for 20% of the U.S. steel consumption, up from 12% in the early 1970s. The U.S. share of world production of raw steel declined from 19% to 14% over the period. Imports of light bar products accounted for less than 9% of U.S. consumption of those products in 1981, according to the U.S. Commerce Department, while imports of wire rod totaled 23% of U.S. consumption. "Wire rod is a very competitive product in the world market because it's very easy to make," Ralph Thompson, the Commerce Department's steel analyst, told the *Charlotte Observer*.

Iron Age stated that exports, as a percent of shipments in 1985, were 34% for Nippon, 26% for British Steel, 30% for Krupp, 49% for USINOR of France, and less than 1% for every American producer on the list. The consensus of steel experts was that imports would average 23% of the market in the last half of the 1980s.

Iverson was one of very few in the steel industry to oppose import restrictions. He saw an outdated U.S. steel industry that had to change.

> About 12% of the steel in the U.S. is still produced by the old open hearth furnace. The Japanese shut down their last open hearth furnace about five years ago. . . . The U.S. produces about 16% of its steel by the continuous casting process. In Japan over 50% of the steel is continuously cast. . . . We Americans have been conditioned to believe in our technical superiority. For many generations a continuing stream of new inventions and manufacturing techniques allowed us to far outpace the rest of the world in both volume and efficiency of production. In many areas this is no longer true and particularly in the steel industry. In the last three decades, almost all the major developments in steel making were made outside the U.S. There were 18 continuous casting units in the world before there was one in this country. I would be negligent if I did not recognize the significant contribution that the government has made toward the technological deterioration of the steel industry. Unrealistic depreciation schedules, high corporate taxes, excessive regulation and jaw-boning for lower steel prices have made it difficult for the steel industry to borrow or generate the huge quantities of capital required for modernization.

By the mid-1980s the integrated mills were moving fast to get back into the game; they were restructuring, cutting capacity, dropping unprofitable lines, focusing products, and trying to become responsive to the market. The President of USX explained: "Steel executives, in trying to act as prudent businessmen, are seeking the lowest-cost solutions to provide what the market wants." Karlis Kirsis, Director of World Steel Dynamics at Paine Webber, told *Purchasing Magazine,* "The industry as we knew it five years ago is no more; the industry as we knew it a year ago is gone."

Purchasing believed that buyers would be seeing a pronounced industry segmentation. There would be integrated producers making mostly flat-rolled and structural grades, reorganized steel companies making a limited range of products, mini-mills dominating the bar and light structural product areas, specialty steel firms seeking niches, and foreign producers. There would be accelerated shutdowns of older plants, elimination of products by some firms, and the installation of new product lines with new technologies by others. There would also be corporate facelifts as executives diversified from steel to generate profits and entice investment dollars. They saw the high-tonnage mills restructuring to handle sheets, plates, structurals, high-quality bars, and large pipe and tubular products, which would allow for a resurgence of specialized mills: cold-finished bar manufacturers, independent strip mills, and mini-mills.

Wheeling-Pittsburgh illustrated the change under way in the industry. Through Chapter 11 reorganization it had cut costs by more than $85/ton. They divided into profit centers, negotiated the lowest hourly wage rate ($18/hour) among unionized integrated steel plants, renegotiated supply contracts, closed pipe and tube mills, and shut 1.6 million tons of blast furnace capacity in favor of an electric furnace with continuous casting.

Paine Webber pointed out the importance of "reconstituted mills," which they called the "People Express" of the industry. These were companies that had reorganized and refocused their resources, usually under Chapter 11. These include Kaiser Steel, The Weirton Works, Jones and Laughlin, Republic, Youngstown, Wheeling, LTV, and others.

Joint ventures had arisen to produce steel for a specific market or region. The Chairman of USX called them "an important new wrinkle in steel's fight for survival" and stated, "If there had been more joint ventures like these two decades ago, the U.S. steel industry might have built only half of the dozen or so hot-strip mills it put up in that time and avoided today's overcapacity." *Purchasing* observed: "The fact is that these combined operations are the result of a laissez-faire attitude within the Justice Department under the Reagan administration following the furor when government restrictions killed the planned USS takeover of National Steel (which later sold 50% interest to a Japanese steelmaker)."

However, the road ahead for the integrated mills would not be easy. While it was estimated they would need $10 billion to improve their facilities, the industry had lost over $7 billion since 1982. *Purchasing* pointed out that tax laws and accounting rules are slowing the closing of inefficient plants. Shutting a 10,000-person plant could require a firm to hold a cash reserve of $100 million to fund health, pension, and insurance liabilities. The Chairman of Armco commented: "Liabilities associated with a plant shutdown are so large that they can quickly devastate a company's balance sheet."

THE MINI-MILL

A new type of mill, the "mini-mill," emerged in the U.S. during the 1970s to compete with the integrated mill. The mini-mill used electric arc furnaces to manufacture a narrow product line from scrap steel. In 1981 the *New York Times* reported:

> The truncated steel mill is to the integrated steel mill what the Volkswagen was to the American auto industry in the 1960s: smaller, cheaper, less complex and more efficient. Although mini-mills cannot produce such products as sheet steel [flat rolled] and heavy construction items,

some industry analysts say it is only a matter of time before technological breakthroughs make this possible.

Since mini-mills came into being in the 1970s, the integrated mills' market share has fallen from about 90% to about 60%, with the loss equally divided between mini-mills and foreign imports. While the integrated steel companies averaged a 7% return on equity, the mini-mills averaged 14%, and some, such as Nucor, achieved about 25%.

The leading mini-mills were Nucor, Florida Steel, Georgetown Steel (Korf Industries), Northstar Steel, and Chaparral. Nucor produced "light bar" products: bars, angles, channels, flats, smooth round, and forging billets. It was beginning to make more alloy steels. Florida Steel made mostly reinforcing bar for construction (rebar) and dominated the Florida market. Korf Industries had two mini-mill subsidiaries, which used modern equipment to manufacture wire-rod.

The mini-mills were not immune to the economic slump in the early eighties. Korf Industries, which owned Georgetown Steel, found its interest charges too large a burden and sought reorganization in 1983. In March of 1983 Georgetown followed the historic wage-cutting contract between the United Steel Workers of America and the major steel companies and asked its union to accept reductions and to defer automatic wage increases. In 1982 Nucor froze wages and executives took a 5% pay cut. Plants went to a four-day schedule in which workers would receive only base rate if they chose to work a fifth day doing clean-up.

Florida Steel, with two-thirds of its sales in Florida, also felt the impact. At its headquarters in Tampa, a staff of over 100 handled accounting, payroll, sales entry, and almost all other services for all its facilities. Their division managers did not have sales responsibilities. Florida Steel experienced a sales decline for 1982 of 22% and an earnings drop from $3.37 per share to a loss of $1.40. The next year was also a year of losses.

Florida Steel employees had faced periodic layoffs during the recession. The firm was non-union (although the Charlotte plant lost an election in 1973) and pay was based on productivity. A small facility at Indian Town, near West Palm Beach, never became productive, even with personnel changes, and had to be closed. A new mini-mill in Tennessee was completed in late 1983.

Mini-mills had tripled their output in the last decade to capture 17% of domestic shipments. Paine Webber predicted the big integrated mills' share of the market would fall to 40%, the mini-mills share would rise to 23%, "reconstituted" mills would increase from 11% to 28%, and specialized mills would increase their share from 1% to 7%. Iverson stated mini-mills could not go beyond a 35% to 40% share due to technical limitations; mini-mills could not produce the flat rolled sheet steel used in cars and appliances.

Iverson told *Metal Center News* in 1983: "We are very interested in the development of a thin slab, which would then allow mini-mills to produce plate and other flat rolled products . . . actually, the thinnest slab that can now be produced is about 6 inches thick . . . (That results in a plant that is too large.) There are a number of people working to develop the process. . . . We have done some work, but our primary efforts at the moment are in connection with other people who are working on it. . . . The likelihood is it would be developed by a foreign company. There are more efforts by foreign steel companies in that direction than in the United States. . . . I'd say probably a minimum of three to five years, or it could take as much as 10 to achieve this."

In 1983 Iverson described the new generation of mini-mills he foresaw: "If you go way back, mini-mills got started by rolling reinforcing bar. With the advent of continuous casting and improvements in rolling mills, mini-mills gradually got into shapes. Now they have moved in two other directions: one being to larger sizes, and the other being a growing metallurgical expertise for improved product quality and production of special bar quality in alloys. Both of these represent expansion of markets for mini-mills."

By 1986 the new competitive environment was apparent. Four mini-mills had closed their doors within the year and Iverson saw that more shutdowns were ahead. The overcapacity of steel bar products and the stagnant market had made it difficult for some companies to generate the cash needed to modernize and expand their product lines. "The mini-mills are going through the same kind of restructuring and rethinking as the integrated mill. They know the problem of overcapacity isn't going to go away quickly. And, for some of the remaining firms to survive, they will have to move into more sophisticated products like special quality and clean-steel bars and heavier structurals and, once the technology is perfected, flat-rolled products. You won't see the market growth by the mini-mills the way it was in the past until the overcapacity issue is resolved and the mills begin entering new product areas."

ORGANIZATION

Nucor, with its 16-person corporate office located in Charlotte, North Carolina, had divisions spread across the U.S. The 11 divisions, one for every plant, each had a general manager, who was also a vice president of the corporation, directly responsible to Mr. Iverson. (See Exhibit 1.) The divisions were of two basic types, joist plants and steel mills. The corporate staff consisted of a single specialist in personnel and a four-person financial function under Mr. Sam Siegel. Iverson, in the beginning, had chosen Charlotte "as the new home base for what he had envisioned as a small cadre of executives who would guide a decentralized operation with liberal authority delegated to managers in the field," according to *South Magazine*.

Iverson gave his views on organization:

> You can tell a lot about a company by looking at its organization charts. . . . If you see a lot of staff, you can bet it is not a very efficient organization. . . . Secondly, don't have assistants. We do not have that title and prohibit it in our company. . . . In this organization nobody reports to the

EXHIBIT 1   **Nucor organization chart**

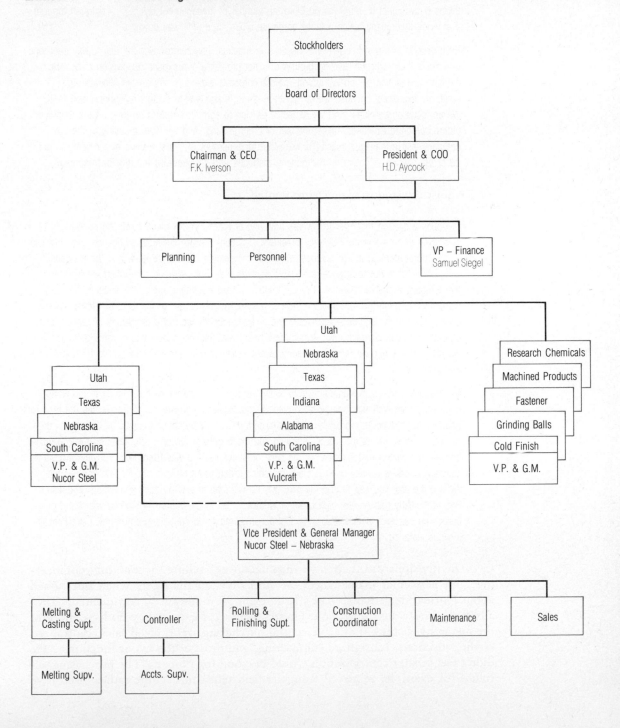

corporate office, the division managers report directly to me.... And one of the most important things is to restrict as much as possible the number of management layers.... I've often thought that when a company builds a fancy corporate office, its on it's way down.

Each division is a profit center and the division manager has control over the day-to-day decisions that make that particular division profitable or not profitable. We expect the division to provide division contribution, which is earnings before corporate expenses. We do not allocate our corporate expenses, because we do not think there is any way to do this reasonably and fairly. We do focus on earnings. And we expect a division to earn 25% return on total assets employed, before corporate expenses, taxes, interest or profit sharing. And we have a saying in the company — if a manager doesn't provide that for a number of years, we are either going to get rid of the division or get rid of the general manager, and it's generally the division manager.

A joist division manager commented:

I've been a division manager four years now and at times I'm still awed by it: the opportunity I was given to be a Fortune 500 vice-president.... I think we are successful because it is our style to pay more attention to our business than our competitors.... We are kind of a "no nonsense" company. That is not to say we don't have time for play, but we work hard when we work and the company is first and foremost in our minds.... I think another one of the successes of our company has been the fact that we have a very minimum number of management levels. We've been careful to avoid getting top heavy and so consequently we put a great deal of responsibility on each individual at each level. It has often been said, jokingly, that if you are the janitor at Vulcraft and you get the right promotions, about four promotions would take you to the top of the company.

Mr. Iverson's style of management is to allow the division manager all the latitude in the world. His involvement with the managers is quite limited. As we've grown, he no longer has the time to visit with the managers more than once or twice a year.... Whereas in many large companies the corporate office makes the major decisions and the people at the operating level sit back to wait for their marching orders, that's not the case at Nucor.... In a way I feel like I run my own company because I really don't get any marching orders from Mr. Iverson. He lets you run the division the way you see fit and the only way he will step in is if he sees something he doesn't like, particularly bad profits, high costs or whatever. But in the years I've worked with him I don't believe he has ever issued one single instruction to me to do something differently. I can't recall a single instance.

The divisions did their own manufacturing, selling, accounting, engineering, and personnel management. A steel division manager, when questioned about Florida Steel, which had a large plant 90 miles away, commented, "I really don't know anything about Florida Steel.... I expect they do have more of the hierarchy. I think they have central purchasing, centralized sales, centralized credit collections, centralized engineering, and most of the major functions." He didn't feel greater centralization would be good for Nucor. "The purchasing activity, for example, removed from the field tends to become rather insensitive to the needs of the field and does not feel the pressures of responsibility. And the division they are buying for has no control over what they pay. . . . Likewise centralized sales would not be sensitive to the needs of their divisions."

South Magazine observed that Iverson had established a characteristic organizational style described as "stripped down" and "no nonsense." "Jack Benny would like this company," observed Roland Underhill, an analyst with Crowell, Weedon and Co. of Los Angeles, "so would Peter Drucker." Underhill pointed out that Nucor's thriftiness doesn't end with its "spartan" office staff or modest offices. "There are no corporate perquisites," he recited. "No company planes. No country club memberships. No company cars."

Fortune reported, "Iverson takes the subway when he is in New York, a Wall Street analyst reports in a voice that suggests both admiration and amazement." The general managers reflected this style in the operation of their individual divisions. Their offices were more like plant offices or the offices of private companies built around manufacturing rather than for public appeal. They were simple, routine, and businesslike.

In 1983 one of Iverson's concerns had been that as Nucor continued to grow, they would have to add another layer of management to their lean structure. In June 1984 he named Dave Aycock President and Chief Operating Officer, while he became Chairman and Chief Executive Officer — they would share one management level. Aycock had most recently been Division Manager of the steel mill at Darlington. But he had been with the company longer than Iverson, having joined Vulcraft in 1955, and had long been recognized as a particularly valued and close advisor to Iverson.

Iverson explained: "The company got to the size that I just wasn't doing the job that I thought should be done by this office. I couldn't talk to the analysts and everyone else I have to talk to, put the efforts into research and development I wanted to, and get to all the units as frequently as I should. That's why I brought Dave in. And, of course, he has been with the company forever." In a February 1985 letter he told stockholders: "These changes are to provide additional emphasis on the expansion of the company's businesses."

"Dave is a very analytical person and very thorough in his thought process," another Division Manager told *33 Metal Producing,* a McGraw-Hill publication. "And Ken, to use an overworked word, is an entrepreneurial type. So, they complement each other. They're both very aggressive men, and make one hell of a good team." Aycock stated: "I am responsible for the operations of all our divisions. To decide where we are going, with what technologies, what our purposes are. And what is our thrust. I help Ken shape where we are going and with what technologies. . . . I've been quite aggressive my whole career at updating, adapting, and developing new technology and new ideas in production and marketing." "Dave's the fellow who now handles most of the day-to-day operations," Iverson commented. "And he handles most of the employees who write to us," — about 10 to 15% of his time.

Division Managers

The general managers met three times a year. In late October they presented preliminary budgets and capital requests. In late February they met to finalize budgets and treat miscellaneous matters. Then, at a meeting in May, they handled personnel matters, such as wage increases and changes of policies or benefits. The general managers as a group considered the raises for the department heads, the next lower level of management. As one of the managers described it:

> In May of each year, all the general managers get together and review all the department heads throughout the company. We have kind of an informal evaluation process. It's an intangible thing, a judgment as to how dedicated an individual is and how well he performs compared to the same position at another plant. Sometimes the numbers don't come out the way a general manager wants to see them, but it's a fair evaluation. The final number is picked by Mr. Iverson. Occasionally there are some additional discussions with Mr. Iverson. He always has an open mind and might be willing to consider a little more for one individual. We consider the group of, say, joist production managers at one time. The six managers are rated for performance. We assign a number, such as +3 to a real cracker jack performer or a −2 to someone who needs improvement. These ratings become a part of the final pay increase granted.

The corporate personnel manager described management relations as informal, trusting, and not "bureaucratic." He felt there was a minimum of paperwork, that a phone call was more common, and that no confirming memo was thought to be necessary. Iverson himself stated:

> Management is not a popularity contest. If everybody agrees with the organization, something is wrong with the organization. You don't expect people in the company to put their arms around each other, and you don't interfere with every conflict. Out of conflict often comes the best answer to a particular problem. So don't worry about it. You are always going to have some conflict in an organization. You will always have differences of opinion, and that's healthy. Don't create problems where there are none.

A Vulcraft manager commented: "We have what I would call a very friendly spirit of competition from one plant to the next. And of course all of the vice presidents and general managers share the same bonus system so we are in this together as a team even though we operate our divisions individually." The general managers are paid a bonus based on a total corporate profit rather than their own divisions' profits. A steel mill manager explained:

> I think it's very important for the general managers to be concerned with contributing to the overall accomplishment of the company. There is a lot of interplay between the divisions with a flow of services, products, and ideas between divisions. Even though we are reasonably autonomous, we are not isolated. . . . We don't like the division managers to make decisions that would take that division away from where we want the whole company to go. But we certainly want the divisions to try new things. We are good copiers; if one division finds something that

works, then we will all try it. I think that's one of our strengths. We have a lot of diverse people looking at ways to do things better.

Iverson revealed his view of management in his disdain for consultants:

They must have a specific job to do because they can't make your decisions. . . . The fellow on the line has to make decisions. . . . First he has to communicate and then he has to have the intestinal fortitude and the personal strength to make the decisions, sometimes under very difficult conditions. . . . A good manager is adaptable and he is sensitive to cultural, geographical, environmental, and business climates. Most important of all he communicates. . . . You never know if someone is a good manager until he manages. And that's why we take people as young as we possibly can, throw responsibility at them and they either work or they don't work. In a sense it's survival of the fittest. But don't kid yourself; that's what industry is all about.

A steel division manager commented in comparing the Nucor manager to the typical manager of a large corporation:

We would probably tend to have managers who have confidence in their abilities and, very importantly, have confidence in other people in their division. And people who are very sensitive to the employees of their division. . . . But, I think if you saw four or five different division managers you'd have four or five different decision-making styles.

A Vulcraft general manager in his early forties who had been promoted to the division manager level nine years earlier said:

The step from department manager to division manager is a big one. I can't think of an instance when a general manager job has been offered to an individual that it has been passed up. Often it means moving from one part of the country to another. There are five department heads in six joist plants, which means there are 30 people who are considered for division manager slots at a joist plant. Mr. Iverson selects the division managers.

His own experience was enlightening:

When I came to this plant four years ago, we had too many people, too much overhead. We had 410 people at the plant and I could see, because I knew how many people we had in the Nebraska plant, we had many more than we needed. That was my yardstick and we set about to reduce those numbers by attrition. . . . We have made a few equipment changes that made it easier for the men, giving them an opportunity to make better bonuses. Of course the changes were very subtle in any given case but overall in four years we have probably helped the men tremendously. With 55 fewer men, perhaps 40–45 fewer in the production area, we are still capable of producing the same number of tons as four years ago.

The divisions managed their activities with a minimum of contact with the corporate staff. Each day disbursements were reported to Siegel's office. Payments flowed into regional lock-boxes. On a weekly basis, joist divisions reported total quotes, sales cancellations, backlog, and production. Steel mills reported tons-rolled, outside shipments, orders, cancellations, and backlog. Mr. Iverson graphed the data. He might talk to the division about every two weeks. On the other hand Iverson was known to bounce ideas off the steel division manager in Darlington, with whom he had worked since joining the company.

The Vulcraft manager commented on the communications with the corporate office: "It's kind of a steady pipeline. I might talk to the corporate office once a day or it might be once a week. But it generally involves, I would not say trivial information, just mundane things. Occasionally I hear from Sam or Ken about serious matters."

Each month the divisions completed a two-page (11″ × 17″) "Operations Analysis," which was sent to all the managers. Its three main purposes were (1) financial consolidation, (2) sharing information among the divisions, and (3) Iverson's examination. The summarized information and the performance statistics for all the divisions were then returned to the managers.

VULCRAFT—THE JOIST DIVISIONS

Half of Nucor's business was the manufacture and sale of open web steel joists and joist girders at six Vulcraft divisions located in Florence, South Carolina; Norfolk, Nebraska; Ft. Payne, Alabama; Grapeland, Texas; St. Joe, Indiana; and Brigham City, Utah. Open web joists, in contrast to solid joists, were made of steel angle iron separated by round bars or smaller angle iron. (See Exhibit 2). These joists cost less and had greater strength in many applications and were used primarily as the roof support systems in larger buildings, such as warehouses and stores.

The joist industry was characterized by high competition among many manufacturers for many small customers. The Vulcraft divisions had over 3,000 customers, none of whom dominated the business. With an estimated 25% of the market, Nucor was the largest supplier in the U.S. It utilized national advertising campaigns and prepared competitive bids on 80% to 90% of buildings using joists. Competition was based on price and delivery performance. Nucor had developed computer programs to prepare designs for customers and to compute bids based on current prices and labor standards. In addition, each Vulcraft plant maintained its own Engineering Department to help customers with design problems or specifications. The Florence manager commented, "Here on the East Coast we have six or seven major competitors; of course, none of them are as large as we are. The competition for any order will be heavy, and we will see six or seven different prices." He added, "I think we have a strong selling force in the marketplace. It has been said to us by some of our competitors that in this particular industry we have the finest selling organization in the country."

Nucor aggressively sought to be the lowest cost producer in the industry. Materials and freight were two important elements of cost. Nucor maintained

EXHIBIT 2   **Illustration of joists**

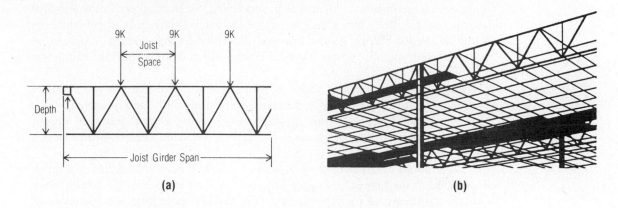

(a)   (b)

its own fleet of almost 100 trucks to ensure on-time delivery to all states, although most business was regional due to transportation costs. Plants were located in rural areas near the markets they served.

The Florence manager stated:

> I don't feel there's a joist producer in the country that can match our cost.... We are sticklers about cutting out unnecessary overhead. Because we put so much responsibility on our people and because we have what I think is an excellent incentive program, our people are willing to work harder to accomplish these profitable goals.

Production

On the basic assembly line used at Nucor, three or four of which might make up any one plant, about six tons per hour would be assembled. In the first stage eight people cut the angles to the right lengths or bent the round bars to the desired form. These were moved on a roller conveyor to six-man assembly stations where the component parts would be tacked together for the next stage, welding. Drilling and miscellaneous work were done by three people between the lines. The nine-man welding station completed the welds before passing the joists on roller conveyors to two-man inspection teams. The last step before shipment was the painting.

In the joist plants, the workers had control over and responsibility for quality. There was an independent quality-control inspector who had the authority to reject the run of joists and cause them to be reworked. The quality control people were not under the incentive system and reported to the Engineering Department.

Daily production might vary widely since each joist was made for a specific job. The wide range of joists made control of the workload at each station difficult; bottlenecks might arise anywhere along the line. Each work station was responsible for identifying such bottlenecks so that the foreman could re-assign people promptly to maintain productivity. Since workers knew most of the jobs on the line, including the more skilled welding job, they could be shifted as needed. Work on the line was described by one general manager as "not machine type but mostly physical labor." He said the important thing was to avoid bottlenecks.

There were four lines of about 28 people each on two shifts at the Florence division. The jobs on the line were rated on responsibility and assigned a base wage, from $6 to $8 per hour. In addition, a weekly bonus was paid on the total output of each line. Each worker received the same percent bonus on his base wage.

The amount of time required to make a joist had been established as a result of experience; the general manager had seen no time studies in his fifteen years with the company. As a job was bid, the cost of each joist was determined through the computer program. The time required depended on the length, number of panels, and depth of the joist.

At the time of production, the labor value of production, the standard, was determined in a similar manner. The general manager stated, "In the last nine or ten years we have not changed a standard." The standards list in use was over 10 years old. Previously, they adjusted the standard if the bonus was too high. He said the technological improvements over the last few years had been small. The general manager reported that the bonus had increased from about 60% nine years earlier to about 100% in 1982 and had stabilized at that point. Exhibits 3 and 4 show data typically computed on performance and used by the manager. He said the difference in performance on the line resulted from the different abilities of the crews.

We don't have an industrial engineering staff. Our Engineering Department's work is limited to the design and the preparation of the paperwork prior to the actual fabrication process. Now, that is

EXHIBIT 3   **Tons per manhour, 52-week moving average**

1977	.163
1978	.179
1979	.192
1980	.195
1981	.194
1982	.208
1983	.215
1984	.214
1985	.228
1986	.225
1987	.218

EXHIBIT 4   **A sample of percentage performance, July 1982**

		Line			
		1	2	3	4
Shift	1st	117	97	82	89
	2nd	98	102	94	107

not to say they don't have any involvement in fabrication. But the efficiency of the plant is entirely up to the manufacturing department. . . . When we had our first group in a joist plant, we produced 3½ tons an hour. We thought that if we ever got to 4 tons, that would be the Millennium. Well, today we don't have anybody who produces less than 6½ tons an hour. This is largely due to improvements that the groups have suggested.

MANAGEMENT

In discussing his philosophy for dealing with the work force, the Florence manager stated:

I believe very strongly in the incentive system we have. We are a non-union shop and we all feel that the way to stay so is to take care of our people and show them we care. I think that's easily done because of our fewer layers of management. . . . I spend a good part of my time in the plant, maybe an hour or so a day. If a man wants to know anything, for example, an insurance question, I'm there and they walk right up to me and ask me questions, which I'll answer the best I know how. . . . You can always tell when people are basically happy. If they haven't called for a meeting themselves or they are not hostile in any way, you can take it they understand the company's situation and accept it. . . . We do listen to our people. . . . For instance last fall I got a call from a couple of workers saying that the people in our Shipping and Receiving area felt they were not being paid properly in relation to production people. So we met with them, discussed the situation and committed ourselves to reviewing the rates of other plants. We assured them that we would get back to them with an answer by the first of the year. Which we did. And there were a few minor changes.

The manager reported none of the plants had any particular labor problems, although there had been some in the past.

In 1976, two years before I came here, there was a union election at this plant which arose out of racial problems. The company actually lost the election to the U.S. Steelworkers. When it came time to begin negotiating the contract, the workers felt, or came to see, that they had little to gain from being in the union. The union was not going to be able to do anything more for them than they were already getting. So slowly the union activity died out and the union quietly withdrew.

He discussed formal systems for consulting with the workers before changes were made:

Of course we're cautioned by our labor counsel to maintain an open pipeline to our employees. We post all changes, company earnings, changes in the medical plan, anything that might affect an employee's job. Mr. Iverson has another philosophy, which is, "Either tell your people everything or tell them nothing." We choose to tell them everything. We don't have any regularly scheduled meetings. We meet whenever there's a need. The most recent examples were a meeting last month to discuss the results of an employee survey and three months before was held our annual dinner meetings off site.

We don't lay our people off and we make a point of telling our people this.

In the economic slump of 1982, we scheduled our line for four days, but the men were allowed to come in the fifth day for maintenance work at base pay. The men in the plant on an average running bonus might make $13 an hour. If their base pay is half that, on Friday they would only get $6–$7 an hour. Surprisingly, many of the men did not want to come in on Friday. They felt comfortable with just working four days a week. They are happy to have that extra day off.

Recently the economic trouble in Texas had hurt business considerably. Both plants had been on decreased schedules for several months. About 20% of the people took the 5th day at base rate, but still no one had been laid off.

In April 1982 the executive committee decided, in view of economic conditions, that a pay freeze was necessary. The employees normally received an increase in their base pay the first of June. The decision was made at that time to freeze wages. The officers of the company, as a show of good faith, accepted a 5% pay cut. In addition to announcing this to the workers with a stuffer in their pay envelopes, meetings were held. Each production line, or incentive group of workers, met in the plant conference room with all supervision — foreman, plant production manager, and division manager. The economic crisis was explained to the employees by the production manager and all questions were answered.

STEEL DIVISIONS

Nucor had steel mills in four locations: Nebraska, South Carolina, Texas, and Utah. The mills were modern "mini-mills," all built within the last 20 years to convert scrap steel into standard angles, flats, rounds, and channels using the latest technology. Sales in 1985 were 1,152,000 tons, a 16% increase over that of

1984. This figure represented about 70% of the mills' output, the remainder being used by other Nucor divisions. In recent years, Nucor had broadened its product line to include a wider range of steel chemistries, sizes, and special shapes. The total capacity of the mills reached 2,100,000 tons in 1985.

A casewriter from Harvard recounted the development of the steel divisions:

> By 1967 about 60% of each Vulcraft sales dollar was spent on materials, primarily steel. Thus, the goal of keeping costs low made it imperative to obtain steel economically. In addition, in 1967 Vulcraft bought about 60% of its steel from foreign sources. As the Vulcraft Division grew, Nucor became concerned about its ability to obtain an adequate economical supply of steel and in 1968 began construction of its first steel mill in Darlington, South Carolina. By 1972 the Florence, South Carolina, joist plant was purchasing over 90% of its steel from this mill. The Fort Payne plant bought about 50% of its steel from Florence. The other joist plants in Nebraska, Indiana and Texas found transportation costs prohibitive and continued to buy their steel from other steel companies, both foreign and domestic. Since the mill had excess capacity, Nucor began to market its steel products to outside customers. In 1972, 75% of the shipments of Nucor steel was to Vulcraft and 25% was to other customers.

Iverson explained in 1984:

> In constructing these mills we have experimented with new processes and new manufacturing techniques. We serve as our own general contractor and design and build much of our own equipment. In one or more of our mills we have built our own continuous casting unit, reheat furnaces, cooling beds and in Utah even our own mill stands. All of these to date have cost under $125 per ton of annual capacity—compared with projected costs for large integrated mills of $1,200–1,500 per ton of annual capacity, ten times our cost. Our mills have high productivity. We currently use less than four manhours to produce a ton of steel. This includes everyone in the operation: maintenance, clerical, accounting, and sales and management. On the basis of our production workers alone, it is less than three manhours per ton. Our total employment costs are less than $60 per ton compared with the average employment costs of the seven largest U.S. steel companies of close to $130 per ton. Our total labor costs are less than 20% of our sales price.

In contrast to Nucor's less than four manhours, similar Japanese mills were said to require more than five hours and comparable U.S. mills over six hours. Nucor's average yield from molten metal to finished products was over 90%, compared with an average U.S. steel industry yield of about 74%, giving energy costs of about $39 per ton compared with their $75 a ton. Nucor ranked 46th on *Iron Age*'s annual survey of world steel producers. They were second on the list of top ten producers of steel worldwide based on tons per employee, at 981 tons. The head of the list was Tokyo Steel at 1,485. U.S. Steel was 7th at 479. Some other results were: Nippon Steel, 453; British Steel, 213; Bethlehem Steel, 329; Kruppstahl, 195; Weirton Steel, 317; and Northstar Steel, 936. Nucor also ranked 7th on the list ranking growth of raw steel production. U.S. Steel was 5th on the same list. U.S. Steel topped the list based on improvement in tons-per-employee, at 56%; Nucor was 7th with a 12% improvement.

THE STEEL-MAKING PROCESS

A steel mill's work is divided into two phases, preparation of steel of the proper "chemistry" and the forming of the steel into the desired products. The typical mini-mill utilized scrap steel, such as junk auto parts, instead of the iron ore that would be used in larger, integrated steel mills. The typical mini-mill had an annual capacity of 200–600 thousand tons, compared with the 7 million tons of Bethlehem Steel's Sparrow's Point, Maryland, integrated plant.

A charging bucket fed loads of scrap steel into electric arc furnaces. The melted load, called a heat, was poured into a ladle to be carried by overhead crane to the casting machine. In the casting machine the liquid steel was extruded as a continuous red-hot solid bar of steel and cut into lengths weighing some 900 pounds called "billets." In the typical plant the billet, about four inches in cross section and about 20 feet long, was held temporarily in a pit where it cooled to normal temperatures. Periodically billets were carried to the rolling mill and placed in a reheat oven to bring them up to 2000°F, at which temperature they would be malleable. In the rolling mill, presses and dies progressively converted the billet into the desired round bars, angles, channels, flats, and other products. After cutting to standard lengths, they were moved to the warehouse.

Nucor's first steel mill, employing more than 500 people, was located in Darlington, South Carolina. The mill, with its three electric arc furnaces, operated 24 hours per day, 5½ days per week. Nucor had made a number of improvements in the melting and casting operations. The former general manager of the Darlington plant had developed a system that involved preheating the ladles, allowing for the faster flow of steel into the caster and resulting in better control of the steel characteristics. Less time and lower capital investment were required. The casting machines were "continuous casters," as opposed to the old batch method. The objective in the "front" of the mill was to keep the casters working. At the time of the Harvard study at Nucor each strand was in operation 90% of the time, while a competitor had announced a "record rate" of 75%, which it had been able to sustain for a week.

Nucor was also perhaps the only mill in the country that regularly avoided the reheating of billets. This saved $10–$12 per ton in fuel usage and losses due to oxidation of the steel. The cost of developing this process had been $12 million. All research projects had not been successful. The company spent approximately $2,000,000 in an unsuccessful effort to utilize resistance-heating. They lost even more on an effort at induction melting. As Iverson told *Metal Producing,* "That costs us a lot of money. Timewise it was very expensive. But you have got to make mistakes and we've had lots of failures." In the rolling mill, the first machine was a roughing mill by Morgarshammar, the first of its kind in the Western Hemisphere. This Swedish machine had been chosen because of its lower cost, higher productivity, and the flexibility. Passing through another five to nine finishing mills converted the billet into the desired finished product. The yield from the billet to finished product was about 93%.

The Darlington design became the basis for plants in Nebraska, Texas, and Utah. The Texas plant had cost under $80 per ton of annual capacity. Whereas the typical mini-mill cost approximately $250 per ton, the average cost of all four of Nucor's mills was under $135 per ton. An integrated mill was expected to cost between $1,200 and $1,500 per ton.

The Darlington plant was organized into 12 natural groups for the purpose of incentive pay: two mills, each had two shifts with three groups — melting and casting, rolling mill, and finishing. In melting and casting there were three or four different standards, depending on the material, established by the department manager years ago based on historical performance. The general manager stated, "We don't change the standards." The caster, the key to the operation, was used at a 92% level — one greater than the claims of the manufacturer. For every good ton of billet above the standard hourly rate for the week, workers in the group received a 4% bonus. For example, with a common standard of 10 tons per run hour and an actual rate for the week of 28 tons per hour, the workers would receive a bonus of 72% of their base rate in the week's pay check.

In the rolling mill there were more than 100 products, each with a different historical standard. Workers received a 4% to 6% bonus for every good ton sheared per hour for the week over the computed standard. The Darlington general manager said the standard would be changed only if there was a major machinery change and that a standard had not been changed since the initial development period for the plant. He commented that, in exceeding the standard the worker wouldn't work harder but would cooperate to avoid problems and moved more quickly if a problem developed: "If there is a way to improve output, they will tell us." Another manager added: "Meltshop employees don't ask me how much it costs Chaparral or LTV to make a billet. They want to know what it costs Darlington, Norfolk, Jewitt, to put a billet on the ground — scrap costs, alloy costs, electrical costs, refactory, gas, etc. Everybody from Charlotte to Plymouth watches the nickels and dimes."

The Darlington manager, who became COO in 1984, stated:

> The key to making a profit when selling a product with no aesthetic value, or a product that you really can't differentiate from your competitors, is cost. I don't look at us as a fantastic marketing organization, even though I think we are pretty good; but we don't try to overcome unreasonable costs by mass marketing. We maintain low costs by keeping the employee force at the level it should be, not doing things that aren't necessary to achieve our goals, and allowing people to function on their own and by judging them on their results.

> To keep a cooperative and productive workforce you need, number one, to be completely honest about everything; number two, to allow each employee as much as possible to make decisions

about that employee's work, to find easier and more productive ways to perform duties; and number three, to be as fair as possible to all employees. Most of the changes we make in work procedures and in equipment come from the employees. They really know the problems of their jobs better than anyone else. We don't have any industrial engineers, nor do we ever intend to, because that's a type of specialist who tends to take responsibility off the top division management and give them a crutch.

To communicate with my employees, I try to spend time in the plant and at intervals have meetings with the employees. Usually if they have a question they just visit me. Recently a small group visited me in my office to discuss our vacation policy. They had some suggestions and, after listening to them, I had to agree that the ideas were good.

THE INCENTIVE SYSTEM

The foremost characteristic of Nucor's personnel system was its incentive plan. Another major personnel policy was providing job security. Also all employees at Nucor received the same fringe benefits. There was only one group insurance plan. Holidays and vacations did not differ by job. The company had no executive dining rooms or restrooms, no fishing lodges, company cars, or reserved parking places.

Absenteeism and tardiness were not problems at Nucor. Each employee had four days of absence before pay was reduced. In addition to these, missing work was allowed for jury duty, military leave, or the death of close relatives. After this, a day's absence cost them bonus pay for that week and lateness of more than a half hour meant the loss of bonus for that day.

Employees were kept informed about the company. Charts showing the division's results in return-on-assets and bonus payoff were posted in prominent places in the plant. The personnel manager commented that as he traveled around to all the plants, he found everyone in the company could tell him the level of profits in their division. The general managers held dinners at least twice a year with their employees. The dinners were held with 50 or 60 employees at a time. After introductory remarks the floor was open for discussion of any work-related problems. The company also had a formal grievance procedure. The Darlington manager couldn't recall the last grievance he had processed.

There was a new employee orientation program and an employee handbook that contained personnel policies and rules. The corporate office sent all news releases to each division, where they were posted on bulletin boards. Each employee in the company also received a copy of the Annual Report. For the last several years the cover of the Annual Report had contained the names of all Nucor employees. Every child of every Nucor employee received up to $1,200 a year for four years if they chose to go on to higher education, including technical schools.

The average hourly worker's pay was $31,000, compared with the average earnings in manufacturing in South Carolina of slightly more than $13,000. The personnel manager believed that pay was not the only thing the workers liked about Nucor. He said that an NBC interviewer, working on the documentary "If Japan Can, Why Can't We," often heard, "I enjoy working for Nucor because Nucor is the best, the most productive, and the most profitable company that I know of."

"I honestly feel that if someone performs well, they should share in the company and if they are going to share in the success, they should also share in the failures," Iverson stated. There were four incentive programs at Nucor, one each for production workers, department heads, staff people such as accountants, secretaries, or engineers, and senior management, which included the division managers. All of these programs were on a group basis.

Within the production program, groups ranged in size from 25 to 30 people and had definable and measurable operations. The company believed that a program should be simple and that bonuses should be paid promptly. "We don't have any discretionary bonuses—zero. It is all based on performance. Now we don't want anyone to sit in judgment, because it never is fair," said Iverson. The personnel manager stated: "Their bonus is based on roughly 90% of historical time it takes to make a particular joist. If during a week they make joists at 60% less than the standard time, they receive a 60% bonus." This was paid with the regular pay the following week. The complete pay check amount, including overtime, was multiplied by the bonus factor. Bonus was not paid when equipment was not operating: "We have the philosophy that when equipment is not operating everybody suffers and the bonus for downtime is zero." The foremen were also part of the group and received the same bonus as the employees they supervised.

The second incentive program was for department heads in the various divisions. The incentive pay here was based on division contribution, defined as the division earnings before corporate expenses and profit sharing are determined. Bonuses were reported to run as high as 51% of a person's base salary in the divisions and 30% for corporate positions.

Officers of the company were under a single profit-sharing plan. Their base salaries were approximately 75% of comparable positions in industry. Once return-on-equity reached 9%, slightly below the average for manufacturing firms, 5% of net earnings before taxes went into a pool that was divided among the officers based on their salaries. Iverson explained: "Now if return-on-equity for the company reaches, say, 20%, which it has, then we can wind up with as much as 190% of our base salaries and 115% on top of that in stock. We get both." In 1982 the return was 9% and the executives received no bonus. Iverson's pay in 1981 was approximately $300,000 but dropped the next year to $110,000. "I think that ranked by total compensation I was the lowest paid CEO in the Fortune 500. I was kind of proud of that, too." In 1986, Iverson's stock was worth over $10 million dollars. The young Vulcraft manager was a millionaire, as well.

There was a third plan for people who were neither production workers nor department managers. Their bonus was based on either the division return-on-assets or the corporate return-on-assets.

The fourth program was for the senior officers. The senior officers had no employment contracts, pension or retirement plans, or other normal perquisites. Their base salaries were set at about 70% of what an individual doing similar work in other companies would receive. More than half of the officer's compensation was reported to be based directly on the company's earnings. Ten percent of pretax earnings over a pre-established level, based on a 12% return on stockholders' equity, was set aside and allocated to the senior officers according to their base salary. Half the bonus was paid in cash and half was deferred.

In lieu of a retirement plan, the company had a profit-sharing plan with a deferred trust. Each year 10% of pretax earnings was put into profit sharing. Fifteen percent of this was set aside to be paid to employees in the following March as a cash bonus and the remainder was put into trust for each employee on the basis of percent of their earnings as a percent of total wages paid within the corporation. The employee was vested 20% after the first year and gained an additional 10% vesting each year thereafter. Employees received a quarterly statement of their balance in profit sharing.

The company had an Employer Monthly Stock Investment Plan to which Nucor added 10% to the amount the employee contributed and paid the commission on the purchase of any Nucor stock. After each five years of service with the company, the employee received a service award consisting of five shares of Nucor stock. Additionally, if profits were good, extraordinary bonus payments would be made to the employees. In 1978, each employee received a $500 payment.

According to Iverson:

> I think the first obligation of the company is to the stockholder and to its employees. I find in this country too many cases where employees are underpaid and corporate management is making huge social donations for self-fulfillment. We regularly give donations, but we have a very interesting corporate policy. First, we give donations where our employees are. Second, we give donations which will benefit our employees, such as to the YMCA. It is a difficult area and it requires a lot of thought. There is certainly a strong social responsibility for a company, but it cannot be at the expense of the employees or the stockholders.

Nucor had no trouble finding people to staff its plants. When the mill in Jewett, Texas, was built in 1975, there were over 5,000 applications for the 400 jobs — many coming from people in Houston and Dallas. Yet everyone did not find work at Nucor what they wanted. In 1975, a Harvard team found high turnover among new production workers after start-up. The cause appeared to be pressure from fellow workers in the group incentive situation. A survival-of-the-fittest situation was found in which those who didn't like to work seldom stuck around. "Productivity increased and turnover declined dramatically once these people left," the Harvard team concluded. Iverson commented: "A lot of people aren't goal-oriented. A lot of them don't want to work that hard, so initially we have a lot of turnover in a plant but then it's so low we don't even measure after that."

The Wall Street Journal reported in 1981:

> Harry Pigg, a sub-district director for the USW in South Carolina, sees a darker side in Nucor's incentive plan. He contends that Nucor unfairly penalizes workers by taking away big bonus payments for absence or tardiness, regardless of the reason. Workers who are ill, he says, try to work because they can't afford to give up the bonus payment. "Nucor whips them into line," he adds. He acknowledges, though, that high salaries are the major barrier to unionizing the company.

Having welcomed a parade of visitors over the years, Iverson had become concerned with their tendency to look for a simple and easy path to success and productivity. "They only do one or two of the things we do. It's not just incentives or the scholarship program; its all those things put together that results in a unified philosophy for the company," he said.

AS 1987 BEGAN

Looking ahead in 1984, Iverson had said: "The next decade will be an exciting one for steel producers. It will tax our abilities to keep pace with technological changes we can see now on the horizon." Imports didn't have to dominate the U.S. economy. He believed the steel industry would continue to play a pivotal role in the growth of American industry. He pointed out comparative advantages of the U.S. steel industry: an abundance of resources, relatively low energy costs, lower transportation costs, and the change in the government's attitude toward business.

The excitement he had predicted had occurred. Imports were a challenge for steel, just as for textiles, shoes, machine tools, and computers. The old steel companies were flexing their muscle and getting back into the game. Overcapacity hadn't left the mini-mill immune; there was no safe haven for anyone. Nucor was no longer a small company, David, with free shots at Goliath.

The honeymoon appeared over. Wall Street worried about what Nucor should do. Cable News Network posed the position of some on Wall Street: "They say basically you guys are selling to the construction companies, you are selling to some fairly depressed industries. They also say, 'Nucor, they were a specialized little niche company. They did what they did very well; but now all of a sudden, they are going out, building these big mills to make huge pieces of steel and they are talking casted cold, all that stuff.' They're worried that you may be getting into deals that are a little too complicated from what they perceive you as being able to do well."

The *New York Times* pointed out that expansion would certainly hurt earnings for the next several years. They quoted a steel consultant: "It is hard to do all that they are trying to do and keep profits up. With the industry in the shape it's in, this is not the time to expand beyond the niche they've established."

With $185 million in cash, Iverson told *Inc.,* "It (going private) has been mentioned to us by a number of brokerage firms and investment houses, but we wouldn't even consider it. It wouldn't be fair to employees, and I don't know whether it would be fair to the stockholders.... You're going to restrict the growth opportunities.... You either grow or die.... Opportunities wouldn't be created for people within the company."

Iverson told CNN: "We've decided that really we want to stay in that niche (steel). We don't want to buy any banks.... All of the growth of the company has been internally generated. We think there are opportunities in the steel industry today.... There are ample opportunities, although they are somewhat harder to find than they used to be."

"Another of my strengths is the ability to stick to my knitting. The reason executives make a lot of mistakes is that sometimes they get bored — they think the grass is greener on the other side so they go out and buy a bank or an oil company or they go into businesses where they have no expertise.... I have never gotten bored with this company. I've done this job so long that I think I have some insight into the needs and the capabilities of the company. I'm not misled into thinking we can do something that we can't."

EXHIBIT 5   Balance sheet data, 1976–1986

	1976	1977	1978	1979	1980
Assets					
Current assets					
Cash	8,156,215	3,346,196	6,286,583	8,716,950	5,753,068
Short-term investments	3,875,000	3,750,000	21,131,652	27,932,854	16,000,000
Accounts receivable	13,493,692	18,897,191	26,580,943	35,203,909	35,537,959
Contracts in process	3,428,026	4,494,418	5,316,522	5,004,091	7,985,985
Inventories	32,643,688	30,410,685	41,548,920	40,007,532	49,599,265
Other current assets	219,423	256,812	245,674	496,854	489,450
	61,816,044	61,155,302	101,110,294	117,362,190	115,365,727
Property, plant, and equipment					
Land and improvements	2,209,289	2,696,502	3,526,812	4,915,078	5,806,711
Buildings and improvements	15,138,400	18,441,047	22,229,110	29,875,783	34,853,546
Plant machinery and equipment	44,212,629	55,992,359	68,677,667	91,865,271	139,182,579
Office and transportation equipment	1,637,493	1,803,511	2,579,600	5,478,870	5,711,199
Construction in process	8,516,708	7,739,163	18,240,643	28,326,555	33,541,819
	71,714,519	86,672,582	115,253,832	160,461,557	219,095,854
Less accumulated depreciation	15,778,779	20,733,060	26,722,157	35,879,558	46,021,581
	55,935,740	65,939,522	88,531,675	124,581,999	173,074,273
Other assets	1,343,797	916,158	3,812,724	1,167,325	2,781,867
Total assets	119,095,581	128,010,982	193,454,693	243,111,514	291,221,867

An economics professor and steel consultant at Middle Tennessee State University told the *Times,* "You're not going to see any growth in the steel market, so the only way to make money is to reduce costs and have new technology to penetrate other companies' business."

The *New York Times* stated: "Critics question whether it is wise to continue expanding production capabilities, as Nucor is doing, when there is already overcapacity in the steel industry and intense competition already exists between the mini-mills." Iverson insisted the strategy would pay off in the long term. He told the *Times,* "The company's strategy makes sense for us. To gain a larger share in an ever-shrinking market, you've got to take something from someone else."

Iverson's position was clear: "We're going to stay in steel and steel products. The way we look at it, this company does only two things well, builds plants economically and runs them efficiently. That is the whole company. We don't have any financial expertise, we're not entrepreneurs, we're not into acquisitions. Steel may not be the best business in the world, but it's what we know how to do and we do it well."

1981	1982	1983	1984	1985	1986
8,704,859	10,668,165	6,384,795	2,863,680	8,028,519	11,008,879
—	34,224,381	72,669,615	109,846,810	177,115,954	117,727,705
42,983,058	34,685,498	51,110,372	58,408,244	60,390,448	61,268,892
5,719,121	3,656,643	7,058,803	8,462,815	10,478,296	9,120,533
72,996,664	48,831,434	56,555,102	73,797,302	78,641,805	96,474,278
978,590	476,527	110,475	74,522	114,125	137,968
131,382,292	132,542,648	193,889,162	253,453,373	334,769,147	295,738,255
12,142,613	12,215,375	12,577,104	12,918,519	12,818,723	15,041,782
53,037,722	53,668,523	55,971,208	58,909,921	61,709,286	75,217,588
245,037,510	244,143,769	258,305,715	277,553,868	279,579,407	331,945,921
6,868,069	9,565,667	9,736,448	8,643,752	14,883,272	16,358,988
1,776,106	3,260,329	2,071,147	1,944,670	7,238,325	13,700,338
318,862,020	322,853,663	338,661,622	359,970,730	376,229,013	452,264,617
66,245,946	83,782,273	107,356,805	131,867,940	150,954,339	181,431,475
252,616,074	239,071,390	231,304,817	228,102,790	225,274,674	270,833,142
783,761	18,903	373,073	632,302	267,367	5,036,247
384,782,127	371,632,941	425,567,052	482,188,465	560,311,188	571,607,644

EXHIBIT 5   **Balance sheet data, 1976–1986 (*cont.*)**

	1976	1977	1978	1979	1980
Liabilities and stockholders' equity					
Current liabilities					
Long-term debt due within one year	438,462	438,462	463,462	1,245,764	1,696,815
Accounts payable	16,220,543	12,077,514	24,150,147	26,414,666	36,640,991
Federal income taxes	5,465,824	4,440,824	15,640,824	15,913,361	4,362,619
Accrued expenses and other current liabilities	8,777,139	13,345,205	15,578,501	19,962,206	23,793,020
	30,901,968	30,302,005	55,832,934	63,535,997	66,493,445
Other liabilities					
Long-term debt due after one year	31,667,308	28,132,692	41,473,077	41,398,138	39,605,169
Deferred federal income taxes	1,819,563	2,619,563	4,019,563	4,919,563	7,519,563
Deferred compensation and other liabilities	621,772	661,317	—	—	—
	34,108,643	31,413,572	45,492,640	46,317,701	47,124,732
Stockholders' equity					
Common stock	885,143	1,261,644	1,795,698	2,721,040	2,758,713
Additional paid-in capital	9,211,839	9,855,410	10,743,090	11,125,185	13,353,856
Retained earnings	44,088,406	55,497,968	79,934,950	119,891,199	161,952,033
Treasury stock	(100,418)	(319,617)	(344,619)	(479,608)	(460,912)
	54,084,970	66,295,405	92,129,119	133,257,816	177,603,690
Total liabilities and stockholders' equity	119,095,581	128,010,982	193,454,693	243,111,514	291,221,867

Source: Nucor Corporation financial reports. Reprinted by permission.

1981	**1982**	**1983**	**1984**	**1985**	**1986**
1,654,784	1,603,462	2,402,462	2,402,462	2,402,462	3,052,462
32,237,889	22,948,867	37,135,084	32,691,249	35,473,011	53,165,551
10,733,627	12,535,096	14,813,909	23,705,195	27,597,464	14,309,565
28,406,013	29,015,281	34,135,340	41,734,778	55,782,891	47,913,395
73,032,313	66,102,706	88,486,795	100,533,684	121,255,828	118,440,973
83,754,231	48,229,615	45,731,000	43,232,384	40,233,769	42,147,654
15,619,563	25,019,563	33,219,563	38,819,563	41,319,563	27,319,563
—	——	—	—	—	—
99,373,794	73,249,178	78,950,563	82,051,947	81,553,332	69,467,217
2,797,948	2,802,796	5,642,727	5,669,757	5,732,382	8,665,397
16,531,759	17,696,568	17,022,043	18,991,334	24,299,195	25,191,988
193,355,403	211,921,654	235,569,108	275,035,788	327,816,850	367,575,659
(309,090)	(139,961)	(104,184)	(94,045)	(346,399)	(17,733,590)
212,376,020	232,281,057	258,129,694	299,602,834	357,502,028	383,699,454
384,782,127	371,632,941	425,567,052	482,188,465	560,311,188	571,607,644

EXHIBIT 6   **Sales, earnings, and statistical data, 1976–1986**

	1976	1977	1978	1979	1980
For the year					
Sales, costs, and earnings					
Net sales	175,768,479	212,952,829	306,939,667	428,681,778	482,420,363
Costs and expenses					
Cost of products sold	142,235,949	168,247,627	227,953,309	315,688,291	369,415,571
Marketing and administrative expenses	14,744,882	19,729,586	28,660,033	36,724,159	38,164,559
Interest expense (income)	2,290,757	2,723,024	1,877,476	1,504,791	(1,219,965)
	159,271,588	190,700,237	258,490,818	353,917,241	406,360,165
Earnings before federal income taxes	16,496,891	22,252,592	48,448,849	74,764,537	76,060,198
Federal income taxes	7,800,000	9,800,000	22,600,000	32,500,000	31,000,000
Net earnings	8,696,891	12,452,592	25,848,849	42,264,537	45,060,198
Net earnings per share	.45	.64	1.30	2.10	2.21
Dividends declared per share	.03	.05	.07	.11	.15
Percentage of earnings to sales	4.9%	5.8%	8.4%	9.9%	9.3%
Return on average equity	17.6%	20.7%	32.6%	37.5%	29.0%
Return on average assets	8.2%	10.1%	16.1%	19.4%	16.9%
Average shares outstanding	19,119,669	19,481,464	19,855,210	20,152,914	20,414,109
Sales per employee	76,421	88,730	115,826	145,316	150,756
At year end					
Working capital	30,914,076	30,853,297	45,277,360	53,826,193	48,872,282
Current ratio	2.0	2.0	1.8	1.8	1.7
Stockholders' equity per share	2.78	3.37	4.59	6.58	8.64
Shares outstanding	19,447,677	19,701,946	20,065,257	20,261,631	20,549,991
Stockholders	24,000	22,000	22,000	23,000	22,000
Employees	2,300	2,500	2,800	3,100	3,300

Source: Nucor Corporation financial reports. Reprinted by permission.

1981	1982	1983	1984	1985	1986
544,820,621	486,018,162	542,531,431	660,259,922	758,495,374	755,228,939
456,210,289	408,606,641	461,727,688	539,731,252	600,797,865	610,378,369
33,524,820	31,720,377	33,988,054	45,939,311	59,079,802	65,900,653
10,256,546	7,899,110	(748,619)	(3,959,092)	(7,560,645)	(5,288,971)
499,991,655	448,226,128	494,967,123	581,711,471	652,317,022	670,990,051
44,828,966	37,792,034	47,564,308	78,548,451	106,178,352	84,238,888
10,100,000	15,600,000	19,700,000	34,000,000	47,700,000	37,800,000
34,728,966	22,192,034	27,864,308	44,548,451	58,478,352	46,438,888
1.67	1.06	1.32	2.11	2.74	2.17
.16	.17	.20	.24	.27	.31
6.4%	4.6%	5.1%	6.7%	7.7%	6.1%
17.8%	10.0%	11.4%	16.0%	17.8%	12.5%
10.3%	5.9%	7.0%	9.8%	11.2%	8.2%
20,756,583	20,912,577	21,066,448	21,169,492	21,345,852	21,405,440
155,663	133,156	148,639	176,069	197,011	181,983
58,349,979	66,439,942	105,402,367	152,919,689	213,513,319	177,297,282
1.8	2.0	2.2	2.5	2.8	2.5
10.17	11.07	12.21	14.10	16.65	18.16
20,890,521	20,987,823	21,135,272	21,241,618	21,472,508	21,131,298
22,000	22,000	21,000	22,000	22,000	22,000
3,700	3,600	3,700	3,800	3,900	4,400

Case 11

VIDEOSHOP—
MARK-TELE, INC.

Cable television began to spread rapidly across the United States during the late 1970s. It was promoted to subscribers predominantly as an entertainment medium that would provide an expanded choice of high-quality television programming.

Some advertising and marketing experts perceived cable television differently. They saw it as opening a revolutionary new dimension in commercial communications. In the short run, cable television would generate new advertising and direct marketing opportunities. As telecommunication technology improved in the long run, cable television could become a direct threat to conventional shopping systems. Most experts, however, forecasted that significant changes in consumer shopping patterns were at least a decade or two away. Mr. Richard Johnson disagreed. He was the managing director of Mark-Tele, Inc., one of the most innovative and aggressive cable television companies.

During the fall of 1981, Mr. Johnson began to prepare a proposal for presentation to his board of directors at its forthcoming winter meeting. The proposal would suggest that Mark-Tele develop several new television channels. These channels would be unconventional. Most cable channels involved an entertainment, educational, or public information format. The proposed new channels would involve innovative commercial formats using telecommunications technology that would allow organizations to market and sell directly to consumers in their own homes. A new marketplace would be created. Mr. Johnson named this concept "VideoShop."

This case was prepared by Professor Michael P. Mokwa of the Arizona State University as a basis for class discussion rather than to illustrate either effective or ineffective handling of a managerial situation. Copyright © 1982 by the author.

THE NEW VENTURE

Several months earlier, Mr. Johnson had created a new ventures task force. The mission of this task force was to generate and study novel programming formats that could be developed into new cable channels in the near term, and possibly into new networks in the long run. These new channels would be used by Mark-Tele to generate additional revenues, to increase its subscription base, and to allocate operating costs more effectively.

The current capacity of the Mark-Tele cable system was fifty-two different channels, but only thirty-one were in use. When Mark-Tele began operations, it had only twelve channels but had grown steadily. Costs had been relatively constant regardless of the number of channels that Mark-Tele operated. Thus, Mr. Johnson perceived Mark-Tele's cost structure as highly fixed, and he foresaw the development of new channels as a means of distributing these costs. Mr. Johnson expected that new channels would draw new subscribers, that subscription rates could be raised as more channels were added, and that subscription revenue could grow faster than corresponding operating costs.

The new ventures task force was carefully selected. It included the operations and sales managers from Mark-Tele, two product development specialists from Mark-Tele's parent company, and a consultant from the communications industry. An excerpt of their report to Mr. Johnson is presented in the Appendix.

The task force recommended that Mark-Tele should develop several new cable channels using the television as the medium for shopping. Each Mark-Tele subscriber could "tune into" these shopping channels. The subscriber could control and execute an entire shopping experience in the home. Products and services could be purchased directly, or the subscriber could gather specific information about a particular product or service and competitive offerings before making an important buying decision. The task force report indicated that eleven different product or service lines appeared viable for the new shopping concept.

Mr. Johnson was thrilled with the new venture idea and the task force report. He wanted to develop and implement the concept quickly. First, he selected a distinctive name for the venture, identifying it as VideoShop. Next, he met informally with some prospective salespeople, distributors and retailers from different product and service fields. Most of these meetings were casual lunches or dinners. Mr. Johnson sensed some strong, but very cautious interest and support from some prospective suppliers. Then, he carefully reviewed and screened the list of product and service lines that had been proposed in the task force report.

Mr. Johnson felt that each of the proposed lines was feasible, but he wanted to focus his efforts on those products and services that appeared (a) to be easiest and most profitable to implement in the near term, and (b) to have the strongest interest among the prospective suppliers with whom he had met. Five lines were selected for development:

1. Catalog sales by regional and national retailers
2. Ticket reservations for concerts, plays and sporting events, as well as reservations at local restaurants
3. Airline ticket reservations and vacation planning
4. A multiple listing service for real estate companies to display homes and commercial property that were for sale in the area or possibly from areas across the country
5. Grocery products

Mr. Johnson expected that he could find outstanding firms from each product or service field to participate in the VideoShop venture under terms that Mark-Tele would set forth. He thought the costs to each firm would be small when compared to the benefits of newly accessible markets.

MARK – TELE'S BACKGROUND

Mark-Tele was founded in 1977, as a wholly owned subsidiary of Intertronics, Inc., a large corporation based in New York City. Intertronics was founded in 1973 as a joint venture among three well-respected, multi-national firms. One firm was primarily in the information processing industry. Another was a publishing and broadcasting conglomerate, and the third was a high-technology producer in electronics. The mission of Intertronics was to design, develop, and implement innovative, applied telecommunications systems for domestic consumer markets. Intertronics received financial support and full technological cooperation from its parent companies, but was operated as an autonomous venture. Intertronics managed each of its subsidiaries using the same orientation.

During 1978, Mark-Tele bid to install cable television systems in several large metropolitan areas in the United States. Late that year, Mark-Tele was granted the right to install a cable television system in a large growing southwestern metropolitan area. Mark-Tele's management was excited to begin operations and to enter this particular area.

The area had more than a sufficient number of households to profitably support a cable television company, according to industry standards. More importantly, the population was growing rapidly. National and international companies were locating headquarters or building large manufacturing facilities in the area. The growth of industry meant a tremendous increase in the number of families relocating into the area. This growth was projected to continue for at least the next fifteen years, thus representing a very attractive cable market for Mark-Tele. Intertronics would use Mark-Tele's location as the test site for a new type of cable television technology. The traditional type of cable used in cable television systems was a "one-way" cable because a "signal" could be directed only from the cable television company *to* the individual households attached to the service.

Recently, Intertronics had developed a "two-way" cable that was capable of transmitting and receiving signals both from the cable television company and from individual households connected to the system. As such, a home could send signals *back* to the cable television company. Two-way cable communication processes were used in a few other areas of the country, but these cable systems required the use of a telephone line along with the one-way cable. The cost of the new two-way cable was nearly four times the cost of the one-way cable. Because Mark-Tele was a test site, it and its subscribers received the cable system at a substantially reduced cost.

To implement the two-way cable, Mark-Tele installed an interactive device to the television set of each of its subscribers. These devices facilitated communication between the Mark-Tele building and individual homes. The interactive devices resembled a small desk-top electronic calculator. These devices were expensive to install, but Intertronics absorbed most of the installation cost. The remaining cost was reflected in slightly higher-than-average monthly subscription charges paid by subscribers. The subscription charge for basic cable services from Mark-Tele was $11 per month. The comparable rate that Mark-Tele would charge for one-way cable would be $8.50 per month.

Mark-Tele's first year of operations concluded with 5,000 subscribers and a small negative net operating profit. In the following year, Mark-Tele subscriptions increased to 38,000, generating a net profit of almost $1.4 million. In 1980, Mark-Tele continued to aggressively attract more subscribers, reaching a 50,000 total. Net profit increased to exceed $2 million. Financial statements for 1979 and 1980 are presented in Exhibit 1.

Research by Mark-Tele suggested that the potential number of homes for the cable network in its market area exceeded 400,000 over the next five years. In ten years, the market potential was forecasted to be nearly 750,000 homes. A demographic profile of current subscribers is presented in Exhibit 2.

Mark-Tele offered many different channel formats. These channels provided a wide variety of programming for virtually any type of viewer. Several of the channels were "pay television." For these, a household would pay an additional charge beyond the basic monthly rate. Pay television services were very successful. The revenue from pay services nearly matched basic subscription revenue for Mark-Tele in 1980. A schedule for the allocation of Mark-Tele's fifty-two-channel capacity is presented in Exhibit 3. Both current and prospective channels are listed.

CABLE TELEVISION TECHNOLOGY

Cable television became increasingly popular during the 1970s. This can be attributed largely to significant advances in computer and communications technologies, as well as regulatory and legal changes, in the telecommunications industry.

EXHIBIT 1   **Income statement, Mark-Tele, Inc.**

Fiscal years ending December 31, 1979 and 1980

	1979*	1980**
REVENUES		
Subscription revenue	$4,560,000	$ 6,600,000
Pay service revenue	4,104,000	5,400,000
Total revenue	$8,664,000	$12,000,000
EXPENSES		
Operation expense (includes salaries)	$3,852,000	$ 5,248,000
Sales expense	1,913,400	2,610,300
Interest expense	136,200	136,200
Depreciation expense	74,800	74,800
Rent expense	46,000	46,000
Equipment maintenance expense	32,500	34,700
Total expense	$6,054,900	$ 8,150,000
Gross profit	$2,609,100	$ 3,850,000
Taxes @ 47%	$1,226,277	$ 1,848,000
Net profit	$1,382,823	$ 2,002,000

*Based upon subscriptions of 38,000 homes with a subscription rate of $10 per month per home and average home "pay service" of $9 per month per home.
**Based upon total subscriptions of 50,000 homes with a subscription rate of $11 per month per home and average home "pay service" of $9 per month per home.

The Mark-Tele cable television system was controlled by a sophisticated configuration of minicomputers with high speed communications between each processor. Three computers, each used for a different task, insured that viewers would have access to the cable network at all times.

The main computer transmitted cable signals to each individual home using the two-way cable lines. The second computer's function was to serve as back-up for the main computer in the event that a system failure might occur. The second computer would be a vital element of the VideoShop system because it could be used as an update system for suppliers to amend information regarding their products or services. This computer also could be used to transmit the orders or reservations placed by "shopping" subscribers directly to prospective suppliers. The third computer functioned as another back-up, if system failures would occur simultaneously in the main computers. A very sophisticated software application integrating the communication network and operating system had been developed to assure 99 percent uptime for the cable system. A diagram sketching the Mark-Tele cable system is presented in Exhibit 4.

The cable system incorporated two different types of storage devices. The first type of storage disk (a magnetic disk) was used to store data, such as billing

EXHIBIT 2   1980 Demographic analysis of Mark-Tele subscribers*

Family size		Age of paying subscriber	
1	17.6%	18–25	22.4%
2	22.8	26–35	19.2
3	10.8	36–45	19.6
4	19.3	46–55	17.7
5	15.1	56–65	7.1
6	5.8	66–75	8.3
7+	8.6	76+	5.7

Family income		Residency	
$0–$8K	1.3%	Home owners	71.6%
$9K–$18K	15.7	Renters	28.4%
$19K–$28K	18.3		
$29K–$35K	17.5		
$36K–$45K	19.6		
$46K–$59K	12.7		
$60K+	14.9		

Number of hours home television active per week		Number of years of education of paying subscribers	
0–7	2.5%	0–8	1.4%
8–14	15.1	9–11	22.5
15–21	17.2	12	21.8
22–28	40.7	13–15	26.3
29–35	20.8	16+ years	28.0
36+ hours	3.7		

*Based upon 50,000 subscribers.

EXHIBIT 3   Channel allocation schedule

Cable channel number	Designated programming/service
1	Mark-Tele channel listing*
2	Program guide*
3	Local transit schedule*
4	Classified ads and yard sales*
5	Weather radar and time*
6	Dow Jones Cable News*
7	Reserved for future use
8**	Home Box Office*
9**	Showtime*

EXHIBIT 3　　　Channel allocation schedule (*cont.*)

Cable channel number	Designated programming/service
10**	The Movie Channel*
11**	Golden Oldies Channel*
12	Reserved for future use
13	Reserved for future use
14	Cable News Network*
15	Reserved for future use
16	UPI News Scan*
17	Government access*
18	Music Television*
19**	Stereo Rock Concert*
20	Educational access*
21	Educational access: New York University*
22	Proposed educational access
23	Proposed interactive channel for lease
24	Proposed interactive channel for lease
25	Proposed interactive channel for lease
26	VideoShop: *Retail Sales Channel*
27	VideoShop: *Entertainment Tickets and Restaurants*
28	VideoShop: *Grocery Products*
29	VideoShop: Reserved
30	VideoShop: Reserved
31	USA Network*
32	WTBS, Atlanta, Channel 17*
33	WOR, New York, Channel 9*
34	K///, Local ABC affiliate
35	Christian Broadcasting Network*
36	ESPN (sports) Network*
37	K///, Local station, Channel 15*
38	K///, Local NBC affiliate, Channel 8*
39	K///, Local CBS affiliate, Channel 11*
40	Proposed channel for lease
41	Concert Connection*
42	WGN, Chicago, Channel 9*
43	Public access: Cultural Bulletin Board*
44**	Proposed games channel
45	Public access: Library Information*
46	Proposed public access
47	Public Broadcasting System
48	Reserved for future banking transactions
49	VideoShop: *Airline Tickets and Travel*
50	VideoShop: *Real Estate Showcase*
51	Reserved for future use
52	Reserved for future use

*Active channel
**Optional pay service

EXHIBIT 4   **Mark-Tele two-way cable system**

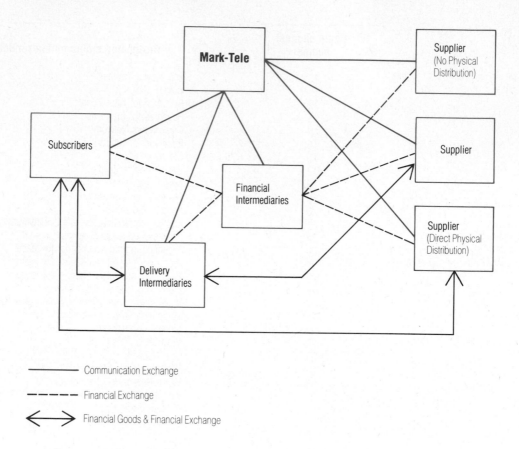

—————— Communication Exchange

------- Financial Exchange

⟨——⟩ Financial Goods & Financial Exchange

information about a particular subscriber. The second type of disk involved an innovative technology that could be used extensively by the VideoShop system. The disk, called a "video disk unit," was capable of storing images or pictures like a movie camera. VideoShop suppliers could store images of their products and services on these disks so that subscribers to the cable system could access the images at any time. Only through the use of the new two-way cable developed by Intertronics would it be possible to incorporate the video disk units (VDU) into a cable network. The two-way cable allowed signals to travel from the main computer to an individual television, and from the television back to the main computer.

Two-way communication was possible through the use of the interactive indexing device attached to each subscriber's television. This indexing device was a small box, about the size of a cigar box. It contained special electronics allowing the device to transmit data back to the main computer. On top of the indexing device, there were twelve keys simply called the keypad. An individual subscriber could use the keypad to call up "menus," sort through a menu, and send data back to the main computer. A menu is a computer term used to describe listings of general categories from which additional information can be drawn.

Using a prospective VideoShop example, a menu for a channel containing airline information could first indicate to a viewer the different airlines from which to choose. The viewer could then push the key on the keypad that corresponds to the airline that he or she was interested in using. The next menu could show all the different cities to which the chosen airline flies. The viewer then could push the key on the keypad that corresponds to the city to which he or she wishes to travel. The following screen could provide the flight numbers and times during which flights are available. From the information on that screen, the user could make a reservation which would be transmitted to the airline's computer through the Mark-Tele computer. Finally, the reservation would be logged, confirmed, and ticket(s) mailed to the viewer. The entire transaction would take only a few minutes to execute. The shopper would control the entire experience in the home environment. It would be simple and efficient.

VIDEOSHOP CHANNELS

Mr. Johnson believed that the most significant factors that would affect the successful acceptance of VideoShop by consumers were: (a) the quality of the picture viewed by the subscribers; (b) the accuracy of the information provided by suppliers to shoppers; (c) the convenience and ease of using the system to shop; (d) the technical reliability of the system; and (e) the delivery, billing, and return policies of suppliers. Mr. Johnson felt strongly that control over suppliers would be vital to assure the success of VideoShop. He thought that Mark-Tele should form a small consumer satisfaction department to conduct VideoShop consumer studies, to review the VideoShop policies and operations of all involved suppliers and to resolve all consumer problems and complaints.

Mr. Johnson felt that the five shopping channels that he had selected from the list generated by the task force would work well, given the nature of the success factors that he perceived to be important. He prepared a brief description for each of the prospective shopping channels and a pro-forma income statement. He would use these to build his presentation for the forthcoming board meeting and to develop a prospectus to sell the VideoShop concept to suppliers. The pro-forma statement is presented in Exhibit 5.

The Catalog Sales Channel(s)

National and regional retailers could use the VideoShop system to sell and promote their entire merchandise lines, including their most current items and

EXHIBIT 5 **Pro-forma income statement VideoShop operation***

REVENUE	
Catalog purchase channel	$300,000
Airline reservation channel	400,000
Ticket sales and restaurant channel	150,000
Multiple listing service channel	36,000
Total Revenue	$886,000
EXPENSES	
Salaries	$240,000
Administrative expense	52,000
Communication expense (telephone lines)	19,200
Depreciation expense	15,700
Interest expense	13,820
Equipment maintenance	4,200
Total expenses	$344,920
Contribution	$541,080

*Based upon 50,000 subscriptions and task force projections.

prices. Shoppers would have the opportunity to view merchandise on the television screen in their own home, avoiding the inconvenience of a shopping trip or the boredom of thumbing through a catalog book. Information about products and prices could be presented in a format similar to catalog books, or innovative action formats could be developed to simulate a store environment or create some novel context.

Retailers would be responsible for developing appropriate videodisk units and keeping information current. Mark-Tele could provide a consulting service to help suppliers produce effective videodisks. Mark-Tele could also reserve the right to reject any material that was felt to be inappropriate. However, Mark-Tele would attempt to be open-minded. For example, products that consumers find embarrassing to purchase at a store could be considered a prime prospect for VideoShop, if presentations were tasteful.

A shopper could use the interactive indexing device to direct and control an entire shopping experience. This could involve viewing information about product features and prices from one retailer, and then quickly switching to another retailer's presentation for comparative information. In addition, a shopper desiring more extensive information could access a brief demonstration or informative advertisement about a product. After the customer selected a product, the interactive device could transmit the order through Mark-Tele's computing system directly to the retailer's processing system. The retailer could present alternative payment programs and specific delivery schedules or instructions. The shopper could charge purchases using national or store credit cards, and could pick up the merchandise directly (but conveniently) or could have it delivered.

Mark-Tele could charge each retailer a service fee based upon a fixed percentage of shoppers' invoice values (before taxes). Individual retailers could be billed monthly and various payment programs could be formulated. The new ventures task force estimated that an average home would purchase a minimum of $300 worth of retail merchandise annually through VideoShop. The task force proposed a service charge rate of 2 percent. Mark-Tele could also generate revenue selling video consulting services to the suppliers.

This shopping and marketing scenario could be the prototype for all the VideoShop channels. Adaptations for different product or service lines and shopping patterns would be relatively easy to implement.

Ticket Sales and Restaurant Reservation Channel

VideoShop could provide detailed information concerning local entertainment alternatives to subscribers. Entertainment organizations could present exciting promotional spots using the video disk technology and sell tickets directly to VideoShop subscribers.

Entertainment shoppers could use video menus to select a particular entertainment form such as movies, theater or sporting events. On another menu, they could view all the relevant alternative events, and then access specific promotional spots about events which interested them. These spots could blend information about performance schedules and locations with features about or highlights of the event. The shopper could select an event and a specific performance, then purchase tickets. Tickets could be sold using conventional diagrams of seating arrangements on innovative graphic formats; or the shopper could actually be presented with the view from a specific seat or area of seating using the video disk technology. When tickets were purchased, these could be paid by credit cards at the time of purchase, or payment could be mailed or made at the time of the event. Likewise, tickets could be mailed or picked up.

Another dimension of this channel could be a restaurant promotion and reservation feature. Restaurant menus and promotional spots could be made accessible for diners. Once diners have chosen a particular restaurant using the memo and spots, they could make a reservation and even select a specific table (if the restaurant developed, as part of its VideoShop system, a seating arrangement routine similar to that of the entertainment organizations).

All VideoShop ticket purchases and reservations could be transmitted directly from the shopper's home through Mark-Tele computers to the restaurant or ticket outlet. Most restaurants and small entertainment organizations would have to purchase or lease a small "intelligence" computing terminal to receive reservations or ticket orders and to keep information updated. Intertronics could supply these.

The task force felt that this channel could generate at least $150,000 in revenue per year, given the current subscriber base. It recommended a $25-

per-month minimum charge to restaurants and a 50¢ service fee per ticket reservation. It was unsure of a fee schedule for entertainment organizations that would only promote events but would not be selling tickets directly through VideoShop. However, the task force thought that rates similar to commercial advertising rates would be appropriate.

Airline Ticket Sales and Travel Accommodations Channel

Discussions with the task force concluded that an airline ticket sales channel could be the easiest for Mark-Tele to implement and operate in the short run, and also could be most lucrative financially. Projected revenue for the first year of operating this channel was $400,000, based upon a very conservative usage rate and an extremely competitive pricing policy.

This channel could allow subscribers to make airline reservations, purchase their tickets, and select travel accommodations using the same fundamental interactive shopping procedures as other VideoShop channels. Shoppers could avoid the aggravating inconveniences of current airline reservation systems, and could quickly do comparative shopping which current systems have inhibited. Research has shown that comparative shopping for airline fares often can save hundreds of dollars. Once a flight has been selected, the subscriber also could make hotel or motel reservations. VideoShop could allow hotels and motels to visually present rooms and surroundings and to promote themselves to *all* travelers.

Perhaps the most important characteristic of this channel could be the potential ease of implementation, once cooperation was secured from the airlines. The format and basic system used within the airlines industry to transmit, display and process schedules, fares and ticket information appeared to be compatible with the Mark-Tele system. Mark-Tele computers and cable lines could be used to link shoppers directly with airline ticket reservation systems, by-passing reservationists and travel agents. Subscribers could select itineraries, then secure reservations and pay using major credit cards. Tickets could be mailed or picked up at airport ticket counters or other service locations.

Mark-Tele could record each ticket purchase and charge the appropriate airline a fixed fee of $4 per ticket. This rate was half the $8-rate charged by most travel agents. The task force believed that a minimum average of two tickets would be purchased by each subscribing household per year. Revenue estimates were not made for the travel accommodations feature of this channel.

Multiple Listing Service Channel

A few large local realtors expressed strong interest in the VideoShop concept. Traditional promotional tools used to stimulate buyers' interest and assist them to make decisions about what properties to see in person included classified newspaper ads, newspaper supplements, brochures, "for sale" signs, the multiple listing catalog and photographs of properties posted on an agency's wall. Most realtors and buyers found these boring. More importantly, these simply did not present most properties effectively. A frequent complaint among realtors and buyers was the high cost in time and dollars wasted traveling to and viewing personally properties that were not represented well in a promotion or informational item. VideoShop could provide an exciting and effective method for presenting realty.

While this VideoShop channel could be accessed by any subscriber, the channel would open a new commercial consumer market for Mark-Tele cable subscriptions—the realty agencies. Many agencies had a television on the premises to entertain clients and their children or to provide a means "to catch the news" when business was slow. Some agencies already had purchased cable service from Mark-Tele.

A general issue was raised by the task force whether to charge a commercial subscriber different fees than a residential subscriber. A more specific issue regarding this channel was whether to limit access to realty agencies and others willing to pay an additional fee for it, or to open it for public access. The task force recommended open access and suggested that a minimum of thirty realty agencies would need to participate. Each could be charged a monthly fee of $100 or an annual fee of $1,000. The realtor would be responsible for producing and maintaining high-quality videodisks with accurate and updated information. Mark-Tele could provide technical assistance and would monitor this channel carefully.

Grocery Products Channel

One of the most exciting prospects for VideoShop could be a grocery products channel. It was the most interesting but difficult channel for which to design a format.

Grocery products are purchased very frequently, and everyone must buy. Consumers have tended to develop relatively consistent grocery shopping patterns. Expenditures on grocery items have been swelling. Many consumers find going shopping to be tedious, laborious, and inconvenient. Others, such as people with handicaps or shut-ins, simply cannot get to stores or cannot shop freely and comfortably in modern superstores. Likewise, grocery producers, wholesalers and retailers have been threatened by escalating cost structures that reduce their margins substantially.

A VideoShop grocery channel, thus, could provide consumers with convenience, comfort, low shopping risks and potential savings. For suppliers, it could generate increased control over operations and costs and higher profits. However, this VideoShop channel would directly attack an expensive, firmly established distribution network and basic, traditional patterns of shopping. Strong resistance from many consumers could be anticipated, and suppliers not involved in the venture could be expected to retaliate competitively. Also, there could be critical barriers to providing shoppers a total assortment of grocery products, including frozen and "fresh" items, and to implementing a cost-effective delivery service or pickup procedure. Undoubtedly, these "bugs" could be worked out. The recommendation for this channel was to maintain its high priority as a channel to develop in the near term, but initially and quickly to invest funds in more design and research before contacting any specific prospective suppliers.

CONCLUSION—A TIME FOR REFLECTION AND/OR ACTION

One more time, Mr. Johnson critically reviewed the task force report and his brief descriptions of prospective VideoShop channels. He felt simultaneously excitement, enthusiasm and some frustration. He and the task force had worked hard and creatively to formulate the idea of VideoShop. They thought that most technological barriers could be overcome, and they projected a very favorable cost structure. Definitely, VideoShop was a concept whose time had arrived! Mark-Tele's board, composed largely of Intertronics personnel, would have to be convinced.

Mark-Tele was a small company, with only a few people and tight resources. It already was a high-investment and high-risk experimental venture, receiving considerable financial support and subsidy from Intertronics. Would Intertronics feel that VideoShop was an extension of the Mark-Tele experiment or a contamination of it? Could the board be convinced to provide more resources and assistance, and what would it expect in return?

If VideoShop received approval and support from the board, Mr. Johnson was not exactly sure in which direction to proceed. While he had identified the primary prospective channels, which specific channel or channels should be developed first? What would be the operational design for a channel, and what type of marketing program would be needed to maximize market awareness and shopper adoption?

Mr. Johnson was also concerned that some of his assumptions and some of those of the task force might be too optimistic, particularly those concerning the costs to suppliers. The task force had recommended that prospective suppliers should incur most of the start-up and maintenance expenses, and the risks. Yet, it appeared that Mark-Tele would skim the VideoShop revenues without much direct cost or risk. Would suppliers accept Mark-Tele's conditions for operations? The entire supply issue would require significant attention. Which specific suppliers would contribute most to VideoShop? Which suppliers would work best with Mark-Tele, and what type of relationships would evolve? How would a marketing program be formulated to reach prospective suppliers?

Suddenly, Mr. Johnson realized that he was vacillating. If Mark-Tele didn't implement VideoShop soon, someone would. VideoShop was a great idea. Mr.

Johnson simply lacked the strategic plan that he could use to convince the board and to market VideoShop to suppliers and shoppers.

Appendix   # New venture task force report proposing a telecommunications shopping system*

We recommend that Mark-Tele design and implement a telecommunication shopping (TCS) system immediately. This proposed new venture appears to be a natural extension of Mark-Tele's experimental mission and an excellent application of Mark-Tele's distinctive technological capabilities in the telecommunications field.

A TCS system would allow a Mark-Tele subscriber to become an active shopper and buyer in the privacy of the home using only the television. Facilitated by Mark-Tele's sophisticated communications and computing technologies, a TCS system subscriber would be able to view and buy a large variety of products and services that conventionally would have required the shopper to leave the home and travel to view and purchase. A TCS system would also serve the suppliers of many different products and services with an opportunity to break away from costly traditional market channels and to inexpensively expand their market coverage and increase sales substantially.

For Mark-Tele, a TCS system would increase revenues, diversify its revenue base and distribute its high fixed costs efficiently. A TCS system could be used as a promotional tool to build and maintain Mark-Tele's local subscription base. Current subscription rates could be raised with the addition of the TCS system, or an additional fee could be charged to subscribers who desire to participate in the TCS system. Suppliers and shopping subscribers would also be charged for services that Mark-Tele would provide in the development and operation of the TCS system. In the longer run, Mark-Tele could potentially develop TCS networks that could be sold to other cable systems. Clearly, early entry into the TCS field would be lucrative financially for Mark-Tele.

In the remainder of this report, we will discuss: (1) significant environmental factors that influence the TCS market; (2) a general strategy for targeting the TCS system; (3) prospective product and service offerings; and (4) developmental issues for promoting the TCS system.

The Environment of TCS

Economic, technological, legal and regulatory, and social trends are emerging in support of a TCS system.

Increased consumer spending is predicted to continue, but gains for retailers will be restricted by inflationary pressures. There will be a slower pace of

*This is an abridged version of the committee's report.

store expansion during the 1980s. Many of the major metropolitan areas are overbuilt with retail space, and developers often are experiencing difficulty obtaining sites and financing. Retailers similarly are experiencing rising rents. Sales growth at many shopping centers has fallen due to slow growth of suburban communities and shrinking distances that consumers are willing to travel to shop as gasoline prices continue to advance.

Retailers are attempting to boost productivity, consolidate store space, and cut costs to improve returns. Inflation has increased operating costs more rapidly than sales during the last ten years. Many retailers have been attracted to discount pricing policies. The catalog showroom has become one of the fastest-growing segments of discount merchandising, featuring national-brand products at discount prices while operating on lower overhead than department stores.

Considering sociocultural trends, women are continuing to enter the work force, thus having less time to engage in shopping for staples, as well as for discretionary purchases. Greater emphasis on recreational activities continues, and individuals are reluctant to sacrifice leisure time to shop in stores. Convenience is emerging as a high priority.

Consumers are emphasizing their self-identity. As such, consumers are demanding more individuality in goods and services, often desiring distinctive products that individual stores may not be able to afford to inventory and display. Definitely, there has been more intense consumer preference for specialty items and services difficult to find in the Mark-Tele market area.

An increase in the number of single-parent and single-person households has led to increased in-home shopping. Nonstore innovations such as pay-by-phone, specialty mail-order catalogs, and toll-free phone ordering have become increasingly popular. Catalog shopping currently offers a full line of merchandise together with prices and features that permit a consumer to comparison shop at home without having to spend time inefficiently searching for products in crowded stores, waiting for sales help or at times being annoyed by overzealous clerks.

In addition, the increasing age of the population, proliferation of retirement communities, and declining mobility of individuals in their later years make catalog shopping very attractive.

There are significant technological advances that will influence the TCS system. In the past, alphanumerics and graphics, but not still or moving "pictures," could be retrieved from a data bank and displayed on a television screen; however, Intertronics' innovative technologies have advanced moving picture capabilities. This new technology has permitted the consumer to control the timing, sequence, and content of information through the use of the keypad. As such, the convenience of purchasing on impulse without need for either a telephone or advance credit arrangements is viable. Purchases can be charged automatically to a bank or credit card account.

Development of videodisks and videocassettes, which to date have been used by viewers to record television programs, has significant promise for advertising and catalog media. Potential exists for suppliers to mail lower-cost video catalogs on a complimentary basis or in lieu of printed direct-mail offerings.

Consumers are being exposed to and are accepting of complex, technical items such as videotape recorders, home computers, and debit cards for use with automatic teller machines. Home computers and the development of "videotex," the generic term for home information-retrieval systems, will provide functions compatible with those of the TCS system. Many consumers will easily develop the technical skills and sophistication needed to actively participate in the TCS system.

The political-legal context is confusing. The Federal Communications Commission has decided that cable franchising is mainly the province of local jurisdictions. All cable companies must interact with local governments to obtain and maintain authority to operate. While Mark-Tele has secured exclusive rights in its metropolitan area, changes in federal and local policy must be monitored, and good rapport with local leaders should be cultivated continuously.

The TCS venture raises questions concerning supplier and financial contractual arrangements. The antitrust implications of arrangements with some large institutions should be studied in more detail on a case-by-case basis. Moreover, movement into the retail sector by Mark-Tele through the TCS system will mean closer scrutiny by federal and local consumer protection agencies such as the Federal Trade Commission and Consumer Product Safety Commission. Finally, Mark-Tele will need to carefully consider protection of the privacy of personal, financial, and transactional data about subscribers of the TCS system. Controls must be established to prevent unauthorized access to information in the system data banks and to guard against unauthorized purchasing.

The General Competitive Context

Industry observers clearly are divided when projecting the evolution of electronic shopping and its acceptance by both consumers and the industry. Consumers appear interested in the potential convenience, extended selections, fuel economies, discount prices and time savings offered by the concept of shopping at home. Furthermore, at least ten thousand firms have expressed interest in the concept of electronic shopping. Currently, all forms of nonstore retailing are growing rapidly, and continued growth is forecasted. Major developments in nonstore retailing will be reviewed.

Mail-order catalogs   General department store merchandisers, catalog showrooms and specialty houses periodically mail catalogs to targeted groups of consumers. An average mail-order house distributes from six to twenty catalog issues yearly at a cost often approaching $2 each. Circulations range from about one hundred thousand to over a million for each mailing. The results have been outstanding. Over $26 billion was spent by consumers on mail-order items in

1978 — an increase of $12 billion in three years. By comparison, in-store retailing sales grew at a rate less than half of the mail-order rate. Mail-order firms' after-tax profits averaged 7 percent during this period.

Specialty firms such as L. L. Bean, Dallas' Horchow Collection, Talbot's of Massachusetts, and Hammacher-Schlemner of New York have become more prominent in the field. Specialty-oriented catalogs are accounting for 75 percent of total mail-order sales, and mail-order catalogs currently contribute 15 percent of the total volume of Christmas season sales.

Telephone- and mail-generated orders, received by traditional store retailers such as Bloomingdale's, J. C. Penney, and Sears are increasing three to five times faster than in-store sales. Sears found that 9.1 percent of its sales came from outside catalogs in 1977 and an additional 11.4 percent from catalog counters in the stores. Montgomery Ward derived 13 percent of its sales from catalogs.

In-flight shopping catalogs used by major airlines are additional evidence of the increasing popularity of nonstore shopping. MasterCard, American Express, and Visa have increased their direct mail offerings to their credit card holders and are expanding their assortments of merchandise.

The catalog showrooms   The catalog showroom is one of the fastest-growing fields of retailing. Catalogs are used to promote and feature jewelry, housewares, appliances, sporting goods and toys at discount prices. Customers visit the showroom to inspect merchandise and to make purchases. Analysts suggest that 85 percent of sales are generated by the catalogs and the remainder by test-selling products promoted on the showroom floor. Sales for 1980 are estimated to be $7.8 billion, an increase of 11 percent from 1979. Forecasts for 1981 suggest a 20-percent gain in sales revenue. The number of showrooms across the country is nearly two thousand.

Noninteractive shopping using the cable   Comp-U-Card International of Stamford, Connecticut, is a seven-year-old telephone merchandising firm. For an annual fee of $18, it offers members a discount on a broad line of durable goods. Members shop around, familiarizing themselves with products and prices. Then, they call Comp-U-Card toll-free for specific information about an item's availability and price. If a purchase decision is made, the consumer provides membership and credit card numbers to an operator, and the merchandise is prepared for delivery. An experimental project has been proposed in which Comp-U-Card would use cable systems and satellite transmission to present product and price information to its subscribers. A transmitted schedule would alert subscribers to the time when particular product information would be presented. Subscribers would continue to use the telephone when ordering. In October 1980, Federated Department Stores acquired a substantial interest in Comp-U-Card.

Telephone purchasing systems using cable presentations are currently operating in Europe. In March 1979, the British Post Office, which runs Britain's telephone system, opened a "viewdata" service called Prestel. Viewers are presented listings of games, restaurants, and consumer product evaluations. Products and services can be purchased on credit by phone. France launched a similar service, called Antiope, in 1979.

A few U.S. companies are testing similar systems. Viewdata Corp., a subsidiary of the Knight-Ridder Newspaper chain, proposes to install a permanent system in southern Florida by 1983. First Bank System of Minneapolis will be testing a "videotex" system in North Dakota similar to the Antiope system of France.

Interactive cable systems and videotex   Since December 1977, Warner Communications and American Express have been involved in a $70-million joint venture testing the QUBE two-way system of Warner Amex Cable in Columbus, Ohio. Currently, the system serves 30,000 of the 105,000 homes in its service area. American Express and Warner Communications propose to build other QUBE systems in such metropolitan areas as Houston, Pittsburgh, and Cincinnati. Both Sears and J. C. Penney currently are testing the QUBE system.

In May 1981, American Telephone & Telegraph (AT&T) endorsed a videotex concept in which a home computer terminal must be purchased. AT&T has set out to develop its own system. AT&T would be a formidable opponent to anyone in the market, considering the firm's capabilities and financial strength. Thus, there are a number of legal actions being undertaken to prevent AT&T's direct entry into the videotex market, fearing it could become a monopoly power. However, strong deregulation sentiments may overcome the opposition and facilitate AT&T's entry into the market.

In summary, the TCS market is embryonic. Growth in nonstore retailing is providing a solid foundation upon which TCS systems can build. Over $100 million already has been invested by U.S. firms to design and test various TCS systems, and at least eighty-three experimental projects are being conducted around the world. As a result, Mark-Tele must be prepared to match formidable competition, and we feel confident that Mark-Tele can.

Target Market Considerations

The TCS system must be carefully tailored and targeted to meet market demands and expectations. There are two different markets that must be considered when developing this venture: (1) the suppliers and (2) the shoppers.

We propose that the TCS system be targeted to the ultimate *user* — the subscribing shopper. A TCS system that is designed well will sell itself to suppliers. Suppliers, therefore, should be considered as a dimension of the "total product" that will be offered to target shoppers. This approach will allow Mark-Tele to retain maximum control and autonomy in the design and implementation of this venture.

The target market—shoppers   A careful review of the size and characteristics of the current and potential Mark-Tele subscription base indicates substantial market potential and buying power. However, critical analysis of shopping and buying behavior is necessary to isolate the most lucrative prospective customer segments and to understand their prospective TCS behavior. Three buying factors appear to be very important: (1) risk perceptions, (2) convenience orientations and (3) buyer satisfaction.

Risk   Buying is a complex experience filled with uncertainty and related risks of unfavorable consequences. Fundamentally, consumers confront the uncertainty of achieving their buying goals and risks such as embarrassment or wasting time, money or effort in a disappointing buying or shopping experience. Consumers usually are not highly conscious of these until they face new, different, or very important buying decisions or situations. In general, shopping is used to reduce uncertainty, risk and potential disappointment. More specifically, consumers shop to help refine their buying goals, to search for and evaluate specific products and terms, to execute transactions, and to favorably reinforce past purchase behaviors.

When consumers consider TCS experiences, they must feel comfortable and in control. All shopping and buying uncertainties, risks and potential negative consequences must be minimized throughout the total TCS experience. Initially, the consumer must learn how to operate/interface with the TCS system. One positive experience should build into others.

During the TCS experience, some traditional risk-reduction tactics such as personal inspection of merchandise or interaction with salespeople will not be available to the shopper. However, there are significant risk-reduction tactics that will be accessible. These include

1. visual and audio comparison of a wide assortment and range of products and services
2. information access and collection controlled by the shopper
3. information availability regarding many product features and all terms of sale and delivery
4. promotional messages that present products and services in attractive, exciting, and believable formats
5. past experiences with the product, service, brand, or supplier
6. personal experiences shared by significant friends, relatives, or peers
7. testimonials from respected celebrities, peers, or experts
8. continuous building of positive shopping experiences with the TCS system

These risk-reduction tactics should be incorporated into the TCS system design and promoted during operations.

In short, we suggest (a) that uncertainty and risk can be significantly reduced by presenting TCS, and its products and services, as personal and uncomplicated; and (b) that shopping confidence can be built by involving shoppers in positive TCS experiences. For example, some exploratory studies have indicated that shoppers feel confident ordering merchandise by television when (1) the product or service is easily recognizable and clearly identified by brand, retailer, size, color and/or other relevant properties; (2) consumers could access the information when they felt ready to actually make the purchase; and (3) consumers had purchased the product or service previously.

Convenience   Shopping is a problem-solving activity. The TCS system offers solutions to many nagging problems encountered when shopping conventionally. Consider the following common aggravations: having to carry merchandise; adapting to limited store hours; poor and confusing displays of merchandise; difficulty in finding desired items; dealing directly with salespeople; spending time and money traveling to the store; crowds of shoppers; boredom and fatigue of going from department to department and store to store. These are some of the inconveniences of conventional shopping systems that TCS can overcome.

A strong need or orientation for convenience is an appropriate base for identifying and understanding the primary target market for the TCS system. The following customer characteristics should be used to identify target market boundaries and to isolate specific segments within the primary target market. In the future, these could be cross-tabulated with other demographic, behavioral, and media characteristics to further refine target segment definitions and to tailor market programs.

Primary target customers for the TCS system are those Mark–Tele subscribers

1.   with greater than average need or desire for convenience
2.   with restricted mobility because children are at home
3.   with appropriate buying power and media (credit cards)
4.   who compile shopping lists regularly
5.   who are frequent catalog shoppers
6.   who rely extensively on newspaper, magazine, or television advertising
7.   who are loyal to specific brands or suppliers
8.   who do not like to travel or find it very difficult to travel
9.   who do not like to deal with crowds
10.   who are handicapped physically
11.   who are actively engaged in time-consuming leisure activities
12.   who are senior citizens

Satisfaction   A consumer must have a satisfying experience each time that the TCS system is used. Otherwise, it is very likely that the consumer will not use TCS again and may discuss the bad experience with other shoppers and discourage their future use of the system. Thus, Mark-Tele must maintain tight control over suppliers. A consumer satisfaction department should be formed within

Mark-Tele. This group should monitor all TCS activities, conduct market research, investigate all consumer complaints and make certain that all consumers are fully informed and satisfied with TCS.

Supplier market implications After selecting general product and service categories and designing a general format for each TCS channel, Mark-Tele should direct attention to the supplier market. At that time, Mark-Tele should evaluate prospective suppliers regarding the relevance of their product or service assortment, their delivery and financial capabilities, the quality of their promotional strategies and their desire to enter into this unconventional market. We feel that Mark-Tele's technical competence and captive subscription base will provide substantial leverage in all negotiations with suppliers. The actual marketing effort should involve personal selling programs custom designed for each prospective target supplier.

Prospective Products and Services

Preliminary research on TCS systems has uncovered a number of product and service lines that are appropriate for our target market and appear to be financially and technically feasible. As this innovative approach to shopping evolves and consumer acceptance and involvement grows, many other products and services could be incorporated. However, the most feasible products and services currently are

1. standard catalog items
2. staple grocery items
3. gifts and specialty items
4. appliances and home entertainment equipment
5. toys, electronic games and equipment, basic sporting goods
6. banking and financial services
7. classified ads
8. multiple listing service of local properties
9. ticket, restaurant, and accommodations reservations
10. educational classes
11. automobiles

We cannot stress too strongly that TCS will involve a high degree of risk perceived by consumers. This must be reduced by offering products and services with which consumers are familiar and comfortable and that involve a minimum number of simple shopping decisions for consumers.

The consumer must *learn* to use the TCS system. Mark-Tele must guide this learning experience and make sure that consumers have consistent, positive shopping experiences that become reinforcing. The following services/features should be incorporated into the TCS system to reduce shopping risks and facilitate consumer satisfaction:

1. Easy to use indexing devices
2. Top quality visual and audio representation
3. Professional promotions
4. Up-to-date information on specials
5. Competitive pricing policies and convenient payment methods
6. TCS availability twenty-four hours per day, seven days per week
7. Maintenance service availability twenty-four hours per day, seven days per week
8. Accurate order taking and fulfilling
9. Prompt delivery or pickup services
10. Quick and equitable handling and resolution of customer complaints
11. Exceptional reliability

Eventually, the TCS product and service assortment could be broadened and channel features changed. However, the products and service lines outlined in this report appear to involve minimal consumer risks, high potential for competitive advantage and target consumer satisfaction and substantial returns for Mark-Tele.

The Competitive Advantage and TCS Promotion

A competitive advantage over conventional suppliers can be achieved by Mark-Tele if the TCS system is designed to serve the needs and expectations of the identified target market by actively considering their prepurchase deliberations, by guiding their purchase activities, and by reinforcing their postpurchase satisfaction. This must be complemented with accurate and reliable order processing and with prompt, efficient logistical support. Above all, Mark-Tele must communicate and promote its distinctive capabilities. We believe that the following distinctive features of the TCS system should be emphasized:

1. The extensive variety and depth of product and service assortments
2. The vast amount of relevant information that is easily accessible and allows consumers to make better choices
3. The excitement, involvement, convenience, and satisfaction of shopping in the privacy of one's home using space-age technology and the simplicity of the television
4. The insignificant, negligible, and indirect costs to consumers, particularly when compared with the opportunities and benefits

We feel that the best medium for promotion of the TCS system will be the television itself. Promotional information should be presented on all television channels other than pay channels. The TCS system initially should be portrayed as a new, exciting service available to all Mark-Tele subscribers. After this campaign, the theme should be changed to focus on *how* the TCS system works *for* and *with* the subscriber/consumer. A final campaign should be developed to re-inforce and to encourage extended usage of the TCS system.

Enclosures and brochures in billing statements should be used extensively in support of the television campaigns to alert subscribers to the availability of the TCS system, to detail operational dimensions, and to discuss changes and additions to the system before these occur. Demonstration projects probably can be executed using the television rather than personal contact.

Mailing, print media and personal selling appear to be appropriate means for reaching prospective subscribers as the cable system expands, as well as a means to retrack and increase penetration of cable services in areas in which these already are available. However, the TCS system should be promoted as only one dimension of the total Mark-Tele cable package to prospective subscribers.

Finally, word of mouth will be a vital factor underlying acceptance and use of TCS. Active stimulation and encouragement of this free, highly effective form of promotion should be implemented and maintained using both creative advertising strategies and other promotional tactics, such as special cable rates to subscribers who get friends or relatives to sign up and use the system.

Conclusion

The recommendation of our committee is that Mark-Tele design and implement the proposed new venture concept — a telecommunication shopping system. We have identified the target customer and viable products and services to satisfy their needs and Mark-Tele's objectives. Development of the supplier market and control over suppliers also has been discussed.

Overall, the distinct advantages of the TCS concept would include (a) the wide variety of products and services that would be available to consumers; (b) the unique and novel process of shopping; (c) the ease, convenience and privacy of shopping and buying; and (d) the special buying incentives, such as comparative sales prices and controlled access to extensive amounts of information regarding products and services.

We recommend immediate action on this proposal to ensure and enact a competitive advantage in this revolutionary marketplace.

Case 12

MUSE AIR

En route to the Love Field airport in Dallas in one of the company's planes, Michael Muse had many things on his mind. He deeply wanted his company, Muse Air Corporation, to be profitable. There was more at stake here than money, it was a matter of pride. "How could anyone have the misfortune to start an airline just a few weeks before the air traffic controller's strike?" Michael asked his father, Lamar Muse, who was in the next seat. "It's just not possible to control everything at all times. You just have to make the best of things," Lamar responded. "Well it's time we took control again," Michael said firmly. "Let's map out our revised strategy for expansion." Lamar knew that he was going to have to review the major factors facing Muse Air to resolve things in Michael's mind.

THE AIRLINE INDUSTRY

Regulation

The major issues facing the airline industry today stem from its continuing struggle to adjust to the changing environment created by the Airline Deregulation Act of 1978. Under deregulation, the control of the Federal Aviation Administration (FAA) and the Civil Aeronautics Board (CAB) over airlines was drastically reduced. As controls over routes and fares were lifted, the industry faced rapidly changing market conditions in which competition increased significantly. The immediate result for the major established airlines was a dramatic drop in corporate earnings as new low-priced entrants forced price wars. The

This case was prepared by Robert McGlashan and Tim Singleton, University of Houston Clear Lake, as a basis for class discussion. Reprinted by permission of North American Case Research Association and the authors.

industry continues to be plagued by financial losses and excess passenger capacity. From 36 certified carriers prior to deregulation, the industry has mushroomed to about 125 airlines today. But the rate of failure has increased also as 28 carriers have gone out of business since 1978.

The primary long-term result of deregulation and increased competition is a stronger and more efficient industry. Overall inflation-adjusted ticket prices, because of discount fares, are now 10%–20% lower than in 1974. Departures at major hub cities in 1983 were up 15.7% and at medium hubs were up 22.5% from 1978. The number of interstate carriers has risen from 36 to 98 with big airlines now controlling 79% of the market, versus 91% before deregulation. Although since 1978, the major carriers have reduced their work forces by 24,000 employees, nearly that many jobs have been created by the smaller airlines.

The FAA continues to exercise regulatory authority over airlines in regard to ground facilities, communication, training of pilots and other personnel, and aircraft safety. Airlines must obtain an operating certificate, subject to compliance with all regulations in these areas. Environmental regulation is also imposed to control noise and engine emissions. Local pressure groups may exert influence on airports to limit flights over certain areas in order to control noise pollution. One special regulation imposed by the International Air Transportation Competition Act of 1979 is the limitation on flights out of Love Field in Dallas. Destinations from Love Field may include locations only in the four states neighboring Texas—Arkansas, Oklahoma, New Mexico and Louisiana.

When the CAB was dissolved on January 1, 1985, the regulatory authority over mergers and interlocking relationships was transferred to the Justice Department, under which the FAA operates. For other businesses, this regulatory authority is the jurisdiction of the Federal Trade Commission. Other responsibilities which the CAB handles, such as selection of carriers for international route operations, have been reassigned to the Department of Transportation. Since both of these departments are in the Executive Branch, there is congressional debate as to whether sufficient control over the airline industry can be retained without the CAB or another congressional agency. Reregulation considerations will continue to surface as the CAB deadline approaches.[1]

Air Traffic Control

Airlines are still dealing with the effects of the August 2, 1981, union strike of the Professional Air Traffic Controllers Organization (PATCO). The air controller's job is to keep airplanes moving at a safe distance from one another as they are passed along from one tower to another. As planes taxi, take off, fly, and land, they stay in touch with the pilots by radio and follow their progress on radar screens. These screens display each plane's location, altitude, speed,

[1] Joan M. Feldman, "Deregulation Loose Ends Spark Debate About Regulation After 1984," *Air Transport World*, 20 (May 1983), 23.

and any problems, such as two planes moving too close together. The screens are all computer-generated.

When 12,000 of the 17,000 controllers walked out at the start of the strike, the traffic control system was thrown into confusion. Under FAA emergency controls, which reduced flight frequencies, nearly 75% of the 22,000 daily flights were kept flying. All the major airlines experienced a decrease in revenues and available slots, both airport and en-route, which reduced flexibility in route structuring despite deregulation. Once the initial pandemonium over the strike abated, the airlines began to tailor their operations to meet the new environment. Steps taken included grounding of the least fuel-efficient planes, concentration on the more important routes, reduction in the work force and restrictions placed on discount fares. A drop in revenue of 12% was reported by TWA and 15% by United Airlines. These figures were typical for the airline industry.

Only since October 30, 1983, has the FAA eliminated most slot restrictions, enabling airlines to determine destinations without having to negotiate and trade for landing slots. Because of continued air traffic control problems in Chicago, Los Angeles, New York, and Denver airports, restrictions have not as yet been lifted in these high density cities. The post-strike rules are slated to expire April 1, 1984, in Denver, but remained in effect in Los Angeles until after the Olympics. Expiration of the rules in New York and Chicago was delayed until January, 1985, however, based on the FAA's assessment of air control's inability to handle unrestricted air traffic at these airports. The temporary preferential route system requires that aircraft fly specific mandatory routes to circumvent congested airspace, but the routes are often considerably longer in distance than airlines would normally fly. Costing time and fuel, these restrictions have affected airlines' cost reduction efforts, especially for the majors who serve longer hauls. It is expected that the FAA will finally eliminate the preferential route system early in 1984.[2] The future of air traffic control is enhanced by the long-awaited decision to modernize the system. The FAA has embarked on a 10-year, ten billion dollar effort to upgrade air traffic control in order to cope with the projected 26.5% growth in aviation by the year 2000.

Cooperative Routing

The flexibility in routing brought about by deregulation has given rise to the hub and spoke system with its central exchange point. This system enables airlines to carry passengers to their final destinations without having to share revenues, as is necessary in interlining agreements. This prederegulation system of interlining is beginning to fall apart as the majors re-evaluate their benefit. Under multilateral, open-ended agreements which have created an integrated national air transportation system, the major airlines provide passengers with

[2]"FAA Nears Ruling on Preferential Routes," *Aviation Week & Space Technology,* 119 (18 April 1983), 34.

interchangeable ticketing and baggage service to final destination. United, American, and Delta are now advising interlining partners that their agreements will be on a bilateral basis with periodic review. The change is contemplated by the majors because of Continental Airlines' action in seeking protection under bankruptcy regulations in 1983. Because Continental did not cease operations completely and resumed service within two days, the bankruptcy court judge ruled that Continental's partners should continue to honor the interline agreement and yet would not be able to collect money owed for services prior to the bankruptcy. At issue, too, is the industry's default protection plan which protects ticket-holders in the event of airline bankruptcy. The end to either system would place new competitive pressures on financially weak airlines.[3]

A new form of cooperative routing has developed in which airlines agree bilaterally to link their route systems in an effort to strengthen their individual hub and spoke networks. Muse Air has such an arrangement with Air Cal. Cooperative routing could be achieved by other means such as arrangements similar to franchise service exchange agreements or outright acquisition of commuter carriers by larger airlines.

Economy

The airline industry is highly affected by the business cycle. The current upturn in the economy has brought increases in revenue passenger miles to help reduce the pressures of overcapacity which plagued the industry throughout the recession of 1981 and 1982. As disposable income grows and air travel increases during the favorable economy, airlines will experience increasing revenues. The temptation in an upturn is to be less vigilant regarding rising costs. Whether these increased revenues translate into increased profits depends on the ability of airlines to keep costs down.

In fact, cost control is the primary key to profitability in the airline industry. With labor cost representing 37% of the total expenses of the established major and national carriers, in contrast to the new entrants' 18%, there is a significant disequilibrium in the industry that market forces will inevitably eliminate. Entering into this equation is the labor relations dilemma facing the industry. Recognizing that a favorable employee attitude is essential to high quality service, how airlines achieve labor cost control directly influences effectiveness as well as efficiency. Two advantages that new entrants have in labor productivity are: (1) established airlines employees and their unions have little understanding or sympathy for the effects of deregulation and (2) employees of new airlines have no allegiance to the preregulation structure and possess the enthusiasm of sharing in a new enterprise. There have been several approaches to labor cost control including employee ownership programs, establishment of new subsidiary carriers, revocation of labor contracts through declaration of bankruptcy, and a two-tiered wage system for old and new employees.

---

[3]"Airline Cooperation Starts to Break Apart," *Business Week,* 29 November 1983, p. 45.

The second major cost factor is fuel availability. The sporadic shortages, political instability in oil producing countries, and decontrol of oil prices are uncontrollable external conditions that directly affect profitability of airlines. When fuel costs rose dramatically in 1979–1980, competitive pressures prevented airlines from passing on those increases to passengers. Although fuel costs have declined for the past three years, they still represent 25% of total airline costs. Fuel efficient aircraft have become an important consideration as a result of high fuel costs.

Beyond operating expenses, the major cost of airlines is the aircraft itself. The high cost of new aircraft has made their acquisition economically prohibitive in spite of their greater fuel efficiency. At current fuel costs, the savings is not sufficient to cover the cost of buying expensive new aircraft. One of the reasons for the high price of aircraft is the fact that manufacturers produce aircraft on an individual job-order basis rather than by mass-production. This nonstandardized production not only increases the original cost but reduces the residual value of aircraft.

Additionally, the fragmentation of the market has reduced opportunities to use larger aircraft. The per-seat cost savings on a 150 versus 100 seat aircraft, for instance, can only be realized if the extra capacity is utilized. This is difficult to achieve in a competitive market already facing overcapacity. Once again, the impact of deregulation seems to be responsible for setting a new trend. In an effort to reduce capacity, airlines are seeking smaller aircraft. The transition to the down-sized transport will be costly to airlines and place new competitive pressures on aircraft manufacturers who have suffered decreased sales for five years. As airlines return to profitability, fleet acquisition will be a priority to gain competitive position.[4]

Reservation System

The distribution of airline ticketing is dominated by travel agents utilizing computerized reservation systems. In fact, 65% of airline reservations are handled by travel agents. Airlines subscribe to one of the majors' computerized systems of which American's Saber is dominant in Texas markets. There are two advantages to the owners or host carriers of the reservation systems. One is a computer bias in which the host is given priority listing among available flights with more information listed than for other airlines. This tends to encourage the choice of the host by travel agents in reserving flights resulting in increased market share for the host. Secondly, it is common for travel agents to book (or plate) tickets to the servicing carrier, which is the computer host. Since there is a four to ten week ticket settlement period, in effect this gives the host utilization of the amounts "plated away" from airline subscribers who are denied cash settlement for that period. It is estimated that the float created by this plating

[4]James Ott, "Airlines Gear for Near Challenges," *Aviation Week & Space Technology*, 118 (14 November 1983), 48.

process amounts to $3 billion and costs the airlines financing that float $360 million a year in new interest expense. The Justice Department has asked CAB to adopt rules to reduce competitive abuses of the computerized systems.[5]

With agent commissions representing 6.7% of total airline operating expenses, the CAB's plan to abolish travel agent exclusivity at the end of 1984 will increase competitive initiatives in retail marketing. By breaking up the travel agent monopoly, new innovations in the distribution of airline ticketing are possible. For instance, direct reservations by individuals through cable television may be implemented, discount houses for airline ticket sales could develop, and business travel departments may gain access to direct reservation systems. New economies may also be realized if the practice of "plating away" from airlines, which attempt to reduce travel agent commissions, is eliminated.[6]

COMPANY HISTORY

The Beginning

Muse Air Corporation was organized in early 1980 by two ex-Southwest Airlines employees, Lamar and Michael Muse. The airline was organized to provide high frequency, single class, low cost air transportation for the general public. It was one of the many new regional airlines entering the market after deregulation of the airline industry.

Lamar Muse, one of Southwest Airlines' founders and former chief executive officer, left Southwest Airlines after a bitter policy dispute in 1978. His two year no-competition agreement with Southwest ran out in October, 1980, when he joined his son, Michael, to operate Muse Air. Michael was a former chief financial officer for Southwest Airlines.

Muse Air began service on July 15, 1981, with two DC-9 Super 80s flying between Dallas and Houston. The plans were to compete directly with Southwest on their most lucrative route. Muse had an aggressive expansion program laid out for the next several years, planning to become a major airline as quickly as possible. Fate had no intention of allowing Muse's plans to run smoothly.

Air Traffic Controllers' Strike

On August 2, 1981, just 18 days after Muse began service, PATCO went out on a nationwide strike, causing the FAA to place restrictions on landing slots.

[5]Michael Cieply, "Hardball," *Forbes*, 132 (28 February 1983), 33.
[6]James Ott, "House Questions Agent Decision," *Week & Space Technology*, 118 (30 May 1983), 57–58.

With the delivery of two McDonnell Douglas DC-9 Super 80s, Muse Air planned to expand its routes to include Midland-Odessa and Tulsa by May, 1982. Even though the FAA planned to increase the air traffic system's capacity to 90% of normal (before strike) by September, 1982, no changes or increases in landing slots were authorized for Dallas or Houston. This was at a time when airline officials were expressing strong dissatisfaction with the FAA's continued use of emergency powers to allocate the additional capacity, instead of switching to normal administrative procedures. Many airlines felt the allocation of additional slots and routes was not being handled fairly.

Planned expansion by Muse into these two new markets in May, 1982, and two additional markets in July, 1982, was being delayed because of Federal Aviation Administration restrictions on operating slots at Love Field in Dallas and Hobby Airport in Houston. Muse Air had applied for permission to provide Houston-Dallas-Tulsa with seven daily round trips and six daily round trips from Dallas to Midland-Odessa. (See Exhibit 1.)

The FAA approved Muse Air for operation of one evening off-peak round trip to Tulsa and denied all other requested slots. The FAA also denied a request for 13 flights daily between Love Field and Austin and 14 flights between Love Field and San Antonio. Muse Air officials argued that the slot restrictions were contrary to the meaning of the deregulation act, tending to favor established carriers over new entrants. Obtaining the slots was vital for Muse Air, not only to prevent grounding of the two DC-9s that were being received, but to boost the load factors systemwide as the result of traffic the new cities would give to its present operation.

The Collapse of Braniff

In May, 1982, Braniff Airlines ceased operations and filed for bankruptcy-court protection under Chapter 11 of the Federal Bankruptcy Code. Braniff needed protection from creditors' lawsuits as it tried to work out a plan to repay all debts. This opened up many slots for other airlines to pick up and expand service. Muse Air was one of the first to present its request to the FAA for some of the Braniff slots.

Of all the new slots received by Muse Air, they were able to finally begin service to Midland-Odessa and Tulsa in late May, 1982. Attention was then turned toward the next planned expansion, that of Austin and San Antonio. Muse Air felt it still had enough Dallas slots to accomplish this expansion on schedule.

The FAA gave Muse Air seven en-route slots and eight airport slots at Dallas on a temporary basis. These slots were former Braniff slots which the FAA later rescinded away and allocated to other airlines by lottery. This left Muse in a position of negotiating for needed slots at Dallas in exchange for slots it did not want, such as at New York LaGuardia. So, again in August, 1982, Muse Air was in a position of having to ground newly acquired aircraft for lack of available slots.

EXHIBIT 1   Muse Air Corporation aircraft delivery schedule

Delivery date	Type	Quantity	Seating	Cities served
July 1981	DC9-80 (Super 80)	2	155	Dallas
				Houston
May 1982	DC9-80	2	155	Midland
				Odessa
				Tulsa
October 1982	DC9-80	2	155	Los Angeles
August 1983	DC9-51 (Super 50)	1	130	*Lubbock
November 1983	DC9-51	2	130	Austin
February 1984	DC9-51	1	130	Ontario, CA
				New
				Orleans
Projected Delivery Date				
April 1984	DC9-51	1	130	New cities
				**Little Rock
				Las Vegas
March 1985	DC9-51	2	130	San
				Antonio
				Chicago
March 1986	DC9-51	2	130	Atlanta
				Florida

*Service discontinued in February 1984.
**Service start-up cancelled February 1984.

Source: 1983 Muse Air annual report and Muse Air news release.

The West Coast

On October 1, 1982, as a way to keep from grounding aircraft, Muse Air began service to Los Angeles, California. This was a complete shift in original expansion plans. While the continuing restrictions on landing rights imposed by the FAA forestalled planned expansion to Austin and San Antonio, the new service to California achieved a break–even level of operations by December, 1982.

During the first part of 1983, Muse Air worked very hard at strengthening existing routes and increasing market share. For the first eight months of 1983, passenger traffic, as measured by revenue passenger miles, was up 195 percent. The fact that gains in traffic outpaced any increase in capacity was due to growing passenger load factors, the percent of seats filled. Growing identity with the traveling public, as much as anything else, was a major reason for these gains. This was accomplished by increasing the number of flights serving a particular market (the Dallas-Houston route was increased to 17 round trip flights daily), and attracting a larger portion of the business community as passengers, since these are the people who travel most frequently.

Continuing Expansion

In late 1983, Muse Air began the expansion again, with service to Lubbock in August and Austin in November, 1983. A major factor that made this possible was the elimination of most FAA slot restrictions on October 30, 1983. Muse's new $3 million dollar terminal at Hobby airport was completed in November, 1983, thus adding another large upgrade to the system.

Muse Air continued with expansion in early 1984, with the opening of the New Orleans market in February. With the Mardi Gras festival in the spring and the World's Fair opening in the summer, this means increased traffic to the New Orleans area. Muse Air fully expected to take advantage of this increased traffic flow and become very quickly established in the area.

Service was also begun to Ontario International in California in February, 1984, plus a selective joint marketing agreement was signed with Air Cal. Through these two "gateway" locations, Muse Air passengers can quickly connect to eight of Air Cal's markets. In essence, this agreement represents a doubling of marketing destinations available to Muse Air customers. All the conveniences of expanded service to eight new West Coast markets was achieved without the costly capital outlays required for opening individual, on-site operations.

In late February of 1984, Muse Air discontinued service to Lubbock as it had proven to be unprofitable for the company. Plans for new service to Little Rock, Arkansas were abandoned the following month. Southwest Airlines moved into Little Rock first and saturated the market with flights.

In response to this, Muse Air opened up nonstop service between Dallas and New Orleans, began service to Las Vegas from Houston in April of 1984 and began special discount fares and Olympic tour packages. At this time, all 11 of its planes were being fully utilized and earning a profit for Muse Air.

COMPANY MANAGEMENT

Management Organization

The organization of Muse Air's top management is a straightforward top-down style. (See Exhibit 2.) Lamar Muse is Chairman of the Board and Michael is President and Chief Executive Officer. Nine vice presidents report to Michael Muse, covering all the major areas of company operation. These people are

EXHIBIT 2   **Muse Air Corporation — corporate organization chart**

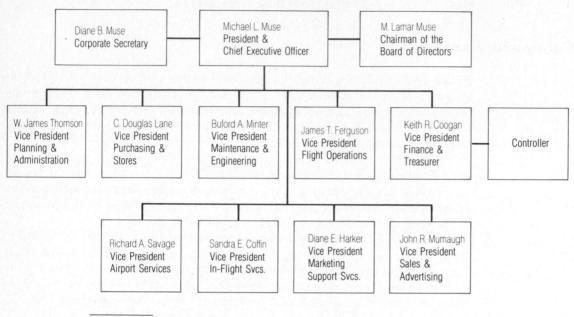

Source: Muse Air Corporation.

- *Vice President–Flight Operations* — Mr. Ferguson served as a senior captain for Texas International Airlines and is now responsible for all operations and pilots.
- *Vice President–Maintenance & Engineering* — Mr. Minter worked previously for Braniff's maintenance department and as Staff Vice President.
- *Vice President–Purchasing & Stores* — Mr. Lane came from Southwest Airlines as Director of Purchasing.
- *Vice President–Planning & Budgeting* — Mr. Thomson is another former Southwest Airlines employee. He was Director of Treasury Operation.
- *Vice President–Finance & Treasurer* — Mr. Coogan, a former Audit Manager for Price Waterhouse, has been with Muse Air two years.
- *Vice President–Airport Services* — Mr. Savage has worked for Texas International, Air Couriers International and TWA, managing airports and airport facilities.
- *Vice President–Sales & Service* — Ms. Harker was a manager of Marketing and Financial support for American Airlines previously.
- *Vice President–In-Flight Services* — Ms. Coffin has worked as a flight attendant and as Director of Training and Support for Eastern Airlines.
- *Vice President–Sales & Advertising* — Mr. Mumaugh worked for United Airlines previously in sales, marketing, in-flight operations, and customer service.

The Muse Air management team contains a great amount of experience and expertise concerning the airline industry from a wide variety of sources and companies.

Employee Benefits

Muse Air has no pension plan for employees but does have a profit-sharing plan. When operating profits exceed a set amount for a quarter, 20% of these excess profits are distributed to the employees as cash. This is only for employees who have been with the company for a set period of time. Muse Air will also adopt a stock purchase plan for employees and highly encourage participation in the program. With the employees having a portion of ownership in the company, they will be more inclined to keep productivity up and costs down.

At present, there is a stock option plan for employees as far down in the company as midmanagement. The employee's position with the company determines how many shares he may purchase and at what price. An employee must have one year of service with Muse Air to participate and can only purchase one third of the option shares within a given year. The employee has five years to purchase all the stocks available to him under the option agreement.

A nonmonetary benefit of Muse Air is the rotation of employees within different ground operation positions. This allows the employees to become well cross-trained in various jobs while keeping their interest rate at a high level. Cross-training helps keep productivity up while keeping costs down for Muse Air since it does not have to keep excess people on the payroll.

AIRCRAFT AND FACILITIES

Muse Air uses the McDonnell Douglas DC-9, Super 80, and DC-9, Super 50, aircraft. These planes both use the cost efficient two engine design and require only two pilots, instead of three, as needed by other aircraft. All planes are set up for single class service with a distinguished, club style atmosphere. The exterior is white with the Muse Air signature in blue on the side of the plane.

The corporate signature of Muse Air as analyzed by Ray Walker, handwriting expert, announces strength and character. The backstroke on the letter "M" shows an awareness of the past, complemented by a powerful forward sweep that indicates confidence in the future. The "A" is an indication of pride. The dot over the "I" is close to the stem, showing an appropriate caution with emphasis on the safety and well-being of others.

Muse Air has implemented a cost efficient work force. Employees are nonunion, which helps keep wage levels moderate. Also, employees are cross-utilized between various jobs, eliminating the work restriction rules that plague many major carriers and raise their effective labor costs. Finally, because Muse

Air is such a young company, there are no long-time employees, meaning lower overall wage levels.

Within the air terminals, Muse Air uses cash register type ticketing and standardized check-in and baggage handling procedures. Operating costs are substantially reduced and passenger arrival-departure time kept to a minimum.

Keeping the comfort and convenience of passengers in mind, all flights are nonsmoking. The DC-9 Super 80 carries 155 passengers while the Super 50 carries 130. This, plus the 3-2 style of seating that has been installed, means more room and comfort for the passengers. The DC-9 gives the passenger a very quiet and smooth ride.

COMPETITION

General

The airline industry is divided into three segments: the major airlines, the national airlines, and the regionals, such as Muse Air. The market share of the majors has been declining since deregulation. At the same time, market share for the regionals has been increasing, picking up what the majors have lost. The load factors of the major airlines have stabilized over the past few years, neither growing nor decreasing. Muse Air's competition consists of three types. The first is Southwest Airlines, with whom Muse Air initiated head-on competition. Second are the regionals that have come into existence following deregulation. Last are the majors who are re-establishing on a much smaller scale, including Braniff and Continental Airlines.

Southwest Airlines

Southwest Airlines provides a single class, high frequency air service to cities in Texas and surrounding states. The company concentrates on short haul markets and stresses high level of aircraft utilization and employee productivity. The principal hubs of Southwest's systems are Dallas' Love Field and Houston's Hobby Airport, with a new hub established in Phoenix. These airports are located substantially closer to downtown business centers than the major airports.

Southwest is considered one of the best run airlines in the country. Revenues and revenue passenger miles rose all during 1983. The airline has a load factor around 62%, well above its break-even point. Southwest expanded into the longer haul routes with the delivery of new Boeing 737-300 aircraft in 1984. With a young and efficient fleet, the company is well positioned to benefit from any improvement in the domestic economic activity.

Regional Airlines

People Express began operating in April, 1981, and intended to triple its size by mid-1985 through the purchase of several Boeing 727s. It also began offering transatlantic service during the summer of 1983, with a leased 747-200. People Express services 17 cities domestically, mostly in the Northeast. It flies from its base at Newark, New Jersey, as far as Houston's Hobby. It was one of the few airlines to report a profit in 1982.

New York Air initiated service in late 1980 in the New York–Boston–Washington D.C. corridor, competing directly with Eastern's shuttle service. Since then it has added cities in the Southeast. The airline experienced an increase of profitability in 1983. New York Air pioneered the concept of business class service at coach class rates. Passengers have been lured with such items as two-by-two seating, more leg room, bagels, and the *New York Times*.

In February, 1984, Air Atlanta began service between Atlanta, Memphis, and New York. The airline is using fewer seats, bigger chairs, more leg room, shorter ticket lines, and waiting areas with telephones and refreshments to lure full fare business passengers. Air Atlanta plans to specialize totally in this market. The planes and waiting areas have been completely redesigned for the business passenger to move on and off the plane quickly. Air Atlanta intends to cater to business passengers.

St. Louis based Air One began operations in April, 1983, with flights to Dallas, Kansas City, Washington D.C., and Newark, NJ. Air One is another airline that caters to the business traveler, offering first class service at coach class prices. In February of 1984, Air One began service between St. Louis and Houston's Hobby, the first of 22 cities it eventually plans to include in its route system. Air One currently has seven Boeing 727s and added five more in late 1984.

Rebirths

Like the phoenix that rose from the ashes, Braniff Airlines began flying again on March 1, 1984. It plans to operate a premium-service, low-cost airline, aimed strictly at the business travel market. From its Dallas hub, Braniff will serve 17 cities, including Houston, Austin, Los Angeles, New Orleans, San Antonio and Tulsa. Braniff is flying from Dallas–Fort Worth Regional Airport and Houston's Intercontinental. Estimates are that it will take several years for the airline to regain the market share it lost in the Houston market.

Braniff restructured itself with the financial backing of the Hyatt Corporation. It has reduced salaries, employees, and operating costs to the bare minimum. Even at these low levels, Braniff needs a 47% load factor to break even. The first stock offering by Braniff indicated moderate public confidence in the reborn airline.

Continental Airlines filed to reorganize under Chapter 11 of the Federal Bankruptcy Code during the third quarter of 1983. In February, 1984, the airline reappeared with bare bones pay scales, unrestricted low air fares, and employees with a stake in the airline's profitability. Like many of the new airlines, Continental is aiming for the single class business market with competitive fares and many special services.

MARKETING STRATEGY

Muse Air endeavors to provide the highest quality airline service to its target market, primarily businessmen and women. The marketing strategy is based on service, price, name recognition, and expansion of routes.

Service

Quality service on Muse Air includes many features: a quiet, comfortable ride on a Super 80 or Super 50 aircraft, with comfortable, large, leather seats in a clean, smoke-free environment; dependable service with convenient close-in airport locations and convenient departure times; the convenience of reserved seating to prevent the crush to board; the best service provided by motivated employees; easy booking for travel agents through American Airlines' computerized SABRE system.

Price

The air transportation market is growing, as the economy improves. Muse Air must gain its share of this market growth. To accomplish this goal, it uses competitive prices to attract customers. In March, 1983, Muse Air offered the "lowest" discounted fare to Los Angeles of $88.

Off peak pricing is used to attract more customers and keep more planes flying at higher occupancy. Muse Air primarily utilizes a two-tier fare structure: business class providing low cost, first class air transportation during prime time; and leisure class providing an economically competitive alternative to various forms of ground transportation.

Muse Air has always had to meet or beat the low fares of its major competitor, Southwest Airlines. The revival of Continental and Braniff Airlines in March, 1984, increased competition on most of the Muse Air routes. This competitive environment may spark another round of price slashing. Braniff has already announced reduced economy fares during March, 1984.

The reborn Continental Airlines precipitated fare discounting as a means to fill seats and gain the customers it lost after filing to reorganize under Chapter 11. Additionally, Delta Air Lines, Pan Am, American, Eastern, and TWA have joined in with their own discounting in order to remain competitive. Of these majors, Delta began service on March 1, 1984, from Houston's Hobby Airport to seven cities including Dallas/Ft. Worth, the major market for Muse Air.

Because of deregulation and the Chapter 11 alternative, the airline industry is becoming more efficient. Everyone is trying to keep costs low, so their rates can be competitive. It is with Southwest that Muse Air must be competitive in order to gain the needed traffic. Muse Air has a lower average cost than Southwest (5.2 cents a seat mile against Southwest's six cents and the industry average of nearly eleven cents). Since overhead is almost identical, Muse Air must differentiate itself from Southwest in order to "break the Southwest habit" to which the frequent flier has become accustomed.

Name Recognition

Lamar Muse feels that name recognition is critical to success. Therefore, Muse Air devotes a lot of effort to promote a premium product with a reserved and sophisticated image.

To enhance the club car image, it provides many in-service extras, including drinks on afternoon flights and a complimentary copy of *The Wall Street Journal*.

To encourage repeat customers, Muse Air has developed several packages and clubs that provide benefits for frequent fliers. For example, the Muse Air Club is for travel coordinators, secretaries, and people in business and government who are responsible for travel arrangements. Club members can earn free trips, participate in monthly drawings for special prizes, and receive the Muse Air magazine and invitations to special receptions.

Muse Air continues to spend heavily for advertising. In 1982, expenditures were over $6 million, or 16% of all operating expenses, for marketing. The initial ad campaign, "Big Daddy Is Back," emphasized their leader, Lamar Muse, and his experience in the airline industry. The next campaign was testimonials from customers.

The latest advertising effort on radio and television is intended to reach a wider group of potential passengers by using people of various ages and occupations. The campaign also attempts to entice the customer with a mystical, indescribable, beautiful experience. The themes are "You just gotta fly it," and "See how beautiful Muse Air can be." Initial response to this campaign has been very positive.

Route Expansion

The fourth component of the Muse Air marketing strategy is expansion of routes. Muse Air began service in July, 1981, between Dallas (Love Field) and Houston (Hobby Airport). As of February, 1984, Muse Air flew 17 round trips daily on the Dallas–Houston route, which is its most popular.

From 1982, Muse Air has expanded service to Midland-Odessa, Texas; Tulsa, Oklahoma; Los Angeles, California; Lubbock, Texas; Austin, Texas; Ontario, California; and New Orleans, Louisiana. As of April 29, 1984, Muse Air was offering service to Las Vegas. See Exhibit 3 for a map of the expanded service area. Plans for future expansion include San Antonio, St. Louis, Chicago, New York, Atlanta, and Florida.

Originally, Muse Air expansion plans were to fly to the South and Midwest. Exhibit 4 is a map of the initial strategic plan of Muse Air as formulated in 1980. There are indications that the westward air travel market is served to overcapacity. Muse may try to return to these original plans to increase profitability. Houston will become the center of operations.

At the end of February, 1984, Muse Air had to cancel plans for beginning service to Little Rock, Arkansas. Muse's service to Little Rock had been announced in January and was to begin April 19, 1984. After the announcement, Southwest Airlines flooded the Little Rock market with new flights, forcing Muse Air out before service began.

EXHIBIT 3   **Proposed expansion of Muse air routes (effective April 29, 1984)**

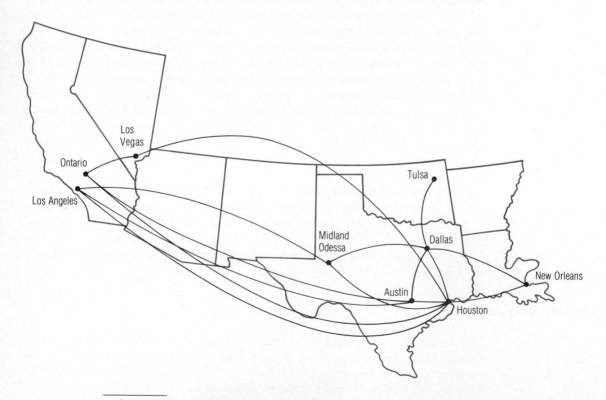

Source: Muse Air Corporation.

EXHIBIT 4   **Muse Air strategic route plan (1980)**

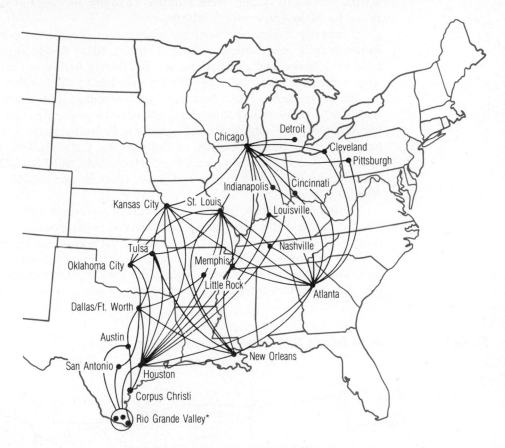

*Includes airports at Brownsville, Harlingen and McAllen, Texas.

Long-range plan of Muse Air is to expand its initial Dallas-Houston
service to cover a total of 24 markets from hubs at Houston, Chicago,
and Atlanta, matching Southwest Airlines' fares in its markets and
undercutting any other competition.

Muse Air will face other competitors as it tries to expand. Delta has already started service to Atlanta from Houston's Hobby airport, the same route proposed by Muse for service in March, 1986.

Not only is Muse Air being crowded out of expansion routes, but existing routes as well. After several months of service, Muse Air discontinued flights to Lubbock, Texas. Delta, American, and Southwest Airlines all service Lubbock. This is the first route that Muse Air has ever had to discontinue.

Besides planned route expansion, an innovative joint marketing program with Air Cal should help Muse Air grow beyond its strictly regional status. The Muse Air/Air Cal joint marketing agreement began February 5, 1984. Muse Air passengers can connect quickly to eight of Air Cal's markets, including San Francisco, Sacramento, San Jose, Palm Springs, and Oakland, California; Seattle, Washington; Portland, Oregon; and Reno, Nevada. See Exhibit 5 for a map of Air Cal routes.

This selective joint marketing agreement represents a doubling of market destinations available to Muse Air customers virtually overnight. All the conveniences of expanded service to eight new West Coast markets were achieved without the costly capital outlays required for opening individual airline on-site operations. According to John Mumaugh, Vice President–Sales and Advertising, this joint marketing program illustrates clearly how deregulation has freed

EXHIBIT 5   Muse Air and Air Cal routes (effective March 1, 1984)

Source: Muse Air Flight Schedule and Flight Summary, effective March 1, 1984.

carriers to pursue creative marketing techniques in a cost-effective manner to ultimately benefit the traveling public.[7]

FINANCES

Equity

The company was initially capitalized in February, 1980, through the issuance of 31,250 shares of common stock to Michael L. Muse for $25,000 in cash. In October, 1980, the company issued and sold an aggregate of 318,750 shares of common stock to five members of the Muse family and Cole, Brumley & Eichner, Inc. for cash payment of $.80 per share. In October, 1980, the company also issued and sold to five members of the Muse family an aggregate of $190,000 principal amount of its 12% convertible subordinated debentures at the face amount. In February, 1981, 237,500 shares of common stock were issued to the five members of the Muse family upon conversion of the debentures. On March 20, 1981, the company's stock was split five-for-four.

On April 30, 1981, the company made a public offering of 2,200,000 shares of common stock with warrants to purchase 1,100,000 shares of common stock priced at $17.50 per unit (one share of common stock and one-half warrant). The proceeds of this offering were used as a deposit and fee relating to the future acquisition of four new DC-9 Super 80 aircraft, the prepayment of a one-year lease on the two Super 80 aircraft that were in operation, the acquisition of aircraft spare parts and engines, the purchase of ground equipment and leasehold improvements, and the unrestricted addition to working capital. The stock was traded in the over-the-counter market under the symbol "MUSE." The warrants provided for the purchase of common stock at $16.00 per share and expired on April 30, 1986, or as early as January 1, 1984, if certain conditions are satisfied and the company chooses to accelerate the expiration date. No warrants have been exercised to date.

On May 24, 1983, the company made another public offering of 1,540,000 shares of common stock at $16.25. The net proceeds of this offering were used to prepay a secured bank note due in July, 1984, and to increase the equity base and working capital position of the company to support future expansion. The common stock commenced trading on the American Stock Exchange under the symbol "MAC" on April 18, 1983 at which time it ceased trading in the over-the-counter market.

With this last equity offering, no further financing was expected in 1984. A cash flow of $12.5 million in 1983 and $25 million in 1984 should pose few difficulties requiring further equity. In addition, the company will likely force the

---

[7]John Mumaugh, "Executive Corner," *Muse Air Monthly* (October 1983), 7.

conversion of the 1.1 million warrants at $16 per share if the common stock trades at or above $24 per share for 30 consecutive trading days. Market capitalization on December 31, 1983, stood at 4,030,113 common shares. The company's balance sheet and statement of operations are included as Exhibits 6 and 7, respectively.

In 1982, Muse sold tax benefits of depreciation and investment tax credits on four of its DC-9 Super 80 aircraft producing net proceeds to the company of approximately $21.6 million. This item was treated as "other" income and accounted for the net earnings of $3.87 per share during fiscal 1982. Without these tax related benefits, the company would have reported a 1982 full year net loss of $3.17 per share.

Capital Stock Valuation

Because of the various crisis situations Muse has encountered, the stock's price has fluctuated widely from a high of 19⅜ to a low of 3½ during its short life (see Exhibit 8). While the stock price has changed with the outlook for the company's future, the book value has steadily increased. Currently, the stock is selling at a 25% discount from book value and about seven times estimated 1984 earnings. As a comparison, Southwest Airlines sells at three times book value and 20 times earnings; Midway and People Express sell at comparable or higher multiples. Also, the earnings leverage is considerable because passenger traffic should increase more rapidly than growth in capacity and net loss carry forwards. Additionally, investment tax credits will be available to offset future income tax.

Based on estimates, Muse Air has the potential to earn $1.50 per share in fiscal year 1984 (see Exhibit 9). If these earnings estimates prove correct and based on a valuation of 12 times earnings, a value for Muse common stock of $18 per share is possible. The potential for substantial price appreciation is within reason. Since warrants move, percentage wise, to a greater extent than does the common, the excellent leverage provided by this vehicle would reward investors even more handsomely.

Muse Air reported its first operating profit of $780,000, or $.17 per share, in the third quarter of 1983. In the 1983 fourth quarter, the company again reported an operating profit of $202,000 or $.04 per share. Both quarters of operating profits helped reduce the 1983 operating net loss to $1,959,000 or $.49 per share. Mr. Michael L. Muse stated that the positive results of the third and fourth quarter " . . . provided Muse Air a solid launching pad for what should prove to be a very successful 1984."[8]

Aircraft Acquisition

The company began service on July 15, 1981, with two Super 80 aircraft leased from McDonnell Douglas Corporation (MDC). The first equity offering in

[8]"Muse Air Reports Substantial Fourth Quarter Operating Profit; Finishes 1983 with Back-To-Back Quarterly Net Profits As Well," Muse Air news release, January 1984.

EXHIBIT 6   Muse Air Corporation — balance sheet

	Year Ended December 31,	
	1983	1982
Assets		
Current assets:		
Cash and temporary investments of $16,931,000 in 1983 and $7,250,000 in 1982	$ 18,404,116	$ 7,488,653
Accounts receivable	6,600,356	3,068,720
Inventories of parts and supplies	513,582	412,833
Prepaid expenses	1,001,455	555,246
Total current assets	26,519,509	11,525,452
Property and equipment at cost:		
Flight equipment — aircraft	130,187,529	109,700,751
Aircraft purchase deposits	8,672,808	
Leasehold improvements	3,454,387	1,026,286
Other flight and ground equipment	14,100,401	9,325,544
	156,415,125	120,052,581
Less: Accumulated depreciation and amortization	(10,593,431)	(3,255,798)
	145,821,694	116,796,783
Other assets, net	445,502	2,470,381
	$172,786,705	$130,792,616
Liabilities and Stockholders' Equity		
Current liabilities:		
Accounts payable	$ 4,352,121	$ 1,081,662
Unearned transportation revenues	1,637,359	681,535
Accrued liabilities	6,957,066	3,389,432
Current maturities of long-term debt	9,615,541	2,460,000
Total current liabilities	22,562,087	7,612,629
Long-term debt less current maturities	83,594,659	76,440,000
Deferred federal income taxes	263,501	715,740
Other long-term liabilities		1,013,790
Total liabilities	106,420,247	85,782,159
Stockholders' equity:		
Common stock, $1.00 par value; 20,000,000 shares authorized; issued and outstanding 4,636,750 shares in 1983 and 3,100,000 shares, $.10 par value, in 1982	4,636,750	310,000
Additional paid-in capital	56,183,993	37,196,245
Retained earnings	5,545,715	7,504,212
Total stockholders' equity	66,366,458	45,010,457
Commitments and contingencies	$172,786,705	$130,792,616

Source: Muse Air Corporation 1983 annual report.

EXHIBIT 7   Muse Air Corporation—statement of operations

	Year Ended December 31,		
	1983	1982	1981
Operating revenues:			
Passenger	$68,976,808	$32,211,861	$ 6,217,593
Other	3,951,150	844,063	78,268
Total operating revenues	72,927,958	33,055,924	6,295,861
Operating expenses:			
Fuel and oil	20,940,064	12,182,590	3,201,335
Flight operations	8,360,307	6,130,036	2,871,844
Marketing	13,292,021	6,112,769	2,251,081
Maintenance	3,827,987	2,211,586	941,113
In-flight service	4,479,305	2,001,974	545,566
Terminal operations	5,109,215	2,889,318	832,069
Insurance and taxes	2,819,025	1,572,725	277,684
General and administrative	2,136,772	1,578,310	714,538
Depreciation and amortization	7,347,628	3,114,827	197,620
Total operating expenses	68,312,324	37,794,135	11,832,850
Operating income (loss)	4,615,634	(4,738,211)	(5,536,989)
Nonoperating income (expense):			
Interest income	1,647,481	897,928	1,569,469
Interest expense (less interest capitalized of $797,967 in 1983 and $1,353,943 in 1982)	(8,556,268)	(4,309,216)	
Other income	499,985	21,835,019	
Other expense	(617,568)	(1,502,186)	
Net non-operating income (expense)	(7,026,370)	16,921,545	1,569,469
Income (loss) before provision for federal income taxes and extraordinary item	(2,410,736)	12,183,344	(3,967,520)
Federal income tax provision (benefit)	(452,239)	2,540,800	
Income (loss) before extraordinary item	(1,958,497)	9,642,534	(3,967,520)
Extraordinary item—utilization of net operating loss carryforwards		1,825,060	
Net income (loss)	$ (1,958,497)	$11,467,594	$ (3,967,520)
Income (loss) per common share:			
Income (loss) before extraordinary item	$ (.49)	$ 3.25	$ (1.86)
Extraordinary item		.62	
Net income (loss)	$ (.49)	$ 3.87	$ (1.86)
Weighted average shares outstanding	4,030,113	2,963,151	2,136,781

Source: Muse Air Corporation 1983 annual report.

EXHIBIT 8 **Muse Air Corporation summary: book value/trading price per share**

Year	Quarter	Book value per share price	Trading price per share *High*	*Low*
1980	4th	$ .81	—	—
1981	1st	—	—	—
	2nd	12.19	15	11½
	3rd	11.26	15¼	7¼
	4th	10.83	12⅝	7⅜
1982	1st	10.35	8⅞	5½
	2nd	9.81	7⅜	3½
	3rd	11.05	9	4⅜
	4th	14.52	13⅝	6⅝
1983	1st	14.09	15	10⅜
	2nd	13.64	19⅜	14¼
	3rd	14.27	17¾	13½
	4th	14.31	16¾	14

Source: 1981, 1982, 1983 Muse Air Corporation annual reports.

EXHIBIT 9 **Muse Air Corporation—statement of operations**

($ thousands except per share amounts)

	1984E	1983	1982	1981
Revenues	$135,000	$72,928	$33,056	$ 6,296
Operating expenses	110,000	68,312	37,794	11,833
Operating income	25,000	4,616	(4,748)	(5,537)
Non-operating income	(16,000)	(7,026)	16,922	1,569
Earnings before taxes	9,000	(2,410)	12,184	(3,968)
Tax liability	2,000	(452)	2,541	—
Earnings before extraordinary item	7,000	(1,958)	9,643	(3,968)
Extraordinary items	—	—	1,825	—
Net income	$ 7,000	$ (1,958)	$11,468	$ (2,941)
Number of primary shares	4,640	4,030	2,963	2,131
Earnings per share:				
Earnings before taxes	$ 1.95	$ (0.49)	$ 4.11	$ (1.86)
Earnings before extraordinary item	—	—	$ 3.25	—
Net income	$ 1.50	$ (0.49)	$ 3.87	$ (1.86)

Source: 1983 Muse Air annual report and analyst estimates.

April, 1981, provided the funds for the lease of these two aircraft as well as the purchase of four new aircraft. In August, 1982, the company repaid the subordinated debt of $4.1 million to MDC from proceeds received from the sale of tax benefits on one of these aircraft.

The company purchased two additional Super 80 aircraft in September, 1982, and one in November, 1982, with $42 million provided from bank financing and with approximately $14 million of the proceeds from the sale of tax benefits associated with these aircraft. In December, 1982, the company leased a sixth Super 80 aircraft under a long-term operating lease agreement from the McDonnell Douglas Finance Corporation (MDFC). As of this date, Muse Air owns five of its Super 80 aircraft and holds a long-term lease for the sixth. Exhibit 1 shows the aircraft delivery schedule.

In August, 1983, Muse Air negotiated the purchase of 10 used McDonnell Douglas DC-9-51 aircraft, five of those from SwissAir and the other five from Austrian Air. The total cost of this acquisition is approximately $100 million. The first two aircraft were delivered in October, 1983, the third in February, 1984. Two more are to be placed in service during late April or early May, 1984. Three additional aircraft are to be delivered in the first quarter of 1985 and the final two in the first quarter of 1986. Muse Air intends to use the smaller aircraft on its shorter hauls with less passenger demand while using the Super 80s on longer and more heavily traveled flights. Approximately $11 million from the second equity offering was used as a deposit on the aircraft with the balance to be financed with bank debt of $65 million as the planes are delivered through 1986.

THE PREDICAMENT

Lamar and Michael Muse were weary from reviewing all of the relevant information pertaining to their situation. The airline industry is going through a time of change. What is the best strategy for Muse Air Corporation to pursue in this rapidly changing environment? Is the time right to expand? Should expansion be regional or national? These were all important questions that Michael Muse felt required definite answers.

Bibliography   "Air 1 starting service to Houston's Hobby," *Houston Chronicle,* 22 February 1984.

"Air Traffic Declines Less Than Expected," *Wall Street Journal,* 3 September 1981, p. 4.

"Air Transport," *Standard & Poor's Industry Surveys* 149 (20 August 1981), A56–A73.

"Air Transport Industry," *The Value Line Investment Survey,* 6 January 1984, 251–52.

"Airline Cooperation Starts to Break Apart," *Business Week,* 28 November 1983, 45.

"Airlines in Turmoil," *Business Week,* 10 October 1983, 98–102.

"Airline Labor Costs Increasing Despite Union Concessions," *Aviation Week & Space Technology* 119 (3 October 1983), 32.

"Airline Wages Are Set for a Long Slide," *Business Week,* 9 April 1984, 127–28.

Banks, Howard. "Airlines," *Forbes* 133 (2 January 1984), 139–43.

Banks, Howard. "Fixing Tickets," *Forbes* 132 (29 August 1983), 42–43.

"Big Daddy's New Airline," *Newsweek* 98 (9 November 1981), 77.

"Braniff is Coming Back to Some Tough Competition," *Business Week,* 27 February 1984, 37–41.

"CAB Urged to Reduce Bias in Reservations Systems," *Aviation Week & Space Technology* 119 (28 November 1983), 34–35.

"Can Western Airlines Fly Back to Profitability?" *Business Week,* 27 February 1984, 114–16.

Cieply, Michael. "Hardball," *Forbes* 132 (28 February 1983), 33.

Clifford, Mark. "A Struggle for Survival," *Financial World* 152 (15 November 1983), 13–18.

Coogan, Keith R. Vice-President of Finance and Treasurer, Houston, Texas. Interview, 21 March 1984.

Donlan, Thomas. "Turbulent Skies," *Barron's,* 17 October 1983, 15.

Donoghue, J. A. "Reservations Systems Likely to Be Disciplined," *Air Transport World* 20 (September 1983), 28–30.

"FAA Nears Ruling on Preferential Routes," *Aviation Week & Space Technology* 119 (18 April 1983), 34–35.

Feldman, Joan M. "Deregulation Loose Ends Spark Debate About Regulation After 1984," *Air Transport World* 20 (May 1983), 23–29.

Harris, William, "Muse Air," *Forbes,* 26 October 1981, 200.

Henderson, Danna K. "Muse Air is making it," *Air Transport World,* September 1983, 54–57.

Kirkpatrick, John. "High Profile," *Dallas Morning News,* 19 June 1983, 4E.

Klempin, Raymond. "Local Airline Activity on the Rise," *Houston Business Journal,* 12 March 1984, 8A.

Kliewer, Terry. "Airline expects big demand," *Houston Post,* 23 February 1984.

Kliewer, Terry and Margaret Downing. "Braniff will make its mark in aviation history March 1," *Houston Post,* 12 February 1984.

"Local Airline Activity on the Rise," *Houston Business Journal,* 12 March 1984, 8A.

Longeway, Barbara. "Continental and Southwest: Agony and Ecstasy," *Houston Chronicle,* 26 February 1984, 4(1).

Longeway, Barbara. "Sentimental Journey: Braniff's first flight rekindles memories," *Houston Chronicle,* 2 March 1984.

Low-Beer, Anthony, and Susan Nakada. "Muse Air Corporation," *Rooney, Pace Inc.* 22 August 1983.

McCartney, Scott. "New Braniff is ready to take to the Skies from 18 Cities," *Houston Chronicle,* 26 February 1984, 4(16).

Meadows, Edward. "The FAA Keeps them Flying," *Fortune* 104 (28 December 1981), 48–52.

Mumaugh, John. "Executive Corner," *Muse Air Monthly,* October 1983, 7.

Mumaugh, John. "Executive Corner," *Muse Air Monthly,* February 1984, 7.

"Muse Air," *Standard & Poor's,* 24 November 1983, Sec. 8605.

"Muse Air Cancels Plans for Little Rock," *Muse Air* news release, 27 March 1984.

"Muse Air Celebrates Inauguration of New Orleans Service,"*Muse Air* news release, 5 February 1984.

"Muse Air Cites Need for Airport Slots," *Aviation Week & Space Technology* 116 (17 May 1982), 41.

Muse Air Corporation 1981 Annual Report.

Muse Air Corporation 1982 Annual Report.

Muse Air Corporation 1983 Annual Report.

"Muse Air Ends Plan for Arkansas Service, Some Fare Increases," *Wall Street Journal,* 29 February 1984, 12.

"Muse Air Expands LAX Service," *Muse Air* news release, 22 January 1984.

"Muse Air Expands Service to Little Rock, Arkansas on April 29," *Muse Air* news release, 21 March 1984.

"Muse Air Expands to Las Vegas April 29," *Muse Air* news release, 21 March 1984.

"Muse Air Expands to New Orleans, La. and Ontario, Ca," *Muse Air* news release, 21 December 1983.

"Muse Air Reports Substantial Fourth Quarter Operating Profit," *Muse Air* news release, January 1984.

"Muse Air to Discontinue Service to Lubbock, Texas," *Wall Street Journal,* 21 February 1984, 32.

"Muse Air to Terminate Lubbock Service," *Muse Air* news release, 17 February 1984.

"Muse Air Says Chairman is Retiring," *Wall Street Journal,* 2 April 1984.

"Muse Expansion Delayed by Slot Problems," *Aviation Week & Space Technology* 116 (12 April 1982), 26.

"Muse Service," *Air Transport Industry* 117 (18 October 1982), 33.

"New Air Tariff Agreement Drafted," *Aviation Week & Space Technology* 116 (8 February 1982), 32.

"New Airline Focuses on Business Travelers," *Houston Post,* 12 February 1984, 16E.

O'Lone, Richard G. "U.S. Manufacturers Project Turnaround," *Aviation Week & Space Technology* 119 (14 March 1983), 167–178.

Ott, James. "Airlines Gear for New Challenges," *Aviation Week & Space Technology* 118 (14 November 1983), 48–50.

Ott, James. "Carriers Intensify Labor Cost Drive," *Aviation Week & Space Technology* 118 (21 November 1983), 27–30.

Ott, James. "House Questions Agent Decision," *Aviation Week & Space Technology* 118 (30 May 1983), 57–58.

Robertson, Thomas S. "Management Lessons from Airlines Deregulation," *Harvard Business Review* 61 (January/February 1983), 40–44.

"The Scramble to Modernize Air Traffic Control," *Business Week* 10 October 1983, 39.

"Service Expansion," *Aviation Week & Space Technology* 116 (8 February 1982), 31.

Shifrin, Carole A. "U.S. Airline Traffic Rises by Estimated 8% in 1983," *Aviation Week & Space Technology* 120 (30 January 1984), 35–36.

"Southwest Airlines," *The Value Line Investment Survey,* 6 January 1984, 271.

Sylvester, David. "Regional Airline Review," *Wheat First Securities Industries Update,* 9 December 1983.

"Upstarts in the Sky," *Business Week* 2692 (15 June 1981), 78–92.

Wewer, Dan R., Jr. "Muse Air Corporation," *Rauscher Pierce Refsnes, Inc.,* 26 September 1983, 1–8.

SHARPCO, INC. (1985)

In 1972, James Sharplin and two brothers decided to open a welding and steel fabrication shop in Monroe, Louisiana. The Sharplins formed a corporation, Sharpco, Inc., bought a parcel of land at the eastern edge of Monroe, and built a small shop building. Most of the initial equity investment was in the form of welding machines, tools, and other items contributed by the three owners. James worked full time at Sharpco while his brothers pursued other interests. The company was profitable from the first year. Sales grew steadily and the shop was expanded several times during the 1970s. In the early 1980s, James exchanged his interest in some commercial property the Sharplins owned for his brothers' shares of Sharpco stock.

Sharpco is engaged in four distinct business areas—all related to heavy equipment, especially crawler tractors (often called "bulldozers" or "caterpillars"). First, the company makes and sells a number of welded steel items for heavy equipment. Second, Sharpco markets new and used crawler tractor parts. Third, James and his workers provide repair service for heavy equipment owners. Finally, Sharpco does high strength repair welding for heavy equipment. Each of these business areas will be discussed further under the heading "Operations."

In January 1985, the business was moved to a new 30,000 square foot facility in what had become a rapidly expanding commercial and industrial area along Interstate Highway 20. Among the more than twenty firms on highway I-20 near Sharpco are heavy equipment dealers representing Deere and Company (makers of John Deere equipment), Case Power and Equipment Company, and Fiat-Allis, Inc. (successor to Allis Chalmers, Inc.). Dealers for the other two major brands of heavy construction equipment, International Harvester and Caterpillar, are located about three miles away. Exhibit 1 shows the location of the new Sharpco plant. Exhibit 2 provides geographic and demographic data relevant to Sharpco's main trade area.

This case was prepared by Arthur Sharplin, McNeese State University, Lake Charles, Louisiana.

EXHIBIT 1   **Sharpco's location**

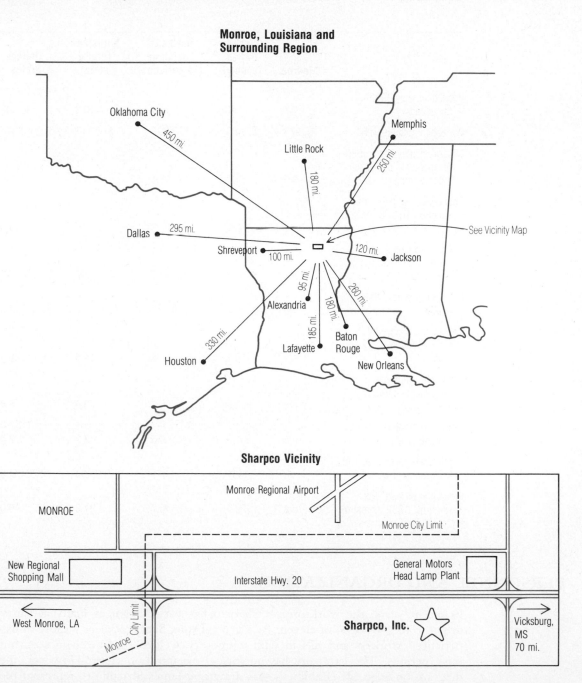

**Monroe, Louisiana and
Surrounding Region**

Oklahoma City — 450 mi.

Little Rock

Memphis — 250 mi.

180 mi.

Dallas — 295 mi.

See Vicinity Map

Shreveport — 100 mi.   120 mi. — Jackson

95 mi.

Alexandria   260 mi.

185 mi.   180 mi.

330 mi.   Baton Rouge

Houston   Lafayette   New Orleans

Sharpco Vicinity

MONROE

Monroe Regional Airport

Monroe City Limit

New Regional Shopping Mall   General Motors Head Lamp Plant

Interstate Hwy. 20

← West Monroe, LA   Monroe City Limit   Sharpco, Inc. ☆   Vicksburg, MS 70 mi. →

EXHIBIT 2   Geographic and demographic data

	Monroe	Ouachita Parish (county)	Northeast Louisiana (16 parishes)	Louisiana (entire state)	United States
Population, July 1982 (thousands)	57	141	434	4,373	230,000
Per capita income, 1981	$6,973	$7,486	$ 5,897	$ 8,113	$ 8,917
Change in population 1980–82 (percent change for entire period)	−0.9	1.2	1.4	4.0	2.8
Change in *real* per capita income, 1979–81 (percent change for entire period)	−5.1	−3.1	−2.9	1.0	−0.4
Value of agricultural production, 1982 (millions)	n/a	$ 14	$ 48	$ 1,407	$ 158,700
Personal income, 1982 (millions)	n/a	$1,380	$16,010	$44,000	$2,578,600
Workforce employed in manufacturing, 1982 (percent)	n/a	18.1	14.9	14.6	20.0
Workforce employed in construction, 1982 (percent)	n/a	8.6	5.7	9.6	5.8
Workforce employed in farming, 1982 (percent)	n/a	1.2	6.6	3.2	2.0
Approximate land area, 1982 (thousands of acres)	n/a	401	6,519	28,494	2,264,960
Proportion of land area in farms, 1982 (percent)	n/a	23.4	40.7	31.3	46.0

PERSONNEL AND ORGANIZATION

In recent years, the workforce at Sharpco has varied from as many as thirty down to its 1985 level of eleven. As a general rule, Sharpco keeps a cadre of experienced workers and fills in with temporary welders and mechanics during busy periods. The company has no formal organization chart. However, the diagram on page 621 (Exhibit 3) was drawn by James Sharplin to represent the organization as it existed in 1985.

EXHIBIT 3   **Informal organization chart — Sharpco**

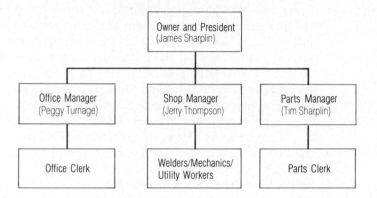

The lines of authority at Sharpco are not rigidly followed. James routinely bypasses each of his direct subordinates and deals directly with workers. "The managers all work as a team," says James. "Any one of us can make a major or minor decision — or write a $10,000 check." Everyone in the organization is expected to pitch in wherever there is a need for extra help and to accept direction from whoever knows most about the particular job being done. The insert below provides brief comments made by James Sharplin concerning each of the key employees.

James Sharplin Discusses Sharpco's Key People   Jerry is thirty years old. He is my mother's grand-nephew. Jerry is dedicated to Sharpco. He has a great deal of ability to get the job done. He is a good welder and the best mechanic we have. The men respect him and that helps make him a good manager. Customers like him; they ask for him. They know they can depend on what he says. During the move, when we were all running just to keep up, Jerry sold two excavator buckets. He worked right through a weekend, even though he had the flu, to get the buckets built. He has a good memory, too. He can usually tell a customer if we have a part without even checking the computer. Jerry's main recreation is hunting. I try to make sure he has some time off during hunting season. When I decided to furnish him a company pickup, I made sure it was something he has always wanted but never felt that he could afford — a four-wheel-drive "mud hog."

Peggy is in her forties. She has taken a number of college courses. Although Peggy does not have a degree, she knows much more than most college graduates. She is as dedicated as any employee I have. She is the most cost-conscious person in the whole organization, including me. After just a year of working with computers she knows more about them than the computer "expert" who sold us the machine. Somehow, Peggy and the computer were an instant match. Peggy is a highly religious lady. I think this accounts in some degree for her diligence and I know I can trust her with anything I have. There has never been the slightest need for me to check up on her. Everyone here respects her and her presence helps keep foul language and rowdy behavior at a minimum. Peggy is usually miles ahead of me with any information I need — like sales statistics. She put the used parts on the computer without any guidance. And the information was in a form she knew I could use. If things move too fast she just works nights and Saturdays. She does all the advertising better than any ad agency could. She comes up with the ideas, does the copy, and just runs it by me for approval. Peggy is a perfectionist.

Tim is twenty-five years old. He is my nephew. Tim is strictly work, family, church, and school. He attends Northeast Louisiana University part time, studying business. Tim has a good number of outside obligations, including school. But whenever I need him he is here. He asked me if he should let his school wait while we get over the move and get things back on an even keel. I told him that he might take one course instead of two, only if he thought it best, but I felt he should continue his education without a break. He works hard — wants to do things right. He grew up on a farm, where he often had neither the time nor the equipment to do quality work. Tim is learning fast. In the long term I think he will be one of our most important people. In fact, he is now. He had to come almost from ground zero — learning welding, learning crawler tractors, learning fabrication. He has done remarkably well in the two years since he came to work here.

There is no formal performance appraisal at Sharpco and no written compensation policy. Sharpco furnishes medical insurance for James, Jerry, and Tim (Peggy is covered under her husband's policy furnished by his employer). The company also pays about one-half the cost of insurance for each worker. The managers are paid on a salary basis. Hourly paid workers make from $6 to $9 an hour, about average for the area. Every year, James says, he ranks the employees in order of what he considers to be their contribution to the company. Then he adjusts the pay of any whose pay seems inequitable. Practically all hiring and firing is done by James personally, although Jerry Thompson has authority to terminate any of his workers.

OPERATIONS

Exhibit 4 shows a typical crawler tractor with the main relevant parts labeled. Practically all of Sharpco's mechanical repair work and most of the parts sales are related to tractor undercarriages, final drives, and steering clutches. The undercarriage is that part of the tractor nearest the ground, including the heavy steel tracks along with rollers, sprockets, and structural members designed to

EXHIBIT 4   **A typical crawler tractor**

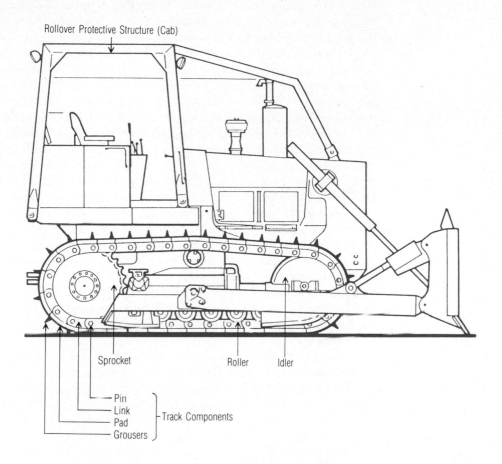

pull the tracks and keep them in alignment. The final drive is a large closed gear box which transmits power to the track. In Exhibit 4 the final drive is hidden from view behind the sprocket. The steering clutches are located above the final drives. They allow either the left or right final drive to be disengaged so that the brake can be applied on the respective side, causing the tractor to turn.

The tracks and related components cannot be insulated from the sand, dirt, and gravel in which a tractor usually operates. Consequently, all of the moving surfaces wear away steadily, especially those which are in contact with one another. The track chain is similar to a large bicycle chain. As the track is pulled by the sprocket around the idler and rollers, the pins wear mainly on just one side. Each pin fits into a bushing which also wears in the direction of the stress. A typical undercarriage will require major repair after 3000 hours of use and overhaul after 1500 additional hours. Major repair consists of removing the tracks and turning each pin and the respective bushing half around so that the least worn surfaces are in contact. To do this, a portable hydraulic press is used to press out one of the pins. This may require two hundred tons of force. Then the tracks, weighing as much as three thousand pounds each, are moved to the track press, where the remaining pins are pressed out, along with the respective bushings. All parts are then inspected and the tracks reassembled with the pins and bushings in their new positions. While the track is off, all undercarriage components are inspected for cracks, leaking oil seals, excessive wear, and other defects. Of course, any needed repairs are made before the tractor is reassembled.

When major overhaul is due, pins and bushings are replaced, idlers and rollers exchanged or reconditioned, and new sprockets are installed. With about every second major overhaul, worn grousers have to be cut off and new ones welded onto the track pads. The entire track chain may also have to be replaced. Less frequently, final drives and steering clutches require repair.

Among the items Sharpco manufactures are roll-over protective structures (cabs) such as that shown on the tractor in Exhibit 4. Many of Sharpco's customers are involved in land clearing. The tractors they use must have heavy steel screens welded or bolted around the cabs to protect the operator from tree limbs. Sharpco makes and installs those screens as well. The cabs and screens are made from ordinary steel. However, most of the items the company makes involve the use of high strength steel, about three times as strong and hard as ordinary steel (and more than twice as costly). Several of these items are shown in Exhibit 5.

The special steel is used for cutting edges and strength members on the blades and buckets. This steel is purchased from major steel distributors and stocked in eight foot by twenty foot sheets, ranging in thickness from three-eighths of an inch to two inches. A portable acetylene cutting torch which runs on a small track is used to cut the steel to shape. Pieces which are to become cutting or digging edges are clamped in a vertical position and the edge beveled at a steep angle using the same kind of automatic torch. Curved pieces of mild steel (used for non-critical parts of digging buckets) and the steel pins and bushings used to attach the buckets to hydraulic excavators and backhoes are furnished by a local machine shop.

After the parts of a digging bucket or land clearing blade are cut and shaped they are welded together just enough to hold them. Then they are carefully inspected prior to final welding. To ensure against failure, Sharpco workers weld all critical points manually, allowing components to cool between layers of weld material. This process requires special high-strength electrodes (welding rods). Less critical welds can be made with semiautomatic machines, which are much faster and easier to operate than manual ones and which use large rolls of wire instead of individual welding electrodes.

Sharpco digging buckets range in size from small standard buckets weighing only three hundred pounds to trapezoidal buckets weighing over a ton and measuring seventeen feet across. A trapezoidal bucket is designed to dig a complete drainage canal as the hydraulic excavator or backhoe to which it is attached

EXHIBIT 5   **Items Sharpco makes using high-strength steel**

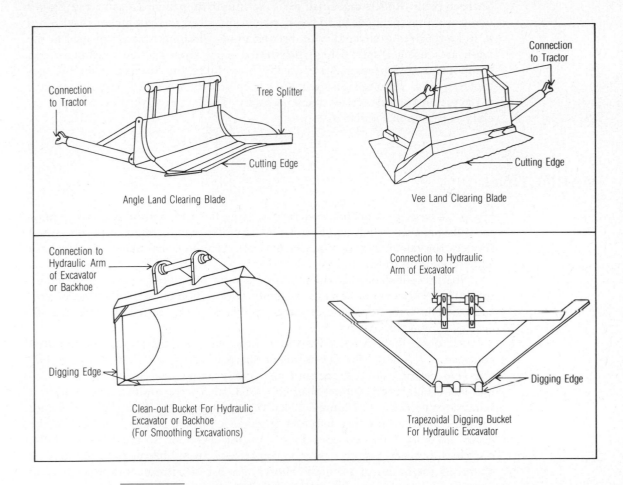

Source: Drawn by Joy Kight.

slowly drives along the intended canal path, scooping out as much as three feet of new ditch with each stroke and laying the dirt aside. Sharpco land clearing blades and rakes weigh up to eight tons. The largest Sharpco vee-blade has two serrated cutting edges, each twenty feet long. Pushed by the largest production model tractor made by Caterpillar or Fiat-Allis, one of these blades clears a swath sixteen feet wide through timber up to thirty inches in diameter.

Blades and buckets require replacement of cutting edges and other wearing surfaces after extended use. Each item is designed so that the worn parts can be cut loose and new ones installed through a procedure similar to the original manufacture.

All of the items Sharpco reconditions or manufactures are painted at the Sharpco plant. Rollers and small parts are simply dipped into a paint vat. Larger items are spray painted. In addition, practically all of the equipment that comes in to be repaired is covered with dirt and mud. Cleaning is accomplished in the wash area using a special high pressure washer. Construction machinery and components to be repaired are usually brought to the Sharpco plant on customer trucks, although Sharpco does keep several trucks of varying sizes to make pickups and deliveries when necessary. The layout of the new Sharpco facility is shown in Exhibit 6.

MARKETING

Sharpco's customers include contractors, large farmers, and other heavy equipment owners, as well as equipment dealers who purchase Sharpco products and services for resale. Several equipment dealers employ Sharpco to repair tracks and recondition rollers and idlers for them.

Sharpco subscribes to a computerized used parts dealer network whereby subscribers exchange price and availability information on needed parts. As a result, the company ships an increasing number of parts, especially used ones, to dealers around the country.

Although the customer list totals more than one thousand, one hundred contractors accounted for two-thirds of Sharpco's 1984 cash flow. For example, one land clearing contractor, with just four tractors, was billed $86,000 during 1984. Eighty percent of Sharpco's 1984 sales were to customers within a hundred-mile radius of Monroe. "That is changing rapidly, though," said Peggy Turnage. "We are getting inquiries from all over the country because of the dealer network." For the months of August, September, and October 1984, ninety equipment owners, mostly contractors, were billed $342,742 out of Sharpco's total sales of $416,557. Shown this list of customers, James Sharplin identified 57 of them as having been regular customers for at least three years.

Sharpco's overall pricing policy, as expressed by James Sharplin, is "whatever the traffic will bear." For new tractor parts, he says, this is normally about 80 or 85 percent of dealer retail price. For used parts, it ranges from 25 to 60 percent of retail, depending upon whether the part in question is a frequently needed one or one which seldom fails. Sharpco prices its digging buckets at or above dealer list prices. According to James Sharplin, this is justified because the Sharpco buckets have a significantly lower failure rate than those equipment dealers furnish. When repair jobs are priced in advance, parts and labor are usually combined. Sharpco tries to stay just below usual original equipment dealer prices on such work. This often results in the loss of jobs to smaller independent service shops, which often price well below what major tractor dealers charge. About one-third of Sharpco's repair work is done on a time and materials basis. Under this kind of billing procedure, customers usually bargain on major components

EXHIBIT 6   Sharpco plant layout

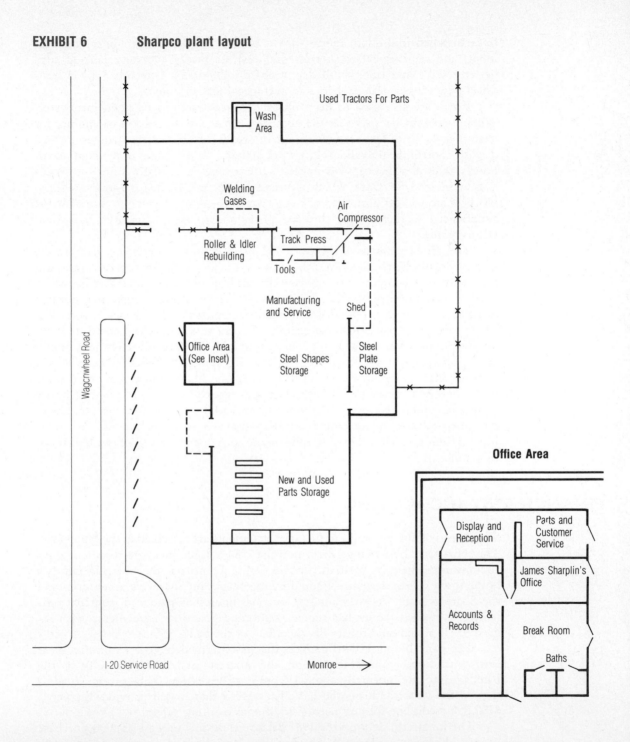

to be installed. But minor items (such as bolts, steel plate for welding reinforcement, and replacement track pads or links) are priced at ninety percent suggested retail, while labor is billed at standard billing rates, currently $26 per hour (local new tractor dealers charge an average of $28 an hour).

Prices are also used to keep Sharpco concentrated in its main businesses. When a customer insists that the company repair a transmission or engine, for example, the price for that work is intentionally elevated. Price changes are also used to control the overall level of work activity. When spurts in demand occur, hourly rates and markups on materials are increased, both for time and materials work and for work which is priced in advance. When demand slackens, workers are laid off until the crew is down to the ten or twelve person cadre of experienced workers. Only then are prices and markups sacrificed to sustain sales volume.

The primary means of promotion is direct mail. Currently the mailings are sent to all customers once a month. James has made plans, however, to program the company's computer to segment the mailing list along several dimensions and to mail more personalized advertisements to differing customer groups. Sharpco also spends about $700 a month on telephone yellow pages advertising. This provides for one-fourth page under "Contractors Equipment and Supplies," one-fourth page under "Welding," and a business card type advertisement briefly listing Sharpco's businesses under "Tractor Equipment & Parts." About once a quarter, Sharpco inserts a series of three two-page advertisements in consecutive issues of *The Contractor's Hotline,* a national weekly newspaper offering heavy equipment and parts for sale to about five thousand equipment owners and dealers. These advertisements cost about $1400 for each three week sequence. James, Jerry Thompson, and Tim Sharplin make infrequent sales calls within about fifty miles of Monroe.

FINANCE AND ACCOUNTING

Summaries of Sharpco's recent financial statements are provided in the Appendix. The short-term borrowings shown on the 1984 balance sheet are represented by 180-day notes held by a small bank in Delhi, Louisiana, the Sharplin family's home town. These notes are secured by mortgages on Sharpco's inventories and the Sharpco plant. As they mature, accrued interest is paid and principal refinanced as needed. James has signed continuing guarantee agreements with regard to all present and future Sharpco debt at the bank.

The bank has agreed to convert the short-term debt to a single five-year loan with fifteen-year amortization and interest established annually at the bank's prime rate, normally about 1½ percent above New York prime. In addition to the five-year loan, the bank has agreed that it will provide Sharpco a $150,000 credit line for any needed additional working capital.

The long-term debt on the 1984 balance sheet includes a $200,000 purchase money obligation on the new Sharpco plant and the land on which it sits. The purchase-money mortgage is subordinated to the bank debt mentioned above. Sharpco's old plant with related long-term debt attached was given in part payment to the developer who built the new plant. By prior agreement with the developer, James Sharplin designed the office area and mechanical features (piping and electrical systems, cranes, etc.) of the new plant and constructed them using Sharpco workers and several subcontractors. This effort was financed with short-term bank borrowing. Upon completion, the new Sharpco facility was appraised at $760,000.

In early 1984, Peggy Turnage computerized the company's accounting records. The computer in use is a Dynabyte featuring 20 megabytes of hard disk storage, a 16-bit microprocessor, and three interactive terminals. The two extra terminals are located in James Sharplin's office and on the customer service counter. The new parts inventory of about 1500 items is carried on a first-in, first-out basis. When a used tractor is purchased for parts the cost of the tractor, plus all labor required to disassemble it, is added to used parts inventory. When a used part is sold, the entire selling price of the part is subtracted from the inventory line item representing the tractor from which it came. A subsidiary file is kept for each tractor, indicating which parts have been sold. So anyone inquiring at one of the terminals can easily determine which used parts are available for sale. James Sharplin has been advised that the accounting procedure he is following significantly understates the used parts inventory. Despite a recommendation from the company's CPA, he has not authorized changing the procedure.

Sharpco's steel inventory is taken at the end of each year and priced at current costs. The steel consists of plates (rectangular flat pieces four or more feet in both width and length) and shapes (long, straight pieces of various cross-sectional configurations—e.g., rounds, angles, beams, and channels). No plate or shape is included in inventory if any part of it has been used. In addition, a large quantity of steel, all entirely usable but of slow-selling shapes and sizes, is not counted because it has been declared "obsolete." As a result of these practices, the steel inventory is shown on company books at perhaps one-half its current market value. In addition, Sharpco owns many land clearing blades, digging buckets and tractor parts which were "traded in" or abandoned by customers but for which no actual credit was given. Many of these items were later restored to usable condition during slack periods. Total value of these, as estimated by James Sharplin, is $15,000.

A job record is prepared for each customer order requiring shop work. One copy is kept in the office and another in a rack in the shop. Each worker is responsible for entering time worked on respective jobs. Parts and other materials issued to jobs are recorded on the office copies of job records. When a job is finished the shop copy of the job record is brought to the office and an invoice is completed.

Several years ago Peggy Turnage compared the time applied to customer jobs to the total time for which employees were paid. She found that fully one-third of employee time was unaccounted for. After telling of that experience, she said, "As soon as I can get the right computer program, I will set up a control system to charge every hour for which we pay employees to a customer job or to cleanup and maintenance."

INTERVIEW WITH JAMES SHARPLIN

The following are excerpts from an interview conducted on February 5, 1985.

Q: James, what do you think is your most important business area?

A: Well, I'd say used tractor parts are going to be our biggest money maker in the long run. When you can buy a D7E [a mid-size Caterpillar tractor] for $10,000, sell $25,000 worth of parts off it and still have two-thirds of it left, that's got to be a good situation. More and more people are looking at saving that ten or fifteen percent, or whatever it is. They don't really care if the part is used or not as long as it is not hurt. The major tractor dealers have done a really good job, but their prices have just continued to climb. We're able to offer the customer a good part at fifty or sixty percent off dealer list. Customers are looking for that. They also know they can depend on us to install the parts we sell and to stand behind them. There is no question, also, that we are better at providing parts and undercarriage service for the whole list of crawler tractors—John Deeres, Caterpillars, Cases—than the average dealer is for just one brand of tractor.

Q: What do you think are the major attributes that you or Sharpco has that will allow you to be successful—just in a general way?

A: We know a great deal more about any undercarriage than dealers do. Of course, dealers have to know the whole tractor and we limit our mechanic work to the undercarriage. The various undercarriages are quite similar, of course, and we've just had a world of experience in that particular area. Also, there's not a better high quality welding shop, especially for construction equipment, in north Louisiana. We know that business. We're good at it.

Q: What do you think about your crew right now, James? How does it stack up?

A: On the whole, they're the best group of workers for this type of business in the Monroe area. We have to pick and choose the jobs that we put individual workers on but we put them on the jobs they're best at doing. Gene Lowe, for instance, is probably the best layout man and general welder that we've got. We use him just for that. But look at Jerry Hodges, who is our fastest welder. We'll let him weld the project out after Gene has cut out the pieces and tacked them together. Charlie LaBorde is real good with customers. So we like to send him out on field jobs, where he'll be in direct contact with the customer. Rodney Gee is another excellent man. He's a kind of handyman. He takes care of our tractor-trailer rig like it was his own. He's a good welder and a good mechanic. He just generally has a great attitude about anything Sharpco wants him to do.

Q: What about the production things you do, the track press, for example, and the roller and idler shop?

A: We run our track press operation quite differently from the way dealers do. We arranged the track press in a room by itself with all the necessary equipment — the turntable, all the tooling. We have it where one man can run the whole operation. It's a two-man job at most dealers. We've kept real good account of the number of hours it takes to do a job and we've steadily improved on that. The track press operator we have now, Juan Hernandez, has run the press for six years. He's by far the best I've ever seen. About a year ago, Juan hurt his back and Jerry Thompson and I filled in for him until he recovered enough to work again. He had major surgery. For at least a month or a month and a half after he came back we wouldn't let him lift anything. Just having him here during that time was a great help because he knew so much about how to set up the machine. We rebuild idlers by building up [with an automatic welder] the wear surfaces and replacing the seals — and they are as good as new. We do not weld on the rollers, though, like some dealers do. To get "new" quality, we replace the worn outer shells of rollers and reuse the shafts, bushings, and collars if they are not hurt. This costs more, and we lose some sales when customers just look at price. But I can't think of a single failure on one of our re-shelled rollers.

Q: Why is the crew so small right now, James?

A: I prefer to keep it small and work just a bit of overtime in order to keep a good steady crew over a long period of time. Besides that, it's so much easier to manage ten people compared to twenty people. I know all these people. I know their problems. I know what makes them tick. I know what will motivate them. When I had twenty or thirty people, I couldn't say that.

Q: What are your long-term plans now for Sharpco, James?

A: Just to continue doing what we're good at and to keep our eyes open for any area where we can do a good job and make money. Grow if it will; but the big thing is to stay profitable and get it to where we can take just a little more time off.

Q: Do you mean where *you* can take a little more time off?

A: No. I mean the key people — Peggy, Jerry, Tim — and myself, of course.

Q: What problems concern you most?

A: Well, the problem is always the same: how to keep expenses down and jack up revenue. I do not ignore human costs but I have to focus mainly on dollars. There seems to be a conspiracy out there to keep us from making money. Besides, if we are profitable enough, I can handle most of the other problems that crop up. One thing I'm going to do, as soon as we get over the move, is to spend most of my time for two or three months with the computer and the accounting system, just getting on top of the numbers. I want to know where the sales and profits are coming from — geographically, of course; but also, what kinds of customers, what parts and services. I want to know where the costs are, too. We already know a lot of that. I just need to study it and set up the reporting system a little better. I also want to figure out the best ways to promote sales of parts, especially used ones, and digging buckets. The farm economy is down and land clearing is about dead. But there is always some construction work going on and people are tending to fix their old equipment rather than buy new stuff. We are broadening our market area, too.

Q: James, how do you feel about your customers? Just tell me what your feelings are.

A: Quite often, in dealing with them in the past from the place we had built over the years and which was at best just adequate for the job, I felt a little inferior. From the instant we moved into our new place I have felt better. For one thing, I'm not apologetic about a price, not timid at all about giving a man a price quick. I offered no apology yesterday when Charles Brooks said, "You're killing me." I sense a new attitude on the part of customers. They seem to be more favorable toward us.

Q: The question I was asking, James, had more to do with whether you develop any kind of personal relationship with your customers.

A: Absolutely, with every one that I possibly can. Any way we can get interaction, joking or talking about common interests, we do. These things help me to remember the customer, of course. But it also gives us something to talk about and ask about the next time we see them. We've developed relationships with people that go back to when we first went in business. Take the Costello brothers. We're able to deal with them and do a great deal of business. Certainly, we give them prices, but I think the work — most of it anyway — would be ours regardless of the price. We know not to get ridiculous and they trust that we won't. Other customers, like Tom Fussel, have just become real close friends over the years. Tom came by here last week and said, "I'm gonna send you a picture of Sharpco when you first went in business. You had three blades in your only building. You didn't even have a door in the back. The shop was so small those three blades completely filled it." He said, "From there to here, you've come a long way — and during that time all the dealers seem to have gone downhill." And he just looked at me and said, "I wonder why that is?"

Appendix   Financial summaries

EXHIBIT A1   ## Sharpco, Inc. — balance sheets

	1981	1982	1983	1984
Assets				
Current assets				
Cash	$ 49,420	$ 8,760	$ 10,205	$ 8,108
Accounts receivable	58,791	56,887	148,531	114,320
Reserve for bad debts	(9,974)	(19,702)	(22,311)	(20,659)
Notes receivable, stockholder	49,427	61,604	79,221	87,637
Inventory	177,322	95,308	144,499	315,108
Total current assets	$324,986	$202,857	$360,145	$504,514
Fixed assets				
Building and improvements	120,766	120,766	188,668	294,491
Machinery and equipment	141,897	141,897	113,444	113,444
Office furniture and equipment	15,856	15,856	13,464	27,943
Vehicles	54,431	62,556	104,021	95,896
Total	332,950	341,075	419,597	531,774
Less accumulated depreciation	163,271	197,074	194,408	138,219
Net depreciated assets	169,679	144,001	225,189	393,555
Land	34,010	47,770	55,530	95,000
Total fixed assets	$203,689	$191,771	$280,719	$488,555
Other assets				
Utility deposits	500	500	950	1,180
TOTAL ASSETS	$529,175	$395,128	$641,814	$994,249

Liabilities and stockholders' equity

	1981	1982	1983	1984
Current liabilities				
Accounts payable	$ 28,458	$ 5,839	$ 48,487	$ 23,124
Accrued expenses	19,819	12,587	13,860	12,602
Withheld and accrued taxes	6,171	5,391	1,467	1,252
Accrued payroll	—	—	—	1,163
Accrued income taxes (overpayment)	11,636	(4,533)	(318)	6,430
Notes payable	171,600	81,281	185,872	268,505
Deposit from customers	9,000	—	—	—
Total current liabilities	$246,684	$100,565	$249,368	$313,076

EXHIBIT A1   **Sharpco, Inc. — balance sheets (*cont.*)**

	1981	1982	1983	1984
Long-term liabilities				
Notes payable	21,293	8,094	59,390	259,009
Stockholders' equity				
Common stock	33,582	33,582	33,582	33,582
Less treasury stock	(11,316)	(11,316)	(11,316)	(11,316)
Retained earnings	238,932	264,203	310,790	399,898
Total stockholders' equity	$261,198	$286,469	$333,056	$422,164
TOTAL LIABILITIES AND STOCKHOLDERS' EQUITY	$529,175	$395,128	$641,814	$994,249

EXHIBIT A2   **Sharpco, Inc. — income statements**

	1981	1982	1983	1984
Revenue				
Welding shop	$278,101	$ 297,547	$ 219,137	$ 268,366
Undercarriage shop	289,344	568,378	642,610	577,298
Direct parts sales	145,304	144,971	197,098	312,915
Steel	82,115	53,460	42,188	44,924
Miscellaneous	10,819	9,048	8,194	17,447
Total revenue	$805,683	$1,073,404	$1,109,227	$1,220,950
Direct costs				
Materials	327,829	565,993	559,097	570,100
Labor	80,117	100,499	112,259	118,684
Subcontractors	5,548	11,339	16,846	13,756
Freight	5,813	5,422	6,757	8,007
Other direct costs	238	77	50	560
Total direct costs	$419,545	$ 683,330	$ 695,009	$ 711,107
Gross profit	386,138	390,074	414,218	509,843
Indirect costs	318,779	359,336	361,599	408,125
Profit before taxes	67,359	30,738	52,619	101,718
Income taxes	11,636	5,467	6,032	12,610
NET PROFIT	$ 55,723	$ 25,271	$ 46,587	$ 89,108

EXHIBIT A3   **Sharpco, Inc. — inventories, December 31, 1984**

Steel	34,685
New parts	162,995
Used parts	100,152
Supplies	548
Finished goods	12,120
Work in progress	4,608
Total	315,108

EXHIBIT A4   **Sharpco, Inc. — sales by month (unadjusted)**

	1981	1982	1983	1984
Jan	55,974	73,463	60,666	51,492
Feb	67,743	91,547	82,996	74,689
Mar	78,002	111,144	69,295	41,780
Apr	73,360	79,510	52,365	70,196
May	85,944	126,957	45,374	151,595
Jun	32,936	77,153	94,390	142,620
Jul	65,898	108,988	137,806	142,505
Aug	69,470	138,695	138,878	116,862
Sep	66,891	95,743	87,621	183,710
Oct	77,054	83,119	149,283	115,987
Nov	76,967	56,725	105,716	49,168
Dec	51,325	24,812	76,682	64,228

CORPORATE-LEVEL STRATEGY:
FORMULATION AND IMPLEMENTATION

Case 14

THE UPJOHN COMPANY

The Upjohn Company is one of the consistently most profitable pharmaceutical companies in the United States. Its sales and earnings have increased steadily over the last ten years, and the company has become a major player in the global pharmaceutical marketplace. This growth, however, has been achieved only in the face of significant environmental pressures, pressures that are becoming stronger. First, there has been increasing price competition in the health care industry from the rapid growth of generic drug companies. Second, there has been an increase in legislative pressures on new drug development both at home and abroad. Third, there has been an increase in global competition as drug companies vie with each other on a worldwide basis. The problem facing Upjohn's management is how to maintain its growth in the domestic and international markets in the face of this increasing competition and regulatory pressure.

OVERVIEW

The Upjohn Company is a global, research-based manufacturer and marketer of pharmaceuticals, agricultural seeds and specialties, and health services. In 1987 it had research, manufacturing, sales, and distribution facilities in more than 200 locations worldwide. The company generated almost $2.3 billion in sales in 1986, its centennial year. This represented a 13.5-percent increase in sales and a growth in earnings per share of 24 percent over 1985. The five-year, compounded growth rate in earnings per share was 11.93 percent at the close of 1986.

The company is divided into two broad industrial segments: first, World-wide Human Health Care Businesses, which concentrates on the development, manufacture, and marketing of drug products globally and accounted for almost 82 percent of total sales in 1986; and second, the Agricultural Division, which

This case was prepared by Douglas D. Moesel, Robert F. Elliott, and Gareth R. Jones, Department of Management, Texas A & M University. Information from Robert D. B. Carlisle, *A Century of Caring: The Upjohn Story,* used by permission of Benjamin Company, Inc.

develops and supplies seeds and drugs for use in agriculture and animal production and which accounted for just over 18 percent of company sales in 1986.
Globally, that year 67 percent of Upjohn's sales revenues were generated in the
United States, 15 percent in Europe, and 18 percent were scattered elsewhere
across the world. By 1986 Upjohn's share of the worldwide pharmaceutical
market was 1.5 percent, and top management's ambition was to achieve a minimum of 2 percent of the market by 1990. The realization of this goal would
move Upjohn from the top fifteen to the top ten drug companies globally.[1]

HISTORY

For the first seventy-three years of its existence, The Upjohn Company was a
family-owned and operated, domestic pharmaceutical company. W. E. Upjohn
was granted a patent on a manufacturing process in 1885, which produced a
"friable" pill. The new pill disintegrated rapidly in the body to speed the release
of medication. This friability contrasted with the hardening of many of the
mass-produced pills of the day, which often passed through the body without
releasing their contents. This process and the secrecy that surrounded it fueled
the early growth of the company Upjohn founded in 1885 and made it difficult
for other companies to imitate the popular product. The founder speeded the
company's growth with a policy of selling his pills at about half the price of the
old-style, mass-produced pill, generating considerable hostility from competitors in doing so. The company expanded its product line quickly, offering 500
products by 1892 and 2,000 by 1900.

By 1900 the new technology of compressed tablets had begun to gain favor
with physicians, and Upjohn had to learn how to imitate the innovations of
other companies. Tablets also disintegrated rapidly in the body but were much
easier to mass-produce. The company began featuring tablets and created a tab-
let department to speed product development.

Upjohn was strongly aware of the need to develop marketing strengths to
complement the company's research and manufacturing skills in manufacturing
process innovations. Realizing early that the profit potential from mass produced tablets would be low, he emphasized the need to develop and market
quality-based, high-price drug products that would give higher profit margins.
Perceiving the company as operating in a luxury market, he had the insight to
switch its focus from pills to tablets and to emphasize product characteristics.
For example, he pioneered the development of pleasantly flavored drugs to suit
consumers' tastes. One result was an important innovation called phenolax, a
sweetly flavored laxative. It proved to be a big seller for more than forty years.

---

[1]Robert D. B. Carlisle, *A Century of Caring: The Upjohn Story* (Elmsford, N.Y.: Benjamin
Company, 1987), p. 226.

In the next two decades Upjohn added a number of promising research areas. In 1912 bacterial vaccines became part of the company's product line. Activity was begun in endocrinology and digitalis extracts for heart failure in 1914. A pleasant-tasting alkalizer called Citrocarbonate was introduced in 1921 and reached $1 million in annual sales by 1926, the first Upjohn product to do so. This product and the intensive sales effort that accompanied marked the emergence of the company as a first-class pharmaceutical house. A succession of other introductions followed, including new flavored versions of cough syrup and cod liver oil. Each of these research efforts was stimulated by a perceived need to respond to the demands of the medical community for improved drug products.

Upjohn was always sensitive to the needs of its main "distributors," the doctors who prescribed its products. An aggressive sales push directed toward pharmacists and doctors helped the company to grow through the tough 1930s and into the years of World War II. The Medical Department was created in 1937 by a member of the founding family, Gifford Upjohn, to upgrade company contacts with physicians. This focus became a hallmark of sales efforts at Upjohn. Through the decades that followed, the company continued to differentiate its products and match its sales strategy to the changing composition of the medical profession.

Much of the company's growth through the 1930s and 1940s was tied to vitamins. Upjohn was the first to produce a standardized combination of vitamins A and D in the United States in 1929. Vitamins accounted for half of the $40 million in sales in 1945 and marked the company as a leader in nutritional supplements. Other products critical to Upjohn's growth included Kaopectate, estrogenic hormone products introduced in the 1930s, and antibiotics and an antidiabetic drug brought out in the 1940s and 1950s.[2]

By 1952 the Research Department had 421 employees, who viewed their research output as second in quality only to Merck & Co. among domestic pharmaceutical companies. The department began to establish broad research areas, which are still important in the 1980s: antibiotics, steroids, antidiabetes agents, nonsteroidal inflammatory drugs, and central nervous system agents.

The progress of the company's research efforts led to increasing demand for customized chemicals to manufacture new drug introductions. The company had purchased standardized chemicals in the past but the growing need for unique materials led to the establishment of Fine Chemicals Manufacturing in 1949 to supply the company with its own products. The chemical division also expanded into external sales, and by 1984, 40 percent of its production was for other companies.

After World War II, the Upjohn Company continued a modest export program, sending most of its foreign sales representatives to Central and South America. The creation of the Export Division in 1952 was the first strong corporate signal that management was committed to competing globally. The

[2]Carlisle, *A Century of Caring*, pp. 13–99.

division was formed in reaction to the globalization strategies of the leading domestic drug companies, which recognized the potential in developing a worldwide market for their products.

In 1958 the twenty-member board of directors, eleven of whom were related directly or by marriage to the founder, voted to recommend public ownership. The following year, the Upjohn Company was formally accepted for listing and trading on the New York Stock Exchange. The decision to go public did not end the involvement of the extended family of the founder, W. E. Upjohn, but it did give the company the additional financial resources it needed to become a stronger force in the global pharmaceutical market.

The company continued to quickly expand its international scope to include sales subsidiaries in Canada, London, and Australia. Through the 1960s and 1970s, it added more subsidiaries and sales offices and built two major production facilities outside the continental United States: one in Belgium in 1963 and the other in Puerto Rico in 1974. By the mid-1980s these plants, in combination with the principal facility in Kalamazoo, Michigan, produced pharmaceuticals for sale in more than 150 countries.

Upjohn's first large venture out of pharmaceuticals came via its entry into animal health products in the late 1940s, when it repackaged several human products, such as antibiotics, for animal use. New products specifically for animals began flowing in 1952, and a sales force to veterinarians was established, growing from one person in 1956 to twenty in 1957. The sales force gradually increased to 130 by the mid-1980s.

Other agricultural products were added over time. After deciding against entry into fertilizers, the company acquired its core seed company, Asgrow Seed Company, in 1968 to develop new improved strains of seeds. It added another top-ten domestic seed company, O's Gold, in 1983. The latter was chosen because its sales force and products complemented Asgrow's. In 1974 Upjohn acquired Cobb Breeding Corporation, a producer of chicken broiler breeders, to continue its expansion into animal drugs. In 1986 the company formed a joint venture with Tyson Foods, Inc., to further expand its broiler operations.

Nonagricultural diversification began in the 1960s. The company started manufacturing polymer chemical products in 1962, with the purchase of the Carwin Company, which was combined with the Fine Chemicals Manufacturing operations. The company entered cosmetics in 1964, when several other pharmaceutical companies were doing likewise. In 1969 it entered home nursing services when it purchased Homemakers, Inc.

The chemicals business was profitable for many years. After profits peaked in 1979, however, rapid decline set in due to a downcycle in the principal markets for chemicals. The polymer chemicals operation was sold in 1985, but Fine Chemicals Manufacturing was retained. The cosmetics business never proved very profitable and was liquidated in 1974. The home nursing service business was renamed Upjohn Healthcare Services. It quickly added new locations and became the market leader in 1974, a position it has held ever since.

UPJOHN'S ENVIRONMENT

By the late 1970s and early 1980s important changes were reshaping competition in the domestic and global pharmaceutical markets. First, more countries were imposing greater regulation on the drug approval process. In the United States the Kefauver-Harris amendments of 1962 placed major new constraints on pharmaceutical manufacturers. They required that companies set forth substantial proof that a drug was safe and effective before the FDA could allow it on the market. The new drug introduction process became considerably longer and more expensive as a result of this legislation, which was viewed by many as the single most important nonscientific event to affect the industry since World War II.

The Kefauver-Harris amendments marked the beginning of substantially increased regulation of the domestic pharmaceutical industry. As drug approval time was lengthened, valuable years of patent protection were being eroded. The Waxman-Hatch Act of 1984 reflected the tremendous growth in domestic political influence of the Generic Pharmaceutical Industry Association (GPIA).

Another major thrust of the bill was to speed the introduction of generic drugs after patent expiration in order to reduce their price. This put increasing pressure on the profits of the company that developed a new drug. Development costs were estimated to approach $100 million for each new drug introduced in 1986.[3] To placate the large drug companies, the bill guaranteed several drug companies, including Upjohn, the exclusive rights for five years beyond normal patent length to market four major drugs each.[4] These patent extensions were to compensate for FDA's slow handling of drug registrations over the previous few years. However, by the end of 1987 approvals for generic copies of patent-expired drugs were being issued at a very rapid pace, and the large drug companies were experiencing increased price competition on many fronts.

Similar legislative pressures were mounting in many other countries. Between 1981 and 1984 the Japanese government ordered price reductions on drugs averaging 40.1 percent.[5] Such legislation marked an industry trend toward—as Upjohn's President and Chief Operating Officer Lawrence C. Hoff put it—a "two-tier industry with innovators in one group and a large number of generic manufacturers in the other segment, competing fiercely on the sole basis of price."[6]

Many countries had begun protectionist campaigns, restricting drug marketing to products manufactured by the domestic industry. Many foreign companies also benefited from development support from their respective governments, allowing them to avoid the full cost of their research efforts. Furthermore, since regulatory procedures, processes, and time orientations differ considerably from

---

[3]Carlisle, *A Century of Caring*, p. 24.
[4]"The Last Word," *Drug and Cosmetic Industry*, 135 (October 1984), p. 126.
[5]Carlisle, *A Century of Caring*, p. 233.
[6]Carlisle, *A Century of Caring*, p. 210.

one country to another, domestic companies often experienced difficulty in obtaining information on how drugs move through foreign regulatory agencies. Although an attempt to achieve standardization of clinical procedures and disseminate intelligence on postmarketing response of users through an international information network was underway in the mid-1980s, it appeared to be years from fruition.

With increasing competition in research, and increasing difficulty and costs in achieving regulatory approval, drug companies began concentrating their research in specific fields of medicine in order to reduce the cost of developing new drugs. To maintain their profitability, companies began specializing in the world's three most lucrative markets for new drugs: heart disease, anti-inflammatory agents and analgesics, and antibiotics. This concentration of resources by major companies in a few specific areas was suggested by an Upjohn spokesperson to be the cause of the scarcity of new drugs classified as breakthrough developments by the FDA in recent years.[7]

However, the slowdown in drug innovation seems to be on the verge of reversal. The advent of biotechnology is expected to fuel a huge surge in the global pharmaceutical products as cures and medications for major diseases begin to appear. The world market for pharmaceutical drugs is projected to reach approximately $300 billion by the end of the century, in contrast to $80 billion in 1986.[8] The seven largest markets were projected to be the United States, Japan, West Germany, France, the United Kingdom, Italy, and Canada. These markets were expected to demand and have the ability to pay for new drugs treating the five major afflictions of developed nations — cancer, heart disease, chronic pain, infectious diseases, and emotional disturbances.

Although the potential for revenues from developing new drugs to suit the specific disease needs of developing nations is huge, such development carries great risks. These countries lack the funds to provide comprehensive health care, although, compared with the cost of hospitalization, pharmaceuticals are expected to be one of the most cost-effective approaches to health care services for such nations. However, the World Health Organization (WHO) is offering research opportunities for major companies through its funding of research to discover cures for six tropical diseases. Upjohn, with the support of these grants, has chosen to concentrate on the five diseases that are parasitic in nature. Although these diseases are endemic to humans, studying them may have application to Upjohn's agricultural and veterinary medicine research.

Other factors also affect the profitability of the pharmaceutical industry. International currency fluctuations influence overseas expansion. For domestic companies, strong overseas earnings are masked by a strong dollar. With downturns in the dollar in 1987, overseas efforts were expected to reflect more favorably on earnings for domestic companies. The industry also seems to be subject

---

[7]The Upjohn Company, *Annual Report* (1986), 9.
[8]Carlisle, *A Century of Caring,* p. 226.

to increasing levels of litigation as companies try to delay entry of competitors new products or to protect essential patent rights.

Upjohn faced such a struggle in 1987 with its breakthrough hair-growth product Regaine, based on the ingredient minoxidil. It filed a claim with the International Trade Commission (ITC) alleging that seven companies in Europe, two in Canada, one in Mexico, and ten in the United States were importing or distributing Minoxidil powder, salts, and concentrates in violation of Upjohn patents.[9] The ITC had one year to complete its probe. In addition, a flood of "baldness cures," by being labeled natural products, had avoided classification as drugs and did not undergo the tests of efficacy required of drugs, but the producers of these cures were trading on the hope generated by reports about minoxidil. The effect that these seemingly useless products would have on the market facing Upjohn's Regaine was uncertain. Regaine was still awaiting final FDA approval in late 1987.

CORPORATE STRATEGY

The company's stated pharmaceutical business strategy to the year 2000 is to ensure that it delivers the greatest volume of quality pharmaceuticals to the greatest number of people while maintaining an appropriate return on investment to assure its continued growth. Three goals seem to be particularly stressed: (1) sales growth (with concurrent market share growth); (2) a continuing growth in return on investment; and (3) competition based on high quality rather than low price. Upjohn plans to achieve these goals by directing the company's resources into areas promising the greatest returns. The aggressive nature of this approach is indicated by Upjohn's quest to become one of the top ten drug companies by 1990. The company estimates that it will need to better the general market growth by at least 3.5 percent per year from 1985 to 1990 in order to attain this position.[10]

Vertical integration has been a part of Upjohn's strategy since its inception. The early process innovations which built the company reflected a desire to improve on the technologies available from external equipment suppliers. Upjohn also pursued backward integration into fine chemicals to support its drug manufacturing activities. To guarantee supplies and quality of inputs, Upjohn Production purchased most of its bulk chemicals from Upjohn Chemicals. By producing its own chemicals, the company could maintain quality control from initial chemical manufacture to the final packaging of its products.

---

[9]"Upjohn Patent Complaint to be Investigated by ITC," *The Wall Street Journal,* May 14, 1987, p. 37.
[10]Carlisle, *A Century of Caring,* p. 226.

Furthermore, rather than remain simply a drug manufacturer, the company developed its own research program in the early 1900s and continually increased its research capabilities after that time to support its marketing efforts. The strong integration of research and manufacturing is the primary characteristic that distinguishes the major-brand drug segment from the generic drug segment.

While most major drug companies were acquiring biotechnical businesses in the mid-1980s as a mixed strategy of backward integration and related diversification, Upjohn decided to develop its own. In 1983 Dr. Ralph E. Christofferson, a long-time consultant, was hired by the company, assigned a budget, given a custom-constructed facility, and instructed to hire the best people in the field. The 150-person staff began working with research professionals in Upjohn's other businesses to show them how the new technology could help applied research efforts in both human health services and agriculture. The group also assisted the Chemicals division in gearing up for manipulation and cloning of genes using biotechnical methods.[11]

However, Upjohn has used acquisitions to achieve its strategic objectives of diversification and expansion in health and agriculture. It built the Agricultural Division and the Worldwide Human Health Care Businesses by related acquisitions. The key to Upjohn's success in diversification has been the degree of research synergy achievable among the individual businesses. Furthermore, potential synergies between its health and agricultural interests are becoming increasingly important. For example, although seeds were not closely related to health services at the time of acquisition, top management may have foreseen the biotechnical revolution of the late 1970s and 1980s, which served to greatly increase the research synergies between development of new plant products and new animal or human products.

The most unrelated business in the company in late 1987 was Upjohn HealthCare Services, Inc. The subsidiary has been kept relatively separate from the rest of the company since its acquisition in 1969 and has continued to lead its market. Given the high growth predicted in the home health care market, it is likely to remain successful.

Consistent with its strategy to serve the global pharmaceutical market, Upjohn has developed a manufacturing operations structure based on three tiers of ownership of manufacturing facilities. This has allowed its management flexibility in responding to changes in worldwide demand and governmental regulations. These tiers are the primary tier, where Upjohn owns and operates the facility; the secondary tier, where joint venture facilities are operated; and the third tier, where Upjohn licenses the use of its technologies or chemical formulas to an independent third-party facility, sometimes retaining marketing rights within the respective market.

The first tier concentrates capital investment and advanced technologies in three primary manufacturing facilities located in Kalamazoo, Belgium, and

[11]Upjohn, *Annual Report*, p. 6.

Puerto Rico. These plants combine state-of-the-art robotics and manufacturing processes to yield manufacturing economies of scale, while allowing strict control over standards of quality. The Belgian location allows reductions in distribution costs for the growing European market, whereas the Puerto Rican site was selected to expand North American production capacity and at the same time receive attractive tax exemptions.

The second tier uses joint venture arrangements, typically stemming from governmental restrictions that require pharmaceuticals sold within a country's borders to be manufactured there. Joint ventures can also arise when a foreign pharmaceutical company develops a successful new drug and seeks a joint marketing arrangement with Upjohn. Joint venturing of the project allows the foreign company to use Upjohn's developmental, production, and marketing expertise, whereas Upjohn typically receives marketing rights for the new product outside of the developing company's native market.

The third-tier production facilities are not owned by Upjohn but are owned and operated by independent third parties utilizing processes and formulas licensed by Upjohn. The same governmental restrictions that explain the use of joint ventures explain the use of third-tier facilities. Besides, it is financially prudent to license rather than own facilities in certain areas of the world because of the risks involved.

Since biomedical research is increasing throughout the world, corporate officers have emphasized the need for a global orientation to research. To facilitate the acquisition of worldwide knowledge, Upjohn is developing research facilities overseas, establishing research centers in Japan and the United Kingdom. Additionally, "Discovery Centers" are being developed, in which Upjohn provides funds and research facilities to university-based scientists near the major centers of learning throughout Europe. This strategy allows Upjohn to achieve a better understanding of worldwide markets, secure access to research funded by foreign governments, gain influence and credibility within foreign markets, and acquire a differing perspective of scientific research through the monitoring of worldwide developments.

Upjohn has used joint ventures not only for manufacturing, but for research purposes as well. Realizing that its major hair-growth product Regaine could use additional developmental expertise for the consumer market, Upjohn announced a joint development project with Procter & Gamble in October 1987.[12] The agreement was to jointly develop ways to make Regaine easier to use and to develop new hair-growth products. Procter & Gamble's experience in formulating creams, gels, and lotions and its knowledge of the hair care market appeared to be the major attractions for Upjohn, even though Procter & Gamble was also sponsoring hair-growth research in England. The companies agreed to share rights to any new hair-growth products they developed.

[12]"Upjohn and P&G to Work on Drug Against Baldness," *The Wall Street Journal,* October 26, 1987, p. 30.

CORPORATE STRUCTURE

Upjohn's corporate structure in 1987 grouped its major business activities into three strategic business units (SBUs) and a central research and development functional unit, known as Scientific Administration. These are shown in Exhibit 1. The SBUs included the Worldwide Human Health Businesses, the Agricultural Division, and Chemicals. The Scientific Administration function is the development unit that serves the SBUs' research and development needs. These and other centrally located support functions report to the Office of the Chairman.

The Chemicals SBU, consisting of 900 employees, primarily serves as a source of fine chemicals for the other two SBUs, predominantly for Worldwide Human Health Care Businesses. It has plants in Kalamazoo and in North Haven, Connecticut. The division also has its own R&D unit, which operates separately from the central R&D group and services the other SBUs' process innovation needs when necessary.

The Agricultural Division SBU is organized by its major subsidiaries, including Asgrow Seeds, and animal health products. Asgrow is further broken down into a domestic unit and a number of international subsidiaries. Animal Health's international business was grouped in both the Agricultural Division and under the Worldwide Human Health Care Businesses SBU's Upjohn International, Inc. unit.

The Worldwide Human Health Businesses SBU structure in 1987 is shown in Exhibit 2. The five principal units included the Upjohn HealthCare Services subsidiary, the Consumer Products Division, Worldwide Pharmaceutical Manufacturing and Engineering, the Domestic Pharmaceutical Marketing Division, and the Upjohn International subsidiary.

Upjohn HealthCare Services, Inc., is the largest private health care provider in the nation, with 300 North American locations in 1986. The head office is located in Kalamazoo, and two regional financial centers serve as other primary hubs. Each location operates fairly autonomously, with 27 field managers and 1,500 staffers supporting the 60,000 care givers and their 200,000 patients.

The Consumer Products Division was established in July 1986 to sell and promote nonprescription drugs, primarily less concentrated versions of prescription drugs approved for consumer sales. It was moved to this higher level in the company to give it greater representation and stronger support throughout the company. The unit was created mainly because of industry predictions that the market for consumer products developed from prescription drugs would reach $50 billion by 2000.

Worldwide Pharmaceutical Manufacturing and Engineering is responsible for all production and facility planning for pharmaceuticals. It is divided into six subunits. These include a special projects group to plan and oversee major construction projects around the world and a licensing group to arrange authoriza-

EXHIBIT 1   **Corporate officers of the Upjohn Company**

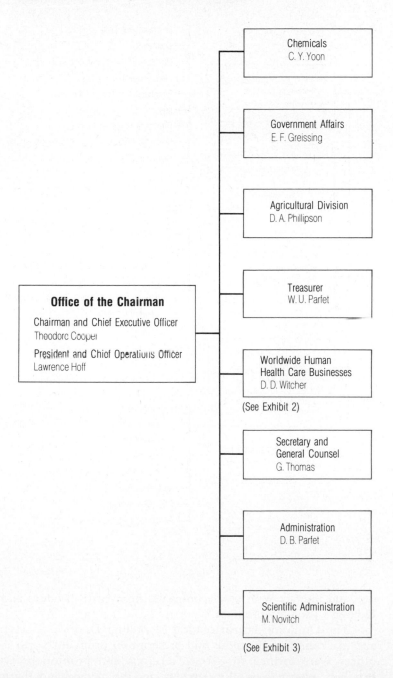

Chemicals
C. Y. Yoon

Government Affairs
E. F. Greissing

Agricultural Division
D. A. Phillipson

Treasurer
W. U. Parfet

Office of the Chairman

Chairman and Chief Executive Officer
Theodore Cooper

President and Chief Operations Officer
Lawrence Hoff

Worldwide Human
Health Care Businesses
D. D. Witcher

(See Exhibit 2)

Secretary and
General Counsel
G. Thomas

Administration
D. B. Parfet

Scientific Administration
M. Novitch

(See Exhibit 3)

EXHIBIT 2   **Worldwide Human Health Care Businesses**

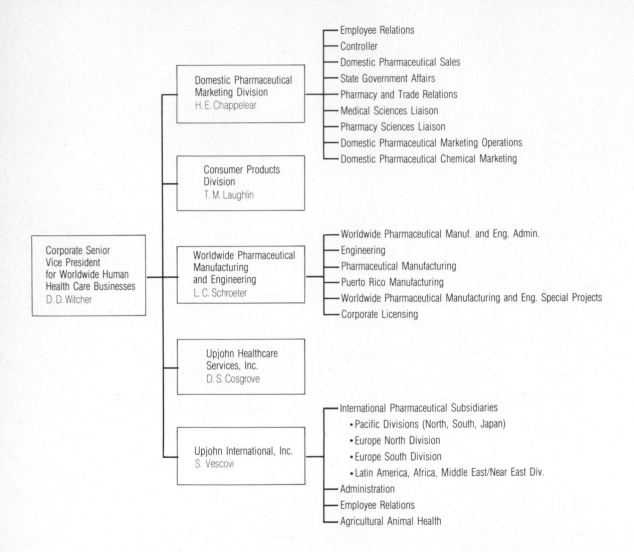

tion and interact with other companies licensed to produce and market one of Upjohn's patented products.

The Domestic Pharmaceutical Marketing Division is responsible for sales and marketing of chemicals and prescription drugs in North America. Special offices were formed to oversee relations and promotions with medical researchers, pharmaceutical researchers, and the medical and pharmaceutical trade.

Upjohn International, Inc. is responsible for sales and marketing of pharmaceuticals and animal health products internationally. It is structured into four geographic regional subsidiary groupings: Pacific, Europe North, Europe South, and Latin America, Africa, and Middle East divisions. Agricultural Animal Health is also a subunit because its international sales force is administered separately from Asgrow's international subsidiaries and is of insufficient size to warrant a separate infrastructure.

Scientific Administration is the lone functional grouping at the corporate level. This research and development group, as shown in Exhibit 3, is structured into subgroups representing agricultural research and development, human health, or "discovery," research, pharmaceutical and consumer drug product development, clinical testing, and a Japanese R&D subunit with its own lab and development groups. A biotechnology and basic research unit works closely with all the other subgroups in providing basic research support and in overseeing academic and government research efforts funded by the company.

Upjohn employed a number of horizontal integration mechanisms to promote synergistic relations between units throughout the corporation. One such effort was the client engineering program formally established in 1980. Engineering assigned its professionals to other units on a semipermanent basis according to the changing needs of each unit. The goal was to achieve better planning and customizing of new facilities to provide maximum use for the occupying units.

The Chemicals R&D group also provided expert services to both the Agricultural Division and Worldwide Human Health Care Businesses through an extensive system of task forces and teams. It was assigned to develop synthetic chemical process and biotechnical and fermentation process innovations and analytical chemical process enhancements upon request from units within each SBU.

New product development efforts are integrated through the use of product development teams. During the development stage, experts from R&D, chemicals, engineering, and manufacturing work together under the leadership of a product manager selected from domestic or international marketing to develop the product, test it clinically, bring it into production, and introduce it to the market.

Another integrative mechanism involves Medical Sciences Liaison domestic directors. Each is assigned to a specific disease group corresponding to a Discovery Research unit, with the responsibility to transfer information from this research unit to other medical researchers and vice versa.

Several key boundary-spanning roles had been created across the company. Examples include government affairs specialists, Medical Sciences Liaison representatives, Medical Specialty representatives, Surgical Specialty representatives, and Pharmacy Sciences Liaison representatives. The regulatory, research, and professional medical groups they target represent critical constituencies for the corporation.

EXHIBIT 3   **Pharmaceutical research & development**

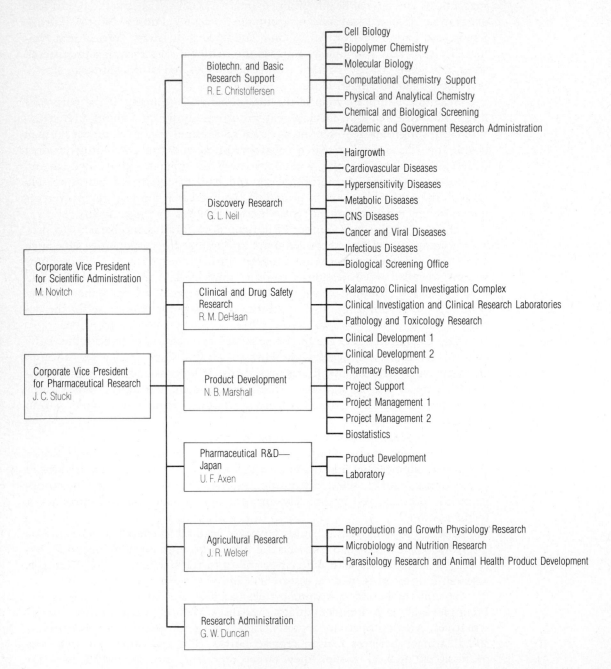

CORPORATE CONTROL

Corporate control at Upjohn centers on the corporate productivity program[13] — a major control effort formalized by Upjohn in 1984. The program established a structured approach to productivity improvement based on a model of each subunit as a production process with inputs, production activities, and outputs for "willing" customers. By early 1987 more than 1,000 organizational subunits had implemented the program. The approach was designed around a series of six steps toward unit productivity improvement.

In the first step, the subunit mission was defined by the subunit manager through a combination of five elements: (1) a statement emphasizing the nature of the subunit's activities and its expected contribution to the next higher organizational unit to which it reported; (2) a summary of products or services the subunit produced; (3) a description of the customers for the subunit; (4) a description of the geographic scope of the subunit's responsibilities; and (5) a description of how the unit's mission related to company profit. Managers were expected to condense these five elements into a single mission statement. The manager at the next higher level then used the statements to check for gaps, overlaps, and duplication of effort within his or her span of control. In addition, cost data were available for each subunit so that the same manager could compare the cost of operating the production subunit with other subunits.

The second step required a process of establishing customer expectation levels for three or four primary outputs (products) and three or four primary customers. The manager of the subunit was responsible for discovering what primary customers expected of the subunit's product or service. This was usually accomplished through meetings, questionnaires, visits, or phone calls. Customer needs and expectations were then set down in written preliminary delivery agreements, which specified terms including the level or amount, timeliness, accuracy, conformity to specifications, and cost effectiveness.

In the third step, subunit managers identified required resources and inputs. Costs of capital, labor, materials, energy, equipment, technology, and service outputs from other subunits were to be determined for each product. Then direct transfer prices for products and services among units were determined through a joint bargaining process, with the option provided, "when practical," to obtain goods and services from outside vendors to encourage internal efficiency.

The fourth step required the subunit manager to select a set of three or four simple measures of subunit productivity. These measures were to include at least one quality measure, one timeliness measure, and one cost measure and were to be applied to three or four major products. Each subunit was thus allowed to select the performance measures that its manager and employees jointly felt best tracked its own performance. The measures had to focus on group rather than individual efforts and to correlate with business success but

[13]Cyrus C. Highlander, "Six Steps to Unit Productivity Improvement: A Corporatewide Effort at Upjohn," *National Productivity Review* (Winter 1986–1987), 20–27.

could not require excessive data gathering. The higher-level manager was directed to concentrate on how these measures improved over time. By tracking subunit performance on productivity measures, corrective action could be taken whenever necessary.

The fifth step was for the subunit manager to set productivity improvement goals for six-to-twelve-month intervals. The goals based on the productivity measures selected were set to be attainable but challenging. The goals were to take into account the goals and objectives of other subunits of the company, especially those of the next-higher level, to avoid conflicts.

The sixth and final step was for the subunit manager to devise and implement improvement plans. This was a list of actions for reaching the productivity-improvement goals. The company insisted that a clear connection be made between productivity improvement in the subunit and increased business profit.

This management-by-objectives approach to productivity was selected because it permitted economies of scale in training, integrated the company's sub-

EXHIBIT 4   **Eleven-year summary: continuing operations**

The Upjohn Company and subsidiaries (dollar amounts in millions, except per-share data)

Years ended December 31		1987	1986	1985
Selected financial data	Operating revenue	**$2,529.6**	$2,291.4	$2,017.2
	Earnings from continuing operations	**305.0**	252.6	203.2
	Earnings per share from continuing operations	**1.63**	1.35	1.10
	Dividends declared per share	**.63**	.507	.447
	Total assets	**3,043.1**	2,665.0	2,376.9
	Long-term debt	**436.3**	423.5	377.3
Operating results	Domestic sales	**$1,556.4**	$1,459.7	$1,322.8
	Foreign sales	**964.6**	820.6	685.7
	Other revenue	**8.6**	11.1	8.7
	Operating revenue	**2,529.6**	2,291.4	2,017.2
	Cost of products and services sold	**820.8**	795.6	731.6
	Research and development	**355.5**	314.1	284.1
	Marketing and administrative	**914.7**	808.3	700.9
	Operating costs and expenses	**2,091.0**	1,918.0	1,716.6
	Operating income	**438.6**	373.4	300.6
	Interest income	**57.3**	53.9	61.9
	Interest expense	**(59.0)**	(58.8)	(70.2)
	Other income (deductions)	**(4.7)**	(12.1)	5.5
	Provision for income taxes	**(127.2)**	(103.8)	(94.6)
	Earnings from continuing operations	**305.0**	252.6	203.2
	(Losses) earnings from discontinued operations			(.2)
	Net earnings	**$ 305.0**	$ 252.6	$ 203.0

units, promoted the efficient transfer of resources and R&D knowledge among subunits and SBUs, and allowed the use of common systems for planning, measuring, and tracking progress. This standardization of control processes also allowed the use of wider spans of control at many managerial levels.

THE FUTURE

As 1989 approaches, Upjohn seems poised for the future, with several new products nearing the end of development or registration approval with the FDA. Its product strategy of high quality and high price is being threatened by a lengthening drug approval process and faster generic drug introductions after patent expiration. Should Upjohn retain the strategy and structure that have helped it reach its present position or should it be contemplating movement into new businesses or a change in strategic orientation to safeguard its position?

1984	1983	1982	1981	1980	1979	1978	1977
$1,901.2	$1,738.8	$1,602.4	$1,610.4	$1,478.1	$1,247.6	$1,107.5	$ 945.8
189.5	180.1	155.0	190.1	155.0	128.1	114.8	77.1
1.03	.99	.86	1.05	.87	.72	.64	.43
.427	.392	.38	.345	.322	.27	.228	.195
2,204.3	2,151.3	1,968.7	1,912.6	1,631.2	1,367.6	1,176.0	1,020.5
382.1	548.5	461.2	458.1	305.7	221.5	214.9	226.2
$1,248.3	$1,111.2	$ 988.0	$ 995.3	$ 888.9	$ 741.6	$ 675.8	$ 596.7
643.3	618.9	607.4	610.3	582.8	501.3	427.6	345.6
9.6	8.7	7.0	4.8	6.4	4.7	4.1	3.5
1,901.2	1,738.8	1,602.4	1,610.4	1,478.1	1,247.6	1,107.5	945.8
703.6	642.5	619.6	634.2	594.7	497.2	423.6	383.6
246.7	218.0	184.8	161.7	139.0	122.1	109.0	95.8
655.2	601.3	567.1	575.1	526.1	443.8	389.4	325.5
1,605.5	1,461.8	1,371.5	1,371.0	1,259.8	1,063.1	922.0	804.9
295.7	277.0	230.9	239.4	218.3	184.5	185.5	140.9
61.5	52.3	48.4	39.6	22.8	17.5	9.4	5.3
(76.5)	(62.3)	(55.5)	(54.4)	(31.9)	(23.7)	(21.2)	(23.4)
(7.3)	(15.6)	(20.2)	5.4	(7.2)	(9.1)	(4.5)	(4.7)
(83.9)	(71.3)	(48.6)	(39.9)	(47.0)	(41.1)	(54.4)	(41.0)
189.5	180.1	155.0	190.1	155.0	128.1	114.8	77.1
(16.2)	(19.9)	(29.0)	(8.3)	15.4	21.4	14.6	14.4
$ 173.3	$ 160.2	$ 126.0	$ 181.8	$ 170.4	$ 149.5	$ 129.4	$ 91.5

EXHIBIT 4   **Eleven-year summary: continuing operations (*cont.*)**

The Upjohn Company and subsidiaries (dollar amounts in millions, except per-share data)

Years ended December 31		1987	1986	1985
Capital resources	Accounts receivable	$ 590.5	$ 513.9	$ 409.7
	Inventories	401.4	364.7	379.3
	Other current assets less (liabilities)	(251.8)	(240.8)	(229.5)
	Working capital	740.1	637.8	559.5
	Net assets of discontinued operations			
	Property, plant and equipment, net	1,114.4	981.5	852.1
	Other assets	513.8	481.6	437.5
	Total	$2,368.3	$2,100.9	$1,849.1
Long-term financing of	Shareholders' equity	$1,673.5	$1,470.2	$1,295.1
capital resources	Long-term debt	436.3	423.5	377.3
	All other	258.5	207.2	176.7
	Total	$2,368.3	$2,100.9	$1,849.1
Major cash flows — cash	Continuing operations	$ 444.4	$ 307.0	$ 253.9
provided (required) by	Property, plant and equipment additions	(212.0)	(201.9)	(152.6)
	(Increase) decrease in investments	(.7)	16.3	34.1
	Long-term borrowings, net	12.8	46.2	(4.8)
	Dividends paid	(108.2)	(92.6)	(80.8)
	All other, net	(43.4)	.5	(89.8)
	Discontinued operations	(12.0)	(9.2)	145.0
	Increase (decrease) in cash	$ 80.9	$ 66.3	$ 105.0
Other data	Common shares outstanding (thousands)	187,061	187,307	186,081
	Employees	20,500	20,700	20,600
	Payroll	$ 654.2	$ 596.9	$ 539.5

Per-share data and shares outstanding reflect a three-for-one stock split effective April 6, 1987, and a two-for-one stock split effective April 7, 1986.

Source: Reprinted by permission of Upjohn Company.

1984	1983	1982	1981	1980	1979	1978	1977
$ 356.1	$ 363.5	$ 340.7	$ 327.2	$ 322.3	$ 262.1	$ 235.3	$ 201.7
344.5	321.0	321.8	349.8	303.4	252.0	224.5	198.0
(367.5)	(238.3)	(270.0)	(270.3)	(279.0)	(140.0)	(124.0)	(82.0)
333.1	446.2	392.5	406.7	346.7	374.1	335.8	317.7
110.3	105.8	103.6	130.6	139.3	118.8	97.5	96.8
760.3	704.8	622.6	556.7	487.7	423.5	386.6	376.8
467.8	487.4	435.8	443.7	295.5	132.3	108.2	41.5
$1,671.5	$1,744.2	$1,554.5	$1,537.7	$1,269.2	$1,048.7	$ 928.1	$ 832.8
$1,134.2	$1,057.3	$ 973.0	$ 965.3	$ 865.8	$ 743.7	$ 639.8	$ 549.0
382.1	548.5	461.2	458.1	305.7	221.5	214.9	226.2
155.2	138.4	120.3	114.3	97.7	83.5	73.4	57.6
$1,671.5	$1,744.2	$1,554.5	$1,537.7	$1,269.2	$1,048.7	$ 928.1	$ 832.8
$ 253.0	$ 141.3	$ 242.6	$ 207.3	$ 140.6	$ 131.3	$ 145.1	$ 120.9
(129.2)	(149.6)	(131.5)	(130.9)	(99.6)	(68.0)	(30.4)	(36.1)
9.8	8.7	7.1	(148.0)	(48.9)	(66.5)	(96.6)	(41.7)
(166.5)	87.4	3.1	152.3	84.2	6.6	(11.2)	1.2
(78.2)	(69.1)	(69.0)	(61.6)	(57.8)	(48.7)	(39.9)	(35.4)
117.9	(13.7)	(5.3)	(15.0)	(8.3)	45.4	17.9	(4.1)
(20.7)	(22.0)	(2.0)	.4	(5.1)	.1	13.9	(5.5)
$ (13.9)	$ (17.0)	$ 45.0	$ 4.5	$ 5.1	$ .2	$ (1.2)	$ (.7)
183,917	182,637	181,362	180,822	179,803	178,639	178,270	177,971
20,210	19,480	19,400	19,300	20,050	19,130	18,110	16,590
$ 501.1	$ 473.7	$ 457.1	$ 460.1	$ 418.4	$ 353.5	$ 303.7	$ 264.3

EXHIBIT 5   **Consolidated statements of earnings**

The Upjohn Company and subsidiaries (dollar amounts in thousands, except per-share data)

For the years ended December 31	1987	1986	1985
Operating revenue			
Net sales	**$2,521,024**	$2,280,325	$2,008,486
Other revenue	**8,555**	11,123	8,719
Total	**2,529,579**	2,291,448	2,017,205
Operating costs and expenses			
Cost of products and services sold	**820,844**	795,614	731,550
Research and development	**355,503**	314,114	284,126
Marketing and administrative	**914,671**	808,305	700,966
Total	**2,091,018**	1,918,033	1,716,642
Operating income	**438,561**	373,415	300,563
Interest income	**57,328**	53,863	61,926
Interest expense	**(58,973)**	(58,779)	(70,229)
Foreign exchange gains (losses)	**3,331**	(5,799)	3,970
All other, net	**(1,526)**	(4,679)	(566)
Earnings from continuing operations before income taxes and minority equity	**438,721**	358,021	295,664
Provision for income taxes	**127,200**	103,800	94,600
Minority equity in earnings (losses)	**6,482**	1,575	(2,129)
Earnings from continuing operations	**305,039**	252,646	203,193
Discontinued operations:			
Loss from operations, net of income taxes			(1,549)
Gain on sale, net of income taxes			1,311
Net earnings	**$ 305,039**	$ 252,646	$ 202,955
Net earnings per common share	**$ 1.63**	$ 1.35	$ 1.10

Per-share data reflect a three-for-one stock split effective April 6, 1987, and a two-for-one stock split effective April 7, 1986.

EXHIBIT 6   **Consolidated balance sheets**

The Upjohn Company and subsidiaries (dollar amounts in thousands)

For the years ended December 31	1987	1986
Current assets:		
Cash and cash items	$ 293,027	$ 212,154
Trade accounts receivable, less allowances of $21,261 (1986: $10,928)	542,100	472,043
Other accounts receivable	48,362	41,809
Inventories	401,403	364,741
Deferred income taxes	54,167	42,825
Other	75,880	68,268
Total current assets	1,414,939	1,201,840
Investments at cost	350,914	350,200
Property, plant and equipment at cost:		
Land	45,314	39,547
Buildings and utilities	662,364	618,844
Equipment	852,215	753,698
Leasehold improvements	7,608	6,958
Construction in process	154,776	93,528
	1,722,277	1,512,575
Less allowance for depreciation	607,886	531,026
Net property, plant and equipment	1,114,391	981,549
Other noncurrent assets	152,887	131,367
Total assets	$3,043,131	$2,664,956
Current liabilities:		
Bank loans, including current maturities of long-term debt	$ 37,890	$ 44,033
Commercial paper		27,754
Accounts payable	147,175	133,244
Compensation and vacation	66,203	54,662
Taxes other than income taxes	24,532	24,351
Income taxes payable	169,113	91,588
Other	229,899	188,408
Total current liabilities	674,812	564,040
Long-term debt	436,292	423,508
Other liabilities	54,659	56,780
Commitments and contingent liabilities		

EXHIBIT 6   **Consolidated balance sheets (*cont.*)**

The Upjohn Company and subsidiaries (dollar amounts in thousands)

For the years ended December 31	1987	1986
Deferred income taxes	**171,256**	132,531
Minority equity in subsidiaries	**32,600**	17,881
Shareholders' equity:		
Preferred stock, one dollar par value; authorized 12,000,000 shares, none issued		
Common stock, one dollar par value; authorized 600,000,000 shares, issued		
188,012,658 shares (1986: 187,306,524 shares)	**188,013**	187,307
Capital in excess of par value	**8,233**	
Retained earnings	**1,578,746**	1,388,377
Currency translation adjustments	**(72,715)**	(105,468)
Less treasury stock at cost, 951,379 shares	**(28,765)**	
Total shareholders' equity	**1,673,512**	1,470,216
Total liabilities and shareholders' equity	**$3,043,131**	$2,664,956

Source: Reprinted by permission of Upjohn Company.

EXHIBIT 7

Consolidated statements of changes in financial position

The Upjohn Company and subsidiaries (dollar amounts in thousands)

For the years ended December 31	1987	1986	1985
Cash provided by continuing operations	**$444,438**	$307,023	$253,937
Capital investment activities provided (required)			
Property, plant and equipment additions	**(211,976)**	(201,920)	(152,637)
Property, plant and equipment retired	**16,462**	6,861	3,974
Currency translation adjustments, net	**(32,547)**	(15,506)	(11,918)
Other noncurrent assets acquired	**(18,156)**	(20,367)	
Construction funds held by trustee		7,171	15,378
	(246,217)	(223,761)	(145,203)
Financing activities provided (required)			
(Increase) decrease in investments	**(714)**	16,295	34,099
(Decrease) increase in short-term debt	**(33,897)**	2,301	(121,533)
Long-term borrowing	**14,247**	200,865	4,405
Reduction of long-term debt	**(1,463)**	(154,657)	(9,160)
Purchase of treasury stock	**(34,750)**		
Other financing activities	**21,695**	15,301	22,124
	(34,882)	80,105	(70,065)
Dividends paid to shareholders	**(108,211)**	(92,639)	(80,765)
Cash (required) provided by discontinued operations	**(11,974)**	(9,218)	144,973
Currency translation adjustments	**37,719**	4,829	2,119
Increase in cash and cash items	**80,873**	66,339	104,996
Cash and cash items, beginning of year	**212,154**	145,815	40,819
Cash and cash items, end of year	**$293,027**	$212,154	$145,815
Cash provided (required) by continuing operations			
Earnings from continuing operations	**$305,039**	$252,646	$203,193
Items not requiring cash			
Depreciation and amortization	**96,040**	81,828	69,566
Deferred income taxes	**27,383**	41,697	22,334
Other	**2,477**	(2,430)	(6,134)
Changes in			
Accounts receivable	**(76,610)**	(104,120)	(53,632)
Inventories	**(36,662)**	14,542	(34,806)
Other current assets	**(7,612)**	31,452	(28,090)
Other assets	**(14,185)**	(47,886)	(19,910)
Payables and accruals	**68,047**	49,681	61,146
Income taxes payable	**77,525**	(14,597)	40,314
Other	**2,996**	4,210	(44)
Cash provided by continuing operations	**$444,438**	$307,023	$253,937

BCI HOLDINGS CORPORATION (FORMERLY BEATRICE COMPANIES INC.)

In June 1984 Beatrice Companies Inc. acquired Esmark, Inc., a food and consumer products conglomerate. Beatrice, the Chicago-based food industry giant was going through a business reorganization, and the acquisition of Esmark was seen as part of the process. Beatrice's performance had declined during the late 1970s, and its suboptimal performance record continued into the 1980s. The business reorganization plan was intended to reverse the trend. The chief executive officer, James Dutt, was optimistic about the synergies that could be reaped from the acquisition of Esmark's new businesses. However, Beatrice's future seemed uncertain, for the rationale behind the new acquisitions was unclear to many observers. Would Dutt's dream of Beatrice as "the world's premier marketer of food and consumer products" materialize?[1] Or would the company turn out to be just another "acquisition junkie," as some analysts believed?

BEATRICE FOODS: ORIGINS

Beatrice Foods Company, was founded as a partnership between George E. Haskell and William W. Bosworth in 1894 in Beatrice, Nebraska, when both

This case was prepared by Gareth R. Jones and Rao Kowtha, Department of Management, Texas A & M University.

[1] Jo Ellen Daily, "Beatrice: An Acquisition Junkie Gets the Shakes," *Business Week,* June 3, 1985, p. 91.

men found themselves jobless after their employer, the Fremont Butter and Egg Company, went bankrupt. Haskell and Bosworth purchased the Beatrice branch of the defunct company and also leased the plant of the Beatrice Creamery Company. They then began buying farm butter, eggs, and poultry and grading and shipping them to local food stores. Business prospered, and soon the company found itself shipping carloads of dairy produce to such distant markets as Boston, New York, and San Francisco. In 1898 the Beatrice Creamery Company was officially incorporated in Nebraska, with a capital of $100,000. Later Bosworth resigned from the company and opened his own business in Beatrice.

Haskell soon recognized the potential economies of scale in developing a regional dairy products business. Under his leadership, Beatrice pioneered the operation and financing of large-scale cream separators in the Prairie States. Its program of cream collection from farmers and a centrally located quality-controlled churning operation soon formed the backbone of the butter industry in the West. Beatrice grew steadily over the years, widening its collection and distribution networks, and to keep pace with the growth of business in the East, the company's general offices were moved to Chicago. In 1924 the company was reincorporated and licensed as a Delaware corporation, with headquarters in Chicago. Clinton E. Haskell, a nephew of the founder, who was elected president in 1928, was the driving force behind the diversified growth of Beatrice Foods in the years to come.

Dairy products were the core business of Beatrice throughout the early years, and the brand name Meadow Gold was used to market all the company's products. To help maintain its industry leadership, Beatrice in 1936 opened a research and new product department and a central quality control laboratory. In 1945 a sanitation program, to ensure plant cleanliness, was instituted throughout Beatrice. When its distribution networks increased, the company also developed extensive cold storage operations to preserve the quality of its products. This ensured its continuing good reputation.

GROWTH IN BEATRICE: 1945–1979

Beatrice's strengths in dairy food production, distribution, and storage provided the company with the skills and expertise to expand its business into new kinds of food products. As a result, Beatrice engaged in a diversification and expansion program, adding to its family new companies producing specialty foods. It placed particular emphasis on food products with a high sales growth potential, such as candy, pickles, and convenience and snack foods. La Choy Food Products, a pioneer in the production of American-Chinese foods, was one of the first companies Beatrice acquired. It was followed by D. L. Clark Co., Leaf, Inc. (maker of Milk Duds), Fisher Nuts Company, and a host of other convenience food companies. These companies were separated from the dairy products operations and organized into the Grocery Division in 1957, to specialize in the production and marketing of convenience foods.

In 1968 the company began developing its Institutional Foods Division with the acquisition of John Sexton & Co., a leading food processor and distributor primarily engaged in selling food and other supplies to hospitals and restaurants. Other acquisitions followed. Peter Eckrich & Sons, Inc., a specialty meat producer was acquired in 1972, and the Specialty Meats Division was thus formed. The division also included Lowrey's Meat Specialties, Inc., Rudolph Foods Company, and County Line Cheese Co., Inc. Meanwhile, the Dairy Products Division continued to expand into such products as yogurt and low-fat dairy foods with the acquisition of Dannon Yogurt (in 1959), and into soft drinks with the acquisition of the Royal Crown Cola Co. bottling operations. The latter acquisition formed the basis of Beatrice's Soft Drinks Division. The central idea that drove Beatrice through these years was growth by the acquisition of food and beverage companies.

The next major step for the company was overseas expansion, when Beatrice realized the potential for applying its strengths in foreign markets. Overseas operations, which started with Beatrice Foods (Malaysia) Ltd. in 1961, were expanded to 28 countries. By 1977 the company owned or had substantial interests in 185 overseas plants and branches. Beatrice's international operations produced dairy foods or candy in every continent except Africa; in Africa the company distributed dairy products. The growth in international operations was realized through a variety of strategies. Beatrice both acquired overseas companies and established its own foreign operations, depending on conditions in the local market and their potential for growth. For example, its entry and subsequent growth in Europe came from acquisitions, as well as from start-ups. Beatrice's management strove to keep up with changing tastes at home and abroad. Generous capital expenditures were common in international operations to build, expand, or modernize new or acquired facilities. The International Division became one of the most profitable for the company, with total sales exceeding $1.1 billion by 1977.

In 1964 a new era started for Beatrice. The company began to diversify into products and businesses outside the food industry, selecting acquisitions according to their sales and earnings growth potential. One of the first such ventures was in the agricultural products business. Sensing the growing demand for protein and leather, Beatrice bought various agricultural product operations and steadily expanded to a total of fifty plants. These plants handled hides, tanned leather, processed animal oils, and inedible tallow, operated wool pulleries, and produced animal protein, feed, and feed supplements.

The company soon entered the consumer goods, chemicals, and financial businesses. For example, in 1973 it acquired Samsonite Corporation, the luggage company, as well as the Southwestern Investment company (SIC), which specialized in consumer and commercial finance. In the chemicals industry, Beatrice bought specialty chemical companies, whose products included high-quality finishes for leathers (Stahl brand); vinyls and textiles (Permuthane); and paper coating and inks, high-performance metal lubricants, and paint and powder coatings (Fiberite). Many other acquisitions followed, such as Stiffel lamps, furniture, and mobile home companies.

By 1973 Beatrice had assumed a divisional form to manage its food and nonfood operations. Besides the five food divisions, Beatrice's new acquisitions were separated into five new divisions: Consumer Products, Institutional and Industrial Products, Luggage and Home Environment Products, Consumer Arts, and Leisure Products.

Beatrice, which had entered the cold storage warehouse business at the turn of the century, expanded those operations. By 1973 the company operated twenty-five cold storage facilities across the country and completed a computerized food distribution center in the Chicago warehouse. Most of these warehouses stored the company's perishable products.

By 1979 net corporate sales reached $7.5 billion, and net earnings stood at $261 million. However, even though Beatrice had steady growth in earnings, the stock market's interest in conglomerates was waning. Beatrice needed to plan its future strategy in order to consolidate its future growth.

DUTT'S REIGN AT BEATRICE

When James Dutt became chief executive officer of Beatrice in 1979, he took over a conglomerate that needed trimming. His mission was to turn Beatrice into a leader in the consumer product and food industries and to improve corporate profitability. His goal was to achieve an 18-percent return on equity. He made his first move by selling off the finance and insurance businesses of SIC for $73 million, arguing that these businesses did not fit in with Beatrice's growth plans.

Next, Dutt aggressively sought to improve Beatrice's market image. During the annual stockholders' meeting in June 1982, he announced his five-year objectives for the company. The Annual Report read: "A key step toward fulfilling the 18 percent return on equity objective is to achieve an annual growth rate of 5 percent, and to increase net earnings by 16 percent per year. To do so, management has identified [key business] segments of the company and will allocate the necessary funds . . . to achieve their full growth potential. A commitment to real growth also means an emphasis on brand marketing. That means among other things, stepping up advertising efforts . . . to continue emphasizing product improvement and innovation."[2] Dutt particularly emphasized diversification, market leadership, and community responsibility. He also stressed export activity and was going to expand overseas operations. A joint venture trading company was opened in Dubai to serve as a conduit for Beatrice products throughout the Persian Gulf area. In addition, joint ventures in Nigeria and the People's Republic of China were being negotiated.

To achieve these goals, Dutt instituted a vigorous asset redeployment program, which resulted in the sale of fifty-six companies, representing about

---

[2]Beatrice Foods Company *Annual Report*, (1981), 6–7.

$1 billion in annual sales. Prominent among these divestitures were Dannon Yogurt and the Royal Crown Cola bottling operations. The initial divestment was followed by the acquisition of a number of small companies. The rationale behind the redeployment effort was to seek acquisitions that would generate returns higher than the corporate average and to divest those businesses that were not producing a return on net assets equal to or in excess of 20 percent. The Dannon divestiture was an example of this policy. Dannon, acquired by Beatrice in 1959, had been a consistent performer until the late 1970s. It enjoyed a 30-percent market share and had net sales of $130 million in 1981. However, management believed that yogurt was a mature product and that even though yogurt appeared related to dairy products, synergies had never been realized.[3] Besides, Dannon's net earnings stood at a mere $3.5 million for 1981, a figure below the desired level of 20 percent ROA. The unit was sold to BSN-Gervais-Dannon for $384 million in 1982.

Some chronic poor performers were left untouched by the divestiture and consolidation campaign, however. John Sexton & Co., for example, could not have reached the return on assets goal even if its current return doubled. The business was retained because the management felt that it was a business "we should be in."[4] This lack of a coherent strategy for managing the corporate portfolio led to a lack of confidence on the part of the stock market. Consequently, when the company paid Northwest Industries, Inc., $580 million for the Coca-Cola Bottling Co. of Los Angeles in January 1982, the investment community did not react too favorably. Despite stout assertions by company officials that these actions were aimed at the long run and that the acquisition fitted well with Beatrice's strategy, many wondered what that strategy was and felt that the price paid, at twenty-two times earnings, was outrageous. Commented an analyst with a leading securities dealer: "Money put into Beatrice stock now is simply going to be dead in the water."[5] To aggravate the situation, earnings for the first quarter, ending on May 31 of that year fell by 7.5 percent—the first such decline in thirty years.

The stock market's skepticism notwithstanding, Beatrice maintained its operating ROE at 14.6 percent for fiscal 1982, and earnings rose by 9 percent. However, the Dairy Products Division—the original business—was experiencing a steady decrease in sales and earnings because consumer consumption of nondairy beverages and products had overtaken the consumption of milk and cheese. Although sales from this division had contributed 34 percent to total corporate sales in 1969, the division contributed only 24 percent by 1982. This downward trend was expected to continue. On the other hand, ethnic and convenience food businesses and the International Food Division were posting significant gains in sales and earnings.

Two other units experiencing problems were Samsonite and Tropicana. Samsonite had been hit by the overall decline in travel due to the oil crisis and

---

[3]Darry G. Kinker, "The Dannon Decision," Case Clearing Association, 1982.
[4]"The Bigness Cult's Grip on Beatrice Foods," *Fortune*, September 20, 1982, p. 124.
[5]"The Bigness Cult's Grip on Beatrice Foods," pp. 122–129.

by an increase in competition from cheaper foreign products. Tropicana, an orange juice producer acquired in 1979 for $490 million, was affected by a freeze in Florida during the previous winter that limited the supply of oranges. The inept efforts of the company to cope with the shortage of fresh juice exposed a major chink in the Beatrice armor. Juice from concentrate was substituted for fresh juice without any discernible phrasing on the carton to inform buyers of the change. The action cost Tropicana substantially in sales and reputation. The matter was of no small concern because fruit juice sales contributed 4.8 percent of Beatrice's total sales volume. Beatrice, it seemed, simply did not have the marketing savvy of its major competitors such as General Foods.

Marketing Problems at Beatrice

Some of the better-known Beatrice brands are Samsonite luggage, Clark candy bars and Eckrich meats. However, most businesses concentrated on regional marketing, and few brands enjoyed national recognition. The name Beatrice itself did not elicit consumer awareness, even though individual brands were well known in their regions and markets. The principal reason for this obscurity was that, unlike most other conglomerates, Beatrice did not have a corporate marketing department. Beatrice was never too well known for its marketing prowess, and Dutt recognized this weakness. He began aggressive marketing programs to stress brand leadership and geographic coverage throughout Beatrice's businesses. As a first step, individual businesses were directed to expand their market coverage. For example, during 1982 Eckrich Meats expanded to Southwestern markets; the Arizona-based Rosarita Foods, which produced Mexican foods, moved into the Eastern markets; and Tropicana increased its distribution to the West Coast. These tactics paid dividends. For example, Eckrich generated 42 percent of its sales for 1982 from areas outside its original Midwest base.

During 1983 Beatrice charted a new plan for its marketing endeavors: to transform itself into a unified, directed marketing company with the ability to penetrate new markets. Advertising to create a unified corporate identity was also on Dutt's agenda. Beatrice traditionally had spent much less than its smaller competitors on advertising. For example, in 1981 advertising expenditures totaled $201 million, which was less than half of what General Foods, a slightly smaller company, spent.

Despite these efforts by Dutt to provide a new marketing identity for Beatrice in order to generate increased sales and revenues across Beatrice's individual food companies, profits continued to show a downward trend. Fiscal 1983 earnings hit an all-time low of $43 million, or 27 cents per share. It seemed that increasing marketing was not enough to improve corporate profitability—that the real problem lay with the company's portfolio of investments. Dutt began to examine the diverse collection of businesses that Beatrice had assembled and to evaluate the way corporate headquarters managed its businesses.

What he found led him to realize that the time for a major overhaul at Beatrice had arrived.

IMPLEMENTING AND MANAGING CHANGE AT BEATRICE

Traditionally, Beatrice had practiced the philosophy of decentralized management, treating each individual business as an autonomous profit center. Only two levels of management stood between a profit center and corporate headquarters, the divisional level and the business-group level, and they similarly took a hands-off approach to interfering in the affairs of each business. Both business-group and corporate-level management performed mainly a portfolio-planning role. As a result, corporate headquarters was staffed with only 300 employees, while more than 100,000 people worked for the company worldwide.

Business-level and operating-strategy decisions were made at the profit center management level. Marketing, purchasing, and production decisions were largely left to the discretion of managers in the individual businesses. These decisions typically included choices concerning personnel, product mix, pricing of products, and markets.

A significant portion of executive compensation at all levels was predicated upon the profit contributions of their businesses. Incentives included stock option plans for all salaried employees of the corporation and performance plans for executives. Executives who met their predetermined performance goals were awarded control over a profit center. The performance of a profit center was tied to overall corporate performance over a three-year period and the corporation's stock price at the end of that period.

Top management firmly believed that this decentralized management style provided the company with a sound and continuing executive development system. Beatrice made little effort to integrate individual business units and build a corporate culture. The company was built from one acquisition to the next, and new businesses that were not used to operating autonomously were quickly indoctrinated into the Beatrice way. The decentralized management style allowed Beatrice to acquire companies quickly, but it did not provide any means by which business units could trade information or knowledge in order to improve corporate profitability.

However, Dutt realized that the diversified growth of the corporation rendered its highly autonomous operating philosophy increasingly unviable. The corporate center was unable to shape any corporate strategy when its businesses were so loosely organized. As a first step in solving this problem, Dutt changed the organization structure used to manage Beatrice's diverse operations. Beatrice's 435 individual profit centers (operating companies) were consolidated into 27 larger, free-standing divisions according to the product markets served by the businesses. Then 6 business groups were created from the 27 individual divisions according to the type of business or industry they were in (Exhibit 1).[5] Divisional managers were made directly responsible to business group managers, who were in turn responsible to corporate managers.

As a result of these changes, businesses inside a division, and divisions inside a group could now share common marketing and distribution channels. The overall thrust for marketing was provided by the Office of the Chairman, headed by Dutt. Group-level managers — each was a senior vice president of the company — were charged with the planning and execution of groupwide business strategies in task forces and teams and were directly responsible to the Office of the Chairman.

The aim behind the reorganization was to allow divisions inside each business group to share resources and trade on each other's marketing knowledge. It also gave group and corporate management more control over divisional performance. While operating decisions were still within the local manager's realm, corporate direction and guidance as to product development and marketing strategies increased. Moreover, control was centralized at corporate headquarters to improve integration among groups and reduce costs. In particular, the centralization process was intended to streamline functions such as purchasing, production, and marketing. For example, the number of advertising agencies the company used was cut from more than 100 to fewer than 10 worldwide firms. The consolidation was undertaken to ensure greater economies in advertising.

Group Structures and Strategies

Beatrice's six operating groups and the divisions inside the groups are discussed below, together with problems confronting the divisions. A summary of the sales and earnings of each group is presented in Exhibits 2 and 3.

Refrigerated Foods   The Refrigerated Foods and Services Group followed the strategy of acquiring strong regional food companies and then giving their products national distribution after acquisition. One of the main problems for the group centered on the price of milk, the basic ingredient used in Beatrice's dairy products. The price paid for raw milk is controlled by Federal Milk Market Orders or state regulatory agencies. These orders and agencies establish the minimum price to be paid for milk. During the 1980s milk lost much of its popularity owing to the increasingly health-conscious consumer market. This decline in demand was to some extent mitigated by the introduction of low-fat milk products (Beatrice introduced low-fat yogurt and other milk products under the name brand Viva after selling Dannon). Although milk had made a comeback in 1983 and 1984 with a 2-percent jump in consumption, sales projections for dairy products were not encouraging. Dairy sales continued to decline

[5]Beatrice Foods Company, Form 10-K Annual Report (1984), p. 74.

EXHIBIT 1   **Beatrice Company's organization — 1984**

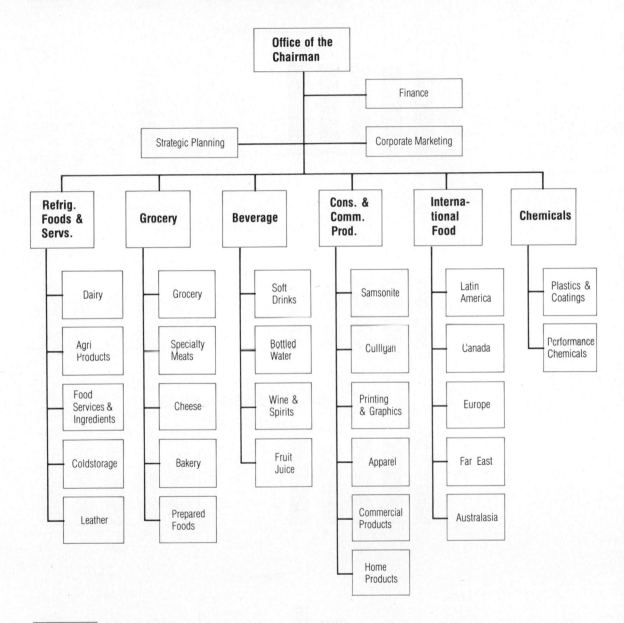

EXHIBIT 2   **Five-year sales and earnings summary (in millions of dollars)**

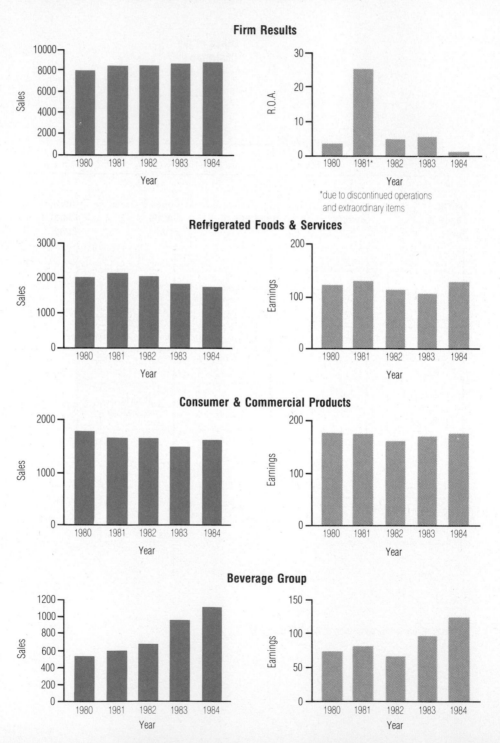

EXHIBIT 2   **Five-year sales and earnings summary (*cont.*)**

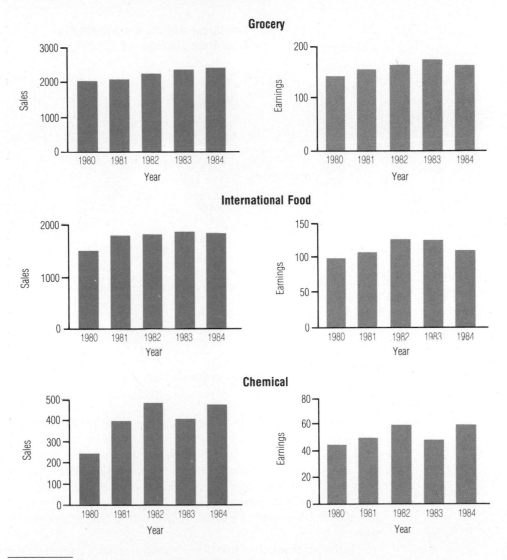

through 1984 as the whole industry struggled to recover from the losses inflicted by a declining demand and surplus raw milk due to the government milk distribution program. Beatrice announced that the Dairy Division would be concentrating on improving productivity and efficiency in the future. The aim was to become a low-cost producer for selected segments of the market. At the same time premium brands such as Louis Sherry ice cream and Swiss Miss chocolate milk were continued.

EXHIBIT 3   **Sales and earnings contributions of segments—1984**

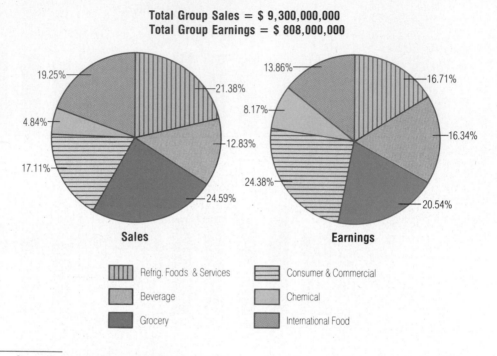

Source: Reprinted by permission of Beatrice Company.

Beverage Group   With Tropicana spearheading its competitive efforts, the fruit juice division had been marketing an extensive line of citrus and other fruit products. The Soft Drinks Division, through wholly owned subsidiaries, bottled and distributed brands such as Coca-Cola, Diet Coke, Dr Pepper and Sprite. The Bottled Water Division consisted of Arrowhead Puritas Waters Inc. and the Great Bear Spring Company. The Wine and Spirits Division markets and distributes imported liquor brands such as Cutty Sark scotch and Marquisat wines.

Lifestyle changes in the 1980s brought about a decline in caffeine consumption and an increase in the consumption of fruit juices. Some industry analysts predicted that the fruit juice market was ready to replace soft drinks and become the trend of the day. However, competition was stiff, with a number of companies, including Procter & Gamble's Citrus Hill brand and Coca-Cola's Minute Maid brand, introducing new fruit juice products.

The soft drinks industry was also hit by the changing demographics as the baby boomers grew older. The industry depended on the under–thirty-five age group for its sales. During the 1980s, however, the number of those between the ages of thirty-five and thirty-nine was expected to increase by 41 percent and the number of those aged forty to forty-four by 50 percent. Caffeine-free and low-sodium versions of soft drinks proliferated, to cater to consumers' changing tastes. Diet soft drinks made up about 21.6 percent of the soft drink industry sales in 1983, estimated at $14.8 billion.[6]

Tropicana, sensing the impending changes and intense competition in the juice market, redesigned its entire product line in 1983. The packaging was changed to make the name Tropicana easily identifiable. Tropicana enjoyed strong popularity with consumers as the only major ready-to-serve orange juice. It had a higher juice content and was positioned in the market as a premium brand. These factors, combined with a renewed focus on marketing, allowed Tropicana to maintain its industry leader status in 1984.

Grocery   The Grocery group consisted of five divisions: Grocery, Prepared Foods, Specialty Meats, Cheese, and Bakery. Grocery was the most visible part of Beatrice, with more than 2,000 products commonly found on the supermarket shelves. The division marketed canned vegetables and sauces, pet foods, frozen foods, and snacks. In addition, it had undertaken a cooperative program with the Dairy Division to market the Swiss Miss chocolate milk. The division concentrated on expanding market share and improving distribution. The pet foods business was doing well with Bonkers, a cat food holding a 30-percent market share.

Prepared Foods had traditionally been involved in the ethnic and packaged foods industry. During the 1980s, its presence in the ethnic food segment expanded. To leverage the division's strengths, all Mexican food lines were consolidated under the brand name of Rosarita, and the product line was expanded to include a variety of sauces. La Choy, the leader in oriental foods, continued to market aggressively and expand its volume.

The stress on ethnic foods could not have come at a more opportune moment. As American consumers began demanding less red meat and more variety in their meals, the popularity of ethnic food surged. However, competition kept increasing, with new brands arriving on the scene. Oriental foods, stagnant for a decade or so, were growing once again in popularity. Innovations such as rice crackers, rice chips, and dinners helped sales significantly. Rosarita, for its part, introduced a line of entrées and dinners in the Mexican food market in recent years. Even in the canned meat and specialty foods segment, Italian, Mexican, and Oriental dishes posted strong gains, with a total of $675 million supermarket sales in 1984.

Eckrich, the flagship brand of the Specialty Meats Division, revitalized its marketing and distribution networks. The intent was to expand a strong Midwestern presence to a nationally distributed brand. However, this business has been experiencing a flat sales volume as the consumption of beef has declined.

The Cheese Division, whose three companies had been brought under a more unified management during the reorganization, has been struggling to

---

[6]"Beverages jump 1.3% to all-time high," *Beverage Industry* (September 1985), 4.

maintain its market share. It faced strong competition from brands such as Treasure Cave and Kraft. New product lines, including shredded natural cheese and flavored cream cheese, were introduced under the County Line brand in 1984. Government surplus distribution programs for cheese products led to a decline in sales. The Bakery Division, which produces cookies, bread, and snack foods also had intense competition—from industry giants like Frito-Lay. The Grocery group, as a whole, emphasized increased market share and sales volume.

Consumer Products   Beatrice put out a broad range of products for consumer and commercial use, including Samsonite luggage, the leader in the $1.4 billion luggage industry; Samsonite furniture; Stiffel lamps, Taylor slush and milk shake machines, and Culligan water treatment services. Exhibit 4 presents the group's structure.

Samsonite found smooth sailing in the international waters since its first overseas expansion in the early 1970s. By 1984, 50 percent of the company's sales came from its international operations. Sales volume of luggage was heavily dependent on the travel conditions and airline baggage restrictions. For example, a new FAA restriction on the allowable volume of carry-on luggage, as well as growth in the business travel segment, spurred the company to develop soft-side and wrinkle-free pieces with greater capacity. It has continued to

EXHIBIT 4   **Consumer & Commercial Products Group**

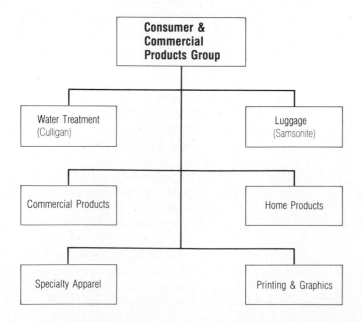

Source: Reprinted by permission of Beatrice Company.

introduce new product ranges and markets luggage products from tote bags to trunks.

Culligan has been doing well by catering to the industrial and residential water treatment markets. Substantial expenditures on product development and marketing slowed the growth of earnings but provided the unit with a strong identity. The Home Products Division includes furniture, Del Mar window coverings, Aristokraft cabinets and Stiffel lamps, companies that have capitalized on the growing home improvement products market. The Commercial Products and Printing & Graphics divisions are in relatively stable industries and enjoy a steady flow of earnings. The group's focus for the 1980s was defined as market penetration and geographic expansion.

International Food   The International Food group has been a profitable performer for the corporation ever since its first foray into the field in 1961. The group is organized into five world regions. Inside each region, businesses are grouped into distinct business areas. For example, the subsidiaries of the European division (the largest) have been grouped as: snacks and confectionery, processed meats, soft drinks and fruit juices, and ice cream and dairy products. The structure has enabled the company to monitor its far-flung operations effectively and to identify market trends on a geographical and product basis. International units are usually managed by resident nationals, who are given great autonomy in their operations, since competition varies from continent to continent and country to country. For example, Beatrice faced substantial competition in Australia, whereas in Latin American countries, its brands were the market leaders and experienced continuous growth and product development. These regions, with their increasing affluence and huge populations, provide fertile growth opportunities.

Beatrice's international operations account for nearly 20 percent of its total sales. New opportunities are opening up in Far Eastern countries such as China. However, the group's earnings are subject to currency fluctuations, which can hurt performance. For example, the troubled economies of Brazil and Venezuela hurt the dollar earnings of the division in 1984, and the decline in the value of the dollar has hurt the group's operating profits.

Chemicals   Fiberite, the market leader in composite materials, continued to experience increased demand from the aerospace industry as the national defense budget swelled. Growth in electronic, business machine, and appliance markets also fueled the demand for Fiberite, and demand is likely to remain stable over the next few years. Performance Chemicals, which included Stahl leather and Permuthane Polymers, also experienced strong demand. The Performance Chemicals Division expanded its distribution to Europe during 1983–1984 and started a joint venture with Mitsubishi Chemical Industries Ltd. in Japan. The group cultivates a well-established set of customers and focuses on research and development activities to continue its strong sales and earnings trend.

BEATRICE'S NEW FACE

According to Dutt, the restructuring of Beatrice in 1984 enabled the company to identify the units that did not fit in with the long-range plans. The company continued to manage the Dairy Division for cash flows and proceeded with the business realignment program through 1984. Reorganization centered on concentrating on the food and consumer products businesses while retaining profitable unrelated businesses. John Sexton & Co. was finally sold off that year. For the first time in the company's history, the management decided to get rid of businesses that were poor fits with the traditional food and consumer product businesses. Increased focus on food businesses was evident as Beatrice sought to realign its portfolio for the future. However, corporate performance continued to decline, and return on investment goals was not being met. In an effort to improve performance, Beatrice once again turned to the acquisition path.

THE ESMARK ACQUISITION

Esmark, Inc., was another company that had grown by diversification outside its core food business during the 1970s. It had net earnings of $107 million in 1982 against total revenues of over $3 billion.[7] Among its well-known products are Swift processed meats and foods, Playtex apparel, Danskin knitwear, and Jhirmack shampoo.

The Swift group consisted of the company's original food processing and marketing businesses. The processed meats and poultry division was the largest business in the group. It supplied its products to both the consumer market and the food service industry. Swift Cheese/Frozen Desserts Division sold a wide variety of cheeses and ice creams. The Dry Grocery Division marketed Peter Pan peanut butter, pet foods, and assorted commodities.

However, Playtex Inc., headquartered in Stamford, Connecticut, was the most consistently profitable unit of the corporation. With an expansive product line of intimate apparel, hosiery, and family products, Playtex operated in seventeen countries and exported to an additional twenty-six countries. In 1982 its earnings exceeded $100 million against revenues of $784 million. The dynamic head of Playtex, Joel Smilow, had been described by *Fortune* magazine as one of the ten toughest bosses in America. Smilow came to Playtex in 1965, from Procter & Gamble, where he had earned a reputation as a marketing genius.

In 1983 Esmark acquired Norton Simon Inc., another conglomerate. With Norton Simon (NSI) came new businesses such as Avis, Inc., Halston Enterprises, Inc., Max Factor & Company, Somerset Group, Inc. and Hunt-Wesson Foods, Inc. Avis is one of the leading companies in the passenger car rental

---

[7]Esmark, Inc., Form 10-K Annual Report (1983), 17.

business. Max Factor was a leading manufacturer of beauty products; Halston was engaged in the fashion clothing business. After the acquisition, the Hunt-Wesson grocery line was combined with the Swift group to achieve marketing synergies. Hunt-Wesson marketed nationally recognized brands of tomato products and cooking oil. Somerset Importers was a nationwide distributor of imported distilled spirits. The company also distilled and distributed bourbon whiskies.

Esmark was one of the most profitable companies in the food industry, and its return on equity had averaged above 25 percent for over a decade. Its operating philosophy was somewhat similar to Beatrice's. Decentralized divisions made business-level operating decisions while corporate managers looked after the broader policy matters and long-range business planning. However, Esmark was different from Beatrice in that close and constant attention was paid to the performance of each operating division. Donald Kelly, the highly respected chief executive of Esmark, managed the company like an investment portfolio. The units that were not performing up to expectations within planning horizons were quickly divested. For example, the entire Energy segment of Esmark (Vickers Petroleum Corp.) was divested in 1980, and a substantial portion of the food business (Canadian operations and Swift Independent Packing Co.) was disposed of in 1981, when its performance declined. This approach contrasted with that at Beatrice, where often years passed before an unprofitable division or business was divested.

With the acquisition of Norton Simon, the size of Esmark assets doubled to $2 billion while long-term debt increased by more than $1.5 billion. In early 1984 the market was rife with rumors that Esmark would be bidding for Beatrice too. However, as it turned out, Beatrice acquired Esmark in June of that year.

Beatrice bought Esmark for $2.8 billion. In justifying the purchase Beatrice pointed to the synergies that could be reaped from this related acquisition. For example, Esmark had a large nationwide marketing network that would serve as a channel for Beatrice's products. It would also bolster Beatrice's marketing efforts at the corporate level and provide synergies across businesses. Additionally, since Esmark was involved in many closely related products and markets, the acquisition would save the high costs and risks associated with developing new products internally. Esmark's national brands would provide Beatrice with many advantages.

Beatrice executives hailed the acquisition of Esmark as critical to the company's efforts to develop strong national brands and distribution capabilities. They felt that Esmark could be easily integrated into an already streamlined Beatrice organization that had been busy selling off assets. The "New Beatrice" would have a vast marketing clout with the addition of Esmark's marketing force. For example, Beatrice's largely regional domestic food business stood to gain from Hunt-Wesson's topnotch 500-member sales organization, with its state-of-the-art inventory system. In addition, Hunt-Wesson's 16 distribution centers were to complement the network of Beatrice food brokers.

While the Swift and Hunt-Wesson divisions of Esmark fit in with the food business of Beatrice, Dutt justified the presence of Playtex and Avis on the grounds of their contribution to Beatrice's overall portfolio and their fit with Beatrice's other businesses. For example, the Consumer Products group would benefit from the addition of another strong performer in Playtex. Avis, Dutt said, gave the company the opportunity to participate in special ventures that represent either good growth potential or synergies with other units.[8] Meanwhile, the international business of Avis and Playtex would benefit and strengthen the International Division. However, Beatrice was buying businesses in which it had no previous management experience and in which marketing, one of Beatrice's traditional weaknesses, was of paramount importance.

The euphoria surrounding the Esmark acquisition served to hide the debt problems of Beatrice for some time. The debt-to-equity ratio of Beatrice was already one of the highest in the industry at 49 percent in 1984. The acquisition of Esmark in June 1984, when the company had to absorb Esmark's debt load of $900 million, more than quadrupled the ratio, to 199 percent by the end of fiscal 1985. Total debt exceeded $4 billion, which Beatrice hoped to reduce by future divestitures. Bankers who financed the merger were convinced at one point that Beatrice could service its debt, even though the annual interest payments of $480 million exceeded the company's 1984 earnings.

Combining the Operations

The acquisition of Esmark prompted another restructuring move. Beatrice was now the largest food marketer in the United States, with expected annual sales of over $13 billion. The task of integrating three major food and consumer goods companies brought about a new need for reorganization. It led to conflict, as the managers in both companies sought to control important operating divisions to preserve their position in the new company. The company was reorganized into four major business segments: U.S. Food, Consumer Products, International Food, and Avis/Other Operations (Exhibit 5).

U.S. Food consisted of the Beverage, Soft Drinks, Grocery, and Refrigerated Food groups. The new Beverage group, headed by John Attwood, (president of the Beatrice Soft Drinks Division) combined bottled water, dairy, soft drink, agricultural products, and warehouse businesses. Dry Grocery combined Hunt's tomato products, Orville Reddenbacher's popcorn, Peter Pan peanut butter and Wesson Oil (all ex-Esmark) with Fisher Nuts, La Choy, Rosarita, and Martha White (Beatrice). The Refrigerated Food Group was composed of Esmark's Swift poultry, processed meats and cheese divisions, as well as Beatrice's cheese products, Eckrich Meats, and Tropicana juices. The Consumer Products group, with Smilow as its president, was further divided into Personal Products and Consumer Durables. Personal Products included the Playtex line and other Esmark brands, while the Consumer Durables group kept Beatrice

[8]Beatrice Companies Inc., Form 10-K Annual Report (1985), p. 22.

EXHIBIT 5   **Beatrice Company's organization — November 1985**

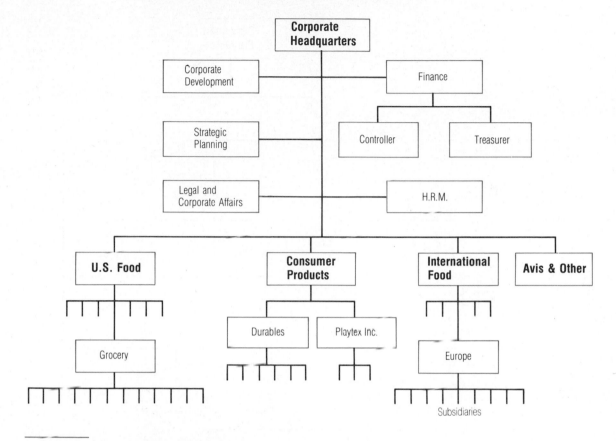

Source: Reprinted by permission of Beatrice Company.

lines such as Samsonite, Culligan, and Stiffel. This is shown in Exhibit 6. Avis, the second largest car rental company in the United States and leader abroad, formed one separate group. The International Food group was largely left untouched.

The Chemicals group was entirely divested during fiscal 1985. Other non-food interests soon followed Chemicals. Wine and spirits, food equipment, foundry, agriproducts, graphic arts, specialty apparel, and cryogenic businesses were all sold off along with the Chemicals group for a total of $1.4 billion. Corporate debt was reduced by approximately $1.3 billion using the proceeds from the sale, bringing down the debt-to-equity ratio to 161 percent in March 1985.[9] The company announced that more debt would be retired over the next two years through income from divestitures.

[9]Beatrice Companies Inc., Prospectus, Special Meeting of Stockholders, March 11, 1986, p. F-46.

EXHIBIT 6   **Consumer products group**

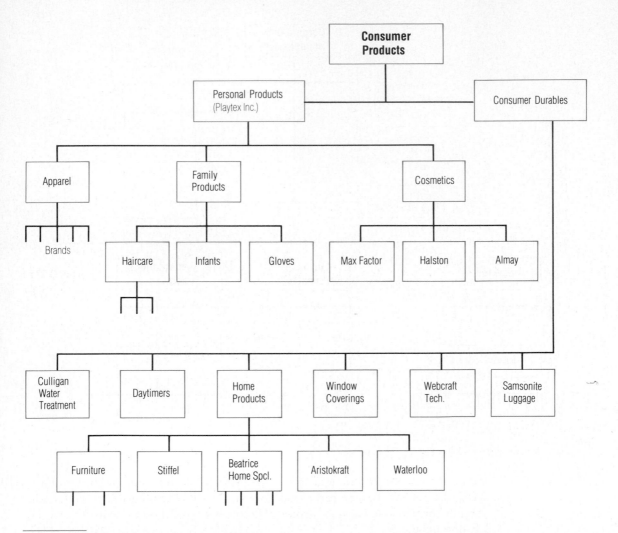

Source: Reprinted by permission of Beatrice Company.

Meanwhile, the stock market reacted sharply to the merger. After the Esmark acquisition, Beatrice shares fell to $25 and were trading at nine times the earnings versus eleven times the earnings for industry stars such as Nabisco Brands, Inc., and Kellogg. Beatrice securities were downgraded to 'A' from 'AA' by the Standard & Poor's Index. Industry analysts commented that Beatrice turns out to be a new company every five years and felt that the market had lost faith in the company's ability to reorganize itself. Many thought that it was not Dutt's strategic vision that prompted the acquisition of Esmark but ego.

Earlier in 1984 Esmark was found to have bought 1.5 percent of Beatrice shares. This led to the perception that Dutt was getting back at Kelly for his attempt to take over Beatrice while at the same time the Esmark takeover neutralized future takeover threats due to Beatrice's huge debt burden.

Management Changes at Beatrice

The company witnessed attrition in the ranks as Dutt grew increasingly impatient and intolerant of dissent over the next few years, when Beatrice's performance failed to improve. In three years La Choy Foods and Tropicana had three presidents each. Of the fifty-eight top corporate officers at the end of fiscal 1980, thirty-seven left the company by 1985. When Esmark's executives started to resign from Beatrice, the situation worsened further, for they were the experts in how to run Beatrice's new businesses. The first casualty was Frederick B. Rentschler, the head of Swift/Hunt-Wesson Foods, which accounted for $1.6 billion of Esmark's $4-billion annual sales. Smilow of Playtex stayed on as the CEO of the Consumer Products group for four months, before quitting in November 1984. Walter Bregman, who succeeded Smilow at Playtex, was forced out in March 1985.

Dutt was still supported and admired by many of Beatrice's directors. However, the Esmark acquisition spelled the end of Dutt's reign. The price of Beatrice stock plummeted when the promised synergies proved to be elusive. Matters came to a head when Senior Vice President Nolan Archibald, a Beatrice veteran and a respected manager, left the company in July 1985 amid a dispute with Dutt.[10] Dutt resigned in early August and was succeeded by William Granger, the former vice chairman brought out of retirement.

THE LEVERAGED BUYOUT

Granger's tenure as the chairman and chief executive of Beatrice was short. Net earnings were low because of lingering merger expenses and the strong performance of the dollar abroad. The debt-to-equity ratio still stood at a staggering 108 percent. To reduce debts further, Granger slated a number of companies from Consumer Products, as well as other companies, for sale. Among them were Danskin, Halston, Orlane, Inc., International Jensen Inc., and Avis. Granger's strategy was that Beatrice's would work toward a 70–30-percent ratio of food to nonfood business in the future, the reason being that the nonfood market is cyclical but the food business is not significantly affected by the economy. He also reorganized the company into three divisions — U.S. Food, Consumer Products, and International Foods — to streamline its operations. The reorganization is shown in Exhibit 7.

[10]Kenneth Dreyfack, "Why Beatrice Had to Dump Dutt," *Business Week,* August 19, 1985, p. 34.

EXHIBIT 7   **Beatrice Company's organization — 1986**

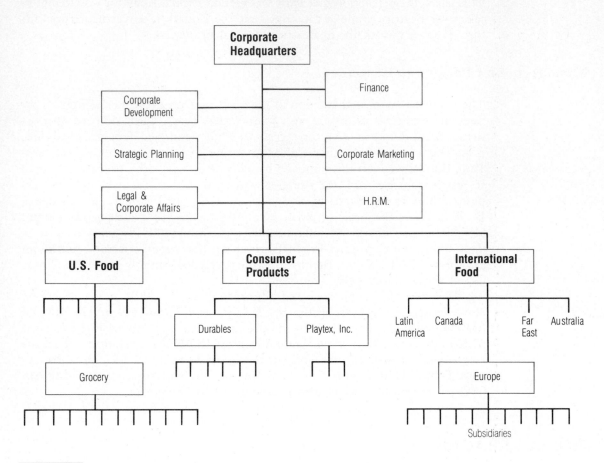

Source: Reprinted by permission of Beatrice Company.

THE MERGER WITH BCI HOLDINGS

Meanwhile, however, Donald Kelly, former chairman of Esmark, was packaging a tender offer for Beatrice with the aid of Kohlberg, Kravis, Roberts & Company (KKR), an investment banking firm. They formed a holding company, BCI Holdings, to bid for Beatrice. Granger, with a weakened management team and in the face of a hostile stock market, offered little resistance to the offer and Beatrice accepted a $40-per-share offer from KKR and Kelly in March 1986. The $6-billion leveraged buyout was the biggest in history, and Beatrice was merged with BCI and was now called BCI Holdings. Kelly commented that he wanted BCI to be private in order to take greater risks and reap greater rewards. However, Kelly's strength was in portfolio management, not in production operations. Industry analysts and executives associated with Esmark operations commented that "Mr. Kelly is not an operating manager. [He] is known for keeping that which works and finding buyers for things that don't."[11]

Thus not surprisingly, soon after the merger, the new management started to sell off companies in order to lower the debt level. The first to go was the Coca-Cola bottling business for $1 billion. Smilow, backed by a group of investors, purchased Playtex Inc. for $1,250 million. The bottled water operations were sold off to France's Perrier Group for $400 million. Rentschler, took over as head of BCI's domestic food operations and carried out a trimming operation at the headquarters by reducing the number of employees from 180 to 60. In June 1987 he succeeded Kelly as the chief executive of BCI Holdings Corp.

Kelly formed another company, E-II Holdings Inc. He remained the chairman of BCI, but was not actively involved in running it. Instead he shifted his focus to altering BCI's portfolio. His plan was to purchase the remaining Beatrice consumer goods companies and manage them. In other words, E-II Holdings would absorb selected businesses of Beatrice. Many specialty food businesses, including Orville Reddenbacher, Hunt's Tomato Sauce and Tropicana, were to be sold off to E-II. Businesses such as Samsonite and Culligan water conditioning were being considered for a spin-off to E-II.

However, not all businesses were to be brought under E-II. Many were divested. Major units sold off in the fifteen months after the merger in March 1986 were Max Factor, the Dairy Products Division (Beatrice's original business), Americold Refrigeration, and Avis. The entire International Food group was also being considered for sale.

Outsiders started to wonder what Beatrice had left. Kelly's intentions became clearer when in May 1987 E-II filed with the Securities and Exchange Commission for an initial public offering of 36 million shares. Industry observers felt that Kelly wanted to liquidate the Beatrice he purchased and build E-II out of its remains. The old Beatrice was gone, as was the old Esmark company. A diversified conglomerate had been sold off to private investors and broken down into smaller companies. The question is, will the new smaller companies operate more efficiently than the old Beatrice conglomerate?

[11]Julie Franz, "Beatrice sell-off due," *Advertising Age*, October 21, 1985, pp. 7 and 108.

EXHIBIT 8   BCI Holdings Corporation — consolidated balance sheet

(in millions)

	As of February 28,	
	1987 (Successor)	1986 (Predecessor)
ASSETS		
Current assets:		
Cash	$ 16	$ 6
Short-term investments, at cost which approximates market	30	141
Receivables, less allowance for doubtful accounts of $14 and $16, respectively	384	346
Inventories	617	631
Net current assets of E-II and discontinued operations	409	656
Other current assets	129	238
Total current assets	1,585	2,018
Net property, plant and equipment	863	774
Intangible assets, principally unallocated purchase cost and goodwill, respectively	2,636	1,171
Net noncurrent assets of E-II and discontinued operations	1,492	2,810
Other noncurrent assets	348	121
	$6,924	$6,894
LIABILITIES AND STOCKHOLDERS' EQUITY		
Current liabilities:		
Short-term debt	$ 4	$ 541
Accounts payable	450	502
Accrued expenses	651	636
Current maturities of long-term debt	125	38
Total current liabilities	1,230	1,717
Long-term debt	4,244	1,147
Noncurrent and deferred income taxes	459	501
Other noncurrent liabilities	683	388
Stockholders' equity:		
Preferred stock	—	—
Preference stock	—	100
Common stock	1	212
Additional capital	418	536
Retained earnings (deficit)	(121)	2,308
Common stock in treasury, at cost	—	(12)
Cumulative foreign currency translation adjustment	10	(3)
Total stockholders' equity	308	3,141
	$6,924	$6,894

Source: Reprinted by permission of Beatrice Company.

EXHIBIT 9   **BCI Holdings Corporation — statement of consolidated earnings**

(in millions, except per-share data)

| | Year ended February 28, | | | |
| | 1987 | | | |
	From April 17 (Successor)	To April 16 (Predecessor)	1986 (Predecessor)	1985 (Predecessor)
Net sales	$4,063	$525	$4,752	$6,015
Cost of sales	2,875	381	3,436	4,455
Gross earnings	1,188	144	1,316	1,560
Selling and administrative expenses	856	112	1,050	1,233
Amortization of intangible assets	55	5	40	31
Integration and restructuring	—	—	—	264
Operating earnings	277	27	226	32
Interest expense	(317)	(14)	(117)	(145)
Change in control expenses	—	(84)	(17)	—
Divestiture gains	—	—	—	700
Miscellaneous income (expense), net	11	—	(17)	28
Earnings (loss) before income taxes and other items	(29)	(71)	75	615
Income tax expense (benefit)	36	(31)	50	258
Earnings (loss) before other items	(65)	(40)	25	357
Earnings from E-II and discontinued operations, net of income tax expense of $64, $15, $174 and $94, respectively	32	14	207	122
Extraordinary items, net of income tax benefit of $32 and $8, respectively	(36)	(10)	—	—
Net earnings (loss)	(69)	$ (36)	$ 232	$ 479
Preferred dividend requirements	(52)			
Net loss applicable to common stockholders	$ (121)			
Weighted-average common shares outstanding	82			
Earnings (loss) per share:				
Before other items	$ (1.43)			
E-II and discontinued operations	.39			
Extraordinary item	(.44)			
Net loss	$ (1.48)			

Source: Reprinted by permission of Beatrice Company.

EXHIBIT 10   **BCI Holdings Corporation — statement of consolidated changes in financial position**

(in millions)

| | Year ended February 28, | | | |
| | 1987 | | | |
	From April 17 (Successor)	To April 16 (Predecessor)	1986 (Predecessor)	1985 (Predecessor)
Cash provided (used) by operations:				
Earnings (loss) before other items	$ (65)	$ (40)	$ 25	$ 357
Items not involving cash:				
Depreciation and amortization of intangibles	141	16	129	139
Net charges due to integration and restructuring	—	—	—	274
Interest expense payable in Exchange Debentures	64	—	—	—
Deferred taxes	—	2	121	258
Other items, net	29	2	24	(6)
Changes in working capital, excluding current debt:				
Divestiture proceeds received in March 1985	—	—	855	(855)
Receivables	(72)	35	2	14
Inventories	(26)	14	42	(95)
Other current assets	52	(22)	6	(98)
Accounts payable and other current liabilities	(64)	(37)	(152)	90
Cash provided (used) by operations before other items	59	(30)	1,052	78
Net cash provided (used) by E-II and discontinued operations	(52)	(27)	11	(75)
Net cash used by extraordinary items	(36)	(10)	—	—
Cash provided (used) by operations	(29)	(67)	1,063	3
Cash provided (used) by investment activities:				
Net expenditures for property, plant and equipment	(94)	(9)	(127)	(61)
Noncurrent assets of purchased businesses	—	—	(7)	(58)
Net proceeds from divested operations and other asset sales	3,385	—	360	592
Other items, net	(11)	(4)	1	(6)
Cash provided (used) by investment activities	3,280	(13)	227	467
Cash provided (used) by financing activities, excluding the Merger:				
Change in debt	(3,770)	134	(1,778)	(455)
Exchange Debentures issued upon exchange of Redeemable Preferred Stock	1,230	—	—	—
Redeemable Preferred Stock retired upon exchange of Exchange Debentures	(1,230)	—	—	—
Proceeds from sale of Beatrice common stock	—	—	434	—
Refund of income taxes	—	—	176	—
Common stock issued upon conversion of preference stock and debentures	—	41	157	34
Preference stock and debentures retired upon conversion into common stock	—	(41)	(157)	(34)
Common stock issued for exercises of stock options and stock warrants	—	20	85	4
Redeemable Preferred Stock issued as dividends and upon conversion of convertible securities	74	—	—	—
Dividends paid in Redeemable Preferred Stock	(52)	—	—	—
Other items, net	106	(23)	(23)	42
Cash provided (used) by financing activities	(3,642)	131	(1,106)	(409)

EXHIBIT 10   **BCI Holdings Corporation — statement of consolidated changes in financial position (*cont.*)**

(in millions)

	Year ended February 28,			
	1987			
	From April 17 (Successor)	To April 16 (Predecessor)	1986 (Predecessor)	1985 (Predecessor)
Effect of Beatrice and Esmark acquisitions in fiscal 1987 and 1985, respectively:				
Funding	7,373	—	—	2,708
Purchase of equity securities	(6,183)	—	—	(2,708)
Debt repaid	(898)	—	—	—
Cash and short-term investments of acquired company	145	—	—	237
Increase in cash and short-term investments resulting from acquisitions	437	—	—	237
Cash provided before cash dividend payments	46	51	184	298
Cash dividends	—	(53)	(195)	(170)
Increase (decrease) in cash and short-term investments	46	(2)	(11)	128
Cash and short-term investments at beginning of period	—	147	158	30
Cash and short-term investments at end of period	$ 46	$145	$ 147	$ 158

Source: Reprinted by permission of Beatrice Company.

EXHIBIT 11   **BCI Holdings Corporation — condensed consolidating financial statements**

(in millions)

	NSI	Swift-Eckrich	Beatrice U.S. Food
CONDENSED CONSOLIDATING INCOME STATEMENT (Fiscal 1987):			
Net sales	$1,712	$1,318	$1,811
Operating expenses	1,498	1,204	1,659
Operating earnings	214	114	152
Intercompany interest income (expense), net	(46)	(31)	(33)
Interest expense, net	(20)	(1)	(66)
Other income (expense)	—	—	9
Earnings (loss) before income taxes and other items	148	82	62
Income tax expense (benefit)	83	43	31
Earnings (loss) before discontinued operations and extraordinary items	65	39	31
Discontinued operations	4	—	41
Extraordinary items	—	—	—
Net earnings (loss)	$ 69	$ 39	$ 72
CONDENSED CONSOLIDATING BALANCE SHEET (As of February 28, 1987):			
Assets:			
Cash and short-term investments	$ 7	$ 1	$ 19
Receivables, net	167	59	123
Inventories	353	101	187
Other current assets	13	1	13
Total current assets	540	162	342
Property, plant and equipment, net	434	208	204
Intangible assets, principally unallocated purchase cost	—	—	—
Other noncurrent assets	18	1	514
Total assets	$ 992	$ 371	$1,060
Liabilities and Stockholders' Equity:			
Short-term debt and current maturities of long-term debt	$ 15	$ —	$ 5
Accounts payable and accrued expenses	313	163	323
Total current liabilities	328	163	328
Long-term debt	228	5	40
Noncurrent and deferred income taxes	39	—	(1)
Other noncurrent liabilities	38	4	13
Net intercompany investments and advances	359	199	680
Stockholders' equity:			
Common stock	—	—	—
Additional capital	—	—	—
Retained earnings (deficit)	—	—	—
Cumulative foreign currency translation adjustment	—	—	—
Total stockholders' equity	—	—	—
Total liabilities and stockholders' equity	$ 992	$ 371	$1,060

Source: Reprinted by permission of Beatrice Company.

BCI Products	BCI International	Parent Company (Holdings)	Eliminations	Holdings Consolidated
$1,243	$2,866	$ —	$ (24)	$8,926
1,125	2,719	174	(24)	8,355
118	147	(174)	—	571
(23)	(11)	258	(114)	—
(45)	(19)	(538)	222	(467)
3	(10)	150	(273)	(121)
53	107	(304)	(165)	(17)
29	61	(238)	53	62
24	46	(66)	(218)	(79)
23	—	7	(55)	20
—	—	(46)	—	(46)
$ 47	$ 46	$ (105)	$(273)	$ (105)
$ 17	$ 113	$ 16	$ —	$ 173
210	267	34	—	860
188	271	—	—	1,100
16	24	102	—	169
431	675	152	—	2,302
247	440	74	—	1,607
—	—	3,130	—	3,130
95	33	203	—	864
$ 773	$1,148	$3,559	$ —	$7,903
$ 20	$ 128	$ 107	$ —	$ 275
180	387	306	—	1,672
200	515	413	—	1,947
28	43	3,982	—	4,326
4	21	420	—	483
109	130	545	—	839
432	439	(2,109)	—	—
—	—	1	—	1
—	—	418	—	418
—	—	(121)	—	(121)
—	—	10	—	10
—	—	308	—	308
$ 773	$1,148	$ 3,559	$ —	$7,903

THE GREYHOUND CORPORATION

In 1981 John Teets succeeded Gerry Trautman as the chief executive officer of The Greyhound Corporation. Although this was an appointment that Teets had worked hard for over the years, he was succeeding a man who had changed Greyhound from a single-business bus transportation company in 1966 to a diversified conglomerate with extensive transportation, manufacturing, food, consumer products, financial, and service interests. The challenge facing Teets was to manage Greyhound's diverse businesses so that he would be able to achieve at least a 15-percent return on equity. However, there were many problems on the horizon that might hinder the achievement of this goal. Some were the direct consequence of Trautman's ambitious expansion and diversification efforts, others resulted from changes in environmental factors and consumer preferences, while still others stemmed from internal inefficiencies that Teets hoped he would be able to remedy. If Teets could not solve these problems and increase Greyhound's profitability, several analysts believed that the company's diverse holdings could be bought by a corporate raider at bargain prices and then split up and sold.[1]

GREYHOUND'S HISTORY AND GROWTH

Trautman was proud of the progress that Greyhound had made under his leadership. More than just making it a larger, more diverse company, he felt that he had placed the company in businesses that would not be as affected by economic

This case was prepared by Gareth R. Jones and James Fiet, Department of Management, Texas A & M University.

[1]K. K. Wiegner, "Old Dog, New Tactics," *Fortune,* February 11, 1985, p. 45.

downturns as its bus lines had been and that would provide a solid base for future profitability.[2] To understand how Trautman's expansionist acquisitions recast Greyhound's strategic orientation, it is helpful to understand Greyhound's history as a bus company.

At the end of 1981, when Trautman turned over the driver's seat to Teets, Greyhound had the second most-recognized trademark and logo in the world, behind only those of Coca-Cola. However, Greyhound had not always been so well known. The company was founded in Hibbing, Minnesota, in 1914. Its first business was providing bus transportation to carry miners to work at the Mesabi Iron Range. As it was the sole provider of bus service for these workers, its early beginnings were immediately successful: in its very first year the new corporation started expanding its routes and acquiring interests in bus companies operating near Chicago. For the next sixteen years the young company continued purchasing adjacent interests in bus companies, extending its route structure from New York to Kansas City. In 1930 the current name of the corporation was adopted, and the now familiar blue running dog logo was painted on its buses.[3] This new logo came to be the symbol of the transcontinental bus carrier that Greyhound was to become.

For the next twenty-seven years Greyhound continued to acquire other bus interests in order to consolidate its routes, and to link its various bus operations. Growth proceeded sometimes by purchase, sometimes by stock swaps, and sometimes by merger, but the result was always the same to the traveling public—it saw more and more of the familiar blue running dog. By 1957 Greyhound had substantially achieved its objective of operating a bus system that could carry passengers to most destinations in the continental United States. It was now a truly national carrier.

In order to continue its growth, Greyhound decided to move into the Canadian market. In 1957 it incorporated Greyhound Lines of Canada, Ltd., as a holding company to allow it to acquire Canadian bus companies. In less than twenty years Greyhound's Canadian subsidiary operated 13,870 miles of bus routes between Toronto and Vancouver via Winnipeg, Calgary, Edmonton, Windsor, and Niagara Falls. It also began to manufacture buses and bus parts in Canada and the United States and operated a tour service. It established its headquarters in Calgary, Alberta, where it operates with more than 3,000 employees.

DIVERSIFYING OUT OF THE BUS BUSINESS

By 1962 Greyhound was facing the prospect of increasingly limited opportunities to expand its route system, which now spanned the continental United States and Canada. Its two bus operations were also generating large sums of

---

[2]A. Stuart, "Greyhound gets ready for a new driver," *Fortune*, December 15, 1980, pp. 58–64.
[3]*Moody's Transportation Manual*, 1987.

excess cash, which could fund Greyhound's expansion into new businesses. The combination of these two factors convinced Greyhound's board of directors to diversify Greyhound's operations outside of the bus transportation industry. As a beginning to its diversification program, Greyhound acquired the Boothe Leasing Company, an enterprise that specialized in equipment leasing, an activity completely unrelated to Greyhound's intercity bus business.

In 1963, to prepare itself for more acquisitions beyond the transportation industry, The Greyhound Corporation became a holding company. Greyhound Lines, Inc., and Greyhound Lines of Canada, Ltd., became the Transportation Services Group of the Greyhound Corporation. That same year the bus manufacturing operations of both the U.S. and Canadian companies were separated from the transportation group, and together with other U.S. acquisitions, were organized into the Transportation Manufacturing Group. Boothe Leasing was renamed Greyhound Leasing and Financial Corporation (GLFC) and became the core around which Greyhound's Financial Group was to be built. Thus by the end of 1963 the company was operating in three major businesses: bus transportation, bus manufacturing, and financial services. The bus manufacturing group supplied all the buses to the transportation group, as well as to other bus companies.

Trautman Spearheads Greyhound's Diversification Drive

When Trautman was appointed CEO in 1966, he wasted no time in implementing Greyhound's new strategy for expansion and growth. A Harvard-trained corporate attorney, he practiced in San Francisco, while serving on Greyhound's board at the company's new headquarters in Phoenix, Arizona. As a former board member, he understood that if Greyhound was to capitalize on its capacity to generate cash for expansion it would have to invest wisely in profitable new acquisitions.[4]

From Trautman's installation as CEO until 1970, Greyhound acquired more than thirty companies and formed a new operating division in the holding company, the Services Group, which specialized in transportation-related businesses. These companies included Border Brokerage Company, Inc., which operated two duty-free shops at the Canadian border, and the Florida Export Group, which also handled duty-free commerce. In addition, the new Services Group included Manncraft Exhibitors, Inc., a company specializing in building displays for major exhibitions; Nassau Air Dispatch, a Caribbean shipping company; and Freeport Flight Services, Inc., a Bahamian aircraft-servicing business. Trautman also brought in a line of cruise ships in the Caribbean, the Bahama Cruise Line company.[5] Then he added Ford Van Lines Inc. of Lincoln, Nebraska,

[4]Stuart, "Greyhound gets ready for a new driver."
[5]Greyhound Corporation, *Annual Reports* (1966–1970).

a company specializing in furniture moving; Red Top Sedan Service, Inc., a Florida limousine service; Texas, New Mexico, Oklahoma Coaches, Inc., and Carey Transportation Inc., two regional intercity bus lines; Trade Winds Transportation Co., Ltd., of Hawaii, another intercity bus carrier; Washington Airport Transport, Inc., a commuter carrier from the suburbs to Dulles Airport; and Gray Line New York Tours Corporation, a sightseeing bus line. Furthermore, he added Hausman Bus Parts, Inc. to the Transportation Manufacturing Group.[6]

Not all the companies that Trautman acquired proved to be as profitable or as manageable as he had hoped. What he was looking for was value, as well as some synergy with his existing transportation activities. However, as the acquisition process continued, the goal of synergy became a secondary objective. When he became dissatisfied with an acquisition, Trautman would divest it as quickly as he had acquired it, and many companies were spun off.

Near the end of his tenure as CEO, Trautman would boast that Greyhound had achieved "diversification within diversification."[7] What he meant was that in his view the operating groups themselves had become diversified, so that individually they were each recession proof, all enhancing the financial strength of the holding company.

The Armour Acquisition

Trautman's boldest maneuver and biggest acquisition came in 1970. He acquired Armour & Co., a large conglomerate that had many diverse business interests in food and consumer products. Trautman's Armour acquisition occurred almost by accident. Certain members of Greyhound's board who also served on the board of directors of Armour & Co. proposed that Greyhound acquire Armour in a friendly takeover. That was intended to be a move to protect the current Armour management from a probable takeover by an unfriendly suitor. In other words, Armour was looking for a white knight to come to its rescue. Trautman was just the man with the will and the bankroll to do it.

Trautman paid $400 million in cash, notes, and stock to take over Armour, which was primarily a large meat-packing company with more than $2 billion of sales in marginally profitable businesses. However, it also had interests in pharmaceuticals, cosmetics, and consumer products, such as soap, through its very profitable Dial Division. Trautman knew that it appeared as though he had overpaid for Armour. However, he soon reduced the price of the acquisition by selling off, for some $225 million, a number of its divisions that he considered to be on the periphery of its core food and consumer businesses. In 1977 he sold off Armour's pharmaceutical division for another $87 million, reducing Greyhound's net investment to $88 million.[8]

[6]Greyhound Corporation, *Annual Reports* (1966–1970).
[7]Greyhound Corporation, *Annual Report* (1980).
[8]"Greyhound: a big sell-off leaves it built for better speed," *Business Week,* July 25, 1983, pp. 88–90.

What remained after these divestitures were Armour's food operations and Armour's Dial unit, around which Trautman built two new operating groups, the Food and Consumer Products Group. The companies in these groups are discussed below. Together, the two groups generated after-tax net income of about $25 million a year. Although this income was only a slim 1 percent of sales, it represented an impressive 28 percent return on Greyhound's net investment.[9] This hefty return was the type of value that Trautman was seeking through his diversification efforts. By acquiring Armour-Dial, he also hoped that his new acquisition would be more recession proof, if not countercyclical to the operation of the bus business. However, in acquiring Armour, Trautman had brought in new businesses that had management problems of their own — in areas where Greyhound had no experience, for instance, the price of pork bellies, cycles for meat packers' contracts, and foreign competition.

ACQUISITIONS AND DIVESTITURES, 1970–1978

For the next eight years, Greyhound under Trautman continued buying businesses and increasing the size of the operating groups in its corporate portfolio. By 1978 Greyhound's holding company consisted of five operating groups: Transportation, Bus Manufacturing, Food and Consumer Products, Services/Food Service, and Financial. Each of these new operating groups in turn acquired many new businesses, so that Greyhound was, as Trautman put it, undergoing "diversification within diversification." Many of these new acquisitions were failures, however. Businesses as diverse as a chicken hatchery, a European acquisition to expand the Financial Group, the Caribbean Gray Cruise Line, Ltd., VAVO Greyhound N. V. of Schoonhoven, Netherlands, Shannon-Greyhound Coaches, Hausman Bus Parts, Inc., and Herbert J. DeGraff Associates all proved unprofitable. Trautman also sold the Industrial Products Group of Armour & Co., and Greyhound Van Lines.[10]

As Greyhound's portfolio of businesses kept changing during this period, Trautman continued to feel that he was shaping a diversified company that would have a powerful base in many lines of business. He was willing to take the risk of acquiring some companies that would be failures as long as the overall health of the company was strengthened. As a symbol of his confidence in Greyhound's diversification strategy, Trautman supported the board's decision to move the corporate headquarters to Phoenix and to build an impressive new corporate headquarters to oversee the company's portfolio. However, Greyhound became more and more distant from its core business, bus transportation.

---

[9]"Greyhound: a big sell-off leaves it built for better speed," pp. 88–90.
[10]Greyhound Corporation, *Annual Reports* (1970–1978).

The Verex Acquisition

Trautman engineered another major acquisition in April 1978 by acquiring 97 percent of the stock of the Verex Corporation, the largest private insurer of residential mortgages in the United States. The Verex acquisition was intended to strengthen the operations of Greyhound's Financial Group, which, together with Greyhound Leasing, seemed to be a promising investment. Verex insured first mortgages on residential real estate, generally having loan-to-value ratios in excess of 80 percent. Verex was headquartered in Minneapolis but wrote insurance business in all fifty states and the District of Columbia.

By 1978 Greyhound had grown nearly as large as it would grow under Trautman's leadership. The collection of businesses that he had assembled — some by acquisition, some by internal growth, and some by selling off pieces of larger businesses — was designed to make Greyhound more resistant to economic downturns. These businesses are summarized in Exhibit 1.

One of the criticisms that was frequently leveled against Trautman's diversification activities concerned the rationale behind the company's growth path. Trautman argued that the basic strength of the company was reflected in its earnings growth while it achieved diversification within diversification. Exhibit 2 summarizes the sources of Greyhound's earnings.

A Closer Look at Some of Greyhound's Operations in 1978

Transportation Group   This group comprised two major divisions, the intercity services group and the travel services group. The Transportation Group operated regularly scheduled passenger bus service between most metropolitan areas in North America and engaged in related operations, such as package shipping, sightseeing services, airport ground transportation, and deluxe tour and charter bus services.

Its Intercity Services Division, which primarily consisted of Greyhound Lines, Inc., and its Canadian subsidiary, provided the largest intercity bus transportation system for passengers, baggage, express parcels, and mail in the United States and Canada. These services were provided in every state in the United States except Hawaii, as well as in most Canadian provinces. The company operated more than 3,000 modern, air-conditioned, and lavatory-equipped buses, which were manufactured by Greyhound's Bus Manufacturing Group. The company also operated a network of 123 company terminals, 63 garages and 2 maintenance centers.

The Travel Services Division provided sightseeing operations in the Canadian Rockies. Other interests of this division were ground transportation services to and from airports at Detroit, Honolulu, Miami, Orlando, and Phoenix. In addition, this division managed connections at these airports with its regularly scheduled intercity bus routes.

EXHIBIT 1	**Greyhound's key operations in 1978**

TRANSPORTATION GROUP

Intercity Services Division:

Greyhound Lines, Inc. — world's largest intercity passenger carrier serving all forty-eight continental states, Mexico, and Canada. Intercity bus service in Canada and to Alaska provided by Greyhound Lines of Canada. Other intercity bus subsidiaries include New Mexico Transportation; Texas, New Mexico & Oklahoma Coaches; and Vermont Transit.

Greyhound Package Express — small package express service for individual and commercial shippers.

Greyhound Group Travel — centralized sales and coordination of all Greyhound charter operations.

Travel Services Division:

Carey Transportation — ground transportation between Manhattan and New York area airports.

Red Top Sedan Services — limousine service at Miami International Airport.

American Sightseeing Tours — charter and sightseeing bus service in Miami area and throughout Florida.

Brewster Transportation — sightseeing and tours in Canadian Rockies.

California Parlor Cars Tours Company — deluxe motor coach tours of California.

Gray Line Companies — sightseeing tours in New York, San Francisco, and Phoenix.

BUS MANUFACTURING GROUP

Motor Coach Industries and *Transportation Manufacturing* — bus manufacturing in Winnipeg, Canada; Pembina, North Dakota; and Roswell, New Mexico.

FOOD AND CONSUMER PRODUCTS GROUP

Armour Fresh Meat Company, Armour Processed Meat Company, and *Armour Poultry and Dairy Products Company* — manufacture and distribute a broad range of fresh, processed, and portion-controlled meats, poultry, and other food products for consumer and institutional use.

Armour-Dial Company — manufactures and markets a wide variety of grocery, personal care, and household products for the consumer.

Armour Handcrafts, Inc. — designs, manufactures, and distributes a wide variety of yarns, handcraft needlepoint, crewel, and wall hanging kits.

Armour International Company — is responsible for overseas marketing of all Armour and Armour-Dial consumer products.

SERVICES/FOOD SERVICES GROUP

Faber Enterprises — restaurants and gift shops in major office buildings and transportation terminals in the Chicago area.

EXHIBIT 1   **Greyhound's key operations in 1978 (*cont.*)**

Greyhound Food Management — coordinator of Greyhound food service operations; Post House restaurants and fast-food operations; Prophet Foods, offering food service for industry, military installations, and other commercial establishments; and restaurant design, engineering, and food service management throughout Belgium.

Greyhound Support Services — provides housekeeping, food service, and other support services for large construction projects for industry and government agencies throughout the world.

Aircraft Service International — ground-handling services for major airlines in the United States and the Caribbean. Also designs, installs, and operates hydrant fueling systems for airports.

Border Brokers — Canada's first and largest customs broker and international freight forwarder.

Greyhound C & D — technical and design services to business and industry by consultants and designers, temporary and permanent office and blue-collar help to business and industry by Greyhound Temporary Personnel.

Dispatch Services — ground-handling services for major airlines at Miami International Airport and Freeport Airport (in the Bahamas).

Florida Export Group — duty-free retail shops at Miami International Airport, a wholesale duty-free business for export, and duty-free shops on cruise ships operating out of Miami and New Orleans.

Greyhound Rent-A-Car — car leasing with unlimited free mileage on a daily, weekly, or monthly basis in major Florida cities and in Atlanta, Denver, Las Vegas, Los Angeles, Mobile, New Orleans, Orange County, Palm Springs, Phoenix, San Francisco, and Tucson.

Research Information Center — full-service marketing research.

Greyhound Convention Services — complete convention and exhibitors' services nationwide, including such key cities as Atlanta, Chicago, Cincinnati, Dallas/Fort Worth, Las Vegas, Los Angeles, Miami, New Orleans, New York, and San Francisco.

FINANCIAL GROUP

Greyhound Computer Corporation — computer leasing and sales in the United States, Canada, Mexico, and Europe.

Greyhound Leasing and Financial Corporation — worldwide industrial equipment leasing.

Pine Top Insurance — engaged in reinsurance operations and in commercial property and excess casualty insurance fields.

Traveler's Express Company — nation's second-largest money order firm.

Verex Corporation — a leading company in residential mortgage insurance and other financial activities.

Source: Greyhound's 1978 Annual Report to Stockholders. Reprinted by permission.

EXHIBIT 2   **Divisional performance — 1978–1981**

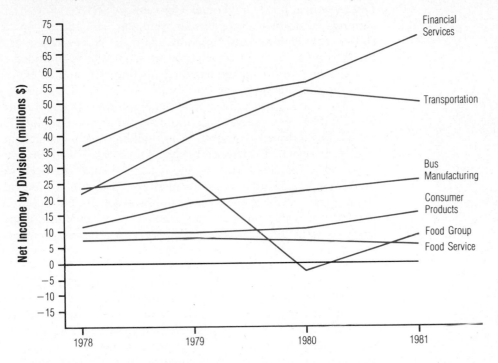

Bus Manufacturing Group The largest manufacturer of intercity buses in North America, this group had operations that were vertically integrated to fabricate bus shells of intercity design, assemble buses, and manufacture bus parts for final assembly. In addition, it warehoused and distributed replacements parts to meet its own requirements and the larger requirements of the bus industry. Greyhound Bus Manufacturing was the principal supplier in the United States of buses to charter operators and sightseeing companies.

Food and Consumer Products Group These companies manufactured and marketed products to independent retailers under private label arrangements, as well as distributed several products under their own trademarks. These trademarks included Dial, Tone, and Pure & Natural soaps, Armour Star and Armour Tree canned meat and meat food products, Dial antiperspirants and shampoos, Appian Way pizza mixes, Parsons' ammonia, Bruce floor care products, Magic sizing and prewash, and Malina handknitting yarns and needle products.

Services/Food Service Group The Services Group provided a broad range of services directed primarily to business markets, although its duty-free shops located at airports and on cruise ships were targeted toward the consumer market. The group also operated two cruise ships through Premier Cruise Lines,

Inc., and other ships through another company, which was the official Walt Disney cruise line. Greyhound Convention Services (GCS) specialized in designing, fabricating, warehousing, shipping, and setting up exhibits for trade shows, conventions and exhibitions. Also, GCS served as a decorating contractor at conventions and trade show sites. Finally, it provided aircraft refueling and cleaning, and baggage handling for domestic and foreign airlines, particularly those operating in the Caribbean.

The Food Service division, generally known as Greyhound Food Management (GFM) Inc., served approximately four hundred locations in industrial plants, bus terminals, airports, office buildings, schools, colleges, and other facilities. It operated cafeterias in the United States and Belgium and provided fast-food restaurants, catering, and machine-vended services. Furthermore, this division operated gift shops, retail shops, drugstores, newsstands, and auto-truck plazas. Another operation in the Food Service Group, Greyhound Support Services, provided housekeeping, food service, and other support services for large construction projects to industry and government agencies throughout the world.

Financial Group This group consisted of Greyhound Computer Corporation, a company specializing in computer leasing and sales in the United States, Canada, Mexico, and Europe; Greyhound Leasing and Financial Corporation, a company specializing in worldwide industrial equipment leasing; Pine Top Insurance, an entity that reinsures commercial property and provides excess casualty insurance for large policyholders; and Verex Corporation, the leading private insurer of highly leveraged residential mortgages for primary lenders.

Another member of the Financial Group, Traveler's Express Company, Inc., merits additional consideration. It specialized in providing traveler's checks and check cashing services in 32,000 retail establishments and financial institutions in the United States and Puerto Rico. This company also provided draft-clearing services for more than 2,300 credit unions and savings and loan associations, making it the largest private sector provider of such services.

Together, these operating divisions were generating combined revenues of nearly $4.5 billion, and Trautman had accomplished his objective of using profits from the bus division to move Greyhound into other businesses.

THE BUS BUSINESS ALMOST GOES OFF THE ROAD

Around the time that he was completing the acquisition of the Verex Corporation, Trautman came across an internal memo that was bitingly critical of Greyhound's transportation operations. It came from one of Greyhound's own disgruntled bus employees, who had just completed a very unpleasant cross-country bus trip. This memo disclosed that the employee had found serious customer service problems, including filthy conditions and poor security at Greyhound terminals. As a result of this memo, Trautman began to investigate numerous letters from customers who complained of service and maintenance problems that had led to unacceptable bus conditions and many bus breakdowns.

Although Trautman had steered Greyhound into mortgage financing, car leasing and rental, financial services, manufacturing consumer products and canned meats, and many other ventures, he could not see from his twentieth-story office what was going wrong in the field with his bus operations. As a result, in early 1978 Trautman hired his own team to investigate the situation and sent them on a secret undercover mission to learn how his bus business was being operated at remote locations. Moreover, he tried to visit as many of these facilities as he could himself during the next couple of months. Trautman found that many of the service and customer satisfaction problems confronting the bus group were real. However, what especially troubled him was that Greyhound's maintenance facilities lacked sufficient spare parts to take care of all but the most serious equipment problems. Consequently, buses were being delayed unnecessarily by problems that ought to have been reasonably anticipated, and in some instances the company was having to provide overnight lodging for stranded passengers.

Then in July 1978 Owen Jones, president of the 14,000-member Amalgamated Council of Greyhound Local Unions, called to ask Trautman to come across the street to his office. As the Greyhound CEO was striding across Clarendon Street in Phoenix, he wondered what had precipitated such an unprecedented request. Trautman knew it was not time to renegotiate the company union contract, but certainly Jones had not called to ask him over to sip tea. The gravity of Jones's call became apparent when he told Trautman that his staff had compiled a list of serious grievances from Greyhound drivers that were not being addressed by the management of Greyhound Lines, so out of exasperation the drivers were sending them to Jones.[11]

Trautman came away from that meeting convinced that the problems he had with the bus line were grimmer than even he was beginning to recognize, and that he had to move quickly if he was to save his bus business. He immediately fired James L. Kerigan as CEO of the bus company and took the title of chairman himself. In September 1978 he promoted a long-time employee, Frank L. Najeotte, to be president and CEO of the bus line, and the two of them worked together to invest $60 million during the next eight months in a concentrated effort to hire more maintenance personnel, upgrade terminal facilities, and polish Greyhound's neglected image.

When the energy crunch hit in April 1979, Greyhound was poised to serve the public's demand for inexpensive transportation—a demand that increased as a result of the steep rise in gasoline prices precipitated by OPEC. Higher crude oil prices pushed gasoline prices for the first time above $1 a gallon and left consumers scurrying to low-cost alternative means of transportation. By the time

---

[11]Stuart, "Greyhound gets ready for a new driver."

the public remembered that Greyhound buses could provide that low-cost transport, Trautman had just finished spending $60 million to renovate and sanitize terminals and enlarge and refurbish Greyhound's extensive fleet of buses. It was almost as if he had known in advance that he would suddenly be able to fill 200 more buses each day during 1979 as compared with 1978. Profits from Greyhound's buses rose from $20 million in 1978 to $39.5 million in 1979, even after the investment of $60 million in improvements.

Besides, 1979 was an excellent year for more reasons than its improved financial performance. The bus line's personnel, and particularly its drivers, felt a renewed commitment to them and to their business from Greyhound's management. As for the public, it too began to pay more attention to Greyhound. Among the memories many people still have of the energy crunch is the recollection of that big Greyhound bus on the billboards with the caption "This vehicle gets over a hundred miles per gallon," referring of course to its fuel usage per passenger mile.

SERIOUS PROBLEMS AT ARMOUR SURPRISE TRAUTMAN

In 1979 Greyhound's Transportation Group and its Financial Group (as a result of the Federal Reserve's push to drive up interest rates to curtail inflation) were enjoying their best earnings year ever. Armour & Co., on the other hand, was barely making a profit, even though this group of related companies had sales in excess of $2 billion a year.

For $500,000, Trautman hired Booze, Allen & Hamilton Inc. to evaluate Armour & Co., and the consulting firm returned with the recommendation that Armour should market its products more aggressively. Whereas in the past Armour had clearly been a production-oriented company, the consultant's recommendation was that much more emphasis be placed on marketing. The best way to accomplish this was to slice Armour Foods into three distinct companies: one for fresh meats, one for processed meat products, and one for poultry. Then, according to the recommendation, substantially higher outlays should be made for advertising and for developing the brand identity of Armour products in the three companies. Finally, to compete with Oscar Mayer & Co., Inc. — the other major food packer, which distributed its products to 80 percent of the nation — Armour, which only covered 50 percent of the country, was urged to expand its distribution network nationwide.

This new marketing strategy proved to be disastrous from the start. Losses occurred immediately in the processed meat division, while earnings plummeted in the other two divisions. Only a favorable year in the wholesale price of poultry kept Armour Foods in the black for 1979. But for the first nine months of 1979, the operating loss at the processed meat division amounted to $26 million. Armour had become the victim of its own ambitions. Its new policies of discarding antiquated accounting systems that worked, raising prices on low-margin products, which alienated established customers, and investing heavily in a distribution system for its products to markets in which it had no brand identity all caused problems. The new policy shifted some resources from the other food units to Armour Foods and created animosity between them and Armour-Dial, with the result that the whole division's future competitive position was at risk.

In an attempt to turn the division around, Trautman fired the management team at Armour Foods, stopped its new marketing orientation, and installed himself temporarily as chairman. His first moves were to return Armour to its formerly profitable private label operation, in which it produced canned meats for large retailers like Safeway. However, the profit picture at Armour did not improve; in fact, it worsened, in spite of Trautman's draconian price cutting and plant closings. The Food Group, of which Armour was the largest company, went from a profit of $22 million in 1979 to a loss of $1.7 million in 1980.

A SILVER LINING FOR GREYHOUND

Even as Armour Foods was losing money, Greyhound as a whole was more profitable than ever. The recession that began in 1979 and the ongoing concern for energy conservation had actually boosted Greyhound's profits to its best year ever in 1981. Greyhound's combined profits had risen from $59.8 million in 1978 to $137.5 million in 1981. In particular, its interest-sensitive Financial Group had seen its income rise from $37 million in 1978 to $70.18 million in 1981. For the Transportation Group, consisting primarily of Greyhound Lines, income grew from $22 million in 1978 to $54 million in 1980, then dropped to $49.7 million in 1981. During this same period, 1978 to 1981, Greyhound's return on equity had soared from 6.3 percent to 14.6 percent, and its earnings per share had more than doubled, from $1.36 to $3.05. (See Exhibit 3.)

Besides these accomplishments, Greyhound was about to achieve $5 billion in sales for the first time. Exhibit 4 indicates the sources of Greyhound's earnings for 1981. It is noteworthy that Greyhound's income from its intercity bus business as a proportion of its total revenues had fallen to 27 percent in 1981, whereas fifteen years before, when Trautman was appointed CEO, bus operations had provided nearly 100 percent of the income.

TRAUTMAN SELECTS TEETS TO TAKE OVER GREYHOUND

Armour's problems came at a very inconvenient time for Trautman because he had planned to retire in 1980. Although the bus business appeared to have been revived, he did not want to leave while Armour, the acquisition of which he was most proud, was in such a serious state. Trautman wanted to solve Ar-

EXHIBIT 3   Selected financial figures — 1978–1981

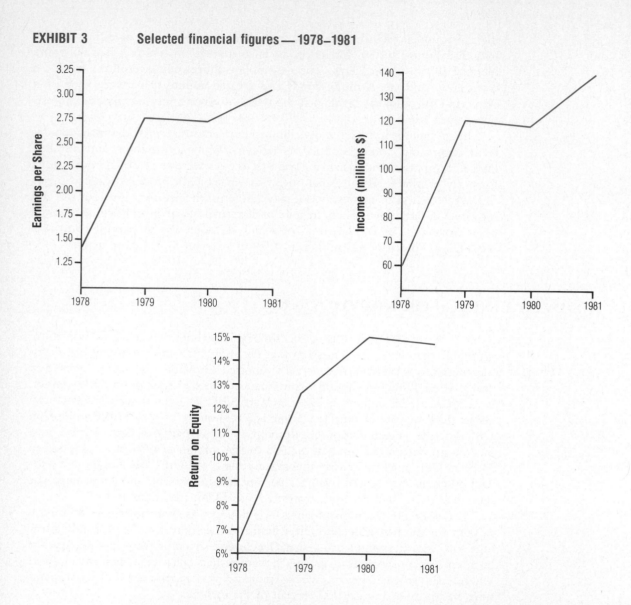

mour's problems while he kept business rolling at Greyhound's other groups and prepared a successor to take over the collection of companies that he had assembled.

So in 1980 Trautman expanded the office of the chairman of the board to include three vice chairmen: Ralph C. Batastini, who managed the Financial Group of companies, which in 1979 had generated 42 percent of Greyhound's earnings; Frank Najeotte, the president of the bus company, who had worked

EXHIBIT 4   **The shape of Greyhound in 1981**

**$135.2 Million in Income
(from $5,164 Million in Revenue)**

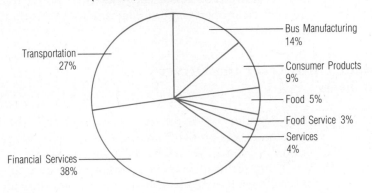

Bus Manufacturing
14%

Consumer Products
9%

Food 5%

Food Service 3%

Services
4%

Transportation
27%

Financial Services
38%

closely with Trautman in its turnaround; and John Teets, who had resuscitated the Food Service business and who had been made CEO of Armour.[12]

Teets was a very different person from Trautman. His background had not included Harvard Business School or law practice. Instead he had learned to become an effective hands-on manager by being as close to the action as possible. He had once worked for his father's construction company but decided that he liked the idea of operating a restaurant better. He borrowed money, started his own restaurant, and quickly made it successful. However, as soon as he had paid back the money he had borrowed and his restaurant was earning a profit, it burned to the ground. In searching for a new business opportunity, Teets answered an advertisement in the newspaper about a position managing a Greyhound food services concession stand at the New York World Fair.

After joining the Food Service Group, Teets did not waste any time distinguishing himself as a tight-fisted cost cutter who could make money on a miserly budget. He seemed to have a talent for squeezing every last penny out of everything he managed. Teets moved up quickly in the group, gaining a reputation as an extremely effective manager. By 1975 he was put in charge of the Food Service Group, which primarily operated a conglomeration of marginally profitable, obscure, franchised restaurants. His aggressive management style produced quick results, and in 1980 he was named the outstanding executive in the food industry. Also in 1980, in addition to his responsibilities as CEO of the Food Service Group, Teets was named as head of Armour in place of Trautman.

In 1981 Armour's major problem, as Teets saw it, was its paying 30–50 percent more in wages and fringe benefits than its competitors. He explained

[12]Paul B. Brown, "Gentlemen, this is a bus!" *Forbes*, September 27, 1982, pp. 70–74.

this to Armour's unions and asked for immediate wage concessions. He told them that if he failed to get these concessions he would have to start closing plants. It was not easy, but after a bitter strike, wage concessions in excess of 15 percent were obtained, and with cost cutting from plant closings and with more efficient operating procedures, it looked as though Armour had bought itself some time.

Trautman Turns Over the Driver's Seat to Teets

With Armour Foods running more efficiently, the bus business still cruising along on excess profits from the recession and energy crunch, and the Financial Group's profits generated by the high interest rate, it looked as though the stage was being set for Trautman's retirement. In fact, all that remained to be done, was to formally select a successor. It was not difficult for Trautman to make up his mind about who should be his successor. He was impressed with Teets's successes in managing the food group and also with the way in which he had dominated Armour's labor unions. Turning over the driver's seat to Teets, he cited three major developments that would contribute to an auspicious future for Greyhound: the improved financial condition of Greyhound's businesses, the selection of new management, and the rejuvenation of Armour. As he put it, these three developments would ensure that Greyhound's advertising slogan, "Greyhound is really going places in the 80's," would be fulfilled.

Problems at Greyhound

On taking over as CEO, Teets confronted two major problems that caused him to feel uneasy about Greyhound's overall profit picture. The first of these problems was Armour's high production cost, which made it a weak competitor. The second was the challenge that Greyhound Lines faced of competing in a newly deregulated bus transportation market. He knew that if he did not find solutions for these two problems they would seriously diminish Greyhound's earnings and make it a likely target for a corporate raider.

Dealing with Armour's High Production Costs

Having been the president of Armour Foods, Teets was very familiar with the division's problems: its high production costs, the reluctance of union leadership and rank-and-file workers to agree with Greyhound's assessment of Armour's problems: and its utter inability to successfully change its marketing orientation in order to compete effectively. In addition, Teets was concerned about Armour's inefficient plants and the volatility of hog and pork belly prices, which cyclically depressed its slim earnings. Though it had turned around its 1980 losses, Armour was still able to earn only $9 million. Furthermore, this profit did not come from continuing operations, but rather from the sale of assets after it closed four of its seventeen plants. This 1981 profit of $9 million still represented a profit margin of less than 0.39 percent on sales of more than $2.3 billion.[13]

Confronting a Deregulated Bus Business

Teets was also concerned about the 1981 passage of House of Representatives bill H. R. 3663, which deregulated the intercity bus business. Greyhound Lines had developed its route system based on the competitive conditions that had existed in the former business environment. However, Teets sensed that future success in the bus business would not be based on the extensiveness of Greyhound's route system, nor on its fifty years' experience of operating in a regulated industry, but on its ability to make money charging competitive fares. While its chief competitor, Continental Trailways, was operating with a less costly wage agreement from the Amalgamated Transit Union (ATU), Greyhound's labor costs were higher, and costs had increased as a result of the $60 million spent in upgrading terminals and maintenance. To the dismay of Greyhound's management team, once again the rules of the competitive game had changed, and the temporary advantage given to Greyhound by the energy crunch was slipping away.[14]

TEETS SEEKS SOLUTIONS

The Challenge to Improve Greyhound's Return on Equity

Although 1981 had clearly been Greyhound's most profitable year, Teets was concerned about whether Greyhound could remain as profitable in what appeared to be a more competitive and uncertain marketplace. Furthermore, even though Greyhound's return on equity had hit 14.6 percent, after dropping from 15.2 percent the previous year, it had only averaged 12.2 percent since 1978. This was less of a return than investors could earn by simply putting their funds in a certificate of deposit or in a more aggressive money fund.

Teets knew that to be safe from a takeover bid Greyhound would have to earn at least a 15-percent return on its shareholders' equity. Achieving this

[13]"Greyhound: a big sell-off leaves it built for better speed," pp. 88–90.
[14]Greyhound Corporation, *Annual Report* (1981).

objective might mean divesting itself of businesses that seemed the least able to attain this return on equity in the next few years, and that could be run better by other companies. In the future, Teets intended to manage the business toward the achievement of an 18-percent return on equity. He proceeded to position the holding company to divest itself of businesses that could not achieve a corporatewide standard of a 15-percent return on equity.[15] At the same time, he was doing everything he could to raise Greyhound's stock price in order to forestall a hostile takeover. Here, he was aided by a bull market that was to last for the next six years. Finally, his actions were intended to generate cash from the sale of underperforming assets. In effect, he was raising cash to give him the flexibility to buy businesses in other industries should he not succeed in revitalizing some of his own businesses that were underperforming.

To immediately raise Greyhound's stock price, Teets ordered the buyback of 2 million of its own shares at an average price of $14.41 per share. This buyback accomplished two objectives. First, Teets was convinced that he was going to be able to raise Greyhound's stock price, and so the buyback was going to be a wise investment. Second, he wanted to send a signal to the stock market that Greyhound's management was not content with the performance of its transportation and food groups and that it intended to initiate prudent changes to improve the situation.

Teets sensed that it was not going to be easy to make Armour a low-cost leader, since it was saddled with a middle management that was less than entrepreneurial, many outmoded plants, and a recalcitrant meat packers' union that intended to protect its high-cost labor pact. In order to begin the divestiture of Armour without sending a clear signal of his intentions to the stock market, Teets reincorporated Armour as an Arizona corporation and issued Greyhound securities to former owners of Armour stock and debentures. Though he announced that these actions were taken to simplify Greyhound's financial filings, this explanation was transparent and unconvincing, given the many filings that Greyhound had to make with its other diverse holdings.

In a move to generate cash, Teets sold $123 million worth of late-model Greyhound buses and subsequently leased them back to Greyhound Lines for periods of ten and eleven years. In Greyhound's Annual Report for 1982, Teets explained these sales as transactions that reduced consolidated debt by $30 million and allowed the corporation to utilize its available tax credits more effectively.

Furthermore, a number of businesses and assets were sold at book value or better, yielding $42 million in cash and notes. As a result of these sales, receivables and inventories were also reduced, which freed up an additional $15.4 million in working capital. Among the businesses sold in 1982 were two Armour turkey-raising facilities and a beef abattoir, the filament yarn business of Armour Handcrafts Inc., Greyhound Rent-A-Car, and various transportation companies such as Walter Transit, Carey Transportation, American Sightseeing Tours,

[15]"Greyhound's new strategy: slimmed down and decentralized, it's after more market share, 15% on equity," *Dun's Business Month* (February 1984), 66–68.

Gray Line of New York and Red Top Sedan Service Inc. In addition, plans were made for selling three hog-slaughtering operations during the summer of 1983. Finally, another $20 million was saved by reducing corporate personnel and by offering early retirement to 300 Greyhound Lines employees. All these changes were intended to enable Greyhound to restructure itself through divestitures and acquisitions to achieve Teets' goal of a 15-percent return on shareholders' equity.

In spite of these cost-cutting measures, Greyhound's net income dropped from $138 million in 1981 to $103 million in 1982. And, in spite of Teets's stated objective of achieving a 15-percent return on shareholders' equity, it dropped from 14.6 percent in 1981 to 10.9 percent in 1982. Most of this decline occurred because Greyhound Line's income dropped from $49.7 million in 1981 to $20.2 million in 1982. As Teets had feared, deregulation and the end of the energy crunch were having a significant and adverse effect on bus business revenues. Furthermore, although Armour's profits had risen from $9 million in 1981 to $13.2 million in 1982, that was still only a slim 0.5-percent profit margin on sales of $2.3 billion.

Greyhound's return on shareholders' equity dropped even further in 1982, to 10.7 percent. In 1983 it fell lower still, to 9 percent, because of the deteriorating competitive position of the transportation and Armour divisions. Clearly, something had to be done.

A Forty-seven-day Strike at Greyhound Lines

With the beginning of deregulated competition in the intercity bus business and declining passenger revenues resulting from the end of the energy crunch, Greyhound found itself paying wages and benefits that were 30–50% higher than those paid by its competitors. Furthermore, its chief competitor, Trailways, negotiated significant wage concessions from the Amalgamated Transit Union, and then immediately passed these on to customers in the form of lower fares. Trailway's action was a frontal assault on Greyhound's most lucrative routes in an attempt to gain market share. In the face of this assault on its market share, Greyhound's response was to match every one of Trailway's price cuts. While Greyhound preserved its market share, it was losing millions of dollars.

As Teets saw it, the bus operation's noncompetitive position was a problem that he could not put on hold. Since essentially all other operating costs besides wages—fuel, taxes, commissions, depreciation—were similar to those of all other carriers, the need to reduce wage costs was imperative. So Teets embarked on a bitter wage negotiation, which resulted in a forty-seven-day strike in 1983. The subsequent agreement included a 7.8-percent wage cut, a freeze on cost-of-living adjustment payments until May 1986, new employee-paid contributions into pension plans of 4 percent of annual gross wages, and larger contributions to health plans. In total, it resulted in an 8-percent cost savings over the next three years. Teets, summed up the agreement by saying, "This contract gives us the parity we were seeking and still makes the employees the best paid in the industry."[16]

Armour Foods Sold

Despite a wage freeze negotiated with the United Food and Commercial Workers Union two years before, in 1981 Armour Food Company still could not overcome the wage discrepancy with its competitors in the meat-packing industry. Furthermore, Teets was concerned that stodgy Armour, with its more than $2.3 billion in sales and only $13 million in net income, would always be dragging down Greyhound's prospects for improved profitability. Therefore he decided to divest Armour. In preparation for the sale that Teets wanted, he separated the Armour Food Company from Armour-Dial, moved public debt to the parent company (so that he could get his price), and exchanged Armour stock for Greyhound stock.

On December 18, 1983, Armour was sold to ConAgra, Inc. The sale price of $166 million comprised cash, notes, and 3.4 million shares of ConAgra common stock, which gave Greyhound a 15-percent interest in a well-managed agricultural products company. This sale price of $166 million was exactly twice what Trautman had paid for Armour and Armour-Dial together, after selling off assets from their original acquisition price of $450 million. But of course, Teets did not sell Armour-Dial; so he got twice Greyhound's money back from a stodgy business that Greyhound did not know how to operate, and at the same time he got the Armour-Dial company for free.

It was Teet's assessment from the beginning that Greyhound would be able to earn far more as a stockholder in ConAgra than it could by trying to operate Armour, as indeed proved true. In the meantime, he was sitting on a large amount of cash to use for a new acquisition.

With the Armour sale, Teets was chopping off nearly half Greyhound's business. (See Exhibit 5.) Nevertheless, with Greyhound's revenues dropping from $5 billion in 1982 to less than $3 billion in 1984 without Armour, the sale gave Teets the opportunity to put Greyhound in better shape than it had been in years. Also, as soon as the Armour sale was consummated, Teets calculated that Greyhound's net return on sales would rise dramatically, from 2 percent in 1982 to an estimated 5.5 percent the following year.

1984: A Year of Unrealized Expectations

After battling the Amalgamated Transit Union and the loss of $25 million in the forty-seven-day strike, Teets expected better performance from the bus business

---

[16]"If anyone won the strike, Greyhound did," *Business Week*, December 19, 1983, pp. 39–40.

EXHIBIT 5   **The shape of Greyhound without Armour (1984)**

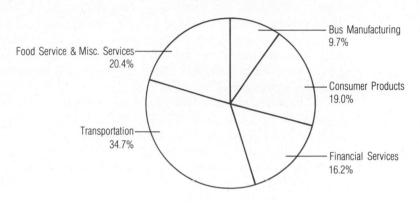

Revenues $2.8 Billion

Bus Manufacturing
9.7%

Consumer Products
19.0%

Financial Services
16.2%

Transportation
34.7%

Food Service & Misc. Services
20.4%

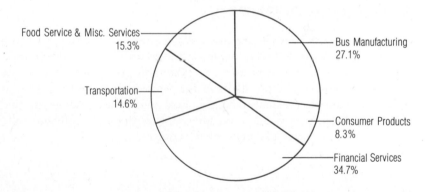

Income $89.5 Million

Bus Manufacturing
27.1%

Consumer Products
8.3%

Financial Services
34.7%

Transportation
14.6%

Food Service & Misc. Services
15.3%

in 1984 than he had been able to achieve in 1983. Anticipating an increase in passenger demand, the bus division raised its advertising budget by more than 33 percent, to $21 million, and simultaneously reduced fares in various markets. It also initiated specialized reductions for college students, Hispanics, retired people, and children. None of these aggressive tactics worked, and Greyhound watched as its share of a declining market decreased.

It was evident that Greyhound Lines had more problems to deal with than just costs. Deregulation had brought about the emergence of lower-cost competitors in regional markets, which were able to be responsive and flexible in pricing and in reacting to Greyhound's actions. As a result, Greyhound lost its competitive edge.[17]

[17]"Greyhound's new strategy," pp. 66–68.

Perhaps a more serious problem than failing to be a low-cost provider of bus services was that 1984 marked the beginning of an era when the need for a national ground transportation system became questionable. One of Greyhound's problems was that it was being challenged by low-cost airlines. People Express flew from Chicago to Los Angeles in four hours for $178. Greyhound riders were paying $129 for a twenty-six-hour ride. In the Texas markets, Texas International airlines brashly advertised that it would exchange a Greyhound bus ticket for a plane ticket. There was no reason for anyone to prefer to ride a bus rather than travel by plane.[18]

If Greyhound could compete as the need for national ground transportation system disappeared, Teets believed that it would be able to do so by hauling passengers from the small towns not served by airlines to major airports. Buses, he concluded, should serve the same function as small feeder airlines, only at a lower cost. It also looked to him as if certain special markets—students and senior citizens, for example, who often travel modest distances on modest budgets—would still present viable opportunities for Greyhound if it could restructure its route system.

1985: The Threat of a Takeover

Clearly, Greyhound and Teets's fortunes were in need of a lift. Far from being a collection of recession-proof businesses that would be individually valuable, as Trautman had planned, Greyhound's principal businesses had become underperformers. As the demand for a national ground transportation system had declined, Teets also had to deal with wide swings in the profitability of his Financial Group, since interest rates first rose and then fell. Under these conditions, Teets planned a new acquisition.

TEETS BUYS PUREX INDUSTRIES

On February 21, 1985, Teets announced the purchase of Purex Industries, Inc., and its thirty household cleaning products, for $264 million. Teets's aim from the beginning with this acquisition was to boost profits in Greyhound's Consumer Products Group (principally composed of the Armour-Dial division) by sharing Dial's sales force and marketing expertise with Purex's products. Purex's products included Purex bleach, Brillo soap pads, Old Dutch cleanser, and Sweetheart and Fels-Naptha soap.

The Purex acquisition drew mixed reviews from Wall Street. First, it did not meet Teets's goal of a 15-percent return, but Teets believed that this could be achieved by 1988, a year after the company as a whole attained it. Second, analysts were unimpressed since Greyhound had not been successful in manag-

[18]Wiegner, "Old Dog, New Tactics," p. 45.

ing Armour. Teets responded that Armour-Dial was capable of marketing consumer products, although it has not been successful at developing its own lines. He cited as evidence the fact that Armour-Dial was marketing the number one deodorant soap in its Dial brand. Analysts did concede that Teets should be able to realize increased profitability by sharing the same sales force between Purex and Armour-Dial. Besides buying Purex's household cleaner business, Greyhound also got Elio's pizza as part of the bargain. Teets was enthusiastic about expanding this frozen pizza business nationwide from its East Coast base. This was to be done using Armour-Dial's sales force.[19]

Among the Greyhound operations with record earnings at the end of 1985 was the Consumer Products Group, which reported its sixth consecutive year of record earnings, with net income up 54 percent, to $41.4 million, from $26.9 million the year before. On its own, Armour-Dial improved its earnings by 14 percent, and to emphasize what Teets hoped would be its new success, it was being renamed Dial. Exhibit 6 summarizes the sources of Greyhound's operating groups' income and earnings in 1986.

THE BUS LINE DIVESTITURE

For Greyhound Lines, the legacy of deregulation was a total inability to be a low-cost provider of bus transportation. Teets said that he did not want to sell the bus transportation group; he said he preferred to make it profitable—after all,

EXHIBIT 6   **The shape of Greyhound in 1986**

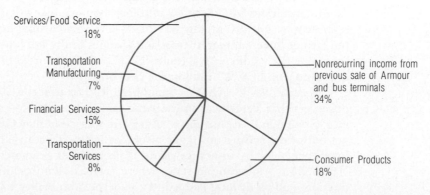

[19]S. Toy and J. H. Dobrzynski, "Will more soap help Greyhound shine?" *Business Week,* March 11, 1985, pp. 73–78.

Greyhound had been in the bus transportation business for more than seventy years. In 1986, in an effort to save the bus lines, he converted 120 company-owned terminals to commission agencies, trimming a huge overhead burden. He also created four stand-alone regional bus companies and a new travel and charter company. Finally, he franchised several of Greyhound's least profitable routes to independent operators, licensing them to use the Greyhound logo and trademark.

However, the one factor that Teets could not control was winning a new labor contract. In February 1986 an offer to freeze wages was rejected by the union. In October, in a deteriorating market, a second offer involving concessions was presented, with the understanding that its rejection would prompt the sale of the company. The offer was subsequently rejected, and fifteen days later Teets announced the sale of Greyhound Lines for approximately $350 million to an investor group headquartered in Dallas. Teets claimed that the actions taken by management in an effort to salvage the bus business were exactly the ones that made it an attractive acquisition for the Currey Group in Dallas.

The sale of Greyhound Lines brought in $290 million in cash and equivalents, including a 25-percent interest in the new holding company established by the investor group. Not included in the sale were twenty-three major downtown parcels of land; Greyhound Lines of Canada; Brewster Transport Company Limited; Texas, New Mexico, Oklahoma Coaches; and the Vermont Transit Co., Inc.[20]

DIVESTITURES IN THE FINANCIAL GROUP

Besides selling Greyhound Lines in 1986, Teets also sold Greyhound Capital Corporation (GCC) and agreed to the pending sale of Verex, Trautman's acquisition. The decision to sell GCC reportedly reflected Teets's conviction that "some businesses just fit better into Greyhound's plans than others." What this statement was really saying was that GCC had become an underperformer in the face of lowered interest rates and changes in the tax laws that disallowed investment tax credits. As a result, GCC was sold for $140 million, realizing a one-time gain of $79.7 million for Greyhound.

In early 1987 Greyhound announced its intention to sell Verex. It seemed to observers that Verex was in the same category as GCC — that is, it did not fit into Greyhound's future plans. Again, it was clear that Greyhound wanted to get out of the private mortgage insurance business because it was suffering high losses generated by insurance claims from business generated before 1985. These claims were originating in states where severe downturns in farming, auto production, and oil drilling had led to a widespread inability to keep up with mortgage payments.

[20]Greyhound Corporation, *Annual Report* (1986).

As a result of these actions, Greyhound reported net income for 1986 of $186 million, compared with $120.1 million for 1985. Earnings for 1986 included several major nonrecurring items, which resulted in a net gain of $102.5 million. These items included gains on the sale of ConAgra shares of $89.5 million and a gain on the sale of Greyhound Capital Corporation of $79.7 million. Exclusive of the nonrecurring items, income for 1986 was $83.7 million, compared with $139.6 million reported in 1985. However, including these extraordinary gains, Teets realized a return on equity of 17.7 percent for 1986.

TEETS NEARS THE COMPLETION OF THE RESTRUCTURING OF GREYHOUND

With the sale of Greyhound Lines, Greyhound Capital, and the pending sale of Verex, Teets said that he was near the end of his task of restructuring Greyhound and shedding those businesses where it looked as though there was insufficient growth potential. In January 1988, after failing to find a buyer for Verex, Greyhound announced that it had stopped taking applications for new mortgage insurance and that it was discontinuing its mortgage insurance business. It also announced that 1987 results would reflect a one-time charge of $45 million after-tax, as a result of reclassifying Verex as a discontinued operation.

By early 1988 Greyhound Corporation was primarily a consumer products and services company. Each of the companies that remained was thought to have the potential to grow internally. Exhibit 7 summarizes the new Greyhound

EXHIBIT 7   **Greyhound's key operations in 1988**

CONSUMER PRODUCTS GROUP

The Dial Corporation — manufactures and markets a wide variety of grocery, personal care, and household products for the consumer under the Dial, Purex, and Armour Star Labels, among other well-known brands.

FINANCIAL GROUP

Greyhound Financial Corporation — engaged in financing commercial and industrial property, primarily income-producing properties such as office buildings and shopping centers, secured loans on receivables from recreational real estate projects, equity note receivables, and similar assets.

TRANSPORTATION MANUFACTURING GROUP

Transportation Manufacturing Corporation and Motor Coach Industries — manufacture busses at plants in Roswell, New Mexico; Pembina, North Dakota; and Winnipeg, Canada.

Universal Coach Parts — sale of bus repair replacement parts.

EXHIBIT 7   **Greyhound's key operations in 1988 (*cont.*)**

SERVICE/FOOD SERIVCE GROUP

Consultants & Designers — technical and design services to business and industry.

Greyhound Airport Services Companies — *Aircraft Service International,* which provides ground handling services for major airlines in the United States and designs, installs, and operates fuel storage and distribution for airports, and *Dispatch Services Group,* which provides ground handling services for major airlines at Miami International Airport and Freeport Airport (in the Bahamas).

Greyhound Exposition Services — provides convention and exhibition services in Las Vegas, Los Angeles, Phoenix, San Diego, and San Francisco.

Greyhound Exhibit Group — designs and manufactures convention and trade show exhibits and displays at facilities in Atlanta, Chicago, Cincinnati, Dallas, Las Vegas, Los Angeles, New York City, Phoenix, and San Francisco.

Greyhound Leisure Services — duty-free retail shops at airports in Miami, Washington, D.C., and Baltimore; a wholesale duty-free business for export; duty-free shops. Cruise ships operating out of Miami and operation of cruise ships out of Port Canaveral by *Premier* Cruise Lines. Also operates a chain of retail gift shops and boutiques in major airports and hotels around the country.

Travelers Express Company — provides money order services to retail establishments and the financial industry, draft-clearing services to financial institutions and corporations, automated teller machine service, and other consumer-oriented payment services.

Faber Enterprises — restaurants and gift shops in major office buildings and transportation terminals in Chicago and Dallas.

Greyhound Food Management — coordinator of Greyhound food service operations; restaurant, fast-food and truck-stop operations; *Restaurant Food Services Division,* offering food services to industry, military installations, and other commercial establishments; *Restaura S.A.,* providing food services management throughout Belgium; *Glacier Park, Inc.,* providing hotel management in Glacier National Park, Montana, and *Cassano's Inc.,* a fast-food pizza chain in Ohio.

Greyhound Support Services — provides housekeeping, food services, and other support services for large remote-site construction projects for industry and government agencies throughout the world and building maintenance services through *Commercial Building Maintenance Company,* San Francisco.

TRANSPORTATION SERVICES GROUP

Greyhound Lines of Canada — intercity bus service, package express, and charter operations in Canada.

Brewster Transport Company — sightseeing and tours in the Canadian Rockies.

Texas, New Mexico & Oklahoma Coaches — tours to Carlsbad Caverns and intercity bus services linking key southwestern cities.

Vermont Transit Company — intercity bus service between cities in Maine, Massachusetts, New Hampshire, New York, and Vermont.

Source: Greyhound's 1988 Annual Report to Stockholders. Reprinted by permission.

Corporation that John Teets had structured. Compare the structure of the company he inherited from Gerry Trautman (Exhibit 1) with the one that existed in January 1988.

At the end of 1981, when Gerry Trautman turned over the driver's seat to John Teets, Trautman promised stockholders that Greyhound was "really going places in the 1980's." But did Trautman envision where John Teets was to take it? Teets has almost completely repositioned Greyhound's businesses and created a company with about half its original assets. The question is, will Teets's new vision of Greyhound and its businesses result in a more profitable company for stockholders?

EXHIBIT 8   Financial briefs

	1987	1986	1985	1984	1983
Revenues (millions)					
Greyhound and consolidated subsidiaries	$2,274	$2,018	$1,924	$1,540	$1,510
Financial Group (not consolidated)	227	263	262	214	182
Combined	$2,501	$2,281	$2,186	$1,754	$1,692
Income (millions)					
Income from continuing operations:					
Greyhound and consolidated subsidiaries	$ 62.6	$ 48.3	$ 73.9	$ 75.5	$ 71.0
Financial Group, exclusive of nonrecurring items	20.2	11.2	10.4	3.3	2.9
Nonrecurring items — $(0.98) and $(0.40) per share		(43.8)	(19.5)		
Income from continuing operations (total)	82.8	15.7	64.8	78.8	73.9
Discontinued operations	(51.5)	173.1	49.4	38.9	12.9
Extraordinary items — $(0.16) and $0.31 per share	(6.2)				14.7
Net income	$ 25.1	$188.8	$114.2	$117.7	$101.5
Income per share (dollars)					
Continuing operations	$ 2.10	$ 0.32	$ 1.34	$ 1.61	$ 1.55
Net income	0.62	4.18	2.36	2.41	2.14
Average outstanding common and equivalent shares (millions)	38.8	44.9	47.9	48.4	47.0

Source: Greyhound Corporation, *Annual Report* (1987). Reprinted by permission.

EXHIBIT 9   Selected financial data

	1987	1986	1985	1984	1983
Operations (000 omitted)[1]					
Sales and revenues:					
Greyhound and consolidated subsidiaries	$2,273,805	$2,017,816	$1,924,245	$1,540,171	$1,510,219
Financial Group (not consolidated)	227,555	262,920	262,243	213,737	181,506
Combined revenues	$2,501,360	$2,280,736	$2,186,488	$1,753,908	$1,691,725
Income of Greyhound and consolidated subsidiaries[2]	$ 62,646	$ 48,315	$ 73,936	$ 75,462	$ 71,047
Net income (loss) of Financial Group[3]	20,158	(32,654)	(9,100)	3,324	2,885
Income from continuing operations	82,804	15,661	64,836	78,786	73,932
Discontinued operations:[4]					
Income (loss) from operations	(39,590)	12,011	49,378	38,923	(8,548)
Gains on sales of businesses	33,099	169,233			21,400
Provisions for losses on discontinued insurance subsidiaries	(45,000)	(8,100)			
Total discontinued operations	(51,491)	173,144	49,378	38,923	12,852
Income before extraordinary items	31,313	188,805	114,214	117,709	86,784
Extraordinary items[5]	(6,211)				14,677
Net income	$ 25,102	$ 188,805	$ 114,214	$ 117,709	$ 101,461
Income (loss) per share (dollars)					
Common and equivalents:					
Continuing operations	$ 2.10	$ 0.32	$ 1.34	$ 1.61	$ 1.55
Discontinued operations	(1.32)	3.86	1.02	0.80	0.28
Extraordinary items	(0.16)				0.31
Net income	$ 0.62	$ 4.18	$ 2.36	$ 2.41	$ 2.14
Assuming full dilution:					
Continuing operations	$ 2.09	$ 0.32	$ 1.32	$ 1.58	$ 1.51
Discontinued operations	(1.31)	3.83	1.00	0.79	0.26
Extraordinary items	(0.16)				0.30
Net income	$ 0.62	$ 4.15	$ 2.32	$ 2.37	$ 2.07
Dividends declared per common share	$ 1.32	$ 1.32	$ 1.26	$ 1.20	$ 1.20
Average outstanding shares (000 omitted):					
Common and equivalents	38,827	44,884	47,933	48,350	47,007
Assuming full dilution	39,213	45,337	49,012	49,626	49,145
People:					
Stockholders of Record	70,930	74,194	84,737	93,543	101,687
Employees (average)	29,694	35,922	36,942	35,392	33,624

EXHIBIT 9   **Selected financial data (*cont.*)**

Financial position (000 omitted)[1]

Total assets	$3,408,769	$2,897,452	$2,863,659	$2,294,343	$2,189,314
Investments in Financial Group subsidiaries	215,271	199,507	216,898	204,932	126,106
Working capital	67,323	189,041	128,556	139,908	153,931
Long-term debt	883,999	605,937	603,947	221,888	261,007
Redeemable preferred stock	6,601	6,599	6,597	6,596	6,595
Other liabilities, deferred items and minority interests	382,390	327,936	232,002	243,061	201,692
Common stock and other equity	937,051	1,027,488	1,130,692	1,118,297	1,085,035
Book value per common share (dollars)	$ 24.80	$ 26.04	$ 24.36	$ 23.57	$ 22.52

[1]Adjusted to present Greyhound Lines, Inc.'s bus operations (sold March 18, 1987) and Greyhound Capital Corporation (sold October 20, 1986) as discontinued, for retroactive restatement upon the adoption in 1987 of SFAS No. 91 by the Financial Group subsidiaries of Greyhound, and to reflect insurance operations as discontinued.

[2]Includes net gains (after-tax) on sales of properties classified as retained assets upon discontinuance of Greyhound Lines, Inc.'s bus operations of $4,890,000 or $0.12 per share in 1987, $24,305,000 or $0.54 per share in 1986, $19,094,000 or $0.40 per share in 1985 and $4,171,000 or $0.09 per share in 1984.

[3]Includes special loss provisions of $43,810,000 (after-tax) or $0.98 per share in 1986, and an unusual loss (after-tax) of $19,440,000 or $0.40 per share in 1985.

[4]Includes a gain on the sale of Greyhound Lines, Inc.'s bus operations in 1987, and in 1986, a gain on sale of Greyhound Capital Corporation of $79,741,000 and a gain of $89,492,000 on the sale of ConAgra Common Stock. Includes the gain on disposal of the Food segment in 1983.

[5]Included in 1987 is a loss on early extinguishment of debt (net of income tax benefit of $4,141,000) or $0.16 per share; and included in 1983 is income consisting of tax benefits of $11,469,000 or $0.24 per share from deduction for tax purposes of U.S. bus operating rights previously written off and gain on extinguishment of debt of $3,208,000 or $0.07 per share.

Source: Greyhound Corporation, *Annual Report* (1987).

EXHIBIT 10   Sales and income of principal business segments

	1987	1986	1985	1984	1983
Sales and revenues (000 omitted)					
Consumer Products	$ 866,465	$ 848,867	$ 843,283	$ 464,524	$ 475,402
Transportation Manufacturing	271,979	193,857	220,891	218,980	259,837
Services	1,135,361	975,092	860,071	856,667	774,980
Consolidated segments	2,273,805	2,017,816	1,924,245	1,540,171	1,510,219
Financial	227,555	262,920	262,243	213,737	181,506
Combined	$2,501,360	$2,280,736	$2,186,488	$1,753,908	$1,691,725
Operating income (loss–000 omitted)					
Consumer Products	$ 69,750	$ 65,350	$ 77,329	$ 42,692	$ 39,237
Transportation Manufacturing	34,368	17,407	32,909	41,145	56,146
Services	90,517	79,577	72,491	88,197	72,458
Financial:					
Before nonrecurring items	17,668	8,483	10,812	5,478	(3,083)
Nonrecurring items[1]		(56,500)	(36,000)		
Total Financial	17,668	(48,017)	(25,188)	5,478	(3,083)
Combined	$ 212,303	$ 114,317	$ 157,541	$ 177,512	$ 164,758
Net income (loss–000 omitted)					
Consumer Products	$ 41,402	$ 34,146	$ 41,364	$ 26,858	$ 22,282
Transportation Manufacturing	18,655	11,068	18,604	27,647	30,162
Services	51,854	42,235	45,813	49,340	46,010
Financial:					
Before nonrecurring items	20,158	11,156	10,340	3,324	2,885
Nonrecurring items[1]		(43,810)	(19,440)		
Total Financial	20,158	(32,654)	(9,100)	3,324	2,885
Income of principal business segments	132,069	54,795	96,681	107,169	101,339
Minority interests	(5,682)	(5,321)	(4,729)	(5,121)	(6,263)
Corporate interest and other costs[2]	(43,583)	(33,813)	(27,116)	(23,262)	(21,144)
Income from continuing operations	82,804	15,661	64,836	78,786	73,932
Discontinued operations[3]	(51,491)	173,144	49,378	38,923	12,852
Income before extraordinary items	31,313	188,805	114,214	117,709	86,784
Extraordinary items[4]	(6,211)				14,677
Net income	$ 25,102	$ 188,805	$ 114,214	$ 117,709	$ 101,461

[1]Special loss provision in 1986 and unusual loss in 1985 (see Notes 3 and 6 of notes to summary combined statements of the Financial Group).
[2]Reduced by net gains on sales of properties classified as retained assets upon discontinuance of Greyhound Lines, Inc.'s bus operations of $4,890,000, $24,305,000, $19,094,000 and $4,171,000 in 1987, 1986, 1985 and 1984, respectively.
[3]See Note B of notes to consolidated financial statements.
[4]Loss on early extinguishment of debt in 1987 and tax benefits of $11,469,000 from deductions for tax purposes of U.S. bus operating rights previously written off and gain on extinguishment of debt of $3,208,000 in 1983.

Source: Greyhound Corporation, *Annual Report* (1987). Reprinted by permission.

EXHIBIT 11   Statement of consolidated financial condition

(000 omitted) Year ended December 31,	1987	1986
Assets		
Current assets		
Cash and short-term investments	$ 20,551	$ 54,457
Receivables	279,679	279,611
Inventories	286,638	203,829
Funds restricted for payment service obligations	613,157	513,063
Prepaid expenses and other current assets	66,026	67,573
Total current assets	1,266,051	1,118,533
Property and equipment		
Land	80,355	73,937
Buildings and leasehold improvements	356,806	263,181
Buses, machinery and other equipment	744,532	598,605
	1,181,693	935,723
Less accumulated depreciation	394,869	330,115
	786,824	605,608
Investments and other assets		
Investments in and long-term receivables due from:		
Financial Group subsidiaries	215,271	199,507
GLI Holding Company and subsidiaries	82,588	
Discontinued operations:		
Insurance subsidiaries	187,651	268,973
Greyhound Lines, Inc. bus operations		143,180
Other investments and assets	208,312	176,230
	693,822	787,890
Deferred income taxes		
Deferred income taxes	79,759	52,740
Intangibles		
Intangibles, including $170,476 not subject to amortization, net of accumulated amortization of $28,583 and $19,260	582,313	332,681
	$3,408,769	$2,897,452

Source: Greyhound Corporation, *Annual Report* (1987). Reprinted by permission.

EXHIBIT 12   Consolidated income statement

(000 omitted) Year ended December 31,	1987	1986	1985
Revenues:			
Sales and revenues	$2,259,015	$2,010,026	$1,908,592
Other income	14,790	7,790	15,653
	2,273,805	2,017,816	1,924,245
Operating costs:			
Cost of sales and revenues	2,079,170	1,855,482	1,741,516
Interest	61,136	69,030	64,927
Unallocated corporate and other costs	23,861	16,627	2,058
Equity in income of affiliates and other income	(5,250)	(1,326)	(3,802)
Minority interests	5,682	5,321	4,729
	2,164,599	1,945,134	1,809,428
Income before income taxes	109,206	72,682	114,817
Income taxes	46,560	24,367	40,881
Income of Greyhound and consolidated subsidiaries	62,646	48,315	73,936
Net income (loss) of Financial Group	20,158	(32,654)	(9,100)
Income from continuing operations	82,804	15,661	64,836
Discontinued operations:			
Income (loss) from operations	(39,590)	12,011	49,378
Gains on sales of businesses	33,099	169,233	
Provisions for losses on discontinued insurance subsidiaries	(45,000)	(8,100)	
Total discontinued operations	(51,491)	173,144	49,378
Income before extraordinary item	31,313	188,805	114,214
Extraordinary charge — early extinguishment of debt, net of tax benefit of $4,141	(6,211)		
Net income	$ 25,102	$ 188,805	$ 114,214
Income (loss) per share (dollars)			
Common and equivalents:			
Continuing operations	$ 2.10	$ 0.32	$ 1.34
Discontinued operations	(1.32)	3.86	1.02
Extraordinary item	(0.16)		
Net income	$ 0.62	$ 4.18	$ 2.36
Assuming full dilution:			
Continuing operations	$ 2.09	$ 0.32	$ 1.32
Discontinued operations	(1.31)	3.83	1.00
Extraordinary item	(0.16)		
Net income	$ 0.62	$ 4.15	$ 2.32
Dividends declared per common share	$ 1.32	$ 1.32	$ 1.26
Average shares outstanding (000 omitted)			
Common and equivalents	38,827	44,884	47,933
Assuming full dilution	39,213	45,337	49,012

Source: Greyhound Corporation, *Annual Report* (1987). Reprinted by permission.

HARCOURT, BRACE, JOVANOVICH

In late 1987 William Jovanovich, CEO of Harcourt, Brace, Jovanovich, found himself at the helm of a firm whose future could at best be described as uncertain. Having for the time being fended off unwanted suitors, Jovanovich had also saddled his firm with an enormous debt burden. HBJ's financial worries were exacerbated by a trend toward globalization and consolidation of the book publishing industry. HBJ was faced with some tough choices as it finished the 1980s and entered the 1990s.

COMPANY BACKGROUND AND DESCRIPTION

Originally incorporated as Harcourt, Brace & Co. in 1919, the company adopted its current name in 1970. It consists of three business segments: publishing, Sea World Enterprises, and communications and services. Acquisitions have played a major role in HBJ's growth.

Historically, the company's strength has been in publishing; the fifth largest book publisher in the country, its primary publications include textbooks, professional journals, and general fiction and nonfiction books. In addition, HBJ publishes and scores aptitude tests and has operations that manufacture and sell school and office graphic supplies. During recent years, however, the firm has retreated somewhat from its publishing emphasis. In 1980 book publishing accounted for 52.4 percent of sales and 61.5 percent of operating profit. In 1985 these figures had declined to 39.4 percent and 35 percent, respectively.[1]

This case was prepared by V. L. Blackburn and C. B. Shrader, Iowa State University.

[1]Peter W. Barnes and Roger Lowestein, "Harcourt Brace to Buy CBS's Book Division," *The Wall Street Journal,* October 27, 1986, p. 4.

Sea World Enterprises operates three marine theme parks in Cleveland, San Diego, and Orlando. It also owns and operates Cypress Gardens, a botanical garden in Winter Haven, Florida. A fourth Sea World was scheduled to open in San Antonio in 1988.

HBJ's Communications and Services Division operates two ABC-affiliated VHF TV stations; publishes farm, business, and professional periodicals, sells accident, health, and life insurance; and operates book clubs.

RECENT DEVELOPMENTS

In 1986 HBJ reversed its recent trend away from book publishing and purchased CBS's Educational and Professional Publishing division for $500 million. The acquisition, which included Holt, Rinehart, and Winston and W. B. Saunders, made HBJ the largest U.S. publisher of elementary and high school textbooks and of medical books.[2] Analysts characterized the acquisition — to the chagrin of Peter Jovanovich, the CEO's son — as a "strategic about-face."[3] Jovanovich maintained that HBJ had been internally developing its book publishing segments all along and suggested that "analysts only look at what you buy, not what you do."

Early in 1987, HBJ made a $50-per-share bid for Harper and Row, topping Theodore L. Cross's bid of $34 per share. Rupert Murdoch was also drawn into the battle, and the spoils finally went to his company, News Corp. Ltd. In the face of HBJ's offer for Harper and Row and its acquisition of the CBS division, rumors abounded that the company was attempting to take on debt to make itself a less likely takeover target.

MANAGEMENT

William Jovanovich has held the position of chief executive officer for more than thirty-two years. He joined the company as a salesman in 1947 and by 1955 had been promoted to his current position. A succession of number-two people have come and gone during his tenure, prompting questions about his management style and potential successor. Asked whether his management style is too autocratic, Jovanovich replies that the suggestion is "a *People* magazine notion that has nothing to do with corporate structure. There's no communal way to run a company. If there's a strong number two man, he goes out and becomes number one elsewhere."

The son of an immigrant coal miner, Jovanovich now surrounds himself with the trappings of his position. A *Forbes* columnist reported seeing in

[2]Barnes and Lowestein, "Harcourt Brace to Buy CBS's Book Division," p. 4.
[3]"HBJ to Buy CBS Text Unit for $500 million," *Publishers Weekly,* November 7, 1986, p. 12.

Jovanovich's office five briefcases with his initials, a Tiffany desk set, and a facsimile set of Leonardo drawings. By way of justification for multiple office locations, Jovanovich observed "I like edifices."

Current speculation suggests that Jovanovich hopes to pass the reins to his son, Peter, who has been named to the office of the president and holds a seat on HBJ's board. Both William and Peter have attempted to quash any such rumors. William Jovanovich has gone so far as to say that there is no question of succession, since he is not retiring. His current contract runs through 1989. Exhibit 1 details HBJ's officers and directors and their corporate affiliations.

EXHIBIT 1   **HBJ directors (showing principal corporate affiliations)**

Theodore M. Black	President, Walter J. Black, Inc.
J. William Brandner	Executive vice-president, Office of the President, and treasurer, Harcourt Brace Jovanovich, Inc.
Ralph D. Caulo	Executive vice-president, Office of the President, Harcourt Brace Jovanovich, Inc.
Trammell Crow	Founder of Trammell Crow Co.; Director, Fidelity Union Life Insurance Co., Dallas
Robert L. Edgell	Vice-chairman, Harcourt Brace Jovanovich, Inc.
Paul Gitlin	Partner, Ernst, Cane, Berner & Gitlin, Attorneys
Maria C. Istomin	Artistic director, John F. Kennedy Center for the Performing Arts, Washington, D.C.
Walter J. Johnson	President, Walter J. Johnson, Inc.
Peter Jovanovich	Executive vice-president, Office of the President, Harcourt Brace Jovanovich, Inc.
William Jovanovich	Chairman and chief executive officer, Harcourt Brace Jovanovich, Inc.
Eugene J. McCarthy	Senator from Minnesota (1958–1970); writer and lecturer
Peter J. Ryan	Partner, Fried, Frank, Harris, Shriver & Jacobson, Attorneys
Virginia B. Smith	Former president, Vassar College; Director, Marine Midland Banks, Inc., and Marine Midland Bank, N.A.
Jack O. Snyder	Executive vice-president, Office of the President, Harcourt Brace Jovanovich, Inc.
Michael R. Winston	Vice-president for academic affairs, Howard University

GENERAL TRENDS IN THE PUBLISHING INDUSTRY

The book publishing industry generates approximately $10 billion in yearly sales, with the top six firms accounting for approximately 30 percent of industry revenues. Although the industry has historically been fragmented, it has faced increasing consolidation in recent years. In particular 1986 was a banner year, with book publishing acquisitions totaling more than $2 billion.[4] The largest of these acquisitions are shown in Exhibit 2. Although acquisitions and consolidation are expected to continue, analysts foresaw that the industry would still be characterized by fragmented specialty publishing, even if six or seven firms held a significant portion of the market.[5]

Explanations for the acquisition fever are numerous. The most controversial argument casts publishing acquisitions in terms of ego gratification: publishing executives want to have acclaimed literary artists under contract because this enhances their own importance. The value of backlists, however, provides probably the most compelling justification for acquisitions. Backlist books by well-known authors such as Hemingway and Fitzgerald sell well (in predictable quantities) year after year, with little advertising or sales support. Also, by combining manufacturing, distribution, and sales force efforts, some publishers are able to increase revenues through merger without realizing commensurate cost increases. Finally, mergers provide a means of jumping traditional entry barriers and expanding the acquiring firm's scope of publishing interests.[6]

A related trend is the gradual globalization of the industry, characterized primarily by foreign entry into the U.S. markets through both internal expansion and acquisition. Saturation of the European market, the value of the dollar

EXHIBIT 2   **Largest book publishing acquisitions of 1986**

Property	Buyer	Price (in millions of dollars)
Scott, Foresman	Time	$520
CBS book publishing operations	Harcourt Brace Jovanovich	$500
Doubleday & Co.	Bertlesmann AG	$475
South-Western Publishing	International Thomson	$270
Silver Burdett	Gulf & Western	$125

Source: Reprinted by permission of *The Wall Street Journal.* © Dow Jones & Company, Inc. 1987. All rights reserved.

[4]Robert J. Cole, "Bids for Harper & Row Spur Publishing Stocks," *The Wall Street Journal,* March 13, 1987, p. D2.
[5]Cole, "Bids for Harper & Row Spur Publishing Stocks," p. D2.
[6]Katherine Bishop, "The Battle of the Booksellers," *New York Times,* March 17, 1987, p. D1.
[7]*Standard & Poor's Industry Survey,* October 1987.

relative to foreign currency, and the internationalization of literary artistry are contributing factors.[7] As shown in Exhibit 2, Betelsman and International Thompson, incorporated in West Germany and Britain, respectively, have recently acquired U.S. companies, as has News Corp. Ltd., a British firm.

When HBJ, Addison-Wesley, Macmillan, Houghton Mifflin, and McGraw-Hill were rumored to be potential takeover targets in 1987, the consensus was that European firms were the most likely and viable threats.

THE BATTLE FOR CONTROL OF HBJ

On May 18, 1987, British Printing and Communications Corporation made a $44-per-share offer for HBJ. This $2 billion offer officially launched the battle for control of HBJ and pitted Robert Maxwell, the socialist CEO of BPCC, against William Jovanovich.[8] Jovanovich immediately characterized the "sudden, unsolicited offer" as "preposterous, both as to intent and value."[9]

To date, the offer represented the largest bid in the active publishing acquisition market. Most analysts, however, believed that it was too low and that additional suitors might be enticed to enter the fray, offering between $50 and $60 per share. In reaction to the offer and in anticipation of a bidding war. HBJ's share price rose $16.125 the day after the announcement, closing at $46.63.

Analysts speculated that Jovanovich would rely on the low bid price and Robert Maxwell's background to justify any defensive moves. After World War II Robert Maxwell held the position of CEO of Pergamon Press. During an attempted takeover bid, Saul Steinberg found that Pergamon's profits had been significantly overstated. The ensuing investigation by the British government led to Mr. Maxwell's being stripped of his board position. He regained this position in 1974 and claimed he was cleared of all previous charges.[10]

In fact, at the time of the bid for HBJ, Jovanovich did refer to Maxwell's background, saying that "Maxwell's dealings since he emerged from the mists of Ruthenia after World War II have not always favored shareholders—as Mr. Saul Steinberg can attest."[11] Jovanovich also seemed offended by the fact that the bid was being made by a much smaller company. In 1986 HBJ earned $74.8 million on revenues of $1.3 billion, and BPCC earned $135 million on $775 million in revenues; thus, BPCC was approximately 60 percent the size of HBJ in terms of sales.

The Defense

In defense against the hostile bid, Jovanovich took immediate, drastic action to ensure his continued control of HBJ. A complicated recapitalization plan was

---

[8]Edwin McDowell, "Maxwell's Harcourt Bid Ends," *New York Times,* May 29, 1987, p. D1.
[9]"HBJ Rejects Maxwell's $1.7 Billion Bid," *Publishers Weekly,* May 29, 1987, p. 18.
[10]"HBJ Rejects Maxwell's $1.7 Billion Bid," p. 18.
[11]"HBJ Rejects Maxwell's $1.7 Billion Bid," p. 18.

announced which increased HBJ's debt to nearly $3 billion. The plan entailed paying a special dividend of $40 per share, at a total cost of $1.6 billion, on July 31. In addition to the cash payment, shareholders received a fraction of a share of new preferred issue with a face value of $13.50, although its market value was estimated at closer to $10 and the value of the existing common stock was expected to drop.[12] HBJ also began a share repurchase program and by the last week in May had bought back 4.8 million shares at a cost of $265.2 million.[13]

Like all recapitalization plans, HBJ's basically resulted in substituting the majority of equity for debt. Also, the combined effect of the share repurchases and the issuance of new preferred stock placed approximately 30 percent of the voting rights in the friendly hands of management, directors, employees, and the First Boston Corporation.

Maxwell reacted by filing suit as a shareholder to block the plan. (At the time of the takeover bid BPCC owned 460,600 shares or almost 2 percent of HBJ's outstanding common stock. It also held $9.49 HBJ debentures.) In the suit Maxwell charged that the planned dividend was illegal under New York state law since it exceeded by $1 billion HBJ's surplus available for dividends and the law precludes paying dividends in excess of surplus. The suit claimed that HBJ ended 1986 with a $500 million surplus, lost $34 million in the first quarter of 1987 and would spend $330 million for share repurchases. In addition Maxwell charged that the issuance of new equity classes and common stock share repurchases would relegate common stockholders to a minority position when control was effectively shifted to management. The net result, according to Maxwell, did not differ substantially from a leveraged buyout.

At 8:30 A.M. on June 8, Maxwell also attempted to win an injunction to prevent the recording of dividend payments on that date or any other specific date. Under HBJ's indenture contract, subordinate debentures are convertible into common stock at the price in effect at the time of conversion.[14] Maxwell filed this injunction to prevent the dividend payment until HBJ provided full disclosure to holders of convertible debentures (totaling $200 million) issued in March 1986.

The judge in the Manhattan district court denied Maxwell's request, indicating that the filing had not been made in a timely manner and that disputes regarding debenture conversion were already being dealt with in a Florida state court. In Florida, Sun Bank, the trustee for debenture holders, was simultaneously involved in litigation with HBJ in an attempt to clarify the conversion price. The Manhattan judge suggested that any further claims Maxwell had as a debenture holder should be handled in conjunction with the Sun Bank case.[15]

In June, BPCC itself made a $1.03 billion rights issue. Maxwell indicated at the time that the proceeds could be used to make a further offer for HBJ if the

[12]John Marcom Jr. and Clifford Krauss, "British Printing Drops Its Offer For Harcourt," *The Wall Street Journal*, May 29, 1987, p. 4.
[13]"Maxwell Sues to Block HBJ's $3 Billion Plan," *Publishers Weekly*, June 12, 1987, p. 23.
[14]"Judge Rules Against Maxwell, Clearing HBJ Proposal," *Publishers Weekly*, June 19, 1987, p. 25.
[15]"Judge Rules Against Maxwell," p. 25.

Florida courts blocked the recapitalization plan. Even if the plan succeeded, however, British analysts believed that BPCC's new financing would allow them to top HBJ's offer. If not, the proceeds from the sale of rights gave BPCC the "resources and flexibility to pursue other opportunities for international expansion."[16]

On July 27, Robert Maxwell announced that BPCC was ending all litigation against HBJ and would soon be bidding for a different U.S. publishing company. In conceding defeat, Maxwell stated that although "BPCC did not achieve its ultimate goal of acquiring HBJ, we are pleased that our efforts have greatly benefited the shareholders of HBJ which included BPCC."[17] On the day of the announcement, Houghton Mifflin, Macmillan, and McGraw-Hill stock prices rose in anticipation of possible bids from Maxwell. William Jovanovich did not make a public statement regarding BPCC's withdrawal announcement.[18]

Analysts' Evaluation

The recapitalization plan announced by HBJ was one of the first of its kind. Analysts immediately began to discuss the implications of such bold defensive tactics. American corporations have become increasingly assertive in their reactions to hostile takeover attempts, as Exhibit 3 shows; it briefly describes some of the more widely used defenses.

EXHIBIT 3 **Descriptions of takeover defenses**

Poison pill
The issuance of securities that can be converted to cash, notes, or equity of the acquirer

Pac Man
Attempting to acquire the threatening firm

Leveraged buyout
Usually implemented by management; making the firm private by using loans secured by its assets and future cash flows

Sale of valued assets
Selling off those assets that are of the most interest to the acquiring firm, thereby reducing the company's value as a target

Self-tender
A share repurchase that reduces the number (percent) of shares available for purchase by the potential acquirer

[16]Barbara Toman, "British Printing Sets $1.03 Billion Issue; Maxwell Sees New Harcourt Bid Possible," *The Wall Street Journal*, June 17, 1987, p. 12.
[17]"Maxwell Concedes Defeat in HBJ Takeover, Aims at Other U.S. Firms," *Publishers Weekly*, August 7, 1987, p. 309.
[18]"Maxwell Concedes Defeat in HBJ Takeover," p. 309.

One of the more popular approaches has been the leveraged buyout. Usually implemented by executives of the target firm, this entails making the company private, using debt secured by its future cash flows and assets. This defense had been criticized by William Jovanovich and others as posing conflicts of interest for managers, who are not subjected to public scrutiny regarding the firm's performance after it becomes privately owned.[19] However, leveraged buyouts legally put the company "into play" (up for sale), which obligates the officers to sell to the highest bidder.

The defense used by HBJ has been termed the "leveraged recapitalization." Like the leveraged buyout, it requires incurring enormous debt loads. In addition, those characteristics that make a firm a good candidate for leveraged buyout also make it a good candidate for leveraged recapitalization. These characteristics include a strong market position, steady cash flows that can be used to service and pay debt, a low debt position prior to the buyout or recapitalization, and undervalued assets that can be sold at a profit to pay debt. Unlike buyouts, recapitalizations do not legally put the firm into play, so management is absolved of its responsibility to sell to the highest bidder. Critics maintain that as a result, managers are able to gain control of the firm's equity for bargain prices without making a personal investment.[20]

Analysts have also criticized leveraged recapitalizations as adding to shareholder risk. Shareholders have so far fared well; Harcourt's share closed up $9 immediately following the announcement. Investment analysts fear, however, that shareholders will become overly optimistic in light of such early success and fail to recognize the potential for disaster. As long as operating earnings meet expectations, stockholders will continue to reap the benefits of recapitalization. When operating margins fall even slightly below expectations, though, stock prices will fall dramatically. Even the slightest economic downturn can precipitate heavy losses for such highly levered firms. In addition, recapitalized companies put themselves at risk of rising interest rates and reduced financial and competitive flexibility.

It is too early to judge the long-term consequences of the leverage recapitalization. When operating margins fall even slightly below expectations, though, stock prices will fall dramatically. Even the slightest economic downturn can precipitate heavy losses for such highly levered firms. In addition, recapitalized companies to survive is contingent on meeting sales and profit expectations. Any shortfall spells disaster for shareholders and creditors, although management has relatively little to lose from a financial standpoint.

HARCOURT'S FUTURE

Ivan Obolensky, a partner with Sterling, Grace and Company, has expressed concern for HBJ's future. "I don't understand where all the euphoria is coming

[19]Marcom and Krauss, "British Printing Drops Its Offer For Harcourt," p. 4.
[20]McDowell, "Maxwell's Harcourt Bid Ends," p. D1.

from. Jovanovich has succeeded, but there's no room for error in meeting his projections."[21]

For the second quarter of 1987, Harcourt, Brace, Jovanovich reported a net loss of $70.8 million versus a net income of $10.9 for the same quarter of 1986. Revenues increased 31 percent to $408.7 million for the second quarter of 1987 from $312 million for the second quarter of 1986. For the total first six months of 1987, HBJ suffered a loss of $98.5 million versus a profit of $3.5 million for the preceding year. These figures clearly point to the high price HBJ has paid for its independence. Prior to the announcement, HBJ shares sold for $10.25.

The success of HBJ's recapitalization plan and in fact HBJ's survival are contingent on the company's ability to achieve its extremely ambitious sales and profit projects. Estimates included in the plan called for net income of $23 million in 1987 (before preferred dividends) and $33 million in 1988. Projections called for more than doubling 1986 revenues — $2.2 billion by 1989. Harcourt officials hastened to point out in SEC filings of second quarter losses that the majority of HBJ's sales and income are realized during the third quarter of the year.[22]

Additional documents filed with the SEC in August 1987 outlined specific plans to reduce costs. They called for a 5 to 10 percent reduction in staff over the next year, which translated into a loss of 800 to 1600 positions. This announcement came on the heels of a July cut of thirty-eight positions in the trade division, eighteen of which were in customer service. HBJ also planned to cancel all philanthropic activities through 1988, freeze some wages and sell executive perquisites, including company-owned planes and condominiums.

HBJ faces some difficult times as a consequence of its overriding commitment to fend off Robert Maxwell's takeover. Although William Jovanovich probably succeeded in making HBJ an unappealing target for other hostile bids, the total cost of independence is yet to be determined. In the face of growing competition and increasing consolidation in the publishing industry, HBJ has sacrificed its financial flexibility and possibly weakened its future competitive position. Its very survival hinges on its ability to generate cash flows from operations or sales of assets sufficient to service and pay debt.

[21]McDowell, "Maxwell's Harcourt Bid Ends," p. D1.
[22]Charles F. McCoy, "Harcourt Posts 2nd-Period Loss of $70.8 Million," *The Wall Street Journal,* August 17, 1987, p. 7.

EXHIBIT 4   Selected balance sheet data

	Year Ended December 31				
	1986	1985	1984	1983	1982
Current assets	$ 458,595,579	$ 285,971,699	$238,531,740	$223,357,459	$198,358,817
Current liabilities	246,642,452	128,866,757	125,281,691	108,728,882	86,833,396
Working capital	211,953,127	157,104,942	113,250,049	114,628,577	111,525,421
Current ratio	1.9 to 1	2.2 to 1	1.9 to 1	2.1 to 1	2.3 to 1
Long-term debt	790,277,858	222,302,939	128,260,571	113,776,471	110,347,903
Total assets (including HBJ Insurance)	2,413,295,148	1,380,857,091	578,707,473	497,233,931	443,780,242
Shareholders' equity	531,477,176	305,906,617	211,946,792	183,593,090	165,500,998
Book value per common share	$13.48	$8.95	$7.42	$6.73	$6.08
Number of common shares outstanding	39,418,557	34,174,239	28,551,444	27,270,927	27,229,143

Per-share amounts, the number of common shares outstanding, and dividends prior to 1986 were restated to reflect the three-for-one stock split in 1986.

EXHIBIT 5   Consolidated sales and revenues

By sources, 1986–1982

	1986		1985		1984		1983		1982	
	Amount	%	Amount	%	Amount	%	Amount	%	Amount	%
Educational Publishing										
	$ 450,013,149	34.6	$400,585,206	40.5	$355,780,595	47.1	$227,315,275	49.4	$273,774,531	46.9
Informational Publishing & Services										
	278,412,316	21.4	247,935,638	25.0	213,581,836	28.3	177,901,179	26.9	168,101,646	28.8
	728,425,465	56.0	648,520,844	65.5	569,362,431	75.4	505,216,454	76.3	441,876,177	75.7
Parks										
	223,239,856	17.2	170,388,155	17.2	143,181,982	19.0	129,366,819	19.5	118,980,621	20.4
Insurance										
	331,549,863	25.5	171,576,097	17.3	42,226,887	5.6	28,093,385	4.2	22,758,135	3.9
Corporate										
	16,889,605	1.3	—	—	—	—	—	—	—	—
	$1,300,104,789	100.0	$990,485,096	100.0	$754,771,300	100.0	$662,676,658	100.0	$583,614,933	100.0

EXHIBIT 6   **Consolidated statements of income (not including HBJ Insurance)**

For the years ended December 31, 1984, 1985, and 1986

	1984	1985	1986
Sales and revenues	$712,544,413	$818,908,999	$968,554,926
Costs and expenses			
Cost of sales	324,651,146	373,097,973	431,093,075
Selling and editorial	200,008,650	236,427,716	274,068,904
General and administrative	111,859,452	120,993,166	143,640,104
Relocation costs[1]	6,624,678		
Income from operations	73,862,358	107,260,294	151,507,156
Interest expense	13,326,603	18,544,415	21,718,605
Income (loss) before taxes	60,535,755	88,715,879	129,788,551
Income taxes (credit)			
Federal	19,225,150	29,926,863	47,632,000
State and local	6,831,140	8,242,000	11,681,000
Net income	$ 34,479,465	$ 50,547,016	$ 70,475,551
Net income per share of common stock	$1.23	$1.62	$1.91

[1]In 1982 the company charged to income $27,700,000 as the estimated cost of relocating its headquarters during the years 1982, 1983, and 1984. The estimate included the costs relating to moving employees and office equipment, the training and recruiting of new employees, employee severances (net of actuarial gains which arise from these terminations), and fees to consultants. The company's relocation was completed during 1984. The actual costs of relocation exceeded the original estimates by $6,624,678 ($.12 per share), owing in part to changes in operations between offices in California (San Diego and San Francisco) and Orlando; also, duplicate rents and wages during the period of moving were considerably higher than anticipated.

EXHIBIT 7   **Consolidated statements of income**

For the years ended December 31, 1983, 1982, and 1981

	1983	1982	1981
Sales and revenues	$648,827,041	$575,254,594	$539,296,454
Costs and expenses			
Cost of sales	297,820,715	271,261,955	251,160,186
Selling and editorial	181,336,740	163,653,634	143,369,330
General and administrative	108,035,640	102,248,290	92,283,937
Relocation costs	—	27,700,000	—
	587,193,095	564,863,879	486,813,453
Income from operations	61,633,946	10,390,715	52,483,001
Relocation costs (net)	—		
Interest expense (net)	10,276,507	12,647,026	12,839,113
Income (loss) before taxes on income	51,357,439	(2,256,311)	39,643,888
Income taxes (credit):			
Federal	17,570,000	(6,811,000)	11,893,000
State and local	6,311,000	1,261,000	3,996,000
	23,881,000	(5,550,000)	15,889,000
Net income	$ 27,476,439	$ 3,293,689	$ 23,754,888
Net income per share of common stock	$3.03	$.36	$2.70

EXHIBIT 8   Consolidated income from operations

By sources, 1986–1982

	1986		1985		1984		1983		1982	
	Amount	%	Amount	%	Amount	%	Amount	%	Amount	%
Educational Publishing										
	$ 53,935,046	35.6	$ 35,746,372	33.3	$36,719,971	49.7	$26,128,447	41.7	$ 14,038,775	128.0
Informational Publishing & Services										
	37,953,557	25.0	31,903,349	29.7	27,587,668	37.4	21,574,211	34.4	14,398,610	131.3
	91,888,603	60.6	67,649,721	63.0	64,307,639	87.1	47,702,658	76.1	28,437,385	259.3
Parks										
	40,089,435	26.5	34,240,931	31.9	24,033,525	32.5	19,207,692	30.7	18,148,471	165.5
Insurance										
	31,754,313	21.0	18,870,150	17.6	4,461,871	6.0	4,707,578	7.5	98,560	.9
Corporate										
	(12,225,195)	(8.1)	(13,500,508)	(12.5)	(12,315,999)	(14.3)	(8,975,747)	(14.3)	(8,018,753)	(73.1)
Relocation Costs										
	—	—	—	—	(6,624,678)	(8.9)	—	—	(27,700,000)	(256.6)
	$151,507,156	100.0	$107,260,294	100.0	$73,862,358	100.0	$62,642,181	100.0	$ 10,965,663	100.0

Case 18

KSM/BEEFALO BREEDING COMPANY: ENTREPRENEURIAL STRATEGIES IN DIVERSIFIED MARKETS

"It seems that every week brings a new dimension to our business," mused George Schweiger, president of KSM Enterprises. "I wonder where we will be a year from now?" Schweiger sat reflectively at his desk gazing out the window of the log home that served as the sales office for the Beaver Log Home distributorship that KSM acquired late in the summer of 1977. He was looking across a snow-covered pasture toward the barns and livestock pens of the Clarence Korte farm. It was on this Illinois farm that Schweiger and Korte launched the Beefalo Breeding Company in April 1977 with the importation of 40 head of half-blood beefalo from California. After less than a year of operation in their two businesses, the management team of Schweiger and Korte were considering diversification into yet another distinct enterprise—fast-food restaurants.

EVENTS LEADING TO THE NEW BUSINESSES

The business experience of George Schweiger, which spans 30 years, has been primarily that of a salesman, promoter, and entrepreneur. For 13 years he was in

This case was prepared by Curtis W. Cook of San Jose State University as a basis for class discussion rather than to illustrate either effective or ineffective handling of an administrative situation. © 1980 by Curtis W. Cook.

the insurance business, for 7 years in the construction business, part of which involved site location/acquisition, contractor negotiations, and equipment installations for the Bonanza Steak House chain of restaurants in the Seattle region. About 11 years ago he relocated in Illinois as the national marketing director for a new firm specializing in outdoor lighting systems. From this position he spun off a new firm involved in custom plastic packaging. Eventually this enterprise diversified toward end products by manufacturing nonprescription pharmaceuticals and cosmetics. Schweiger's function in the above two businesses was in sales management. Five years ago he switched into brokerage consulting, specializing in diamonds and bulk Scotch whiskey. After two years in the brokerage business, he organized a company to develop an organic fertilizer produced from a bacteria blend of decomposing sawdust. It was through this agricultural venture that he developed a working relationship with Clarence Korte, an experienced organic farmer and dairy rancher.

Clarence Korte, after retiring from military service in 1956, joined his brother Ralph to start the Korte Construction Company. Currently, this construction firm is one of the largest in Southern Illinois, with several multimillion dollar contracts for industrial and commercial buildings. However, in 1962 Clarence decided to leave management involvement in Korte Construction and return to his family's tradition in farming. In partnership with his brother, Clarence developed a large Holstein dairy herd and converted to all-organic farming on the 520-acre farm near Pocahantas, about 40 miles east of St. Louis. In November 1976 fire destroyed most of the physical plant of the dairy operation, causing an estimated $350,000 loss. Rather than rebuild for dairy production, the Kortes liquidated all dairy assets in February 1977. Clarence was intrigued by the economic and nutritional superiorities of beefalo (a bison-bovine hybrid) over conventional beef cattle. In conjunction with George Schweiger, the Kortes decided to venture into this new breed of livestock. Thus, Beefalo Breeding Company was formed and the start of a herd buildup began in spring of 1977.

While the calamity of a fire provided the circumstances that cleared the way for entry into beefalo production, the log home business began more as a marketing outgrowth of another product line sold through KSM Enterprises. KSM was also established in 1977 when Schweiger, who has a penchant for novel products, brought to the new firm the distributorship for a European-produced low-temperature radiant heating system. The product is a system-conductive foil sealed in sheet plastic that is stapled to ceiling framing prior to installation of drywall, plasterboard, or acoustical tile. Out of a desire to have a means of displaying and demonstrating the product, the possibility of selling and/or constructing homes was considered. Management quickly narrowed the search to becoming a distributor for some manufacturer of precut log homes, and Beaver Log Homes of Grand Island, Nebraska, was selected.

Thus, by the end of their first year of investment/management association, Schweiger and Korte had established their two principal businesses as log home sales and beefalo breeding/production. Yet serious challenges remained as to the desired direction and rate of future growth, with capital availability a chronic constraint.

MANAGERIAL ROLES

In seeking to define alternatives relative to these challenges, the two principals in these joint enterprises have informally evolved specialized roles. Clarence Korte, with experience in construction and livestock/farming management, concentrates on production-related tasks. This involves not only management of the livestock operation but also supervision of erecting log structures and constructing whatever finishing touches are desired by the purchaser of a log home or barn.

George Schweiger tends to the sales and financial side of the business. Included in his role are direct selling/merchandising of both log homes and beefalo as well as promoting investments in beefalo under a variety of tax-sheltered programs. Schweiger acknowledges that he is a dreamer and promoter of ideas and novel concepts:

> Probably the greatest problem I have is going from one thing to another. I am looking for the new products, the different ideas. I have always maintained that talent is the cheapest commodity that can be obtained. Sure, good talent is expensive, but in relationship to its performance it is a value. My feeling has always been that if I can get it together, so to speak, then I'll find somebody else more qualified than I to manage it. . . . So I tend to be a dreamer. If a potential product is there, it can be made to work given the proper infusion of capital and management expertise. If I have any expertise at all, I think it is in the field of taking ideas and converting them into different types of presentations for development of a business.

KSM ENTERPRISES AND THE BEAVER LOG HOME CONTRACT

KSM Enterprises Inc. was incorporated on March 1, 1977, with 300,000 no-par shares authorized (although franchise taxes were paid on only 100,000 shares). An initial equity capitalization of approximately $87,000 was obtained with investments from Korte equal to 29.2 percent of the total, Schweiger with 26.5 percent, one "silent" investor with 32.0 percent, and six others totaling 12.3 percent. As of December 31, 1977, book value was 87 cents per share. During its formative period, KSM relied on borrowed funds to provide partial financing of physical facilities and periodically to supply working capital. One year from date of incorporation, debt financing totaled approximately $35,000.

Schweiger brought to KSM the radiant heating system with which he had been involved for about eight months prior to incorporation. In deciding to expand the product line to include the home in which the heating system could be installed, he did not want the newly established KSM to compete directly with more experienced companies. Speaking in February 1978, Schweiger explained:

> We just didn't want to go out and start building stick built homes so we started to explore the log home market and found that everything indicated that it was probably the fastest-growing segment of the building market. We felt that there was an opportunity here. Three years ago, there probably wasn't a log home — other than Abe Lincoln's cabin up at Salem — within a 50-mile radius of here. Today there are probably a dozen.

With a determination to enter into a distinctly different segment of the construction industry, after researching the product, production methods, and financial capabilities of 15 log-home manufacturers, management decided to negotiate with Beaver Log Homes. When asked why Beaver Log Homes was selected over other manufacturers, Schweiger stated:

> Principally, because our studies of other companies indicated to us that both from the standpoint of the finished product as well as the overall financial strength and capabilities of the firm, Beaver offered to us and to the consumer the best log home on the market today for the price. There is a superior log home to Beaver, cut from Michigan White Cedar, but it is not the home for the average buyer. So we just felt that Beaver was by far the best company to deal with.

The contract gave KSM dealership rights to all of southern Illinois, including the right for KSM to contract for subdealers in communities throughout that part of the state. One contract provision required KSM to build either a log home or log office building to serve as a demonstration model. Since the Korte farm land was adjacent to I-70 (a major interstate connecting the St. Louis metropolitan region to points east), management decided to erect a log office facility adjacent to the interstate where it would be clearly visible from both directions, even though exits and the closest commercial activities are approximately two miles from the site. The nearest community with light industrial firms is Highland, about five miles to the southwest.

Under terms of the contract with Beaver, KSM will receive a 27.5 percent discount from list price if they equal or exceed the purchase of 50,000 lineal feet of logs annually. Additionally, quarterly quotas are to be met or the margin will be reduced. For each quarter that quotas are met, an additional 2 percent production bonus (beyond 27.5 percent) is awarded.

Marketing of Log Homes

Beaver sells log homes principally on the basis of logs precut for several types of basic floor plans, both one- and two-story homes. For an average-sized Beaver Log Home requiring 2,359 lineal feet of logs, suggested retail price for logs is about $8,300. Custom design is possible as log construction is not limited to size or shape of floor design, although height is limited without cross-tie structural support. Clarence Korte, for example, built and custom designed a 3,100-square-foot home for his family. Logs are cut and number coded (to match blueprint designs) at the mill in Claremore, Oklahoma, and transported directly by truck to the building site.

KSM sells on cash basis, with 30 percent down payment required either from the individual purchaser or the subdealer at the time the contract is signed. The remainder is due at the time logs are delivered. KSM will help prospective customers work with local banks or savings and loans to arrange mortgage financing. For individuals purchasing within about a 100-mile radius of Highland, Illinois, KSM will erect the log home shell on the owner's foundation if the owner/builder so desires. Clarence Korte assembles and supervises a crew of laborers for this purpose on an as-needed basis. KSM will also provide whatever finishing the customer desires. Once a contract is signed, the normal delivery schedule is 45 days for delivery, with 15 days variance according to the mill's cutting schedule.

KSM engages in little newspaper advertising. The parent does advertise in some trade magazines and popular home-related magazines (e.g., *Better Homes and Gardens*). KSM primarily relies on local home shows as a means of achieving exposure and creating interest. For such purposes, an 8 by 10 foot display booth (constructed of Beaver logs) is erected at the show site. The principal costs of such promotional activity is the show promotional fee and the labor cost of someone to work at the booth distributing free brochures, talking to those who pass by, and to interested parties, selling a $3 book of Beaver plans and specifications for standard model homes. Promotional fees are for advertising of the home show, typically for radio spots which might run from $280 to $560 for 40 to 120 spots that promote both the show and the sponserer (in this case, KSM's Beaver Homes).

Because of the vastness of the franchised sales territory, KSM management intends to sell primarily through contracts with builders/dealers who represent one to three county areas. KSM will discount logs to subdealers or contract builders from 5 percent to 22.5 percent off list price, depending on expected sales volume of the dealer. Such a practice would reduce the pressures on Schweiger to personally be responsible for direct selling to individual home owners.

For KSM to qualify for the 27.5 percent operating margin discount, approximately 24 "average size" homes of 2,050 lineal feet need to be sold annually with about 20 per year necessary to break even. Such an average size (based on Beaver sales statistics) represents a value of $7,000 to $8,000 each. Logs represent 18 to 25 percent of the total cost of the house, with 20 percent considered a "rule of thumb." Other cost factors include foundation or basement, plumbing, heating systems, electrical, doors and windows, etc.

After the first six months of the Beaver dealership, KSM had sold three homes. By February 1979 (after one and one half years), a total of 18 log buildings had been sold; bids were out on 15 additional plans.

BEEFALO AS A NEW MEAT SOURCE

Beefalo are a hybrid bison/bovine cross developed to impart the growth advantages of bison (buffalo) into meat production animals that would have color, confirmation (shape), and edible characteristics similar to beef cattle. A successful breed was first announced in 1973 by developer D. C. "Bud" Basolo, after years of experimentation and breeding up to arrive at a pureblood sire. A pureblood beefalo is defined as ⅜ American Bison and ⅝ domestic bovine (typically ⅜ Charolais and ⅖ Hereford). Several production advantages are claimed for beefalo over beef:

1. Beefalo calves are smaller at birth (approximately 45 to 65 pounds compared to 80 to 105 pounds for cattle). Thus, less assistance and care are necessary at birth, resulting in lower losses (deaths), especially on open ranges.

2. Beefalo are believed heartier than cattle, able to withstand greater temperature extremes and less prone to sickness. Historically, buffalo herds roamed from Canada to Mexico and prior to man, their principal adversary was the predator (wolves, coyotes, etc.). Calves are able to run approximately four hours after birth regardless of weather conditions.

3. Beefalo mature more quickly than beef. Animals mature to a slaughter weight (approximately 1,000 to 1,100 pounds) in about 12 months compared to about 18 months for beef.

4. Beefalo convert feed to flesh more efficiently than beef and require less grain for finishing. A test conducted by Dr. Gary C. Smith at Texas A & M University in 1976 statistically confirmed the superior productive efficiency of 486 head of beefalo compared to bovine control groups. Among some of Dr. Smith's findings, one pen of cattle on a feed ration of 14 percent roughage and 86 percent concentrate (corn, rolled oats, soy meal, etc.) over a 120-day period for finishing prior to slaughter gained an average 2.55 pounds per day at a feed cost of 47 cents per pound. Beefalo, which were on a 26 percent roughage ration, averaged a gain of 2.71 pounds per day at the same 47 cents cost. Those beefalo on a 36 percent roughage produced an average daily gain of 0.5 to 0.7 of a pound more (3.21 to 3.41) at a cost of 37 cents per pound.

5. Beefalo yield a proportionately higher percentage of meat to live weight. This results from more energy being converted into muscle tissue rather than fat. In the Texas A & M study, all beefalo carcasses were federally graded in yield grade 2, the most favored yield grade of producers since excess fat is minimal yet the meat tissue is bright in color and well conformed (blocky rather than thin and rangy). As a percentage of dressed carcass to live weight, the beefalo averaged 63 percent compared to a typical 59 to 61 percent yield for steers or English-bred cattle. Dr. Smith commented, "Based on my experience of 15 years' work in this field, they [beefalo] have

remarkable dressing percentages and it is due to the fact that they are muscular, extremely muscular in relation to other cattle."

Considered as food for human consumption, beefalo test out favorably in terms of nutritional value relative to beef. The following data from Certified Labs Inc., 19 Hudson St., New York (USDA Certified Laboratory #3677) are representative of comparative analysis of beefalo (ground) and ground beef as purchased in supermarkets:

	Lot Dec 484 Ground Beefalo	Lot Dec 483 Ground Beef
Protein	20.35%	16.67%
Fat	3.65%	24.80%
Calories	32.4/ounce	82.4/ounce
Cholesterol	5.19 Mg./ounce	150.5 Mg./ounce

Beefalo Breeding Company's Production Operations

Within one year of their inception, Beefalo Breeding Company developed the largest herd of beefalo in the Midwest. Most of the 520 acres on the Korte Brothers Farm are devoted to organic farming of feed grains for feed fattening and finishing of livestock. Since 1970 the farm has been entirely organic, eliminating the use of chemical fertilizers, herbicides, and pesticides. The farm carries organic certification and is one of two selected by Dr. Barry Commoner of Washington University for comparative studies between chemical and ecological farming. This farm has a capacity for producing grain and alfalfa capable of finishing approximately 800 head per year, on the basis of a quarterly turnover (90-day finishing). The Korte Farm itself is not intended for extensive grazing, as all but about 65 acres is cultivated farmland. Currently there are four grain storage tanks adjacent to the feedlot, each capable of holding approximately 65 tons of feed.

The company is incorporated separately from KSM, with Schweiger and the Korte brothers as the stockholders. It is a member of both the World Beefalo Association (California) and the American Beefalo Association (Kentucky), organizations concerned with registering breeders and developing performance data on the various beefalo blood lines. Beefalo Breeding Company is under a management/feeding contract with the Korte Farm for the feeding and care of the herd. Under terms of the arrangement, the corporation pays Korte 27.5 cents per pound of weight gain, which provides an adequate return to the Korte Farm. If Holsteins or Herefords were being fattened instead of beefalo, a fee of at least 35 cents per pound would be necessary for the farm to obtain a similar return. This difference is because of the genetic advantage of beefalo, which have the same digestive tract as buffalo, a more efficient converter of feed.

Beefalo Breeding Company prefers to place 800 to 850 pound beefalo (after grass feeding) into the feedlot for 60 to 90 days. A 12 to 15 bushel hot-feed ration (of rolled, oats, corn, crushed wheat, soy meal, etc.) will produce white marbling and exterior fat suitable to yield a choice quality grade (the most-used grade in major supermarkets) and a quantity yield grade of 2.

To accommodate grassland feeding, Beefalo Breeding Company bought a 670-acre ranch located in south-central Missouri, near Salem (valued at $300,000). The 540 acres of pasture land in this ranch, once improved, will be capable of supporting a 300 to 350 head beefalo cow-calf operation. While the first year of business saw a buildup to 135 animals at the Illinois facility, in April 1978, the first 124 head were delivered to the Missouri ranch. This herd was purchased from a breeder in Pauls Valley, Oklahoma, at a cost of $38,000 delivered, financed through an open-end bank note.

Marketing Beefalo

While beefalo is subject to the same grading process as beef, in February 1978, the Meat Division of the USDA issued basic guidelines to their field graders that would certify beefalo as a separate class of animals from beef. Having this classification enables beefalo to be marketed as distinct from beef, although in practice it can be sold through supermarkets as beef since the consumer would not discern the difference.

Since beefalo are a relatively new breed of livestock, on a national basis herd sizes remain small. To build up herds, most breeders retain heifers for calf production and sell off as slaughter animals young bulls/bullocks (most breeding is through artificial insemination from registered pureblood bulls). This scarcity of slaughter animals enables beefalo producers generally to command a premium price for their meat, usually about 10 cents/pound over comparable beef carcass grades. Organically produced and certified meat of any kind also usually commands a higher price because of presumed health advantages.

By late March 1978, Beefalo Breeding Company had 30 head ready for slaughter (1,100 to 1,200 pounds each), the first in any quantity for retail sale. At this time the Chicago Board of Trade price quote for choice beef was in the $46 to $48 range, live weight basis. Schweiger and Korte both expressed disillusion with conventional meat distribution systems, since the producer essentially is a price taker. For this reason they explored alternative marketing approaches. Schweiger remarked:

> We are not in accord with the current marketing methods of the agricultural industry. We think they are controlled too much by speculators. If we can control our production cost and go directly to the consumer with the finished product, we can reap the profits currently enjoyed by the speculators as opposed to the producers.

Since Beefalo Breeding had not previously slaughtered more than one or two animals at a time, they had no regular clientele or distribution procedures.

Several alternatives were thus explored. Schweiger phoned Nelson Name Service in Minneapolis to see if they could compile lists of all the health food stores and Weight Watchers Clubs in Illinois. Packages of frozen select retail cuts (i.e., steaks, roasts, ground beefalo) could be sold to health food stores. To Weight Watchers the intent would be to sell halves or quarters of beefalo, either in fresh carcass form or cut and frozen. Beefalo Breeding Company also was contacted by a New York beefalo firm asking if it would be possible to purchase slaughter-ready livestock. Although the New York firm was smaller in actual numbers of beefalo, they had an established promotional and distribution system (selling direct to consumers in halves and quarters).

Schweiger also contacted area supermarket chains to explore the feasibility of a special beefalo promotion. In talking with the manager of meat operations with the National Supermarket chain (which had a large share of market in the St. Louis area), the idea was readily acceptable. However, to be able to use beefalo as a promotional item, National would require at least 300 head since they followed a policy of uniform advertising within a metropolitan market.

Another option was to have approximately 80 percent of the carcass ground into hamburger patties to build up a supply pending the opening of Beefalo Barns Restaurants (details noted in future section). The remaining 20 percent (steaks only) would be packaged in 10-pound units, frozen, and sold through local promotion.

However, because these animals had to go to slaughter (additional feeding would result in minimal salable weight gain), Schweiger in April made arrangements to supply five IGA markets (local independents) in Peoria, Illinois, with 14 head for a special sale. The price was 10 cents/pound dressed weight over choice beef. Additionally, in a reciprocal arrangement with a Springfield, Illinois, radio station, Beefalo Breeding Company sold livestock directly to a Springfield packer, with the radio station advertising the availability of beefalo halves and quarters. The advertising was at no direct cost to the company since Clarence Korte had supplied an electrical power generator to the radio station when an ice storm in late March knocked out their power source and forced them off the air. Schweiger saw these market sources more as temporary, although he recognized residual value in (a) exposing the public to beefalo, (b) possibly attracting some wealthy investors into tax-sheltered partnerships of herds under management contract to Beefalo Breeding Company, or (c) attracting potential investors to the fast-food concept of Beefalo Barns.

THE NEED FOR OUTSIDE CAPITAL

While developing markets (at a premium price) for fattened livestock consumed part of Schweiger's time, most of his energy during 1978 was devoted to developing a variety of prospecti for attracting equity investors or debt capital. Additional capital was desired for three purposes: (a) building up herd size to fully utilize the feedlot capacity and/or provide adequate meat supply for six restaurants, (b) to launch a fast-food restaurant operation through general partnerships, franchising, and/or stock placement, and (c) to lease and/or purchase additional pasture land where beefalo would graze until reaching an appropriate feedlot weight.

Schweiger worked with two firms that might be able to attract investors interested in the tax-sheltering prospects of livestock. He held several meetings during 1978 with the St. Louis office senior tax partner of Peat, Marwick, and Mitchell and with a principal in the Investment Planning Group of Clayton, Missouri. The intent of working with these firms was to pull together a group of investors with sufficient capital for one or more large herds of beefalo. Schweiger explained the basics of one of his proposals:

> If we had a herd [of 100], we would sell an absentee owner group the animals and manage the herd under the contract. With this arrangement we would not need anyone's money [for working capital]. We would have all our own. The basic annual fee would be $350 per year per cow. There would be a $300 maintenance cost on the cow plus a $50 breeding fee. We would maintain the cow with her calf until the calf was weaned, and then prorate the remaining number of months (to anniversary date of contract) against the $300 maintenance fee for the offspring. We would assume all feeding costs and charge outside veterinarian fees. If the investing group wanted insurance, it would be their responsibility. The annual management-maintenance fees would be paid in advance.

> A 100-head partnership program would require a total capital investment of $204,000. If we had one partner in a 40 to 50 percent tax bracket, let's say with a 5 percent participation, he would initially invest $10,200. In the first year he would write off 85 percent of his capital contribution against his income tax (for paper loses since there is no revenue inflow). In the second year against his cash contribution, he will write off 188 percent against his taxes, the fourth year 444 percent, and from the fourth year on the partnership is actually in an income-producing position. But from an investor's viewpoint, the front end years provide a tremendous write-off against personal income tax. The net result of a seven-year program, based on current prices of animals, would be a net cash accumulation in excess of $2 million if the herd is liquidated. Although programmed to terminate at the end of the seventh year, in reality there would be no good reason to liquidate unless the limited partners wanted their capital to invest in another program that would have an accelerated depreciation schedule.

Finding it difficult to put together tax-sheltered partnerships in the magnitude mentioned above, Schweiger toward year-end 1978 began promoting smaller programs, based on a minimum of 10 head. Such programs would involve a first-year cash outlay of approximately $11,000 for 10 heifers (females). This proposal included many of the features of previous ones (i.e., describing beefalo, the principle of breeding up, advantages of starting with half-blood heifers, risk factors, and management), although in less detail. Exhibits 1 to 4 present some of the agreement forms and financial projections for this type of program.

EXHIBIT 1   **Beefalo purchase agreement**

THIS AGREEMENT made and entered into on the _____ day of _____ 19_____ , by and between Clarence A. Korte and George D. Schweiger, d/b/a Beefalo Breeding Company, ("Seller") R.R. #1, Pocahontas, Illinois, 62275, and _____ ("Buyer"), whose mailing address is _____ .

WITNESSETH:

In consideration of the mutual covenants, terms and conditions contained herein, the parties hereto do hereby agree as follows:

1. Seller agrees to sell to Buyer _____ head of one-half (½) blood registered Beefalo Breeding cattle (hereinafter referred to as the "Breeding Herd") which animals are more particularly described in Exhibit "A" attached hereto and made a part hereof. All animals purchased shall be subject to the approval of Buyer at the time of delivery.

2. Buyer and Seller are entering into a certain Management and Marketing Agreement of even date herewith, relating to the management, maintenance and breeding of the Breeding Herd and all progeny resulting therefrom.

3. The animals in the Breeding Herd are represented and warranted to be breeders capable of being registered in either or both the World Beefalo Association (WBA) or the American Beefalo Association (ABA) and, at the option of Buyer shall be registered in the Association elected by Buyer.

4. Seller shall successfully breed each female in the Breeding Herd with semen from a pureblood Beefalo bull, should any animal fail, after a reasonable time to settle, Seller shall replace it with a comparable animal. Any replacement or substitution of animals in the Breeding Herd shall carry the same warranties as set forth herein.

5. Buyer agrees to pay a total purchase price of one thousand five hundred ($1,500.00) dollars for each female in Breeding Herd for a total purchase price of $ _____

   a. The sum of six hundred ($600.00), dollars per female in the Breeding Herd shall be paid on the date hereof;

   b. The balance of nine hundred ($900.00) dollars per female in the Breeding Herd shall be paid on or before January 1, 19_____ , provided, however, that Buyer may have the option, in lieu of making such payment, to execute and deliver to Seller a Promissory Note in the form attached hereto as Exhibit _____ in the principal amount of such balance. The Promissory Note, until the balance of the purchase price is paid, shall accrue interest at the rate of nine (9%) percent per annum, and such principal shall be paid upon the earlier of:

      1. Sale, with the consent of Buyer, of female animals (except culls) from Buyers herd which are the animals purchased hereunder or their progeny (or sale of any animals in liquidation of the herd), such payment to be limited to the proceeds of such sale.

      2. Seven years from date of the execution hereof.

6. The outstanding balance of principal and interest thereon shall be secured by a security interest in all animals purchased hereunder and their progeny. Buyer agrees to execute from time to time such Financing Statements or other documents as Seller may request to perfect such security interest in the State of Illinois, Missouri, and elsewhere; including, without limitation, any Uniform Commercial Code Financing Statements or renewals thereof. Buyer appoints Seller as Buyer's attorney-in-fact to execute and file any such documents.

7. In the event Seller shall default under the Management and Marketing Agreement and as a result of such default Buyer as Owner terminates said Agreement, Buyer shall nevertheless remain obligated to satisfy the Note.

EXHIBIT 1   **Beefalo purchase agreement (*cont.*)**

8. In the event that Buyer terminates this Agreement during the first three calendar years, he will pay to the Company 50% of the progeny value as additional fees. Determination of the value of the progeny shall be made by an independent third party selected and mutually agreed upon by both parties hereto.

9. All representations, conditions, warranties and agreements set forth herein shall survive delivery of title and Buyer acknowledges that there have been no representations, expressed or implied except as setforth herein.

10. This Purchase Agreement, the Management and Marketing Agreement, the Security Agreement and the Note constitute the entire understanding between the parties hereto with respect to the subject matter hereof. Any changes, amendments or deletions must be in writing and signed by the parties to this Agreement.

This Agreement shall be interpreted in accordance with the laws of the State of Illinois.

IN WITNESS WHEREOF the parties have set their hands and seals this _____ day of _____ 19_____ .

Buyer _____   Seller _____

EXHIBIT 2   **Management and marketing agreement**

THIS AGREEMENT is made and entered into on this _____ day of _____ 19_____ by and between Clarence A. Korte and George D. Schweiger, d/b/a Beefalo Breeding company, hereinafter referred to as "Company" and _____ whose mailing address is _____

Hereinafter referred to as "Owner."

WITNESSETH:

WHEREAS, Owner is the sole owner and operator of the Beefalo breeding livestock, hereinafter referred to as "livestock" or "animals" described in Exhibit A, which is attached hereto and made a part hereof, and,

WHEREAS, The Company is presently operating Beefalo breeding ranches in Illinois and Missouri and is experienced in the breeding management and marketing of Beefalo livestock, and,

WHEREAS, Owner desires Company to manage, breed and sell said Livestock under the terms and conditions of this Management and Marketing Agreement.

NOW THEREFORE, in consideration of the mutual promises and covenants contained herein, the parties agree as follows/

1. Owner represents that he is the sole owner of the Livestock (Exhibit A), subject only to the terms of the Beefalo Purchase Agreement, and a promissory note and Security Agreement referred to therein.

2. Company shall provide all management and shall maintain, care for, feed and take whatever other steps are reasonably necessary for the well-being of the Livestock and their progeny. The maintenance of the Livestock under this Agreement shall include the breeding, feeding, calving, normal veterinarian services, raising and growing out of progeny, and the keeping of breeding and identification records in connection with the Livestock. Company agrees to maintain, care for and breed the Livestock in accordance with the standard practices for a purebred Beefalo operation and in accordance with the instruction of Owner.

3. Company shall furnish owners semiannual reports regarding the status of the Livestock subject to this Agreement. In addition Company will furnish Owner, as soon as reasonably possible, data concerning any accident, illness or sickness causing the death of any of the Livestock, and a post-mortem report with regard to such animal.

EXHIBIT 2 **Management and marketing agreement (*cont.*)**

---

4. At the option of Owner and at Owner expense, Company will prepare applications for registration in Owners name of all progeny complying with the regulations covering said registration in either or both the World Beefalo Association (WBA) or the American Beefalo Association (ABA) and shall use its best efforts to obtain a lifetime membership in the Association of the Owner's choosing. Fees for membership in or the registration of progeny shall be paid by Owner and are not included in the fee due Company described in paragraph 8.

5. In order to assist Owner in its operation of its Livestock, Company shall be available periodically to consult with Owner in connection with the maintenance, care, and growth of the animals subject to this Agreement. Such advice and counsel shall be in connection with the general and special maintenance of the Livestock, the sale of progeny, the retention of progeny, the selling, culling and replacement of Livestock in the Herd, and such other matters which are incident to the husbandry of Beefalo Livestock.

6. All Livestock subject to this Agreement shall be kept and maintained at such place or places as Company determines in its sole discretion, and during the term of this Agreement, Company shall, at all times, maintain control and jurisdiction over said animals; provided Company shall advise Owner of the location thereof and they shall be available for Owner's inspection at reasonable times.

7. Company shall not be responsible or liable for any loss or damage to any of the Beefalo Livestock subject to this Agreement, on account of any accident, disease, or death, or by reason of any acts of any employee, servant, or agent of the Company, except in the event of gross negligence or willful misconduct by Company or its employees, servants or agents. However, Company shall have the right to replace or substitute any animal lost for any reason from the original Beefalo Breeding Herd, said replacement or substitution to be of comparable quality to animal(s) replaced or substituted.

8. In consideration of the Company's responsibilities, obligations and warranties hereunder, as a fee for the management of the Breeding Herd, Owner agrees to pay the Company as follows:
   (1) The sum of four hundred ($400.00) dollars for each breeding female in the herd, said sum payable upon the date first set forth above.
   (2) The sum of four hundred ($400.00) dollars for each breeding female in the herd, said sum payable on the date of the first anniversary of this Agreement.
   (3) The sum of four hundred ($400.00) dollars for each breeding female in the herd, said sum payable on the date of the second anniversary of this Agreement.
   (4) In addition to the fees set forth above, (para. 8 1, 2 & 3), the Company shall receive fifty percent (50%) of all net proceeds (gross sales less expenses) derived from the sale of any animals or other income from Owner's Herd during the term of this Agreement and the Beefalo Purchase Agreement as full payment for management, maintenance, breeding and other services provided by the Company.
   Company and Owner agree that the net proceeds realized from the sale of animals from the Herd, income from semen sales or other income, shall be distributed between the parties as set forth below:
   a. Company shall receive fifty percent (50%) of all net income as provided in paragraph 8, Art. 4 above.
   b. Owner shall receive fifty percent (50%) of all net income, provided, however, that from such amount Owner shall pay to Company any interest due on the Note for the current or prior years.

9. The Company may collect and sell semen obtained from bulls in the Owner's Breeding Herd. Bulls and semen from Owner's Breeding Herd may be used by Company on all cattle owned or managed by Company at no cost to Company.

10. This Management Agreement shall be effective commencing the date of execution and shall continue for a period of seven years from said date, provided however, that this Agreement shall be

EXHIBIT 2   **Management and marketing agreement (*cont.*)**

renewed at then prevailing rates being charged new Herd owners and, otherwise, on the same terms and conditions for one additional seven-year period from and after such termination date unless either party notifies the other, in writing prior to 90 days preceding the termination date, of its intent to terminate this Agreement. Notwithstanding the forgoing, Owner may at any time cancel this contract by 90 days' written notice to Company. Upon termination of this Agreement for any reason, all amounts owing to either party in accordance with the terms of this Agreement shall be paid on the same basis as if the Agreement were continued to the end of the quarter following the quarter in which notice is given. Owner shall be responsible for the removal of the Livestock from the place or places in which they are maintained as of the effective date of the termination, and as of such date Company shall have no further responsibilities in connection with such Livestock.

11. All notices required or permitted under the terms of this Agreement shall be delivered in person or by certified mail, postage prepaid, addressed as follows:

If to Company:

BEEFALO BREEDING COMPANY
R.R. 1
Pocahontas, Illinois 62275

If to Owner:

12. This Agreement shall be binding upon the parties hereto, their heirs, executors and administrators.

13. Any insurance with regard to the Livestock subject to this Agreement shall be paid by Owner, provided however, the Company shall use its best efforts to secure such coverage as requested by Owner.

14. The obligations of Owner under this Agreement are secured by a Security Agreement of even date herewith, and a default hereunder shall constitute a default under the Security Agreement.

15. Company shall not be required to advance any sums on behalf of Owner, but if it does, Owner shall repay the same promptly on demand and repayment thereof shall be secured by the security interest in the livestock.

16. Owner is fully aware of the speculative nature of purchasing and managing breeding cattle and represents that his or its financial circumstances are consistent with this investment and that he or it is a sophisticated investor and by reason of his or its business and financial experience, he or it has the capacity to protect his or its own interests in connection with his or its investment.

17. This Agreement constitutes the entire agreement of the parties hereto.

IN WITNESS WHEREOF, the parties hereto have set their hands on the date and year first above written.

OWNER(s)   BEEFALO BREEDING COMPANY

By _____   By _____

EXHIBIT 3   **Three-year cash investment: purchase of 10 Beefalo Breeding heifers**

Down payment		$ 6,000.00
Management expense		4,000.00
Interest (prepaid)		810.00
Cash paid out 19_____		$10,810.00
Tax effects:		
Depreciation (seven-year life — half year)	$2,142.90	
Management expense	4,000.00	
Interest expense	810.00	
Investment tax credit (10%)*	3,000.00	
Total equivalent deductions		$10,252.90

Second Year

Management expense		
Interest expense		
Cash paid out 19_____		$ 4,810.00
Tax effect		
Depreciation	$3,673.50	
Management expense	4,000.00	
Interest expense	810.00	
Total deductions		$ 8,483.50

Third Year

Management expense		$ 7,000.00
Interest expense		810.00
		$ 7,810.00
Income (estimated sales $6,000 ÷ 50%)		3,000.00
Cash paid out 19_____		$ 4,810.00
Tax effect:		
Depreciation	$2,623.90	
Management expense	4,000.00	
Interest expense	810.00	
Total deductions		$ 7,633.90

*Investment tax credit assumes a 50 percent tax bracket and a tax credit being the equivalent to $3,000 of standard deductions.
Balance of depreciation is $6,559.70.
No direct cash investment after third year.

EXHIBIT 4   **Economic projection: seven-year program**

Assumptions:

1. 100% live calf crop in the first year and an 80 percent calf crop thereafter. That 50% are male and 50% are female and all females are bred and calve annually.

2. The original herd increases to 126 head and the average price is $1,800 per head and herd liquidation takes place at the end of seven years.

3. That 40 percent of sales is ordinary income and 60 percent is capital gains.

Economics:	Ordinary income	Capital gains	Total
Total sales	$90,000	$136,800	$226,800
Expenses:			
Cost of herd	15,000		15,000
Management and marketing			
Original fees	14,000		14,000
50 percent of sales	45,000	68,400	113,400
Interest	5,670		5,670
Total	$79,670	$ 68,400	$148,070
Net profit before taxes	$10,330	$ 68,400	$ 78,730
Net tax liability (below)*			$ 17,345
Net after-tax profit			$ 61,385
Taxes			
Net profit before tax	$10,330	$ 68,400	$ 78,730
60 percent capital gain exclusion		41,040	41,040
Taxable	$10,330	$ 27,360	$ 37,690
Tax on above (50%)			$ 18,845
Investment tax credit			1,500
Net tax liability (above)			$ 17,345

*For the purposes of this computation it has been assumed that the 50% management fee would be deducted against the proceeds to which it relates. Accordingly, a substantial portion ($68,400) has been deducted against capital gains income. Had this instead been reflected as an ordinary deduction the net tax liability of $17,345 would have been a net refund of $3,175 or additional net aftertax profits of $20,520.

The analysis of economic benefits is based on assumptions concerning future events and present tax laws (which may be changed). Some assumptions may not occur which could have substantial effect. Therefore the actual results obtained may vary considerably from the projections.

THE BEEFALO BARNS (FAST-FOOD) CONCEPT

Most of the conventional marketing alternatives available to Beefalo Breeding Company represent variations of the beef distribution system. The company is committed to breed and produce beefalo, but seeks a market outlet that preserves the identity of beefalo and provides a premium price. When asked if his proposed development of a new fast-food chain was viewed as a means of controlling disposition of the end product, Schweiger responded:

No, I see the restaurant alternative as a completely separate program with beefalo the catalyst for a restaurant chain — for a franchised chain — as opposed to setting up one or two restaurants just to get into the restaurant business. The ultimate limitation with the restaurant concept is that it cannot enjoy the accelerated growth that potentially might be there because there simply are not the animals to support it. This year we wouldn't assemble more than 50,000 head of beefalo even if we contacted every breeder in the country. But we can put together sufficient number of animals to supply six restaurants over the next 12 to 18 months.

The concept that Schweiger began exploring early in 1978 was to develop distinctiveness in fast foods both through product and building design. His idea was to extend the log home concept into a restaurant building structure constructed of Beaver logs. The menu would feature beefalo burgers in several sizes as a means of achieving product differentiation. The integration of the product and the structure would build promotion and furnishings around a western theme. Schweiger did not, however, foresee thrusting a marketing appeal to specific segments, such as the health-conscious consumer. He commented, "Anyone who stops at a fast-food restaurant is a market for us. We're not after only the teenage market, the older age market, the after-hours disco crowd, or anything like that." However he later noted that the health aspects of beefalo might be a major selling point. "This is the message we want to get to the American people. If you're going to eat red meat, then why not eat something that's good for you."

To identify his project, Schweiger initially used the name "Beefalo Inns," then later changed to "Beefalo Barns." He spoke of the need to approach the naming of the restaurant from a scientific view, but suggested that tentatively the "Barn" concept captured the architectural style with its gabled roof atop the log structure. He was further thinking about freeway locations for the first Beefalo Barns in order to quickly expose people to the idea. "If we use freeway locations, people are adventuresome, so they're going to try it. The type of building housing our restaurant is a totally new concept in fast-food buildings. We also have a meat product that probably 99 percent of the American public still have not tasted. But it is being more widely known and advertised every day."

The principal feature of Beefalo Barns would be a variety of burgers. Schweiger would prefer to use all fresh meat, to achieve further product distinctiveness similar to Wendy's. He would use the Burger Chef concept of a condiment bar to allow customers to add what they like. Steaks might possibly be offered; if so, the selections probably would be a six-ounce ground beefalo steak and an eight-ounce rib eye. Prices would be competitive, but probably 10 percent over McDonald's or Burger Chef. "Basically what we want to shoot for is $1.70 average ticket covering patties, fries, drink, and apple turnover."

Schweiger estimated that at least two restaurants would be necessary to test the feasibility of continued expansion. Although the first facility probably would be wholly owned, he projected moving quickly to joint venturing or franchising. "I would see getting into the fast-food business as a vehicle for a national franchise. To me, who needs the hassle of operating simply one restaurant." Six facilities were seen as a feasible target for the first year, with additional facilities limited only by the number of animals available for slaughter. He thought that one way of assuring adequate meat supply would be to involve other breeders as limited partners, stockholders, or franchisees. Schweiger noted that there are approximately 50 beefalo breeders in Kentucky and Tennessee, so that might be a natural area in which to expand. Nationally, there are breeders in the 48 continental states. (Two pages of a 10-page proposal circulated to interested breeders and parties are reproduced as Exhibits 5 and 6, which include the introduction and pro forma income statement.)

During 1978 Schweiger entered into negotiations with property holders of several potential sites. (See map in Exhibit 7). One site was at the Pocahontas exit off I-70, about two miles from the KSM sales office and Korte Farm. Preliminary studies indicated a year-around average traffic count under the interstate overpass at 11,000 cars per day in 1976, with a summer average of 13,900. The exit traffic (coming off the interstate) was 4,000 cars per day, of which 20 percent was considered to be local traffic. Year-around passenger count per vehicle was 1.7, while during the months of May through September it was 2.5. Based on these figures, Schweiger calculated that roughly 3,700 persons per day might be looking for food or other services such as gasoline. He commented: "If we can tap 15 percent of the potential traffic May through September, we can pay all of our bills, gross $150,000, and lock up the place for six months (the nontourist season) if need be."

EXHIBIT 5   **Sample page of Beefalo Barn proposal**

Introduction

Beefalo Barn offers a new and exciting approach to the fast-food industry. The serving of "beefalo" exclusively in the atmosphere of early American log buildings offers a unique dining experience for the consumer.

The format of the Beefalo Barns will combine the features of several fast-food restaurants and will offer both eat-in and carryout service.

The success of the so-called fast-food industry and the forecast for future growth is a phenomenon in the business world. When one considers that in 1960, just 18 years ago, there were virtually no fast-food chains, it is difficult to realize the tremendous impact these outlets have had and the amount of the consumer's food dollar that is going into their cash registers.

Most people are familiar with the golden arches of McDonald's or the goatee of Colonel Sanders, but few realize the true magnitude of their operations. McDonald's alone uses the hamburger from 20,000 head of cattle per week, Kentucky Fried Chicken uses about 7 percent of our total poultry production, and these are but two of a long and growing list of chains, e.g., Wendy's, A & W, French's, Taco Bell, Zantigo, Burger Chef, Dairy Queen, Burger King, Pizza Hut, etc.

Combined annual sales of the fast-food industry today exceed $20 billion and represent about 35 percent of all food dollars.

We, at Beefalo Barns, strongly believe that there is room for one more, one that is built around a new meat called "beefalo." We hope as you evaluate the balance of the material in this brochure that you will come to the same conclusion and will join with us in this new venture.

EXHIBIT 6   **Sample page of Beefalo Barn proposal**

BEEFALO BARN: Pro forma income and expense statement

Gross sales	100%	$200,000		$300,000		$400,000
Gross sales	100%	$200,000		$300,000		$400,000
Food costs	32	64,000		96,000		128,000
Gross profit	68	136,000		204,000		272,000
Operating expenses:						
Labor	22%	44,000	21%	63,000	20%	80,000
Employee taxes, benefits	3.0	6,000	3.0	9,000	3.0	12,000
Paper goods	4.0	8,000	4.0	12,000	4.0	16,000
Utilities	2.0	4,000	2.2	6,600	2.5	10,000
Laundry	.5	1,000	.6	1,800	.7	2,800
Advertising	1.5	3,000	1.8	5,400	2.0	8,000
Office supplies	.3	600	.4	1,200	.5	2,000
Telephone	.6	1,200	.6	1,800	.6	2,400
Legal and accounting	.5	1,000	.8	2,400	.7	2,800
Insurance	1.5	3,000	1.5	4,500	1.5	6,000
Maintenance and repairs	1.0	2,000	1.0	3,000	1.0	4,000
Miscellaneous	1.0	2,000	1.0	3,000	1.0	4,000
Total	38.4	75,000	37.9	113,700	37.5	160,000
Fixed cost:						
Land and building*		16,000		16,000		16,000
Equipment and fixtures†		14,000		14,000		14,000
Total	15.0	30,000	10.0	30,000	7.5	30,000
Total costs	85.4	169,000	79.9	239,700	77.0	318,000
Net income	14.6%	$ 31,000	20.1%	$ 60,300	23.0%	$ 82,000

*Land and building cost can vary substantially from unit to unit.
†Equipment and fixtures are assuming a five-year lease.

Negotiations were entered into for a second site, also adjacent to I-70, but several miles to the east at the Illinois 143 exit. This property is owned by King Oil Company, which operates a truck stop at the off-ramp location (the only commercial establishment at the exit). The oil company tentatively would be willing to construct the building with site improvements (exclusive of interior equipment) and lease the facility to Beefalo Barns for a 10 percent return to King (lease payments estimated at $6,000 to $7,000 annually). Schweiger thought such terms to be advantageous.

I don't see how we can go wrong in putting in the equipment and opening this location because it certainly reduces the sales volume necessary to meet the lease obligation. The other advantage obviously is that it eliminates a lot of front-end cash requirements on our part. Where we were nominally looking at probably $60 to $100,000 cash up front, we are probably looking at $25 to $40,000 maximum with this type of arrangement. As a pilot program, obviously the lower you can keep your cash requirements, the better off you are going to be.

EXHIBIT 7   **Proposed Beefalo Barns locations**

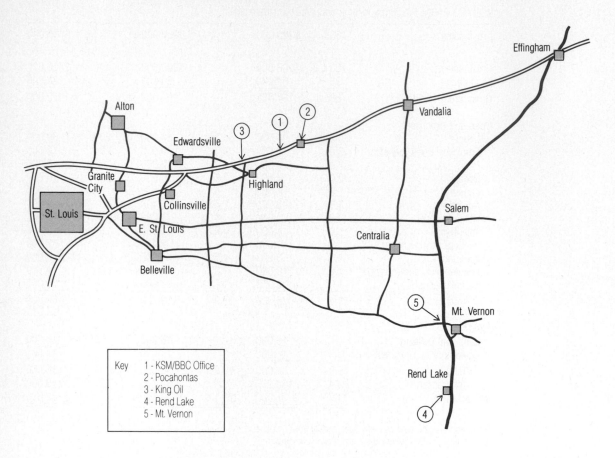

Key   1 - KSM/BBC Office
       2 - Pocahontas
       3 - King Oil
       4 - Rend Lake
       5 - Mt. Vernon

   The King Oil site probably would be operated year round because of the steady flow of trucks and cars that normally stop for refueling. Among other sites where investor contact had been made was one in conjunction with a sports complex at Rend Lake (seasonal resort area) and a downtown location in Mt. Vernon (year round). Schweiger indicated that a group of Illinois and St. Louis investors expressed an interest in owning the Beefalo Barn at the Mt. Vernon site:

   Tentatively we would set up ownership on a limited partnership basis, and we [Beefalo Barns, Inc.] would be the general partners. We would probably establish 50 units at $2,100 per unit, with a two-unit minimum to comply with Illinois Security Statutes of limiting the partnership to 25 or fewer investors. Of the $105,000 we would raise, $100,000 would be applied to the partnership capital account and $5,000 would cover organizational expenses. We would then as a partnership acquire the land, build the facility, lease the equipment, and provide the operating capital. With such an arrangement, we would probably go in as general partners at 30 to

40 percent participation, with no capital contributions. The limited partners would pick up 60 to 70 percent with their capital contribution. As general partners we would not participate in any partnership profits until all limited partners had received back their capital contributions. Once they have 100 percent return, then we participate on a proportional basis.

Management believes they would be unable to require large franchise fees, should this be the direction of expansion. In the absence of an established record, they are considering not charging a franchise fee, per se, but charging a predetermined fee based on franchise performance. A tentative front-end fee of $5,000 was discussed to cover Beefalo Barn's expenses for assistance in site location, building design, equipment lineup, etc. The franchisee would have total obligation for purchasing equipment, land, and building. Beefalo Barns would then charge a royalty fee based on dollar sales of beefalo purchased through the parent firm.

The Beefalo Barn Restaurant would use a 36 by 48 feet Beaver log building, with seating capacity for 66 people (see Exhibit 8). Decor would be in a western motif with wooden tables, wagon-wheel light fixtures, cattle brand displays, etc. Service equipment would use standard models (not customized), with a gas-fired fry grill used for cooking. Schweiger anticipated relying heavily on experienced managers (or formally trained food-service managers from one of the special schools in Dallas, Las Vegas, or Purdue) for operation of the restaurants. Some standards would be established regarding personnel, sanitation, and food storage/preparation. But largely, individual restaurant managers would have responsibility and authority to manage their operation in response to local conditions. For example, deciding whether to open for breakfast and the specification of breakfast menu items would be the manager's prerogative.

Schweiger emphasized that quality control is the primary factor on which success is dependent:

To me, the most critical factor in the whole thing is the movement of meat from the feedlot, through the slaughterhouse, to the retail outlet. To start out, we're only going to have one to three stores and we're going to be starting from scratch. So we've got two things to worry about initially — to control the quality of that meat and keep spoilage down, and yet, to maintain adequate supplies at the restaurant, because the last thing you need to do is to run out.

THE FUTURE

By early 1979, the future direction for KSM and Beefalo Breeding Company remained uncertain. During mid-1978, the Beefalo Barns idea was very central to the thinking of Schweiger. It presented not only an outlet for beefalo in which maximum value could be added to the product, but also an opportunity to branch out into another business. Six months later, however, no commitments had been made to start the first restaurant. In the interim, Schweiger had been

EXHIBIT 8 **Beefalo Barn restaurant layout (seating — 66)**

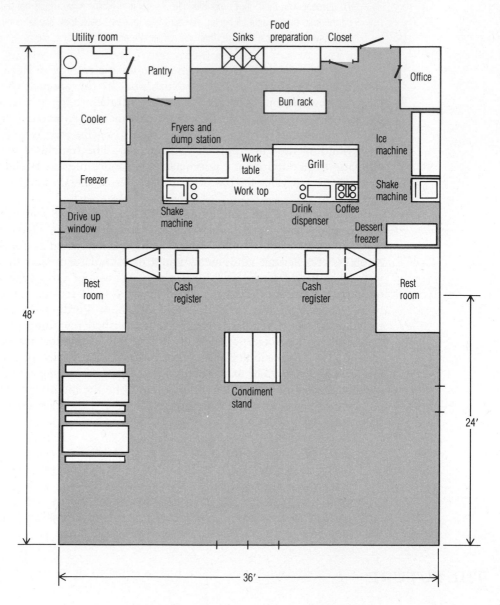

closely involved with a group of investors in Southern California, who were considering not only the tax-sheltering possibilities of beefalo, but who also expressed interest in the concept of marketing beefalo through restaurants (tentatively located either in California or Colorado). This group potentially could assemble a multimillion dollar capital investment fund within 72 hours. Their major reservation to date about starting a restaurant chain was concern over the availability of a guaranteed supply of beefalo. They estimated at least 1,000 cows producing calves for meat would be necessary to sustain the scale of operation this group felt necessary to make attractive a major investment.

In the first year in which beefalo were available for meat production, about $50,000 was generated through red meat sales. The most recent sale involved 4,200 pounds of ground beefalo to an Oklahoma public school system for institutional feeding (cafeterias). By February 1979, Beefalo Breeding Company was caring for approximately 500 head of beefalo, about two-thirds of which involved herd management contracts for outside investors. Seventy-five head had recently arrived at the Missouri ranch from a prominent California beefalo producer. It was expected that a management contract for another 250-head herd would be finalized within 60 days. In anticipation of herd expansion, on February 15 Schweiger was meeting with representatives holding property east of Jefferson City, Missouri, to work out terms for a 15-year lease of 600 to 880 acres of pasture, capable of supporting 400 head.

Schweiger continued to feel himself stretched thin in terms of being able to devote ample time to his various programs. Much of his time was involved in negotiating and attempting to persuade various individuals and groups in one or more facets of his existing or proposed businesses. He talked at one time of taking on an assistant, but finding a relatively young person who could function as a jack-of-all-trades with a high tolerance for uncertainty was difficult. Hiring such a person at this time also was complicated by limited cash flow, since herd buildup required keeping cows out of the marketing stream for breeding purposes.

In discussing his dilemma with a class of M.B.A. students, Schweiger remarked:

> I'm not reasonably sure at this time which of our business activities ought to be emphasized. Which way do I go? Should I spend most of my time raising capital for buying beefalo herds and in finding high-paying outlets for carcass beefalo? If so, what would be my best approach to marketing? What do I do with the Beefalo Barns idea, or the Beaver Homes? What are the trade-offs and payoffs? I'm open to your suggestions.

Case 19

EASTMAN KODAK COMPANY

Eastman Kodak Company was incorporated in New Jersey on October 24, 1901, as successor to the business originally established by George Eastman in September 1880, known as the Eastman Dry Plate Company.[1] The Dry Plate Company was formed to develop a new type of dry photographic plate, which was more portable and easier to use than other plates in the rapidly developing photography field. To mass-produce these dry plates uniformly, Eastman later patented a plate-coating machine and began to manufacture the plates commercially. Eastman's continuing interest in the infant photographic industry led to his development in 1884 of silver halide paper-based photographic roll film. Eastman capped this invention with his introduction of the first portable camera in 1888. This camera, naturally, used his own patented film, and the film was also developed using his own proprietary method. Thus Eastman had gained control of all the stages of the photographic process. His breakthroughs made possible the development of photography as a mass leisure activity. The popularity of the "recorded images" business was immediate, and sales boomed. Eastman's inventions had revolutionized the photographic industry, and his company was uniquely placed to lead the world in the development of photographic technology.

From the beginning, Kodak used four main principles to guide the growth of its business: mass production to lower production costs; maintaining the lead in technological developments; extensive product advertising; and the development of a multinational business to exploit the world market. Although common now, these goals were revolutionary at the time. By 1901 the Eastman Kodak Company of today was established on these principles. Kodak's yellow

This case was prepared by Gareth R. Jones, Department of Management, Texas A & M University. Annual report data excerpts reprinted with the permission of Eastman Kodak. Kodak has not reviewed or approved the case study content.

[1]"Eastman Kodak Co.," *Moody's Industrial Manual* (1986), Vol. 1, p. 3016.

EXHIBIT 1   **Percent return on average shareowners' equity**

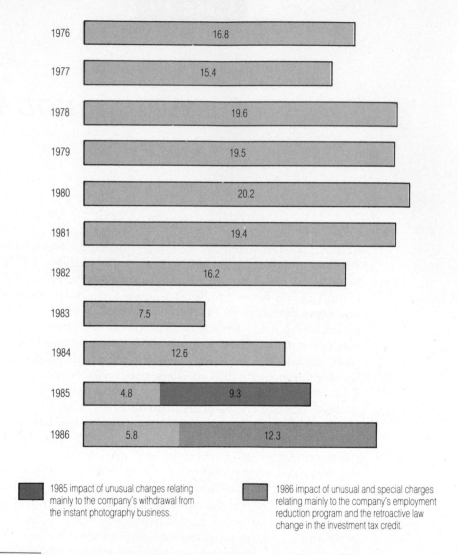

Year	Value
1976	16.8
1977	15.4
1978	19.6
1979	19.5
1980	20.2
1981	19.4
1982	16.2
1983	7.5
1984	12.6
1985	4.8 / 9.3
1986	5.8 / 12.3

■ 1985 impact of unusual charges relating mainly to the company's withdrawal from the instant photography business.

☐ 1986 impact of unusual and special charges relating mainly to the company's employment reduction program and the retroactive law change in the investment tax credit.

Source: Reprinted courtesy of Eastman Kodak Company. Copyright 1987 by Eastman Kodak.

boxes could be found in every country in the world. Its pre-eminence in world markets was unmatched as Kodak operated research, manufacturing, and distribution networks throughout Europe and the world. Its leadership in the development of advanced color film for simple, easy-to-use cameras and in quality film processing was maintained by constant research and development in all its many research laboratories. Finally, its huge volume of production allowed it to obtain economies of scale in turning out its film products. It was also its own supplier of the plastics and chemicals needed to produce film and made most of the component parts for its cameras.

These strengths gave Kodak a superior position in the world photography industry. Kodak became one of the most profitable American corporations, and its return on shareholders' equity averaged 18 percent for many years (see Exhibit 1). To maintain its competitive advantage, it continued to invest heavily in research and development in silver halide photography, remaining principally in the photographic business. In this business, the name Kodak became a household word across the world, signifying unmatched quality, as the company used its resources to expand world sales and become a multinational enterprise. Approximately 40 percent of Kodak's revenues come from sales outside the United States.

Since the early 1970s, however, and especially in the 1980s, Kodak has run into major problems, reflected in the drop in return on equity, as shown in Exhibit 1. Its pre-eminence in the photography industry has been increasingly threatened on many fronts as the nature of the industry and industry competition has changed. First, major changes have taken place within the photography business, and second, new methods of recording images and memories beyond silver halide technology have emerged.

THE NEW INDUSTRY ENVIRONMENT

By the 1970s Kodak began to face an uncertain environment in all its product markets. First, the color film and paper market from which Kodak made 75 percent of its profits experienced growing competition from the Japanese, when led by Fuji Photo Film Co., Ltd., they entered the market. Fuji invested in huge, low-cost manufacturing plants, using the latest technology to mass-produce film in large volume. The low production costs it achieved, combined with an aggressive competitive price-cutting strategy, squeezed Kodak's profit margin. Finding no apparent differences in quality and obtaining more vivid colors with the Japanese product, consumers began to switch to the cheaper Japanese film, and this shift drastically reduced Kodak's market share.

Besides greater industry competition, another liability for Kodak was that it had done little internally to improve its own productivity to counteract rising costs. Its supremacy in the marketplace had made it complacent, and consequently it had not introduced productivity or quality improvements as fast as it might have. Furthermore, Kodak still produced film in many different countries in the world, rather than in a single country—like Fuji in Japan—and this also gave it a cost disadvantage. Thus the combination of efficient production by Fuji and Kodak's own management style allowed the Japanese to become the cost leaders—to charge lower prices and still maintain profit margins.[2]

To add insult to injury, Fuji snatched the sponsorship of the 1984 Olympic games in Los Angeles from Kodak because Kodak's negotiators had dragged their feet in the bargaining process. In order to counteract this blunder, Kodak was forced to adopt an aggressive pricing and promotion campaign to maintain its market share, and this further reduced its profit margin.[3] Kodak reportedly spent some $10 million on advertising airtime during the games—much more than sponsorship of the games would have cost. Kodak purchased early the official film rights of the 1988 games in Seoul, South Korea, for $10 million to avoid this problem.[4]

Kodak was also facing competition on other product fronts. Its cameras had an advantage because of their ease of use as compared to complex 35 mm single lens reflex models. They were also inexpensive. However, the quality of their prints could not compare with those of 35 mm cameras. In 1970 Kodak had toyed with the idea of producing a simple-to-use 35 mm camera but had abandoned it. In the late 1970s, however, the Japanese did develop an easy-to-use 35 mm pocket camera, featuring such innovations as auto flash, focus and rewind. The quality of the prints produced by these cameras was far superior to the grainy prints produced by the smaller instamatic and disc cameras, and consumers began to switch to these products in large numbers. In turn, this shift led to the need for new kinds of film, which Kodak was slow to introduce, thus adding to its product problems.

Kodak's shrinking market share due to increased competition from the Japanese was not its only problem. In the early 1980s Kodak introduced several less-than-successful products. For instance, in 1982 Kodak introduced a new disc camera as a replacement for the pocket instamatic camera. The disc camera used a negative even smaller than the instamatic and was smaller and easier to use. Four and a half million units were shipped to the domestic market by Christmas the first year, but almost a million of the units still remained on retailers' shelves in the new year. The disc cameras had been outsold by pocket 35 mm cameras, which produced higher-quality pictures.[5] The disc camera also sold poorly in the European and Japanese markets. Yet Kodak's research showed that 90 percent of disc camera users were satisfied with the camera and especially liked its high "yield rate" of 93 percent printable pictures, compared with 75 percent for the pocket instamatic.

[2]Thomas Moore, "Embattled Kodak Enters the Electronic Age," *Fortune,* August 22, 1983, pp. 120–128.
[3]Alex Taylor, "Kodak Scrambles to Refocus," *Fortune,* March 3, 1986, pp. 34–38.
[4]Taylor, "Kodak Scrambles," p. 38.
[5]"Kodak's New Lean and Hungry Look," p. 33.

A final blow on the camera front came to Kodak when it lost its patent suit with Polaroid Corp. Kodak had originally forgone the instant photography business in the 1940s, when it turned down Edwin Land's offer to develop his instant photography process. Polaroid Corp. developed it, and of course instant photography was wildly successful, capturing a significant share of the photographic market. In response, Kodak set out to develop its own instant camera in the 1960s, to compete with Polaroid's. According to testimony in the patent trial, Kodak spent $94 million perfecting its system, only to scrub it when Polaroid introduced the new SX-70 camera in 1972. Kodak then rushed to produce a competing instant camera, hoping to capitalize on the $6.5 billion in sales of instant cameras. However, on January 9, 1986, a federal judge ordered Kodak out of the instant photography business for violating seven of Polaroid's patents in its rush to produce an instant camera. The estimated cost to Kodak for closing its instant photography operation and exchanging the 16.5 million cameras sold to consumers is expected to reach $800 million. In 1985 Kodak reported that it had exited the industry at a cost of $494 million.[6] However, the total costs of this misadventure will be uncertain until the damages suit is settled in court. The total could reach $1 billion if Polaroid asks for compensation for the losses in revenue it suffered in its battle with Kodak for market share. Polaroid could triple that amount if it proves that Kodak "willfully and deliberately" infringed on its patents.[7]

On its third product front, photographic processing, Kodak also experienced problems. It faced stiff competition from foreign manufacturers of photographic paper and from new competitors in the film processing market. Increasingly, film processors were turning to cheaper sources of paper to reduce the costs of film processing. Once again the Japanese had developed cheaper sources of paper and were eroding Kodak's market share. At the same time many new independent film processing companies had emerged and printed film at far cheaper rates than Kodak's own official developers. These independent laboratories had opened to service the needs of drugstores and supermarkets and frequently offered twenty-four–hour service. They used the cheaper paper to maintain their cost advantage and were willing to accept lower profit margins in return for a higher volume of sales. As a result, Kodak lost markets for its chemical and paper products — products that contributed significantly to its revenues and profits.

Thus the photographic industry surrounding Kodak had changed dramatically. Competition had increased in all product areas, and Kodak, while still the largest producer, faced increasing threats to its profitability as it was forced to reduce its prices to match the competition. To cap the problem, by 1980 the market was all but saturated: 95 percent of all U.S. households owned at least

---

[6]Charles K. Ryan, *Eastman Kodak, Company Outline*. Merrill Lynch, Pierce, Fenner & Smith Incorporated, May 7, 1986.
[7]Taylor, "Kodak Scrambles," pp. 34–38.

one camera. Increased competition in a mature market was not an enviable position for a company used to high profitability and growth.

The second major problem that Kodak had to confront was due not to increased competition in existing product markets but to the emergence of new industries that provided alternative means for producing and recording images beyond the photographic one. The introduction of videotape recorders, and later video cameras, gave consumers an alternative way to use their dollars to produce images, particularly moving images. Video basically destroyed the old, film-based home movie business of which Kodak had a virtual monopoly. Since Sony's introduction of the Betamax machine in 1975, the video industry has grown into a multibillion dollar business.[8] VCRs and 16 mm video cameras are increasingly hot-selling items as their prices fall with the growth in demand and the standardization of technology. More recently, 8 mm video cameras have been emerging — obviously, much smaller than the 16 mm version. The introduction of laser and compact discs has also been a significant development. The vast amount of data that can be recorded on these discs gives them a great advantage in reproducing images through electronic means, and it may be only a matter of time before compact disc cameras become available. It increasingly appears as if the whole nature of the recording industry is changing from chemical methods of reproduction to electronic methods. This transformation, of course, will undermine Kodak's whole edge in the market because its preeminence in the technical field lies in silver halide photography.

These changes in the competitive environment have caused enormous difficulties for Kodak. Between 1972 and 1982 profit margins from sales declined from 15.7 percent to 10.7 percent. In 1983, despite a raging bull market, Kodak stock, once outstanding, fell 12.5 percent, making it the worst performer among the thirty blue-chip issues in the Dow Jones industrial average. The stock price had dropped to less than half of its value in 1973. When earnings plummeted by 51 percent from $1,162 million in 1982 to $565 million in 1983, the seriousness of Kodak's deteriorating situation became apparent.[9] Kodak's glossy image lost its luster.

The person in charge of Kodak during this critical period has been Colby Chandler, its chief executive officer. Chandler, who took over as chairman in July 1983, was regarded by some as an unlikely person to head Kodak in its deteriorating situation. An avid farmer in his spare time, he has a management style very different from that of past Kodak leaders. However, Chandler quickly saw the need for change. In a statement to shareholders in 1984, he announced that

> This is a time of transition in every part of our company. It is a time to eliminate those functions we can do without and to emphasize those that bring us new growth. It is a time to look to the energy and experience of our people — to their resourcefulness, resilience, and self-reliance. It is

---

[8]John Greenwald, "Aiming for a Brighter Picture," *Time,* January 9, 1984, 49.
[9]Barbara Buell, "Kodak Is Trying to Break Out of Its Shell," *Business Week,* June 10, 1985, pp. 92–95.

a time for our company to do more and to do it more quickly, because today we are being challenged as we have never been before.[10]

To restore Kodak's prestige and profitability, Chandler put forward three principal corporate goals: (1) to enter and become a principal player in electronic imaging technologies; (2) to maintain Kodak's position as one of the twenty-five most profitable U.S. companies; and (3) to increase and restore shareholders' equity to 20 percent (ROE for 1985 was 9.7 percent).[11] To achieve these goals he made dramatic changes in Kodak's strategy and structure.

STRATEGIC CHANGE AT KODAK

The changes in strategy made by Chandler were twofold: he strove to increase Kodak's control of its existing businesses, and he spearheaded attempts by Kodak to diversify into new businesses.

Kodak's strategy in its existing businesses was to try to fill the gaps in its product line by introducing new products it either made itself or bought from Japanese manufacturers and sold under the Kodak name. For example, in attempting to maintain market share in the camera business, Kodak introduced a new line of disc cameras to replace the instamatic lines. However, in addition, Kodak entered into an agreement with Chinon of Japan to produce a range of 35 mm automatic cameras under the Kodak name. This would capitalize on the Kodak name and give Kodak a presence in this market to maintain its camera and film sales. The venture has succeeded; Kodak has sold 500,000 cameras and has 15 percent of the market. In addition, Kodak has developed a whole new range of "DX" coded films to match the new 35 mm camera market—films that possess the vivid color qualities of Fuji film. Kodak had not developed vivid film color earlier because of its belief that consumers wanted "realistic" color from their photographs. Kodak also entered the electronic imaging industry via a joint venture with Matsushita. Matsushita produced a range of 8 mm video cameras under the Kodak name. However, sales of these cameras never took off (some blame the outdated design of the camera), and in 1987 Kodak announced that it was withdrawing from the market.

Beyond the film and camera businesses, Kodak has made major moves to solidify its hold on the film processing market. Kodak has attempted to stem the inflow of foreign photographic paper by gaining control over the processing market. In 1986 it acquired Texas-based Fox Photo Inc. for $96 million, becoming the largest wholesale photograph finisher. This acquisition allowed Kodak to secure a large stable customer for its chemical and paper products. Also in 1986 Kodak introduced new improved one-hour film processing labs to compete

[10]Cornelius J. Murphy, "Kodak's Global Factory," *Planning Review,* 13 (May 1985), 3.
[11]Taylor, "Kodak Scrambles," pp. 34–38.

with other photographic developers. To accompany the new labs, Kodak has popularized the Kodak "color watch system," which requires that these labs use only Kodak paper and chemicals.[12] Kodak hopes that this will stem the flow of business to one-hour minilabs and also establish the quality standards of processing in the field.

As a result of all these moves, Kodak has gained strong control over the processing end of the market and is making large inroads into the film and camera end as well. Kodak has especially been helped here by the decline in the value of the dollar, which has forced Fuji film to raise its prices. Consequently, Kodak too has been able to increase its prices. All these measures have increased Kodak's visibility in the market and allowed it to regain strength in its existing businesses. By spending heavily on research and joint ventures with Japanese companies, Kodak is making sure that it stays abreast of technological advances coming out of Japan.

However, despite these improvements, Kodak was limited by its involvement solely in the photographic industry. In this industry, sales increase only 5 percent a year, and Kodak already has 80 percent of the market, so the potential for growth is very limited. Given this fact and the growth in the use of other imaging techniques, which poses a threat to Kodak, Chandler's second strategy thrust was to embark on an immediate policy of acquisition and diversification.

Acquisitions, Joint Ventures, and Internal Venturing

To meet the needs of its customers in the future, Kodak realized that it would require expertise in a broader range of technologies to satisfy customer's recording and imaging needs. Furthermore, it saw the imaging business increasing and a large number of different types of markets emerging in this field, including business and industrial customers. For example, electronic imaging has become very important in the medical sciences and in all technical and research activities, especially since the advent of the computer. Consequently, Kodak is targeting electronics, communications, computer science, and various hard-copy-output technologies as being increasingly important to its imaging products of the future. Kodak's goal of reinvesting profits to build and extend its businesses can be seen in its move toward acquisitions and joint ventures. Since the silver-based film technology is slowly giving way to electronics, Chandler, in an effort to keep the company growing, is linking new technologies with Kodak's expertise in pictures, graphics, and chemicals. To buy time until it can market its own products, Kodak is marketing the products of others. Among recent products is an electronic publishing system for corporate documents and an automated microfilm-imaging system. The Ektaprint Electronic Publishing System has the ability to edit, print, and update text and graphics for publications. The com-

12Taylor, "Kodak Scrambles," pp. 34–38.

puter comes from Sun Microsystems Inc. The software, enhanced by Kodak, is produced by Interleaf Inc., while the printer is manufactured by Canon, Inc. (one of Kodak's Japanese competitors).[13] Kodak has also announced a new $500,000 imaging system that locates microfilm and scans it for computer use. This product is directed at the banking and insurance company markets. Kodak has joined with Corning Glass Works' biotechnology efforts to develop commercial foods from the dairy by-product whey, using enzyme and fermentation technology.[14]

Aimed at maintaining Kodak's reputation as a growing innovative company, Chandler's unprecedented acquisition and investment drive has cost more than $300 million. Kodak has purchased companies as diverse as computer work stations and anticancer drugs. It has been aggressively acquiring companies to fill in its product lines and obtain technical expertise. After taking more than a decade to make its first four acquisitions, the company completed seven acquisitions in 1985 and more than ten in 1986. Among the acquisitions is Spin Physics, Inc., which Kodak obtained in 1972 for about $8 million and which manufactures high technology magnetic heads for high-density data storage. Atex, Inc., acquired in 1981, makes newspaper and magazine publishing systems. Eikonix Corp., acquired in 1985, manufactures digital processing equipment, and Garlic Corp., also acquired in 1985, develops advanced digital magnetic recording heads for disc drives.[15] Another 1985 acquisition — for $175 million — was Verbatim Corporation, a major producer of floppy discs. This acquisition made Kodak one of the three big producers in the floppy disc industry and brought Kodak into direct competition with 3M.

Besides making acquisitions, Kodak began to enter into joint ventures in the biotechnical industry, both to build its business and to enter new businesses. In February 1980 Halcom International Inc. and Kodak signed an agreement to combine new process technologies developed by each company to produce acetic anhydride from carbon monoxide and methanol. In April 1985 Kodak and ICN Pharmaceuticals, Inc. jointly announced the formation of a research institute that will explore new biomedical compounds aimed at stopping the spread of viral infections and slowing the aging process. Kodak and ICN will invest a total of $45 million over a period of six years to form and operate The Nucleic Acid Research Institute, a joint venture that will be located at ICN's Costa Mesa, California, facility. The institute will dedicate much of its research exclusively to preclinical studies of new antiviral and antiaging substances.

In February 1986 Kodak and Immunex Corp. announced the formation of Immunology Ventures, a joint venture partnership to research, develop, and manufacture lymphokine therapeutic and related products. The joint venture will be equally owned by Immunex and Kodak. Kodak will receive from Immunex the rights to manufacture certain lymphokine therapeutics and a proprietary process for the bulk manufacture and purification of recombinant

[13]Barbara Buell, "Kodak Scrambles to Fill the Gap," *Business Week*, February 8, 1986, p. 30.
[14]"Kodak Seeks Profit in Whey," *Business Week*, January 13, 1986, p. 42.
[15]Taylor, "Kodak Scrambles," pp. 34–38.

proteins. The aggregate capital contribution over the next three years is expected to equal more than $30 million. Immunology Ventures will also collaborate in research and development activities within both Immunex and Kodak's Life Sciences Division.[16]

Kodak has also formed a battery venture with Matsushita. Matsushita produces a range of alkaline batteries for Kodak, and the gold-topped battery is being extensively advertised in opposition to Duracell Inc.'s copper-topped battery. However, Kodak internally ventured a new lithium battery, which lasts six times as long as conventional batteries, and this is seen to be an opportunity for future growth, especially because of its extensive use in cameras. Kodak also markets a wide range of videocassettes, produced in Japan, for electronic imaging, in order to fill this gap in its product portfolio.

Since Kodak's beginnings, research has been the cornerstone of the company's growth. Kodak is now concentrating on imaging sciences, not just on photographic imaging, and is conducting research intended to lead to innovative products based on silver halide, electrophotography, and electronic methods. Its established research expertise has positioned Kodak as a potential leader in imaging products and provides the base for expansion into such businesses as chemicals and the life sciences. For example, Kodak's interest in life sciences derives from its scientific skills in chemistry, biology, and physics.

To manage its expanding base of technologies, Kodak recently initiated a reorganization of research to encourage internal venturing. First, it created a corporate research organization, or new venture division whose primary concentration is new technological directions that will form the basis for future businesses. Second, it attempted to link this division with the company's business groups, to enable them to more easily integrate research and development into the design, manufacture, and marketing of their products. This should make Kodak more market oriented.

As a result of these new developments, Kodak is a very different company than it was just a few years ago. It now turns out 50,000 products, as compared with 30,000 just eight years ago.[17] In order to handle the range of its products and businesses, Kodak divides its activities into three major product areas, or divisions, within the company. Then, inside each product area, different individual businesses manage the various product lines. Kodak's major divisions and the business units inside each division are discussed below.

Photographic and Information Management Division

The largest division of the company is the Photographic and Information Management Division (PIMD). This division is responsible for the production and

---

[16]"Eastman Kodak Co.," *Moody's Industrial Manual* (1986), Vol. 1, p. 3016.
[17]T. Govatos, Photo Notes-Industry Report. Datext (1986).

distribution of Kodak's familiar products and services for the worldwide marketplace. The division accounts for approximately 80 percent of corporate sales. It includes photographic products for consumers and professionals; video imaging systems and magnetic materials; business equipment and graphics imaging systems designed to span the rapidly growing fields of printing and information management; and health-related products critical to medical analysis and diagnosis.[18]

Inside the division, there are eighteen different individual businesses, which are members of one of three strategic business units. These business units comprise the businesses that have common interests, such as technology, products offered, or market served. The three business units in this division are Commercial and Information Systems, Photographic Products Group, and Diversified Technologies.

Commercial and Information Systems   This unit consists of the businesses that serve a wide range of customer needs for image-intensive information processing. Recent growth of this unit has been due to several acquisitions, including Atex Inc., Eikonix Corp., and Diconix, Inc. Atex, a subsidiary since 1981, sells versatile electronic publishing and text-editing systems to newspapers and magazines worldwide, as well as to government agencies and law firms. Its list of customers includes leading newspapers in such cities as Boston, Chicago, Dallas, Houston, Miami, New York, and Philadelphia; national magazines such as *Time, Newsweek, U.S. News & World Report, Forbes, Reader's Digest,* and *National Geographic;* and government customers such as the U.S. Supreme Court and the U.S. Government Printing Office. Eikonix Corp., is a leader in the design, development, and production of precision digital imaging systems. Included in its range of commercial products are devices that scan and convert images into digital form and equipment to edit and manipulate color photographs and transparencies to produce color separations for printing and graphic arts applications. The Eikonix Designmaster 8000 allows users to proceed directly from artwork to printing plates with unmatched quality and flexibility.

Further growth within the Commercial and Information Systems unit is a result of the Ektaprint line of copier-duplicators. The copiers have achieved good sales growth and reached new standards for quality, reliability, and productivity in the very competitive high-volume segment of the copier marketplace. Kodak further enhanced its position as a world-class imaging leader with the announcement of two new image management packages: the Kodak Ektaprint Electronic Publishing System (KEEPS) and the Kodak Image Management System (KIMS). KEEPS is designed for use where there is a need for high-quality documents formed from text, graphics, and other images. The documents are reproduced by software designed specifically for electronic publishing. KIMS electronically stores, retrieves, and distributes existing documents. The system enables users with large, active data bases to view and manipulate information stored on microfilm and magnetic or optical disks.[19]

[18]Eastman Kodak Company, *Annual Report* (1985), 5.
[19]Eastman Kodak, *Annual Report* (1985), 5.

Kodak reported $498 million in electronic sales in 1984, which was slightly less than 5 percent of its total revenues. The company has established itself in the electronic areas of artificial intelligence, computer systems, consumer electronics, medical electronics, peripherals, telecommunications, and test and measuring equipment markets. Kodak hopes to gain a strong foothold in these businesses to make up for losses in its traditional business. However, it is entering areas where it faces strong competition from established companies such as Digital Equipment, Sony, and IBM.[20]

Photographic Products Group   The largest of the three operating groups in this division, this group contains the company's original businesses, including consumer products, motion picture and audiovisual products, photofinishing, and consumer electronics. The unit is responsible for strengthening Kodak's position in its existing businesses. It was the developer of the new line of 35 mm products featuring easy-to-use cameras and improved films. The new Kodacolor VR-G 100 and VR-G 400 films offer consumers photos with richer, brighter colors and strengthen the link between the company's films and cameras.

Diversified Technologies   This unit includes products marketed outside the traditional photographic and commercial areas. Within it is the newly acquired Verbatim Corporation, a recognized leader in the manufacture and sale of flexible diskettes for microcomputers. Verbatim Corporation sells in the mass-memory marketplace under the brand names DataLife and ValuLife and gives Kodak a position in the markets for magnetic and optical media. Other technologies within this unit include clinical products such as Kodak Ektachem analyzers, used in the health sciences for improving the display, storage, processing, and retrieval of diagnostic images.[21]

Eastman Chemicals Division

The second major division is the Eastman Chemical Division (ECD). Established more than sixty-five years ago as a supplier of raw materials for Kodak's film and processing businesses, it was responsible for developing many of the chemicals and plastics that have made Kodak the leader in the photographic industry. Now the division is a major supplier of chemicals, fibers, and plastics to thousands of customers worldwide. Kodak is enjoying increased growth in its plastic material and resins unit because of outstanding performance and enthusiastic customer acceptance of Kodak PET (polyethylene terephthalate) polymer used in soft drink bottles and other food and beverage containers. The growth in popularity of sixteen-ounce PET bottles spurred a record year for both revenue and volume.

[20]Kodak's New Image: "Electronics Imaging," *Electron Business* (January 1986), 38–43.
[21]C. H. Chandler, "Eastman Kodak Opens Windows of Opportunity," *The Journal of Business Strategy,* 7 (1986), 5–9.

In 1986 three new businesses were established within this division: Specialty Printing Inks, Performance Plastics, and Animal Nutrition Supplements. They all share the common objective of enabling the division to move more quickly into profitable new market segments where there is the potential for growth.[22]

Life Sciences Division

Kodak's newest division, the Life Sciences Division (LSD) was created in 1984, with the mission to develop and commercialize new products deriving from Kodak's distinctive competencies in chemistry and biotechnology. LSD has three objectives. The first objective is to focus on newer, less developed markets in an effort to concentrate resources in markets with fewer competitors and high profit potential. Newer areas include developing nutritional supplements that can be delivered orally or intravenously, as well as nutrition products for sale over the counter to consumers. Second, the division is interested in developing innovative ways to control the absorption of pharmaceutical drugs into the body so that the drug remains therapeutically effective for the optimum amount of time. The third objective involves developing new applications for existing products and processes. Kodak has about 500,000 chemical formulations in its files on which it can base new product developments. This is a rich untapped resource.

Within the Life Science Division are the Bio-Products Division and the Laboratory and Specialty Products Division, which are engaging in joint research with biotechnology companies such as the Cetus Corporation, Amgen, and Immunex. The divisions are pursuing an aggressive strategy to scale up and commercialize products based on biotechnology derived from in-house as well as outside contract research. Ventures that the Bio-Products Division has entered into include an agreement with Advanced Genetic Sciences for the commercial production of SNOWMAX, an ice-nucleating product useful in making artificial snow for ski areas. The Laboratory and Specialty Products Division has entered into agreements with several organizations to gain marketing rights to products in the cancer field. The most notable are the agreements entered into with NeoRx and Cytogen for the rights to imaging and therapy products derived from monoclonal antibodies conjugated with radioisotopes.[23]

CHANGING THE CORPORATE STRUCTURE

As he tackled changes in strategy, Chandler also directed his efforts at reshaping Kodak's management style and organizational structure to make the organization

---

[22]Eastman Kodak Company, *Annual Report* (1986), 19.
[23]Eastman Kodak, *Annual Report* (1986), 24.

more flexible and attuned to the competitive environment. Kodak's dominance in the industry meant that previously it did not have to worry about outside competition—a situation that had given rise to an organizational culture emphasizing traditional, conservative values rather than entrepreneurial values. Kodak was often described as a conservative plodding monolith because all decision making had been centralized at the top of the organization among a clique of senior managers. Furthermore, the company had been operating along functional lines, with research, production, and sales and marketing functions being operated separately in different divisions. The result of all these factors was a lack of communication and slow, inflexible decision making that led to delays in making new product decisions. The separate functional operations also led to bad interdivisional relations when the company attempted to transfer resources between divisions because managers protected their own turf at the expense of corporate goals.

Another factor encouraging Kodak's conservative orientation was its promotion policy. Seniority and loyalty to "mother Kodak" counted nearly as much as ability when it came to promotions. The company has been led by only twelve presidents since its beginnings in the 1880s.[24] Long after Eastman's suicide in 1932, Kodak followed his cautious ways. "If George didn't do it, his successors didn't either."[25] Kodak's technical orientation also contributed to its problems. Traditionally, its engineers and scientists had dominated decision making, and marketing had been neglected. They were perfectionists who spent enormous amounts of time developing, analyzing, testing, assessing, and retesting its new products, but little time was given to determining if the products satisfied consumer needs. This technical orientation led to problems such as management passing up the invention of xerography, leaving the new technology to be developed by a small Rochester company named Haloid Co. (later Xerox). Similarly, it had passed up the instant camera business. Kodak's lack of a marketing orientation allowed competitors to overtake it in several areas that were natural extensions of its photography business, such as 35 mm cameras and video recorders.

Kodak's early management style, while profitable through the 1960s because of the company's privileged competitive position, was thus creating difficulties. With its monopoly in the photographic film and paper industry gone, Kodak was in trouble. Chandler had to alter Kodak's management orientation. He began with some radical changes in the company's culture and structure.

Firmly committed to cost-cutting efforts, Chandler orchestrated a massive downsizing of the work force to eliminate the fat that had accumulated from Kodak's prosperous past. Traditionally, Kodak had prided itself as being one of the most "Japanese" of all U.S. companies, which hired college graduates and gave them a permanent career. Now it had to go against one of its founding

[24]Barbara Buell, "A Gust of Fresh Air for the Stodgy Giant of Rochester," *Business Week*, June 10, 1985, p. 93.
[25]Moore, "Embattled Kodak," *Fortune*, August 22, 1983, pp. 120–128.

principles and reduce its work force. Kodak's policy of lifetime employment was swept out the door when declining profitability led to large employee layoff.[26] Chandler instituted a special early retirement program, froze pay raises, and made the company's first layoffs in more than a decade. By 1985 the "yellow box factory" had dropped from 12,600 of its original 136,000 employees. To further reduce costs in 1986, divisions were required to cut employment by an additional 10 percent and to cut budgetary expenditures by 5 percent.

While these measures had an effect on the organization's culture, Chandler still needed to reshape its structure. In an effort to meet his goals, he began the transition in 1985 by shedding the old, stratified corporate structure for what he called a more "entrepreneurial" approach. The first step taken was to reorganize the company's $8.3-billion Photographic Division into the seventeen operating units referred to in the previous section and to establish the four divisions as the backbone of Kodak's new structure. Each of the seventeen line-of-business units now contains all the functions necessary for the success of the enterprise, including marketing, financial, planning, product development, and manufacturing specialists. Each unit is treated as an independent profit center and managed by a young executive with authority over everything from design to production. All units have a common goal of improving the level of quality and efficiency inside each division and eliminating problems in the transfer of resources and technology among divisions. The purpose behind this change was to eliminate the old divisional orientation that had led to competition within Kodak and reduced integration in the company. Kodak hopes that the changes in organizational control and structure will promote innovation, speed reaction time, and establish clear profit goals.[27] With this restructuring, Kodak also reduced its top-heavy management in order to decentralize decision making to lower levels in the hierarchy. This may be a sign that the company is at last shedding its image of having a paternalistic approach to management.[28]

In further attempts to bring costs more into line with those of foreign competitors who benefit from lower wage rates, favored government treatment, and currency advantages, Kodak also instituted new control systems. It directed its operating units in February 1986 to reduce operating and expense budgets. In the company's move to meet quality while at the same time keeping costs low, manufacturing plants have introduced stringent specifications, which have increased quality and efficiency. To compete effectively in a global marketplace, Kodak is using quality as the yardstick to measure its success.[29]

The company has developed quality-training programs to help managers improve organizational effectiveness, to allow supervisors to enhance unit performance, and to enable employees to take a quality approach to problem

[26]Buell, "A Gust of Fresh Air," p. 93.
[27]Buell, "A Gust of Fresh Air," p. 93.
[28]"Yellow at the Edges," *The Economist*, December 7, 1984, p. 90.
[29]Eastman Kodak, *Annual Report* (1985), p. 12.

solving. Kodak's major worldwide programs are reducing variability in raw materials and finished emulsions, enhancing the control of key product features, and speeding product commercialization, while quality projects are leading to increased data integrity and machine efficiency, enhanced employee morale, and decreased maintenance costs, waste, and inventory. In marketing, a team approach to quality at Eastman Chemicals Division has identified more than 100 projects to improve customer relations and reduce the overall cost of doing business. Virtually every job in the company is being redefined in terms of the value its occupants add to the operation in terms of quality, as seen by customers in the marketplace.[30]

With its new risk-taking attitude, Kodak has also attempted to create a structure and culture to encourage internal venturing. It formed a "venture board" to help underwrite small projects and make conventional venture capital investments. In addition, the company created an "office of submitted ideas," to screen outside projects. Last year alone, Kodak received more than 3,000 proposals, although only 30 made it through the screening process.[31] This aggressive research program led to a breakthrough in tabular silver halide grains, which improve the light-gathering process of film. The discovery resulted in the new line of 35 mm products.

In the film and processing market, Chandler took the battle to Fuji's doorstep. To whittle away Fuji's 70-percent market share in Japan, Kodak opened a new technical center for customers and distributors and in 1985 announced plans to build a Japanese research facility. In an aggressive campaign to increase Kodak's visibility, Chandler created a new subsidiary just for Japan, tripled the normal staff, and worked the public relations people overtime. Kodak sponsored judo championships on television, as well as sumo wrestling tournaments, and even has a listing on the Tokyo Stock Exchange.[32]

Kodak also reorganized its worldwide facilities to reduce costs. International divisions were turning out identical products at higher cost than their counterparts in the United States. In a plan to coordinate worldwide production to increase productivity and lower costs, Kodak reshuffled some of its foreign production. It streamlined European production by reducing the extent of its operations and by avoiding duplication of research and production; it also brought some foreign manufacturing home. As a result, Kodak gained $55 million in productivity savings. However, the rise of the dollar boosted the cost of export products to foreign customers, and consequently, export expenses offset most of the gains.[33] Now that the dollar has fallen, these problems have been reversed, and Kodak's international operations have regained their profitability.

[30]Eastman Kodak, *Annual Report* (1986), p. 15.
[31]Taylor, "Kodak Scrambles," pp. 34–38.
[32]James B. Treece, Barbara Buell, and Jane Sasseen, "How Kodak Is Trying to Move Mount Fuji," *Business Week,* December 2, 1985, pp. 62–64.
[33]Eastman Kodak, *Annual Report* (1985).

KODAK'S FUTURE

Whether Kodak has succeeded in its efforts to reorganize its strategy and structure has yet to be seen. Some analysts are confident that the changes Kodak has made will restore its profitability, but others think that Kodak has done too little too late. There are many problems that Kodak must deal with.

First, Kodak faces challenges with its new acquisitions. Managing these ventures with a new entrepreneurial style rather than through its centralized, conservative approach of the past will not be easy. Already, difficulties have crept in. One example is Kodak's managing of Atex Inc., the manufacturer of desk-top publishing systems that Kodak bought in 1981. Because of Kodak's overbearing management style, the top executives and employees of Atex left the company, creating serious management problems for Kodak. The Atex executives claimed that Kodak executives were hard-working but bureaucratic and did not understand the competitive nature of computer technology. One must react to the computer marketplace weekly, and Atex executives could not handle Kodak's slow pace.[34]

What effects the reorganization of PIMD into seventeen operating units will have on performance remains to be seen. There seems to be a new sense of purpose and a quicker response time in divisional activities. There is also increased willingness to take risks and make investments in other companies and undertake joint ventures to speed entry into markets such as electronic products, midsize copiers, and magnetic products. Even with all this reorganization, however, Kodak still faces flat profits, for it has moved into some very uncertain environments, where the company has little experience and extremely formidable rivals. Kodak must face competition from RCA and GE in consumer electronics, and Memorex and 3M in magnetic tape and floppy disks. It must combat foreign competition from Fuji and Konica, and from Nikon Inc., Canon, and Minolta Corp. in still cameras. It has already lost the battle with Matsushita, Sony, and Toshiba in video cameras and recorders.

Venturing into the volatile electronics business is obviously a gamble. However, Kodak had little choice, since its existing business was mature, and amateur and professional photography was a saturated market. In addition, video will increasingly undercut many of Kodak's consumer and commercial applications, further slowing industry growth. Electronic imaging technology will probably never match the quality of silver-based film, however, and a competitive electronic still camera remains in the future.

Financially, Kodak is still one of the top twenty-five U.S. companies. It is financially sound, with total assets of $12.5 billion. Management has set a goal of regaining a 20-percent return on equity over the next four years. Investors predict earnings of $6.40 per share by 1990, based on a 17-percent ROE. Kodak's market position is also a major advantage. The Kodak brand is one of the most

[34]Moore, "Embattled Kodak," pp. 120–128.

recognized in the world. Its prominent position in the film and photographic paper industry and the quality reputation of the company through brand recognition are readily transferred to commercial, industrial, and other consumer products. Kodak will likely become a major player in magnetic tape and floppy disks, as well as copiers and information systems, given its planned acquisition of IBM's copier business.

Research has always been the foundation of Kodak. Research and development gave direction to corporate growth and brought about the emergence of new product lines. Kodak's success depends on the ability of its research departments to continue innovating and making improvements for current products and to successfully market them in competitive environments. Kodak must translate its technical competences into successful new products, if it is to regain its former profitability. The future will tell whether its divisions can develop the entrepreneurial attitude necessary to survive in the global market. For example, the Life Sciences Division expects to be a major source of revenues and earnings by 1990. This seems very possible, for there is a growing need for nutritional and agriculture products to help feed the world's increasing population. Kodak will have a strong market position if it can continue to be on the edge of innovation.

On the down side, concerns for Kodak include industry change. Partly because of the advent of electronic media such as videocassette recorders and the ability of cameras to capture images on floppy disks, the rate of growth in the traditional film industry has slowed significantly in recent years. The growth rate is 4–5 percent annually, compared with the old growth rate of 8 percent. The traditional film market has been the strong point for Kodak. However, over the next few years, Kodak will be a major player in the electronic imaging industry, which should sustain a growth rate of about 25 percent annually.

Kodak also has the problem that new businesses mean lower profit margins. New ventures and market entries for Kodak, such as electronic imaging, magnetic tape, and floppy disks, are in highly competitive industries and traditionally carry a much lower profit margin than chemical photography. Besides, new businesses are very expensive to enter, and thus Kodak's long-term earnings are heavily dependent on the future growth of these industries and on its ability to profit from this growth.

The biggest question is, can Kodak learn to play the different and tougher competitive game? The market has changed, and Kodak must play in businesses where it is no longer a worldwide leader and where it has neither a technological advantage nor a significant cost advantage. Kodak's move toward diversification and the strengthening of its primary business, however late, indicates that it has the motivation to compete in the new industry environment. The question now is whether Kodak's moves under Chandler will prove successful and whether Kodak can manage its new strategy and structure.

The Eastman Kodak Company and subsidiary companies' consolidated statements are summarized in Exhibits 2–8.

EXHIBIT 2   **Summary of the year in figures**

(Dollar amounts and shares in millions, except per share figures)

	1986	1985	Change
Sales	$ 11,550	$ 10,631	+ 9%
Earnings from operations	$ 724*	$ 561**	+29%
Net earnings	$ 374*	$ 332**	+13%
—percent of sales	3.2%	3.1%	
—per common share	$ 1.66*	$ 1.46**	
Cash dividends declared	$ 551	$ 553	
—per common share	$ 2.44	$ 2.43	
Average number of common shares outstanding	225.7	227.3	
Shareowners at close of year	172,713	184,231	
Total net assets (shareowners' equity)	$ 6,388	$ 6,562	− 3%
Additions to properties	$ 1,438	$ 1,495	− 4%
Depreciation	$ 956	$ 831	+15%
Wages, salaries, and employee benefits	$ 4,912	$ 4,482	+10%
Employees at the close of year			
—in the United States	83,600	89,200	− 6%
—worldwide	121,450	128,950	− 6%

*After deducting unusual charges of $520 million and certain other special charges of $134 million which in total reduced earnings from operations by $654 million. Net earnings were reduced by $373 million because of all special charges and an additional $50 million as a result of the retroactive repeal of the U.S. investment tax credit for a total reduction of $1.87 per share.
**After deducting unusual charges of $563 million which reduced net earnings by $302 million and net earnings per share by $1.33.

Source: Reprinted courtesy of Eastman Kodak Company. Copyright 1987 by Eastman Kodak.

EXHIBIT 3   **Consolidiated statement of earnings**

	1986	1985	1984
	(in millions, except per share data)		
Sales			
Sales to: Customers in the United States	$ 6,915	$ 6,854	$ 6,887
Customers outside the United States	4,635	3,777	3,713
Total sales	11,550	10,631	10,600
Costs			
Cost of goods sold	7,613	7,129	6,887
Sales, advertising, distribution, and administrative expenses	2,693	2,378	2,166
Unusual charges	520	563	—
Total costs and expenses	10,826	10,070	9,053
Earnings			
Earnings from operations	724	561	1,547
Investment income	129	129	140
Interest expense	200	183	114
Other income and (charges)	(55)	23	51
Earnings before income taxes	598	530	1,624
Provision for United States, foreign, and other income taxes	224	198	701
Net earnings	$ 374	$ 332	$ 923
Average number of common shares outstanding[1]	225.7	227.3	242.6
Net earnings per share[1]	$ 1.66	$ 1.46	$ 3.80

[1]Per share data and average number of common shares outstanding for 1984 have been restated to give effect to the 3-for-2 partial stock split in 1985.

Source: Reprinted courtesy of Eastman Kodak Company. Copyright 1987 by Eastman Kodak.

EXHIBIT 4   Consolidated statement of retained earnings

	1986	1985	1984
	(in millions, except per share data)		
Retained earnings			
Retained earnings at beginning of year	$6,710	$6,931	$6,586
Net earnings	374	332	923
Total	7,084	7,263	7,509
Cash dividends declared at $2.44 per share ($2.43 in 1985; $2.40 in 1984)[1]	551	553	578
Retained earnings at end of year	$6,533	$6,710	$6,931

[1]Per share data and average number of common shares outstanding for 1984 have been restated to give effect to the 3-for-2 partial stock split in 1985.

Source: Reprinted courtesy of Eastman Kodak Company. Copyright 1987 by Eastman Kodak.

EXHIBIT 5   Consolidated statement of financial condition

Assets	Dec. 28, 1986	Dec. 29, 1985
	(dollars in millions)	
Current assets		
Cash	$ 145	$ 161
Marketable securities	468	652
Receivables	2,563	2,346
Inventories	2,072	1,940
Deferred income tax charges	348	397
Prepaid charges applicable to future operations	215	181
Total current assets	5,811	5,677
Properties		
Land, buildings, machinery, and equipment at cost	12,919	12,047
Less: accumulated depreciation	6,643	6,070
Net properties	6,276	5,977
Other assets		
Long-term receivables and other noncurrent assets	815	488
Total assets	$12,902	$12,142

Source: Reprinted courtesy of Eastman Kodak Company. Copyright 1987 by Eastman Kodak.

EXHIBIT 6 Liabilities and shareowners' equity

	Dec. 28, 1986	Dec. 29, 1985
	(dollars in millions)	
Current liabilities		
Payables	$ 3,440	$ 2,989
Taxes — income and other	209	156
Dividends payable	142	180
Total current liabilities	3,791	3,325
Other liabilities and deferred credits		
Long-term borrowings	911	988
Other long-term liabilities	603	219
Deferred income tax credits	1,209	1,048
Total liabilities and deferred credits	6,514	5,580
Shareowners' equity		
Common stock, par value $2.50 per share 500,000,000 shares authorized; issued at December 28, 1986 — 248,705,111 at December 29, 1985 — 248,582,250	622	621
Additional capital paid in or transferred from retained earnings	314	312
Retained earnings	6,533	6,710
	7,469	7,643
Less: Treasury stock (22,671,873 shares) at cost	1,081	1,081
Total shareowners' equity	6,388	6,562
Total liabilities and shareowners' equity	$12,902	$12,142

Source: Reprinted courtesy of Eastman Kodak Company. Copyright 1987 by Eastman Kodak.

EXHIBIT 7   **Consolidated statement of changes in financial position**

	1986	1985	1984
	(in millions)		
Funds provided by:			
Net earnings	$ 374	$ 332	$ 923
Depreciation and amortization	975	838	760
Other noncash charges and credits, net	284	(4)	153
Total from earnings	1,633	1,166	1,836
Increase (decrease) in long-term borrowings	(77)	579	68
Increase in other liabilities	851	1,035	48
Total funds provided	2,407	2,780	1,952
Funds used for:			
Additions to properties	1,438	1,495	970
Dividends to shareowners	551	553	578
Increase in: Receivables	217	296	271
Inventories	132	182	48
Treasury stock purchases	—	353	728
Other items, net	269	99	(92)
Total funds used	2,607	2,978	2,503
Decrease in cash & marketable securities	200	198	551
Cash and marketable securities, beginning of year	813	1,011	1,562
Cash and marketable securities, end of year	$ 613	$ 813	$1,011

Source: Reprinted courtesy of Eastman Kodak Company. Copyright 1987 by Eastman Kodak.

EXHIBIT 8   **Kodak in review**

(Dollar amounts and shares in millions except per share figures)

		1986
Management's discussion and analysis	**Sales**	**$ 11,550**
	Earnings from operations	**724***
	Earnings before income taxes	**598**
	Net earnings	**374***
Earnings and dividends	Net earnings — percent of sales	3.2%
	— percent return on average shareowners' equity	5.8%
	— per common share[1][2]	1.66*
	Cash dividends declared — on common shares	551
	— per common share[2]	2.44
	Common shares outstanding at close of year	225.8
	Shareowners at close of year	172,713
	Earnings retained	(177)
Balance sheet data	Current assets	$ 5,811
	Properties at cost	12,919
	Accumulated depreciation	6,643
	Total assets	12,902
	Current liabilities	3,791
	Long-term obligations	911
	Total liabilities and deferred credits	6,514
	Total net assets (shareowners' equity)	6,388
Supplemental information	Sales — Imaging	$ 9,408
	— Chemicals	2,378
	Research and development expenditures	1,059
	Additions to properties	1,438
	Depreciation	956
	Taxes (excludes payroll, sales, and excise taxes)	329
	Wages, salaries, and employee benefits	4,912
	Employees at close of year — in the United States	83,600
	— worldwide	121,450
Subsidiary companies outside the U.S.	Sales	$ 4,387
	Earnings from operations	400
	Eastman Kodak Company equity in net earnings (loss)	167

[1]Based on average number of shares outstanding.
[2]Data prior to 1985 have been restated to give effect to the 3-for-2 partial stock split paid in 1985.

 *After deducting unusual charges of $520 million and certain other special charges of $134 million which in total reduced earnings from operations by $654 million. Net earnings were reduced by $373 million because of all special charges and an additional $50 million as a result of the retroactive repeal of the U.S. investment tax credit for a total reduction of $1.87 per share.
**After deducting unusual charges of $563 million which reduced net earnings by $302 million and net earnings per share by $1.33.

Source: Reprinted courtesy of Eastman Kodak Company. Copyright 1987 by Eastman Kodak.

1985	1984	1983	1982	1981	1980	1979	1978	1977	1976
$ 10,631	$ 10,600	$ 10,170	$ 10,815	$ 10,337	$ 9,734	$ 8,028	$ 7,013	$ 5,967	$ 5,438
561**	1,547	1,027	1,860	2,060	1,896	1,649	1,646	1,188	1,127
530	1,624	1,020	1,872	2,183	1,963	1,707	1,681	1,201	1,169
332**	923	565	1,162	1,239	1,154	1,001	902	643	651
3.1%	8.7%	5.6%	10.7%	12.0%	11.9%	12.5%	12.9%	10.8%	12.0%
4.8%	12.6%	7.5%	16.2%	19.4%	20.2%	19.5%	19.6%	15.4%	16.8%
1.46**	3.80	2.28	4.75	5.11	4.77	4.13	3.73	2.66	2.69
553	578	587	581	566	517	468	376	339	334
2.43	2.40	2.37	2.37	2.33	2.13	1.93	1.55	1.40	1.38
225.7	233.4	248.4	248.3	243.7	242.1	242.1	242.1	242.1	242.1
184,231	189,972	200,005	203,788	220,513	234,009	242,227	250,853	247,803	239,528
(221)	345	(22)	581	673	637	533	526	304	317
$ 5,677	$ 5,131	$ 5,420	$ 5,289	$ 5,063	$ 5,246	$ 4,522	$ 4,000	$ 3,192	$ 2,899
12,047	10,775	10,049	9,344	7,963	6,861	6,041	5,515	5,142	4,780
6,070	5,386	4,801	4,286	3,806	3,426	3,081	2,778	2,484	2,212
12,142	10,778	10,928	10,622	9,446	8,754	7,554	6,801	5,904	5,524
3,325	2,306	2,172	2,146	2,119	2,247	1,741	1,563	1,239	1,202
988	409	416	350	93	79	75	76	84	84
5,580	3,641	3,408	3,081	2,676	2,726	2,163	1,943	1,573	1,498
6,562	7,137	7,520	7,541	6,770	6,028	5,391	4,858	4,331	4,026
$ 8,531	$ 8,380	$ 8,097	$ 8,935	$ 8,258	$ 7,904	$ 6,458	$ 5,674	$ 4,754	$ 4,348
2,348	2,464	2,285	2,151	2,349	2,070	1,777	1,532	1,374	1,247
976	838	746	710	615	520	459	389	351	335
1,495	970	889	1,500	1,190	902	603	442	426	497
831	758	652	575	452	399	361	342	323	292
297	793	543	801	1,026	881	770	836	614	571
4,482	4,148	4,340	4,446	4,099	3,643	3,177	2,776	2,448	2,309
89,200	85,600	86,000	93,300	91,900	84,400	80,800	79,600	77,900	80,200
128,950	123,900	125,500	136,500	136,400	129,500	126,300	124,800	123,700	127,000
$ 3,429	$ 3,367	$ 3,410	$ 4,279	$ 4,017	$ 4,125	$ 3,305	$ 2,735	$ 2,280	$ 2,109
169	113	60	302	450	446	482	411	266	242
(9)	25	(65)	72	188	254	289	220	121	111

Case 20

TEXANA PETROLEUM CORPORATION

During the summer of 1966, George Prentice, the newly designated Executive Vice President for domestic operations of the Texana Petroleum Corporation, was devoting much of his time to thinking about improving the combined performance of the five product divisions reporting to him. (See Exhibit 1.) His principal concern was that corporate profits were not reflecting the full potential contribution which could result from the close technological interdependence of the raw materials utilized and produced by these divisions. The principal difficulty, as Prentice saw it, was that the division general managers reporting to him were not working well together:

> As far as I see it, the issue is where do we make the money for the corporation? Not how do we beat the other guy. Nobody is communicating with anybody else at the general manager level. In fact they are telling a bunch of secrets around here.

RECENT CORPORATE HISTORY

The Texana Petroleum Corporation was one of the early major producers and marketers of petroleum products in the southwest United States. Up until the early 1950s, Texana had been almost exclusively in the business of processing and refining crude oil and in selling petroleum products through a chain of company operated service stations in the southwestern United States and in Central and South America. By 1950 company sales had risen to approximately $500 million, with accompanying growth in profits. About 1950, however,

EXHIBIT 1   **Texana Petroleum Company — partial organization chart, 1966**

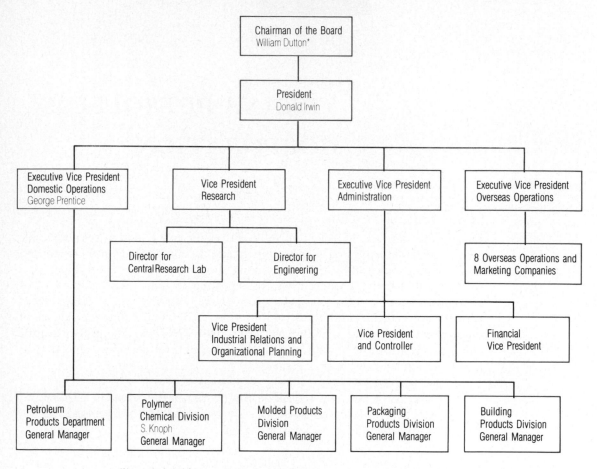

*Names included for persons mentioned in the case.

Texana faced increasingly stiff competition at the retail service station level from several larger national petroleum companies. As a result, sales volume declined sharply during the early 1950s and by 1955 sales had fallen to only $300 million and the company was operating at just above the break-even point.

At this time, because of his age, Roger Holmes, who had been a dominant force in the company since its founding, retired as President and Chief Executive Officer. He was replaced by Donald Irwin, 49, who had been a senior executive with a major chemical company. William Dutton, 55, was appointed Chairman of the Board to replace the retiring Board Chairman. Dutton had spent his entire career with Texana. Prior to his appointment as Chairman, he had been Senior Vice President for Petroleum Products, reporting to Holmes.

Irwin and Dutton, along with other senior executives, moved quickly to solve the problems facing Texana. They gradually divested the company's retail outlets and abandoned the domestic consumer petroleum markets. Through both internal development and acquisition they expanded and rapidly increased the company's involvement in the business of processing petroleum for chemical and plastics products. In moving in this direction they were rapidly expanding on initial moves made by Texana in 1949, when the company built its first chemical processing plant and began marketing these products. To speed the company's growth in these areas, Irwin and Dutton selected aggressive general managers for each division and gave them a wide degree of freedom in decision making. Top management's major requirement was that each division general manager create a growing division with a satisfactory return on investment capital. By 1966 top management had reshaped the company so that in both the domestic and foreign market it was an integrated producer of chemicals and plastic materials. In foreign operations the company continued to operate service stations in Latin America and in Europe. This change in direction was successful and by 1966 company sales had risen to $750 million, with a healthy rise in profit.

In spite of this success, management believed that there was a need for an increase in return on invested capital. The financial and trade press, which had been generous in its praise of the company's recovery, was still critical of the present return on investment, and top management shared this concern. Dutton, Irwin, and Prentice were in agreement that one important method of increasing profits was to take further advantage of the potential cost savings which could come from increased coordination between the domestic operating divisions, as they developed new products, processes, and markets.

DOMESTIC ORGANIZATION, 1966

The product division's reports to Mr. Prentice represented a continuum of producing and marketing activities from production and refining of crude oil to the marketing of several types of plastics products to industrial consumers. Each division was headed by a general manager. While there was some variation in the internal organizational structure of the several divisions, they were generally set up along functional lines (manufacturing, sales, research and development). Each division also had its own controller and engineering activities, although these were supported and augmented by the corporate staff. While divisions had their own research effort, there was also a Central Research Laboratory at the corporate level, which carried on longer-range research of a more fundamental nature that was outside the scope of the activities of any of the product divisions.

The *Petroleum Products Division* was the remaining nucleus of the company's original producing and refining activities. It supplied raw materials to the Polymer and Chemicals Division and also sold refining products under long-term contracts to other petroleum companies. In the early and mid-1950s this division's management had generated much of the company's revenue and profits through its skill in negotiating these agreements. In 1966 top corporate management felt that this division's management had accepted its role as a supplier to the rest of the corporation, and felt that there were harmonious relations between it and its sister divisions.

The *Polymer and Chemicals Division* was developed internally during the late 1940s and early 50s as management saw its share of the consumer petroleum market declining. Under the leadership of Seymour Knoph (who had been General Manager for several years) and his predecessor (who was in 1966 Executive Vice President–Administration) the division had rapidly developed a line of chemical and polymer compounds derived from petroleum raw materials. Most of the products of this division were manufactured under licensing agreement or were materials the formulation of which was well understood. Nevertheless, technical personnel in the division had developed an industry-wide reputation for their ability to develop new and improved processes. Top management of the division took particular pride in this ability. From the beginning, the decisions of what products to manufacture were based to a large extent upon the requirements of the Molded and Packaging Products Divisions. However, Polymer and Chemicals Division executives had always attempted to market these same products to external customers, and had been highly successful. These external sales were extremely important to Texana since they assured a large enough volume of operation to process a broad product line of polymer chemicals profitably. As the other divisions had grown, they had required a larger proportion of the division's capacity, which meant that Polymer and Chemicals Division managers had to reduce their commitment to external customers.

The *Molded Products Division* was also an internally developed division, which had been formed in 1951. Its products were a variety of molded plastic products ranging from toys and household items to automotive and electronic parts. This division's major strengths were its knowledge of molding technology and particularly its marketing ability. While it depended upon the Polymer and Chemicals Division for its raw materials, its operations were largely independent of those of the Packaging Products and Building Products Divisions.

The *Packaging Products Division* was acquired in 1952. Its products were plastic packaging materials, including films, cartons, bottles, etc. All of these products were marketed to industrial customers. Like the Molded Products Division, the Packaging Division depended on the Polymer and Chemicals Division as a source of raw materials, but was largely independent of other end-product divisions.

The *Building Products Division* was acquired in 1963 to give Texana a position in the construction materials market. The division produced and marketed a variety of insulation roofing materials and similar products to the building trade. It was a particularly attractive acquisition for Texana, because prior to the acquisition it had achieved some success with plastic products for insulation and roofing materials. Although the plastic products accounted for less than

20 percent of the total division sales in 1965, plans called for these products to account for over 50 percent of division sales in the next five years. Its affiliation with Texana gave this division a stronger position in plastic raw materials through the Polymer and Chemicals Division.

Selection and Recruitment of Management Personnel

The rapid expansion of the corporation into these new areas had created the need for much additional management talent, and top management had not hesitated to bring new men in from outside the corporation, as well as advancing promising younger men inside Texana. In both the internally developed and acquired divisions, most managers had spent their career inside the division, although some top division managers were moved between divisions or into corporate positions.

In speaking about the type of men he had sought for management positions, Donald Irwin described his criterion in a financial publication:

> We don't want people around who are afraid to move. The attraction of Texana is that it gives the individual responsibilities which aren't diluted. It attracts the fellow who wants a challenge.

Another corporate executive described Texana managers:

> It's a group of very tough-minded, but considerate, gentlemen with an enormous drive to get things done.

Another manager, who had been with Texana for his entire career, and who considered himself to be different from most Texana managers, described the typical Texana manager as follows:

> Texana attracts a particular type of person. Most of these characteristics are personal characteristics rather than professional ones. I would use terms such as cold, unfeeling, aggressive, and extremely competitive, but not particularly loyal to the organization. He is loyal to dollars, his own personal dollars. I think this is part of the communication problem. I think this is done on purpose. The selection procedures lead in this direction. I think this is so because of contrast with the way the company operated ten years ago. Of course I was at the plant level at that time. But today the attitude I have described is also in the plants. Ten years ago the organization was composed of people who worked together for the good of the organization, because they wanted to. I don't think this is so today.

Location of Division Facilities

The Petroleum Products, Polymer and Chemicals, and the Packaging Products Divisions had their executive offices located on separate floors of the Texana headquarters building in the Chicago "Loop." The plants and research and development facilities of these divisions were spread out across Oklahoma, Texas, and Louisiana. The Molded Products Division had its headquarters, research and development facilities, and a major plant in an industrial suburb of Chicago. This division's other plants were at several locations in the Middle West and East Coast. The Building Products Division's headquarters and major production and technical facilities were located in Fort Worth, Texas. All four divisions shared sales offices in major cities from coast to coast.

Evaluation and Control of Division Performance

The principal method of controlling and evaluating the operations of these divisions was the semiannual review of division plans and the approval of major capital expenditures by the executive committee.[1] In reviewing performance against plans, members of the executive committee placed almost sole emphasis on the division's actual return on investment against budget. Corporate executives felt that this practice, together with the technological interdependence of the divisions, created many disputes about transfer pricing.

In addition to these regular reviews, corporate executives had frequent discussions with division executives about their strategies, plans, and operations. It had been difficult for corporate management to strike the proper balance in guiding the operations for the divisions. This problem was particularly acute with regard to the Polymer and Chemicals Division, because of its central place in the corporation's product line. One corporate staff member explained his view of the problem:

> This whole matter of communications between the corporate staff and the Polymer and Chemicals Division has been a fairly difficult problem. Corporate management used to contribute immensely to this by trying to get into the nuts and bolts area within the Polymer and Chemicals organization, and this created serious criticisms; however, I think they have backed off in this manner.

A second corporate executive, in discussing this matter for a trade publication report, put the problem this way:

> We're trying to find the middle ground. We don't want to be a holding company, and with our diversity we can't be a highly centralized corporation.

Executive Vice President– Domestic Operations

In an effort to find this middle ground the position of Executive Vice President– Domestic Operations was created in early 1966, and George Prentice was its

[1]The executive committee consisted of Messrs. Dutton, Irwin, and Prentice, as well as the Vice President of Research, Executive Vice President–Administration, and the Executive Vice President of Foreign Operations.

first occupant. Prior to this change, there had been two Senior Domestic Vice Presidents — one in charge of the Petroleum and Polymer and Chemicals Divisions and the other in charge of the end-use divisions. Mr. Prentice had been Senior Vice President in charge of the end-use divisions before the new position was created. He had held that position for only two years, having come to it from a highly successful marketing career with a competitor.

At the time of his appointment one press account described Mr. Prentice as "hard-driving, aggressive, and ambitious — an archetype of the self-actuated dynamo Irwin has sought out."

Shortly after taking his new position Prentice described the task before him:

> I think the corporation wants to integrate its parts better and I am here because I reflect this feeling. We can't be a bunch of entrepreneurs around here. We have got to balance discipline with entrepreneurial motivation. This is what we were in the past, just a bunch of entrepreneurs and if they came in with ideas we would get the money, but now our dollars are limited, and especially the Polymer and Chemical boys haven't been able to discipline themselves to select from within ten good projects. They just don't seem to be able to do this, and so they come running in here with all ten good projects which they say we have to buy, and they get upset when we can't buy them all.

> This was the tone of my predecessors (Senior Vice Presidents). All of them were very strong on being entrepreneurs. I am going to run it different. I am going to take a marketing and capital orientation. As far as I can see, there is a time to compete and a time to collaborate, and I think right now there has been a lack of recognition in the Polymer and Chemicals executive suite that this thing has changed.

Other Views of Domestic Interdivisional Relations

Executives within the Polymer and Chemicals Divisions, in the end-use divisions, and at the corporate level, shared Prentice's view that the major breakdown in interdivisional relations was between the Polymer and Chemicals Division and the end-use divisions. Executives in the end-use divisions made these typical comments about the problem:

> I think the thing we have got to realize is that we are wedded to the Polymer and Chemicals Division whether we like it or not. We are really tied up with them. And just as we would with any outside supplier or with any of our customers, we will do things to maintain their business. But because they feel they have our business wrapped up they do not reciprocate in turn. Now let me emphasize that they have not arbitrarily refused to do the things that we are requiring, but there is a pressure on them for investment projects and we are low man on the pole. And I think this could heavily jeopardize our chances for growth.

> I would say our relationships are sticky, and I think this is primarily because we think our reason for being is to make money, so we try to keep Polymer and Chemicals as an arm's length

supplier. For example, I cannot see just because it is a Polymer and Chemicals product, accepting millions of pounds of very questionable material. It takes dollars out of our pocket, and we are very profit-centered.

The big frustration, I guess, and one of our major problems, is that you can't get help from them [Polymer and Chemicals]. You feel they are not interested in what you are doing, particularly if it doesn't have a large return for them. But as far as I am concerned this has to become a joint venture relationship, and this is getting to be real sweat with us. We are the guys down below yelling for help. And they have got to give us some relief.

My experience with the Polymer and Chemicals Division is that you cannot trust what they say at all, and even when they put it in writing you can't be absolutely sure that they are going to live up to it.

Managers within the Polymer and Chemicals Division expressed similar sentiments:

Personally, right now I have the feeling that the divisions' interests are growing farther apart. It seems that the divisions are going their own way. For example, we are a Polymer producer but the molding division wants to be in a special area, so that means they are going to be less of a customer to us, and there is a whole family of plastics being left out that nobody's touching, and this is bearing on our program. . . . We don't mess with the Building Products Division at all, either. They deal in small volumes. Those that we are already making we sell to them, those that we don't make we can't justify making because of the kinds of things we are working with. What I am saying is that I don't think the corporation is integrating, but I think we ought to be, and this is one of the problems of delegated divisions. What happens is that an executive heads this up and goes for the place that makes the most money for the division, but this is not necessarily the best place from a corporate standpoint.

We don't have as much contact with sister divisions as I think we should. I have been trying to get a liaison with guys in my function but it has been a complete flop. One of the problems is that I don't know who to call on in these other divisions. There is no table of organization, nor is there any encouragement to try and get anything going. My experience has been that all of these operating divisions are very closed organizations. I know guys up the line will say that I am nuts about this. They say to just call over and I will get an answer. But this always has to be a big deal, and it doesn't happen automatically, and hurts us.

The comments of corporate staff members describe these relationships and the factors they saw contributing to the problem:

Right now I would say there is an iron curtain between the Polymer and Chemicals Division and the rest of the corporation. You know, we tell our divisions they are responsible, autonomous groups, and the Polymer and Chemicals Division took it very seriously. However, when you are a three-quarter-billion-dollar company, you've got to be coordinated, or the whole thing is going to fall apart—it can be no other way. The Domestic Executive Vice President thing has been a big step forward to improve this, but I would say it hasn't worked out yet.

The big thing that is really bothering [the Polymer and Chemicals Division] is that they think they have to go develop all new markets on their own. They are going to do it alone independently, and this is the problem they are faced with. They have got this big thing, that they want to prove that they are a company all by themselves and not rely upon packaging or anybody else.

Polymer and Chemicals Division executives talked about the effect of this drive for independence of the divisional operating heads on their own planning efforts:

The Polymer and Chemicals Division doesn't like to communicate with the corporate staff. This seems hard for us, and I think the [a recent major proposal] was a classic example of this. That plan, as it was whipped up by the Polymer and Chemicals Division has massive implications for the corporation both in expertise and in capital. In fact, I think we did this to be a competitive one-up on the rest of our sister divisions. We wanted to be the best-looking division in the system, but we carried it to an extreme. In this effort, we wanted to show that we had developed this concept completely on our own. . . . Now I think a lot of our problems with it stemmed from this intense desire we have to be the best in this organization.

Boy, a big doldrum around here was shortly after Christmas (1965) when they dropped out a new plant, right out of our central plan, without any appreciation of the importance of this plant to the whole Polymer and Chemicals Division's growth. . . . Now we have a windfall and we are back in business on this new plant. But for a while things were very black and everything we had planned and everything we had built our patterns on were out. In fact, when we put this plan together, it never really occurred to us that we were going to get it turned down, and I'll bet we didn't even put the plans together in such a way as to really reflect the importance of this plant to the rest of the corporation.

A number of executives in the end-use divisions attributed the interdivisional problems to different management practices and assumptions within the Polymer and Chemicals Division. An executive in the packaging division made this point:

We make decisions quickly and at the lowest possible level, and this is tremendously different from the rest of Texana. I don't know another division like this in the rest of the corporation.

Look at what Sy Knoph has superfluous to his operation compared to ours. These are the reasons for our success. You've got to turn your guys loose and not breathe down their necks all the time. We don't slow our people down with staff. Sure, you may work with a staff, the wheels may grind, but they sure grind slow.

Also, we don't work on detail like the other divisions do. Our management doesn't feel they need the detail stuff. Therefore, they're [Polymer and Chemical] always asking us for detail which we can't supply, our process doesn't generate it and their process requires it, and this always creates problems with the Polymer and Chemicals Division. But I'll be damned if I am going to have a group of people running between me and the plant, and I'll be goddamned if I am going to clutter up my organization with all the people that Knoph has got working for him. I don't want this staff, but they are sure pushing it on me.

This comment from a molding division manager is typical of many about the technical concerns of the Polymer and Chemicals Division management:

Historically, even up to the not-too-distant past, the Polymer and Chemicals Division was considered a snake pit as far as the corporate people were concerned. This was because the corporate people were market-oriented and Polymer and Chemicals Division was technically run and very much a manufacturing effort. These two factors created a communication barrier, because to really understand the Polymer and Chemicals Division problems, they felt that you had to have a basic appreciation of the technology and all the interrelationships.

Building on this strong belief, the Polymer and Chemicals Division executives in the past have tried to communicate in technical terms, and this just further hurt the relationship, and it just did not work. Now they are coming up with a little bit more business or commercial orientation, and they are beginning to appreciate that they have got to justify the things they want to do in a business or commercial orientation, and they are beginning to appreciate that they have got to justify the things they want to do in a business sense rather than just a technical sense. This also helps the problem of maintaining their relationships with the corporation as most of the staff is nontechnical; however, this has changed a little bit in that more and more technical people have been coming on and this has helped from the other side.

They work on the assumption in the Polymer and Chemicals Division that you have to know the territory before you can be an effective manager. You have got to be an operating guy to contribute meaningfully to their problems. However, their biggest problem is this concentration on technical solutions to their problems. This is a thing that has boxed them in the most trouble with the corporation and the other sister divisions.

These and other executives also pointed to another source of conflict between the Polymer and Chemicals Division and other divisions. This was the question of whether the Polymer and Chemicals Division should develop into a more independent marketer, or whether it should rely more heavily on the end-use divisions to "push" its products to the market.

Typical views of this conflict are the following comments by end-use division executives:

The big question I have about Polymer and Chemicals is what is their strategy going to be? I can understand them completely from a technical standpoint, this is no problem. I wonder what is the role of this company? How is it going to fit into what we and others are doing? Right now, judging from the behavior I've seen, Polymer and Chemicals could care less about what we are doing in terms of integration of our markets or a joint approach to them.

I think it is debatable whether the Polymer and Chemicals Division should be a new product company or not. Right now we have an almost inexhaustible appetite for what they do and do well. As I see it, the present charter is fine. However, that group is very impatient, aggressive, and they want to grow, but you have got to grow within guidelines. Possibly the Polymer and Chemicals Division is just going to have to learn to hang on the coattails of the other divisions, and do just what they are doing now, only better.

I think the future role of the Polymer and Chemicals Division is going to be, at any one point in time for the corporation, that if it looks like a product is needed, they will make it. . . . They are going to be suppliers because I will guarantee you that if the moment comes and we can't buy it elsewhere, for example, then I darn well know they are going to make it for us regardless of what their other commitments are. They are just going to have to supply us. If you were to put the Polymer and Chemicals Division off from the corporation, I don't think they would last a year. Without their huge captive requirements, they would not be able to compete economically in the commercial areas they are in.

A number of other executives indicated that the primary emphasis within the corporation on return on investment by divisions tended to induce, among other things, a narrow, competitive concern on the part of the various divisional managements. The comment of this division executive was typical:

As far as I can see it, we [his division and Polymer and Chemicals] are 180 degrees off on our respective charters. Therefore, when Sy Knoph talks about this big project we listen nicely and then we say, "God bless you, lots of luck," but I am sure we are not going to get involved in it. I don't see any money in it for us. It may be a gold mine for Sy but it is not for our company; and as long as we are held to the high profit standards we are, we just cannot afford to get involved. I can certainly see it might make good corporate sense for us to get it, but it doesn't make any sense in terms of our particular company. We have got to be able to show the returns in order to get continuing capital and I just can't on that kind of project. I guess what I am saying is that under the right conditions we could certainly go in but not under the present framework; we would just be dead in terms of dealing with the corporate financial structure. We just cannot get the kinds of returns on our capital that the corporation has set to get new capital. In terms of the long run, I'd like very much to see what the corporation has envisioned in terms of a hook-up between us, but right now I don't see any sense in going on. You know my career is at stake here, too.

Another divisional executive made this point more succinctly:

Personally I think that a lot more could be done from a corporate point of view and this is frustrating. Right now all these various divisions seem to be viewed strictly as an investment by the corporate people. They only look at us as a banker might look at us. This hurts us in terms of evolving some of these programs because we have relationships which are beyond financial relationships.

The remarks of a corporate executive seemed to support this concern:

One of the things I worry about is where is the end of the rope on this interdivisional thing. I'm wondering if action really has to come from just the division. You know, in this organization when they decide to do something new it always has been a divisional proposal — they were coming to us for review and approval. The executive committee ends up a review board; not us, working downward. With this kind of pattern the talent of the corporate people is pretty well seduced into asking questions and determining whether a thing needs guidelines. But I think we ought to be the idea people as well, thinking about where we are going in the future, and if we think we ought to be getting into some new area, then we tell the divisions to do it. The stream has got to work both ways. Now it is not.

Case 21

THE THERMOMETER CORPORATION OF AMERICA: DIVISION OF FIGGIE INTERNATIONAL, INC.

It was late November of 1982, when Harry Figgie, Jr., Chairman of Figgie International, and Joe Skadra, group vice president and treasurer, were meeting in the company's new headquarters complex in Richmond, Virginia. Figgie International (FI) was a diversified company which had 40 different businesses ranging from fire engines to clothing. Included in these businesses was the manufacture of thermometers which was conducted under the name of Thermometer Corporation of America (TCA). The TCA plant was located in Springfield, Ohio, a city of 86,000 in the west-central part of the state.

FI recently received a proposal from Ohio Thermometer Co. (OTC) dated November 17, 1982, and entitled "An Analysis of a Merger and Future Between TCA and OTC" (see Appendix). The proposal was presented by Charles L. Wappner and Jerome P. Bennett, president and vice president, respectively (and co-owners), of OTC. OTC was a competitor in the thermometer business and was also located in Springfield, Ohio. Figgie and Skadra arranged this meeting to discuss the November 17 proposal. Their conversation began as follows:

Figgie: As you know, I met with Charlie [Wappner] and Jerry [Bennett] on November 17th at their request. At that meeting they presented their proposal, which calls for Figgie [International] to purchase OTC.

This case was prepared by Per Jenster, Henry Odell, and Ken Burger, McIntire School of Commerce, University of Virginia. Reprinted by permission of North American Case Research Association and the authors. ©1985. All rights reserved.

Skadra: As I recall, they [OTC] tried to acquire TCA from us back in 1978.

Figgie: Yes, but at that time we felt that the growth potential for TCA was too good to consider divesting. I have kept in touch with Charlie and Jerry since then, so their proposal wasn't a complete surprise.

Skadra: How did the meeting go?

Figgie: The atmosphere was very friendly. I pointed out, as best I could, that while we regard ourselves as a good parent company to work with, a number of changes would have to be made if we assimilated OTC. I'm sure from the comments they made that they understand this and would be willing to work with us.

Skadra: Living and working in the same community, they must know Bill Kieffer [TCA president].

Figgie: They know him and apparently have considerable respect for him and for his abilities as a manager, as do we. In the proposal they specifically refer to his [Kieffer's] "running a lean operation." This tells me that if a merger of TCA and OTC were to take place, they would be willing to accept Kieffer as their leader.

Skadra: In terms of return on investment, TCA has been one of our top businesses — until recently.

Figgie: True enough, but we haven't been able to get the sales growth we had hoped for. Bill [Kieffer] has, on several occasions, asked me for help in acquiring businesses that would help us expand the thermometer business and help him in getting that growth.

Skadra: I remember looking at a couple that just couldn't be justified.

Figgie: Despite the recent decline in sales at TCA I still think it has potential, and I don't want to consider selling it. We have a proven manager in Bill and a good operation. But we're not fully utilizing the managerial capabilities of Bill and his team.

Skadra: The proposal indicates a number of possible synergies that might be realized by combining the two operations. We'll certainly have to identify those before negotiating.

Figgie: Yes, and I also keep thinking about that idle manufacturing plant we have in Springfield, which is now being used for storage.

Skadra: As I recall, that plant has 65,000 square feet on one floor.

Figgie: Charlie said that their present plant has 100,000 square feet on one floor. Apparently it's not being fully used now. Charlie and Jerry own it personally.

Skadra: From a quick look at the figures, their asking price of $1,500,000 (Exhibit 1) seems very high. I'd like to take a closer look at the whole situation, especially the financial aspect.

Figgie: I agree. Let's analyze the offer from a strategic and financial standpoint, looking at all the angles.

Skadra: Since both TCA and OTC have had declining sales and profits in the last couple of years, I think we should pay special attention to costs.

EXHIBIT 1   **Proposed terms of sale of assets of Ohio Thermometer to Figgie International**

	Net sound value
Lloyd-Thomas appraised values May 31, 1982:	
Machinery	$ 555,985
Furniture and fixtures	135,361
Office furniture and fixtures	39,921
Office machines	19,808
Industrial power trucks	10,758
Dies*	213,473
Tools and trucks*	4,000
	979,306
Inventories complete at cost September 30, 1982 values	513,740
Total value	$1,493,046

Acceptable Terms: $1,493,000 cash at closing or at your option: $500,000 cash at closing and balance in acceptable securities or notes.

a) Jerry Bennett and Charles Wappner would agree to stay for at least two years.

b) We would agree to lease our 100,000-sq.-ft. factory and office building to Figgie International for two years at $5,000 per month on a net net basis.

c) Our NCR 8271 computer system is leased from U.S. Leasing. There are 30 months remaining at a rental of $1,672 per month. We would agree to transfer this lease to Figgie International if desired.

*Owners' valuation.

BACKGROUND

In late 1963, Harry E. Figgie, Jr., acquired the controlling interest in "Automatic" Sprinkler Corporation of America, a family-owned firm with sales of $22 million. Figgie recalled:

> On January 2, 1964, I drove 90 miles to Youngstown, Ohio, to take over a company I'd never seen. Their top officer said to me, 'You've got to be the dumbest man alive.' I said, 'I'm the second dumbest. You sold it!'

Since then Figgie and his executive team had expanded the corporation to a multidivisional firm with sales of $770 million in 1981. This growth came about through an aggressive acquisition phase to obtain what Figgie referred to as a "critical mass" of $300 million in annual sales. To do this, he applied a management concept of a lean organization with a small, highly mobile corporate staff. According to Harry Figgie:

EXHIBIT 2 Figgie International, Inc. balance sheet and income statement data

Income data (million $)

Year ended Dec. 31	Revs.	Oper. inc.	% Oper. inc. of revs.	Cap. exp.	Depr.	Int. exp.	Net bef. taxes	Eff. tax rate	Net inc.	% Net inc. of revs.
1982[1]	708	51.0	7.2%	31.9	14.9	21.4	38.6	32.4%	26.1	3.7%
1981[2,3]	770	72.3	9.4%	28.1	14.5	22.2	48.1	46.6%	25.7	3.3%
1980[2]	760	65.2	8.6%	22.4	13.8	23.6	40.3	48.8%	20.6	2.7%
1979	691	62.0	9.0%	24.0	16.1	21.3	33.8	48.0%	17.6	2.5%
1978	628	52.4	8.3%	29.1	12.9	16.8	30.4	49.0%	15.5	2.5%
1977	568	40.5	7.1%	34.4	9.7	12.5	21.8	47.1%	11.5	2.0%
1976	518	41.4	8.0%	12.7	8.1	9.5	25.7	48.7%	13.1	2.5%
1975	480	40.2	8.4%	13.5	7.7	9.9	23.7	48.2%	12.2	2.5%
1974	476	41.4	8.6%	14.8	6.6	13.3	22.9	48.6%	11.2	2.4%

Balance sheet data (million $)

Dec. 31	Current assets				Total assets	Ret. on assets	Long-term debt	Common equity	Total cap.	% LT debt of cap.	Ret. on equity
	Cash	Assets	Liab.	Ratio							
1982[1]	15.6	268	111	2.4	465	5.5%	122	164	343	35.7%	15.9%
1981	6.8	298	131	2.3	475	5.4%	127	146	335	37.8%	17.6%
1980	10.6	318	141	2.3	485	4.3%	140	128	335	41.7%	15.7%
1979	7.0	316	143	2.2	478	3.8%	145	111	326	44.5%	15.2%
1978	9.8	285	111	2.6	436	3.8%	154	98	315	48.7%	14.7%
1977	9.2	256	108	2.4	376	3.5%	117	90	260	45.0%	11.5%
1976	8.8	217	63	3.4	312	4.3%	110	88	244	45.0%	13.8%
1975	15.2	213	63	3.4	300	4.0%	112	79	232	48.2%	13.9%
1974	14.8	228	80	2.9	309	3.8%	113	72	224	50.6%	14.1%

[1] Estimated.
[2] Reflects acquisitions.
[3] Reflects accounting change.

In those days, it was not uncommon for the team to look over as many as 50 companies a month. In one rush of buying (in 1967), they closed 5 deals in just 25 days.

This phase ended in 1970, after Figgie had acquired more than 50 new divisions. Among these acquisitions was Mid-Con, Inc., a minor conglomerate consisting of a number of smaller companies in the Ohio Valley, one of which was the Thermometer Corporation of America. Most of the other small firms obtained in this particular acquisition had been divested since then.

During the next 10 years the company grew from $356 million in sales to $770 million through internal growth. Harry Figgie recalled:

Such growth was not without problems as we chewed up working capital and sent our debt-to-equity ratio up to 1.36 to 1 [1979].

In 1981, the company changed its name to Figgie International, Inc. and prepared itself for a new period of aggressive growth. As the recession hit the company in 1982 and overall sales dropped about 8%, cost reduction became Harry Figgie's number-one priority in 1982 (see Exhibit 2 for Balance Sheet and Income Statement Data).

FIGGIE INTERNATIONAL, INC.

In a recent interview in *The Craftsman,* an internal publication of FI, Harry Figgie discussed his ambitious plan of growth for the future. The plan entailed a new phase of acquisitions that would build on the company's present business groups. Figgie's goals for the future included:

- Further reduce the company's debt-to-equity ratio.
- Top $1 billion in sales and start building toward $2 billion through an aggressive acquisition program.
- Continue to emphasize internal consolidation, bringing the minimum divisional size up to $25 million in sales.
- Pursue high technology and bring robotics and CAE/CAD/CAM into the workplace by adapting new techniques and strategies.
- Remain faithful to the company's commitment of producing quality products at competitive prices.

Harry E. Figgie, Jr. and His Management Philosophy

Most people would probably say that Harry Figgie was well prepared when he took over the small, troubled Automatic Sprinkler Corp. in 1964. After earning his B.S. in metallurgical engineering at Case Institute of Technology, Harry Figgie earned an M.B.A. at Harvard Business School, a J.D. at Cleveland Marshall Law School, and a M.S. in industrial engineering at Case. Later, as a partner with Booz, Allen & Hamilton, a management consulting firm, Harry Figgie was exposed to a wide range of business situations in smaller and medium-size firms. The experience he gained in management consulting, as well as in his capacity as chairman and chief operating officer of Figgie International, had made him known as one of the foremost cost-reduction authorities in the world. In his book, *The Cost Reduction and Profit Improvement Handbook,* he stresses the importance of a lean organization:

> The first point to remember about the concept of cost reduction is that it can be used interchangeably with the term "profit improvement." If profit improvement is the glass of water half full, then cost reduction is the glass half empty [p. 1] . . .
> As will be demonstrated, a 10% reduction in costs can increase profits by 25% to 50%, or more if the savings can be preserved . . . [p. 3]

Harry Figgie's management concept also placed responsibility for profit-making decisions at the basic profit-center level, that was, the division president. Accordingly, each president had "entrepreneurial" control of his division's profit and growth performance. He reported to a group vice president, who in turn, reported directly to Figgie. One subdivision president commented:

> I have full responsibility for my division, but will receive help from corporate headquarters if I ask. And you'd better ask before the trouble arrives; they [corporate headquarters] don't like surprises. . . . Figgie International is our banker and advisor.

Organization

Figgie International was divided into 5 groups: Consumer, Fire Protection/Safety, Machinery, Technical, and Service. The contribution by group is shown in Exhibit 3.

The Consumer Group included Rawlings sporting goods (baseballs, baseball gloves, basketballs, footballs, golf clubs, and related equipment), Adirondack baseball bats, Fred Perry sportswear (tennis clothing and other sportswear), home fire alarms, vacuum-cleaners, and thermometers (TCA).

The Fire Protection/Safety Group consisted of custom-made fire engines, sprinkler systems, chemical fire extinguishers, aerial-type water delivery systems for fire-fighting apparatus, protective breathing equipment, and security systems and equipment.

The Machinery and Products Group encompassed capping, sorting and sealing machinery, high-speed automatic bottling equipment, road-building and maintenance equipment, hydraulic pumps, vibrating road rollers, material-handling systems, battery-powered vehicles, and mortar and concrete mixers.

EXHIBIT 3   **Contribution by business group**

Business group (1982)*	Sales	Profits
Consumer	18%	8%
Fire protection/safety	43%	41%
Machinery and products	19%	−6%
Technical	19%	21%
Services	1%	36%

*Sales to the U.S. Government accounted for an estimated 21% of the total in 1982.

The Technical Products Group consisted primarily of aircraft and missile components, aircraft display instruments and armament control systems, telemetry and electronic instrumentation systems, and electronic access control and monitoring systems.

The Service Group included sales financing, computer software, real estate, and natural resources investments.

Management Systems

Cash was managed centrally at Figgie International, and divisions submitted all receivable collections to headquarters. Conversely, cash for payables was sent to divisions upon request. Corporate capital and headquarters expenses were paid for in two ways: "payment for debt services" (assets less current liabilities at FI's cost of capital rate [Beta = 1.10]), and "incremental costs of working capital" which were charged at slightly over prime for changes in working capital calculated on a monthly basis.

The capital budgeting procedure ran parallel to the allocation of working capital. Here, a division manager could make discretionary decisions up to $1,000, and a group vice president up to $5,000. All other capital investments had to be encompassed in the budget or submitted for Harry Figgie's approval.

Planning was also an integral part of the management process. In line with the management philosophy of keeping things simple, divisional presidents presented with their group officer the annual business plan between October 1 and November 30 to Harry Figgie and the corporate staff. The plan included a detailed budget for the coming year and a summary for the following four years. As one corporate officer noted: "Three things can happen to a plan at the annual meeting, and two are not good." Operational performance (actual) and a rolling five-month forecast were reported by divisions on a monthly basis.

The reward system was a central part of the management system at Figgie International, and was highly integrated with the planning and budgeting process. The division presidents receive bonuses based on their achievement of pretax return on sales (50%) and pretax return on assets (50%).

THERMOMETER CORPORATION OF AMERICA (TCA)

The operations of TCA were in a 35,000-square-foot, two-story plant in the southern part of the city of Springfield. The office consisted of 2,500 square feet on the second floor. A wide variety of thermometer products was manufactured, including scientific and houseware products. The main manufacturing processes included:

1. The blowing of glass tubes to modify them by adding bulbs, or joining tubes of different diameters. Standard lathes had been customized so that the glass tubes could be heated and rotated as the blowing took place.
2. Etching of glass tubes was needed to provide the degree markings for the scientific and other special-use thermometers. The tubes were coated with wax and a special machine formed slits through which acid could reach the glass surface.
3. Calibration of the thermometer required the right combination of tube bore and bulb size, amount of liquid enclosed (mercury or alcohol-based), and degree marking (etched on the glass or printed on an enclosure in the tube or on a mounting). The operators worked with controlled-temperature baths and made the adjustments.

Since the operations did not lend themselves to automation, the machines required full-time operators to load each piece and perform the operations. Considerable manual skills were required, especially in the glass-blowing. Most operations required the glass to be in a heated, semi-molten state so that the machines could process it. Heating attachments, some of which have been designed by TCA, maintained the processing temperature.

Many of the machines were "dedicated" for a particular operation and were not changed. As a result such machines, remaining idle for much of the time, were typically older machines, but were deemed to be as effective as newer models. The plant was operating at 40% of capacity. About 50% of the total cost of sales was raw materials and purchased parts.

There were 31 hourly paid employees in the plant, most of whom were women. They belonged to the United Auto Workers union. The average hourly wage rate was $4.39 plus $1.48 in fringe benefits. There had been one brief strike in recent years. The relationship between management and workers seemed good; many of the employees had been with TCA for many years, and turnover was low.

Salaried workers were shown in the organization chart (Exhibit 4). A manual accounting system was used, which Mr. Kieffer considered adequate for generating needed information for his operating purposes and for the required reports to FI headquarters. He indicated that he would want to study the situation very carefully and find just the right hardware before shifting to computerization.

Financial information is shown in Exhibits 5, 6, 7, and 8.

EXHIBIT 4   **Thermometer Corporation of America — organization chart — November 1982**

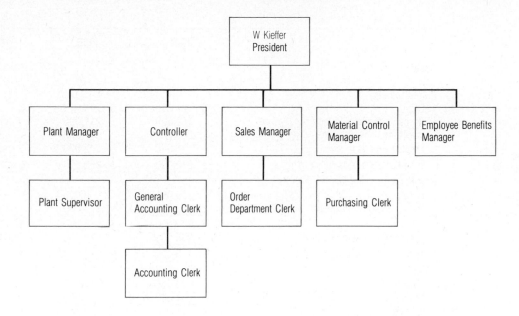

EXHIBIT 5   Thermometer Corporation of America — comparative balance sheets at December 31, 1981, 1980, and 1979

	1981	1980	1979
Assets			
Current assets			
Cash	$ (27,000)	$ —	$ —
Accounts Receivable (net)	162,000	211,000	193,000
Inventory	869,000	642,000	638,000
Prepaid expenses	6,000	2,000	1,000
Total current assets	$1,010,000	$ 855,000	$ 832,000
Property and equipment			
Land	9,000	9,000	9,000
Machinery and equipment	1,192,000	1,176,000	1,164,000
Total	$1,201,000	$1,185,000	$1,173,000
Less: accumulated depreciation	1,088,000	1,072,000	1,046,000
Total property and equipment	$ 113,000	$ 113,000	$ 127,000
Other assets			
Patents	36,000	42,000	47,000
Other assets	1,000	1,000	1,000
Total other assets	$ 37,000	$ 43,000	$ 48,000
Total assets	$1,160,000	$1,011,000	$1,007,000
Liabilities and stockholder's equity			
Current liabilities			
Accounts payable	$ 100,000	$ 78,000	$ 23,000
Unpaid withheld taxes	33,000	30,000	25,000
Accrued expenses	225,000	186,000	165,000
Total current liabilities	$ 358,000	$ 294,000	$ 213,000
Long-term debt	0	0	0
Total liabilities	$ 358,000	$ 294,000	$ 213,000
Stockholder's equity			
Original investment	$ 151,000	$ 151,000	$ 151,000
Retained earnings	1,121,000	1,015,000	93,000
Intra-company current	(470,000)	(449,000)	550,000
Total stockholder's equity	$ 802,000	$ 717,000	$ 794,000
Total liabilities and stockholder's equity	$1,160,000	$1,011,000	$1,007,000

EXHIBIT 6   **Thermometer Corporation of America — comparative income statements for the years ended December 31, 1981, 1980, and 1979**

	1981	1980	1979
Net sales	$1,677,000	$1,730,000	$1,762,000
Cost of sales	1,096,000	1,193,000	1,220,000
Gross profit	581,000	537,000	542,000
Operating expenses			
Selling	134,000	123,000	124,000
Administrative	172,000	153,000	160,000
Debt service	72,000	80,000	78,000
Other	7,000	(3,000)	8,000
Total operating expenses	385,000	353,000	370,000
Income (loss) from operations	196,000	184,000	172,000
Provision for income taxes	90,000	85,000	79,000
Net income (loss)	$ 106,000	$ 99,000	$ 93,000

EXHIBIT 7   **Thermometer Corporation of America — schedule of cost of goods sold for the year ended December 31, 1981**

	1981
Materials	$ 467,992
Direct labor	211,066
Manufacturing expenses:	
Indirect labor	$ 60,497
Supervision	59,760
Vacation and holiday	39,996
Payroll taxes	42,439
Industrial welfare	550
Employees insurance	43,534
Supplies	32,110
Maintenance and repairs	10,269
Truck	5,896
Freight	41,816
Utilities	49,161
Depreciation	12,352
Insurance	39,450
Taxes	—
Scrap	17,584
Travel	221
Rentals	17,018
Miscellaneous	—
	$ 472,653
Burden (absorbed)	(363,601)
Burden from inventory	307,593
Total cost of goods manufactured	$ 416,645
Decrease in finished goods inventory	—
Cost of goods sold	$1,095,703

EXHIBIT 8   **Thermometer Corporation of America — schedule of selling and administrative expenses for the year ended December 31, 1981**

	1981
Selling expenses	
Salaries	$ 9,586
Commissions	61,295
Travel	715
Advertising	31,172
Samples	2,917
Telephone	4,037
Show expense	20,460
Payroll taxes	899
Depreciation	2,439
Supplies	131
Miscellaneous	—
	$133,651
Administrative expenses	
Salaries	$110,433
Payroll taxes	9,301
Pension	11,000
Travel	4,278
Office supplies	3,892
Telephone	2,422
Legal and professional	2,800
Depreciation	1,595
Dues and subscriptions	3,572
Insurance	1,274
Bank charges	4,106
Contributions	914
Data processing	4,238
Rent — autos	3,643
Amortization patents	5,700
Bad debt expense	3,000
Miscellaneous	386
	$172,554

OHIO THERMOMETER COMPANY (OTC)

OTC was located in a one-story, 100,000-square-foot building in Springfield. The plant was about 5 miles from the TCA plant. The current operations (equipment and storage) used 60% of the floor space. The primary product was dial thermometers of 12″ and 18″ diameters. The primary parts were the coated steel dial face (which was printed with the thermometer readings and other desired backgrounds), the aluminum outer band, brass bushings and shaft, temperature indicator, clear acryllic plastic dial cover (lens), and the bimetallic coil (which moved the indicator as the temperature varied). OTC used more durable materials than competitors. The total material purchases including raw materials and purchased parts, such as coils and indicators, were about 50% of the total cost of sales.

The plant operations were divided into three areas. One area contained the punch presses, which cut out the dial faces and the outer bands from sheet metal. A second area held the printing line with various printing presses and a drying oven connected by a circular conveyor belt. The third area was where the assembly took place. The punch presses were the only metalworking equipment used and were standard models.

There were 70 hourly paid shop employees who belonged to the International Association of Machinists union. The average wage rate was $4.92 per hour. Fringe benefits were $1.60 per hour. The work in the plant was not highly skilled. As shown in Exhibit 6, the plant had five supervisors.

OTC had an art department, which generated a wide variety of advertising for printing on the dial face. The equipment provided photographic and silk-screening capabilities.

Exhibit 9 shows 23 salaried employees, including the three officers, Charlie Wappner (president), Jerry Bennett (vice president — sales), and V. Bennett (secretary). V. Bennett was Wappner's sister and Bennett's wife and filled the position of secretary on a part-time basis at a salary of $3,000 annually. Aside from these corporate officers the average annual salaries were as follows:

1. Managers and engineers $25,000
2. Supervisors, technicians, and artists $18,000
3. Clerks, computer operators, and secretaries $14,000

Fringe benefits were about 35% of salaries.

The NCR 8271 computer (leased) was used for accounting, inventory, and production control. It had far larger capabilities than were needed for the operation.

Financial information is shown in Exhibits 10, 11, 12, and 13.

Wappner stated that since July 1, 1982, several steps had been taken to increase profits. A 6% price increase was in effect. Improvements had been made in plant operations. Some overhead items, such as retirement benefits, had been reduced. As a result of these changes, Wappner was projecting income from operations for the fiscal year ending June 30, 1983, at $130,000.

EXHIBIT 9   **Ohio Thermometer organization chart — November 1982**

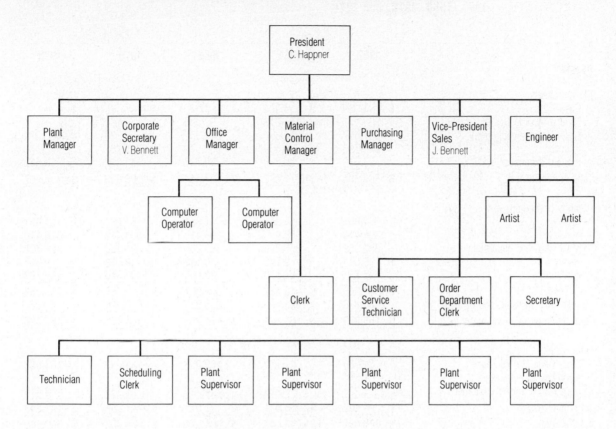

EXHIBIT 10   The Ohio Thermometer Company—comparative balance sheets at June 30, 1982, 1981, 1980, 1979, and 1978

	1982	1981	1980	1979	1978
Assets					
Current assets					
Cash	$ 7,939	$ 4,934	$ 4,330	$ —	$ —
Federal income tax refundable	—	55,216	90,546	—	—
Accounts receivable (net)	247,057	282,055	339,342	559,238	481,374
Inventory	626,796	708,409	853,579	903,762	795,181
Prepaid expenses	24,513	20,808	19,737	45,392	23,552
Total current assets	$ 906,305	$1,071,422	$1,307,534	$1,508,892	$1,300,607
Property and equipment					
Land	51,851	51,851	51,851	51,851	51,851
Building	308,418	308,418	308,418	308,418	308,418
Machinery and equipment	380,362	356,235	353,300	320,180	281,792
Trucks	9,518	9,518	9,518	9,518	9,518
Furniture	97,717	87,570	86,480	85,320	83,790
Total	$ 847,866	$ 813,592	$ 809,567	$ 775,287	$ 735,369
Less: Accumulated depreciation	691,896	663,478	635,337	610,816	577,634
Total property and equipment	$ 155,970	$ 150,114	$ 174,230	$ 164,471	$ 157,735
Other assets					
Cash value life insurance	21,860	21,679	109,958	135,833	135,833
Advances to employees	1,544	12,912	10,635	—	—
Deposits on leased equipment	1,202	2,220	2,220	5,256	5,410
Total other assets	$ 24,406	$ 36,811	$ 122,813	$ 141,089	$ 141,243
Total assets	$1,086,881	$1,258,347	$1,604,577	$1,814,452	$1,599,585
Liabilities & stockholder's equity					
Current liabilities					
Notes payable	$ 300,000	$ 175,000	$ 185,000	$ 175,000	$ 85,000
Current maturities on L-T debt	9,993	10,290	8,728	5,753	5,255
Accounts payable	418,671	519,981	418,566	506,937	450,094
Accrued expenses	73,390	67,136	83,414	106,679	132,510
Total current liabilities	$ 802,054	$ 772,407	$ 695,708	$ 794,369	$ 672,859
Long-term debt	20,473	53,374	159,173	187,464	196,197
Total liabilities	$ 822,527	$ 825,781	$ 854,881	$ 981,833	$ 869,056
Stockholder's equity					
Common stock	250,000	250,000	250,000	250,000	250,000
Retained earnings	111,634	279,846	596,976	679,399	577,809
Less: Treasury stock	97,280	97,280	97,280	97,280	97,280
Total stockholder's equity	$ 264,354	$ 432,566	$ 749,696	$ 832,619	$ 730,529
Total liabilities and stockholder's equity	$1,086,881	$1,258,347	$1,604,577	$1,814,452	$1,599,585

EXHIBIT 11   The Ohio Thermometer Company—comparative income statements for the years ended June 30, 1982, 1981, 1980, 1979, and 1978

	1982	1981	1980	1979	1978
Net Sales	$3,654,311	$3,649,931	$4,286,345	$4,735,234	$4,367,128
Cost of Sales	2,788,718	2,882,232	3,337,012	3,538,663	3,248,270
Gross Profit	865,593	767,699	949,333	1,196,571	1,118,858
Operating Expenses:					
Selling	513,136	593,627	654,647	615,489	525,870
Administrative	441,451	472,730	435,530	422,065	334,121
Interest	63,317	56,546	40,668	30,706	18,461
Bad Debts	15,206	15,241	—	—	—
Other	—	—	(4,976)	(4,474)	41,950
Total Operating Expenses	1,033,110	1,138,144	1,125,869	1,063,786	920,402
Income (Loss) from Operations	(167,517)	(370,445)	(176,536)	132,785	198,456
Provision for Income Taxes	—	—	—	30,000	78,000
Tax Benefit of Net Oper. Loss Carrybacks	—	54,010	70,546	—	—
Net Income (Loss) before Special Items	(167,517)	(316,435)	(105,990)	102,785	120,456
Insurance Proceeds on Deceased Officer	—	—	23,762	—	—
Net Income (Loss)	$ (167,517)	$ (316,435)	$ (82,228)	$ 102,785	$ 120,456

EXHIBIT 12   **The Ohio Thermometer Company — schedules of cost of goods sold for the years ended June 30, 1982, and 1981**

	1982	1981
Materials	$1,423,055	$1,462,728
Direct labor	$ 513,231	$ 555,098
Manufacturing expenses		
Indirect labor	$ 63,303	$ 59,041
Production office	3,157	4,034
Engineers	41,780	41,984
Supervision	120,874	112,258
Vacation and holiday	88,482	91,659
Retirement	29,372	33,198
Payroll taxes	81,298	87,391
Industrial welfare	210	2,527
Employees insurance	109,956	94,604
Supplies	104,784	106,549
Maintenance and repairs	66,883	69,858
Truck	2,645	2,780
Freight	16,465	17,090
Utilities	58,373	50,676
Depreciation — Building	9,850	9,850
Depreciation — Other	14,918	11,312
Insurance	5,125	7,234
Taxes	5,616	5,788
Dues and subscriptions	420	1,148
Travel	222	267
Rent	490	442
Miscellaneous	2,236	2,187
	$ 826,459	$ 811,877
Total cost of goods manufactured	$2,762,745	$2,829,703
Decrease in finished goods inventory	25,973	52,529
Cost of goods sold	$2,788,718	$2,882,232

EXHIBIT 13   **The Ohio Thermometer Company — schedules of selling and administrative expenses for the years ended June 30, 1982 and 1981**

	1982	1981
Selling expenses		
Salaries	$135,936	$157,883
Commissions	159,211	202,616
Travel	18,088	23,873
Advertising	20,662	15,219
Prospect	10	32
Samples	3,657	6,392
Freight	167,595	179,743
Telephone	5,818	4,780
Dues and subscriptions	2,159	3,089
	$513,136	$593,627
Administrative expenses		
Executive salaries	$ 99,611	$ 88,299
Office salaries	124,401	126,898
Payroll taxes	36,584	24,862
Executive pension	28,293	60,638
Director fees	3,300	2,400
Travel	9,139	4,625
Postage	5,872	6,132
Office supplies	30,610	50,332
Telephone	8,109	7,194
Legal and professional	19,077	19,133
Depreciation	3,649	6,980
Dues and subscriptions	2,056	2,354
Insurance	17,007	14,468
Life insurance on officers	10,398	8,564
Contributions	3,520	753
Taxes	15,458	21,961
Rent — Computer	20,064	20,064
Rent — Autos	4,303	7,073
	$441,451	$472,730

THE THERMOMETER INDUSTRY

Market Structure

In the early '80s, the thermometer industry was composed of two major segments: the consumer market and the industrial market. The ratio of industrial to consumer sales for the total thermometer market was approximately 20%–80%. TCA maintained an interest in both segments with about the same split as the total industry. OTC, however, was predominantly focused in the consumer segment, especially the weather components of that market which comprised over 80% of their total thermometer sales.

Marketing information for the industrial sector was generally not available on a per-company basis or by type of thermometer instrument. This situation was due to the fact that the production of thermometers in most companies was but a small part of a huge product line of all types of recorders, gauges, and instruments. As a result, it was virtually impossible to isolate meaningful information on the industrial market.

Therefore, the majority of information was on competitive activities within the consumer market. The product lines in this market included weather, houseware/decorator, cooking, and a miscellaneous line which included medical, automobile, and other small uses of thermometers as shown in Exhibit 14. The total market for thermometers (consumer and industrial) was estimated at $100 million in 1982.

Market Conditions

The sale of consumer thermometer lines generally fluctuated with the economy. A number of items within the decorator line, for example, were positioned as gift items, and sales corresponded to the general consumer buying mood, especially during holidays.

Products within all categories ranged from low-price, mainly discount items to high-quality, high-price specialty items. Most of the seven major competitors within the consumer market had at least one strong product which acted as the anchor for the rest of their lines.

Distribution of consumer thermometer products was generally accomplished through retailers of all types, including department/variety, hardware, discount, drug, grocery, and showroom and catalog stores. Retail outlets that commonly carry thermometer products are shown at Exhibit 15. Because of shelf-space limitations and high costs of dealing with multiple vendors, most retail outlets preferred to do business with vendors who represent manufacturers that produce a wide variety of thermometers. Historically, most retailers limited the number to three or, at most, four separate vendors. Most would welcome the opportunity to reduce that number if a manufacturer could expand to include thermometers from more of the standard lines.

EXHIBIT 14 **Examples of products included in each of the product lines**

Weather
  12″ and 18″ dials — plain and decorated
  Window units
  Remote reading units
  Wall weather units
  Patio units

Houseware — decorator
  Gift lines
  Clock component
  Oven-refrigerator units

Cooking
  Meat units
  Candy units
  Thermo spoon/fork units
  Cheese/yogurt units

Miscellaneous
  Mercury units
  Car units
  Dairy and poultry units
  Laboratory/hobby units

EXHIBIT 15 **Examples of retail outlets by type**

Discounters	Department & Variety
K-Mart	Sears
Woolworth	Montgomery Ward
Target	Penny's
G. C. Murphy	Alden's
Shopko	Hammacher-Schlemmer
Fedco	Hoffritz
Wilson's	Mercantile
Frank's Nursery	Allied
Hill's	Ben Franklin
Western Auto	Neiman-Marcus
Rink's	
Meijer-Thrifty Acres	

EXHIBIT 15   **Examples of retail outlets by type (*cont.*)**

Hardware	Drug Stores
American	Walgreen
Ace	Super X
Cotter-True Value	Skaggs
Geo. Worthington — Sentry	Eckerds
HWI	Rexall
S & T	Cunningham
Bostwick-Braun — Pro	Skillern
Clark-Siviter	Osco
S. B. Hubbard	Fays
Stratton-Baldwin	K & B
Woodward-Wight	Affiliated
Farwell, Ozmun, Kirk	Long's
Our Own Hardware	Zahn
Coast to Coast	Kerr
United	McKesson
Central	Thrifty
	Payless

Catalog & Show Rooms	
E. F. MacDonald	Brookstone
Top Value	Bolinds
Premium Corporation	Harriet Carter
L. L. Bean	Miles Kimball
Century	Eastern Mountain Sports
Southern States	Orvis Stitchery
Edward Don	Edmund Scientific
Joan Cook	Gander Mountain
Sportsman's Guide	Gokey's
Johnny Appleseed	Taylor Gifts

Foods	Distributors
Certified	Dutch Peddler
Kroger's	Washington
T.G. & Y.	Peyton's
Lucky (Ch.)	Mid States
Von's	Invento — H & S
Publix	Benny's
Safeway	Manor Sales
National Tea	Edwin Jay
Gemco	Comer-Hanby
Albertson's	Superior Merchandise
Western Grocers	Ely
National Grocers	Ideal School Supply
Lucky (L.A.)	Orchard Supply
Super Valu	Mid States Distributing
Spartan's	

EXHIBIT 15   **Examples of retail outlets by type (*cont.*)**

Advertising and Premium

General Motors	Jack Daniels
Ford	Standard Oil
Coca-Cola	Firestone
Pepsi	Calverts
Seagrams	Dupont
National Distributors	Cargill
Seven Up	Goodrich
Dr Pepper	RCA
E. H. Lilley	Fram
Monroe	Homelite
R. C. Cola	Chrysler
Coors	Briggs Stratton
Anderson Anco	Bolens
Bendix	Stihl
Plough	

Competitive Situation

The largest share of the thermometer market was held by *Taylor* with 30%. Not only did this company have a balanced array of products which spanned all of the consumer lines, it was also strongly positioned in the industrial market. Their industrial line included all types of sensing, recording, and control devices.

Taylor had used its expertise in the industrial sector to develop specialized, high-quality products which competed at the high end of the consumer market. Decorator units included "top-of-the-line" thermometers and hydrometers as well as recording devices for amateur meteorologists. Taylor had positioned most of its products as specialty items or heterogenous shopping-good items.

Springfield held the second largest share of the market with 15%. This company concentrated on the price-sensitive consumer. It emphasized high volume, limited product lines, low raw material costs, and large production runs to hold down production costs. Springfield had strong positions in the weather, cooking, and decorator components of the consumer market.

Airguide had a narrow product line with 6% market share. Its initial entry into the consumer market was through its compass line. Since then, the company had diversified into consumer weather thermometers. Airguide actively pursued international markets and currently imported many of its products.

Cooper maintained fourth position in the consumer market with 5%. This company had products in the weather segment; however, its main strength was its line of bimetal cooking thermometers. Patents on manufacturing processes provide a competitive edge in terms of best quality combined with the lowest production costs in the industry for these types of thermometers.

OTC occupied fifth position by virtue of its strength in round–dial thermometers with 3.5%. Springfield had captured the low end of this segment. OTC produced higher quality products and had an established reputation as the most reliable name in this segment of the market. In addition, OTC had captured the market dealing in promotional and scenic display thermometers (12″ and 18″ round–dial types). Its Achilles' heel was the lack of competitive products across all parts of the consumer market. Over 80% of OTC's total thermometer sales were concentrated in their dial thermometers. They did manufacture thermometers for miscellaneous uses such as automobiles, but these areas were considered to be rather limited in terms of growth potential. OTC had, however, compensated for its lack of a wide product selection by developing one of the best vendor representative groups in the consumer thermometer industry. This network of vendor representatives provided excellent breadth and depth of reach into all retail markets.

TCA struggled in sixth place in the total consumer market with 1.5%. Most of its revenues (80%) originated from weather and cooking thermometers. In addition, TCA maintained a small presence in the industrial market (15% of revenues) as well as the housewares and miscellaneous markets.

Although TCA had managed to maintain product lines which crossed all consumer markets, it had failed to dominate in any of these markets. Consequently, it was experiencing low market share across the board and had no flagship product that could ultimately provide a dominant level of consumer awareness and interest in its products. TCA also appeared to have somewhat weak representation in the marketplace due to its inability to develop a strong, comprehensive vendor network.

Chaney was seventh among the top competitors with one percent and was really focused in only two areas. Its major strength was based on strong candy and meat thermometer products. The company did offer weather instruments, but none of its weather products were well known.

Exhibit 16 summarizes the relative positions of each of the seven top competitors in the consumer market and indicates which segments are served by their products.

Distribution Channels

Most of the companies had comparable channel configurations. For example, all of the seven competing manufacturers used vendor systems in which manufacturers' reps contacted all types of retail outlets.

Taylor, Springfield, and OTC had the strongest network of reps. Since most retail outlets preferred to do business with only those companies that carried broad, well-established product lines, it was difficult for the other companies to break into the retail marketplace. Thus, TCA used a combination of manufacturers' reps and its own sales reps to maintain a stronger presence in the marketplace. Normally their sales force reps concentrated on key accounts based on geographical location and size.

EXHIBIT 16   **Relative market position and breadth of product lines**

Company	% of total thermometer market	Segments of consumer sector			
		Weather	Houseware & decorator	Cooking	Misc.
Taylor	30.0	Y	Y	Y	Y
Springfield	15.0	Y	Y	Y	N
Airguide	6.0	Y	N	N	Y
Cooper	5.0	Y	Y	Y	N
OTC	3.5	Y	N	Y	Y
TCA	1.5	Y	Y	Y	Y
Chaney	1.0	Y	N	Y	N

CONCLUDING DIALOGUE

The conversation between Figgie and Skadra continued:

Figgie: Jerry Bennett told me that he thought the addition of TCA products for his present OTC manufacturers' reps would immediately increase the rate of sales by $500,000 annually. He also thinks that within five years the combined companies would have a sales potential of $10,000,000.

Skadra: Very optimistic! He sounds like a salesman.

Figgie: I had a chance later to talk with Bill Kieffer. He has concerns about working with the OTC plant personnel. He thinks they are used to doing things in their own way and may be difficult to change. And he thinks that their processes can be made more efficient.

Skadra: Do you think we can assimilate Charlie and Jerry into TCA without losing their interest and effort?

Figgie: We'll have to do some thinking about that.

Skadra: By agreeing to cut their salaries by a combined total of $72,000 per year and by agreeing to work for two years they are demonstrating support for the continuing operation.

Figgie: Charlie and Jerry have apparently taken title to the building in their own names and would like to rent the building to us as part of a merger.

Skadra: With FI's vacant plant, we may have an alternative to renting from them.

Figgie: Springfield is a small town; we have little chance of leasing the idle plant. How much do you estimate we would have to spend for improvements to make the plant usable for manufacturing?

Skadra: About $100,000.

Figgie: The possible loss carry-forward does not justify assuming the risk of potential liabilities that would accompany the purchase of the stock of OTC Corporation.

There are a number of factors to consider here, Joe. Will you and your staff take a good look at the November 17th offer and prepare a complete counter-proposal with supporting justification. Also I'd like to have a strategy for conducting the negotiations.

EXHIBIT 17   Economic indices

Title	Unit of measure	Fourth quarter 1982	October 1982	Est. of November 1982	Est. of December 1982	Average		
						1980	1981	1982 (est.)
Twelve leading indicators	1967 = 100	131.4	130.6	130.8	132.8	131.2	133.3	128.4
Four coincident indicators	do.	128.3	128.5	128.3	128.2	140.3	141.3	132.2
Six lagging indicators	do.	165.1	168.4	165.0	161.9	176.8	187.7	177.4
Total unemployed	Thousands	11,839	11,576	11,906	12,036	7,448	8,080	10,678
Unemployment rate, total	Percent	10.7	10.5	10.7	10.8	7.1	7.9	9.7
New private housing units started, total	A.r., thous.	1,253	1,126	1,404	1,229	1,292	1,087	1,061
Chg. in business inventories, 1972 dol.	do.	(17.7)				(2.9)	8.2	(8.5)
Change in money supply	Percent	1.29	1.72	1.41	0.74	.052	0.52	0.69
Federal funds rate	Percent	9.29	9.71	9.20	8.95	13.36	16.38	12.26
Treasury bill rate	do.	7.93	7.75	8.04	8.01	11.61	14.08	10.72
Bank rates on short-term business loans	do.	11.26				15.17	19.56	14.69
Average prime rate charged by banks	do.	11.96	12.52	11.85	11.50	15.27	18.87	14.86
Consumer prices (CPI), all items	1967 = 100	293.4	294.1	293.6	292.4	246.8	272.4	289.1
Producer price index (PPI), all commodities	do.	300.3	299.9	300.4	300.6	268.8	293.4	299.3

Title	Unit of measure	Average				First quarter 1982	Second quarter 1982	Third quarter 1982	Fourth quarter 1982 (est.)
		1979	1980	1981	(Est.) 1982				
GNP in 1972 dollars	A.r., thous.	1,483.0	1,474.0	1,502.6	1,475.5	1,470.7	1,478.4	1,481.1	1,471.7
GNP in current dollars	do.	2,413.0	2,633.1	2,937.7	3,057.5	2,995.5	3,045.2	3,088.2	3,101.3
Personal saving rate	Percent	5.2	5.8	6.4	6.5	6.6	6.7	6.9	5.8

Appendix	## An analysis of a merger and future between TCA and OTC presented to Harry E. Figgie, Jr., by Jerome P. Bennett and Charles L. Wappner, November 17, 1982

We at Ohio Thermometer are of the opinion that our company's growth is tied to the economy. When times are good, sales are good and when times are bad, sales drop. The reason is our product base. Ohio Thermometer is very weak in the inexpensive category, kitchen or cooking category, and almost non-existent in the gift and decorator field. Without these three areas it is impossible for us to replace another thermometer company. We don't have the necessary capital to tool for all of these areas, hence our need for TCA's products. We feel, as competitors to TCA, that they have the same problems in the housewares field, only more severe. They have been unable to come up with a dial that is competitive with Ohio's, consequently they have no ammunition to replace any other company. Companies such as TCA are being replaced by Springfield or Taylor. Ohio Thermometer is, however, not being replaced mainly because everybody has to have our dials. We can't see TCA making much movement in the housewares industry because of the above problems. We feel TCA is also tied to the economy in this particular area.

In other areas of thermometry Ohio Thermometer has the advertising thermometer business locked up. This is an area that's up and expanding and profitable. TCA is in the auto field and scientific area, which are areas that we don't get into, so we really don't know how they are doing in those areas. They also have a gourmet thermometer line that we feel has tremendous potential, but they lack the customer base that we have. If they had our customer base, those items could perform miracles. In addition to the mentioned areas, Ohio has the Detroit automobile business under control, in our pocket, and we are the dominant people in the poultry industry.

Put the two companies together and you wind up with the most balanced thermometer company in the country. Together the companies would be the answer to many of our customers' problems. Most purchasing agents at this time want to cut down the list of vendors. In the thermometer field, if you talk to them, they say they must carry Taylor because of their name, and they must have Ohio because of their dials. Most have Springfield and they usually have a fourth vendor, which is either Chaney, Cooper, or TCA, but very, very seldom do they ever have a fifth vendor, so they take their pick between one of the three, either Chaney, Cooper, or TCA. With a combined company, TCA and Ohio, we certainly would be in a position to eliminate the fourth vendor and very possibly eliminate the third vendor. I am not too sure that, at certain areas, that you couldn't really take a good shot at Taylor. We know Chaney's and Cooper's customers and we know their weaknesses and we know their strengths. I think a combined company would have a field day or a Marianna's turkey shoot in the foreseeable future.

Looking at both sides, if Ohio could buy TCA, and I might add we have tried to do this in 1978, at this point it would probably stretch our finances. We feel that our borrowing would be somewhere close to $1,000,000. This would cover our current borrowing, allow $500,000 to be paid to Figgie International, with the rest going towards working capital. We would have to have some other type of financing for the remainder of the purchase price of TCA, and pay these off over a number of years. Could we get this financing? Questionable.

If Figgie International takes over Ohio these problems are eliminated and with Kieffer running a lean operation, we see immediate profits and probably large profits.

I, personally, feel that by taking the best sales reps from Ohio and the best sales reps from TCA and combining them; figures don't lie; we would have one of the strongest sales operations in the thermometer field. I feel that because of our contacts and our personal relationships with all of our customers, that we would keep all of them and be able to expand the entire base thermometer business. In addition, we sell to almost all of TCA's housewares accounts, so I can't see where we would lose any of that business. Quite frankly, with the two companies, the housewares end of the business would be a bonanza to the customers, at the same time solving their problems of too many vendors.

Our four or five year sales forecast would be in the 10 million dollar plus range. Even if the economy didn't bounce back, we could still project many inroads in the thermometer business and even if the economy stays as it is today, we would project a 10% to 15% to 20% sales increase per year. Again, with these sales and with the idea of running a lean company, there would be enough profit to go into the thermometer business with new items in depth. We look at weather stations that Taylor sells in the $300 to $400 range and it makes our mouths water. We sell to the same accounts that they sell to, only we can't compete with them, as we don't have the product.

Lastly, whether together or separately, both TCA and Ohio are going to have to get into the electronics area. Obviously TCA would have the jump on us, because they could use other Figgie operations. However, individually, we doubt that they would have the necessary profits to make the expenditures to do this.

A HAPPY MARRIAGE!!

Intangibles That Ohio Has to Sell

1. *Dial thermometer business*
    Making TCA the major factor in the dial thermometer business with $2,750,000 in existing business, this is the heart of the thermometer business today.
2. *Advertising thermometer business*
    This would make TCA the major and dominant supplier in the advertising and point of sale thermometer business with $550,000 of existing business. Ohio now supplies almost all of the major corporations with their advertising thermometer needs, controlling an estimated 95% of this business.

3. *Industrial and special products*

This would make TCA the dominant company in the automobile thermometer business and the major supplier of thermometers and instruments to the poultry industry, both in the United States and Canada.

4. *Customer base*

Ohio now has a very broad base of customers because all major accounts carry Ohio dials. The list of Ohio's customers is attached. This would automatically expose all TCA products to the major discounters, distributors, department and variety stores, hardware chains, drug chains, food chains, and catalog and catalog showrooms.

5. *Ohio Expertise in thermometer business*

Ohio Thermometer is about to start its 50th year in the thermometer business. Over the years we have consistently ranked number one or two with Taylor Instrument in accuracy and quality, according to past published consumer reports.

6. *Sales operation*

In looking over our customer base, it should be obvious that Ohio has the dominant sales rep organization between the two companies. In addition, Bennett and Reeder know the buyers on a first name basis at the major accounts such as K-Mart, Sears, Penney's, etc. We feel this will automatically prevent the loss of customers and would actually increase the thermometer base. Almost all accounts that Ohio now sells are TCA's accounts, which would add to protecting our business.

USX: RESTRUCTURING FOR SURVIVAL

OVERVIEW

On July 9, 1986, United States Steel Corp. announced the decision to change the name of the company to USX. The change reflected the fact that it was no longer primarily a steel company. In 1979 more than 73 percent of U.S. Steel's revenues came from steel. By 1986 steel accounted for only 24 percent of the company's revenues. Oil and gas operations accounted for 60 percent of revenues, while the remaining 16 percent came from a collection of diversified businesses. This diversification strategy was closely linked to the name of David Roderick, chairman of the board since 1979, and was part of Roderick's response to the enormous problems faced by the American steel industry. Other elements of Roderick's strategy included a 50-percent reduction in steel-making capacity, layoffs that decreased the work force in the steel business from 120,000 to just 20,000, and investments designed to modernize what capacity remained and to boost labor productivity. In the process, the company that once held 60 percent of the U.S. market saw its share slip to only 16 percent by mid-1987.

Roderick's strategy has not been without its critics. The 1982 acquisition of Marathon Oil Company for $6 billion and the 1985 acquisition of Texas Oil & Gas Corporation for $3 billion seemed to many to be poor moves. Like the steel industry, the oil and gas industry is cyclical. U.S. Steel bought Marathon near the peak in oil prices and paid what many saw as an excessive price. Four years later the oil and gas industry was as depressed as the steel industry, doubling USX's woes. The acquisition of Texas Oil and Gas further enraged many shareholders, since it doubled outstanding common shares to 258 million, while boosting U.S. Steel's exposure to the declining oil and gas market. Due in part to the dilution in U.S. Steel's shares and in part to the weaknesses in both oil and steel,

This case was prepared by Charles W. L. Hill, University of Washington.

U.S. Steel stock plunged. Between 1982 when U.S. Steel bought Marathon Oil and mid-1986, when it became USX, the company's stock declined 11 percent, while the Standard & Poor's 400 industrials jumped by 114 percent. In mid-1986 USX's market value stood at only half of the book value of its assets. To make matters worse, in August 1986 contract negotiations with the United Steelworkers of America broke down and a six-month strike began.

Against this troubling background, in mid-1986 a number of corporate raiders, including Holmes à Court, T. Boone Pickens Jr., Carl C. Icahn, and Irwin Jacobs, began to look closely at USX. Icahn built up an 11.4-percent stake in the company and talked about making a $31-per-share offer. Icahn summarized his view of USX's strategy as follows: "Make no mistake, a strongly knit corporate aristocracy exists in America.... The top man, what's more, usually finds expanding his power more important than rewarding owners. When Mobile and USX had excess cash, did they enrich shareholders? Of course not. They bought Marcor and Marathon—disastrous investments, but major increases in the size of the manor."[1] However, Icahn pulled out of USX in the wake of Wall Street's insider trading scandals, and the company retained its independence.

After the turmoil of 1986, things picked up for USX in 1987. The steelworkers' strike ended in February with a compromise agreement. The steel market exhibited unexpectedly strong demand throughout 1987, and modest price rises helped USX's steel operations to show a profit. Aided by the strong dollar and years of capacity and cost cutting, U.S. companies found themselves gaining market share from foreign producers for the first time in a decade. Moreover, oil and gas prices also staged a modest recovery from the lows reached in 1986, improving the overall outlook for USX.

BACKGROUND

U.S. Steel was formed in 1901, when J. P. Morgan merged the steel-making empires of Andrew Carnegie, Judge Elbert Gary, and William H. Moore to form the world's first billion-dollar company. The formation of U.S. Steel was a successful attempt to gain control of steel inputs and steel-making capacity. The newly formed U.S. Steel controlled more than 60 percent of American steel-making capacity. The company used its substantial market power to curtail output and raise prices. Thus, for example, U.S. Steel was able to raise the price of a ton of steel rails from $2 to $28 over a ten-year period.

The corporation that J. P. Morgan created dominated the American steel industry for the next seventy years. In retrospect, however, U.S. Steel's dominance did not serve the company well. Secure as the price leader of a powerful domestic oligopoly, U.S. Steel lacked any incentive to maximize its efficiency.

---

[1] Carl C. Icahn, "What Ails Corporate America," *Business Week*, October 27, 1986, p. 101.

The company developed a rigid bureaucracy, dominated by production men who ignored the recommendations of the marketing staff and paid little attention to customer needs. A highly centralized and militaristic management style impeded change and discouraged any criticism of top management policies. Lower and middle level managers were given little autonomy and even the most routine of decisions had to be approved by top managers. Moreover, there was a shared perception that promotion was on the basis of seniority rather than ability. This discouraged the pursuit of greater efficiencies and meant that few managers were willing to criticize long-established operating procedures. In sum, the culture of U.S. steel was an inflexible one that encouraged inertia.[2]

The inflexible and dogmatic culture of U.S. Steel permeated all aspects of the company's business. The strategy of U.S. Steel during this period was to supply all types of steel for all purposes. This "supermarket mentality" paid no attention to the profitability of different product lines. Thus U.S. Steel clung to a wire division even though the unit had been losing money for twenty years. The company responded to the rising import tide of the 1960s and 1970s not by trying to reduce capacity and operating costs, but with appeals for protectionism. When the Environmental Protection Agency attacked U.S. Steel for its violation of pollution regulations, the company responded with an advertising campaign that attacked the agency. Perhaps most telling of all, when Roderick's predecessor, Edgar Speer, received a report suggesting that his pet project, a plan to build a multibillion-dollar steel mill on the shores of Lake Erie, would jeopardize the corporation financially, Speer ordered repeated follow-up studies aimed at justifying the concept.

By 1979 the company was in deep trouble. U.S. Steel lost $293 million on sales of $12,492.1 million, and its market share fell to 20 percent in the face of tough competition from foreign producers and domestic minimills. Many of its operating facilities were hopelessly out of date. At a time when most of the large integrated producers had switched to the more efficient basic oxygen furnace steel-making method, U.S. Steel had the industry's highest proportion of antiquated open hearth furnaces. Not surprisingly, its cost structure was one of the highest in the global industry, while the quality of its finished steel was among the lowest.

It was against this background that in 1979 Roderick was appointed chairman of the board to replace the ailing Speer. Unlike previous U.S. Steel chairmen, Roderick rose through the finance function rather than the production function of the company. According to one board member, Roderick was appointed partly because he was not a production man and could bring a fresh perspective to the company. His approach has indeed proved to be fresh and innovative. He is perceived as being more open than previous CEOs. One way in which this has been visible is that he consulted middle managers regarding what they thought to be U.S. Steel's weaknesses. After they identified two problem

---

[2]"The Toughest Job in Business: How They Are Remaking U.S. Steel," *Business Week*, February 25, 1985, pp. 50–56.

areas—the performance evaluation system and internal communications—he then took the further step of providing the opportunity for these managers to voice their opinions to top management. Top management, therefore, was made aware of concerns that they may not have heard otherwise, and have taken steps to respond to them.[3]

THE STEEL INDUSTRY

Production Processes

Before the 1970s most steel in the United States was made using the open hearth furnace (OHF). In the OHF, molten iron from a blast furnace, scrap steel, and limestone are loaded into a shallow steel-making area known as a hearth, which is open to the sweep of flames that emanate alternatively from opposite ends of the furnace. The percentage of steel made in OHFs peaked at 80 percent in 1968 and by 1985 had fallen to a mere 7.3 percent.

The technology that replaced OHFs is called the basic oxygen furnace (BOF). (See Exhibit 1.) The BOF uses as its primary raw material molten pig iron from a blast furnace. Scrap steel is also loaded into the BOF and can account for as much as 33 percent of the total metal content. The fuel is oxygen, which is blown into the roof of the furnace through a lance. Newer BOF technology also involves feeding the oxygen in through the bottom of the furnace. The advantage of the BOF over the older open hearth furnace is speed. A BOF can make 300 tons of steel in 45 minutes, whereas open hearth furnaces required several hours. The BOF has a rather large minimum efficient scale of between 200 to 300 tons of capacity. This translates into an annual production capacity of 3 million to 5 million tons of steel.

Once made, molten steel is either poured into ingots, which must then be sent to steel mills for rolling into semifinished shapes, or poured directly into a continuous caster. The continuous caster forms molten steel directly into semifinished shapes. It has the advantage of by-passing the reheating required before the rolling of ingots, saving substantially on energy costs, and of producing steel of a consistent and high quality. However, despite the advantages of continuous casting, U.S. companies have been slow to adopt the technology. Casters are difficult and expensive to install into existing plants, requiring outlays of between $150 million and $200 million. Many U.S. companies have lacked the capital necessary to make such investments. In 1978 only 15 percent of American steel was made using continuous casting. By 1986 the figure had increased to 55 percent, and by the end of 1987 it had risen to around 70 percent.

---

[3]"U.S. Steel's Roderick: A Chairman Who Doesn't Flinch," *Business Week,* February 25, 1985, p. 55.

EXHIBIT 1   **Steel-making methods**

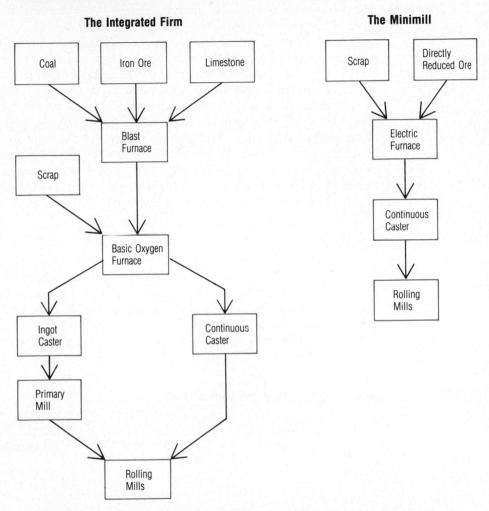

The Integrated Firm   The Minimill

Source: Adapted from D. F. Barnett and R. W. Crandell, *Up from the Ashes: The Rise of the Steel Mill in the United States*, 1986, p. 4. By permission of The Brookings Institution.

A third steel–making technology, the electric arc furnace, is used primarily by minimills. (See Exhibit 1.) Electric arc furnaces were first used for the production of alloys, stainless steel, and tool steels but since the 1940s have been used to produce lower-quality steel from scrap, such as bars, wires and rod, and medium to light structural shapes. Minimills simply load scrap steel into an electric furnace to produce molten steel. The heat of the melting steel is precisely controlled by an electric current that arcs from one electrode to another inside the furnace. Most minimills use continuous casting for all their output.

The minimum efficient scale of production for electric arc furnaces, at between 200,000 and 400,000 tons per annum, is much lower than the minimum efficient scale of the basic oxygen furnace.

A disadvantage of electric arc furnaces is that they are unable to produce large structural pieces and flat-rolled steel, which account for a major portion of steel production. However, this may be changing. In 1987 Nucor Corporation, the largest minimill operator, announced that it had bought a new German technology that will allow it to produce a very thin rolled steel for oil drums and the like. Ultimately, Nucor hopes to adapt the technology to make the high-grade sheet steel used in autos. A further disadvantage of electric arc furnaces is that they depend on the availability of affordable scrap steel. Normally, the price of scrap steel is lower than the cost of making iron in a blast furnace. However, in times of rapid recovery scrap steel prices can inflate dramatically, eliminating much of the cost advantage enjoyed by electric arc furnaces.

Productive Capacity

The U.S. steel industry is divided into two sectors: integrated companies and minimills. There are fourteen integrated companies (shown in Exhibit 2) with a steel-making capacity ranging from 26 million tons at USX to 1 million tons of steel per year. There are around 40 minimill companies, with capacity ranging from 2.5 million tons per annum at Nucor to less than 100,000 tons per year

EXHIBIT 2   **Integrated U.S. steel companies, 1985**

Company	Capacity (millions of tons)
USX	26.2
LTV	19.1
Bethlehem Steel Corp.	18.0
Inland Steel Company	9.3
Armco Inc.	6.8
National Steel Corp.	5.6
Wheeling–Pittsburgh Steel Corporation	4.5
Weirton Steel	4.0
Ford Motor Company (Range Steel Company)	3.6
California Steel & Tube	2.1
McLouth Steel Products Corporation	2.0
CF&I Steel Corporation	2.0
The Interlake Corporation	1.4
Sharon Steel Corporation	1.0

Source: Reprinted from D. F. Barnett and R. W. Crandell, *Up from the Ashes: The Rise of the Steel Mill in the United States,* 1986, p. 4. By permission of The Brookings Institution.

among the smaller manufacturers. Total U.S. steel-making capacity in 1986 was 127 million tons per year, 100 million tons of which came from integrated companies and the remainder from minimills. With production of 80.5 million tons of steel in 1986, the industry utilized only 63 percent of its capacity. The excess capacity problem was most severe among the integrated companies, despite years of plant closings. Between 1977 and 1985 the major integrated companies reduced their capacity by more than 40 million tons, but this still has left substantial excess. Added to the domestic capacity problem, there is also a problem of global excess capacity. Recent estimates suggest that as much as one fifth of the world's steel-making capacity is lying idle.

Demand Conditions

Since 1974 the world's steel industry has been characterized by sluggish demand conditions. Slow economic growth, the use of substitute materials, and rising energy costs have kept world demand below 1974 levels. Steel production in the United States peaked at 151 million tons in 1973, fell to around 130 million tons by the end of the 1970s, and then collapsed to around 70 million tons in the early 1980s as the rising dollar, a flood of imports, and economic recession hit the industry hard. Since then there has been a moderate recovery: 1986 production reached over 80 million tons, and similar levels are predicted for 1987. However, much of the steel industry's rebound in 1986 and 1987 appeared to be due to inventory rebuilding. After the onset of the strike at USX in mid-1986, users allowed their inventories to decline with little interruption until early 1987. When USX's re-entry into the market in March 1987 failed to cause widely expected price declines, users began to rebuild inventories, a process that has been largely responsible for keeping shipments at a high level throughout 1987.

Demand for steel derives from its many uses. The bulk of steel is sold to seven major market segments.

Steel service centers These middlemen supply the needs of thousands of U.S. manufacturers and fabricators and in 1986 commanded 24 percent of the steel industry's shipments.

Automotive companies In 1986 the second-largest market segment, automotive companies, took 16.5 percent of domestic steel production. Demand for steel has historically always been closely tied to demand for autos. The use of plastics in cars grew by 33 percent between 1976 and 1986, with steel being the loser.

Construction This market accounted for 12.3 percent of domestic steel output in 1986. The outlook for the construction market is poor. The industry has been in a slump since construction's heyday in the late 1970s. Many of the problems can be traced to favorable tax laws, which encouraged overbuilding in the early 1980s and led to excess capacity in the commercial building market.

Oil and gas   Once an important steel market, this segment has decreased its demand for steel from 7.2 percent of shipments in 1981 to a little more than 1 percent of total industry shipments in 1986. The demand for steel in this sector is very sensitive to the number of oil-drilling rigs in operation. Since the collapse of oil prices in 1985, activity in the drilling industry has been at a postwar low.

Containers   Containers, packaging, and other shipment materials accounted for about 6 percent of total steel demand in 1986. The dramatic shift in consumer food and beverage markets to aluminum, paper, and even glass, as well as resin-based strapping for shipping products, has decimated demand for tin plate in the last ten years. Total shipments to this segment have fallen by more than 21 percent since 1981, and the market is predicted to continue shrinking, although at a slower rate.

Capital goods industries   Between 1984 and 1986 shipments to this segment dropped from 5.3 million tons to 4.2 million tons. A pickup in export demand for construction equipment and other heavy machinery would allow for a modest improvement in this sector.

Appliances   Shipments to this segment amounted to 1.6 million tons in 1986, up 9.5 percent from 1985 due to a boom in home building.

Imports

Many of the problems faced by the American steel industry have been blamed on foreign imports. Imports first became a problem in 1959 after a strike that shut down the industry for four months. Having gained a foothold in the U.S. market, during the next decades imports rose to take nearly 20 percent of the market, up from an average of less than 2.5 percent in the three years before the strike. By 1984 imports held 26 percent of the U.S. market. Estimates for 1985 suggest that U.S. producers had substantially higher production costs in their most efficient plants when compared with producers in West Germany, Japan, South Korea, and Brazil. For example, it cost $403 to produce a ton of finished steel in the United States, $324 in West Germany, $286 in Japan, $270 in South Korea, and $274 in Brazil. Much of the difference could be explained by higher labor costs. In early 1985 these stood at $22.50 per man-hour in the United States, $11.90 in West Germany, $11.70 in Japan, $2.85 in South Korea, and $2.90 in Brazil.[4]

In response to the plight of the American steel industry, in 1985 the White House engineered an agreement with seven steel-making countries to voluntarily limit steel imports to 18.5 percent of the U.S. market by 1989. By late 1987

[4]For details, see Donald Barnett and Robert Crandall, *Up from the Ashes: The Rise of the Steel Minimill in the United States* (Washington, D.C.: The Brookings Institution, 1986).

the dollar had also fallen 40 percent from its 1985 high, substantially reducing, if not eliminating, the cost advantage of many foreign exporters. As a consequence of these two developments, steel imports fell by 28 percent between 1985 and 1987. However, the dollar's fall does not hit all countries equally. Some exporting countries, such as Brazil and South Korea, tie the value of their currency to the dollar. Moreover, a large number of developing countries produce steel and are going after business in the United States. Most of these countries are not covered by the voluntary agreements.

Minimills

The minimill sector of the U.S. industry is relatively new. Minimill entry has been relatively easy, especially in the lower-product grades, due to the relatively low capital costs of minimill plants. The first minimills were established in the 1960s, and by the end of that decade they held some 5 percent of the U. S. market. To begin with, the product line of minimills was limited to low-quality steel bars used in construction and manufacturing. However, technological advances improved the efficiency of minimills and increased the range of products that they could manufacture. They diversified into more and more sophisticated products, such as wire rods, higher-quality bars, and medium-sized structural shapes, taking market share from the integrated mills along the way. By 1987 minimills held about 25 percent of the U.S. market.

Minimills have been able to compete successfully not only with domestic integrated companies, but with foreign integrated competition as well. There are a number of reasons for this.

1. The minimills are nonunion establishments. As a consequence, their labor costs are $6-per-hour below those of unionized plants.

2. Many minimills have pursued a product niche strategy and specialized in a few products. Specialization results in longer production runs and increases both productivity and capacity utilization.

3. Minimills use some of the most up-to-date equipment available. From their inception, minimills were built on the assumption of a short economic life, and they have been replaced or modernized rapidly. Each new generation of minimills has embodied the latest production techniques. In contrast, no new plants have been constructed in the integrated sector since the early 1960s, and existing plants have been only partly reorganized to eliminate excess capacity. As a consequence, the number of man-hours per ton required to produce wire rods at the typical minimill is half of that in a typical U.S. integrated minimill, and 60 percent of that in a Japanese integrated mill.

4. Minimills use low-cost scrap steel as their raw material rather than iron ore. Low-cost scrap has always been plentiful in the United States.

5. Electric arc furnaces are more fuel efficient than basic oxygen and open hearth furnaces, resulting in energy saving of as much as $60 per ton.

Plant Closings and Modernization

The integrated companies reacted to the twin threats of low-cost imports and minimills by eliminating excess productive capacity and modernizing what remained. Between 1982 and 1987 the industry cut capacity from 154 million tons per year to 112 million tons per year. Most of these reductions came from the integrated companies. USX, saddled with some of the oldest facilities, has cut capacity by nearly 50 percent, to 19 million tons. As a consequence of the plant closings, most of the remaining capacity is relatively up-to-date. Billions of dollars have been invested in cost-saving techniques such as continuous casting. There have also been massive labor reductions. During the 1980s more than 200,000 workers left the payroll of integrated companies. In addition labor practices have changed dramatically, with the union putting aside many of its old objections against flexible working arrangements.

The result of these changes has been an impressive rise in productivity. For the industry as a whole, productivity increased by 27.4 percent between 1981 and 1987. At USX, it now takes a mere 3.25 man-hours to produce and ship a ton of steel; in 1981 it took 9.2 man-hours.

Despite these changes for the better, problems remain. Many industry experts agree that a further 20 million tons must be cut from the capacity of integrated mills. However, this is not an easy task, for two reasons: (1) In a unionized company, the costs of severance pay and early retirement can be enormous, averaging between $75,000 and $100,000 per worker. (2) Even when a steel company closes a mill, local groups and plant employees sometimes buy it to preserve jobs. In early 1987 USX closed its Geneva Works in Provo, Utah, with 2.6 million tons of capacity. Local investors promptly bought the plant and are now operating it, so the capacity remains.

THE OIL AND GAS INDUSTRY

Market Conditions, 1985–1987

The price of oil has virtually always been controlled—first by Standard Oil Co., and later by the Texas Railroad Commission, the large international oil companies, and finally by OPEC. The oil price increases engineered by OPEC in 1973–1974, and again in 1979–1980, encouraged conservation measures. As a consequence, U.S. consumption of energy per dollar of GNP declined by some 28 percent between 1970 and 1986. Automobiles account for 45 percent of petroleum consumption in the United States, and the average business fleet mileage improved from 13.1 miles per gallon in 1973 to 17.9 miles per gallon in 1985, as automakers downsized their engines.

Increased oil production worldwide and greater fuel efficiency enabled the United States to reduce its reliance on crude oil imported from OPEC. In 1985 the United States imported 1.32 million barrels per day of OPEC crude, down from 5.643 million barrels per day in 1977. As a consequence of such developments, OPEC's share of world oil production dropped to less than 30 percent in 1985, down from a peak of 48 percent in 1979. In an effort to recapture its slipping market share, Saudi Arabia, the largest OPEC producer and owner of one-fourth of the free world's oil reserves, began flooding the market with crude oil in late 1985. Other OPEC producers followed the Saudis' lead. The result was a fall in world oil prices from $30 per barrel to less than $10 per barrel by mid-1986.

The U.S. oil industry, one of the world's high-cost producers, slumped into a deep recession. Thousands of marginal wells were shut as the price of oil fell below operating costs, which often ran as high as $15 per barrel. By December 1986 domestic production had dropped off by 680,000 barrels per day, or 7 percent, while imports from OPEC surged by 53 percent, as domestic users switched to low-cost OPEC oil.

Although to the Saudis oil at $10 per barrel was still a good economic prospect (the operating costs of Saudi wells are among the world's lowest at around $2 per barrel), the free market price was politically untenable. The damage to U.S. oil interests and the political problems such damage creates cannot be ignored by the Saudis, who depend on the United States for military support in the Persian Gulf. After political pressure from both the United States and Saudi Arabia's disgruntled OPEC partners, King Fahd of Saudi Arabia led the cartel back to fixed-price contracts in February 1987. The new agreement called for OPEC to cut oil production by 7 percent and raise prices to $18 per barrel. For most of 1987 the agreement had the effect of stabilizing oil prices in the $18–$20 range. However, disarray broke out again in OPEC toward the end of 1987, and oil prices slumped to $15 per barrel.

Market Conditions in the Future

Industry forecasts suggest that U.S. demand for crude oil will continue to grow at around 1 percent per year between now and the year 2000, adding 3 million barrels per day to the current consumption rate of 15.7 million barrels per day. Domestic reserves, however, are nearing depletion. It is estimated that all known recoverable reserves in the United States will be virtually depleted by the year 2010. Thus, as oil demand rises, U.S. requirements will have to be met by higher imports. Crude oil and product imports could increase from 26 percent of demand in 1985 to as much as 56 percent by the year 2000. Furthermore, the bulk of the increase is likely to come from areas vulnerable to disruptions. A recent study by Conoco estimates that OPEC producers will probably supply as

EXHIBIT 3   **Market share of leading oil and gas companies, 1985**

	Production			
	Crude oil		Natural gas	
Company	Market share (%)	Rank	Market share (%)	Rank
Exxon	7.22	1	4.63	2
Standard Oil	6.77	2	na	na
Arco	6.09	3	2.95	7
Texaco	6.02	4	4.60	3
Chevron	5.52	5	4.66	1
Shell	4.98	6	3.66	6
Amoco	3.77	7	4.15	4
Marathon	1.51	12	0.84	17
Texas Oil and Gas	na	na	1.21	14
	Reserves			
Exxon	7.49	2	9.29	1
Standard Oil	7.28	3	3.73	5
Arco	7.55	1	3.17	7
Texaco	4.86	7	3.00	8
Chevron	5.74	5	4.01	3
Shell	6.95	4	3.65	6
Amoco	4.90	6	5.12	2
Marathon	1.61	11	0.93	17
Texas Oil and Gas	0.29	20	0.95	16
	Refining capacity			
Exxon	8.13	2	8.73	2
Standard Oil	4.50	7	4.95	8
Arco	4.44	8	6.22	6
Texaco	5.92	5	6.94	5
Chevron	12.73	1	11.25	1
Shell	6.91	3	7.37	3
Amoco	6.65	4	6.95	4
Marathon	3.34	9	3.34	10
Texas Oil and Gas	na	na	na	na

Source: Reprinted from *National Petroleum News Factbook*, 1987, page 138, by permission of Hunter Publishing Company.

much as 60 percent of world demand by 2000 and that, depending on price and production, they may be supplying as much as 75 percent. Most of the OPEC producers are based in the Middle East, an area that remains politically unstable. The ongoing war between Iran and Iraq could easily flare up into the next energy crunch. As for crude oil prices, Conoco's study suggests that they will hover around the $18–$20-per-barrel range until the early 1990s, before rising to the $40–$50 range by 2000.

In the even longer run, serious questions about oil remain. At the present consumption rate of 20 million barrels per year, worldwide reserves of some 700 billion barrels of oil will last for only 35 years. Admittedly, many promising areas remain to be explored, such as the 1.5-million-acre coastal plain in North Alaska and California's coastal waters. However, environmental concerns have limited exploration in these areas to date.

The Structure of the U.S. Market

Exhibit 3 gives details of the 1986 market share of a number of different oil and gas companies with regard to production, proven reserves, and refining capacity. Exhibit 4 gives details of the retail outlets owned by the same selection of leading oil companies.

A number of distinct trends have characterized the retail market in recent years. First, the number of retail service outlets has shrunk by almost half since 1972. There were 117,000 gas stations at the end of 1987, compared with 226,000 at the end of 1972. Some observers predict that the service station population will shrink to 100,000 outlets by 1990. Second, those stations that remain are on the average larger and better run; they also tend to sell many nonpetroleum products. Third, a number of the majors have increased their position in recent years

EXHIBIT 4   **Retail outlets of leading oil companies, 1986**

Firm	Number of outlets	Rank	Number of states
Exxon	14,468	2	37
Standard Oil	7,623	9	29
Arco	1,719	21	6
Texaco	18,939	1	46
Chevron	13,879	3	33
Shell	11,133	6	41
Amoco	12,337	5	30
Mobil	12,619	4	40
Marathon	2,395	16	6

Source: Reprinted from *National Petroleum News Factbook*, 1987, page 130, by permission of Hunter Publishing Company.

through mergers. For example, Chevron Corporation jumped from number six to number two in retail rankings between 1984 and 1985 with its acquisition of Gulf Oil Corp. Fourth, there has been a marked growth in the convenience store industry and the amount of gasoline sold by convenience stores. Sales of gasoline through convenience stores increased by 73 percent between 1981 and 1985, accounting for 17 percent of all gasoline sold in the United States in 1985.

STRATEGY AT USX

Since David Roderick became chairman in 1979, USX has had three main strategic objectives: (1) to reduce steel-making capacity and modernize what remains to become competitive; (2) to diversify into new business in an attempt to reduce USX's dependence on steel operations; and (3) to sell off nonstrategic assets. Underlying these objectives has been Roderick's belief that the company should be managed for the *long-term* benefit of *all* shareholders, and "not for the next 30 days." After years of poor earnings performance, however, many shareholders wonder how long the long term really is.

Restructuring Steel

Roderick's first step was to employ William Roesch, a forward-thinking steel executive from Kaiser Steel Corporation, to head USX's steel operations, U.S. Steel International, Inc. Roesch brought with him a change of attitude. His view was that USS should no longer strive to be the number one producer. Instead, its objective should be to become the most profitable company in the steel industry. After a 1980 customer survey found that less than 10 percent of steel customers considered USS the highest quality supplier in the industry, Roesch also initiated a campaign to improve the quality of delivered steel.

Before Roesch could make an impact, however, he died. Roesch was replaced by Thomas Graham, a former LTV Corporation manager, whom many regarded as the best operator in the industry. Graham faced a formidable task. USS's market share had recently fallen from 20 percent to 15.5 percent, primarily because it had lost 20–30 percent of its sales to General Motors due to high prices and poor quality. The company was hopelessly overstaffed, carried far too much obsolete capacity, and had persisted in continuing unprofitable product lines. Consequently, USS was losing $125 on every ton of steel that it produced.

Graham began by replacing managers who could not adjust to the new era of minimills and imports. Many of the company's old timers were replaced by younger men. He cut out unnecessary corporate staff, including a fifty-four-member export staff (as a high-cost producer in the global marketplace, USS had no exports) and a twenty-five-member economic forecasting unit. He also dramatically shortened lines of communication, reducing the number of management layers between the senior vice president for sales and his sales force from six to two.

Next, USS got out of the product lines where it could not compete with minimills, such as the wire-making business. In the process, USS halved the number of its product lines to six—including flat-rolled, tubular, and plate steel—all products that minimills cannot currently manufacture.

The biggest change, however, has been in capacity and work-force levels. Between 1979 and 1986 USS had shut down more than 50 percent of its productive capacity and reduced its work force by 100,000, to 20,000. Most of the cuts have come from plants operating with open hearth furnaces. USS's remaining plants in 1986 are detailed in Exhibit 5. Major capital expenditures are currently being restricted to only three key plants: Gary Works, Baytown, and Fairfield. The remaining plants are clearly question marks.

As a consequence of the changes discussed above, USS has succeeded in cutting the man-hours required to produce a ton of steel from 8.5 in 1982 to under 4 in 1987, and the company hopes to whittle them down to 3.5. However, the path has not always been easy. A 1986 attempt to get pay cuts from the steel unions led to a six-month strike at USS. The strike ended in February 1987 with a compromise agreement that gave USS the pay cuts it had wanted, but in return for profit-sharing agreements. Immediately after the strike ended, USS revealed plans to cut its steel-making capacity by a further 27 percent, down to 19 million tons per year, and to lay off 3,400 workers in addition to the 1,346 jobs specifically eliminated in the new contract. Plant closings include the complete shutdown of the Provo plant in Utah, and partial shutdowns of a number of other facilities.

USS is starting to gain access to nonunion steel makers through a Michigan-based joint venture with Worthington Industries. USS has also entered into joint ventures with South Korea's Pohang Iron & Steel Corporation, Ltd. and the Ford Motor Company. The Korean venture involves a $300-million modernization of its Pittsburg, California, sheet steel finishing plant, which is to use low-cost steel imported from Korea. The Ford venture is designed to improve the position of Ford's Rouge Steel Company, an electrogalvanizing plant in Dearborn, Michigan. The plant coats steel from both Range Steel, and from USS's Gary operation. For USS, the move promotes closer ties with an important customer.

Diversification

USX's diversification began in earnest when the company acquired Marathon Oil for $6.6 billion in early 1982. Marathon, the twelfth largest U.S. oil company, has an important, 49-percent stake in the giant Yates oil field in Texas and a 38-percent stake in the Brae field in Britain's North Sea. At the time of the acquisition, the price of oil stood at $33 per barrel. Marathon was predicting that oil prices would increase to about $48 per barrel by 1987, doubling Marathon's

EXHIBIT 5   **USS plants in 1986**

Plant location	Capacity (millions of tons)	Type of furnace	Comments
Clairton, Pennsylvania	0.0	None	A coking facility
Monongahela Valley, Pennsylvania	2.9	Basic oxygen	No continuous casting
Fairfield, Alabama	2.9	Basic oxygen	Needs further continuous casting
Fairless Hills, Pennsylvania	3.6	Open hearth	Old facilities, no slab caster, old hot strip mill
Provo, Utah	3.0	Open hearth	Old facilities, no continuous caster, poor finishing facilities
Pittsburg, California	0.0	None	Rolling mill
Gary, Indiana	7.0	Basic oxygen	Needs second continuous caster
Lorain, Ohio	2.8	Basic oxygen	Needs additional continuous casting
Baytown, Texas	1.2	Electric arc	Modern plant
South Chicago, Illinois	0.7	Electric arc	Small plant

Source: Reprinted from D. F. Barnett and R. W. Crandell, *Up from the Ashes: The Rise of the Steel Mill in the United States,* 1986, pp. 50–51. By permission of The Brookings Institution.

cash flow between 1982 and 1986. That did not happen. Instead oil prices collapsed to $10 per barrel in 1986 and recovered to only $18 per barrel in 1987. The impact on USX was devastating. Instead of being able to offset depressed steel earnings by booming oil earnings, USX found itself facing a sharp downturn in both its major industries. Among other things, this raised questions as to how USX would pay off the $5.9-billion debt that it took on to pay for the Marathon acquisition.

Critics were also quick to point out that Marathon had a fundamental problem: a poor record in replacing domestic reserves. From 1980 to 1983 it replaced only 35 percent of its production, compared with the 69-percent average of fifteen major competitors. In addition, Marathon's average cost of finding oil and gas in the United States was 61 percent higher than the industry's average. However, Marathon has made an attempt to boost exploration and production efforts, although the economics of the oil market made new exploration a poor prospect in the mid-1980s.

Despite shareholder concerns about the Marathon deal, in 1985 USS made a further acquisition in the oil and gas industry—that of Texas Oil & Gas (TXO), for $3.7 billion. The deal, based on a stock swap plan, required USS to double outstanding shares to 258 million, dramatically diluting the stake of USS's shareholders in the company. Moreover, at a time when energy prices were falling, it was difficult for many shareholders to see the logic behind the deal.

Management, however, presented the deal as part of a sound long-term strategy that would ultimately benefit all shareholders. Although TXO's earnings have slumped in the face of anemic demand and overproduction in the gas industry, TXO is an efficient operation, with exploration costs far below the industry norm and a good record for replacing reserves. When the gas industry recovers, TXO might be able to boost its sales by at least 50 percent simply by tapping current unused capacity. USX's management seems to be counting on TXO's earnings to mushroom when the gas surplus ends.

Between October 1985, when the deal was announced, and August 1986, USX's stock dropped 55 percent, while Wall Street surged ahead. Then corporate raiders began to take an interest in USX. Although no formal takeover bid was ever made, corporate raider Carl Icahn built up an 11.4-percent stake in USX and forced management to defend its restructuring strategy.

Divestments

Between 1980 and 1986 USX sold off $4.7 billion worth of assets. Included in the asset sales have been the sale of USS Chemicals through a public stock offering as Aristech Chemical Corporation; the sale of U.S. Steel Supply Division; timberland in Michigan; coal reserves; and iron ore reserves. The objective has been twofold: to sell off assets that do not fit in with USX's long-term strategy, and to use asset sales to pay off the debt burden of the Marathon Oil and TXO acquisitions. In the process, USX has become far less of a vertically integrated operation. As Roderick has observed, the fully integrated steel company is a thing of the past. To quote Roderick, "How much iron ore does Taiwan own? How much coal do the minimills own?"[5]

MANAGEMENT AND ORGANIZATION

USX corporation is now organized into four operating units: Marathon Oil Company, USS (the steel-making arm), U.S. Diversified Group, and Texas Oil

[5]John Merwin, "Not for the Next 30 Days," *Forbes*, July 13, 1987, pp. 72–80.

and Gas Corp. The main activities of each of these units are detailed in Exhibit 6. In marked contrast to the 1979 days, decision making has been decentralized within the organization and each business unit operates in a largely autonomous fashion. The decentralization seems to be working. For example, under the old centralized structure, managers of the $400-million steel service center business (now a division of USS) were spending hours each day on the phone with the Pittsburgh, Penn. head office getting approval for price and delivery terms. Now they make those decisions themselves and spend more time with customers. The result has been near-record sales and profits, despite the depressed steel market. Another aspect of the autonomy is that each major operating unit gets to keep all the profits it generates. Thus, for example, Marathon Oil does not have to make contributions from its earnings to the parent company to help offset losses elsewhere.

In contrast to the old U.S. Steel, Marathon has always been an informal and decentralized organization. In an attempt to get USS to adopt more of Marathon's operating culture, there are plans to move managers between the two opera-

EXHIBIT 6	USX in 1986

Oil and gas Sales $8,963 million	*Marathon Oil.* Integrated worldwide oil and gas company. Ranked 12th in U.S. liquid hydrocarbon production in 1986. Principal domestic producing areas: Texas, Wyoming, Gulf of Mexico, and Alaska. Also operates in the North Sea, Abu Dhabi, and Indonesia. Marathon branded operations: approximately 2,400 stations in 5 states. Emro Marketing Company outlets: approximately 1,300 in 18 states. Four domestic refineries, plus a refinery in West Germany. *Texas Oil and Gas.* Leading domestic driller of natural gas wells. Operations include purchasing natural gas, gathering gas from company-owned wells and those of others, processing gas, selling and delivering gas to utilities, large pipeline companies, and domestic users. Owns 51 gas-gathering systems and 22 gas-processing plants. Pipeline systems total 9,216 miles. Operates 36 drilling rigs.
Steel Sales $3,708 million	*USS.* Largest domestic integrated steel producer. Plants located in Alabama, California, Illinois, Indiana, Ohio, Pennsylvania, Texas, and Utah. Domestic ore operations located in Minnesota. Plants produce a variety of semifinished and finished steel products. Raw steel production capability: 19.1 million tons annually. Continuous casting capability: 35 percent of annual net tonnage.
Diversified businesses Sales $2,811 million	*Diversified businesses.* Operations in the manufacturing of oil field equipment and the distribution of oil field supplies and services; engineering, construction, and consulting services; domestic transportation; agricultural chemicals; real estate; and the management of mineral resources. Also include operations in domestic and international mining and Great Lakes transportation.

Source: Reprinted by permission from the USX 1986 Annual Report.

tions, especially in such staff functions as accounting and public relations. The objective is to further break down USS's old-style bureaucratic culture.

However, to date there have been fewer signs of cultural convergence than of tension between USS and Marathon. For example, USS assumed that it would get all of Marathon's tubular drilling steel business, but Marathon executives have insisted that they cannot show favoritism to USS and have continued to place orders where the price is lowest — which often means with steel companies other than USS. Similarly, even when adding white-collar workers, Marathon has refused to hire displaced steel executives, causing one steel executive to complain that Marathon "isn't part of the family."

USX'S FINANCES

Details of USX's finances for 1984–1986 are summarized in Exhibit 7. For USX, 1986 was a disastrous year with net losses of more than $1.8 billion. However, the signs are that 1987 will generate at least a partial recovery. Value line estimates suggest that USX will show a net profit of $415 million in 1987, followed by $610 million in 1988. Long-term debt, however, is predicted to increase to $6.5 billion in 1987, before declining back to $6 billion in 1988.

EXHIBIT 7   **USX: summary of financial statement**

	1986	1985	1984
	(dollars in millions except per share data)		
Sales	$14,938	$20,779	$21,092
Net income (loss)	(1,833)	598	793
Dividends			
Preferred	92	121	119
Common	269	161	141
Net income reinvested in business			
Increase (dècrease)	(2,194)	316	533
Long-term debt	5,697	6,074	6,983
Working capital	18	530	560
Stockholders' equity	5,634	7,698	6,932
Total capitalization	16,611	15,188	15,435
Per common share			
Net income (loss)	$ (7.46)	$ 1.94	$ 2.81
Book value	18.24	26.48	25.26

Source: Reprinted by permission from the USX 1986 Annual Report.

THE FUTURE

On the face of it, each of USX's strategic objectives had been to some extent achieved by 1987. USX's steel-making capacity had been reduced by 50 percent, more than 75 percent of the company's revenues were generated by nonsteel activities (primarily oil and gas), and USX has sold off $4.7 billion in assets, from coal reserves to timberland. Despite enormous losses in 1986, Roderick is now upbeat about USX's prospects. To quote him, "There's just no question. This company is going to be a cash cow. . . . In 1988 and 1989 we ought to have excess cash of $1 billion each year, after our capital investments. We can do a lot of things — buy back stock, make acquisitions, or reduce debt."[6] Roderick is also reportedly searching for further diversification opportunities to add to the steel and oil businesses. It is said that the next diversification move might be into food processing or financial services. There is also talk of the possibility of spinning off all or part of the steel-making business to shareholders.

[6]Merwin, "Not for the Next 30 Days," pp. 72–80.

Case 23

WALSH PETROLEUM

John Walsh sighed as he looked again at the financial statements his accountant had delivered that morning. When John's father died two years ago, his accountant had advised against selling the business. "It's a good business, John," he said, "and I think you could do a lot to improve it."

While Walsh Petroleum, Inc. had increased profits in 1985, John still considered them unacceptably low. Company sales had declined for the third straight year, and while John realized that other oil distributors faced the same problems, he had to wonder what type of future he could expect if he stayed with the family business. Now 31 years old and just married, maybe he should consider selling the business and starting another career before he got too old.

COMPANY HISTORY

Walsh Petroleum was founded in 1957 by John's mother and father as commission agents in the oil business. By 1976, the senior Walsh converted the company to a conventional oil distributorship. Both the family and the company were well respected in the local community, and the company grew steadily. The 1970s and early 1980s were a period of relative prosperity for Walsh Petroleum. Dollar sales in 1982 were four times higher than sales in 1977 (although most of this increase was a result of increased unit sales prices). Nonetheless, profits were at their highest level in 1982. A year later, sales gallonage started a decline that had continued unabated. In 1984, John's father died, leaving John's mother and John to manage the firm.

This case was prepared by George A. Overstreet, Jr., Stewart C. Malone, and Bernard A. Morin. The authors gratefully acknowledge the financial support of the General Electric Foundation and the McIntire School of Commerce at the University of Virginia in the preparation of this case. As well, the cooperation and assistance of the two closely held corporations represented herein are deeply appreciated.

COMPANY OPERATIONS

Walsh Petroleum distributed oil products throughout a seven-county area of the southeastern United States. Their marketing area was semi-rural, but contained two county seats with populations of 15,000 and 25,000. The area's proximity to a growing, major metropolitan city was expected to result in higher-than-average population growth over the next ten years, but in no way was the area likely to become a suburb of the city. The firm represented a major branded oil company and carried a full line of petroleum products. There were three basic classes of customers for Walsh:

Reseller Accounts

Walsh served as a distributor of oil products to ten reseller locations, most of which were local gas stations. Gaining new reseller customers depended more on financial considerations than marketing techniques, since gasoline and oil products were generally considered commodities, and most distributors offered similar types of services. When a new gas station was about to be constructed (an event that had been occurring with decreasing frequency over the past twenty years), the operator would contact several distributors such as Walsh. The distributor would formulate a proposal based on expected sales gallonage. In return for an exclusive, long-term contract to supply the location with gasoline and oil products, the distributor provided the station with fuel storage tanks, pumps, remote consoles, and a canopy. Walsh's profit margin per gallon declined as the reseller's volume climbed, based on a sliding scale. If up to 50,000 gallons a month were delivered, he received 4.5¢ over delivered cost (including freight). If 50,000 to 65,000 gallons a month were delivered, he received 4.0¢ per gallon. For 65,000–75,000 gallons he received 3.65¢, and for over 75,000 gallons he received 3.5¢ per gallon. Over the course of the contract the station operator could switch suppliers if he/she was willing to make a settlement on the equipment provided by the original distributor.

John had recently audited the profitability of his reseller accounts and found that many of the accounts yielded over a 20% after-tax Internal Rate of Return (IRR).[1] New reseller contracts also tended to be very lucrative, but there were relatively few high-gallonage locations left in Walsh's trading area, and only two or three new reseller accounts were out for bid each year. The capital requirements for such investments had grown over the years and ranged from $60,000 to $100,000.

In addition to the ten contract locations, Walsh operated a reseller location itself, on which it had constructed a convenience store (C-store). This diversification move was initiated by Mr. Walsh, Sr., in 1983. The C-store facility was located on 3.0 acres with 300 feet of road frontage on a 4-lane U.S. high-

---

[1]See Exhibit 10 for a discounted cash flow analysis of a recent reseller investment.

way. The property had been appraised at $356,000 and included not only the convenience store but also the bulk storage facilities (144,000 gallons). Mrs. Walsh personally owned the site and leased it to Walsh Petroleum at $4,000 per month ($2,500 for the bulk storage plant and $1,500 for the C-store). The property had a $100,000 note payable over five years at 9%.

Home Heating Oil

Active accounts numbered 624, of which 325 were classified as automatic (with refills scheduled by the distributor). While the home heating oil business was relatively profitable, it was also highly seasonal, and, thus, efficient utilization of equipment and personnel was viewed as a problem. Some other distributors had taken on equipment sales and service, as well as related businesses such as air conditioning, in order to balance the seasonality of fuel oil sales. John had concluded that heating oil sales would have to double in order to justify the equipment investment and personnel training for an in-house sales/service department.

Commercial/Agricultural Accounts

Approximately 120 businesses and/or farms maintained their own tanks and pumps for which Walsh supplied oil products. While these accounts had generally shown some degree of loyalty to their petroleum supplier, there was no contractual relationship that would prevent them from changing suppliers.

Within Walsh Petroleum's trading area, there were currently three other gasoline and oil distributors. Competitive pressures were moderate for existing gasoline reseller and home heating oil accounts, but John had recently noticed an increased level of competition for the one or two new reseller locations that were constructed each year. None of the four distributors possessed a large competitive advantage over the others. Each competitor had about the same level of sales, and all possessed a similar amount of financial resources. Since gasoline and oil products have a significant freight cost-to-value ratio, distributors of these products generally had a trading radius of approximately 75 miles around their terminal or distribution point. While the local competitors did not really worry John, some of the distributors that served the nearby metropolitan area were significantly larger than Walsh, and a move by one of these larger competitors into Walsh's trading area could well upset the competitive equilibrium that had evolved over the years.

FAMILY AND MANAGEMENT

Mrs. Walsh assumed the chairmanship of the company following the death of her husband, and she held 52% of the voting stock of the corporation (the remaining 48% being held equally by John and his two younger brothers). Having worked with her husband for several years, she was very knowledgeable about the firm's operations. While she held the title of chairman, Mrs. Walsh's duties consisted of supervising the convenience store adjacent to the distributorship and maintaining relationships with the fuel oil customers. A prominent citizen of the local community, Mrs. Walsh also served on the town council.

John Walsh had been employed as a geologist with an energy consulting firm in Denver prior to 1982. When he was visiting home one weekend, he mentioned to his father that he was concerned that his career would be hurt by the recent recession in the oil drilling business. Later that weekend, while having coffee together in the local donut shop, John Sr. said, "John, our business here is changing rapidly, too. If you have any interest in joining the family business, you better make up your mind soon, because I may just sell the business rather than put up with all the changes that are occurring."

John returned to Denver, but after several months he decided that the opportunity at Walsh Petroleum might offer a better future than his current job. John returned home in late 1982 and began to learn the business from his father. Not only did John assume many of the administrative duties, but he also managed the marketing relationships with the major accounts.

John's two younger brothers were not active in the management of the business at the time, although each held 16% of the corporate stock. Richard was 26 years old and was employed in another city. Daniel was a sophomore in college.

Aside from John and his mother, Walsh Petroleum employed three clerks and four driver/maintenance workers. The three clerks handled much of the administrative paperwork for both the oil distributorship and the convenience store. Convenience stores have a multitude of vendors, all of whom expect payment within ten days. Managing the payables took a great deal of time, and Walsh's bookkeeping clerk had complained on more than one occasion that she couldn't keep up with the workload. All of the accounting was done manually, and John planned to install a computer system in the near future.

In addition, there were two full-time and three part-time workers at the convenience store. Salaries and benefits for these workers corresponded to industry averages, and all employees were non-unionized. During the first quarter of 1986, John purchased a new tractor/trailer for $60,000 (9,000-gallon capacity). In addition, Walsh had three older "bobtail" trucks for short deliveries (2,000-gallon capacity), and two used service delivery vans.

THE OIL DISTRIBUTION INDUSTRY

Few industries have experienced the volatility and changes connected with the oil business in the past 15 years. In 1973, the Arab oil embargo resulted in a 119% increase in the price of crude oil during a twelve-month period. While demand fell slightly from 1973 to 1981, prices were expected to continue climbing.

Spurred by higher prices, oil exploration and refinery construction continued to increase. In 1981, President Reagan decontrolled gasoline and crude oil prices. The acquisition price of crude oil began to drop, and demand also fell as the world economy entered a recession.

The changes that occurred upstream in the oil production industry had a large impact on the independent petroleum market in the following ways:

1. Between 1974 and 1985, American auto manufacturers doubled the miles per gallon of new cars, from 13.2 MPG to 26.4 MPG.
2. During the same period, gasoline consumption of passenger cars declined from approximately 75 billion gallons to 65 billion gallons.
3. The number of service stations (defined as outlets with 50% or more dollar volume from the sale of petroleum products) fell from 226,459 in 1972 to 121,000 in 1985.

In addition to these changes, oil distributors also faced declining margins, increased real estate costs, and a proliferation of environmental regulations.

News for distributors had not been all bad. The past two years had seen firmer gross profit margins and increased gallonage pumped. Although the market had not recovered to the volume levels of the late 1970s and early 1980s, gasoline gallonage used by motorists increased 1.5% in 1983, 1.5% in 1984, and 3.4% in 1985.[2] A significant portion of the increased demand had to be attributed to the oversupply of world crude and, hence, to lower prices during each of the last three years (−3.3% for 1983, −1.6% for 1984, and −1.6% for 1985).

Independent petroleum marketers are entrepreneurs involved in the sale and distribution of refined petroleum and ancillary products. While the exact number of the companies was unknown, one trade association report estimated their number to be between 11,000 and 12,000 in 1985.[3] In terms of size, the trade association membership is broken down in Exhibit 1.

Independent petroleum marketers have responded to the pressures in their industry in one of two ways: diversification or consolidation (mergers and acquisitions). Exhibit 2 shows the number of diversified operations for companies belonging to the major trade association.

Aside from diversifying into other areas, the number of acquisitions had increased in the past few years, spurred by industry decontrol. Independent marketers, particularly larger ones with the capital available to make acquisitions, had acquired other distributors to take advantage of economies of scale in storage, distribution, and other areas such as billing and general administrative services. A 1984 study found that 56 of 135 marketers had purchased one or more marketing companies within the last five years, and 24 of the 56 had purchased

[2] *1986 State of the Convenience Store Industry,* National Association of Convenience Stores, Inc., Alexandria, VA (1986), p. 7.
[3] *1985 Petroleum Marketing Databook,* Petroleum Marketing Education Foundation, Alexandria, VA (1985), p. 12.

EXHIBIT 1   **Percentage of marketers by size distribution**

Millions of gallons sold	1984	1982
Less than 1.0 MM gallons	13.8	18.0
1.0– 2.49	23.8	26.3
2.5– 4.99	21.9	20.8
5.0– 7.49	12.2	9.7
7.5– 9.99	6.6	6.7
10.0–14.99	9.3	7.1
15.0–19.99	3.8	2.8
20.0–24.99	2.2	1.8
25.0–29.99	1.7	1.4
30.0–39.99	1.8	1.5
40.0–49.99	1.1	1.2
50.0 and above	1.8	2.7
Average volume	7.80	7.12
Median volume	3.91	3.18

Source: *1985 Petroleum Marketing Databook,* Petroleum Marketing Education Foundation, Alexandria, VA (1985), p. 12. Reprinted by permission of the Petroleum Marketing Education Foundation.

EXHIBIT 2   **1984 Diversified operations**

Operations	Number of operations
Auto repair/maintenance center	7,081
Auto/truck/trailer rentals	638
Beverage only stores	228
Car washes	2,961
Convenience stores	14,235
Fast-food operations	1,002
Heating/air conditioning service	3,189
Kerosene heater sales	1,275
Lube centers	1,549
Plumbing service	501
Tires/tires, battery, and accessory stores	3,507
Truck stops	1,734
Towing service	911
Coal sales	164
Other	1,000

Source: *1985 Petroleum Marketing Databook,* Petroleum Marketing Education Foundation, Alexandria, VA (1985), p. 15. Reprinted by permission of the Petroleum Marketing Education Foundation.

more than one.[4] Most of the acquisition activity occurred among marketers with assets greater than $1MM. Of the 90 firms in this category in the sample, 46 had acquired one or more businesses during the period.

As a result of increasing profit pressure, a number of operating changes had occurred on the distribution level.[5] First, the total number of distributor-owned transportation vehicles had declined dramatically from 106,868 in 1982 to 96,972 in 1984. Second, distributors had decreased the amount of their storage facilities from a 2.3 billion-gallon capacity in 1982 to 1.7 billion in 1984. Finally, credit terms to distributors had tightened. In 1982, net 30-day payment terms were reported by 21% of trade association members, while in 1984 this percentage had dropped to 8.2%. These changes and others had led gasoline and oil distributors to redefine the term "good customer." Whereas in the 1960s and 1970s, distributors were willing to inventory product and deliver relatively small amounts of gasoline on small "bobtail" trucks, the new market realities made these practices less attractive. Instead of inventorying product, successful distributors would now send a large transport truck (9,000-gallon capacity) to the terminal, or distribution point, and transport the gasoline directly to one service station. Since it was inefficient to have the large truck tied up making multiple deliveries, the customer emphasis was on the volume gas station with tank capacity large enough to handle one large delivery. The "mom-and-pop" gasoline retailer was now considered undesirable. John Walsh stated, "In 1980 we considered a good account one that pumped 20,000–25,000 gallons per month, while in 1986 we consider a good account to be in the range of 40,000–50,000 gallons per month."

In addition to the deregulation of gasoline and crude oil prices in 1981, another regulatory development that affected oil distributors was the issuance of EPA regulations regarding leakage of gasoline from underground steel storage tanks. According to one authority, as many as 30% of steel tanks currently in the ground might be leaking.[6] Since both past and present owners of property with underground tanks could be held legally liable for leakage pollution, many companies were completely removing older tanks (more than 10–15 years old) at a cost of approximately $1,000 for a 1,000- to 3,000-gallon tank. The cost of removing and then reinstalling a similar-size tank cost approximately $6,000. If there was a minor leak, clean-up costs would be approximately $5,000 extra. Liability insurance for tank leakage had become exceedingly expensive and difficult to obtain, especially for older, single-wall steel tanks.

The Current Situation

From his study of trade journals and attendance at industry conferences, John Walsh had concluded that basic industry trends portended a bleak future for

[4] *1984 Petroleum Marketing Databook*, Petroleum Marketing Education Foundation, Alexandria, VA (1984), p. 19.
[5] *1985 Petroleum Marketing Databook*, Petroleum Marketing Education Foundation, Alexandria, VA (1985), pp. 15–16.
[6] Plenn, Steffen W., *Underground Tankage: The Liability of Leaks,* Petroleum Marketing Education Foundation, Alexandria, VA (1986), pp. 9–12.

Walsh Petroleum unless some substantial changes were made in the company's strategy. It seemed apparent to John that his company had to do something different or get out of the business. Being relatively young, John was confident that he could start a career elsewhere, but he enjoyed living in his hometown of Lancaster and liked the idea of being his own boss. Furthermore, his mother was currently receiving an annual salary of $50,000 in addition to rent she received on the C-store. If they sold the company, would the proceeds generate sufficient income to replace his mother's current income?

If they decided not to sell the business, John wondered how the business could be changed. He had received an offer to purchase a competitor, Valley Oil, only weeks before.

The Valley Oil Alternative

In many respects, it seemed as though Valley Oil faced the same problems as Walsh. The two companies sold basically the same product lines, although Valley's percentage of heating fuel sales was higher than Walsh's. This aspect of Valley was attractive to John, since heating fuel commanded higher margins than gasoline (25¢ per gallon versus 8¢ to 10¢ per gallon), and customers were a little less sensitive to price than gasoline resellers. Overall, though, Valley's unit sales were declining and unit profit margins were being squeezed. Many of Valley's contract resellers were low-volume accounts and had experienced declining sales volume. Furthermore, their underground tanks were old.

The owner of Valley had died recently, and Valley's current 55-year-old CEO wanted to get out of the business. Valley's CEO had sent along a copy of the company's recent financial statements, which John had given to a consultant to value Valley Oil for him (see Appendix). Valley's CEO said that while the company wasn't for sale on the open market yet, he felt that an $800,000 offer would buy the company. John's consultant didn't think Valley was worth that much, but John was skeptical of the consultant's conclusions because the consultant did not have experience in the petroleum business.

John thought that acquiring Valley Oil could offer some unique advantages—advantages that many other potential acquirers could not realize. First, many of the selling and administrative expenses that Valley incurred could be performed by Walsh's personnel. A potential buyer from outside the industry would probably have substantially higher operating costs than John would have.

Rather than beginning his analysis with what employees he would be able to eliminate from Valley's payroll, John decided to examine how many people he would have to add to Walsh Petroleum to serve Valley's customers. He figured that initially he would need at least two additional clerks to handle the scheduling and the billing for Valley accounts. Two additional full-time drivers would be needed for deliveries and two seasonal drivers for fuel oil. Salaries for clerks and drivers were estimated at $9,000 and $18,000 a year, respectively, and fringe benefits would probably add about 35%. John thought he could get someone to manage the new business at $30,000 (benefits included). John also felt that if he could get his computerized accounting system up and running within a year for approximately $40,000, he might be able eventually to eliminate one of the clerks. John was also pleased with the thought that the acquisition of Valley would allow him to spread the significant up-front investment in hardware and software over a greater number of accounts, and by adding a delivery scheduling module to the computer system he should be able to schedule his deliveries more efficiently. In addition, John's accountant recommended that he use a conservative tax rate of 30% in his analysis of Valley.

Even with the operating savings John might be able to utilize, Valley would probably be an attractive acquisition to some of the large distributors in the nearby city. Compared to the fierce competition in that city, John's trading area would probably look very attractive to them. While John's knowledge of the local market gave him an advantage, the larger, city-based distributors could achieve many of the operating cost savings that John was contemplating. By purchasing Valley, John felt his gross profit margin would improve due to a reduced level of competition.

The more John thought about the possibility of combining Walsh and Valley, the more likely it seemed that he wouldn't need most of Valley's physical assets to service the accounts he would be acquiring. John had scheduled a lunch with Valley's CEO to discuss the possibility of the acquisition. John's hopes of only acquiring Valley's customers were quickly dashed. Valley's CEO stated that if he was getting out of the business, he was going to sell the whole business as a unit, not hold a "rummage sale." Moreover, he seemed firm about the price of $800,000. The rise in Valley's gross profit margin in 1985 had continued through the first half of 1986 because of the unprecedented drop in oil prices and "sticky" retail prices. However, John knew that Valley's CEO would want to sell the business this year before long-term capital gains rates expired.

A big issue in John's mind was how to finance the acquisition. Neither he nor his mother had enough liquid funds outside the business to acquire Valley. Valley's owners indicated that they might be willing to hold a note, but they would require certain covenants regarding Walsh Petroleum's financial condition in order to protect their position. Also, personal guarantees from John, his mother, and his brothers would be required. John decided to try to get Valley's owners to finance 75% of the acquisition price over 10 years. While he would have to pay a premium over the prime rate, in his opinion it might still be a good investment.

THE C-STORE ALTERNATIVE

One of the relative bright spots in Walsh Petroleum's operation had been the C-store. C-stores originated as a convenient alternative to the traditional grocery store, and the premise that consumers would pay higher than grocery store prices in exchange for convenience proved correct. Since customers typically bought only a few items, checkout lines were very short. C-stores carried a relatively limited product line of items generally regarded as necessities. Milk, bread, and beer and wine made up a substantial percentage of C-store sales. Although a majority of the products sold in C-stores carried a very similar product mix, opportunities did exist for C-store operators to differentiate themselves. A number of operators offered video rentals, hot food service (hot dogs, pizza, etc.), and other amenities. Geographic location was also a critical success factor. Customers selected a C-store based on its proximity to their home or their daily route or travel.

Many motor fuel operators had taken the traditional gas station, closed the maintenance bays, and remodeled them into small convenience stores (800–1200 sq. ft.) with gasoline pumps out front. Likewise, convenience store operators, such as Southland (7-Eleven), added self-service gas pumps. According to the National Association of Convenience Stores, gasoline margins averaged 7.3%, while non-gasoline margins averaged 32.2%.[7]

In early 1982, the Walshes had commissioned a marketing consulting group to conduct a feasibility study of a C-store location adjacent to the fuel oil distributorship. The location had approximately 300 feet of frontage on a major highway, and the traffic count looked as though it would make the operation feasible. Mr. Walsh, Sr. had remodeled an existing two-bay station, and within two years the unit was meeting and then exceeding the marketing consultants' projections.

Walsh Petroleum currently owned an unoccupied two-bay service station on a corner lot with good access from all directions and a stable traffic flow in a growing, nearby community. In the past the Walshes had leased the property to a number of service station operators. None of them had been able to make a success of the operation, and it was John's opinion that the day of the "traditional" two-bay station was past its prime. Customers wanted either the pricing and convenience of a self-service station or a super-premium station that provided clearly superior maintenance and service. The turnover of operators was consuming much of Walsh's time, and the station would often sit empty.

John had felt that it might be possible to demolish the station and erect a C-store with self-serve gasoline pumps on the site. To investigate this possibility, John commissioned the same market research firm that had provided the feasibility study for the original C-store to analyze the new location. This firm had developed a forecasting model that would generate fairly accurate sales estimates for both gasoline and in-store sales for a C-store. Among the many variables included in the model was highway traffic flow, store size and layout, and distance to the nearest existing C-store, as well as a variety of demographic data on the area. John's corner lot had a traffic count of 14,000 vehicles per day on the main road and 4,000 vehicles a day on the side street. The resulting sales forecast for gasoline was 915,000 gallons with a 24-month maturity and 410,000 gallons in year 1. Kerosene sales were forecast at 7,500 gallons in year 1 and 10,000 gallons per annum thereafter. Inside sales items totaled $213,000 (year 1),

[7]"Why the C-store Image Race Could Lead to a Shakeout," *National Petroleum News*, September 1987, p. 40.

$428,000 (year 2), and matured at $530,000 in year 3. Expected margins were 50¢ a gallon for kerosene, 8¢ a gallon for gasoline, and 32% for inside sales.

At the same time, an architectural firm had been retained as a design consultant. Exhibit 3 shows the costs that had been estimated under John's close supervision. Another option John had was to build a C-store using his major oil supplier's generic C-store design plan. The generic design included a smaller C-store (40 × 50 feet) under a 90 × 40 feet canopy with pumps on either side of the store (35 feet from pump to entrance). The advantage to this design was that the major oil company would refund Walsh 2¢ per gallon on all gallons sold (up to 150,000 gallons per month) for 36 months and provide a detailed site plan without charge. John felt he would lose some inside sales with their fatter margins and he wouldn't get to build his own C-store identity and goodwill. The overall cost would be approximately the same for the two options, and John was uncertain which choice was best from a marketing point of view.

EXHIBIT 3   **C-store estimated costs**

Appraised value of lot	$100,000
Building (≈$60 for 2400 sq. feet of C-store)	144,400
Market research	1,000
Equipment costs:	
Gas equipment	150,000
Food equipment	60,000
Canopy	17,500
Capitalized site plan (consultant)	20,000
Inventory:	
Food	40,000
Fuel	14,500
Net operating capital	20,000
TOTAL	$567,400
Salvage value:	
Gas equipment	$ 13,500
Food equipment	6,000
Canopy	1,750
Capitalized site plan	0
Asset lives:	
Gas equipment	5 years
Food equipment	7 years
Canopy	10 years
Site plan and building	31.5 years

Depreciation method:
Gas, food and canopy equip.—Dou. decl. bal.
Site plan and building—straight line

Based on those of his other store, John estimated the operating expenses per annum for the new store as follows: salaries and benefits for a 126-hour week at $80,000, utilities at $14,000, property taxes at $2,000, and other miscellaneous expenses at $20,000.

While the research pertaining to the original C-store had been highly accurate, John wondered how reliable the model could be in forecasting future sales for the proposed C-store. Since even the major highways were relatively undeveloped in his rural market, there were certainly some desirable road frontage locations near his site. As a matter of fact, there was a one-acre site directly across the street that could be used for a C-store location. While he had considered buying the property as a defensive move, he felt he really couldn't afford to buy it at $150,000.

John felt that the threat of new C-store competitors was very real. Even though a half-million dollar investment for a C-store was a substantial investment to John, this sum might look like a real bargain to the major C-store chains that had been paying up to a million dollars for prime suburban locations. Surely, John reasoned, a competing C-store within a mile or two of his location would adversely affect the validity of his financial projections. The design consultant had added a drive-in window at a cost of approximately $25,000 to differentiate the store and build customer loyalty. John felt a drive-in window would add 15% annually to projected inside sales.

At a recent petroleum distributors conference, John discussed his C-store plans with several fellow distributors. Most felt that the generic C-store designs offered by the major oil companies were too small to provide the maximum level of in-store sales, particularly in a rural market. They questioned the wisdom of the drive-in window, suggesting a car-wash operation instead.

While John felt the C-store alternative had potential, he also was aware that the move had its risks. Nationally, the number of C-stores had increased rapidly. At the end of 1981, there were 38,000 C-stores, and only 16,416 of these sold gasoline. Just four years later, the C-store population had reached 61,000, with 33,500 selling gasoline.[8]

There was general agreement in the industry that the danger of C-store saturation was greatest in suburban areas, but that substantial opportunities remained in both urban and rural markets. One rural operator, who competed successfully in towns with as few as 1,000 residents, said, "For the rest of the industry, the mark-up on gas is six to eight cents a gallon, while we get eight to ten cents. Often we are the only gas station in town."[9] While gas margins would be higher in rural areas, C-stores often increased margins on other products as well. Fast foods and video rentals were extremely profitable in the absence of strong competitors. Pizza, for example, carried a 70% profit margin. One C-store/pizza vendor said that the pizza concept probably wouldn't work

[8]"Why the C-store Image Race Could Lead to a Shakeout," p. 41.
[9]"Rural vs. Urban: A Site Selection Dilemma," *Convenience Store News*, BAT Publications, New York, NY, July 13–August 2, 1987, p. 54.

in cities where people could go to a Pizza Hut, "but out in the rural area, there's no place else to get a good pizza."[10]

Until recently, most of the competitors in the C-store industry were convenience store chains, such as Southland, and locations operated by independent oil distributors. There were increasing indications that the big oil refiners were entering the industry in force. Eight refiner/supplier oil companies, such as Texaco, Mobil, and Exxon, were ranked in the top 50 C-store operators. Many industry observers expected that the entry of the big-oil–owned C-stores would touch off a price war in the industry, particularly in the in-store segment. The rationale behind this expectation was that oil companies would lower in-store merchandise mark-ups in order to increase pump gallonage. However, the major oil companies had tended to concentrate on the urban areas, leaving the rural markets to the distributors.

THE FUTURE OF WALSH OIL

During one of the recent executive education programs John had attended, a few sessions had been devoted to evaluating investment opportunities. He knew that he should try to determine an appropriate hurdle rate to use. There were some discussions at these sessions about calculating a cost of capital, but that seemed too academic and complicated. Instead, he went to the library and looked up various interest rates and decided to add a couple of percentage points to them. He figured that a small company like his would have to pay somewhere between 2 and 5 percent over the going rate. The interest rates as of August 1986 are listed in Exhibit 4.

As he reviewed his notes from the training sessions, John found that real estate investments were evaluated differently than other types of investments. Rather than using the total acquisition price as a measure of cash outflow, real estate investments were analyzed on the basis of equity cash outflow to determine the payback. One of John's friends in the real estate business told him that rather than using the purchase price of the acquisition as a measure of its cost, he should use the down payment, or the immediate cash outflow, as the cost measure and calculate a levered rate of return on investment.

EXHIBIT 4　　　**Selected interest rates — August 1986**

Prime rate charged by banks	7.75%
U.S. Treasury bonds — ten years	7.17%
Corporate bonds — Aaa seasoned	8.72%
Home mortgages — FHLBB	10.26%

[10]Ibid., p. 54.

John scheduled an initial meeting with his banker to see what type of financing he might be able to obtain. While the banker expressed interest in the C-store, he didn't feel that the bank would be willing to lend funds for the acquisition of Valley Oil. "John, it's just too risky for us," he said. "Valley's assets just aren't liquid enough to qualify as high-quality collateral. With those old tanks and trucks, we would never get our money out. Now the C-store is something I could sell to the loan committee. It's my guess that we could finance 80% of the land and building at 11.5% for 15 years.[11] In addition, we could finance 80% of the equipment including the site plan over 7 years at a 9.75% fixed rate."

The banker paused, as if unsure how to proceed. "You know, John, what I'm about to bring up is somewhat sensitive," he said, "so just tell me to stop if I'm out of line. I've watched you work like a dog over the past year to turn your business around, but at some point you have to start thinking about yourself. You can work like hell for thirty years and still only be a minority stockholder. If your mother and two brothers wanted to sell out at some point in the future, all your efforts, not to mention your career, are down the drain."

"Here's an alternative you might just think about," said the banker. "Walsh Petroleum owns the C-store site you are talking about developing. Why don't you buy the land personally and construct the C-store on it? We here at the bank would lend you the money, although we would probably have to have Walsh Petroleum guarantee the loan. You could then lease the C-store back to Walsh Petroleum, and start building up some personal equity for yourself through the real estate investment."

As John Walsh pondered his alternatives, one thing seemed certain to him—he would have to take action very soon. Many of his friends he met at the trade association meetings seemed to be complacent about the pressures on their industry at this time, but as John glanced at the financial statements again, he knew that a few more years like these past two would threaten not only his family's financial security, but his own as well. After all, he was really the only member of the family whose income was directly related to the future of Walsh Petroleum. He remembered the discussion of these issues at a recent dinner with his mother and brothers.

"John, I agree with the idea of expanding the business, and I think it would have pleased your dad," said Mrs. Walsh, "but you have to remember that Walsh Petroleum is really all I have. If we take on too much debt, and get into trouble, I don't know what I'll do in my old age."

"I see your point, Mom," said John, "but the fact is that I'm the only one in the family who is devoting the rest of my life to running the business. You already own C-store #1, and Richard and Daniel either don't want to be in the business or aren't sure yet. I don't want to sound selfish, but my interest in the business is only 16%. I don't want to wake up when I'm fifty and find that I've

---

[11] It should be noted that the bank is refinancing land that Walsh currently owns.

spent my whole life running this business for the rest of the family and have relatively little to show for it."

Richard puffed on his pipe and said, "John, I'm not sure the C-store alternative is a good idea for the family business. Sure, it's a good deal for you personally, but the rest of us have to guarantee your loan at the bank. I think Walsh Petroleum should give serious consideration to the Valley Oil deal."

"And why do you think that Valley is better than the C-store?" asked John.

"The main reason," Richard replied, "is that Walsh Petroleum is primarily a gasoline distributor. The original C-store was a great idea of Dad's, but the oil business is this family's cash cow. This is an opportunity to take out a competitor. We all agree there aren't a whole lot of new people going into this business, but if a big gasoline distributor in the region buys Valley, then Walsh Petroleum has got some major problems on its hands. The increased competition could certainly lower our gross margin one to two cents a gallon, and we all know that there are two large distributors that are interested in Valley."

"But, Richard, can't you see that we're in a declining industry?" said John. "If you looked at those financials I sent you, it should be obvious that our gallonage has been declining for several years."

"What do you think, Daniel?" asked Mrs. Walsh. "After all, it's as much your business as it is John's or Richard's."

"I think that John and Richard both have good points," said Daniel. "While John is the only one of us three in the business now, I may want to join the company when I finish school, and I really don't care to be a clerk in a convenience store. And while John certainly has a right to try to accumulate some wealth, I don't know that using the family business's credit rating to guarantee his personal investments is really fair to the rest of us. After all, John is at least getting a decent salary, and Richard and I don't even receive any dividends."

"Wait a second, Dan," said John, somewhat resentfully. "I'm not riding a gravy train here. My thirty-thousand-dollar salary at Walsh is no higher than what my market worth is, and especially the way things are going, my upside potential is much lower than I could get working for someone else. Even more importantly, the family couldn't find anyone else to do this job for any less than what I'm getting."

The family discussion had ended without resolving anything, but John was certain the business would be worth substantially less if he was unable to turn the operation around. Aside from the purely financial considerations, John knew that the major oil companies were now evaluating their distributors on sales levels and sales growth. A distributor in an attractive market who wasn't showing the appropriate level of sales or sales growth might soon find itself without a supply contract.

Further, while John was anxious to stop the decline in the company's financial performance, he also felt strongly that the business's plan he developed now should lay the foundation for the business growth for the next five to ten years. The questions in his mind were, "How do we do it, and is it worth the trouble?"

EXHIBIT 5   Walsh Petroleum statement of income for the years ended 1981–1985

	Year 1981	Year 1982	Year 1983	Year 1984	Year 1985
Gallons					
Premium	386,144	687,087	584,076	617,420	593,777
Unleaded	1,193,536	1,236,757	830,002	898,065	841,184
Regular	1,930,719	2,656,736	1,660,004	1,290,969	1,039,110
Lube	24,847	17,793	18,184	16,660	15,725
Heating oil	491,583	409,267	327,845	373,609	335,054
Diesel	375,478	373,704	338,249	348,420	327,098
Kerosene	79,769	96,215	99,733	138,555	125,182
Other products	1,810	414	713	5,301	10,682
Total	4,483,886	5,477,973	3,858,806	3,688,999	3,287,812
Sales					
Premium	322,225	533,091	551,540	517,510	533,998
Unleaded	1,195,855	1,493,304	1,020,024	1,019,856	881,903
Regular	2,385,763	2,967,718	1,633,912	1,187,458	854,324
Lube	84,438	64,681	66,005	60,491	58,988
Heating oil	533,368	478,842	368,498	411,344	364,539
Diesel	397,663	410,090	332,637	345,317	310,858
Kerosene (gasohol in '80)	92,252	119,845	117,952	162,359	147,066
Other products	53,960	10,757	48,261	140,259	177,768
Net sales	5,065,524	6,078,328	4,138,829	3,844,594	3,329,444
Cost of sales					
Beginning inventory	77,420	84,927	84,804	136,862	131,592
Purchases net of discounts	4,725,693	5,691,682	3,885,577	3,528,264	2,942,582
	4,803,113	5,776,609	3,970,381	3,665,126	3,074,174
Ending inventory	84,927	84,804	136,862	131,592	149,007
Cost of sales	4,718,186	5,691,805	3,833,519	3,533,534	2,925,167
Gross profit	347,338	386,523	305,310	311,060	404,277
Selling, general & admin. expenses					
Licenses & non-income taxes	22,447	22,462	18,472	22,604	8,917
Vehicle expense	23,362	41,510	36,837	43,950	32,583
Officers' salaries	68,248	63,370	53,970	52,952	50,780
Other salaries and wages	78,763	92,138	121,160	135,692	140,623
Other expense	132,880	135,589	136,903	127,892	150,957
Depreciation	46,524	68,676	72,842	73,404	69,441
Interest	0	0	0		
On borrowing needs	6,457	7,410	11,232	11,999	9,299
Operating income (loss)	(31,343)	(44,632)	(146,106)	(157,433)	(58,323)
Earnings on marketable securities	4,456	2,853	3,009	2,943	3,739
Other income (hauling fees)	83,587	112,425	103,109	144,878	85,038
Earnings before taxes	56,700	70,646	(39,988)	(9,612)	30,454
Provision for federal income taxes	6,590	11,870	(15,294)	(2,229)	2,485
Net income	50,110	58,776	(24,694)	(7,383)	27,969

Note: Inventory is recorded on a lifo basis.

EXHIBIT 6   **Walsh Petroleum balance sheet for the years ended 1981–1985**

	Year 1981	Year 1982	Year 1983	Year 1984	Year 1985
Assets					
Current assets					
Cash	36,305	7,704	38,510	55,652	14,003
Marketable securities	0	0	0	0	0
Accounts rec	262,047	254,809	190,673	143,802	155,839
Inventories	84,927	84,804	136,862	131,592	149,007
Refundable taxes	3,964	0	27,194	2,665	200
Prepaid exp	5,756	7,121	13,698	8,625	9,609
Notes receivable	0	0	0	0	9,368
Other current assets	0	0	0	0	116,607[1]
Total current assets	392,999	354,438	406,937	342,336	454,633
Property plant and equipment[2]					
Land	25,201	28,134	25,489	34,893	30,544
Buildings	0	0	0	0	0
Equipment	154,029	140,493	163,011	130,797	144,965
Vehicles	51,930	60,678	42,367	37,032	24,604
Furniture and fixtures	5,544	3,730	3,449	4,102	3,425
Total	236,704	233,035	234,316	206,824	203,538
Less accumulated depreciation	0	0	0	0	0
Net property plant and equipment	236,704	233,035	234,316	206,824	203,538
Other assets					
Long-term investments	677	1,202	1,202	1,202	1,202
Deposits and licenses	0	0	0	0	0
Cash surrender value — officers' life insurance	30,970	35,117	690	3,116	0
Loan fees — net	370	277	195	0	0
Advances to affiliated companies	0	0	0	0	0
Total other assets	32,017	36,596	2,087	4,318	1,202
Total assets	661,720	624,069	643,340	553,478	659,373
Liabilities					
Current liabilities					
Accounts payable	264,812	155,012	157,254	80,624	98,505
Notes payable	0	0	50,000	30,000	0
Current portion of long-term debt	18,163	18,315	18,204	17,900	50,675
Construction loan payable	0	0	0	0	0
Income taxes payable	334	4,506	0	235	2,485
Advances from officers	0	0	0	0	0
Accrued expenses	42,834	45,944	55,125	44,424	40,724
Other current liabilities	0	0	522	846	0
Total current liabilities	326,143	223,777	281,105	174,029	192,389

EXHIBIT 6   **Walsh Petroleum balance sheet for the years ended 1981–1985 (*cont.*)**

	Year 1981	Year 1982	Year 1983	Year 1984	Year 1985
Long-term debt	19,849	10,305	0	0	0
Other long-term debt[3]	14,572	30,054	26,992	51,592	0
Total liabilities	360,564	264,136	308,097	225,621	192,389
Owners' equity	301,157	359,933	335,240	327,856	466,984
Total liabilities & owners' equity	661,721	624,069	643,337	553,477	659,373

Note: Walsh has limited underground tank liability due to placing tanks in reseller's name, and having installed double-walled tanks at the bulk plant over the past five years.
[1]Key man life insurance payoff (cash).
[2]In 1985 the approximate market values were as follows: land, $100,000; equipment, $100,000; vehicles, $18,000.
[3]Equipment demand note payable net of current maturities at prime +1.

EXHIBIT 7   **Walsh unit sales trends (1984–1987)**

Unit	Type	Avg. gal./month (000's)		
		1984	1985	1986 (est.)
1	4,000 sq ft rural grocery, owner change in 1984	6.0	10.5	10.8
2	Village 2-bay, financial problems, cash only, pool hall	11.7	16.8	14.3
3	5,000 sq ft rural grocery in low-growth area	—	—	8.2
4	C-store in growing rural area	—	6.7	18.1
5	2-bay station with marina service, new C-store competition	20.3	17.9	20.7
6	Rehab 2-bay on front of bulk plant property, owned by mother and leased to corporation, good location on four-lane with crossover access, growth area	28.4	35.3	37.5
7	3-bay station in low-growth rural area, father and son	9.9	9.9	10.1
8	1,500 sq ft rural grocery with new owner, business recovery	14.0	9.1	11.6
9	3,000 sq ft rural C-store with interceptor location, sell on consignment with Walsh controlling price, considering canopy to be leased by Walsh from owner	17.6	18.8	20.0
10	3,000 sq ft rural C-store with interceptor location	21.9	22.4	22.7

EXHIBIT 8   **Walsh Petroleum ratio analysis for the years ended 1981–1985**

Ratio analysis	Year 1981	Year 1982	Year 1983	Year 1984	Year 1985
Dupont analysis					
Return on sales	0.99%	0.97%	−0.60%	−0.19%	0.84%
× Asset turnover	7.66	9.74	6.43	6.95	5.05
= Return on assets	7.57%	9.42%	−3.84%	−1.33%	4.24%
× Financial leverage	2.20	1.73	1.92	1.69	1.41
= Return on equity	16.64%	16.33%	−7.37%	−2.25%	5.99%
Gallonage Dupont					
Return on sales	1.12	1.07	−0.64	−0.20	0.85
× Asset turnover	6.78	8.78	6.00	6.67	4.99
= Return on assets	7.57%	9.42%	−3.84%	−1.33%	4.24%
× Financial leverage	2.20	1.73	1.92	1.69	1.41
= Return on equity	16.64%	16.33%	−7.37%	−2.25%	5.99%
Activity					
Fixed asset turnover	21.40	26.08	17.66	18.59	16.36
Sales growth (dollars)	13.48%	19.99%	−31.91%	−7.11%	−13.40%
Sales growth (gallons)	—	22.17%	−29.56%	−4.40%	−10.88%
Profitability					
Gross margin	6.86%	6.36%	7.38%	8.09%	12.14%
Salaries ratio (offic. salar. ÷ sales)	1.35%	1.04%	1.30%	1.38%	1.53%
S, G, & A ratio (S, G, & A + sales)	6.43%	5.84%	8.88%	9.96%	11.53%
Working capital usage					
Days payable	19.08	9.31	13.87	7.65	10.80
Collection period (days)	18.88	15.30	16.82	13.65	17.08
Days inventory	6.12	5.09	12.07	12.49	16.34
Cash cycle [(collect. + inv.) − day's pay]	5.92	11.09	15.02	18.49	22.62
Leverage					
Total debt/assets	54.49%	42.32%	47.89%	40.76%	29.18%
Long-term debt/assets	0.03	0.02	0.00	0.00	0.00
Liquidity					
Current ratio	1.20	1.58	1.45	1.97	2.36
Acid test ratio	0.94	1.20	0.96	1.21	1.59

EXHIBIT 9 Reseller investment analysis: assumptions

Investment		
Underground costs		
Storage tanks & UG Lines	0	
Electr. tank mon. & probes	0	
Submersible pumps	0	
Installation	0	
Fuel inventory	0	
Total	0	

Aboveground costs	
Dispensers	$25,000
Remote console	3,500
Canopy	8,000
Signage	1,500
Installation	32,000
Total	$70,000

Asset lives	
Canopy	10 yrs.
All other	5 yrs.

Financing to retailer	
% equity	100.00%
Principal	$25,000
Interest rate	9.00%
Term	60 mo.

	Year 1	Year 2	Year 3	Year 4	Year 5	Year 6	Year 7	Year 8	Year 9	Year 10
Operating costs										
Property taxes	500	500	500	500	500	500	500	500	500	500
Maintenance	0	2,000	2,000	2,000	2,000	2,000	2,000	2,000	2,000	2,000
Revenues/gallon										
Gasoline	$0.045	$0.045	$0.045	$0.045	$0.045	$0.045	$0.045	$0.045	$0.045	$0.045
Diesel	$0.045	$0.045	$0.045	$0.045	$0.045	$0.045	$0.045	$0.045	$0.045	$0.045
Kerosene	$0.300	$0.300	$0.300	$0.300	$0.300	$0.300	$0.300	$0.300	$0.300	$0.300
Sales mix										
Gasoline	90.00%	90.00%	90.00%	90.00%	90.00%	90.00%	90.00%	90.00%	90.00%	90.00%
Diesel	5.00%	5.00%	5.00%	5.00%	5.00%	5.00%	5.00%	5.00%	5.00%	5.00%
Kerosene	5.00%	5.00%	5.00%	5.00%	5.00%	5.00%	5.00%	5.00%	5.00%	5.00%
Total gallons	450,000	450,000	450,000	450,000	450,000	450,000	450,000	450,000	450,000	450,000
Tax rate	30.00%	30.00%	30.00%	30.00%	30.00%	30.00%	30.00%	30.00%	30.00%	30.00%
Discount rate	12.00%									

Note: Arrangement here centers around placing the underground tanks in the reseller's name to avoid liability. Walsh loans $25,000 to the reseller for this purpose, as noted above. Terms of the loan, and the arrangement in general, are subject to negotiation.

EXHIBIT 10 Reseller investment analysis: cash flow analysis

	Initial	Year 1	Year 2	Year 3	Year 4	Year 5	Year 6	Year 7	Year 8	Year 9	Year 10
Revenues											
Gas		18,225	18,225	18,225	18,225	18,225	18,225	18,225	18,225	18,225	18,225
Diesel		1,013	1,013	1,013	1,013	1,013	1,013	1,013	1,013	1,013	1,013
Kerosene		6,750	6,750	6,750	6,750	6,750	6,750	6,750	6,750	6,750	6,750
Total		25,988	25,988	25,988	25,988	25,988	25,988	25,988	25,988	25,988	25,988
Operating costs											
Taxes		500	500	500	500	500	500	500	500	500	500
Maintenance		2,000	2,000	2,000	2,000	2,000	2,000	2,000	2,000	2,000	2,000
Depreciation		26,400	16,160	9,952	6,176	3,869	524	419	336	268	215
Total		26,900	18,660	12,452	8,676	6,369	3,024	2,919	2,836	2,768	2,715
Interest earned		2,082	1,693	1,267	802	293					
Pretax income		1,169	9,020	14,803	18,114	19,911	22,963	23,068	23,152	23,219	23,273
Less: taxes		351	2,706	4,441	5,434	5,973	6,889	6,920	6,946	6,966	6,982
Net income		818	6,314	10,362	12,680	13,938	16,074	16,148	16,206	16,253	16,291
Plus:											
Depreciation		26,400	16,160	9,952	6,176	3,869	524	419	336	268	215
Principal repayments		4,146	4,535	4,960	5,425	5,934					
Less:											
Initial principal	(25,000)										
Below-ground cost	0										
Above-ground cost	(70,000)										
	(95,000)										
Cash flow		31,364	27,009	25,274	24,281	23,742	16,599	16,567	16,542	16,522	16,506
Present value of annual cash flows	(95,000)	28,004	21,531	17,990	15,431	13,472	8,409	7,494	6,681	5,958	5,314
Cumulative present value position	(95,000)	(66,996)	(45,465)	(27,475)	(12,044)	1,427	9,837	17,331	24,012	29,970	35,284

IRR 22.02%
NPV 35,284

EXHIBIT 11   **Motor fuel marketers — industry average of firms with assets of $500M–$1MM**

Statement of income for the years 1980–1985 ($000's)

	1980	1981	1982	1983	1984	1985
Gallons						
Premium	3,936.0	2,920.0	3,189.0	3,532.0	542.4	380.8
Unleaded	0.0	0.0	0.0	0.0	1,286.3	1,193.4
Regular	0.0	0.0	0.0	0.0	1,385.2	2,241.8
Lube	0.0	0.0	0.0	0.0	0.0	0.0
Heating oil	746.0	245.0	295.0	342.0	287.0	366.3
Diesel	777.0	853.0	920.0	982.0	1,558.4	1,241.1
Kerosene	0.0	0.0	0.0	0.0	59.2	71.3
Other products	47.0	40.0	65.0	30.0	104.2	62.0
Total	5,506.0	4,058.0	4,469.0	4,886.0	5,222.7	5,556.7
Sales						
Premium	0	0	0	0	0	0
Unleaded	0	0	0	0	0	0
Regular	0	0	0	0	0	0
Lube	0	0	0	0	0	0
Heating oil	0	0	0	0	0	0
Diesel	0	0	0	0	0	0
Kerosene (gasohol in '80)	0	0	0	0	0	0
Other products	0	0	0	0	0	0
Net sales	5,775.9	4,930.7	5,427.6	5,241.6	5,646.4	5,086.5
Cost of sales						
Beginning inventory	0.0	158.5	135.4	140.4	143.5	97.7
Purchases net of discounts	5,402.0	4,510.2	5,000.1	4,816.5	5,117.3	4,595.7
	5,402.0	4,668.7	5,135.5	4,956.9	5,260.8	4,693.4
Ending inventory	158.5	135.4	140.4	143.5	97.7	76.4
Cost of sales	5,243.2	4,533.3	4,995.1	4,813.4	5,163.1	4,617.0
Gross profit	532.7	397.4	432.5	428.2	483.3	469.5
Selling, general & admin. expenses						
Licenses & non-income taxes	25.9	32.4	28.0	19.8	20.4	22.5
Vehicle expense	69.9	65.2	61.7	58.4	58.5	63.6
Officers' salaries	49.1	40.6	42.9	40.8	55.4	50.4
Other salaries and wages	152.0	104.5	115.2	118.6	96.5	126.2
Other expense	140.4	81.8	109.7	115.2	144.2	125.9
Depreciation	39.3	37.4	37.9	44.3	53.1	50.6
Interest	0.0	0.0	0.0	0.0	0.0	0.0
On borrowing needs	19.2	22.4	22.0	16.0	18.5	26.2
Operating income (loss)	36.9	13.1	15.1	15.1	36.7	4.1
Earnings on marketable securities	0.0	0.0	0.0	0.0	0.0	0.0
Other income (expense)	38.0	30.4	26.0	35.3	20.3	32.1
Earnings before taxes	74.9	43.5	41.1	50.4	57.0	36.2
Provision for federal income taxes	19.4	11.0	8.8	11.8	12.9	11.6
Net income	55.5	32.5	32.3	38.6	44.1	24.6

EXHIBIT 12   **Motor fuel marketers — industry average of firms with assets of $500M–$1MM**

Balance sheet as of 12/31 1980–1985 ($000's)

	Year 1980	Year 1981	Year 1982	Year 1983	Year 1984	Year 1985
Assets						
Current assets						
Cash	79.7	54.2	67.5	87.2	64.7	34.2
Marketable securities	19.4	14.5	12.8	17.6	6.4	14.8
Accounts rec	247.5	224.0	235.2	263.0	264.0	194.4
Inventories	158.5	135.4	140.4	143.5	97.7	76.4
Refundable taxes	0.0	0.0	0.0	0.0	0.0	0.0
Prepaid exp	0.0	0.0	0.0	0.0	0.0	0.0
Notes receivable	0.0	0.0	0.0	0.0	18.0	23.7
Other current assets	20.0	30.1	21.1	16.6	26.6	47.9
Total current assets	525.1	458.2	477.0	527.9	477.4	391.4
Property plant and equipment						
Land	0	0	0	0	0	0
Buildings	0	0	0	0	0	0
Equipment	0	0	0	0	0	0
Vehicles	0	0	0	0	0	0
Furniture and fixtures	0	0	0	0	0	0
Total	0	0	0	0	0	0
Less accumulated depreciation	0	0	0	0	0	0
Net property plant and equipment	287.1	225.4	215.5	248.8	244.9	218.7
Other assets						
Long-term investments	0.0	0.0	0.0	0.0	10.7	28.9
Deposits and licenses	0	0	0	0	0	0
Cash surrender value — officers' life insurance	0	0	0	0	0	0
Loan fees — net	0	0	0	0	0	0
Advances to affiliated companies	0	0	0	0	0	0
Total other assets	25.4	20.6	25.5	29.1	23.2	43.9
Total assets	837.6	704.2	718.0	805.8	745.5	654.0

EXHIBIT 12   **Motor fuel marketers — industry average of firms with assets of $500M–$1MM (*cont.*)**

Balance sheet as of 12/31 1980–1985 ($000's)

	Year 1980	Year 1981	Year 1982	Year 1983	Year 1984	Year 1985
Liabilities						
Current liabilities						
Accounts payable	237.3	200.1	190.3	203.2	166.9	121.0
Notes payable	27.5	29.6	46.1	35.7	68.7	109.8
Current portion of long-term debt	30.9	15.9	15.4	12.7	0.0	0.0
Construction loan payable	0.0	0.0	0.0	0.0	0.0	0.0
Income taxes payable	0.0	0.0	0.0	0.0	6.9	1.5
Advances from officers	0.0	0.0	0.0	0.0	0.0	0.0
Accrued expenses	0.0	0.0	0.0	0.0	0.0	0.0
Other current liabilities	67.3	38.4	39.5	43.3	63.4	66.5
Other financing needed	0.0	0.0	0.0	0.0	0.0	0.0
Total current liabilities	363.0	284.0	291.3	294.9	305.9	298.8
Long-term debt	157.4	130.7	105.1	122.3	98.7	85.9
Other long-term debt	2.7	2.9	8.7	4.3	0.0	0.0
Total liabilities	523.1	417.6	405.1	421.5	404.6	384.7
Owners' equity	314.5	286.6	313.0	384.3	340.9	269.4
Total liabilities & owners' equity	837.6	704.2	718.1	805.8	745.5	654.1

Source: Data reprinted by permission of the Petroleum Marketing Education Foundation.

EXHIBIT 13   **Motor fuel marketers — industry average of firms with assets of $500M–$1MM**

Ratio analysis

Ratio analysis	Year 1980	Year 1981	Year 1982	Year 1983	Year 1984	Year 1985
Dupont analysis						
Return on sales	0.96%	0.66%	0.60%	0.74%	0.78%	0.48%
× Asset turnover	6.90	7.00	7.56	6.50	7.57	7.78
= Return on assets	6.63%	4.62%	4.50%	4.79%	5.92%	3.76%
× Financial leverage	2.66	2.46	2.29	2.10	2.19	2.43
= Return on equity	17.65%	11.34%	10.32%	10.04%	12.94%	9.13%
Gallonage Dupont						
Return on sales	1.01	0.80	0.72	0.79	0.84	0.44
× Asset turnover	6.57	5.76	6.22	6.06	7.01	8.50
= Return on assets	6.63%	4.62%	4.50%	4.79%	5.92%	3.76%
× Financial leverage	2.66	2.46	2.29	2.10	2.19	2.43
= Return on equity	17.65%	11.34%	10.32%	10.04%	12.94%	9.13%
Activity						
Fixed asset turnover	20.12	21.88	25.19	21.07	23.06	23.26
Sales growth (dollars)	−14.63%	10.08%	−3.43%	7.72%	−9.92%	
Sales growth (gallons)	−26.30%	10.13%	9.33%	6.89%	6.40%	
Profitability						
Gross margin	9.22%	8.06%	7.97%	8.17%	8.56%	9.23%
Salaries ratio	0.85%	0.82%	0.79%	0.78%	0.98%	0.99%
S, G, & A ratio	7.57%	6.58%	6.59%	6.73%	6.64%	7.64%
Working capital usage						
Days payable	15.00	14.81	12.80	14.15	10.79	8.68
Collection period (days)	15.64	16.58	15.82	18.31	17.07	13.95
Day inventory	10.02	10.02	9.44	9.99	6.32	5.48
Cash cycle	10.66	11.79	12.46	14.16	12.59	10.75
Leverage						
Total debt/assets	62.45%	59.30%	56.41%	52.31%	54.27%	58.81%
Long-term debt/assets	0.19	0.19	0.15	0.15	0.13	0.13
Times interest EBIT	2.92	1.58	1.69	1.94	2.98	1.16
Liquidity						
Current ratio	1.45	1.61	1.64	1.79	1.56	1.31
Acid test ratio	1.01	1.14	1.16	1.30	1.24	1.05

Source: Data reprinted by permission of the Petroleum Marketing Education Foundation.

Appendix   Valuation of Valley Oil Co.

PURPOSE AND METHODOLOGY

Fair market value is defined as "the price at which the property would change hands between a willing buyer and a willing seller when the former is not under any compulsion to buy and the latter is not under any compulsion to sell, both parties having reasonable knowledge of relevant facts" (Rev. Rul. 59–60).

Revenue Ruling 59–60 also outlines many techniques appropriate in the determination of fair market value. Among these are the following:

- the economic outlook in general and the condition and outlook of the specific industry in particular;
- the nature of the business and the history of the enterprise from its inception;
- the book value of the stock and the financial condition of the business;
- the earning capacity of the company; and
- whether or not the enterprise has goodwill or other intangible value.[1]

Bearing these points in mind, the analysis will consider the following:

I. Condition of industry
II. Condition of company
   A. Life cycle and market
   B. Financial trends and earnings capacity
   C. Income-based value
   D. Goodwill potential
III. Adjusted asset value
IV. Conclusion

I. CONDITION OF INDUSTRY

At present, the picture in the petroleum marketing industry is glum; according to a National Petroleum News study, industry observers see a fallout rate of over 17% for the 1985–87 period. Through 1990, the rate is even higher; observers expect little more than two-thirds of the jobbers will still be in business by 1990.[2] Over the past decade, jobber returns have been falling drastically. According to data collected by the Petroleum Marketing Education Foundation,

---

[1]Burke, Frank M. *Valuation and Valuation Planning for Closely Held Businesses* (Prentice-Hall: Englewood Cliffs, N.J., 1981), pp. 27–77.
[2]Reid, Marvin. "To Stay In or Sell Out," *National Petroleum News*, August 1985, p. 45.

after-tax return on equity has fallen from almost 20% in 1979–80 to only 6.9% in 1984–85 (see Exhibit A1). This falling return comes from two main sources. First, as demand remains weak and the age of assets increases, total asset turnover, an asset productivity measure, falls significantly. Second, because of the pressure put on prices by deregulation and by the elimination of benefits from refiners,[3] profit margins have dropped drastically. Although margins improved in 1985, and so far in 1986, these are the result of a market phenomenon, sticky retail prices during periods of unprecedented price decline. In other words, the improvement is a temporary result of the reluctance of marketers to pass price declines on to the consumer. Upon return to normal equilibrium, one finds that the marketer is squeezed from both sides, volume and margin.

Given these factors, it seems logical to place the petroleum marketing industry late in the life cycle. The industry has shown several classic examples of mature (stage three) behavior:

- Sales, as a percent of assets, have trended down dramatically, showing both old, deteriorating assets and market overcrowding.
- Fallout has reached an all-time high, with a definite buyer's market developing.[4]
- Prices have declined to unprecedented lows.
- The market is composed of fewer, but larger, firms.

This placement in the mature stage of the cycle suggests that, barring revolutionary changes in the industry, nothing but decline can be foreseen.

EXHIBIT A1   **Industry Dupont analysis**

Year	Profit margin	×	Total asset turns	×	Financial leverage multiplier	=	ROE
1976–1977	1.03		4.85		2.33		11.6
1977–1978	0.87		5.40		2.55		12.0
1978–1979	0.92		5.20		2.49		11.9
1979–1980	1.24		6.25		2.57		19.9
1980–1981	0.97		7.21		2.66		18.6
1981–1982	0.58		7.44		2.47		10.7
1982–1983	0.55		7.80		2.51		10.8
1983–1984	0.59		6.87		2.39		9.7
1984–1985	0.47		6.12		2.37		6.8

[3]Reid, Marvin. "To Stay In or Sell Out," *National Petroleum News*, August 1985, p. 46.
[4]*Ibid.*, p. 47.

II. CONDITION OF COMPANY

A. Life Cycle and Market

Valley Oil finds itself in the middle of this declining industry. Its position in the life cycle does not seem to be much better; in fact, Valley appears to have advanced into the early decline stage. Several factors contribute to this assessment:

- Sales/total assets have declined from over 5.8 in 1983 to only 5.31 in 1985. On a gallonage basis, where price fluctuations have less impact, there has still been a close to fifty percent decline since 1979.
- Assets (e.g., trucks, tanks, equipment) tend to be quite old. Exhibit A9 illustrates this characteristic for the tanks.
- Sales, on both an absolute dollar and a gallonage basis, are declining steadily. Although the actual percentage varies from year to year, the overall trend is distinct.

What does this imply for Valley? First, the firm must cope with trying to maintain market share and profitability in an environment where the potential for both is shrinking. Second, the firm must attempt this in spite of its own inherent limitations; it is burdened with older, shrinking-volume resellers, as well as aged vehicles and tanks.

B. Financial Trends and Earnings Capacity

The firm's financial statements do not yield a picture any more bright. First, the downward trend in sales is disturbing. Second, excluding the first half of 1985, the same trend has applied to margin. The combination of these two factors places a vise grip on profitability. In fact, if it were not for the margin windfall in the first half of this year, Valley would have taken a major blow.

C. Income-based Value

In any discounted, income-based valuation, two factors must be determined: the discount rate and the earnings base. Theoretically, the discount rate can be assumed to be the rate of return which an investor could earn on a portfolio of similar risk assets. As a starting point, one can consider that for the week of August 1, the Standard and Poor's 10-bond utility average yielded 9.03%. This range of 9% is consistent with performance over recent months and actually low for the past decade. Working from this starting point, one can logically assume that there would have to be some risk premium; therefore, a minimum capitalization rate would be 10%. As illustrated in Exhibit A2, one can use a

EXHIBIT A2 **Weighted average earnings for evaluation purposes**

Year	Weight factor	Income	W × I
1981	1	(1,536)	(1,536)
1982	2	38,032	76,064
1983	3	40,920	122,760
1984	4	42,219	168,876
1985	5	36,951	184,755
	15		550,919

Weighted Average Earnings = $36,728

weighted average of the last five years as an earnings base. This both eliminates any unusual blip in the last year and takes into account the overall trend.

When this average earnings figure is capitalized at 10%, an income-based valuation of $367,280 is determined. Using a more reasonable discount rate of 12% yields a value of $306,067.

D. Goodwill Potential

A study by David Nelson, a consultant to the Petroleum Marketing Education Foundation, shows that, of 37 sales studied in 1983, 19 received "goodwill." This ratio was down from 13 out of 18 in 1981.[5] In addition to the quantitative evidence suggesting that large blue sky premiums are a thing of the past, there are several logical arguments to support this point:

- More and more firms are entering the market on the selling side, suggesting a definite oversupply.[6]
- The firm is completely unleveraged, yet it can barely support its current operating costs. Margins are insufficient to cover fixed costs, leaving hauling fees and finance charges as the only means of profit.

Given that the industry trend is toward little or no blue sky, that Valley would be one of many firms entering the market, and that its margins do not even indicate profitable gallonage, it seems unreasonable to attach any goodwill to the earnings base or to an asset valuation.

[5]Reid, Marvin. "To Stay In or Sell Out," *National Petroleum News,* August 1985, p. 47.
[6]*Ibid.*

III. ADJUSTED ASSET VALUE

Another step that must be taken in any valuation is an assessment of the asset value of the company. If this market-related asset value is higher than the income-based value, then the business has negative operating value and is worth more liquidated.

When this step is taken with Valley, the analysis is fairly simple. (See Exhibit A3 for complete analysis). All of the current assets can be liquidated at their book value except for accounts receivables. These must be carried across to market less a 10% bad debt adjustment. This brings the value of total current assets to $620,557.

Adjustments for the fixed assets are a bit more complex. First, the land/buildings account must be adjusted to $100,000 market value. Equipment, with the exception of tanks, is valued at about $20,000 (79 pumps @ $250). The vehicles have an appraised market value of $156,500. The market value for furniture and fixtures is $7,050, giving a total market value to long-term assets of

EXHIBIT A3   **Valley Oil Co. — adjusted asset valuation**

	Book	Market
Assets		
Cash	26,558	26,558
A/R	421,308	421,308
Inventory	153,135	137,821
Refundable taxes	3,888	3,888
Prepaids	25,883	25,883
Notes receivable	5,099	5,099
Land/building	79,942	100,000
Equipment	247,258	20,000
Vehicles*	310,000	156,500
Furniture and fixtures	37,896	7,050
Less: account depreciation	(475,238)	—
Total asset value	835,729	904,107
Liabilities		
A/P	(196,670)	(196,670)
Income taxes payable	(6,899)	(6,899)
Total liabilities value	(203,569)	(203,569)
Less: Contingent tank liability	—	(90,000)
Total value	632,160	610,538

*One two-year-old tractor/trailer (9,000-gallon capacity), two older "bobtail" trucks (2,000-gallon capacity), and one older service van.

$283,550. The next step to be followed is to deduct any liabilities. These are deducted at book value of $203,569.

The final step in the adjusted asset valuation is to consider any hidden assets or liabilities. These can take several forms:

- Undervalued real estate which could actually bring much more than its book value;
- Exclusive distribution contracts or other market-related, hidden assets; and
- Contingent liabilities such as pending lawsuits or potential lawsuits from sources such as leaking underground tanks.

The first of these is ruled out by the fact that Valley owns only one piece of real estate, which was recently appraised and is included in the valuation at its appraised value of $100,000. Neither does the second factor enter into the value — Valley has no unique market-related advantages.

The question of contingent liabilities is important; the possibility that one or more of the approximately 90 tanks could develop or already possess a leak is far from remote. According to Steffen Plenn, author of *Underground Tankage: The Liability of Leaks,* as many as thirty percent of the steel tanks currently in the ground may be leaking. What's worse, that number is expected to rise. The volatile nature of this problem is most clearly seen in its propensity to wind up in court. Plenn explains that these leaks, when discovered, are disasters of a magnitude that will not avoid court.[7] The most serious implication, however, is that the liability has historically extended to all owners of the tanks, both past and present, vis-a-vis the concept of joint and several liability. Thus, in the process of any rationally executed liquidation, the seller would have to remove each of the older tanks. In the case of Valley, this cost would amount to approximately $90,000.[8] Deducting this contingent tank liability (cost of removal) from the previously computed values yields a liquidation value of $610,538.

IV. CONCLUSION

This now presents us with two different values for consideration:

1. The income-based value of $367,280 and
2. The adjusted asset liquidation basis of $610,538.

---

[7]Plenn, Steffen W., *Underground Tankage: The Liability of Leaks* (Petroleum Marketing Education Foundation: Alexandria, VA, 1986), pp. 9–12.
[8]Ascertained in conversation with a local contractor. Confirmed by recent removals of similar tanks.

Realizing that

- the liquidation value exceeds the income-based value;
- there is a trend toward decreasing blue sky premiums;
- goodwill is usually paid for growing or unusually profitable gallons, of which Valley has none;
- there is a significant contingent liability attached to the tanks, all of which cannot be eliminated by tank removal (due to potential for previous leaks); and, finally,
- Valley is a declining firm in a mature industry,

we recommend use of the adjusted asset liquidation value of $610,538 as our best estimate of market value.

EXHIBIT A4   **Valley Oil Co. — income statement information**

For the years ended 1984 and 1985

	1984	1985
Other expenses		
Advertising	6,254	6,921
Office expense	7,066	10,566
Utilities	5,033	4,806
Insurance	15,360	37,855
Telephone	3,327	4,310
Rent*	27,163	27,940
Professional fees	7,483	10,503
Repairs	34,445	32,026
Directors' fees	4,800	4,800
Travel	5,982	10,178
Dues and subscriptions	4,786	4,442
Contributions	1,520	4,403
Sales promotion	5,705	5,736
Miscellaneous	—	673
Pension plan expense	1,072	—
Employee benefits	28,834	33,448
Bad debts	28,091	25,552
Total	186,921	224,159

*Rent on bulk plant and corporate office.

EXHIBIT A5   Valley Oil Co. — statement of income for the years ended 1981–1985

	1981	1982	1983	1984	1985
Gallons*					
Premium	NA	NA	NA	NA	382,869
Unleaded	NA	NA	NA	NA	1,152,730
Regular	3,956,353	3,316,151	4,004,842	3,101,595	1,418,560
Lube	NA	NA	NA	NA	NA
Heating oil	978,113	1,004,000	1,057,131	1,137,072	1,267,011
Diesel	NA	NA	NA	NA	NA
Kerosene	286,870	286,430	262,802	310,066	315,739
Other products	NA	NA	NA	NA	NA
Total	5,221,336	4,606,581	5,324,775	4,548,733	4,536,909
Sales					
Premium	NA	NA	NA	NA	358,038
Unleaded	NA	NA	NA	NA	1,038,871
Regular	NA	NA	NA	3,061,113	1,222,758
Lube	NA	NA	NA	95,781	100,922
Heating oil	NA	NA	NA	1,172,390	871,031
Diesel	NA	NA	NA	NA	355,966
Kerosene	NA	NA	NA	364,573	359,583
Other products	NA	NA	NA	NA	92,493
Net sales	4,734,881	4,332,049	4,657,833	4,234,277	4,279,681
Cost of sales					
Beginning inventory	211,832	210,000	192,449	153,639	160,344
Purchases net of discounts	4,292,934	3,873,798	4,138,784	3,752,969	3,714,003
	4,504,766	4,083,798	4,331,233	3,906,608	3,874,347
Ending inventory	210,000	192,449	153,639	160,344	153,135
Cost of sales	4,294,766	3,891,349	4,177,594	3,746,264	3,721,212
Gross profit	440,115	440,700	480,239	488,013	558,469
Selling, general & admin. expenses					
Licenses & non-income taxes	23,584	24,450	25,943	25,810	22,252
Vehicle expense	100,471	61,397	85,365	74,066	81,748
Officers' salaries	45,500	49,414	48,700	51,000	53,100
Other salaries and wages	155,843	142,087	154,104	148,434	162,161
Other expense	145,081	168,015	168,076	186,921	224,159
Depreciation	44,428	38,032	36,920	54,639	61,015
Interest	10,025	3,496	5,272	7,144	11,203
On borrowing needs	0	0	0	0	0
Operating income (loss)	(84,817)	(46,191)	(44,141)	(60,001)	(57,169)
Earnings on marketable securities	8,746	14,493	5,134	6,426	8,103
Other income (hauling income)	72,552	74,672	90,703	96,501	95,066
Earnings before taxes	(3,519)	42,974	51,696	42,926	46,000
Provision for federal income taxes	(1,983)	4,942	10,776	707	9,049
Net income	(1,536)	38,032	40,920	42,219	36,951

*From 1981 to 1984, gallonage data is available only as aggregate gasoline sales — these are entered as regular. Likewise, during the entire five-year period, heating oil and diesel are combined under heating oil. During the same time period, dollar values are often unavailable.

EXHIBIT A6   Valley Oil Co. — balance sheet for the years ended 1981–1985

	Year 1981	Year 1982	Year 1983	Year 1984	Year 1985
Assets					
Current assets					
Cash	64,468	31,922	24,076	10,000	26,558
Marketable securities	0	0	0	0	0
Accounts rec	656,187	579,313	471,803	470,120	421,308
Inventories	210,000	192,449	153,639	160,344	153,135
Refundable taxes	33,054	0	0	9,920	3,888
Prepaid exp	2,636	1,535	1,526	1,766	25,883
Notes receivable	1,804	40,277	14,481	59,342	5,099
Other current assets	0	0	0	0	0
Total current assets	968,149	845,496	665,525	711,492	635,871
Property plant and equipment					
Land	79,942	79,942	79,942	79,942	79,942
Buildings	0	0	0	0	0
Equipment	207,463	216,139	208,116	207,873	227,444
Vehicles	247,339	274,634	253,153	279,634	255,355
Furniture and fixtures	5,032	21,588	22,393	24,388	30,464
Total	539,776	592,303	563,604	591,837	593,205
Less accumulated depreciation	392,800	430,332	427,310	392,465	422,781
Net property plant and equipment	146,976	161,971	136,294	199,372	170,424
Other assets					
Long-term investments	0	0	0	0	0
Deposits and licenses	0	0	0	0	0
Cash surrender value — officers' life insurance	0	0	0	0	0
Loan fees — net	0	0	0	0	0
Advances to affiliated companies	0	0	0	0	0
Total other assets	0	0	0	0	0
Total assets	1,115,125	1,007,467	801,819	910,864	806,295

EXHIBIT A6   **Valley Oil Co. — balance sheet for the years ended 1981–1985 (*cont.*)**

	Year 1981	Year 1982	Year 1983	Year 1984	Year 1985
Liabilities					
Current liabilities					
Accounts payable	670,524	474,892	272,434	295,092	196,670
Notes payable	0	45,000	0	50,000	0
Current portion of long-term debt	0	0	0	0	0
Construction loan payable	0	0	0	0	0
Income taxes payable	0	4,942	5,832	0	6,899
Advances from officers	0	0	0	0	0
Accrued expenses	0	0	0	0	0
Other current liabilities	0	0	0	0	0
Other financing needed	0	0	0	0	0
Total current liabilities	670,524	524,834	278,266	345,092	203,569
Long-term debt	0	0	0	0	0
Other long-term debt	0	0	0	0	0
Total liabilities	670,524	524,834	278,266	345,092	203,569
Owners' equity	444,601	482,633	523,553	565,772	602,726
Total liabilities & owners' equity	1,115,125	1,007,467	801,819	910,864	806,295

EXHIBIT A7   Valley Oil Co. — selected ratios for the years ended 1981–1985

Ratio analysis	Year 1981	Year 1982	Year 1983	Year 1984	Year 1985
Dupont analysis					
Return on sales	−0.03%	0.88%	0.88%	1.00%	0.86%
× Asset turnover	4.25	4.30	5.81	4.65	5.31
= Return on assets	−0.14%	3.78%	5.10%	4.64%	4.58%
× Financial leverage	2.51	2.09	1.53	1.61	1.34
= Return on equity	−0.35%	7.88%	7.82%	7.46%	6.13%
Activity					
Fixed asset turnover	32.22	26.75	34.17	21.24	25.11
Sales growth (dollars)	−16.28%	−8.51%	7.52%	−9.09%	1.07%
Sales growth (gallons)	−30.65%	−11.77%	15.59%	−14.57%	−0.26%
Profitability					
Gross margin	9.30%	10.17%	10.31%	11.53%	13.05%
Salaries ratio (officers' salaries + sales)	0.96%	1.14%	1.05%	1.20%	1.24%
S, G, & A ratio (S, G, & A + sales)	9.94%	10.28%	10.35%	11.48%	12.70%
Working capital usage					
Days payable	51.69	40.01	21.35	25.44	16.77
Collection period (days)	50.58	48.81	36.97	40.52	35.93
Days inventory	16.19	16.21	12.04	13.82	13.06
Cash cycle [(collect. pd. + inv.) − day's pay.]	15.08	25.01	27.66	28.91	32.22
Leverage					
Total debt/assets	60.13%	52.09%	34.70%	37.89%	25.25%
Long-term debt/assets	0.00	0.00	0.00	0.00	0.00
Times interest EBIT	−7.46	−12.21	−7.37	−7.40	−4.10
Liquidity					
Current ratio	1.44	1.61	2.39	2.06	3.12
Acid test ratio	1.13	1.24	1.84	1.60	2.37

EXHIBIT A8   **Valley Oil Co. — annual station gallons (1985)**

Stations*	
1	346,279
2	160,316
3	128,620
4	111,702
5	105,036
6	116,286
7	37,894
8	19,746
9	121,440
10**	244,802
11	304,772
12	189,422
13	196,152
14	148,226
15	47,118
16	130,472
17	100,106
18	220,440
Total	2,728,829

*Reseller locations with contracts ranging from 2–5 years.
**Wholly owned by Valley Oil with appraised value of $100,000 (good potential, 4-lane interceptor, C-store location).

EXHIBIT A9   **Valley Oil Co. — capacity and age of tanks**

Sites*	Capacity	Age	Type	Product
1	4000	12	steel	gas
	4000	12	"	"
	3000	25	"	"
	4000	25	"	"
	3000	25	"	"
2	2000	7	"	"
	2000	7	"	"
	1000	2	"	"
3	1000	8	"	"
	1000	8	"	"
4	1000	10	"	"
	1000	10	"	"
	1000	10	"	"
5	2000	20	"	"
	1000	20	"	"
	1000	20	"	"
6	1000	12	"	"
	1000	10	"	diesel
	1000	10	"	"
7	1000	15	"	gas
	1000	15	"	"
	2000	10	"	"
	1000	1	"	"
	1000	1 month	"	"
8	1000	25	"	"
	2000	3	"	"
	2000	3	"	"
	2000	3	"	"
9	2000	10	"	"
	4000	11	"	"
	3000	11	"	"
	3000	11	"	"
	1000	11	"	"
10	1000	12	"	"
	1000	5	"	"
11	1000	15	"	diesel
	1000	15	"	gas
12	10000	15	"	"
	4000	15	"	"
	4000	15	"	"
	1000	15	"	kerosene
13	1000	12	"	gas
	1000	12	"	"
	1000	12	"	"

EXHIBIT A9   Valley Oil Co.—capacity and age of tanks (*cont.*)

Sites*	Capacity	Age	Type	Product
14	2000	14	"	"
	1000	14	"	"
15	1000	12	"	"
	1000	12	"	diesel
	2000	12	"	fuel oil
16	10000	10	"	gas
	2000	10	"	"
17	2000	10	"	"
18	1000	5	"	"
	1000	5	"	"
19	1000	9	"	"
	1000	9	"	"
	1000	9	"	"
20	10000	35	"	diesel
21	20000	15	"	fuel oil
	20000	15	"	"
	20000	15	"	"
	20000	15	"	
	20000	15	"	gas
	20000	15	"	"
	20000	15	"	"
	20000	15	"	"
	10000	15	"	"
	6266	35	"	kerosene
	6266	35	"	"
	5631	35	"	"
	6266	35	"	"
	6266	35	"	"
	6266	35	"	"
	6769	35	"	"
22	4000	10	"	gas
	4000	10	"	"
	3000	10	"	"
	3000	25	"	"
	3000	25	"	"
23	1000	20	"	"
	1000	20	"	"
24	2000	7	"	"
	1000	7	"	"
	1000	7	"	kerosene
	1000	7	"	kerosene
25	2000	11	"	gas
	2000	11	"	"

*Sites include reseller locations, large individual users, and bulk plant (No. 21).

CITICORP—BRITISH NATIONAL LIFE ASSURANCE

Ira Rimerman, Group Executive, Consumer Services Group, International, Citicorp, was in his third-floor office at Citicorp's headquarters in New York City on January 16, 1986, when he received notice from the Board of Citicorp that his MEP (Major Expenditure Proposal) to acquire the British National Life Assurance Company, Ltd. (BNLA), in England had been approved. For a total investment of $33.3 million, Citicorp was now in the life underwriting business.[1]

Although pleased with the Board's approval, there were several issues on Mr. Rimerman's mind as he thought back over the last few months when his staff analyzed and developed suggestions for a business strategy for BNLA, including key policies, tactics, and organizational changes.

CITICORP'S HISTORY

Citicorp's corporate history spanned 175 years, from its inception as a small commerical bank in New York City in 1812 through its growth into one of the

This case was prepared by Professors John M. Gwin, Per V. Jenster, and William K. Carter for the sixth McIntire Commerce Invitational (MCI VI) held at the University of Virginia on February 11–14, 1987. We gratefully acknowledge the General Electric Foundation for its support of the MCI and of the preparation of this case. We are also grateful to Citicorp for its willing cooperation in this project.

[1]All financial information related to BNLA has been changed for proprietary reasons.

EXHIBIT 1   **Citicorp and subsidiaries**

Revenues earned and rates of return achieved

	Revenues (billions)	ROA	ROE
1981	$4.0	.46%	13%
1982	$5.1	.59%	16%
1983	$5.8	.67%	16%
1984	$6.6	.62%	15%
1985	$8.5	.62%	15%

ROE = (net income − preferred dividends) / average common equity
ROA = net income / average total assets

Source: 1985 Annual Report of Citicorp.

world's largest financial services intermediaries. A recurring historical theme seemed to be the firm's ability to correctly identify the developing trends in the marketplace and to devise appropriate strategies for taking advantage of them.

The firm first emerged as a significant bank in the latter part of the nineteenth century by responding successfully to the transition of the United States from an agricultural to an industrial economy. Since the mid-1960s, the firm had transcended the corporate treasurer and the metropolitan New Yorker as its sole funding sources and found ways to attract the more than $1.5 trillion consumer savings market in the United States.

During the 1960s and 1970s, Citicorp completed two separate but integral strategic efforts that revolutionized the company and influenced the whole financial services industry. First, in 1967, the firm formed a bank holding company, which permitted it to broaden its geographic and product bases. Second, in the early 1970s, it redefined its business from a US commercial bank with branches abroad to a global financial services enterprise with the United States as its home base. By 1980, the firm had further broadened its scope by defining its business as that of providing services and information to solve financial needs. Exhibits 1 and 2A, 2B, and 2C provide a summary of the firm's financial profile.

CITICORP'S STRATEGY

The firm's strategic plan called for three separate kinds of world-class banks, all of which could leverage off an unrivaled global network. By the mid-1980s, the Investment Bank, also known as the Capital Markets Group, enabled the firm to fully intermediate the capital flows of the world, with over $6 billion in transactions in the swap market. The Institutional Bank was the principal supplier of financial service mechanisms to corporations and governments

EXHIBIT 2A   **Citicorp and subsidiaries**

Consolidated balance sheet (in billions of dollars)

	12–31–85	12–31–84
ASSETS		
Cash, deposits with banks, and securities	$ 40	$ 31
Commercial loans	$ 58	$ 59
Consumer loans	55	43
Lease financing	3	2
Allowance for credit losses	1	1
Net	$115	$103
Premises and other assets	18	17
Total	$173	$151
LIABILITIES		
Deposits	$105	$ 90
Borrowings and other liabilities	42	39
Long-term debt	16	13
Capital notes and redeemable preferred	2	2
	$165	$144
STOCKHOLDERS' EQUITY		
Preferred stock	1	1
Common stock	1	1
Additional paid-in capital	1	1
Retained earnings	5	4
	$ 8	$ 7
TOTAL	$173	$151

Source: 1985 Annual Report of Citicorp.

worldwide. Finally, the Individual Bank served the individual consumer on a worldwide basis.

Walter B. Wriston, former chairman of Citicorp/Citibank, explained the firm's strategy:

> Over time, it seemed to us, the institution without access to the consumer would slowly become an institution without adequate funding. In addition, consumer-led economic recoveries are becoming more the rule than the exception and we looked for ways to participate. For all of these reasons, you have often heard about this consumer transition and the identification of the consumer as a key to our strategy in the middle '70s. It was usually described as risky but there are also risks in doing nothing.[2]

[2] *The Citi of Tomorrow: Today,* Walter B. Wriston's address to the Bank and Financial Analysts Association, New York, March 7, 1984.

EXHIBIT 2B

Citicorp and subsidiaries

Consolidated income statement (in billions of dollars, except per-share amounts)

	1985	1984	1983
Interest revenue	$19.5	$18.2	$15.2
Less: Interest expense	14.0	13.9	11.2
Provision for credit losses	1.3	.6	.5
Net	$ 4.2	$ 3.7	$ 3.5
Other revenues	3.0	2.3	1.8
	$ 7.2	$ 6.0	$ 5.3
Operating expenses	5.5	4.5	3.7
Income before income taxes	$ 1.7	$ 1.5	$ 1.6
Income taxes	.7	.6	.7
Net income	$ 1.0	$ .9	$ .9
Earnings per share:			
Common and equivalent	$ 7.12	$ 6.45	$ 6.48
Fully diluted	7.11	6.36	6.15

EXHIBIT 2C

Citibank and subsidiaries

Consolidated balance sheet (in billions of dollars)

	12–31–1985	12–31–1984
ASSETS		
Cash, deposits with banks, and securities	$ 40	$ 28
Loans and lease financing, net	75	69
Premises and other assets	16	15
Total	$131	$112
LIABILITIES		
Deposits	$ 92	$ 78
Borrowings and other liabilities	29	26
Long-term debt	3	2
	$124	$106
STOCKHOLDERS' EQUITY		
Capital stock	1	1
Additional paid-in capital	1	1
Retained earnings	5	4
	$ 7	$ 6
Total	$131	$112

Source: 1985 Annual Report of Citicorp.

The holding company structure was used to overcome the geographic constraints of the domestic businesses. It also allowed for a few acquisitions and for the creation of de novo units to build a global network which, among other things, featured a unique competitive franchise for bank cards within the Individual Bank. Wriston also remarked:

> It costs about $150 per year to service an individual through a branch system. That number plummets to $20 if we use the credit card as our primary delivery vehicle. In short, through fees and merchant discounts, the card as a stand-alone product is a profitable endeavor. By the 1990s, it may well become the core delivery mechanism when augmented by automatic teller machines and home banking.... We envision a world of 35 million Citicorp customers producing earnings of $30 per customer.... We had big plans for this group when it started and we can now see a time by which it will become a billion dollar business.

The 1980s also dictated a new philosophy, which differed from traditional bank practice and from the media's bias for focusing on size as a measure of success. Commercial asset growth on the books of Citicorp was discouraged. In fact, management stretched its imagination to take assets off the firm's books, not to put them on. In 1983, more than $2 billion in loans generated in the United States by the Institutional Bank was sold to others by the Investment Bank. That number was expected to reach $20 billion by 1989. Wriston further explained:

> Our stockholders benefit, since we keep part of the spread while someone else keeps the assets (and the risk). But in order to make this a viable business, you must have both the asset generating capability and the distribution capability nationwide and worldwide.

The worldwide orientation was further encouraged as cross-border lending started to slow down. Citicorp predicted that individual countries would be forced to develop their own indigenous capital markets. Thus, there was an opportunity to develop a "multi-domestic" strategy which would enable Citicorp to offer full financial services in 60–80 countries before 1990.

The Five I's

In the early 1980s, Citicorp added two more "I's" to the strategic thrust which had initially included development of the Investment Bank, the Individual Bank, and the Institutional Bank. The two embryonic "I's" were the Information and Insurance businesses. According to Wriston,

> We want to be in the information business simply because we are in the information business. Information about money has become almost as important as money itself. As bankers, we are familiar with the time value of money. As investors, we must think of the time value of information. The core of any decision making process is information. The fact that you know

something relevant before, or more clearly than your competitors may lead you to act sooner, to your advantage. Herein lies the problem, determining what is relevant. Hence, the packaging of information and its distribution will be critical.... We eventually intend to become a main competitor, as a preeminent distributor of financial data-base services worldwide. This is only possible with a truly global system, one through which information is distributed with electrons rather than the mail.[3]

The rationale for entering the insurance business was simple: insurance services accounted for fully 40% of all financial services in 1985. Citicorp would therefore not be a truly effective financial services enterprise without offering these products. Insurance was also a natural adjunct to the consumer business, considering the outmoded and expensive agency method of distribution that dominated the industry. Moreover, the firm was already a major factor in credit insurance. For example, one-third of its second-mortgage customers bought credit life insurance.

The Banking Holding Company Act of 1956, and specifically Regulation Y, Section 4(c)–8 for the Board of Governors of the Federal Reserve System, prohibited banks from engaging in life insurance underwriting (with certain exceptions). Thus, the firm's insurance strategy was primarily aimed at an overseas expansion. This expansion was made possible by the Federal Reserve Board's ruling, requested by Citicorp, which enabled the firm to establish a fully competitive insurance operation in the United Kingdom. The Board concluded:

The general activity of underwriting life insurance in the United Kingdom can be considered usual in connection with banking or other financial operations in the United Kingdom.

This shift in the Board's attitude enabled Citicorp to consider expansion into insurance, to identify the UK as a potential country in which to do so, and ultimately to pursue BNLA for acquisition.

Citicorp's goals for the five I's as of 1986 can be summarized as follows[4]:

1. Institutional
    Trim work force from 20,000 to 17,000
    Pull back from middle markets overseas
    Push investment banking products more
    Clean up loan portfolio, reduce write-offs

2. Investment
    Build credible corporate finance group, especially in mergers and acquisitions
    Hold onto investment banking talent

[3]Consistent with these plans, Citicorp acquired Quotron, a firm specializing in informational data bases.
[4]Source: Citicorp and *Business Week*, December 8, 1986.

Wire 90 trading rooms around the globe
Improve coordination between London, Tokyo, and New York

3. Individual
Continue to grow fast in retail banking
Make all acquired S&L's profitable
Push international consumer business

4. Information
Leave Quotron alone to calm customers
Develop new products

5. Insurance
Push for easing limits on banks
Grow overseas
Cross-sell more insurance products through customer base

The 1985 sector performance is displayed in Exhibit 3.

CITICORP'S STRUCTURE AND OBJECTIVES

The Investment Bank, the Institutional Bank, and the Individual Bank were each organized into a sector and headed by a sector executive. Activities related to insurance and information were under the auspices of group executives within the three sectors, until such time as they justified the creation of their own sectors.

Each of the three sectors was composed of several groups, divisions, and business families, headed by a group executive, with business managers reporting to him or her. The organization of the Individual Bank, which is of particular interest in this case, was somewhat different from the other Banks. As dictated in John S. Reed's (chairman of Citicorp since 1985) memorandum of March 9, 1976 (internally known as the "Memo from the Beach"), the business manager was responsible for the day-to-day operation, whereas a division executive's responsibility was strategic in nature.

This meant that a branch manager in, say, Hong Kong, would report to an area manager, then a country manager, a division manager, a group executive, a vice-chairman or sector executive, and then the chairman. In effect, the flat structure placed only three layers of management between the most junior branch manager and the Policy Committee (thirty senior executives) of Citicorp.

In January 1986, Reed issued a set of guidelines developed by the Policy Committee, which included Citicorp's objectives for the next ten years (Exhibit 4) and its values (Exhibit 5). Exhibit 6 (A and B) displays the organizational structure of the Individual Bank and Consumer Services Group International.

EXHIBIT 3   **Citicorp and subsidiaries**

Sector performance (in millions of dollars)

	1985	1984	% change
INDIVIDUAL BANK			
Net revenue	$4,120	$3,107	33
Operating expenses	3,614	2,735	32
Other income and expense	102	(12)	n.a.
Income before taxes	608	360	69
Net income	$ 340	$ 222	53
ROA	.61%	.51%	
ROE	15.3 %	12.7 %	
INSTITUTIONAL BANK			
Net revenue	$2,168	$2,068	5
Operating expenses	1,500	1,275	18
Income before taxes	668	793	(16)
Net income	$ 392	$ 454	(14)
ROA	.54%	.64%	
ROE	13.6 %	15.9 %	
INVESTMENT BANK			
Net revenue	$1,589	$1,241	28
Operating expenses	803	587	37
Income before taxes	786	654	20
Net income	$ 425	$ 343	24
ROA	1.34%	1.33%	
ROE	33.5 %	33.2 %	
UNALLOCATED			
(Certain corporate-level items which are not allocated among sectors)			
Revenue	$ 28	$ (79)	n.a.
Operating expenses	148	116	28
Additional provision for credit losses	226	68	132
Income before taxes	(346)	(263)	(32)
Net income	(159)	(129)	(23)

Source: 1985 Annual Report of Citicorp.

EXHIBIT 4   **Citicorp objectives**

January 29, 1986

Citicorp's objective is to continue to build the world's leading financial services organization by creating value for our stockholders, customers, staff members and the communities where we live and work. Creation of value is dependent on building an internal environment based on integrity, innovation, teamwork and a commitment to unquestioned financial strength.

Value for the shareholder

— 12–18% compound growth in earnings per share

— Improving return on equity to 17–18% (maintaining the internal hurdle at 20%)

— A strong balance sheet, including a 10% capital position and a AA+ credit rating

— Performance profile (earnings, market position, returns) improving within the top 30 companies in the world

— Improving market position for our businesses, defined by explicit market share reporting

— Well-diversified geographic and business earnings, assets, and liabilities

Value for our customer

Maintain and build our two customer sets, institutional and individual, through customer service excellence, professionalism, product innovation, and the energy of our response to customer needs. Regularly monitor progress through external and internal surveys.

Value for our staff

Maintain an open, challenging, rewarding, and healthy working environment characterized by excellence and fairness in dealing with our employees. Business unit management is responsible for maintaining this working environment, and will support and adhere to the People Management beliefs outlined in the attached statement. We will regularly monitor such support and adherence with specific, measurable, goals.

Value for the communities in which we operate

Management of each business unit and/or geographic location is part of the community within which we operate and has an obligation:

— to contribute to community values.
— to participate in appropriate ways.
— to work to change the legal and regulatory environment to enhance our "opportunity space."
— to deal with our communities in an open, straightforward manner.

EXHIBIT 5   **Excellence in people management**

What We Believe

The Basics

While people management is a part of our business, there are certain non-negotiable assumptions we make about how we will deal with the people who make up Citicorp. These basics must take precedence in everything we do.

> Respect for individuals
> Treating people with dignity, openness, honesty, and fairness

Citicorp Values

In addition to our other specific Citicorp values (Innovation, Integrity, and Service Excellence), we have a set of values related to people management. These are things we feel strongly about, and which are driven by the needs of our business.

> *Meritocracy.* Emphasizing excellence of performance, professionalism, and effectiveness as the determining factors for selection, retention, rewards, and advancement. Recognizing good performance wherever and whenever it occurs. Appropriately exiting consistent nonperformers.

> *Independent Initiative.* Promoting personal freedom to act and allowing people to succeed and to learn from failure.

> *Listening.* Creating an environment where we really hear what people say. Working together so that people throughout the organization have an impact.

> *Development.* Consciously building experience and talent of our people with the goal of professional growth. Creating a balance between developmental experiences and current contribution.

Working Style

Our working styles will vary in different business situations and environments. The following describe the ways in which we approach people management, each applied as appropriate to individual business conditions.

> *Teamwork.* Building effective business-driven partnerships within the organization. Achieving a balance between cooperation and entrepreneurial spirit.

> *Integration.* Helping new people and new businesses to effectively and appropriately become part of the Citicorp culture.

THE INTERNATIONAL OPPORTUNITY

In the 1985 Annual Report,[5] the board stated:

> We recognize that, ultimately, our success will be directly attributable to our ability to offer our consumers worldwide preeminent service for each of their relationships with us. Our view is that

---

[5]Citicorp 1985 Annual Report, p. 11.

EXHIBIT 6A   **Individual bank**

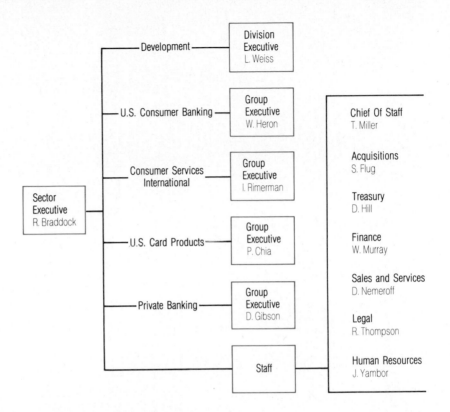

by pursuing service excellence across all of our efforts, we enhance our standing with our customers and thereby the likelihood that they will choose us for a growing share of their financial needs.

Internationally, Citicorp expanded its presence in a number of markets during 1985, while maintaining returns well in excess of corporate standards. In that year, Citicorp completed significant acquisitions in Italy (Banca Centro Sud), Belgium (Banque Sud Belge), and Chile (Corporacion Financiera Atlas), as well as consumer businesses in Colombia, Guam, and India.

Richard S. Braddock, sector executive of the Individual Bank and director of Citicorp and Citibank, explained:

> We view our opportunities in the international marketplace as substantial, not only because our share tends to be relatively small in most places, but also because we have the opportunity to apply lessons learned from market to market and to expand attractive and proven product packages.[6]

[6]Citicorp 1985 Annual Report, p. 11.

EXHIBIT 6B   Consumer Services Group-International (individual bank)

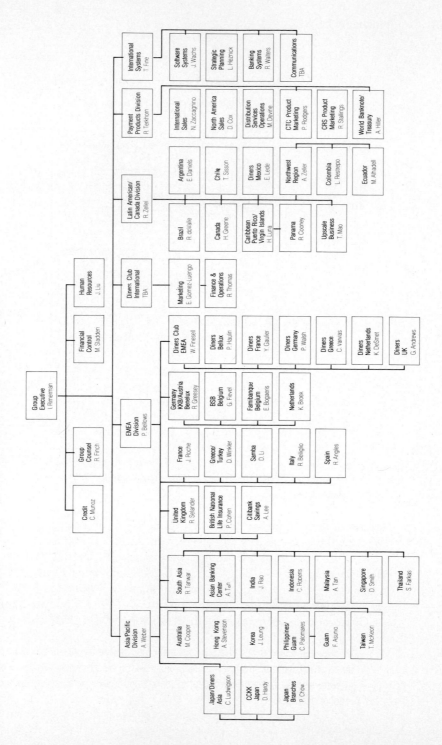

The Consumer Service Group, International (CSGI)

The Consumer Service Group, International, within the Individual Bank, was organized in separate divisions: the Asia-Pacific division had its headquarters in Tokyo; Europe-Middle East-Africa (EMEA) division, in London; the Western division, in Rio de Janeiro; Payment Products Division (Diners Club), in Chicago; and Systems Division, in New York. The group employed 26,000 people in 70 businesses, located in 40 countries.

John Liu, Senior Human Resource Officer, Consumer Services Group, International, summarized how Citicorp's culture was reflected by the Group:

> We want to be part of the largest low-cost provider of financial service in the world. As such we don't focus only on banks such as Chase Manhattan. Rather, we look also at Sears, AMEX, and others who provide financial services. This is the stretch we hold in front of us.
>
> In order to help achieve this, we have to find new ways of doing things. Taking insurance as an example, Citicorp practices its decentralized operational mode, sometimes referred to as the "thousand flowers" approach.
>
> In insurance, to use a metaphor, we want to have a thousand flowers bloom. Over time, we'll put the flowers together in a bouquet, and if we don't like the shape of it, we'll take this or that flower away. However, today we just started our picking and that is why you'll find insurance activities in the Institutional Bank (commercial insurance), the Investment Bank (brokerage insurance activities), and with us in the Individual Bank (life underwriting, mortgage insurance, etc.). It's all emerging slowly out of our philosophy, and the BNLA acquisition is the first major life underwriting acquisition we have ever had.
>
> As part of this stretch, the corporation applies certain hurdle rates to guide this vision. We have a stated hurdle rate, internally, such as a ROE of no less than 20%. Additionally, we also have a ROA hurdle rate of 90 basis points. In our group, we use our own internal hurdle rates as a way of managing our businesses. One such hurdle rate which comes to mind is to target a ratio of 1.5 between consumer net revenue and delivery expenses.
>
> Within the Group, we want to more than double our earnings over the next five years. We want to do this partly through acquisitions, of which we must have done at least 10 over the past three years and added more than 6,000 people. Although we still will make acquisitions, we clearly must slow down and develop these new businesses.
>
> The acquisitions have not been hostile and for the most part have been either "hospitalized" or unprofitable businesses. This has given us certain advantages, but also created challenges when it comes to integrating a new business into our organization.[7]

The unique culture and reward system of CSGI is reflected in Exhibit 7, which summarizes the results of an organizational survey of its senior managers.

[7]Interview with John Liu.

EXHIBIT 7   Summary of organizational surveys conducted by the case writers

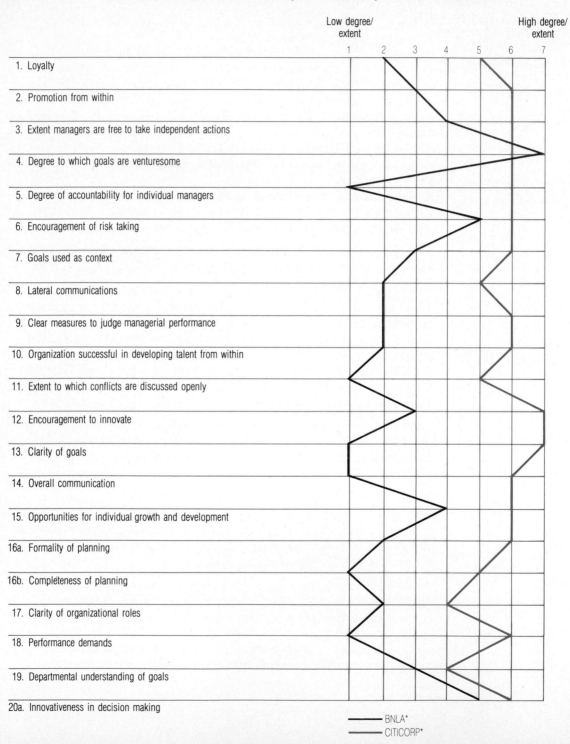

	Low degree/extent						High degree/extent
	1	2	3	4	5	6	7
1. Loyalty							
2. Promotion from within							
3. Extent managers are free to take independent actions							
4. Degree to which goals are venturesome							
5. Degree of accountability for individual managers							
6. Encouragement of risk taking							
7. Goals used as context							
8. Lateral communications							
9. Clear measures to judge managerial performance							
10. Organization successful in developing talent from within							
11. Extent to which conflicts are discussed openly							
12. Encouragement to innovate							
13. Clarity of goals							
14. Overall communication							
15. Opportunities for individual growth and development							
16a. Formality of planning							
16b. Completeness of planning							
17. Clarity of organizational roles							
18. Performance demands							
19. Departmental understanding of goals							
20a. Innovativeness in decision making							

——— BNLA*
——— CITICORP*

EXHIBIT 7   **Summary of organizational surveys conducted by the case writers (*cont.*)**

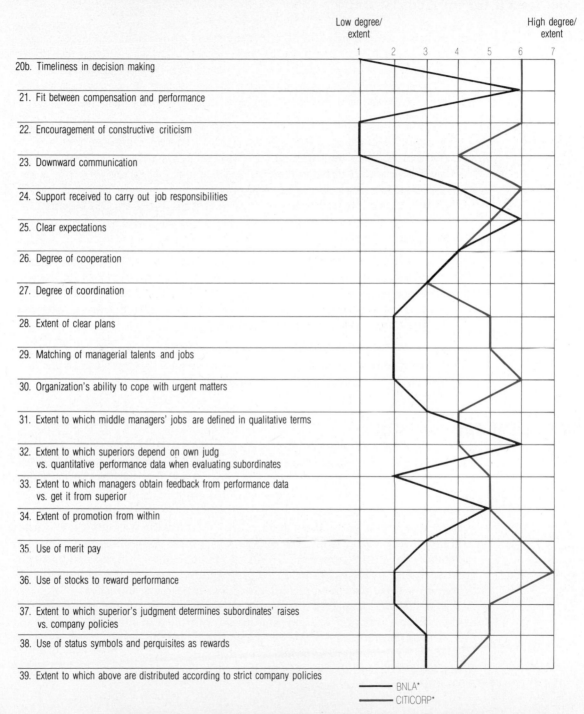

Low degree/extent — 1 2 3 4 5 6 7 — High degree/extent

20b. Timeliness in decision making

21. Fit between compensation and performance

22. Encouragement of constructive criticism

23. Downward communication

24. Support received to carry out job responsibilities

25. Clear expectations

26. Degree of cooperation

27. Degree of coordination

28. Extent of clear plans

29. Matching of managerial talents and jobs

30. Organization's ability to cope with urgent matters

31. Extent to which middle managers' jobs are defined in qualitative terms

32. Extent to which superiors depend on own judg vs. quantitative performance data when evaluating subordinates

33. Extent to which managers obtain feedback from performance data vs. get it from superior

34. Extent of promotion from within

35. Use of merit pay

36. Use of stocks to reward performance

37. Extent to which superior's judgment determines subordinates' raises vs. company policies

38. Use of status symbols and perquisites as rewards

39. Extent to which above are distributed according to strict company policies

———— BNLA*
———— CITICORP*

*Questionnaires were completed by managers and outside observers. Items of the questionnaire are summarized and labeled for proprietary reasons; values indicate average scores.

The Search for an Acquisition

Liu further explained how the BNLA acquisition came about:

> About three years ago, we started a drive to get into insurance and encouraged our people in the UK, Australia, Germany, and Belgium to start to look into insurance. As you know, there are three ways you can get into a new business: You can a) acquire, b) start a de novo unit, or c) do a joint venture.
>
> In England, which was one of the largest and most profitable markets (relatively) for life insurance, we initially identified Excelsior Life Assurance[8] as a possibility in early 1984. As an insurance company of substantial size in the UK, the acquisition would immediately bring us into this market on a large scale. However, the more we analyzed the numbers, the more concerned we got. This was a significant investment, and we had little knowledge about life insurance. So when our joint-venture partner (a large U.S. insurance company) withdrew, we reconsidered our options.
>
> Then Citicorp's UK Country Manager and the European Division Manager of the United Kingdom sponsored (identified) BNLA as a potential candidate for our move into life underwriting insurance. After the identification of the candidate, an acquisition team was put together. The team consisted of people from across our UK businesses as well as outside consultants and were all selected for their specific skills as they related to this opportunity.
>
> One of the important issues for us is now to decide how to integrate the business—should we fully integrate, keep it at an arm's-length distance, or somewhere in between, and how should we do it. With this decision also comes the question of what type of person to put into the driver's seat.

The United Kingdom (UK)

The UK economy is the sixth-largest in the world and is in transition, as is the U.S. economy, from an industrial to a service orientation. By 1985, the UK had the lowest level of legal/regulatory control for domestic and international financial activity of any developed country. However, UK regulation of life insurance underwriting, particularly with regard to reserves, was among the most stringent in the world. The government was considered politically stable, and the conservatives in power were committed to controlling inflation and government spending to provide a platform for economic growth. Even though 12% of the work force was unemployed, there was little social unrest.

The UK was expected to remain self-sufficient in oil for the remainder of the century. Inflation was expected to be controlled in the 5–7% range, and there were expected to be no major changes in either the political system or the regulatory environment. Expected growth figures for UK GNP for 1986 and 1987 were 1.5% and 2.6%, respectively. Inflation was expected to be around 5.0% for the same two periods.

[8]The name has been changed to protect confidentiality.

The UK Life Assurance Market

The UK life assurance market was considered large and growing. Growth in new premiums went from $1.9 BN in 1980 to $4.7 BN in 1983. During the same period average growth of premium income, rose from $7.8 BN to $13.2 BN, and total sums insured grew an average of 17%, to $295 BN. There were 289 licensed underwriters in the UK. The relative size of the top twelve companies is presented in Exhibit 8.

Analyses showed that life assurance in the UK was seen as both a protection instrument and a consumer investment. The policies accumulated cash value and also yielded dividends to policyholders. There were basically three types of underwriters in the marketplace: industrial, orthodox, and linked life.

The industrial companies offered small value policies which were targeted at the lower socio-economic groups. The premiums were collected in person, usually monthly, by employed agents, who did little actual "selling." The policies carried high administrative overheads and were, therefore, relatively poor values for the consumer. This sector of the market was dominated by Prudential, which wrote 65% of the new policies issued each year. This type of insurance had a vast customer base, with over 70 million policies in existence. At the same time, this type of policy had a declining market share, and smaller companies were retrenching because of overhead inefficiencies.

EXHIBIT 8   **Major players in the life market**

World-wide premium income

	Classification	Ranking	$ MM Value	% of Total	% Increase on '82/'81	% Increase on '81/'80	Size of life fund (end '82) $BN
Prudential	Stock	1	1656	13	12	16	9.4
Legal and General	Stock	2	775	6	15	10	6.6
Standard Life	Mutual	3	630	5	13	20	6.3
Norwich Union	Mutual	4	565	4	19	13	3.8
Hambro Life	Stock	5	464	4	20	32	2.1
Commercial Union	Stock	6	444	4	12	15	3.8
Eagle Star	Stock/Sub	7	414	3	21	28	2.2
Abbey Life	Stock/Sub	8	353	3	8	63	1.4
Sun Life	Stock	9	328	3	2	25	2.1
Scottish Amicable	Mutual	10	319	3	24	38	2.5
G.R.E.	Stock	11	318	3	14	27	2.8
Pearl	Stock	12	311	2	8	10	1.9
Subtotal			6577	53	13	21	44.9 (56%)
Others	13/48		4924	40	15	21	
Balance			823	7	5	15	36.1 (44%)
			12324	100	15	21	81.0

Note: $1.20 = £1.

The orthodox life companies offered larger value policies which catered to the more affluent customer. This type of policy was distributed through "independent" professionals who usually had some other relationship with the customer. These independent agents could be insurance brokers, solicitors (attorneys), accountants, banks, or estate agents. It was fairly common in the UK for all of these groups to offer insurance as a part of their service portfolio to their clients. These independent agents typically offered policies from three to six different underwriters. The firms which offered orthodox policies had traditionally not "marketed" to their consumer base for fear of offending the professional intermediary. There were different "classes" of agents who covered specific market segments.

The linked life policy was relatively new, and was introduced in the 1960s as an alternative to the orthodox life policy. It targeted the same consumer as the orthodox policy, but was sold normally by a commission-paid, self-employed sales force, much like insurance representatives in the United States. Policyholders of linked life insurance did not "participate" in the profits of the underwriter through dividends, but their investments were placed in a number of funds (similar to mutual funds) managed by the underwriter. Thus, the linked life policyholder took investment risk/return, and the underwriter provided a death guarantee. The range of products offered by the three types of underwriters is depicted in Exhibit 9.

Trends in the UK market indicated that the role of single premium life assurance was expanding. This type policy was one in which a single payment

EXHIBIT 9   Product range

	Nonprofit/ participating	Relative importance (low/high)	Industrial	Traditional	Linked
PROTECTION					
Whole life	NP	L	—	✓	—
	P	L	✓	✓	✓
Term	NP	H	✓	✓	✓
Permanent health	NP	M	—	✓	—
SAVINGS					
Endowment	NP	L	—	✓	—
	P	H	✓	✓	✓
Pensions	NP	L	—	✓	—
	P	H	✓	✓	✓
Annuities	NP	M	—	✓	✓
Single premium bonds	P	H	—	✓	✓
GROUP SCHEMES					
Pension (can include term and PH insurance)	N/A	H	—	✓	✓

was made to the underwriter at the beginning of the policy life, and no further premiums were due. Before the creation of the single premium policy, most life policy premiums were paid yearly over the life of the policy. Logically, there was no single premium industrial underwriting, given the socio-economic status of most policyholders. The target for the single premium policies was the "banked homeowner" — a person who had a relationship with a bank, and owned his or her home.

In addition to the expansion of the single premium policy, there had been a decline in share of the industrial policy from 13% of total insurance in 1980 to 6% in 1983. The growth sectors of the market were linked life and personal pensions (which were similar to the Individual Retirement Account in the United States).

Premium income had generally become increasingly volatile, because single premium income had grown from 12% of total premium income in 1980 to 22% in 1983. Since 1968, the growth segments for premium income were linked life, personal pensions, and mortgage endowment. In 1983, the government introduced "Mortgage Interest Relief at Source" (MIRAS), which caused mortgage repayments on insurance-linked mortgages to appear more competitive than conventional mortgages, thus causing an increase in the mortgage endowment business. In March 1984, the British government abolished Life Assurance Premium Relief (LAPR).

In their attempt to expand their share of the market, traditional companies had begun moving into the linked life segment. Major growth was expected in pension-related policies as the most efficient (from a tax perspective) savings medium. Allied Dunbar and Guardian Royal Exchange exemplified a movement to "full financial services."

For the future, the desire of the government to increase the "portability" of pensions could open a major new market. At this time, personal pensions were sold only by life assurance companies (by law). The removal of this restriction was under consideration and would bring new banks into the market. There was some concern that the government policy of "fiscal neutrality" between savings mediums could cause further amendment to tax laws, but this was not expected in the short term.

In the future marketplace, it would be possible for banks to exploit their customer bases and "sell" insurance, instead of being passive providers. Building Societies (very similar to US savings and loan institutions, and responsible for writing most home mortgages in the UK) did not currently have legislative permission to function as insurance brokers as did the banks. It was expected that the Societies would request that power in 1986–87, which would bring more new players to the market. There would be an increase in the pensions business to reach the large self-employed group in the UK. Exhibit 10 offers a view of the current and future importance of key segments in the UK market.

In summary, the UK life underwriting market was the seventh largest in the world, and was growing. Life assurance in the UK filled a dual role for the consumer — protection and savings/investment. The market was led by large

EXHIBIT 10   Intermediaries' view of key market segments

	Currently important	Likely to increase in importance
Self-employed	90	65
People on medium incomes	82	46
Owners/directors of small companies	80	57
People on high incomes	79	53
Young couples	78	57
Middle-aged couples	72	43
Women	68	51
People with free capital	66	39
Retired couples	46	38

and well-established players, but there were major market opportunities for other well-managed companies. The market was differentiated by distribution methods, and the long-term profit stream generated by most firms led to high investor confidence and high share prices. UK premium income in 1982 totaled $28 billion, of which $12 billion was in life assurance underwriting. The market was predominantly UK-owned, as were the major players, though a company did not necessarily need to be a general insurance firm to compete successfully in either market. Each market involved different legislative bases, different distribution channels, and different skills. UK firms were significant in world markets, particularly non-life, where they received over 50% of the premium income.

The UK Financial Services Market

There were five major categories of financial services in the UK: transaction accounts, savings, shelter (home) financing, lending, and protection. Exhibit 11 is a chart of the major players and other entrants in these markets. The total savings market had grown from $124 billion in 1980 to $193.6 billion in 1983. The relative share figures for the major institutions in the savings market are shown in Exhibit 12. Shelter finance had grown from $62.8 billion to $108.8 billion in the same period. A synopsis of the growth and change in the unsecured loan market is shown in Exhibit 13.

Banks were leading the expansion into the related areas of mortgage financing, estate agency (trust), stock brokering, and life assurance underwriting. Building Societies now offered checkbook access to savings and ATM networks. Legislation intended to equalize competitive roles in the market had been passed. Technological advancements were expected at this point, but were not yet in place. The market would continue to change rapidly due to continuing deregulation and increasing technological sophistication. Traditional barriers were falling, and banks were leading the way into other sectors of the economy

EXHIBIT 11   **Elements of the market**

	Major players	Other entrants
Transaction accounts	Clearing banks	—
Savings	Building societies Life assurance companies	Banks
Shelter finance	Building societies	Banks Finance houses
Lending	Banks	Finance houses In-store credit
Protection	Life assurance companies General insurance companies	—

EXHIBIT 12   **Market movements — savings**

"50% of deposits with insurance companies"

	1980	1983
Insurance funds	45%	50%
Building societies	28%	28%
Banks	13%	7½%
National savings	7%	7%
Shares, etc.	7%	7½%
TOTAL MARKET	$124 BN	$193.6 BN

Note: $1.20 = 1 for all years.
Compound growth = 16% per annum (RPI 8.3% compound).
Insurance funds ($97 million at end of 1983) are not accessible.

EXHIBIT 13   **Market movements — unsecured loans**

"Not participating as a principal — but providing cover to repay"

	1980	1983
Finance houses	34%	29%
Bank loans	29%	37%
Bank credit cards	18%	21%
In-store cards	11%	9%
Other	8%	4%
TOTAL MARKET	$7.1 BN	$13.2 BN

Compound growth 23%.
An estimated 30% of bank and finance house loans are covered by life/disability insurance to cover repayments.
New developments from 1982 on larger loans give bullet repayments covered by endowment insurance.
Statistics exclude "loan backs" from long-term savings under an insurance policy.

to satisfy consumer demand. Insurance was an integral part of the market and was supported by past and present government and fiscal policy.

Citicorp in the UK

The Consumer Services Group (UK) was dominated by Citibank Savings, a mature business operating in four specific markets:

Finance House: Indirect financing for autos and home improvement.

Mortgage Banking: Consumer mortgages through association with insurance firm partners.

Retail Cards: Private label card operation for London's High Street retailers, as well as the European Banking Centre, Travellers Checks, and Diners Club.

Consumer Banking: Cross-selling a portfolio of products to consumers, such as personal loans, checking (transaction) accounts, mortgages, and insurance.

Citibank Savings had 39 branches in the UK, 19 of which were recognized as direct branches within the consumer bank.

UK Life Assurance Consumers

UK life assurance consumers were underinsured relative to those of other developed nations. The total life coverage as a percent of yearly average wage as compared for seven industrialized nations was:

UK   88%
France   147%
Sweden   148%
Australia   178%
United States 183%
Canada   184%
Japan   325%

The product was seen by UK consumers as intangible and offering no present benefit. The contracts were viewed as a "mass of small print" and were inflexible once purchased. The purchase pattern was characterized as infrequent and having a high unit cost, and the consumer had a "low knowledge base" about the product. The benefits perceived were "peace of mind," a response to issues of social responsibility, and investment/tax avoidance. 74% of UK households had life coverage, which included 45% of all adults (predominantly men). A chart of UK consumer behavior regarding purchase by product type is presented as Exhibit 14. The major reasons for purchase were "protection" and "house purchase." In general, no major alternatives were considered, and the decision to buy insurance coverage was a joint one in the family. The amount of coverage was generally based on affordability rather than need, and shopping among companies was minimal. Exhibit 15 characterizes the major segments of the market; required company attributes from the consumers' view are shown in Exhibit 16.

The life assurance market was not as mature as its size might indicate. Most consumers were underinsured, and over half the adult population had no coverage at all. There was a key role to be played for protection products (distinct from investment products). Linked life companies concentrated on "investment policies," and the benefits to the policyholder were neither fixed nor guaranteed

EXHIBIT 14   **UK consumer behavior**

Key product group	Holding %	Recent purchase %[1]	Future purchase %[2]
Endowment mortgage	9	17	9
Mortgage protection	16	24	16
Protection cover	35	42	19
Endowment cover	42	63	39
TOTAL (including multi-purchase)	74	100	57

[1]Purchased in the last 12 months.
[2]Expected purchase in the next 12 months.

EXHIBIT 15   **Consumer "types"**

	Medium	Purchase	Timing	Knowledge	Mindset
Thinking young couple	Broker Direct to company	Buys	Regular	Sophisticated	Protection
Young family man	Agent Salesman	Sold	Spasmodic	Low — trusting	Protection/ savings
Mid-age man	Any	Sold	Spasmodic	Low — wants known company	Protection/ savings
Self-employed	Salesman Broker	Sold	Spasmodic	Learns quickly Decision maker	Savings
Late arrivals	Direct (coupon response)	Indirectly sold	Once	Low	Protection (burial policy)

EXHIBIT 16   **Required company attributes**

What to look for in a company (excl. industrial)

	Spontaneous	Prompted
Well known	33%	60%
Good reputation	27%	51%
Good investment performance	23%	30%
Good salespeople	15%	56%
Long established	8%	43%

by the company, but were invested in a separate range of funds (at the risk/return of the consumer). In this sense, linked life firms worked very much like mutual fund companies in the US. Their sources of income were profits from insurance underwriting, a 5% bid/offer differential on investments in the funds, and a 3/4% fund management fee. The products were sold through a direct sales force, which was normally paid only by commission.

In the UK market, 15% of adults had a linked life policy (33% of adults with life assurance coverage). The policies were most popular in the under-55 age range, and in London and the southeast of England.

THE HISTORY OF BRITISH NATIONAL LIFE ASSURANCE

British National Life Assurance was a spinoff company from the British National Insurance Society. It was created in 1982 by Sir William Baltimore[9] as a subsidiary of EXCO Corporation[10] (a large US company), when EXCO Corporation had decided to diversify into financial services. British National Insurance remained a property and casualty life underwriter, while BNLA became the life underwriting business of EXCO Corporation. The Managing Director of the new firm was Ernest Smith,[11] a true English gentleman and skilled manager. The Sales Director was Frank Jones,[12] a charismatic and skilled salesman with considerable experience in the insurance business.

EXCO Corporation took very little interest in the performance of BNLA and allowed Mr. Smith and Mr. Jones to manage the company as they saw fit. In essence, Mr. Jones controlled sales and marketing, and Mr. Smith controlled public relations and administration.

[9]The name has been changed to protect confidentiality.
[10]The name has been changed to protect confidentiality.
[11]The name has been changed to protect confidentiality.
[12]The name has been changed to protect confidentiality.

In the interim, Sir William Baltimore retired from EXCO Corporation. He subsequently became Director of Insurance Development (on a consulting basis) for Citicorp's Consumer Services Group International EMEA Division, headquartered in London.

The consumers' view of the Citicorp/BNLA merger was that it offered wider financial services as a result, and a bank-owned insurance company was seen positively. Negative reaction to the fact that it was American-owned could be foreseen.

In January 1986, BNLA employed 392 people, 142 at its headquarters and 250 comprising the sales force from 22 branches. Each branch had a branch manager and an administrative assistant. An organizational chart and staff analysis are provided in Exhibits 17 and 18.

There were 47,600 policyholders and $305 million in life insurance in force. However, BNLA policy lapses and salesperson turnover were twice the industry average. The commission-only sales force was the major distribution method for BNLA products, and its productivity was some 75% below average. The sales force was inappropriately trained, and the commission structure resulted in low pay relative to the competition.

BNLA spent considerable sums of money training a sales force that was paid poorly relative to industry averages. Mr. Jones subscribed to the philosophy that a high-quality product would essentially sell itself, and that, therefore, high commissions were unnecessary. His view was that sales goals would be achieved, in the long run, as a result of high training levels and high-quality products. This became known in the organization as "Frank's Philosophy." This philosophy also constrained promotional activities to direct selling only. The marketing department was therefore mostly engaged in arranging flashy conventions and gimmicks for the sales force.

Communication between top management and the organization was generally considered poor or non-existing. Bad news, such as the lack of profits, the low sales force performance, and information about the negative cash flows was never passed along to the management team. Although annual budgets were compiled, their content was never shared with departments. Conversely, no formal system existed for monthly reporting on departmental activities. Smith believed that financial reporting should be kept to a minimum, although all required disclosures were always filed on time. The financial officer had a small mini-computer at his disposal. Moreover, the firm had taken steps to automate the office environment at its headquarters by establishing a word-processing pool.

Toward the end of 1984, EXCO Corporation decided that it was not going to make a go of BNLA (or of financial services generally), and put the company up for sale. The company knew that it was "on the block," and employee morale took a nose dive. This enhanced the "rudderless" sense of the company, as performance became even less an issue and "Frank's Philosophy" became the guiding force in the firm. A culture-reward system profile of BNLA is shown in Exhibit 7.

EXHIBIT 17   **BNLA organization chart**

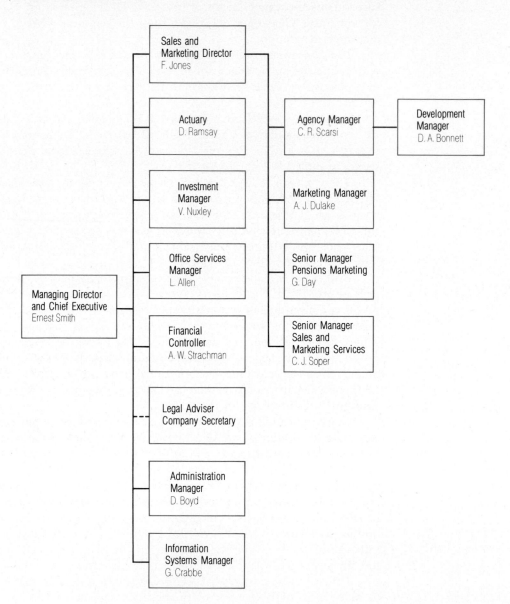

EXHIBIT 18   **British National Life — staff analysis**

Department	Jan. 1986
Actuarial	5
Administration	21
Operations:	
Office services	10
Data processing	21
Finance	16
Investment	3
Personnel and training	—
Legal	1
Marketing	13
Sales	9
Credit insurance (from Nov. 1986)	—
Managing Director	2
Branch managers	22
Branch administrators	19
Subtotal	142
Salaried sales force	n.a.
Total	**142**
Sales associates	**250**

BNLA Product/Market Posture

At the time of the Citicorp acquisition, BNLA was a linked life firm which offered six basic products to the market:

1. Plan-for-Life — a highly flexible policy offered the consumer control over the content of his or her plan. The consumer decided what proportion of the premium to devote to savings or protection, and this could be changed as needs and circumstances warranted.

2. Plan-for-Capital — a regular savings plan with high investment content and minimum life coverage. It was ideal for someone who wanted to save dynamically for eight to ten years. The proceeds were free from basic rate income tax (the "off the top" rate in the UK), from personal capital gains tax, and, after ten years, from higher-rate tax as well. This product was quite similar to the Individual Retirement Account in its tax treatment. It differed in its small insurance cover.

3. Plan-for-Investment — a lump-sum plan to invest in the company's different funds. The capital invested was allocated a set number of units, depending

on the current value of the fund. At any time, the plan had a value equivalent to the bid (sell) value of the price of units multiplied by the number of units held. This fund was very similar to the mutual funds offered through brokerage houses in the US, except there were certain tax advantages not offered in US mutual funds.

4. Plan-for-Retirement—a retirement annuity policy which was suitable for the self-employed and those who had no private pension scheme—a unit-linked product, but with outstanding tax advantages. This plan was similar to the Keogh plans in the US, but was free of investment limits.

5. Plan-for-Executive—an individual pension plan suitable for senior members of a trading company (brokerage house) who wished to add to their retirement benefits. This was a very specialized policy, and was, once again, similar to the IRA, except that both the executive and his or her employer could contribute.

6. Plan-for-Pension Preservation—a specialized plan conforming to legislation passed in 1970 which allowed the transfer of vested pension funds from a previous employer into this plan without tax penalties.

In addition to these plans, a brokerage provided access to general insurance, such as motor, house contents (homeowners), and building insurance (UK insurance companies are not permitted to act as insurance brokers). The BNLA product line was generally complete and well rounded, and fulfilled the all-around needs of the consumer, from protection and investment to retirement planning.

BNLA—A Financial Perspective

Accounting standards in the US required earnings on a life insurance policy to be recognized evenly over the years of premium payments. UK life insurance regulations, in contrast, required maintenance of prudent reserves that resulted in a new life assurance company's generating losses or very low profits during its early years. The function of the regulations was to severely restrict dividend payments and thereby protect policyholders. US accounting was significantly less conservative; when the balance sheet of a UK life firm was recast to comply with US accounting, the reported equity generally increased considerably.

Citicorp's customary financial goals and targets were designed for traditional banking businesses and did not lend themselves to evaluating an investment in a life insurance company. For that reason, Citicorp measured BNLA performance against a hurdle rate of 20% ROE on BNLA's recorded equity. Based on Citicorp's projections at the time of the acquisition, BNLA was expected to produce negative ROEs in 1985 and 1986 (see Exhibit 19A) and to achieve the 20% hurdle rate for the first time in 1991. To comply with US accounting, BNLA's recorded equity at the time of the acquisition was adjusted as follows (in millions; please note that all BNLA financial data have been changed for proprietary reasons):

Book values of assets	$77.1	
Book amount of liabilities	66.9	
Book value of equity	$10.2	
Adjustments to comply with US accounting:		
Write-downs of assets	−3.5	
	$ 6.7	
Reduction of reserves	+6.5	
Adjusted equity	$13.2	
Portion acquired	100%	
Purchased equity	$13.2	
Purchase price	13.7	$13.7
Goodwill	$ 0.5	
Additional capital infusion		19.6
TOTAL INVESTMENT[13]		$33.3

Exhibits 19A, 19B, 19C, and 19D present summary financial data on BNLA, including forecasts. For 1985, production of new life policies was 40% below forecast. Operating expenses were 50% higher than forecast and about 50% higher than the industry norms for a firm at this stage of development. This is fairly consistent with expense levels of previous years.

THE ACQUISITION

During the time when Citicorp UK was actively seeking an insurance company to acquire, Bob Selander was the new country manager of Citicorp's UK business. The acquisition of an insurance company was a part of the strategic plan he inherited from his predecessor. Sir William Baltimore had previously developed a list of potential acquisitions for consideration.

The first possibility which came to light was Excelsior Life Assurance — one of the largest life assurance firms in the UK. Sir William Baltimore had been a director of Excelsior Life Assurance and knew its inner workings very well. Upon his recommendations and with the joint-venture participation of another life assurance firm, an acquisition plan was put together. Late in the process, the joint-venture partner withdrew from the deal, and Citicorp decided that Excelsior Life Assurance was too large to acquire alone. The search was reopened.

---

[13]Investment was made in pounds sterling, and was fully hedged via the forward market.

EXHIBIT 19A   **BNLA operating forecast, including required synergies**

Restated according to US accounting principles (in millions)

	1985	1986	1987	1988	1989
Premiums, net	$19.9	$47.0	$74.5	$109.9	$153.1
Reinsurance	0	2.7	8.5	12.5	15.0
Investment income	3.2	8.4	12.9	19.8	30.4
Total revenues	$23.1	$58.1	$95.9	$142.2	$198.5
Benefits paid	$ 3.1	$ 4.2	$ 7.2	$ 13.3	$ 34.1
Increase in reserves	12.0	40.5	66.4	96.4	119.3
Commissions	2.9	6.7	11.6	17.2	23.4
Operating expenses	5.5	7.8	7.4	9.1	12.5
Total expenses	$23.5	$59.2	$92.6	$136.0	$189.3
Income before taxes*	$ (0.4)	$ (1.1)	$ 3.3	$ 6.2	$ 9.2
Income taxes	0	0	0.8	2.8	4.3
Net income	$ (0.4)	$ (1.1)	$ 2.5	$ 3.4	$ 4.9
ROE:					
On BNLA equity	(7%)	(5%)	7%	9%	12%
By Citicorp formulas	(30%)	(40%)	6%	11%	16%

*Reconciled with BNLA's stand-alone forecast, under UK accounting principles, as follows:

	1985	1986	1987	1988	1989
UK pretax income, without synergies	$ (0.7)	$ (3.9)	$ (2.4)	$ (0.6)	$ 1.5
Adjustment for US accounting rules		(0.1)	(0.1)	(0.1)	(0.1)
Impact of synergies		1.1	4.0	4.9	5.6
Impact of capital infusion	0.3	1.8	1.8	2.0	2.2
Income before taxes, as reported above	$ (0.4)	$ (1.1)	$ 3.3	$ 6.2	$ 9.2

Source: Citicorp MEP; the data have been altered for proprietary reasons.

After considering several moderately sized firms, it was decided that the goodwill portion of the purchase price for a moderately sized firm would never allow such an acquisition to make Citicorp's internal hurdle rates. The search was moved to smaller firms. From a list of 12 life assurance firms, BNLA emerged as the most desirable candidate. Exhibits 20 and 21 discuss Citicorp's rationale for the acquisition. Not only was BNLA of a size that permitted the acquisition to be managed, but there was fairly little to be paid for the goodwill of the company. In short, the price was right, and the potential was there. Negotiations with EXCO Corporation and with Ernest Smith continued for some time, and finally, the purchase price was agreed upon. Citicorp had its UK life assurance company.

EXHIBIT 19B   **BNLA forecast balance sheets, including required synergies**

Restated according to US accounting principles (in millions, as of December 31 of each year)

	1985	1986	1987	1988	1989
Securities	$91	$126	$177	$257	$363
Reinsurance receivable	0	1	7	13	15
Other assets	4	8	21	38	59
Total assets	$95	$135	$205	$308	$436
Insurance reserves	$62	$103	$169	$266	$385
Other liabilities	1	1	3	6	10
Common stock	32	32	32	32	32
Retained earnings	0	(1)	1	4	10
Total	$95	$137	$205	$308	$437

Source: Citicorp MEP; the data have been altered for proprietary reasons.

EXHIBIT 19C   **BNLA historical balance sheets**

According to UK accounting principles (in millions, as of December 31 of each year; all balances restated at an exchange rate of 1 pound sterling = $1.4)

	1984	1983
Securities	$56	$38
Other assets	4	1
Total assets	$60	$39
Insurance reserves	$56	$31
Other liabilities	1	5
Capital	3	3
Total	$60	$39

Source: Citicorp MEP; the data have been altered for proprietary reasons.

EXHIBIT 19D   **BNLA historical income statements**

According to UK accounting principles (in millions; all balances restated at an exchange rate of 1 pound sterling = $1.4)

	1984	1983
Premiums, net	$31	$ 5
Investment income	4	3
Total revenues	$35	$ 8
Benefits paid	$ 3	$ 3
Increase in reserves	25	7
Commissions	1	1
Operating expenses	9	1
Total expenses	$38	$12
Income before taxes	($ 3)	($ 4)
Income taxes	0	0
Net income	($ 3)	($ 4)

Note: Caution should be exercised in comparing BNLA financial data with that of Citicorp, or even with that of other UK life assurance companies. This is because, first, there were some significant differences between traditional banking businesses and a UK life insurance operation, especially in rules governing the accounting recognition of earnings and in UK tax and regulatory requirements. Second, these differences were exaggerated in the case of a relatively new, rapidly growing UK life assurance company, where the reported amount of equity may have been as large as 60% of reported assets because of the conservatism inherent in regulatory requirements. Third, it was also difficult to make meaningful financial comparisions among different UK life companies. An immature firm had a financial picture bearing little resemblance to that of an older, established competitor, which may have reported equity as low as 2% of total assets.

Source: Citicorp MEP; the data have been altered for proprietary reasons.

EXHIBIT 20   **Memorandum**

TO: Group Executive
FROM: Divisional Executive
RE: UK Insurance Acquisition MEP
DATE: 14th August 1985

As you know, in 1981 Citibank submitted an application to the Fed seeking permission to expand its line of insurance activities in the UK to write whole life in addition to its traditional base of credit life. This action was felt appropriate given that in the UK expanded insurance activities are considered a normal part of the banking sector with most large UK banks engaged in such activities through wholly owned insurance subsidiaries. Therefore for Citibank to enjoy equal footing with the competition, approval would be necessary since these activities are not otherwise permitted under Citibank's U.S. charter.

EXHIBIT 20   **Memorandum (*cont.*)**

Upon receiving permission from the Fed in early '84 we were then confronted with the business decision of how best to tackle this new opportunity. A team from within Citibank Savings was formed to evaluate the market place and make a recommendation on how to proceed. In this effort they were assisted by a senior insurance consultant from the UK who had a prior relationship with Citibank. A broad range of companies were evaluated as possible acquisition candidates and several points became clear. A direct sales force (versus mass solicitation) was considered key as well as the company's ownership structure (i.e., if publically owned how could a takeover be effected).

Considerations of size became important because additional Fed approval would be required for any take-over. A unique opportunity confronted us to acquire a major UK insurer, PQ Life Assurance, but the cost of such an acquisition was put at a figure several hundred million dollars higher than the desired size of investment. This acquisition which would have been a joint venture was approved internally within Citibank but closure with our proposed partners failed.

We then shifted our thinking back to internal "de novo" growth and in so doing have re-evaluated several smaller acquisition candidates which had surfaced previously. Acquiring a smaller company may be regarded as "accelerated de novo" and we are actively pursuing the acquisition of British National Life Assurance Company at a cost of $13.7MM (goodwill of $0.5MM) with a further capital increase of $19.6MM bringing the total investment to $33.3MM. If we were to pursue the internal de novo growth route we would also require additional capital of about $19.6MM as our current capitalization of $3MM supports the credit life business only. These capital levels are prescribed by the UK insurance regulatory bodies in order to meet minimum solvency margins.

The following analysis compares forecasted earnings through acquisition versus internal growth. On a cumulative basis through 1990 the acquisition route produces over $17MM in incremental earnings.

It is important to note that there is a lag in profitability in an emerging life assurance business due to the slow build up of premium income (net of commissions) which in the earlier years is not sufficient to cover the fixed costs of the distribution system. The difference in profitability between the two alternatives below is simply a reflection of this curve and that once a steady state is achieved both propositions would yield the same results.

PCE $MM	De novo	Acquisition	B/(W)
1985	$(.5)	$(1.3)	$ (.6)
1986	(1.3)	(2.9)	(1.6)
1987	(3.6)	.4	4.0
1988	(3.5)	1.3	4.8
1989	(2.5)	2.5	5.0
1990	(1.3)	4.9	6.2
	(12.7)	4.9	17.8

This MEP assumes no tax credit against the operating losses in 1985 and 1986. In 1987, the first full year of profitability, the loss carryforward is absorbed. In any event no current UK taxes will likely be payable at least until 1990 and the tax expense is therefore all U.S. deferred.

Your approval of the attached MEP is recommended.

Note: All numbers in this document have been changed for proprietary reasons.

EXHIBIT 21   **Citibank inter-office communication**

TO	Office:	Kensington	SUBJECT	British National	
	Person:	Divisional Executive		*Life Acquisition*	
FROM	Office:	Hammersmith	REFERENCE	AAA/dcb	
	Person:	UK Country	DATE	13th August 1985	
		Business Managers			

Attached is an MEP covering the proposed acquisition of 100% of British National Life Assurance Company Limited (BNL) for a price not to exceed US$13.7MM. We have also included a $19.6MM capital injection in this MEP as we anticipate this being the incremental requirement under UK statutory provisions prior to adequate earnings levels being achieved. Injection of this capital will also improve the company's earnings performance allowing earlier consolidation for tax purposes.

Rationale

Life insurance continues to be viewed as a key element to our Individual Bank strategy in the UK. Consumers view life insurance not only as protection, but also as a tax planning and investment opportunity. 50% of total UK consumer savings are invested in insurance company managed funds. In order to meet the full financial needs of the UK consumer, we must offer life insurance related services. In order to do so, we filed in 1981 and received U.S. Federal Reserve Board approval in 1984 to sell and underwrite life insurance through our UK subsidiaries. To date these have been involved only in the credit life related areas complementary to our Citibank Savings lending activities.

We have been pursuing a full service life insurance sales and underwriting firm to broaden our presence in the UK consumer market. Due to extremely high premiums, the acquisition of a large company giving us an immediate and substantial presence has been eliminated as an option. Instead, we have decided to develop our existing insurance operations and look at BNL as an opportunity to accelerate our de novo expansion. BNL gives us an existing infrastructure, including systems, investment management, and a direct sales force; a reasonably capable management team and an appropriate product line. Utilizing BNL and our existing customer base we anticipate substantial sales/revenue synergies which could not otherwise be realized by a de novo development in less than two years.

Based on our projections, a de novo development of a direct sales insurance business involving the hiring of management, systems and product development and branch/sales force recruitment and training would require 18–24 months and US$3.5MM in expenses before any sales occur. Cumulative, after tax losses through 1990 on a start-up, would be US$12.7MM. This compares with the BNL acquisition cumulative profits of US$4.9MM through 1990.

The success of the acquisition is dependent on our providing BNL with sales prospects from our existing UK customer portfolio. This will enhance sales force performance by increasing new policy sales per salesperson by 50% in 1986 and up to 100% in 1990. The resultant sales per salesperson in 1990 are expected to be at the level currently achieved by mature direct sales forces in the life insurance industry.

Company Background

The origins of BNL date back to 1920, but true development started with the relaunch of the company as a direct selling, unit linking life company in January 1983, and today has 34M policyholders with $218MM insurance in force. 1984 premiums were $4.2MM generated through a direct sales force of 247 operating out of 22 branch offices. Its premium income in 1984 was $17.2MM single and $3.2MM regular.

A wholly-owned subsidiary of XYZ Corporation [This company's identity is altered to protect confidentiality], the firm is now being sold as part of XYZ's efforts to refocus on its non-financial business activities.

EXHIBIT 21   **Citibank inter-office communication (*cont.*)**

Financial Expectations

BNL presently loses approximately $3.1MM pre-tax due to start-up expenses and the higher costs in the growth phase of a life insurance company. With our purchase of BNL, the company will be able to offer insurance to the 1MM consumers with whom we have an established relationship in the UK. We expect this to nearly double sales and lead to a 5th year achievement of our corporate hurdle rates. Cumulative losses prior to breakeven in year three will amount to US$4MM. Of the $1.3MM premium, goodwill is anticipated to $.5MM after allowing for a $.8MM adjustment to revalue policyholder liabilities. Details are contained in the attached MEP.

Regulatory and Other Considerations

Any agreement will be subject to UK/US regulatory approvals where we do not anticipate any objections to the acquisition given the small size and our existing permssions.

The purchase will be subject to our audit and acceptance of:

- BNL's operating system, controls, and procedures
- a review of contracts, leases, and other documentation
- personnel, legal, and regulatory compliance
- a review of their investment portfolio
- the financial statements and tax returns (Peat Marwick will handle)
- current policyholder portfolio (we will retain an outside actuarial consultant for valuation purposes)

Additionally, we will require management continuity and will negotiate employment contracts with several key managers to ensure continuity after our acquisition.

The company's headquarters are approximately one hour's drive from our Hammersmith offices so I envision no management complications due to location.

The company will initially be managed independently from our other Individual Bank activities focusing on the necessary adjustments to ensure Citicorp standards are met. The building of sales momentum is the next priority with further synergies to be explored at a later date. Given the apparent strength of the BNL management team, minimal personnel moves into BNL are anticipated. The existing Managing Director will report to me and I will retain the insurance expertise currently on my staff.

I recommend your approval.

Note: All numbers in this document have been changed for proprietary reasons.

CLUB MÉDITERRANÉE

Sipping a cognac and smoking one of his favorite cigars on his way back to Paris from New York on the Concorde, Serge Trigano was reviewing the new organization structure that was to be effective November 1981. In the process he was listing the operational problems and issues that were yet to be resolved. Son of the chief executive of "Club Med," Serge Trigano was one of the joint managing directors and he had just been promoted from director of operations to general manager of the American zone, responsible for operations and marketing for the whole American market. Having experienced a regional organization structure that was abandoned some four years ago, he wanted to make sure that this time the new structure would better fit the objectives of Club Med and allow its further development in a harmonious way.

COMPANY BACKGROUND AND HISTORY

Club Med was founded in 1950 by a group of friends led by Gérard Blitz. Initially it was a nonprofit organization set up for the purpose of going on vacation together in some odd place. The initial members were essentially young people who liked sports and especially the sea. The first "village," a tent village, was a camping site in the Balearic Isles. After four years of activities, Gilbert Trigano was appointed the new managing director. Gilbert Trigano came to Club Med from a family business involved in the manufacture of tents in France, a major supplier to Club Med. With this move, and in the same year, the holiday village concept was expanded beyond tent villages to straw hut villages, the first of which was opened in 1954. Further expanding its activities, in 1956 Club Med

This case was prepared by Professor Jacques Horovitz as a basis for class discussion rather than to illustrate either effective or ineffective handling of an administrative situation. Copyright 1981 by IMEDE (International Management Development Institute), Lausanne, Switzerland. Reproduced by permission.

opened its first ski resort at Leysin, Switzerland. In 1965 its first bungalow village was opened, and in 1968 the first village started its operation in the American zone. Club Med's main activity was, and still is today, to operate a vacation site for tourists who would pay a fixed sum (package) to go on vacation for a week, two weeks, or a month and for whom all the facilities were provided in the village. Club Med has always had the reputation of finding beautiful sites which were fairly new to tourists (for instance, Moroccan tourism was "discovered" by Club Med) and which offered many activities, especially sports activities, to its members.[1] In 1981 Club Med operated 90 villages in 40 different countries on five continents. In addition to its main activity it had extended to other sectors of tourism in order to be able to offer a wider range of services. In 1976 Club Med acquired a 45 percent interest in an Italian company (Valtur) which had holiday villages in Italy, Greece, and Tunisia, mainly for the Italian market. In 1977 Club Med took over Club Hotel, which had built up a reputation over the last 12 years as a leader in the seasonal ownership time-sharing market. The result of this expansion had been such that in 1980 more than 770,000 people had stayed in the villages of Club Med or its Italian subsidiary, whereas there were 2,300 in 1950. Most members were French in 1950, and in 1980 only 45 percent were French. In addition, 110,000 people had stayed in the apartments or hotels managed by its time-sharing activity. Actually, in 1980, Club Med sales were about 2.5 billion French francs (FF) and its cash flow around FF170 million. (See Exhibit 1 for the last 10 years' financial performance.) Exhibits 2–4 show the number of people who had stayed at the holiday centers of Club Med, the number of beds it had as of 1980, and the nationality of its members. The present case focuses exclusively on the organization struc-

EXHIBIT 1   Financial performance (thousands of French francs)

Years	Sales	Net income	Cash flow	EPS
1969–70	313,000	NA	NA	5.31
1970–71	363,000	NA	NA	5.73
1971–72	427,000	13,400	25,100	7.41
1972–73	502,000	22,500	37,000	10.88
1973–74	600,000	27,300	42,800	12.78
1974–75	791,000	40,000	56,790	16.08
1975–76	1,060,000	51,800	70,900	20.78
1976–77	1,350,000	67,870	103,645	20.98
1977–78	1,616,000	72,135	114,578	23.78
1978–79	1,979,000	85,900	138,300	28.42
1979–80	2,462,000	111,600	173,100	36.91

[1]When going on vacation to any of Club Med's villages, one becomes a "member" of Club Med.

EXHIBIT 2   **Growth in number of club members**

Year	Number of members
1950	2,300
1955	10,000
1960	45,000
1965	90,000
1970	293,000
1975	432,000
1980	770,000*

*Includes Valtur.

EXHIBIT 3   **Number of facilities, 1981**

	Number of holiday centers	Number of beds
Club Med and Valtur	102	60,500
Hotels	7	1,000
Apartment buildings	24	11,000
Total	133	72,500

EXHIBIT 4   **Members of Club Med according to country of origin, 1979***

France	301,000	43.1%
United States/Canada	124,000	17.8
Belgium	41,600	6.0
Italy	34,400	4.9
West Germany	34,100	4.9
Switzerland	18,500	2.6
Austria	6,800	1.0
Australia	18,400	26.0
Others	84,900	12.1
Conferences and seminars	34,700	5.0[†]
	698,500	100.0%

*Excluding Valtur.
[†]Most seminars are in France for French customers.

ture of the holiday village operations and not on the time-sharing activities of the company.

SALES AND MARKETING

In 1981 Club Med was international, with vacation sites all over the world, and so were its customers. They came from different continents, backgrounds, market segments, and did not look for the same thing in a vacation package. Club Med offered different types of villages and a wide range of activities to accommodate all the people who chose to go on a package deal.[2] The club offered ski villages in ski resorts for those who liked to ski; straw hut villages with very Spartan comfort on the Mediterranean, mainly for young bachelors; and hotel and bungalow resort villages with all comforts open throughout the year, some with special facilities for families and young children. An average client who went to a straw hut village on the Mediterranean usually did not go to a plush village at Cap Skirring in Senegal (and the price was different too), although the same type of person might go to both.

A family with two or three children who could afford the time and money needed to travel to a relatively nearby village was, however, less likely to go to a village in Malaysia due to the long journey and the cost of transportation. Broadly speaking, diverse kinds of holiday seekers were represented among the Club's customers. However, there was a larger proportion of office workers, executives, and professional people and a small proportion of workers and top management. The sales and marketing of the Club, which began in Europe, had expanded to include two other important markets: the American zone, including the United States, Canada, and South America, and the Far Eastern Zone, including Japan and Australia. The Club's sales network covered 29 countries. Sales were either direct through the Club-owned offices, 23 of which existed at the moment (see Exhibit 5 for countries where the Club owns commercial offices as well as villages and operations) or indirect through travel agencies (in France Havas was the main retailer). Originally all the villages were aimed at the European market; in 1968 with the opening of its first village in America, the Club broke into the American market and opened an office in New York. Since then the American market had grown more or less independently. Eighty percent of the beds in the villages located in the American geographical area were sold to Club members in the United States and Canada. Sixty-five percent of French sales, which represent 47 percent of the Club's turnover, were direct by personal visits to the office, by telephone, or by letter. However, in the United States, direct sales accounted for only 5 percent of the total, the remaining 95 percent being sold through travel agencies. These differences were partly

---

[2]Most villages offered by Club Med are rented by the company or run under a management contract.

EXHIBIT 5 Countries of operations before new structure

Country	Separate commercial office	Country manager	Country manager supervising commercial operations	Villages
Germany	X			
Switzerland	X	X		X
Turkey			X	X
Italy	X	X		X
Venezuela	X			
Belgium	X			X
Mexico			X	X
United States	X	X		
Bahamas		X ⎫ Same as United States		X
Haiti		X ⎭		X
Brazil			X	X
Japan	X			
Great Britain	X			
Tunisia			X	X
Morocco		X		X
Holland	X			
Greece	X	X		X
Israel			X	X
Malaysia	X	X		X
France	X	X		
New Zealand	X			
Australia	X			X
Egypt		X		X
Singapore	X			
Canada	X			
Tahiti		X		X
South Africa	X			
Spain	X	X		X
Senegal		X		X
Ivory Coast		X		
Mauritius		X Same as Reunion		X
Sri Lanka		X Same as Mauritius		X
Guadeloupe		X ⎫ Same as United States		X
Martinique		X ⎭		X
Reunion Island		X		X
Dominican Republic		X Same as United States		X
United Arab Emirates				X

explained by national preferences but also by a deliberate choice on the part of the Club. Until the appointment of Serge Trigano to lead the U.S. zone, all sales and marketing officers reported to a single worldwide marketing director. (The capital structure of Club Med is shown in Exhibit 6.)

THE VILLAGE

Club Med had around 90 villages, and it was growing fast. In the next three years (1981–84) about 20 new villages were scheduled to open. At Club Med a village was typically a hotel, bungalows, or huts in usually a very nice area offering vacationers a series of several activities, among which were swimming, tennis, sailing, waterskiing, windsurfing, archery, gymnastics, snorkling, deep sea diving, horseback riding, applied arts, yoga, golf, boating, soccer, circuits, excursions, bike riding, and skiing. There were also usually on site a shop, a hairdresser, even some cash changing, car renting, and so on, and a baby or mini club in many places. Club Med was well known for having chosen sites which were the best in any country where they were, not only from a geographical point of view but also from an architectural point of view and the facilities provided. Exhibit 7 shows the number of villages which were open during the winter or summer season by type.

Essentially there were three types of villages. Hut villages were the cheapest, open only during the summer season. All the hut villages had been built early in Club Med's history and were on the Mediterranean. They did not offer all the comfort that the wealthy traveler was used to (common showers). Then there were bungalows or hotels or "hard type" villages which were more comfortable with private bathrooms. Most were still double-bedded which meant that two single men or women would have to share the same bedroom. In a vil-

EXHIBIT 6   **Providers of capital to Club Med, 1981**

Compagnie Financière Group (Rothschild)	7.0%
Banque de Paris et des Pays Bas	6.0
REDEC Group	5.0
Credit Lyonnais	7.5
Union des Assurances de Paris	7.5
The IFI International Group	7.0
The Company Personnel's Common Investment Fund	5.0
	45.0
Public	55.0
	100%

EXHIBIT 7 **Number of villages by type and season**

	Sea			Mountain	Total
	Huts	Bungalows	Hotels	**Mountain**	**Total**
Summer season	14	31	26	10	81
Winter season	0	19	11	23	53

Source: Club Méditerranée Trident N123/124, Winter 1980–81, Summer 1981.

lage there were two types of people: the GMs, or "gentils membres," who were the customers and came usually for one, two, three, or four weeks on a package deal to enjoy all the facilities and activities of any village, and the GOs, or "gentils organisateurs," who helped people make this vacation the best. There were GOs for sports, for applied arts, for excursions, for food, for the bar, as disk jockeys, as dancing instructors, for the children or babies in the miniclubs, for maintenance, for traffic, for accounting, for receptions, and so forth.[3] On average there were 80 to 100 GOs per village.

There was a third category of people who were behind the scenes: the service people, usually local people hired to maintain the facilities and the garden, to clean up, and so on (about 150 service people per village). They could also be promoted to GOs.

Every season (either after the summer season from May to September or the winter season in April, or every six months) all the GOs would be moved from one village to another; that was one of the principles of the Club since its inception so that nobody would stay for more than six months in any particular site. The village chief of maintenance was an exception. He stayed one full year; if a village was closed in the winter, he remained for the painting, the repair, and so forth. The service people (local people) were there all the year round or for six months, if the village was only open in the summer (or winter for ski resorts). Exhibit 8 shows a typical organization structure of a village from the GO's point of view.

Under the chief of the village there were several coordinators: one for entertainment, responsible for all of the day and night activities (shows, music, night club, plays, games, and so on); the sports chief who coordinated all the sports activities in any particular village; the maintenance chief who would see to the maintenance of the village, either when there was a breakdown or just to repaint the village or keep the garden clean, grow new flowers, etc., and who was assisted by the local service people; and the food and beverage chief who

[3]Although the GOs were specialized by "function," they had also to be simply "gentils organisateurs," i.e., making the GM's life easy and participating in common activities, such as arrival cocktails, shows, and games.

EXHIBIT 8   **Organization chart of a typical village**

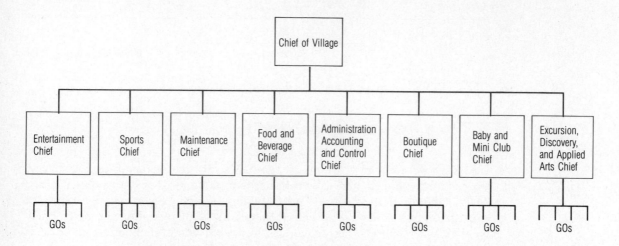

coordinated the cooking in the different restaurants as well as the bar. Usually there was a bazaar for miscellaneous items, a garment boutique and a hairdresser under a boutique's coordinator. There was a coordinator for the baby club (if existent) within the village to provide the children with some special activities; this coordinator was also responsible for the medical part of the village (nurses and doctor). Many times there was a doctor on site, especially when a village was far from a big town. A coordinator of excursions and applied arts was on duty to help the GM to go somewhere or propose accompanied excursions (one, two, three days) for those who wanted it, or to assist a GO in making a silk scarf or pottery. There was a coordinator of administration, accounting, and control who dealt with cash, telephone, traffic, planning and reception, basic accounting, salaries for GOs and service personnel, taxes, and so forth. The food and beverage service and maintenance operations were heavy users of local service personnel.

COMPANY ORGANIZATION STRUCTURE

Exhibit 9 shows the organization structure of Club Med's holiday village activity just before Serge Trigano's appointment as director of the U.S. zone. (The rest—time-sharing activities—are additional product-market subsidiaries.)

There were several joint managing directors who participated in the management committee. Essentially the structure was a functional one, with a joint managing director for marketing and sales, another one for operations, and several other function heads like accounting, finance, and tax. Exhibit 10 shows how the operations part of the organization was structured.

EXHIBIT 9   **Organization chart before November 1981, holiday villages activity only**

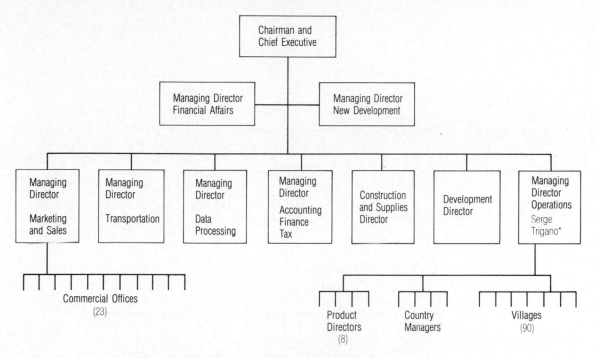

*Until his recent appointment as managing director, American zone.

Essentially the structure was composed of three parts. As there was an entertainment chief in the village, there was a director of entertainment at the head office and the same for sports. There were several product directors who mirrored the structure of the village. There were country managers in certain countries where the club had several villages in operation, and then there were the 90 villages. All reported to Serge Trigano.

The Role of the Product Directors

Product directors were responsible for the product policy. They made decisions with respect to the policy of Club Med in all the villages, such as the type of activities that should be in each village and the maintenance that should be done. They recruited and trained the various GOs needed for their domain (e.g., sports GOs, entertainment GOs, administration GOs, cooks). They staffed the villages by deciding with the director of operations which chief of village would go where and how many people would go with him. They made investment

EXHIBIT 10   Organization chart—operations just before the new move in November 1981

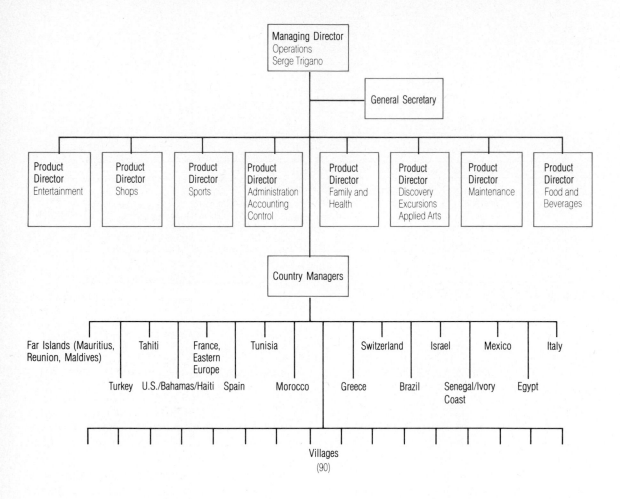

proposals for each village for maintenance, new activities, extension, or renovation purposes. They also assumed the task of preparing the budgets and
controlling application of policies in the villages by traveling extensively as
"ambassadors" of the head office to the villages. Each one of them was assigned
a certain number of villages. When visiting the village, he would go there representing not his particular product but Club Med's product as a whole. Also,
each of them, including the director of operations, was assigned, on a rotating
basis, the task of answering emergency phone calls from any village and making
emergency decisions or taking action if necessary. Exhibit 11 presents examples
of product organization. In the new regional structure their role and place were
questioned.

EXHIBIT 11   **Examples of product management**

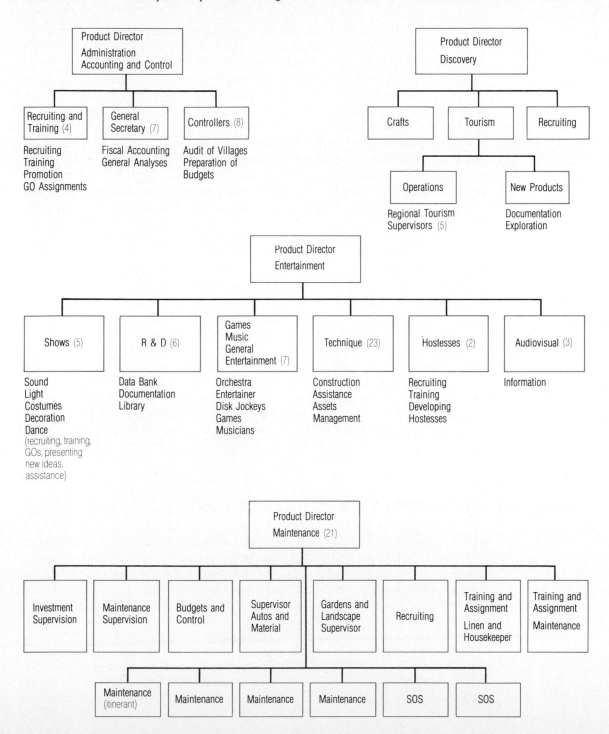

The Role of the Country Manager

Country managers were mainly the ambassadors of Club Med in the countries where Club Med had village(s). Usually they were located in countries with more than one village. They would handle political relations themselves, maintaining lasting relationships with elected bodies, mayors, civil servants, regional offices, and so forth. They would introduce to the new team coming every six months what the country had to offer, its constraints, local mores, the local people to be invited, local artists to be invited, the traps to be avoided, the types of suppliers, the type of local events that might be of interest for the village (so that the village would not forget, for instance, national holidays). They would try to get Club Med more integrated politically and socially in the host country, in particular in less developed countries where there was a gap between the abundance and richness of the club as compared to its immediate environment. They also had an assistance role, such as getting work permits for GOs and also finding suppliers; sometimes, in fact, the country manager had a buyer attached to his staff who would purchase locally for the different villages to get economies of scale. In addition, the country managers personally recruited and maintained lists of the service personnel available to Club Med. They would go and negotiate the salaries, wages, and working conditions of the service personnel with the unions so that the village was free of being involved every six months in a renegotiation. Also, they might have an economic role by helping develop local production or culture as the Club was a heavy buyer of local food and products. They could also act as a development antenna looking for new sites or receiving proposals from local investors and submit them to head office. They would also handle legal and tax problems when Club Med had a local legal entity as well as maintain relationships with the owners of the land, hotels, or bungalows when Club Med—as was often the case—was only renting the premises.

PROBLEMS WITH THE CURRENT STRUCTURE

The current structure had been set up about four years ago. It had also been Club Med's structure before 1971, but in between (1971–76) there had been a change in the operations side only which had involved setting up area managers; instead of having one director of operations, there had been five directors who had under their control several countries and villages. From 1971 to 1976 there had been no country managers and each of the area managers had had about 10 or 15 villages under his supervision. This structure was changed in 1976 because it seemed to have created several Club Meds in one. The area managers had started to try to get the best chiefs of village and people for their area. As a result GOs were not moving around every six months from one area of the world to another as was the policy, and also area managers started giving different types of services to their customers so that, for instance, a Frenchman going to one of the zones one year and to another the next year would find a different Club Med. These reasons had led to the structure presented in Exhibit 9 for the operations. But until now marketing had always been worldwide.

Of course the structure in operation until now had created the reverse problem: it seemed to Serge Trigano and others that it was too centralized. In fact Serge Trigano had a span of control (which is rarely achieved in industry) of 90 chiefs of villages plus 8 product directors and 14 country managers, all reporting to him from all over the world. There was an overload of information, too much detail, and too many issues being entrusted to him, which would be worse as time would go by since Club Med was growing and doubling its capacity every five years. Beside the problem of centralization and information overload, another problem seemed to appear because Club Med's operations had not adapted enough to the international character of its customers. Most of the GOs were still recruited in France whereas now 15–20 percent of the customers came from the American zone. France was not even the best location to find GOs, who often needed to speak at least one other language. They had to be unmarried, under 30; they had to change countries every six months, with no roots; and they had to work long hours and be accessible 24 hours a day, seven days a week for a relatively low salary. The feeling was that maybe one could find happier and more enthusiastic people in Australia or Brazil than in France. Too much centralization, information overload, and lack of internationalization in operations were among the big problems in the current structure.

Also, there was a feeling that a closer local coordination between marketing and operations could give better results since customers seemed to concentrate on one zone (American in the United States, European in Europe) because of transportation costs, and a coordination might lead to a better grasp of customer needs, price, product, offices, and so on. For example, when Club Med was smaller and only in Europe, departure from its villages was done only once a week. As a result, reception at the village was also once a week. Lack of local coordination between operations and marketing had created arrivals and departures almost every day in certain villages, overburdening the GO's staff and disrupting the organization of activities. As another illustration, the American customer was used to standard hotel services (bathroom, towels, etc.), which may be different than in Europe. Closer local ties might help respond better to local needs.

Centralization had also created bottlenecks in assignments and supervision of people. Every six months everybody — all GOs — were coming back to Paris from all over the world to be assigned to another village. Five or ten years ago this was in fact a great happening that allowed everybody to discuss matters with the product people, see headquarters, and find friends who had been in other villages, but now with 5,000 GOs coming almost at the same time — and wanting to speak to the product directors — reassigning them was becoming somewhat hectic. It was likely to be even worse in the future because of the growth of the company.

PLANNING AND CONTROL

The planning cycle could be divided into two main parts: first, there was a three-year plan started two years ago, which involved the product directors and the country managers. Each product director would define his objectives for the next three years and the action programs that would go with it and propose investments that he would like to make for his product in each of the 90 villages. All the product directors would meet to look at the villages one by one and see how the investment fit together, as well as consider the staffing number of GOs and service personnel in broad terms for the next three years. Of course the big chunk of the investment program was the maintenance of the facilities since 55 percent of the investment program concerned such maintenance programs. The rest was concerned with additions or modifications of the villages, such as new tennis courts, theater, or restaurant, revamping a boutique, and so on. The country managers were involved in that same three-year plan. First of all they would give the product directors their feelings and suggestions for investments as well as for staffing the villages. In addition, they would provide some objectives and action programs in how they would handle personnel problems, political problems, economic problems, cultural and social integration, sales of Club Med in their country, and development.

Besides this three-year operational plan, there was the one-year plan which was divided into two six-month plans. For each season a budget was prepared for each of the villages. This budget was mostly prepared by the product director for administration accounting, and it concerned the different costs, such as goods consumed, personnel charges, and rents. This budget was given to the chief of the village when he left with his team. In addition to this operational budget, there was an investment budget every six months in more detail than the three-year plan. This investment budget was prepared by the maintenance director under the guidance and proposal from the different product directors. It was submitted to the operations director and then went directly to the chief executive of the company. It had not been unusual (before the three-year plan) for the investment budget proposals of product directors to the maintenance director to run three times as high as what would in fact be given and allowed by the chief executive.

On the control side, there was a controller in each of the villages (administrator chief of accounting and control), as well as central controllers who would be assigned a region and would travel from one village to the other. But the local controller and his team in fact were GOs like any other ones and they were changing from one village to another every six months. There was a kind of "fact and rule book" that was left in the village so that the next team would understand the particular ways and procedures of the village. But mostly speaking, each new team would start all over again each time it was coming with a new budget and standard, rules, and procedures from the central head office, as well as with the help of the fact and rule book. These two tools—the three-year plan and the six-month (season) budgets—were the main planning and control tools used.

OBJECTIVES AND POLICIES

Five objectives seemed to be important to Serge Trigano when reviewing the structure. One was that the club wanted to continue to grow and double its capacity every five years, either by adding new villages or increasing the size of the current ones (see Exhibit 12).

The second objective, which had always guided Club Med, was that it would have to continue to innovate, not to be a hotel chain but to be something different as it had always been and to continue to respond to the changing needs of the customers.

A third objective stemmed from the fact that Club Med was no longer essentially French. The majority of its customers (GMs) in fact did not come from France; as a result, it would have to continue to internationalize its employees, its structure, its ways of thinking, training, and so on (see Exhibit 13).

The fourth objective was economic. Costs were increasing, but not all of these costs could be passed on to the gentils membres unless the club wanted to stop its growth. One way of not raising prices to the customer was to increase productivity by standardization, better methods, and procedures.

The fifth objective was to keep the basic philosophy of Club Med: to keep the village concept an entity protected as much as possible from the outside world but integrated in the country in which it was; to keep the package concept for GMs; and, finally, to continue social mixing. Whatever your job or your social position, at Club Med, you were recognized only by two things: the color of your bathing suit and the beads you wore around your neck, which allowed you to pay for your scotch, orange juice, and so on, at the bar. Part of the philosophy, in addition, was to make sure that the GOs' nomadism would continue: change every season.

THE PROPOSED NEW STRUCTURE

With these objectives in mind, the new structure to be effective November 1981 had just been sketched as shown in Exhibit 14. The idea would be to move the operations and marketing closer together in three zones. One would be America (North and South); another Europe and Africa; and the third (in the long run when this market would be more developed), the Far East. In each area a director would manage the operations side, that is, the villages and the marketing side—promotion, selling, pricing, distributing Club Med's concept. In fact, most of the American GMs were going to the American zone villages; most of the European GMs to the European zone; and most of the Asian GMs to the Asian zone—mainly because the cost of transportation from one zone to another was prohibitive.

This was the general idea, and now it had to be pushed further. Among the main interesting and troublesome aspects of the new structure were the following: how to avoid with this structure separating Club Med into three different

EXHIBIT 12   **The club growth in numbers**

	1969–70	1970–71	1971–72	1972–73	1973–74	1974–75	1975–76	1976–77	1977–78	1978–79	1979–80
Membership objective	255,000	293,000	299,000	318,000	339,000	408,000	475,000	540,000	578,000	615,000	698,500
Villages	25	55	55	60	61	69	70	74	74	78	83
Beds		33,900	34,300	36,400	37,000	49,300	50,400	53,800	55,600	58,600	64,600
Number of hotel nights—winter		881,000	948,000	1,018,000	1,044,000	1,240,000	1,628,000	1,790,000	1,940,000	2,011,000	2,250,000
Number of hotel nights—summer		2,651,000	2,801,000	2,850,000	2,920,000	3,210,000	3,400,000	3,550,000	3,710,000	3,970,000	4,265,000
Occupancy rate (percent)		68.07%	69.52%	66.81%	66.76%	69.63%	70.70%	71.19%	71.65%	72.87%	72.88%
Number of permanent employees	793	938	950	978	977	1,035	1,157	1,132	1,192	1,286	1,297
Number of GOs in villages (summer season)*											6,000
Number of service personnel in villages (summer season)*											10,000
Number of employees in Paris (operations only)											250
Number of employees, country management											100

*Number is approximate.

EXHIBIT 13   Evolution of general managers by nationality

	1972–73	1978–79
France	60.0%	47.2%
United States	7.7	17.8
Belgium	8.7	6.0
Italy	7.5	5.6
West Germany	7.4	4.9
Switzerland	2.4	1.0
Others	5.7	12.2
	100%	100%

EXHIBIT 14   The proposed structure

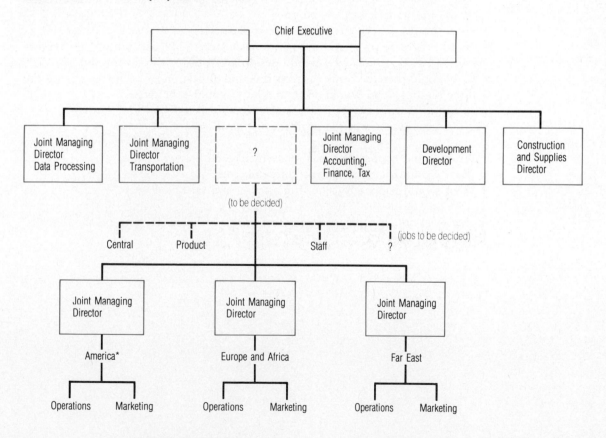

*Serge Trigano's new position.

entities with three different types of products? Should such occurrence be avoided? It seemed that this should not be allowed; that's why the structure which had been there four years ago with five regions failed. It had transformed Club Med into five mini Club Meds, although even at that time the five area managers did not have marketing and sales responsibility. In addition to this major issue of how to preserve the unity and uniqueness of Club Med with a geographic structure, several other questions were of great importance:

- Who would decide what activities would take place in a village?
- Who would decide the investments to be made in a village?
- Who would staff a village?
- Would there be a central hiring and training of all GOs or only some of them?
- How would the geographic managers be evaluated in terms of performance?
- If they wanted to continue with the GOs and give them the right and possibility to move every six months from one part of the world to another, how would the transfer of GOs be done?
- How should the transfer of GOs be coordinated?
- Should there be some common basic procedures, like accounting and reporting, and in that case, who would design and enforce those procedures?
- How could there be some coordination and allocation of resources among the three regions; who would do it; and how would it be done?

Also of importance was the problem of transition.

- What would happen to the country managers?
- What would happen to the product directors?
- What would happen to central marketing and sales?

These were some of the questions that bothered Serge Trigano on the flight to Paris from New York.

DAIMLER-BENZ — THE GLOBAL TRUCK INDUSTRY

Dr. Gerhard Liener, Daimler-Benz's managing director for acquisitions and foreign operations, was analyzing the international strategy of the firm's truck group, headquartered in Stuttgart, West Germany. It was January 29, 1986, and he wondered how long his company would be able to maintain its strength in the face of increased global competition posed by European and American truck companies, international joint ventures, and the lurking threat of Japanese export of large commercial vehicles.

HISTORY OF DAIMLER-BENZ

Daimler–Benz was the product of a merger between two German automobile manufacturers, Benz et Cie and Daimler Motoren Gesellschaft, in 1926. Karl Benz and Gottlieb Daimler, both pioneers in the automotive industry, set up their respective companies in 1883 and 1890. Both firms manufactured expensive cars as well as commercial vehicles and large engines for locomotives, ships, and zeppelins.

Shortly after the merger, Daimler–Benz began to grow rapidly. Production increased from 10,829 vehicles in 1927 to over 42,000 by 1938. Innovations in diesel power, success in racing, and a revival of the German economy all contributed to this growth. Unfortunately, this expansion was abruptly halted

This case was prepared by Professor Per V. Jenster of the McIntire School of Commerce, University of Virginia, and Professors Alfred Kotzle and Franz X. Bea of the University of Tubingen. Copyright 1986. The authors acknowledge the support provided by the McIntire Foundation.

when most of the company's production facilities were destroyed in World War II. Daimler-Benz was quick to rebuild, however, and by 1950 production had exceeded the pre-war high.

In the years that followed, Daimler-Benz saw even more phenomenal growth. Output increased from 104,000 units in 1956 to over 300,000 units by 1969. A commitment to quality was the trademark of this company, which produced a highly specialized line of commercial vehicles. Expansion and acquisitions internationally kept the supply of vehicles growing with the demand for them. By 1985 Daimler-Benz produced 541,039 cars (up 13.1 percent over 1984) and 220,213 commercial vehicles (up 4.4 percent from 1984), of which 65,407 (down 3.8 percent) were trucks over 6 tons. The total concern achieved 1985 revenues of DM 51,900 million (up 19 percent), of which DM 37,079 million came from cars and commercial vehicles. Daimler-Benz exported 53.6 percent of its production.

DAIMLER-BENZ AND THE TRUCK INDUSTRY

Over the years, the commercial vehicle market had evolved into a complex and competitive arena. With an emphasis on quality and reliability. Daimler-Benz was the largest producer of diesel trucks in the world, as well as Europe's largest commercial vehicle producer. Daimler-Benz had a long tradition of truck assembly overseas which had been forced by "local content" rules, i.e., rules specifying that a certain part of the value added process must reside locally. For this and other reasons, Daimler-Benz over the years established truck and bus plants in Brazil and Argentina, as well as in Turkey, Spain, Yugoslavia, Indonesia, Saudi Arabia, Nigeria, and Hampton, Virginia. Additionally, there were twenty-three assembly plants worldwide in which Daimler-Benz had no ownership.

Daimler-Benz had increasingly realized the strategic importance of a global presence, and this had led them to pursue acquisition candidates in America, the world's largest market for commercial vehicles. This process resulted in the 1977 acquisition of Euclid (a heavy equipment manufacturing subsidiary of White), which was divested in 1983; Freightliner, Inc., Oregon, 1981; and a 49% stake in Fabrica De Autotransportes Mexicana (FAMSA), Mexico, in 1985. Dr. Liener explained this effort to *Financial Times:* "We must think of our sons," suggesting that the long-term health and development of the truck group was at stake.

FAMSA employed 865 office and factory workers and had a production capacity of 15,000 commercial vehicles, although the expected 1986 sales would not exceed 4,000 vehicles due to the poor Mexican economy. When asked why Daimler-Benz chose Mexico for this operation, Mr. Hans-Jurgen Hinrichs, sales director of FAMSA, clarified that "the white spot on the map annoyed us." He suggested that "Daimler-Benz's policy of trying to be everywhere in the world, even when the prospects in the short term don't appear to be too great," would continue to pay dividends of the type the group collected when its patience and persistence in the Middle East was rewarded in the startling truck sales boom after the mid-1970s oil price rise. It was also acknowledged that there were still some gaps in Daimler-Benz's world coverage, but that it had been talking seriously to the Chinese about truck sales and assembly there.

COMPETITION

The nature of the competitive environment had changed over the last ten years. Daimler-Benz was now facing a three-pronged assault from Western Europe, Japan, and the United States in the international truck industry. Exhibit 1 presents the 1984 production of heavy-duty trucks by the major manufacturers.

The idea of international competition was actually much more complex than the Europe–United States–Japan triad might suggest, due to the fact that ownership interests often crossed national boundaries. For instance, many of America's largest truck producers were under European control. Renault had a large stake in Mack Trucks, which itself had many subsidiaries in foreign markets. The Swedish Volvo's recent purchase of White Motor Corp., and Daimler-Benz's 1981 purchase of Freightliner, Inc. gave these large European firms a very strong foothold in the U.S. market. Similarly, Iveco, a Fiat subsidiary, was increasing its presence in the United States as well.

In 1985, the first signs of Japanese interest in the European truck market had become apparent. Hino, Mitsubishi, Isuzu, Mazda, and Toyota all displayed commercial vehicles at the Brussels motor show at the beginning of the year. And while all except Hino had been making increasing inroads into Europe's light commercial vehicles, Hino's exhibits were in weight ranges up to 15 tons.

In the United States, Japanese truck producers were moving swiftly into market niches that the domestic manufacturers had abandoned, thinking they would be too expensive to supply with American vehicles. Significantly, the Japanese are being aided and abetted in this process by the U.S. producers. For example, Nissan Diesel signed an agreement to supply a new generation of medium-weight trucks to International Harvester, now Navistar, and distribute them through Navistar's 850 dealers. At the same time, Nissan planned to sell through its own distribution company based in Texas.

General Motors, which held nearly 40 percent of the shares in Isuzu, decided to start selling Isuzu Class 3 light-weight trucks through its own network of 250 dealers in twenty states. Ironically, GM seemed to be filling out gaps in its own range because it believed that Hino and Toyota would aggressively attack the diesel sectors (Classes 3–8) in the States. For its U.S. venture, Hino had linked up with Mitsui, the major Japanese trading house, which also had long been associated with Toyota but had also been selling trucks through its own distribution network. Between the two distribution networks, they saved more

EXHIBIT 1   **Heavy trucks: International production by major manufacturers, 1984**

Daimler-Benz: 65,000 units	(units)
(66,000 units in 1983)	
Produced in:	(units)
Germany	38,000
USA/Canada	20,000
Brazil	6,000
Argentina	1,000

I.H.C. (Navistar): 36,000 units	(units)
(23,000 units in 1983)	
Produced in:	(units)
USA/Canada	35,000
Australia	1,000

Volvo: 36,000 units	(units)
(30,000 units in 1983)	
Produced in:	(units)
Sweden	26,000
USA	10,000

Paccar: 32,000 units	(units)
(19,000 units in 1983)	
Produced in:	(units)
USA/Canada	30,500
Mexico	1,000
Great Britain	500

Mack: 29,000 units	(units)
(14,000 units in 1983)	
Produced in:	(units)
USA/Canada	29,000

Mitsubishi: 22,000 units	(units)
(17,000 units in 1983)	
Produced in:	(units)
Japan	22,000

Saab-Scania: 22,000 units	(units)
(17,000 units in 1983)	
Produced in:	(units)
Sweden	22,000

Hino: 21,000 units	(units)
(15,000 units in 1983)	
Produced in:	(units)
Japan	21,000

Ford: 21,000 units	(units)
(12,000 units in 1983)	
Produced in:	(units)
USA	19,500
Great Britain	1,000
Brazil	500

General Motors: 20,000 units	(units)
(13,000 units in 1983)	
Produced in:	(units)
USA	18,000
Korea	1,000
Great Britain	500
Brazil	500

Nissan: 19,000 units	(units)
(17,000 units in 1983)	
Produced in:	(units)
Japan	19,000

Fiat IVECO: 19,000 units	(units)
(19,000 units in 1983)	
Produced in:	(units)
Italy	14,000
Germany	3,000
France	750
Argentina	1,000
Brazil	250

Isuzu: 17,000 units	(units)
(15,000 units in 1983)	
Produced in:	(units)
Japan	17,000

Renault R. V. I.: 17,000 units	(units)
(20,000 units in 1983)	
Produced in:	(units)
France	15,000
Spain	1,500
Great Britain	500

M.A.N.: 12,000 units	(units)
(12,000 units in 1983)	
Produced in:	(units)
Germany	11,000
Austria	1,000

than twenty dealerships on sales in excess of 1,000 trucks per year, with an expected increase of 4,000 by 1990.

By the same token, General Motors and Ford each had many subsidiaries in Europe, and especially in the United Kingdom, producing commercial vehicles which had large shares of their markets as well. Paccar, which manufactured Kenworth and Peterbilt trucks, had affiliates in Europe, Africa, and the Middle East. Navistar and Mack also sold a large number of their vehicles to foreign customers.

It was apparent from the large number of subsidiaries, acquisitions, joint ventures, and assembly plants located throughout the world, that the European and U.S. truck manufacturers found it effective for several reasons to maintain a strong global presence, with production and assembly taking place in multiple locations. The Japanese produced and exported trucks at an increasing rate without relying on foreign manufacturing subsidiaries or joint ventures.

Export of commercial vehicles from Japan increased by nearly 40 percent from 1979 to 1980. More important, while North America was the largest market for these vehicles, sales to EEC countries increased by 34 percent that year, and sales to other European countries jumped a staggering 92 percent. "Led by the traditional Japanese powers, Toyota, Nissan, and others, this nation is making the true run at the world truck market." (*Financial Times,* Nov. 29, 1985.)

FREIGHTLINER INC.

On July 31, 1981, Daimler-Benz completed its acquisition of Freightliner Corp., previously a subsidiary of Consolidated Freightways Inc. (CFI). The $300 million transaction gave Daimler-Benz full ownership of Freightliner's four truck-assembly plants located in Portland, Oregon; Mt. Holly, North Carolina; Indianapolis, Indiana; and Burnaby, British Columbia, Canada, along with Freightliner's parts-manufacturing plants in Portland, Oregon; Gastonia, North Carolina; and Fremont, California. Freightliner's two Vancouver financial subsidiaries, Freightliner of Canada, Ltd., and Freightliner Financial Services, Ltd., were also included in the deal.

Freightliner, headquartered in Portland, Oregon, manufactured and sold mainly heavy-duty trucks of the Class 8 variety, signifying a gross weight of at least 33,000 pounds. The Freightliner acquisition gave Daimler-Benz an immediate 10 percent share of the Class 8 truck market to add to its existing lines of Class 6 and 7 trucks, sold through Mercedes-Benz of North America. Freightliner had also been previously involved in sales of medium-duty trucks as a result of its truck-marketing ties with Volvo. As a result of the Daimler-Benz acquisition, however, this collaboration was terminated.

Freightliner was formed by Consolidated Freightway Inc. in 1939 in order to design and build trucks more suitable to the long-haul traffic in the West,

EXHIBIT 2   **U.S. market shares for class 8 trucks**

	1980		1985
IHC	20.4	IHC (Navistar)	21.3
Mack	19.5	Mack	19.1
Paccar	15.4	Paccar	16.3
GMC	14.4	*Freightliner*	13.5
Ford	12.0	Ford	11.6
Freightliner	9.0	GMC	9.0
White	9.0	White	8.2
Others	1.3	Others	0.7

where the majority of CFI's driving was done. During the 1950s, Freightliner began to sell to other truckers as well, with sales to CFI gradually making up a smaller percentage of total revenue.

Freightliner's trucks were marketed by White Motor for over twenty years, but were never distributed in the eastern U.S.A. In 1977, Freightliner set up its own organization of 207 dealers after White Motor began to lose market share. In order to achieve increased sales, it was decided that improved eastern service was needed, and to help accomplish this a new plant was opened in Mt. Holly, North Carolina, in 1979. This was followed by the closing of their Chino, California, assembly plant in September 1980. The closing was blamed partly on the sharp decrease in demand for heavy-duty trucks experienced after the peak reached in 1979. This decrease in demand caused a sales drop of 36 percent early in 1980, which led to the dismissal of Freightliner's president, William Critzer.

Critzer's successor was Ronald Burbank, who had just been named chief operating officer of CFI. He continued on as president and chief executive officer after the acquisition by Daimler-Benz; and aided by a rise in heavy-duty truck demand, an improved product range, and strong sales efforts, he was able to expand sales greatly, thus reaching full capacity in 1984. However, their inability fully to meet demand caused the U.S. market share to decline somewhat in 1984, whereas their Canadian share continued to increase.

The demand for heavy-duty trucks declined slightly in 1985 to 134,000 vehicles from 138,000 in 1984 (compared to 80,000 in 1983), whereas 145,000 medium-heavy vehicles were sold in both years. Despite the growing competition, Freightliner was able to sell 20,809 (against 20,526 in 1984) heavy-duty vehicles in North America, producing sales of $1.6 billion. This meant an improvement in Freightliner's U.S. market share from 12.8 percent to 13.5 percent, whereas the Canadian share dropped to 12.3 percent from 13.2 percent. Exhibit 2 provides an overview of the market share for the various U.S. competitors. Freightliner furthermore saw a 10 percent reduction in employees, to 5,439 from 6,059 in 1984.

THE FUTURE OF DAIMLER-BENZ

Daimler-Benz had weathered the 1980–1983 world recession that sent sales of most truck manufacturers plummeting, and sales at Daimler-Benz had even been relatively stable. Its expansion policy had been one of wise acquisitions and cautious movement into new markets. Its reputation for quality, value and innovation had up until now been unequaled. The question for Dr. Liener was how to sustain the strategic position in a global industry where competition was increasing.

Selected References

"Daimler-Benz Conglomerates," *Fortune,* October 17, 1986.

"West German Industry Fights Back," *Financial Times,* October 15, 1985.

"The Global Truck Industry," *Financial Times,* October 15, 1985.

Daimler-Benz AG Annual Report, 1985.

Daimler-Benz AG Annual Report, 1986.

Kenneth Gooding, "Another Entry for the High-Tech Race," *Financial Times,* October 15, 1985.

"Branchen analysen," April 1987, Bayerische Hypotheken und Wechsel-Bank AG, Munchen.

Graham Turner, "Inside Europe's Giant Companies: Daimler-Benz Goes Top of the League," *Long Range Planning,* Vol. 19, No. 5, pp. 12–17, 1986.

Rolf Bühner, *Strategie und Organisation,* Gabler, Wiesbaden, 1985.

Crash-Programm für den Superkonzern," Manager Magazin, May 1988, pp. 37–63.

FORD OF EUROPE

In mid-1983, the Management Committee of Ford of Europe (the company's senior decision-making committee) was once again examining the trends, opportunities, and threats offered by the European market (see Exhibits 1, 2, 3, and 4). The principal threat perceived by management was the growing Japanese presence in Europe. Japanese manufacturers had increased their car sales in Western Europe from 750,000 units in 1979 to almost one million units in 1983 and they were beginning to establish a manufacturing foothold in Europe. Nissan, for example, was just beginning to produce automobiles in Italy, it would soon increase its production of vehicles for Europe from a Spanish plant, and, most worrisome, the company was expected to announce imminently a decision to proceed with a previously shelved plan to construct a new and very large assembly plant in the United Kingdom. Although Ford competed very successfully against the other European producers—and for the first time had captured the number one European market share position in the second quarter of 1983—Japanese producers' plants in Europe would constitute a new and severe challenge. What especially worried Ford was the possibility that Nissan's new U.K. plant would import major automobile components into Europe from Japan, assemble them into finished vehicles, and then claim that the vehicles were European in origin and thus not subject to any existing European–Japanese trade agreements or understandings.

This worry had led Ford executives back in 1981 to consider seriously local content regulations as a way of reducing this risk and helping to stem the growth of the Japanese producers' share of the European market. Local content regulations, most commonly employed by developing countries against multinational firms based in developed countries, defined the percentage of a product

This case was prepared by H. Landis Gabel and Anthony E. Hall, of INSEAD (European Institute of Business Administration). The case study was developed after discussions with certain Ford personnel but it does not necessarily reflect the actual scope or manner of deliberations undertaken by Ford management or the conclusions of Ford management.
© H. Landis Gabel and Anthony E. Hall, 1985.

EXHIBIT 1   **Ford Motor Company and consolidated subsidiaries — consolidated balance sheet at December 31, 1982**

	1982	1981
	($ millions)	
Assets		
Current assets		
Cash and cash items	$ 943.7	$ 1,176.5
Marketable securities (including $500 million of commercial paper of Ford Motor Credit Company in 1981), at cost and accrued interest (approximates market)	611.7	923.5
Receivables	2,376.5	2,595.8
Inventories	4,123.3	4,642.9
Other current assets	743.7	838.2
Total current assets	8,798.9	10,176.9
Equities in net assets of unconsolidated subsidiaries and affiliates	2,413.4	2,348.2
Property		
Land, plant and equipment, at cost	17,014.9	16,395.7
Less accumulated depreciation	9,546.9	8,959.4
Net land, plant and equipment	7,468.0	7,436.3
Unamortized special tools	2,668.3	2,410.1
Net property	10,136.3	9,846.4
Other assets	613.1	649.9
Total assets	$21,961.7	$23,021.4

EXHIBIT 1   **Ford Motor Company and consolidated subsidiaries — consolidated balance sheet at December 31, 1982 (*cont.*)**

	1982	1981
	($ millions)	
Liabilities and stockholders' equity		
Current liabilities		
Accounts payable		
Trade	$ 3,117.5	$ 2,800.2
Other	1,002.1	1,089.8
Total accounts payable	4,119.6	3,890.0
Income taxes	383.0	208.9
Short-term debt	1,949.1	2,049.0
Long-term debt payable within one year	315.9	128.7
Accrued liabilities	3,656.4	3,663.7
Total current liabilities	10,424.0	9,940.3
Long-term debt	2,353.3	2,709.7
Other liabilities	1,922.7	1,856.2
Deferred income taxes	1,054.1	1,004.8
Minority interests in net assets of consolidated subsidiaries	130.1	148.2
Guarantees and commitments	—	—
Stockholders' equity		
Capital stock, par value $2.00 a share		
Common stock, shares issued: 1982 — 108,870,062; 1981 — 107,859,065	217.8	215.7
Class B stock, shares issued: 1982 — 11,717,738; 1981 — 12,717,003	23.4	25.5
Capital in excess of par value of stock	522.4	526.1
Foreign-currency translation adjustments	(623.2)	—
Earnings retained for use in the business	5,937.1	6,594.9
Total stockholders' equity	6,077.5	7,362.2
Total liabilities and stockholders' equity	$21,961.7	$23,021.4

Source: Ford of Europe.

EXHIBIT 2   **Ford Motor Company and consolidated subsidiaries — ten-year financial summary**

(millions of dollars)

Summary of operations	1982[1]	1981
Sales	$37,067.2	38,247.1
Total costs	37,550.8	39,502.9
Operating income (loss)	(483.6)	(1,255.8)
Interest income	562.7	624.6
Interest expense	745.5	674.7
Equity in net income of unconsolidated subsidiaries and affiliates	258.5	167.8
Income (loss) before income taxes	(407.9)	(1,138.1)
Provision (credit) for income taxes	256.6[3]	(68.3)[3]
Minority interests	(6.7)	(9.7)
Income (loss) before cumulative effect of an accounting change	(657.8)	(1,060.1)
Cumulative effect of an accounting change[4]	—	—
Net income (loss)	(657.8)	(1,060.1)
Cash dividends	—	144.4
Retained income (loss)	$ (657.8)	(1,204.5)
Income before minority interests as percentage of sales	*	*
Stockholders' equity at year-end	$ 6,077.5	7,362.2
Assets at year-end	$21,961.7	23,021.4
Long-term debt at year-end	$ 2,353.3	2,709.7
Average number of shares of capital stock outstanding (in millions)	120.4	120.3
A share (in dollars)		
Income (loss) before cumulative effect of an accounting change	$ (5.46)	(8.81)
Cumulative effect of an accounting change[4]	—	—
Net income (loss)[5]	$ (5.46)	(8.81)
Net income assuming full dilution	—	—
Cash dividends	—	$ 1.20
Stockholders' equity at year-end	$ 50.40	61.06
Common stock price range (NYSE)	$ 41½	26
	$ 16¾	15¾

1980	1979	1978	1977	1976[2]	1975	1974	1973
37,085.5	43,513.7	42,784.1	37,841.5	28,839.6	24,009.1	23,620.6	23,015.1
39,363.8	42,596.7	40,425.6	35,095.9	27,252.7	23,572.7	23,015.4	21,446.1
(2,278.3)	917.0	2,358.5	2,745.6	1,586.9	436.4	605.2	1,569.0
543.1	693.0	456.0	299.1	232.6	155.8	171.4	189.9
432.5	246.8	194.8	192.7	216.6	301.0	281.5	174.7
187.0	146.2	159.0	150.0	136.3	107.0	58.5	48.5
(1,980.7)	1,509.4	2,778.7	3,002.0	1,739.2	398.2	553.6	1,632.7
(435.4)[3]	330.1	1,175.0	1,325.6	730.6	151.9	201.5	702.1
(2.0)	10.0	14.8	3.6	25.5	18.8	25.0	24.1
(1,543.3)	1,169.3	1,588.9	1,672.8	983.1	227.5	327.1▲	906.5▲
—	—	—	—	—	95.2	—	—
(1,543.3)	1,169.3	1,588.9	1,672.8	983.1	322.7	327.1	906.5
312.7	467.6	416.6	359.3	263.4	242.6	298.1	317.1
(1,856.0)	701.7	1,172.3	1,313.5	719.7	80.1	29.0	589.4
*	2.7%	3.7%	4.4%	3.5%	1.4%	1.5%	4.0%
8,567.5	10,420.7	9,686.3	8,456.9	7,107.0	6,376.5	6,267.5	6,405.1
24,347.6	23,524.6	22,101.4	19,241.3	15,768.1	14,020.2	14,173.6	12,954.0
2,058.8	1,274.6	1,144.5	1,359.7	1,411.4	1,533.9	1,476.7	977.0
120.3	119.9	119.0	118.1	117.6	116.6	116.8	124.1
(12.83)	9.75	13.35	14.16	8.36	1.95	2.80▲	7.31▲
—	—	—	—	—	0.82	—	—
(12.83)	9.75	13.35	14.16	8.36	2.77	2.80	7.31
—	$9.15	12.42	13.08	7.74	2.65	2.69▲	6.86▲
2.60	3.90	3.50	3.04	2.24	2.08	2.56	2.56
71.05	86.46	80.77	71.15	60.14	54.09	53.58	51.66
35¾	45⅜	51⅞	49¼	49½	36¼	43½	65⅞
18⅛	29⅜	39	41⅜	34⅞	25⅞	23	30⅞

EXHIBIT 2   **Ford Motor Company and consolidated subsidiaries — ten-year financial summary (*cont.*)**

Summary of operations	1982[1]	1981
▲*Pro forma* amounts assuming the investment tax credits accrued after 1970 flowed through to income in		
Net income (in millions)	—	—
Net income a share	—	—
Assuming full dilution	—	—
Facility and Tooling Data		
Capital expenditures for expansion, modernization and replacement of facilities (excluding special tools)	$ 1,605.8	1,257.4
Depreciation	$ 1,200.8	1,168.7
Expenditures for special tools	$ 1,361.6	970.0
Amortization of special tools	$ 955.6	1,010.7
Employee Data — Worldwide		
Payroll	$ 8,863.0	9,380.1
Total labor costs	$11,756.7	12,238.3
Average number of employees	379,229	404,788
Employee Data — U.S. Operations		
Payroll	$ 5,352.7	5,507.5
Average hourly labor costs per hour worked[7] (in dollars)		
Earnings	$ 13.57	12.75
Benefits	9.80	8.93
Total	$ 23.37	21.68
Average number of employees	155,901	170,806

Share data have been adjusted to reflect the five-for-four stock split that became effective May 24, 1977.
*1982, 1981, and 1980 results were a loss.
[1]See Note 1 of Notes to Financial Statements.
[2]Change to LIFO reduced net income by $81 million.
[3]See Note 5 of Notes to Financial Statements.
[4]Cumulative effect of change (as of January 1, 1975) to flow-through method of accounting for investment tax credit.
[5]See Note 7 of Notes to Financial Statements.
[6]Excludes effect of UAW strike.
[7]Excludes data for subsidiary companies.

Source: Ford of Europe.

1980	1979	1978	1977	1976[2]	1975	1974	1973
the year the assets were placed in service:							
—	—	—	—	—	—	$363.9	938.9
—	—	—	—	—	—	$ 3.12	7.57
—	—	—	—	—	—	$ 2.98	7.10
1,583.8	2,152.3	1,571.5	1,089.6	551.0	614.2	832.5	891.7
1,057.2	895.9	735.5	628.7	589.7	583.8	530.8	485.1
1,184.7	1,288.0	970.2	672.7	503.7	342.2	618.7	594.3
912.1	708.5	578.2	487.7	431.0	435.3	392.7	463.1
9,519.0	10,169.1	9,774.9	8,338.3	6,639.2	5,629.2	5,892.6	5,769.2
12,417.3	13,227.2	12,494.0	10,839.2	8,653.3	7,165.7	7,317.3	7,108.2
426,735	494,579	506,531	479,292	443,917[6]	416,120	464,731	474,318
5,248.5	6,262.6	6,581.2	5,653.4	4,380.4	3,560.5	3,981.9	4,027.0
11.45	10.35	9.73	8.93	8.03	7.10	6.61	6.12
8.54	5.59	4.36	3.91	3.98	3.86	2.88	2.31
19.99	15.94	14.09	12.84	12.01	10.96	9.49	8.43
179,917	239,475	256,614	239,303	219,698[6]	203,691	235,256	249,513

EXHIBIT 3   Ford Motor Company and consolidated subsidiaries—ten-year summary of vehicle factory sales

	1982	1981	1980	1979	1978	1977	1976	1975	1974	1973
U.S. and Canadian Cars and Trucks[1]										
Cars										
United States	1,270,519	1,385,174	1,397,431	2,044,461	2,632,190	2,625,485	2,197,039	1,867,713	2,336,415	2,685,423
Canada	118,721	148,515	162,576	236,437	248,285	247,427	210,049	225,293	258,980	231,598
Total cars	1,389,240	1,533,689	1,560,007	2,280,898	2,880,475	2,872,912	2,407,088	2,093,006	2,595,395	2,917,021
Trucks[2]										
United States	803,484	716,648	753,195	1,183,016	1,458,132	1,345,282	1,017,736	809,360	991,447	1,086,281
Canada	70,120	104,136	109,006	160,160	153,955	149,756	131,186	131,104	143,079	98,326
Total trucks	873,604	820,784	862,201	1,343,176	1,612,087	1,495,038	1,148,922	940,464	1,134,526	1,184,607
Total cars and trucks	2,262,844	2,354,473	2,422,208	3,624,074	4,492,562	4,367,950	3,556,010	3,033,470	3,729,921	4,101,628
Cars and Trucks Outside the United States and Canada[2]										
Germany	797,850	737,383	657,258	880,325	847,529	891,390	815,279	636,799	496,780	728,514
Britain	423,073	418,629	468,472	555,496	433,191	563,384	515,368	468,255	559,534	615,276
Spain	229,839	254,006	266,522	252,917	247,408	212,855	16,448	—		
Brazil	145,110	125,346	165,703	169,631	158,935	129,466	169,707	172,235	177,698	144,739
Australia	141,990	127,181	93,490	115,148	107,389	112,376	108,549	124,600	131,393	130,881
Mexico	90,478	107,312	84,668	74,703	68,009	49,216	45,498	55,909	54,649	44,242
South Africa	59,171	66,962	52,671	40,447	46,201	34,156	33,638	36,878	40,155	35,473
Argentina	52,764	78,671	106,463	89,669	52,702	52,466	35,318	39,793	53,810	61,373
Other countries	51,790	43,225	10,995	7,894	8,139	9,042	8,629	9,833	14,993	8,902
Total outside United States and Canada	1,992,065	1,958,715	1,906,242	2,186,230	1,969,503	2,054,351	1,748,434	1,544,302	1,529,012	1,769,400
Total worldwide—cars and trucks	4,254,909	4,313,188	4,328,450	5,810,304	6,462,065	6,422,301	5,304,444	4,577,772	5,258,933	5,871,028
Tractors[2]										
United States	24,258	31,517	35,286	51,361	35,789	39,650	34,643	38,342	41,090	40,223
Overseas	48,905	57,757	62,415	82,267	59,448	90,880	83,177	73,981	68,202	61,624
Total worldwide—tractors	73,163	89,274	97,701	133,628	95,237	130,530	117,820	112,323	109,292	101,847
Total worldwide factory sales	4,328,072	4,402,462	4,426,151	5,943,932	6,557,302	6,552,831	5,422,264	4,690,095	5,368,225	5,972,875

[1]Factory sales are by source of manufacture, except that Canadian exports to the United States are included in U.S. vehicle sales and U.S. exports to Canada are included as Canadian vehicle sales. Prior year data have been restated for reclassification of Club Wagons from cars to trucks.
[2]Includes units manufactured by other companies and sold by Ford.

EXHIBIT 4   **Ford Shares of Major Car and Truck Markets**

	Cars				Trucks			
	1982		**1981**		**1982**		**1981**	
	Industry unit sales	Ford market share	Industry unit sales	Ford market share	Industry unit sales	Ford market share	Industry unit sales	Ford market share
United States	7,955,970	16.9%	8,514,956	16.6%	2,584,989	30.6%	2,281,879	31.4%
Canada	713,005	15.8	903,536	15.2	205,409	26.7	287,290	30.2
Germany	2,091,297	11.3	2,264,634	11.8	187,789	8.1	214,261	7.7
United Kingdom	1,552,926	30.5	1,484,250	30.9	229,346	36.6	213,832	30.5
Other European markets[1]	6,171,231	8.2	5,913,692	7.8	874,626	6.1	842,626	7.0
Brazil	556,596	17.6	448,256	19.2	134,621	23.2	132,677	17.9
Mexico	288,253	12.9	342,724	15.9	181,948	27.7	230,939	25.6
Argentina	114,455	33.9	172,640	31.8	29,484	54.1	56,965	46.4
Other Latin American markets[1]	288,423	15.9	439,635	11.1	171,138	17.5	249,266	13.8
Australia	454,250	26.0	453,806	23.0	162,104	13.0	152,476	13.1
South Africa	283,427	14.5	301,528	16.7	142,696	10.3	152,013	10.7
All other markets[1]	4,673,287	2.0	4,630,160	1.8	3,288,457	1.0	3,437,096	0.8
Worldwide total[1]	25,143,120	12.5%	25,869,817	12.4%	8,192,607	14.6%	8,252,320	14.0%

[1] 1982 data estimated.

Source: Ford of Europe.

that must be produced in a specified geographical region as a precondition of sale in that region.

Although local content regulations had been discussed occasionally in the Management Committee for the past two years, no conclusions had been reached, and pressure was building to push the discussion through to a definitive policy stance. If the Committee were to decide to favor local content regulations, it would then have to decide on strategy and tactics. Regulations could take various forms, some of which might be more advantageous to Ford than others. And, of course, Ford would have to decide how to represent its position to the governmental bodies that would have to introduce, monitor, and enforce the regulations.

FORD OF EUROPE

Ford's European headquarters are based at Warley near Brentwood in southeast England. The sixth floor of its 2,500-person office building houses Ford of Europe's executive suites, where trade policy is a frequent—and often emotional—topic of conversation. The Ford Motor Company had a long tradition of favoring unrestricted international trade. Henry Ford declared in 1928, "I don't believe in anything else than free trade all 'round." Indeed, he exported the sixth car he made (to Canada). But the international trade environment of the 1920s was not that of the 1970s and 1980s, and although Henry Ford II was a strong free-trader like his grandfather, Ford U.S. had altered its official policy position in 1980 away from free trade toward fair trade with an element of protectionism. The management of Ford of Europe could follow this lead by lobbying for local content regulations, but they did not feel obliged to do so. They

EXHIBIT 5   **Automobile production by producer, 1975, 1980, 1982**

Producer	1975	1980	1982
		(thousands of units)	
1. General Motors (United States)	4,649	4,753	4,069
2. Toyota (Japan)	2,336	3,293	3,144
3. Gr. Nissan (Nissan–Fuji)	2,280	3,117	2,958
4. Volkswagen–Audi	1,940	2,529	2,108
5. Renault-RVI (France)	1,427	2,132	1,965
6. Ford (United States)	2,500	1,888	1,817
7. Peugeot–Talbot–Citroën (France)	659	1,408	1,574
8. Ford (Europe)	1,099	1,395	1,450
9. Fiat–Autobianchi–Lancia–OM	1,231	1,554	1,170
10. Toyo–Kogyo (Mazda)	642	1,121	1,110
11. Honda	413	956	1,020
12. Mitsubishi	520	1,104	969
13. Chrysler Co. (United States–Canada)	1,508	882	967
14. Open (General Motors)	675	833	961
15. Lada (Fiat–U.S.S.R.)	690	825	800
16. Daimler-Benz	556	717	700
17. Suzuki	184	468	603
18. General Motors (Canada)	598	763	560
Talbot (France, United Kingdom, Europe)	719	642	—
19. British Leyland	738	525	494
20. Isuzu	244	472	404
21. BMW	221	341	378
22. Ford Canada	481	434	374
23. Volvo (Sweden–Netherlands)	331	285	335
24. Seat (Fiat)	332	297	246
25. Polski Fiat	135	330	240
26. Moskvitch	300	230	205
27. American Motors	463	252	194
28. Alfa Romeo	191	221	189
29. Vauxhall	190	151	164
30. Saporoskje (U.S.S.R.)	130	150	150

Source: *L'Argus de l'Automobile.* Reprinted by permission.

were sufficiently independent of their American parent that the decision was theirs to make.

Ford of Europe was a product of the Ford Motor Company's traditional internationalism. It was created in 1967 when the managing director of Ford of Germany, John Andrews, convinced Henry Ford II of the need to coordinate the design, development, production, and marketing operations of the Ford European national operating companies within the framework of the European Economic Community (EEC).

Ford now has 25 manufacturing sites in six European countries, and it is the most geographically integrated car producer in Europe. In the last five years the company spent more than $5 billion on automation and common design of its European cars, with the objective of making at least half the parts used in its European line interchangeable. Ford's European integration and focus and its image as a national producer in each national market gives it an important advantage in the growing trend of nationalistic car buying. The company proudly claims that 95 percent of the content of its European cars is European in origin.

Ford of Europe had sales of $9.9 billion in 1981 and would have ranked 34th on the FORTUNE 500 listing. From 1980 through 1982 — one of the worst periods for the auto industry since the 1950s — Ford of Europe earned $1 billion in profit. (See Exhibit 5 for production information on world automobile manufacturers.)

THE GROWING JAPANESE PRESENCE IN EUROPE

Ford of Europe had identified Japanese automotive products as the principal threat in the 1980s. To respond to that threat, Ford's European companies launched a major education and development program in the late 1970s called "After Japan." The program had started with trips by management to Japan to tour Japanese automobile assembly plants. By 1983, "After Japan" was well established with emphasis on robotics, quality circles, "just in time" inventory controls, and other work practices imported from Japan. Already, over 700 robots were at work in Ford's European plants with 1,500 planned by 1986.

Ford's top management believed, however, that it would still take at least five to ten years for their European plants to establish the cost and productivity levels necessary to match the landed price of Japanese imports. The Japanese cost advantage has been estimated to be about $1,500 ex-works per automobile.

A series of bilateral trade agreements between individual European countries and Japan currently capped Japanese automobile imports into Europe. A reciprocal trade treaty between Italy and Japan (ironically initiated by the Japanese in the 1950s) restricted exports to each other's market to 2,200 units annually. Japan's shares of the French and U.K. markets were informally limited to 3 percent and 11 percent, respectively. The French quota was imposed by

President Valéry Giscard d'Estaing in 1976 after an abrupt increase in Japan's share of the French market. The U.K. quota was negotiated with the Japanese Ministry of International Trade and Industry (MITI) in 1978 after a previous, less formal agreement on export restraint failed. The Benelux countries and West Germany were technically open to the Japanese after the lapse of a 1981 informal one-year agreement in those countries establishing a maximum share of 10 percent of each market for the Japanese. Although there was no evidence that the Japanese were moving quickly to exploit this opening into Europe, Ford executives feared that the whole structure of trade understandings was very fragile.[1]

It was not only by exporting vehicles that the Japanese were making their presence felt in Europe, threatening European producers, and promoting European government concern. In 1981, British Leyland launched its Triumph "Acclaim." The Acclaim was a Honda "Ballade" assembled under license from Honda. Mechanical components were imported from Japan, and a royalty was paid to Honda on each car. The Acclaim was introduced to plug a gap in British Leyland's model range, and it precipitated a considerable outcry by some European governments. For example, although British Leyland argued that 70 percent of the car was British in origin, the Italian government refused to allow the first consignment of Acclaims to enter their country from Britain in 1982. The Italians classified the car as Japanese and thus subject to the strict quota agreement between Italy and Japan. British Leyland successfully mobilized support from the U.K. government and the EEC, and the Italians eventually backed down. Nonetheless, the nature of the future battle was becoming clear.

In August 1983, the French government announced that starting in 1984 the Acclaim would be subject to the French "voluntary" agreement with Japan; or rather 40 percent of it would be. That was the percentage that the French government deemed to be of Japanese origin. Again the threat to the Acclaim was withdrawn after a visit to Paris by U.K. Trade Minister, Cecil Parkinson, in August 1983.

The United Kingdom also experienced a similar situation on the import side. In 1983 a Mitsubishi automobile named the "Lonsdale" was imported for the first time into the United Kingdom from Australia, where it was assembled from Japanese components. Strong industry concern was again expressed about hidden loopholes in the network of orderly marketing agreements, but no action was taken.

Japanese components were also beginning to appear on the European market in the 1980s in what had been until then strictly European automobiles. In

---

[1]Ford also perceived an import threat from the emerging automobile industries of Eastern Europe. Many of the countries of Eastern Europe had established their industries with the help of Western European producers (e.g., Fiat in the Soviet Union and Poland, and Renault in Romania). The cars now produced in Eastern Europe were of outdated design, however, and with rapidly growing domestic demand, Eastern European countries were not expected to be a challenge in Western European markets on a scale close to that of the Japanese.

Milan, Innocenti replaced the old British Leyland miniengine in its small car with a Japanese Daihatsu engine. And in 1981 General Motors started to purchase gearboxes from Japan for its "Cavalier" (U.K.) and "Rekord" (Germany) models. General Motors was thought by many industry observers to be pursuing a policy of increasing the percentage of Japanese components in its European and U.S. models.

In addition to their direct export of vehicles, and their indirect exports through cooperative agreements with some European producers, the Japanese were beginning to explore direct foreign investment in Europe. Nissan (Datsun) had for some time been actively looking at sites for overseas automobile assembly plants. In 1981, Nissan commissioned the consulting firm of McKinsey and Co. to undertake a feasibility study for the location of an assembly plant in the United Kingdom. It was to produce up to 200,000 units annually by 1986, rising possibly to 500,000 by 1990. Employment on a greenfield site was to be 4,000–5,000, rising to perhaps 12,000 workers. The scheme would be eligible for government grants of £50–100 million.

Included in the negotiations between Nissan and the U.K. government was a discussion of the degree of voluntary local content. It was widely rumored at the time that Nissan was prepared to accept an EEC content level of 60 percent by value from the outset, rising to 80 percent later. The U.K. Department of Industry was rumored to want these percentages to apply to the ex-works price, after classifying Nissan's profit after tax on the operation as an import. British Leyland and Ford lobbied hard for an immediate 80 percent local content. Further uncertainty revolved around the impact of the new plant on the understanding between the U.K. Society of Motor Manufacturers and Traders and the Japanese Association of Motor Assemblers, which restrained the Japanese share of the U.K. market to 11 percent. The project had been temporarily shelved in 1982 because of uncertainty about future car sales, possible hostility from European governments (notably Italy and France), and fears of poor labor relations. It now threatened to come off the shelf.

Although the U.K. project was at least temporarily stalled, the first cars had just begun to roll off the line from a factory in southern Italy that Nissan built jointly with Alfa Romeo.[2] The production rate planned was 60,000 units annually. The Italian government was said to be satisfied that no more than 20 percent of the value of the cars was being imported into Italy.

Finally, Nissan was sending four-wheel-drive vehicles into the EEC from a Spanish plant in which it held a two-thirds share. Next year, panel vans would follow.[3]

---

[2] This plant was a 50/50 joint venture in which Alfa Romeo mechanical components were installed in a Nissan "Cherry" body coming from Japan. Alfa Romeo ran the assembly operation. Half the finished vehicles went to Alfa Romeo and half to Nissan.
[3] In 1980 Nissan bought 36 percent of Motor Iberica and later increased that share to 66 percent.

THE U.S. SITUATION

Much of what might be envisioned in Europe's future was already taking place in the United States. Japanese imports had been taking a progressively larger and larger share of the market until a voluntary limit of 1.68 million vehicles was negotiated between Washington and Toyko in 1981. That agreement was due to expire in March 1984, and there was widespread speculation that the Japanese wanted at least a substantially higher ceiling in the future. In the meantime, Ford's share of the U.S. market had dropped alarmingly from 26 percent in 1976 to 16 percent in 1982. Analysts blamed much of this on a 1975 decision by Henry Ford II to postpone a major U.S.-based small car program. (A U.S.-based "Fiesta" had been planned.) Ford reengineered and restyled their existing "Pinto" line instead and relied on that for the small car market.

Regardless of the question of fault, Ford's deteriorating position in the late 1970s led the company in 1980 to reverse its historic free-trade policy, arguing for what was called "fair trade" instead. Fair trade was defined by its proponents as trade between countries with similar social and industrial infrastructures and similar national trade policies (for example, similar wage rates, indirect tax burdens, and export incentives).

In November 1980, Ford and the United Auto Workers Union lost a petition they had filed in June with the U.S. International Trade Commission[4] seeking protection from imports. A three-to-two majority of the commissioners ruled that imports were not the major cause of the industry's problems. The causes, according to the majority, were the recession and Detroit's own mistakes.

Ford had requested in its statement to the International Trade Commission that imports from Japan be limited to 1.7 million cars — the 1976 import level. Ford's setback by the Commission was short-lived, however. In April 1981, President Reagan announced the voluntary export restraint agreement with the Ministry of International Trade and Industry. Automobile imports would not exceed 1.68 million units for the next three years.

In spite of the voluntary export restraint, Ford continued lobbying for legislative relief from the pressure of Japanese imports. Ford favored a policy that combined a continuing cap on Japanese imports, a better yen/dollar exchange rate, and tax incentives. The United Auto Workers Union, fearful of the threat to American jobs, was lobbying hard for domestic content legislation.

In February 1983, a bill was introduced in Congress entitled the "Fair Practices in Automotive Products Act" (see Exhibit 6). If passed, the bill would impose a graduated minimum domestic content percentage for automobile importers dependent on the total volume of the importer's sales. The percentages ranged from zero for foreign producers with U.S. sales of fewer than 100,000

---

[4]The International Trade Commission is an advisory commission that determines whether a given industry has been substantially injured by foreign imports, and if so, makes recommendations to the President. Traditionally, the Commission has been viewed as a valuable ally in the executive branch of the government of beleaguered U.S. industries. Thus its decision in this case was a surprise to everyone.

EXHIBIT 6   **Selected testimony on "Fair Practices and Procedures in Automotive Products Act of 1983"**

Over one million jobs have been lost in the auto industry and its supplier industries since 1978. In many parts of our country, this has contributed to unemployment unheard of since the Great Depression.

Quite simply, this bill requires that the more cars a company wants to sell in our country, the more they would be required to build here. If a company takes advantage of the biggest automobile market in the world, it ought to make some effort to put some of its manufacturing in that market — the economic times demand it, and so does the American worker.

These are tough times — and much of the industrial base of our country has eroded. Without reviving this base, our national security is jeopardized and economic recovery will be stifled. We must act now, before our jobs and industrial base are permanently lost.

Congressman Richard Ottinger (D–N.Y.) (Sponsor of the Bill)

It is our belief that this legislation will (1) have a negative effect on U.S. employment, (2) impose substantial costs on consumers, (3) violate our international agreements, (4) invite retaliation by our trading partners against United States exports, (5) undermine the competitiveness of the domestic auto manufacturers, and (6) discourage foreign investment in the United States.

When the Congressional Budget Office reviewed this legislation last September, it determined that, by 1990, this legislation would create 38,000 auto jobs but 104,000 jobs would be lost in the U.S. export sector. This would mean a net loss in American jobs of 66,000.

The direct effect of H.R. 1234 would be to increase substantially the automobile prices paid by American consumers by reducing both the number of automobile imports and the competitive pressures that they exert on domestic manufacturers.

A 1980 Commission staff analysis — commenting on a proposal to reduce foreign car imports from 2.4 million to 1.7 million units per year — estimated that prices of small cars would increase by between $527 and $838 per unit, and increase total consumer expenditures on the purchase of automobiles by $1.9 to $3.6 billion per year.

Statements by opposing Congressmen

units per year to an upper limit of 90 percent for those with annual sales of more than 500,000 units.

The conflicting positions on trade policy of General Motors (GM) on the one hand and Ford, Chrysler, and the American Motor Company on the other were brought into the open by the proposed bill. General Motors lobbied against the bill, arguing that any moves toward protectionism could cause a cascade of restrictive measures that would threaten global traders such as itself. Said Thomas R. Atkinson, GM's Director of International Economic Policy (*New York Herald Tribune,* June 29, 1983):

Local content and other performance regulations decrease our flexibility as a corporation, and force us to do things we otherwise might not be doing. We wish these laws had never been invented, and would not like to see them increased or created in countries where they don't exist now.

General Motor's position was particularly suspect in the eyes of the other major U.S. manufacturers, given the 1982 announcement by GM and Toyota of

EXHIBIT 6   **Selected testimony on "Fair Practices and Procedures in Automotive Products Act of 1983" (*cont.*)**

(The Bill) would severely damage America's trading position, flout our international obligations under the General Agreement on Tariffs and Trade (GATT), subject us to challenge under bilateral Treaties of Friendship, Commerce and Navigation with many of our trading partners, and be of great cost to the American consumer and to the nation.

Secretary of State George Schultz

In addition to competitive pressures on price, foreign competition has also provided important incentives for U.S. manufacturers to engage in research efforts and to invest in new technologies. American car makers have been moving rapidly toward smaller "world cars" that are very similar to those produced abroad, and United States companies are already importing engines, transmissions, and other components. Confronted with the enormous cost of downsizing American cars and the lower production costs of many foreign companies, United States auto makers are reportedly planning even greater reliance on foreign sources for major components. The enactment of legislation requiring vehicles sold in the United States to be 90 percent "American-made" by 1987 would disrupt established supply lines and aggravate the demands upon scarce domestic capital resources now faced by the United States automobile industry and the economy as a whole. The resulting supply effects would increase car prices, leading to reduced sales and employment in the auto industry.

United States Federal Trade Commission

The difficulties of our industry ultimately will not be resolved in legislative halls, but rather in the marketplace where success is earned by offering superior products at competitive prices. Rather than seek shelter from competition — even temporarily — in laws and regulations, U.S. automakers must continue their efforts to meet and exceed foreign competition.

General Motors Corporation

a cooperative plan to produce 450,000 small cars annually by 1985 from a mothballed GM plant in Fremont, California. General Motors and Toyota would have equal shares in the venture, and half the output would be sold under the Toyota name, half under the GM name (to replace GM's "Chevette"). Ford and other U.S. manufacturers were strongly opposed to the deal, fearing that it was a precedent that could end up threatening the native U.S. industry. The implications of a joint venture by the world's first and third largest automobile manufacturers were obvious to all their competitors.

Of course, there were other risks involved in the proposed U.S. domestic content law that went beyond those cited by GM. The more restrictive the import regulations in the United States, for example, the greater the pressure on Europe from Japanese exports diverted from U.S. shores. And some analysts within Ford felt that the bill would stimulate Japanese direct investment in the United States, perhaps constituting a greater threat to the U.S. manufacturers than some limited degree of imports. On this point the interest of the U.S. labor unions and manufacturers could conflict. Finally, there was the general realization that the government could exact a "price" in return for protectionist favors granted the industry.

As of this writing, the bill was being debated in Congress, where it was felt to have a reasonable chance of passage. Whether it would pass the Senate and survive a threatened presidential veto would likely depend on Japanese export pressure. A Data Resources International analyst argued that the passage of the bill would be a real possibility if the Japanese were to take much more than their current 20 percent of the U.S. market.

LOCAL CONTENT REGULATIONS

Local content regulations have long been a device used by developing countries to force multinational companies to increase the rate at which they transfer technology and employment to their local operations. With respect to automobiles, these regulations typically require that a certain percentage of a vehicle's content be produced in the country of sale. This percentage may be defined by value or by weight. Weight is generally thought to be a stricter criterion because it is not susceptible to manipulation by transfer pricing. Yet it can lead to only low-technology, high-weight items being produced locally (e.g., steel castings and chassis components).

Although simple in concept, local content regulations can often be quite complicated in practice. The treatment of overhead and profit is often a problem. Some countries apply the regulations on the basis of fleet averaging, others to specific models. Mexico, where at least 50 percent of the value of all cars sold must be produced locally, strengthened its regulations by also requiring that the value of all component imports must be matched by component exports for each assembler. This led to a flurry of investments by Chrysler and Ford in engine facilities in Mexico.

Until recently, Spain had a 95 percent domestic content rule. All component imports were assessed a 30 percent customs duty, and 50 percent of all local manufacturing operations had to be Spanish owned. All this was changed in the 1975 negotiations between the Spanish government and Ford over Ford's "Bobcat" (or "Fiesta") project in Valencia. Contemplating the attractive prospect of a plant producing 225,000 cars annually, the Spanish government settled for 100 percent Ford ownership, 75 percent Spanish content, and 5 percent import duty on component parts. Concessions on import duty were also granted for machine tools and equipment unavailable in Spain. But two-thirds of automobile production had to be exported from Spain, and Ford's sales in Spain could not exceed 10 percent of the previous year's total Spanish market size. General Motors arranged a similar deal for a plant in Zaragoza, Spain, producing 280,000 small "S cars" ("Corsas") annually. Spanish accession to the EEC would phase out much of its protective legislation.

Local content regulations did not exist in any EEC or European Free Trade Association (EFTA) country except Portugal and Ireland. (The European Community's trade regime did have a scheme for defining local assembly with the EFTA countries for the purpose of trade classification—60 percent of value added had to be locally produced.) Nevertheless, there was a variety of statutory powers in the EEC and the General Agreement on Tariffs and Trade (GATT) that could protect specific industries. For example, Regulation No. 926 of the EEC allowed for the protection of specific industries and could be triggered by the Commission of the EEC after advice from the Council of Ministers.

At the GATT level, any member country could ask for temporary protection from imports from another member (under Articles 19–23) if those imports severely endangered national industry. These "escape clause" articles were difficult for EEC countries to use, however, because each country delegated responsibility for all trade negotiations to the EEC Commission in Brussels. Thus the European automobile industry would have to coordinate campaigns in a number of EEC member countries before it could approach the EEC Commission. Even then, there was no guarantee that the Commission would agree to take a case to the GATT. Not surprisingly, existing import restrictions were essentially bilateral diplomatic agreements—varying widely from country to country—rather than statutory enactments.

FORD'S DELIBERATIONS

At least on the surface, informal local content regulations in Europe looked very attractive to Ford's executives. The Japanese threat was surely very real. Production levels in Europe in 1980 were about the same as they had been in 1970, and in the last decade, while European exports to non-European markets fell 42 percent, Japanese worldwide exports rose 426 percent. Ford's market analysts forecast slow growth for the European market in the future, indicating that higher Japanese sales in Europe would come directly from those of the established European producers. The existing structure of voluntary agreements to limit Japanese imports into individual European countries was fragile. Although "voluntary" was clearly a euphemism, any cracks in the agreements could quickly lead to more Japanese imports before new and possibly more lenient agreements were negotiated. West Germany and Belgium were thought to be the weak spots.

If a European local content rule were to be established on the basis of local sales (i.e., if a specified percentage of each manufacturer's European sales had to be produced in Europe), then the existing system of individual national voluntary trade agreements would become redundant. Alternatively, if a local content rule were to be applied to local production (i.e., if a specified percentage of the content of each manufacturer's cars assembled in Europe had to be sourced in Europe), then some controls on automobile imports would still be needed. A local content rule of this type would prevent the Japanese from circumventing the intent of import controls by importing the bulk of their components from Japan while establishing only token assembly operations in Europe.

Yet there were many potential negative consequences for European producers if local content regulations spread across Europe. It was not obvious that European producers should object to Japanese imports, even at a substantially higher level than at present, if the alternative was to be new Japanese greenfield plants in Europe. Even if they complied scrupulously with local content rules, these new plants, employing the most advanced production technology and work methods, could be tough competitors, unshackled from any form of constraint. At the very least, they would add production capacity to a market already suffering from 20 percent excess capacity. A price war was certainly not impossible to imagine. And Ford, among others, was worried about the impact that these plants could have on fleet sales, particularly in the high-margin U.K. market, if nationalistic customers began to think of Nissan, for example, as a "national" producer.

Another problem was that local content rules could limit Ford's own manufacturing flexibility. The key new concept in the automobile industry in the 1970s was that of a "world car." A world car is assembled in local markets (tailored to local consumers' tastes) from a common set of components. Each component is produced in very high volume at one site, where it can be done least expensively, and then shipped around the world to the scattered assembly plants. Local content rules and world cars were seemingly incompatible.

Ford's "Erika" project (the 1981 "Escort") was the first of the world cars. In actual practice, the world car concept was of questionable success. The Escort that was marketed in the United States differed so much in style and design from its European sibling that there was little parts commonality, and transportation costs ate away at the efficiency gains from large-scale production of the common parts. The result was that although there was some international trade in components within Ford, most movement of parts was either within Europe or within the United States.

General Motors had similar problems with its "J car" (the Vauxhall "Cavalier" in the United Kingdom and Opel "Rekord" in West Germany) and "X car" (the Vauxhall "Royale" in the United Kingdom and Opel "Senator" in Germany). General Motors seemed to have been more successful than Ford, however, in standardizing components, and whereas Ford had primarily maintained an approach of European sourcing for European markets, GM had already moved to exploit its global reach.

To make matters even more complex, Ford had a 25 percent share in Toyo Kogyo (Mazda) and thus an option of working with Mazda to import inexpensive Japanese vehicles. Indeed, a Mazda pickup truck was sold in the United States and Greece as a Ford truck, and the very successful Ford "Laser" in the Far East was a version of the Mazda 626 made in Japan. (In July 1983, Ford was threatening such a policy to counteract the proposed GM–Toyota production plant in California.)

TECHNICAL ASPECTS OF LOCAL CONTENT REGULATIONS

If the management of Ford of Europe were to support local content regulations, they felt they would have to answer four technical questions:

1. How should "local" be defined geographically?
2. How was local content to be measured?
3. To what should local content regulations be applied — individual cars, models, or a producer's entire fleet?
4. What should the minimum percentage of local content be?

The company had already done some thinking about each question.

Of all the producers, Ford was the most geographically integrated in Europe. It would therefore be important to encompass most or all of Europe in the term "local." A definition restricted to the EEC would exclude Ford's big Valencia plant in Spain and a 200,000-unit per year plant contemplated for Portugal. These plants represented critical low-cost sources for small cars for the other European markets. (Both Spain and Portugal had applied for admission to the EEC, however.) Ford regarded a nation-state definition as impractical and intolerable.

Defining local content was a very difficult task. One proposal was to define content by weight. This had the advantage of being difficult to manipulate by transfer pricing, but it might allow the importation of high-value, high-technology components that were light in weight.

The other common definition of local content was by value. Essentially the percentage of local content was established by subtracting the value of the imported components as declared on customs documentation from 1) the distributor's price, 2) the ex-works price, or 3) the ex-works price minus the labor and overhead content of the car. Then the local content residue was divided by the corresponding denominator.

Clearly the percentage of the imported components gets larger from 1) to 3) as the value of the domestic content gets smaller. Ford had not decided its position with regard to this issue, except that it did not want specific components identified for mandatory local production. It was also possible to devise other hybrid methods of valuing local content, but they were generally not under discussion.

Regarding the question of to what should the local content rules be applied, Ford favored applying them to the average of a producer's entire line of cars, rather than to each individual car or model. The former would jeopardize Ford's current importation from South Africa of small quantities of their P100 pickup truck (based on the "Cortina").

There was also a related question of whether automobile production or regional sales should form the basis of measurement. Ford preferred that a specified percentage of a producer's European sales be made in Europe, since such a rule was insurance against circumvention of the current import quotas. A production-based local content rule would only prevent circumvention of the intent of import quotas by token local final assembly.

Finally there was the question of what the appropriate percentage should be. Figures currently under discussion ranged from 60 to 80 percent, although the percentage clearly depended on the format of the specific proposals. Of particular significance in terms of these percentages was that a 60 percent rule might allow importation of engines and major parts of the drive train that would all be excluded by an 80 percent rule. Also, it might be very difficult for the Japanese to start up a new plant with an immediate 80 percent local content (even if that percentage were to be achieved with more time). Start-up at 60 percent would be substantially easier.

THE POLITICAL OPTIONS

Should Ford decide to support local content regulations and then find answers to the technical questions, it would still have to determine the best way to carry its case to the appropriate government body. And here again, the way was not clear.

Ford definitely did not want to act on its own. It would be much better to act in concert with the other European producers. (Despite the all-American image of the founder and his name, Ford of Europe unquestionably considered itself "European.") Not only was this desirable on general principles, but for one quite specific reason Ford preferred not to lobby the EEC directly. It had recently fought and was currently fighting other battles with the European Commission. In 1982, the Commission had issued an interim order to Ford under Article 85 of the Treaty of Rome (an antitrust statute) requiring the company to offer right-hand-drive cars to the West German market. The background to this directive was that most European automobile producers charged significantly higher prices in the United Kingdom than on the Continent. To prevent consumers from ordering right-hand-drive cars in Germany and importing them to the United Kingdom, Ford had refused to make the models available on the Continent. This provoked a consumer reponse to which the EEC Commission reacted.

In June 1983 the Commission issued a draft regulation applicable to the distribution systems of all motor manufacturers operating in Europe. The regulation aimed at harmonizing vehicle availability and prices across Europe. Any model of vehicle sold in any EEC member state would have to be made available in all other member states. And if price differences exceeded 12 percent (net of taxes) between any EEC markets, new importers (not authorized by the manufacturer) could enter the market. Ford, along with all other European motor manufacturers, was opposing this proposal vigorously.

Although Ford preferred to have a common industry position to press on the governmental authorities, there was little likelihood of unanimity among the

European producers even on the most basic question of whether local content rules were desirable. General Motors was an almost certain opponent of local content rules despite the fact that it too might welcome relief from Japanese competition. Fiat, Renault, and British Leyland, on the other hand, might be strong allies who could perhaps rally the support of their respective governments. They appeared to have much to gain from local content rules because they had most of their operations in Europe and they purchased most of their components locally.

There were a number of sourcing arrangements, however, which could undermine the support of some of these firms. Japanese cars assembled in Australia were entering the United Kingdom with a certificate of origin from Australia. British Leyland's Acclaim was of questionable origin. Fiat was bringing in "Pandas" from Brazil, and Volkswagen "Beetles" came into Europe from Mexico. Renault had extensive operations in the United States that could alter the company's outlook. And on July 27, 1983, the *Wall Street Journal* reported that Fiat was being indicted by the Italian authorities for selling cars made in Spain and Brazil under the guise of Italian manufacture. Fiat denied the charge.

Ford executives believed, nonetheless, that with the exception of GM, Ford was likely to find general support within the industry. In fact, in a 1981 draft paper, the CLCA[5] stated:

> The establishment of Japanese motor vehicle manufacturing plants should be subject to the following durable conditions:
>
> a. the CIF value of the components not originating from the EEC should not exceed 20 percent of the price ex-works of the vehicle.
>
> b. the manufacturing and assembly of mechanical components (engines, gearboxes and drivetrain) should be performed within the EEC.

THE EUROPEAN COMMISSION

Ford executives believed that the European Commission was prepared to take some action on the automobile imports issue. In January 1983 the Commission had held discussions with the Japanese in Toyko and had obtained a nonbinding commitment to moderate vehicle exports to the EEC. The Commission was currently monitoring the agreement. Beyond this it was unclear what action the European Commission was considering. In principle, the EEC should be expected to favor relatively free trade between its member countries and the rest of the world. The history of international trade since World War II — a history in which the EEC featured prominently — was one of declining tariffs (from an

[5]Comité de Liaison des Constructeurs Associations. The CLCA was basically a political liaison committee of the national automotive trade associations of France, the United Kingdom, Germany, Belgium, Holland, and Italy.

average of 20 percent on manufactured goods in the 1950s to 8 percent in the mid-1970s), dramatically growing trade volumes, and greater interdependence of national economies. Two other principles dear to the EEC were that all member countries maintain a *common* trade policy vis-à-vis non-EEC countries, and that there be no barriers to trade between member countries. Clearly, the existing set of nonuniform bilateral trade agreements with the Japanese offended these principles.

Although the principles underlying the EEC were relatively unambiguous, the EEC often resorted to protective policies, and it was not immune to pressures to maintain jobs in the automotive sector. But granted this observation, it was still not evident just how job preservation might best be achieved. Formal local content rules would be inconsistent with EEC law and would violate the GATT. Thus any local content measures would have to be informal, such as those that currently existed between the Japanese and the British. Would the EEC prefer to see a uniform (albeit informal) external quota and internal production-based local content rule? Or would it rather see a uniform internal sales-based content rule and no quota? Would its preference in either case be less restrictive than the status quo, shaky though it might be? And was it realistic to expect that an informal negotiating process could create a common position among the different EEC member states? A weak, contentious, and nonuniform set of local content rules established and enforced by each EEC member country could be the worst of all the imaginable alternatives.

The Japanese, of course, would have some influence on EEC thinking on this matter. Any EEC action would probably come in the context of trade negotiations — not simply unilaterally imposed trade sanctions. And what position might the Japanese take? It is conceivable that they might agree to some reasonable export restraints into the EEC in return for open markets within the EEC. That would give them access to the two big markets from which they were currently virtually excluded — France and Italy. But would those two countries agree? Each would face greater Japanese competition in its home market but less in its export markets in other EEC countries.

The executives on the Management Committee considered their alternatives. If they were to have any role in determining the public policies that would undoubtedly have a significant impact on their company, they would have to act quickly.

Reference   *New York Herald Tribune,* June 27, 1983.

EXHIBIT 7   **Analysis of automobile construction cost**

		Percentage of ex-works price
Freight		2
Administration, selling cost, warranty, and profit		7
Production and assembly overheads		22
Variable manufacturing costs:		69
Engine	10.4	
Gearbox	4.8	
Axles	6.9	
Other mechanical parts	8.3	
Body stamping	5.5	
Body assembly	6.9	
Accessories and seating	7.6	
Final assembly and painting	18.6	
	69.0	
Total		100%

Notes
1. The labor content of variable manufacturing costs accounts for 14 percent of the total ex-works price.
2. For a typical medium-sized salon at a production level of 200,000 annually.
3. Final retail price is usually 22 percent higher than the ex-works price.

Source: Yves Doz, "Internationalization of Manufacturing in the Automobile Industry," unpublished paper, and Ford of Europe estimates.

EXHIBIT 8   EEC market share analysis 1973/1980/1982 (percent of total registrations)

	Germany	Belgium	Denmark	France	United Kingdom	Italy	Holland	Total[6]
Fiat[1]	7.2/3.6/4.3	9.1/5.4/5.7	7.1/8.7/4.9	4.8/3.7/4.9	3.0/3.3/3.0	64.6/49.4/51.7	8.8/4.1/5.5	16.9/12.2/14.9
Ford[2]	12.8/10.4/11.3	14.7/8.5/8.6	11.7/10.6/16.1	4.6/3.7/6.5	24.2/30.7/30.1	3.6/4.8/5.6	9.3/9.1/10.4	11.5/11.4/12.1
General Motors[3]	21.6/16.9/18.2	13.4/10.2/10.3	12.8/11.6/14.3	2.5/1.8/2.5	9.8/8.8/12.0	3.3/3.5/3.7	13.0/15.3/16.1	10.4/9.1/9.5
Renault	7.1/4.7/3.9	9.7/8.9/9.4	5.3/1.9/1.0	28.9/40.5/39.1	3.6/5.8/4.1	3.3/10.5/11.1	7.5/8.7/8.0	10.6/14.3/14.4
Peugeot[4]	6.7/4.7/4.0	24.3/15.2/13.8	11.6/8.6/7.4	51.8/36.4/30.2	12.4/5.1/4.4	10.2/11.0/8.5	27.8/12.9/11.8	20.6/14.1/12.2
Volkswagen[5]	24.9/21.7/23.5	10.3/8.9/10.4	19.1/5.1/5.3	2.4/4.0/4.9	4.1/3.4/4.5	3.8/4.4/5.3	8.4/7.5/8.2	9.9/9.6/10.0
Nissan	—/2.1/2.0	—/3.8/3.7	—/5.0/5.2	—/0.9/0.9	—/6.1/5.9	—/0.03/0.01	—/5.3/4.6	—/2.5/2.2
Honda	—/1.8/1.5	—/4.4/3.3	—/2.4/0.9	—/0.4/0.4	—/1.5/1.1	—/0.03/0.01	—/5.5/3.5	—/1.4/1.0
Mazda	—/1.9/1.9	—/3.2/3.6	—/8.9/9.4	—/0.7/0.7	—/1.0/1.0	—/0.02/0.01	—/3.9/3.7	—/1.4/1.3
Mitsubishi (Colt)	—/1.7/1.9	—/3.5/3.4	—/3.4/1.2	—/0.2/0.2	—/0.7/0.6	—/0.02/0.02	—/4.8/3.5	—/1.1/0.9
Toyota	—/2.4/1.9	—/9.1/6.1	—/8.2/7.1	—/0.7/0.7	—/2.3/1.8	—/0.02/0.03	—/6.0/4.4	—/2.1/1.5
For 1973 all Japanese vehicles	0.8	13.4	7.1	0.6	4.6	0.1	10.1	2.5

[1]Fiat includes Lancia and Autobianchi.
[2]Ford includes all sourced vehicles (e.g., Spain and Belgium).
[3]General Motors includes both Vauxhall and Opel.
[4]Peugeot includes 1973 Chrysler and Citroën, bought in 1979 and 1974, respectively.
[5]Includes Audi.
[6]Ireland and Luxembourg figures (about 100,000 units) are not included.

Source: L'Argus de l'Automobile. Reprinted by permission.

EXHIBIT 9   **Share of Japanese Exports in Registrations by Importing Country in Europe**

Country	1966	1970	1975	1979	1981
Belgium	0.3%	4.9%	16.5%	18.0%	28%
France	0	0.2	1.6	2.2	2
Germany	0	0.1	1.7	5.6	10
Italy	0	0	0.1	0.1	—
Netherlands	0.6	3.2	15.5	19.5	26
United Kingdom	0.1	0.4	9.0	10.8	10
Denmark	0.5	3.4	14.7	18.1	28
Ireland	0	0	8.9	25.2	30
Austria	0	0.9	5.4	12.4	23
Switzerland	0.1	5.6	8.4	16.0	26
Portugal	0	10.7	11.8	7.8	11
Finland	14.4	18.3	20.8	23.9	26
Norway	1.9	11.4	28.4	24.2	36
Sweden	0.2	0.7	6.5	10.0	14

Source: From *The World Car: The Future of the Automobile Industry* by S. W. Sinclair. © 1983. Reprinted with permission of Facts on File, Inc., New York.

EXHIBIT 10   **Restrictions on Japanese car sales in developed countries, 1981–1982**

United Kingdom	10–11 percent market share ceiling, dating from 1975 package to nationalize British Leyland
Federal Republic of Germany	Growth limit of 10 percent per annum on 1980 sales (252,000 units)
Netherlands	No increase on 1980 level
Luxembourg	No increase on 1980 level
Italy	Quota of 2,200 units
France	3 percent market share ceiling
Belgium	Reduction of 7 percent on 1980 sales
EEC as a whole	Common external tariff is 10.9 percent
Canada	Shipments of "around 174,000" units as against 158,000 in 1980
Australia	All imports restricted to 20 percent of market; tariff of 57 percent; local content must be 85 percent to count as home-produced
United States	Shipments of 1.68 million for 1981 (Japanese fiscal year); subsequent shipment limits to be calculated taking account of U.S. market conditions; tariff is 2.9 percent
Denmark, Greece, Ireland	No restrictions
Japan	No quotas or tariffs on assembled cars, but internal taxes, depending on engine size; distribution and administrative checking systems alleged to operate as nontariff barriers

Note: The Benelux and Canadian restrictions are supposed to last only for 1981. The others appear to be more permanent.

Source: From *The World Car: The Future of the Automobile Industry* by S. W. Sinclair. © 1983. Reprinted with permission of Facts on File, Inc., New York.

EXHIBIT 11   **Foreign sourcing—Recently announced commitments by U.S. automobile manufacturers to purchase foreign-made components for use in domestic vehicles production**

Automobile manufacture	Description of component	Intended use	Manufacturing source	Approximate number of components	Period
General Motors	2-8 lit V-6	Cars	GM Mexico	<400,000/year	1982–
	2-0 lit L-4 with transmission	Minitrucks	Isuzu (Japan)	100,000/year	1981–
	1-8 lit diesel L-4	Chevette	Isuzu (Japan)	Small numbers	1982–
	1-8 lit L-4	J-car	GM Brazil	250,000/year	1979–
	THM 180 automatic transmission	Chevette	GM Strasbourg (France)	~250,000/year	1979–
Ford	2-2 lit L-4	Cars	Ford Mexico	<400,000/year	1983–
	Diesel L-4	Cars	Toyo Kogyo	150,000/year	1983–
	2-0 lit L-4	Minitrucks	Toyo Kogyo	<100,000/ycar	1982–
	2-3 lit L-4	Cars	Ford Brazil	~50,000/year	1979–
	Diesel 6 cyl.	Cars	BMW/Steyr	100,000/year	1983–
	Turbo-diesel/4 cyl.	Cars	BMW/Steyr	—	1985–
	Manual transaxles	Front-disc cars	Toyo Kogyo	100,000/year	1980–
	Aluminum cylinder heads	1-6 lit L-4	Europe, Mexico	—	1980–
	Electronic engine control devices	Cars	Toshiba	100,000+/year	1978–
	Ball joints	Cars	Musashi Seimibu	1,000,000/year	1980–84
Chrysler	L-6 and V-8 engines	Cars	Chrysler Mexico	<100,000/year	Early 1970
	2-2 lit L-4	K-body	Chrysler Mexico	<270,000/year	1981
	2-6 lit L-4	K-body	Mitsubishi	1 million	1981–85
	1-7 lit L-4	L-body (Omni)	Volkswagen	1–2 million	1978–82
	1-6 lit L-4	L-body	Talbot (Peugeot)	400,000 total	1982–84
	2-0 lit Diesel V-6	K-body	Peugeot	100,000/year	1982–
	1-4 lit L-4	A-body (Omni replacement)	Mitsubishi	300,000/year	1984–
	Aluminum cylinder heads	2-2 lit L-4	Fiat		
AMC	Car components and power train	AMC-Renault	Renault in France and Mexico	300,000/year	1982–
VW of America	Radiators, stampings	Rabbit	VW Mexico	250,000/year	1979–
	L-4 diesel and gas	Cars	VW Mexico	300,000+/year	1982–

Source: Reprinted by permission from Supplement No. 2/1981, *Bulletin of the European Communities.*

Index